ANTHOLOGY OF THE AMERICAN SHORT STORY

Contents

Publisher: Patricia Coryell
Editor in Chief: Carrie Brand
Senior Marketing Manager: To
Senior Development Editor: Jan
Senior Project Editor: Samantha
Art and Design Manager: Gary
Cover Design Director: Tony Sai
Composition Buyer: Chuck Dutt
New Title Project Manager: Susan
Editorial Assistant: Katilyn Crow
Marketing Assistant: Bettina Chiu
Editorial Assistant: Andrew Laske

Cover image: Bridgton Farm, by G

Text credits begin on page 971, whi

Copyright © 2008 by Houghton Mi

No part of this work may be reprod
tronic or mechanical, including photo
or retrieval system without the prior
less such copying is expressly permitte
profit transcription in Braille, Hought
further uses of copyrighted selections
from the selections' individual copyright
lege Permissions, Houghton Mifflin Co

Printed in the U.S.A.

Library of Congress Control Number: 20

Preface

When I was a small boy, my mother's father, Axel Fjeldseth, would come to live with us in the winter, not wanting to endure the darkest months of northern Minnesota alone on a remote farm. Every evening after dinner, he would fill his cup with coffee, lean forward in an attitude of intimacy, and tell a story. His accounts were filled with reminiscences of his youth, with humorous adventures involving his seven children, with doubtful tales of bear hunting or catching pike too heavy to lift into the boat. Outside in the frigid night, a blizzard might be raging, with the wind whistling around the house and the snow drifting into fantastic designs, but inside we lived entirely in my grandfather's tale. No one enjoyed all of this more than I did, unless it was grandfather himself, for he came alive in the telling, his quick eyes searching the faces of his listeners, his emotions ranging from intensity in tragic fare to uproarious good fun in the comedic episodes. He adored the stories he told; he cherished the telling of them, even if he had told them a hundred times; he loved that his listeners were entertained by them. There was no television in those days, and, in our house at least, oral tales and family legends were a major source of amusement, instructing the children in what to value, what to avoid, and how to live.

I inherited the garrulous proclivities of my grandfather, to the dismay of my friends and loved ones, and I absorbed his deep interest in stories, especially after he taught me to read them, opening the door to fascinating new worlds and characters. This obsession continued throughout high school and college, and in due course it brought me to Pennsylvania State University for graduate work. The library at Penn State is named for the first professor of American literature, Fred Lewis Pattee, the author of *The Development of the American Short Story*, the earliest comprehensive study of short fiction in the United States, published in 1923. There, in his library, among his books, I deepened my admiration for the genre, and my enthusiasm has never waned. Narratives have sustained my life, enriching it beyond measure, entertaining and instructing me during my own long winter nights.

It has always been my intention to assemble a comprehensive anthology of the American story, a desire reaching back four decades to my earliest publications on the genre, and I am delighted to bring one forth now with the distinguished firm of Houghton Mifflin. Other scholars have edited fine collections of stories, and the academy has been enriched by them, but they follow the established assumption that the earliest indigenous short fiction is Washington Irving's "Rip Van Winkle," published in 1819. This is a marvelous tale, to be sure, but not at all the inception of the form. One contribution this anthology makes is to correct the neglect of an important component of American literary history, the early story, those works published between 1747 and 1819. These preliminary attempts at fiction are not always an aesthetic success, but they help demonstrate the progressive skill in handling the "art" of the story, the methodology of storytelling, which did not come easily. Some aspects of narrative seem crude and uneven, but the subjects treated are as important now as they were in the period surrounding the Revolutionary War: the formation and definition of an American identity (what values, assumption, ethics are typical of the new culture of the United States), the representation of ethnicity and race (especially Native Americans and African Americans), and the portrayal of gender roles in a period of change. Indeed, although selections in this book cover a broad range of ideas, these three concepts are the central unifying ideas of the entire collection.

Organization

The stories collected in this book range from 1747 to 2005. They are listed chronologically to present the development of the art of the genre and the flow of ideas and themes that emerged over two centuries, and they are organized into five historical sections reflecting major cultural transitions that changed literary interests. Each part begins with an introduction discussing historical and social events, major developments in literature, and the ways in which the selected stories contribute to the advance of the form.

    Part 1, "An Overview of the American Short Story," provides an introduction to the genre, its history, and its varying types, along with a brief survey of the growth of short fiction in America. Part 2, "Irving and the Predecessors of the American Story," covers the period from Benjamin Franklin to Washington Irving, presenting stories virtually unknown even to senior scholars of literature. Part 3, "American Romanticism," offers works that differ greatly from those of the previous age, informed by Transcendental ideas expressed in symbolism and allegory. This section culminates with some of the finest works of short fiction ever published. Part 4, "Realism and Naturalism," introduces "Local Colorism" along with the major writers of the period, including many women who were taking their place in the literary hierarchy and a spectrum of minority authors who were being heard for the first time. The great surge of experimentation and exploration that characterized the post–World War I era is contained in Part 5, "Modernism and Experimentation," covering the Jazz Age, the Lost Generation, and the writers of the Great Depression. Part 6, "The Contemporary Expansion of the Genre," demonstrates the great racial and ethnic diversity of writers at the end of the twentieth century and celebrates the enormous freshness and inventiveness of their stories. The work by minority women has been particularly remarkable during the last decades of the twentieth century. Appendix A, "List of Sources," collects the publication information that is also provided with the headnote to each story. Appendix B, "Selected Books for the Study of the American Short Story," points the way to important scholarship on the subject, those books that have been at the center of the intellectual investigation of this rich literary tradition.

Principles of Inclusion

A fundamental guideline for developing this comprehensive volume was to include works that were originally published in English and in America. The only compromise on that standard is Benjamin Franklin's "The Speech of Miss Polly Baker," which originally appeared in London in 1747 but was quickly reprinted here. Since this marvelous account constitutes what might be considered the first story by an American, I decided to include it, even though publication in London preceded that in New York by a few months. All of the other selections appeared first in this country.

Beyond the early section, which does not duplicate any anthology of short fiction ever published, the remaining stories in the book have been chosen to include works that in some way represent transitional moments in the development of the form: some subject, theme, manner of telling, or device that is significant in literary history. The tales by Mark Twain and Bret Harte, for example, signal the beginning of the Local Color movement. In addition, I have tried to balance "standard" works with fresh selections that have not appeared in previous collection, such as the pieces by Alice Dunbar-Nelson, Anzia Yesierska, Hisaye Yamamoto, Sandra Cisneros, Tim O'Brien, and Yiyun Li, to mention only some of the new works in the volume. Many of these stories are by women and ethnic minorities, but that was not the sole reason they were chosen. In each case, these stories represent some new contribution to the stream of American fiction. They are works of impressive artistic integrity that also expand the various issues that have been central to American literary history.

Acknowledgments

The construction of a major anthology is necessarily a process of collaboration, of interaction with other scholars and students over decades of mutual engagement in literature. My life has been enriched by being surrounded by dear friends and esteemed colleagues, many of whom have come to be part of my family. They have contributed to my understanding of American literature in deeply important ways, especially those in the American Literature Association: Alfred Bendixen (Texas A&M University), George Monteiro (Brown University), Linda Wagner-Martin (University of North Carolina), Gloria Cronin (Brigham Young University), Jeanne Reesman (University of Texas at San Antonio), Alfred

Samuels (University of Utah), Gary Scharnhorst (University of New Mexico), and many others.

Beverly Lyon Clark (Wheaton College), John Clendenning (California State University, Northridge), Keith Newlin (University of North Carolina, Wilmington), Margaret Crumpton Winter (California State University, Stanislaus), Robert M. Luscher (University of Nebraska, Kearney), Jeanne Campbell Reesman (University of Texas, San Antonio), Gary Scharnhorst (University of New Mexico), Mary De Jong (Pennsylvania State University), Clark Maddux (Tennessee State University), Donald D. Kummings (University of Wisconsin, Parkside), Marion S. McAvey (Becker College), Evelyn Funda (Utah State University), Charles Marvin (University of Missouri, Columbia), Mimi R. Gladstein (University of Texas, El Paso), and John Hildebidle (M.I.T.) all read early drafts of the manuscript and offered insightful, and contradictory, advice on how to make the book better. I am grateful to them for sharing their expertise, their professional integrity, and their honesty, however chastening.

My work at the University of Georgia benefits immensely from the John Olin Eidson Distinguished Professorship in American Literature, which provides time and resources to assist my research. One of the greatest pleasures in my life is continuous association with the graduate students working under my direction, and they have contributed in major ways to the development of this volume. Especially deserving of mention are Katherine Brown, Steven Florczyk, and Nicole Camastra, all of whom will write their own books in due course.

This volume was encouraged by Michael Gillespie, who, in his capacity as an editor at Houghton Mifflin, flew to Athens to ask me to do it, and his constant support and confidence were instrumental in the many months during which I read hundreds of stories, eventually assembling a rough draft five times longer than was practical. After his departure from the company, Lisa Kimball ably assumed his position, and I am indebted to her skill in solving problems, large and small, and for keeping the process moving. Jane Acheson, in charge of development, was unfailingly efficient, knowledgeable, and congenial, and the book is better for her involvement. The forbearance of my wife, Gwen, is beyond measure, for she listened, with inhuman patience and good will, to my telling of all of these stories and more. There are some pretty good ones.

James Nagel
University of Georgia

ANTHOLOGY OF THE
AMERICAN SHORT STORY

1

An Overview of the American Short Story

The short story succeeded in America as it had nowhere else. In England, the written form originated in the early eighteenth century. It took a few decades for it to be imported to the New World, but once there it flourished, finding expression in hundreds of brief narratives by the end of the century and in tens of thousands by the completion of the next. In England, it remained, then as now, a subordinate form to the novel, which dominated as the appropriate venue for serious work. By the era of Realism in America, however, short fiction had come to the fore. All of the important modernist writers wrote in the mode, producing work among the best in the language, and in contemporary times the form has become even more important. By the end of the twentieth century, remarkably, emerging writers from a broad spectrum of differing ethnic groups have chosen to write short fiction, often producing more volumes of them than novels. In an important sense, American stories are an examination of a diverse and complex society, and the writers who produced them recorded the salient ideas, conflicts, feelings, disasters, and successes that a people experienced. It is an invaluable cultural history, a powerful record of a nation.

The Origins of the Story

All known cultures developed, early in their existence, some form of art, some expression in music, and some way of telling narratives to one another, myths that explained the origin of the universe, tales that exemplified the values most treasured by the group, or accounts of honorable ancestors whose lives deserved to be emulated by succeeding generations. The oral tradition was a dominant form among Native peoples when Europeans arrived in North America, and the new immigrants brought with them written forms of stories that had themselves derived from earlier spoken modes.

In American fiction, the *yarn* is most closely tied to oral tradition. Its methods imply a speaker addressing an audience gathered nearby. There is a great deal of emphasis on the narrator, who interacts with the listeners and is interrupted frequently with questions and extraneous remarks. Nevertheless, the story advances, despite some question about whether or not the speaker believes his own story. The audience doubts it and suspects the whole thing is an elaborate hoax. Mark Twain's "The Celebrated Jumping Frog of Calaveras County" falls into this category, which commonly features hyperbole, outrageous events, ironic humor, and implausible conclusions. Yarns were told in the vernacular, capturing local dialects, and language itself was an important part of the mode. They became popular as part of *Southwestern humor,* usually reporting the exploits of famous hunters or frontiersmen, but other regions had their own form of exaggerated oral accounts.

Related to the yarn, but with a better-organized plot, was the *tale,* often called a "tall tale." The genre is normally humorous, featuring preposterous situations, unbelievable characters, and outcomes that challenge credulity. Immensely popular, in the nineteenth century they rewarded common people with a literary form all their own, since citizens of all classes could be entertained by them, and the magazines of the time could not get enough. By the end of the 1890s, however, the mode had lost popularity, although the strategy of a dramatized narrator continued to influence written fiction, especially in the stories of minority writers in the decades that followed.

The yarn and the tale owe a great deal to the ancient traditions of written narratives. Among the earliest of such genres was the *fable,* often featuring animals as characters, each emphasizing, or satirizing, some dominant human trait. Such stories are thus known as *beast fables.* Ancient Egyptian records, dating back to 4000 BC, indicate that the sons of Cheops entertained their father with these prose narratives. Sometime around 600 BC, Aesop recorded his collection of fables, humorous didactic narratives that are told in prose or verse and intended to indoctrinate children with instructive values. Long before contact with Europeans, Native American oral tales were often in the form of fables, with animal characters exemplifying human traits: courage, trickery, perseverance, or sacrifice. Later, Joel Chandler Harris used the tradition for his Uncle Remus stories, as did Charles Chesnutt in his Conjure tales.

Among the most ancient of forms is the *parable,* a didactic narrative in prose, occasionally in verse, that presents an illustration of some spiritual or moral concept. The most famous parables are those from the Christian Bible, in which Jesus is said to have illustrated his lessons with accounts of the Good Samaritan and the prodigal son. The genre is older than Christianity, however, and originates with the Greek rhetoricians, who defined it as distinct from the fable by excluding animals as characters. The plot of a parable is simpler, presenting a character in an ethical dilemma, facing the consequences of an earlier action, or confronting a common transitional moment in which a decision will alter the course of a life. Plato utilized the mode in *The Republic,* which was well known to early American writers, but the Bible was probably a greater influence on them. Puritan clergymen used the form in sermons and lessons, but in the Age of Reason, the era during which written short fiction arose, the tradition lost favor.

Myths are also ancient narratives, originating in oral conventions throughout the world, explaining natural phenomena, the creation of the universe, the ways of the gods, the glories of ancestral figures. Greek and Norse myths are among European examples, along with those originating in Christian lore, and they have been sustained in opera and the theater and transformed in modern film. Native American myths continue to inform many tribal ceremonies even in the twenty-first century, illustrating the way in which they can fuse themselves within the cultural knowledge of a people, perpetuating their evocative power generation after generation. Related to this convention is the *legend,* which tends to be more closely related to history than supernatural events. Legends tend to improve with the telling, the exploits becoming more sensational over time, as in accounts of military or athletic heroics. In America, a new catalogue of legends needed to be developed, and many of them, Plymouth Rock, the romance of John Smith with Pocahontas, George Washington throwing a coin across the Potomac, have been sustained over the centuries.

Written stories, in various forms, have a long history and a rich tradition. More recent than ancient myths and Biblical parables, other kinds of short fiction appeared that were widely popular. Some time around the tenth century, the Arabian *Thousand and One Nights* collected an enormous number of stories, including the voyages of Sinbad the sailor, Aladdin and his lamp, and Ali-Baba and the forty thieves. In Europe, the first translation was in French in the early eighteenth century, and the English translation followed in 1840. Other such collections of short fiction include the *Gesta Romanorum* (or *Deeds of the Romans*) from the fourteenth century, anecdotes and tales in Latin that were immensely admired and went on to influence Geoffrey Chaucer and William Shakespeare. Far from describing only the Romans, the book is a collection of accounts from numerous cultures, including Asian and European.

Early Narrative Forms in the New World

The earliest British story in the modern tradition is regarded as Daniel Defoe's "A True Relation of the Apparition of One Mrs. Veal" in 1706, after which there was a slow but steady appearance in England of short fictional narratives. Their inception in the New World came somewhat later and essentially followed the development of newspapers and magazines, but it is significant that their inauguration came during the Enlightenment, a rational age focused on the material world and not on the hereafter.

As a result, the literature of the eighteenth century is decidedly that of the everyday world: conflicts are *moral,* having to do with relationships among people, rather than *theological,* relating to sin and dealing with the deity. Several different forms flow together to influence short fiction, the most common of which is the *sketch,* a work of expository prose describing a scene or character. Sketches were widely admired, but they contained little by way of plot, usually had no conflict, and thus concluded without resolution. They did contain dialogue appropriate to a region, however, which influenced more complex fiction to follow. Washington Irving's *The Sketch Book* of 1819 is among the best-known collections, and two of the pieces, "Rip Van Winkle" and "The Legend of Sleepy Hollow," became international sensations.

Another component of the prehistory of the American story is the *anecdote,* a brief narrative, often humorous, relating something that happened to an actual person in a real place. Oral in nature, ephemeral in substance, the form is not didactic. Too brief to develop a theme, the point of the genre is simply to relay an event and its outcome. The sketch describes a person, the anecdote an action. It is an ancient tradition, reaching back to Plutarch's *Lives of Famous Greeks and Romans,* for example. In America, readers were fascinated by anecdotes, and early newspapers featured them in every issue. By the time of the Revolutionary War, the new magazines were using them for filler between articles, extending the popularity of the genre. As monthlies developed in the last half of the nineteenth century, the form found continued expression, and it attracts readers even in the twenty-first century.

The most difficult of the fictional genres to define is, in fact, the *story,* perhaps because it is eclectic, inventive, and highly personal. It comes from different periods and intellectual backgrounds, and the expression of fiction is quite different in each. As a general matter, it can be said that the genre consists of brief prose narratives structured around a central character confronted with a conflict. Stories, tightly organized, rarely develop subplots. Dialogue is integrated with action, style with point of view, imagery with setting. Brevity is thought to prevent the substantial development of more than one figure, although secondary characters are valuable for their interaction with the protagonist. The central plot is one of conflict and resolution, a simple matter in work depicting physical action, more subtle in the psychological internalization of discord, more complex in fiction showing the social implications of a moral crisis. Edgar Allan Poe provided the standard expectations for the form, arguing for the unity of all effects: narrative voice, style, plot, character, imagery, and theme. Although there has been a great deal of experimentation within the genre, and a plethora of theoretical commentary, no one has improved upon Poe's maxim.

The Early Story in America

In many ways, the earliest period of short fiction in America is the most intriguing for literary history in that it is here, in the years from 1747 to 1819, that the essential elements of a "story" are established. At first, writers had great difficulty in integrating exposition with dialogue, description with action, character depiction with plot development. Some early efforts were entirely dialogue, others exposition without speech. When characters did converse, what came out of their mouths was formal English, the language Britain considered appropriate for literary expression.

But even in these attempts, there is an improvement of narrative skill and a movement toward a realistic presentation of humanity, including the capturing of the vernacular, sometimes with startling effect. In the progression from diaries, biography, and historical anecdotes, fictional episodes gradually emerged, constituting a decidedly secular tradition. If somewhat given to melodramatic plots, early stories captured the issues of the age, a turbulent era of war and profound social and political adjustment.

Even in such exciting times, the aesthetic of fiction developed to include the use of flashbacks to cover simultaneous action in two locations, frames to enclose an internal plot, and the implementation of the epistolary technique, borrowed from the novel, to advance action and establish motivation. These devices reveal a sophistication of thinking about the form, and such methods were used to depict characters in the war, the rejection of British social norms for the fledgling society, the plight of Native Americans in the new nation, and, perhaps most dramatic of all, the suffering of African slaves. This is weighty material for a rudimentary art form, but these important matters were the central subjects of the early story.

Romanticism

The period of American Romanticism brought an impressive maturing of the genre as it progressed from its uncertain handling of narrative to highly sophisticated fiction by the end of the period in 1865. In subject as well as art, it broadened its scope and deepened its approach, and the most pressing issues of the day were addressed: women's rights, the integration of Native Americans into the developing society, the abolition of slavery, and the drift toward the inevitable Civil War.

The anonymous authorship of the earlier age made it difficult to gauge the social context of authorship, but in Romanticism it was clear that women writers were becoming an important literary force, even editing the most prestigious of magazines. At the same time, the first known African American stories began to appear. Some writers were still developing the new culture, while others, Poe among them, reached back into history for *Gothic* materials to energize their tales. Two important humor traditions emerged, *Downeast* and *Southwest,* contributing comic tales and capturing the vernacular of specific regions. The rejection of the rationalistic philosophy of the previous era and the development of *Transcendentalism* transformed assumptions of reality, which was assumed to be spiritual in a pantheistic sense, so that the deity was in nature where a sensitive intuition could communicate with it. *Symbolism* and *allegory* became the means of expressing such ideas, and Nathaniel Hawthorne emerged as a master of the mode. Perhaps the crowning achievement of the period was Herman Melville's "Benito Cereno," a work that is long enough to be called a *novella*. It was not only an artistic *tour de force* but addressed subjects of enormous concern, the importation of slaves and the definition of evil, and the result was arresting, dramatic, and haunting.

Romanticism was a vibrant literary period, filled with innovation, controversy, and impressive achievement in short fiction. Indeed, as early as 1832 the English were sufficiently fascinated with American stories that Mary Russell Mitford published three volumes of them in London. Even at this early stage, it was clear that the form in the new world had a vitality that had already impressed its European readership.

American Realism

The period of American Realism began in the cataclysmic turmoil of the Civil War and ended with the international devastation of World War I. These somber events led to a transition in thinking about the country and its place in global affairs. Gone was the optimism that inspired the Romantics to believe in the inevitable improvement of the human race, and this collapse brought with it the end of symbolism and allegory as fictional modes. Realistic stories are the stuff of everyday life, not of spiritual abstractions. Waves of immigrants more than doubled the population and brought new religions, cultures, and traditions. The major cities swelled with constant arrivals who spoke little English, had limited skills, and, initially, fared poorly in the economy. For the first time, urban poverty became a common topic, as Jacob Riis's *How the Other Half Lives* documented. Simultaneously, westward expansion beckoned as the Homestead Act promised 160 acres of land to each family who would clear it and live on it for five years. Millions did so, and their lives became the subject of powerful novels and stories. The growth of the newspaper syndicate, followed by hundreds of popular monthly magazines, created a fresh market for the story, and the writers were ready.

Beginning with the work of Bret Harte and Mark Twain, *Local Color* fiction sprung to prominence, depicting the various regions of the continent and capturing the characters, dialects, and folkways of specific locations. Realism gave readers a "slice of life," often depicting an ethical crisis at the center of the plot. *Naturalism,* a movement that presumes that there are deterministic forces beyond the control of the characters, showed the inescapable consequences of poverty, greed, lust, or fate. There was an emphasis on biological impulses inspired by the evolutionary theories of Charles Darwin. By the end of the century, women writers constituted fully half of the authors appearing from the leading publishing houses, and African American, Asian, Latino, Jewish, and Native writers were contributing important short fiction to the leading magazines. The country was maturing and changing at a rapid pace, as was short fiction. Much of the best literature of the age appeared in that genre, classics still read a century later.

The Modernist Era

The great surge of enthusiasm that energized Realism continued into the Modernist era, with yet more magazines clamoring for stories and with the institution of major literary awards to recognize achievements in the form. It was a turbulent period, begun with disillusionment and despair in the wake of the world war, relieved by the buoyant jazz age of the 1920s, crushed by the Great Depression of the 1930s, embroiled in another war even more devastating than the first one, and concluding with the social transformations of the 1950s.

Never before in American history had so much taken place in such a brief time span, and it had its impact on literature. The Lost Generation, those writers and intellectuals shocked by World War I and disgusted by prohibition and conservative social behavior at home, fled to London and then Paris, lured by an open lifestyle and cultural stimulation. So many expatriates fled to France that whole subcultures of English-language bookstores, newspapers, and taverns emerged. Ernest Hemingway was there, writing about the war and drinking at the American Bar at the Ritz Hotel, as was F. Scott Fitzgerald, living comfortably near the Opera while recording the Jazz Age. Only a few years later, back at home, John Steinbeck created his monumental work about the deprivations of the Great Depression.

Throughout the early twentieth century, there was a good deal of experimentation with story form, reaching back to the polyphonic prose of the *Imagist* movement (1914 to 1918), fiction written in accord with poetic techniques. Out of this emerged *Minimalism*, which would be an influence until the end of the century. Freudian psychology was all the rage, Marxist economic theories attracted large segments of the population, and new waves of immigration brought fresh ideas to a still-developing country. Women writers continued to rival their male counterparts for dominance in the field, and new authors of every ethnic identity emerged to contribute to the growth of what had become a major genre in American letters.

Contemporary Diversity

The contemporary era has been filled with contradictions, including the civil rights movement and race rioting in the major cities, a renewed women's movement and the resurgence of the stay-at-home mother, major advances for immigrants, greater freedom of sexual preferences, and much broader access to academic institutions. By the end of the century more than half of all graduating high school students were moving on to higher education. The nation endured the Vietnam War, the most socially disruptive military conflict in the century, but out of it came a new stream of literary energy, especially in fiction.

The broad ethnic spectrum of American writers, dominated for a century by white and African American authors, expanded to include Jewish, Asian, Native American, Latino, and Caribbean immigrants, who have brought fresh ideas to literature. Their work broadened the form of the story by experimentation and innovation, but in a sense the normative aesthetics of narrative remained in place while subject and characterization underwent revitalizing transformation. In the early years of the twenty-first century, the genre is showing signs of becoming a dominant fictional form, with scores of volumes of interlinked stories competing with traditional novels in popularity, with major magazines and publishing houses clamoring for contributions, and with distinguished new prizes being awarded every year.

Gender, Race, and American Identity

Throughout the development of short fiction in America, several central subjects dominated and served as threads linking over two centuries of ideas together. It is not insignificant that the first story, Benjamin Franklin's "The Speech of Miss Polly Baker," deals directly with the issue of gender. The social and legal codes of the day are called into question in a manner that is both serious and comic, and the light satiric tone of the piece allows it to delight at the same time as it informs.

Many of the early stories dealt with courtship, honorable conduct in marriage, and even sexuality, often with humorous results. "The Story of the Captain's Wife and an Aged Woman," which should be regarded as a classic, concerns infidelity and its consequences, an issue central to the construction of new societal standards of conduct in a time when English values had been rejected. These ideas manifest in fiction concerning people from very different backgrounds, from Lydia Maria Child's "The Indian Wife," to Frances Ellen Watkins Harper's "The Two Offers" (the first known story by an African American), to Mary Wilkins Freeman's "The Revolt of 'Mother.'" Charles Chesnutt's "The Wife of His Youth" places the theme in a special context, writing about the moral obligation of freed slaves to recognize marriages that took place prior to emancipation. Other writers, from divergent traditions, also addressed the concept: John M. Oskison depicting Native American polygamy, María Cristina Mena's cross-cultural romance, Sui Sin Far's subtle revelations of manipulation in "Mrs. Spring Fragrance." In more modern times, Ernest Hemingway wrote about the issue of abortion, Hisaye Yamamoto the idea of repressed desires, Sandra Cisneros the tragedy of rape, Yiyun Li the depth of homosexual love.

Beyond relations between the sexes, however, other dimensions of gender were also addressed, often with riveting effects, as in Willa Cather's depiction of the submerged life in "A Wagner Matinée," a subject John Steinbeck further explored in "The Chrysanthemums," as did Tillie Olson in "Help Her to Believe," later reprinted as "I Stand Here Ironing." Tim O'Brien's "The Sweetheart of the Song Tra Bong" portrays the horror of war by having a young woman as the focus of moral corruption, and Judith Ortiz Cofer, in "Nada," shows the emotional consequences of military conflict on a mother who loses a son. Gish Jen's "Who's Irish?" deals with ethnic prejudices being transcended by female friendship. These are powerful expansions of the gender theme that has played an important role in the national literature.

The subjects of racial and national identity have also been central issues from the 1770s, acknowledging the complexity of a society unique among the nations of the world. In the years after the Revolutionary War, scores of stories emerged dealing with Native Americans, for example, represented in those years as noble savages, characters of unsullied honor, dignity, and loyalty. "Adventure of a Young English Officer among the Abenakee Savages," perhaps the first work of short fiction to find original publication in North America, portrays a chief of such qualities, one who speaks the King's English but whose compassion is poignant even at a remove of more than two centuries. Other tales of the day presented similar characters, including William Richardson's "The Indians: A Tale," Lydia Maria Child's "The Indian Wife," and, late in the nineteenth century, John M. Oskison's "The Problem of Old Harjo," one of the earliest works by a member of the Cherokee nation. Late in the twentieth century, Native American writers emerged as among the most important practitioners of the story, including Leslie Marmon Silko, Louise Erdrich, Sherman Alexie, and Susan Power, all portraying Indians engaged in the struggle to remain true to their heritage and yet function in a highly technological contemporary age.

African Americans have traveled much the same road, emerging first as subjects for literature at the time of the Revolutionary War. During this era, the issue was the abolition of slavery, and there were roughly a hundred stories on this idea published before 1800, but black writers quickly began to publish stories dealing with their own issues. Beginning with Frances Ellen Watkins Harper in 1859 and soon joined by Charles Chesnutt, Alice Dunbar-Nelson, Paul Lawrence Dunbar, and Jessie Faucet, these authors made substantial contributions to the growth of short fiction throughout the Realistic movement. This expansion of authorship accelerated in the twentieth century, with Jean Toomer and Arna Bontemps contributing remarkable work in the early half of the century, as did James Baldwin, Alice Walker, and Jamaica Kincaid in the last half, among scores of others.

By the twentieth century, American writers came from so many cultural backgrounds that it is nearly impossible to separate them into discrete categories. Maria Cristina Mena was among the earliest Latino authors, and late in the century Sandra Cisneros and Judith Ortiz Cofer continued her early work with great distinction. Among Asian writers, the contribution of Sui Sin Far was renewed by a host of important new writers, Hisaye Yamamoto, Frank Chin, Amy Tan, Gish Jen, and Yiyun Li among them. Writers of Jewish descent, reaching back to the work of Anzia Yezierska, became major figures in letters, especially in the form of the novel, but Tillie Olson and Philip Roth contributed significantly to the story tradition.

It would be an egregious simplification to ignore the fact that among authors commonly identified as white, there were profound differences in background, religion, and cultural values. Region may influence language, characterization, and theme, producing contrasts between the work of William Faulkner and Ernest Hemingway, for example. Sometimes it is a rural-urban contrast, as with Hamlin Garland's tales of the middle border compared to F. Scott Fitzgerald's fiction of social striving in the tony suburbs of the major cities. Often it is a matter of literary sensibility, the deft humor of James Thurber set against the stern seriousness of Jack London's Naturalistic fiction or the poignant sensitivity of Willa Cather's representations of prairie women. The Roman Catholic assumptions of Kate Chopin's Louisiana stories or Flannery O'Connor's South contrast dramatically with those of writers from Protestant or non-Christian traditions. Collectively, however, writers of varying ethnic backgrounds, religious orientation, and countries of national origin have combined to produce the rich complexity of the American story, a tradition of tragedy, power, insight, and sensitivity that has helped to define American identity.

2

Irving and the Predecessors
of the American Story

In *The Development of the American Short Story* (1923), Fred Lewis Pattee maintains that the genre in the United States began in 1819 with Washington Irving. Pattee knew more American literature than anyone else at the time, and he is justly regarded as the great patriarch of the field, but he was only partly correct. Certainly "Rip Van Winkle" was the first such work to attract wide international attention, and its adaptation of an ancient myth to present a Catskill setting gave it a stature quite beyond any previous short narrative. As Pattee points out, Irving significantly advanced the form when he eliminated didacticism and introduced his own humor, style, and intriguing portraits of localized characters. It should also be recognized, however, that there were hundreds of brief fictional narratives before Irving, and any serious study of literary history must take them into account, however unsophisticated some aspects of the new literature might appear to modern sensibilities.

It is important that the genre in the United States began at almost precisely the same time as the country itself. Even in colonial times, there were biographical and historical reports of life in the new land, from the founding of Jamestown in 1607 to the landing of the *Mayflower* in Plymouth in 1620. These prose accounts of early hardships in the new world were recorded in diaries and journals. Of special significance is the origin of the Massachusetts Bay Colony in 1630. The proper Bostonians almost immediately founded Harvard College and established a printing press to disseminate the work of their highly educated citizens. Their initial literary productions were largely in the form of sermons, poetic meditations on scripture, and historical records, all in book form.

A newspaper was begun in 1704 and a magazine, *The Boston Gazette*, in 1719. *The New-York Weekly Journal* followed in 1733, two monthly periodicals in 1741, and several new ones were added in each subsequent decade so that there were forty by the outbreak of the Revolution, most of them based in New York, Philadelphia, or Boston. It was understandable that the magazines exhibited a regional focus in that nearly all of them were published above the Mason-Dixon line. It was not until

1797, for example, that a Southern magazine emerged, the *South-Carolina Weekly Museum* in Charleston. By the close of the century, however, scores of magazines were distributed throughout the United States providing an outlet for a popular new form of literature, short fiction.

It was predictable that life in the colonies would undergo the same kind of intellectual transformations that were taking place in Europe. In the eighteenth century, immigration to America changed: the number of new arrivals increased dramatically, doubling the population; and the people who were coming in such numbers were no longer primarily English. Germans were the largest group, but some areas of the colonies were heavily French, others Dutch, one Swedish. They brought with them new ways of thinking about the world. The narrow faith of Puritanism gradually gave way to a new emphasis on reason, including scientific methodology. In the context of the inquiries by Copernicus, Galileo, and Newton, it was no longer possible to believe in a geocentric universe. New developments in medicine, including William Harvey's discovery of the circulation of blood, changed the way the human body was regarded. James Hutton's studies demonstrated the geological evolution of the earth's surface, and other advances in biology, geology, and chemistry called into question earlier assumptions about the nature of life on earth.

In theology, the new thinking was that a religion based on the concepts of human depravity and a wrathful God could not be divinely inspired. The Deists countered by suggesting that people were fundamentally good, benevolent, caring. They should love truth and practice virtue, exhibiting kindness toward others and respecting their ability to reason. The citizens of a democratic society would discuss things logically, not gather to hear the pronouncements of the ruling class. The era of dependence upon spiritual revelation as a means to knowledge, of miracles and Biblical authority, had come to an end. Intellectual inquiry was elevated above religious authority, and each human mind was assumed to be capable of the processes of deliberation, an idea that led directly to the principle of democracy, of the participation of the people in their own governance.

The literature of Puritan New England emphasized the workings of God in the world, the extent to which His hand could be seen behind virtually every situation. In contrast, short fiction, as it emerged during the Age of Reason, was essentially a secular literature, based on the assumption that people are free to make choices about their lives and thus are responsible for their actions. Even the earliest stories focused on the foibles of all-too-human characters, caught in everyday circumstances, making decisions on the basis of their best judgment.

The Origin of the Short Story

As with the novel, the American story was influenced by developments in British literature. The origin of the genre in England is normally dated from the appearance of Daniel Defoe's "A True Relation of the Apparition of One Mrs. Veal" in 1706. When the story begins in the New World depends upon the definition of terms, but

Benjamin Franklin's "The Speech of Miss Polly Baker" is often regarded as the first work of short fiction. It was published in London in 1747 and quickly reprinted in numerous places in the colonies. A humorous narrative in the form of a dramatized monologue before a judge, it also demonstrates how speech, even when rendered in the vernacular, can be used in fiction to advance important religious, moral, and social ideas.

A marvelous social satire, "Polly Baker" contains biting irony about self-righteous magistrates and a judgmental society that, even in a Deistic age, still maintained sexual attitudes from the Puritan past. The story is, in some respects, rudimentary as a fictional narrative: For one thing, the plot is revealed in an expository preamble; Miss Baker's speech, brilliantly crafted, is nonetheless a "monologue" without dramatic interaction with those who hear it. What makes the story work is the persuasiveness of the logic, the eloquence of the rhetoric (rather beyond what might be expected of the good Polly), the indirect revelations of hypocrisy in society, and the climatic argument that convinced even a judge of her virtue. It is, in almost every sense, representative of the Age of Reason, in which rational discussion based on a systematic presentation of evidence is the noblest exercise of the human mind and spirit. That Polly, a disgraced woman, here engages a learned court in debate and emerges victorious suggests the most profound democratic themes: that gender places no parameters on the functioning of the intellect; that intelligence need not parallel social standing; that a woman punished by society might nevertheless be a loving mother worthy of respect and admiration. Nathaniel Hawthorne would later build *The Scarlet Letter* on some of these ideas, but Franklin introduced them a century earlier.

War and Romance

This unique effort aside, stories of any length did not appear from American writers until 1775, concurrent with the beginning of the Revolutionary War. Once short fiction began to be published, however, it came in a torrent, and much of it was of considerable merit. Indeed, it could be said that the story flourished in America as it did nowhere else, and it quickly became a dominant form of serious literature.

Since short fiction began at the same time as the war, many of the early stories combined military action with the more sentimental matter of romance. "The Calamities of War, and the Effects of Unbridled Passion," which appeared in 1784, handles love and war with a sprightly plot, stock characters, believable dialogue, and central motifs of historical significance. The portrait of the young soldier, Martius, serves as a model of patriotism, bravery, and compassion for the men of the age. The plot links military adventure to romance through Martius's bride, Sophia, a strong-minded and resourceful woman who accompanies her husband to the front, where he is killed in combat. Before he dies, however, he expresses compassion and forgiveness for the man who shot him, Sophia's brother. This coincidence reflects a war in which families were torn apart, with members fighting on opposing sides, and the fiction of the period emphasized reconciliation and a renewed commitment to common purpose. In this case, that endeavor for Sophia and her brother is raising an infant son, who will be brought up to emulate his father's virtues.

Stories bringing together the Revolutionary War with sentimental romance ran the risk of portraying superficial relationships, clichéd plots, and stereotyped characters. The "vile seducer" was one such character featured in a vast number of stories of seduction and abandonment. "Amelia; or, The Faithless Briton" (1787) dealt with a heroine undone by a wounded British soldier her family has nursed back to health. Amelia is rewarded for her tender mercies only by betrayal and condescension linked to English social hierarchy, one of the customs the new America was dedicated to rejecting. A poignant romance plot thus promoted the drafting of a new set of public values for the fledgling nation. Beyond the sentimental tragedy of the action, the story uses a frame with expository narration, a narrative device that would gradually disappear from the genre; it is one of the earliest narratives to use flashbacks to present simultaneous events; and a letter plays an important role in the plot, an echo of the epistolary device used in early novels.

Thomas Bellamy's "The Fatal Effects of Seduction, Exemplified in a Letter from the Reformed Edmund, to His Friend" (1789) also uses correspondence to teach a moral lesson about responsibility in sexual matters, but it is less skillful in advancing the action: many events are not portrayed but merely reported. The didactic theme is strong, however, and it plays a role in establishing a new code of conduct for the emerging nation. "Three Days after Marriage: or, the History of Ned Easy and Mrs. Manlove. A Story Founded in Fact" introduces a twist into the standard romance plot in that it is not the man who is sexually aggressive but the woman. It begins with a wedding, an interlude of prolonged consummation, and a totally exhausted husband seeking relief from his demanding wife. Although it depends largely upon comic events for its effect, the use of personified characters (Ned Easy, Mrs. Manlove) underscores the humor. Nevertheless, the portrayal of feminine passion and a light tone are used to address a serious subject in the decades after the war, the formation of new ethical codes guiding courtship and marriage.

Perhaps the best work of fiction of the period is "The Story of the Captain's Wife and an Aged Woman" by Ruri Colla, in all probability an assumed name. Although there is a supernatural element in the tale the young wife tells to explain her pregnancy to her seafaring husband, it is not certain whether any part of her account actually happened. It may be a clever ruse to cause her husband to admit his own infidelity and thus excuse her own. In any event, the frame narration is skillfully presented, the plot moves swiftly and without undue sentiment, the characters are intriguing, and few writers of the period presented the infidelity theme more adroitly.

Stories of Native Americans

One of the most common characters in the early stories is the Native American, a figure nearly always romanticized as a Noble Savage of honesty, bravery, generosity, and deeply honorable temperament. The most popular early short fiction was "Adventure of a Young English Officer among the Abenakee Savages," published just before the war in the *Royal American Magazine* in 1775. America was still a colony, and this periodical emphasized its status within the empire. Typical issues would feature the King's address to Parliament, news from London, essays of local interest, anecdotes, and the occasional fictional narrative. In this story, the plot reaches back to the hostilities of the French and Indian War of 1756 to 1764, during which an English unit has been defeated by a band of Abenakee, a tribe living in Maine and southern Quebec. An officer is about to be killed when the chief intervenes and saves his life. The Indian is a grieving father whose son was killed in combat, and he reveals that he no longer has any joy in life. Identifying with the English parent of the young officer, he wishes to spare that unknown man the pain and disillusionment he has himself suffered. After he has restored the wounded officer to health, he sends him back to England, where the soldier can give his father the joy the Indian will never have. It is a remarkable early story for its emotion and portrayal of interracial compassion, even if some of its fictional techniques are uncertain. Native American speech is rendered in formal English: the chief says to the officer, "Seest thou yon beauteous luminary, the sun in all its splendor? Does the sight of it afford thee any pleasure?" But the plot is strong, as is the characterization of the Indian father, who, significantly, is the protagonist. It is the Abenakee who bears the grief, has the conflict, undergoes psychological change, and exhibits humane compassion, treating the officer as a surrogate son and developing empathy for the young man's absent father. Little is revealed about the Englishman, who is essentially uninteresting and without conflict. It should be noted, however, in this period just before the Revolutionary War, that he is a positive British character, honorable and intelligent and a sterling representative of the realm.

A more typical story is "Indian Fidelity" from 1788, which begins not with a title but with the assertion that "the following instance of Indian fidelity, deserves to be held in perpetual remembrance." The central character is a Native American in upstate New York who promises to deliver a message from his chief to Major Schuyler. Meanwhile, the major has taken ill and returns down the river toward Albany. The messenger arrives with the letter and insists on giving it personally to him, not realizing he has left the post. The Indian walks many days to fulfill his obligation and hand the document directly to Schuyler. The narrative ends with a didactic passage, typical of the methodology of the time. Although there is not much character development, and the Indian speaks formal British English, it is notable for its portrait of a steadfast Native American and for the humanitarian message in the conclusion that urges the audience to move away from racial stereotypes.

William Richardson's "The Indians: A Tale" appeared in 1798. The status of the author, a Professor of Humanity at the University of Glasgow, lent authenticity to the account. The plot depicts a traditional captivity situation: a young woman is taken prisoner by the Hurons and grows to admire their customs and values. The story is important for its portrayal of Indians as noble and just as well as for the acceptance of Native values by the white woman: She prays to nature, to the waves of Lake Ontario, and not to the Christian god. It is also notable that the tribe is allied with the French, since most fiction portrayed a close link between indigenous peoples and the British. The story is also a good example of the difficulties writers were having with how to advance a plot. Here the action does not so much "happen" as it is reported in dialogue. For example, the protagonist gives a flashback in first person when she tells Ononthio the account of her capture. But he was there and personally witnessed the events and thus does not need to be told about them. Later, Ononthio offers some remarkably perceptive psychological observations: "Yet capricious inconsistent mortals, timid at once and presumptuous, tremble with the imagination of danger, and complain as if their sufferings were real. They create miseries to themselves, and arrogantly charge them on the Almighty. Beware, my daughter, beware of rebellion against the Almighty Spirit." The idea that people are afraid of things they imagine and thus create their own suffering is remarkable in the fiction of the eighteenth century.

Stories of Slavery and Abolition

The second most common subject is the slave experience, an issue covered from the capture of a noble person in Africa, to the voyage to America, to cruel treatment in slavery, to death. All of this is presented in the elevated language and plot devices appropriate to high drama. The white slave traders are greedy, unscrupulous, and devoid of the ethics of polite society. The black characters are invariably dignified; they act out of high purpose; in most stories they speak formal British English; and they exhibit bravery, loyalty, honesty, and integrity beyond any other characters in the literature of the period. In one instance, for example, a newly freed slave rushes back to save the child of his master from a burning building, anticipating the events of Stephen Crane's "The Monster," published at the end of the nineteenth century. A few stories attempt to render speech in dialect, one of the first early renditions of the vernacular in literature.

An "Anecdote," published in the *American Museum* in 1790, depicts not only colloquial speech but the clever and humane logic of an apparently free black man accused of the crime of purchasing stolen goods. Allowed to plead his case, and speaking in his own dialect, he persuades the judge to define the crime as buying stolen property. The protagonist then demonstrates that the master of a slave has, in effect, purchased appropriated assets as well, since children belong to their parents and were taken by the slavers and bought by the masters. The logic is inescapable, and the case is dismissed. Beyond the plot, however, this brief narrative depicts the realistic speech of the African while at the same time presenting the judge with both a moral and legal conflict. Moreover, the reasoning of the black defendant proves superior to that of the white judge, a fact not lost on a receptive audience of the time. Indeed, the Northern states came earlier than is generally recognized to abolition: Antislavery movements were established in Philadelphia in 1775 and in the 1780s in Massachusetts, Connecticut, and Rhode Island. Vermont abolished slavery outright in its constitution of 1777, and by the turn of the century New York and New Jersey had followed suit. The short narratives about abolition that appeared in this period contributed to the public understanding of one of the truly important issues of the day, leading the United States Congress to ban the importation of slaves in 1808.

A related subject was the passage to America on a slave ship, the subject of "Intrepidity of a Negro Woman," which ran in the *Massachusetts Magazine* in 1791. It told of a noble African woman who gives birth during passage to the new world and, rather than see her child subjected to the cruelty she has already experienced, she throws it overboard, a dramatic plot device that became central to later abolitionist fiction, including Harriet Beecher Stowe's *Uncle Tom's Cabin*. This account not only demonstrates the tragic costs of involuntary servitude, it does so in a plot that is dramatic and shocking. The use of a white narrator who witnessed the events establishes several points: the authenticity of the narrative; the lingering psychological effect the matter has had on him; and the sympathy white people should feel for Africans so brutally treated as to sacrifice their children out of love. This theme is poignantly presented, but there is no attempt at dialogue, extended description, or the use of other artistic devices to support the central idea.

"The Wretched Taillah: An African Story," published in the *Massachusetts Magazine* in 1792, is representative of early abolitionist stories set in Africa. The Black characters are of noble birth and high moral principle; they act out of altruistic motives in a moment of crisis; they are handsome physically, spiritually, and morally. Their word is their bond, and they assume the same high standards of everyone they meet, which puts them at a disadvantage in dealing with the slave traders who intrude into their idyllic world. This idealized portrait underscores the tragedy of their betrayal into a future of predictable misery. Obviously didactic works of this type nevertheless contribute to the development of the genre. Short fiction quickly became a vehicle for social improvement, and the direct protest against slave owners who "call themselves civilized" was a stinging indictment of some parts of the United States. The invocation of the Deity in the conclusion broadens the protest from the social realm to the spiritual, calling for divine justice where human decency seems to have failed.

The first issue of *The Weekly Magazine of Original Essays, Fugitive Pieces, and Interesting Intelligence* in 1798 carried a brief story entitled "The Negro," which offered an account of the happy life of an African warrior, his capture, and his wretched life of slavery in America. Although this plot was already standard fare, several matters are of special interest in this case. Lost love is a major issue since the slave has left behind in Africa the beloved Yoncha, whom he will never see again. This circumstance inspires the white narrator to imagine prolonged separation from his own wife. Black feelings have become equivalent to those of his people. Slave life prompts the protagonist to long for death as an escape, an idea reiterated by the narrator in a concluding didactic passage calling outright for abolition, a common theme of the stories of the Early National period. It should also be noted that the African first appears as a distinct character with individualizing personalities and desires in these early American stories.

Ultimately, the themes of these works are not only abolitionist but antiracist as well, showing the intelligence and decency of black and white people alike. The implication is that the new American society must encompass citizens of many races. Beyond abolition, the early stories dealt with tales on many other subjects, didactic narratives on "The Fatal Effects of Gaming," for example, and allegories about the fledgling United States such as "The Farmer and His Thirteen Sons" or "Story of the Thirteen Partners" that present models for cooperation among the states.

None of these subjects had a great number of early stories devoted to them, but all of them moved, in their uncertain ways, toward the realization of early storytelling that was to come in the fiction of Washington Irving. He was in England in June of 1818 when he wrote "Rip Van Winkle," the first American story after the Revolution to win international approval and sustained attention from the general reading public. The plot was not original, however, since much of it was adapted from numerous tales of legendary sleepers reaching back to the Greek legend of Epimenides, who slept in a cave for fifty-seven years, and Grimms' *Teutonic Mythology,* which includes a tale about a blacksmith who goes into the mountains and encounters some strange creatures who are lawn bowling. But the most immediate source was a tale in Otmar's *Volkesagen* (1800) about Peter Klaus, who was a goatherd from Sittendorf. In search of a lost goat, he wanders into the mountains and encounters twelve knights bowling, and he is put to the task of setting pins. When he drinks from a tankard, he falls asleep and wakes up some twenty years later, and his beard has grown a foot. Everything in the community has changed, and his daughter does not recognize him. He tells his account and is welcomed back into society.

Irving gave the plot an American setting with issues unique to the new world. During Rip's long sleep, for example, the Revolutionary War has taken place, and, in a sense, he and the country are reborn together. Rather than the drowsy society of the colonial monarchy, he finds a new democracy in which the people are energized, argumentative, and involved in the affairs of their society. Irving invented an "author" for his *Sketch Book,* Geoffrey Crayon, who has ostensibly found the account of Rip's adventure among the papers of Diedrich Knickerbocker. Irving thus placed himself at several removes from the telling of the story. Still, he gives the material his characteristic satiric humor and charm, an ironic narrative method free of didacticism, and a unique skill in drawing fascinating characters of a specific time and place. Perhaps for that reason, as well as the mythic appeal of a character fallen from time, "Rip Van Winkle" has remained popular for both scholars and general readers for nearly two centuries.

"Rip Van Winkle" did not represent the full maturity of the story form, however, a fruition that was to come in the period of Romanticism. Irving's fiction has humor, charm, and mythic fascination, but the plot lacks conflict: it has drama but not human interaction. It is more sketch than story, befitting an element of *The Sketch Book,* but it is nevertheless a truly significant advance in the development of American short fiction.

Conclusion

By the time "Rip Van Winkle" appeared in 1819, a range of important subjects had already been addressed in the early stories. The issues of courtship and sexual politics were significant because they were central to the development of a new social ethic for the emerging nation. British mores had, in a sense, been rejected, and a new set of social codes was developing. Honorable sexual dealings seemed vitally important in a deistic age that had scorned the rigid codes of Puritanism and yet wished to retain the family structure that made for an orderly society. The concern for Native Americans was natural for an immigrant people living among an indigenous population that had no desire to assimilate into white culture.

The abolition of slavery, which was a central controversy at the time of the drafting of the Articles of Confederation in 1777 and the Constitution in 1789, emerged as a central concern in literature and American life, finally erupting in Civil War in 1861. The inevitability of that war is evident even in the earliest of these stories. Even though the racial identities of the anonymous authors are not known for certain, the central humanitarian themes they offered could hardly be more forcefully stated. Short fiction about love, adventure, and heroism had already become common by 1819, and more subtle issues of conflicting moral imperatives, truth-illusion quandaries, and the quest for a new national identity had been introduced, if not fully developed.

In artistry, the story made slower strides than it did in its range of subjects. Early writers, most of them anonymous to protect their reputations, were not deft in the handling of narrative point of view, in driving plot forward to sustain interest, or in presenting believable dialogue, although some notable advances took place. Tales began to introduce complex narrative devices, including flashbacks and simultaneous action, but for the most part the telling of fiction was still rudimentary.

Although the culture still clung to the idea that elevated language was appropriate for serious literature, from Franklin onward writers experimented with rendering realistic dialects, including that of minority groups. As a general proposition, however, it should be said that by 1819 short fiction had already become a vibrant literary force, one that had produced hundreds of fictional narratives published in scores of magazines, which were beginning to flourish with the burgeoning population of the United States. Any genuine understanding of the history of fiction in America would be incomplete without an accounting of their contributions to the early short story.

Benjamin Franklin

The Speech of Miss Polly Baker

"The Speech of Miss Polly Baker" appeared in London in *The General Advertiser* in April 1747 and was quickly reprinted in numerous newspapers throughout Britain and America. Satire was extremely popular in the Age of Reason, and Benjamin Franklin's humorous attack on the social values of his day was deeply appreciated for its wit and common sense. Although not a story in the formal sense, since the action is presented in the prologue, it is a powerful utilization of dialogue, or rather monologue, to reveal the logical workings of a character's mind while capturing the dialect of the time. That Polly is a lower-class woman who argues her case with great intelligence and persuasiveness has much to say about the needless limitations on gender roles in the eighteenth century and on the assumption that social standing was an indication of inherent worth. "Polly Baker," written by a largely unknown author who was in his early forties, remains a classic work of the period and forms part of the prehistory of the development of the short story.

Benjamin Franklin, "The Speech of Miss Polly Baker," *The General Advertiser* (April 15, 1747): 1.

Before a Court of Judicature, at Connecticut near Boston in New England: where she was prosecuted the Fifth Time, for having a Bastard Child: Which influenced the Court to dispense with her Punishment, and induced one of her Judges to marry her the next day.

May it please the Honourable Bench, to indulge me in a few Words: I am a poor unhappy Woman, who have no Money to fee Lawyers to plead for me, being hard to put it to get a tolerable Living. I shall not trouble your Honours with long Speeches for I have not the Presumption to expect, that you may, by any Means, be prevailed on to deviate in your Sentence from the Law, in my Favour. All I humbly hope is, that your Honours would charitably move the Governor's Goodness on my Behalf, that my Fine may be remitted. This is the Fifth Time, Gentlemen, that I have been dragg'd before your Court on the same Account; twice I have paid heavy Fines, and twice have been brought to Publick Punishment, for want of Money to pay those Fines. This may have been agreeable to the Laws, and I don't dispute it; but since Laws are sometimes unreasonable in themselves, and therefore repealed, and others bear too hard on the Subject in particular Circumstances, and therefore there is left a Power somewhat to dispense with the Execution of them; I take the Liberty to say, That I think this Law, by which I am punished, is both unreasonable in itself, and particularly severe with regard to me, who have always lived an inoffensive Life in the Neighbourhood where I was born, and defy my Enemies (if I have any) to say I ever wrong'd Man, Woman, or Child. Abstracted from the Law, I cannot conceive (may it please your

Honours) what the Nature of my Offense is. I have brought Five fine Children into the World, at the Risque of my Life; I have maintain'd them well by my own Industry, without burthening the Township, and would have done it better, if it had not been for the heavy Charges and Fines I have paid. Can it be a Crime (in the Nature of Things I mean) to add to the Number of the King's Subjects, in a new County that really wants People? I own it, I should think it a Praise-worthy, rather than a punishable Action. I have debauched no other Woman's Husband, nor enticed any Youth; these Things I never was charg'd with, nor has any one the least Cause of Complaint against me, unless, perhaps, the Minister, or Justice, because I have had Children without being married, by which they have missed a Wedding Fee. But, can ever this be a Fault of mine? I appeal to your Honours. You are pleased to allow I don't want Sense: but I must be stupified to the last Degree, not to prefer the Honourable State of Wedlock, to the Condition I have lived in. I always was, and still am willing to enter into it; and doubt not my behaving well in it, having all the industry, Frugality, Fertility, and Skill in Oeconomy, appertaining to a good Wife's Character. I defy any Person to say, I ever refused an Offer of that Sort. On the contrary, I readily consented to the only Proposal of Marriage that ever was made me, which was when I was a Virgin; but too easily confiding in the Person's Sincerity that made it, I unhappily lost my own Honour, by trusting to his; for he got me with Child, and then forsook me. That very Person you all know; he is now become a Magistrate of this County; and I had Hopes he would have appeared this Day on the Bench, and have endeavoured to moderate the Court in my Favour; then I should have scorn'd to have mention'd it, but I must now complain of it, as unjust and unequal, That my Betrayer and Undoer, the first Cause of all my Faults and Miscarriages (if they must be deemed such) should be advanc'd to Honour and Power in the Government, that punishes my Misfortunes with Stripes and Infamy. I should be told, 'tis like, That were there no Act of Assembly in the Case, the Precepts of Religion are violated by my Transgressions. If mine, then, is a religious Offense, leave it to religious Punishments. You have already excluded me from the Comforts of your Church Communion. Is not that sufficient? You believe I have offended Heaven, and must suffer eternal Fire: Will not that be sufficient? What Need is there, then, of your additional Fines and Whipping? I own, I do not think as you do; for, if I thought what you call a Sin, was really such, I could not presumptuously commit it. But, how can it be believed, that Heaven is angry at my having Children, when to the little done by me towards it, God has been pleased to add his Divine Skill and admirable Workmanship in the Formation of their Bodies, and crown'd it, by furnishing them with rational and immortal Souls. Forgive me, Gentlemen, if I talk a little extravagantly on these Matters; I am no Divine, but if you, Gentlemen, must be making Laws, do not turn natural and useful Actions into Crimes, by your Prohibitions. But take into your wise Consideration, the great and growing Number of Batchelors in the Country, many of whom from the mean Fear of the Expences of a Family, have never sincerely and honourably courted a Woman in their Lives; and by their Manner of Living, leave unproduced (which is little better than Murder) Hundreds of their Posterity to the Thousandth Generation. Is not this a greater Offense against the Publick Good, than mine? Compel them, then, by law, either to Marriage, or to pay double the Fine of Fornication every Year. What must poor young Women do, when Custom have forbid to solicit the Men, and who cannot force themselves upon Husbands, when the Laws take no Care to provide them any; and yet severely punish them if they do their Duty without them; the Duty of the first and great Command of Nature, and of Nature's God, *Encrease and Multiply.* A Duty, from the steady Performance of which, nothing has been able to deter me; but for its Sake, I have hazarded the Loss of the Publick Esteem, and have frequently endured Publick Disgrace and Punishment; and therefore ought, in my humble Opinion, instead of a Whipping, to have a Statue erected to my Memory.

Anonymous

Adventure of a Young English Officer
among the Abenakee Savages

"Adventure of a Young English Officer among the Abenakee Savages" was reprinted many times in the eighteenth century, and it became the most popular of the early tales of Native Americans, perhaps because of its deeply humane portrayal of an Abenakee elder. It was published in the *Royal American Magazine* in 1775 when America was still a British colony, hence the sympathetic depiction of a young English soldier. The time of the action is during the French and Indian War, in which the English fought both the French forces of eastern Canada and the Indians allied with them. But the war is only the background for the drama of a grieving Indian who feels compassion for the father of his English prisoner. In historical context, the story is extraordinary for featuring an Abenakee as protagonist, the character who undergoes psychological turmoil and growth. The officer is flat, with little development, and he provides the occasion for internal struggle without participating in it. His captor is a far more interesting character, one the audience of the day would identify with and understand. The presentation of dialogue is marked by the use of formal British English for all of the characters, with no attempt to render a different dialect for the chief. Despite these problems, the emotional conclusion is handled dramatically, without expository comment, providing a model for more realistic stories to follow in the next century.

Anonymous, "Adventure of a Young English Officer among the Abenakee Savages," *Royal American Magazine* 2 (February 1775): 59–61.

During the last war in America, a band of savages having surprised and defeated a party of the English, such of those as were not actually killed on the spot had very little chance of getting away from enemies who were much more quick of foot than they, and who, pursuing them with unrelenting fury, used those whom they overtook with a barbarity almost without example, even in those countries.

A young English officer, pressed by two Savages who were making at him with uplifted hatchets, had not the least hope of escaping death, and tho't of nothing now but to sell his life as dear as he could. Just then, an old Savage, armed with a bow, drew near him, in act to pierce him with an arrow; but after taking aim at him, all on a sudden he drops his point, and runs to throw himself between the young Englishman and the two Barbarians who were going to massacre him. These drew back out of respect to the motions of the old man, who, with signs of peace, took the officer by the hand, after removing his apprehensions by friendly gestures, and carried him home with him to his hut. There he treated him with great humanity and gentleness, less like his slave than his companion. He taught him the Abenakee language, and the coarse arts in use among those people. They lived very well satisfied with each other. One only point of the old man's deportment could not but give the young officer some uneasiness; he would some times surprize the savage fixing his eyes upon him, when, after looking long and stedfastly [sic] at him, he would let fall some tears.

However, on the return of the spring the Abenakees took the field again, and proceeded in quest of the English.

The old man, who had still remains of vigour enough to bear the fatigues of war, went along with his countrymen, not forgetting to take his prisoner with him. They made a march of above two hundred leagues, through the trackless wilds and forests of that country, till at length they came within view of a plain, in which they discovered an English camp. This the old Savage showed to his young companion, at the same time eyeing him wishfully, and marking his countenance. "There (says he) are thy brothers waiting to give us battle. What sayest thou? I preserved thee from death. I have taught thee to build canoes; to make bows and arrows; to catch the deer of the forest; to wield the hatchet; with all our arts of war. What wast thou when I took thee home to my dwelling? Thy hands were as the hands of a mere child; they could serve thee but little for thy defence, and less yet for providing thee means of sustenance. Thy soul was in the dark; thou wert a stranger to all necessary knowledge. To me thou owest life, the means of life, every thing——Couldest thou then be ungrateful enough to go over to join thy countrymen, and to lift the hatchet against us?"

The young Englishman made answer that he should, it was true, have a just repugnance to the carrying arms against those of his own nation, but that he would never turn them against the Abenakees, whom, so long as he should live, he would consider as his brothers.

At this the Savage dejected his head and lifting up his hands he covered his face with them, as it were in a deep meditation. After he had remained some time in this attitude, he looked earnestly at the English officer and said to him in a tone of grief, mixed with tenderness, "Have thou a father?" "He was alive," answered the young man, "when I left my country." "Oh, how unhappy must he be," said the Savage. After a moment's pause he added, "Dost thou not know that I too was once a father? Alas! I am no longer one. No, I am no longer a father! I saw my son fall in battle. He fought by the side of me. I saw him die like a man, die covered with wounds as he fell. But I revenged him."

As he pronounced these words with the most pathetic emphasis, he shuddered; he seemed to breathe with pain, choaked [sic] with inward groans, which he was endeavoring to stifle. His eyes looked wild, but no tears came from them. Little by little the violence of his agitations ceased. He grew calm, and turning towards the east, he pointed to the rising sun, and said to the young Englishman, "Seest thou yon beauteous luminary, the sun in all its splendor? Does the sight of it afford thee any pleasure?"

"Undoubtedly," answered the officer, "who can behold so fine a sky without delight?"

"And yet to me it no longer gives any!" says the Savage. After pronouncing these few words he turned, and casting his eye on a bush in full flower, "See!" said he, "young man, does not that gay appearance of flowers give thee a sort of joy to look at it?"

"It does, indeed," replied the officer.

"And yet," says the old man, "it delights not me!" adding, with some degree of impetuosity, "Depart — haste — fly to yon camp of thy friends. Get home, that thy father may still see, with pleasure, the rising of the sun and the flowers of the spring."

Anonymous
Indian Fidelity

"Indian Fidelity," which appeared in the *Columbian Magazine* in 1788, is a simple tale with a powerful theme: that Native American people are noble, steadfast, and entirely worthy of respect. Early fiction in general offered a positive portrait of the indigenous population, often glamorizing them beyond human capability for virtue, but such depictions were part of the effort to create harmony between European immigrants and local peoples. Typical of early attempts at short stories, the narrative combines action with exposition and dialogue but arrives at a didactic conclusion, lest the main point be lost. It should be noted that there is no attempt to capture dialect: the Indian speaks British English.

Anonymous, "Indian Fidelity," *Columbian Magazine, or Monthly Miscellany* 2 (August 1788): 421-22.

The Following instance of Indian Fidelity deserves to be had in perpetual remembrance

A company of gentlemen belonging to Massachusetts and New York, who have lately purchased a large tract of land of this commonwealth (Massachusetts) lying westward of New York, and within the territories of the six nations, sent up a committee into the Indian country, this present summer, to treat with the natives about a quit claim. The Indians heard of their coming, and mistaking them for another company, who were aiming at the same purchase, sent them word to come no farther, lest they should be involved in difficulty. The gentlemen had advanced a considerable way into the Indian country, and were loath to return without effecting their design; one of them, Major Schuyler, wrote a letter to the commandant at Niagara, explaining their intentions and requesting his influence with the Indians to remove their misapprehensions. One of the Indian messengers undertook to carry the letter to Niagara and bring back an answer.

The gentlemen tarried where they were. In the meantime Major Schuyler was taken sick and was sent down the river towards Albany. The messenger returned, and the gentlemen asked him if he had got an answer. He told them (by the interpreter) that he had, but looking round said "I do not see the man to whom I promised to deliver it." They related to him the circumstance of his illness and absence but told him that they were all engaged in the same business, had one heart, and that the letter was intended for them all, and wished he would deliver it. He refused.

They consulted among themselves and offered him 50 dollars as a reward for his service and an inducement to deliver them the letter. He spurned at the proposal. They consulted again and concluded that as they were sufficiently numerous to overpower him and the others who were present they would take it by force; but first permitted the interpreter to explain to him the whole matter, the difficulty they were in, the loss of time, etc., acquainting him with their determination to have the letter. The Indian grew stern, clenched the letter in one hand, drew his knife with the other, and solemnly declared that if they should get the letter by violence he would not survive the disgrace but would plunge the weapon into his own breast. They desisted from their purpose and reasoned with him again, but he was inflexible. Then they asked him whether he was willing, after having taken so long a journey, to go a hundred miles farther for the sake of delivering the letter to Major Schuyler. He answered, "Yes, I do not value fatigue, but will never be guilty of a breach of trust." Accordingly he went and had the satisfaction of completing his engagement. The letter was favourable to their views, and they have entered into a treaty for the land.

Americans! Is this the people whom you accuse of *perfidy?* When you have removed them from their native seats, will you place in their stead a people of better principles and manners?

Anonymous
The Calamities of War and the Effects of Unbridled Passion

"The Calamities of War" illustrates one approach to the developing form of the story, a melodramatic tale of military conflict that justifies its depiction of violence and death by offering lessons to be drawn from the events. Indeed, it begins not with action or dialogue but with an intrusive didactic paragraph on the destructiveness of war. It then moves into the action involving Martius; his wife, Sophia; and her brother. In the background are the Revolutionary War, still a popular subject in the fiction of 1784; Philadelphia as the capitol of the United States; and George Washington as "our illustrious Commander in Chief." Of special interest are the pitting of close relatives against each other, a common topic a century later during the American Civil War, and a woman's ability to bear the tension and tragedy of front-line action. Sophia demonstrates, quite dramatically, that she can. The forgiveness of the young couple for her brother also suggests a paradigm for conciliation within society, for in order for the new country to move ahead its gaze had to be turned to the future rather than to the past. The final moralizing reflections, unfortunately, seem ill-suited to the events that precede them, for at issue is not so much a "passion to excess" but a devotion to the wrong cause. Artistically, the use of first person is here squandered in that there is no character development of the speaker, who seems not to have been a participant in, nor an observer of, the action depicted.

Anonymous, "The Calamities of War and the Effects of Unbridled Passion," *Boston Magazine* (February 1784): 127–29.

War, however unavoidably entered into, and humanely carried on, must from its very nature, occasion many distressing scenes, many heart-rending partings. The voice of patriotism informs us, there is something ennobling, and which raises us above the fear of death, in the idea of suffering in the cause of freedom, and dying for the public good. But when the father, husband, or son is snatched from us, our feelings will not permit us to give such speculative reasonings their full force, but we esteem ourselves peculiarly unfortunate, in being compelled to sustain so great a share of the common calamity. Such are the consequences of war considered in the best light, but when malice, rancour, and revenge add their baneful influence, when the leaden death comes aimed from the hands of a brother, or still more shocking, from that of a son, the distress must be greatly aggravated; it would be in vain to attempt to describe the horrors of such a war; it may then indeed be called the reign of the furies.

The following tale may serve to illustrate the foregoing remarks. Martius, an amiable and accomplished youth residing in the capital, came of age precisely at the time, when the port bill and the violence of the soldiery made the designs of the British Ministry plain to every jealous lover of freedom; being interrupted in his commercial views, he instantly determined to exert himself in the immediate service of his country. Having obtained a subaltern commission, he endear'd himself to our illustrious Commander in Chief, by his exertions in disciplining the irregular multitude which had flocked together at the first cry of distress, and by his active, firm and intrepid conduct displayed in several actions, was thought worthy of being promoted, by gradual advances, to the command of a troop of horse. This station at the same time that it enlarged the sphere of his duty, served to call forth those great military powers which he possessed, and there were few actions, where secrecy, firmness, and skill were displayed, in which he bore not an active part.

Thus far we have considered him in a military character, in the domestic line he was not less worthy of imitation.

Martius and Sophia had lived in the greatest intimacy from their childhood, constant companions in youth, when the passions are undisguised; a mutual tenderness had subsisted between them, which, increasing with their years, had ripened into Love. To her tall and graceful form, nature had join'd a most pleasing countenance, which with a mild blue rolling eye, and a complexion the just combination of the lily and rose, heightened with a constant smile, confirmed the truth of the assertion, that beauty and her attendant graces have fixed their residence in this capital. With the consent of their immediate connections on both sides, they were led willing victims to the altar of Hymen, and we may assert that a more accomplished and affectionate couple has never graced his temple.

Soon after their marriage his duty obliged him to join his corps, and he used every argument to persuade her to continue with her friends; he represented to her, to what shocks her feelings and delicacy would be exposed in attending a camp, that whenever he was absent from her, and especially when in action, so apprehensive would she be of danger and fearful for his safety, that her mind would be kept in a continual state of alarm. On her side, she urged that the most afflicting certainty could not be equal to that cruel state of suspence, in which at a distance from him, she must unavoidably be involved; that the thought of administering in the least to his comfort of convenience, in her mind fully over ballanced [sic] any hardships she must be exposed. "Let me accompany you," said she, "if you are fortunate it will be an agreable [sic] tour, if not, if any misfortune should befall you, I will by my conduct endeavour to prove, that the virtues of resolution and patience under sufferings are not confined to your sex." Indeed she met with many hardships to exercise her patience, but one particularly affecting, served to put her fortitude and magnanimity to the hardest proof. One day as Martius was upon his station, advanc'd from the main army, he was surprised at the sudden appearance of a body of horsemen, who by their uniform, he knew were of those men, who, from mistaken notions of loyalty, had taken up arms against their country; nor was the surprise less on their part, they had inadvertently approached nearer the outpost than they had intended, their party being small, they instantly betook themselves to flight, and Martius and his followers, urged on by a thirst for military glory, hastily pursued them; the foremost of the pursuers had almost came up with the rear of the pursued, when a young man, who appeared to be their leader, with the fury of a tyger turning upon his hunters, suddenly facing round, discharged his carbine in the breast of Martius!!

His faithful followers would have revenged the fall of their favourite chief, by the immediate death of the whole party, who were compelled to submit themselves prisoners at discretion, but our hero, with a feeble voice, charged them to abstain from violence.

They then conveyed the almost breathless body of their friend to the door of his tent, and the youth, by whom he had received the mortal wound, softened by the noble manner in which he had restrained the just indignation of his followers, and already repenting of his rash act, accompanied them.

The melancholy sight of an officer carried by two soldiers, drew the attention of Sophia, and she freely bestowed her pity upon the unfortunate sufferer, but little did she suppose that she herself was so nearly concerned in the calamity; language cannot express her feelings when her bosom friend was laid almost lifeless at her feet, and his last sigh, which was poured out upon her bosom, seem'd to rend her very heart asunder; but how was she shocked when in the person of the youth who had occasioned her distress, she recollected an only brother. He had early in life warmly espoused the cause of the British government, and with the rancor common to those whose friendship is changed into the bitterest enmity, had fought every opportunity of distressing his countrymen; the warmth of his passions had led him into the unjustifiable action which had thus involved his sister in distress, and the same ungovernable temper would now have led him to an act which could only aggravate her sufferings and entail on him everlasting ruin; viewing himself as the cause of these complicated calamities, he suddenly snatched a pistol, and would have finished his life by his own hand, but was restrained by his sister's entreaties and the influence of the surrounding multitude. Here then was an occasion for the display of female fortitude and magnanimity, to pay the tribute of her tears and sorrow to the memory of her husband; and at the same time, to avoid driving to despair, by her excessive grief, a brother, who in spite of his faults, she loved; this was a difficult task, but which by her prudence and self-command she effected.

We will not detain the readers attention of this distressing subject longer than to add, that Sophia spends her time in an agreeable retirement, instilling into the mind of an infant son, the only image of her lost Martius, the virtues which his parent so eminently possessed, and to him also her brother endeavours to supply the place of a lost father, by his instructions, and by warning him against indulging any passion to excess, as it will infallibly be a means of rendering him and his connections unhappy through life.

Anonymous
Amelia; or, The Faithless Briton.
An Original Novel, Founded upon Recent Events

"Amelia," published only four years after the end of the Revolutionary War, presents a female protagonist in a seduced and abandoned plot with an international setting. Thematically, it represents a common attitude during the years of conflict, an indictment of the morals of English society and its betrayal of an innocent and trusting America. As is standard in sentimental fiction, confidence and generosity are rewarded by deceit and rejection, and the ending can only be in death. But the action moves with good pace, and it includes a key letter, an artistic nod to the era of epistolary fiction. The dialogue is rich and realistic, a rare quality in early tales of this type. Of special interest is the use of flashbacks to present simultaneous action in two locations, a device that would not become common in the genre for over a century.

Anonymous, "Amelia, or, The Faithless Briton. An Original Novel, Founded upon Recent Events," *Columbian Magazine, or Monthly Miscellany* 1 (October 1787): 676–82; supplement to vol. 1 (October 1787): 877–80.

The revolutions of government and subversions of empire, which have swelled the theme of national historians, have, likewise, in every age, furnished anecdote to the biographer, and incident to the novelist. The objects of policy or ambition are generally, indeed, accomplished at the expense of private ease and prosperity; while the triumph of arms, like the funeral festivity of a savage tribe, serves to announce some recent calamity — the waste of prosperity, or the fall of families.

Thus, the great events of the late war which produced the separation of the British empire, and established the sovereignty of America, were chequered with scenes of private sorrow, and the success of the contending forces were alternately fatal to the peace and order of domestic life. The lamentations of the widow and the orphan mingled with the song of victory; and the sable mantle with which the hand of friendship clothed the bier of the gallant Montgomery, cast a momentary gloom upon the trophies his valour had achieved.

Though the following tale then, does not exhibit the terrible magnificence of warlike operations, or scrutinize the principles of national politics, it recites an episode that too frequently occurs in the military drama, and contains a history of female affliction, that claims, from its authenticity, at least, an interest in the feeling heart. It is the first of a series of novels, drawn from the same source, and intended for public communication through the medium of the *Columbian Magazine:* but as the author's object is merely to glean those circumstances in the progress of the revolution which the historian has neither leisure nor disposition to commemorate, and to produce, from the annals of private life, something to entertain and something to improve his readers, the occasion will yield little to hope from the applause of the public, and nothing to dread from its candor.

Horatio Blyfield was a respectable inhabitant of the state of New York. Success had rewarded his industry in trade with an ample fortune; and his mind, uncontaminated by envy and ambition, freely indulged itself in the delicious enjoyments of the father and the friend. In the former character he superintended the education of a son and daughter, left to his sole care by the death of their excellent mother; and in the latter his benevolence and counsel were uniformly exercised for the relief of the distressed, and the information of the illiterate.

His mercantile intercourse with Great-Britain afforded an early opportunity of observing the disposition of that kingdom with respect to her colonies; and his knowledge of the habits, tempers, and opinions of the American citizens furnished him with a painful anticipation of anarchy and war. The texture of his mind, indeed, was naturally calm and passive, and the ordinary effects of a life of sixty years duration, had totally eradicated all those passions which rouse men to opposition and qualify them for enterprize. When, therefore, the gauntlet was thrown upon the theatre of the new world, and the spirit of discord began to rage, Horatio, like the Roman Atticus, withdrew from public clamour to a sequestered cottage, in the interior district of Long-Island; and, consecrating the youthful ardour of his son, Honorius, to the service of his country, the fair Amelia was the only companion of his retreat.

Amelia had then attained her seventeenth year. The delicacy of her form was in unison with the mildness of her aspect, and the exquisite harmony of her soul was responsive to the symmetry of her person. The pride of parental attachment had graced her with every accomplishment that depends upon tuition; and it was the singular fortune of Amelia, to be at once the admiration of our sex, and the favourite of her own. From such a daughter Horatio could not but receive every solace of which his generous feelings were susceptible in a season of national calamity; but the din of arms that frequently interrupted the silence of the neighboring forests, and the disastrous intelligence which his son occasionally transmitted from the standard of the union, superseded the cheerful avocations of the day, and dispelled the peaceful slumbers of the night.

After a retirement of many months, on a morning fatal to the happiness of Horatio's family, the sound of artillery announced a battle, and the horsemen who were observed galloping across the grounds, proved that the scene of action could not be remote. As soon, therefore, as the tumults of hostility had subsided, Horatio advanced with his domestics, to administer comfort and assistance to the wounded, and to provide a decent interment for the mangled victims of the conflict. In traversing the deadly field, he perceived an officer, whose exhausted strength just served for the articulation of a groan, and his attention was immediately directed to the preservation of this interesting object, who alone, of the number that had fallen, yielded a hope that his compassionate exertions might be crowned with success. Having bathed, and bound up his wounds, the youthful soldier was borne to the cottage, where, in a short time, a stronger pulse, and a freer respiration, afforded a flattering presage of returning life.

Amelia, who had anxiously waited the arrival of her father, beheld, with a mixed sensation of horror and pity, the spectacle which now accompanied him. She had never before seen the semblance of death, which therefore afflicted her with all the terrors of imagination; and, notwithstanding the pallid countenance of the wounded guest, he possessed an elegance of person, which, according to the natural operations of female sensibility, added something, perhaps, to her commiseration for his misfortunes. When, however, these first impressions had passed away, the tenderness of her nature expressed itself in the most assiduous actions for his ease and accommodation, and the increasing symptoms of his recovery filled her mind with joy and exultation.

The day succeeding that on which he was introduced to the family of Horatio, his servant, who had made an ineffectual search for his body among the slain, arrived at the cottage, and discovered him to be Doliscus, the only son and heir of a noble family in England.

When Doliscus had recovered from the senseless state to which he had been reduced (chiefly, indeed, by the great effusion of blood) the first exercise of his faculties was the acknowledgement of obligation, and the profession of gratitude. To Horatio he spoke in terms of reverence and respect; and to Amelia in the more animated language of admiration, which melted at length into the gentle tone of flattery and love. But Doliscus had been reared in the school of dissipation; and, with all the qualifications which allure and captivate the female heart, he had learned to consider virtue only as an obstacle to pleasure, and beauty merely as an incentive to the gratification of passion. His experience soon enabled him to discover something in the solicitude of the artless Amelia beyond the dictates of compassion and hospitality; and, even before his wounds were closed, he conceived the infamous project of violating the purity and tranquillity of a family, to which he was indebted for the prolongation of his existence, and the restoration of his health. From that very innocence, however, which betrayed her feelings, while she was herself ignorant of their source, he anticipated the extremest difficulty and danger. To improve the evident predilection of her mind into a fixed and ardent attachment, required not, indeed, a very strenuous display of his talents and address; but the sacrifice of her honour (which an unsurmountable antipathy to the matrimonial engagements made necessary to the accomplishment of his purpose) was a task that he justly foresaw, could be only executed by the detestable agency of perfidy and fraud. With these views then, he readily accepted the solicitations of his unsuspecting host, and even contrived to protract his cure, in order to furnish a plea for his continuance at the cottage.

Amelia, when, at length, the apprehensions for his safety were removed, employed all the charms of music and conversation to dissipate the languor, which his indisposition had produced, and to prevent the melancholy with which retirement is apt to affect a disposition accustomed to the gay and busy transactions of the world. She experienced an unusual pleasure, indeed, in the discharge of these benevolent offices; for, in the company of Doliscus, she insensibly forgot the anxiety she was wont to feel for the fate of her absent brother; and the sympathy which she had hitherto extended to all the sufferers of the war, was now monopolized by a single object. Horatio's attachment to the solitude of his library afforded frequent opportunities for this infatuating intercourse, which the designing Doliscus gradually diverted from general to particular topics — from observations upon public manners and events, to insinuations of personal esteem and partiality. Amelia was incapable of deceit, and unacquainted with suspicion. The energy, but, at the same time, the respect, with which Doliscus addressed her, was grateful to her feelings; his rank and fortune entitled him to consideration, and the inestimable favours that had been conferred upon him offered a specious security for his truth and fidelity. The acknowledgment of reciprocal regard was therefore an easy acquisition, and Doliscus triumphed in the modest, but explicit avowal, before Amelia was apprized of its importance and extent. From that moment, however, he assumed a pensive and dejected carriage. He occasionally affected to start from the terrors of a deep reverie; and the vivacity of his temper, which had never yielded to the anguish of his wounds, seemed suddenly to have expired under the weight of secret and intolerable affliction. Amelia, distressed and astonished, implored an explanation of so mysterious a change in his deportment; but his reiterated sighs, which were, for a while, the only answers she received, tended equally to encrease her curiosity and her sorrow.

At length he undertook to disclose the source of his pretended wretchedness; and, having prefaced the hypocritical tale with the most solemn protestations of his love and constancy, he told the trembling Amelia that, were it even possible to disengage himself from an alliance which had been early contracted for him with a noble heiress of London, still the pride of family, and the spirit of loyalty, which governed his father's actions, would oppose a union unaccompanied by the accumulation of dignity, and formed with one whose connexions were zealous in the arduous resistance to the authority of Britain. "While he lives," added Doliscus, "it is not in my power to chuse the means of happiness — and yet, as the time approaches when it will be inconsistent with the duty and honor of a soldier to enjoy any longer the society of Amelia, how can I reflect upon my situation without anguish and despair!" The delicate frame of Amelia was agitated with the sensations which this picture had excited; and, for the first time, she became acquainted with the force of love, and the dread of separation from its object. Doliscus traced the sentiments of her heart in the silent, but certain indications of her countenance, and when tears had melted the violence of her first emotion into a soft and sympathetic grief, the treacherous suitor thus prosecuted his scheme against her peace and innocence. "But it is impossible to resolve upon perpetual misery! One thing may yet be done to change the scene, without incurring a father's resentment and reproach: — Can my Amelia consent to sacrifice a sentiment of delicacy, to ensure a life of happiness?" Her complexion brightened, and her eye inquisitively turned towards him. "The parade of public marriage," he continued, "neither adds strength or energy to the obligation; for, form is the superfluous offspring of fashion, not the result of reason. The poor peasant whose nuptial contract is only witnessed by the hallowed minister that pronounces it, is as blest as the prince who weds in all the ostentation of a court, and furnishes an additional festival to a giddy nation. My Amelia has surely no vanity to gratify with idle pageantry; and as the privacy of the marriage does not take from its sanctity, I will venture to propose — nay, look not with severity; at the neighbouring farm we may be met by the chaplain of my regiment, and love and honour shall record a union, which prudence fetters with a temporary secrecy."

Hope, fear, the sense of decorum, and the incitements of a passion, pure, but fervent, completed the painful perturbation of Amelia's heart, and, in this critical moment of her fate, deprived her of speech and recollection.

An anxious interval of silence took place; but when, at length, the power of expression returned, Amelia urged the duty which she owed to a parent, the scandal which the world imputed to clandestine marriages, and the fatal consequences that might arise from the obscurity of the transaction. But Doliscus, steady to his purpose, again deprecated the folly of pursuing the shadow in preference to the substance, of preserving fame at the expence of happiness, and of relinquishing the blessings of connubial life, for the sake of its formalities. He spoke of Horatio's inflexible integrity, which could not brook even the appearance of deception, and of his punctilious honour, which could not submit even to the appearance of intrusion upon the domestic arrangements of another, as insurmountable arguments for denying him the knowledge of their union. Finally, he described, in the warmest colouring of passion and fancy, the effects of Amelia's refusal upon the future tenour of his life, and bathing her hand with his obedient tears, practised all the arts of flattery and frenzy. The influence of love supersedes every other obligation. Amelia acknowledged its dominion, and yielded to the persuasion of the exulting Doliscus. The marriage ceremony was privately repeated; — but how will it excite the indignation of the virtuous reader, when he understands that the sacred character of the priest was personated by a soldier whom Doliscus had suborned for this iniquitous occasion! Ye spirits of seduction! whose means are the prostitution of faith, and whose end is the destruction of innocence — tremble at impending judgment, for "there is no mercy in heaven for such unheard-of crimes as these."

But a short time had elapsed after this fatal step, when the mandate of the commanding officer obliged Doliscus to prepare for joining his corps. A silent, but pungent sense of indiscretion added to the anguish which Amelia felt in the hour of separation; and not all his strong assurances of inviolable truth and attachment, with the soothing prospect of an honourable avowal of their union, could efface the melancholy impressions of her mind. The farmer, at whose house the fictitious marriage had been rehearsed, was employed to manage their future correspondence; and Doliscus, finally, left the cottage with vows of love and gratitude at his lips; but schemes of fraud and perjury in his heart. The small distance from New York, where he was quartered, rendered it easy to maintain an epistolary intercourse; which became, during its continuance, the only employment, and the only gratification of Amelia's existence. Its continuance, however, exceeded not a few weeks. Doliscus soon assumed a formal and dispassionate style, the number of his letters gradually diminished, and every allusion to that marriage, which was the last hope and consolation of Amelia, he cautiously avoided. But an event that demanded the exercise of all her fortitude, now forced itself upon Amelia's thoughts. She was pregnant; yet could neither resort for council and comfort to the father whom she had deceived, or obtain it from the lover by whom she had been seduced. In the tenderest and most delicate terms she communicated her situation to Doliscus, emphatically called upon him to rescue her reputation from obloquy, and solicitously courted his return to the cottage, or, at least, that he would disclose to Horatio the secret of their union. To prevent any accident, the farmer was prevailed upon to be the bearer of the paper which contained these sentiments, and, on his return, produced the following epistle:

> Madam,
>   The sudden death of my father will occasion me to embark for
> England to-morrow. It is not therefore possible to visit the cottage

before my departure; but you may be assured that I still entertain the warmest gratitude for the favours which were there conferred upon me by the virtuous Horatio and his amiable daughter.

Although I do not perfectly comprehend the meaning of some expressions you have employed, I perceive that you stand in need of a confidential person, to whom you may reveal the consequence of an indiscreet attachment; and from my knowledge of his probity (of which you are likewise a judge) no man seems more conveniently situated, or better calculated for that office, than the worthy farmer who has delivered your letter. To him, therefore, I have recommended you; and lest any pecuniary assistance should be necessary on this occasion, I have intrusted him with a temporary supply, directing him in which manner he may, from time to time, obtain a sum adequate to your exigencies.

The hurry of package and adieus, compels me abruptly to subscribe myself, madam, your most devoted, humble servant,

Doliscus

"Gracious God!" exclaimed Amelia, and fell senseless to the ground. For a while, a convulsive motion shook her frame, but, gradually subsiding, the flame of life seemed to be extinct, and all her terrors at an end. The poor farmer, petrified with horror and amazement, stood gazing on the scene: But the exertions of his homely spouse, at length restored Amelia to existence and despair.

It has often been observed that despondency begets boldness and enterprize; and the female heart, which is susceptible of the gentlest sentiment, is likewise capable of the noblest fortitude. Amelia perceived all the baseness of the desertion meditated by Doliscus; she foresaw all its ruinous consequences upon Horatio's peace, her own character, and the fate of the innocent being which she bore, and, wiping the useless tears from her cheek, she resolved publicly to vindicate her honour, and assert her rights. Animated then, with the important purpose, supported by the presumption of her marriage, and hoping yet to find Doliscus in New York, she immediately repaired to that city — but, alas! he was gone! This disappointment, however, did not defeat, nor could any obstacle retard the prosecution of her design: A ship that sailed the succeeding day wafted her to Britain, friendless and forlorn.

Innumerable difficulties and inconveniences were encountered by the inexperienced traveller, but they vanished before the object of her pursuit; and even her entrance into London, that chaos of clamour and dissipation, produced no other sensations than those which naturally arose from her approach to the dwelling of Doliscus.

Amelia recollected that Doliscus had often described the family residence to be situated in Grosvenor place, and the stage, in which she journeyed, stopping in the evening at a public house in Piccadilly, she determined, without delay, to pay him her unexpected and unwelcome visit. The embarrassed and anxious manner with which she enquired for his house, exposed her to unjust surmise and senseless ribaldry; but her grief rendered her incapable of observation, and her purity was superior to insult.

Doliscus had arrived about a fortnight earlier than Amelia. The title, influence, and fortune, which devolved upon him in consequence of his father's death, had swelled his youthful vanity to excess, and supplied him with a numerous retinue of flatterers and dependants. At the moment that he was listening in ecstacy to that servile crew, the victim of his arts, the deluded daughter of the man to whom he was indebted for the preservation of his life, stood trembling at his door. A gentle rap, after an awful pause of some minutes, procured her admission. Her memory recognized the features of the servant that opened the door; but it was not the valet who had attended Doliscus at the cottage — she remembered not where or when she had seen him.

After considerable solicitation the porter consented to call Doliscus from his company, and conducted Amelia into an antechamber to wait his arrival. A roar of laughter succeeded the delivery of her message, and the word *assignation,* which was repeated on all sides, seemed to renovate the wit and hilarity of the table. The gay and gallant host, inflamed with Champaign, was not displeased at the imputation, but observed that as a lady was in the cafe, it was unnecessary to apologize for a short desertion of his friends and wine.

At the sight of that lady, however, Doliscus started. Amelia's countenance was pale and haggard with fatigue and sorrow; her person was oppressed with the burthen which she now bore in its last stage, and her eye, fixed stedfastly upon him, as he entered the room, bespoke the complicated anguish and indignation of her feelings. Her aspect so changed, and her appearance so unexpected, added to the terrors of a guilty conscience, and, for a moment, Doliscus thought the visitation supernatural. But Amelia's wrongs having inspired her with courage, she boldly reproached him with his baseness and perfidy, and demanded a public and unequivocal acknowledgment of their marriage. In vain he endeavoured to soothe and divert her from her purpose; in vain to persuade her to silence and delay; his arts had lost their wonted influence, while the restoration of her injured fame and honour absorbed every faculty of her mind.

At length he assumed a different tone, a more authoritative manner. "Madam," exclaimed he. "I am not to be thus duped or controled: I have a sense of pity indeed for your indiscretion, but none for your passion: I would alleviate your afflictions, but I will not submit to your frenzy." "Wretch!" retorted Amelia, "but that I owe something to a father's peace, I should despise to call thee husband." "Husband!" cried Doliscus, with a sneer; "Husband! why truly I remember a rural masquerade, at which an honest soldier, now my humble porter, played the parson, and you the blushing bride — but, pr'ythee do not talk of husband."

This discovery only was wanting for the consummation of Amelia's misery.

It was sudden and fatal as the lightning's blast — she sunk beneath the stroke. A deadly stupor seized upon her senses, which was sometimes interrupted with a boisterous laugh, and sometimes with a nervous ejaculation.

Doliscus, unaffected by compassion or remorse, was solicitous only to employ this opportunity for Amelia's removal, and having conveyed her into a coach, a servant was directed to procure lodgings for her in some quarter of the city. She spoke not a word during the transaction, but gazing with apparent indifference upon the objects that surrounded her, she submitted to be transported to hithersoever they pleased to conduct her. After winding through a drear and dirty passage in the neighbourhood of St. Giles's, the carriage stopped at a hovel which belonged to a relation of the servant that accompanied her, and he having communicated in a short whisper the object of his visit, an old and decrepid beldam led Amelia into a damp and narrow room, whose scant and tattered furniture proved the wretchedness of its inhabitants.

A premature birth was the natural consequence of the conflict which had raged in Amelia's mind. She had entered the apartment but a few moments, when the approach of that event gave a turn to her passions, and called her drooping faculties once more into action. Without comfort, without assistance, in the hour of extreme distress (save the officious services of her antiquated host) she was delivered of a son; but the fond sensibility of the mother obtained an instantaneous superiority over every other consideration; though, alas! this solitary gratification too, continued not long; her infant expired after a languid existence of three days, serving only to increase the bitterness of Amelia's portion.

Amelia cast her eye towards heaven as the breath deserted the body of her babe; — it was not a look of supplication, for what had she to hope, or what to dread? — neither did it indicate dissatisfaction or reproach, for she had early learned the duty of reverence and resignation — but it was an awful appeal to the throne of grace, for the vindication of the act by which she had resolved to terminate her woes. A phial of laudanum, left by a charitable apothecary, who had visited her in her sickness, presented the means, and she wanted not the fortitude to employ them. Deliberately, then, pouring the baneful draught into a glass, she looked wistfully for a while upon the infant corpse that lay extended on the bed, then bending her knee, uttered, in a firm and solemn voice, the melancholy effusions of her soul. "Gracious Father: when thy justice shall pronounce upon the deed which extricates me from the calamities of the world, let thy mercy contemplate the cause that urged me to the perpetration. I have been deluded into error; but am free from guilt; I have been solicitous to preserve my innocence and honour; but am exposed to infamy and shame. The treachery of him to whom I entrusted my fate, has reduced me to despair — the declining day of him from whom I received my being, has been clouded with my indiscretions, and there is no cure left for the sorrows that consume me, but the dark and silent grave. Visit me not then, in thy wrath, oh Father! but let the excess of my sufferings in this world, expiate the crime which wafts me into the world to come — may thy mercy yield comfort to Horatio's heart, and teach Doliscus the virtue of repentance!"

She rose and lifted the glass. At that instant, a noise on the stairs attracted her attention, and a voice anxiously pronouncing — "It must be so! — nay, I will see her" — arrested the dreadful potion in its passage to her lips. "It is my Amelia!" exclaimed Horatio, as he hastily entered the room.

Amelia started, and looked for some moments intently on her father, then rushed into his arms, and anxiously concealed the shame and agony of her countenance, in that bosom, from which alone she now dreaded a reproach, or hoped for consolation. He, too, beheld with horror the scene that was presented to his view: He pressed his deluded miserable daughter to his heart, while a stream of tears ran freely down his cheeks; till, at length, his imagination, infected with the objects that surrounded him, conceived the dreadful purpose of the draught, which had fallen from Amelia's hand, and anticipated a sorrow, even beyond the extremity of his present feelings. When, however, he collected sufficient courage to resolve his fears, and it was ascertained, that the meditated act had not been perpetrated, a momentary sensation of joy illuminated his mind, like the transient appearance of the moon, amidst the gloomy horrors of a midnight storm.

When the first impressions of this mournful interview had passed away, Horatio spoke comfort to his daughter. "Come, my child, the hand of heaven, that afflicted us with worldly cares, has been stretched out to guard you from everlasting wretchedness: That Providence which proves how vain are the pursuits of this life, has bestowed upon us the means of seeking the permanent happiness of that which is to come. Cheer up, my Amelia! The errors of our conduct may expose us to the scandal of the world, but it is guilt alone which can violate the inward tranquillity of the mind." He then took her hand, and attempted to lead her to the door. "Let us withdraw from this melancholy scene, my love!" — "Look there!" said Amelia, pointing to the corpse, "Look there." "Ah!" said Horatio, in a faultering accent. "But it is the will of heaven!" "Then it is right," cried Amelia — "give the poor victim a little earth, sir! is it not sad to think of? — and I am satisfied." She now consented to quit the room, and was conveyed in a carriage to the inn, at which Horatio (who immediately returned to superintend the interment of the child) had stopped on his arrival.

It is now proper to inform the reader, that after Amelia had left the cottage, and the alarm of her elopement had spread around the neighbourhood, the farmer hastened to communicate to Horatio the transactions which he had witnessed, and the suspicions which his wife had conceived of Amelia's situation. The wretched father sickened at the tale. But it was the sentiment of compassion and not of resentment, that oppressed his soul. There are men, indeed, so abject in their subjection of the opinion of the world, that they can sacrifice natural affection to artificial pride, and doom to perpetual infamy and wretchedness a child, who might be reclaimed from error by parental admonition, or raised from despair by the fostering hand of friendship. Horatio, however, entertained a different sense: He regarded not the weakness of human virtue as an object of accusation, but liberally distinguished between the crimes and the errors of mankind; and, when he could not alleviate the afflicted, or correct the vicious, he continued to lament, but he forebore to reprobate. "My poor Amelia! How basely has her innocence been betrayed! — But I must follow her: — may be, her injuries have distracted her, and she has fled, she knows not whither! — Come! Not a moment shall be lost: I will overtake my child, wherever her sorrows may lead her; for, if I cannot procure redress for her wrongs, I will, at least, administer comfort to her miseries." Such was the language of Horatio, as soon as he could exercise the power of utterance. A few days enabled him to arrange his affairs, and having learned the route which Amelia had taken, he embarked in the first vessel for England. The peculiar object of his voyage, and the nature of his misfortunes, determined him to conceal himself from the knowledge of his friends and correspondents; and a lucky chance discovered the wretched abode of his Amelia, the very instant of his arrival in London.

"Can you tell me my good host, where Doliscus, the lord — resides?" said Horatio as he entered the inn. "Marry, that I can," replied the landlord, "his porter is just now talking with my wife, and if you will step into the next room, perhaps he will show you the way to the house." Horatio advanced towards the room door, and, upon looking through a glass pannel in the door, he beheld the identical servant that had attended Doliscus at the cottage in eager conversation with the hostess. He paused. "She is delivered; but the child is dead:" — said the servant. Horatio started; his imagination eagerly interpreted these words to have been spoken of Amelia, and he could scarcely restrain the anguish of his feelings from loud exclamation and complaint. "My lord's conscience grows unusually troublesome," continued the servant; "he has ordered me again to enquire after her health, and to provide for the funeral of the child — would she were safe in America! for, to be sure, her father is the best old man that ever lived!" "It is well!" cried Horatio. "Did you call, sir?" said the hostess, opening the door. The servant took this opportunity of withdrawing, and Horatio silently followed him at a distance, till he arrived at the habitation of Amelia, in the critical moment which enabled him to save the life he had given, and to rescue his deluded daughter from the desperate sin of suicide.

When Horatio returned to the inn, after discharging the last solemn duties to the departed infant, the landlord presented a letter to him, which a servant had just left at the bar, and asked if he was the person to whom it was addressed. As soon as Horatio had cast eye upon the superscription, he exclaimed, "why mystery is this? A letter left for my son Honorius at an inn in London." He eagerly seized the paper, and retiring into an adjoining chamber, he perused its contents with increased amazement and agitation.

Sir,

I am sensible that the injuries of which you complain, will neither admit of denial or expiation. Your note was delivered; a few minutes after, some circumstances had been communicated to me respecting the unhappy Amelia, that awakened a sentiment of remorse, and prepared me for a ready compliance with your summons. To-morrow morning, at five o'clock, I shall attend at the place which you have appointed.

Doliscus

The voice of Honorius inquiring for the letter, roused Horatio from the reverie into which its contents had plunged him. The honour of his son, the villainy of his antagonist, and Amelia's sufferings, contending with feelings of the father, and the forbearance of the christian, at last prevailed with him to suffer the hostile interview to which Doliscus had thus consented. When therefore, Honorius entered the room, and the natural expressions of tenderness and surprize were mutually exchanged, they freely discoursed of the lamentable history of Amelia, and warmly execrated that treachery which had accomplished the ruin of her peace and fame. Nor had Doliscus confined his baseness to this object. The chance of war had thrown Honorius into his power shortly after his departure from the cottage, and discovering his affinity to Amelia, the persevering hypocrite artfully insinuated to the commander in chief, that Honorius meditated an escape, and obtained an order for his imprisonment on board a frigate, which sailing suddenly for England, he was lodged upon his arrival, in the common gaol, appropriated for the confinement of American prisoners. Here it was, however, that he acquired the information of Amelia's elopement, and heard the cause to which it was imputed, from the captured master of an American vessel, who had formerly been employed in the service of Horatio, and had received the communication from the lips of his ancient patron, in the first moments of his grief. The fate which had unexpectedly led him to Britain, Honorius now regarded as the minister of revenge. He frowned away the tear which started at the recital of his sister's wrongs, as if ashamed to pity till he had redressed them; and feeling, upon this occasion, an additional motive for soliciting his freedom, he employed the interest of Horatio's name, which notwithstanding the political feuds that prevailed, was sufficient, at length, to procure his discharge upon parole. Having easily learned the abode of Doliscus, he immediately addressed that note to him, which produced the answer delivered to Horatio.

When Honorius was informed that Amelia was, at that time, beneath the same roof, he expressed an eager desire immediately to embrace his afflicted sister; but Horatio strongly represented the impropriety of an interview till the event of the assignation with Doliscus was ascertained, and it was, therefore, agreed for the present, to conceal his arrival from her knowledge.

Absorbed in the melancholy of her thoughts, Amelia had not uttered a sylla-ble since the removal from her dreary habitation, but suffered the busy atten-tions of the servants of the inn, with a listless indifference. The agitation of her mind, indeed, had hitherto rendered her insensible to the weakness of her frame; but exhausted nature, at length produced the symptoms of an approaching fever, and compelled her, reluctantly, to retire to her bed. When Horatio entered the room, the fever had considerably increased; he therefore requested the assis-tance of a neighbouring physician, who pronounced her situation to be critically dangerous. In the evening, the unusual vivacity of her eyes, the incoherence of her speech, and repeated peals of loud and vacant laughter, proved the disor-dered state of her understanding, and increased the apprehensions of her atten-dants. "A few hours will decide her fate," said the Doctor, as he left the room. "My poor Amelia!" cried Horatio, raising her hand to his lips — she looked sternly at him for a moment, then relaxing the severity of her features, she again burst into a boisterous laugh, which terminated in a long and heavy sigh, as if her spirits were exhausted with the violence of her exertions.

The task which Horatio had now to perform was difficult indeed! The virtue and fortitude of his soul could hardly sustain a conflict against the grief and passion that consumed him, while on the one hand, he beheld the distraction of his daugh-ter, and, on the other, anticipated the danger of his son. He resolved, however, to keep Amelia's indisposition a secret from Honorius, with whom he arranged the dreadful business of the morning, and, having fervently bestowed his blessing there, he returned to pass the night in prayer and watching by Amelia's side.

Honorius retired to his chamber, but not to rest. It was not, however, the danger of the approaching combat, which occasioned a moment's anxiety or re-flection; for his courage was superior to every consideration of personal safety. But that courage had hitherto been regulated by a sense of obligation consistent with the precepts of religion — he had often exerted it to deserve the glorious meed of a soldier, but he scorned to employ it for the contemptible reputation of a duellist; it had taught him to serve his country, but not to offend his God. "If there is a cause which can justify the act, is it not mine? 'Tis not a punctilious ho-nour, a visionary insult, or a petulant disposition that influences my conduct," said Honorius, as he mused upon the subject. "A sister basely tricked of her in-nocence and fame, a father ungratefully plundered of his peace and hopes, in the last stage of an honourable life, and myself (but that is little) treacherously transported to a remote inhospitable land — these are my motives; and heaven, Doliscus, be the judge between us!"

As soon as the dawn appeared, Honorius repaired to the place of appoint-ment, where a few minutes before the hour, Doliscus likewise arrived. He was attended by a friend, but perceiving his antagonist alone, he required his com-panion to withdraw to a distant spot, from which he might observe the event, and afford assistance to the vanquished party.

"Once more we meet, sir," said Doliscus, "upon the business of death; but that fortune which failed you in your country's cause, may be more propitious in your own." — "What pity it is," exclaimed Honorius, "that thou should'st be a villain, for thou art brave!" "Nay, I come to offer a more substantial revenge for the wrongs I have committed, than merely the imputation of so gross an epithet — take it, sir — it is my life." They instantly engaged. Doliscus for a while defended himself with superior address, but laying himself suddenly open to the pass of his antagonist, he received his sword in the left breast, a little below the seat of the heart!

"Nobly done," cried Doliscus as he fell, "it is the vengeance of Amelia; and oh! may it serve to expiate the crime of her betrayer." His friend, who had attentively viewed the scene, advanced, when he saw him on the ground; and, assisted by Honorius, bore him to a carriage which had been directed to attend within call. He was then conveyed to the house of an eminent surgeon, who having ordered the necessary accommodations, examined the wound, and pronounced it to be mortal. "Fly, sir," said Doliscus, turning to Honorius at this intelligence — "your country will afford you an asylum, and protect you from the consequences of my fate. I beseech you embitter not my last moments with the reflection of your danger — but bear with you to the injured Amelia, the story of my repentance, and, if you dare, ask her to forgive me." The resentments of Honorius were subdued; he presented his hand to the dying Doliscus, in whose eye a gleam of joy was kindled at the thought, but it was quickly superseded by a cold and sudden tremor; he attempted, but in vain, to speak; he seized the offered hand; he pressed it eagerly to his lips, and in the moment of that expressive action, he expired.

Honorius now hastened to inform Horatio of this fatal event, and to contrive the means of escape. But when he returned to the inn, confusion and distress were pictured on every face; a wild, but harmonious voice, occasionally broke forth into melancholy strains, and the name of Amelia was repeatedly pronounced in accents of tenderness and compassion. — "How is it, my son?" cried Horatio eagerly. "Doliscus is no more!" replied Honorius. "Would he had lived another day! I wished not the ruin of his soul." "But he repented, sir." "Then heaven be merciful!" exclaimed Horatio.

Here their conversation was interrupted by the melodious chauntings of Amelia.

> I'll have none of your flow'rs, though so blooming and sweet;
> Their scent, it may poison, and false is their hue;
> I tell you begone! for I ne'er shall forget,
> That Doliscus was lovely and treacherous too.

Honorius listened attentively to the song; it vibrated in his ear, and swelled the aching artery of his heart. "Come on!" said Horatio, leading him to Amelia's chamber. They found her sitting on the bed, with a pillow before her, over which she moved her fingers, as if playing on a harpsichord. Their entrance disturbed her for a moment, but she soon resumed her employment.

> He said and swore he lov'd me true? —
> Was it a lover's part!
> To ruin good Horatio's peace, and break
>   Amelia's heart?

A heavy sigh followed these lines, which were articulated in a wistful and sympathetic tone, and she sunk exhausted on her bed. In a few minutes, however, she started from this still and silent state, and having gazed with a wild and aching eye around the room, she uttered a loud and piercing cry — it was the awful signal of her dissolution — and her injured spirit took its everlasting flight.

The reader will excuse a minute description of the succeeding scenes. The alarm raised by the death of Doliscus compelled Honorius to quicken his departure, and he joined the standard of America a few hours before the battle of Monmouth, in which, for the service of his country, he sacrificed a life that misfortune had then taught him to consider of no other use or estimation.

As for the venerable Horatio, having carried with him to the cottage the remains of his darling child, in a melancholy solitude he consumes the time; his only business, meditation and prayer; his only recreation, a daily visit to the monument, which he has raised in commemoration of Amelia's fate; and all his consolation resting in this assurance, that whatever may be the sufferings of virtue HERE, its portion must be happiness H E R E A F T E R.

Thomas Bellamy

The Fatal Effects of Seduction, Exemplified in a Letter from the Reformed Edmund, to His Friend

Nothing is known of Thomas Bellamy, which may have been a pseudonym, a common practice in late eighteenth-century America, where the story was still morally suspect as a genre. This brief narrative from 1789 is historically notable for its use of the epistolary technique, popular in English in early novels, and for its overtly didactic theme. It is also significant for illustrating the difficulties writers had in telling stories: many of the salient events of this tale occur "off stage," including the seduction; the death of Maria, the maiden in question; and the reformation of Edmund's ethical conduct. As fiction matured as a form, these matters would have been portrayed directly rather than simply reported. But the story does present, in first person, an exaggerated narrative of the lament of Charles for what he did to Maria and the enormous price he was willing to pay to assuage his guilt.

Thomas Bellamy, "The Fatal Effects of Seduction, Exemplified in a Letter from the Reformed Edmund, to His Friend." *Gentlemen and Ladies Town and Country Magazine* 6 (June 1789): 250–51.

Our fears are completed! My poor brother, after sinking into the deepest melancholy, is now no more!

Buried in the mazy windings of a gloomy wood, stands an habitation formed only for the retreat of those, who in times long past, withdrew from all the comforts of society, to close the remnant of their days in uninterrupted retirement. I had heard the unhappy particulars of his conduct, from a gentleman, who has kindly exerted every power of argument and improved sense, to restore our lost Charles, to the deserted paths of reason. But, alas! His endeavours proved abortive; this worthy friend informs me that he has lately been witness to a scene of frenzy that must affect us all; as near as possible, receive, in his own words, the relation:

"Defeated in every attempt to restore your brother to himself and to the world, I abandoned all hopes, and had not seen him for three days; on the morning of the fourth, his old servant James, came to me, and desired I would attend his dear master, who, since my departure, had immured himself in a small building, wherein is placed an image that seems to represent the injured Maria, again alive. I immediately flew to my wretched friend. But, O God! What a scene presented itself! In a spot that seemed to forbid the approach of every social being, stood, I may say, the monument of the departed saint, who had fallen a victim to his arts; the awful solemnity of silence reigned around, disturbed at intervals by deep and piercing sighs, proceeding from the bleeding heart of the wretched man within. I approached the door and, unobserved, beheld him weeping over the waxen image of perfect beauty. I saw him rise and address that power whose afflicting hand was on him. Then, grasping a small dagger, he pronounced with sullen firmness, 'If, I am guilty of an act of desperation, forgive me heaven! Pity my delusion! For justice seems to whisper, "Strike the blow!" Sorrow clouds my days, society abandons me! I only close a life, painful to myself, and useless to mankind. Rest, Shade of Innocence, in peace! A Saint! Where I can never come: For the last time, faint resemblance of what Maria once was! I again behold thee! Farewell imperfect images of thy adored original! Whom my honour might have rendered happy, but whom my villainy destroyed.'

At this instant, the destructive weapon had usurped the seat of life, when, rapidly advancing, I plucked from his desperate hand the instrument of death! His eyes were sullenly fixed upon me, and uttering, 'Is *this* retreat invaded!' he fell on the ground bereft of life or motion. I hastened to the house, and sent James for every assistance; the afflicted faithful old man soon returned with the worthy Dr. G——, but all was over. He came only to unite his tears with mine: they fell, and bedewed the departed victim of despair.

And, now, oh! My friend! Let not the sad relation fail to make that impression on a heart, which I knew to be susceptible of those feelings which do honour to human nature. Let not our beloved friend die in vain! I invite you to my peaceful cot, where, with my loved Amanda, I pass a life of innocence and simplicity. Heavens blessed light is ushered in with prayers to that Being, who bestowed it. Our two dear infants join, as does the evening descend without, repeating the grateful talk. Moderate and unbroken slumbers succeed, sweetened by health and peace, while religion presents the happy prospect of future and unsullied felicity. Friendship without guile; friendship that feels for your eternal welfare, entreats you to come and join our train. Think of poor Charles, and then, if you hesitate a moment, in quitting the destructive path you walk in, I give you up forever! But you have a heart to feel, and I nourish every hope. Oh! May this unhappy man, with whom we have murdered many a guilty hour, prove an awful lesson! Consider, what he might have been, what he was! And, alas, what he is! Think of mysterious Providence, and reform. Expecting your presence in a few days, I remain,

> Your affectionate
> Edmund"

Anonymous
Three Days after Marriage: or, the History of Ned Easy and Mrs. Manlove. A Story Founded in Fact

"Three Days after Marriage," which appeared in the *Gentlemen and Ladies Town and Country Magazine* in 1789, is a ribald tale of matrimony and adultery with a complicated twist. In this case it is the woman who has the greater lust and capacity for libertine adventure and the husband who seeks relief from the extraordinary demands upon his sexual prowess presented by his bride. His solution to the dilemma is inventive and effective. The use of personified characters indicates from the beginning the humorous tone of the story, but the plot drives this early exploration of the switch in gender roles of the standard matrimonial narrative.

Anonymous, "Three Days after Marriage: or, the History of Ned Easy and Mrs. Manlove. A Story Founded in Fact," *Gentlemen and Ladies Town and Country Magazine* 6 (February 1789): 19–21.

It has been received as a general, and almost invariable maxim, amongst the fair sex, that *a reformed rake makes the best husband;* and almost every female fancies she has sufficient powers and attractions to work this reformation.

How often this schism in libertinage takes place, we cannot precisely determine; but, if we may judge from observation and experience, very few debauchees have been reclaimed this century, except amongst the Methodists and other Puritans, who can convert sinners by *renovation* just when they please.

Ned Easy fell directly under the description of a professed rake; he plumed himself upon having debauched more girls than the officers of the three regiments of guards: he laughed at marriage, and left cuckolds to go to heaven their own way. Such extraordinary amorous feats bespoke an uncommon athletic constitution, and, at the same time, an engaging person to recommend him: both these he possessed, with no small share of address, which a great command of words enabled him to recommend very energetically; add to this his father left him a clear estate of five hundred a year; but as his generosity kept pace with his gallantry, the dirty acres were soon mortgaged, after having opened fine prospects from his villa, which was before surrounded with useless timber, that, in his opinion, only served to give his house that *air sombre,* which impartial foreigners discover in almost every street in Paris.

Having thus conveyed the fee simple of his state, and his wants increasing with his poverty, he began seriously to think it was high time to *bee-tap* his fortune by the cobbling business of marriage — a dose he had always considered as very hard to swallow.

When his affairs took this disagreeable turn, he had just formed a connexion with a young lady of good family, and some expectancies; but not being in possession of the one thing needful, all thoughts of a connubial plan were dismissed the moment they presented themselves to his fancy. Lavinia entertained a very sincere regard for Ned, as she was not without hopes that, by perseverance and assiduity, she might remove all his objections to the conjugal vow. She presented him with her miniature picture, which he embraced with rapture, and constantly wore it pendant next his heart.

This prelude to the fair one's expected happiness was but of short duration. An execution took place in Easy's house, and he was obliged to make a retreat to the country. In this retreat he made acquaintance with Mrs. Manlove, a widow lady still in her prime, rather inclined to the *em bon point,* but not incumbured with it. She had married at eighteen for convenience, an old bachelor, who, at his death, left her in possession of fifty thousand pounds; and, she had resolved that in her next connubial alliance, she would indulge, and to her genius freely give. Ned seemed by nature destined to captivate the widow: he was the man after her own heart, every circumstance conspired mutually to promote their nuptials, which, in a decent period, took place. The buxom widow and the handsome Ned were in every one's mouth: the women envied Mrs. Manlove, the men considered Easy as their professed rival.

The marriage solemnized and consummated with mutual satisfaction, four and twenty hours of perfect felicity ensued, in which Mrs. Easy thought she had made the happiest choice in the world, and that Ned had been born and destined for her. This pleasing delirium continued all the succeeding day and the following night. But, on the third morning, Ned displayed some yawnings, and threw out a few inuendoes that separate beds would be far more commodious during the warm weather. These unexpected hints gave Mrs. Easy the alarm, and she began to upbraid her husband with want of affection, accusing him with being a hypocrite, and a traitor, who had married her only for the sake of her money; saying this she flew to her bureau, and brought forth all his letters, in which his vows of eternal love were depicted in the most forcible terms. "Here," she said, "monster, some of your base expressions."

"Most Angelic Fair,

'Till I beheld you my heart was invulnerable to the shafts of love — but you have rivetted my chains so completely, that nothing but death can free me from them."

"Again."

"Divine Arabella,

No longer doubt the sincerity of my passion, the truth of those vows which, on my knees I have so often repeated, intreating you to be inseparably mine. Vouchsafe then, most amiable of your sex, one kind thought towards a wretch, who, without thee, must remain completely miserable — but, with thee, perfectly and eternally happy."

"Once more, villain, hear thy base, thy deceitful falsehoods."

"HEAVENS! incomparable enchantress! what joy! what rapture did I feel last night, on perusing your kind billet. I almost devoured it with a thousand, and a thousand kisses. Tears involuntarily flowed as a tribute to your kindness. I considered that delectable scrip of paper as my passport to Elysium, where uninterrupted felicity eternally reigns — never — ever to be interrupted by the most transient cloud of cold indifference. Oh! what a thought was there! Forbid it beauty — Forbid it love!"

Whilst Mrs. Easy was thus giving Ned extracts from his own epistles, in the most energetic and impassioned manner, he was amusing himself, without paying her the least attention, in contemplating the charms of his late lovely mistress, in her miniature portrait. This behaviour so enraged her that she threw all the letters into the fire, then flying furiously at her husband, snatched the picture from him and trampled it under her feet.

Ned's surprize and consternation were so great at this unexpected attack, that he was deprived of the power of defending himself or his favourite portrait. After Mrs. Easy had performed this achievement, she flew out of the room, leaving him to ruminate upon his wife's behaviour, and the first fruits of connubial felicity in spring, which served him as a pretty sample of his autumnal vintage.

After recovering from his astonishment, he began to consider of the most probable means to get rid of such a wanton vixen. He was convinced that her passions were inordinate, and that she would go any lengths to gratify them. A lucky thought struck him; as revenge would certainly operate in her breast, and as she would not fail seizing the first favourable opportunity of comuting [sic] him. At this moment ensign Pleaseall entered, to congratulate his friend Easy upon his nuptials; but more particularly to borrow a cool hundred, having been broke down, the night before at the hazard table. Ned did not deny him the money; but said he had a particular favour to request of him in turn. The son of Mars, flushed with the success of his application, said he lived but to serve him. Ned then told him what he had to propose depended upon the strictest honour, and utmost secrecy. This promised and assented to, he acquainted Pleaseall with the scene which had just passed between him and his wife, and that he was resolved to be divorced from her; then added, if he would assist in bringing a separation about, he would present him with five hundred pounds, half of which was at his service that instant. The bait was too alluring in Pleaseall's present circumstances, and he assented to the proposal.

In fine the Ensign agreed to throw himself, upon every occasion, into Mrs. Easy's way, and seize the first opportunity of furnishing Ned with such testimonies of his wife's infidelity, as would produce the desired effects.

Mrs. Easy's bosom still glowed with jealousy, rage, and resentment, and she was even meditating some means of ample revenge upon her husband. Pleaseall met with her in this critical moment, and had sufficient address to carry his project into execution. Ned had planted his witnesses so effectually that they had oral as well as ocular demonstration of all that passed. We may therefore expect that the lawyers will in a short time reap the advantages of Ned's well planned project of getting rid of a *termagant wife three days after marriage.*

Ruri Colla
The Story of the Captain's Wife and an Aged Woman

In "The Captain's Wife" the pseudonymous Ruri Colla uses a traditional frame narrative to address a common problem of eighteenth-century New England, the issue of young wives married to seafaring men who are absent on long voyages. During the years of separation, there was concern for the fidelity of both of the partners in marriage, a matter that gave rise to a common tale at the time entitled "Whalers' Bastards." Ruri Colla's story presents human yearning and constancy with a great deal of fictional skill, a craftsmanship quite beyond the norm for the age. Without direct didacticism nor sentimentality, it presents a compelling plot with realistic characters confronting a familiar moral problem, one readers of the day would have understood. The suggestion of a supernatural element as one possible interpretation of the story does not diminish the verisimilitude of the conflict. Indeed, this narrative is one of the few literary creations of the period that rivals the tales of Edgar Allen Poe and Nathaniel Hawthorne for artistic sophistication and for what later became known as Romantic Ambiguity.

Ruri Colla, "The Story of the Captain's Wife and an Aged Woman," *Gentlemen and Ladies Town and Country Magazine* 6 (October 1789): 483–85; 6 (November 1789): 520–21.

There is not perhaps, in the whole system of vices any one to which human nature is more prone than this, viz. the censuring and condemning others for those very things which we practice ourselves; and tis no very uncommon thing, to see a person suffer his resentment to rise to an exceeding high pitch against his neighbor for treating him, or only a suspicion that he has treated him, in the same way that he himself has before treated that very same person, and for which he has never felt himself disposed to make any kind of satisfaction; but this must be as wrong as it is common; for notwithstanding it is wrong in A to injure B, after that B has injured A, when he has conducted in the same manner towards him, and has made him no kind of satisfaction therefor; or at least such a resentment must fit with an exceeding *ill grace* on B, and prove the exceeding criminality of his conduct, it being what he most pointedly condemns himself. People would do well to consider before they are so lavish with their censures of others, to pause a moment, and ask themselves this serious question, "do not I practice the same things myself, for which I am just going to load my neighbor with reproaches?" If this idea could be reduced to practise it would have two very good effects; one is, scandal would in a measure, cease to be the topics of conversation; the other is, many people would leave off the practice of certain vices, that they might have the opportunity of exposing the follies of others.

I have no where met with a more striking instance of the above-mentioned vice than in the following narration, which I some years ago had from a then aged clergyman of this Commonwealth, and which, though some parts of it appear of the incredible kind, yet he affirmed it to have been a fact, and that it took place while he was at his studies, before he entered on the work of the ministry, in one of the capital towns on the American Continent, where he had his place of abode; the story I believe was never before committed to print, which consideration has induced me to insert it here.

A woman of the age of about twenty one years, the wife of a sea-captain (whose husband had been absent on a voyage, a very considerable time longer than was expected he would have been gone when he left home) began to be exceedingly anxious for his safety, and as a succession of days and weeks brought her no intelligence of him, she grew quite inconsolable. Day after day, she spent her time walking down on the different wharfes, inquiring of all who had lately arrived, if they had any tydings from her husband; fruitless were all her enquiries, which fixed a solemn gloom on her countenance.

One day as she was returning from her unavailing enquiries, she met an aged woman, who looking stedfastly [sic] in her face, said, "Child what makes you appear so melancholy?" The afflicted woman told her it was the absence of her husband, whom she never expected to see more. The old woman perceiving the depth of her distress spoke smilingly to her, saying, "Child be not so troubled; your husband is alive, he is well; in time he will return in safety; follow my advice; say nothing; you meet me on that wharf this evening a little before the close of the day light, and you shall see your husband, and be returned to this place before morning."

The woman was struck with amazement at this proposal and, though she gave but a small degree of credence to the assertion, yet her desire was so great to see him, that her wishes got the better of her belief, and she promised to meet the old woman accordingly; on which they parted and the wife retired to her home.

After returning home she began to ruminate on what was past, and the whole appeared to her so strange, that she concluded to pay no regard to the appointment; yet when the time appointed came, her desires prevailed upon her to repair to the place appointed, where she no sooner arrived than she met the old woman with a half-bushel measure under her arm. "Follow me," said she, and stepping through between two stores to the backtide of the wharf, she put the half-bushel into the water, which was immediately transformed to a sail boat, with the sails all standing; the old woman taking her by the hand led her into the boat; they shoved off from the wharf, a smart breeze springing up, they soon lost sight of the town, the harbour, and the land. The consternation of the lady was such to this adventure, that she was nearly in a suspension of ideas, but according to her best judgment in about two hour's time they made an harbour, on which a fine town was situated; they landed at a wharf, and walked up a street about ten rods, when the old woman, turning up to a door, said to the lady in a low voice, "here child is your husband, in this house, go in, you will find him — meet me two hours before day, at the boat."

The lady, full of astonishment entered the house, where, to her increased surprize, she beheld her husband sitting at the table at supper. He cast his eyes upon her and viewed her with the greatest degree of attention, while eating his supper, during which, his wife observed in his hand a knife and fork, of a very curious and singular form.

Supper being finished, he arose from the table and took a seat by her, saying "woman; perhaps my conduct may appear odd, and perhaps offensive to you — but I trace in your countenance every feature of my wife; I therefore propose spending the night with you, if it is in my power to purchase the favour. I wish therefore you would inform me of your terms." The lady blushing replied, "this is a negotiation which I am totally unacquainted with, yet Sir, if you will deliver me the curious knife and fork, with which you eat your supper, I will grant you, your request." He told her the knife and fork were of insignificant value indeed — he could not hesitate of giving her one hundred times the value of them. But the knife and fork he wished to keep, on account of an intimate friend, who had made a present of them. But the woman insisted they were her only terms, which if he did not mean to comply with, she hoped he would give her no more trouble on the occasion. He, seeing she was determined, gave her the knife and fork, on which they retired.

At two or three hours before day, the husband falling asleep, she arose softly, left the house, and repaired to the boat, where she met the old woman. They entered on board, and in about two or three hours time were at the wharf from whence they first sailed, being then about half way between break of day, and the rising of the sun, from whence she returned to her own house.

About seven months from this her husband returned into port, and before he reached his house some officious friend informed him of the pregnancy of his wife.

Words are scarcely capable of conveying an idea of the rage into which he flew on this occasion. He stamped and stormed like a mad-man, swearing by all that was great or good, that he would never set his eyes on her again — that a breach of the marriage covenant — that incontinency was a crime in its nature unpardonable, and which never could be forgiven.

That he would as fast as possible make sale of his estate — leave his native country, and return no more. That he would leave the unfaithful partner of his bed, to the free and full possession of her favourite, or else satisfy himself with the heart's-blood of them both.

However, he took lodgings at a friend's house, and so vigilant was he, that his wife's inconsistent attempts to fall in his company, all proved fruitless. Day after day did she rack her inventions in fabricating schemes to bring herself into his company, but all to no kind of effect.

More than a week had transpired when she went to an uncle of his, and agreed with him to make an entertainment, and that her husband should be one of the guests, and she was to be there *incog.* until the guests had sat down at table. The guests were invited and accepted — the day arrived — the guests made their appearance, dinner was brought upon the table; those who were bidden sat down. It so happened that our sea Captain had a plate sat before him which was unaccompanied with a knife and fork. Notice was taken of it by the master of the feast, who called on a waiter to supply the Captain, when on a sudden from a door right behind him, issued his wife, and laid on his plate the remarkable knife and fork which she received of him in the *foreign port.*

The Captain seeing the knife and fork, recognized them in a moment, which summoned up nearly the whole mass of his blood into his face, and by his looks there was the utmost danger of its bursting through the skin — from the *vivid* colour of the rose, his face assumed the lifeless colour of the lilly, which again was changed to the blooming red, and thus alternately did his countenance assume different aspects.

It was some time before his confusion would admit of him speaking, at length he arose from the table (while the company neglected the plentiful provision which was made for them, to gaze upon the Captain), and turning round to his wife, he thus addressed her: "Pray, in the name of goodness, inform me where you procured this remarkable knife and fork?" "Do you wish (reply'd his wife) I should satisfy your curiosity at this time?" "Yes, by all means," (reply'd he). "Well, then," said the wife, "do you not remember that between seven and eight months ago, you in a foreign port, parted with such a knife and fork to a woman, for the sake of her company a night?" The Captain in confusion, after some hesitation, answered in the affirmative. "Well," said the wife, "that woman was no other than she who addresses you." With that she gave them a relation of the whole adventure. The Captain (whose confusion rather encreased) stood motionless for a few moments, while the company was all attention — at length he broke silence, and thus addressed her: "Dear, loving and much injured wife, with the deepest contrition I now make you my double acknowledgements, first, for the incontinence which I in my heart was actually guilty of towards you; and secondly, for my ill-usage of you for the false suspicion of a crime of — I hope you will treat me in a different way from that in which I have conducted towards you, and overlook that real guilt which I had proposed never to have acquainted you of. I am myself a guilty culprit, convicted by your own confession. I lye wholly at your mercy, and I hope you will extend that clemency towards me which I deny'd to you." The wife with a softness peculiar to herself, answered him, "Tho' your conduct to me (all things considered) has been rather hard hearted, yet I have no disposition to act the same or unfeeling part towards you — you have my hearty forgiveness, since matters are as they are; and I hope from this you will not again take it upon yourself to divorce yourself from your wife without first examining whether she is guilty or not, and never hereafter to condemn another for those practices which you follow yourself."

The company was exceedingly pleased with her answer — another seat and plate was provided — they all sat down and made a very merry as well as a very good dinner; after which they arose in good humour, each one repairing to his respective home — the Captain and his wife to theirs, and nothing more was said by either of them with regard to the unaccountable adventure of theirs.

Whether the foregoing relation was true in *fact*, or not, I pretend not to say (tho' the character of the relater was well established in the moral world) yet it strongly enforces the observations made in the foregoing part of this paper, and every one would do well to consider that while he condemns others for those things which he practices himself, he cuts the same ridiculous and dispicable [sic] figure with the Captain in the foregoing narrative; and that when at any time he has been exposing the vices of his neighbors, he should conclude with this observation, *I am the man;* and he may rest assured, that if he does not make the observation himself, those in the company will not fail to do it, if they are acquainted with him.

Anonymous

Anecdote [An Argument against the Ownership of Slaves]

"Anecdote," taken from the *American Museum* of 1790, is certainly a minor work that is nonetheless of historical importance. For one thing, the subject is the injustice of slavery, a frequent topic of conversation and political action in the abolitionist Northeast after the Revolutionary War. The brief narrative presents in dramatic form an argument that raged throughout the debates over the Articles of Confederation a decade earlier and that had just concluded with an unsettling compromise in the Constitution of the United States, ratified the year before this story appeared. The concern about the injustice of slavery would be prolonged in American history for over seventy years before it finally erupted in the Civil War. But there are more subtle touches in the anecdote as well. The first paragraph establishes an ironic tone and a posture that is undermined by the ensuing events. The attempt to render dialect is also unusual for the time, and it is here awkwardly done, although it is notable that so much of the action takes place in dialogue. The dismissal of the case by the judge is overtly didactic, attempting to teach a wide audience about the fundamental injustice of slavery. Still, such anecdotes ran almost daily in the northern newspapers and magazines.

Anonymous, "Anecdote," *American Museum* 7, no. 6 (June 1790): 332–33.

A Negro fellow being strongly suspected to have stolen goods in his possession, was taken before a certain justice of peace in Philadelphia, and charged with the offence. The fellow was so hardened as to acknowledge the fact, and, to add to his crime, had the audacity to make the following speech: "Massa justice, me know me got dem tings from Tom dere — and me tinke Tom teal dem too — but what den, massa? Dey be only a piccaninny cork-screw and a piccaninny knife — one cost sixpence and tudda a shilling — and me pay Tom for dem honestly, massa."

"A very pretty story truly — you knew they were stolen, and yet allege in excuse you paid honestly for them. I'll teach you better law than that, sirrah! Don't you know, Cesar, the receiver is as bad as the thief? You must be severely whipt, you black rascal you!"

"Very well, massa! If de black rascal be wipt for buying tolen goods, me hope de white rascal be wipt too for same ting, when me catch him, as well as Cesar."

"To be sure," rejoined his worship.

"Well den," says Cesar, "here be Tom's massa — hold him fast, constable, he buy Tom as I buy de picaninny knife and de piccaninny corkscrew. He know very well poor Tom be tolen from his old fadder and mudder, & de knife and the corkscrew have neder."

Whether it was that his worship, as well as Tom's master, were smote in the same instant with the justice or the severity of Cesar's application, we know not: but after a few minutes pause, Cesar was dismissed, and the action discharged.

Anonymous
Intrepidity of a Negro Woman

This brief anecdote ran in the *Massachusetts Magazine* in 1791, an example of the abolitionist fiction that was a dominant subject of the period. The debate over the issue had played a central role in the meetings of representatives of the thirteen states for both the Articles of Confederation and the Constitution of the United States, but the North was unable to command sufficient votes to prevail in the controversy. Nevertheless, the region went on to eradicate slavery state by state, but the antislavery forces lost none of their moral outrage over the general concept of the practice. This account is of interest not only for this dominant theme but for dramatizing the moral cost of the traffic in human beings. It is also notable for the skill of its narration, for the speaker is, by implication, a white person who was apparently present on a slave ship during the middle passage to America. He tells the incident at some later point, unable to get the memory of the horrifying details out of his head. Although there is no dialogue, which might have better rounded out the characterizations, there is strong dramatic action and an unforgettable conclusion.

Anonymous, "Intrepidity of a Negro Woman," *Massachusetts Magazine* 3 (December 1791): 728.

Some hundreds of Negroes were spread upon the deck, all of whom had their feet in irons. Their hands were disengaged because it was the hour in which their miserable nourishment was distributed to them. There did I see grief express itself in all its varied forms; some deluged the planks with their tears; others fiercely demanded vengeance from Heaven; and others, with motionless eyes, looked towards their native land, which they could no longer perceive. On one side a husband sustained his fainting wife, whose weeping infant in vain sucked the breasts which were dried up with sufferings; on another, a son, driven to raging, madness, tore out his teeth with gnawing the chains which crushed his father's limbs. Around us were planted armed murderers, with smiles on their lips and audacity on their fronts.

Nothing was wanting to complete this scene but an instance of that dumb ferocity, that last courage of despair, of which man is capable, when his soul has become steeled beneath the torments of injustice. A female Negro gave us this example. She was pregnant, and the pains of labour seized her; by a gesture she gave intimation of it to our guards; they removed her from the crowd and placed her on a sail on the after part of the vessel; without uttering a single cry, without a moan, without shedding a tear, she delivered herself. Scarcely did she perceive her infant, when she seized it, gazed on it with a fierce eye, looked around her, saw herself little observed; crawled to the edge of the ship; gave her son the first and last kiss, and precipitated herself with him into the waves. Then the alarms of disappointed avarice took the place of humanity. Urban swore, stormed, threatened the guards. They slacked sail — some sailors threw themselves into the sea. Useless efforts! The irons of the poor Negro had plunged her beyond their reach; they took up the infant, but it was dead.

Anonymous
The Wretched Taillah: An African Story

"The Wretched Taillah" was published in the *Massachusetts Magazine* in 1792 as part of the growing sentiment against slavery, a matter expressed directly by the narrator in an invocation to God to intercede and bring justice to the world. The African characters are, as was standard in the tradition, of high moral fiber and elevated social rank. They are intelligent, honorable, trusting, generous, and noble, in contrast to the disreputable slave traders who prey upon them. The individuation of the Africans personalizes the tragedy, since people of unique desires, emotions, and loyalties are forcibly separated from their families forever. Such accounts were not subtle in their didacticism, and the central protest against social and racial injustice is twice iterated directly by the narrator. The explicit invocation of God creates a religious dimension to a plot with intense dramatic action.

Anonymous, "The Wretched Taillah: An African Story," *Massachusetts Magazine* 4 (April 1792): 250–51.

On the banks of the Gambia was born the beautiful Taillah. Her shape was tall, regular, and elegant. Her soul seemed formed for the highest state of refinement, and had she been born of a different complexion, in this or any civilized country, she would have been esteemed, admired, and caressed. But, alas, how different her destiny! Strange that those who call themselves civilized, without one tear of pity, can wantonly involve in misery, souls of a more dignified nature than theirs!

Taillah was the only daughter of Tantee, prince of the fertile plains stretched along the south side of the river Gambia. Of a fierce and cruel disposition, war was his only delight and employment. The northern side of the river was possessed by Fidlao, a prince less powerful but in whose soul, although uncultivated by science, humanity and every social virtue flourished. With anguish of soul he beheld the fertile plains watered by the Gambia, still more fertilized by the heaps of his slaughtered countrymen. But overtures of peace to Tantee were in vain, while those Americans whose traffick is the human species, gladly purchased the captives. Tantee conducted his wars with vigour, and frequently with success. To defend his subjects was Fidlao's only desire. He never could think of vending any of Tantee's subjects to the Americans, whom he ever considered as the prime cause of all their desolating wars, and as the scourges of the God of his ancestors on his species. In a battle, fought by the two princes, Fidlao was defeated and his son, Tildah, the inheritor of all his father's virtues, was taken and immediately bound hands and feet, and cast into a dungeon, hung around by the curtain of darkness and despair. Not a ray of light to cheer his body, nor a faint glimmering of hope to support his drooping soul — Fidlao seeing that all was lost, in a fit of despair thrust a dagger into his breast, heaping curses on Tantee, and the inhuman purchasers of his friends and countrymen.

The next day was kept a festival by the subjects of Tantee: but to Taillah it was a day of sorrow. The generous supporters of humanity, and the defenders of liberty, were sunk into wretchedness and oblivion, while cruel barbarity, oppression, and tyranny stept forth and reaped the rewards of virtue. The ghosts of her wantonly butchered countrymen haunted her imagination; the thoughts of her father's vending the unfortunate captives to the Americans tortured her soul with anguish. The misfortunes of a young, brave, humane, and virtuous prince wrought so strongly on her feelings that she determined to effect his escape or become a sacrifice for virtue in distress. She went immediately to the keeper of the dungeon and by bribery at last gained admission to the gloomy confinement of Tildah. The prince, perceiving a ray of light from her torch, and supposing the message was for his murder, cried out with joy: "O God of the ancestors of Fidlao, I thank thee for this prospect of a speedy end to all my miseries. Death is all I desire. Tantee has seized my kingdom, and what have I left? Separate me not from my murdered friends, separate me not from the good Fidlao. Hear my prayers, O God of the ancestors of Fidlao, for I have served thee with a pure heart. I am wretched, but, not vicious." As he thus spoke, he heard these gentle accents: "Tildah, worthy Tildah, where art thou?" What was his astonishment when he saw before him the beautiful Taillah melting into tears of pity! She gave him some refreshment, unbound him, and retired, promising to return in the evening and effect his escape. She took the keeper of the dungeon to her apartment, and showing him her treasures, offered them all if he would permit the prince to depart and report that he was dead, which was daily expected to happen.

It was too tempting. He complied. She brought him from the dungeon, and they, with a trusty female servant, took a boat and fell down the river. In searching along the coast for a place of reception, they were driven to an uninhabited island. Here they resolved to fix their residence, free from the horrid scenes of war, cruelty, and devastation. Their hearts beat in perfect concord, and all was harmony and love. Each revolving year was witness of their happiness.

Four years had now elapsed since Tildah had bid adieu to misery, when, walking on the shore after a violent storm, he perceived a white person on a piece of timber. He immediately took his boat and brought him on shore. He found that he was the captain of a ship from an American port, for the express purpose of enslaving his fellow countrymen. He had ever been accustomed to consider persons of this complexion as monsters of inhumanity, whose happiness consisted in making others miserable. But he was in distress, and the heart of Tildah melted into pity. He led him to his cottage and treated him as a brother. The American tarried with Tildah a year, and had a son by the female servant. At length, being anxious to revisit his native country, he prevailed on Tildah to convey him in his boat to the *embouchure* of the Gambia, hoping there to find some American vessel. He promised Tildah, in the most sacred manner, that he would never make known the place of his retirement. Tildah returned safe to his anxious Taillah. The captain found a vessel, almost ready to sail for the West Indies, waiting to purchase only a few more slaves. This perjured villain, breaking through every bond of humanity and gratitude, informed the captain of Tildah's retirement. They sailed directly for the island and seized the noble Tildah, and the beautiful Taillah with four children, together with the female servant and her infant, and cast them into the hold of the ship. O God! Why slept thy thunder and crushed not the execrated heads of such monsters of ingratitude and inhumanity?

Anonymous
The Negro

One of the most intriguing of the abolitionist early stories, "The Negro" appeared in *The Weekly Magazine of Original Essays, Fugitive Pieces, and Interesting Intelligence* in 1798. Although there is a frame that presents an opening and closing argument for the elimination of slavery, the heart of the narrative is a first-person retrospective account of happy life in Africa. Learning of the longing of the slave for his beloved Yoncha, the white narrator is driven to reflect on his feeling for his own wife, Eliza, thus establishing a parallel set of human emotions and family values across racial lines. Essentially, the slave supplies the particulars of his life, and the narrator draws the moral lesson. Unlike other polemical fiction, this story is almost entirely dialogue, with the speech on both sides elevated and formal, with no attempt to differentiate dialects between the two men. The suggestion that white gods are stronger than African ones lends to slavery a religious sanction that rarely appears in the fiction of the day, but the loss of love and happiness, the longing for death as an escape from bondage, and the didactic conclusion all became standard fare for abolitionist short fiction in this period.

Anonymous, "The Negro," *The Weekly Magazine of Original Essays, Fugitive Pieces, and Interesting Intelligence* 1 (February 3, 1798): 11-12.

"Alas! I am very faint and very feeble," said a voice which misery seemed to have rendered almost inarticulate. They were the words of a poor negro, who, oppressed by the heat of the sun (for the day was hot and sultry), in a languid posture was enjoying a short respite from his labours. "Detested be that avarice which deals in cargoes of wretchedness and thrives by the traffic of despair!" "Perhaps," said I, "this child of sorrow has been torn from a father — a mother. Nature must have pleaded very loudly against his captivity," for I thought I could perceive the tears of affection standing in his eyes. "Or perhaps he has loved — one who returned his vows with an equal passion, and for whom his heart beat high with rapture. Perhaps he has looked forward, with eager expectation, to the days he seemed destined to pass with the companion of his youth; and now" — I thought on thee, Eliza, the partner of my life, and I endeavoured to divert my thoughts from the gloomy road they were pursuing — but in vain. My captive spoke still louder.

"I once was happy," said he. "When I lived beyond these great waters, I heard not the yells of despair; the gale rung not with the shrieks of the wretched. Our hut was in a cool valley, beneath the shade of the lofty palm-trees. My labours then were sweet, for I feared neither stripes nor master. My work in the fields provided my father with food, and he repaid with smiles the toil of his son. All was joy, all was pleasure. Strong and cheerful, I hailed the breezes of the morning; at noon I bathed in the stream; and in the evening joined the happy dance in the meadow. But now —"

"I loved, alas! the beauteous Yoncha. She was the theme of every song, the envy of surrounding virgins. For her love I fought and made two heroes bow at my feet. The maid of my heart trembled for my safety and hailed my victory with the smiles of rapture. I brought her the clustered bananas. From my hand, she said they were more luscious. For her I climbed the airy cocoa-tree and threw into her lap the milky fruit. In the chase, she nerved my arm with strength and inspired my breast with courage. Then I smiled on danger; I heeded not death. I attacked the indignant foe in his den. Though his eyes glistened with anger, I pierced him, and he bled for Yoncha. I carried home the spoils of the battle and placed them in her bower. But now, alas! she bleeds for her lost warrior. She hears not his groans. He pines in slavery; he lingers for the stroke of death. Ah, me! the deep ocean divides us. Methinks the breezes that play on the surface of the waters might waft her a sigh, or a prayer. I have often asked them, but they seem not to regard me."

"We were dancing on the green in the evening, and we dreaded not the hour of danger. But the tall ship anchored in the stream, and treachery lurked for our captivity. In vain we wept. The whites heed not the sighs of the negro. They know not the treasure I have left behind me. She may yet be safe. I recall the scenes of pleasure I partook with her, and memory adds new horrors to despair."

"I have toiled till my hand is feeble. I must, therefore, expect more lashes. The white men are very powerful, for their Gods are stronger than ours. They are not appeased by the sighs of the negro. Our labours are bitter, but they furnish a rich sweet for our masters."

And are thy sighs, wretched negro! thus served up as a repast to our luxury? Shall we not reject the drug thy sorrows have prepared? Shall we drown thy cries in the roar of the carousal, while thy tears are mantling in the bowl, and mixing it with the gall of human anguish? No! Be assured, injured captives, your sighs have been wafted to a corner of the globe where humanity seldom cries in vain. She has pleaded the cause of millions, and the period of your sorrows is fast approaching.

William Richardson
The Indians: A Tale

In 1798, William Richardson was a professor of humanities at the University of Glasgow, giving "The Indians: A Tale" an academic imprimatur rare in the literature of the period. The story is English in its formal language and in the portrayal of the central female character, Marano, and her brother Sidney, but it was published in Philadelphia and involves patently American situations and settings. It features a strong plot told by a third-person narrator, and there is a flashback to an important scene, a temporal shift that was still experimental in short fiction. Despite the stilted language, the story is of historic interest for the portrayal of Native Americans as a people who were noble and just, a staple of the captivity narrative popular at the time. Also common in the tradition was the female protagonist who adopts the values of her noble captors. The didactic conclusion was also standard fare, in part for its role in justifying the role of fiction in polite society.

William Richardson, "The Indians: A Tale," *Philadelphia Monthly Magazine; or, Universal Repository* 1 (January 1798): 23-27; 1 (February 1798): 74-77.

Marano, amiable in her sorrow, sat alone by a shelving rock. She sought in solitude to indulge the anguish of her soul. She leaned on her snowy arm. Her tresses flowed careless to the gale. The blooming beauty of her complexion was flushed with weeping. Her blue eyes were full of tender anxiety. And her bosom heaved with repeated sighs.

"When will he return!" she said, "my beloved Oneyo! The husband of my affections! How I long to behold him! Ye waves of Ontario, convey him to his native shore; restore him to his friends, restore him to my tender embrace. O when shall I behold him? When will the swift canoe come bounding over the lake, and waft the hero to his gladsome isle! Yes, thou happy isle? Thy rocks, thy resounding glades and thy forests shall then rejoice. Gladness shall be in the village. The elders shall come forth to receive him. The festival shall be prepared. Ah me! Peradventure he hath perished! Or now expires in some bloody field! Impetuous in his valour, and eager in the ardour of youth, perchance he rushes on the foe and falls!"

While Marano thus indulged her inquietude, the venerable Ononthio was drawing nigh to console her. He had perceived the uneasiness of her soul, and had followed her unobserved from the village. He was the father of Oneyo, one of the elders of the nation, revered for his wisdom, and beloved for his humanity. Temperate in his youth, and active in his old age, he was vigorous and cheerful. The furrows on his brow were not those of anxiety, but of time. His gait was stately, and his aspect gracious. He loved Marano with the affection of a father. "Be comforted," he said, "give not thy soul to despondency. The great Spirit who rides in the whirlwind, and speaks from the passing thunder, the father and governor of all things, will protect thee. But to merit his favour, be resigned to his will. It is impious to anticipate misery, and render ourselves unhappy before we are actually afflicted. Yet capricious inconsistent mortals, timid at once and presumptuous, tremble with the imagination of danger, and complain as if their sufferings were real. They create miseries to themselves, and arrogantly charge them on the Almighty. Beware, my daughter, beware of rebellion against the Almighty Spirit. If you repine inconsiderately, if you complain without actual cause, you rebel. He hath commanded us to be happy, he is ever offended with our disobedience; but if we encourage groundless anxiety, we disobey. By destroying your own tranquility, you are no less an enemy to the general system of happiness he hath ordained, than if you injured the peace of another. Be comforted. Oneyo may soon return loaded with the spoils of the Briton, and extolled by the gallant warriors of France."

"To see my husband return in safety," she replied, "is the sum of my desires. To see him loaded with the spoils of the Briton will be no addition to my joy." The Indian seemed astonished. "Have you forgotten," she continued, "that I myself am a Briton? That I was carried violently from my father's house, when the Outagami ravaged our land, and carried terror to the gates of Albany? My parents perished. I was yet a child; but I remember the bloody carnage. My brother of riper years was rescued; but I became the prey of their fury. Since that time, many years are elapsed; yet at the name of Briton, my bosom glows with peculiar transport."

"I fondly imagined," answered the Indian, "that you loved us. We named you after the manner of our tribe. But your affections are estranged, and you languish for the land of your fathers. I called you my daughter; but, Marano, you would leave me." Uttering these words, he looked tenderly upon her. "You would leave me," he repeated, and a tear rose in his eye. Marano was affected. She clasped his hand and pressed it to her rosy lips. "No, I will never leave thee. My heart is thine and my beloved Oneyo's. I revere thee. Can I forget my compassion? Can I forget the dreadful day when the Outagami, in an assembly of their nation, decreed me a sacrifice to their god Areskoui? You was [were] present at an embassy from your people. Oneyo in the bloom of early years had accompanied his father. He was beside you. He sighed when he beheld me weeping. Alas! I was feeble, friendless, and beset with foes. Oneyo intreated you to relive me. Your own heart was affected, you interposed in [on] my behalf, you redeemed me and called me your's. Oneyo hastened to my deliverance, he loosened my fetters, and clasped me to his breast. Our affection grew with our years. You beheld it with kind indulgence, and ratified our wishes with your consent. I have heard of European refinements, of costly raiment and lofty palaces; yet to me the simplicity of these rocks and forests seems far more delightful. But if Oneyo returns not, I am undone. Many moons have arisen since with the flower of our tribe he departed. The matrons are already wailing for their sons. Oneyo, alas! is impetuous, and the warriors of Albion are undaunted. The blood of their foes has already tinged the Ohio; Canada trembled at their approach, and may ere now have become the prize of their valour. Ah me! if thy son hath fallen, grief will subdue thee; I know the tenderness of thine affection, it will pull thee down to the grave. Who then will be a comforter to me? Who will be my friend? Among a strange people I have no father to protect me, no brother to counsel and give me aid."

Ononthio was about to reply, when an Indian from the village accosted them. He told them with a sorrowful aspect, that the hopes of their tribe were blasted, for that some Indians of a neighboring nation, having returned from Canada, brought certain intelligence of the total overthrow of their friends; that they had with difficulty escaped; that Oneyo was seen fierce and intrepid in the heat of the battle; that he was surrounded by the foe, and must have fallen a victim to their fury.

Marano was overwhelmed. Ononthio heaved a sigh. But the hapless condition of his daughter, and the desire of yielding her consolation, suspended and relieved his sorrow. "If my son hath fallen," he said, "he hath fallen as became a warrior. His praise shall be preserved by his kindred, and descend to posterity in the warsong. His name shall terrify the European, when the chieftains of future times, rushing fierce from their forest, shall surround his habitations at midnight, and raise the yell of death in his ear. Oneyo shall not die unrevenged."

"He shall not," interrupted the Indian. "The messengers of our misfortunes hovered, after the discomfiture of their allies, around the walls of Quebec. They surprised a party of the foe; they have brought captives to our island. The elders of the nation are now assembled; they have doomed them a sacrifice to the memory of the dead; and defer their execution only till your arrival." "Alas," said Marano, "the sacrifice of a captive will afford me small consolation. Will the death of the foe restore life to my husband? Or heal his ghastly wounds? Or re-animate his breathless bosom? Leave me to my woe. Leave me to wail on these lonely mountains. Here I will not long be a sojourner. I will away to my love. I will meet him beyond the deserts, in some blissful valley where no bloody foe shall invade us. Leave me to my sorrow, for I will not live." She entreated in vain: The Indian was urgent, and Ononthio seconded his solicitation.

That nation of Indians of which Oneyo was a leader, inhabited an island in the lake Ontario. They were therefore no sooner informed of the death of Oneyo and of their brethren, than they abandoned themselves to loud lamentation. The matrons, with rent garments and disheveled tresses, ran forth into the fields, and filled the air with their wailing. They then crowded around the captives, whom, in the bitterness of their woe, they loaded with keen invectives. The elders were assembled: The boiling caldron into which the victims, after suffering every species of torment, were to be precipitated, was suspended over a raging fire; the knives, tomahawks, and other implements of cruelty, were exhibited in dreadful array; and the prisoners, loaded with heavy fetters, were conducted to the place of sacrifice.

Though Marano was deeply afflicted, the screams of the Indians, and the horrid preparations of torture, drew her attention to the prisoners. She regarded them with an eye of pity. Their leader, in the prime of youth, was comely, vigorous, and graceful. The sullenness of undaunted and indignant valour was pourtrayed by nature in his fearless aspect. His eye full of ardour and invincible firmness surveyed the preparations of death with indifference, and shot defiance on the foe. His followers, though valiant, seemed incapable of the same obstinate resolution; their features betrayed symptoms of dismay; but turning to their leader, they were struck with his unshaken boldness; they resumed their native courage, and armed their minds with becoming fortitude. Marano sighed. The sense of her own misfortune was for a moment suspended. "Peradventure," said she in her soul, "this valiant youth, like Oneyo, may be lamented. Some tender maiden to whom his faith has been plighted, may now languish for his return. Some aged parent, whose infirmities he relieved and supported, may be sighing anxious for his safety. Or some orphan sister, helpless and forsaken like me, may by his death be made desolate." She then reflected on her own condition, and on the variety of her misfortunes. Carried into captivity in her early years, she was a stranger to her people, and to her kindred. Her husband no longer existed: And he who had been to her as a father, overcome by age and calamity, was now declining into the grave. Yet, alive to compassion, she was moved for the unhappy victims. She admired the magnanimity of their leader, and, in regarding him, she felt unusual emotions, and a pang that she could not express. She longed to accost him. He was of her nation! Could she behold him perish, and not endeavour to save him! Could she behold him tortured and not shed a tear for his suffering! Meantime one of the elders of the nation made a signal to the multitude. Immediate silence ensued. Then, with a look of stern severity, he thus addressed himself to the captive! "The caldron boils, the axe is sharpened. Be prepared for torture and painful death. The spirit of the deceased is yet among us: He lingers on the mountains, or hovers amid the winds. He expects a sacrifice, and shall not chide our delay. Have you a parent or a friend? They shall never behold thee. Prepare for torture and painful death." "Inflict your tortures," he replied: "my soul contemns them. I have no parents to lament for Sidney. In Albany they were massacred, massacred by inhuman Indians. I had a sister — I lost her. She was carried into captivity, and became the victim of your savage fury. I have friends; but they are fearless, for they are Britons. Inflict your tortures; my soul contemns them; but remember, the day of vengeance shall overtake you."

Marano was astonished. Of Albany! Reft of his parents by the sword! And of a sister! Suffice it to say, he was her brother. Mutual was their amazement, their affection mutual. She fell on his throbbing breast. He received her into his arms. His soul was softened. Marano for a time was speechless. At length weeping, and in broken accents, "And have I found thee! A brother to solace and support me! Who will soothe me with sympathising tenderness! Who will guide me through the weary wilderness of my sorrow! Who will be to me as a parent! I was desolate and forlorn; my soul languished and was afflicted; but now I will endure with patience." Then turning to the astonished multitude, "He is my brother! Born of the same parents. If I have ever merited your favour, O save him from destruction." They were deeply affected. "Be not dismayed," said Ononthio. He spoke with the consent of the elders. "Be not dismayed. The brother of Marano shall be to us as Oneyo." Then addressing himself with an air of dignity to the stranger, "Young man, I have lost a son, Marano a husband, and our nation a gallant warrior. He was slain by the people of your land, and we were desirous of gratifying his spirit before it passes the mountains, by offering a sacrifice to its memory. But you are the brother of Marano; by her intercession we have changed our design, and adopt you into our tribe. Be a brother to our people, and to me a son. Supply the place of the dead; and as you possess his valour, and steady boldness, may you inherit his renown." So saying, he presented to him the Kalumet of peace, and a girdle of Wampum.

Meantime the arrival of some canoes, filled with armed warriors, attracted the notice of the assembly. They were transported with extacy and surprise when they descried the ensign of their nation, and recognized some of their brethren whom they imagined slain. The hopes of Marano were revived. She enquired eagerly for Oneyo. "He perished," answered an Indian. She grew pale, her voice faultered, faint and speechless, she fell back on the throbbing breast of

Ononthio. "He perished," continued the Indian, "and with him the prime of our warriors. The armies of France and Briton were marshalled beneath the walls of Quebec. Direful was the havock of battle. The earth trembled with the shock of the onset. The air was tortured with repeated peals. The commanders of both armies were slain. Their fall was glorious, for their souls were undaunted. Resentment inflamed the combatants. Keen and obstinate was the encounter. Albion at length prevailed. Her sons, like a rapid torrent, overthrew the ranks of their adversaries. We counselled Oneyo to retire. Raging against the foe, and performing feats of amazing valour, we saw him environed beyond all hopes of retreat. We saw the impetuosity of a youthful warrior, who brandished a bloody sword, rushing on to destroy him. We hastened from the field of death. We tarried sometime in the adjacent forests, and observed the progress of the foe. The walls of our allies were overthrown. The sword of Albion will pursue us, and our shield, our gallant warriors, our Oneyo, is no more."

This melancholy recital filled the audience with lamentation; but their sorrow was interrupted by the sudden astonishment of the narrator. Casting his eye accidentally on the Briton, "Seize him, tear him," he exclaimed; "his was the lifted sword I beheld! It was he cleft the breast of our chieftain! It was he that destroyed him."

The resentment of the assembly was again inflamed. "I am innocent of his blood," said the captive. But his declaration, and the entreaties of Ononthio in his behalf, were lost in furious screams and invectives. They dragged him again to the place of sacrifice. Marano, distracted with contending woes, "Spare him! spare him!" exclaimed; "he is my brother," fixing her eyes on him with a look of exquisite anguish, "whose hands are red with the blood of my husband! and was there none but thee to destroy him." "Tear him!" exclaimed the multitude. Marano clasped him to her bosom, and turning to the outrageous and menacing croud, with a wild and frantic demeanour, "Bloody, bloody, though he be, I will defend him or perish! Let the same javelin transfix us both! Smite, and our kindred gore shall be mingled." The transcendant greatness of her calamity, who had lost a husband by the hand of a brother, and the resistless energy of her features, expressive of woe, tenderness, and despair, awed the violence of the assembly, and disposed them to pity. Ononthio took advantage of the change. He waved his hand with parental love and authority. His hoary locks gave dignity to his gesture. The usual benignity of his countenance was softened with sorrow. He spoke the language of his soul, and was eloquent; spoke the language of feeling, and was persuasive. They listened to him with profound veneration, were moved, and deferred the sacrifice. He then comforted Marano, and conveyed the captives to a place of security. When they were apart from the multitude, "Tell me," said he to the Briton, "are you guiltless of the death of my son!" "I know not," he replied, for he had resumed the pride of indignant courage, "I know not whom I may have slain. I drew my sword against the foes of my country, and I am not answerable for the blood I have spilt." "Young man," said Ononthio, full of solicitude and parental tenderness, "O reflect on a father's feelings. I had an only son. He was valiant. He was the prop and solace of my old age: if he hath gone down to darkness and the grave, I have no longer any joy in existence. But if he lives, and lives by thy clemency, the prayers of an old man shall implore blessings upon thee, and the Great Spirit shall reward thee." While he was yet speaking a tear rose in his eye, his voice faultered, he sighed, "O tell me if my son survives."

"I slew him not," he replied. "I know not that I slew thy son. To his name and quality I was a stranger. In the heat of the encounter a gallant Indian assailed me. He was tired and exhausted. I disarmed him, and my sword was lifted against his life, 'Briton,' said he, with a resolute tone, 'think not that death dismays me. I have braved perils and the sword. I am not a suppliant for myself. I have an aged parent whose life depends on mine: the wife of my bosom is a stranger among my people and I alone can protect her.' Generous youth, I replied, go comfort and protect thy friends. I sent him forthwith from the field. I never inquired into his condition, for in preserving him I obeyed my heart." Marano and Ononthio were overjoyed. But reflecting that many days had elapsed since the discomfiture of their allies, and that hitherto they had received no intelligence of Oneyo, their joy suffered abatement.

Meantime Ononthio counselled his daughter to conduct the strangers to a distant retreat, and preserve them there, till, by his influence and authority, he had appeased the violence of his brethren. "Judge not unfavourably of my nation," said he, "from this instance of impetuosity. They follow the immediate impulse of nature, and are often extravagant. But the vehemence of passion will soon abate, and reason will assume her authority. You see nature unrestrained but not perverted; luxuriant, but not corrupt. My brethren are wrathful; but to latent or lasting enmity they are utter strangers."

It was already night. The Indians were dispersed to their hamlets. The sky was calm, and unclouded. The full orbed moon, in serene and solemn majesty, arose in the east. Her beams were reflected in a blaze of silver radiance from the smooth and untroubled breast of the lake. The grey hills and awful forests were solitary and silent. No noise was heard, save the roaring of a distant cascade, save the interrupted wailings of matrons who lamented the untimely deaths of their sons. Marano, with the captives issuing unperceived from the village, pursued their way along the silent shore, till they arrived at a narrow unfrequented recess. It was open to the lake, bounded on either side by abrupt and shelving precipices, arrayed with living verdure, and parted by a winding rivulet. A venerable oak overshadowed the fountain and rendered the scene more solemn. The other captives were overcome with fatigue, and finding some withered leaves in an adjoining cavern, they indulged themselves in repose. Marano conversed long with her brother, she poured out her soul in his sympathizing bosom, she was comforted and relieved. While she leaned on his breast, while his arm was folded gently around her, a balmy slumber surprised them. Their features, even in sleep, preserved the character of their souls. A smile played innocent on the lips of Marano, her countenance was ineffably tender, and her tresses lay careless on her snowy bosom. The features of Sidney, of a bolder and more manly expression, seemed full of benignity and complacence. Calm and unruffled was their repose; they enjoyed the happy visions of innocence, and dreamed not of impending danger.

The moon, in unrivalled glory, had now attained her meridian, when the intermitting noise of rowers came slowly along the lake. A canoe soon appeared, and the dipping oars, arising at intervals from the water, shone gleaming along the deep. The boatmen, silent and unobserved, moored their vessel on the sandy beach, and a young man, of a keen and animated aspect, arrayed in the shaggy skin of a bear, armed with a bow and a javelin, having left his companions, was advancing along the shore. It was Oneyo. Having received wounds in the battle, he had been unable to prosecute his return, and had tarried with some Indians in the neighbourhood of Montreal. By the skilful application of herbs and balsams his cure was at length effectuated, and he returned impatient to his nation.

"I will return secretly," he said. "I will enjoy the sorrow and regret of Marano and of my brethren who doubtless believe me dead. I will enjoy the extacy of their affection, and their surprise on my unexpected arrival. My lovely Marano now laments unconsoled. I will hasten to relieve her, and press her with weeping joy, to my faithful transported bosom."

Such were the sentiments of anticipated rapture that occupied the soul of Oneyo when he discovered Marano in the arms of a stranger. He stood motionless in an agony of grief, anger, and astonishment. Pale and trembling he uttered some words incoherently. He again advanced, again recognized her, then turning abruptly, in bitter anguish, smiting his breast, "Faithless inconstant," he cried, "and is this my expected meeting! In the arms of a stranger! Arrogant invader of my felicity! He shall perish! His blood shall expatiate his offence!" Fury flashed in his eye, he grasped his javelin, he aimed the blow, and recognized his deliverer. Surprise and horror seized him. Injured by my deliverer! By him whom my soul revered! And shall I dip my hands in his blood! My life he preserved. Would to heaven he had slain me! Thus injured and betrayed, Oneyo shall not live. "Thou Great Universal Spirit, whose path is in the clouds! whose voice is in the thunder! and whose eye pierces the heart! O conduct me to the blissful valley, for Oneyo will not live." He sighed. "One look, one parting look of my love. O I believed her faithful, for her I lived, for her I die." He advanced towards her, he gazed on her with anguish and regret. "She will not weep for me! Faithless and inconstant. She will exult! Exult to behold me bleeding! And shall it be? For this have I cherished her? Lavished my soul on her? To be betrayed! To give her love to a stranger?" He paused, trembled, his countenance grew fierce, his eye wild, he grasped his javelin — Marano named him: her voice was soft and plaintive, her visions were of Oneyo. "O come," she said, "hasten to thy love. Tarry not, my Oneyo! How I long to behold thee." "For this" said he, "I'll embrace thee." He embraced her; she awaked, discovered her husband, and flew eagerly into his arms. He flung from her in fierce indignation. "Away," he cried, "go cherish thy stranger. Away, perfidious!" She followed him trembling and aghast. "He is my brother." "Thy brother — Stranger," said he to the Briton, who now approached him, "you preserved my life. You are generous and valiant. Tell me then, am I to salute thee as a friend, and give full vent to my gratitude? Or must I view thee as a guileful seducer, and lift my javelin against thy life?"

The Briton, perceiving his error, answered him with brevity and composure: he related to him the circumstances of his captivity, and in confirmation appealed to the testimony of his father. The Indian was satisfied. He embraced them. They returned by morning to the village. Ononthio received them with decent gladness, and the day was crowned with rejoicing.

Washington Irving
Rip Van Winkle

Washington Irving was born in New York City in 1783 and educated in the law, a profession he practiced only briefly. When he was in his early twenties, he, his brother William, and James Kirke Paulding established *Salmagundi,* a satirical magazine, which he edited for a number of years. His reputation was made, however, with the publication of *A History of New York* in 1809, a humorous book marked by its Horatian satire and ironic tone. The purported author of the volume was the pseudonymous Diedrich Knickerbocker, and the use of a putative author was a device Irving would sustain throughout his career. He was in England in June of 1818 when he wrote "Rip Van Winkle," the first American story to win international approbation and sustained attention from the general reading public. It appeared in *The Sketch Book of Geoffrey Crayon, Gent.,* and Crayon claims to have discovered the tale among the papers of the late Knickerbocker, who has written a book of "scrupulous accuracy." The fantastic story he tells, however, melds realistic elements of village life with a folktale based on legends of prodigious sleepers that reach from the German tale of Peter Klaus to the ancient Greek myth of Epimenides. Irving makes this account uniquely American by having the Revolutionary War take place while Rip is in his slumbers, completely missing the most momentous event yet to take place on the continent. The literary skill of the telling, the wry humor and gentle satire, the force of the mythic materials, and the elegance of the style combine to make "Rip Van Winkle" a truly important document in literary history.

Washington Irving, "Rip Van Winkle," *The Sketch Book of Geoffrey Crayon, Gent.* (New York: Putnam, 1848), 27-41.

The following Tale was found among the papers of the late Diedrich Knicker-bocker, an old gentleman of New-York, who was very curious in the Dutch History of the province, and the manners of the descendants from its primitive settlers. His historical researches, however, did not lie so much among books as among men; for the former are lamentably scanty on his favorite topics; whereas he found the old burghers, and still more, their wives, rich in that legendary lore, so invaluable to true history. Whenever, therefore, he happened upon a genuine Dutch family, snugly shut up in its low-roofed farmhouse, under a spreading sycamore, he looked upon it as a little clasped volume of black-letter, and studied it with the zeal of a bookworm.

The result of all these researches was a history of the province, during the reign of the Dutch governors, which he published some years since. There have been various opinions as to the literary character of his work, and, to tell the truth, it is not a whit better than it should be. Its chief merit is its scrupulous accuracy, which, indeed, was a little questioned, on its first appearance, but has since been completely established; and it is now admitted into all historical collections, as a book of unquestionable authority.

The old gentleman died shortly after the publication of his work, and now, that he is dead and gone, it cannot do much harm to his memory, to say, that his time might have been much better employed in weightier labors. He, however, was apt to ride his hobby his own way; and though it did now and then kick up the dust a little in the eyes of his neighbors, and grieve the spirit of some friends from whom he felt the truest deference and affection, yet his errors and follies are remembered "more in sorrow than in anger," and it begins to be suspected, that he never intended to injure or offend. But however his memory may be appreciated by critics, it is still held dear by many folk, whose good opinion is well worth having; particularly by certain biscuit-bakers, who have gone so far as to imprint his likeness on their new-year cakes, and have thus given him a chance for immortality, almost equal to the being stamped on a Waterloo medal, or a Queen Anne's farthing.

> By Woden, God of Saxons,
> From whence comes Wensday, that is Wodensday,
> Truth is a thing that ever I will keep
> Unto thylke day in which I creep into
> My sepulchre.
>   — Cartwright.

Whoever has made a voyage up the Hudson, must remember the Kaatskill mountains. They are a dismembered branch of the great Appalachian family, and are seen away to the west of the river, swelling up to a noble height, and lording it over the surrounding country. Every change of season, every change of weather, indeed every hour of the day, produces some change in the magical hues and shapes of these mountains; and they are regarded by all the good wives, far and near, as perfect barometers. When the weather is fair and settled, they are clothed in blue and purple, and print their bold outlines on the clear evening sky; but sometimes, when the rest of the landscape is cloudless, they will gather a hood of gray vapors about their summits, which, in the last rays of the setting sun, will glow and light up like a crown of glory.

At the foot of these fairy mountains, the voyager may have descried the light smoke curling up from a village, whose shingle roofs gleam among the trees, just where the blue tints of the upland melt away into the fresh green of the nearer landscape. It is a little village of great antiquity, having been founded by some of the Dutch colonists, in the early times of the province, just about the beginning of the government of the good Peter Stuyvesant (may he rest in peace!) and there were some of the houses of the original settlers standing within a few years, built of small yellow bricks brought from Holland, having latticed windows and gable fronts, surmounted with weathercocks.

In that same village, and in one of these very houses (which to tell the precise truth, was sadly time-worn and weather-beaten), there lived many years since, while the country was yet a province of Great Britain, a simple, good-natured fellow, of the name of Rip Van Winkle. He was a descendant of the Van Winkles who figured so gallantly in the chivalrous days of Peter Stuyvesant, and accompanied him to the seige of fort Christina. He inherited, however, but little of the martial character of his ancestors. I have observed that he was a simple good-natured man; he was moreover a kind neighbor, and an obedient henpecked husband. Indeed, to the latter circumstance might be owing that meekness of spirit which gained him such universal popularity; for those men are most apt to be obsequious and conciliating abroad, who are under the discipline of shrews at home. Their tempers, doubtless, are rendered pliant and malleable in the fiery furnace of domestic tribulation, and a curtain lecture is worth all the sermons in the world for teaching the virtues of patience and long-suffering. A termagant wife may, therefore, in some respects, be considered a tolerable blessing; and if so, Rip Van Winkle was thrice blessed.

Certain it is, that he was a great favorite among all the good wives of the village, who, as usual with the amiable sex, took his part in all family squabbles, and never failed, whenever they talked those matters over in their evening gossipings, to lay all the blame on Dame Van Winkle. The children of the village, too, would shout with joy whenever he approached. He assisted at their sports, made their playthings, taught them to fly kites and shoot marbles, and told them long stories of ghosts, witches, and Indians. Whenever he went dodging about the village, he was surrounded by a troop of them hanging on his skirts, clambering on his back, and playing a thousand tricks on him with impunity; and not a dog would bark at him throughout the neighborhood.

The great error in Rip's composition was an insuperable aversion to all kinds of profitable labor. It could not be from the want of assiduity or perseverance; for he would sit on a wet rock, with a rod as long and heavy as a Tartar's lance, and fish all day without a murmur, even though he should not be encouraged by a single nibble. He would carry a fowling-piece on his shoulder for hours together, trudging through woods and swamps, and up hill and down dale, to shoot a few squirrels or wild pigeons. He would never refuse to assist a neighbor, even in the roughest toil, and was a foremost man at all country frolics for husking Indian corn or building stone fences. The women of the village, too, used to employ him to run their errands, and to do such little odd jobs as their less obliging husbands would not do for them; — in a word, Rip was ready to attend to anybody's business but his own; but as to doing family duty, and keeping his farm in order, he found it impossible.

In fact, he declared it was of no use to work on his farm; it was the most pestilent little piece of ground in the whole country; every thing about it went wrong, and would go wrong in spite of him. His fences were continually falling to pieces; his cow would either go astray, or get among the cabbages; weeds were sure to grow quicker in his fields than anywhere else; the rain always made a point of setting in just as he had some out-door work to do; so that though his patrimonial estate had dwindled away under his management, acre by acre, until there was little more left than a mere patch of Indian corn and potatoes, yet it was the worst conditioned farm in the neighborhood.

His children, too, were as ragged and wild as if they belonged to nobody. His son Rip, an urchin begotten in his own likeness, promised to inherit the habits, with the old clothes of his father. He was generally seen trooping like a colt at his mother's heels, equipped in a pair of his father's cast-off galligaskins, which he had much ado to hold up with one hand, as a fine lady does her train in bad weather.

Rip Van Winkle, however, was one of those happy mortals, of foolish, well-oiled dispositions, who take the world easy, eat white bread or brown, whichever can be got with least thought or trouble, and would rather starve on a penny than work for a pound. If left to himself, he would have whistled life away in perfect contentment; but his wife kept continually dinning in his ears about his idleness, his carelessness, and the ruin he was bringing on his family.

Morning, noon, and night, her tongue was incessantly going, and every thing he said or did was sure to produce a torrent of household eloquence. Rip had but one way of replying to all lectures of the kind, and that, by frequent use, had grown into a habit. He shrugged his shoulders, shook his head, cast up his eyes, but said nothing. This, however, always provoked a fresh volley from his wife, so that he was fain to draw off his forces, and take to the outside of the house — the only side which, in truth, belongs to a henpecked husband.

Rip's sole domestic adherent was his dog Wolf, who was as much henpecked as his master; for Dame Van Winkle regarded them as companions in idleness, and even looked upon Wolf with an evil eye as the cause of his master's going so often astray. True it is, in all points of spirit befitting an honorable dog, he was as courageous an animal as ever scoured the woods — but what courage can withstand the ever-during and all-besetting terrors of a woman's tongue? The moment Wolf entered the house, his crest fell, his tail drooped to the ground, or curled between his legs, he sneaked about with a gallows air, casting many a sidelong glance at Dame Van Winkle, and at the least flourish of a broomstick or ladle, he would fly to the door with yelping precipitation.

Times grew worse and worse with Rip Van Winkle, as years of matrimony rolled on: a tart temper never mellows with age, and a sharp tongue is the only edge tool that grows keener with constant use. For a long while he used to console himself, when driven from home, by frequenting a kind of perpetual club of the sages, philosophers, and other idle personages of the village, which held its sessions on a bench before a small inn, designated by a rubicund portrait of his majesty George the Third. Here they used to sit in the shade, of a long lazy summer's day, talking listlessly over village gossip, or telling endless sleepy stories about nothing. But it would have been worth any statesman's money to have heard the profound discussions that sometimes took place, when by chance an old newspaper fell into their hands, from some passing traveller. How solemnly they would listen to the contents, as drawled out by Derrick Van Bummel, the schoolmaster, a dapper learned little man, who was not to be daunted by the most gigantic word in the dictionary; and how sagely they would deliberate upon public events some months after they had taken place.

The opinions of this junto were completely controlled by Nicholas Vedder, a patriarch of the village, and landlord of the inn, at the door of which he took his seat from morning till night, just moving sufficiently to avoid the sun, and keep in the shade of a large tree; so that the neighbors could tell the hour by his movements as accurately as by a sun-dial. It is true, he was rarely heard to speak, but smoked his pipe incessantly. His adherents, however (for every great man has his adherents), perfectly understood him, and knew how to gather his opinions. When any thing that was read or related displeased him, he was observed to smoke his pipe vehemently, and to send forth short, frequent, and angry puffs; but when pleased, he would inhale the smoke slowly and tranquilly, and emit it in light and placid clouds, and sometimes taking the pipe from his mouth, and letting the fragrant vapor curl about his nose, would gravely nod his head in token of perfect approbation.

From even this strong hold the unlucky Rip was at length routed by his termagant wife, who would suddenly break in upon the tranquillity of the assemblage, and call the members all to nought; nor was that august personage, Nicholas Vedder himself, sacred from the daring tongue of this terrible virago, who charged him outright with encouraging her husband in habits of idleness.

Poor Rip was at last reduced almost to despair, and his only alternative to escape from the labor of the farm and clamor of his wife, was to take gun in hand, and stroll away into the woods. Here he would sometimes seat himself at the foot of a tree, and share the contents of his wallet with Wolf, with whom he sympathized as a fellow-sufferer in persecution. "Poor Wolf," he would say, "thy mistress leads thee a dog's life of it; but never mind, my lad, whilst I live thou shalt never want a friend to stand by thee!" Wolf would wag his tail, look wistfully in his master's face, and if dogs can feel pity, I verily believe he reciprocated the sentiment with all his heart.

In a long ramble of the kind, on a fine autumnal day, Rip had unconsciously scrambled to one of the highest parts of the Kaatskill mountains. He was after his favorite sport of squirrel-shooting, and the still solitudes had echoed and re-echoed with the reports of his gun. Panting and fatigued, he threw himself, late in the afternoon, on a green knoll covered with mountain herbage, that crowned the brow of a precipice. From an opening between the trees, he could overlook all the lower country for many a mile of rich woodland. He saw at a distance the lordly Hudson, far, far below him, moving on its silent but majestic course, with the reflection of a purple cloud, or the sail of a lagging bark, here and there sleeping on its glassy bosom, and at last losing itself in the blue highlands.

On the other side he looked down into a deep mountain glen, wild, lonely, and shagged, the bottom filled with fragments from the impending cliffs, and scarcely lighted by the reflected rays of the setting sun. For some time Rip lay musing on this scene; evening was gradually advancing; the mountains began to throw their long blue shadows over the valleys; he saw that it would be dark long before he could reach the village; and he heaved a heavy sigh when he thought of encountering the terrors of Dame Van Winkle.

As he was about to descend he heard a voice from a distance hallooing, "Rip Van Winkle! Rip Van Winkle!" He looked round, but could see nothing but a crow winging its solitary flight across the mountain. He thought his fancy must have deceived him, and turned again to descend, when he heard the same cry ring through the still evening air, "Rip Van Winkle! Rip Van Winkle!" — at the same time Wolf bristled up his back, and giving a low growl, skulked to his master's side, looking fearfully down into the glen. Rip now felt a vague apprehension stealing over him: he looked anxiously in the same direction, and perceived a strange figure slowly toiling up the rocks, and bending under the weight of something he carried on his back. He was surprised to see any human being in this lonely and unfrequented place, but supposing it to be some one of the neighborhood in need of his assistance, he hastened down to yield it.

On nearer approach, he was still more surprised at the singularity of the stranger's appearance. He was a short square-built old fellow, with thick bushy hair, and a grizzled beard. His dress was of the antique Dutch fashion — a cloth jerkin strapped round the waist — several pair of breeches, the outer one of ample volume, decorated with rows of buttons down the sides, and bunches at the knees. He bore on his shoulder a stout keg, that seemed full of liquor, and made signs for Rip to approach and assist him with the load. Though rather shy and distrustful of this new acquaintance, Rip complied with his usual alacrity, and mutually relieving one another, they clambered up a narrow gully, apparently the dry bed of a mountain torrent. As they ascended, Rip every now and then heard long rolling peals, like distant thunder, that seemed to issue out of a deep ravine or rather cleft between lofty rocks, toward which their rugged path conducted. He paused for an instant, but supposing it to be the muttering of one of those transient thunder-showers which often take place in mountain heights, he proceeded. Passing through the ravine, they came to a hollow, like a small amphitheatre, surrounded by perpendicular precipices, over the brinks of which, impending trees shot their branches, so that you only caught glimpses of the azure sky, and the bright evening cloud. During the whole time, Rip and his companion had labored on in silence; for though the former marvelled greatly what could be the object of carrying a keg of liquor up this wild mountain, yet there was something strange and incomprehensible about the unknown, that inspired awe, and checked familiarity.

On entering the amphitheatre, new objects of wonder presented themselves. On a level spot in the centre was a company of odd-looking personages playing at nine-pins. They were dressed in a quaint outlandish fashion: some wore short doublets, others jerkins, with long knives in their belts, and most of them had enormous breeches, of similar style with that of the guide's. Their visages, too, were peculiar; one had a large beard, broad face, and small piggish eyes; the face of another seemed to consist entirely of nose, and was surmounted by a white sugar-loaf hat, set off with a little red cock's tail. They all had beards, of various shapes and colors. There was one who seemed to be the commander. He was a stout old gentleman, with a weather-beaten countenance; he wore a laced doublet, broad belt and hanger, high-crowned hat and feather, red stockings, and high-heeled shoes, with roses in them. The whole group reminded Rip of the figures in an old Flemish painting, in the parlor of Dominie Van Shaick, the village parson, and which had been brought over from Holland at the time of the settlement.

What seemed particularly odd to Rip, was, that though these folks were evidently amusing themselves, yet they maintained the gravest faces, the most mysterious silence, and were, withal, the most melancholy party of pleasure he had ever witnessed. Nothing interrupted the stillness of the scene but the noise of the balls, which, whenever they were rolled, echoed along the mountains like rumbling peals of thunder.

As Rip and his companion approached them, they suddenly desisted from their play, and stared at him with such fixed statue-like gaze, and such strange, uncouth, lack-lustre countenances, that his heart turned within him, and his knees smote together. His companion now emptied the contents of the keg into large flagons, and made signs to him to wait upon the company. He obeyed with fear and trembling; they quaffed the liquor in profound silence, and then returned to their game.

By degrees, Rip's awe and apprehension subsided. He even ventured, when no eye was fixed upon him, to taste the beverage, which he found had much of the flavor of excellent Hollands. He was naturally a thirsty soul, and was soon tempted to repeat the draught. One taste provoked another, and he reiterated his visits to the flagon so often, that at length his senses were overpowered, his eyes swam in his head, his head gradually declined, and he fell into a deep sleep.

On waking, he found himself on the green knoll whence he had first seen the old man of the glen. He rubbed his eyes — it was a bright sunny morning. The birds were hopping and twittering among the bushes, and the eagle was wheeling aloft, and breasting the pure mountain breeze. "Surely," thought Rip, "I have not slept here all night." He recalled the occurrences before he fell asleep. The strange man with the keg of liquor — the mountain ravine — the wild retreat among the rocks — the wo-begone party at nine-pins — the flagon — "Oh! that flagon! that wicked flagon!" thought Rip — "what excuse shall I make to Dame Van Winkle?"

He looked round for his gun, but in place of the clean well-oiled fowling-piece, he found an old fire-lock lying by him, the barrel encrusted with rust, the lock falling off, and the stock worm-eaten. He now suspected that the grave roysters of the mountain had put a trick upon him, and having dosed him with liquor, had robbed him of his gun. Wolf, too, had disappeared, but he might have strayed away after a squirrel or partridge. He whistled after him, and shouted his name, but all in vain; the echoes repeated his whistle and shout, but no dog was to be seen.

He determined to revisit the scene of the last evening's gambol, and if he met with any of the party, to demand his dog and gun. As he rose to walk, he found himself stiff in the joints, and wanting in his usual activity. "These mountain beds do not agree with me," thought Rip, "and if this frolic should lay me up with a fit of the rheumatism, I shall have a blessed time with Dame Van Winkle." With some difficulty he got down into the glen; he found the gully up which he and his companion had ascended the preceding evening; but to his astonishment a mountain stream was now foaming down it, leaping from rock to rock, and filling the glen with babbling murmurs. He, however, made shift to scramble up its sides, working his toilsome way through thickets of birch, sassafras, and witch-hazel; and sometimes tripped up or entangled by the wild grape vines that twisted their coils or tendrils from tree to tree, and spread a kind of network in his path.

At length he reached to where the ravine had opened through the cliffs to the amphitheatre; but no traces of such opening remained. The rocks presented a high impenetrable wall, over which the torrent came tumbling in a sheet of feathery foam, and fell into a broad deep basin, black from the shadows of the surrounding forest. Here, then, poor Rip was brought to a stand. He again called and whistled after his dog; he was only answered by the cawing of a flock of idle crows, sporting high in the air about a dry tree that overhung a sunny precipice; and who, secure in their elevation, seemed to look down and scoff at the poor man's perplexities. What was to be done? The morning was passing away, and Rip felt famished for want of his breakfast. He grieved to give up his dog and gun; he dreaded to meet his wife; but it would not do to starve among the mountains. He shook his head, shouldered the rusty firelock, and with a heart full of trouble and anxiety, turned his steps homeward.

As he approached the village, he met a number of people, but none whom he knew, which somewhat surprised him, for he had thought himself acquainted with every one in the country round. Their dress, too, was of a different fashion from that to which he was accustomed. They all stared at him with equal marks of surprise, and whenever they cast their eyes upon him, invariably stroked their chins. The constant recurrence of this gesture, induced Rip, involuntarily, to do the same, when, to his astonishment, he found his beard had grown a foot long!

He had now entered the skirts of the village. A troop of strange children ran at his heels, hooting after him, and pointing at his gray beard. The dogs, too, not one of which he recognized for an old acquaintance, barked at him as he passed. The very village was altered: it was larger and more populous. There were rows of houses which he had never seen before, and those which had been his familiar haunts had disappeared. Strange names were over the doors — strange faces at the windows — every thing was strange. His mind now misgave him; he began to doubt whether both he and the world around him were not bewitched. Surely this was his native village, which he had left but the day before. There stood the Kaatskill mountains — there ran the silver Hudson at a distance — there was every hill and dale precisely as it had always been — Rip was sorely perplexed — "That flagon last night," thought he, "has addled my poor head sadly!"

It was with some difficulty that he found the way to his own house, which he approached with silent awe, expecting every moment to hear the shrill voice of Dame Van Winkle. He found the house gone to decay — the roof fallen in, the windows shattered, and the doors off the hinges. A half-starved dog, that looked like Wolf, was skulking about it. Rip called him by name, but the cur snarled, showed his teeth, and passed on. This was an unkind cut indeed. — "My very dog," sighed poor Rip, "has forgotten me!"

He entered the house, which, to tell the truth, Dame Van Winkle had always kept in neat order. It was empty, forlorn, and apparently abandoned. This desolateness overcame all his connubial fears — he called loudly for his wife and children — the lonely chambers rang for a moment with his voice, and then all again was silence.

He now hurried forth, and hastened to his old resort, the village inn — but it too was gone. A large rickety wooden building stood in its place, with great gaping windows, some of them broken, and mended with old hats and petticoats, and over the door was painted, "The Union Hotel, by Jonathan Doolittle." Instead of the great tree that used to shelter the quiet little Dutch inn of yore, there now was reared a tall naked pole, with something on the top that looked like a red night-cap, and from it was fluttering a flag, on which was a singular assemblage of stars and stripes — all this was strange and incomprehensible. He recognized on the sign, however, the ruby face of King George, under which he had smoked so many a peaceful pipe, but even this was singularly metamorphosed. The red coat was changed for one of blue and buff, a sword was held in the hand instead of a sceptre, the head was decorated with a cocked hat, and underneath was painted in large characters, GENERAL WASHINGTON.

There was, as usual, a crowd of folk about the door, but none that Rip recollected. The very character of the people seemed changed. There was a busy, bustling, disputatious tone about it, instead of the accustomed phlegm and drowsy tranquillity. He looked in vain for the sage Nicholas Vedder, with his broad face, double chin, and fair long pipe, uttering clouds of tobacco smoke, instead of idle speeches; or Van Bummel, the schoolmaster, doling forth the contents of an ancient newspaper. In place of these, a lean bilious-looking fellow, with his pockets full of handbills, was haranguing vehemently about rights of citizens — election — members of Congress — liberty — Bunker's hill — heroes of seventy-six — and other words which were a perfect Babylonish jargon to the bewildered Van Winkle.

The appearance of Rip, with his long, grizzled beard, his rusty fowling-piece, his uncouth dress, and an army of women and children at his heels, soon attracted the attention of the tavern politicians. They crowded round him, eying him from head to foot, with great curiosity. The orator bustled up to him, and drawing him partly aside, inquired, "on which side he voted?" Rip stared in vacant stupidity. Another short but busy little fellow pulled him by the arm, and rising on tiptoe, inquired in his ear, "whether he was Federal or Democrat." Rip was equally at a loss to comprehend the question; when a knowing, self-important old gentleman, in a sharp cocked hat, made his way through the crowd, putting them to the right and left with his elbows as he passed, and planting himself before Van Winkle, with one arm a-kimbo, the other resting on his cane, his keen eyes and sharp hat penetrating, as it were, into his very soul, demanded in an austere tone, "what brought him to the election with a gun on his shoulder, and a mob at his heels, and whether he meant to breed a riot in the village?"

"Alas! gentlemen," cried Rip, somewhat dismayed, "I am a poor, quiet man, a native of the place, and a loyal subject of the King, God bless him!"

Here a general shout burst from the bystanders — "a tory! a tory! a spy! a refugee! hustle him! away with him!"

It was with great difficulty that the self-important man in the cocked hat restored order; and having assumed a tenfold austerity of brow, demanded again of the unknown culprit, what he came there for, and whom he was seeking. The poor man humbly assured him that he meant no harm, but merely came there in search of some of his neighbors, who used to keep about the tavern.

"Well — who are they? — name them."

Rip bethought himself a moment, and inquired, "Where's Nicholas Vedder?"

There was silence for a little while, when an old man replied, in a thin, piping voice, "Nicholas Vedder? why, his is dead and gone these eighteen years! There was a wooden tomb-stone in the church-yard that used to tell all about him, but that's rotten and gone too."

"Where's Brom Dutcher?"

"Oh, he went off to the army in the beginning of the war; some say he was killed at the storming of Stony-Point — others say he was drowned in the squall, at the foot of Antony's Nose. I don't know — he never came back again."

"Where's Van Bummel, the schoolmaster?"

"He went off to the wars, too; was a great militia general, and is now in Congress."

Rip's heart died away, at hearing of these sad changes in his home and friends, and finding himself thus alone in the world. Every answer puzzled him, too, by treating of such enormous lapses of time, and of matters which he could not understand: war — Congress — Stony-Point! — he had no courage to ask after any more friends, but cried out in despair, "Does nobody here know Rip Van Winkle?"

"Oh, Rip Van Winkle!" exclaimed two or three. "Oh to be sure! that's Rip Van Winkle yonder, leaning against the tree."

Rip looked, and beheld a precise counterpart of himself as he went up the mountain; apparently as lazy and certainly as ragged. The poor fellow was now completely confounded. He doubted his own identity, and whether he was himself or another man. In the midst of his bewilderment, the man in the cocked hat demanded who he was, and what was his name?

"God knows," exclaimed he at his wit's end; "I'm not myself — I'm somebody else — that's me yonder — no — that's somebody else, got into my shoes — I was myself last night, but I fell asleep on the mountain, and they've changed my gun, and every thing's changed, and I'm changed, and I can't tell what's my name, or who I am!"

The by-standers began now to look at each other, nod, wink significantly, and tap their fingers against their foreheads. There was a whisper, also, about securing the gun, and keeping the old fellow from doing mischief; at the very suggestion of which, the self-important man with the cocked hat retired with some precipitation. At this critical moment a fresh comely woman pressed through the throng to get a peep at the gray-bearded man. She had a chubby child in her arms, which, frightened at his looks, began to cry. "Hush, Rip," cried she, "hush, you little fool; the old man won't hurt you." The name of the child, the air of the mother, the tone of her voice, all awakened a train of recollections in his mind.

"What is your name, my good woman?" asked he.

"Judith Gardenier."

"And your father's name?"

"Ah, poor man, Rip Van Winkle was his name; but it's twenty years since he went away from home with his gun, and never has been heard of since — his dog came home without him; but whether he shot himself, or was carried away by the Indians, nobody can tell. I was then but a little girl."

Rip had but one question more to ask; but he put it with a faltering voice:

"Where's your mother?"

Oh, she too had died but a short time since: she broke a blood-vessel in a fit of passion at a New-England pedler.

There was a drop of comfort, at least, in this intelligence. The honest man could contain himself no longer. He caught his daughter and her child in his arms. "I am your father!" cried he — "Young Rip Van Winkle once — old Rip Van Winkle now! — Does nobody know poor Rip Van Winkle?"

All stood amazed, until an old woman, tottering out from among the crowd, put her hand to her brow, and peering under it in his face for a moment, exclaimed, "Sure enough! it is Rip Van Winkle — it is himself. Welcome home again, old neighbor — Why, where have you been these twenty long years?"

Rip's story was soon told, for the whole twenty years had been to him but as one night. The neighbors stared when they heard it; some were seen to wink at each other, and put their tongues in their cheeks; and the self-important man in the cocked hat, who, when the alarm was over, had returned to the field, screwed down the corners of his mouth, and shook his head — upon which there was a general shaking of the head throughout the assemblage.

It was determined, however, to take the opinion of old Peter Vanderdonk, who was seen slowly advancing up the road. He was a descendant of the historian of that name, who wrote one of the earliest accounts of the province. Peter was the most ancient inhabitant of the village, and well versed in all the wonderful events and traditions of the neighborhood. He recollected Rip at once, and corroborated his story in the most satisfactory manner. He assured the company that it was a fact, handed down from his ancestor the historian, that the Kaatskill mountains had always been haunted by strange beings. That it was affirmed that the great Hendrick Hudson, the first discoverer of the river and country, kept a kind of vigil there every twenty years, with his crew of the Half-moon, being permitted in this way to revisit the scenes of his enterprise, and keep a guardian eye upon the river and the great city called by his name. That his father had once seen them in their old Dutch dresses playing at nine-pins in a hollow of the mountain; and that he himself had heard, one summer afternoon, the sound of their balls, like distant peals of thunder.

To make a long story short, the company broke up, and returned to the more important concerns of the election. Rip's daughter took him home to live with her; she had a snug, well-furnished house, and a stout cheery farmer for a husband, whom Rip recollected for one of the urchins that used to climb upon his back. As to Rip's son and heir, who was the ditto of himself, seen leaning against the tree, he was employed to work on the farm, but evinced an hereditary disposition to attend to any thing else but his business.

Rip now resumed his old walks and habits; he soon found many of his former cronies, though all rather the worse for the wear and tear of time; and preferred making friends among the rising generation, with whom he soon grew into great favor.

Having nothing to do at home, and being arrived at that happy age when a man can be idle with impunity, he took his place once more on the bench, at the inn door, and was reverenced as one of the patriarchs of the village, and a chronicle of the old times "before the war." It was some time before he could get into the regular track of gossip, or could be made to comprehend the strange events that had taken place during his torpor. How that there had been a revolutionary war — that the country had thrown off the yoke of old England — and that, instead of being a subject of his majesty George the Third, he was now a free citizen of the United States. Rip, in fact, was no politician; the changes of states and empires made but little impression on him; but there was one species of despotism under which he had long groaned, and that was — petticoat government. Happily, that was at an end; he had got his neck out of the yoke of matrimony, and could go in and out whenever he pleased, without dreading the tyranny of Dame Van Winkle. Whenever her name was mentioned, however, he shook his head, shrugged his shoulders, and cast up his eyes; which might pass either for an expression of resignation to his fate, or joy at his deliverance.

He used to tell his story to every stranger that arrived at Mr. Doolittle's hotel. He was observed, at first, to vary on some points every time he told it, which was doubtless owing to his having so recently awaked. It at last settled down precisely to the tale I have related, and not a man, woman, or child in the neighborhood, but knew it by heart. Some always pretended to doubt the reality of it, and insisted that Rip had been out of his head, and that this was one point on which he always remained flighty. The old Dutch inhabitants, however, almost universally gave it full credit. Even to this day, they never hear a thunder-storm of a summer afternoon about the Kaatskill, but they say Hendrick Hudson and his crew are at their game of nine-pins: and it is a common wish of all henpecked husbands in the neighborhood, when life hangs heavy on their hands, that they might have a quieting draught out of Rip Van Winkle's flagon.

Note. — The foregoing tale, one would suspect, had been suggested to Mr. Knickerbocker by a little German superstition about the Emperor Frederick *der Rothbart* and the Kypphaüser mountain: the subjoined note, however, which he had appended to the tale, shows that it is an absolute fact, narrated with his usual fidelity.

"The story of Rip Van Winkle may seem incredible to many, but nevertheless I give it my full belief, for I know the vicinity of our old Dutch settlements to have been very subject to marvellous events and appearances. Indeed, I have heard many stranger stories than this, in the villages along the Hudson, all of which were too well authenticated to admit of a doubt. I have even talked with Rip Van Winkle myself, who, when last I saw him, was a very venerable old man, and so perfectly rational and consistent on every other point, that I think no conscientious person could refuse to take this into the bargain; nay, I have seen a certificate on the subject taken before a country justice, and signed with a cross, in the justice's own handwriting. The story, therefore, is beyond the possibility of doubt.

D.K."

3

American Romanticism

The period of American Romanticism was a time of contradictions: social continuity and yet enormous change; humanitarian reform and the persistence of slavery in the Southern states; a rigorous intellectualism along with a new regard for intuition and spiritual transcendence. The population of the United States, swelled by immigration, grew from roughly nine million in 1820 to over thirty million in 1865. The original thirteen states more than doubled in number, and westward expansion gained momentum with each passing decade. It was an epoch of transformation, but nevertheless writers stressed a core set of assumptions that gave coherence to a highly fragmented society: a belief in political freedom, an emphasis on the dignity and sovereignty of the individual, a confidence that free enterprise would benefit the whole of society, and a faith in the manifest destiny of the United States. Specialized social and intellectual systems also emerged, especially Transcendentalism, a New England movement that was highly idealistic and spiritual, influenced by pantheistic spiritual assumptions from Europe and, mystical ideas about the transmigration of the soul from Indian philosophy.

Abolition became a more organized political force partly as a reaction to the Missouri Compromise of 1820, a situation in which Missouri petitioned for admission to the Union at a time when there were an equal number of free and slave states. The balance would have to tip one way or another, and tensions flared, threatening sectional violence until the issue was solved with the admission of Maine (which had been part of Massachusetts) as a free state to balance Missouri. This accommodation preserved a tenuous stability, but an insistence that slaves be freed grew throughout the North, a sentiment that spread as England and France abolished slavery in their territories.

Reformist sentiment strengthened in America with each major event, especially the founding of the New England Anti-slavery Society in 1831, the establishment of the Underground Railroad, and the inflammatory Fugitive Slave Law of 1850. The *Dred Scott* decision of the Supreme Court in 1857, which denied citizenship to African Americans, stressing that they "had no rights which the white man was bound to respect," and the insurrection of John Brown in 1859 further reinforced the Reformist movement. Even more dramatic, the Abolitionist Party was transformed into the Republican Party, electing Abraham Lincoln in 1861.

The Southern states seceded, an act that had been looming since the Revolutionary War. The attack by the Confederacy on Fort Sumter, and General Lee's forays into Northern Virginia and Pennsylvania, soon followed. Eventually, the tide of war turned and the South surrendered in 1865. The Civil War brought a change in sensibility so dramatic, and with such profound implications for literature, that the conclusion of the conflict is generally regarded as the end of the Romantic movement, although some ideological vestiges persisted, especially the elevation of the common person and the sanctity of nature.

Other social changes developed as well. The meeting of suffragists in Seneca Falls in 1848 indicated that the push for equality for women was gaining momentum throughout society. That movement built upon gender themes introduced in the earliest American stories, but the writers of the Romantic period added some new ideas: suffrage, economic equality, psychological health, and moral justice. A flood of short fiction appeared addressed to these subjects, often set against a background of domestic upheaval. Although authors at the end of the century would produce more powerful work on this theme, Romantic fiction established the context for important social changes in the lives of women.

Throughout this period the short story underwent tremendous modification, expanding its range of subjects, refining its aesthetic, deepening its psychological presentations, and increasing its popularity among the reading public, which was growing rapidly. Scores of magazines began to appear, and the birth of the "gift book" tradition in 1826 began the publication of volumes for the coffee table. *The Atlantic Souvenir* was the first, quickly followed by *The Token* and a host of similar publications, which inspired publisher Louis A. Godey in 1830 to found the first sustained magazine in the country, *Godey's Magazine*, later known as *Godey's Lady's Book*. For several decades this monthly provided a major outlet for stories and tales of all kinds.

In many ways, short fiction reflected societal events: the Revolutionary War was no longer a central issue, but emphasis on the politics of gender persisted, especially in the work of such women writers as Elizabeth Stoddard, Harriet Prescott Spofford, and the first African American practitioner of the short story, Frances Ellen Watkins Harper. The prominence of the ethnic themes popular just after the founding of the country continued as Lydia Maria Child wrote about Native Americans at the same time Harriet Beecher Stowe was promoting the abolition of slavery in her short stories as well as in *Uncle Tom's Cabin*. The emphasis on new American myths flourished throughout the period, the best of which was a haunting tale by William Austin, "Peter Rugg, the Missing Man," a story that rivaled the popularity of the sketches of Washington Irving from the decade before.

To these concerns writers added two significant humor traditions, Downeast and Southwest. The "Downeasters" of Maine and northern New England took their name from the fact that the prevailing trade winds blew north and east along the coast from New York and Boston. Yankee comic instincts were for ironic understatement and regional dialect. Southwestern humor, on the other hand, depended on exaggeration, hyperbole, for its effects. A host of characters were developed who could wrestle bears and kill alligators and jump the Mississippi, all speaking the vernacular with colorful phrases and regional intonations. Thomas Bangs Thorpe was among the most successful writers of this tradition.

The best authors of the period introduced dramatic new subjects for the short story. Edgar Allan Poe, for example, used controlled vengeance at the heart of many of his revenge plots. He also developed the method of Romantic ambiguity, presenting events with several possible interpretations, including Gothic supernaturalism and psychological aberration. Nathaniel Hawthorne used allegory as a mode, the last period of short fiction to do so, and Herman Mellville's work reached for universal significance, as in the portrayal of anguish in "Bartleby the Scrivener."

Romanticism was a period rich in innovation and technical developments. The early methods of presenting a story evolved into complex strategies of narration, subtle psychological characterizations, and ironic implications. Narrative line became better controlled, allowing for the emphasis on a central theme, and writers brought together all of the elements of fiction in support of a central idea. Indeed, from the theoretical contributions of Poe developed the tradition of the story as a tightly controlled artistic unit with all aspects contributing to the unifying concept. Short fiction, because it is so brief, usually presented a single main character, developed one major theme, and introduced and resolved a single conflict. By contrast, long stories, such as "Benito Cereno," grew from the French tradition of the *novella*. Its pages allowed for more complex development of characters and motifs, but in general, work in the genre remained of magazine length, designed to be read at a single sitting.

Brevity was a hallmark of the form even from the earliest years of the period. William Austin's "Peter Rugg, the Missing Man" in 1824 drew on historic materials to formulate a new American myth of the eternal wanderer, cursed by his own oath, the victim of hasty pride. He is lost somewhere in time with his daughter and horse, forever attempting to reach Boston. Austin's tale relied not only on plot for its significance but also on the skill of narration, in which multiple speakers all provide accounts of their encounters with Rugg on the roads of New England. Only in the aggregate do the events create a coherent tale about Peter Rugg, doomed by his own oath. The tale inspired scores of later works, from Hawthorne's "A Virtuoso's Collection," to Stephen Vincent Benet's "John Brown's Body," Louise Imogen Guiney's "Peter Rugg, the Bostonian," and Edward Everett Hale's "Man without a Country" (1863). Austin had discovered powerful material for his finest story, a myth that persisted for centuries.

Thomas Bangs Thorpe's "The Big Bear of Arkansas," which appeared in the *Spirit of the Times* in 1841, was immensely popular and established in the reading public an eagerness for more pieces of humorous exaggeration. In fact, it employs what became two literary traditions: *Southwestern humor* (typified by hyperbole, a sophisticated narrator who records a fantastic tale told by a backwoods character, and the use of the vernacular for artistic purposes) and *Local Color* (which presented the mores and personalities associated with certain regions of the country). Thorpe places the recitation of the tale on a Mississippi riverboat where people of different social classes would intermingle. The frame narrator, a highly educated man from the East, sets out the context for the performance and then turns the tale over to Jim Doggett. He speaks in a language that is humorous in its malapropisms and ungrammatical formulations and yet wonderful for the drama and "life" that make incredible events seem arresting. The numerous allusions to Biblical and classical parallels, the destruction of the wilderness, and the suggestion of spiritual dimensions in bear hunting all anticipate one of the great stories in American literature, William Faulkner's "The Bear."

Francis Harper's "The Two Offers" is important as the first short story by an African American woman. In some respects it is artistically rudimentary: the most important events are not dramatized but are summarized by a disembodied first-person narrator. The central themes, the pressure on young women to marry and have children, the destructiveness of alcohol, and the obligations of men to their families, are all driven home directly through exposition, although they are implicit in the action as well. However, the eloquence of the language, the adroit rendering of dialogue, and the tenderness of the sentiments combine to make the story memorable, and the relationship between the two central women anticipates the work of Sarah Orne Jewett later in the century. It is also significant that racial issues do not dominate the central themes of the conflict, an indication of the broad social concerns that filled Harper's adult life.

What is remarkable about Harriet Spofford's "Circumstance" in 1860 is the sustained tension of the threat to a woman's life at the center of the plot and the skill of describing the woods and fields of New England. The interplay of death images with the portrait of domestic life, set against musical references, performs a vital role in the suspense of the situation. Elizabeth Stoddard's "The Prescription," which appeared in *Harper's New Monthly Magazine* in 1864, deals with emotional illness within a marriage. A dominating husband has driven a young wife to despair, and she seeks the advice of a kindly physician. His prescription is essentially that she get away for a time and find herself. She does so. This marriage problem became popular in fiction three decades later in Charlotte Perkins Gilman's "The Yellow Wallpaper" and in numerous stories by Kate Chopin, as well as in her celebrated novel *The Awakening*. There is a physician who is significant in each case, a notable fact in the Romantic age, during which people distrusted the rationality of the eighteenth century. But here, the doctor is perceptive, sympathetic, and understanding. That self-assertiveness for women would transform society had been an issue since the Seneca Falls conference of 1848, but the end of the nineteenth century saw its rise to prominence as an important theme in fiction.

The status of Lydia Maria Child in literary history derives from her expansion of the fiction of social engagement. Building on American stories of the eighteenth century, Child wrote extensively about the collision between Native American life and European cultures, often with tragic consequences, as in "The Indian Wife." Her earlier novel, *Hobomok: A Tale of Early Times* (1824), dealt with the Cherokees in Georgia and the issues of assimilation and intermarriage. She contributed to the fervor of abolitionist sentiment in writing both fiction and essays about African American issues and calling for an immediate end to slavery, especially in *An Appeal in Favor of That Class of American Called Africans* in 1833. Later she served as editor of the *National Anti-Slavery Standard* in New York. Perhaps her most persistent theme was women's rights, however, and she wrote impressively about the wasted talent and intelligence of young women denied access to education and employment, ideas developed in *The History of the Condition of Women* (1836).

An appreciation of Harriet Beecher Stowe's "The Two Altars" (1851) rests almost entirely on an understanding of historical context. Born into a deeply religious New England family, Stowe grew up in the antislavery atmosphere that had been building steadily since the Revolutionary War and the drafting of the constitution in the century before. The passage of the Fugitive Slave Law in 1850, which stated that runaway slaves who had escaped to safety in the North be captured and returned to servitude in the South, intensified sectional animosities. The law provided that anyone aiding an escaped slave would be subject to six months in prison and a fine of $1,000. That law only served to inflame abolitionist passions and led to the formation of the Underground Railroad, a network of assistance that allowed runaways to find freedom in Canada. As art, the story does not represent a significant advance of the genre, but the structural pairing of the two halves of the story, each treating the theme of liberty, provides an ironic impact that was not lost on the audience of the time.

Herman Melville's "Benito Cereno" from 1855 is, in many ways, the most important short story in American Romanticism, largely because of its technical sophistication and rich thematic multiplicity. On the simplest level it is a tale of naval adventure with its origins in an actual historical source, Captain Amasa Delano's *Narrative of Voyages and Travels in the Northern and Southern Hemispheres: Comprising Three Voyages Round the World; Together with a Voyage of Survey and Discovery, in the Pacific and Oriental Islands* (1817). Delano's *Narrative* was, significantly, published in Boston, the center of the strongest abolitionist activity. The plot of "Benito Cereno" is taken directly from Delano's book. However, Melville's skill is in transforming legal documents into literary art, something he does with style, manipulation of narrative point of view, the creation of constantly building suspense, and limitations of information. Melville wrote often of adventure at sea, from his early novels *Typee* and *Omoo*, to his masterpiece *Moby-Dick*, to a great narrative left unpublished at his death, "Billy Budd." But none of these works have the tight dramatic structure he crafted at the heart of "Benito Cereno." This story is essentially organized in three distinct sections: the discovery of the slave ship and the progressive realization by Delano as to her true situation; the court documents containing the depositions in the case; and the conclusion. Although the legal testimonies would seem to establish the "truth" in the case, tying Melville's fictionalization of the material to verifiable events, in a sense they only serve to further complicate the elusive thematic center of the novella.

The subject of "Benito Cereno" is one that preoccupied the American short story from its beginning in 1775: the corruption of slavery and the moral horror that emanates from it on nearly every level, destroying slave owner, slave, and ship captain. Melville here does not present a simple abolitionist propaganda tale, however. Instead, he reveals the levels of evil that derive from slavery and the "middle passage" across the Atlantic. The slave owner has been killed by the time the action begins, so the attention shifts to Babo, the leader of the rebellion; Benito Cereno, the captain of the slaver; and to Delano, who observes and interprets the significance of his experience. Scholars have, over time, regarded each character as the protagonist in varying interpretations, but it is Delano's mind that is the source of much of the information presented. He has the realization that suddenly makes the situation clear, and this revelation occurs only after many false assessments of the circumstances. An empirical method of understanding thus becomes its own important theme, and it is here more richly developed than in any other short fiction of the age. But even that theme is less significant than the ghastly presentation of the horrors of a slave ship and the psychological damage that results from the capture of innocent Africans. It is not surprising that Melville presented his account primarily from the point of view of Captain Amasa Delano, from Massachusetts, the focal point of abolitionist activity.

Even Melville's earliest forays into short fiction resulted in some truly brilliant works, including "Bartleby, the Scrivener," which he wrote in 1853 and published late that year in *Putnam's Monthly Magazine*. In one of the most frequently analyzed stories in American literature, with many conflicting interpretations, two issues resonate throughout the critical discussions: the origin and significance of the titular character's decision to withdraw from the world; and the impact Bartleby has had on the narrator, the lawyer who employs him. Bartleby's "problem" seems to involve either a philosophical realization of the emptiness and loneliness of human existence or some kind of emotional aberration, a schizophrenic withdrawal of unknown origin, although the experience in the dead letter office is proffered as a possible explanation. Not enough data is presented about Bartleby to make a conclusive answer possible, and the tension of that irresolution lingers.

The more complex issue is the mind of the narrator, whether he is an insensitive legal functionary, living an emotionally protective life and hence someone who failed to connect with Bartleby and hastened him to his grave; or, a person who was transformed by his encounter with the scrivener, changed emotionally through his empathetic participation in his employee's tragedy. The narrator's willingness to relate intimate details of the experience, including not only his weak attempts at humor but deeper revelations about how Bartleby became an obsession for him, suggests that the events have touched him in an important way. Overall, the story would seem to be a confession of how the narrator was not equal to the problem he faced, lacking either the insight or the strength to deal with it, and thus failing not only Bartleby but himself. The telling would seem, in this context, an attempt at escaping guilt through self-revelation, profound stuff for American fiction only a century removed from its first rudimentary expressions in the genre.

Augustus Baldwin Longstreet's "The Horse Swap," originally published in 1833, is important not only as an example of the Southwestern humor tradition that was developing during the period of Romanticism but also for the many ways in which it represents a transition to the Local Color movement of regional fiction depicting the mores, language, culture, and humor of a given area. In capturing the vernacular and character types of the South, Longstreet also established aspects of the coming Realistic movement that was to produce some of the most important fiction of the last half of the century. The term "local color" was not at all one of disparagement but rather a designation of a set of artistic methods, among them using a sophisticated narrator who portrays backwoods or rustic folk in highly dramatic situations, as in the trading of horses. Thorpe's tall tale about "The Big Bear of Arkansas" relied on exaggeration for effect. Longstreet's story involves the accurate presentation of local dialects, folkways, conflicts, and traditions from an outside perspective, a city slicker. Bret Harte became famous writing stories of this type, and, to some extent, the best work of Mark Twain, William Faulkner, Sarah Orne Jewett, and a host of other important writers sustained the literary tradition that Longstreet helped establish three decades before it flourished in national magazines.

Nathaniel Hawthorne's "Young Goodman Brown" is important in that it illustrates several ideological transformations that took place in American Romanticism. That Hawthorne used a setting in a Puritan community reflects not only a temporal shift but a revisiting of his own family history, complete with actual names: his ancestor had presided over the Salem witch trials and had sentenced men and women to death for possession. But beyond biographical matters, his allegory reflects the new assumption, in a dramatic break with the Age of Reason, that reality is fundamentally spiritual and that the physical universe is merely a reflection, a symbol, of a transcendent higher plane. The use of personification (the wife's name is "Faith") makes characters into types who function both as literal beings and as representations of inner human qualities: when Goodman Brown loses his Faith, he is emotionally doomed. The story is also an example of Hawthorne's portrayals of the effects of hidden sin, which nearly always destroys the happiness of those who affect purity but harbor guilt, the central theme of *The Scarlet Letter*. In "Rappaccini's Daughter," originally published in 1844, Hawthorne crafted a plot based on the Romantic distrust of the Age of Reason and its presumed obsession with cold logic as opposed to human feelings. In this case, the issue involves a rivalry between two scientists in Padua, and two innocent young people are entwined in the consequences of this competition. The conflict is enriched by the complexity of the characters. For example, Rappaccini possesses simultaneously mad genius and fatherly affection; his daughter reveals both purity and deadly corruption. In this celebrated tale, Hawthorne also illustrates how the Romantic story contributed psychological insight and thematic complexity to the growth of American literature.

Edgar Allan Poe's "The Fall of the House of Usher" (1839) and "The Cask of Amontillado" (1846) mark a significant advance in the art of the genre. They illustrate the author's principles of coherence and congruence, of crafting fiction so that all of its elements contribute toward the same end, aesthetics working to underscore ideas. Part of Poe's genius was that he redesigned the surface elements of traditional Gothic tales (terror, suspense, mysterious settings) and used them to develop psychological themes. Toward those ends his subtle manipulation of point of view, of elegant style, and the pacing of plot all sustain a single effect. His themes, although varied, often explore the psychological effects of violence, the torment of hidden guilt, or the desperate need to release a haunting memory of responsibility, all at issue in "The Cask of Amontillado." "The Fall of the House of Usher," perhaps his best-known work, is notable for its deft handling of point of view and for the many possible interpretations it permits. Scholars have disagreed whether the events related are the product of an insane narrator who suffers from hallucinations, the result of a literal foray into supernatural realms, or a symbolic exercise in illustrating the human mind at war with itself. Poe derived the plot, at least in part, from Dr. Samuel Warren's *Passages from the Diary of a Late Physician,* published in 1835, in which a young woman in a cataleptic state is presumed dead, is buried, and returns to her family during a raging storm. Poe made the most of his Gothic materials to craft a haunting narrative of intense psychological drama. Nothing is extraneous in Poe's best stories, and his skill in writing fiction greatly advanced the genre of the Romantic story.

Even a cursory overview of the Romantic period reveals that it was an era of enormous changes in literature. In the space of four decades, the art of the story developed from the often awkward presentation of a narrative line to a highly integrated form in which aesthetics and ideas supported one another and even small details contributed to the unified effect of the whole. The authors of the time, drawing from the origins of the story in America, addressed the most crucial issues of the day: abolition, women's rights, Native Americans, social reform, and a deepening psychological insight that is astonishing in a pre-Freudian age. Women writers had taken the stage in literary endeavors, never to relinquish it, and the first African American writers of fiction were now publishing in the major venues.

By the end of the period, the American story had begun to attract international attention, so much so that, beginning in 1832, the English playwright Mary Russell Mitford published in London three volumes of American stories and sketches. In 1846, on home soil, Rufus Wilmot Griswold brought out *The Prose Writers of America,* also containing a good deal of short fiction. The rapid development of the story form was an astonishing transformation in a fledgling culture still struggling to define itself, and yet Romantic writers produced works of momentous substance and artistic grace that were quickly recognized throughout the world.

William Austin
Peter Rugg, the Missing Man

On September 10, 1824, a day filled with excitement in Boston because of the visit of the celebrated French war hero Lafayette, the *New England Galaxy* published what looked like a letter to the editor but carrying the title "Some Account of Peter Rugg, the Missing Man, Late of Boston, New England, in a Letter to Mr. Herman Krauff." It was signed by "Jonathan Dunwell," about whom nothing was known. It was not a genuine correspondence but a short story, and for seventeen years the true author, a local attorney and politician named William Austin, concealed his identity. A descendent of early immigrants to the area, he had lived his early life in Massachusetts, graduating from Harvard in 1798 before going to London to study law in 1802. He then established his practice in Charlestown and served as a justice of the peace and as a state senator. His fiction is limited to five stories, the most notable of which is "Peter Rugg," remarkable for its fusion of local details with elements that oscillate between reality, psychological projection, and the supernatural. In this respect his tale anticipates the later work of Hawthorne and Poe. Rugg, cursed by his own oath, is forever lost on his mission to reach Boston, becoming yet another mythic questor reaching back to the Wandering Jew, the Flying Dutchman, and a host of other doomed adventurers. Rugg's life offered a didactic admonition against the tempting of fate with hasty vows, and the haunting drama of his plight made this tale the most frequently read short fiction of its age.

William Austin, "Peter Rugg, the Missing Man," *Literary Papers of William Austin, with a Biographical Sketch by His Son, James Walker Austin* (Boston: Little, Brown, 1890), 3–17. Originally published in the *New England Galaxy* 7 (September 10, 1824): 32.

From Jonathan Dunwell of New York, to Mr. Herman Krauff.

Sir, — Agreeably to my promise, I now relate to you all the particulars of the lost man and child which I have been able to collect. It is entirely owing to the humane interest you seemed to take in the report, that I have pursued the inquiry to the following result.

You may remember that business called me to Boston in the summer of 1820. I sailed in the packet to Providence, and when I arrived there I learned that every seat in the stage was engaged. I was thus obliged either to wait a few hours or accept a seat with the driver, who civilly offered me that accommodation. Accordingly, I took my seat by his side, and soon found him intelligent and communicative. When we had travelled about ten miles, the horses suddenly threw their ears on their necks, as flat as a hare's. Said the driver, "Have you a surtout with you?"

"No," said I; "why do you ask?"

"You will want one soon," said he. "Do you observe the ears of all the horses?"

"Yes; and was just about to ask the reason."

"They see the storm-breeder, and we shall see him soon."

At this moment there was not a cloud visible in the firmament. Soon after, a small speck appeared in the road.

"There," said my companion, "comes the storm-breeder. He always leaves a Scotch mist behind him. By many a wet jacket do I remember him. I suppose the poor fellow suffers much himself, — much more than is known to the world."

Presently a man with a child beside him, with a large black horse, and a weather-beaten chair, once built for a chaise-body, passed in great haste, apparently at the rate of twelve miles an hour. He seemed to grasp the reins of his horse with firmness, and appeared to anticipate his speed. He seemed dejected, and looked anxiously at the passengers, particularly at the stage-driver and myself. In a moment after he passed us, the horses' ears were up, and bent themselves forward so that they nearly met.

"Who is that man?" said I; "he seems in great trouble."

"Nobody knows who he is, but his person and the child are familiar to me. I have met him more than a hundred times, and have been so often asked the way to Boston by that man, even when he was travelling directly from that town, that of late I have refused any communication with him; and that is the reason he gave me such a fixed look."

"But does he never stop anywhere?"

"I have never known him to stop anywhere longer than to inquire the way to Boston; and let him be where he may, he will tell you he cannot stay a moment, for he must reach Boston that night."

We were now ascending a high hill in Walpole; and as we had a fair view of the heavens, I was rather disposed to jeer the driver for thinking of his surtout, as not a cloud as big as a marble could be discerned.

"Do you look," said he, "in the direction whence the man came; that is the place to look. The storm never meets him; it follows him."

We presently approached another hill; and when at the height, the driver pointed out in an eastern direction a little black speck about as big as a hat. "There," said he, "is the seed-storm. We may possibly reach Polley's before it reaches us, but the wanderer and his child will go to Providence through rain, thunder, and lightning."

And now the horses, as though taught by instinct, hastened with increased speed. The little black cloud came on rolling over the turnpike, and doubled and trebled itself in all directions. The appearance of this cloud attracted the notice of all the passengers, for after it had spread itself to a great bulk it suddenly became more limited in circumference, grew more compact, dark, and consolidated. And now the successive flashes of chain lightning caused the whole cloud to appear like a sort of irregular net-work, and displayed a thousand fantastic images. The driver bespoke my attention to a remarkable configuration in the cloud. He said every flash of lightning near its centre discovered to him, distinctly, the form of a man sitting in an open carriage drawn by a black horse. But in truth I saw no such thing; the man's fancy was doubtless at fault. It is a very common thing for the imagination to paint for the senses, both in the visible and invisible world.

In the mean time the distant thunder gave notice of a shower at hand; and just as we reached Polley's tavern the rain poured down in torrents. It was soon over, the cloud passing in the direction of the turnpike toward Providence. In a few moments after, a respectable-looking man in a chaise stopped at the door. The man and child in the chair having excited some little sympathy among the passengers, the gentleman was asked if he had observed them. He said he had met them; that the man seemed bewildered, and inquired the way to Boston; that he was driving at great speed, as though he expected to outstrip the tempest; that the moment he had passed him, a thunder-clap broke directly over the man's head, and seemed to envelop both man and child, horse and carriage. "I stopped," said the gentleman, "supposing the lightning had struck him, but the horse only seemed to loom up and increase his speed; and as well as I could judge, he travelled just as fast as the thunder-cloud."

While this man was speaking, a pedler with a cart of tin merchandise came up, all dripping; and on being questioned, he said he had met that man and carriage, within a fortnight, in four different States; that at each time he had inquired the way to Boston; and that a thunder-shower like the present had each time deluged his wagon and his wares, setting his tin pots, etc. afloat, so that he had determined to get a marine insurance for the future. But that which excited his surprise most was the strange conduct of his horse, for long before he could distinguish the man in the chair, his own horse stood still in the road, and flung back his ears. "In short," said the pedler, "I wish never to see that man and horse again; they do not look to me as though they belonged to this world."

This was all I could learn at that time; and the occurrence soon after would have become with me, "like one of those things which had never happened," had I not, as I stood recently on the door-step of Bennett's hotel in Hartford, heard a man say, "There goes Peter Rugg and his child! he looks wet and weary, and farther from Boston than ever." I was satisfied it was the same man I had seen more than three years before; for whoever has once seen Peter Rugg can never after be deceived as to his identity.

"Peter Rugg!" said I; "and who is Peter Rugg?"

"That," said the stranger, "is more than any one can tell exactly. He is a famous traveller, held in light esteem by all innholders, for he never stops to eat, drink, or sleep. I wonder why the government does not employ him to carry the mail."

"Ay," said a by-stander, "that is a thought bright only on one side; how long would it take in that case to send a letter to Boston, for Peter has already, to my knowledge, been more than twenty years travelling to that place."

"But," said I, "does the man never stop anywhere; does he never converse with any one? I saw the same man more than three years since, near Providence, and I heard a strange story about him. Pray, sir, give me some account of this man."

"Sir," said the stranger, "those who know the most respecting that man, say the least. I have heard it asserted that Heaven sometimes sets a mark on a man, either for judgment or a trial. Under which Peter Rugg now labors, I cannot say; therefore I am rather inclined to pity than to judge."

"You speak like a humane man," said I; "and if you have known him so long, I pray you will give me some account of him. Has his appearance much altered in that time?"

"Why, yes. He looks as though he never ate, drank, or slept; and his child looks older than himself; and he looks like time broken off from eternity, and anxious to gain a resting-place."

"And how does his horse look?" said I.

"As for his horse, he looks fatter and gayer, and shows more animation and courage than he did twenty years ago. The last time Rugg spoke to me he inquired how far it was to Boston. I told him just one hundred miles."

"'Why,' said he, 'how can you deceive me so? It is cruel to mislead a traveller. I have lost my way; pray direct me the nearest way to Boston.'

"I repeated, it was one hundred miles.

"'How can you say so?' said he; 'I was told last evening it was but fifty, and I have travelled all night.'

"'But,' said I, 'you are now travelling from Boston. You must turn back.'

"'Alas,' said he, 'it is all turn back! Boston shifts with the wind, and plays all around the compass. One man tells me it is to the east, another to the west; and the guide-posts too, they all point the wrong way.'

"'But will you not stop and rest?' said I; 'you seem wet and weary.'

"'Yes,' said he, 'it has been foul weather since I left home.'

"'Stop, then, and refresh yourself.'

"'I must not stop; I must reach home to-night, if possible: though I think you must be mistaken in the distance to Boston.'

"He then gave the reins to his horse, which he restrained with difficulty, and disappeared in a moment. A few days afterward I met the man a little this side of Claremont, winding around the hills in Unity, at the rate, I believe, of twelve miles an hour."

"Is Peter Rugg his real name, or has he accidentally gained that name?"

"I know not, but presume he will not deny his name; you can ask him, — for see, he has turned his horse, and is passing this way."

In a moment a dark-colored high-spirited horse approached, and would have passed without stopping, but I had resolved to speak to Peter Rugg, or whoever the man might be. Accordingly I stepped into the street; and as the horse approached, I made a feint of stopping him. The man immediately reined in his horse. "Sir," said I, "may I be so bold as to inquire if you are not Mr. Rugg? for I think I have seen you before."

"My name is Peter Rugg," said he. "I have unfortunately lost my way; I am wet and weary, and will take it kindly of you to direct me to Boston."

"You live in Boston, do you; and in what street?"

"In Middle Street."

"When did you leave Boston?"

"I cannot tell precisely; it seems a considerable time."

"But how did you and your child become so wet? It has not rained here to-day."

"It has just rained a heavy shower up the river. But I shall not reach Boston to-night if I tarry. Would you advise me to take the old road or the turnpike?"

"Why, the old road is one hundred and seventeen miles, and the turnpike is ninety-seven."

"How can you say so? You impose on me; it is wrong to trifle with a traveller; you know it is but forty miles from Newburyport to Boston."

"But this is not Newburyport; this is Hartford."

"Do not deceive me, sir. Is not this town Newburyport, and the river that I have been following the Merrimack?"

"No, sir; this is Hartford, and the river the Connecticut."

He wrung his hands and looked incredulous. "Have the rivers, too, changed their courses, as the cities have changed places? But see! the clouds are gathering in the south, and we shall have a rainy night. Ah, that fatal oath!"

He would tarry no longer; his impatient horse leaped off, his hind flanks rising like wings; he seemed to devour all before him, and to scorn all behind.

I had now, as I thought, discovered a clew to the history of Peter Rugg; and I determined, the next time my business called me to Boston, to make a further inquiry. Soon after, I was enabled to collect the following particulars from Mrs. Croft, an aged lady in Middle Street, who has resided in Boston during the last twenty years. Her narration is this:

Just at twilight last summer a person stopped at the door of the late Mrs. Rugg. Mrs. Croft on coming to the door perceived a stranger with a child by his side, in an old weather-beaten carriage, with a black horse. The stranger asked for Mrs. Rugg, and was informed that Mrs. Rugg had died at a good old age, more than twenty years before that time.

The stranger replied, "How can you deceive me so? Do ask Mrs. Rugg to step to the door."

"Sir, I assure you Mrs. Rugg has not lived here these twenty years; no one lives here but myself, and my name is Betsey Croft."

The stranger paused, looked up and down the street, and said, "Though the paint is rather faded, this looks like my house."

"Yes," said the child, "that is the stone before the door that I used to sit on to eat my bread and milk."

"But," said the stranger, "it seems to be on the wrong side of the street. Indeed, everything here seems to be misplaced. The streets are all changed, the people are all changed, the town seems changed, and what is strangest of all, Catherine Rugg has deserted her husband and child. Pray," continued the stranger, "has John Foy come home from sea? He went a long voyage; he is my kinsman. If I could see him, he could give me some account of Mrs. Rugg."

"Sir," said Mrs. Croft, "I never heard of John Foy. Where did he live?"

"Just above here, in Orange-tree Lane."

"There is no such place in this neighborhood."

"What do you tell me! Are the streets gone? Orange-tree Lane is at the head of Hanover Street, near Pemberton's Hill."

"There is no such lane now."

"Madam, you cannot be serious! But you doubtless know my brother, William Rugg. He lives in Royal Exchange Lane, near King Street."

"I know of no such lane; and I am sure there is no such street as King Street in this town."

"No such street as King Street! Why, woman, you mock me! You may as well tell me there is no King George. However, madam, you see I am wet and weary, I must find a resting-place. I will go to Hart's tavern, near the market."

"Which market, sir? for you seem perplexed; we have several markets."

"You know there is but one market near the town dock."

"Oh, the old market; but no such person has kept there these twenty years."

Here the stranger seemed disconcerted, and uttered to himself quite audibly: "Strange mistake; how much this looks like the town of Boston! It certainly has a great resemblance to it; but I perceive my mistake now. Some other Mrs. Rugg, some other Middle Street. — Then," said he, "madam, can you direct me to Boston?"

"Why, this is Boston, the city of Boston; I know of no other Boston."

"City of Boston it may be; but it is not the Boston where I live. I recollect now, I came over a bridge instead of a ferry. Pray, what bridge is that I just came over?"

"It is Charles River bridge."

"I perceive my mistake: there is a ferry between Boston and Charlestown; there is no bridge. Ah, I perceive my mistake. If I were in Boston my horse would carry me directly to my own door. But my horse shows by his impatience that he is in a strange place. Absurd, that I should have mistaken this place for the old town of Boston! It is a much finer city than the town of Boston. It has been built long since Boston. I fancy Boston must lie at a distance from this city, as the good woman seems ignorant of it."

At these words his horse began to chafe, and strike the pavement with his forefeet. The stranger seemed a little bewildered, and said, "No home to-night;" and giving the reins to his horse, passed up the street, and I saw no more of him.

It was evident that the generation to which Peter Rugg belonged, had passed away.

This was all the account of Peter Rugg I could obtain from Mrs. Croft; but she directed me to an elderly man, Mr. James Felt, who lived near her, and who had kept a record of the principal occurrences for the last fifty years. At my request she sent for him; and after I had related to him the object of my inquiry, Mr. Felt told me he had known Rugg in his youth, and that his disappearance had caused some surprise; but as it sometimes happens that men run away, — sometimes to be rid of others, and sometimes to be rid of themselves, — and Rugg took his child with him, and his own horse and chair, and as it did not appear that any creditors made a stir, the occurrence soon mingled itself in the stream of oblivion; and Rugg and his child, horse, and chair were soon forgotten.

"It is true," said Mr. Felt, "sundry stories grew out of Rugg's affair, whether true or false I cannot tell; but stranger things have happened in my day, without even a newspaper notice."

"Sir," said I, "Peter Rugg is now living. I have lately seen Peter Rugg and his child, horse, and chair; therefore I pray you to relate to me all you know or ever heard of him."

"Why, my friend," said James Felt, "that Peter Rugg is now a living man, I will not deny; but that you have seen Peter Rugg and his child, is impossible, if you mean a small child; for Jenny Rugg, if living, must be at least — let me see — Boston massacre, 1770 — Jenny Rugg was about ten years old. Why, sir, Jenny Rugg, if living, must be more than sixty years of age. That Peter Rugg is living, is highly probable, as he was only ten years older than myself, and I was only eighty last March; and I am as likely to live twenty years longer as any man."

Here I perceived that Mr. Felt was in his dotage, and I despaired of gaining any intelligence from him on which I could depend.

I took my leave of Mrs. Croft, and proceeded to my lodgings at the Marlborough Hotel.

"If Peter Rugg," thought I, "has been travelling since the Boston massacre, there is no reason why he should not travel to the end of time. If the present generation know little of him, the next will know less, and Peter and his child will have no hold on this world."

In the course of the evening, I related my adventure in Middle Street.

"Ha!" said one of the company, smiling, "do you really think you have seen Peter Rugg? I have heard my grandfather speak of him, as though he seriously believed his own story."

"Sir," said I, "pray let us compare your grandfather's story of Mr. Rugg with my own."

"Peter Rugg, sir, — if my grandfather was worthy of credit, — once lived in Middle Street, in this city. He was a man in comfortable circumstances, had a wife and one daughter, and was generally esteemed for his sober life and manners. But unhappily, his temper, at times, was altogether ungovernable, and then his language was terrible. In these fits of passion, if a door stood in his way, he would never do less than kick a panel through. He would sometimes throw his heels over his head, and come down on his feet, uttering oaths in a circle; and thus in a rage, he was the first who performed a somerset, and did what others have since learned to do for merriment and money. Once Rugg was seen to bite a tenpenny nail in halves. In those days everybody, both men and boys, wore wigs; and Peter, at these moments of violent passion, would become so profane that his wig would rise up from his head. Some said it was on account of his terrible language; others accounted for it in a more philosophical way, and said it was caused by the expansion of his scalp, as violent passion, we know, will swell the veins and expand the head. While these fits were on him, Rugg had no respect for heaven or earth. Except this infirmity, all agreed that Rugg was a good sort of a man; for when his fits were over, nobody was so ready to commend a placid temper as Peter.

"One morning, late in autumn, Rugg, in his own chair, with a fine large bay horse, took his daughter and proceeded to Concord. On his return a violent storm overtook him. At dark he stopped in Menotomy, now West Cambridge, at the door of a Mr. Cutter, a friend of his, who urged him to tarry the night. On Rugg's declining to stop, Mr. Cutter urged him vehemently. 'Why, Mr. Rugg,' said Cutter, 'the storm is overwhelming you. The night is exceedingly dark. Your little daughter will perish. You are in an open chair, and the tempest is increasing.' '*Let the storm increase,*' said Rugg, with a fearful oath, '*I will see home to-night, in spite of the last tempest, or may I never see home!*' At these words he gave his whip to his high-spirited horse and disappeared in a moment. But Peter Rugg did not reach home that night, nor the next; nor, when he became a missing man, could he ever be traced beyond Mr. Cutter's, in Menotomy.

"For a long time after, on every dark and stormy night the wife of Peter Rugg would fancy she heard the crack of a whip, and the fleet tread of a horse, and the rattling of a carriage passing her door. The neighbors, too, heard the same noises, and some said they knew it was Rugg's horse; the tread on the pavement was perfectly familiar to them. This occurred so repeatedly that at length the neighbors watched with lanterns, and saw the real Peter Rugg, with his own horse and chair and the child sitting beside him, pass directly before his own door, his head turned toward his house, and himself making every effort to stop his horse, but in vain.

"The next day the friends of Mrs. Rugg exerted themselves to find her husband and child. They inquired at every public house and stable in town; but it did not appear that Rugg made any stay in Boston. No one, after Rugg had passed his own door, could give any account of him, though it was asserted by some that the clatter of Rugg's horse and carriage over the pavements shook the houses on both sides of the streets. And this is credible, if indeed Rugg's horse and carriage did pass on that night; for at this day, in many of the streets, a loaded truck or team in passing will shake the houses like an earthquake. However, Rugg's neighbors never afterward watched. Some of them treated it all as a delusion, and thought no more of it. Others of a different opinion shook their heads and said nothing.

"Thus Rugg and his child, horse, and chair were soon forgotten; and probably many in the neighborhood never heard a word on the subject.

"There was indeed a rumor that Rugg was seen afterward in Connecticut, between Suffield and Hartford, passing through the country at headlong speed. This gave occasion to Rugg's friends to make further inquiry; but the more they inquired, the more they were baffled. If they heard of Rugg one day in Connecticut, the next they heard of him winding round the hills in New Hampshire; and soon after a man in a chair, with a small child, exactly answering the description of Peter Rugg, would be seen in Rhode Island inquiring the way to Boston.

"But that which chiefly gave a color of mystery to the story of Peter Rugg was the affair at Charlestown bridge. The toll-gatherer asserted that sometimes, on the darkest and most stormy nights, when no object could be discerned, about the time Rugg was missing, a horse and wheel-carriage, with a noise equal to a troop, would at midnight, in utter contempt of the rates of toll, pass over the bridge. This occurred so frequently that the toll-gatherer resolved to attempt a discovery. Soon after, at the usual time, apparently the same horse and carriage approached the bridge from Charlestown square. The toll-gatherer, prepared, took his stand as near the middle of the bridge as he dared, with a large three-legged stool in his hand; as the appearance passed, he threw the stool at the horse, but heard nothing except the noise of the stool skipping across the bridge. The toll-gatherer on the next day asserted that the stool went directly through the body of the horse, and he persisted in that belief ever after. Whether Rugg, or whoever the person was, ever passed the bridge again, the toll-gatherer would never tell; and when questioned, seemed anxious to waive the subject. And thus Peter Rugg and his child, horse, and carriage, remain a mystery to this day."

This, sir, is all that I could learn of Peter Rugg in Boston.

Lydia Maria Child
The Indian Wife

Lydia Maria Child's "The Indian Wife" was first published in *The Legendary* in 1828, a magazine that was to survive only two issues. It was later reprinted in *The Coronal* (1832) and then *Fact and Fiction* (1846), testimony of its popularity among readers of the day. Child was immensely admired as a writer of fiction, an essayist, and as an editor. Her work was nearly always reformist, addressing social issues such as abolition, women's rights, the place of Native Americans in society, and anti-Semitism, about which she wrote a series of poignant articles. "The Indian Wife" followed the success of her first novel, *Hobomok: A Tale of the Early Times,* set in Georgia and focusing on relations between white settlers and the Cherokee. Her story takes place in what is now Minneapolis, at the confluence of the Mississippi and Minnesota rivers, where a falls drops off nearly fifty feet. The Dakota called the location "Minirora," curling water, and Child based her tale on a legend about a tragic event that took place when French immigrants were first coming to the area.

Lydia Maria Child, "The Indian Wife," *The Legendary* 1 (1828): 197–207.

—— May slighted woman turn,
And as a vine the oak hath shaken off,
Bend lightly to her tendencies again?
Oh, no! by all her loveliness, by all
That makes life poetry and beauty, no!
Make her a slave; steal from her rosy cheek
By needless jealousies; let the last star
Leave her a watcher by your couch of pain;
Wrong her by petulance, suspicion, all
That makes her cup a bitterness — yet give
One evidence of love, and earth has not
An emblem of devotedness like hers.
But oh! estrange her once, it boots not how,
By wrong or silence, anything that tells
A change has come upon your tenderness —
And there is not a high thing out of heaven
Her pride o'ermastereth not.

— Willis

Tahmiroo was the daughter of a powerful Sioux chieftain; and she was the only being ever known to turn the relentless old man from a savage purpose. Something of this influence was owing to her infantile beauty; but more to the gentleness of which that beauty was the emblem. Her's was a species of loveliness

rare among Indian girls. Her figure had the flexile grace so appropriate to protected and dependant woman in refined countries; her ripe, pouting lip, and
dimpled cheek wore the pleading air of aggrieved childhood; and her dark eye
had such an habitual expression of timidity and fear, that the young Sioux called
her the "Startled Fawn."

I know not whether her father's broad lands, or her own appealing beauty,
was the most powerful cause of admiration; but certain it is, Tahmiroo was the
unrivalled belle of the Sioux. She was a creature all formed for love. Her downcast eye, her trembling lip, and her quiet, submissive motion, all spoke its language; yet various young chieftains had in vain sought her affections, and when
her father urged her to strengthen his power by an alliance, she answered him
only by her tears.

This state of things continued until 1765, when a company of French traders
came to reside there, for the sake of deriving profit from the fur trade. Among
them was Florimond de Rancé, a young, indolent Adonis, whom pure ennui had
led from Quebec to the Falls of St Anthony. His fair, round face, and studied fop-
pery of dress might have done little toward gaining the heart of the gentle Sioux;
but there was a deference and courtesy in his manner, which the Indian never
pays to degraded woman, and Tahmiroo's deep sensibilities were touched by it.
A more careful arrangement of her rude dress, an anxiety to speak his language
fluently, and a close observance of European customs soon betrayed the subtle
power, which was fast making her its slave. The ready vanity of the Frenchman
quickly perceived it. At first he encouraged it with that sort of undefined pleasure, which man always feels in awakening strong affection in the hearts of even
the most insignificant. Then the idea that, though an Indian, she was a princess,
and that her father's extensive lands on the Missouri were daily becoming of
more and more consequence to his ambitious nation, led him to think of marriage with her as a desirable object. His eyes and his manner had said this, long
before the old chief began to suspect it; and he allowed the wily Frenchman to
twine himself almost as closely around his heart, as he had around the more
yielding soul of his darling child.

Though exceedingly indolent by nature, Florimond de Rancé had acquired
skill in many graceful arts, which excited the wonder of the savages. He fenced
well enough to foil the most expert antagonist, and in hunting, his rifle was sure
to carry death to the game. These accomplishments, and the facility with which
his pliant nation conform to the usages of savage life, made him a universal favorite, and at his request, he was formally adopted as one of the tribe. But conscious as he was of his power, it was long before he dared to ask for the daughter
of the haughty chief. When he did make the daring proposition, it was received
with a still and terrible wrath, that might well frighten him from his purpose.
Rage showed itself only in the swelling veins and clenched hand of the old chief.
With the boasted coldness and self-possession of an Indian, he answered, "There

are Sioux girls enough for the poor pale faces that come among us. A king's daughter weds the son of a king. Eagles must sleep in an eagle's nest."

In vain Tahmiroo knelt and supplicated. In vain she promised that Florimond de Rancé would adopt all his enmities and all his friendships; that in hunting, and in war, he would be an invaluable treasure. The chief remained inexorable. Then Tahmiroo no longer joined in the dance, and the old men noticed that her rich voice was silent, when they passed her wigwam. The light of her beauty began to fade, and the bright vermillion current, which mantled under her brown cheek, became sluggish and pale. The languid glance she cast on the morning sun and the bright earth, entered into her father's soul. He could not see his beautiful child thus gradually wasting away. He had long averted his eyes, whenever he saw Florimond de Rancé; but one day, when he crossed his hunting path, he laid his hand on his shoulder, and pointed to Tahmiroo's dwelling. Not a word was spoken. The proud old man, and the blooming lover entered it together. Tahmiroo was seated in the darkest corner of the wigwam, her head leaning on her hand, her basket work tangled beside her, and a bunch of flowers, the village maidens had brought her, scattered and withering at her feet. The chief looked upon her, with a vehement expression of love, which none but stern countenances can wear. "Tahmiroo," he said, in a subdued tone, "go to the wigwam of the stranger, that your father may again see you love to look on the rising sun, and the opening flowers." There was mingled joy and modesty in the upward glance of the "Startled Fawn" of the Sioux; and when Florimond de Rancé saw the light of her mild eye, suddenly and timidly veiled by its deeply fringed lid, he knew that he had lost none of his power.

The marriage song was soon heard in the royal wigwam, and the young adventurer became the son of a king.

Months and years past on, and found Tahmiroo the same devoted, submissive being. Her husband no longer treated her with the uniform gallantry of a lover. He was not often harsh; but he adopted something of the coldness and indifference of the nation he had joined. Tahmiroo sometimes wept in secret; but so much of fear had lately mingled with her love, that she carefully concealed her grief from him who had occasioned it. When she watched his countenance, with that pleading, innocent look, which had always characterized her beauty, she sometimes would obtain a glance such as he had given her in former days, and then her heart would leap like a frolicsome lamb, and she would live cheerfully on the remembrance of that smile, through many wearisome days of silence and neglect. Never was woman, in her heart breaking devotedness, satisfied with such slight testimonials of love, as was this gentle Sioux girl. If Florimond chose to fish, she would herself ply the oars, rather than he should suffer fatigue; and the gaudy canoe her father had given her, might often be seen gliding down the stream, while Tahmiroo dipped her oars in unison with her soft, rich voice, and the indolent Frenchman lay sunk in luxurious repose. She had learned his religion; but for herself she never prayed. The cross he had given her was always raised in supplication for him; and if he but looked unkindly on her, she kissed it, and invoked its aid, in agony of soul. She fancied the sounds of his native land might be dear to him, and she studied his language with a patience and perseverance to which the savage has seldom been known to submit. She tried to imitate the dresses she had heard him describe; and if he looked with a pleased eye on any ornament she wore, it was always reserved to welcome his return. Yet, for all this lavishness of love, she asked but kind, approving looks, which cost the giver nothing. Alas, for the perverseness of man, in scorning the affection he ceases to doubt! The little pittance of love for which poor Tahmiroo's heart yearned so much, was seldom given. Her soul was a perpetual prey to anxiety and excitement; and the quiet certainty of domestic bliss was never her allotted portion. There were, however, two beings, on whom she could pour forth her whole flood of tenderness, without reproof or disappointment. She had given birth to a son and daughter, of uncommon promise. Victoire, the eldest, had her father's beauty, save in the melting dark eye, with its plaintive expression, and the modest drooping of its silken lash. Her cheeks had just enough of the Indian hue to give them a warm, rich coloring; and such was her early maturity, that at thirteen years of age, her tall figure combined the graceful elasticity of youth, with the staid majesty of womanhood. She had sprung up at her father's feet, with the sudden luxuriance of a tropical flower; and her matured loveliness aroused all the dormant tenderness and energy within him. It was with mournful interest he saw her leaping along the chase, with her mother's bounding, sylphlike joy; and he would sigh deeply when he observed her oar rapidly cutting the waters of the Missouri, while her boat flew over the surface of the river like a wild bird in sport — and the gay young creature would wind round among the eddies, or dart forward, with her hair streaming on the wind, and her lips parted with eagerness. Tahmiroo did not understand the nature of his emotions. She thought, in the simplicity of her heart, that silence and sadness were the natural expressions of a white man's love; but when he turned his restless gaze from his daughter to her, she met an expression which troubled her. Indifference had changed into contempt; and woman's soul, whether in the drawingroom or the wilderness, is painfully alive to the sting of scorn. Sometimes her placid nature was disturbed by a strange jealousy of her own child. "I love Victoire only because she is the daughter of Florimond," thought she; "and why, oh! why does he not love me for being the mother of Victoire?"

It was too evident, that De Rancé wished his daughter should be estranged from her mother, and her mother's people. With all members of the tribe, out of his own family, he sternly forbade her having any intercourse; and even there he kept her constantly employed in taking dancing lessons from himself, and obtaining various branches of learning from an old Catholic priest, whom he had solicited to reside with him for that purpose. But this kind of life was irksome to the Indian girl, and she was perpetually escaping the vigilance of her father, to try her arrow in the woods, or guide her pretty canoe over the waters. De Rancé had long thought it impossible to gratify his ambitious views for his daughter, without removing her from the attractions of her savage home, and each day's experience convinced him more and more of the truth of this conclusion.

To favor his project he assumed an affectionate manner towards his wife; for he well knew that one look or word of kindness would at any time win back all her love. When the deep sensibilities of her warm heart were roused, he would ask for leave to sell her lands; and she, in her prodigality of tenderness, would have given him anything, even her own life, for such smiles as he then bestowed. The old chief was dead, and there was no one to check the unfeeling rapacity of the Frenchman. Tracts after tracts of Tahmiroo's valuable land were sold, and the money remitted to Quebec, whither he had the purpose of conveying his children, on the pretence of a visit, but in reality with the firm intent of never again beholding his deserted wife.

A company of Canadian traders happened to visit the Falls of St Anthony, just at this juncture, and Florimond de Rancé took the opportunity to apprise Tahmiroo of his intention to educate Victoire at one of the convents in Quebec. The Sioux pleaded with all the earnestness of a mother's eloquence; but she pleaded, in vain. Victoire and her father joined the company of traders, on their return to Canada. Tahmiroo knelt and fervently besought that she might accompany them. She would stay out of sight, she said; they should not be ashamed of her, among the great white folks at the east; and if she could but live where she could see them every day, she should die happier.

"Ashamed of you! and you the daughter of a Sioux king!" exclaimed Victoire proudly, and, with a natural impulse of tenderness, fell on her mother's neck, and wept.

"Victoire, 't is time to depart!" said her father sternly. The sobbing girl tried to release herself; but she could not. Tahmiroo embraced her with the energy of despair; for, after all her doubts and jealousies, Victoire was the darling child of her bosom — she was so much the image of Florimond when he first said he loved her. "Woman! let her go!" exclaimed De Rancé, exasperated by the length of the parting scene. Tahmiroo raised her eyes anxiously to his face, and she saw that his arm was raised to strike her.

"I am a poor daughter of the Sioux; oh! why did you marry me?" exclaimed she, in a tone of passionate grief.

"For your father's lands," said the Frenchman coldly.

This was the drop too much. Poor Tahmiroo with a piercing shriek fell on the earth, and hid her face in the grass. She knew not how long she remained there. Her highly wrought feelings had brought on a dizziness of the brain; and she was conscious only of a sensation of sickness, accompanied by the sound of receding voices. When she recovered, she found herself alone with Louis, her little boy, then about six years old. The child had wandered there, after the traders had departed, and having in vain tried to waken his mother, he had laid himself down at her side, and slept on his bow and arrows. From that hour Tahmiroo was changed. Her quiet, submissive air gave place to a stern and lofty manner; and she, who had always been so gentle, became as bitter and implacable as the most blood thirsty of her tribe. In little Louis all the strong feelings of her soul were centered; but even her affection for him was characterized by a strange and unwonted fierceness. Her only care seemed to be to make him like his grandfather, and to instil a deadly hatred of white men; and the boy learned his lessons well. He was the veriest little savage that ever let fly an arrow. To his mother alone he yielded anything like submission; and the Sioux were proud to hail the haughty child as their future chieftain.

Such was the aspect of things on the shores of the Mississippi, when Florimond de Rancé came among them, after an absence of three years. He was induced to make this visit, partly from a lingering curiosity to see his boy, and partly from the hopes of obtaining more land from the yielding Tahmiroo. He affected much contrition for his past conduct, and promised to return with Victoire, before the year expired. Tahmiroo met him with the most chilling indifference, and listened to him with a vacant look, as if she heard him not. It was only when he spoke to her boy, that he could arouse her from this apparent lethargy. On this subject she was all suspicion. She had a sort of undefined dread that he too would be carried away from her; and she watched over him like a she wolf, when her young is in danger.

Her fears were not unfounded; for Florimond de Rancé did intend, by demonstrations of fondness, and glowing descriptions of Quebec, to kindle in the mind of his son a desire to accompany him.

Tahmiroo thought the hatred of white men, which she had so carefully instilled, would prove a sufficient shield; but many weeks had not elapsed, before she saw that Louis was fast yielding himself up to the fascinating power, which had enthralled her own youthful spirit. With this discovery came horrible thoughts of vengeance; and more than once, she had nearly nerved her soul to murder the father of her son; but she could not. Something in his features still reminded her of the devoted young Frenchman who had carried her quiver through the woods, and kissed the moccasin he stooped to lace, and she could not kill him.

The last cutting blow was soon given to the heart of the Indian Wife. Young Louis, full of boyish curiosity, expressed a wish to go with his father, though he, at the same time, promised a speedy return. He had always been a stubborn boy; and she felt now as if her worn-out spirit would vainly contend against his wilfulness. With that sort of resigned stupor, which often indicates approaching insanity, she yielded to his request, exacting, however, a promise that he would sail a few miles down the Mississippi with her, the day before his departure.

The day arrived. Florimond de Rancé was at a distance on business. Tahmiroo decked herself in the garments and jewels she had worn on the day of her marriage, and selected the gaudiest wampum belts for the little Louis.

"Why do you put these on?" said the boy.

"Because Tahmiroo will no more see her son in the land of the Sioux," said she, mournfully, "and when her father meets her in the Spirit Land, he will know the beads he gave her."

She took the wondering boy by the hand, and led him to the river side. There lay the canoe her father had given her when she left him for "the wigwam of the Stranger." It was faded and bruised now, and so were all her hopes. She looked back on the hut, where she had spent her brief term of wedded happiness, and its peacefulness seemed a mockery of her misery. And was she — the lone, the wretched, the desperate, and deserted one — was she the "Startled Fawn" of the Sioux, for whom contending chiefs had asked in vain ? The remembrance of all her love and all her wrongs came up before her memory, and death seemed more pleasant to her than the gay dance she once loved so well. But then her eye rested on her boy — and, O God! with what an agony of love! It was the last vehement struggle of a soul all formed for tenderness. "We will go to the Spirit Land together," she exclaimed. "He cannot come there to rob me!"

She took Louis in her arms, as if he had been a feather, and springing into the boat, she guided it toward the Falls of St Anthony. "Mother, mother! the canoe is going over the rapids!" screamed the frightened child. "My father stands on the waves and beckons me!" she said. The boy looked at the horribly fixed expression of her face, and shrieked aloud for help.

The boat went over the cataract. Louis de Rancé was seen no more. He sleeps with the "Startled Fawn" of the Sioux, in the waves of the Mississippi! The story is well remembered by the Indians of the present day; and when a mist gathers over the Falls, they often say, "Let us not hunt to day. A storm will certainly come; for Tahmiroo and her son are going over the Falls of St Anthony."

Augustus Baldwin Longstreet
The Horse Swap

Augustus Baldwin Longstreet's "The Horse Swap," one of the most famous of the popular tales of wily horse traders, was originally published in the *Milledgeville Southern Reader* in 1833 and included *Georgia Scenes* two years later. The author, an attorney educated at Yale who was also an ordained minister, was at various times in his life a judge, a politician, an editor, and president of four colleges, including Emory University and the University of Mississippi. It is not surprising that for his most celebrated story he created a narrator, Lyman Hall, who is cultured and urbane, distinctly apart from the backwoods world and rustic characters he describes. This device, of a discordant relationship between the teller and the people he depicts, became customary in the Local Color movement after the Civil War. Longstreet here portrays a male world of loafers, con men, city slickers, and animal dealers, who approach their subject with a studied inscrutability. There is apparently an ethic to swapping horses: boasting and posturing are permitted; lying is forbidden; concealment is an art. The rich dialogue is rendered in the vernacular, giving texture and humor to the unfolding drama of making a deal.

Augustus Baldwin Longstreet, "The Horse Swap," *Georgia Scenes, Characters, Incidents &c. in the First Half Century of the Republic* (Augusta: S. R. Sentinel Office, 1835), 23–31.

———

During the session of the Supreme Court, in the village of —— , about three weeks ago, when a number of people were collected in the principal street of the village, I observed a young man riding up and down the street, as I supposed, in a violent passion. He galloped this way, then that, and then the other; spurred his horse to one group of citizens, then to another, then dashed off at half speed, as if fleeing from danger; and, suddenly checking his horse, returned first in a pace, then in a trot, and then in a canter. While he was performing these various evolutions, he cursed, swore, whooped, screamed, and tossed himself in every attitude which man could assume on horseback. In short, he *cavorted* most magnanimously (a term which, in our tongue, expresses all that I have described, and a little more), and seemed to be setting all creation at defiance. As I like to see all that is passing, I determined to take a position a little nearer to him, and to ascertain, if possible, what it was that affected him so sensibly. Accordingly, I approached a crowd before which he had stopped for a moment, and examined it with the strictest scrutiny. But I could see nothing in it that seemed to have anything to do with the cavorter. Every man appeared to be in good humour, and all minding their own business. Not one so much as noticed the principal figure. Still he went on. After a semicolon pause, which my appearance seemed to produce (for he eyed me closely as I approached), he fetched a whoop, and swore that "he could out-swap any live man, woman, or child that ever walked these hills, or that ever straddled horseflesh since the days of old daddy Adam. Stranger," said he to me, "did you ever see the *Yellow* Blossom from Jasper?"

"No," said I, "but I have often heard of him."

"I'm the boy," continued he; "perhaps a *leetle*, jist a *leetle*, of the best man at a horse-swap that ever trod shoe-leather."

I began to feel my situation a little awkward, when I was relieved by a man somewhat advanced in years, who stepped up and began to survey the *"Yellow Blossom's"* horse with much apparent interest. This drew the rider's attention, and he turned the conversation from me to the stranger.

"Well, my old coon," said he, "do you want to swap *hosses?"*

"Why, I don't know," replied the stranger; "I believe I've got a beast I'd trade with you for that one, if you like him."

"Well, fetch up your nag, my old cock; you're jist the lark I wanted to get hold of. I am perhaps a *leetle*, jist a *leetle*, of the best man at a horse-swap that ever stole *cracklins* out of his mammy's fat gourd. Where's your *hoss?"*

"I'll bring him presently; but I want to examine your horse a little."

"Oh! look at him," said the Blossom, alighting and hitting him a cut; "look at him. He's the best piece of *hoss*flesh in the thirteen united univarsal worlds. There's no sort o' mistake in little Bullet. He can pick up miles on his feet, and fling 'em behind him as fast as the next man's *hoss*, I don't care where he comes from. And he can keep at it as long as the sun can shine without resting."

During this harangue, little Bullet looked as if he understood it all, believed it, and was ready at any moment to verify it. He was a horse of goodly countenance, rather expressive of vigilance than fire; though an unnatural appearance of fierceness was thrown into it by the loss of his ears, which had been cropped pretty close to his head. Nature had done but little for Bullet's head and neck; but he managed, in a great measure, to hide their defects by bowing perpetually. He had obviously suffered severely for corn; but if his ribs and hip bones had not disclosed the fact, *he* never would have done it; for he was in all respects as cheerful and happy as if he commanded all the corn-cribs and fodder-stacks in Georgia. His height was about twelve hands; but as his shape partook somewhat of that of the giraffe, his haunches stood much lower. They were short, strait, peaked, and concave. Bullet's tail, however, made amends for all his defects. All that the artist could do to beautify it had been done; and all that horse could do to compliment the artist, Bullet did. His tail was nicked in superior style, and exhibited the line of beauty in so many directions, that it could not fail to hit the most fastidious taste in some of them. From the root it dropped into a graceful festoon; then rose in a handsome curve; then resumed its first direction; and then mounted suddenly upward like a cypress knee to a perpendicular of about two and half inches. The whole had a careless and bewitching inclination to the right. Bullet obviously knew where his beauty lay, and took all occasions to display it to the best advantage. If a stick cracked, or if any one moved suddenly about him, or coughed, or hawked, or spoke a little louder than common, up went Bullet's tail like lightning; and if the *going up* did not please, the *coming down* must of necessity, for it was as different from the other movement as was its direction. The first was a bold and rapid flight upward, usually to an angle of forty-five degrees. In this position he kept his interesting appendage until he satisfied himself that nothing in particular was to be done; when he commenced dropping it by half inches, in second beats, then in triple time, then faster and shorter and faster and shorter still, until it finally died away imperceptibly into its natural position. If I might compare sights to sounds, I should say its *settling* was more like the note of a locust than anything else in nature.

Either from native sprightliness of disposition, from uncontrollable activity, or from an unconquerable habit of removing flies by the stamping of the feet, Bullet never stood still; but always kept up a gentle fly-scaring movement of his limbs, which was peculiarly interesting.

"I tell you, man," proceeded the Yellow Blossom, "he's the best live hoss that ever trod the grit of Georgia. Bob Smart knows the hoss. Come here, Bob, and mount this hoss, and show Bullet's motions." Here Bullet bristled up, and looked as if he had been hunting for Bob all day long, and had just found him. Bob sprang on his back. "Boo-oo-oo!" said Bob, with a fluttering noise of the lips; and away went Bullet, as if in a quarter race, with all his beauties spread in handsome style.

"Now fetch him back," said Blossom. Bullet turned and came in pretty much as he went out.

"Now trot him by." Bullet reduced his tail to *"customary;"* sidled to the right and left airily, and exhibited at least three varieties of trot in the short space of fifty yards.

"Make him pace!" Bob commenced twitching the bridle and kicking at the same time. These inconsistent movements obviously (and most naturally) disconcerted Bullet; for it was impossible for him to learn, from them, whether he was to proceed or stand still. He started to trot, and was told that wouldn't do. He attempted a canter, and was checked again. He stopped, and was urged to go on. Bullet now rushed into the wide field of experiment, and struck out a gait of his own, that completely turned the tables upon his rider, and certainly deserved a patent. It seemed to have derived its elements from the jig, the minuet, and the cotillon. If it was not a pace, it certainly had *pace* in it, and no man would venture to call it anything else; so it passed off to the satisfaction of the owner.

"Walk him!" Bullet was now at home again; and he walked as if money was staked on him.

The stranger, whose name, I afterward learned, was Peter Ketch, having examined Bullet to his heart's content, ordered his son Neddy to go and bring up Kit. Neddy soon appeared upon Kit; a well-formed sorrel of the middle size, and in good order. His *tout ensemble* threw Bullet entirely in the shade, though a glance was sufficient to satisfy any one that Bullet had the decided advantage of him in point of intellect.

"Why, man," said Blossom, "do you bring such a hoss as that to trade for Bullet? Oh, I see you've no notion of trading."

"Ride him off, Neddy!" said Peter. Kit put off at a handsome lope.

"Trot him back!" Kit came in at a long, sweeping trot, and stopped suddenly at the crowd.

"Well," said Blossom, "let me look at him; maybe he'll do to plough."

"Examine him!" said Peter, taking hold of the bridle close to the mouth; "he's nothing but a tacky. He an't as *pretty* a horse as Bullet, I know; but he'll do. Start 'em together for a hundred and fifty *mile*; and if Kit an't twenty mile ahead of him at the coming out, any man may take Kit for nothing. But he's a monstrous mean horse, gentleman; any man may see that. He's the scariest horse, too, you ever saw. He won't do to hunt on, no how. Stranger, will you let Neddy have your rifle to shoot off him? Lay the rifle between his ears, Neddy, and shoot at the blaze in that stump. Tell me when his head is high enough."

Ned fired, and hit the blaze; and Kit did not move a hair's breadth.

"Neddy, take a couple of sticks, and beat on that hogshead at Kit's tail."

Ned made a tremendous rattling, at which Bullet took fright, broke his bridle, and dashed off in grand style; and would have stopped all farther negotiations by going home in disgust, had not a traveller arrested him and brought him back; but Kit did not move.

"I tell you, gentlemen," continued Peter, "he's the scariest horse you ever saw. He an't as gentle as Bullet, but he won't do any harm if you watch him. Shall I put him in a cart, gig, or wagon for you, stranger? He'll cut the same capers there he does here. He's a monstrous mean horse."

During all this time Blossom was examining him with the nicest scrutiny. Having examined his frame and limbs, he now looked at his eyes.

"He's got a curious look out of his eyes," said Blossom.

"Oh yes, sir," said Peter, "just as blind as a bat. Blind horses always have clear eyes. Make a motion at his eyes, if you please, sir."

Blossom did so, and Kit threw up his head rather as if something pricked him under the chin than as if fearing a blow. Blossom repeated the experiment, and Kit jerked back in considerable astonishment.

"Stone blind, you see, gentlemen," proceeded Peter; "but he's just as good to travel of a dark night as if he had eyes."

"Blame my buttons," said Blossom, "if I like them eyes."

"No," said Peter, "nor I neither. I'd rather have 'em made of diamonds; but they'll do, if they don't show as much white as Bullet's."

"Well," said Blossom, "make a pass at me."

"No," said Peter; "you made the banter, now make your pass."

"Well, I'm never afraid to price my hosses. You must give me twenty-five dollars boot."

"Oh, certainly; say fifty, and my saddle and bridle in. Here, Neddy, my son, take away daddy's horse."

"Well," said Blossom, "I've made my pass, now you make yours."

"I'm for short talk in a horse-swap, and therefore always tell a gentleman at once what I mean to do. You must give me ten dollars."

Blossom swore absolutely, roundly, and profanely, that he never would give boot.

"Well," said Peter, "I didn't care about trading; but you cut such high shines, that I thought I'd like to back you out, and I've done it. Gentlemen, you see I've brought him to a hack."

"Come, old man," said Blossom, "I've been joking with you. I begin to think you do want to trade; therefore, give me five dollars and take Bullet. I'd rather lose ten dollars any time than not make a trade, though I hate to fling away a good hoss."

"Well," said Peter, "I'll be as clever as you are, just put the five dollars on Bullet's back, and hand him over; it's a trade."

Blossom swore again, as roundly as before, that he would not give boot; and, said he, "Bullet wouldn't hold five dollars on his back, no how. But, as I bantered you, if you say an even swap, here's at you."

"I told you," said Peter, "I'd be as clever as you, therefore, here goes two dollars more, just for trade sake. Give me three dollars, and it's a bargain."

Blossom repeated his former assertion; and here the parties stood for a long time, and the by-standers (for many were now collected) began to taunt both parties. After some time, however, it was pretty unanimously decided that the old man had backed Blossom out.

At length Blossom swore he "never would be backed out for three dollars after bantering a man;" and, accordingly, they closed the trade.

"Now," said Blossom, as he handed Peter the three dollars, "I'm a man that, when he makes a bad trade, makes the most of it until he can make a better. I'm for no rues and after-claps."

"That's just my way," said Peter; "I never goes to law to mend my bargains."

"Ah, you're the kind of boy I love to trade with. Here's your hoss, old man. Take the saddle and bridle off him, and I'll strip yours; but lift up the blanket easy from Bullet's back, for he's a mighty tender-backed hoss."

The old man removed the saddle, but the blanket stuck fast. He attempted to raise it, and Bullet bowed himself, switched his tail, danced a little, and gave signs of biting.

"Don't hurt him, old man," said Blossom, archly; "take it off easy. I am, perhaps, a leetle of the best man at a horse-swap that ever catched a coon."

Peter continued to pull at the blanket more and more roughly, and Bullet became more and more *cavortish*: insomuch that, when the blanket came off, he had reached the *kicking* point in good earnest.

The removal of the blanket disclosed a sore on Bullet's back-bone that seemed to have defied all medical skill. It measured six full inches in length and four in breadth, and had as many features as Bullet had motions. My heart sickened at the sight; and I felt that the brute who had been riding him in that situation deserved the halter.

The prevailing feeling, however, was that of mirth. The laugh became loud and general at the old man's expense, and rustic witticisms were liberally bestowed upon him and his late purchase. These Blossom continued to provoke by various remarks. He asked the old man "if he thought Bullet would let five dollars lie on his back." He declared most seriously that he had owned that horse three months, and had never discovered before that he had a sore back, "or he never should have thought of trading him," &c., &c.

The old man bore it all with the most philosophic composure. He evinced no astonishment at his late discovery, and made no replies. But his son Neddy had not disciplined his feelings quite so well. His eyes opened wider and wider from the first to the last pull of the blanket; and, when the whole sore burst upon his view, astonishment and fright seemed to contend for the mastery of his countenance. As the blanket disappeared, he stuck his hands in his breeches pockets, heaved a deep sigh, and lapsed into a profound revery, from which he was only roused by the cuts at his father. He bore them as long as he could; and, when he could contain himself no longer, he began, with a certain wildness of expression which gave a peculiar interest to what he uttered: "His back's mighty bad off; but dod drot my soul if he's put it to daddy as bad as he thinks he has, for old Kit's both blind and *deef*, I'll be dod drot if he eint."

"The devil he is," said Blossom.

"Yes, dod drot my soul if he *eint*. You walk him, and see if he *eint*. His eyes don't look like it; but he'd *jist as leve go agin* the house with you, or in a ditch, as any how. Now you go try him." The laugh was now turned on Blossom; and many rushed to test the fidelity of the little boy's report. A few experiments established its truth beyond controversy.

"Neddy," said the old man, "you oughtn't to try and make people discontented with their things. Stranger, don't mind what the little boy says. If you can only get Kit rid of them little failings, you'll find him all sorts of a horse. You are a *leetle* the best man at a horse-swap that ever I got hold of; but don't fool away Kit. Come, Neddy, my son, let's be moving; the stranger seems to be getting snappish."

Nathaniel Hawthorne
Young Goodman Brown

"Young Goodman Brown" was originally published in the *New England Magazine* in 1835 before it was included in *Mosses from an Old Manse* in 1846. It has long been regarded as the quintessential Romantic story in that it uses personification, symbolism, and allegory to develop themes that relate not only to Puritan American culture but to human psychology and morality as well. One of the most popular of the conflicting interpretations is that it is an allegory representing Goodman Brown's adolescent dream of perpetual innocence, his assumption that he can live in a world of eternal purity, a place of love without any hint of lust, an Eden with no snake to tempt him and no apple to bring him knowledge of the human condition. When he recognizes the potential for sin within himself, a stunning discovery, he loses his capacity to believe in the goodness of other people, and his life and happiness are destroyed. To some extent his situation mirrors that of America itself, the New World intent on preserving its innocence free from the taint of the dark European past of political and sexual intrigue.

Nathaniel Hawthorne, "Young Goodman Brown," *Mosses from an Old Manse* (Boston: Houghton, Mifflin and Company, 1846), 1: 69–84.

Young Goodman Brown came forth at sunset, into the street of Salem village, but put his head back, after crossing the threshold, to exchange a parting kiss with his young wife. And Faith, as the wife was aptly named, thrust her own pretty head into the street, letting the wind play with the pink ribbons of her cap, while she called to Goodman Brown.

"Dearest heart," whispered she, softly and rather sadly, when her lips were close to his ear, "pr'ythee, put off your journey until sunrise, and sleep in your own bed to-night. A lone woman is troubled with such dreams and such thoughts, that she's afeard of herself, sometimes. Pray, tarry with me this night, dear husband, of all nights in the year!"

"My love and my Faith," replied young Goodman Brown, "of all nights in the year, this one night must I tarry away from thee. My journey, as thou callest it, forth and back again, must needs be done 'twixt now and sunrise. What, my sweet, pretty wife, dost thou doubt me already, and we but three months married!"

"Then God bless you!" said Faith, with the pink ribbons, "and may you find all well, when you come back."

"Amen!" cried Goodman Brown. "Say thy prayers, dear Faith, and go to bed at dusk, and no harm will come to thee."

So they parted; and the young man pursued his way, until, being about to turn the corner by the meeting-house, he looked back and saw the head of Faith still peeping after him, with a melancholy air, in spite of her pink ribbons.

"Poor little Faith!" thought he, for his heart smote him. "What a wretch am I, to leave her on such an errand! She talks of dreams, too. Methought, as she spoke, there was trouble in her face, as if a dream had warned her what work is to be done to-night. But, no, no! 't would kill her to think it. Well; she's a blessed angel on earth; and after this one night, I'll cling to her skirts and follow her to Heaven."

With this excellent resolve for the future, Goodman Brown felt himself justified in making more haste on his present evil purpose. He had taken a dreary road, darkened by all the gloomiest trees of the forest, which barely stood aside to let the narrow path creep through, and closed immediately behind. It was all as lonely as could be; and there is this peculiarity in such a solitude, that the traveller knows not who may be concealed by the innumerable trunks and the thick boughs overhead; so that, with lonely footsteps, he may yet be passing through an unseen multitude.

"There may be a devilish Indian behind every tree," said Goodman Brown to himself; and he glanced fearfully behind him, as he added, "What if the devil himself should be at my very elbow!"

His head being turned back, he passed a crook of the road, and looking forward again, beheld the figure of a man, in grave and decent attire, seated at the foot of an old tree. He arose, at Goodman Brown's approach, and walked onward, side by side with him.

"You are late, Goodman Brown," said he. "The clock of the Old South was striking, as I came through Boston; and that is full fifteen minutes agone."

"Faith kept me back awhile," replied the young man, with a tremor in his voice, caused by the sudden appearance of his companion, though not wholly unexpected.

It was now deep dusk in the forest, and deepest in that part of it where these two were journeying. As nearly as could be discerned, the second traveller was about fifty years old, apparently in the same rank of life as Goodman Brown, and bearing a considerable resemblance to him, though perhaps more in expression than features. Still, they might have been taken for father and son. And yet, though the elder person was as simply clad as the younger, and as simple in manner too, he had an indescribable air of one who knew the world, and would not have felt abashed at the governor's dinner-table, or in King William's court, were it possible that his affairs should call him thither. But the only thing about him, that could be fixed upon as remarkable, was his staff, which bore the likeness of a great black snake, so curiously wrought, that it might almost be seen to twist and wriggle itself like a living serpent. This, of course, must have been an ocular deception, assisted by the uncertain light.

"Come, Goodman Brown!" cried his fellow-traveller, "this is a dull pace for the beginning of a journey. Take my staff, if you are so soon weary."

"Friend," said the other, exchanging his slow pace for a full stop, "having kept covenant by meeting thee here, it is my purpose now to return whence I came. I have scruples, touching the matter thou wot'st of."

"Sayest thou so?" replied he of the serpent, smiling apart. "Let us walk on, nevertheless, reasoning as we go, and if I convince thee not, thou shalt turn back. We are but a little way in the forest, yet."

"Too far, too far!" exclaimed the goodman, unconsciously resuming his walk. "My father never went into the woods on such an errand, nor his father before him. We have been a race of honest men and good Christians, since the days of the martyrs. And shall I be the first of the name of Brown, that ever took this path and kept" —

"Such company, thou wouldst say," observed the elder person, interrupting his pause. "Well said, Goodman Brown! I have been as well acquainted with your family as with ever a one among the Puritans; and that's no trifle to say. I helped your grandfather, the constable, when he lashed the Quaker woman so smartly through the streets of Salem. And it was I that brought your father a pitch-pine knot, kindled at my own hearth, to set fire to an Indian village, in king Philip's war. They were my good friends, both; and many a pleasant walk have we had along this path, and returned merrily after midnight. I would fain be friends with you, for their sake."

"If it be as thou sayest," replied Goodman Brown, "I marvel they never spoke of these matters. Or, verily, I marvel not, seeing that the least rumor of the sort would have driven them from New England. We are a people of prayer, and good works to boot, and abide no such wickedness."

"Wickedness or not," said the traveller with the twisted staff, "I have a very general acquaintance here in New England. The deacons of many a church have drunk the communion wine with me; the selectmen, of divers towns, make me their chairman; and a majority of the Great and General Court are firm supporters of my interest. The governor and I, too — but these are state-secrets."

"Can this be so!" cried Goodman Brown, with a stare of amazement at his undisturbed companion. "Howbeit, I have nothing to do with the governor and council; they have their own ways, and are no rule for a simple husbandman like me. But, were I to go on with thee, how should I meet the eye of that good old man, our minister, at Salem Village? Oh, his voice would make me tremble, both Sabbath-day and lecture-day!"

Thus far, the elder traveller had listened with due gravity, but now burst into a fit of irrepressible mirth, shaking himself so violently, that his snake-like staff actually seemed to wriggle in sympathy.

"Ha! ha! ha!" shouted he, again and again; then composing himself, "Well, go on, Goodman Brown, go on; but, prithee, don't kill me with laughing!"

"Well, then, to end the matter at once," said Goodman Brown, considerably nettled, "there is my wife, Faith. It would break her dear little heart; and I'd rather break my own!"

"Nay, if that be the case," answered the other, "e'en go thy ways, Goodman Brown. I would not, for twenty old women like the one hobbling before us, that Faith should come to any harm."

As he spoke, he pointed his staff at a female figure on the path, in whom Goodman Brown recognized a very pious and exemplary dame, who had taught him his catechism in youth, and was still his moral and spiritual adviser, jointly with the minister and Deacon Gookin.

"A marvel, truly, that Goody Cloyse should be so far in the wilderness, at night-fall!" said he. "But, with your leave, friend, I shall take a cut through the woods, until we have left this Christian woman behind. Being a stranger to you, she might ask whom I was consorting with, and whither I was going."

"Be it so," said his fellow-traveller. "Betake you to the woods, and let me keep the path."

Accordingly, the young man turned aside, but took care to watch his companion, who advanced softly along the road, until he had come within a staff's length of the old dame. She, meanwhile, was making the best of her way, with singular speed for so aged a woman, and mumbling some indistinct words, a prayer, doubtless, as she went. The traveller put forth his staff, and touched her withered neck with what seemed the serpent's tail.

"The devil!" screamed the pious old lady.

"Then Goody Cloyse knows her old friend?" observed the traveller, confronting her, and leaning on his writhing stick.

"Ah, forsooth, and is it your worship, indeed?" cried the good dame. "Yea, truly is it, and in the very image of my old gossip, Goodman Brown, the grandfather of the silly fellow that now is. But, would your worship believe it? my broomstick hath strangely disappeared, stolen, as I suspect, by that unhanged witch, Goody Cory, and that, too, when I was all anointed with the juice of smallage and cinque-foil and wolf's-bane" —

"Mingled with fine wheat and the fat of a new-born babe," said the shape of old Goodman Brown.

"Ah, your worship knows the recipe," cried the old lady, cackling aloud. "So, as I was saying, being all ready for the meeting, and no horse to ride on, I made up my mind to foot it; for they tell me, there is a nice young man to be taken into communion to-night. But now your good worship will lend me your arm, and we shall be there in a twinkling."

"That can hardly be," answered her friend. "I may not spare you my arm, Goody Cloyse, but here is my staff, if you will."

So saying, he threw it down at her feet, where, perhaps, it assumed life, being one of the rods which its owner had formerly lent to the Egyptian Magi. Of this fact, however, Goodman Brown could not take cognizance. He had cast up his eyes in astonishment, and looking down again, beheld neither Goody Cloyse nor the serpentine staff, but his fellow-traveller alone, who waited for him as calmly as if nothing had happened.

"That old woman taught me my catechism!" said the young man; and there was a world of meaning in this simple comment.

They continued to walk onward, while the elder traveller exhorted his companion to make good speed and persevere in the path, discoursing so aptly, that his arguments seemed rather to spring up in the bosom of his auditor, than to be suggested by himself. As they went, he plucked a branch of maple, to serve for a walking-stick, and began to strip it of the twigs and little boughs, which were wet with evening dew. The moment his fingers touched them, they became strangely withered and dried up, as with a week's sunshine. Thus the pair proceeded, at a good free pace, until suddenly, in a gloomy hollow of the road, Goodman Brown sat himself down on the stump of a tree, and refused to go any farther.

"Friend," said he, stubbornly, "my mind is made up. Not another step will I budge on this errand. What if a wretched old woman do choose to go to the devil, when I thought she was going to Heaven! Is that any reason why I should quit my dear Faith, and go after her?"

"You will think better of this by-and-by," said his acquaintance, composedly. "Sit here and rest yourself awhile; and when you feel like moving again, there is my staff to help you along."

Without more words, he threw his companion the maple stick, and was as speedily out of sight as if he had vanished into the deepening gloom. The young man sat a few moments by the road-side, applauding himself greatly, and thinking with how clear a conscience he should meet the minister, in his morning-walk, nor shrink from the eye of good old Deacon Gookin. And what calm sleep would be his, that very night, which was to have been spent so wickedly, but purely and sweetly now, in the arms of Faith! Amidst these pleasant and praise-worthy meditations, Goodman Brown heard the tramp of horses along the road, and deemed it advisable to conceal himself within the verge of the forest, conscious of the guilty purpose that had brought him thither, though now so happily turned from it.

On came the hoof-tramps and the voices of the riders, two grave old voices, conversing soberly as they drew near. These mingled sounds appeared to pass along the road, within a few yards of the young man's hiding-place; but owing, doubtless, to the depth of the gloom, at that particular spot, neither the travellers nor their steeds were visible. Though their figures brushed the small boughs by the way-side, it could not be seen that they intercepted, even for a moment, the faint gleam from the strip of bright sky, athwart which they must have passed. Goodman Brown alternately crouched and stood on tip-toe, pulling aside the branches, and thrusting forth his head as far as he durst, without discerning so much as a shadow. It vexed him the more, because he could have sworn, were such a thing possible, that he recognized the voices of the minister and Deacon Gookin, jogging along quietly, as they were wont to do, when bound to some ordination or ecclesiastical council. While yet within hearing, one of the riders stopped to pluck a switch.

"Of the two, reverend Sir," said the voice like the deacon's, "I had rather miss an ordination-dinner than to-night's meeting. They tell me that some of our community are to be here from Falmouth and beyond, and others from Connecticut and Rhode Island; besides several of the Indian powows, who, after their fashion, know almost as much deviltry as the best of us. Moreover, there is a goodly young woman to be taken into communion."

"Mighty well, Deacon Gookin!" replied the solemn old tones of the minister. "Spur up, or we shall be late. Nothing can be done, you know, until I get on the ground."

The hoofs clattered again, and the voices, talking so strangely in the empty air, passed on through the forest, where no church had ever been gathered, nor solitary Christian prayed. Whither, then, could these holy men be journeying, so deep into the heathen wilderness? Young Goodman Brown caught hold of a tree, for support, being ready to sink down on the ground, faint and over-burthened with the heavy sickness of his heart. He looked up to the sky, doubting whether there really was a Heaven above him. Yet, there was the blue arch, and the stars brightening in it.

"With Heaven above, and Faith below, I will yet stand firm against the devil!" cried Goodman Brown.

While he still gazed upward, into the deep arch of the firmament, and had lifted his hands to pray, a cloud, though a wind was stirring, hurried across the zenith, and hid the lightening stars. The blue sky was still visible, except directly overhead, where this black mass of cloud was seeping swiftly northward. Aloft in the air, as if from the depth of the cloud, came a confused and doubtful sound of voices. Once, the listener fancied that he could distinguish the accents of town's-people of his own, men and women, both pious and ungodly, many of whom he had met at the communion-table, and had seen others rioting at the tavern. The next moment, so indistinct were the sounds, he doubted whether he had heard aught but the murmur of the old forest, whispering without a wind. Then came a stronger swell of those familiar tones, heard daily in the sunshine, at Salem village, but never, until now, from a cloud of night. There was one voice, of a young woman, uttering lamentations, yet with an uncertain sorrow, and entreating for some favor, which, perhaps, it would grieve her to obtain. And all the unseen multitude, both saints and sinners, seemed to encourage her onward.

"Faith!" shouted Goodman Brown, in a voice of agony and desperation; and the echoes of the forest mocked him, crying — "Faith! Faith!" as if bewildered wretches were seeking her, all through the wilderness.

The cry of grief, rage, and terror, was yet piercing the night, when the unhappy husband held his breath for a response. There was a scream, drowned immediately in a louder murmur of voices, fading into far-off laughter, as the dark cloud swept away, leaving the clear and silent sky above Goodman Brown. But something fluttered lightly down through the air, and caught on the branch of a tree. The young man seized it, and beheld a pink ribbon.

"My Faith is gone!" cried he, after one stupefied moment. "There is no good on earth; and sin is but a name. Come, devil! for to thee is this world given."

And maddened with despair, so that he laughed loud and long, did Goodman Brown grasp his staff and set forth again, at such a rate, that he seemed to fly along the forest-path, rather than to walk or run. The road grew wilder and drearier, and more faintly traced, and vanished at length, leaving him in the heart of the dark wilderness, still rushing onward, with the instinct that guides mortal man to evil. The whole forest was peopled with frightful sounds; the creaking of the trees, the howling of wild beasts, and the yell of Indians; while, sometimes the wind tolled like a distant church-bell, and sometimes gave a broad roar around the traveller, as if all Nature were laughing him to scorn. But he was himself the chief horror of the scene, and shrank not from its other horrors.

"Ha! ha! ha!" roared Goodman Brown, when the wind laughed at him. "Let us hear which will laugh loudest! Think not to frighten me with your deviltry! Come witch, come wizard, come Indian powow, come devil himself! and here comes Goodman Brown. You may as well fear him as he fear you!"

In truth, all through the haunted forest, there could be nothing more frightful than the figure of Goodman Brown. On he flew, among the black pines, brandishing his staff with frenzied gestures, now giving vent to an inspiration of horrid blasphemy, and now shouting forth such laughter, as set all the echoes of the forest laughing like demons around him. The fiend in his own shape is less hideous, than when he rages in the breast of man. Thus sped the demoniac on his course, until, quivering among the trees, he saw a red light before him, as when the felled trunks and branches of a clearing have been set on fire, and throw up their lurid blaze against the sky, at the hour of midnight. He paused, in a lull of the tempest that had driven him onward, and heard the swell of what seemed a hymn, rolling solemnly from a distance, with the weight of many voices. He knew the tune; It was a familiar one in the choir of the village meeting-house. The verse died heavily away, and was lengthened by a chorus, not of human voices, but of all the sounds of the benighted wilderness, pealing in awful harmony together. Goodman Brown cried out; and his cry was lost to his own ear, by its unison with the cry of the desert.

In the interval of silence, he stole forward, until the light glared full upon his eyes. At one extremity of an open space, hemmed in by the dark wall of the forest, arose a rock, bearing some rude, natural resemblance either to an altar or a pulpit, and surrounded by four blazing pines, their tops a flame, their stems untouched, like candles at an evening meeting. The mass of foliage, that had overgrown the summit of the rock, was all on fire, blazing high into the night, and fitfully illuminating the whole field. Each pendant twig and leafy festoon was in a blaze. As the red light arose and fell, a numerous congregation alternately shone forth, then disappeared in shadow, and again grew, as it were, out of the darkness, peopling the heart of the solitary woods at once.

"A grave and dark-clad company!" quoth Goodman Brown.

In truth, they were such. Among them, quivering to-and-fro, between gloom and splendor, appeared faces that would be seen, next day, at the council-board of the province, and others which, Sabbath after Sabbath, looked devoutly heavenward, and benignantly over the crowded pews, from the holiest pulpits in the land. Some affirm, that the lady of the governor was there. At least, there were high dames well known to her, and wives of honored husbands, and widows, a great multitude, and ancient maidens, all of excellent repute, and fair young girls, who trembled lest their mothers should espy them. Either the sudden gleams of light, flashing over the obscure field, bedazzled Goodman Brown, or he recognized a score of the church-members of Salem village, famous for their especial sanctity. Good old Deacon Gookin had arrived, and waited at the skirts of that venerable saint, his reverend pastor. But, irreverently consorting with these grave, reputable, and pious people, these elders of the church, these chaste dames and dewy virgins, there were men of dissolute lives and women of spotted fame, wretches given over to all mean and filthy vice, and suspected even of horrid crimes. It was strange to see, that the good shrank not from the wicked, nor were the sinners abashed by the saints. Scattered, also, among their pale-faced enemies, were the Indian priests, or powows, who had often scared their native forest with more hideous incantations than any known to English witchcraft.

"But, where is Faith?" thought Goodman Brown; and, as hope came into his heart, he trembled.

Another verse of the hymn arose, a slow and mournful strain, such as the pious love, but joined to words which expressed all that our nature can conceive of sin, and darkly hinted at far more. Unfathomable to mere mortals is the lore of fiends. Verse after verse was sung, and still the chorus of the desert swelled between, like the deepest tone of a mighty organ. And, with the final peal of that dreadful anthem, there came a sound, as if the roaring wind, the rushing streams, the howling beasts, and every other voice of the unconverted wilderness, were mingling and according with the voice of guilty man, in homage to the prince of all. The four blazing pines threw up a loftier flame, and obscurely discovered shapes and visages of horror on the smoke-wreaths, above the impious assembly. At the same moment, the fire on the rock shot redly forth, and formed a glowing arch above its base, where now appeared a figure. With reverence be it spoken, the apparition bore no slight similitude, both in garb and manner, to some grave divine of the New England churches.

"Bring forth the converts!" cried a voice, that echoed through the field and rolled into the forest.

At the word, Goodman Brown stepped forth from the shadow of the trees, and approached the congregation, with whom he felt a loathful brotherhood, by the sympathy of all that was wicked in his heart. He could have well nigh sworn, that the shape of his own dead father beckoned him to advance, looking downward from a smoke-wreath, while a woman, with dim features of despair, threw

out her hand to warn him back. Was it his mother? But he had no power to retreat one step, nor to resist, even in thought, when the minister and good old
Deacon Gookin seized his arms, and led him to the blazing rock. Thither came
also the slender form of a veiled female, led between Goody Cloyse, that pious
teacher of the catechism, and Martha Carrier, who had received the devil's
promise to be queen of hell. A rampant hag was she! And there stood the pros-
elytes, beneath the canopy of fire.

"Welcome, my children," said the dark figure, "to the communion of your
race! Ye have found, thus young, your nature and your destiny. My children, look
behind you!"

They turned; and flashing forth, as it were, in a sheet of flame, the fiend-
worshippers were seen; the smile of welcome gleamed darkly on every visage.

"There," resumed the sable form, "are all whom ye have reverenced from
youth. Ye deemed them holier than yourselves, and shrank from your own sin,
contrasting it with their lives of righteousness, and prayerful aspirations heavenward. Yet, here are they all, in my worshipping assembly! This night it shall be
granted you to know their secret deeds; how hoary-bearded elders of the church
have whispered wanton words to the young maids of their households; how
many a woman, eager for widow's weeds, has given her husband a drink at bedtime, and let him sleep his last sleep in her bosom; how beardless youths have
made haste to inherit their father's wealth; and how fair damsels — blush not,
sweet ones! — have dug little graves in the garden, and bidden me, the sole
guest, to an infant's funeral. By the sympathy of your human hearts for sin, ye
shall scent out all the places — whether in church, bed-chamber, street, field, or
forest — where crime has been committed, and shall exult to behold the whole
earth one stain of guilt, one mighty blood-spot. Far more than this! It shall be
yours to penetrate, in every bosom, the deep mystery of sin, the fountain of all
wicked arts, and which inexhaustibly supplies more evil impulses than human
power — than my power, at its utmost! — can make manifest in deeds. And
now, my children, look upon each other."

They did so; and, by the blaze of the hell-kindled torches, the wretched man
beheld his Faith, and the wife her husband, trembling before that unhallowed altar.

"Lo! There ye stand, my children," said the figure, in a deep and solemn tone,
almost sad, with its despairing awfulness, as if his once angelic nature could yet
mourn for our miserable race. "Depending upon one another's hearts, ye had
still hoped that virtue were not all a dream! Now are ye undeceived! — Evil is
the nature of mankind. Evil must be your only happiness. Welcome, again, my
children, to the communion of your race!"

"Welcome!" repeated the fiend-worshippers, in one cry of despair and triumph.

And there they stood, the only pair, as it seemed, who were yet hesitating on
the verge of wickedness, in this dark world. A basin was hollowed, naturally, in

the rock. Did it contain water, reddened by the lurid light? or was it blood? or, perchance, a liquid flame? Herein did the Shape of Evil dip his hand, and prepare to lay the mark of baptism upon their foreheads, that they might be partakers of the mystery of sin, more conscious of the secret guilt of others, both in deed and thought, than they could now be of their own. The husband cast one look at his pale wife, and Faith at him. What polluted wretches would the next glance show them to each other, shuddering alike at what they disclosed and what they saw!

"Faith! Faith!" cried the husband. "Look up to Heaven, and resist the Wicked One!"

Whether Faith obeyed, he knew not. Hardly had he spoken, when he found himself amid calm night and solitude, listening to a roar of the wind, which died heavily away through the forest. He staggered against the rock, and felt it chill and damp, while a hanging twig, that had been all on fire, besprinkled his cheek with the coldest dew.

The next morning, young Goodman Brown came slowly into the street of Salem village, staring around him like a bewildered man. The good old minister was taking a walk along the graveyard, to get an appetite for breakfast and meditate his sermon, and bestowed a blessing, as he passed, on Goodman Brown. He shrank from the venerable saint, as if to avoid an anathema. Old Deacon Gookin was at domestic worship, and the holy words of his prayer were heard through the open window. "What God doth the wizard pray to?" quoth Goodman Brown. Goody Cloyse, that excellent old Christian, stood in the early sunshine, at her own lattice, catechising a little girl, who had brought her a pint of morning's milk. Goodman Brown snatched away the child, as from the grasp of the fiend himself. Turning the corner by the meeting-house, he spied the head of Faith, with the pink ribbons, gazing anxiously forth, and bursting into such joy at sight of him, that she skipt along the street, and almost kissed her husband before the whole village. But Goodman Brown looked sternly and sadly into her face, and passed on without a greeting.

Had Goodman Brown fallen asleep in the forest, and only dreamed a wild dream of a witch-meeting?

Be it so, if you will. But, alas! it was a dream of evil omen for young Goodman Brown. A stern, a sad, a darkly meditative, a distrustful, if not a desperate man, did he become, from the night of that fearful dream. On the Sabbath-day, when the congregation were singing a holy psalm, he could not listen, because an anthem of sin rushed loudly upon his ear, and drowned all the blessed strain. When the minister spoke from the pulpit, with power and fervid eloquence, and with his hand on the open bible, of the sacred truths of our religion, and of saint-like lives and triumphant deaths, and of future bliss or misery unutterable, then did Goodman Brown turn pale, dreading lest the roof should thunder down upon the grey blasphemer and his hearers. Often, awaking suddenly at midnight, he shrank from the bosom of Faith, and at morning or eventide, when the family knelt down at prayer, he scowled, and muttered to himself, and gazed sternly at his wife, and turned away. And when he had lived long, and was borne to his grave, a hoary corpse, followed by Faith, an aged woman, and children and grand-children, a goodly procession, besides neighbors, not a few, they carved no hopeful verse upon his tombstone; for his dying hour was gloom.

Edgar Allan Poe
The Fall of the House of Usher

Perhaps the most famous of Edgar Allan Poe's short fiction, "The Fall of the House of Usher" was published in *Burton's Gentleman's Magazine* in 1839. The author was co-editor of this short-lived periodical, and he greatly increased its circulation by including his own works in its issues. "Usher" was an enormous success and an illustration of Poe's theory of composition that all elements of a story should contribute to its central idea, giving it both coherence and congruence. From its first line to its last, this Gothic tale combines style, imagery, narration, allusions, structure, and theme for dramatic effect. For example, the Usher mansion is inextricably entwined with the family within, and it externalizes the decay and instability that become progressively more evident in Roderick Usher as the plot develops. Both the house and the residents collapse and die at the same time. But the artistic success of the narrative stems from its thematic vibrancy, the multiplicity of its complex pattern of ideas, and the varying interpretations the text makes possible. "The Fall of the House of Usher" has been read as a literal tale of the supernatural, as an irrational fantasy by the narrator, as a psychological exploration of the unconscious mind, and as an illustration of the frustration of the Romantic artist in search of the Sublime. The range of these interpretive strategies illustrates the richness of Poe's fiction at its best.

Edgar Allan Poe, "The Fall of the House of Usher," *Burton's Gentleman's Magazine* 5 (September 1839): 145–52.

During the whole of a dull, dark and soundless day in the autumn of the year, when the clouds hung oppressively low in the heavens, I had been passing alone, on horseback, through a singularly dreary tract of country; and at length found myself, as the shades of the evening drew on, within view of the melancholy House of Usher. I know not how it was — but, with the first glimpse of the building, a sense of insufferable gloom pervaded my spirit. I say insufferable; for the feeling was unrelieved by any of that half-pleasurable, because poetic, sentiment, with which the mind usually receives even the sternest natural images of the desolate or terrible. I looked upon the scene before me — upon the mere house, and the simple landscape features of the domain — upon the bleak walls — upon the vacant eye-like windows — upon a few rank sedges — and upon a few white trunks of decayed trees — with an utter depression of soul which I can compare to no earthly sensation more properly than to the after-dream of the reveller upon opium — the bitter lapse into common life — the hideous dropping off of the veil. There was an iciness, a sinking, a sickening of the heart — an unredeemed dreariness of thought which no goading of the imagination could torture into aught of the sublime. What was it — I paused to think — what was it that so unnerved me in the contemplation of the House of Usher? It was a mystery all insoluble; nor could I grapple with the shadowy fancies that crowded upon me as I pondered. I was forced to fall back upon the unsatisfactory conclusion, that while, beyond doubt, there *are* combinations of very simple natural objects which have the power of thus affecting us, still the reason, and the analysis, of this power, lie among considerations beyond our depth. It was possible, I reflected, that a mere different arrangement of the particulars of the scene, of the details of the picture, would be sufficient to modify, or perhaps to annihilate its capacity for sorrowful impression; and, acting upon this idea, I reined my horse to the precipitous brink of a black and lurid tarn that lay in unruffled lustre by the dwelling, and gazed down — but with a shudder even more thrilling than before — upon the re-modelled and inverted images of the gray sedge, and the ghastly tree-stems, and the vacant and eye-like windows.

Nevertheless, in this mansion of gloom I now proposed to myself a sojourn of some weeks. Its proprietor, Roderick Usher, had been one of my boon companions in boyhood; but many years had elapsed since our last meeting. A letter, however, had lately reached me in a distant part of the country — a letter from him — which, in its wildly importunate nature, had admitted of no other than a personal reply. The MS. gave evidence of nervous agitation. The writer spoke of acute bodily illness — of a pitiable mental idiosyncrasy which oppressed him — and of an earnest desire to see me, as his best, and indeed, his only personal friend, with a view of attempting, by the cheerfulness of my society, some alleviation of his malady. It was the manner in which all this, and much more, was said — it was the apparent *heart* that went with his request — which allowed me no room for hesitation — and I accordingly obeyed, what I still considered a very singular summons, forthwith.

Although, as boys, we had been even intimate associates, yet I really knew little of my friend. His reserve had been always excessive and habitual. I was aware, however, that his very ancient family had been noted, time out of mind, for a peculiar sensibility of temperament, displaying itself, through long ages, in many works of exalted art, and manifested, of late, in repeated deeds of munificent yet unobtrusive charity, as well as in a passionate devotion to the intricacies, perhaps even more than to the orthodox and easily recognizable beauties, of musical science. I had learned, too, the very remarkable fact, that the stem of the Usher race, all time-honored as it was, had put forth, at no period, any enduring branch; in other words, that the entire family lay in the direct line of descent, and had always, with very trifling and very temporary variation, so lain. It was this deficiency, I considered, while running over in thought the perfect keeping of the character of the premises with the accredited character of the people, and while speculating upon the possible influence which the one, in the long lapse of centuries, might have exercised upon the other — it was this deficiency, perhaps, of collateral issue, and the consequent undeviating transmission, from sire to son, of the patrimony with the name, which had, at length, so identified the two as to merge the original title of the estate in the quaint and equivocal appellation of the "House of Usher" — an appellation which seemed to include, in the minds of the peasantry who used it, both the family and the family mansion.

I have said that the sole effect of my somewhat childish experiment, of looking down within the tarn, had been to deepen the first singular impression. There can be no doubt that the consciousness of the rapid increase of my superstition — for why should I not so term it? — served mainly to accelerate the increase itself. Such, I have long known, is the paradoxical law of all sentiments having terror as a basis. And it might have been for this reason only, that, when I again uplifted my eyes to the house itself, from its image in the pool, there grew in my mind a strange fancy — a fancy so ridiculous, indeed, that I but mention it to show the vivid force of the sensations which oppressed me. I had so worked upon my imagination as really to believe that around about the whole mansion and domain there hung an atmosphere peculiar to themselves and their immediate vicinity — an atmosphere which had no affinity with the air of heaven, but which had reeked up from the decayed trees, and the gray walls, and the silent tarn, in the form of an inelastic vapor or gas — dull, sluggish, faintly discernible, and leaden-hued. Shaking off from my spirit what *must* have been a dream, I scanned more narrowly the real aspect of the building. Its principal feature seemed to be that of an excessive antiquity. The discoloration of ages had been great. Minute fungi overspread the whole exterior, hanging in a fine tangled web-work from the eaves. Yet all this was apart from any extraordinary dilapidation. No portion of the masonry had fallen; and there appeared to be a wild inconsistency between its still perfect adaptation of parts, and the utterly porous, and evidently decayed condition of the individual stones. In this there was much that reminded me of the specious totality of old wood-work which has rotted for long years in some neglected vault, with no disturbance from the breath of the external air. Beyond this indication of extensive decay, however, the fabric gave little token of instability. Perhaps the eye of a scrutinizing observer might have discovered a barely perceptible fissure, which, extending from the roof of the building in front, made its way down the wall in a zig-zag direction, until it became lost in the sullen waters of the tarn.

Noticing these things, I rode over a short causeway to the house. A servant in waiting took my horse, and I entered the Gothic archway of the hall. A valet, of stealthy step, thence conducted me, in silence, through many dark and intricate passages in my progress to the studio of his master. Much that I encountered on the way contributed, I know not how, to heighten the vague sentiments of which I have already spoken. While the objects around me — while the carvings of the ceilings, the sombre tapestries of the walls, the ebon blackness of the floors, and the phantasmagoric armorial trophies which rattled as I strode, were but matters to which, or to such as which, I had been accustomed from my infancy — while I hesitated not to acknowledge how familiar was all this — I still wondered to find how unfamiliar were the fancies which ordinary images were stirring up. On one of the staircases, I met the physician of the family. His countenance, I thought, wore a mingled expression of low cunning and per-plexity. He accosted me with trepidation and passed on. The valet now threw open a door and ushered me into the presence of his master.

The room in which I found myself was very large and excessively lofty. The windows were long, narrow, and pointed, and at so vast a distance from the black oaken floor as to be altogether inaccessible from within. Feeble gleams of encrimsoned light made their way through the trellised panes, and served to ren-der sufficiently distinct the more prominent objects around; the eye, however, struggled in vain to reach the remoter angles of the chamber, of the recesses of the vaulted and fretted ceiling. Dark draperies hung upon the walls. The general furniture was profuse, comfortless, antique, and tattered. Many books and mu-sical instruments lay scattered about, but failed to give any vitality to the scene. I felt that I breathed an atmosphere of sorrow. An air of stern, deep, and irre-deemable gloom hung over and pervaded all.

Upon my entrance, Usher arose from a sofa upon which he had been lying at full length, and greeted me with a vivacious warmth which had much in it, I at first thought of an overdone cordiality — of the constrained effort of the en-nuyé man of the world. A glance, however, at his countenance convinced me of his perfect sincerity. We sat down; and for some moments, while he spoke not, I gazed upon him with a feeling half of pity, half of awe. Surely, man had never before so terribly altered, in so brief a period, as had Roderick Usher! It was with difficulty that I could bring myself to admit the identity of the wan being before me with the companion of my early boyhood. Yet the character of his face had been at all times remarkable. A cadaverousness of complexion; an eye large, liq-uid, and luminous beyond comparison; lips somewhat thin and very pallid, but of a surpassingly beautiful curve; a nose of a delicate Hebrew model, but with a breadth of nostril unusual in similar formations; a finely moulded chin, speaking in its want of prominence, of a want of moral energy; hair of a more than web-like softness and tenuity; these features, with an inordinate expansion above the regions of the temple, made up altogether a countenance not easily to be for-gotten. And now in the mere exaggeration of the prevailing character of these features, and of the expression they were wont to convey, lay so much of change that I doubted to whom I spoke. The now ghastly pallor of the skin, and the now miraculous lustre of the eye, above all things startled and even awed me. The silken hair, too, had been suffered to grow all unheeded, and as, in its wild gossamer texture, it floated rather than fell about the face, I could not, even with effort, connect its arabesque expression with any idea of simple humanity.

In the manner of my friend I was at once struck with an incoherence — an inconsistency; and I soon found this to arise from a series of feeble and futile struggles to overcome an habitual trepidancy, an excessive nervous agitation. For something of this nature I had indeed been prepared, no less by his letter, than by reminiscences of certain boyish traits, and by conclusions deduced from his peculiar physical conformation and temperament. His action was alternately vivacious and sullen. His voice varied rapidly from a tremulous indecision (when the animal spirits seemed utterly in abeyance) to that species of energetic concision — that abrupt, weighty, unhurried, and hollow-sounding enunciation — that leaden, self-balanced and perfectly modulated gutteral utterance, which may be observed in the moments of the intensest excitement of the lost drunkard, or the irreclaimable eater of opium.

It was thus that he spoke of the object of my visit, of his earnest desire to see me, and of the solace he expected me to afford him. He entered, at some length, into what he conceived to be the nature of his malady. It was, he said, a constitutional and a family evil, and one for which he despaired to find a remedy — a mere nervous affection, he immediately added, which would undoubtedly soon pass off. It displayed itself in a host of unnatural sensations. Some of these, as he detailed them, interested and bewildered me — although, perhaps, the terms, and the general manner of the narration had their weight. He suffered much from a morbid acuteness of the senses; the most insipid food was alone endurable; he could wear only garments of certain texture; the odors of all flowers were oppressive; his eyes were tortured by even a faint light; and there were but peculiar sounds, and these from stringed instruments, which did not inspire him with horror.

To an anomalous species of terror I found him a bounden slave. "I shall perish," said he, "I *must* perish in this deplorable folly. Thus, thus, and not otherwise, shall I be lost. I dread the events of the future, not in themselves, but in their results. I shudder at the thought of any, even the most trivial, incident, which may operate upon this intolerable agitation of soul. I have, indeed, no abhorrence of danger, except in its absolute effect — in terror. In this unnerved — in this pitiable condition — I feel that I must inevitably abandon life and reason together in my struggles with some fatal demon of fear."

I learned, moreover, at intervals, and through broken and equivocal hints, another singular feature of his mental condition. He was enchained by certain superstitious impressions in regard to the dwelling which he tenanted, and from which, for many years, he had never ventured forth — in regard to an influence whose supposititious force was conveyed in terms too shadowy here to be restated — an influence which some peculiarities in the mere form and substance of his family mansion, had, by hint of long sufferance, he said, obtained over his spirit — an effect whcih the *physique* of the gray walls and turrets, and of the dim tarn into which they all looked down, had, at length, brought about upon the *morale* of his existence.

He admitted, however, although with hesitation, that much of the peculiar gloom which thus afflicted him could be traced to a more natural and far more palpable origin — to the severe and long-continued illness — indeed to the evidently approaching dissolution — of a tenderly beloved sister; his sole companion for long years — his last and only relative on earth. "Her decease," he said, with a bitterness which I can never forget, "would leave him (him the hopeless and the frail) the last of the ancient race of the Ushers." As he spoke, the lady Madeline (for so was she called) passed slowly through a remote portion of the apartment, and, without having noticed my presence, disappeared. I regarded her with an utter astonishment not unmingled with dread. Her figure, her air, her features — all, in their very minutest development were those — were identically (I can use no other sufficient term) were identically those of the Roderick Usher who sat beside me. A feeling of stupor oppressed me, as my eyes followed her retreating steps. As a door, at length, closed upon her exit, my glance sought instinctively and eagerly the countenance of the brother — but he had buried his face in his hands, and I could only perceive that a far more than ordinary wanness had overspread the emaciated fingers through which trickled many passionate tears.

The disease of the lady Madeline had long baffled the skill of her physicians. A settled apathy, a gradual wasting away of the person, and frequent although transient affections of a partially cataleptical character, were the unusual diagnosis. Hitherto she had steadily borne up against the pressure of her malady, and had not betaken herself finally to bed; but, on the closing in of the evening of my arrival at the house she succumbed, as her brother told me at night with inexpressible agitation, to the prostrating power of the destroyer — and I learned that the glimpse I had obtained of her person would thus probably be the last I should obtain — that the lady, at least while living, would be seen by me no more.

For several days ensuing, her name was unmentioned by either Usher or myself; and, during this period, I was busied in earnest endeavor to alleviate the melancholy of my friend. We painted and read together — or I listened, as if in a dream, to the wild improvisations of his speaking guitar. And thus, as a closer and still closer intimacy admitted me more unreservedly into the recesses of his spirit, the more bitterly did I perceive the futility of all attempt at cheering a mind from which darkness, as if an inherent positive quality, poured forth upon all objects of the moral and physical universe, in one unceasing radiation of gloom.

I shall ever bear about me, as Moslem in their shrouds at Mecca, a memory of the many solemn hours I thus spent alone with the master of the House of Usher. Yet I should fail in any attempt to convey an idea of the exact character of the studies, or of the occupations, in which he involved me, or led me the way. An excited and highly distempered ideality threw a sulphurous lustre over all. His long improvised dirges will ring for ever in my ears. Among other things, I bear painfully in mind a certain singular perversion and amplification of the wild air of the last waltz of Von Weber. From the paintings over which his elaborate fancy brooded, and which grew, touch by touch, into vaguenesses at which I shuddered the more thrillingly, because I shuddered knowing not why, from these paintings (vivid as these images now are before me) I would in vain endeavor to educe more than a small portion which should lie within the compass of merely written words. By the utter simplicity, by the nakedness, of his designs, he arrested and over-awed attention. If ever mortal painted an idea, that mortal was Roderick Usher. For me at least — in the circumstances then surrounding me — there arose out of the pure abstractions which the hypochondriac contrived to throw upon his canvas, an intensity of intolerable awe, no shadow of which felt I ever yet in the contemplation of the certainly glowing yet too concrete reveries of Fuseli.

One of the phantasmagoric conceptions of my friend, partaking not so rigidly of the spirit of abstraction, may be shadowed forth, although feebly, in words. A small picture presented the interior of an immensely long and rectangular vault or tunnel, with low walls, smooth, white, and without interruption or device. Certain accessory points of the design served well to convey the idea that this excavation lay at an exceeding depth below the surface of the earth. No outlet was observed in any portion of its vast extent, and no torch, or other artificial source of light was discernible — yet a flood of intense rays rolled throughout, and bathed the whole in a ghastly and inappropriate splendor.

I have just spoken of that morbid condition of the auditory nerve which rendered all music intolerable to the sufferer, with the exception of certain effects of stringed instruments. It was, perhaps, the narrow limits to which he thus confined himself upon the guitar, which gave birth, in great measure, to the fantastic character of his performances. But the fervid *facility* of his impromptus could not be so accounted for. They must have been, and were, in the notes, as well as in the words of his wild fantasies, (for he not unfrequently accompanied himself with rhymed verbal improvisations,) the result of that intense mental collectedness and concentration to which I have previously alluded as observable only in particular moments of the highest artificial excitement. The words of one of these rhapsodies I have easily borne away in memory. I was, perhaps, the more forcibly impressed with it, as he gave it, because, in the under or mystic current

of its meaning, I fancied that I perceived, and for the first time, a full consciousness on the part of Usher, of the tottering of his lofty reason upon her throne.
The verses, which were entitled "The Haunted Palace," ran very nearly, if not
accurately, thus:

I.
In the greenest of our valleys,
    By good angels tenanted,
Once a fair and stately palace —
    Snow-white palace — reared its head.
In the monarch Thought's dominion —
    It stood there!
Never seraph spread a pinion
    Over fabric half so fair.

II.
Banners yellow, glorious, golden,
    On its roof did float and flow;
(This — all this — was in the olden
    Time long ago)
And every gentle air that dallied,
    In that sweet day,
Along the ramparts plumed and pallid,
    A winged odor went away.

III.
Wanderers in that happy valley
    Through two luminous windows saw
Spirits moving musically
    To a lute's well-tuned law,
Round about a throne, where sitting
    (Porphyrogene!)
In state his glory well befitting,
    The sovereign of the realm was seen.

IV.
And all with pearl and ruby glowing
    Was the fair palace door,
Through which came flowing, flowing, flowing,
    And sparkling evermore,
A troop of Echoes whose sole duty
    Was but to sing,
In voices of surpassing beauty,
    The wit and wisdom of their king.

v.

But evil things, in robes of sorrow,
   Assailed the monarch's high estate;
(Ah, let us mourn, for never morrow
   Shall dawn upon him, desolate!)
And, round about his home, the glory
   That blushed and bloomed
Is but a dim-remembered story
   Of the old time entombed.

vi.

And travellers now within that valley,
   Through the red-litten windows, see
Vast forms that move fantastically
   To a discordant melody;
While, like a rapid ghastly river,
   Through the pale door,
A hideous throng rush out forever,
   And laugh — but smile no more.

I well remember that suggestions arising from this ballad led us into a train of thought wherein there became manifest an opinion of Usher's which I mention not so much on account of its novelty, (for other men have thought thus,) as on account of the pertinacity with which he maintained it. This opinion, in its general form, was that of the sentience of all vegetable things. But, in his disordered fancy, the idea had assumed a more daring character, and trespassed, under certain conditions, upon the kingdom of inorganization. I lack words to express the full extent, or the earnest *abandon* of his persuasion. The belief, however, was connected (as I have previously hinted) with the gray stones of the home of his forefathers. The condition of the sentience had been here, he imagined, fulfilled in the method of collocation of these stones — in the order of their arrangement, as well as in that of the many fungi which overspread them, and of the decayed trees which stood around — above all, in the long undisturbed endurance of this arrangement, and in its reduplication in the still waters of the tarn. Its evidence — the evidence of the sentience — was to be seen, he said, (and I here started as he spoke,) in *the gradual yet certain condensation of an atmosphere of their own about the waters and the walls.* The result was discoverable, he added, in that silent, yet importunate and terrible influence which for centuries had moulded the destinies of his family, and which made *him* what I now saw him — what he was. Such opinions need no comment, and I will make none.

Our books — the books which, for years, had formed no small portion of the mental existence of the invalid — were, as might be supposed, in strict keeping with this character of phantasm. We pored together over such works as the

Ververt et Chartreuse of Gresset; the Belphegor of Machiavelli; the Selenography of Brewster; the Heaven and Hell of Swedenborg; the Subterranean Voyage of Nicholas Klimm de Holberg; the Chiromancy of Robert Flud, of Jean d'Indaginé, and of De la Chambre; the Journey into the Blue Distance of Tieck; and the City of the Sun of Campanella. One favorite volume was a small octavo edition of the Directorium Inquisitorium, by the Dominican Eymeric de Gironne; and there were passages in Pomponius Mela, about the old African Satyrs and Œgipans, over which Usher would sit dreaming for hours. His chief delight, however, was found in the earnest and repeated perusal of an exceedingly rare and curious book in quarto Gothic — the manual of a forgotten church — the *Vigilae Mortuorum secundum Chorum Ecclesiae Maguntinae.*

I could not help thinking of the wild ritual of this work, and of its probable influence upon the hypochondriac, when, one evening, having informed me abruptly that the lady Madeline was no more, he stated his intention of preserving her corpse for a fortnight, previously to its final interment, in one of the numerous vaults within the main walls of the building. The wordly reason, however, assigned for this singular proceeding, was one which I did not feel at liberty to dispute. The brother had been led to his resolution (so he told me) by considerations of the unusual character of the malady of the deceased, of certain obtrusive and eager inquiries on the part of her medical men, and of the remote and exposed situation of the burial ground of the family. I will not deny that when I called to mind the sinister countenance of the person whom I met upon the staircase, on the day of my arrival at the house, I had no desire to oppose what I regarded as at best but a harmless, and not by any means an unnatural precaution.

At the request of Usher, I personally aided him in the arrangements for the temporary entombment. The body having been encoffined, we two alone bore it to its rest. The vault in which we placed it (and which had been so long unopened that our torches, half smothered in its oppressive atmosphere, gave us little opportunity for investigation) was small, damp, and utterly without means of admission for light; lying, at great depth, immediately beneath that portion of the building in which was my own sleeping apartment. It had been used, apparently, in remote feudal times, for the worst purposes of a donjon-keep, and, in later days, as a place of deposit for powder, or other highly combustible substance, as a portion of its floor, and the whole interior of a long archway through which we reached it, were carefully sheathed with copper. The door, of massive iron, had been, also, similarly protected. Its immense weight caused an unusually sharp grating sound, as it moved upon its hinges.

Having deposited our mournful burden upon tressels within this region of horror, we partially turned aside the yet unscrewed lid of the coffin, and looked upon the face of the tenant. The exact similitude between the brother and sister even here again startled and confounded me. Usher, divining, perhaps, my thoughts, murmured out some few words from which I learned that the deceased and himself had been twins, and that sympathies of a scarcely intelligible nature had always existed between them. Our glances, however, rested not long upon the dead — for we could not regard her unawed. The disease which had thus entombed the lady in the maturity of youth, had left, as usual in all maladies of a strictly cataleptical character, the mockery of a faint blush upon the bosom and the face, and that suspiciously lingering smile upon the lip which is so terrible in death. We replaced and screwed down the lid, and, having secured the door of iron, made our way, with toil, into the scarcely less gloomy apartments of the upper portion of the house.

And now, some days of bitter grief having elapsed, an observable change came over the features of the mental disorder of my friend. His ordinary manner had vanished. His ordinary occupations were neglected or forgotten. He roamed from chamber to chamber with hurried, unequal, and objectless step. The pallor of his countenance had assumed, if possible, a more ghastly hue — but the luminousness of his eye had utterly gone out. The once occasional huskiness of his tone was heard no more; and a tremulous quaver, as if of extreme terror, habitually characterized his utterance — There were times, indeed, when I thought his unceasingly agitated mind was laboring with an oppressive secret, to divulge which he struggled for the necessary courage. At times, again, I was obliged to resolve all into the mere inexplicable vagaries of madness, as I beheld him gazing upon vacancy for long hours, in an attitude of the profoundest attention, as if listening to some imaginary sound. It was no wonder that his condition terrified — that it infected me. I felt creeping upon me, by slow yet certain degrees, the wild influences of his own fantastic yet impressive superstitions.

It was, most especially, upon retiring to bed late in the night of the seventh or eighth day after the entombment of the lady Madeline, that I experienced the full power of such feelings. Sleep came not near my couch — while the hours waned and waned away. I struggled to reason off the nervousness which had dominion over me. I endeavored to believe that much, if not all of what I felt, was due to the phantasmagoric influence of the gloomy furniture of the room — of the dark and tattered draperies, which, tortured into motion by the breath of a rising tempest, swayed fitfully to and fro upon the walls, and rustled uneasily about the decorations of the bed. But my efforts were fruitless. An irrepressible tremor gradually pervaded my frame; and, at length, there sat upon my very heart an incubus of utterly causeless alarm. Shaking this off with a gasp and a struggle, I uplifted myself upon the pillows, and, peering earnestly within the intense darkness of the chamber, harkened — I know not why, except that an instinctive spirit prompted me — to certain low and indefinite sounds which came, through the pauses of the storm, at long intervals, I know not whence. Overpowered by an intense sentiment of horror, unaccountable yet unendurable, I threw on my clothes with haste, for I felt that I should sleep no more during the night, and endeavored to arouse myself from the pitiable condition into which I had fallen, by pacing rapidly to and fro through the apartment.

I had taken but few turns in this manner, when a light step on an adjoining staircase arrested my attention. I presently recognized it as that of Usher. In an instant afterwards he rapped, with a gentle touch, at my door, and entered, bearing a lamp. His countenance was, as usual, cadaverously wan — but there was a species of mad hilarity in his eyes — an evidently restrained hysteria in his whole demeanor. His air appalled me — but any thing was preferable to the solitude which I had so long endured, and I even welcomed his presence as a relief.

"And you have not seen it?" he said abruptly, after having stared about him for some moments in silence — "you have not then seen it? — but, stay! you shall." Thus speaking, and having carefully shaded his lamp, he hurried to one of the gigantic casements, and threw it freely open to the storm.

The impetuous fury of the entering gust nearly lifted us from our feet. It was, indeed, a tempestuous yet sternly beautiful night, and one wildly singular in its terror and its beauty. A whirlwind had apparently collected its force in our vicinity; for there were frequent and violent alterations in the direction of the wind; and the exceeding density of the clouds (which hung so low as to press upon the turrets of the house) did not prevent our perceiving the life-like velocity with which they flew careering from all points against each other, without passing away into the distance. I say that even their exceeding density did not prevent our perceiving this — yet we had no glimpse of the moon or stars — nor was there any flashing forth of lightning. But the under surfaces of the huge masses of agitated vapor, as well as all terrestrial objects immediately around us, were glowing in the unnatural light of a faintly luminous and distinctly visible gaseous exhalation which hung about and enshrouded the mansion.

"You must not — you shall not behold this!" said I, shudderingly, to Usher, as I led him, with a gentle violence, from the window to a seat. "These appearances, which bewilder you, are merely electrical phenomena not uncommon — or it may be that they have their ghastly origin in the rank miasma of the tarn. Let us close this casement — the air is chilling and dangerous to your frame. Here is one of your favorite romances. I will read, and you shall listen — and so we will pass away this terrible night together."

The antique volume which I had taken up was the "Mad Trist" of Sir Launcelot Canning — but I had called it a favorite of Usher's more in sad jest than in earnest; for, in truth, there is little in its uncouth and unimaginative prolixity which could have had interest for the lofty and spiritual ideality of my friend. It was, however, the only book immediately at hand; and I indulged a vague hope that the excitement which now agitated the hypochondriac might find relief (for the history of mental disorder is full of similar anomalies) even in the extremeness of the folly which I should read. Could I have judged, indeed, by the wild, overstrained air of vivacity with which he harkened, or apparently harkened, to the words of the tale, I might have well congratulated myself upon the success of my design.

I had arrived at that well-known portion of the story where Ethelred, the hero of the Trist, having sought in vain for peaceable admission into the dwelling of the hermit, proceeds to make good an entrance by force. Here, it will be remembered, the words of the narrative run thus —

"And Ethelred, who was by nature of a doughty heart, and who was now mighty withal, on account of the powerfulness of the wine which he had drunken, waited no longer to hold parley with the hermit, who, in sooth, was of an obstinate and maliceful turn, but, feeling the rain upon his shoulders, and fearing the rising of the tempest, uplifted his mace outright, and, with blows, made quickly room in the plankings of the door for his gauntleted hand, and now pulling therewith sturdily, he so cracked, and ripped, and tore all asunder, that the noise of the dry and hollow-sounding wood alarummed and reverberated throughout the forest."

At the termination of this sentence I started, and, for a moment, paused; for it appeared to me (although I at once concluded that my excited fancy had deceived me) — it appeared to me that, from some very remote portion of the mansion or of its vicinity, there came, indistinctly, to my ears, what might have been, in its exact similarity of character, the echo (but a stifled and dull one certainly) of the very cracking and ripping sound which Sir Launcelot had so particularly described. It was, beyond doubt, the coincidence alone which had arrested my attention; for, amid the rattling of the sashes of the casements, and the ordinary commingled noises of the still increasing storm, the sound, in itself, had nothing, surely, which should have interested or disturbed me. I continued the story.

"But the good champion Ethelred, now entering within the door, was sore enraged and amazed to perceive no signal of the maliceful hermit; but, in the stead thereof, a dragon of a scaly and prodigious demeanor, and of a fiery tongue, which sate in guard before a palace of gold, with a floor of silver; and upon the wall there hung a shield of shining brass with this legend enwritten —

Who entereth herein, a conqueror hath bin,
Who slayeth the dragon, the shield he shall win.

And Ethelred uplifted his mace, and struck upon the head of the dragon, which fell before him, and gave up his pesty breath, with a shriek so horrid and harsh, and withal so piercing, that Ethelred had fain to close his ears with his hands against the dreadful noise of it, the like whereof was never before heard."

Here again I paused abruptly, and now with a feeling of wild amazement — for there could be no doubt whatever that, in this instance, I did actually hear (although from what direction it proceeded I found it impossible to say) a low and apparently distant, but harsh, protracted, and most unusual screaming or grating sound — the exact counterpart of what my fancy had already conjured up as the sound of the dragon's unnatural shriek as described by the romancer.

Oppressed, as I certainly was, upon the occurrence of this second and most extraordinary coincidence, by a thousand conflicting sensations, in which wonder and extreme terror were predominant, I still retained sufficient presence of mind to avoid exciting, by any observation, the sensitive nervousness of my companion. I was by no means certain that he had noticed the sounds in question; although, assuredly, a strange alteration had, during the last few minutes, taken place in his demeanor. From a position fronting my own, he had gradually brought round his chair, so as to sit with his face to the door of the chamber, and thus I could but partially perceive his features, although I saw that his lips trembled as if he were murmuring inaudibly. His head had dropped upon his breast — yet I knew that he was not asleep, from the wide and rigid opening of the eye, as I caught a glance of it in profile. The motion of his body, too, was at variance with this idea — for he rocked from side to side with a gentle yet constant and uniform sway. Having rapidly taken notice of all this, I resumed the narrative of Sir Launcelot, which thus proceeded: —

"And now, the champion, having escaped from the terrible fury of the dragon, bethinking himself of the brazen shield, and of the breaking up of the enchantment which was upon it, removed the carcass from out of the way before him, and approached valorously over the silver pavement of the castle to where the shield was upon the wall; which in sooth tarried not for his full coming, but fell down at his feet upon the silver floor, with a mighty great and terrible ringing sound."

No sooner had these syllables passed my lips, than — as if a shield of brass had indeed, at the moment, fallen heavily upon a floor of silver — I became aware of a distinct, hollow, metallic, and clangorous, yet apparently muffled reverberation. Completely unnerved, I started convulsively to my feet, but the measured rocking movement of Usher was undisturbed. I rushed to the chair in which he sat. His eyes were bent fixedly before him, and throughout his whole countenance there reigned a more than stony rigidity. But, as I laid my hand upon his shoulder, there came a strong shudder over his frame; a sickly smile quivered about his lips; and I saw that he spoke in a low, hurried, and gibbering murmur, as if unconscious of my presence. Bending closely over his person, I at length drank in the hideous import of his words.

"Not hear it? — yes, I hear it, and *have* heard it. Long — long — long — many minutes, many hours, many days, have I heard it — yet I dared not — oh, pity me, miserable wretch that I am! — I dared not — I *dared* not speak! *We have put her living in the tomb!* Said I not that my senses were acute? — I *now* tell you that I heard her first feeble movements in the hollow coffin. I heard them — many, many days ago — yet I dared not — *I dared not speak!* And now — to-night — Ethelred — ha! ha! — the breaking of the hermit's door, and the death-cry of the dragon, and the clangor of the shield — say, rather, the rending of the coffin, and the grating of the iron hinges, and her struggles within the coppered archway of the vault! Oh whither shall I fly? Will she not be here anon? Is she not hurrying to upbraid me for my haste? Have I not heard her footsteps on the stair? Do I not distinguish that heavy and horrible beating of her heart? Madman!" — here he sprung violently to his feet, and shrieked out his syllables, as if in the effort he were giving up his soul — "Madman! *I tell you that she now stands without the door!*"

As if in the superhuman energy of his utterance there had been found the potency of a spell — the huge antique pannels to which the speaker pointed, threw slowly back, upon the instant, their ponderous and ebony jaws. It was the work of the rushing gust — but then without those doors there *did* stand the lofty and enshrouded figure of the lady Madeline of Usher. There was blood upon her white robes, and the evidence of some bitter struggle upon every portion of her emaciated frame. For a moment she remained trembling and reeling to and fro upon the threshold — then, with a low moaning cry, fell heavily inward upon the person of her brother, and in her horrible and now final death-agonies, bore him to the floor a corpse, and a victim to the terrors he had dreaded.

From that chamber, and from that mansion, I fled aghast. The storm was still abroad in all its wrath as I found myself crossing the old causeway. Suddenly there shot along the path a wild light, and I turned to see whence a gleam so unusual could have issued — for the vast house and its shadows were alone behind me. The radiance was that of the full, setting, and blood-red moon, which now shone vividly through that once barely-discernible fissure, of which I have before spoken, as extending from the roof of the building, in a zig-zag direction, to the base. While I gazed, this fissure rapidly widened — there came a fierce breath of the whirlwind — the entire orb of the satellite burst at once upon my sight — my brain reeled as I saw the mighty walls rushing asunder — there was a long tumultuous shouting sound like the voice of a thousand waters — and the deep and dank tarn at my feet closed sullenly and silently over the fragments of the *"House of Usher."*

> *Note.* — The ballad of "The Haunted Palace," introduced in this tale, was published separately, some months ago, in the Baltimore *Museum*.

Thomas Bangs Thorpe
The Big Bear of Arkansas

Perhaps the foremost example of the humor of the Old Southwest, the most southern and western section of the United States prior to the Louisiana Purchase, Thorpe's "The Big Bear of Arkansas" appeared in the popular *Spirit of the Times* in

1841 before being included in *The Big Bear of Arkansas and Other Sketches* in 1845. Utilizing what became standard techniques in the tradition, it features an urbane narrator out of place in a country atmosphere of garrulous ruffians. He records, in the vernacular, a hyperbolic tale of fantastic hunting adventures told to him by Jim Doggett, one that takes place in Arkansas, "the creation State," one "without a fault." Regional pride is typical of the mode, as is the capturing of local dialects, mores, and character types. But Thorpe invests this fantastic account with a motif that suggests a deeper layer of significance, the passing of the American wilderness, the destruction of the very natural world that had made the continent seem Edenic in its innocence. It is that sense of loss that lends an elegiac tone to this otherwise comic narrative.

Thomas Bangs Thorpe, "The Big Bear of Arkansas," *Spirit of the Times* 11 (March 27, 1841): 43–51.

A steamboat on the Mississippi frequently, in making her regular trips, carries between places varying from one to two thousand miles apart; and as these boats advertise to land passengers and freight at "all intermediate landings," the heterogeneous character of the passengers of one of these upcountry boats can scarcely be imagined by one who has never seen it with his own eyes. Starting from New Orleans in one of these boats, you will find yourself associated with men from every State in the Union, and from every portion of the globe; and a man of observation need not lack for amusement or instruction in such a crowd, if he will take the trouble to read the great book of character so favorably opened before him. Here may be some jostling together the wealthy Southern planter, and the pedlar of tin-ware from New England — the Northern merchant, and the Southern jockey — a venerable bishop, and a desperate gambler — the land speculator, and the honest farmer — professional men of all creeds and characters — Wolvereens, Suckers, Hoosiers, Buckeyes, and Corncrackers, beside a "plentiful sprinkling" of the half-horse and half-alligator species of men, who are peculiar to "old Mississippi," and who appear to gain a livelihood simply by going up and down the river. In the pursuit of pleasure or business, I have frequently found myself in such a crowd.

On one occasion, when in New Orleans, I had occasion to take a trip of a few miles up the Mississippi, and I hurried on board the well-known, "high-pressure-and-beat-every-thing" steamboat "Invincible," just as the last note of the last bell was sounding, and when the confusion and bustle that is natural to a boat's getting under way had subsided, I discovered that I was associated in as heterogeneous a crowd as was ever got together. As my trip was to be of a few hours duration only, I made no endeavors to become acquainted with my fellow passengers, most of whom would be together many days. Instead of this, I took out of my pocket the "latest paper," and more critically than usual examined its contents; my fellow passengers at the same time disposed of themselves in little groups. While I was thus busily employed in reading, and my companions were more busily still employed in discussing such subjects as suited their humors best, we were startled most unexpectedly by a loud Indian whoop, uttered in the "social hall," that part of the cabin fitted off for a bar; then was to be heard a loud crowing, which would not have continued to have interested us — such sounds being quite common in that *place of spirits* — had not the hero of these windy accomplishments stuck his head into the cabin and hallooed out, "Hurra for the Big Bar of Arkansaw!" and then might be heard a confused hum of voices, unintelligible, save in such broken sentences as "horse," "screamer," "lightning is slow," etc. As might have been expected, this continued interruption attracted the attention of every one in the cabin; all conversation dropped, and in the midst of this surprise the "Big Bar" walked into the cabin, took a chair, put his feet on the stove, and looking back over his shoulder, passed the general and familiar salute of "Strangers, how are you?" He then expressed himself as much at home as if he had been at "the Forks of Cypress," and "prehaps a little more so." Some of the company at this familiarity looked a little angry, and some astonished, but in a moment every face was wreathed in a smile. There was something about the intruder that won the heart on sight. He appeared to be a man enjoying perfect health and contentment — his eyes were as sparkling as diamonds, and good natured to simplicity. Then his perfect confidence in himself was irresistibly droll. "Prehaps," said he, "gentlemen," running on without a person speaking, "prehaps you have been to New Orleans often; I never made *the first visit before,* and I don't intend to make another in a crow's life. I am thrown away in that ar place, and useless, that ar a fact. Some of the gentlemen thar called me *green* — well, prehaps I am, said I, *but I arn't so at home;* and if I aint off my trail much, the heads of them perlite chaps themselves weren't much the hardest, for according to my notion, they were *real know-nothings,* green as a pumpkin-vine — couldn't, in farming, I'll bet, raise a crop of turnips — and as for shooting, they'd miss a barn if the door was swinging, and that, too, with the best rifle in the country. And then they talked to me 'bout hunting, and laughed at my calling the principal game in Arkansaw poker, and high-low-jack. 'Prehaps,' said I, 'you prefer checkers and rolette;' at this they laughed harder than ever, and asked me if I lived in the woods, and didn't know what *game* was? At this I rather think I laughed. 'Yes,' I roared, and says, 'Strangers, if you'd asked me *how we got our meat* in Arkansaw, I'd a told you at once, and given you a list of varmints that would make a caravan, beginning with the bar, and ending off with the cat; that's *meat* though, not game.' Game, indeed, that's what city folks call it, and with them it means chippen-birds, and shite-pokes; maybe such trash live in my diggings, but I arn't noticed them yet — a bird any way is too trifling.

I never did shoot at but one, and I'd never forgiven myself for that had it weighed less than forty pounds; I wouldn't draw a rifle on anything less than that; and when I meet with another wild turkey of the same weight I will drap him."

"A wild turkey weighing forty pounds?" exclaimed twenty voices in the cabin at once.

"Yes, strangers, and wasn't it a whopper? You see, the thing was so fat that he couldn't fly far, and when he fell out of the tree, after I shot him, on striking the ground he bust open behind, and the way the pound gobs of tallow rolled out of the opening was perfectly beautiful."

"Where did all that happen?" asked a cynical looking hoosier.

"Happen! happened in Arkansaw; where else could it have happened, but in the creation State, the finishing-up country; a State where the *sile* runs down to the centre of the 'arth, and government gives you a title to every inch of it. Then its airs, just breath them, and they will make you snort like a horse. It's a State without a fault, it is."

"Excepting mosquitoes," cried the hoosier.

"Well, stranger, except them; for it ar a fact that they are rather *enormous,* and do push themselves in somewhat troublesome. But, stranger, they never stick twice in the same place, and give them a fair chance for a few months, and you will get as much above noticing them as an alligator. They can't hurt my feelings, for they lay under the skin; and I never knew but one case of injury resulting from them, and that was to a Yankee: and they take worse to foreigners, anyhow, than they do to natives. But the way they used that fellow up! first they punched him until he swelled up and busted, then he sup-per-a-ted, as the doctor called it, until he was raw as beef; then he took the ager, owing to the warm weather, and finally he took a steamboat and left the country. He was the only man that ever took mosquitoes at heart that I know of. But mosquitoes is natur, and I never find fault with her; if they ar large, Arkansaw is large, her varmints ar large, her trees ar large, her rivers ar large, and a small mosquitoe would be of no more use in Arkansaw than preaching in a cane-brake."

This knock-down argument in favor of big mosquitoes used the hoosier up, and the logician started on a new track, to explain how numerous bear were in his "diggings," where he represented them to be "about as plenty as blackberries, and a little plentifuler."

Upon the utterance of this assertion, a timid little man near me enquired if the bear in Arkansaw ever attacked the settlers in numbers.

"No," said our hero, warming with the subject, "no, stranger, for you see it ain't the natur of bar to go in droves, but the way they squander about in pairs and single ones is edifying. And then the way I hunt them — the old black rascals know the crack of my gun as well as they know a pig's squealing. They grow thin in our parts, it frightens them so, and they do take the noise dreadfully, poor things. That gun of mine is perfect *epidemic among bar* — if not watched closely, it will go off as quick on a warm scent as my dog Bowie-knife will; and then that dog, whew! why the fellow thinks that the world is full of bar, he finds them so easy. It's lucky he don't talk as well as think, for with his natural modesty, if he should suddenly learn how much he is acknowledged to be ahead of all other dogs in the universe, he would be astonished to death in two minutes. Strangers, that dog knows a bar's way as well as a horse-jockey knows a woman's; he always barks at the right time — bites at the exact place — and whips without getting a scratch. I never could tell whether he was made expressly to hunt bar, or whether bar was made expressly for him to hunt; any way, I believe they were ordained to go together as naturally as Squire Jones says a man and woman is, when he moralizes in marrying a couple. In fact, Jones once said, said he, 'Marriage according to law is a civil contract of divine origin, it's common to all countries as well as Arkansaw, and people take to it as naturally as Jim Doggett's Bowie-knife takes to bar.'"

"What season of the year do your hunts take place?" enquired a gentlemanly foreigner, who, from some peculiarities of his baggage, I suspected to be an Englishman, on some hunting expedition, probably, at the foot of the Rocky Mountains.

"The season for bar hunting, stranger," said the man of Arkansaw, "is generally all the year round, and the hunts take place about as regular. I read in history that varmints have their fat season, and their lean season. That is not the case in Arkansaw, feeding as they do upon the *spontenacious* productions of the sile, they have one continued fat season the year round — though in winter things in this way is rather more greasy than in summer, I must admit. For that reason bar with us run in warm weather, but in winter they only waddle. Fat, fat! it's an enemy to speed — it tames everything that has plenty of it. I have seen wild turkies, from its influence, as gentle as chickens. Run a bar in this fat condition, and the way it improves the critter for eating is amazing; it sort of mixes the ile up with the meat until you can't tell t'other from which. I've done this often. I recollect one perty morning in particular, of putting an old he fellow on the stretch, and considering the weight he carried, he run well. But the dogs soon tired him down, and when I came up with him wasn't he in a beautiful sweat — I might say fever; and then to see his tongue sticking out of his mouth a feet, and his sides sinking and opening like a bellows, and his cheeks so fat he couldn't look cross. In this fix I blazed at him, and pitch me naked into a briar patch if the steam didn't come out of the bullet hole ten foot in a straight line. The fellow, I reckon, was made on the high-pressure system, and the lead sort of bust his biler."

"That column of steam was rather curious, or else the bear must have been *warm*," observed the foreigner, with a laugh.

"Stranger, as you observe, that bar was WARM, and the blowing off of the steam show'd it, and also how hard the varmint had been run. I have no doubt if he had kept on two miles farther his insides would have been stewed; and I expect to meet with a varmint yet of extra bottom, who will run himself into a skin full of bar's-grease: it is possible, much onlikelier things have happened."

"Where abouts are these bear so abundant?" enquired the foreigner, with increasing interest.

"Why, stranger, they inhabit the neighborhood of my settlement, one of the prettiest places on Old Mississippi — a perfect location, and no mistake; a place that had some defects until the river made the 'cut-off' at 'Shirt-tail bend,' and that remedied the evil, as it brought my cabin on the edge of the river — a great advantage in wet weather, I assure you, as you can now roll a barrel of whiskey into my yard in high water, from a boat, as easy as falling off a log; it's a great improvement, as toting it by land in a jug, as I used to do, *evaporated* it too fast, and it became expensive. Just stop with me, stranger, a month or two, or a year if you like, and you will appreciate my place. I can give you plenty to eat, for beside hog and hominy, you can have bar ham, and bar sausages, and a mattrass of bar-skins to sleep on, and a wildcat-skin, pulled off hull, stuffed with corn-shucks, for a pillow. That bed would put you to sleep if you had the rheumatics in every joint in your body. I call that ar bed a *quietus*. Then look at my land, the government ain't got another such a piece to dispose of. Such timber, and such bottom land, why you can't preserve anything natural you plant in it, unless you pick it young, things thar will grow out of shape so quick. I once planted in those diggings a few potatoes and beets, they took a fine start, and after that an ox team couldn't have kept them from growing. About that time I went off to old Kentuck on bisiness, and did not hear from them things in three months, when I accidentally stumbled on a fellow who had stopped at my place, with an idea of buying me out. 'How did you like things?' said I. 'Pretty well,' said he; 'the cabin is convenient, and the timber land is good; but that bottom land ain't worth the first red cent.' 'Why?' said I. ''Cause,' said he. ''Cause what?' said I. '''Cause it's full of cedar stumps and Indian mounds,' said he, 'and *it can't be cleared*.' 'Lord,' said I, 'them ar "cedar stumps" is beets, and them ar "Indian mounds" ar tater hills,' — as I expected the crop was overgrown and useless; the sile is too rich, *and planting in Arkansaw is dangerous*. I had a good sized sow killed in that same bottom land; the old thief stole an ear of corn, and took it down where she slept at night to eat; well, she left a grain or two on the ground, and lay down on them; before morning the corn shot up, and the percussion killed her dead. I don't plant any more; natur intended Arkansaw for a hunting ground, and I go according to natur."

The questioner, who thus elicited the description of our hero's settlement, seemed to be perfectly satisfied, and said no more; but the "Big Bar of Arkansaw" rambled on from one thing to another with a volubility perfectly astonishing, occasionally disputing with those around him, particularly with a "live sucker" from Illinois, who had the daring to say that our Arkansaw friend's stories "smelt rather tall."

In this manner the evening was spent, but conscious that my own assocation with so singular a personage would probably end before morning, I asked him if he would not give me a description of some particular bear hunt — adding that I took great interest in such things, though I was no sportsman. The desire seemed to please him, and he squared himself round towards me, saying, that he could give me an idea of a bar hunt that was never beat in this world, or in any other. His manner was so singular, that half of his story consisted in his excellent way of telling it, the great peculiarity of which was, the happy manner he had of emphasizing the prominent parts of his conversation. As near as I can recollect, I have italicized them, and given the story in his own words.

"Stranger," said he, "in bar hunts *I am numerous,* and which particular one as you say I shall tell puzzles me. There was the old she devil I shot at the hurricane last fall — then there was the old hog thief I popped over at the Bloody Crossing, and then —— Yes, I have it, I will give you an idea of a hunt, in which the greatest bar was killed that ever lived, *none excepted;* about an old fellow that I hunted, more or less, for two or three years, and if that ain't a *particular bar hunt,* I ain't got one to tell. But in the first place, stranger let me say, I am pleased with you, because you ain't ashamed to gain information by asking, and listening, and that's what I say to Countess's pups every day when I'm home — and I have got great hopes of them ar pups, because they are continually *nosing* about, and though they stick it sometimes in the wrong place, they gain experience anyhow, and may learn something useful to boot. Well, as I was saying about this big bar, you see when I and some more first settled in our region, we were drivin to hunting naturally; we soon liked it, and after that we found it an easy matter to make the thing our business. One old chap who had pioneered 'afore us, gave us to understand that we had settled in the right place. He dwelt upon its merits until it was affecting, and showed us, to prove his assertions, more marks on the sassafras trees than I ever saw on a tavern door 'lection time. 'Who keeps that ar reckoning?' said I. 'The bar,' said he. 'What for?' said I. 'Can't tell,' said he, 'but so it is, the bar bite the bark and wood too, at the highest point from the ground they can reach, and you can tell, by the marks,' said he, 'the length of the bar to an inch.' 'Enough,' said I, 'I've learned something here a'ready, and I'll put it in practice.' Well, stranger, just one month from that time I killed a bar, and told its exact length before I measured it by those very marks — and when I did that I swelled up considerable — I've been a prouder man ever since. So I went on, larning something every day, until I was reckoned a buster, and allowed to be decidedly the best bar hunter in my district; and that is a reputation as much harder to earn than to be reckoned first man in Congress, as an iron ram-rod is harder than a toadstool. Did the varmints grow over cunning by being fooled with by greenhorn hunters, and by this means get troublesome, they send for me as a matter of course, and thus I do my own hunting, and most of my neighbors'. I walk into the varmints though, and it has become about as much the same to me as drinking. It is told in two sentences — a bar is started, and he is killed. The thing is somewhat monotonous now — I know just how much they will run, where they will tire, how much they will growl, and what a thundering time I will have in getting them home. I could give you this history of the chase with all particulars at the commencement, I know the signs so well. *Stranger, I'm certain.* Once I met with a match, though, and I will tell you about it, for a common hunt would not be worth relating.

"On a fine fall day, long time ago, I was trailing about for bar, and what should I see but fresh marks on the sassafras trees, about eight inches above any in the forests that I knew of. Says I, them marks is a hoax, or it indicates the d —— t bar that was ever grown. In fact, stranger, I couldn't believe it was real, and I went on. Again I saw the same marks, at the same height, and *I knew the thing lived.* That conviction came home to my soul like an earthquake. Says I, here is something a-purpose for me — that bar is mine, or I give up the hunting business. The very next morning what should I see but a number of buzzards hovering over my cornfield. The rascal has been there, said I, for that sign is certain; and, sure enough, on examining, I found the bones of what had been as beautiful a hog the day before, as was ever raised by a Buck-eye. Then I tracked the critter out of the field to the woods, and all the marks he left behind, showed me that he was *the Bar.*

"Well, stranger, the first fair chase I ever had with that big critter, I saw him no less than three distinct times at a distance, the dogs run him over eighteen miles, and broke down, my horse gave out, and I was as nearly used up as a man can be, made on *my* principle, *which is patent.* Before this adventure, such things were unknown to me as possible; but, strange as it was, that bar got me used to it, before I was done with him, — for he got so at last, that he would leave me on a long chase *quite easy.* How he did it, I never could understand. That a bar runs at all, is puzzling; but how this one could tire down, and bust up a pack of hounds and a horse, that were used to overhauling every thing they started after in no time, was past my understanding. Well, stranger, that bar finally got so sassy, that he used to help himself to a hog off my premises whenever he wanted one; — the buzzards followed after what he left, and so between *bar and buzzard,* I rather think I was *out of pork.* Well, missing that bar so often, took hold of my vitals, and I wasted away. The thing had been carried too far, and it reduced me in flesh faster than an ager. I would see that bar in everything I did, — *he hunted me,* and that, too, like a devil, which I began to think he was. While in this fix, I made preparations to give him a last brush, and be done with it. Having completed every thing to my satisfaction, I started at sun-rise, and to my great joy, I discovered from the way the dogs run, that they were near him — finding his trail was nothing, for that had become as plain to the pack as a turnpike-road. On we went, and coming to an open country, what should I see but the bar very leisurely ascending a hill, and the dogs close at his heels, either a match for him this time in speed, or else he did not care to get out of their way — I don't know which. But, wasn't he a beauty though? I loved him like a brother. On he went, until coming to a tree, the limbs of which formed a crotch about six feet from the ground, — into this crotch he got and seated himself, — the dogs yelling all around it — and there he sat eyeing them, as quiet as a pond in low water. A green-horn friend of mine, in company, reached shooting distance before me, and blazed away, hitting the critter in the centre of his forehead. The bar shook his head as the ball struck it, and then he walked down from that tree as gently as a lady would from a carriage. 'Twas a beautiful sight to see him do that, — he was in such a rage, that he seemed to be as little afraid of the dogs, as if they had been sucking pigs; and the dogs warn't slow in making a ring around him at a respectful distance, I tell you; even Bowie-knife himself stood off. Then the way his eyes flashed — why the fire of them would have singed a cat's hair; in fact, that bar was in a *wrath all over.* Only one pup came near him, and he was brushed out so totally with the bar's left paw, that he entirely disappeared; and that made the old dogs more cautious still. In the mean time, I came up, and taking deliberate aim as a man should do, at his side, just back of his foreleg, *if my gun did not snap,* call me a coward, and I won't take it personal. Yes, stranger, *it snapped,* and I could not find a cap about my person. While in this predicament, I turned round to my fool friend — says I, 'Bill,' says I, 'you're an ass — you're a fool — you might as well have tried to kill that bar by barking the tree under his belly, as to have done it by hitting him in the head. Your shot has made a tiger of him, and blast me, if a dog gets killed or wounded when they come to blows, I will stick my knife into your liver. I will —— ' my wrath was up. I had lost my caps, my gun had snapped, the fellow with me had fired at the bar's head, and I expected every moment to see him close in with the dogs, and kill a dozen of them at least. In this thing I was mistaken, for the bar leaped over the ring formed by the dogs, and giving a fierce growl, was off — the pack of course in full cry after him. The run this time was short, for coming to the edge of a lake the varmint jumped in, and swam to a little island in the lake, which it reached just a moment before the dogs. I'll have him now, said I, for I had found my caps in the *lining of my coat* — so, rolling a log into the lake, I paddled myself across to the island, just as the dogs had cornered the bar in a thicket. I rushed up and fired — at the same time the critter leaped over the dogs and came within three feet of me, running like mad; he jumped into the lake, and tried to mount the log I had just deserted, but every time he got half his body on it, it would roll over and send him under; the dogs, too, got around him, and pulled him about, and finally Bowie-knife clenched with him, and they sunk into the lake together. Stranger, about this time I was excited, and I stripped off my coat, drew my knife, and intended to have taken a part with Bowie-knife myself when the bar rose to the surface. But the varmint staid under — Bowie-knife came up alone, more dead than alive, and with the pack came ashore. Thank God, said I, the old villain has got his deserts at last. Determined to have the body, I cut a grape-vine for a rope, and dove down where I could see the bar in the water, fastened my queer rope to his leg, and fished him, with great difficulty, ashore. Stranger, may I be chawed to death by young alligators, if the thing I looked at wasn't a *she bar, and not the old critter after all.* The way matters got mixed on that island was onaccountably curious, and thinking of it made me more than ever convinced that I was hunting the devil himself. I went home that night and took to my bed — the thing was killing me. The entire team of Arkansaw in bar-hunting, acknowledged himself used up, and the fact sunk into my feelings like a snagged boat will in the Mississippi. I grew as cross as a bar with two cubs and a sore tail. The thing got out 'mong my neighbors, and I was asked how come on that individ-u-al that never lost a bar when once started? and if that same individ-u-al didn't wear telescopes when he turned a she bar, of ordinary size, into an old he one, a little larger than a horse? Prehaps, said I, friends — getting wrathy — perhaps you want to call somebody a liar. Oh, no, said they, we only heard such things as being *rather common* of late, but we don't believe one word of it; oh, no, — and then they would ride off and laugh like so many hyenas over a dead nigger. It was too much, and I determined to catch that bar, go to Texas, or die — and I made my preparations accordin'. I had the pack shut up and rested. I took my rifle to pieces, and iled it. I put caps in every pocket about my person, *for fear of the lining.* I then told my neighbors, that on Monday morning — naming the day — I would start THAT BAR, and bring him home with me, or they might divide my settlement among them, the owner having disappeared. Well, stranger, on the morning previous to the great day of my hunting expedition, I went into the woods near my house, taking my gun and Bowie-knife along, just *from habit,* and there sitting down also from habit, what should I see, getting over my fence, but *the bar!* Yes, the old varmint was within a hundred yards of me, and the way he walked *over that fence,* — stranger, he loomed up like a *black mist,* he seemed so large, and he walked right towards me. I raised myself, took deliberate aim, and fired. Instantly the varmint wheeled, gave a yell, and *walked through the fence* like a falling tree would through a cobweb. I started after, but was tripped up by my inexpressibles, which either from habit, or the excitement of the moment, were about my heels, and before I had really gathered myself up, I heard the old varmint groaning in a thicket near by, like a thousand sinners, and by the time I reached him he was a corpse. Stranger, it took five niggers and myself to put that carcase on a mule's back, and old long ears waddled under his load, as if he was foundered in every leg of his body, and with a common whopper of a bar, he would have trotted off, and enjoyed himself. 'Twould astonish you to know how big he was, — I made a *bed spread of his skin,* and the way it used to cover my bar mattrass, and leave several feet on each side to tuck up, would have delighted you. It was in fact a creation bar, and if it had lived in Sampson's time, and had met him, in a fair fight, it would have licked him in the twinkling of a dice-box.

But, stranger, I never liked the way I hunted, *and missed him.* There was some-thing curious about it, I could never understand, — and I never was satisfied at his giving in so *easy at last.* Prehaps, he had heard of my preparations to hunt him the next day, so he jist come in, like Capt. Scott's coon, to save his wind to grunt with in dying; but that ain't likely. My private opinion is, that that bar was an *unhuntable bar, and died when his time come.*"

When the story was ended, our hero sat some minutes with his auditors in a grave silence; I saw there was a mystery to him connected with the bear whose death he had just related, that had evidently made a strong impression on his mind. It was also evident that there was some superstitious awe connected with the affair, — a feeling common with all "children of the wood," when they meet with any thing out of their every day experience. He was the first one, however, to break the silence, and jumping up he asked all present to "liquor" before go-ing to bed, — a thing which he did, with a number of companions, evidently to his heart's content.

Long before day, I was put ashore at my place of destination, and I can only follow with the reader, in imagination, our Arkansas friend, in his adventures at the "Forks of Cypress" on the Mississippi.

Nathaniel Hawthorne
Rappaccini's Daughter

Nathaniel Hawthorne's "Rappaccini's Daughter" was published in the *United States Magazine and Democratic Review* in 1844 before being included in *Mosses from an Old Manse* two years later. Widely regarded as his most complex portrait of moral ambiguity, this theme is united with the historical conflict between the head and the heart, between the world of empirical science in a "material" universe and the humanistic concerns of emotion, intuition, and religion. The Romantic period, it should be remembered, followed the Age of Reason, and there were deep mis-givings about the wisdom of probing into the mysteries of life and death, especially in the practice of medicine. But rather than produce stock characters exemplifying the conflict, Hawthorne here presents multifaceted individuals: Doctor Rappac-cini, a scientist who loves his daughter but uses her as part of a scientific experi-ment; Beatrice, both an emblem of feminine purity and a deadly attraction whose very breath destroys life; and Baglioni, a "humanistic" scientist who meddles into matters he does not fully understand and destroys what is most precious. At the center of the action is Giovanni, at once an "innocent," a rational student enrolled at the University of Padua, and a sentimentalist who kills the woman he loves. The skill with which Hawthorne advances the plot that entwines these characters in their complex interaction is remarkable, as is the enigmatic conclusion, in which it is difficult to sort out the moral responsibility for what takes place.

Nathaniel Hawthorne, "Rappaccini's Daughter," *Mosses from an Old Manse* (Boston: Houghton, Mifflin and Company, 1846), 1: 85–118.

A young man, named Giovanni Guasconti, came, very long ago, from the more southern region of Italy, to pursue his studies at the University of Padua. Giovanni, who had but a scanty supply of gold ducats in his pocket, took lodgings in a high and gloomy chamber of an old edifice, which looked not unworthy to have been the palace of a Paduan noble, and which, in fact, exhibited over its entrance the armorial bearings of a family long since extinct. The young stranger, who was not unstudied in the great poem of his country, recollected that one of the ancestors of this family, and perhaps an occupant of this very mansion, had been pictured by Dante as a partaker of the immortal agonies of his Inferno. These reminiscences and associations, together with the tendency to heartbreak natural to a young man for the first time out of his native sphere, caused Giovanni to sigh heavily, as he looked around the desolate and ill-furnished apartment.

"Holy Virgin, signor," cried old dame Lisabetta, who, won by the youth's remarkable beauty of person, was kindly endeavoring to give the chamber a habitable air, "what a sigh was that to come out of a young man's heart! Do you find this old mansion gloomy? For the love of heaven, then, put your head out of the window, and you will see as bright sunshine as you have left in Naples."

Guasconti mechanically did as the old woman advised, but could not quite agree with her that the Lombard sunshine was as cheerful as that of southern Italy. Such as it was, however, it fell upon a garden beneath the window, and expended its fostering influences on a variety of plants, which seemed to have been cultivated with exceeding care.

"Does this garden belong to the house?" asked Giovanni.

"Heaven forbid, signor! — unless it were fruitful of better pot-herbs than any that grow there now," answered old Lisabetta. "No: that garden is cultivated by the own hands of Signor Giacomo Rappaccini, the famous Doctor, who, I warrant him, has been heard of as far as Naples. It is said that he distils these plants into medicines that are as potent as a charm. Oftentimes you may see the signor Doctor at work, and perchance the signora his daughter, too, gathering the strange flowers that grow in the garden."

The old woman had now done what she could for the aspect of the chamber, and, commending the young man to the protection of the saints, took her departure.

Giovanni still found no better occupation than to look down into the garden beneath his window. From its appearance, he judged it to be one of those botanic gardens, which were of earlier date in Padua than elsewhere in Italy, or in the world. Or, not improbably, it might once have been the pleasure-place of an opulent family; for there was the ruin of a marble fountain in the centre, sculptured with rare art, but so wofully shattered that it was impossible to trace the original design from the chaos of remaining fragments. The water, however, continued to gush and sparkle into the sunbeams as cheerfully as ever. A little gurgling sound ascended to the young man's window, and made him feel as if a fountain were an immortal spirit, that sung its song unceasingly, and without heeding the vicissitudes around it; while one century embodied it in marble, and another scattered the perishable garniture on the soil. All about the pool into which the water subsided, grew various plants, that seemed to require a plentiful supply of moisture for the nourishment of gigantic leaves, and, in some instances, flowers gorgeously magnificent. There was one shrub in particular, set in a marble vase in the midst of the pool, that bore a profusion of purple blossoms, each of which had the lustre and richness of a gem; and the whole together made a show so resplendent that it seemed enough to illuminate the garden, even had there been no sunshine. Every portion of the soil was peopled with plants and herbs, which, if less beautiful, still bore tokens of assiduous care; as if all had their individual virtues, known to the scientific mind that fostered them. Some were placed in urns, rich with old carving, and others in common garden-pots; some crept serpent-like along the ground, or climbed on high, using whatever means of ascent was offered them. One plant had wreathed itself round a statue of Vertumnus, which was thus quite veiled and shrouded in a drapery of hanging foliage, so happily arranged that it might have served a sculptor for a study.

While Giovanni stood at the window, he heard a rustling behind a screen of leaves, and became aware that a person was at work in the garden. His figure soon emerged into view, and showed itself to be that of no common laborer, but a tall, emaciated, sallow, and sickly-looking man, dressed in a scholar's garb of black. He was beyond the middle term of life, with grey hair, a thin grey beard, and a face singularly marked with intellect and cultivation, but which could never, even in his more youthful days, have expressed much warmth of heart.

Nothing could exceed the intentness with which this scientific gardener examined every shrub which grew in his path; it seemed as if he was looking into their inmost nature, making observations in regard to their creative essence, and discovering why one leaf grew in this shape, and another in that, and wherefore such and such flowers differed among themselves in hue and perfume. Nevertheless, in spite of the deep intelligence on his part, there was no approach to intimacy between himself and these vegetable existences. On the contrary, he avoided their actual touch, or the direct inhaling of their odors, with a caution that impressed Giovanni most disagreeably; for the man's demeanor was that of one walking among malignant influences, such as savage beasts, or deadly snakes, or evil spirits, which, should he allow them one moment of license, would wreak upon him some terrible fatality. It was strangely frightful to the young man's imagination, to see this air of insecurity in a person cultivating a garden, that most simple and innocent of human toils, and which had been alike the joy and labor of the unfallen parents of the race. Was this garden, then, the Eden of the present world? — and this man, with such a perception of harm in what his own hands caused to grow, was he the Adam?

The distrustful gardener, while plucking away the dead leaves or pruning the too luxuriant growth of the shrubs, defended his hands with a pair of thick gloves. Nor were these his only armor. When, in his walk through the garden, he came to the magnificent plant that hung its purple gems beside the marble fountain, he placed a kind of mask over his mouth and nostrils, as if all this beauty did but conceal a deadlier malice. But finding his task still too dangerous, he drew back, removed the mask, and called loudly, but in the infirm voice of a person affected with inward disease:

"Beatrice! — Beatrice!"

"Here am I, my father! What would you?" cried a rich and youthful voice from the window of the opposite house; a voice as rich as a tropical sunset, and which made Giovanni, though he knew not why, think of deep hues of purple or crimson, and of perfumes heavily delectable — "Are you in the garden!"

"Yes, Beatrice," answered the gardener, "and I need your help."

Soon there emerged from under a sculptured portal the figure of a young girl, arrayed with as much richness of taste as the most splendid of the flowers, beautiful as the day, and with a bloom so deep and vivid that one shade more would have been too much. She looked redundant with life, health, and energy; all of which attributes were bound down and compressed, as it were, and girdled tensely, in their luxuriance, by her virgin zone. Yet Giovanni's fancy must have grown morbid, while he looked down into the garden; for the impression which the fair stranger made upon him was as if here were another flower, the human sister of those vegetable ones, as beautiful as they — more beautiful than the richest of them — but still to be touched only with a glove, nor to be approached without a mask. As Beatrice came down the garden-path, it was observable that she handled and inhaled the odor of several of the plants, which her father had most sedulously avoided.

"Here, Beatrice," said the latter, — "see how many needful offices require to be done to our chief treasure. Yet, shattered as I am, my life might pay the penalty of approaching it so closely as circumstances demand. Henceforth, I fear, this plant must be consigned to your sole charge."

"And gladly will I undertake it," cried again the rich tones of the young lady, as she bent towards the magnificent plant, and opened her arms as if to embrace it. "Yes, my sister, my splendor, it shall be Beatrice's task to nurse and serve thee; and thou shalt reward her with thy kisses and perfume breath, which to her is as the breath of life!"

Then, with all the tenderness in her manner that was so strikingly expressed

in her words, she busied herself with such attentions as the plant seemed to require; and Giovanni, at his lofty window, rubbed his eyes, and almost doubted
whether it were a girl tending her favorite flower, or one sister performing the
duties of affection to another. The scene soon terminated. Whether Doctor
Rappaccini had finished his labors in the garden, or that his watchful eye had
caught the stranger's face, he now took his daughter's arm and retired. Night
was already closing in; oppressive exhalations seemed to proceed from the
plants, and steal upward past the open window; and Giovanni, closing the lattice,
went to his couch, and dreamed of a rich flower and beautiful girl. Flower and
maiden were different and yet the same, and fraught with some strange peril in
either shape.

But there is an influence in the light of morning that tends to rectify whatever errors of fancy, or even of judgment, we may have incurred during the sun's
decline, or among the shadows of the night, or in the less wholesome glow of
moonshine. Giovanni's first movement on starting from sleep, was to throw
open the window, and gaze down into the garden which his dreams had made so
fertile of mysteries. He was surprised, and a little ashamed, to find how real and
matter-of-fact an affair it proved to be, in the first rays of the sun, which gilded
the dew-drops that hung upon leaf and blossom, and, while giving a brighter
beauty to each rare flower, brought everything within the limits of ordinary experience. The young man rejoiced, that, in the heart of the barren city, he had
the privilege of overlooking this spot of lovely and luxuriant vegetation. It
would serve, he said to himself, as a symbolic language, to keep him in communion with nature. Neither the sickly and thought-worn Doctor Giacomo
Rappaccini, it is true, nor his brilliant daughter, were now visible; so that Giovanni could not determine how much of the singularity which he attributed to
both, was due to their own qualities, and how much to his wonder-working
fancy. But he was inclined to take a most rational view of the whole matter.

In the course of the day, he paid his respects to Signor Pietro Baglioni, professor of medicine in the University, a physician of eminent repute, to whom
Giovanni had brought a letter of introduction. The professor was an elderly personage, apparently of genial nature, and habits that might almost be called
jovial; he kept the young man to dinner, and made himself very aggreeable by
the freedom and liveliness of his conversation, especially when warmed by a
flask or two of Tuscan wine. Giovanni, conceiving that men of science, inhabitants of the same city, must needs be on familiar terms with one another, took
an opportunity to mention the name of Dr. Rappaccini. But the professor did
not respond with so much cordiality as he had anticipated.

"Ill would it become a teacher of the divine art of medicine," said Professor
Pietro Baglioni, in answer to a question of Giovanni, "to withhold due and well-
considered praise of a physician so eminently skilled as Rappaccini. But, on the
other hand, I should answer it but scantily to my conscience, were I to permit a

worthy youth like yourself, Signor Giovanni, the son of an ancient friend, to imbibe erroneous ideas respecting a man who might hereafter chance to hold your life and death in his hands. The truth is, our worshipful Doctor Rappaccini has as much science as any member of the faculty — with perhaps one single exception — in Padua, or all Italy. But there are certain grave objections to his professional character."

"And what are they?" asked the young man.

"Has my friend Giovanni any disease of body or heart, that he is so inquisitive about physicians?" said the Professor, with a smile. "But as for Rappaccini, it is said of him — and I, who know the man well, can answer for its truth — that he cares infinitely more for science than for mankind. His patients are interesting to him only as subjects for some new experiment. He would sacrifice human life, his own among the rest, or whatever else was dearest to him, for the sake of adding so much as a grain of mustard-seed to the great heap of his accumulated knowledge."

"Methinks he is an awful man, indeed," remarked Guasconti, mentally recalling the cold and purely intellectual aspect of Rappaccini. "And yet, worshipful Professor, is it not a noble spirit? Are there many men capable of so spiritual a love of science?"

"God forbid," answered the Professor, somewhat testily — "at least, unless they take sounder views of the healing art than those adopted by Rappaccini. It is his theory, that all medicinal virtues are comprised within those substances which we term vegetable poisons. These he cultivates with his own hands, and is said even to have produced new varieties of poison, more horribly deleterious than Nature, without the assistance of this learned person, would ever have plagued the world with. That the Signor Doctor does less mischief than might be expected, with such dangerous substances, is undeniable. Now and then, it must be owned, he has effected — or seemed to effect — a marvellous cure. But, to tell you my private mind, Signor Giovanni, he should receive little credit for such instances of success — they being probably the work of chance — but should be held strictly accountable for his failures, which may justly be considered his own work."

The youth might have taken Baglioni's opinions with many grains of allowance, had he known that there was a professional warfare of long continuance between him and Doctor Rappaccini, in which the latter was generally thought to have gained the advantage. If the reader be inclined to judge for himself, we refer him to certain black-letter tracts on both sides, preserved in the medical department of the University of Padua.

"I know not, most learned Professor," returned Giovanni, after musing on what had been said of Rappaccini's exclusive zeal for science — "I know not how dearly this physician may love his art; but surely there is one object more dear to him. He has a daughter."

"Aha!" cried the Professor with a laugh. "So now our friend Giovanni's secret is out. You have heard of this daughter, whom all the young men in Padua are wild about, though not half a dozen have ever had the good hap to see her face. I know little of the Signora Beatrice, save that Rappaccini is said to have instructed her deeply in his science, and that, young and beautiful as fame reports her, she is already qualified to fill a professor's chair. Perchance her father destines her for mine! Other absurd rumors there be, not worth talking about, or listening to. So now, Signor Giovanni, drink off your glass of Lacryma."

Guasconti returned to his lodgings somewhat heated with the wine he had quaffed, and which caused his brain to swim with strange fantasies in reference to Doctor Rappaccini and the beautiful Beatrice. On his way, happening to pass by a florist's, he bought a fresh bouquet of flowers.

Ascending to his chamber, he seated himself near the window, but within the shadow thrown by the depth of the wall, so that he could look down into the garden with little risk of being discovered. All beneath his eye was a solitude. The strange plants were basking in the sunshine, and now and then nodding gently to one another, as if in acknowledgment of sympathy and kindred. In the midst, by the shattered fountain, grew the magnificent shrub with its purple gems clustering all over it; they glowed in the air, and gleamed back again out of the depths of the pool, which thus seemed to overflow with colored radiance from the rich reflection that was steeped in it. At first, as we have said, the garden was a solitude. Soon, however, — as Giovanni had half-hoped, half-feared, would be the case, — a figure appeared beneath the antique sculptured portal, and came down between the rows of plants, inhaling their various perfumes, as if she were one of those beings of old classic fable, that lived upon sweet odors. On again beholding Beatrice, the young man was even startled to perceive how much her beauty exceeded in his recollection of it; so brilliant, so vivid in its character, that she glowed amid the sunlight, and, as Giovanni whispered to himself, positively illuminated the more shadowy intervals of the garden path. Her face being now more revealed than on the former occasion, he was struck by its expression of simplicity and sweetness; qualities that had not entered into his idea of her character, and which made him ask anew, what manner of mortal she might be. Nor did he fail again to observe, or imagine, an analogy between the beautiful girl and the gorgeous shrub that hung its gem-like flowers over the fountain; a resemblance which Beatrice seemed to have indulged a fantastic humor in heightening, both by the arrangement of her dress and the selection of its hues.

Approaching the shrub, she threw open her arms, as with a passionate ardor, and drew its branches into an intimate embrace; so intimate, that her features were hidden in its leafy bosom, and her glistening ringlets all intermingled with the flowers.

"Give me thy breath, my sister," exclaimed Beatrice; "for I am faint with common air! And give me this flower of thine, which I separate with gentlest fingers from the stem, and place it close beside my heart."

With these words, the beautiful daughter of Rappaccini plucked one of the richest blossoms of the shrub, and was about to fasten it in her bosom. But now, unless Giovanni's draughts of wine had bewildered his senses, a singular incident occurred. A small orange-colored reptile, of the lizard or chameleon species, chanced to be creeping along the path, just at the feet of Beatrice. It appeared to Giovanni — but, at the distance from which he gazed, he could scarcely have seen anything so minute — it appeared to him, however, that a drop or two of moisture from the broken stem of the flower descended upon the lizard's head. For an instant, the reptile contorted itself violently, and then lay motionless in the sunshine. Beatrice observed this remarkable phenomenon, and crossed herself, sadly, but without surprise; nor did she therefore hesitate to arrange the fatal flower in her bosom. There it blushed, and almost glimmered with the dazzling effect of a precious stone, adding to her dress and aspect the one appropriate charm, which nothing else in the world could have supplied. But Giovanni, out of the shadow of his window, bent forward and shrank back, and murmured and trembled.

"Am I awake? Have I my senses?" said he to himself. "What is this being? — beautiful, shall I call her? — or inexpressibly terrible?"

Beatrice now strayed carelessly through the garden, approaching closer beneath Giovanni's window, so that he was compelled to thrust his head quite out of its concealment, in order to gratify the intense and painful curiosity which she excited. At this moment, there came a beautiful insect over the garden wall; it had perhaps wandered through the city and found no flowers nor verdure among those antique haunts of men, until the heavy perfumes of Doctor Rappaccini's shrubs had lured it from afar. Without alighting on the flowers, this winged brightness seemed to be attracted by Beatrice, and lingered in the air and fluttered about her head. Now here it could not be but that Giovanni Guasconti's eyes deceived him. Be that as it might, he fancied that while Beatrice was gazing at the insect with childish delight, it grew faint and fell at her feet! — its bright wings shivered! it was dead! — from no cause that he could discern, unless it were the atmosphere of her breath. Again Beatrice crossed herself and sighed heavily, as she bent over the dead insect.

An impulsive movement of Giovanni drew her eyes to the window. There she beheld the beautiful head of the young man — rather a Grecian than an Italian head, with fair, regular features, and a glistening of gold among his ringlets, gazing down upon her like a being that hovered in mid-air. Scarcely knowing what he did, Giovanni threw down the bouquet which he had hitherto held in his hand.

"Signora," said he, "there are pure and healthful flowers. Wear them for the sake of Giovanni Guasconti!"

"Thanks, Signor," replied Beatrice, with her rich voice, that came forth as it were like a gush of music; and with a mirthful expression half childish and half woman-like. "I accept your gift, and would fain recompense it with this precious purple flower, but if I toss it into the air, it will not reach you. So Signor Guasconti must even content himself with my thanks."

She lifted the bouquet from the ground, and then as if inwardly ashamed at having stepped aside from her maidenly reserve to respond to a stranger's greeting, passed swiftly homeward through the garden. But, few as the moments were, it seemed to Giovanni when she was on the point of vanishing beneath the sculptured portal, that his beautiful bouquet was already beginning to wither in her grasp. It was an idle thought; there could be no possibility of distinguishing a faded flower from a fresh one, at so great a distance.

For many days after this incident, the young man avoided the window that looked into Doctor Rappaccini's garden, as if something ugly and monstrous would have blasted his eye-sight, had he been betrayed into a glance. He felt conscious of having put himself, to a certain extent, within the influence of an unintelligible power, by the communication which he had opened with Beatrice. The wisest course would have been, if his heart were in any real danger, to quit his lodgings and Padua itself, at once; the next wiser, to have accustomed himself, as far as possible, to the familiar and day-light view of Beatrice; thus bringing her rigidly and systematically within the limits of ordinary experience. Least of all, while avoiding her sight, should Giovanni have remained so near this extraordinary being, that the proximity and possibility even of intercourse, should give a kind of substance and reality to the wild vagaries which his imagination ran riot continually in producing. Guasconti had not a deep heart — or at all events, its depths were not sounded now — but he had a quick fancy, and an ardent southern temperament, which rose every instant to a higher fever-pitch. Whether or no Beatrice possessed those terrible attributes — that fatal breath — the affinity with those so beautiful and deadly flowers — which were indicated by what Giovanni had witnessed, she had at least instilled a fierce and subtle poison into his system. It was not love, although her rich beauty was a madness to him; nor horror, even while he fancied her spirit to be imbued with the same baneful essence that seemed to pervade her physical frame; but a wild offspring of both love and horror that had each parent in it, and burned like one and shivered like the other. Giovanni knew not what to dread; still less did he know what to hope; yet hope and dread kept a continual warfare in his breast, alternately vanquishing one another and starting up afresh to renew the contest. Blessed are all simple emotions, be they dark or bright! It is the lurid intermixture of the two that produces the illuminating blaze of the infernal regions.

Sometimes he endeavored to assuage the fever of his spirit by a rapid walk through the streets of Padua, or beyond its gates; his footsteps kept time with the throbbings of his brain, so that the walk was apt to accelerate itself to a race.

One day, he found himself arrested; his arm was seized by a portly personage who had turned back on recognizing the young man, and expended much breath in overtaking him.

"Signor Giovanni! — stay, my young friend!" cried he. "Have you forgotten me? That might well be the case, if I were as much altered as yourself."

It was Baglioni, whom Giovanni had avoided, ever since their first meeting, from a doubt that the professor's sagacity would look too deeply into his secrets. Endeavoring to recover himself, he stared forth wildly from his inner world into the outer one, and spoke like a man in a dream.

"Yes; I am Giovanni Guasconti. You are Professor Pietro Baglioni. Now let me pass!"

"Not yet — not yet, Signor Giovanni Guasconti," said the Professor, smiling, but at the same time scrutinizing the youth with an earnest glance. — "What; did I grow up side by side with your father, and shall his son pass me like a stranger, in these old streets of Padua? Stand still, Signor Giovanni; for we must have a word or two before we part."

"Speedily, then, most worshipful Professor, speedily!" said Giovanni, with feverish impatience. "Does not your worship see that I am in haste?"

Now, while he was speaking, there came a man in black along the street, stooping and moving feebly, like a person in inferior health. His face was all overspread with a most sickly and sallow hue, but yet so pervaded with an expression of piercing and active intellect, that an observer might easily have overlooked the merely physical attributes, and have seen only this wonderful energy. As he passed, this person exchanged a cold and distant salutation with Baglioni, but fixed his eyes upon Giovanni with an intentness that seemed to bring out whatever was within him worthy of notice. Nevertheless, there was a peculiar quietness in the look, as if taking merely a speculative, not a human interest, in the young man.

"It is Doctor Rappaccini!" whispered the Professor, when the stranger had passed. — "Has he ever seen your face before?"

"Not that I know," answered Giovanni, starting at the name.

"He *has* seen you! — he must have seen you!" said Baglioni, hastily. "For some purpose or other, this man of science is making a study of you. I know that look of his! It is the same that coldly illuminates his face, as he bends over a bird, a mouse, or a butterfly, which in pursuance of some experiment, he has killed by the perfume of a flower; — a look as deep as nature itself, but without nature's warmth of love. Signor Giovanni, I will stake my life upon it, you are the subject of one of Rappaccini's experiments!"

"Will you make a fool of me?" cried Giovanni, passionately. "*That*, Signor Professor, were an untoward experiment."

"Patience, patience!" replied the imperturbable Professor. "I tell thee, my poor Giovanni, that Rappaccini has a scientific interest in thee. Thou hast fallen into fearful hands! And the Signora Beatrice? What part does she act in this mystery?"

But Guasconti, finding Baglioni's pertinacity intolerable, here broke away, and was gone before the Professor could again seize his arm. He looked after the young man intently, and shook his head.

"This must not be," said Baglioni to himself. "The youth is the son of my old friend, and shall not come to any harm from which the arcana of medical science can preserve him. Besides, it is too insufferable an impertinence in Rappaccini thus to snatch the lad out of my own hands, as I may say, and make use of him for his infernal experiments. This daughter of his! It shall be looked to. Perchance, most learned Rappaccini, I may foil you where you little dream of it!"

Meanwhile, Giovanni had pursued a circuitous route, and at length found himself at the door of his lodgings. As he crossed the threshold, he was met by old Lisabetta, who smirked and smiled, and was evidently desirous to attract his attention; vainly, however, as the ebullition of his feelings had momentarily subsided into a cold and dull vacuity. He turned his eyes full upon the withered face that was puckering itself into a smile, but seemed to behold it not. The old dame, therefore, laid her grasp upon his cloak.

"Signor! — Signor!" whispered she, still with a smile over the whole breadth of her visage, so that it looked not unlike a grotesque carving in wood, darkened by centuries — "Listen, Signor! There is a private entrance into the garden!"

"What do you say?" exclaimed Giovanni, turning quickly about, as if an inanimate thing should start into feverish life. — "A private entrance into Doctor Rappaccini's garden!"

"Hush! hush! — not so loud!" whispered Lisabetta, putting her hand over his mouth. "Yes; into the worshipful Doctor's garden, where you may see all his fine shrubbery. Many a young man in Padua would give gold to be admitted among those flowers."

Giovanni put a piece of gold into her hand.

"Show me the way," said he.

A surmise, probably excited by his conversation with Baglioni, crossed his mind, that this interposition of old Lisabetta might perchance be connected with the intrigue, whatever were its nature, in which the Professor seemed to suppose that Doctor Rappaccini was involving him. But such a suspicion, though it disturbed Giovanni, was inadequate to restrain him. The instant he was aware of the possibility of approaching Beatrice, it seemed an absolute necessity of his existence to do so. It mattered not whether she were angel or demon; he was irrevocably within her sphere, and must obey the law that whirled him onward, in ever lessening circles, towards a result which he did not attempt to foreshadow. And yet, strange to say, there came across him a sudden doubt, whether this intense interest on his part were not delusory — whether it were really of so deep and positive a nature as to justify him in now thrusting himself into an incalculable position — whether it were not merely the fantasy of a young man's brain, only slightly, or not at all, connected with his heart!

He paused — hesitated — turned half about — but again went on. His withered guide led him along several obscure passages, and finally undid a door, through which, as it was opened, there came the sight and sound of rustling leaves, with the broken sunshine glimmering among them. Giovanni stepped forth, and forcing himself through the entanglement of a shrub that wreathed its tendrils over the hidden entrance, he stood beneath his own window, in the open area of Doctor Rappaccini's garden.

How often is it the case, that, when impossibilities have come to pass, and dreams have condensed their misty substance into tangible realities, we find ourselves calm, and even coldly self-possessed, amid circumstances which it would have been a delirium of joy or agony to anticipate! Fate delights to thwart us thus. Passion will choose his own time to rush upon the scene, and lingers sluggishly behind, when an appropriate adjustment of events would seem to summon his appearance. So was it now with Giovanni. Day after day, his pulses had throbbed with feverish blood, at the improbable idea of an interview with Beatrice, and of standing with her, face to face, in this very garden, basking in the oriental sunshine of her beauty, and snatching from her full gaze the mystery which he deemed the riddle of his own existence. But now there was a singular and untimely equanimity within his breast. He threw a glance around the garden to discover if Beatrice or her father were present, and perceiving that he was alone, began a critical observation of the plants.

The aspect of one and all of them dissatisfied him; their gorgeousness seemed fierce, passionate, and even unnatural. There was hardly an individual shrub which a wanderer, straying by himself through a forest, would not have been startled to find growing wild, as if an unearthly face had glared at him out of the thicket. Several, also, would have shocked a delicate instinct by an appearance of artificialness, indicating that there had been such commixture, and, as it were, adultery of various vegetable species, that the production was no longer of God's making, but the monstrous offspring of man's depraved fancy, glowing with only an evil mockery of beauty. They were probably the result of experiment, which, in one or two cases, had succeeded in mingling plants individually lovely into a compound possessing the questionable and ominous character that distinguished the whole growth of the garden. In fine, Giovanni recognized but two or three plants in the collection, and those of a kind that he well knew to be poisonous. While busy with these contemplations, he heard the rustling of a silken garment, and turning, beheld Beatrice emerging from beneath the sculptured portal.

Giovanni had not considered with himself what should be his deportment; whether he should apologize for his intrusion into the garden, or assume that he was there with the privity, at least, if not by the desire, of Doctor Rappaccini or his daughter. But Beatrice's manner placed him at his ease, though leaving him still in doubt by what agency he had gained admittance. She came lightly along the path, and met him near the broken fountain. There was surprise in her face, but brightened by a simple and kind expression of pleasure.

"You are a connoisseur in flowers, Signor," said Beatrice with a smile, alluding to the bouquet which he had flung her from the window. "It is no marvel, therefore, if the sight of my father's rare collection has tempted you to take a nearer view. If he were here, he could tell you many strange and interesting facts as to the nature and habits of these shrubs, for he has spent a life-time in such studies, and this garden is his world."

"And yourself, lady" — observed Giovanni — "if fame says true — you, likewise, are deeply skilled in the virtues indicated by these rich blossoms, and these spicy perfumes. Would you deign to be my instructress, I should prove an apter scholar than under Signor Rappaccini himself."

"Are there such idle rumors?" asked Beatrice, with the music of a pleasant laugh. "Do people say that I am skilled in my father's science of plants? What a jest is there! No; though I have grown up among these flowers, I know no more of them than their hues and perfume; and sometimes, methinks I would fain rid myself of even that small knowledge. There are many flowers here, and those not the least brilliant, that shock and offend me, when they meet my eye. But, pray, Signor, do not believe these stories about my science. Believe nothing of me save what you see with your own eyes."

"And must I believe all that I have seen with my own eyes?" asked Giovanni pointedly, while the recollection of former scenes made him shrink. "No, Signora, you demand too little of me. Bid me believe nothing, save what comes from your own lips."

It would appear that Beatrice understood him. There came a deep flush to her cheek; but she looked full into Giovanni's eyes, and responded to his gaze of uneasy suspicion with a queen-like haughtiness.

"I do so bid you, Signor!" she replied. "Forget whatever you may have fancied in regard to me. If true to the outward senses, still it may be false in its essence. But the words of Beatrice Rappaccini's lips are true from the heart outward. Those you may believe!"

A fervor glowed in her whole aspect, and beamed upon Giovanni's consciousness like the light of truth itself. But while she spoke, there was a fragrance in the atmosphere around her rich and delightful, though evanescent, yet which the young man, from an indefinable reluctance, scarcely dared to draw into his lungs. It might be the odor of the flowers. Could it be Beatrice's breath, which thus embalmed her words with a strange richness, as if by steeping them in her heart? A faintness passed like a shadow over Giovanni, and flitted away; he seemed to gaze through the beautiful girl's eyes into her transparent soul, and felt no more doubt or fear.

The tinge of passion that had colored Beatrice's manner vanished; she became gay, and appeared to derive a pure delight from her communion with the youth, not unlike what the maiden of a lonely island might have felt, conversing with a voyager from the civilized world. Evidently her experience of life had been confined within the limits of that garden. She talked now about matters as simple as the day-light or summer-clouds, and now asked questions in reference to the city, or Giovanni's distant home, his friends, his mother, and his sisters; questions indicating such seclusion, and such lack of familiarity with modes and forms, that Giovanni responded as if to an infant. Her spirit gushed out before him like a fresh rill, that was just catching its first glimpse of the sunlight, and wondering at the reflections of earth and sky which were flung into its bosom. There came thoughts, too, from a deep source, and fantasies of a gem-like brilliancy, as if diamonds and rubies sparkled upward among the bubbles of the fountain. Ever and anon, there gleamed across the young man's mind a sense of wonder, that he should be walking side by side with the being who had so wrought upon his imagination — whom he had idealized in such hues of terror — in whom he had positively witnessed such manifestations of dreadful attributes — that he should be conversing with Beatrice like a brother, and should find her so human and so maiden-like. But such reflections were only momentary; the effect of her character was too real, not to make itself familiar at once.

In this free intercourse, they had strayed through the garden, and now, after many turns among its avenues, were come to the shattered fountain, beside which grew the magnificent shrub with its treasury of glowing blossoms. A fragrance was diffused from it, which Giovanni recognized as identical with that which he had attributed to Beatrice's breath, but incomparably more powerful. As her eyes fell upon it, Giovanni beheld her press her hand to her bosom, as if her heart were throbbing suddenly and painfully.

"For the first time in my life," murmured she, addressing the shrub, "I had forgotten thee!"

"I remember, Signora," said Giovanni, "that you once promised to reward me with one of these living gems for the bouquet, which I had the happy boldness to fling to your feet. Permit me now to pluck it as a memorial of this interview."

He made a step towards the shrub, with extended hand. But Beatrice darted forward, uttering a shriek that went through his heart like a dagger. She caught his hand, and drew it back with the whole force of her slender figure. Giovanni felt her touch thrilling through his fibres.

"Touch it not!" exclaimed she, in a voice of agony. "Not for thy life! It is fatal!"

Then, hiding her face, she fled from him, and vanished beneath the sculptured portal. As Giovanni followed her with his eyes, he beheld the emaciated figure and pale intelligence of Doctor Rappaccini, who had been watching the scene, he knew not how long, within the shadow of the entrance.

No sooner was Guasconti alone in his chamber, than the image of Beatrice came back to his passionate musings, invested with all the witchery that had been gathering around it ever since his first glimpse of her, and now likewise imbued with a tender warmth of girlish womanhood. She was human: her nature was endowed with all gentle and feminine qualities; she was worthiest to be worshipped; she was capable, surely, on her part, of the height and heroism of love. Those tokens, which he had hitherto considered as proofs of a frightful peculiarity in her physical and moral system, were now either forgotten, or, by the subtle sophistry of passion, transmuted into a golden crown of enchantment, rendering Beatrice the more admirable, by so much as she was the more unique. Whatever had looked ugly, was now beautiful; or, if incapable of such a change, it stole away and hid itself among those shapeless half-ideas, which throng the dim region beyond the daylight of our perfect consciousness. Thus did Giovanni spend the night, nor fell asleep, until the dawn had begun to awake the slumbering flowers in Doctor Rappaccini's garden, whither his dreams doubtless led him. Up rose the sun in his due season, and flinging his beams upon the young man's eyelids, awoke him to a sense of pain. When thoroughly aroused, he became sensible of a burning and tingling agony in his hand — in his right hand — the very hand which Beatrice had grasped in her own, when he was on the point of plucking one of the gem-like flowers. On the back of that hand there was now a purple print, like that of four small fingers, and the likeness of a slender thumb upon his wrist.

Oh, how stubbornly does love — or even that cunning semblance of love which flourishes in the imagination, but strikes no depth of root into the heart — how stubbornly does it hold its faith, until the moment come, when it is doomed to vanish into thin mist! Giovanni wrapt a handkerchief about his hand, and wondered what evil thing had stung him, and soon forgot his pain in a reverie of Beatrice.

After the first interview, a second was in the inevitable course of what we call fate. A third; a fourth; and a meeting with Beatrice in the garden was no longer an incident in Giovanni's daily life, but the whole space in which he might be said to live; for the anticipation and memory of that ecstatic hour made up the remainder. Nor was it otherwise with the daughter of Rappaccini. She watched for the youth's appearance, and flew to his side with confidence as unreserved as if they had been playmates from early infancy — as if they were such playmates still. If, by any unwonted chance, he failed to come at the appointed moment, she stood beneath the window, and sent up the rich sweetness of her tones to float around him in his chamber, and echo and reverberate throughout his heart — "Giovanni! Giovanni! Why tarriest thou? Come down!" — And down he hastened into that Eden of poisonous flowers.

But, with all this intimate familiarity, there was still a reserve in Beatrice's demeanor, so rigidly and invariably sustained, that the idea of infringing it scarcely occurred to his imagination. By all appreciable signs, they loved; they had looked love, with eyes that conveyed the holy secret from the depths of one soul into the depths of the other, as if it were too sacred to be whispered by the way; they had even spoken love, in those gushes of passion when their spirits darted forth in articulated breath, like tongues of long-hidden flame; and yet there had been no seal of lips, no clasp of hands, nor any slightest caress, such as love claims and hallows. He had never touched one of the gleaming ringlets of her hair; her garment — so marked was the physical barrier between them — had never been waved against him by a breeze. On the few occasions when Giovanni had seemed tempted to overstep the limit, Beatrice grew so sad, so stern, and withal wore such a look of desolate separation, shuddering at itself, that not a spoken word was requisite to repel him. At such times, he was startled at the horrible suspicions that rose, monster-like, out of the caverns of his heart, and stared him in the face; his love grew thin and faint as the morning-mist; his doubts alone had substance. But when Beatrice's face brightened again, after the momentary shadow, she was transformed at once from the mysterious, questionable being, whom he had watched with so much awe and horror; she was now the beautiful and unsophisticated girl, whom he felt that his spirit knew with a certainty beyond all other knowledge.

A considerable time had now passed since Giovanni's last meeting with Baglioni. One morning, however, he was disagreeably surprised by a visit from the Professor, whom he had scarcely thought of for whole weeks, and would willingly have forgotten still longer. Given up, as he had long been, to a pervading excitement, he could tolerate no companions, except upon condition of their perfect sympathy with his present state of feeling. Such sympathy was not to be expected from Professor Baglioni.

The visitor chatted carelessly, for a few moments, about the gossip of the city and the University, and then took up another topic.

"I have been reading an old classic author lately," said he, "and met with a story that strangely interested me. Possibly you may remember it. It is of an Indian prince, who sent a beautiful woman as a present to Alexander the Great. She was as lovely as the dawn, and gorgeous as the sunset; but what especially distinguished her was a certain rich perfume in her breath — richer than a garden of Persian roses. Alexander, as was natural to a youthful conqueror, fell in love at first sight with this magnificent stranger. But a certain sage physician, happening to be present, discovered a terrible secret in regard to her."

"And what was that?" asked Giovanni, turning his eyes downward to avoid those of the Professor.

"That this lovely woman," continued Baglioni, with emphasis, "had been nourished with poisons from her birth upward, until her whole nature was so imbued with them, that she herself had become the deadliest poison in existence. Poison was her element of life. With that rich perfume of her breath, she blasted the very air. Her love would have been poison! — her embrace death! Is not this a marvellous tale?"

"A childish fable," answered Giovanni, nervously starting from his chair. "I marvel how your worship finds time to read such nonsense, among your graver studies."

"By the bye," said the Professor, looking uneasily about him, "what singular fragrance is this in your apartment? Is it the perfume of your gloves? It is faint, but delicious, and yet, after all, by no means agreeable. Were I to breathe it long, methinks it would make me ill. It is like the breath of a flower — but I see no flowers in the chamber."

"Nor are there any," replied Giovanni, who had turned pale as the Professor spoke; "nor, I think, is there any fragrance, except in your worship's imagination. Odors, being a sort of element combined of the sensual and the spiritual, are apt to deceive us in this manner. The recollection of a perfume — the bare idea of it — may easily be mistaken for a present reality."

"Aye; but my sober imagination does not often play such tricks," said Baglioni; "and were I to fancy any kind of odor, it would be that of some vile apothecary drug, wherewith my fingers are likely enough to be imbued. Our worshipful friend Rappaccini, as I have heard, tinctures his medicaments with odors richer than those of Araby. Doubtless, likewise, the fair and learned Signora Beatrice would minister to her patients with draughts as sweet as a maiden's breath. But wo to him that sips them!"

Giovanni's face evinced many contending emotions. The tone in which the Professor alluded to the pure and lovely daughter of Rappaccini was a torture to his soul; and yet, the intimation of a view of her character, opposite to his own, gave instantaneous distinctness to a thousand dim suspicions, which now grinned at him like so many demons. But he strove hard to quell them, and to respond to Baglioni with a true lover's perfect faith.

"Signor Professor," said he, "you were my father's friend — perchance, too, it is your purpose to act a friendly part towards his son. I would fain feel nothing towards you save respect and deference. But I pray you to observe, Signor, that there is one subject on which we must not speak. You know not the Signora Beatrice. You cannot, therefore, estimate the wrong — the blasphemy, I may even say — that is offered to her character by a light or injurious word."

"Giovanni! — my poor Giovanni!" answered the Professor, with a calm expression of pity, "I know this wretched girl far better than yourself. You shall hear the truth in respect to the poisoner Rappaccini, and his poisonous daughter. Yes; poisonous as she is beautiful! Listen; for even should you do violence to my grey hairs, it shall not silence me. That old fable of the Indian woman has become a truth, by the deep and deadly science of Rappaccini, and in the person of the lovely Beatrice!"

Giovanni groaned and hid his face.

"Her father," continued Baglioni, "was not restrained by natural affection from offering up his child, in this horrible manner, as the victim of his insane zeal for science. For — let us do him justice — he is as true a man of science as ever distilled his own heart in an alembic. What, then, will be your fate? Beyond a doubt, you are selected as the material of some new experiment. Perhaps the result is to be death — perhaps a fate more awful still! Rappaccini, with what he calls the interest of science before his eyes, will hesitate at nothing."

"It is a dream!" muttered Giovanni to himself, "surely it is a dream!"

"But," resumed the professor, "be of good cheer, son of my friend! It is not yet too late for the rescue. Possibly, we may even succeed in bringing back this miserable child within the limits of ordinary nature, from which her father's madness has estranged her. Behold this little silver vase! It was wrought by the hands of the renowned Benvenuto Cellini, and is well worthy to be a love-gift to the fairest dame in Italy. But its contents are invaluable. One little sip of this antidote would have rendered the most virulent poisons of the Borgias innocuous. Doubt not that it will be as efficacious against those of Rappaccini. Bestow the vase, and the precious liquid within it, on your Beatrice, and hopefully await the result."

Baglioni laid a small, exquisitely wrought silver phial on the table, and withdrew, leaving what he had said to produce its effect upon the young man's mind.

"We will thwart Rappaccini yet!" thought he, chuckling to himself, as he descended the stairs. "But, let us confess the truth of him, he is a wonderful man! — a wonderful man indeed! A vile empiric, however, in his practice, and therefore not to be tolerated by those who respect the good old rules of the medical profession!"

Throughout Giovanni's whole acquaintance with Beatrice, he had occasionally, as we have said, been haunted by dark surmises as to her character. Yet, so thoroughly had she made herself felt by him as a simple, natural, most affectionate and guileless creature, that the image now held up by Professor Baglioni, looked as strange and incredible, as if it were not in accordance with his own original conception. True, there were ugly recollections connected with his first glimpses of the beautiful girl; he could not quite forget the bouquet that withered in her grasp, and the insect that perished amid the sunny air, by no ostensible agency save the fragrance of her breath. These incidents, however, dissolving in the pure light of her character, had no longer the efficacy of facts, but were acknowledged as mistaken fantasies, by whatever testimony of the senses they might appear to be substantiated. There is something truer and more real, than what we can see with the eyes, and touch with the finger. On such better evidence, had Giovanni founded his confidence in Beatrice, though rather by the necessary force of her high attributes, than by any deep and generous faith on his part. But, now, his spirit was incapable of sustaining itself at the height to which the early enthusiasm of passion had exalted it; he fell down, grovelling among earthly doubts, and defiled therewith the pure whiteness of Beatrice's image. Not that he gave her up; he did but distrust. He resolved to institute some decisive test that should satisfy him, once for all, whether there were those dreadful peculiarities in her physical nature, which could not be supposed to exist without some corresponding monstrosity of soul. His eyes, gazing down afar, might have deceived him as to the lizard, the insect, and the flowers. But if he could witness, at the distance of a few paces, the sudden blight of one fresh and healthful flower in Beatrice's hand, there would be room for no further question. With this idea, he hastened to the florist's, and purchased a bouquet that was still gemmed with the morning dew-drops.

It was now the customary hour of his daily interview with Beatrice. Before descending into the garden, Giovanni failed not to look at his figure in the mirror; a vanity to be expected in a beautiful young man, yet, as displaying itself at that troubled and feverish moment, the token of a certain shallowness of feeling and insincerity of character. He did gaze, however, and said to himself, that his features had never before possessed so rich a grace, nor his eyes such vivacity, nor his cheeks so warm a hue of superabundant life.

"At least," thought he, "her poison has not yet insinuated itself into my system. I am no flower to perish in her grasp!"

With that thought, he turned his eyes on the bouquet, which he had never once laid aside from his hand. A thrill of indefinable horror shot through his frame, on perceiving that those dewy flowers were already beginning to droop; they wore the aspect of things that had been fresh and lovely, yesterday. Giovanni grew white as marble, and stood motionless before the mirror, staring at his own reflection there, as at the likeness of something frightful. He remembered Baglioni's remark about the fragrance that seemed to pervade the chamber. It must have been the poison in his breath! Then he shuddered — shuddered at himself! Recovering from his stupor, he began to watch, with curious eye, a spider that was busily at work, hanging its web from the antique cornice of the apartment, crossing and re-crossing the artful system of interwoven lines, as vigorous and active a spider as ever dangled from an old ceiling. Giovanni bent towards the insect, and emitted a deep, long breath. The spider suddenly ceased its toil; the web vibrated with a tremor originated in the body of the small artizan. Again Giovanni sent forth a breath, deeper, longer, and imbued with a venomous feeling out of his heart; he knew not whether he were wicked or only desperate. The spider made a convulsive gripe with his limbs, and hung dead across the window.

"Accursed! Accursed!" muttered Giovanni, addressing himself. "Hast thou grown so poisonous, that this deadly insect perishes by thy breath?"

At that moment, a rich, sweet voice came floating up from the garden: —

"Giovanni! Giovanni! It is past the hour! Why tarriest thou! Come down!"

"Yes," muttered Giovanni again. "She is the only being whom my breath may not slay! Would that it might!"

He rushed down, and in an instant, was standing before the bright and loving eyes of Beatrice. A moment ago, his wrath and despair had been so fierce that he could have desired nothing so much as to wither her by a glance. But, with her actual presence, there came influences which had too real an existence to be at once shaken off; recollections of the delicate and benign power of her feminine nature, which had so often enveloped him in a religious calm; recollections of many a holy and passionate outgush of her heart, when the pure fountain had been unsealed from its depths, and made visible in its transparency to his mental eye; recollections which, had Giovanni known how to estimate them, would have assured him that all this ugly mystery was but an earthly illusion, and that, whatever mist of evil might seem to have gathered over her, the real Beatrice was a heavenly angel. Incapable as he was of such high faith, still her presence had not utterly lost its magic. Giovanni's rage was quelled into an aspect of sullen insensibility. Beatrice, with a quick spiritual sense, immediately felt that there was a gulf of blackness between them, which neither he nor she could pass. They walked on together, sad and silent, and came thus to the marble fountain, and to its pool of water on the ground, in the midst of which grew the shrub that bore gem-like blossoms. Giovanni was affrighted at the eager enjoyment — the appetite, as it were — with which he found himself inhaling the fragrance of the flowers.

"Beatrice," asked he abruptly, "whence came this shrub!"

"My father created it," answered she, with simplicity.

"Created it! created it!" repeated Giovanni. "What mean you, Beatrice?"

"He is a man fearfully acquainted with the secrets of nature," replied Beatrice; "and, at the hour when I first drew breath, this plant sprang from the soil, the offspring of his science, of his intellect, while I was but his earthly child. Approach it not!" continued she, observing with terror that Giovanni was drawing nearer to the shrub. "It has qualities that you little dream of. But I, dearest Giovanni, — I grew up and blossomed with the plant, and was nourished with its breath. It was my sister, and I loved it with a human affection: for — alas! hast thou not suspected it? there was an awful doom."

Here Giovanni frowned so darkly upon her that Beatrice paused and trembled. But her faith in his tenderness reassured her, and made her blush that she had doubted for an instant.

"There was an awful doom," she continued, — "the effect of my father's fatal love of science — which estranged me from all society of my kind. Until Heaven sent thee, dearest Giovanni, Oh! how lonely was thy poor Beatrice!"

"Was it a hard doom?" asked Giovanni, fixing his eyes upon her.

"Only of late have I known how hard it was," answered she tenderly. "Oh, yes; but my heart was torpid, and therefore quiet."

Giovanni's rage broke forth from his sullen gloom like a lightning-flash out of a dark cloud.

"Accursed one!" cried he, with venomous scorn and anger. "And finding thy solitude wearisome, thou hast severed me, likewise, from all the warmth of life, and enticed me into thy region of unspeakable horror!"

"Giovanni!" exclaimed Beatrice, turning her large bright eyes upon his face. The force of his words had not found its way into her mind; she was merely thunder-struck.

"Yes, poisonous thing!" repeated Giovanni, beside himself with passion. "Thou hast done it! Thou hast blasted me! Thou hast filled my veins with poison! Thou hast made me as hateful, as ugly, as loathsome and deadly a creature as thyself, — a world's wonder of hideous monstrosity! Now — if our breath be happily as fatal to ourselves as to all others — let us join our lips in one kiss of unutterable hatred, and so die!"

"What has befallen me?" murmured Beatrice, with a low moan out of her heart. "Holy Virgin pity me, a poor heartbroken child!"

"Thou! Dost thou pray?" cried Giovanni, still with the same fiendish scorn. "Thy very prayers, as they come from thy lips, taint the atmosphere with death. Yes, yes; let us pray! Let us to church, and dip our fingers in the holy water at the portal! They that come after us will perish as by a pestilence. Let us sign crosses in the air! It will be scattering curses abroad in the likeness of holy symbols!"

"Giovanni," said Beatrice calmly, for her grief was beyond passion, "Why dost thou join thyself with me thus in those terrible words? I, it is true, am the horrible thing thou namest me. But thou! — what hast thou to do, save with one other shudder at my hideous misery, to go forth out of the garden and mingle with thy race, and forget that there ever crawled on earth such a monster as poor Beatrice?"

"Dost thou pretend ignorance?" asked Giovanni, scowling upon her. "Behold! This power have I gained from the pure daughter of Rappaccini!"

There was a swarm of summer-insects flitting through the air, in search of the food promised by the flower-odors of the fatal garden. They circled round Giovanni's head, and were evidently attracted towards him by the same influence which had drawn them, for an instant, within the sphere of several of the shrubs. He sent forth a breath among them, and smiled bitterly at Beatrice, as at least a score of the insects fell dead upon the ground.

"I see it! I see it!" shrieked Beatrice. "It is my father's fatal science! No, no, Giovanni; it was not I! Never, never! I dreamed only to love thee, and be with thee a little time, and so to let thee pass away, leaving but thine image in mine heart. For, Giovanni — believe it — though my body be nourished with poison, my spirit is God's creature, and craves love as its daily food. But my father! — he has united us in this fearful sympathy. Yes; spurn me! — tread upon me! — kill me! Oh, what is death, after such words as thine? But it was not I! Not for a world of bliss would I have done it!"

Giovanni's passion had exhausted itself in its outburst from his lips. There now came across him a sense, mournful, and not without tenderness, of the intimate and peculiar relationship between Beatrice and himself. They stood, as it were, in an utter solitude, which would be made none the less solitary by the densest throng of human life. Ought not, then, the desert of humanity around them to press this insulated pair closer together? If they should be cruel to one another, who was there to be kind to them? Besides, thought Giovanni, might there not still be a hope of his returning within the limits of ordinary nature, and leading Beatrice — the redeemed Beatrice — by the hand? Oh, weak, and selfish, and unworthy spirit, that could dream of an earthly union and earthly happiness as possible, after such deep love had been so bitterly wronged as was Beatrice's love by Giovanni's blighting words! No, no; there could be no such hope. She must pass heavily, with that broken heart, across the borders — she must bathe her hurts in some fount of Paradise, and forget her grief in the light of immortality — and *there* be well!

But Giovanni did not know it.

"Dear Beatrice," said he, approaching her, while she shrank away, as always at his approach, but now with a different impulse — "dearest Beatrice, our fate is not yet so desperate. Behold! There is a medicine, potent, as a wise physician has assured me, and almost divine in its efficacy. It is composed of ingredients the most opposite to those by which thy awful father has brought this calamity upon thee and me. It is distilled of blessed herbs. Shall we not quaff it together, and thus be purified from evil?"

"Give it to me!" said Beatrice, extending her hand to receive the little silver phial which Giovanni took from his bosom. She added, with a peculiar emphasis: "I will drink — but do thou await the result."

She put Baglioni's antidote to her lips; and, at the same moment, the figure of Rappaccini emerged from the portal, and came slowly towards the marble fountain. As he drew near, the pale man of science seemed to gaze with a triumphant expression at the beautiful youth and maiden, as might an artist who should spend his life in achieving a picture or a group of statuary, and finally be satisfied with his success. He paused — his bent form grew erect with conscious power, he spread out his hand over them, in the attitude of a father imploring a blessing upon his children. But those were the same hands that had thrown poison into the stream of their lives! Giovanni trembled. Beatrice shuddered very nervously, and pressed her hand upon her heart.

"My daughter," said Rappaccini, "thou art no longer lonely in the world! Pluck one of those precious gems from thy sister shrub, and bid thy bridegroom wear it in his bosom. It will not harm him now! My science, and the sympathy between thee and him, have so wrought within his system, that he now stands apart from common men, as thou dost, daughter of my pride and triumph, from ordinary women. Pass on, then, through the world, most dear to one another, and dreadful to all besides!"

"My father," said Beatrice, feebly — and still, as she spoke, she kept her hand upon her heart — "wherefore didst thou inflict this miserable doom upon thy child?"

"Miserable!" exclaimed Rappaccini. "What mean you, foolish girl? Dost thou deem it misery to be endowed with marvellous gifts, against which no power nor strength could avail an enemy? Misery, to be able to quell the mightiest with a breath? Misery, to be as terrible as thou art beautiful? Wouldst thou, then, have preferred the condition of a weak woman, exposed to all evil, and capable of none?"

"I would fain have been loved, not feared," murmured Beatrice, sinking down upon the ground. "But now it matters not; I am going, father, where the evil, which thou hast striven to mingle with my being, will pass away like a dream — like the fragrance of these poisonous flowers, which will no longer taint my breath among the flowers of Eden. Farewell, Giovanni! Thy words of hatred are like lead within my heart — but they, too, will fall away as I ascend. Oh, was there not, from the first, more poison in thy nature than in mine?"

To Beatrice — so radically had her earthly part been wrought upon by Rappaccini's skill — as poison had been life, so the powerful antidote was death. And thus the poor victim of man's ingenuity and of thwarted nature, and of the fatality that attends all such efforts of perverted wisdom, perished there, at the feet of her father and Giovanni. Just at that moment, Professor Pietro Baglioni looked forth from the window, and called loudly, in a tone of triumph mixed with horror, to the thunder-stricken man of science: —

"Rappaccini! Rappaccini! And is *this* the upshot of your experiment?"

Edgar Allan Poe
The Cask of Amontillado

Edgar Allan Poe's "The Cask of Amontillado" was first published in *Godey's Lady's Book* in November of 1846, and it has been an important American story ever since. In one dimension it illustrates the author's artistic principals of coherence and congruence, of having all the elements of fiction work together for common effect, all contributing to the underlying theme of the work. In this instance, for example, the first-person narrative method is that of dramatic irony in that the polite, patrician language of the narrator conflicts with the calculated cruelty at the center of his intentions. "Amontillado" is most often read as a confessional piece in which the aristocratic Montressor, speaking half a century after the events, finally seeks to unburden a guilt that has haunted him all these years. The depth of that concept is revealed only in the last line of this elegantly crafted short fiction.

Edgar Allan Poe, "The Cask of Amontillado," *Godey's Lady's Book* 33 (November 1846): 216–18.

The thousand injuries of Fortunato I had borne as I best could, but when he ventured upon insult I vowed revenge. You, who so well know the nature of my soul, will not suppose, however, that I gave utterance to a threat. *At length* I would be avenged; this was a point definitively settled — but the very definitiveness with which it was resolved precluded the idea of risk. I must not only punish but punish with impunity. A wrong is unredressed when retribution overtakes its redresser. It is equally unredressed when the avenger fails to make himself felt as such to him who has done the wrong.

It must be understood that neither by word nor deed had I given Fortunato cause to doubt my good will. I continued, as was my wont, to smile in his face, and he did not perceive that my smile *now* was at the thought of his immolation.

He had a weak point — this Fortunato — although in other regards he was a man to be respected and even feared. He prided himself upon his connoisseurship in wine. Few Italians have the true virtuoso spirit. For the most part their enthusiasm is adopted to suit the time and opportunity, to practice imposture upon the British and Austrian *millionaires*. In painting and gemmary, Fortunato, like his countrymen, was a quack, but in the matter of old wines he was sincere. In this respect I did not differ from him materially; — I was skilful in the Italian vintages myself, and bought largely whenever I could.

It was about dusk, one evening during the supreme madness of the carnival season, that I encountered my friend. He accosted me with excessive warmth, for he had been drinking much. The man wore motley. He had on a tight-fitting partistriped dress, and his head was surmounted by the conical cap and bells. I was so pleased to see him that I thought I should never have done wringing his hand.

I said to him — "My dear Fortunato, you are luckily met. How remarkably well you are looking to-day. But I had received a pipe of what passes for Amontillado, and I have my doubts."

"How?" said he. "Amontillado? A pipe? Impossible! And in the middle of the carnival."

"I have my doubts," I replied; "and I was silly enough to pay the full Amontillado price without consulting you in the matter. You were not to be found, and I was fearful of losing a bargain."

"Amontillado!"

"I have my doubts."

"Amontillado!"

"And I must satisfy them."

"Amontillado!"

"As you are engaged, I am on my way to Luchresi. If any one has a critical turn it is he. He will tell me — "

"Luchresi cannot tell Amontillado from Sherry."

"And yet some fools will have it that his taste is a match for your own."

"Come, let us go."

"Whither?"

"To your vaults."

"My friend, no; I will not impose upon your good nature. I perceive you have an engagement. Luchresi — "

"I have no engagement; — come."

"My friend, no. It is not the engagement, but the severe cold with which I perceive you are afflicted. The vaults are insufferably damp. They are encrusted with nitre."

"Let us go, nevertheless. The cold is merely nothing. Amontillado! You have been imposed upon. And as for Luchresi, he cannot distinguish Sherry from Amontillado."

Thus speaking, Fortunato possessed himself of my arm; and putting on a mask of black silk and drawing a *roquelaire* closely about my person, I suffered him to hurry me to my palazzo.

There were no attendants at home; they had absconded to make merry in honour of the time. I had told them that I should not return until the morning, and had given them explicit orders not to stir from the house. These orders were sufficient, I well knew, to insure their immediate disappearance, one and all, as soon as my back was turned.

I took from their sconces two flambeaux, and giving one to Fortunato, bowed him through several suites of rooms to the archway that led into the vaults. I passed down a long and winding staircase, requesting him to be cautious as he followed. We came at length to the foot of the descent, and stood together upon the damp ground of the catacombs of the Montresors.

The gait of my friend was unsteady, and the bells upon his cap jingled as he strode.

"The pipe," said he.

"It is farther on," said I; "but observe the white web-work which gleams from these cavern walls."

He turned towards me, and looked into my eyes with two filmy orbs that distilled the rheum of intoxication.

"Nitre?" he asked at length.

"Nitre," I replied. "How long have you had that cough?"

"Ugh! ugh! ugh! — ugh! ugh! ugh! — ugh! ugh! ugh! — ugh! ugh! ugh! — ugh! ugh! ugh!"

My poor friend found it impossible to reply for many minutes.

"It is nothing," he said, at last.

"Come," I said, with decision, "we will go back; your health is precious. You are rich, respected, admired, beloved; you are happy, as once I was. You are a man to be missed. For me it is no matter. We will go back; you will be ill, and I cannot be responsible. Besides, there is Luchresi — "

"Enough," he said; "the cough is a mere nothing; it will not kill me. I shall not die of a cough."

"True — true," I replied; "and, indeed, I had no intention of alarming you unnecessarily — but you should use all proper caution. A draught of this Medoc will defend us from the damps."

Here I knocked off the neck of a bottle which I drew from a long row of its fellows that lay upon the mould.

"Drink," I said, presenting him the wine.

He raised it to his lips with a leer. He paused and nodded to me familiarly, while his bells jingled.

"I drink," he said, "to the buried that repose around us."

"And I to your long life."

He again took my arm, and we proceeded.

"These vaults," he said, "are extensive."

"The Montresors," I replied, "were a great and numerous family."

"I forget your arms."

"A huge human foot d'or, in a field azure; the foot crushes a serpent rampant whose fangs are imbedded in the heel."

"And the motto?"

"Nemo me impune lacessit."

"Good!" he said.

The wine sparkled in his eyes and the bells jingled. My own fancy grew warm with the Medoc. We had passed through long walls of piled skeletons, with casks and puncheons intermingling, into the inmost recesses of the catacombs. I paused again, and this time I made bold to seize Fortunato by an arm above the elbow.

"The nitre!" I said; "see, it increases. It hangs like moss upon the vaults. We are below the river's bed. The drops of moisture trickle among the bones. Come, we will go back ere it is too late. Your cough —— "

"It is nothing," he said; "let us go on. But first, another drought of the Medoc."

I broke and reached him a flaçon of De Grâve. He emptied it at a breath. His eyes flashed with a fierce light. He laughed and threw the bottle upwards with a gesticulation I did not understand.

I looked at him in surprise. He repeated the movement — a grotesque one.

"You do not comprehend?" he said.

"Not I," I replied.

"Then you are not of the brotherhood."

"How?"

"You are not of the masons."

"Yes, yes," I said; "yes, yes."

"You? Impossible! A mason?"

"A mason," I replied.

"A sign," he said, "a sign."

"It is this," I answered, producing from beneath the folds of my *roquelaire* a trowel.

"You jest," he exclaimed, recoiling a few paces. "But let us proceed to the Amontillado."

"Be it so," I said, replacing the tool beneath the cloak and again offering him my arm. He leaned upon it heavily. We continued our rout in search of the Amontillado. We passed through a range of low arches, descended, passed on, and descending again, arrived at a deep crypt, in which the foulness of the air caused our flambeaux rather to glow than flame.

At the most remote end of the crypt there appeared another less spacious. Its walls had been lined with human remains, piled to the vault overhead, in the fashion of the great catacombs of Paris. Three sides of this interior crypt were still ornamented in this manner. From the fourth side the bones had been thrown down, and lay promiscuously upon the earth, forming at one point a mound of some size. Within the wall thus exposed by the displacing of the bones, we perceived a still interior crypt or recess, in depth about four feet, in width three, in height six or seven. It seemed to have been constructed for no especial use within itself, but formed merely the interval between two of the colossal supports of the roof of the catacombs, and was backed by one of their circumscribing walls of solid granite.

It was in vain that Fortunato, uplifting his dull torch, endeavoured to pry into the depth of the recess. Its termination the feeble light did not enable us to see.

"Proceed," I said; "herein is the Amontillado. As for Luchresi ——— "

"He is an ignoramus," interrupted my friend, as he stepped unsteadily forward, while I followed immediately at his heels. In an instant he had reached the extremity of the niche, and finding his progress arrested by the rock, stood stupidly bewildered. A moment more and I had fettered him to the granite. In its surface were two iron staples, distant from each other about two feet, horizontally. From one of these depended a short chain, from the other a padlock. Throwing the links about his waist, it was but the work of a few seconds to secure it. He was too much astounded to resist. Withdrawing the key I stepped back from the recess.

"Pass your hand," I said, "over the wall; you cannot help feeling the nitre. Indeed, it is *very* damp. Once more, let me *implore* you to return. No? Then I must positively leave you. But I will first render you all the little attentions in my power."

"The Amontillado!" ejaculated my friend, not yet recovered from his astonishment.

"True," I replied; "the Amontillado."

As I said these words I busied myself among the pile of bones of which I have before spoken. Throwing them aside, I soon uncovered a quantity of building stone and mortar. With these materials and with the aid of my trowel, I began vigorously to wall up the entrance of the niche.

I had scarcely laid the first tier of the masonry when I discovered that the intoxication of Fortunato had in great measure worn off. The earliest indication I had of this was a low moaning cry from the depth of the recess. It was *not* the cry of a drunken man. There was then a long and obstinate silence. I laid the second tier, and the third, and the fourth; and then I heard the furious vibration of the chain. The noise lasted for several minutes, during which, that I might hearken to it with the more satisfaction, I ceased my labours and sat down upon the bones. When at last the clanking subsided, I resumed the trowel, and finished without interruption the fifth, the sixth, and the seventh tier. The wall was now nearly upon a level with my breast. I again paused, and holding the flambeaux over the mason-work, threw a few feeble rays upon the figure within.

A succession of loud and shrill screams, bursting suddenly from the throat of the chained form, seemed to thrust me violently back. For a brief moment I hesitated, I trembled. Unsheathing my rapier, I began to grope with it about the recess; but the thought of an instant reassured me. I placed my hand upon the solid fabric of the catacombs, and felt satisfied. I reapproached the wall. I replied to the yells of him who clamoured. I reechoed, I aided, I surpassed them in volume and in strength. I did this, and the clamourer grew still.

It was now midnight, and my task was drawing to a close. I had completed the eighth, the ninth and the tenth tier. I had finished a portion of the last and the eleventh; there remained but a single stone to be fitted and plastered in. I struggled with its weight; I placed it partially in its destined position. But now there came from out the niche a low laugh that erected the hairs upon my head. It was succeeded by a sad voice, which I had difficulty in recognizing as that of the noble Fortunato. The voice said —

"Ha! ha! ha! — he! he! he! — a very good joke, indeed — an excellent jest. We will have many a rich laugh about it at the palazzo — he! he! he! — over our wine — he! he! he!"

"The Amontillado!" I said.

"He! he! he! — he! he! he! — yes, the Amontillado. But is it not getting late? Will not they be awaiting us at the palazzo — the Lady Fortunato and the rest? Let us be gone."

"Yes," I said, "let us be gone."

"For the love of God, Montresor!"

"Yes," I said, "for the love of God!"

But to these words I hearkened in vain for a reply. I grew impatient. I called aloud —

"Fortunato!"

No answer. I called again —

"Fortunato!"

No answer still. I thrust a torch through the remaining aperture and let it fall within. There came forth in return only a jingling of the bells. My heart grew sick; it was the dampness of the catacombs that made it so. I hastened to make an end of my labour. I forced the last stone into its position; I plastered it up. Against the new masonry I re-erected the old rampart of bones. For the half of a century no mortal has disturbed them. *In pace requiescat!*

Harriet Beecher Stowe
The Two Altars; or, Two Pictures in One

Harriet Beecher Stowe's "The Two Altars; or, Two Pictures in One" is not as well known as her fiction in the Local Color mode collected in *Oldtown Fireside Stories* (1872), and it is overshadowed by the success of her antislavery novels, especially *Uncle Tom's Cabin* (1851) and *Dred: A Tale of the Great Dismal Swamp* (1856). Nevertheless, it is an important document in literary history, written in response to the passage of the Fugitive Slave Law in 1850, which required that runaway slaves be returned to the South for further servitude. Stowe's religious background, and her experiences in abolitionist New England, provided her with the central themes of her humanitarian fiction, ideas well represented in the two parts of "The Two Altars." The first section shows the sacrifices a white family is willing to endure on behalf of the young men fighting for freedom during the Revolutionary War; the second segment portrays a black family, living in Boston, torn asunder by the impact of the new law that requires that the husband and father be returned to slavery, never to see his family again. The injustice inherent in the contrast between the two family situations is dramatic, as is the ironic emphasis on the concept of liberty.

Harriet Beecher Stowe, "The Two Altars; or, Two Pictures in One," *The New-York Evangelist and New-York Presbyterian* 22, no. 24 (June 12, 1851): 3–4; 22, no. 25 (June 19, 1851): 97–98.

I. The Altar of Liberty, or 1776

The well-sweep of the old house on the hill was relieved dark and clear, against the reddening sky, as the early winter sun was going down in the west. It was a brisk, clear, metallic evening; the long drifts of snow blushed crimson red on their tops, and lay in shades of purple and lilac in the hollows; and the old wintry wind brushed shrewdly along the plain, tingling people's noses, blowing open their cloaks, puffing in the back of their necks, and showing other unmistakable indications that he was getting up steam for a real roistering night.

"Hurrah! How it blows!" said little Dick Ward, from the top of the mossy wood-pile.

Now Dick had been sent to said wood-pile, in company with his little sister Grace, to pick up chips, which, everybody knows, was in the olden time considered a wholesome and gracious employment, and the peculiar duty of the rising generation. But said Dick, being a boy, had mounted the wood-pile, and erected there a flagstaff, on which he was busily tying a little red pocket-handkerchief, occasionally exhorting Grace "to be sure and pick up fast."

"Oh, yes, I will," said Grace; "but you see the chips have got ice on 'em, and make my hands so cold!"

"Oh, don't stop to suck your thumbs! Who cares for ice? Pick away, I say, while I set up the flag of liberty."

So Grace picked away as fast as she could, nothing doubting but that her cold thumbs were in some mysterious sense an offering on the shrine of liberty; while soon the red handkerchief, duly secured, fluttered and snapped in the brisk evening wind.

"Now you must hurrah, Gracie, and throw up your bonnet," said Dick, as he descended from the pile.

"But won't it lodge down in some place in the wood-pile?" suggested Grace thoughtfully.

"Oh, never fear; give it to me, and just holler now, Gracie, 'Hurrah for liberty!' and we'll throw up your bonnet and my cap; and we'll play, you know, that we are a whole army and I'm General Washington."

So Grace gave up her little red hood, and Dick swung his cap, and up they both went into the air; and the children shouted, and the flag snapped and fluttered, and altogether they had a merry time of it. But then the wind — good-for-nothing, roguish fellow! — made an ungenerous plunge at poor Grace's little hood, and snipped it up in a twinkling, and whisked it off, off, off, — fluttering and bobbing up and down, quite across a wide, waste, snowy field, — and finally lodged it on the top of a tall, strutting rail, that was leaning, very independently quite another way from all the other rails of the fence.

"Now see, do see!" said Grace; "there goes my bonnet! What will Aunt Hitty say?" and Grace began to cry.

"Don't you cry, Gracie; you offered it up to liberty, you know: it's glorious to give up everything for liberty."

"Oh, but Aunt Hitty won't think so."

"Well, don't cry, Gracie, you foolish girl! Do you think I can't get it? Now, only play that that great rail is a fort, and your bonnet is a prisoner in it, and see how quick I'll take the fort and get it!" and Dick shouldered a stick, and started off.

"What upon *airth* keeps those children so long? I should think they were *making* chips!" said Aunt Mehetabel; "the fire's just a-going out under the tea-kettle."

By this time Grace had lugged her heavy basket to the door, and was stamping the snow off her little feet, which were so numb that she needed to stamp, to be quite sure they were yet there. Aunt Mehetabel's shrewd face was the first that greeted her as the door opened.

"Gracie — What upon *airth!* — wipe your nose, child; your hands are frozen. Where alive is Dick? — and what's kept you out all this time? — and where's your bonnet?"

Poor Grace, stunned by this cataract of questions, neither wiped her nose nor gave any answer, but sidled up into the warm corner where grandmamma was knitting, and began quietly rubbing and blowing her fingers, while the tears silently rolled down her cheeks, as the fire made the former ache intolerably.

"Poor little dear!" said grandmamma, taking her hands in hers; "Hitty sha'n't scold you. Grandma knows you've been a good girl, — the wind blew poor Gracie's bonnet away;" and grandmamma wiped both eyes and nose, and gave her, moreover, a stalk of dried fennel out of her pocket, whereat Grace took heart once more.

"Mother always makes fools of Roxy's children," said Mehetabel, puffing zealously under the tea-kettle. "There's a little maple sugar in that saucer up there, mother, if you will keep giving it to her," she said, still vigorously puffing. "And now, Gracie," she said, when, after a while, the fire seemed in tolerable order, "will you answer my question? Where is Dick?"

"Gone over in the lot to get my bonnet."

"How came your bonnet off?" said Aunt Mehetabel. "I tied it on firm enough."

"Dick wanted me to take it off for him, to throw up for liberty," said Grace.

"Throw up for fiddlestick! Just one of Dick's cut-ups; and you was silly enough to mind him!"

"Why, he put up a flagstaff on the wood-pile, and a flag to liberty, you know, that papa's fighting for," said Grace more confidently, as she saw her quiet, blue-eyed mother, who had silently walked into the room during the conversation.

Grace's mother smiled, and said encouragingly, "And what then?"

"Why, he wanted me to throw up my bonnet and he his cap, and shout for liberty; and then the wind took it and carried it off, and he said I ought not to be sorry if I did lose it, — it was an offering to liberty."

"And so I did," said Dick, who was standing as straight as a poplar behind the group; "and I heard it in one of father's letters to mother that we ought to offer up everything on the altar of liberty and so I made an altar of the wood-pile."

"Good boy!" said his mother; "always remember everything your father writes. He has offered up everything on the altar of liberty, true enough; and I hope you, son, will live to do the same."

"Only, if I have the hoods and caps to make," said Aunt Hitty, "I hope he won't offer them up every week, — that's all!"

"Oh, well, Aunt Hitty, I've got the hood; let me alone for that. It blew clear over into the Daddy Ward pasture lot, and there stuck on the top of the great rail; and I played that the rail was a fort, and besieged it, and took it."

"Oh, yes! you're always up to taking forts, and anything else that nobody wants done. I'll warrant, now, you left Grace to pick up every blessed one of them chips."

"Picking up chips is girls' work," said Dick; "and taking forts and defending the country is men's work."

"And pray, Mister Pomp, how long have you been a man?" said Aunt Hitty.

"If I ain't a man, I soon shall be; my head is 'most up to my mother's shoulder, and I can fire off a gun, too. I tried, the other day, when I was up to the store. Mother, I wish you'd let me clean and load the old gun, so that, if the British should come" —

"Well, if you are so big and grand, just lift me out that table, sir," said Aunt Hitty; "for it's past supper-time."

Dick sprang, and had the table out in a trice, with an abundant clatter, and put up the leaves with quite an air. His mother, with the silent and gliding motion characteristic of her, quietly took out the table-cloth and spread it, and began to set the cups and saucers in order, and to put on the plates and knives, while Aunt Hitty bustled about the tea.

"I'll be glad when the war's over, for one reason," said she. "I'm pretty much tired of drinking sage tea, for one, I know."

"Well, Aunt Hitty, how you scolded that peddler, last week, that brought along that real tea!"

"To be sure I did. S'pose I'd be taking any of his old tea, bought of the British? — fling every teacup in his face first."

"Well, mother," said Dick, "I never exactly understood what it was about the tea, and why the Boston folks threw it all overboard."

"Because there was an unlawful tax laid upon it, that the government had no right to lay. It wasn't much in itself; but it was a part of a whole system of oppressive meanness, designed to take away our rights, and make us slaves of a foreign power."

"Slaves!" said Dick, straightening himself proudly. "Father a slave!"

"But they would not be slaves! They saw clearly where it would all end, and they would not begin to submit to it in ever so little," said the mother.

"I wouldn't, if I was they," said Dick.

"Besides," said his mother, drawing him towards her, "it wasn't for themselves alone they did it. This is a great country, and it will be greater and greater; and it's very important that it should have free and equal laws, because it will by and by be so great. This country, if it is a free one, will be a light of the world, — a city set on a hill, that cannot be hid; and all the oppressed and distressed from other countries shall come here to enjoy equal rights and freedom. This, dear boy, is why your father and uncles have gone to fight, and why they do stay and fight, though God knows what they suffer and" — And the large blue eyes of the mother were full of tears; yet a strong, bright beam of pride and exultation shone through those tears.

"Well, well, Roxy, you can always talk, everybody knows," said Aunt Hitty, who had been not the least attentive listener of this little patriotic harangue; "but, you see, the tea is getting cold, and yonder I see the sleigh is at the door, and John's come; so let's set up our chairs for supper."

The chairs were soon set up, when John, the eldest son, a lad of about fifteen, entered with a letter. There was one general exclamation, and stretching out of hands towards it. John threw it into his mother's lap; the tea-table was forgotten, and the tea-kettle sang unnoticed by the fire, as all hands crowded about mother's chair to hear the news. It was from Captain Ward, then in the American army at Valley Forge. Mrs. Ward ran it over hastily, and then read it aloud. A few words we may extract.

"There is still," it said, "much suffering. I have given away every pair of stockings you sent me, reserving to myself only one; for I will not be one whit better off than the poorest soldier that fights for his country. Poor fellows! it makes my heart ache sometimes to go round among them, and see them with their worn clothes and torn shoes, and often bleeding feet, yet cheerful and hopeful, and every one willing to do his very best. Often the spirit of discouragement comes over them, particularly at night, when, weary, cold, and hungry, they turn into their comfortless huts, on the snowy ground. Then sometimes there is a thought of home, and warm fires, and some speak of giving up; but next morning out come Washington's general orders, — little short note, but 's wonderful the good it does; and then they all resolve to hold on, come what may. There are commissioners going all through the country to pick up supplies. If they come to you, I need not to tell you what to do. I know all that will be in your hearts."

"There, children, see what your father suffers," said the mother, "and what it costs these poor soldiers to gain our liberty."

"Ephraim Scranton told me that the commissioners had come as far as the Three Mile Tavern, and that he rather 'spected they'd be along here to-night," said John, as he was helping round the baked beans to the silent company at the tea-table.

"To-night? — do tell, now!" said Aunt Hitty. "Then it's time we were awake and stirring. Let's see what can be got."

"I'll send my new overcoat, for one," said John. "That old one isn't cut up yet, is it, Aunt Hitty?"

"No," said Aunt Hitty, "I was laying out to cut it over next Wednesday, when Desire Smith could be here to do the tailoring."

"There's the south room," said Aunt Hitty, musing; "that bed has the two old

Aunt Ward blankets on it, and the great blue quilt, and two comforters. Then mother's and my room, two pair — four comforters — two quilts — the best chamber has got" —

"Oh, Aunt Hitty, send all that's in the best chamber! If any company comes, we can make it up off from our beds," said John. "I can send a blanket or two off from my bed, I know, — can't but just turn over in it, so many clothes on, now."

"Aunt Hitty, take a blanket off from our bed," said Grace and Dick at once.

"Well, well, we'll see," said Aunt Hitty, bustling up.

Up rose grandmamma, with great earnestness now, and going into the next room, and opening a large cedar-wood chest, returned, bearing in her arms two large snow-white blankets, which she deposited flat on the table, just as Aunt Hitty was whisking off the table-cloth.

"Mortal! mother, what are you going to do?" said Aunt Hitty.

"There," she said, "I spun those, every thread of 'em, when my name was Mary Evans. Those were my wedding-blankets, made of real nice wool, and worked with roses in all the corners. I've got *them* to give!" and grandmamma stroked and smoothed the blankets, and patted them down, with great pride and tenderness. It was evident she was giving something that lay very near her heart; but she never faltered.

"La! mother, there's no need of that," said Aunt Hitty. "Use them on your own bed, and send the blankets off from that; they are just as good for the soldiers."

"No, I sha'n't!" said the old lady, waxing warm; "'t isn't a bit too good for 'em. I'll send the very best I've got, before they shall suffer. Send 'em the *best!*" and the old lady gestured oratorically.

They were interrupted by a rap at the door, and two men entered, and announced themselves as commissioned by Congress to search out supplies for the army. Now the plot thickens. Aunt Hitty flew in every direction, — through entry passage, meal-room, milk-room, down cellar, up chamber, — her cap border on end with patriotic zeal; and followed by John, Dick, and Grace, who eagerly bore to the kitchen the supplies that she turned out, while Mrs. Ward busied herself in quietly sorting and arranging, in the best possible traveling order, the various contributions that were precipitately launched on the kitchen floor.

Aunt Hitty soon appeared in the kitchen with an armful of stockings, which, kneeling on the floor, she began counting and laying out.

"There," she said, laying down a large bundle on some blankets, "that leaves just two pair apiece all round."

"La!" said John, "what's the use of saving two pair for me? I can do with one pair, as well as father."

"Sure enough," said his mother; "besides, I can knit you another pair in a day."

"And I can do with one pair," said Dick.

"Yours will be too small, young master, I guess," said one of the commissioners.

"No," said Dick; "I've got a pretty good foot of my own, and Aunt Hitty will always knit my stockings an inch too long, 'cause she says I grow so. See here, — these will do;" and the boy shook his triumphantly.

"And mine, too," said Grace, nothing doubting, having been busy all the time in pulling off her little stockings.

"Here," she said to the man who was packing the things into a wide-mouthed sack; "here's mine," and her large blue eyes looked earnestly through her tears.

Aunt Hitty flew at her. "Good land! the child's crazy. Don't think the men could wear your stockings, — take 'em away!"

Grace looked around the room with an air of utter desolation, and began to cry. "I wanted to give them something," said she. "I'd rather go barefoot on the snow all day than not send 'em anything."

"Give me the stockings, my child," said the old soldier tenderly. "There, I'll take 'em, and show 'em to the soldiers, and tell them what the little girl said that sent them. And it will do them as much good as if they could wear them. They've got little girls at home, too." Grace fell on her mother's bosom completely happy, and Aunt Hitty only muttered, —

"Everybody does spile that child; and no wonder, neither!"

Soon the old sleigh drove off from the brown house, tightly packed and heavily loaded. And Grace and Dick were creeping up to their little beds.

"There's been something put on the altar of Liberty to-night, hasn't there, Dick?"

"Yes, indeed," said Dick; and, looking up to his mother, he said, "But, mother, what did you give?"

"I?" said the mother musingly.

"Yes, you, mother; what have you given to the country?"

"All that I have, dears," said she, laying her hands gently on their heads, — "my husband and my children!"

II. The Altar of ——— , or 1850

The setting sun of chill December lighted up the solitary front window of a small tenement on — Street, in Boston, which we now have occasion to visit. As we push gently aside the open door, we gain sight of a small room, clean as busy hands can make it, where a neat, cheerful young mulatto woman is busy at an ironing-table. A basket full of glossy-bosomed shirts, and faultless collars and wrist-bands, is beside her, into which she is placing the last few items with evident pride and satisfaction. A bright black-eyed boy, just come in from school, with his satchel of books over his shoulder, stands, cap in hand, relating to his mother how he has been at the head of his class, and showing his school tickets, which his mother, with untiring admiration, deposits in the little real china teapot, which, as being their most reliable article of gentility, is made the deposit of all the money and most especial valuables of the family.

"Now, Henry," says the mother, "look out and see if father is coming along the street;" and she begins filling the little black tea-kettle, which is soon set singing on the stove.

From the inner room now daughter Mary, a well-grown girl of thirteen, brings the baby, just roused from a nap, and very impatient to renew his acquaintance with his mamma.

"Bless his bright eyes! — mother will take him," ejaculates the busy little woman, whose hands are by this time in a very floury condition, in the incipient stages of wetting up biscuit, — "in a minute;" and she quickly frees herself from the flour and paste, and, deputing Mary to roll out her biscuit, proceeds to the consolation and succor of young master.

"Now, Henry," says the mother, "you'll have time, before supper, to take that basket of clothes up to Mr. Sheldin's; put in that nice bill that you made out last night. I shall give you a cent for every bill you write out for me. What a comfort it is, now, for one's children to be gettin' learnin' so!"

Henry shouldered the basket and passed out the door, just as a neatly dressed colored man walked up with his pail and whitewash brushes.

"Oh, you've come, father, have you? Mary, are the biscuits in? You may as well set the table now. Well, George, what's the news?"

"Nothing, only a pretty smart day's work. I've brought home five dollars, and shall have as much as I can do, these two weeks;" and the man, having washed his hands, proceeded to count out his change on the ironing-table.

"Well, it takes you to bring in the money," said the delightful wife; "nobody but you could turn off that much in a day."

"Well, they do say — those that's had me once — that they never want any other hand to take hold in their rooms. I s'pose it's a kinder practice I've got, and kinder natural!"

"Tell ye what," said the little woman, taking down the family strong box, — to wit, the china teapot aforenamed, — and pouring the contents on the table, "we're getting mighty rich now! We can afford to get Henry his new Sunday cap, and Mary her mousseline-de-laine dress — Take care, baby, you rogue!" she hastily interposed, as young master made a dive at a dollar bill, for his share in the proceeds.

"He wants something, too, I suppose," said the father; "let him get his hand in while he's young."

The baby gazed, with round, astonished eyes, while mother, with some difficulty, rescued the bill from his grasp; but, before any one could at all anticipate his purpose, he dashed in among the small change with such zeal as to send it flying all over the table.

"Hurrah! Bob's a smasher!" said the father, delighted; "he'll make it fly, he thinks;" and, taking the baby on his knee, he laughed merrily as Mary and her mother pursued the rolling coin all over the room.

"He knows now, as well as can be that he's been doing mischief," said the delighted mother, as the baby kicked and crowed uproariously; "he's such a forward child, now, to be only six months old! Oh, you've no idea, father, how mischievous he grows;" and therewith the little woman began to roll and tumble the little mischief-maker about, uttering divers frightful threats, which appeared to contribute, in no small degree, to the general hilarity.

"Come, come, Mary," said the mother at last, with a sudden burst of recollection; "you mustn't be always on your knees fooling with this child! Look in the oven at them biscuits."

"They're done exactly, mother, — just the brown!" and, with the word, the mother dumped baby on to his father's knee, where he sat contentedly munching a very ancient crust of bread, occasionally improving the flavor thereof by rubbing it on his father's coat-sleeve.

"What have you got in that blue dish there?" said George, when the whole little circle were seated around the table.

"Well, now, what do you suppose?" said the little woman, delighted; "a quart of nice oysters, — just for a treat, you know. I wouldn't tell you till this minute," said she, raising the cover.

"Well," said George, "we both work hard for our money, and we don't owe anybody a cent; and why shouldn't we have our treats, now and then, as well as rich folks?"

And gayly passed the supper hour; the tea-kettle sung, the baby crowed, and all chatted and laughed abundantly.

"I'll tell you," said George, wiping his mouth; "wife, these times are quite another thing from what it used to be down in Georgia. I remember then old mas'r used to hire me out by the year; and one time, I remember, I came and paid him in two hundred dollars, — every cent I'd taken. He just looked it over, counted it, and put it in his pocket-book, and said, 'You are a good boy, George,' — and he gave me half a dollar!"

"I want to know, now!" said his wife.

"Yes, he did, and that was every cent I ever got of it; and, I tell you, I was mighty bad off for clothes, them times."

"Well, well, the Lord be praised, they're over, and you are in a free country now!" said the wife, as she rose thoughtfully from the table, and brought her husband the great Bible. The little circle were ranged around the stove for evening prayers.

"Henry, my boy, you must read — you are a better reader than your father — thank God, that let you learn early!"

The boy, with a cheerful readiness, read, "The Lord is my Shepherd," and the mother gently stilled the noisy baby to listen to the holy words. Then all kneeled, while the father, with simple earnestness, poured out his soul to God.

They had but just risen — the words of Christian hope and trust scarce died on their lips — when, lo! The door was burst open, and two men entered; and one of them, advancing, laid his hand on the father's shoulder. "This is the fellow," said he.

"You are arrested in the name of the United States!" said the other.

"Gentlemen, what is this?" said the poor man, trembling.

"Are you not the property of Mr. B., of Georgia?" said the officer.

"Gentlemen, I've been a free, hard-working man these ten years."

"Yes; but you are arrested, on suit of Mr. B., as his slave."

Shall we describe the leave-taking, — the sorrowing wife, the dismayed children, the tears, the anguish, that simple, honest, kindly home, in a moment so desolated? Ah, ye who defend this because it is law, think for one hour what if this that happens to your poor brother should happen to you!

§§

It was a crowded court-room, and the man stood there to be tried — for life? — no; but for the life of life — for liberty!

Lawyers hurried to and fro, buzzing, consulting, bringing authorities, — all anxious, zealous, engaged, — for what? To save a fellow man from bondage? No; anxious and zealous lest he might escape; full of zeal to deliver him over to slavery. The poor man's anxious eyes follow vainly the busy course of affairs, from which he dimly learns that he is to be sacrificed — on the altar of the Union; and that his heart-break and anguish, and the tears of his wife, and the desolation of his children are, in the eyes of these well-informed men, only the bleat of a sacrifice, bound to the horns of the glorious American altar!

§§

Again it is a bright day, and business walks brisk in this market. Senator and statesman, the learned and patriotic, are out, this day, to give their countenance to an edifying and impressive and truly American spectacle, — the sale of a man! All the preliminaries of the scene are there: dusky-browed mothers, looking with sad eyes while speculators are turning round their children, looking at their teeth, and feeling of their arms; a poor, old, trembling woman, helpless, half blind, whose last child is to be sold, holds on to her bright boy with trembling hands. Husbands and wives, sisters and friends, all soon to be scattered like the chaff of the threshing-floor, look sadly on each other with poor nature's last tears; and among them walk briskly glib, oily politicians, and thriving men of law, letters, and religion, exceedingly sprightly and in good spirits — for why? — it isn't *they* that are going to be sold; it's only somebody else. And so they are very comfortable, and look on the whole thing as quite a matter-of-course affair, and, as it is to be conducted to-day, a decidedly valuable and judicious exhibition.

And now, after so many hearts and souls have been knocked and thumped this way and that way by the auctioneer's hammer, comes the *instructive* part of the whole; and the husband and father, whom we saw in his simple home, reading and praying with his children, and rejoicing in the joy of his poor ignorant heart that he lived in a free country, is now set up to be admonished of his mistake.

Now there is a great excitement, and pressing to see, and exultation and approbation; for it is important and interesting to see a man put down that has tried to be a *free man*.

"That's he, is it? Couldn't come it, could he?" says one.

"No; and he will never come it, that's more," says another triumphantly.

"I don't generally take much interest in scenes of this nature," says a grave representative; "but I came here to-day for the sake of the principle!"

"Gentlemen," says the auctioneer, "we've got a specimen here that some of your Northern abolitionists would give any price for; but they sha'n't have him! no! we've looked out for that. The man that buys him must give bonds never to sell him to go North again!"

"Go it!" shout the crowd; "good! good! hurrah!" An impressive idea!" says the Senator; "a noble maintaining of principle!" and the man is bid off, and the hammer falls with a last crash on his heart, his hopes, his manhood, and he lies a bleeding wreck on the altar of Liberty!

Such was the altar in 1776; such is the altar in 1850!

Herman Melville
Bartleby, the Scrivener

Herman Melville's "Bartleby, the Scrivener," one of the most frequently taught works in American literature, was first published in *Putnam's Monthly Magazine* in 1853 before appearing three years later in *The Piazza Tales*. These two publications constitute the existing "text" in that no manuscript has been discovered and it was not reprinted during Melville's lifetime. One of the author's early attempts at short fiction, the first draft was written during the summer of 1853 and may have been based on family circumstances, since Melville had many lawyers to draw from, including his brother Allan, who had an office at 10 Wall Street in New York. A complex narrative, it has been much analyzed, and most controversies focus on two central issues: the cause and meaning of Bartleby's progressive retreat from the world, and the narrator's psychological growth and deepening on the basis of his encounter with this strange person. Indeed, ultimately the story seems more about the person who tells it than about Bartleby himself, about whom little is known. But the lawyer has been profoundly affected by the events, and that seems to be the motivation for the telling of them. Given the retrospective point of view, it is clear that all of the action has taken place before the narrator speaks the first line, so the story becomes a meditation on the meaning of it all, the result of which is summarized in the final sentence.

Herman Melville, "Bartleby, the Scrivener," *Putnam's Monthly Magazine* 2, no. 11 (November 1853): 546–57; 2, no. 12 (December 1853): 609–15.

I am a rather elderly man. The nature of my avocations for the last thirty years has brought me into more than ordinary contact with what would seem an interesting and somewhat singular set of men, of whom as yet nothing that I know of has ever been written: — I mean the law-copyists or scriveners. I have known very many of them, professionally and privately, and if I pleased, could relate divers histories, at which good-natured gentlemen might smile, and sentimental souls might weep. But I waive the biographies of all other scriveners for a few passages in the life of Bartleby, who was a scrivener the strangest I ever saw or heard of. While of other law-copyists I might write the complete life, of Bartleby nothing of that sort can be done. I believe that no materials exist for a full and satisfactory biography of this man. It is an irreparable loss to literature. Bartleby was one of those beings of whom nothing is ascertainable, except from the original sources, and in his case those are very small. What my own astonished eyes saw of Bartleby, *that* is all I know of him, except, indeed, one vague report which will appear in the sequel.

Ere introducing the scrivener, as he first appeared to me, it is fit I make some mention of myself, my *employees,* my business, my chambers, and general surroundings; because some such description is indispensable to an adequate understanding of the chief character about to be presented.

Imprimis: I am a man who, from his youth upwards, has been filled with a profound conviction that the easiest way of life is the best. Hence, though I belong to a profession proverbially energetic and nervous, even to turbulence, at times, yet nothing of that sort have I ever suffered to invade my peace. I am one of those unambitious lawyers who never addresses a jury, or in any way draws down public applause; but in the cool tranquillity of a snug retreat, do a snug business among rich men's bonds and mortgages and title-deeds. All who know me, consider me an eminently *safe* man. The late John Jacob Astor, a personage little given to poetic enthusiasm, had no hesitation in pronouncing my first grand point to be prudence; my next, method. I do not speak it in vanity, but simply record the fact, that I was not unemployed in my profession by the late John Jacob Astor; a name which, I admit, I love to repeat, for it hath a rounded and orbicular sound to it, and rings like unto bullion. I will freely add, that I was not insensible to the late John Jacob Astor's good opinion.

Some time prior to the period at which this little history begins, my avocations had been largely increased. The good old office, now extinct in the State of New-York, of a Master in Chancery, had been conferred upon me. It was not a very arduous office, but very pleasantly remunerative. I seldom lose my temper;

much more seldom indulge in dangerous indignation at wrongs and outrages; but I must be permitted to be rash here and declare, that I consider the sudden and violent abrogation of the office of Master in Chancery, by the new Constitution, as a —— premature act; inasmuch as I had counted upon a life-lease of the profits, whereas I only received those of a few short years. But this is by the way.

My chambers were up stairs at No. — Wall-street. At one end they looked upon the white wall of the interior of a spacious sky-light shaft, penetrating the building from top to bottom. This view might have been considered rather tame than otherwise, deficient in what landscape painters call "life." But if so, the view from the other end of my chambers offered, at least, a contrast, if nothing more. In that direction my windows commanded an unobstructed view of a lofty brick wall, black by age and everlasting shade; which wall required no spy-glass to bring out its lurking beauties, but for the benefit of all near-sighted spectators, was pushed up to within ten feet of my window panes. Owing to the great height of the surrounding buildings, and my chambers being on the second floor, the interval between this wall and mine not a little resembled a huge square cistern.

At the period just preceding the advent of Bartleby, I had two persons as copyists in my employment, and a promising lad as an office-boy. First, Turkey; second, Nippers; third, Ginger Nut. These may seem names, the like of which are not usually found in the Directory. In truth they were nicknames, mutually conferred upon each other by my three clerks, and were deemed expressive of their respective persons or characters. Turkey was a short, pursy Englishman of about my own age, that is, somewhere not far from sixty. In the morning, one might say, his face was of a fine florid hue, but after twelve o'clock, meridian — his dinner hour — it blazed like a grate full of Christmas coals; and continued blazing — but, as it were, with a gradual wane — till 6 o'clock, P. M. or thereabouts, after which I saw no more of the proprietor of the face, which gaining its meridian with the sun, seemed to set with it, to rise, culminate, and decline the following day, with the like regularity and undiminished glory. There are many singular coincidences I have known in the course of my life, not the least among which was the fact, that exactly when Turkey displayed his fullest beams from his red and radiant countenance, just then, too, at that critical moment, began the daily period when I considered his business capacities as seriously disturbed for the remainder of the twenty-four hours. Not that he was absolutely idle, or averse to business then; far from it. The difficulty was, he was apt to be altogether too energetic. There was a strange, inflamed, flurried, flighty recklessness of activity about him. He would be incautious in dipping his pen into his inkstand. All his blots upon my documents were dropped there after twelve o'clock, meridian. Indeed, not only would he be reckless and sadly given to making blots in the afternoon, but some days he went further, and was rather noisy. At such times, too, his face flamed with augmented blazonry, as if cannel coal had been heaped on anthracite. He made an unpleasant racket with his chair; spilled his sand-box; in mending his pens, impatiently split them all to pieces, and threw them on the floor in a sudden passion; stood up and leaned over his table, boxing his papers about in a most indecorous manner, very sad to behold in an elderly man like him. Nevertheless, as he was in many ways a most valuable person to me, and all the time before twelve o'clock, meridian, was the quickest, steadiest creature too, accomplishing a great deal of work in a style not easy to be matched — for these reasons, I was willing to overlook his eccentricities, though indeed, occasionally, I remonstrated with him. I did this very gently, however, because, though the civilest, nay, the blandest and most reverential of men in the morning, yet in the afternoon he was disposed, upon provocation, to be slightly rash with his tongue, in fact, insolent. Now, valuing his morning services as I did, and resolved not to lose them; yet, at the same time made uncomfortable by his inflamed ways after twelve o'clock; and being a man of peace, unwilling by my admonitions to call forth unseemly retorts from him; I took upon me, one Saturday noon (he was always worse on Saturdays), to hint to him, very kindly, that perhaps now that he was growing old, it might be well to abridge his labors; in short, he need not come to my chambers after twelve o'clock, but dinner over, had best go home to his lodgings and rest himself till teatime. But no; he insisted upon his afternoon devotions. His countenance became intolerably fervid, as he oratorically assured me — gesticulating with a long ruler at the other end of the room — that if his services in the morning were useful, how indispensable, then, in the afternoon?

"With submission, sir," said Turkey on this occasion, "I consider myself your right-hand man. In the morning I but marshal and deploy my columns; but in the afternoon I put myself at their head, and gallantly charge the foe, thus!" — and he made a violent thrust with the ruler.

"But the blots, Turkey," intimated I.

"True, — but, with submission, sir, behold these hairs! I am getting old. Surely, sir, a blot or two of a warm afternoon is not to be severely urged against gray hairs. Old age — even if it blot the page — is honorable. With submission, sir, we *both* are getting old."

This appeal to my fellow-feeling was hardly to be resisted. At all events, I saw that go he would not. So I made up my mind to let him stay, resolving, nevertheless, to see to it, that during the afternoon he had to do with my less important papers.

Nippers, the second on my list, was a whiskered, sallow, and, upon the whole, rather piratical-looking young man of about five and twenty. I always deemed him the victim of two evil powers — ambition and indigestion. The ambition was evinced by a certain impatience of the duties of a mere copyist, an unwarrantable usurpation of strictly professional affairs, such as the original drawing up of legal documents. The indigestion seemed betokened in an occasional nervous testiness and grinning irritability, causing the teeth to audibly grind to-gether over mistakes committed in copying; unnecessary maledictions, hissed, rather than spoken, in the heat of business; and especially by a continual discon-tent with the height of the table where he worked. Though of a very ingenious mechanical turn, Nippers could never get this table to suit him. He put chips un-der it, blocks of various sorts, bits of pasteboard, and at last went so far as to at-tempt an exquisite adjustment by final pieces of folded blotting-paper. But no invention would answer. If, for the sake of easing his back, he brought the table lid at a sharp angle well up towards his chin, and wrote there like a man using the steep roof of a Dutch house for his desk: — then he declared that it stopped the circulation in his arms. If now he lowered the table to his waistbands, and stooped over it in writing, then there was a sore aching in his back. In short, the truth of the matter was, Nippers knew not what he wanted. Or, if he wanted any thing, it was to be rid of a scrivener's table altogether. Among the manifes-tations of his diseased ambition was a fondness he had for receiving visits from certain ambiguous-looking fellows in seedy coats, whom he called his clients. In-deed I was aware that not only was he, at times considerable of a ward-politician, but he occasionally did a little business at the Justices' courts, and was not un-known on the steps of the Tombs. I have good reason to believe, however, that one individual who called upon him at my chambers, and who, with a grand air, he insisted was his client, was no other than a dun, and the alleged title-deed, a bill. But with all his failings, and the annoyances he caused me, Nippers, like his compatriot Turkey, was a very useful man to me; wrote a neat, swift hand; and, when he chose, was not deficient in a gentlemanly sort of deportment. Added to this, he always dressed in a gentlemanly sort of way; and so, incidentally, re-flected credit upon my chambers. Whereas with respect to Turkey, I had much ado to keep him from being a reproach to me. His clothes were apt to look oily and smell of eating-houses. He wore his pantaloons very loose and baggy in summer. His coats were execrable; his hat not to be handled. But while the hat was a thing of indifference to me, inasmuch as his natural civility and deference, as a dependent Englishman, always led him to doff it the moment he entered the room, yet his coat was another matter. Concerning his coats, I reasoned with him; but with no effect. The truth was, I suppose, that a man with so small an income, could not afford to sport such a lustrous face and a lustrous coat at one and the same time. As Nippers once observed, Turkey's money went chiefly for red ink. One winter day I presented Turkey with a highly-respectable looking coat of my own, a padded gray coat, of a most comfortable warmth, and which buttoned straight up from the knee to the neck. I thought Turkey would appre-ciate the favor, and abate his rashness and obstreperousness of afternoons. But no. I verily believe that buttoning himself up in so downy and blanket-like a coat had a pernicious effect upon him; upon the same principle that too much oats are bad for horses. In fact, precisely as a rash, restive horse is said to feel his oats, so Turkey felt his coat. It made him insolent. He was a man whom prosperity harmed.

Though concerning the self-indulgent habits of Turkey I had my own private surmises, yet touching Nippers I was well persuaded that whatever might be his faults in other respects, he was, at least, a temperate young man. But indeed, nature herself seemed to have been his vintner, and at his birth charged him so thoroughly with an irritable, brandy-like disposition, that all subsequent potations were needless. When I consider how, amid the stillness of my chambers, Nippers would sometimes impatiently rise from his seat, and stooping over his table, spread his arms wide apart, seize the whole desk, and move it, and jerk it, with a grim, grinding motion on the floor, as if the table were a perverse voluntary agent, intent on thwarting and vexing him; I plainly perceive that for Nippers, brandy and water were altogether superfluous.

It was fortunate for me that, owing to its peculiar cause—indigestion—the irritability and consequent nervousness of Nippers, were mainly observable in the morning, while in the afternoon he was comparatively mild. So that Turkey's paroxysms only coming on about twelve o'clock, I never had to do with their eccentricities at one time. Their fits relieved each other like guards. When Nippers' was on, Turkey's was off; and *vice versa*. This was a good natural arrangement under the circumstances.

Ginger Nut, the third on my list, was a lad some twelve years old. His father was a carman, ambitious of seeing his son on the bench instead of a cart, before he died. So he sent him to my office as student at law, errand boy, and cleaner and sweeper, at the rate of one dollar a week. He had a little desk to himself, but he did not use it much. Upon inspection, the drawer exhibited a great array of the shells of various sorts of nuts. Indeed, to this quick-witted youth the whole noble science of the law was contained in a nut-shell. Not the least among the employments of Ginger Nut, as well as one which he discharged with the most alacrity, was his duty as cake and apple purveyor for Turkey and Nippers. Copying law papers being proverbially a dry, husky sort of business, my two scriveners were fain to moisten their mouths very often with Spitzenbergs to be had at the numerous stalls nigh the Custom House and Post Office. Also, they sent Ginger Nut very frequently for that peculiar cake — small, flat, round, and very spicy — after which he had been named by them. Of a cold morning when business was but dull, Turkey would gobble up scores of these cakes, as if they were mere wafers — indeed they sell them at the rate of six or eight for a penny — the scrape of his pen blending with the crunching of the crisp particles in his mouth. Of all the fiery afternoon blunders and flurried rashnesses of Turkey, was his once moistening a ginger-cake between his lips, and clapping it on to a mortgage for a seal. I came within an ace of dismissing him then. But he mollified me by making an oriental bow, and saying — "With submission, sir, it was generous of me to find you in stationery on my own account."

Now my original business — that of a conveyancer and title hunter, and drawer-up of recondite documents of all sorts — was considerably increased by receiving the master's office. There was now great work for scriveners. Not only must I push the clerks already with me, but I must have additional help. In answer to my advertisement, a motionless young man one morning, stood upon my office threshold, the door being open, for it was summer. I can see that figure now — pallidly neat, pitiably respectable, incurably forlorn! It was Bartleby.

After a few words touching his qualifications, I engaged him, glad to have among my corps of copyists a man of so singularly sedate an aspect, which I thought might operate beneficially upon the flighty temper of Turkey, and the fiery one of Nippers.

I should have stated before that ground glass folding-doors divided my premises into two parts, one of which was occupied by my scriveners, the other by myself. According to my humor I threw open these doors, or closed them. I resolved to assign Bartleby a corner by the folding-doors, but on my side of them, so as to have this quiet man within easy call, in case any trifling thing was to be done. I placed his desk close up to a small side-window in that part of the room, a window which originally had afforded a lateral view of certain grimy back-yards and bricks, but which, owing to subsequent erections, commanded at present no view at all, though it gave some light. Within three feet of the panes was a wall, and the light came down from far above, between two lofty buildings, as from a very small opening in a dome. Still further to a satisfactory arrangement, I procured a high green folding screen, which might entirely isolate Bartleby from my sight, though not remove him from my voice. And thus, in a manner, privacy and society were conjoined.

At first Bartleby did an extraordinary quantity of writing. As if long famishing for something to copy, he seemed to gorge himself on my documents. There was no pause for digestion. He ran a day and night line, copying by sun-light and by candle-light. I should have been quite delighted with his application, had he been cheerfully industrious. But he wrote on silently, palely, mechanically.

It is, of course, an indispensable part of a scrivener's business to verify the accuracy of his copy, word by word. Where there are two or more scriveners in an office, they assist each other in this examination, one reading from the copy, the other holding the original. It is a very dull, wearisome, and lethargic affair. I can readily imagine that to some sanguine temperaments it would be altogether intolerable. For example, I cannot credit that the mettlesome poet Byron would have contentedly sat down with Bartleby to examine a law document of, say five hundred pages, closely written in a crimpy hand.

Now and then, in the haste of business, it had been my habit to assist in comparing some brief document myself, calling Turkey or Nippers for this purpose. One object I had in placing Bartleby so handy to me behind the screen, was to avail myself of his services on such trivial occasions. It was on the third day, I think, of his being with me, and before any necessity had arisen for having his own writing examined that, being much hurried to complete a small affair I had in hand, I abruptly called to Bartleby. In my haste and natural expectancy of instant compliance, I sat with my head bent over the original on my desk, and my right hand sideways, and somewhat nervously extended with the copy, so that immediately upon emerging from his retreat, Bartleby might snatch it and proceed to business without the least delay.

In this very attitude did I sit when I called to him, rapidly stating what it was I wanted him to do — namely, to examine a small paper with me. Imagine my surprise, nay, my consternation, when without moving from his privacy, Bartleby in a singularly mild, firm voice, replied, "I would prefer not to."

I sat awhile in perfect silence, rallying my stunned faculties. Immediately it occurred to me that my ears had deceived me, or Bartleby had entirely misunderstood my meaning. I repeated my request in the clearest tone I could assume. But in quite as clear a one came the previous reply, "I would prefer not to."

"Prefer not to," echoed I, rising in high excitement, and crossing the room with a stride. "What do you mean? Are you moon-struck? I want you to help me compare this sheet here — take it," and I thrust it towards him.

"I would prefer not to," said he.

I looked at him steadfastly. His face was leanly composed; his gray eye dimly calm. Not a wrinkle of agitation rippled him. Had there been the least uneasiness, anger, impatience or impertinence in his manner; in other words, had there been any thing ordinarily human about him, doubtless I should have violently dismissed him from the premises. But as it was, I should have as soon thought of turning my pale plaster-of-paris bust of Cicero out of doors. I stood gazing at him awhile, as he went on with his own writing, and then reseated myself at my desk. This is very strange, thought I. What had one best do? But my business hurried me. I concluded to forget the matter for the present, reserving it for my future leisure. So calling Nippers from the other room, the paper was speedily examined.

A few days after this, Bartleby concluded four lengthy documents, being quadruplicates of a week's testimony taken before me in my High Court of Chancery. It became necessary to examine them. It was an important suit, and great accuracy was imperative. Having all things arranged I called Turkey, Nippers and Ginger Nut from the next room, meaning to place the four copies in the hands of my four clerks, while I should read from the original. Accordingly Turkey, Nippers and Ginger Nut had taken their seats in a row, each with his document in hand, when I called to Bartleby to join this interesting group.

"Bartleby! quick, I am waiting."

I heard a slow scrape of his chair legs on the uncarpeted floor, and soon he appeared standing at the entrance of his hermitage.

"What is wanted?" said he mildly.

"The copies, the copies," said I hurriedly. "We are going to examine them. There" — and I held towards him the fourth quadruplicate.

"I would prefer not to," he said, and gently disappeared behind the screen.

For a few moments I was turned into a pillar of salt, standing at the head of my seated column of clerks. Recovering myself, I advanced towards the screen, and demanded the reason for such extraordinary conduct.

"*Why* do you refuse?"

"I would prefer not to."

With any other man I should have flown outright into a dreadful passion, scorned all further words, and thrust him ignominiously from my presence. But there was something about Bartleby that not only strangely disarmed me, but in a wonderful manner touched and disconcerted me. I began to reason with him.

"These are your own copies we are about to examine. It is labor saving to you, because one examination will answer for your four papers. It is common usage. Every copyist is bound to help examine his copy. Is it not so? Will you not speak? Answer!"

"I prefer not to," he replied in a flute-like tone. It seemed to me that while I had been addressing him, he carefully revolved every statement that I made; fully comprehended the meaning; could not gainsay the irresistible conclusion; but, at the same time, some paramount consideration prevailed with him to reply as he did.

"You are decided, then, not to comply with my request — a request made according to common usage and common sense?"

He briefly gave me to understand that on that point my judgment was sound. Yes: his decision was irreversible.

It is not seldom the case that when a man is browbeaten in some unprecedented and violently unreasonable way, he begins to stagger in his own plainest faith. He begins, as it were, vaguely to surmise that, wonderful as it may be, all the justice and all the reason is on the other side. Accordingly, if any disinterested persons are present, he turns to them for some reinforcement for his own faltering mind.

"Turkey," said I, "what do you think of this? Am I not right?"

"With submission, sir," said Turkey, with his blandest tone, "I think that you are."

"Nippers," said I, "what do *you* think of it?"

"I think I should kick him out of the office."

(The reader of nice perceptions will here perceive that, it being morning, Turkey's answer is couched in polite and tranquil terms, but Nippers replies in ill-tempered ones. Or, to repeat a previous sentence, Nippers's ugly mood was on duty, and Turkey's off.)

"Ginger Nut," said I, willing to enlist the smallest suffrage in my behalf, "what do *you* think of it?"

"I think, sir, he's a little *luny*," replied Ginger Nut with a grin.

"You hear what they say," said I, turning towards the screen, "come forth and do your duty."

But he vouchsafed no reply. I pondered a moment in sore perplexity. But once more business hurried me. I determined again to postpone the consideration of this dilemma to my future leisure. With a little trouble we made out to examine the papers without Bartleby, though at every page or two, Turkey deferentially dropped his opinion that this proceeding was quite out of the common; while Nippers, twitching in his chair with a dyspeptic nervousness, ground out between his set teeth occasional hissing maledictions against the stubborn oaf behind the screen. And for his (Nippers's) part, this was the first and the last time he would do another man's business without pay.

Meanwhile Bartleby sat in his hermitage, oblivious to every thing but his own peculiar business there.

Some days passed, the scrivener being employed upon another lengthy work. His late remarkable conduct led me to regard his ways narrowly. I observed that he never went to dinner; indeed that he never went any where. As yet I had never of my personal knowledge known him to be outside of my office. He was a perpetual sentry in the corner. At about eleven o'clock though, in the morning, I noticed that Ginger Nut would advance toward the opening in Bartleby's screen, as if silently beckoned thither by a gesture invisible to me where I sat. The boy would then leave the office jingling a few pence, and reappear with a handful of ginger-nuts which he delivered in the hermitage, receiving two of the cakes for his trouble.

He lives, then, on ginger-nuts, thought I; never eats a dinner, properly speaking; he must be a vegetarian then; but no; he never eats even vegetables, he eats nothing but ginger-nuts. My mind then ran on in reveries concerning the probable effects upon the human constitution of living entirely on ginger-nuts. Ginger-nuts are so called because they contain ginger as one of their peculiar constituents, and the final flavoring one. Now what was ginger? A hot, spicy thing. Was Bartleby hot and spicy? Not at all. Ginger, then, had no effect upon Bartleby. Probably he preferred it should have none.

Nothing so aggravates an earnest person as a passive resistance. If the individual so resisted be of a not inhumane temper, and the resisting one perfectly harmless in his passivity; then, in the better moods of the former, he will endeavor charitably to construe to his imagination what proves impossible to be solved by his judgment. Even so, for the most part, I regarded Bartleby and his ways. Poor fellow! thought I, he means no mischief; it is plain he intends no insolence; his aspect sufficiently evinces that his eccentricities are involuntary. He is useful to me. I can get along with him. If I turn him away, the chances are he will fall in with some less indulgent employer, and then he will be rudely treated, and perhaps driven forth miserably to starve. Yes. Here I can cheaply purchase a delicious self-approval. To befriend Bartleby; to humor him in his strange wilfulness, will cost me little or nothing, while I lay up in my soul what will eventually prove a sweet morsel for my conscience. But this mood was not invariable with me. The passiveness of Bartleby sometimes irritated me. I felt strangely goaded on to encounter him in new opposition, to elicit some angry spark from him answerable to my own. But indeed I might as well have essayed to strike fire with my knuckles against a bit of Windsor soap. But one afternoon the evil impulse in me mastered me, and the following little scene ensued:

"Bartleby," said I, "when those papers are all copied, I will compare them with you."

"I would prefer not to."

"How? Surely you do not mean to persist in that mulish vagary?"

No answer.

I threw open the folding-doors near by, and turning upon Turkey and Nippers, exclaimed in an excited manner —

"He says, a second time, he won't examine his papers. What do you think of it, Turkey?"

It was afternoon, be it remembered. Turkey sat glowing like a brass boiler, his bald head steaming, his hands reeling among his blotted papers.

"Think of it?" roared Turkey; "I think I'll just step behind his screen, and black his eyes for him!"

So saying, Turkey rose to his feet and threw his arms into a pugilistic position. He was hurrying away to make good his promise, when I detained him, alarmed at the effect of incautiously rousing Turkey's combativeness after dinner.

"Sit down, Turkey," said I, "and hear what Nippers has to say. What do you think of it, Nippers? Would I not be justified in immediately dismissing Bartleby?"

"Excuse me, that is for you to decide, sir. I think his conduct quite unusual, and indeed unjust, as regards Turkey and myself. But it may only be a passing whim."

"Ah," exclaimed I, "you have strangely changed your mind then — you speak very gently of him now."

"All beer," cried Turkey; "gentleness is effects of beer — Nippers and I dined together to-day. You see how gentle I am, sir. Shall I go and black his eyes?"

"You refer to Bartleby, I suppose. No, not to-day, Turkey," I replied; "pray, put up your fists."

I closed the doors, and again advanced towards Bartleby. I felt additional incentives tempting me to my fate. I burned to be rebelled against again. I remembered that Bartleby never left the office.

"Bartleby," said I, "Ginger Nut is away; just step round to the Post Office, won't you? (it was but a three minutes walk,) and see if there is any thing for me."

"I would prefer not to."

"You *will* not?"

"I *prefer* not."

I staggered to my desk, and sat there in a deep study. My blind inveteracy returned. Was there any other thing in which I could procure myself to be ignominiously repulsed by this lean, penniless wight? — my hired clerk? What added thing is there, perfectly reasonable, that he will be sure to refuse to do?

"Bartleby!"

No answer.

"Bartleby," in a louder tone.

No answer.

"Bartleby," I roared.

Like a very ghost, agreeably to the laws of magical invocation, at the third summons, he appeared at the entrance of his hermitage.

"Go to the next room, and tell Nippers to come to me."

"I prefer not to," he respectfully and slowly said, and mildly disappeared.

"Very good, Bartleby," said I, in a quiet sort of serenely severe self-possessed tone, intimating the unalterable purpose of some terrible retribution very close at hand. At the moment I half intended something of the kind. But upon the whole, as it was drawing towards my dinner-hour, I thought it best to put on my hat and walk home for the day, suffering much from perplexity and distress of mind.

Shall I acknowledge it? The conclusion of this whole business was, that it soon became a fixed fact of my chambers that a pale young scrivener, by the name of Bartleby, had a desk there; that he copied for me at the usual rate of four cents a folio (one hundred words); but he was permanently exempt from examining the work done by him, that duty being transferred to Turkey and Nippers, one of compliment doubtless to their superior acuteness; moreover, said Bartleby was never on any account to be dispatched on the most trivial errand of any sort; and that even if entreated to take upon him such a matter, it was generally understood that he would prefer not to — in other words, that he would refuse point-blank.

As days passed on, I became considerably reconciled to Bartleby. His steadiness, his freedom from all dissipation, his incessant industry (except when he chose to throw himself into a standing revery behind his screen), his great stillness, his unalterableness of demeanor under all circumstances, made him a valuable acquisition. One primo thing was this, — *he was always there;* — first in the morning, continually through the day, and the last at night. I had a singular confidence in his honesty. I felt my most precious papers perfectly safe in his hands. Sometimes to be sure I could not, for the very soul of me, avoid falling into sudden spasmodic passions with him. For it was exceeding difficult to bear in mind all the time those strange peculiarities, privileges, and unheard of exemptions, forming the tacit stipulations on Bartleby's part under which he remained in my office. Now and then, in the eagerness of dispatching pressing business, I would inadvertently summon Bartleby, in a short, rapid tone, to put his finger, say, on the incipient tie of a bit of red tape with which I was about compressing some papers. Of course, from behind the screen the usual answer, "I prefer not to," was sure to come; and then, how could a human creature with the common infirmities of our nature, refrain from bitterly exclaiming upon such perverseness — such unreasonableness. However, every added repulse of this sort which I received only tended to lessen the probability of my repeating the inadvertence.

Here it must be said, that according to the custom of most legal gentlemen occupying chambers in densely-populated law buildings, there were several keys to my door. One was kept by a woman residing in the attic, which person weekly scrubbed and daily swept and dusted my apartments. Another was kept by Turkey for convenience sake. The third I sometimes carried in my own pocket. The fourth I knew not who had.

Now, one Sunday morning I happened to go to Trinity Church, to hear a celebrated preacher, and finding myself rather early on the ground, I thought I would walk round to my chambers for a while. Luckily I had my key with me; but upon applying it to the lock, I found it resisted by something inserted from the inside. Quite surprised, I called out; when to my consternation a key was turned from within; and thrusting his lean visage at me, and holding the door ajar, the apparition of Bartleby appeared, in his shirt sleeves, and otherwise in a strangely tattered dishabille, saying quietly that he was sorry, but he was deeply engaged just then, and — preferred not admitting me at present. In a brief word or two, he moreover added, that perhaps I had better walk round the block two or three times, and by that time he would probably have concluded his affairs.

Now, the utterly unsurmised appearance of Bartleby, tenanting my law-chambers of a Sunday morning, with his cadaverously gentlemanly *nonchalance,* yet withal firm and self-possessed, had such a strange effect upon me, that incontinently I slunk away from my own door, and did as desired. But not without sundry twinges of impotent rebellion against the mild effrontery of this unaccountable scrivener. Indeed, it was his wonderful mildness chiefly, which not only disarmed me, but unmanned me, as it were. For I consider that one, for the time, is a sort of unmanned when he tranquilly permits his hired clerk to dictate to him, and order him away from his own premises. Furthermore, I was full of uneasiness as to what Bartleby could possibly be doing in my office in his shirt sleeves, and in an otherwise dismantled condition of a Sunday morning. Was any thing amiss going on? Nay, that was out of the question. It was not to be thought of for a moment that Bartleby was an immoral person. But what could he be doing there? — copying? Nay again, whatever might be his eccentricities, Bartleby was an eminently decorous person. He would be the last man to sit down to his desk in any state approaching to nudity. Besides, it was Sunday; and there was something about Bartleby that forbade the supposition that he would by any secular occupation violate the proprieties of the day.

Nevertheless, my mind was not pacified; and full of a restless curiosity, at last I returned to the door. Without hindrance I inserted my key, opened it, and entered. Bartleby was not to be seen. I looked round anxiously, peeped behind his screen; but it was very plain that he was gone. Upon more closely examining the place, I surmised that for an indefinite period Bartleby must have ate, dressed, and slept in my office, and that too without plate, mirror, or bed. The cushioned seat of a rickety old sofa in one corner bore the faint impress of a lean, reclining form. Rolled away under his desk, I found a blanket; under the empty grate, a blacking box and brush; on a chair, a tin basin, with soap and a ragged towel; in a newspaper a few crumbs of ginger-nuts and a morsel of cheese. Yes, thought I, it is evident enough that Bartleby has been making his home here, keeping bachelor's hall all by himself. Immediately then the thought came sweeping across me, What miserable friendlessness and loneliness are here revealed! His poverty is great; but his solitude, how horrible! Think of it. Of a Sunday, Wall-street is deserted as Petra; and every night of every day it is an emptiness. This building too, which of week-days hums with industry and life, at nightfall echoes with sheer vacancy, and all through Sunday is forlorn. And here Bartleby makes his home; sole spectator of a solitude which he has seen all populous — a sort of innocent and transformed Marius brooding among the ruins of Carthage!

For the first time in my life a feeling of overpowering stinging melancholy seized me. Before I had never experienced aught but a not-unpleasing sadness. The bond of a common humanity now drew me irresistibly to gloom. A fraternal melancholy! For both I and Bartleby were sons of Adam. I remembered the bright silks and sparkling faces I had seen that day, in gala trim, swan-like sailing down the Mississippi of Broadway; and I contrasted them with the pallid copyist, and thought to myself, Ah, happiness courts the light, so we deem the world is gay; but misery hides aloof, so we deem that misery there is none. These sad fancyings — chimeras, doubtless, of a sick and silly brain — led on to other and more special thoughts, concerning the eccentricities of Bartleby. Presentiments of strange discoveries hovered round me. The scrivener's pale form appeared to me laid out, among uncaring strangers, in its shivering winding sheet.

Suddenly I was attracted by Bartleby's closed desk, the key in open sight left in the lock.

I mean no mischief, seek the gratification of no heartless curiosity, thought I; besides, the desk is mine, and its contents too, so I will make bold to look within. Every thing was methodically arranged, the papers smoothly placed. The pigeon holes were deep, and removing the files of documents, I groped into their recesses. Presently I felt something there, and dragged it out. It was an old bandanna handkerchief, heavy and knotted. I opened it, and saw it was a savings' bank.

I now recalled all the quiet mysteries which I had noted in the man. I remembered that he never spoke but to answer; that though at intervals he had considerable time to himself, yet I had never seen him reading — no, not even a newspaper; that for long periods he would stand looking out, at his pale window behind the screen, upon the dead brick wall; I was quite sure he never visited any refectory or eating house; while his pale face clearly indicated that he never drank beer like Turkey, or tea and coffee even, like other men; that he never went any where in particular that I could learn; never went out for a walk, unless indeed that was the case at present; that he had declined telling who he was, or whence he came, or whether he had any relatives in the world; that though so thin and pale, he never complained of ill health. And more than all, I remembered a certain unconscious air of pallid — how shall I call it? — of pallid haughtiness, say, or rather an austere reserve about him, which had positively awed me into my tame compliance with his eccentricities, when I had feared to ask him to do the slightest incidental thing for me, even though I might know, from his long-continued motionlessness, that behind his screen he must be standing in one of those dead-wall reveries of his.

Revolving all these things, and coupling them with the recently discovered fact that he made my office his constant abiding place and home, and not forgetful of his morbid moodiness; revolving all these things, a prudential feeling began to steal over me. My first emotions had been those of pure melancholy and sincerest pity; but just in proportion as the forlornness of Bartleby grew and grew to my imagination, did that same melancholy merge into fear, that pity into repulsion. So true it is, and so terrible too, that up to a certain point the thought or sight of misery enlists our best affections; but, in certain special cases, beyond that point it does not. They err who would assert that invariably this is owing to the inherent selfishness of the human heart. It rather proceeds from a certain hopelessness of remedying excessive and organic ill. To a sensitive being, pity is not seldom pain. And when at last it is perceived that such pity cannot lead to effectual succor, common sense bids the soul be rid of it. What I saw that morning persuaded me that the scrivener was the victim of innate and incurable disorder. I might give alms to his body; but his body did not pain him; it was his soul that suffered, and his soul I could not reach.

I did not accomplish the purpose of going to Trinity Church that morning. Somehow, the things I had seen disqualified me for the time from church-going. I walked homeward, thinking what I would do with Bartleby. Finally, I resolved upon this; — I would put certain calm questions to him the next morning, touching his history, &c., and if he declined to answer them openly and unreservedly (and I supposed he would prefer not), then to give him a twenty dollar bill over and above whatever I might owe him, and tell him his services were no longer required; but that if in any other way I could assist him, I would be happy to do so, especially if he desired to return to his native place, wherever that might be, I would willingly help to defray the expenses. Moreover, if, after reaching home, he found himself at any time in want of aid, a letter from him would be sure of a reply.

The next morning came.

"Bartleby," said I, gently calling to him behind his screen.

No reply.

"Bartleby," said I, in a still gentler tone, "come here; I am not going to ask you to do any thing you would prefer not to do — I simply wish to speak to you."

Upon this he noiselessly slid into view.

"Will you tell me, Bartleby, where you were born?"

"I would prefer not to."

"Will you tell me, *any thing* about yourself?"

"I would prefer not to."

"But what reasonable objection can you have to speak to me? I feel friendly towards you."

He did not look at me while I spoke, but kept his glance fixed upon my bust of Cicero, which as I then sat, was directly behind me, some six inches above my head.

"What is your answer, Bartleby?" said I, after waiting a considerable time for a reply, during which his countenance remained immovable, only there was the faintest conceivable tremor of the white attenuated mouth.

"At present I prefer to give no answer," he said, and retired into his hermitage.

It was rather weak in me I confess, but his manner on this occasion nettled me. Not only did there seem to lurk in it a certain calm disdain, but his perverseness seemed ungrateful, considering the undeniable good usage and indulgence he had received from me.

Again I sat ruminating what I should do. Mortified as I was at his behavior, and resolved as I had been to dismiss him when I entered my office, nevertheless I strangely felt something superstitious knocking at my heart, and forbidding me to carry out my purpose, and denouncing me for a villain if I dared to breathe one bitter word against this forlornest of mankind. At last, familiarly drawing my chair behind his screen, I sat down and said: "Bartleby, never mind then about revealing your history; but let me entreat you, as a friend, to comply as far as may be with the usages of this office. Say now you will help to examine papers to-morrow or next day: in short, say now that in a day or two you will begin to be a little reasonable: — say so, Bartleby."

"At present I would prefer not to be a little reasonable," was his mildly cadaverous reply.

Just then the folding-doors opened, and Nippers approached. He seemed suffering from an unusually bad night's rest, induced by severer indigestion than common. He overheard those final words of Bartleby.

"*Prefer not*, eh?" gritted Nippers — "I'd *prefer* him, if I were you, sir," addressing me — "I'd *prefer* him; I'd give him preferences, the stubborn mule! What is it sir, pray, that he *prefers* not to do now?"

Bartleby moved not a limb.

"Mr. Nippers," said I, "I'd prefer that you would withdraw for the present."

Somehow, of late I had got into the way of involuntarily using this word "prefer" upon all sorts of not exactly suitable occasions. And I trembled to think that my contact with the scrivener had already and seriously affected me in a mental way. And what further and deeper aberration might it not yet produce? This apprehension had not been without efficacy in determining me to summary means.

As Nippers, looking very sour and sulky, was departing, Turkey blandly and deferentially approached.

"With submission sir," said he, "yesterday I was thinking about Bartleby here, and I think that if he would but prefer to take a quart of good ale every day, it would do much towards mending him, and enabling him to assist in examining his papers."

"So you have got the word too," said I, slightly excited.

"With submission, what word, sir," asked Turkey, respectfully crowding himself into the contracted space behind the screen, and by so doing, making me jostle the scrivener. "What word, sir?"

"I would prefer to be left alone here," said Bartleby, as if offended at being mobbed in his privacy.

"*That's* the word, Turkey," said I — "*that's* it."

"Oh, *prefer?* oh yes — queer word. I never use it myself. But, sir, as I was saying, if he would but prefer —"

"Turkey," interrupted I, "you will please withdraw."

"Oh certainly, sir, if you prefer that I should."

As he opened the folding-door to retire, Nippers at his desk caught a glimpse of me, and asked whether I would prefer to have a certain paper copied on blue paper or white. He did not in the least roguishly accent the word prefer. It was plain that it involuntarily rolled from his tongue. I thought to myself, surely I must get rid of a demented man, who already has in some degree turned the tongues, if not the heads of myself and clerks. But I thought it prudent not to break the dismission at once.

The next day I noticed that Bartleby did nothing but stand at his window in his dead-wall revery. Upon asking him why he did not write, he said that he had decided upon doing no more writing.

"Why, how now? what next?" exclaimed I, "do no more writing?"

"No more."

"And what is the reason?"

"Do you not see the reason for yourself," he indifferently replied.

I looked steadfastly at him, and perceived that his eyes looked dull and glazed. Instantly it occurred to me, that his unexampled diligence in copying by his dim window for the first few weeks of his stay with me might have temporarily impaired his vision.

I was touched. I said something in condolence with him. I hinted that of course he did wisely in abstaining from writing for a while; and urged him to embrace that opportunity of taking wholesome exercise in the open air. This, however, he did not do. A few days after this, my other clerks being absent, and being in a great hurry to dispatch certain letters by the mail, I thought that, having nothing else earthly to do, Bartleby would surely be less inflexible than usual, and carry these letters to the post-office. But he blankly declined. So, much to my inconvenience, I went myself.

Still added days went by. Whether Bartleby's eyes improved or not, I could not say. To all appearance, I thought they did. But when I asked him if they did, he vouchsafed no answer. At all events, he would do no copying. At last, in reply to my urgings, he informed me that he had permanently given up copying.

"What!" exclaimed I; "suppose your eyes should get entirely well — better than ever before — would you not copy then?"

"I have given up copying," he answered, and slid aside.

He remained as ever, a fixture in my chamber. Nay — if that were possible — he became still more of a fixture than before. What was to be done? He would do nothing in the office: why should he stay there? In plain fact, he had now become a millstone to me, not only useless as a necklace, but afflictive to bear. Yet I was sorry for him. I speak less than truth when I say that, on his own account, he occasioned me uneasiness. If he would but have named a single relative or friend, I would instantly have written, and urged their taking the poor fellow away to some convenient retreat. But he seemed alone, absolutely alone in the universe. A bit of wreck in the mid Atlantic. At length, necessities connected with my business tyrannized over all other considerations. Decently as I could, I told Bartleby that in six days' time he must unconditionally leave the office. I warned him to take measures, in the interval, for procuring some other abode. I offered to assist him in this endeavor, if he himself would but take the first step towards a removal. "And when you finally quit me, Bartleby," added I, "I shall see that you go not away entirely unprovided. Six days from this hour, remember."

At the expiration of that period, I peeped behind the screen, and lo! Bartleby was there.

I buttoned up my coat, balanced myself; advanced slowly towards him, touched his shoulder, and said, "The time has come; you must quit this place; I am sorry for you; here is money; but you must go."

"I would prefer not," he replied, with his back still towards me.

"You *must*."

He remained silent.

Now I had an unbounded confidence in this man's common honesty. He had frequently restored to me sixpences and shillings carelessly dropped upon the floor, for I am apt to be very reckless in such shirt-button affairs. The proceeding then which followed will not be deemed extraordinary.

"Bartleby," said I, "I owe you twelve dollars on account; here are thirty-two; the odd twenty are yours. — Will you take it?" and I handed the bills towards him.

But he made no motion.

"I will leave them here then," putting them under a weight on the table. Then taking my hat and cane and going to the door I tranquilly turned and added — "After you have removed your things from these offices, Bartleby, you will of course lock the door — since every one is now gone for the day but you — and if you please, slip your key underneath the mat, so that I may have it in the morning. I shall not see you again; so good-bye to you. If hereafter in your new place of abode I can be of any service to you, do not fail to advise me by letter. Good-bye, Bartleby, and fare you well."

But he answered not a word; like the last column of some ruined temple, he remained standing mute and solitary in the middle of the otherwise deserted room.

As I walked home in a pensive mood, my vanity got the better of my pity. I could not but highly plume myself on my masterly management in getting rid of Bartleby. Masterly I call it, and such it must appear to any dispassionate thinker. The beauty of my procedure seemed to consist in its perfect quietness. There was no vulgar bullying, no bravado of any sort, no choleric hectoring, and striding to and fro across the apartment, jerking out vehement commands for Bartleby to bundle himself off with his beggarly traps. Nothing of the kind. Without loudly bidding Bartleby depart — as an inferior genius might have done — I *assumed* the ground that depart he must; and upon that assumption built all I had to say. The more I thought over my procedure, the more I was charmed with it. Nevertheless, next morning, upon awakening, I had my doubts, — I had somehow slept off the fumes of vanity. One of the coolest and wisest hours a man has, is just after he awakes in the morning. My procedure seemed as sagacious as ever, — but only in theory. How it would prove in practice — there was the rub. It was truly a beautiful thought to have assumed Bartleby's departure; but, after all, that assumption was simply my own, and none of Bartleby's. The great point was, not whether I had assumed that he would quit me, but whether he would prefer so to do. He was more a man of preferences than assumptions.

After breakfast, I walked down town, arguing the probabilities *pro* and *con*. One moment I thought it would prove a miserable failure, and Bartleby would be found all alive at my office as usual; the next moment it seemed certain that I should see his chair empty. And so I kept veering about. At the corner of Broadway and Canal-street, I saw quite an excited group of people standing in earnest conversation.

"I'll take odds he doesn't," said a voice as I passed.

"Doesn't go? — done!" said I, "put up your money."

I was instinctively putting my hand in my pocket to produce my own, when I remembered that this was an election day. The words I had overheard bore no reference to Bartleby, but to the success or non-success of some candidate for the mayoralty. In my intent frame of mind, I had, as it were, imagined that all Broadway shared in my excitement, and were debating the same question with me. I passed on, very thankful that the uproar of the street screened my momentary absent-mindedness.

As I had intended, I was earlier than usual at my office door. I stood listening for a moment. All was still. He must be gone. I tried the knob. The door was locked. Yes, my procedure had worked to a charm; he indeed must be vanished. Yet a certain melancholy mixed with this: I was almost sorry for my brilliant success. I was fumbling under the door mat for the key, which Bartleby was to have left there for me, when accidentally my knee knocked against a panel, producing a summoning sound, and in response a voice came to me from within — "Not yet; I am occupied."

It was Bartleby.

I was thunderstruck. For an instant I stood like the man who, pipe in mouth, was killed one cloudless afternoon long ago in Virginia, by summer lightning; at his own warm open window he was killed, and remained leaning out there upon the dreamy afternoon, till some one touched him, when he fell.

"Not gone!" I murmured at last. But again obeying that wondrous ascendancy which the inscrutable scrivener had over me, and from which ascendancy, for all my chafing, I could not completely escape, I slowly went down stairs and out into the street, and while walking round the block, considered what I should next do in this unheard-of perplexity. Turn the man out by an actual thrusting I could not; to drive him away by calling him hard names would not do; calling in the police was an unpleasant idea; and yet, permit him to enjoy his cadaverous triumph over me, — this too I could not think of. What was to be done? or, if nothing could be done, was there any thing further that I could *assume* in the matter? Yes, as before I had prospectively assumed that Bartleby would depart, so now I might retrospectively assume that departed he was. In the legitimate carrying out of this assumption, I might enter my office in a great hurry, and pretending not to see Bartleby at all, walk straight against him as if he were air. Such a proceeding would in a singular degree have the appearance of a home-thrust. It was hardly possible that Bartleby could withstand such an application of the doctrine of assumptions. But upon second thoughts the success of the plan seemed rather dubious. I resolved to argue the matter over with him again.

"Bartleby," said I, entering the office, with a quietly severe expression, "I am seriously displeased. I am pained, Bartleby. I had thought better of you. I had imagined you of such a gentlemanly organization, that in any delicate dilemma a slight hint would suffice — in short, an assumption. But it appears I am deceived. Why," I added, unaffectedly starting, "you have not even touched that money yet," pointing to it, just where I had left it the evening previous.

He answered nothing.

"Will you, or will you not, quit me?" I now demanded in a sudden passion, advancing close to him.

"I would prefer *not* to quit you," he replied, gently emphasizing the *not*.

"What earthly right have you to stay here? Do you pay any rent? Do you pay my taxes? Or is this property yours?"

He answered nothing.

"Are you ready to go on and write now? Are your eyes recovered? Could you copy a small paper for me this morning? or help examine a few lines? or step round to the post-office? In a word, will you do any thing at all, to give a coloring to your refusal to depart the premises?"

He silently retired into his hermitage.

I was now in such a state of nervous resentment that I thought it but prudent to check myself at present from further demonstrations. Bartleby and I were alone. I remembered the tragedy of the unfortunate Adams and the still more unfortunate Colt in the solitary office of the latter; and how poor Colt, being dreadfully incensed by Adams, and imprudently permitting himself to get wildly excited, was at unawares hurried into his fatal act — an act which certainly no man could possibly deplore more than the actor himself. Often it had occurred to me in my ponderings upon the subject, that had that altercation taken place in the public street, or at a private residence, it would not have terminated as it did. It was the circumstance of being alone in a solitary office, up stairs, of a building entirely unhallowed by humanizing domestic associations — an uncarpeted office, doubtless, of a dusty, haggard sort of appearance; — this it must have been, which greatly helped to enhance the irritable desperation of the hapless Colt.

But when this old Adam of resentment rose in me and tempted me concerning Bartleby, I grappled him and threw him. How? Why, simply by recalling the divine injunction: "A new commandment give I unto you, that ye love one another." Yes, this it was that saved me. Aside from higher considerations, charity often operates as a vastly wise and prudent principle — a great safeguard to its possessor. Men have committed murder for jealousy's sake, and anger's sake, and hatred's sake, and selfishness' sake, and spiritual pride's sake; but no man that ever I heard of, ever committed a diabolical murder for sweet charity's sake. Mere self-interest, then, if no better motive can be enlisted, should, especially with high-tempered men, prompt all beings to charity and philanthropy. At any rate, upon the occasion in question, I strove to drown my exasperated feelings towards the scrivener by benevolently construing his conduct. Poor fellow, poor fellow! thought I, he don't mean any thing; and besides, he has seen hard times, and ought to be indulged.

I endeavored also immediately to occupy myself, and at the same time to comfort my despondency. I tried to fancy that in the course of the morning, at such time as might prove agreeable to him, Bartleby, of his own free accord, would emerge from his hermitage, and take up some decided line of march in the direction of the door. But no. Half-past twelve o'clock came; Turkey began to glow in the face, overturn his inkstand, and become generally obstreperous; Nippers abated down into quietude and courtesy; Ginger Nut munched his noon apple; and Bartleby remained standing at his window in one of his profoundest dead-wall reveries. Will it be credited? Ought I to acknowledge it? That afternoon I left the office without saying one further word to him.

Some days now passed, during which, at leisure intervals I looked a little into "Edwards on the Will," and "Priestley on Necessity." Under the circumstances, those books induced a salutary feeling. Gradually I slid into the persuasion that these troubles of mine touching the scrivener, had been all predestinated from eternity, and Bartleby was billeted upon me for some mysterious purpose of an all-wise Providence, which it was not for a mere mortal like me to fathom. Yes, Bartleby, stay there behind your screen, thought I; I shall persecute you no more; you are harmless and noiseless as any of these old chairs; in short, I never feel so private as when I know you are here. At least I see it, I feel it; I penetrate to the predestinated purpose of my life. I am content. Others may have loftier parts to enact; but my mission in this world, Bartleby, is to furnish you with office-room for such period as you may see fit to remain.

I believe that this wise and blessed frame of mind would have continued with me, had it not been for the unsolicited and uncharitable remarks obtruded upon me by my professional friends who visited the rooms. But thus it often is, that the constant friction of illiberal minds wears out at last the best resolves of the more generous. Though to be sure, when I reflected upon it, it was not strange that people entering my office should be struck by the peculiar aspect of the unaccountable Bartleby, and so be tempted to throw out some sinister observations concerning him. Sometimes an attorney having business with me, and calling at my office, and finding no one but the scrivener there, would undertake to obtain some sort of precise information from him touching my whereabouts; but without heeding his idle talk, Bartleby would remain standing immovable in the middle of the room. So after contemplating him in that position for a time, the attorney would depart, no wiser than he came.

Also, when a Reference was going on, and the room full of lawyers and witnesses and business was driving fast; some deeply occupied legal gentleman present, seeing Bartleby wholly unemployed would request him to run round to his (the legal gentleman's) office and fetch some papers for him. Thereupon,

Bartleby would tranquilly decline, and yet remain idle as before. Then the lawyer would give a great stare, and turn to me. And what could I say? At last I was made aware that all through the circle of my professional acquaintance, a whisper of wonder was running round, having reference to the strange creature I kept at my office. This worried me very much. And as the idea came upon me of his possibly turning out a long-lived man, and keep occupying my chambers, and denying my authority; and perplexing my visitors; and scandalizing my professional reputation; and casting a general gloom over the premises; keeping soul and body together to the last upon his savings (for doubtless he spent but half a dime a day), and in the end perhaps outlive me, and claim possession of my office by right of his perpetual occupancy: as all these dark anticipations crowded upon me more and more, and my friends continually intruded their relentless remarks upon the apparition in my room; a great change was wrought in me. I resolved to gather all my faculties together, and for ever rid me of this intolerable incubus.

Ere revolving any complicated project, however, adapted to this end, I first simply suggested to Bartleby the propriety of his permanent departure. In a calm and serious tone, I commended the idea to his careful and mature consideration. But having taken three days to meditate upon it, he apprised me that his original determination remained the same; in short, that he still preferred to abide with me.

What shall I do? I now said to myself, buttoning up my coat to the last button. What shall I do? what ought I to do? what does conscience say I *should* do with this man, or rather ghost. Rid myself of him, I must; go, he shall. But how? You will not thrust him, the poor, pale, passive mortal, — you will not thrust such a helpless creature out of your door? you will not dishonor yourself by such cruelty? No, I will not, I cannot do that. Rather would I let him live and die here, and then mason up his remains in the wall. What then will you do? For all your coaxing, he will not budge. Bribes he leaves under your own paperweight on your table; in short, it is quite plain that he prefers to cling to you.

Then something severe, something unusual must be done. What! surely you will not have him collared by a constable, and commit his innocent pallor to the common jail? And upon what ground could you procure such a thing to be done? — a vagrant, is he? What! he a vagrant, a wanderer, who refuses to budge? It is because he will *not* be a vagrant, then, that you seek to count him *as* a vagrant. That is too absurd. No visible means of support: there I have him. Wrong again: for indubitably he *does* support himself, and that is the only unanswerable proof that any man can show of his possessing the means so to do. No more then. Since he will not quit me, I must quit him. I will change my offices; I will move elsewhere; and give him fair notice, that if I find him on my new premises I will then proceed against him as a common trespasser.

Acting accordingly, next day I thus addressed him: "I find these chambers too far from the City Hall; the air is unwholesome. In a word, I propose to remove my offices next week, and shall no longer require your services. I tell you this now, in order that you may seek another place."

He made no reply, and nothing more was said.

On the appointed day I engaged carts and men, proceeded to my chambers, and having but little furniture, every thing was removed in a few hours. Throughout, the scrivener remained standing behind the screen, which I directed to be removed the last thing. It was withdrawn; and being folded up like a huge folio, left him the motionless occupant of a naked room. I stood in the entry watching him a moment, while something from within me upbraided me.

I re-entered, with my hand in my pocket — and — my heart in my mouth.

"Good-bye, Bartleby. I am going — good-bye, and God some way bless you; and take that," slipping something in his hand. But it dropped upon the floor, and then, — strange to say — I tore myself from him whom I had so longed to be rid of.

Established in my new quarters, for a day or two I kept the door locked, and started at every footfall in the passages. When I returned to my rooms after any little absence, I would pause at the threshold for an instant, and attentively listen, ere applying my key. But these fears were needless. Bartleby never came nigh me.

I thought all was going well, when a perturbed looking stranger visited me, inquiring whether I was the person who had recently occupied rooms at No. — Wall-street.

Full of forebodings, I replied that I was.

"Then sir," said the stranger, who proved a lawyer, "you are responsible for the man you left there. He refuses to do any copying; he refuses to do anything; he says he prefers not to; and he refuses to quit the premises."

"I am very sorry, sir," said I, with assumed tranquillity, but an inward tremor, "but, really, the man you allude to is nothing to me — he is no relation or apprentice of mine, that you should hold me responsible for him."

"In mercy's name, who is he?"

"I certainly cannot inform you. I know nothing about him. Formerly I employed him as a copyist; but he has done nothing for me now for some time past."

"I shall settle him then, — good morning, sir."

Several days passed, and I heard nothing more; and though I often felt a charitable prompting to call at the place and see poor Bartleby, yet a certain squeamishness of I know not what withheld me.

All is over with him, by this time, thought I at last, when through another week no further intelligence reached me. But coming to my room the day after, I found several persons waiting at my door in a high state of nervous excitement.

"That's the man — here he comes," cried the foremost one, whom I recognized as the lawyer who had previously called upon me alone.

"You must take him away, sir, at once," cried a portly person among them, advancing upon me, and whom I knew to be the landlord of No. — Wall-street. "These gentlemen, my tenants, cannot stand it any longer; Mr. B ——" pointing to the lawyer, "has turned him out of his room, and he now persists in haunting the building generally, sitting upon the banisters of the stairs by day, and sleeping in the entry by night. Every body is concerned; clients are leaving the offices; some fears are entertained of a mob; something you must do, and that without delay."

Aghast at this torrent, I fell back before it, and would fain have locked myself in my new quarters. In vain I persisted that Bartleby was nothing to me — no more than to any one else. In vain: — I was the last person known to have any thing to do with him, and they held me to the terrible account. Fearful then of being exposed in the papers (as one person present obscurely threatened) I considered the matter, and at length said, that if the lawyer would give me a confidential interview with the scrivener, in his (the lawyer's) own room, I would that afternoon strive my best to rid them of the nuisance they complained of.

Going up stairs to my old haunt, there was Bartleby silently sitting upon the banister at the landing.

"What are you doing here, Bartleby?" said I.

"Sitting upon the banister," he mildly replied.

I motioned him into the lawyer's room, who then left us.

"Bartleby," said I, "are you aware that you are the cause of great tribulation to me, by persisting in occupying the entry after being dismissed from the office?"

No answer.

"Now one of two things must take place. Either you must do something, or something must be done to you. Now what sort of business would you like to engage in? Would you like to re-engage in copying for some one?"

"No; I would prefer not to make any change."

"Would you like a clerkship in a dry-goods store?"

"There is too much confinement about that. No, I would not like a clerkship; but I am not particular."

"Too much confinement," I cried, "why you keep yourself confined all the time!"

"I would prefer not to take a clerkship," he rejoined, as if to settle that little item at once.

"How would a bar-tender's business suit you? There is no trying of the eyesight in that."

"I would not like it at all; though, as I said before, I am not particular."

His unwonted wordiness inspired me. I returned to the charge.

"Well then, would you like to travel through the country collecting bills for the merchants? That would improve your health."

"No, I would prefer to be doing something else."

"How then would going as a companion to Europe, to entertain some young gentleman with your conversation, — how would that suit you?"

"Not at all. It does not strike me that there is any thing definite about that. I like to be stationary. But I am not particular."

"Stationary you shall be then," I cried, now losing all patience, and for the first time in all my exasperating connection with him fairly flying into a passion. "If you do not go away from these premises before night, I shall feel bound — indeed I *am* bound — to — to — to quit the premises myself!" I rather absurdly concluded, knowing not with what possible threat to try to frighten his immobility into compliance. Despairing of all further efforts, I was precipitately leaving him, when a final thought occurred to me — one which had not been wholly unindulged before.

"Bartleby," said I, in the kindest tone I could assume under such exciting circumstances, "will you go home with me now — not to my office, but my dwelling — and remain there till we can conclude upon some convenient arrangement for you at our leisure? Come, let us start now, right away."

"No: at present I would prefer not to make any change at all."

I answered nothing; but effectually dodging every one by the suddenness and rapidity of my flight, rushed from the building, ran up Wall-street towards Broadway, and jumping into the first omnibus was soon removed from pursuit. As soon as tranquillity returned I distinctly perceived that I had now done all that I possibly could, both in respect to the demands of the landlord and his tenants, and with regard to my own desire and sense of duty, to benefit Bartleby, and shield him from rude persecution. I now strove to be entirely care-free and quiescent; and my conscience justified me in the attempt; though indeed it was not so successful as I could have wished. So fearful was I of being again hunted out by the incensed landlord and his exasperated tenants, that, surrendering my business to Nippers, for a few days I drove about the upper part of the town and through the suburbs, in my rockaway; crossed over to Jersey City and Hoboken, and paid fugitive visits to Manhattanville and Astoria. In fact I almost lived in my rockaway for the time.

When again I entered my office, lo, a note from the landlord lay upon the desk. I opened it with trembling hands. It informed me that the writer had sent to the police, and had Bartleby removed to the Tombs as a vagrant. Moreover, since I knew more about him than any one else, he wished me to appear at that place, and make a suitable statement of the facts. These tidings had a conflicting effect upon me. At first I was indignant; but at last almost approved. The landlord's energetic, summary disposition, had led him to adopt a procedure which I do not think I would have decided upon myself; and yet as a last resort, under such peculiar circumstances, it seemed the only plan.

As I afterwards learned, the poor scrivener, when told that he must be conducted to the Tombs, offered not the slightest obstacle, but in his pale unmoving way, silently acquiesced.

Some of the compassionate and curious bystanders joined the party; and headed by one of the constables arm in arm with Bartleby, the silent procession filed its way through all the noise, and heat, and joy of the roaring thoroughfares at noon.

The same day I received the note I went to the Tombs, or to speak more properly, the Halls of Justice. Seeking the right officer, I stated the purpose of my call, and was informed that the individual I described was indeed within. I then assured the functionary that Bartleby was a perfectly honest man, and greatly to be compassionated, however unaccountably eccentric. I narrated all I knew and closed by suggesting the idea of letting him remain in as indulgent confinement as possible till something less harsh might be done — though indeed I hardly knew what. At all events, if nothing else could be decided upon, the alms-house must receive him. I then begged to have an interview.

Being under no disgraceful charge, and quite serene and harmless in all his ways, they had permitted him freely to wander about the prison, and especially in the inclosed grass-platted yards thereof. And so I found him there, standing all alone in the quietest of the yards, his face towards a high wall, while all around, from the narrow slits of the jail windows, I thought I saw peering out upon him the eyes of murderers and thieves.

"Bartleby!"

"I know you," he said, without looking round, — "and I want nothing to say to you."

"It was not I that brought you here, Bartleby," said I, keenly pained at his implied suspicion. "And to you, this should not be so vile a place. Nothing reproachful attaches to you by being here. And see, it is not so sad a place as one might think. Look, there is the sky, and here is the grass."

"I know where I am," he replied, but would say nothing more, and so I left him.

As I entered the corridor again, a broad meat-like man, in an apron, accosted me, and jerking his thumb over his shoulder said—"Is that your friend?"

"Yes."

"Does he want to starve? If he does, let him live on the prison fare, that's all."

"Who are you?" asked I, not knowing what to make of such an unofficially speaking person in such a place.

"I am the grub-man. Such gentlemen as have friends here, hire me to provide them with something good to eat."

"Is this so?" said I, turning to the turnkey.

He said it was.

"Well then," said I, slipping some silver into the grub-man's hands (for so they called him). "I want you to give particular attention to my friend there;

let him have the best dinner you can get. And you must be as polite to him as possible."

"Introduce me, will you?" said the grub-man, looking at me with an expression which seem to say he was all impatience for an opportunity to give a specimen of his breeding.

Thinking it would prove of benefit to the scrivener, I acquiesced; and asking the grub-man his name, went up with him to Bartleby.

"Bartleby, this is Mr. Cutlets; you will find him very useful to you."

"Your sarvant, sir, your sarvant," said the grub-man, making a low salutation behind his apron. "Hope you find it pleasant here, sir; — spacious grounds — cool apartments, sir — hope you'll stay with us some time — try to make it agreeable. May Mrs. Cutlets and I have the pleasure of your company to dinner, sir, in Mrs. Cutlets' private room?"

"I prefer not to dine to-day," said Bartleby, turning away. "It would disagree with me; I am unused to dinners." So saying he slowly moved to the other side of the inclosure, and took up a position fronting the dead-wall.

"How's this?" said the grub-man, addressing me with a stare of astonishment. "He's odd, aint he?"

"I think he is a little deranged," said I, sadly.

"Deranged? deranged is it? Well now, upon my word, I thought that friend of yourn was a gentleman forger; they are always pale and genteel-like, them forgers. I can't help pity 'em — can't help it, sir. Did you know Monroe Edwards?" he added touchingly, and paused. Then, laying his hand pityingly on my shoulder, sighed, "he died of consumption at Sing-Sing. So you weren't acquainted with Monroe?"

"No, I was never socially acquainted with any forgers. But I cannot stop longer. Look to my friend yonder. You will not lose by it. I will see you again."

Some few days after this, I again obtained admission to the Tombs, and went through the corridors in quest of Bartleby; but without finding him.

"I saw him coming from his cell not long ago," said a turnkey, "may be he's gone to loiter in the yards."

So I went in that direction.

"Are you looking for the silent man?" said another turnkey passing me. "Yonder he lies — sleeping in the yard there. 'Tis not twenty minutes since I saw him lie down."

The yard was entirely quiet. It was not accessible to the common prisoners. The surrounding walls, of amazing thickness, kept off all sounds behind them. The Egyptian character of the masonry weighed upon me with its gloom. But a soft imprisoned turf grew under foot. The heart of the eternal pyramids, it seemed, wherein, by some strange magic, through the clefts, grass-seed, dropped by birds, had sprung.

Strangely huddled at the base of the wall, his knees drawn up, and lying on his side, his head touching the cold stones, I saw the wasted Bartleby. But nothing stirred. I paused; then went close up to him; stooped over, and saw that his dim eyes were open; otherwise he seemed profoundly sleeping. Something prompted me to touch him. I felt his hand, when a tingling shiver ran up my arm and down my spine to my feet.

The round face of the grub-man peered upon me now. "His dinner is ready. Won't he dine to-day, either? Or does he live without dining?"

"Lives without dining," said I, and closed the eyes.

"Eh! — He's asleep, aint he?"

"With kings and counsellors," murmured I.

★　★　★　★　★　★　★

There would seem little need for proceeding further in this history. Imagination will readily supply the meagre recital of poor Bartleby's interment. But ere parting with the reader, let me say, that if this little narrative has sufficiently interested him, to awaken curiosity as to who Bartleby was, and what manner of life he led prior to the present narrator's making his acquaintance, I can only reply, that in such curiosity I fully share, but am wholly unable to gratify it. Yet here I hardly know whether I should divulge one little item of rumor, which came to my ear a few months after the scrivener's decease. Upon what basis it rested, I could never ascertain; and hence, how true it is I cannot now tell. But inasmuch as this vague report has not been without a certain strange suggestive interest to me, however sad, it may prove the same with some others; and so I will briefly mention it. The report was this: that Bartleby had been a subordinate clerk in the Dead Letter Office at Washington, from which he had been suddenly removed by a change in the administration. When I think over this rumor, I cannot adequately express the emotions which seize me. Dead letters! does it not sound like dead men? Conceive a man by nature and misfortune prone to a pallid hopelessness, can any business seem more fitted to heighten it than that of continually handling these dead letters, and assorting them for the flames? For by the cart-load they are annually burned. Sometimes from out the folded paper the pale clerk takes a ring: — the finger it was meant for, perhaps, moulders in the grave; a bank-note sent in swiftest charity: — he whom it would relieve, nor eats nor hungers any more; pardon for those who died despairing; hope for those who died unhoping; good tidings for those who died stifled by unrelieved calamities. On errands of life, these letters speed to death.

Ah Bartleby! Ah humanity!

Herman Melville
Benito Cereno

Herman Melville's "Benito Cereno" first appeared in *Putnam's Monthly Magazine* in 1855 before being included in *The Piazza Tales* the following year. He had written this novella during the winter of 1854–1855 based on Chapter 18 of Captain Amasa Delano's *Narrative of Voyages and Travels in the Northern and Southern Hemispheres: Comprising Three Voyages Round the World; Together with a Voyage of Survey and Discovery, in the Pacific and Oriental Islands,* published in Boston in 1817. Melville worked very closely with the historical facts of the case but added the fictional elements of a point of view closely identified with Delano's mind, a restructuring of dramatic elements, the invention of dialogue and thought, and the introduction of an artistic style almost totally absent from the dry historical records of the court trial. Perhaps the most important story published during the period of American Romanticism, Melville infused his narrative with issues that blazed throughout the era: the problem of slavery and its grotesque damage to society, morality, and the human psyche; the uncertainties of the interpretation of empirical data; and the extent to which carefully wrought fiction can impact social change and understanding.

Herman Melville, "Benito Cereno," *The Piazza Tales* (New York: Dix & Edwards, 1856), 109–270.

In the year 1799, Captain Amasa Delano, of Duxbury, in Massachusetts, commanding a large sealer and general trader, lay at anchor with a valuable cargo, in the harbor of St. Maria — a small, desert, uninhabited island toward the southern extremity of the long coast of Chili. There he had touched for water.

On the second day, not long after dawn, while lying in his berth, his mate came below, informing him that a strange sail was coming into the bay. Ships were then not so plenty in those waters as now. He rose, dressed, and went on deck.

The morning was one peculiar to that coast. Everything was mute and calm; everything gray. The sea, though undulated into long roods of swells, seemed fixed, and was sleeked at the surface like waved lead that has cooled and set in the smelter's mould. The sky seemed a gray surtout. Flights of troubled gray fowl, kith and kin with flights of troubled gray vapors among which they were mixed, skimmed low and fitfully over the waters, as swallows over meadows before storms. Shadows present, foreshadowing deeper shadows to come.

To Captain Delano's surprise, the stranger, viewed through the glass, showed no colors; though to do so upon entering a haven, however uninhabited in its shores, where but a single other ship might be lying, was the custom among peaceful seamen of all nations. Considering the lawlessness and loneliness of the spot, and the sort of stories, at that day, associated with those seas, Captain Delano's surprise might have deepened into some uneasiness had he not been a person of a singularly undistrustful good nature, not liable, except on extraordinary and repeated incentives, and hardly then, to indulge in personal alarms, any way involving the imputation of malign evil in man. Whether, in view of what humanity is capable, such a trait implies, along with a benevolent heart, more than ordinary quickness and accuracy of intellectual perception, may be left to the wise to determine.

But whatever misgivings might have obtruded on first seeing the stranger, would almost, in any seaman's mind, have been dissipated by observing that, the ship, in navigating into the harbor, was drawing too near the land; a sunken reef making out off her bow. This seemed to prove her a stranger, indeed, not only to the sealer, but the island; consequently, she could be no wonted freebooter on that ocean. With no small interest, Captain Delano continued to watch her — a proceeding not much facilitated by the vapors partly mantling the hull, through which the far matin light from her cabin streamed equivocally enough; much like the sun — by this time hemisphered on the rim of the horizon, and, apparently, in company with the strange ship entering the harbor — which, wimpled by the same low, creeping clouds, showed not unlike a Lima intriguante's one sinister eye peering across the Plaza from the Indian loop-hole of her dusk *saya-y-manta*.

It might have been but a deception of the vapors, but, the longer the stranger was watched the more singular appeared her manœuvres. Ere long it seemed hard to decide whether she meant to come in or no — what she wanted, or what she was about. The wind, which had breezed up a little during the night, was now extremely light and baffling, which the more increased the apparent uncertainty of her movements.

Surmising, at last, that it might be a ship in distress, Captain Delano ordered his whale-boat to be dropped, and, much to the wary opposition of his mate, prepared to board her, and, at the least, pilot her in. On the night previous, a fishing-party of the seamen had gone a long distance to some detached rocks out of sight from the sealer, and, an hour or two before daybreak, had returned, having met with no small success. Presuming that the stranger might have been long off soundings, the good captain put several baskets of the fish, for presents, into his boat, and so pulled away. From her continuing too near the sunken reef, deeming her in danger, calling to his men, he made all haste to apprise those on board of their situation. But, some time ere the boat came up, the wind, light though it was, having shifted, had headed the vessel off, as well as partly broken the vapors from about her.

Upon gaining a less remote view, the ship, when made signally visible on the verge of the leaden-hued swells, with the shreds of fog here and there raggedly furring her, appeared like a white-washed monastery after a thunder-storm, seen perched upon some dun cliff among the Pyrenees. But it was no purely fanciful resemblance which now, for a moment, almost led Captain Delano to think that nothing less than a ship-load of monks was before him. Peering over the bulwarks were what really seemed, in the hazy distance, throngs of dark cowls; while, fitfully revealed through the open port-holes, other dark moving figures were dimly descried, as of Black Friars pacing the cloisters.

Upon a still nigher approach, this appearance was modified, and the true character of the vessel was plain — a Spanish merchantman of the first class, carrying negro slaves, amongst other valuable freight, from one colonial port to another. A very large, and, in its time, a very fine vessel, such as in those days were at intervals encountered along that main; sometimes superseded Acapulco treasure-ships, or retired frigates of the Spanish king's navy, which, like superannuated Italian palaces, still, under a decline of masters, preserved signs of former state.

As the whale-boat drew more and more nigh, the cause of the peculiar pipe-clayed aspect of the stranger was seen in the slovenly neglect pervading her. The spars, ropes, and great part of the bulwarks, looked woolly, from long unacquaintance with the scraper, tar, and the brush. Her keel seemed laid, her ribs put together, and she launched, from Ezekiel's Valley of Dry Bones.

In the present business in which she was engaged, the ship's general model and rig appeared to have undergone no material change from their original warlike and Froissart pattern. However, no guns were seen.

The tops were large, and were railed about with what had once been octagonal net-work, all now in sad disrepair. These tops hung overhead like three ruinous aviaries, in one of which was seen perched, on a ratlin, a white noddy, a strange fowl, so called from its lethargic, somnambulistic character, being frequently caught by hand at sea. Battered and mouldy, the castellated forecastle seemed some ancient turret, long ago taken by assault, and then left to decay. Toward the stern, two high-raised quarter galleries — the balustrades here and there covered with dry, tindery sea-moss — opening out from the unoccupied state-cabin, whose dead-lights, for all the mild weather, were hermetically closed and calked — these tenantless balconies hung over the sea as if it were the grand Venetian canal. But the principal relic of faded grandeur was the ample oval of the shield-like stern-piece, intricately carved with the arms of Castile and Leon, medallioned about by groups of mythological or symbolical devices; uppermost and central of which was a dark satyr in a mask, holding his foot on the prostrate neck of a writhing figure, likewise masked.

Whether the ship had a figure-head, or only a plain beak, was not quite certain, owing to canvas wrapped about that part, either to protect it while undergoing a re-furbishing, or else decently to hide its decay. Rudely painted or chalked, as in a sailor freak, along the forward side of a sort of pedestal below the canvas, was the sentence, *"Seguid vuestro jefe,"* (follow your leader); while upon the tarnished head-boards, near by, appeared, in stately capitals, once gilt, the ship's name, "SAN DOMINICK," each letter streakingly corroded with tricklings of copper-spike rust; while, like mourning weeds, dark festoons of sea-grass slimily swept to and fro over the name, with every hearse-like roll of the hull.

As, at last, the boat was hooked from the bow along toward the gangway amidship, its keel, while yet some inches separated from the hull, harshly grated as on a sunken coral reef. It proved a huge bunch of conglobated barnacles adhering below the water to the side like a wen — a token of baffling airs and long calms passed somewhere in those seas.

Climbing the side, the visitor was at once surrounded by a clamorous throng of whites and blacks, but the latter outnumbering the former more than could have been expected, negro transportation-ship as the stranger in port was. But, in one language, and as with one voice, all poured out a common tale of suffering; in which the negresses, of whom there were not a few, exceeded the others in their dolorous vehemence. The scurvy, together with the fever, had swept off a great part of their number, more especially the Spaniards. Off Cape Horn they had narrowly escaped shipwreck; then, for days together, they had lain tranced without wind; their provisions were low; their water next to none; their lips that moment were baked.

While Captain Delano was thus made the mark of all eager tongues, his one eager glance took in all faces, with every other object about him.

Always upon first boarding a large and populous ship at sea, especially a foreign one, with a nondescript crew such as Lascars or Manilla men, the impression varies in a peculiar way from that produced by first entering a strange house with strange inmates in a strange land. Both house and ship — the one by its walls and blinds, the other by its high bulwarks like ramparts — hoard from view their interiors till the last moment: but in the case of the ship there is this addition; that the living spectacle it contains, upon its sudden and complete disclosure, has, in contrast with the blank ocean which zones it, something of the effect of enchantment. The ship seems unreal; these strange costumes, gestures, and faces, but a shadowy tableau just emerged from the deep, which directly must receive back what it gave.

Perhaps it was some such influence, as above is attempted to be described, which, in Captain Delano's mind, heightened whatever, upon a staid scrutiny, might have seemed unusual; especially the conspicuous figures of four elderly grizzled negroes, their heads like black, doddered willow tops, who, in venerable contrast to the tumult below them, were couched, sphynx-like, one on the starboard cat-head, another on the larboard, and the remaining pair face to face on the opposite bulwarks above the main-chains. They each had bits of unstranded old junk in their hands, and, with a sort of stoical self-content, were picking the junk into oakum, a small heap of which lay by their sides. They accompanied the task with a continuous, low, monotonous chant; droning and druling away like so many gray-headed bag-pipers playing a funeral march.

The quarter-deck rose into an ample elevated poop, upon the forward verge of which, lifted, like the oakum-pickers, some eight feet above the general throng, sat along in a row, separated by regular spaces, the cross-legged figures of six other blacks; each with a rusty hatchet in his hand, which, with a bit of brick and a rag, he was engaged like a scullion in scouring; while between each two was a small stack of hatchets, their rusted edges turned forward awaiting a like operation. Though occasionally the four oakum-pickers would briefly address some person or persons in the crowd below, yet the six hatchet-polishers neither spoke to others, nor breathed a whisper among themselves, but sat intent upon their task, except at intervals, when, with the peculiar love in negroes of uniting industry with pastime, two and two they sideways clashed their hatchets together, like cymbals, with a barbarous din. All six, unlike the generality, had the raw aspect of unsophisticated Africans.

But that first comprehensive glance which took in those ten figures, with scores less conspicuous, rested but an instant upon them, as, impatient of the hubbub of voices, the visitor turned in quest of whomsoever it might be that commanded the ship.

But as if not unwilling to let nature make known her own case among his suffering charge, or else in despair of restraining it for the time, the Spanish captain, a gentlemanly, reserved-looking, and rather young man to a stranger's eye, dressed with singular richness, but bearing plain traces of recent sleepless cares and disquietudes, stood passively by, leaning against the main-mast, at one moment casting a dreary, spiritless look upon his excited people, at the next an unhappy glance toward his visitor. By his side stood a black of small stature, in whose rude face, as occasionally, like a shepherd's dog, he mutely turned it up into the Spaniard's, sorrow and affection were equally blended.

Struggling through the throng, the American advanced to the Spaniard, assuring him of his sympathies, and offering to render whatever assistance might be in his power. To which the Spaniard returned for the present but grave and ceremonious acknowledgments, his national formality dusked by the saturnine mood of ill-health.

But losing no time in mere compliments, Captain Delano, returning to the gangway, had his basket of fish brought up; and as the wind still continued light, so that some hours at least must elapse ere the ship could be brought to the anchorage, he bade his men return to the sealer, and fetch back as much water as the whale-boat could carry, with whatever soft bread the steward might have, all the remaining pumpkins on board, with a box of sugar, and a dozen of his private bottles of cider.

Not many minutes after the boat's pushing off, to the vexation of all, the wind entirely died away, and the tide turning, began drifting back the ship helplessly seaward. But trusting this would not long last, Captain Delano sought, with good hopes, to cheer up the strangers, feeling no small satisfaction that, with persons in their condition, he could — thanks to his frequent voyages along the Spanish main — converse with some freedom in their native tongue.

While left alone with them, he was not long in observing some things tending to heighten his first impressions; but surprise was lost in pity, both for the Spaniards and blacks, alike evidently reduced from scarcity of water and provisions; while long-continued suffering seemed to have brought out the less good-natured qualities of the negroes, besides, at the same time, impairing the Spaniard's authority over them. But, under the circumstances, precisely this condition of things was to have been anticipated. In armies, navies, cities, or families, in nature herself, nothing more relaxes good order than misery. Still, Captain Delano was not without the idea, that had Benito Cereno been a man of greater energy, misrule would hardly have come to the present pass. But the debility, constitutional or induced by hardships, bodily and mental, of the Spanish captain, was too obvious to be overlooked. A prey to settled dejection, as if long mocked with hope he would not now indulge it, even when it had ceased to be a mock, the prospect of that day, or evening at furthest, lying at anchor, with plenty of water for his people, and a brother captain to counsel and befriend, seemed in no perceptible degree to encourage him. His mind appeared unstrung, if not still more seriously affected. Shut up in these oaken walls, chained to one dull round of command, whose unconditionality cloyed him, like some hypochondriac abbot he moved slowly about, at times suddenly pausing, starting, or staring, biting his lip, biting his finger-nail, flushing, paling, twitching his beard, with other symptoms of an absent or moody mind. This distempered spirit was lodged, as before hinted, in as distempered a frame. He was rather tall, but seemed never to have been robust, and now with nervous suffering was almost worn to a skeleton. A tendency to some pulmonary complaint appeared to have been lately confirmed. His voice was like that of one with lungs half gone — hoarsely suppressed, a husky whisper. No wonder that, as in this state he tottered about, his private servant apprehensively followed him. Sometimes the negro gave his master his arm, or took his handkerchief out of his pocket for him; performing these and similar offices with that affectionate zeal which transmutes into something filial or fraternal acts in themselves but menial; and which has gained for the negro the repute of making the most pleasing body-servant in the world; one, too, whom a master need be on no stiffly superior terms with, but may treat with familiar trust; less a servant than a devoted companion.

Marking the noisy indocility of the blacks in general, as well as what seemed the sullen inefficiency of the whites it was not without humane satisfaction that Captain Delano witnessed the steady good conduct of Babo.

But the good conduct of Babo, hardly more than the ill-behavior of others, seemed to withdraw the half-lunatic Don Benito from his cloudy languor. Not that such precisely was the impression made by the Spaniard on the mind of his visitor.

The Spaniard's individual unrest was, for the present, but noted as a conspicuous feature in the ship's general affliction. Still, Captain Delano was not a little concerned at what he could not help taking for the time to be Don Benito's unfriendly indifference towards himself. The Spaniard's manner, too, conveyed a sort of sour and gloomy disdain, which he seemed at no pains to disguise. But this the American in charity ascribed to the harassing effects of sickness, since, in former instances, he had noted that there are peculiar natures on whom prolonged physical suffering seems to cancel every social instinct of kindness; as if, forced to black bread themselves, they deemed it but equity that each person coming nigh them should, indirectly, by some slight or affront, be made to partake of their fare.

But ere long Captain Delano bethought him that, indulgent as he was at the first, in judging the Spaniard, he might not, after all, have exercised charity enough. At bottom it was Don Benito's reserve which displeased him; but the same reserve was shown towards all but his faithful personal attendant. Even the formal reports which, according to sea-usage, were, at stated times, made to him by some petty underling, either a white, mulatto or black, he hardly had patience enough to listen to, without betraying contemptuous aversion. His manner upon such occasions was, in its degree, not unlike that which might be supposed to have been his imperial countryman's, Charles V., just previous to the anchoritish retirement of that monarch from the throne.

This splenetic disrelish of his place was evinced in almost every function pertaining to it. Proud as he was moody, he condescended to no personal mandate. Whatever special orders were necessary, their delivery was delegated to his body-servant, who in turn transferred them to their ultimate destination, through runners, alert Spanish boys or slave boys, like pages or pilot-fish within easy call continually hovering round Don Benito. So that to have beheld this undemonstrative invalid gliding about, apathetic and mute, no landsman could have dreamed that in him was lodged a dictatorship beyond which, while at sea, there was no earthly appeal.

Thus, the Spaniard, regarded in his reserve, seemed the involuntary victim of mental disorder. But, in fact, his reserve might, in some degree, have proceeded from design. If so, then here was evinced the unhealthy climax of that icy though conscientious policy, more or less adopted by all commanders of large ships, which, except in signal emergencies, obliterates alike the manifestation of sway with every trace of sociality; transforming the man into a block, or rather into a loaded cannon, which, until there is call for thunder, has nothing to say.

Viewing him in this light, it seemed but a natural token of the perverse habit induced by a long course of such hard self-restraint, that, notwithstanding the present condition of his ship, the Spaniard should still persist in a demeanor, which, however harmless, or, it may be, appropriate, in a well-appointed vessel, such as the San Dominick might have been at the outset of the voyage, was anything but judicious now. But the Spaniard, perhaps, thought that it was with cap-

tains as with gods: reserve, under all events, must still be their cue. But probably
this appearance of slumbering dominion might have been but an attempted disguise to conscious imbecility — not deep policy, but shallow device. But be all
this as it might, whether Don Benito's manner was designed or not, the more
Captain Delano noted its pervading reserve, the less he felt uneasiness at any
particular manifestation of that reserve towards himself.

Neither were his thoughts taken up by the captain alone. Wonted to the
quiet orderliness of the sealer's comfortable family of a crew, the noisy confusion of the San Dominick's suffering host repeatedly challenged his eye. Some
prominent breaches, not only of discipline but of decency, were observed. These
Captain Delano could not but ascribe, in the main, to the absence of those subordinate deck-officers to whom, along with higher duties, is intrusted what may
be styled the police department of a populous ship. True, the old oakum-pickers
appeared at times to act the part of monitorial constables to their countrymen,
the blacks; but though occasionally succeeding in allaying trifling outbreaks now
and then between man and man, they could do little or nothing toward establishing general quiet. The San Dominick was in the condition of a transatlantic
emigrant ship, among whose multitude of living freight are some individuals,
doubtless, as little troublesome as crates and bales; but the friendly remonstrances of such with their ruder companions are of not so much avail as the unfriendly arm of the mate. What the San Dominick wanted was, what the
emigrant ship has, stern superior officers. But on these decks not so much as a
fourth-mate was to be seen.

The visitor's curiosity was roused to learn the particulars of those mishaps
which had brought about such absenteeism, with its consequences; because,
though deriving some inkling of the voyage from the wails which at the first moment had greeted him, yet of the details no clear understanding had been had.
The best account would, doubtless, be given by the captain. Yet at first the visitor was loth to ask it, unwilling to provoke some distant rebuff. But plucking up
courage, he at last accosted Don Benito, renewing the expression of his benevolent interest, adding, that did he (Captain Delano) but know the particulars of
the ship's misfortunes, he would, perhaps, be better able in the end to relieve
them. Would Don Benito favor him with the whole story.

Don Benito faltered; then, like some somnambulist suddenly interfered with,
vacantly stared at his visitor, and ended by looking down on the deck. He maintained this posture so long, that Captain Delano, almost equally disconcerted,
and involuntarily almost as rude, turned suddenly from him, walking forward to
accost one of the Spanish seamen for the desired information. But he had hardly
gone five paces, when, with a sort of eagerness, Don Benito invited him back, re-
gretting his momentary absence of mind, and professing readiness to gratify him.

While most part of the story was being given, the two captains stood on the
after part of the main-deck, a privileged spot, no one being near but the servant.

"It is now a hundred and ninety days," began the Spaniard, in his husky whisper, "that this ship, well officered and well manned, with several cabin passengers — some fifty Spaniards in all — sailed from Buenos Ayres bound to Lima, with a general cargo, hardware, Paraguay tea and the like — and," pointing forward, "that parcel of negroes, now not more than a hundred and fifty, as you see, but then numbering over three hundred souls. Off Cape Horn we had heavy gales. In one moment, by night, three of my best officers, with fifteen sailors, were lost, with the main-yard; the spar snapping under them in the slings, as they sought, with heavers, to beat down the icy sail. To lighten the hull, the heavier sacks of mata were thrown into the sea, with most of the water-pipes lashed on deck at the time. And this last necessity it was, combined with the prolonged detentions afterwards experienced, which eventually brought about our chief causes of suffering. When ——"

Here there was a sudden fainting attack of his cough, brought on, no doubt, by his mental distress. His servant sustained him, and drawing a cordial from his pocket placed it to his lips. He a little revived. But unwilling to leave him unsupported while yet imperfectly restored, the black with one arm still encircled his master, at the same time keeping his eye fixed on his face, as if to watch for the first sign of complete restoration, or relapse, as the event might prove.

The Spaniard proceeded, but brokenly and obscurely, as one in a dream.

—"Oh my God! rather than pass through what I have, with joy I would have hailed the most terrible gales; but ——"

His cough returned and with increased violence; this subsiding, with reddened lips and closed eyes he fell heavily against his supporter.

"His mind wanders. He was thinking of the plague that followed the gales," plaintively sighed the servant; "my poor, poor master!" wringing one hand, and with the other wiping the mouth. "But be patient, Señor," again turning to Captain Delano, "these fits do not last long; master will soon be himself."

Don Benito reviving, went on; but as this portion of the story was very brokenly delivered, the substance only will here be set down.

It appeared that after the ship had been many days tossed in storms off the Cape, the scurvy broke out, carrying off numbers of the whites and blacks. When at last they had worked round into the Pacific, their spars and sails were so damaged, and so inadequately handled by the surviving mariners, most of whom were become invalids, that, unable to lay her northerly course by the wind, which was powerful, the unmanageable ship, for successive days and nights, was blown northwestward, where the breeze suddenly deserted her, in unknown waters, to sultry calms. The absence of the water-pipes now proved as fatal to life as before their presence had menaced it. Induced, or at least aggravated, by the more than scanty allowance of water, a malignant fever followed the scurvy; with the excessive heat of the lengthened calm, making such short work of it as to sweep away, as by billows, whole families of the Africans, and a yet larger number, proportionably, of the Spaniards, including, by a luckless fatality, every remaining officer on board. Consequently, in the smart west winds eventually following the calm, the already rent sails, having to be simply dropped, not furled, at need, had been gradually reduced to the beggars' rags they were now. To procure substitutes for his lost sailors, as well as supplies of water and sails, the captain, at the earliest opportunity, had made for Baldivia, the southernmost civilized port of Chili and South America; but upon nearing the coast the thick weather had prevented him from so much as sighting that harbor. Since which period, almost without a crew, and almost without canvas and almost without water, and, at intervals, giving its added dead to the sea, the San Dominick had been battle-dored about by contrary winds, inveigled by currents, or grown weedy in calms. Like a man lost in woods, more than once she had doubled upon her own track.

"But throughout these calamities," huskily continued Don Benito, painfully turning in the half embrace of his servant, "I have to thank those negroes you see, who, though to your inexperienced eyes appearing unruly, have, indeed, conducted themselves with less of restlessness than even their owner could have thought possible under such circumstances."

Here he again fell faintly back. Again his mind wandered; but he rallied, and less obscurely proceeded.

"Yes, their owner was quite right in assuring me that no fetters would be needed with his blacks; so that while, as is wont in this transportation, those negroes have always remained upon deck — not thrust below, as in the Guinea-men — they have, also, from the beginning, been freely permitted to range within given bounds at their pleasure."

Once more the faintness returned — his mind roved — but, recovering, he resumed:

"But it is Babo here to whom, under God, I owe not only my own preservation, but likewise to him, chiefly, the merit is due, of pacifying his more ignorant brethren, when at intervals tempted to murmurings."

"Ah, master," sighed the black, bowing his face, "don't speak of me; Babo is nothing; what Babo has done was but duty."

"Faithful fellow!" cried Captain Delano. "Don Benito, I envy you such a friend; slave I cannot call him."

As master and man stood before him, the black upholding the white, Captain Delano could not but bethink him of the beauty of that relationship which could present such a spectacle of fidelity on the one hand and confidence on the other. The scene was heightened by the contrast in dress, denoting their relative positions. The Spaniard wore a loose Chili jacket of dark velvet; white small-clothes and stockings, with silver buckles at the knee and instep; a high-crowned sombrero, of fine grass; a slender sword, silver mounted, hung from a knot in his sash — the last being an almost invariable adjunct, more for utility than ornament, of a South American gentleman's dress to this hour. Excepting when his occasional nervous contortions brought about disarray, there was a certain precision in his attire curiously at variance with the unsightly disorder around; especially in the belittered Ghetto, forward of the main-mast, wholly occupied by the blacks.

The servant wore nothing but wide trowsers, apparently, from their coarseness and patches, made out of some old topsail; they were clean, and confined at the waist by a bit of unstranded rope, which, with his composed, deprecatory air at times, made him look something like a begging friar of St. Francis.

However unsuitable for the time and place, at least in the blunt-thinking American's eyes, and however strangely surviving in the midst of all his afflictions, the toilette of Don Benito might not, in fashion at least, have gone beyond the style of the day among South Americans of his class. Though on the present voyage sailing from Buenos Ayres, he had avowed himself a native and resident of Chili, whose inhabitants had not so generally adopted the plain coat and once plebeian pantaloons; but, with a becoming modification, adhered to their provincial costume, picturesque as any in the world. Still, relatively to the pale history of the voyage, and his own pale face, there seemed something so incongruous in the Spaniard's apparel, as almost to suggest the image of an invalid courtier tottering about London streets in the time of the plague.

The portion of the narrative which, perhaps, most excited interest, as well as some surprise, considering the latitudes in question, was the long calms spoken of, and more particularly the ship's so long drifting about. Without communicating the opinion, of course, the American could not but impute at least part of the detentions both to clumsy seamanship and faulty navigation. Eying Don Benito's small, yellow hands, he easily inferred that the young captain had not got into command at the hawse-hole, but the cabin-window; and if so, why wonder at incompetence, in youth, sickness, and gentility united?

But drowning criticism in compassion, after a fresh repetition of his sympathies, Captain Delano, having heard out his story, not only engaged, as in the first place, to see Don Benito and his people supplied in their immediate bodily needs, but, also, now further promised to assist him in procuring a large permanent supply of water, as well as some sails and rigging; and, though it would involve no small embarrassment to himself, yet he would spare three of his best seamen for temporary deck officers; so that without delay the ship might proceed to Conception, there fully to refit for Lima, her destined port.

Such generosity was not without its effect, even upon the invalid. His face lighted up; eager and hectic; he met the honest glance of his visitor. With gratitude he seemed overcome.

"This excitement is bad for master," whispered the servant, taking his arm, and with soothing words gently drawing him aside.

When Don Benito returned, the American was pained to observe that his hopefulness, like the sudden kindling in his cheek, was but febrile and transient.

Ere long with a joyless mien, looking up towards the poop, the host invited his guest to accompany him there, for the benefit of what little breath of wind might be stirring.

As, during the telling of the story, Captain Delano had once or twice started at the occasional cymballing of the hatchet-polishers, wondering why such an interruption should be allowed, especially in that part of the ship, and in the ears of an invalid; and moreover, as the hatchets had anything but an attractive look, and the handlers of them still less so, it was, therefore, to tell the truth, not without some lurking reluctance, or even shrinking, it may be, that Captain Delano, with apparent complaisance, acquiesced in his host's invitation. The more so, since, with an untimely caprice of punctilio, rendered distressing by his cadaverous aspect, Don Benito, with Castilian bows, solemnly insisted upon his guest's preceding him up the ladder leading to the elevation; where, one on each side of the last step, sat for armorial supporters and sentries two of the ominous file. Gingerly enough stepped good Captain Delano between them, and in the instant of leaving them behind, like one running the gauntlet, he felt an apprehensive twitch in the calves of his legs.

But when, facing about, he saw the whole file, like so many organ-grinders, still stupidly intent on their work, unmindful of everything beside, he could not but smile at his late fidgety panic.

Presently, while standing with his host, looking forward upon the decks below, he was struck by one of those instances of insubordination previously alluded to. Three black boys, with two Spanish boys, were sitting together on the hatches, scraping a rude wooden platter, in which some scanty mess had recently been cooked. Suddenly, one of the black boys, enraged at a word dropped by one of his white companions, seized a knife, and, though called to forbear by one of the oakum-pickers, struck the lad over the head, inflicting a gash from which blood flowed.

In amazement, Captain Delano inquired what this meant. To which the pale Don Benito dully muttered, that it was merely the sport of the lad.

"Pretty serious sport, truly," rejoined Captain Delano. "Had such a thing happened on board the Bachelor's Delight, instant punishment would have followed."

At these words the Spaniard turned upon the American one of his sudden, staring, half-lunatic looks; then, relapsing into his torpor, answered, "Doubtless, doubtless, Señor."

Is it, thought Captain Delano, that this hapless man is one of those paper captains I've known, who by policy wink at what by power they cannot put down? I know no sadder sight than a commander who has little of command but the name.

"I should think, Don Benito," he now said, glancing towards the oakum-picker who had sought to interfere with the boys, "that you would find it advantageous to keep all your blacks employed, especially the younger ones, no matter at what useless task, and no matter what happens to the ship. Why, even with my little band, I find such a course indispensable. I once kept a crew on my quarter-deck thrumming mats for my cabin, when, for three days, I had given up my ship — mats, men, and all — for a speedy loss, owing to the violence of a gale, in which we could do nothing but helplessly drive before it."

"Doubtless, doubtless," muttered Don Benito.

"But," continued Captain Delano, again glancing upon the oakum-pickers and then at the hatchet-polishers, near by, "I see you keep some, at least, of your host employed."

"Yes," was again the vacant response.

"Those old men there, shaking their pows from their pulpits," continued Captain Delano, pointing to the oakum-pickers, "seem to act the part of old dominies to the rest, little heeded as their admonitions are at times. Is this voluntary on their part, Don Benito, or have you appointed them shepherds to your flock of black sheep?"

"What posts they fill, I appointed them," rejoined the Spaniard, in an acrid tone, as if resenting some supposed satiric reflection.

"And these others, these Ashantee conjurors here," continued Captain Delano, rather uneasily eying the brandished steel of the hatchet-polishers, where, in spots, it had been brought to a shine, "this seems a curious business they are at, Don Benito?"

"In the gales we met," answered the Spaniard, "what of our general cargo was not thrown overboard was much damaged by the brine. Since coming into calm weather, I have had several cases of knives and hatchets daily brought up for overhauling and cleaning."

"A prudent idea, Don Benito. You are part owner of ship and cargo, I presume; but none of the slaves, perhaps?"

"I am owner of all you see," impatiently returned Don Benito, "except the main company of blacks who belonged to my late friend, Alexandro Aranda."

As he mentioned this name, his air was heart-broken; his knees shook; his servant supported him.

Thinking he divined the cause of such unusual emotion, to confirm his surmise, Captain Delano, after a pause, said: "And may I ask, Don Benito, whether — since awhile ago you spoke of some cabin passengers — the friend, whose loss so afflicts you, at the outset of the voyage accompanied his blacks?"

"Yes."

"But died of the fever?"

"Died of the fever. Oh, could I but ——"

Again quivering, the Spaniard paused.

"Pardon me," said Captain Delano, lowly, "but I think that, by a sympathetic experience, I conjecture, Don Benito, what it is that gives the keener edge to your grief. It was once my hard fortune to lose, at sea, a dear friend, my own brother, then supercargo. Assured of the welfare of his spirit, its departure I could have borne like a man; but that honest eye, that honest hand — both of which had so often met mine — and that warm heart; all, all — like scraps to the dogs — to throw all to the sharks! It was then I vowed never to have for fellow-voyager a man I loved, unless unbeknown to him, I had provided every requisite, in case of a fatality, for embalming his mortal part for interment on shore. Were your friend's remains now on board this ship, Don Benito, not thus strangely would the mention of his name affect you."

"On board this ship?" echoed the Spaniard. Then, with horrified gestures, as directed against some spectre, he unconsciously fell into the ready arms of his attendant, who, with a silent appeal toward Captain Delano, seemed beseeching him not again to broach a theme so unspeakably distressing to his master.

This poor fellow now, thought the pained American, is the victim of that sad superstition which associates goblins with the deserted body of man, as ghosts with an abandoned house. How unlike are we made! What to me, in like case, would have been a solemn satisfaction, the bare suggestion, even, terrifies the Spaniard into this trance. Poor Alexandro Aranda! What would you say could you here see your friend — who, on former voyages, when you, for months, were left behind, has, I dare say, often longed, and longed, for one peep at you — now transported with terror at the least thought of having you anyway nigh him.

At this moment, with a dreary grave-yard toll, betokening a flaw, the ship's forecastle bell, smote by one of the grizzled oakum-pickers, proclaimed ten o'clock, through the leaden calm; when Captain Delano's attention was caught by the moving figure of a gigantic black, emerging from the general crowd below, and slowly advancing towards the elevated poop. An iron collar was about his neck, from which depended a chain, thrice wound round his body; the terminating links padlocked together at a broad band of iron, his girdle.

"How like a mute Atufal moves," murmured the servant.

The black mounted the steps of the poop, and, like a brave prisoner, brought up to receive sentence, stood in unquailing muteness before Don Benito, now recovered from his attack.

At the first glimpse of his approach, Don Benito had started, a resentful shadow swept over his face; and, as with the sudden memory of bootless rage, his white lips glued together.

This is some mulish mutineer, thought Captain Delano, surveying, not without a mixture of admiration, the colossal form of the negro.

"See, he waits your question, master," said the servant.

Thus reminded, Don Benito, nervously averting his glance, as if shunning, by anticipation, some rebellious response, in a disconcerted voice, thus spoke: —

"Atufal, will you ask my pardon, now?"

The black was silent.

"Again, master," murmured the servant, with bitter upbraiding eyeing his countryman, "Again, master; he will bend to master yet."

"Answer," said Don Benito, still averting his glance, "say but the one word, *pardon,* and your chains shall be off."

Upon this, the black, slowly raising both arms, let them lifelessly fall, his links clanking, his head bowed; as much as to say, "no, I am content."

"Go," said Don Benito, with inkept and unknown emotion.

Deliberately as he had come, the black obeyed.

"Excuse me, Don Benito," said Captain Delano, "but this scene surprises me; what means it, pray?"

"It means that that negro alone, of all the band, has given me peculiar cause of offense. I have put him in chains; I ——"

Here he paused; his hand to his head, as if there were a swimming there, or a sudden bewilderment of memory had come over him; but meeting his servant's kindly glance seemed reassured, and proceeded: —

"I could not scourge such a form. But I told him he must ask my pardon. As yet he has not. At my command, every two hours he stands before me."

"And how long has this been?"

"Some sixty days."

"And obedient in all else? And respectful?"

"Yes."

"Upon my conscience, then," exclaimed Captain Delano, impulsively, "he has a royal spirit in him, this fellow."

"He may have some right to it," bitterly returned Don Benito, "he says he was king in his own land."

"Yes," said the servant, entering a word, "those slits in Atufal's ears once held wedges of gold; but poor Babo here, in his own land, was only a poor slave; a black man's slave was Babo, who now is the white's."

Somewhat annoyed by these conversational familiarities, Captain Delano turned curiously upon the attendant, then glanced inquiringly at his master; but, as if long wonted to these little informalities, neither master nor man seemed to understand him.

"What, pray, was Atufal's offense, Don Benito?" asked Captain Delano; "if it was not something very serious, take a fool's advice, and, in view of his general docility, as well as in some natural respect for his spirit, remit him his penalty."

"No, no, master never will do that," here murmured the servant to himself, "proud Atufal must first ask master's pardon. The slave there carries the padlock, but master here carries the key."

His attention thus directed, Captain Delano now noticed for the first, that, suspended by a slender silken cord, from Don Benito's neck, hung a key. At once, from the servant's muttered syllables, divining the key's purpose, he smiled and said: — "So, Don Benito — padlock and key — significant symbols, truly."

Biting his lip, Don Benito faltered.

Though the remark of Captain Delano, a man of such native simplicity as to be incapable of satire or irony, had been dropped in playful allusion to the Spaniard's singularly evidenced lordship over the black; yet the hypochondriac seemed some way to have taken it as a malicious reflection upon his confessed inability thus far to break down, at least, on a verbal summons, the entrenched will of the slave. Deploring this supposed misconception, yet despairing of correcting it, Captain Delano shifted the subject; but finding his companion more than ever withdrawn, as if still sourly digesting the lees of the presumed affront above-mentioned, by-and-by Captain Delano likewise became less talkative, oppressed, against his own will, by what seemed the secret vindictiveness of the morbidly sensitive Spaniard. But the good sailor, himself of a quite contrary disposition, refrained, on his part, alike from the appearance as from the feeling of resentment, and if silent, was only so from contagion.

Presently the Spaniard, assisted by his servant somewhat discourteously crossed over from his guest; a procedure which, sensibly enough, might have been allowed to pass for idle caprice of ill-humor, had not master and man, lingering round the corner of the elevated skylight, began whispering together in low voices. This was unpleasing. And more; the moody air of the Spaniard, which at times had not been without a sort of valetudinarian stateliness, now seemed anything but dignified; while the menial familiarity of the servant lost its original charm of simple-hearted attachment.

In his embarrassment, the visitor turned his face to the other side of the ship. By so doing, his glance accidentally fell on a young Spanish sailor, a coil of rope in his hand, just stepped from the deck to the first round of the mizzen-rigging. Perhaps the man would not have been particularly noticed, were it not that, during his ascent to one of the yards, he, with a sort of covert intentness, kept his eye fixed on Captain Delano, from whom, presently, it passed, as if by a natural sequence, to the two whisperers.

His own attention thus redirected to that quarter, Captain Delano gave a slight start. From something in Don Benito's manner just then, it seemed as if the visitor had, at least partly, been the subject of the withdrawn consultation going on — a conjecture as little agreeable to the guest as it was little flattering to the host.

The singular alternations of courtesy and ill-breeding in the Spanish captain were unaccountable, except on one of two suppositions — innocent lunacy, or wicked imposture.

But the first idea, though it might naturally have occurred to an indifferent observer, and, in some respect, had not hitherto been wholly a stranger to Captain Delano's mind, yet, now that, in an incipient way, he began to regard the stranger's conduct something in the light of an intentional affront, of course the idea of lunacy was virtually vacated. But if not a lunatic, what then? Under the circumstances, would a gentleman, nay, any honest boor, act the part now acted by his host? The man was an impostor. Some low-born adventurer, masquerading as an oceanic grandee; yet so ignorant of the first requisites of mere gentlemanhood as to be betrayed into the present remarkable indecorum. That strange ceremoniousness, too, at other times evinced, seemed not uncharacteristic of one playing a part above his real level. Benito Cereno — Don Benito Cereno — a sounding name. One, too, at that period, not unknown, in the surname, to supercargoes and sea captains trading along the Spanish Main, as belonging to one of the most enterprising and extensive mercantile families in all those provinces; several members of it having titles; a sort of Castilian Rothschild, with a noble brother, or cousin, in every great trading town of South America. The alleged Don Benito was in early manhood, about twenty-nine or thirty. To assume a sort of roving cadetship in the maritime affairs of such a house, what more likely scheme for a young knave of talent and spirit? But the Spaniard was a pale invalid. Never mind. For even to the degree of simulating mortal disease, the craft of some tricksters had been known to attain. To think that, under the aspect of infantile weakness, the most savage energies might be couched — those velvets of the Spaniard but the silky paw to his fangs.

From no train of thought did these fancies come; not from within, but from without; suddenly, too, and in one throng, like hoar frost; yet as soon to vanish as the mild sun of Captain Delano's good-nature regained its meridian.

Glancing over once more towards his host — whose side-face, revealed above the skylight, was now turned towards him — he was struck by the profile, whose clearness of cut was refined by the thinness, incident to ill-health, as well as ennobled about the chin by the beard. Away with suspicion. He was a true offshoot of a true hidalgo Cereno.

Relieved by these and other better thoughts, the visitor, lightly humming a tune, now began indifferently pacing the poop, so as not to betray to Don Benito that he had at all mistrusted incivility, much less duplicity; for such mistrust would yet be proved illusory, and by the event; though, for the present, the circumstance which had provoked that distrust remained unexplained. But when that little mystery should have been cleared up, Captain Delano thought he might extremely regret it, did he allow Don Benito to become aware that he had indulged in ungenerous surmises. In short, to the Spaniard's black-letter text, it was best, for awhile, to leave open margin.

Presently, his pale face twitching and overcast, the Spaniard, still supported by his attendant, moved over towards his guest, when, with even more than his usual embarrassment, and a strange sort of intriguing intonation in his husky whisper, the following conversation began: —

"Señor, may I ask how long you have lain at this isle?"

"Oh, but a day or two, Don Benito."

"And from what port are you last?"

"Canton."

"And there, Señor, you exchanged your sealskins for teas and silks, I think you said?"

"Yes. Silks, mostly."

"And the balance you took in specie, perhaps?"

Captain Delano, fidgeting a little, answered —

"Yes; some silver; not a very great deal, though."

"Ah — well. May I ask how many men have you, Señor?"

Captain Delano slightly started, but answered —

"About five-and-twenty, all told."

"And at present, Señor, all on board, I suppose?"

"All on board, Don Benito," replied the Captain, now with satisfaction.

"And will be to-night, Señor?"

At this last question, following so many pertinacious ones, for the soul of him Captain Delano could not but look very earnestly at the questioner, who, instead of meeting the glance, with every token of craven discomposure dropped his eyes to the deck; presenting an unworthy contrast to his servant, who, just then, was kneeling at his feet, adjusting a loose shoe-buckle; his disengaged face meantime, with humble curiosity, turned openly up into his master's downcast one.

The Spaniard, still with a guilty shuffle, repeated his question:

"And — and will be to-night, Señor?"

"Yes, for aught I know," returned Captain Delano — "but nay," rallying himself into fearless truth, "some of them talked of going off on another fishing party about midnight."

"Your ships generally go — go more or less armed, I believe, Señor?"

"Oh, a six-pounder or two, in case of emergency," was the intrepidly indifferent reply, "with a small stock of muskets, sealing-spears, and cutlasses, you know."

As he thus responded, Captain Delano again glanced at Don Benito, but the latter's eyes were averted; while abruptly and awkwardly shifting the subject, he made some peevish allusion to the calm, and then, without apology, once more, with his attendant, withdrew to the opposite bulwarks, where the whispering was resumed.

At this moment, and ere Captain Delano could cast a cool thought upon what had just passed, the young Spanish sailor, before mentioned, was seen descending from the rigging. In act of stooping over to spring inboard to the deck, his voluminous, unconfined frock, or shirt, of coarse woolen, much spotted with tar, opened out far down the chest, revealing a soiled under garment of what seemed the finest linen, edged, about the neck, with a narrow blue ribbon, sadly faded and worn. At this moment the young sailor's eye was again fixed on the whisperers, and Captain Delano thought he observed a lurking significance in it, as if silent signs, of some Freemason sort, had that instant been interchanged.

This once more impelled his own glance in the direction of Don Benito, and, as before, he could not but infer that himself formed the subject of the conference.

He paused. The sound of the hatchet-polishing fell on his ears. He cast another swift side-look at the two. They had the air of conspirators. In connection with the late questionings, and the incident of the young sailor, these things now begat such return of involuntary suspicion, that the singular guilelessness of the American could not endure it. Plucking up a gay and humorous expression, he crossed over to the two rapidly, saying: — "Ha, Don Benito, your black here seems high in your trust; a sort of privy-counselor, in fact."

Upon this, the servant looked up with a good-natured grin, but the master started as from a venomous bite. It was a moment or two before the Spaniard sufficiently recovered himself to reply; which he did, at last, with cold constraint: — "Yes, Señor, I have trust in Babo."

Here Babo, changing his previous grin of mere animal humor into an intelligent smile, not ungratefully eyed his master.

Finding that the Spaniard now stood silent and reserved, as if involuntarily, or purposely giving hint that his guest's proximity was inconvenient just then, Captain Delano, unwilling to appear uncivil even to incivility itself, made some trivial remark and moved off; again and again turning over in his mind the mysterious demeanor of Don Benito Cereno.

He had descended from the poop, and, wrapped in thought, was passing near a dark hatchway, leading down into the steerage, when, perceiving motion there, he looked to see what moved. The same instant there was a sparkle in the shadowy hatchway, and he saw one of the Spanish sailors, prowling there hurriedly placing his hand in the bosom of his frock, as if hiding something. Before the man could have been certain who it was that was passing, he slunk below out of sight. But enough was seen of him to make it sure that he was the same young sailor before noticed in the rigging.

What was that which so sparkled? thought Captain Delano. It was no lamp — no match — no live coal. Could it have been a jewel? But how come sailors with jewels? — or with silk-trimmed under-shirts either? Has he been robbing the trunks of the dead cabin-passengers? But if so, he would hardly wear one of the stolen articles on board ship here. Ah, ah — if, now, that was, indeed, a secret sign I saw passing between this suspicious fellow and his captain awhile since; if I could only be certain that, in my uneasiness, my senses did not deceive me, then ——

Here, passing from one suspicious thing to another, his mind revolved the strange questions put to him concerning his ship.

By a curious coincidence, as each point was recalled, the black wizards of Ashantee would strike up with their hatchets, as in ominous comment on the white stranger's thoughts. Pressed by such enigmas and portents, it would have been almost against nature, had not, even into the least distrustful heart, some ugly misgivings obtruded.

Observing the ship, now helplessly fallen into a current, with enchanted sails,

drifting with increased rapidity seaward; and noting that, from a lately intercepted projection of the land, the sealer was hidden, the stout mariner began to
quake at thoughts which he barely durst confess to himself. Above all, he began
to feel a ghostly dread of Don Benito. And yet, when he roused himself, dilated
his chest, felt himself strong on his legs, and coolly considered it — what did all
these phantoms amount to?

Had the Spaniard any sinister scheme, it must have reference not so much to
him (Captain Delano) as to his ship (the Bachelor's Delight). Hence the present
drifting away of the one ship from the other, instead of favoring any such possible scheme, was, for the time, at least, opposed to it. Clearly any suspicion,
combining such contradictions, must need be delusive. Beside, was it not absurd
to think of a vessel in distress — a vessel by sickness almost dismanned of her
crew — a vessel whose inmates were parched for water — was it not a thousand
times absurd that such a craft should, at present, be of a piratical character; or
her commander, either for himself or those under him, cherish any desire but
for speedy relief and refreshment? But then, might not general distress, and
thirst in particular, be affected? And might not that same undiminished Spanish
crew, alleged to have perished off to a remnant, be at that very moment lurking
in the hold? On heart-broken pretense of entreating a cup of cold water, fiends
in human form had got into lonely dwellings, nor retired until a dark deed had
been done. And among the Malay pirates, it was no unusual thing to lure ships
after them into their treacherous harbors, or entice boarders from a declared enemy at sea, by the spectacle of thinly manned or vacant decks, beneath which
prowled a hundred spears with yellow arms ready to upthrust them through the
mats. Not that Captain Delano had entirely credited such things. He had heard
of them — and now, as stories, they recurred. The present destination of the
ship was the anchorage. There she would be near his own vessel. Upon gaining
that vicinity, might not the San Dominick, like a slumbering volcano, suddenly
let loose energies now hid?

He recalled the Spaniard's manner while telling his story. There was a gloomy
hesitancy and subterfuge about it. It was just the manner of one making up his
tale for evil purposes, as he goes. But if that story was not true, what was the
truth? That the ship had unlawfully come into the Spaniard's possession? But in
many of its details, especially in reference to the more calamitous parts, such as
the fatalities among the seamen, the consequent prolonged beating about, the
past sufferings from obstinate calms, and still continued suffering from thirst; in
all these points, as well as others, Don Benito's story had corroborated not only
the wailing ejaculations of the indiscriminate multitude, white and black, but
likewise — what seemed impossible to be counterfeit — by the very expression
and play of every human feature, which Captain Delano saw. If Don Benito's
story was, throughout, an invention, then every soul on board, down to the
youngest negress, was his carefully drilled recruit in the plot: an incredible

inference. And yet, if there was ground for mistrusting his veracity, that inference was a legitimate one.

But those questions of the Spaniard. There, indeed, one might pause. Did they not seem put with much the same object with which the burglar or assassin, by day-time, reconnoitres the walls of a house? But, with ill purposes, to solicit such information openly of the chief person endangered, and so, in effect, setting him on his guard; how unlikely a procedure was that? Absurd, then, to suppose that those questions had been prompted by evil designs. Thus, the same conduct, which, in this instance, had raised the alarm, served to dispel it. In short, scarce any suspicion or uneasiness, however apparently reasonable at the time, which was not now, with equal apparent reason, dismissed.

At last he began to laugh at his former forebodings; and laugh at the strange ship for, in its aspect, someway siding with them, as it were; and laugh, too, at the odd-looking blacks particularly those old scissors-grinders, the Ashantees; and those bed-ridden old knitting women, the oakum-pickers; and almost at the dark Spaniard himself, the central hobgoblin of all.

For the rest, whatever in a serious way seemed enigmatical, was now good-naturedly explained away by the thought that, for the most part, the poor invalid scarcely knew what he was about; either sulking in black vapors, or putting idle questions without sense or object. Evidently for the present, the man was not fit to be intrusted with the ship. On some benevolent plea withdrawing the command from him, Captain Delano would yet have to send her to Conception, in charge of his second mate, a worthy person and good navigator — a plan not more convenient for the San Dominick than for Don Benito; for, relieved from all anxiety, keeping wholly to his cabin, the sick man, under the good nursing of his servant, would, probably, by the end of the passage, be in a measure restored to health; and with that he should also be restored to authority.

Such were the American's thoughts. They were tranquilizing. There was a difference between the idea of Don Benito's darkly pre-ordaining Captain Delano's fate, and Captain Delano's lightly arranging Don Benito's. Nevertheless, it was not without something of relief that the good seaman presently perceived his whale-boat in the distance. Its absence had been prolonged by unexpected detention at the sealer's side, as well as its returning trip lengthened by the continual recession of the goal.

The advancing speck was observed by the blacks. Their shouts attracted the attention of Don Benito, who, with a return of courtesy, approaching Captain Delano, expressed satisfaction at the coming of some supplies, slight and temporary as they must necessarily prove.

Captain Delano responded; but while doing so, his attention was drawn to something passing on the deck below: among the crowd climbing the landward bulwarks, anxiously watching the coming boat, two blacks, to all appearances accidentally incommoded by one of the sailors, violently pushed him aside, which the sailor someway resenting, they dashed him to the deck, despite the earnest cries of the oakum-pickers.

"Don Benito," said Captain Delano quickly, "do you see what is going on there? Look!"

But, seized by his cough, the Spaniard staggered, with both hands to his face, on the point of falling. Captain Delano would have supported him, but the servant was more alert, who, with one hand sustaining his master, with the other applied the cordial. Don Benito restored, the black withdrew his support, slipping aside a little, but dutifully remaining within call of a whisper. Such discretion was here evinced as quite wiped away, in the visitor's eyes, any blemish of impropriety which might have attached to the attendant, from the indecorous conferences before mentioned; showing , too, that if the servant were to blame, it might be more the master's fault than his own, since when left to himself, he could conduct thus well.

His glance called away from the spectacle of disorder to the more pleasing one before him, Captain Delano could not avoid again congratulating his host upon possessing such a servant, who, though perhaps a little too forward now and then, must upon the whole be invaluable to one in the invalid's situation.

"Tell me, Don Benito," he added, with a smile — "I should like to have your man here, myself — what will you take for him? Would fifty doubloons be any object?"

"Master wouldn't part with Babo for a thousand doubloons," murmured the black, overhearing the offer, and taking it in earnest and, with the strange vanity of a faithful slave, appreciated by his master, scorning to hear so paltry a valuation put upon him by a stranger. But Don Benito, apparently hardly yet completely restored, and again interrupted by his cough, made but some broken reply.

Soon his physical distress became so great, affecting his mind, too, apparently, that, as if to screen the sad spectacle, the servant gently conducted his master below.

Left to himself, the American, to while away the time till his boat should arrive, would have pleasantly accosted some one of the few Spanish seamen he saw; but recalling something that Don Benito had said touching their ill conduct, he refrained; as a shipmaster indisposed to countenance cowardice or unfaithfulness in seamen.

While, with these thoughts, standing with eye directed forward towards that handful of sailors, suddenly he thought that one or two of them returned the glance and with a sort of meaning. He rubbed his eyes, and looked again; but again seemed to see the same thing. Under a new form, but more obscure than any previous one, the old suspicions recurred, but, in the absence of Don Benito, with less of panic than before. Despite the bad account given of the sailors, Captain Delano resolved forthwith to accost one of them. Descending the poop, he made his way through the blacks, his movement drawing a queer cry from the oakum-pickers, prompted by whom, the negroes, twitching each other aside, divided before him; but, as if curious to see what was the object of this deliberate visit to their Ghetto, closing in behind, in tolerable order, followed the white stranger up. His progress thus proclaimed as by mounted kings-at-arms, and escorted as by a Caffre guard of honor, Captain Delano, assuming a good-humored, off-handed air, continued to advance; now and then saying a blithe word to the negroes, and his eye curiously surveying the white faces, here and there sparsely mixed in with the blacks, like stray white pawns venturously involved in the ranks of the chess-men opposed.

While thinking which of them to select for his purpose, he chanced to observe a sailor seated on the deck engaged in tarring the strap of a large block, a circle of blacks squatted round him inquisitively eying the process.

The mean employment of the man was in contrast with something superior in his figure. His hand, black with continually thrusting it into the tar-pot held for him by a negro, seemed not naturally allied to his face, a face which would have been a very fine one but for its haggardness. Whether this haggardness had aught to do with criminality, could not be determined; since, as intense heat and cold, though unlike, produce like sensations, so innocence and guilt, when, through casual association with mental pain, stamping any visible impress, use one seal — a hacked one.

Not again that this reflection occurred to Captain Delano at the time, charitable man as he was. Rather another idea. Because observing so singular a haggardness combined with a dark eye, averted as in trouble and shame, and then again recalling Don Benito's confessed ill opinion of his crew, insensibly he was operated upon by certain general notions which, while disconnecting pain and abashment from virtue, invariably link them with vice.

If, indeed, there be any wickedness on board this ship, thought Captain Delano, be sure that man there has fouled his hand in it, even as now he fouls it in the pitch. I don't like to accost him. I will speak to this other, this old Jack here on the windlass.

He advanced to an old Barcelona tar, in ragged red breeches and dirty night-cap, cheeks trenched and bronzed, whiskers dense as thorn hedges. Seated between two sleepy-looking Africans, this mariner, like his younger shipmate, was employed upon some rigging — splicing a cable — the sleepy-looking blacks performing the inferior function of holding the outer parts of the ropes for him.

Upon Captain Delano's approach, the man at once hung his head below its previous level; the one necessary for business. It appeared as if he desired to be thought absorbed, with more than common fidelity, in his task. Being addressed, he glanced up, but with what seemed a furtive, diffident air, which sat strangely enough on his weatherbeaten visage, much as if a grizzly bear, instead of growling and biting, should simper and cast sheep's eyes. He was asked several questions concerning the voyage — questions purposely referring to several particulars in

Don Benito's narrative, not previously corroborated by those impulsive cries greeting the visitor on first coming on board. The questions were briefly answered, confirming all that remained to be confirmed of the story. The negroes about the windlass joined in with the old sailor; but, as they became talkative, he by degrees became mute, and at length quite glum, seemed morosely unwilling to answer more questions, and yet, all the while, this ursine air was somehow mixed with his sheepish one.

Despairing of getting into unembarrassed talk with such a centaur, Captain Delano, after glancing round for a more promising countenance, but seeing none, spoke pleasantly to the blacks to make way for him; and so, amid various grins and grimaces, returned to the poop, feeling a little strange at first, he could hardly tell why, but upon the whole with regained confidence in Benito Cereno.

How plainly, thought he, did that old whiskerando yonder betray a consciousness of ill desert. No doubt, when he saw me coming, he dreaded lest I, appraised by his Captain of the crews general misbehavior, came with sharp words for him, and so down with his head. And yet — and yet, now that I think of it, that very old fellow, if I err not, was one of those who seemed so earnestly eying me here awhile since. Ah, these currents spin one's head round almost as much as they do the ship. Ha, there now's a pleasant sort of sunny sight; quite sociable, too.

His attention had been drawn to a slumbering negress, partly disclosed through the lacework of some rigging, lying with youthful limbs carelessly disposed, under the lee of the bulwarks, like a doe in the shade of woodland rock. Sprawling at her lapped breasts, was her wide-awake fawn, stark naked, its black little body half lifted from the deck, crosswise with its dam's; its hands, like two paws, clambering upon her; its mouth and nose ineffectually rooting to get at the mark; and meantime giving a vexatious half-grunt, blending with the composed snore of the negress.

The uncommon vigor of the child at length roused the mother. She started up, at a distance facing Captain Delano. But as if not at all concerned at the attitude in which she had been caught, delightedly she caught the child up, with maternal transports, covering it with kisses.

There's naked nature, now; pure tenderness and love, thought Captain Delano, well pleased.

This incident prompted him to remark the other negresses more particularly than before. He was gratified with their manners: like most uncivilized women, they seemed at once tender of heart and tough of constitution; equally ready to die for their infants or fight for them. Unsophisticated as leopardesses; loving as doves. Ah! thought Captain Delano, these, perhaps, are some of the very women whom Ledyard saw in Africa, and gave such a noble account of.

These natural sights somehow insensibly deepened his confidence and ease. At last he looked to see how his boat was getting on; but it was still pretty remote. He turned to see if Don Benito had returned; but he had not.

To change the scene, as well as to please himself with a leisurely observation of the coming boat, stepping over into the mizzen-chains, he clambered his way into the starboard quarter-gallery — one of those abandoned Venetian-looking water-balconies previously mentioned — retreats cut off from the deck. As his foot pressed the half-damp, half-dry sea-mosses matting the place, and a chance phantom cats-paw — an islet of breeze, unheralded, unfollowed — as this ghostly cats-paw came fanning his cheek; as his glance fell upon the row of small, round dead-lights — all closed like coppered eyes of the coffined — and the state-cabin door, once connecting with the gallery, even as the dead-lights had once looked out upon it, but now calked fast like a sarcophagus lid; and to a purple-black tarred-over, panel, threshold, and post; and he bethought him of the time, when that state-cabin and this state-balcony had heard the voices of the Spanish king's officers, and the forms of the Lima viceroy's daughters had perhaps leaned where he stood — as these and other images flitted through his mind, as the cats-paw through the calm, gradually he felt rising a dreamy inquietude, like that of one who alone on the prairie feels unrest from the repose of the noon.

He leaned against the carved balustrade, again looking off toward his boat; but found his eye falling upon the ribbon grass, trailing along the ship's water-line, straight as a border of green box; and parterres of sea-weed, broad ovals and crescents, floating nigh and far, with what seemed long formal alleys between, crossing the terraces of swells, and sweeping round as if leading to the grottoes below. And overhanging all was the balustrade by his arm, which, partly stained with pitch and partly embossed with moss, seemed the charred ruin of some summer-house in a grand garden long running to waste.

Trying to break one charm, he was but becharmed anew. Though upon the wide sea, he seemed in some far inland country; prisoner in some deserted château, left to stare at empty grounds, and peer out at vague roads, where never wagon or wayfarer passed.

But these enchantments were a little disenchanted as his eye fell on the corroded main-chains. Of an ancient style, massy and rusty in link, shackle and bolt, they seemed even more fit for the ship's present business than the one for which she had been built.

Presently he thought something moved nigh the chains. He rubbed his eyes, and looked hard. Groves of rigging were about the chains; and there, peering from behind a great stay, like an Indian from behind a hemlock, a Spanish sailor, a marlingspike in his hand, was seen, who made what seemed an imperfect gesture towards the balcony, but immediately as if alarmed by some advancing step along the deck within, vanished into the recesses of the hempen forest, like a poacher.

What meant this? Something the man had sought to communicate, unbeknown to any one, even to his captain. Did the secret involve aught unfavorable to his captain? Were those previous misgivings of Captain Delano's about to be verified? Or, in his haunted mood at the moment, had some random, unintentional motion of the man, while busy with the stay, as if repairing it, been mistaken for a significant beckoning?

Not unbewildered, again he gazed off for his boat. But it was temporarily hidden by a rocky spur of the isle. As with some eagerness he bent forward, watching for the first shooting view of its beak, the balustrade gave way before him like charcoal. Had he not clutched an outreaching rope he would have fallen into the sea. The crash, though feeble, and the fall, though hollow, of the rotten fragments, must have been overheard. He glanced up. With sober curiosity peering down upon him was one of the old oakum-pickers, slipped from his perch to an outside boom; while below the old negro, and, invisible to him, reconnoitering from a port-hole like a fox from the mouth of its den, crouched the Spanish sailor again. From something suddenly suggested by the man's air, the mad idea now darted into Captain Delano's mind, that Don Benito's plea of indisposition, in withdrawing below, was but a pretense: that he was engaged there maturing his plot, of which the sailor, by some means gaining an inkling, had a mind to warn the stranger against; incited, it may be, by gratitude for a kind word on first boarding the ship. Was it from foreseeing some possible interference like this, that Don Benito had, beforehand, given such a bad character of his sailors, while praising the negroes; though, indeed, the former seemed as docile as the latter the contrary? The whites, too, by nature, were the shrewder race. A man with some evil design, would he not be likely to speak well of that stupidity which was blind to his depravity, and malign that intelligence from which it might not be hidden? Not unlikely, perhaps. But if the whites had dark secrets concerning Don Benito, could then Don Benito be any way in complicity with the blacks? But they were too stupid. Besides, who ever heard of a white so far a renegade as to apostatize from his very species almost, by leaguing in against it with negroes? These difficulties recalled former ones. Lost in their mazes, Captain Delano, who had now regained the deck, was uneasily advancing along it, when he observed a new face; an aged sailor seated cross-legged near the main hatchway. His skin was shrunk up with wrinkles like a pelican's empty pouch; his hair frosted; his countenance grave and composed. His hands were full of ropes, which he was working into a large knot. Some blacks were about him obligingly dipping the strands for him, here and there, as the exigencies of the operation demanded.

Captain Delano crossed over to him, and stood in silence surveying the knot; his mind, by a not uncongenial transition, passing from its own entanglements to those of the hemp. For intricacy, such a knot he had never seen in an American ship, nor indeed any other. The old man looked like an Egyptian priest, making Gordian knots for the temple of Ammon. The knot seemed a combination of double-bowline-knot, treble-crown-knot, back-handed-well-knot, knot-in-and-out-knot, and jamming-knot.

At last, puzzled to comprehend the meaning of such a knot, Captain Delano addressed the knotter: —

"What are you knotting there, my man?"

"The knot," was the brief reply, without looking up.

"So it seems; but what is it for?"

"For some one else to undo," muttered back the old man, plying his fingers harder than ever, the knot being now nearly completed.

While Captain Delano stood watching him, suddenly the old man threw the knot towards him, saying in broken English — the first heard in the ship — something to this effect: "Undo it, cut it, quick." It was said lowly, but with such condensation of rapidity, that the long, slow words in Spanish, which had preceded and followed, almost operated as covers to the brief English between.

For a moment, knot in hand, and knot in head, Captain Delano stood mute; while, without further heeding him, the old man was now intent upon other ropes. Presently there was a slight stir behind Captain Delano. Turning, he saw the chained negro, Atufal, standing quietly there. The next moment the old sailor rose, muttering, and, followed by his subordinate negroes, removed to the forward part of the ship, where in the crowd he disappeared.

An elderly negro, in a clout like an infant's, and with a pepper and salt head, and a kind of attorney air, now approached Captain Delano. In tolerable Spanish, and with a good-natured, knowing wink, he informed him that the old knotter was simple-witted, but harmless; often playing his odd tricks. The negro concluded by begging the knot, for of course the stranger would not care to be troubled with it. Unconsciously, it was handed to him. With a sort of congé, the negro received it, and, turning, his back, ferreted into it like a detective custom-house officer after smuggled laces. Soon, with some African word, equivalent to pshaw, he tossed the knot overboard.

All this is very queer now, thought Captain Delano, with a qualmish sort of emotion; but, as one feeling incipient sea-sickness, he strove, by ignoring the symptoms, to get rid of the malady. Once more he looked off for his boat. To his delight, it was now again in view, leaving the rocky spur astern.

The sensation here experienced, after at first relieving his uneasiness, with unforeseen efficacy soon began to remove it. The less distant sight of that well-known boat — showing it, not as before, half blended with the haze, but with outline defined, so that its individuality, like a man's, was manifest; that boat, Rover by name, which, though now in strange seas, had often pressed the beach of Captain Delano's home, and, brought to its threshold for repairs, had familiarly lain there, as a Newfoundland dog; the sight of that household boat evoked a thousand trustful associations, which, contrasted with previous suspicions, filled him not only with lightsome confidence, but somehow with half humorous self-reproaches at his former lack of it.

"What, I, Amasa Delano — Jack of the Beach, as they called me when a lad — I, Amasa; the same that, duck-satchel in hand, used to paddle along the water-side to the school-house made from the old hulk — I, little Jack of the Beach, that used to go berrying with cousin Nat and the rest; I to be murdered here at the ends of the earth, on board a haunted pirate-ship by a horrible Spaniard? Too nonsensical to think of! Who would murder Amasa Delano? His conscience is clean. There is some one above. Fie fie, Jack of the Beach! you are a child indeed; a child of the second childhood, old boy; you are beginning to dote and drule, I'm afraid."

Light of heart and foot, he stepped aft, and there was met by Don Benito's servant, who, with a pleasing expression, responsive to his own present feelings, informed him that his master had recovered from the effects of his coughing fit, and had just ordered him to go present his compliments to his good guest, Don Amasa, and say that he (Don Benito) would soon have the happiness to re-join him.

There now, do you mark that? again thought Captain Delano, walking the poop. What a donkey I was. This kind gentleman who here sends me his kind compliments, he, but ten minutes ago, dark-lantern in hand, was dodging round some old grind-stone in the hold, sharpening a hatchet for me, I thought. Well, well; these long calms have a morbid effect on the mind, I've often heard, though I never believed it before. Ha! glancing towards the boat; there's Rover; good dog; a white bone in her mouth. A pretty big bone though, seems to me. — What? Yes, she has fallen afoul of the bubbling tide-rip there. It sets her the other way, too, for the time. Patience.

It was now about noon, though, from the grayness of everything, it seemed to be getting towards dusk.

The calm was confirmed. In the far distance, away from the influence of land, the leaden ocean seemed laid out and leaded up, its course finished, soul gone, defunct. But the current from landward, where the ship was, increased; silently sweeping her further and further towards the tranced waters beyond.

Still, from his knowledge of those latitudes, cherishing hopes of a breeze, and a fair and fresh one, at any moment, Captain Delano, despite present prospects, buoyantly counted upon bringing the San Dominick safely to anchor ere night. The distance swept over was nothing; since, with a good wind, ten minutes' sailing would retrace more than sixty minutes, drifting. Meantime, one moment turning to mark "Rover" fighting the tide-rip, and the next to see Don Benito approaching, he continued walking the poop.

Gradually he felt a vexation arising from the delay of his boat; this soon merged into uneasiness; and at last — his eye falling continually, as from a stage-box into the pit, upon the strange crowd before and below him, and, by-and-by, recognizing there the face — now composed to indifference — of the Spanish sailor who had seemed to beckon from the main-chains — something of his old trepidations returned.

Ah, thought he — gravely enough — this is like the ague: because it went off, it follows not that it won't come back.

Though ashamed of the relapse, he could not altogether subdue it; and so, exerting his good-nature to the utmost, insensibly he came to a compromise.

Yes, this is a strange craft; a strange history, too, and strange folks on board. But — nothing more.

By the way of keeping his mind out of mischief till the boat should arrive, he tried to occupy it with turning over and over, in a purely speculative sort of way, some lesser peculiarities of the captain and crew. Among others, four curious points recurred:

First, the affair of the Spanish lad assailed with a knife by the slave boy; an act winked at by Don Benito. Second, the tyranny in Don Benito's treatment of Atufal, the black; as if a child should lead a bull of the Nile by the ring in his nose. Third, the trampling of the sailor by the two negroes; a piece of insolence passed over without so much as a reprimand. Fourth, the cringing submission to their master, of all the ship's underlings, mostly blacks; as if by the least inadvertence they feared to draw down his despotic displeasure.

Coupling these points, they seemed somewhat contradictory. But what then, thought Captain Delano, glancing towards his now nearing boat — what then? Why, Don Benito is a very capricious commander. But he is not the first of the sort I have seen; though it's true he rather exceeds any other. But as a nation — continued he in his reveries — these Spaniards are all an odd set; the very word Spaniard has a curious, conspirator, Guy-Fawkish twang to it. And yet, I dare say, Spaniards in the main are as good folks as any in Duxbury, Massachusetts. Ah good! At last "Rover" has come.

As, with its welcome freight, the boat touched the side, the oakum-pickers, with venerable gestures, sought to restrain the blacks, who, at the sight of three gurried water-casks in its bottom, and a pile of wilted pumpkins in its bow, hung over the bulwarks in disorderly raptures.

Don Benito, with his servant, now appeared; his coming perhaps, hastened by hearing the noise. Of him Captain Delano sought permission to serve out the water, so that all might share alike, and none injure themselves by unfair excess. But sensible, and, on Don Benito's account, kind as this offer was, it was received with what seemed impatience; as if aware that he lacked energy as a commander, Don Benito, with the true jealousy of weakness, resented as an affront any interference. So, at least, Captain Delano inferred.

In another moment the casks were being hoisted in, when some of the eager negroes accidentally jostled Captain Delano, where he stood by the gangway; so that, unmindful of Don Benito, yielding to the impulse of the moment, with good-natured authority he bade the blacks stand back; to enforce his words making use of a half-mirthful, half-menacing gesture. Instantly the blacks paused, just where they were, each negro and negress suspended in his or her posture, exactly as the word had found them — for a few seconds continuing so — while, as between the responsive posts of a telegraph, an unknown syllable ran from man to man among the perched oakum-pickers. While the visitor's attention was fixed by this scene, suddenly the hatchet-polishers half rose, and a rapid cry came from Don Benito.

Thinking that at the signal of the Spaniard he was about to be massacred, Captain Delano would have sprung for his boat, but paused, as the oakum-pickers, dropping down into the crowd with earnest exclamations, forced every white and every negro back, at the same moment, with gestures friendly and familiar, almost jocose, bidding him, in substance, not be a fool. Simultaneously the hatchet-polishers resumed their seats, quietly as so many tailors, and at once, as if nothing had happened, the work of hoisting in the casks was resumed, whites and blacks singing at the tackle.

Captain Delano glanced towards Don Benito. As he saw his meagre form in the act of recovering-itself from reclining in the servant's arms, into which the agitated invalid had fallen, he could not but marvel at the panic by which himself had been surprised, on the darting supposition that such a commander, who, upon a legitimate occasion, so trivial, too, as it now appeared, could lose all self-command, was, with energetic iniquity, going to bring about his murder.

The casks being on deck, Captain Delano was handed a number of jars and cups by one of the steward's aids, who, in the name of his captain, entreated him to do as he had proposed — dole out the water. He complied, with republican impartiality as to this republican element, which always seeks one level, serving the oldest white no better than the youngest black; excepting, indeed, poor Don Benito, whose condition, if not rank, demanded an extra allowance. To him, in the first place, Captain Delano presented a fair pitcher of the fluid; but, thirsting as he was for it, the Spaniard quaffed not a drop until after several grave bows and salutes. A reciprocation of courtesies which the sight-loving Africans hailed with clapping of hands.

Two of the less wilted pumpkins being reserved for the cabin table, the residue were minced up on the spot for the general regalement. But the soft bread, sugar, and bottled cider, Captain Delano would have given the whites alone, and in chief Don Benito; but the latter objected; which disinterestedness not a little pleased the American; and so mouthfuls all around were given alike to whites and blacks; excepting one bottle of cider, which Babo insisted upon setting aside for his master.

Here it may be observed that as, on the first visit of the boat, the American had not permitted his men to board the ship, neither did he now; being unwilling to add to the confusion of the decks.

Not uninfluenced by the peculiar good-humor at present prevailing, and for the time oblivious of any but benevolent thoughts, Captain Delano, who, from recent indications, counted upon a breeze within an hour or two at furthest, dispatched the boat back to the sealer, with orders for all the hands that could be spared immediately to set about rafting casks to the watering-place and filling them. Likewise he bade word be carried to his chief officer, that if, against present expectation, the ship was not brought to anchor by sunset, he need be under no concern; for as there was to be a full moon that night, he (Captain Delano) would remain on board ready to play the pilot, come the wind soon or late.

As the two Captains stood together, observing the departing boat — the servant, as it happened, having just spied a spot on his master's velvet sleeve, and silently engaged rubbing it out — the American expressed his regrets that the San Dominick had no boats; none, at least, but the unseaworthy old hulk of the long-boat, which, warped as a camel's skeleton in the desert, and almost as bleached, lay pot-wise inverted amidships, one side a little tipped, furnishing a subterranean sort of den for family groups of the blacks, mostly women and small children; who, squatting on old mats below, or perched above in the dark dome, on the elevated seats, were descried, some distance within, like a social circle of bats, sheltering in some friendly cave; at intervals, ebon flights of naked boys and girls, three or four years old, darting in and out of the den's mouth.

"Had you three or four boats now, Don Benito," said Captain Delano, "I think that, by tugging at the oars, your negroes here might help along matters some. Did you sail from port without boats, Don Benito?"

"They were stove in the gales, Señor."

"That was bad. Many men, too, you lost then. Boats and men. Those must have been hard gales, Don Benito."

"Past all speech," cringed the Spaniard.

"Tell me, Don Benito," continued his companion with increased interest, "tell me, were these gales immediately off the pitch of Cape Horn?"

"Cape Horn? — who spoke of Cape Horn?"

"Yourself did, when giving me an account of your voyage," answered Captain Delano, with almost equal astonishment at this eating of his own words, even as he ever seemed eating his own heart, on the part of the Spaniard. "You yourself, Don Benito, spoke of Cape Horn," he emphatically repeated.

The Spaniard turned, in a sort of stooping posture, pausing an instant, as one about to make a plunging exchange of elements, as from air to water.

At this moment a messenger-boy, a white, hurried by, in the regular performance of his function carrying the last expired half hour forward to the forecastle, from the cabin time-piece, to have it struck at the ship's large bell.

"Master," said the servant, discontinuing his work on the coat sleeve, and addressing the rapt Spaniard with a sort of timid apprehensiveness, as one charged with a duty, the discharge of which, it was foreseen, would prove irksome to the very person who had imposed it, and for whose benefit it was intended, "master told me never mind where he was, or how engaged, always to remind him, to a minute, when shaving-time comes. Miguel has gone to strike the half-hour afternoon. It is *now*, master. Will master go into the cuddy?"

"Ah — yes," answered the Spaniard, starting, as from dreams into realities; then turning upon Captain Delano, he said that ere long he would resume the conversation.

"Then if master means to talk more to Don Amasa," said the servant, "why not let Don Amasa sit by master in the cuddy, and master can talk, and Don Amasa can listen, while Babo here lathers and strops."

"Yes," said Captain Delano, not unpleased with this sociable plan, "yes, Don Benito, unless you had rather not, I will go with you."

"Be it so, Señor."

As the three passed aft, the American could not but think it another strange instance of his host's capriciousness, this being shaved with such uncommon punctuality in the middle of the day. But he deemed it more than likely that the servant's anxious fidelity had something to do with the matter; inasmuch as the timely interruption served to rally his master from the mood which had evidently been coming upon him.

The place called the cuddy was a light deck-cabin formed by the poop, a sort of attic to the large cabin below. Part of it had formerly been the quarters of the officers; but since their death all the partitionings had been thrown down, and the whole interior converted into one spacious and airy marine hall; for absence of fine furniture and picturesque disarray of odd appurtenances, somewhat answering to the wide, cluttered hall of some eccentric bachelor-squire in the country, who hangs his shooting-jacket and tobacco-pouch on deer antlers, and keeps his fishing-rod, tongs, and walking-stick in the same corner.

The similitude was heightened, if not originally suggested, by glimpses of the surrounding sea; since, in one aspect, the country and the ocean seem cousins-german.

The floor of the cuddy was matted. Overhead, four or five old muskets were stuck into horizontal holes along the beams. On one side was a claw-footed old table lashed to the deck; a thumbed missal on it, and over it a small, meagre crucifix attached to the bulk-head. Under the table lay a dented cutlass or two, with a hacked harpoon, among some melancholy old rigging, like a heap of poor friars' girdles. There were also two long, sharp-ribbed settees of Malacca cane, black with age, and uncomfortable to look at as inquisitors' racks, with a large, misshapen arm-chair, which, furnished with a rude barber's crotch at the back, working with a screw, seemed some grotesque engine of torment. A flag locker was in one corner, open, exposing various colored bunting, some rolled up, others half unrolled, still others tumbled. Opposite was a cumbrous washstand, of black mahogany, all of one block, with a pedestal, like a font, and over it a railed shelf, containing combs, brushes, and other implements of the toilet. A torn hammock of stained grass swung near; the sheets tossed, and the pillow wrinkled up like a brow, as if who ever slept here slept but illy, with alternate visitations of sad thoughts and bad dreams.

The further extremity of the cuddy, overhanging the ship's stern, was pierced with three openings, windows or port-holes, according as men or cannon might peer, socially or unsocially, out of them. At present neither men nor cannon were seen, though huge ring-bolts and other rusty iron fixtures of the wood-work hinted of twenty-four-pounders.

Glancing towards the hammock as he entered, Captain Delano said, "You sleep here, Don Benito?"

"Yes, Señor, since we got into mild weather."

"This seems a sort of dormitory, sitting-room, sail-loft, chapel, armory, and private closet all together, Don Benito," added Captain Delano, looking round.

"Yes, Señor; events have not been favorable to much order in my arrangements."

Here the servant, napkin on arm, made a motion as if waiting his master's good pleasure. Don Benito signified his readiness, when, seating him in the Malacca arm-chair, and for the guest's convenience drawing opposite one of the settees, the servant commenced operations by throwing back his master's collar and loosening his cravat.

There is something in the negro which, in a peculiar way, fits him for avocations about one's person. Most negroes are natural valets and hair-dressers; taking to the comb and brush congenially as to the castinets, and flourishing them apparently with almost equal satisfaction. There is, too, a smooth tact about them in this employment, with a marvelous, noiseless, gliding briskness, not ungraceful in its way, singularly pleasing to behold, and still more so to be the manipulated subject of. And above all is the great gift of good-humor. Not the mere grin or laugh is here meant. Those were unsuitable. But a certain easy cheerfulness, harmonious in every glance and gesture; as though God had set the whole negro to some pleasant tune.

When to this is added the docility arising from the unaspiring contentment of a limited mind, and that susceptibility of blind attachment sometimes inhering in indisputable inferiors, one readily perceives why those hypochondriacs, Johnson and Byron — it may be, something like the hypochondriac Benito Cereno — took to their hearts, almost to the exclusion of the entire white race, their serving men, the negroes, Barber and Fletcher. But if there be that in the negro which exempts him from the inflicted sourness of the morbid or cynical mind, how, in his most prepossessing aspects, must he appear to a benevolent one? When at ease with respect to exterior things, Captain Delano's nature was not only benign, but familiarly and humorously so. At home, he had often taken rare satisfaction in sitting in his door, watching some free man of color at his work or play. If on a voyage he chanced to have a black sailor, invariably he was on chatty and half-gamesome terms with him. In fact, like most men of a good, blithe heart, Captain Delano took to negroes, not philanthropically, but genially, just as other men to Newfoundland dogs.

Hitherto, the circumstances in which he found the San Dominick had repressed the tendency. But in the cuddy, relieved from his former uneasiness, and, for various reasons, more sociably inclined than at any previous period of the day, and seeing the colored servant, napkin on arm, so debonair about his master, in a business so familiar as that of shaving, too, all his old weakness for negroes returned.

Among other things he was amused with an odd instance of the African love of bright colors and fine shows, in the black's informally taking from the flag-locker a great piece of bunting of all hues, and lavishly tucking it under his master's chin for an apron.

The mode of shaving among the Spaniards is a little different from what it is with other nations. They have a basin, specifically called a barber's basin, which on one side is scooped out, so as accurately to receive the chin, against which it is closely held in lathering; which is done, not with a brush, but with soap dipped in the water of the basin and rubbed on the face.

In the present instance salt-water was used for lack of better; and the parts lathered were only the upper lip, and low down under the throat, all the rest being cultivated beard.

The preliminaries being somewhat novel to Captain Delano, he sat curiously eying them, so that no conversation took place, nor, for the present, did Don Benito appear disposed to renew any.

Setting down his basin, the negro searched among the razors, as for the sharpest, and having found it, gave it an additional edge by expertly strapping it on the firm, smooth, oily skin of his open palm; he then made a gesture as if to begin, but midway stood suspended for an instant, one hand elevating the razor, the other professionally dabbling among the bubbling suds on the Spaniard's lank neck. Not unaffected by the close sight of the gleaming steel, Don Benito nervously shuddered; his usual ghastliness was heightened by the lather, which lather, again, was intensified in its hue by the contrasting sootiness of the negro's body. Altogether the scene was somewhat peculiar, at least to Captain Delano, nor, as he saw the two thus postured, could he resist the vagary, that in the black he saw a headsman, and in the white a man at the block. But this was one of those antic conceits, appearing and vanishing in a breath, from which, perhaps, the best regulated mind is not always free.

Meantime the agitation of the Spaniard had a little loosened the bunting from around him, so that one broad fold swept curtain-like over the chair-arm to the floor, revealing, amid a profusion of armorial bars and ground-colors — black, blue, and yellow — a closed castle in a blood red field diagonal with a lion rampant in a white.

"The castle and the lion," exclaimed Captain Delano — "why, Don Benito, this is the flag of Spain you use here. It's well it's only I, and not the King, that sees this," he added, with a smile, "but" — turning towards the black — "it's all one, I suppose, so the colors be gay;" which playful remark did not fail somewhat to tickle the negro.

"Now, master," he said, readjusting the flag, and pressing the head gently further back into the crotch of the chair; "now, master," and the steel glanced nigh the throat.

Again Don Benito faintly shuddered.

"You must not shake so, master. See, Don Amasa, master always shakes when I shave him. And yet master knows I never yet have drawn blood, though it's true, if master will shake so, I may some of these times. Now master," he continued. "And now, Don Amasa, please go on with your talk about the gale, and all that; master can hear, and, between times, master can answer."

"Ah yes, these gales," said Captain Delano; "but the more I think of your voyage, Don Benito, the more I wonder, not at the gales, terrible as they must have been, but at the disastrous interval following them. For here, by your account, have you been these two months and more getting from Cape Horn to St. Maria, a distance which I myself, with a good wind, have sailed in a few days. True, you had calms, and long ones, but to be becalmed for two months, that is, at least, unusual. Why, Don Benito, had almost any other gentleman told me such a story, I should have been half disposed to a little incredulity."

Here an involuntary expression came over the Spaniard, similar to that just before on the deck, and whether it was the start he gave, or a sudden gawky roll of the hull in the calm, or a momentary unsteadiness of the servant's hand, however it was, just then the razor drew blood, spots of which stained the creamy lather under the throat: immediately the black barber drew back his steel, and, remaining in his professional attitude, back to Captain Delano, and face to Don Benito, held up the trickling razor, saying, with a sort of half humorous sorrow, "See, master — you shook so — here's Babo's first blood."

No sword drawn before James the First of England, no assassination in that timid King's presence, could have produced a more terrified aspect than was now presented by Don Benito.

Poor fellow, thought Captain Delano, so nervous he can't even bear the sight of barber's blood; and this unstrung, sick man, is it credible that I should have imagined he meant to spill all my blood, who can't endure the sight of one little drop of his own? Surely, Amasa Delano, you have been beside yourself this day. Tell it not when you get home, sappy Amasa. Well, well, he looks like a murderer, doesn't he? More like as if himself were to be done for. Well, well, this day's experience shall be a good lesson.

Meantime, while these things were running through the honest seaman's mind, the servant had taken the napkin from his arm, and to Don Benito had said — "But answer Don Amasa, please, master, while I wipe this ugly stuff off the razor, and strop it again."

As he said the words, his face was turned half round, so as to be alike visible to the Spaniard and the American, and seemed, by its expression, to hint, that he was desirous, by getting his master to go on with the conversation, considerately to withdraw his attention from the recent annoying accident. As if glad to snatch the offered relief, Don Benito resumed, rehearsing to Captain Delano, that not only were the calms of unusual duration, but the ship had fallen in with obstinate currents; and other things he added, some of which were but repetitions of former statements, to explain how it came to pass that the passage from Cape Horn to St. Maria had been so exceedingly long; now and then mingling with his words, incidental praises, less qualified than before, to the blacks, for their general good conduct. These particulars were not given consecutively, the servant, at convenient times, using his razor, and so, between the intervals of shaving, the story and panegyric went on with more than usual huskiness.

To Captain Delano's imagination, now again not wholly at rest, there was something so hollow in the Spaniard's manner, with apparently some reciprocal hollowness in the servant's dusky comment of silence, that the idea flashed across him, that possibly master and man, for some unknown purpose, were acting out, both in word and deed, nay, to the very tremor of Don Benito's limbs, some juggling play before him. Neither did the suspicion of collusion lack apparent support, from the fact of those whispered conferences before mentioned. But then, what could be the object of enacting this play of the barber before him? At last, regarding the notion as a whimsy, insensibly suggested, perhaps, by the theatrical aspect of Don Benito in his harlequin ensign, Captain Delano speedily banished it.

The shaving over, the servant bestirred himself with a small bottle of scented waters, pouring a few drops on the head, and then diligently rubbing; the vehemence of the exercise causing the muscles of his face to twitch rather strangely.

His next operation was with comb, scissors, and brush; going round and round, smoothing a curl here, clipping an unruly whisker-hair there, giving a graceful sweep to the temple-lock, with other impromptu touches evincing the hand of a master; while, like any resigned gentleman in barber's hands, Don Benito bore all, much less uneasily, at least, than he had done the razoring; indeed, he sat so pale and rigid now, that the negro seemed a Nubian sculptor finishing off a white statue-head.

All being over at last, the standard of Spain removed, tumbled up, and tossed back into the flag-locker, the negro's warm breath blowing away any stray hair which might have lodged down his master's neck; collar and cravat readjusted; a speck of lint whisked off the velvet lapel; all this being done; backing off a little space, and pausing with an expression of subdued self-complacency, the servant for a moment surveyed his master, as, in toilet at least, the creature of his own tasteful hands.

Captain Delano playfully complimented him upon his achievement; at the same time congratulating Don Benito.

But neither sweet waters, nor shampooing, nor fidelity, nor sociality, delighted the Spaniard. Seeing him relapsing into forbidding gloom, and still remaining seated, Captain Delano, thinking that his presence was undesired just then, withdrew, on pretense of seeing whether, as he had prophesied, any signs of a breeze were visible.

Walking forward to the main-mast, he stood awhile thinking over the scene, and not without some undefined misgivings, when he heard a noise near the cuddy, and turning, saw the negro, his hand to his cheek. Advancing, Captain Delano perceived that the cheek was bleeding. He was about to ask the cause, when the negro's wailing soliloquy enlightened him.

"Ah, when will master get better from his sickness; only the sour heart that sour sickness breeds made him serve Babo so; cutting Babo with the razor, because, only by accident, Babo had given master one little scratch; and for the first time in so many a day, too. Ah, ah, ah," holding his hand to his face.

Is it possible, thought Captain Delano; was it to wreak in private his Spanish spite against this poor friend of his, that Don Benito, by his sullen manner, impelled me to withdraw? Ah this slavery breeds ugly passions in man. — Poor fellow!

He was about to speak in sympathy to the negro, but with a timid reluctance he now reentered the cuddy.

Presently master and man came forth; Don Benito leaning on his servant as if nothing had happened.

But a sort of love-quarrel, after all, thought Captain Delano.

He accosted Don Benito, and they slowly walked together, They had gone but a few paces, when the steward — a tall, rajah-looking mulatto, orientally set off with a pagoda turban formed by three or four Madras handkerchiefs wound about his head, tier on tier — approaching with a saalam, announced lunch in the cabin.

On their way thither, the two captains were preceded by the mulatto, who, turning round as he advanced, with continual smiles and bows, ushered them on, a display of elegance which quite completed the insignificance of the small bare-headed Babo, who, as if not unconscious of inferiority, eyed askance the graceful steward. But in part, Captain Delano imputed his jealous watchfulness to that peculiar feeling which the full-blooded African entertains for the adulterated one. As for the steward, his manner, if not bespeaking much dignity of self-respect, yet evidenced his extreme desire to please; which is doubly meritorious, as at once Christian and Chesterfieldian.

Captain Delano observed with interest that while the complexion of the mulatto was hybrid, his physiognomy was European — classically so.

"Don Benito," whispered he, "I am glad to see this usher-of-the-golden-rod of yours; the sight refutes an ugly remark once made to me by a Barbadoes planter; that when a mulatto has a regular European face, look out for him; he is a devil. But see, your steward here has features more regular than King George's of England; and yet there he nods, and bows, and smiles; a king, indeed — the king of kind hearts and polite fellows. What a pleasant voice he has, too?"

"He has, Señor."

"But tell me, has he not, so far as you have known him, always proved a good, worthy fellow?" said Captain Delano, pausing, while with a final genuflexion the steward disappeared into the cabin; "come, for the reason just mentioned, I am curious to know."

"Francesco is a good man," a sort of sluggishly responded Don Benito, like a phlegmatic appreciator, who would neither find fault nor flatter.

"Ah, I thought so. For it were strange, indeed, and not very creditable to us white-skins, if a little of our blood mixed with the African's, should, far from improving the latter's quality, have the sad effect of pouring vitriolic acid into black broth; improving the hue, perhaps, but not the wholesomeness."

"Doubtless, doubtless, Señor, but" — glancing at Babo — "not to speak of negroes, your planter's remark I have heard applied to the Spanish and Indian intermixtures in our provinces. But I know nothing about the matter," he listlessly added.

And here they entered the cabin.

The lunch was a frugal one. Some of Captain Delano's fresh fish and pumpkins, biscuit and salt beef, the reserved bottle of cider, and the San Dominick's last bottle of Canary.

As they entered, Francesco, with two or three colored aids, was hovering over the table giving the last adjustments. Upon perceiving their master they withdrew, Francesco making a smiling congé, and the Spaniard, without condescending to notice it, fastidiously remarking to his companion that he relished not superfluous attendance.

Without companions, host and guest sat down, like a childless married couple, at opposite ends of the table, Don Benito waving Captain Delano to his place, and, weak as he was, insisting upon that gentleman being seated before himself.

The negro placed a rug under Don Benito's feet, and a cushion behind his back, and then stood behind, not his master's chair, but Captain Delano's. At first, this a little surprised the latter. But it was soon evident that, in taking his position, the black was still true to his master; since by facing him he could the more readily anticipate his slightest want.

"This is an uncommonly intelligent fellow of yours, Don Benito," whispered Captain Delano across the table.

"You say true, Señor."

During the repast, the guest again reverted to parts of Don Benito's story, begging further particulars here and there. He inquired how it was that the scurvy and fever should have committed such wholesale havoc upon the whites, while destroying less than half of the blacks. As if this question reproduced the whole scene of plague before the Spaniard's eyes, miserably reminding him of his solitude in a cabin where before he had had so many friends and officers round him, his hand shook, his face became hueless, broken words escaped; but directly the sane memory of the past seemed replaced by insane terrors of the present. With starting eyes he stared before him at vacancy. For nothing was to be seen but the hand of his servant pushing the Canary over towards him. At length a few sips served partially to restore him. He made random reference to the different constitution of races, enabling one to offer more resistance to certain maladies than another. The thought was new to his companion.

Presently Captain Delano, intending to say something to his host concerning the pecuniary part of the business he had undertaken for him, especially — since he was strictly accountable to his owners — with reference to the new suit of sails, and other things of that sort; and naturally preferring to conduct such affairs in private, was desirous that the servant should withdraw; imagining that Don Benito for a few minutes could dispense with his attendance. He, however, waited awhile; thinking that, as the conversation proceeded, Don Benito, without being prompted, would perceive the propriety of the step.

But it was otherwise. At last catching his host's eye, Captain Delano, with a slight backward gesture of his thumb, whispered, "Don Benito, pardon me, but there is an interference with the full expression of what I have to say to you."

Upon this the Spaniard changed countenance; which was imputed to his resenting the hint, as in some way a reflection upon his servant. After a moment's pause, he assured his guest that the black's remaining with them could be of no disservice; because since losing his officers he had made Babo (whose original office, it now appeared, had been captain of the slaves) not only his constant attendant and companion, but in all things his confidant.

After this, nothing more could be said; though, indeed, Captain Delano could hardly avoid some little tinge of irritation upon being left ungratified in so inconsiderable a wish, by one, too, for whom he intended such solid services. But it is only his querulousness, thought he; and so filling his glass he proceeded to business.

The price of the sails and other matters was fixed upon. But while this was being done, the American observed that, though his original offer of assistance had been hailed with hectic animation, yet now when it was reduced to a business transaction, indifference and apathy were betrayed. Don Benito, in fact, appeared to submit to hearing the details more out of regard to common propriety, than from any impression that weighty benefit to himself and his voyage was involved.

Soon, his manner became still more reserved. The effort was vain to seek to draw him into social talk. Gnawed by his splenetic mood, he sat twitching his beard, while to little purpose the hand of his servant, mute as that on the wall, slowly pushed over the Canary.

Lunch being over, they sat down on the cushioned transom; the servant placing a pillow behind his master. The long continuance of the calm had now affected the atmosphere. Don Benito sighed heavily, as if for breath.

"Why not adjourn to the cuddy," said Captain Delano; "there is more air there." But the host sat silent and motionless.

Meantime his servant knelt before him, with a large fan of feathers. And Francesco coming in on tiptoes, handed the negro a little cup of aromatic waters, with which at intervals he chafed his master's brow; smoothing the hair along the temples as a nurse does a child's. He spoke no word. He only rested his eye on his master's, as if, amid all Don Benito's distress, a little to refresh his spirit by the silent sight of fidelity.

Presently the ship's bell sounded two o'clock; and through the cabin windows a slight rippling of the sea was discerned; and from the desired direction.

"There," exclaimed Captain Delano, "I told you so, Don Benito, look!"

He had risen to his feet, speaking in a very animated tone, with a view the more to rouse his companion. But though the crimson curtain of the stern-window near him that moment fluttered against his pale cheek, Don Benito seemed to have even less welcome for the breeze than the calm.

Poor fellow, thought Captain Delano, bitter experience has taught him that one ripple does not make a wind, any more than one swallow a summer. But he is mistaken for once. I will get his ship in for him, and prove it.

Briefly alluding to his weak condition, he urged his host to remain quietly where he was, since he (Captain Delano) would with pleasure take upon himself the responsibility of making the best use of the wind.

Upon gaining the deck, Captain Delano started at the unexpected figure of Atufal, monumentally fixed at the threshold, like one of those sculptured porters of black marble guarding the porches of Egyptian tombs.

But this time the start was, perhaps, purely physical. Atufal's presence, singularly attesting docility even in sullenness, was contrasted with that of the hatchet-polishers, who in patience evinced their industry; while both spectacles showed, that lax as Don Benito's general authority might be, still, whenever he chose to exert it, no man so savage or colossal but must, more or less, bow.

Snatching a trumpet which hung from the bulwarks, with a free step Captain Delano advanced to the forward edge of the poop, issuing his orders in his best Spanish. The few sailors and many negroes, all equally pleased, obediently set about heading the ship towards the harbor.

While giving some directions about setting a lower stu'n'-sail, suddenly Captain Delano heard a voice faithfully repeating his orders. Turning, He saw Babo, now for the time acting, under the pilot, his original part of captain of the slaves. This assistance proved valuable. Tattered sails and warped yards were soon brought into some trim. And no brace or halyard was pulled but to the blithe songs of the inspirited negroes.

Good fellows, thought Captain Delano, a little training would make fine sailors of them. Why see, the very women pull and sing too. These must be some of those Ashantee negresses that make such capital soldiers, I've heard. But who's at the helm. I must have a good hand there.

He went to see.

The San Dominick steered with a cumbrous tiller, with large horizontal pullies attached. At each pully-end stood a subordinate black, and between them, at the tiller-head, there sponsible post, a Spanish seaman, whose countenance evinced his due share in the general hopefulness and confidence at the coming of the breeze.

He proved the same man who had behaved with so shame-faced an air on the windlass.

"Ah, — it is you, my man," exclaimed Captain Delano — "well, no more sheep's-eyes now; — look straight forward and keep the ship so. Good hand, I trust? And want to get into the harbor, don't you?"

The man assented with an inward chuckle, grasping the tiller-head firmly. Upon this, unperceived by the American, the two blacks eyed the sailor intently.

Finding all right at the helm, the pilot went forward to the forecastle, to see how matters stood there.

The ship now had way enough to breast the current. With the approach of evening, the breeze would be sure to freshen.

Having done all that was needed for the present, Captain Delano, giving his last orders to the sailors, turned aft to report affairs to Don Benito in the cabin; perhaps additionally incited to rejoin him by the hope of snatching a moment's private chat while the servant was engaged upon deck.

From opposite sides, there were, beneath the poop, two approaches to the cabin; one further forward than the other, and consequently communicating with a longer passage. Marking the servant still above, Captain Delano, taking the nighest entrance — the one last named, and at whose porch Atufal still stood — hurried on his way, till, arrived at the cabin threshold, he paused an instant, a little to recover from his eagerness. Then, with the words of his intended business upon his lips, he entered. As he advanced toward the seated Spaniard, he heard another footstep, keeping time with his. From the opposite door, a salver in hand, the servant was likewise advancing.

"Confound the faithful fellow," thought Captain Delano; "what a vexatious coincidence."

Possibly, the vexation might have been something different, were it not for the brisk confidence inspired by the breeze. But even as it was, he felt a slight twinge, from a sudden indefinite association in his mind of Babo with Atufal.

"Don Benito," said he, "I give you joy; the breeze will hold, and will increase. By the way, your tall man and time-piece, Atufal, stands without. By your order, of course?"

Don Benito recoiled, as if at some bland satirical touch, delivered with such adroit garnish of apparent good breeding as to present no handle for retort.

He is like one flayed alive, thought Captain Delano; where may one touch him without causing a shrink?

The servant moved before his master, adjusting a cushion; recalled to civility, the Spaniard stiffly replied: "you are right. The slave appears where you saw him, according to my command; which is, that if at the given hour I am below, he must take his stand and abide my coming."

"Ah now, pardon me, but that is treating the poor fellow like an ex-king indeed. Ah, Don Benito," smiling, "for all the license you permit in some things, I fear lest, at bottom, you are a bitter hard master."

Again Don Benito shrank; and this time, as the good sailor thought, from a genuine twinge of his conscience.

Again conversation became constrained. In vain Captain Delano called attention to the now perceptible motion of the keel gently cleaving the sea; with lack-lustre eye, Don Benito returned words few and reserved.

By-and-by, the wind having steadily risen, and still blowing right into the harbor, bore the San Dominick swiftly on. Rounding a point of land, the sealer at distance came into open view.

Meantime Captain Delano had again repaired to the deck, remaining there some time. Having at last altered the ship's course, so as to give the reef a wide berth, he returned for a few moments below.

I will cheer up my poor friend, this time, thought he.

"Better and better, Don Benito," he cried as he blithely re-entered: "there will soon be an end to your cares, at least for awhile. For when, after a long, sad voyage, you know, the anchor drops into the haven, all its vast weight seems lifted from the captain's heart. We are getting on famously, Don Benito. My ship is in sight. Look through this side-light here; there she is; all a-taunt-o! The Bachelor's Delight, my good friend. Ah, how this wind braces one up. Come, you must take a cup of coffee with me this evening. My old steward will give you as fine a cup as ever any sultan tasted. What say you, Don Benito, will you?"

At first, the Spaniard glanced feverishly up, casting a longing look towards the sealer, while with mute concern his servant gazed into his face. Suddenly the old ague of coldness returned, and dropping back to his cushions he was silent.

"You do not answer. Come, all day you have been my host; would you have hospitality all on one side?"

"I cannot go," was the response.

"What? it will not fatigue you. The ships will lie together as near as they can, without swinging foul. It will be little more than stepping from deck to deck; which is but as from room to room. Come, come, you must not refuse me."

"I cannot go," decisively and repulsively repeated Don Benito.

Renouncing all but the last appearance of courtesy, with a sort of cadaverous sullenness, and biting his thin nails to the quick, he glanced, almost glared, at his guest, as if impatient that a stranger's presence should interfere with the full indulgence of his morbid hour. Meantime the sound of the parted waters came more and more gurglingly and merrily in at the windows; as reproaching him for his dark spleen; as telling him that, sulk as he might, and go mad with it, nature cared not a jot; since, whose fault was it, pray?

But the foul mood was now at its depth, as the fair wind at its height.

There was something in the man so far beyond any mere unsociality or sourness previously evinced, that even the forbearing good-nature of his guest could no longer endure it. Wholly at a loss to account for such demeanor, and deeming sickness with eccentricity, however extreme, no adequate excuse, well satisfied, too, that nothing in his own conduct could justify it, Captain Delano's pride began to be roused. Himself became reserved. But all seemed one to the Spaniard. Quitting him, therefore, Captain Delano once more went to the deck.

The ship was now within less than two miles of the sealer. The whale-boat was seen darting over the interval.

To be brief, the two vessels, thanks to the pilot's skill, ere long in neighborly style lay anchored together.

Before returning to his own vessel, Captain Delano had intended communicating to Don Benito the smaller details of the proposed services to be rendered. But, as it was, unwilling anew to subject himself to rebuffs, he resolved, now that he had seen the San Dominick safely moored, immediately to quit her, without further allusion to hospitality or business. Indefinitely postponing his ulterior plans, he would regulate his future actions according to future circumstances. His boat was ready to receive him; but his host still tarried below. Well, thought Captain Delano, if he has little breeding, the more need to show mine. He descended to the cabin to bid a ceremonious, and, it may be, tacitly rebukeful adieu. But to his great satisfaction, Don Benito, as if he began to feel the weight of that treatment with which his slighted guest had, not indecorously, retaliated upon him, now supported by his servant, rose to his feet, and grasping Captain Delano's hand, stood tremulous; too much agitated to speak. But the good augury hence drawn was suddenly dashed, by his resuming all his previous reserve, with augmented gloom, as, with half-averted eyes, he silently reseated himself on his cushions. With a corresponding return of his own chilled feelings, Captain Delano bowed and withdrew.

He was hardly midway in the narrow corridor, dim as a tunnel, leading from the cabin to the stairs, when a sound, as of the tolling for execution in some jail-yard, fell on his ears. It was the echo of the ship's flawed bell, striking the hour, drearily reverberated in this subterranean vault. Instantly, by a fatality not to be withstood, his mind, responsive to the portent, swarmed with superstitious suspicions. He paused. In images far swifter than these sentences, the minutest details of all his former distrusts swept through him.

Hitherto, credulous good-nature had been too ready to furnish excuses for reasonable fears. Why was the Spaniard, so superfluously punctilious at times, now heedless of common propriety in not accompanying to the side his departing guest? Did indisposition forbid? Indisposition had not forbidden more irksome exertion that day. His last equivocal demeanor recurred. He had risen to his feet, grasped his guest's hand, motioned toward his hat; then, in an instant, all was eclipsed in sinister muteness and gloom. Did this imply one brief, repentant relenting at the final moment, from some iniquitous plot, followed by remorseless return to it? His last glance seemed to express a calamitous, yet acquiescent farewell to Captain Delano forever. Why decline the invitation to visit the sealer that evening? Or was the Spaniard less hardened than the Jew, who refrained not from supping at the board of him whom the same night he meant to betray? What imported all those day-long enigmas and contradictions, except they were intended to mystify, preliminary to some stealthy blow? Atufal, the pretended rebel, but punctual shadow, that moment lurked by the threshold without. He seemed a sentry, and more. Who, by his own confession, had stationed him there? Was the negro now lying in wait?

The Spaniard behind — his creature before: to rush from darkness to light was the involuntary choice.

The next moment, with clenched jaw and hand, he passed Atufal, and stood unharmed in the light. As he saw his trim ship lying peacefully at anchor, and almost within ordinary call; as he saw his household boat, with familiar faces in it, patiently rising and falling on the short waves by the San Dominick's side; and then, glancing about the decks where he stood, saw the oakum-pickers still gravely plying their fingers; and heard the low, buzzing whistle and industrious hum of the hatchet-polishers, still bestirring themselves over their endless occupation; and more than all, as he saw the benign aspect of nature, taking her innocent repose in the evening; the screened sun in the quiet camp of the west shining out like the mild light from Abraham's tent; as charmed eye and ear took in all these, with the chained figure of the black, clenched jaw and hand relaxed. Once again he smiled at the phantoms which had mocked him, and felt something like a tinge of remorse, that, by harboring them even for a moment, he should, by implication, have betrayed an atheist doubt of the ever-watchful Providence above.

There was a few minutes' delay, while, in obedience to his orders, the boat was being hooked along to the gangway. During this interval, a sort of saddened satisfaction stole over Captain Delano, at thinking of the kindly offices he had that day discharged for a stranger. Ah, thought he, after good actions one's conscience is never ungrateful, however much so the benefited party may be.

Presently, his foot, in the first act of descent into the boat, pressed the first round of the side-ladder, his face presented inward upon the deck. In the same moment, he heard his name courteously sounded; and, to his pleased surprise, saw Don Benito advancing — an unwonted energy in his air, as if, at the last moment, intent upon making amends for his recent discourtesy. With instinctive good feeling, Captain Delano, withdrawing his foot, turned and reciprocally advanced. As he did so, the Spaniard's nervous eagerness increased, but his vital energy failed; so that, the better to support him, the servant, placing his master's hand on his naked shoulder, and gently holding it there, formed himself into a sort of crutch.

When the two captains met, the Spaniard again fervently took the hand of the American, at the same time casting an earnest glance into his eyes, but, as before, too much overcome to speak.

I have done him wrong, self-reproachfully thought Captain Delano; his apparent coldness has deceived me; in no instance has he meant to offend.

Meantime, as if fearful that the continuance of the scene might too much unstring his master, the servant seemed anxious to terminate it. And so, still presenting himself as a crutch, and walking between the two captains, he advanced with them towards the gangway; while still, as if full of kindly contrition, Don Benito would not let go the hand of Captain Delano, but retained it in his, across the black's body.

Soon they were standing by the side, looking over into the boat, whose crew turned up their curious eyes. Waiting a moment for the Spaniard to relinquish his hold, the now embarrassed Captain Delano lifted his foot, to overstep the threshold of the open gangway; but still Don Benito would not let go his hand. And yet, with an agitated tone, he said, "I can go no further; here I must bid you adieu. Adieu, my dear, dear Don Amasa. Go — go!" suddenly tearing his hand loose, "go, and God guard you better than me, my best friend."

Not unaffected, Captain Delano would now have lingered; but catching the meekly admonitory eye of the servant, with a hasty farewell he descended into his boat, followed by the continual adieus of Don Benito, standing rooted in the gangway.

Seating himself in the stern, Captain Delano, making a last salute, ordered the boat shoved off. The crew had their oars on end. The bowsmen pushed the boat a sufficient distance for the oars to be lengthwise dropped. The instant that was done, Don Benito sprang over the bulwarks, falling at the feet of Captain Delano; at the same time calling towards his ship, but in tones so frenzied, that none in the boat could understand him. But, as if not equally obtuse, three sailors, from three different and distant parts of the ship, splashed into the sea, swimming after their captain, as if intent upon his rescue.

The dismayed officer of the boat eagerly asked what this meant. To which, Captain Delano, turning a disdainful smile upon the unaccountable Spaniard, answered that, for his part, he neither knew nor cared; but it seemed as if Don Benito had taken it into his head to produce the impression among his people that the boat wanted to kidnap him. "Or else — give way for your lives," he wildly added, starting at a clattering hubbub in the ship, above which rang the tocsin of the hatchet-polishers; and seizing Don Benito by the throat he added, "this plotting pirate means murder!" Here, in apparent verification of the words, the servant, a dagger in his hand, was seen on the rail overhead, poised, in the act of leaping, as if with desperate fidelity to befriend his master to the last; while, seemingly to aid the black, the three white sailors were trying to clamber into the hampered bow. Meantime, the whole host of negroes, as if inflamed at the sight of their jeopardized captain, impended in one sooty avalanche over the bulwarks.

All this, with what preceded, and what followed, occurred with such involutions of rapidity, that past, present, and future seemed one.

Seeing the Negro coming, Captain Delano had flung the Spaniard aside, almost in the very act of clutching him, and, by the unconscious recoil, shifting his place, with arms thrown up, so promptly grappled the servant in his descent, that with dagger presented at Captain Delano's heart, the black seemed of purpose to have leaped there as to his mark. But the weapon was wrenched away, and the assailant dashed down into the bottom of the boat, which now, with disentangled oars, began to speed through the sea.

At this juncture, the left hand of Captain Delano, on one side, again clutched the half-reclined Don Benito, heedless that he was in a speechless faint, while his right foot, on the other side, ground the prostrate negro; and his right arm pressed for added speed on the after oar, his eye bent forward, encouraging his men to their utmost.

But here, the officer of the boat, who had at last succeeded in beating off the towing sailors, and was now, with face turned aft, assisting the bowsman at his oar, suddenly called to Captain Delano, to see what the black was about; while a Portuguese oarsman shouted to him to give heed to what the Spaniard was saying.

Glancing down at his feet, Captain Delano saw the freed hand of the servant aiming with a second dagger — a small one, before concealed in his wool — with this he was snakishly writhing up from the boat's bottom, at the heart of his master, his countenance lividly vindictive, expressing the centred purpose of his soul; while the Spaniard, half-choked, was vainly shrinking away, with husky words, incoherent to all but the Portuguese.

That moment, across the long-benighted mind of Captain Delano, a flash of revelation swept, illuminating, in unanticipated clearness, his host's whole mysterious demeanor, with every enigmatic event of the day, as well as the entire past voyage of the San Dominick. He smote Babo's hand down, but his own heart smote him harder. With infinite pity he withdrew his hold from Don Benito. Not Captain Delano, but Don Benito, the black, in leaping into the boat, had intended to stab.

Both the black's hands were held, as, glancing up towards the San Dominick, Captain Delano, now with scales dropped from his eyes, saw the negroes, not in misrule, not in tumult, not as if frantically concerned for Don Benito, but with mask torn away, flourishing hatchets and knives, in ferocious piratical revolt. Like delirious black dervishes, the six Ashantees danced on the poop. Prevented by their foes from springing into the water, the Spanish boys were hurrying up to the topmost spars, while such of the few Spanish sailors, not already in the sea, less alert, were descried, helplessly mixed in, on deck, with the blacks.

Meantime Captain Delano hailed his own vessel, ordering the ports up, and the guns run out. But by this time the cable of the San Dominick had been cut; and the fag-end, in lashing out, whipped away the canvas shroud about the beak, suddenly revealing, as the bleached hull swung round towards the open ocean, death for the figure-head, in a human skeleton; chalky comment on the chalked words below, *"Follow your leader."*

At the sight, Don Benito, covering his face, wailed out: "'Tis he, Aranda! my murdered, unburied friend!"

Upon reaching the sealer, calling for ropes, Captain Delano bound the negro, who made no resistance, and had him hoisted to the deck. He would then have assisted the now almost helpless Don Benito up the side; but Don Benito, wan as he was, refused to move, or be moved, until the negro should have been first put below out of view. When, presently assured that it was done, he no more shrank from the ascent.

The boat was immediately dispatched back to pick up the three swimming sailors. Meantime, the guns were in readiness, though, owing to the San Dominick having glided somewhat astern of the sealer, only the aftermost one could be brought to bear. With this, they fired six times; thinking to cripple the fugitive ship by bringing down her spars. But only a few inconsiderable ropes were shot away. Soon the ship was beyond the gun's range, steering broad out of the bay; the blacks thickly clustering round the bowsprit, one moment with taunting cries towards the whites, the next with upthrown gestures hailing the now dusky moors of ocean — cawing crows escaped from the hand of the fowler.

The first impulse was to slip the cables and give chase. But, upon second thoughts, to pursue with whale-boat and yawl seemed more promising.

Upon inquiring of Don Benito what firearms they had on board the San

Dominick, Captain Delano was answered that they had none that could be used; because, in the earlier stages of the mutiny, a cabin-passenger, since dead, had secretly put out of order the locks of what few muskets there were. But with all his remaining strength, Don Benito entreated the American not to give chase, either with ship or boat; for the negroes had already proved themselves such desperadoes, that, in case of a present assault, nothing but a total massacre of the whites could be looked for. But, regarding this warning as coming from one whose spirit had been crushed by misery the American did not give up his design.

The boats were got ready and armed. Captain Delano ordered his men into them. He was going himself when Don Benito grasped his arm.

"What! have you saved my life, Señor, and are you now going to throw away your own?"

The officers also, for reasons connected with their interests and those of the voyage, and a duty owing to the owners, strongly objected against their commander's going. Weighing their remonstrances a moment, Captain Delano felt bound to remain; appointing his chief mate — an athletic and resolute man, who had been a privateer's-man — to head the party. The more to encourage the sailors, they were told, that the Spanish captain considered his ship good as lost; that she and her cargo, including some gold and silver, were worth more than a thousand doubloons. Take her, and no small part should be theirs. The sailors replied with a shout.

The fugitives had now almost gained an offing. It was nearly night; but the moon was rising. After hard, prolonged pulling, the boats came up on the ship's quarters, at a suitable distance laying upon their oars to discharge their muskets. Having no bullets to return, the negroes sent their yells. But, upon the second volley, Indian-like, they hurtled their hatchets. One took off a sailor's fingers. Another struck the whale-boat's bow, cutting off the rope there, and remaining stuck in the gunwale like a woodman's axe. Snatching it, quivering from its lodgment, the mate hurled it back. The returned gauntlet now stuck in the ship's broken quarter-gallery, and so remained

The negroes giving too hot a reception, the whites kept a more respectful distance. Hovering now just out of reach of the hurtling hatchets, they, with a view to the close encounter which must soon come, sought to decoy the blacks into entirely disarming themselves of their most murderous weapons in a hand-to-hand fight, by foolishly flinging them, as missiles, short of the mark, into the sea. But, ere long, perceiving the stratagem, the negroes desisted, though not before many of them had to replace their lost hatchets with handspikes; an exchange which, as counted upon, proved, in the end, favorable to the assailants.

Meantime, with a strong wind, the ship still clove the water; the boats alternately falling behind, and pulling up, to discharge fresh volleys.

The fire was mostly directed towards the stern, since there, chiefly, the negroes, at present, were clustering. But to kill or maim the negroes was not the object. To take them, with the ship, was the object. To do it, the ship must be boarded; which could not be done by boats while she was sailing so fast.

A thought now struck the mate. Observing the Spanish boys still aloft, high as they could get, he called to them to descend to the yards, and cut adrift the sails. It was done. About this time, owing to causes hereafter to be shown, two Spaniards, in the dress of sailors, and conspicuously showing themselves, were killed; not by volleys, but by deliberate marksman's shots; while, as it afterwards appeared, by one of the general discharges, Atufal, the black, and the Spaniard at the helm likewise were killed. What now, with the loss of the sails, and loss of leaders, the ship became unmanageable to the negroes.

With creaking masts, she came heavily round to the wind; the prow slowly swinging into view of the boats, its skeleton gleaming in the horizontal moonlight, and casting a gigantic ribbed shadow upon the water. One extended arm of the ghost seemed beckoning the whites to avenge it.

"Follow your leader!" cried the mate; and, one on each bow, the boats boarded. Sealing-spears and cutlasses crossed hatchets and hand-spikes. Huddled upon the long-boat amidships, the negresses raised a wailing chant, whose chorus was the clash of the steel.

For a time, the attack wavered; the negroes wedging themselves to beat it back; the half-repelled sailors, as yet unable to gain a footing, fighting as troopers in the saddle, one leg sideways flung over the bulwarks, and one without, plying their cutlasses like carters' whips. But in vain. They were almost overborne, when, rallying themselves into a squad as one man, with a huzza, they sprang inboard, where, entangled, they involuntarily separated again. For a few breaths' space, there was a vague, muffled, inner sound, as of submerged sword-fish rushing hither and thither through shoals of black-fish. Soon, in a reunited band, and joined by the Spanish seamen, the whites came to the surface, irresistibly driving the negroes toward the stern. But a barricade of casks and sacks, from side to side, had been thrown up by the mainmast. Here the negroes faced about, and though scorning peace or truce, yet fain would have had respite. But, without pause, overleaping the barrier, the unflagging sailors again closed. Exhausted, the blacks now fought in despair. Their red tongues lolled, wolf-like, from their black mouths. But the pale sailors' teeth were set; not a word was spoken; and, in five minutes more, the ship was won.

Nearly a score of the negroes were killed. Exclusive of those by the balls, many were mangled; their wounds — mostly inflicted by the long-edged sealing-spears, resembling those shaven ones of the English at Preston Pans, made by the poled scythes of the Highlanders. On the other side, none were killed, though several were wounded; some severely, including the mate. The surviving negroes were temporarily secured, and the ship, towed back into the harbor at midnight, once more lay anchored.

Omitting the incidents and arrangements ensuing, suffice it that, after two days spent in refitting, the ships sailed in company for Conception, in Chili, and thence for Lima, in Peru; where, before the vice-regal courts, the whole affair, from the beginning, underwent investigation.

Though, midway on the passage, the ill-fated Spaniard, relaxed from constraint, showed some signs of regaining health with free-will; yet, agreeably to his own foreboding, shortly before arriving at Lima, he relapsed, finally becoming so reduced as to be carried ashore in arms. Hearing of his story and plight, one of the many religious institutions of the City of Kings opened an hospitable refuge to him, where both physician and priest were his nurses, and a member of the order volunteered to be his one special guardian and consoler, by night and by day.

The following extracts, translated from one of the official Spanish documents, will, it is hoped, shed light on the preceding narrative, as well as, in the first place, reveal the true port of departure and true history of the San Dominick's voyage, down to the time of her touching at the island of St. Maria.

But, ere the extracts come, it may be well to preface them with a remark.

The document selected, from among many others, for partial translation, contains the deposition of Benito Cereno; the first taken in the case. Some disclosures therein were, at the time, held dubious for both learned and natural reasons. The tribunal inclined to the opinion that the deponent, not undisturbed in his mind by recent events, raved of some things which could never have happened. But subsequent depositions of the surviving sailors, bearing out the revelations of their captain in several of the strangest particulars, gave credence to the rest. So that the tribunal, in its final decision, rested its capital sentences upon statements which, had they lacked confirmation, it would have deemed it but duty to reject.

I, Don Jose de Abos and Padilla, His Majesty's Notary for the Royal Revenue, and Register of this Province, and Notary Public of the Holy Crusade of this Bishopric, etc.

Do certify and declare, as much as is requisite in law, that, in the criminal cause commenced the twenty-fourth of the month of September, in the year seventeen hundred and ninety-nine, against the negroes of the ship San Dominick, the following declaration before me was made:

Declaration of the first witness, **Don Benito Cereno.**

The same day, and month, and year, His Honor, Doctor Juan Martinez de Rozas, Councilor of the Royal Audience of this Kingdom, and learned in the law of this Intendency, ordered the captain of the ship San Dominick, Don Benito Cereno, to appear; which he did in his litter, attended by the monk Infelez; of whom he received the oath, which he took by God, our Lord, and a sign of the

Cross; under which he promised to tell the truth of whatever he should know and should be asked; — and being interrogated agreeably to the tenor of the act commencing the process, he said, that on the twentieth of May last, he set sail with his ship from the port of Valparaiso, bound to that of Callao; loaded with the produce of the country beside thirty cases of hardware and one hundred and sixty blacks, of both sexes, mostly belonging to Don Alexandro Aranda, gentleman, of the city of Mendoza; that the crew of the ship consisted of thirty-six men, beside the persons who went as passengers; that the negroes were in part as follows:

§§

[Here, in the original, follows a list of some fifty names, descriptions, and ages, compiled from certain recovered documents of Aranda's, and also from recollections of the deponent, from which portions only are extracted.]

§§

*   — One, from about eighteen to nineteen years, named Jose, and this was the man that waited upon his master, Don Alexandro, and who speaks well the Spanish, having served him four or five years;   *   *   *   a mulatto, named Francesco, the cabin steward, of a good person and voice, having sung in the Valparaiso churches, native of the province of Buenos Ayres, aged about thirty-five years.   *   *   *   A smart Negro, named Dago, who had been for many years a grave-digger among the Spaniards, aged forty-six years.   *   *   *   Four old negroes, born in Africa, from sixty to seventy, but sound, calkers by trade, whose names are as follows: — the first was named Muri, and he was killed (as was also his son named Diamelo); the second, Nacta; the third, Yola, likewise killed; the fourth, Ghofan; and six full-grown negroes, aged from thirty to forty-five, all raw, and born among the Ashantees — Matiluqui, Yan, Lecbe, Mapenda, Yambaio, Akim; four of whom were killed;   *   *   *   a powerful negro named Atufal, who being supposed to have been a chief in Africa, his owner set great store by him.   *   *   *   And a small negro of Senegal, but some years among the Spaniards, aged about thirty, which negro's name was Babo;   *   *   *   that he does not remember the names of the others, but that still expecting the residue of Don Alexandro's papers will be found, will then take due account of them all, and remit to the court;   *   *   *   and thirty-nine women and children of all ages.*

§§

[The catalogue over, the deposition goes on]

§§

*   *   *   *   That all the negroes slept upon deck, as is customary in this navigation, and none wore fetters, because the owner, his friend Aranda, told him that they were all tractable;   *   *   *   that on the seventh day after leaving port, at three o'clock in the morning, all the Spaniards being asleep except the two officers on the watch, who were the boatswain, Juan Robles, and the carpenter, Juan*

Bautista Gayete, and the helmsman and his boy, the negroes revolted suddenly, wounded dangerously the boatswain and the carpenter, and successively killed eighteen men of those who were sleeping upon deck, some with hand-spikes and hatchets, and others by throwing them alive overboard, after tying them; that of the Spaniards upon deck, they left about seven, as he thinks, alive and tied, to manœuvre the ship, and three or four more, who hid themselves, remained also alive. Although in the act of revolt the negroes made themselves masters of the hatchway, six or seven wounded went through it to the cockpit, without any hindrance on their part; that during the act of revolt, the mate and another person, whose name he does not recollect, attempted to come up through the hatchway, but being quickly wounded, were obliged to return to the cabin; that the deponent resolved at break of day to come up the companion-way, where the negro Babo was, being the ringleader, and Atufal, who assisted him, and having spoken to them, exhorted them to cease committing such atrocities, asking them, at the same time, what they wanted and intended to do, offering, himself, to obey their commands; that notwithstanding this, they threw, in his presence, three men, alive and tied, overboard; that they told the deponent to come up, and that they would not kill him; which having done, the negro Babo asked him whether there were in those seas any negro countries where they might be carried, and he answered them, No; that the negro Babo afterwards told him to carry them to Senegal, or to the neighboring islands of St. Nicholas; and he answered, that this was impossible, on account of the great distance, the necessity involved of rounding Cape Horn, the bad condition of the vessel, the want of provisions, sails, and water; but that the negro Babo replied to him he must carry them in any way; that they would do and conform themselves to everything the deponent should require as to eating and drinking; that after a long conference, being absolutely compelled to please them, for they threatened to kill all the whites if they were not, at all events, carried to Senegal, he told them that what was most wanting for the voyage was water; that they would go near the coast to take it, and thence they would proceed on their course; that the negro Babo agreed to it; and the deponent steered towards the intermediate ports, hoping to meet some Spanish or foreign vessel that would save them; that within ten or eleven days they saw the land, and continued their course by it in the vicinity of Nasca; that the deponent observed that the negroes were now restless and mutinous, because he did not effect the taking in of water, the negro Babo having required, with threats, that it should be done, without fail, the following day; he told him he saw plainly that the coast was steep, and the rivers designated in the maps were not to be found, with other reasons suitable to the circumstances; that the best way would be to go to the island of Santa Maria, where they might water easily, it being a solitary island, as the foreigners did; that the deponent did not go to Pisco, that was near, nor make any other port of the coast because the negro Babo had intimated to him several times, that he would kill all the whites the very moment he should perceive any city, town, or settlement of any kind on the shores to which they should be carried: that having determined to go to the island of Santa Maria, as the deponent had planned, for the purpose of trying whether, on the passage or near the island itself, they could find any vessel that should favor them, or whether he could escape from it in a boat to the neighboring coast of Arruco, to adopt the necessary means he immediately changed his course, steering for the island; that the negroes Babo and Atufal held daily conferences, in which they discussed what was necessary for their design of returning to Senegal, whether they were to kill all the Spaniards, and particularly the deponent; that eight days after parting from the coast of Nasca, the deponent being on the watch a little after day-break, and soon after the negroes had their meeting, the negro Babo came to the place where the deponent was, and told him that he had determined to kill his master, Don Alexandro Aranda, both because he and his companions could not otherwise be sure of their liberty, and that to keep the seamen in subjection, he wanted to prepare a warning of what road they should be made to take did they or any of them oppose him; and that, by means of the death of Don Alexandro, that warning would best be given; but, that what this last meant, the deponent did not at the time comprehend, nor could not, further than that the death of Don Alexandro was intended; and moreover the negro Babo proposed to the deponent to call the mate Raneds, who was sleeping in the cabin, before the thing was done, for fear, as the deponent understood it, that the mate, who was a good navigator, should be killed with Don Alexandro and the rest; that the deponent, who was the friend, from youth, of Don Alexandro, prayed and conjured, but all was useless; for the negro Babo answered him that the thing could not be prevented, and that all the Spaniards risked their death if they should attempt to frustrate his will in this matter, or any other; that, in this conflict, the deponent called the mate, Raneds, who was forced to go apart, and immediately the negro Babo commanded the Ashantee Martinqui and the Ashantee Lecbe to go and commit the murder; that those two went down with hatchets to the berth of Don Alexandro; that, yet half alive and mangled, they dragged him on deck; that they were going to throw him overboard in that state, but the negro Babo stopped them, bidding the murder be completed on the deck before him, which was done, when, by his orders, the body was carried below, forward; that nothing more was seen of it by the deponent for three days; * * * that Don Alonzo Sidonia, an old man, long resident at Valparaiso, and lately appointed to a civil office in Peru, whither he had taken passage, was at the time sleeping in the berth opposite Don Alexandro's; that awakening at his cries, surprised by them, and at the sight of the negroes with their bloody hatchets in their hands, he threw himself into the sea through a window which was near him, and was drowned, without it being in the power of the deponent to assist or take him up; * * * that a short time after killing Aranda, they brought upon deck his german-cousin, of middle-age, Don Francisco Masa, of Mendoza, and the young Don Joaquin, Marques de

Aramboalaza, then lately from Spain, with his Spanish servant Ponce, and the three young clerks of Aranda, José Mozairi, Lorenzo Bargas, and Hermenegildo Gandix, all of Cadiz; that Don Joaquin and Hermenegildo Gandix, the negro Babo, for purposes hereafter to appear, preserved alive; but Don Francisco Masa, José Mozairi, and Lorenzo Bargas, with Ponce the servant, beside the boatswain, Juan Robles, the boatswain's mates, Manuel Viscaya and Roderigo Hurta, and four of the sailors, the negro Babo ordered to be thrown alive into the sea, although they made no resistance, nor begged for anything else but mercy; that the boatswain, Juan Robles, who knew how to swim, kept the longest above water, making acts of contrition, and, in the last words he uttered, charged this deponent to cause mass to be said for his soul to our Lady of Succor: ★ ★ ★ *that, during the three days which followed, the deponent, uncertain what fate had befallen the remains of Don Alexandro, frequently asked the negro Babo where they were, and, if still on board, whether they were to be preserved for interment ashore, entreating him so to order it; that the negro Babo answered nothing till the fourth day, when at sunrise, the deponent coming on deck, the negro Babo showed him a skeleton, which had been substituted for the ship's proper figurehead — the image of Christopher Colon, the discoverer of the New World; that the negro Babo asked him whose skeleton that was, and whether, from its whiteness, he should not think it a white's; that, upon discovering his face, the negro Babo, coming close, said words to this effect: "Keep faith with the blacks from here to Senegal, or you shall in spirit, as now in body, follow your leader," pointing to the prow;* ★ ★ ★ *that the same morning the negro Babo took by succession each Spaniard forward, and asked him whose skeleton that was, and whether, from its whiteness, he should not think it a white's; that each Spaniard covered his face; that then to each the negro Babo repeated the words in the first place said to the deponent;* ★ ★ ★ *that they (the Spaniards), being then assembled aft, the negro Babo harangued them, saying that he had now done all; that the deponent (as navigator for the negroes) might pursue his course, warning him and all of them that they should, soul and body, go the way of Don Alexandro, if he saw them (the Spaniards) speak or plot anything against them (the negroes) — a threat which was repeated every day; that, before the events last mentioned, they had tied the cook to throw him overboard, for it is not known what thing they heard him speak, but finally the negro Babo spared his life, at the request of the deponent; that a few days after, the deponent, endeavoring not to omit any means to preserve the lives of the remaining whites, spoke to the negroes peace and tranquillity, and agreed to draw up a paper, signed by the deponent and the sailors who could write, as also by the negro Babo, for himself and all the blacks, in which the deponent obliged himself to carry them to Senegal, and they not to kill any more, and he formally to make over to them the ship, with the cargo, with which they were for that time satisfied and quieted.* ★ ★ *But the next day, the more surely to guard against the sailors' escape, the negro Babo commanded all* the boats to be destroyed but the long-boat, which was unseaworthy, and another, a cutter in good condition, which knowing it would yet be wanted for towing the water casks, he had it lowered down into the hold.

᯽

[Various particulars of the prolonged and perplexed navigation ensuing here follow, with incidents of a calamitous calm, from which portion one passage is extracted, to wit:]

᯽

— That on the fifth day of the calm, all on board suffering much from the heat, and want of water, and five having died in fits, and mad, the negroes became irritable, and for a chance gesture, which they deemed suspicious — though it was harmless — made by the mate, Raneds, to the deponent in the act of handing a quadrant, they killed him; but that for this they afterwards were sorry, the mate being the only remaining navigator on board except the deponent.

᯽

— That omitting other events, which daily happened, and which can only serve uselessly to recall past misfortunes and conflicts, after seventy-three days' navigation, reckoned from the time they sailed from Nasca, during which they navigated under a scanty allowance of water, and were afflicted with the calms before mentioned, they at last arrived at the island of Santa Maria, on the seventeenth of the month of August, at about six o'clock in the afternoon, at which hour they cast anchor very near the American ship, Bachelor's Delight, which lay in the same bay, commanded by the generous Captain Amasa Delano; but at six o'clock in the morning, they had already descried the port, and the negroes became uneasy, as soon as at distance they saw the ship, not having expected to see one there; that the negro Babo pacified them, assuring them that no fear need be had; that straight-way he ordered the figure on the bow to be covered with canvas, as for repairs, and had the decks a little set in order; that for a time the negro Babo and the negro Atufal conferred; that the negro Atufal was for sailing away, but the negro Babo would not, and, by himself, cast about what to do; that at last he came to the deponent, proposing to him to say and do all that the deponent declares to have said and done to the American captain;   *   *   *

    *   *   *   *   that the negro Babo warned him that if he varied in the least, or uttered any word, or gave any look that should give the least intimation of the past events or present state, he would instantly kill him, with all his companions, showing a dagger, which he carried hid, saying something which, as he understood it, meant that that dagger would be alert as his eye; that the negro Babo then announced the plan to all his companions, which pleased them; that he then, the better to disguise the truth, devised many expedients, in some of them uniting deceit and defense; that of this sort was the device of the six Ashantees before named, who were his bravoes; that them he stationed on the break of the poop, as if to clean certain hatchets (in cases, which were part of the cargo), but in reality to use them, and distribute them at need, and at a given word he told them;

that, among other devices, was the device of presenting Atufal, his right hand man, as chained, though in a moment the chains could be dropped; that in every particular he informed the deponent what part he was expected to enact in every device, and what story he was to tell on every occasion, always threatening him with instant death if he varied in the least: that, conscious that many of the negroes would be turbulent, the negro Babo appointed the four aged negroes, who were calkers, to keep what domestic order they could on the decks; that again and again he harangued the Spaniards and his companions, informing them of his intent, and of his devices, and of the invented story that this deponent was to tell; charging them lest any of them varied from the story; that these arrangements were made and matured during the interval of two or three hours, between their first sighting the ship and the arrival on board of Captain Amasa Delano; that this happened about half-past seven o'clock in the morning, Captain Amasa Delano coming in his boat, and all gladly receiving him; that the deponent, as well as he could force himself, acting then the part of principal owner, and a free captain of the ship, told Captain Amasa Delano, when called upon, that he came from Buenos Ayres, bound to Lima, with three hundred negroes; that off Cape Horn, and in a subsequent fever, many negroes had died; that also, by similar casualties, all the sea officers and the greatest part of the crew had died.

❦❦

[And so the deposition goes on, circumstantially recounting the fictitious story dictated to the deponent by Babo, and through the deponent imposed upon Captain Delano; and also recounting the friendly offers of Captain Delano, with other things but all of which is here omitted. After the fictitious story, etc. the deposition proceeds:]

❦❦

— that the generous Captain Amasa Delano remained on board all the day, till he left the ship anchored at six o'clock in the evening, deponent speaking to him always of his pretended misfortunes, under the fore-mentioned principles, without having had it in his power to tell a single word, or give him the least hint, that he might know the truth and state of things; because the negro Babo, performing the office of an officious servant with all the appearance of submission of the humble slave, did not leave the deponent one moment; that this was in order to observe the deponent's actions and words, for the negro Babo understands well the Spanish; and besides, there were thereabout some others who were constantly on the watch, and likewise understood the Spanish;

   * * * that upon one occasion, while deponent was standing on the deck conversing with Amasa Delano, by a secret sign the negro Babo drew him (the deponent) aside, the act appearing as if originating with the deponent; that then, he being drawn aside, the negro Babo proposed to him to gain from Amasa Delano full particulars about his ship, and crew, and arms; that the deponent asked "For what?" that the negro Babo answered he might conceive; that, grieved at the prospect of what might overtake the generous Captain Amasa Delano, the

deponent at first refused to ask the desired questions, and used every argument to induce the negro Babo to give up this new design; that the negro Babo showed the point of his dagger; that, after the information had been obtained the negro Babo again drew him aside, telling him that that very night he (the deponent) would be captain of two ships, instead of one, for that, great part of the American's ship's crew being to be absent fishing, the six Ashantees, without any one else, would easily take it; that at this time he said other things to the same purpose; that no entreaties availed; that, before Amasa Delano's coming on board, no hint had been given touching the capture of the American ship: that to prevent this project the deponent was powerless; ＊　＊　＊　—that in some things his memory is confused, he cannot distinctly recall every event; ＊　＊　＊　— that as soon as they had cast anchor at six of the clock in the evening, as has before been stated, the American Captain took leave, to return to his vessel; that upon a sudden impulse, which the deponent believes to have come from God and his angels, he, after the farewell had been said, followed the generous Captain Amasa Delano as far as the gunwale, where he stayed, under pretense of taking leave, until Amasa Delano should have been seated in his boat; that on shoving off, the deponent sprang from the gunwale into the boat, and fell into it, he knows not how, God guarding him; that —

§⁊

[Here, in the original, follows the account of what further happened at the escape, and how the San Dominick was retaken, and of the passage to the coast; including in the recital many expressions of "eternal gratitude" to the "generous Captain Amasa Delano." The deposition then proceeds with recapitulatory remarks, and a partial renumeration of the negroes, making record of their individual part in the past events, with a view to furnishing, according to command of the court, the data whereon to found the criminal sentences to be pronounced. From this portion is the following;]

§⁊

— That he believes that all the negroes, though not in the first place knowing to the design of revolt, when it was accomplished, approved it. ＊　＊　＊　That the negro, José, eighteen years old, and in the personal service of Don Alexandro, was the one who communicated the information to the negro Babo, about the state of things in the cabin, before the revolt; that this is known, because, in the preceding midnight, he use to come from his berth, which was under his master's, in the cabin, to the deck where the ringleader and his associates were, and had secret conversations with then negro Babo, in which he was several times seen by the mate; that, one night, the mate drove him away twice; ＊　＊　that this same negro José was the one who, without being commanded to do by the negro Babo, as Lecbe and Martinqui were, stabbed his master, Don Alexandro, after he had been dragged half-lifeless to the deck; ＊　＊　that the mulatto steward, Francesco, was of the first band of revolters, that he was, in all things, the creature and tool of the negro Babo; that, to make his court, he just before a repast in the cabin, proposed, to the negro Babo, poisoning a dish for the generous Captain

Amasa Delano; this is known and believed, because the negroes have said it; but that the negro Babo, having another design, forbade Francesco;   *   *   that the Ashantee Lecbe was one of the worst of them; for that, on the day the ship was retaken, he assisted in the defense of her, with a hatchet in each hand, with one of which he wounded, in the breast, the chief mate of Amasa Delano, in the first act of boarding; this all knew; that, in sight of the deponent, Lecbe struck, with a hatchet, Don Francisco Masa, when, by the negro Babo's orders, he was carrying him to throw him overboard, alive, beside participating in the murder, before mentioned, of Don Alexandro Aranda, and others of the cabin-passengers; that, owing to the fury with which the Ashantees fought in the engagement with the boats, but this Lecbe and Yan survived; that Yan was bad as Lecbe; that Yan was the man who, by Babo's command willing prepared the skeleton of Don Alexandro, in a way the negroes afterwards told the deponent, but which he, so long as reason is left him, can never divulge; that Yan and Lecbe were the two who, in a calm by night, riveted the skeleton to the bow; this also the negroes told him; that the negro Babo was he who traced the inscription below it; that the negro Babo was the plotter from first to last; he ordered every murder, and was the helm and keel of the revolt; that Atufal was his lieutenant in all; but Atufal, with his own hand, committed no murder; nor did the negro Babo;   *   *   that Atufal was shot, being killed in the fight with the boats, ere boarding;   *   *   that the negresses, of age, were knowing to the revolt, and testified themselves satisfied at the death of their master, Don Alexandro; that, had the Negroes not restrained them, they would have tortured to death, instead of simply killing, the Spaniards slain by command of the negro Babo; that the negresses used their utmost influence to have the deponent made away with; that, in the various acts of murder, they sang songs and danced — not gaily, but solemnly; and before the engagement with the boats, as well as during the action, they sang melancholy songs to the negroes, and that this melancholy tone was more inflaming than a different one would have been, and was so intended; that all this is believed, because the negroes have said it.

   — that of the thirty-six men of the crew, exclusive of the passengers (all of whom are now dead), which the deponent had knowledge of, six only remained alive, with four cabin-boys and ship-boys, not included with the crew;   *   *   — that the negroes broke an arm of one of the cabin-boys and gave him strokes with hatchets.

ᔐᔅ

[Then follow various random disclosures referring to various periods of time. The following are extracted;]

ᔐᔅ

   — That during the presence of Captain Amasa Delano on board, some attempts were made by the sailors, and one by Hermenegildo Gandix, to convey hints to him of the true state of affairs; but that these attempts were ineffectual,

owing to fear of incurring death, and furthermore, owing to the devices which of-
fered contradictions to the true state of affairs, as well as owing to the generosity
and piety of Amasa Delano incapable of sounding such wickedness; ★ ★ ★
that Luys Galgo, a sailor about sixty years of age, and formerly of the king's navy,
was one of those who sought to convey tokens to Captain Amasa Delano; but his
intent, though undiscovered, being suspected, he was, on a pretense, made to retire
out of sight, and at last into the hold, and there was made away with. This the
negroes have since said; ★ ★ ★ *that one of the ship-boys feeling, from Cap-*
tain Amasa Delano's presence, some hopes of release, and not having enough pru-
dence, dropped some chance-word respecting his expectations, which being
overheard and understood by a slave-boy with whom he was eating at the time, the
latter struck him on the head with a knife, inflicting a bad wound, but of which
the boy is now healing; that likewise, not long before the ship was brought to an-
chor, one of the seamen, steering at the time, endangered himself by letting the
blacks remark some expression in his countenance, arising from a cause similar to
the above; but this sailor, by his heedful after conduct, escaped; ★ ★ ★ *that*
these statements are made to show the court that from the beginning to the end of
the revolt, it was impossible for the deponent and his men to act otherwise than
they did; ★ ★ ★ *— that the third clerk, Hermenegildo Gandix, who before*
had been forced to live among the seamen, wearing a seaman's habit, and in all re-
spects appearing to be one for the time; he, Gandix, was killed by a musket ball
fired through mistake from the boats before boarding; having in his fright run up
the mizzen-rigging, calling to the boats — "don't board," lest upon their boarding
the negroes should kill him; that this inducing the Americans to believe he some
way favored the cause of the negroes, they fired two balls at him, so that he fell
wounded from the rigging, and was drowned in the sea; ★ ★ ★ *— that the*
young Don Joaquin, Marques de Aramboalaza, like Hermenegildo Gandix,
the third clerk, was degraded to the office and appearance of a common seaman;
that upon one occasion when Don Joaquin shrank, the negro Babo commanded
the Ashantee Lecbe to take tar and heat it, and pour it upon Don Joaquin's hands;
★ ★ ★ *— that Don Joaquin was killed owing to another mistake of the Amer-*
icans, but one impossible to be avoided, as upon the approach of the boats, Don
Joaquin, with a hatchet tied edge out and upright to his hand, was made by the
negroes to appear on the bulwarks; whereupon, seen with arms in his hands and
in a questionable attitude, he was shot for a renegade seaman; ★ ★ ★ *— that*
on the person of Don Joaquin was found secreted a jewel, which, by papers that
were discovered, proved to have been meant for the shrine of our Lady of Mercy in
Lima; a votive offering, beforehand prepared and guarded, to attest his gratitude,
when he should have landed in Peru, his last destination, for the safe conclusion of
his entire voyage from Spain; ★ ★ ★ *— that the jewel, with the other effects*
of the late Don Joaquin, is in the custody of the brethren of the Hospital de Sac-
erdotes, awaiting the disposition of the honorable court; ★ ★ ★ *— that, ow-*
ing to the condition of the deponent, as well as the haste in which the boats

*departed for the attack, the Americans were not forewarned that there were,
among the apparent crew, a passenger and one of the clerks disguised by the negro
Babo;   *   *   *   — that, beside the negroes killed in the action, some were killed
after the capture and re-anchoring at night, when shackled to the ring-bolts on
deck; that these deaths were committed by the sailors, ere they could be prevented.
That so soon as informed of it, Captain Amasa Delano used all his authority,
and, in particular with his own hand, struck down Martinez Gola, who, having
found a razor in the pocket of an old jacket of his, which one of the shackled negroes had on, was aiming it at the negro's throat; that the noble Captain Amasa
Delano also wrenched from the hand of Bartholomew Barlo a dagger, secreted at
the time of the massacre of the whites, with which he was in the act of stabbing
a shackled negro, who, the same day, with another negro, had thrown him down
and jumped upon him;   *   *   *   — that, for all the events, befalling through so
long a time during which the ship was in the hands of the negro Babo, he cannot
here give account; but that, what he has said is the most substantial of what occurs to him at present, and is the truth under the oath which he has taken; which
declaration he affirmed and ratified, after hearing it read to him.*

*He said that he is twenty-nine years of age, and broken in body and mind;
that when finally dismissed by the court, he shall not return home to Chili, but
betake himself to the monastery on Mount Agonia without; and signed with his
honor, and crossed himself, and, for the time, departed as he came, in his litter,
with a monk Infelez, to the Hospital de Sacerdotes.*   BENITO CERENO.
DOCTOR ROZAS.

If the Deposition have served as the key to fit into the lock of the complications which precede it, then, as a vault whose door has been flung back, the San
Dominick's hull lies open today.

Hitherto the nature of this narrative, besides rendering the intricacies in the
beginning unavoidable, has more or less required that many things, instead of
being set down in the order of occurrence, should be retrospectively, or irregularly given; this last is the case with the following passages, which will conclude
the account:

During the long, mild voyage to Lima, there was, as before hinted, a period
during which the sufferer a little recovered his health, or, at least in some degree,
his tranquillity. Ere the decided relapse which came, the two captains had many
cordial conversations — their fraternal unreserve in singular contrast with former withdrawments.

Again and again it was repeated, how hard it had been to enact the part
forced on the Spaniard by Babo.

"Ah, my dear friend," Don Benito once said, "at those very times when you
thought me so morose and ungrateful, nay, when, as you now admit, you half
thought me plotting your murder, at those very times my heart was frozen; I

could not look at you, thinking of what, both on board this ship and your own, hung, from other hands, over my kind benefactor. And as God lives, Don Amasa, I know not whether desire for my own safety alone could have nerved me to that leap into your boat, had it not been for the thought that, did you, unenlightened, return to your ship, you, my best friend, with all who might be with you, stolen upon, that night, in your hammocks, would never in this world have wakened again. Do but think how you walked this deck, how you sat in this cabin, every inch of ground mined into honey-combs under you. Had I dropped the least hint, made the least advance towards an understanding between us, death, explosive death — yours as mine — would have ended the scene."

"True, true," cried Captain Delano, starting, "you have saved my life, Don Benito, more than I yours; saved it, too, against my knowledge and will."

"Nay, my friend," rejoined the Spaniard, courteous even to the point of religion, "God charmed your life, but you saved mine. To think of some things you did — those smilings and chattings, rash pointings and gesturings. For less than these, they slew my mate, Raneds; but you had the Prince of Heaven's safe-conduct through all ambuscades."

"Yes, all is owing to Providence, I know: but the temper of my mind that morning was more than commonly pleasant, while the sight of so much suffering, more apparent than real, added to my good-nature, compassion, and charity, happily interweaving the three. Had it been otherwise, doubtless, as you hint, some of my interferences might have ended unhappily enough. Besides, those feelings I spoke of enabled me to get the better of momentary distrust, at times when acuteness might have cost me my life, without saving another's. Only at the end did my suspicions get the better of me, and you know how wide of the mark they then proved."

"Wide, indeed," said Don Benito, sadly; "you were with me all day; stood with me, sat with me, talked with me, looked at me, ate with me, drank with me; and yet, your last act was to clutch for a monster, not only an innocent man, but the most pitiable of all men. To such degree may malign machinations and deceptions impose. So far may even the best man err, in judging the conduct of one with the recesses of whose condition he is not acquainted. But you were forced to it; and you were in time undeceived. Would that, in both respects, it was so ever, and with all men."

"You generalize, Don Benito; and mournfully enough. But the past is passed; why moralize upon it? Forget it. See, yon bright sun has forgotten it all, and the blue sea, and the blue sky; these have turned over new leaves."

"Because they have no memory," he dejectedly replied; "because they are not human."

"But these mild trades that now fan your cheek, do they not come with a human-like healing to you? Warm friends, steadfast friends are the trades."

"With their steadfastness they but waft me to my tomb, Señor," was the foreboding response.

"You are saved," cried Captain Delano, more and more astonished and pained; "you are saved: what has cast such a shadow upon you?"

"The negro."

There was silence, while the moody man sat, slowly and unconsciously gathering his mantle about him, as if it were a pall.

There was no more conversation that day.

But if the Spaniard's melancholy sometimes ended in muteness upon topics like the above, there were others upon which he never spoke at all; on which, indeed, all his old reserves were piled. Pass over the worst, and, only to elucidate, let an item or two of these be cited. The dress, so precise and costly, worn by him on the day whose events have been narrated, had not willingly been put on. And that silver-mounted sword, apparent symbol of despotic command, was not, indeed, a sword, but the ghost of one. The scabbard, artificially stiffened, was empty.

As for the black — whose brain, not body, had schemed and led the revolt, with the plot — his slight frame, inadequate to that which it held, had at once yielded to the superior muscular strength of his captor, in the boat. Seeing all was over, he uttered no sound, and could not be forced to. His aspect seemed to say, since I cannot do deeds, I will not speak words. Put in irons in the hold, with the rest, he was carried to Lima. During the passage, Don Benito did not visit him. Nor then, nor at any time after, would he look at him. Before the tribunal he refused. When pressed by the judges he fainted. On the testimony of the sailors alone rested the legal identity of Babo.

Some months after, dragged to the gibbet at the tail of a mule, the black met his voiceless end. The body was burned to ashes; but for many days, the head, that hive of subtlety, fixed on a pole in the Plaza, met, unabashed, the gaze of the whites; and across the Plaza looked towards St. Bartholomew's church, in whose vaults slept then, as now, the recovered bones of Aranda: and across the Rimac bridge looked towards the monastery, on Mount Agonia without; where, three months after being dismissed by the court, Benito Cereno, borne on the bier, did, indeed, follow his leader.

Frances Ellen Watkins Harper
The Two Offers

Frances Harper's "The Two Offers" is credited with being the first short fiction written by an African American woman. Published in 1859 in a magazine reserved exclusively for black authors, it is remarkably free of racial issues, focusing instead on a host of subjects that, along with the abolition of slavery, formed the substance of her distinguished lecturing career: the temperance movement, equal rights for women, and the restructuring of marriage to constitute an equal partnership. Born to free parents in the South, Harper knew well the suffering and indignity of slavery, and she early devoted herself to its iradication. Although trained in "domestic science," which she taught at Union Seminary, her eloquence and natural gifts on stage created a new career for her as a lecturer, and for two years she was hired to speak on behalf of the Maine Antislavery Society, addressing audiences throughout the north. She was chosen to speak before the World Congress of Representative Women at the Columbia Exposition hosted by Chicago in 1893, a speech in which she advocated universal suffrage for all Americans. Earlier, in 1854, she began publishing volumes of poetry, verse written in the sentimental tradition of genteel emotions and didactic themes, and she emerged as the most important African American poet of her age, largely on the basis of her extraordinary skill in utilizing the dialect of common people for artistic purposes. That ability served her well in the drafting of her first story, "The Two Offers," which is notable for its eloquent style and sensitive observations about courtship, marriage, and the obligations of family life. In 1892 she published *Iola Leroy; or, Shadows Uplifted,* a widely popular novel that appealed to both white and African American audiences. As a lecturer, poet, novelist, and short-story writer, Harper established herself as an important figure in literary history.

Frances Ellen Watkins Harper, "The Two Offers," *Anglo-African Magazine* 1 (September 1859): 288–91; 1 (October 1859): 311–13.

"What is the matter with you, Laura, this morning? I have been watching you this hour, and in that time you have commenced a half dozen letters and torn them all up. What matter of such grave moment is puzzling your dear little head, that you do not know how to decide?"

"Well, it is an important matter: I have two offers for marriage, and I do not know which to choose."

"I should accept neither, or to say the least, not at present."

"Why not?"

"Because I think a woman who is undecided between two offers, has not love enough for either to make a choice; and in that very hesitation, indecision, she has a reason to pause and seriously reflect, lest her marriage, instead of being an affinity of souls or a union of hearts, should only be a mere matter of bargain and sale, or an affair of convenience and selfish interest."

"But I consider them both very good offers, just such as many a girl would gladly receive. But to tell you the truth, I do not think that I regard either as a woman should the man she chooses for her husband. But then if I refuse, there is the risk of being an old maid, and that is not to be thought of."

"Well, suppose there is, is that the most dreadful fate that can befall a woman? Is there not more intense wretchedness in an ill-assorted marriage — more utter loneliness in a loveless home, than in the lot of the old maid who accepts her earthly mission as a gift from God, and strives to walk the path of life with earnestness and unfaltering steps?"

"Oh! what a little preacher you are. I really believe that you were cut out for an old maid; that when nature formed you, she put in a double portion of intellect to make up for a deficiency of love; and yet you are kind and affectionate. But I do not think that you know anything of the grand, over-mastering passion, or the deep necessity of woman's heart for loving."

"Do you think so?" resumed the first speaker; and bending over her work she quietly applied herself to the knitting that had lain neglected by her side, during this brief conversation; but as she did so, a shadow flitted over her pale and intellectual brow, a mist gathered in her eyes, and a slight quivering of the lips, revealed a depth of feeling to which her companion was a stranger.

But before I proceed with my story, let me give you a slight history of the speakers. They were cousins, who had met life under different auspices. Laura Lagrange, was the only daughter of rich and indulgent parents, who had spared no pains to make her an accomplished lady. Her cousin, Janette Alston, was the child of parents, rich only in goodness and affection. Her father had been unfortunate in business, and dying before he could retrieve his fortunes, left his business in an embarrassed state. His widow was unacquainted with his business affairs, and when the estate was settled, hungry creditors had brought their claims and the lawyers had received their fees, she found herself homeless and almost penniless, and she who had been sheltered in the warm clasp of loving arms, found them too powerless to shield her from the pitiless pelting storms of adversity. Year after year she struggled with poverty and wrestled with want, till her toil-worn hands became too feeble to hold the shattered chords of existence, and her tear-dimmed eyes grew heavy with the slumber of death. Her daughter had watched over her with untiring devotion, had closed her eyes in death, and gone out into the busy, restless world, missing a precious tone from the voices of earth, a beloved step from the paths of life. Too self reliant to depend on the charity of relations, she endeavored to support herself by her own exertions, and she had succeeded. Her path for a while was marked with struggle and trial, but instead of uselessly repining, she met them bravely, and her life became not a thing of ease and indulgence, but of conquest, victory, and accomplishments. At the time when this conversation took place, the deep trials of her life had passed away. The achievements of her genius had won her a position in the literary world, where she shone as one of its bright particular stars. And with her fame came a competence of worldly means, which gave her leisure for improvement, and the riper development of her rare talents. And she, that pale intellectual woman, whose genius gave life and vivacity to the social circle, and whose presence threw a halo of beauty and grace around the charmed atmosphere in which she moved, had at one period of her life, known the mystic and solemn strength of an all-absorbing love. Years faded into the misty past, had seen the kindling of her eye, the quick flushing of her cheek, and the wild throbbing of her heart, at tones of a voice long since hushed to the stillness of death. Deeply, wildly, passionately, she had loved. Her whole life seemed like the pouring out of rich, warm and gushing affections. This love quickened her talents, inspired her genius, and threw over her life a tender and spiritual earnestness. And then came a fearful shock, a mournful waking from that "dream of beauty and delight." A shadow fell around her path; it came between her and the object of her heart's worship; first a few cold words, estrangement, and then a painful separation; the old story of woman's pride — digging the sepulchre of her happiness, and then a new-made grave, and her path over it to the spirit world; and thus faded out from that young heart her bright, brief and saddened dream of life. Faint and spirit-broken, she turned from the scenes associated with the memory of the loved and lost. She tried to break the chain of sad associations that bound her to the mournful past; and so, pressing back the bitter sobs from her almost breaking heart, like the dying dolphin, whose beauty is born of its death anguish, her genius gathered strength from suffering and wondrous power and brilliancy from the agony she hid within the desolate chambers of her soul. Men hailed her as one of earth's strangely gifted children, and wreathed the garlands of fame for her brow, when it was throbbing with a wild and fearful unrest. They breathed her name with applause, when through the lonely halls of her stricken spirit, was an earnest cry for peace, a deep yearning for sympathy and heart-support.

But life, with its stern realities, met her; its solemn responsibilities confronted her, and turning, with an earnest and shattered spirit, to life's duties and trials, she found a calmness and strength that she had only imagined in her dreams of poetry and song. We will now pass over a period of ten years, and the cousins have met again. In that calm and lovely woman, in whose eyes is a depth of tenderness, tempering the flashes of her genius, whose looks and tones are full of sympathy and love, we recognize the once smitten and stricken Janette Alston. The bloom of her girlhood had given way to a higher type of spiritual beauty, as if some unseen hand had been polishing and refining the temple in which her lovely spirit found its habitation; and this had been the fact. Her inner life had grown beautiful, and it was this that was constantly developing the outer. Never, in the early flush of womanhood, when an absorbing love had lit up her eyes and glowed in her life, had she appeared so interesting as when, with a countenance which seemed overshadowed with a spiritual light, she bent over the death-bed of a young woman, just lingering at the shadowy gates of the unseen land.

"Has he come?" faintly but eagerly exclaimed the dying woman. "Oh! how I have longed for his coming, and even in death he forgets me."

"Oh, do not say so, dear Laura, some accident may have detained him," said Janette to her cousin; for on that bed, from whence she will never rise, lies the once-beautiful and light-hearted Laura Lagrange, the brightness of whose eyes has long since been dimmed with tears, and whose voice had become like a harp whose every chord is tuned to sadness — whose faintest thrill and loudest vibrations are but the variations of agony. A heavy hand was laid upon her once warm and bounding heart, and a voice came whispering through her soul, that she must die. But, to her, the tidings was a message of deliverance — a voice, hushing her wild sorrows to the calmness of resignation and hope. Life had grown so weary upon her head — the future looked so hopeless — she had no wish to tread again the track where thorns had pierced her feet, and clouds overcast her sky; and she hailed the coming of death's angel as the footsteps of a welcome friend. And yet, earth had one object so very dear to her weary heart. It was her absent and recreant husband; for, since that conversation, she had accepted one of her offers, and become a wife. But, before she married, she learned that great lesson of human experience and woman's life, to love the man who bowed at her shrine, a willing worshipper. He had a pleasing address, raven hair, flashing eyes, a voice of thrilling sweetness, and lips of persuasive eloquence; and being well versed in the ways of the world, he won his way to her heart, and she became his bride, and he was proud of his prize. Vain and superficial in his character, he looked upon marriage not as a divine sacrament for the soul's development and human progression, but as the title-deed that gave him possession of the woman he thought he loved. But alas for her, the laxity of his principles had rendered him unworthy of the deep and undying devotion of a purehearted woman; but, for awhile, he hid from her his true character, and she blindly loved him, and for a short period was happy in the consciousness of being beloved; though sometimes a vague unrest would fill her soul, when, overflowing with a sense of the good, the beautiful, and the true, she would turn to him, but find no response to the deep yearnings of her soul — no appreciation of life's highest realities — its solemn grandeur and significant importance. Their souls never met, and soon she found a void in her bosom, that his earth-born love could not fill. He did not satisfy the wants of her mental and moral nature — between him and her there was no affinity of minds, no intercommunion of souls.

Talk as you will of woman's deep capacity for loving, of the strength of her affectional nature. I do not deny it; but will the mere possession of any human love, fully satisfy all the demands of her whole being? You may paint her in poetry or fiction, as a frail vine, clinging to her brother man for support, and dying when deprived of it; and all this may sound well enough to please the imaginations of school-girls, or love-lorn maidens. But woman — the true woman — if you would render her happy, it needs more than the mere development of her affectional nature. Her conscience should be enlightened, her faith in the true and right established, and scope given to her Heaven-endowed and God-given faculties. The true aim of female education should be, not a development of one or two, but all the faculties of the human soul, because no perfect womanhood is developed by imperfect culture. Intense love is often akin to intense suffering, and to trust the whole wealth of a woman's nature on the frail bark of human love, may often be like trusting a cargo of gold and precious gems, to a bark that has never battled with the storm, or buffetted the waves. Is it any wonder, then, that so many life-barks go down, paving the ocean of time with precious hearts and wasted hopes? that so many float around us, shattered and dismasted wrecks? that so many are stranded on the shoals of existence, mournful beacons and solemn warnings for the thoughtless, to whom marriage is a careless and hasty rushing together of the affections? Alas that an institution so fraught with good for humanity should be so perverted, and that state of life, which should be filled with happiness, become so replete with misery. And this was the fate of Laura Lagrange. For a brief period after her marriage her life seemed like a bright and beautiful dream, full of hope and radiant with joy. And then there came a change — he found other attractions that lay beyond the pale of home influences. The gambling saloon had power to win him from her side, he had lived in an element of unhealthy and unhallowed excitements, and the society of a loving wife, the pleasures of a well-regulated home, were enjoyments too tame for one who had vitiated his tastes by the pleasures of sin. There were charmed houses of vice, built upon dead men's loves, where, amid a flow of song, laughter, wine, and careless mirth, he would spend hour after hour, forgetting the cheek that was paling through his neglect, heedless of the tear-dimmed eyes, peering anxiously into the darkness, waiting, or watching his return.

The influence of old associations was upon him. In early life, home had been to him a place of ceilings and walls, not a true home, built upon goodness, love and truth. It was a place where velvet carpets hushed his tread, where images of loveliness and beauty invoked into being by painter's art and sculptor's skill, pleased the eye and gratified the taste, where magnificence surrounded his way and costly clothing adorned his person; but it was not the place for the true culture and right development of his soul. His father had been too much engrossed in making money, and his mother in spending it, in striving to maintain a fashionable position in society, and shining in the eyes of the world, to give the proper direction to the character of their wayward and impulsive son. His mother put beautiful robes upon his body, but left ugly scars upon his soul; she pampered his appetite, but starved his spirit. Every mother should be a true artist, who knows how to weave into her child's life images of grace and beauty, the true poet capable of writing on the soul of childhood the harmony of love and truth, and teaching it how to produce the grandest of all poems — the poetry of a true and noble life. But in his home, a love for the good, the true and right, had been sacrificed at the shrine of frivolity and fashion. That parental authority which should have been preserved as a string of precious pearls, unbroken and unscattered, was simply the administration of chance. At one time obedience was enforced by authority, at another time by flattery and promises, and just as often it was not enforced [at] all. His early associations were formed as chance directed, and from his want of home-training, his character received a bias, his life a shade, which ran through every avenue of his existence and darkened all his future hours. Oh, if we would trace the history of all the crimes that have o'ershadowed this sin-shrouded and sorrow-darkened world of ours, how many might be seen arising from the wrong home influences, or the weakening of the home ties. Home should always be the best school for the affections, the birth-place of high resolves, and the altar upon which lofty aspirations are kindled, from whence the soul may go forth strengthened, to act its part aright in the great drama of life, with conscience enlightened, affections cultivated, and reason and judgment dominant. But alas for the young wife. Her husband had not been blessed with such a home. When he entered the arena of life, the voices from home did not linger around his path as angels of guidance about his steps; they were not like so many messages to invite him to deeds of high and holy worth. The memory of no sainted mother arose between him and deeds of darkness; the earnest prayers of no father arrested him in his downward course: and before a year of his married life had waned, his young wife had learned to wait and mourn his frequent and uncalled-for absence. More than once had she seen him come home from his midnight haunts, the bright intelligence of his eye displaced by the drunkard's stare, and his manly gait changed to the inebriate's stagger; and she was beginning to know the bitter agony that is compressed in the mournful words, a drunkard's wife. And then there came a bright but brief episode in her experience; the angel of life gave to her existence a deeper meaning and loftier significance: she sheltered in the warm clasp of her loving arms, a dear babe, a precious child, whose love filled every chamber of her heart, and felt the fount of maternal love gushing so new within her soul. That child was hers. How overshadowing was the love with which she bent over its helplessness, how much it helped to fill the void and chasms in her soul. How many lonely hours were beguiled by its winsome ways, its answering smiles and fond caresses. How exquisite and solemn was the feeling that thrilled her heart when she clasped the tiny hands together and taught her dear child to call God "Our Father."

What a blessing was that child. The father paused in his headlong career, awed by the strange beauty and precocious intellect of his child; and the mother's life had a better expression through her ministrations of love. And then there came hours of bitter anguish, shading the sunlight of her home and hushing the music of her heart. The angel of death bent over the couch of her child and beaconed it away. Closer and closer the mother strained her child to her wildly heaving breast, and struggled with the heavy hand that lay upon its heart. Love and agony contended with death, and the language of the mother's heart was,

> Oh, Death, away! that innocent is mine;
> I cannot spare him from my arms
> To lay him, Death, in thine.
> I am a mother, Death; I gave that darling birth
> I could not bear his lifeless limbs
> Should moulder in the earth.

But death was stronger than love and mightier than agony and won the child for the land of crystal founts and deathless flowers, and the poor, stricken mother sat down beneath the shadow of her mighty grief, feeling as if a great light had gone out from her soul, and that the sunshine had suddenly faded around her path. She turned in her deep anguish to the father of her child, the loved and cherished dead. For awhile his words were kind and tender, his heart seemed subdued, and his tenderness fell upon her worn and weary heart like rain on perishing flowers, or cooling waters to lips all parched with thirst and scorched with fever; but the change was evanescent, the influence of unhallowed associations and evil habits had vitiated and poisoned the springs of his existence. They had bound him in their meshes, and he lacked the moral strength to break his fetters, and stand erect in all the strength and dignity of a true manhood, making life's highest excellence his ideal, and striving to gain it.

And yet moments of deep contrition would sweep over him, when he would resolve to abandon the wine-cup forever, when he was ready to forswear the handling of another card, and he would try to break away from the associations that he felt were working his ruin; but when the hour of temptation came his strength was weakness, his earnest purposes were cobwebs, his well-meant resolutions ropes of sand, and thus passed year after year of the married life of Laura Lagrange. She tried to hide her own agony from the public gaze, to smile when her heart was almost breaking. But year after year her voice grew fainter and sadder, her once light and bounding step grew slower and faltering. Year after year she wrestled with agony, and strove with despair, till the quick eyes of her brother read, in the paling of her cheek and the dimning eye, the secret anguish of her worn and weary spirit. On that wan, sad face, he saw the death-tokens, and he knew the dark wing of the mystic angel swept coldly around her path. "Laura," said her brother to her one day, "you are not well, and I think you need our mother's tender care and nursing. You are daily losing strength, and if you will go I will accompany you." At first, she hesitated, she shrank almost instinctively from presenting that pale sad face to the loved ones at home. That face was such a tell-tale; it told of heart-sickness, of hope deferred, and the mournful story of unrequited love. But then a deep yearning for home sympathy woke within her a passionate longing for love's kind words, for tenderness and heart-support, and she resolved to seek the home of her childhood, and lay her weary head upon her mother's bosom, to be folded again in her loving arms, to lay that poor, bruised and aching heart where it might beat and throb closely to the loved ones at home. A kind welcome awaited her. All that love and tenderness could devise was done to bring the bloom to her cheek and the light to her eye; but it was all in vain; her's was a disease that no medicine could cure, no earthly balm would heal. It was a slow wasting of the vital forces, the sickness of the soul. The unkindness and neglect of her husband, lay like a leaden weight upon her heart, and slowly oozed away its life-drops. And where was he that had won her love, and then cast it aside as a useless thing, who rifled her heart of its wealth and spread bitter ashes upon its broken altars? He was lingering away from her when the death-damps were gathering on her brow, when his name was trembling on her lips! lingering away! when she was watching his coming, though the death films were gathering before her eyes, and earthly things were fading from her vision. "I think I hear him now," said the dying woman, "surely that is his step;" but the sound died away in the distance. Again she started from an uneasy slumber, "that is his voice! I am so glad he has come." Tears gathered in the eyes of the sad watchers by that dying bed, for they knew that she was deceived. He had not returned. For her sake they wished his coming. Slowly the hours waned away, and then came the sad, soul-sickening thought that she was forgotten, forgotten in the last hour of human need, forgotten when the spirit, about to be dissolved, paused for the last time on the threshold of existence, a weary watcher at the gates of death. "He has forgotten me," again she faintly murmured, and the last tears she would ever shed on earth sprung to her mournful eyes, and clasping her hands together in silent anguish, a few broken sentences issued from her pale and quivering lips. They were prayers for strength and earnest pleading for him who had desolated her young life, by turning its sunshine to shadows, its smiles to tears. "He has forgotten me," she murmured again, "but I can bear it, the bitterness of death is passed, and soon I hope to exchange the shadows of death for the brightness of eternity, the rugged paths of life for the golden streets of glory, and the care and turmoils of earth for the peace and rest of heaven." Her voice grew fainter and fainter, they saw the shadows that never deceive flit over her pale and faded face, and knew that the death angel waited to soothe their weary one to rest, to calm the throbbing of her bosom and cool the fever of her brain. And amid the silent hush of their grief the freed spirit, refined through suffering, and brought into divine harmony through the spirit of the living Christ, passed over the dark waters of death as on a bridge of light, over whose radiant arches hovering angels bent. They parted the dark locks from her marble brow, closed the waxen lids over the once bright and laughing eye, and left her to the dreamless slumber of the grave. Her cousin turned from that death-bed a sadder and wiser woman. She resolved more earnestly than ever to make the world better by her example, gladden by her presence, and to kindle the fires of her genius on the altars of universal love and truth. She had a higher and better object in all her writings than the mere acquisition of gold, or acquirement of fame. She felt that she had a high and holy mission on the battle-field of existence, that life was not given her to be frittered away in nonsense, or wasted away in trifling pursuits. She would willingly espouse an unpopular cause but not an unrighteous one. In her the downtrodden slave found an earnest advocate; the flying fugitive remembered her kindness as he stepped cautiously through our Republic, to gain his freedom in a monarchial land, having broken the chains on which the rust of centuries had gathered.

Little children learned to name her with affection, the poor called her blessed, as she broke her bread to the pale lips of hunger. Her life was like a beautiful story, only it was clothed with the dignity of reality and invested with the sublimity of truth. True, she was an old maid, no husband brightened her life with his love, or shaded it with his neglect. No children nestled lovingly in her arms called her mother. No one appended Mrs. to her name; she was indeed an old maid, not vainly striving to keep up an appearance of girlishness, when departed was written on her youth. Not vainly pining at her loneliness and isolation, the world was full of warm, loving hearts and her own beat in unison with them. Neither was she always sentimentally sighing for something to love, objects of affection were all around her, and the world was not so wealthy in love that it had no use for her's; in blessing others she made a life and benediction, and as old age descended peacefully and gently upon her, she had learned one of life's most precious lessons, that true happiness consists not so much in the fruition of our wishes as in the regulation of desires and the full development and right culture of our whole natures.

Harriet Prescott Spofford
Circumstance

Harriet Prescott Spofford published nearly 300 stories in the course of her writing career, many of them among the best of the period. "Circumstance," which first appeared in *The Atlantic Monthly* in 1860 and was included in *The Amber Gods and Other Stories* in 1864, is notable for the sustained tension of the plot and for the rich description of nature. Spofford was born in Calais, Maine, in 1849, and her New England heritage served her well in depicting the verdant woods and fields of her native region. That she places a woman in peril in the wilderness is an indication of her emphasis on female characters and their interactions with the world around them, a situation she often revisited in her fiction. Despite the Gothic suggestions of the opening, and the benevolent coincidence of the conclusion, the sharp descriptions and dramatic conflict at the heart of the action have given the story a place in literary history.

Harriet Prescott Spofford, "Circumstance," *The Atlantic Monthly* 5 (May 1860): 558–65.

She had remained, during all that day, with a sick neighbor, — those eastern wilds of Maine in that epoch frequently making neighbors and miles synonymous, — and so busy had she been with care and sympathy that she did not at first observe the approaching night. But finally the level rays, reddening the snow, threw their gleam upon the wall, and, hastily donning cloak and hood, she bade her friends farewell and sallied forth on her return. Home lay some three miles distant, across a copse, a meadow, and a piece of woods, — the woods being a fringe on the skirts of the great forests that stretch far away into the North. That home was one of a dozen log-houses lying a few furlongs apart from each other, with their half-cleared demesnes separating them at the rear from a wilderness untrodden save by stealthy native or deadly panther tribes.

She was in a nowise exalted frame of spirit, — on the contrary, rather depressed by the pain she had witnessed and the fatigue she had endured; but in certain temperaments such a condition throws open the mental pores, so to speak, and renders one receptive of every influence. Through the little copse she walked slowly, with her cloak folded about her, lingering to imbibe the sense of shelter, the sunset filtered in purple through the mist of woven spray and twig, the companionship of growth not sufficiently dense to band against her the sweet home-feeling of a young and tender wintry wood. It was therefore just on the edge of the evening that she emerged from the place and began to cross the meadow-land. At one hand lay the forest to which her path wound; at the other the evening star hung over a tide of failing orange that slowly slipped down the earth's broad side to sadden other hemispheres with sweet regret. Walking rapidly now, and with her eyes wide-open, she distinctly saw in the air before her what was not there a moment ago, a winding-sheet, — cold, white, and ghastly, waved by the likeness of four wan hands, — that rose with a long inflation and fell in rigid folds, while a voice, shaping itself from the hollowness above, spectral and melancholy, sighed, — "The Lord have mercy on the people! The Lord have mercy on the people!" Three times the sheet with its corpse-covering outline waved beneath the pale hands, and the voice, awful in its solemn and mysterious depth, sighed, "The Lord have mercy on the people!" Then all was gone, the place was clear again, the gray sky was obstructed by no deathly blot; she looked about her, shook her shoulders decidedly, and, pulling on her hood, went forward once more.

She might have been a little frightened by such an apparition, if she had led a life of less reality than frontier settlers are apt to lead; but dealing with hard fact does not engender a flimsy habit of mind, and this woman was too sincere and earnest in her character, and too happy in her situation, to be thrown by antagonism merely upon superstitious fancies and chimeras of the second-sight. She did not even believe herself subject to an hallucination, but smiled simply, a little vexed that her thought could have framed such a glamour from the day's occurrences, and not sorry to lift the bough of the warder of the woods and enter and disappear in their somber path. If she had been imaginative, she would have hesitated at her first step into a region whose dangers were not visionary; but I suppose that the thought of a little child at home would conquer that propensity in the most habituated. So, biting a bit of spicy birch, she went along. Now and then she came to a gap where the trees had been partially felled, and here she found that the lingering twilight was explained by that peculiar and perhaps electric film which sometimes sheathes the sky in diffused light for very many hours before a brilliant aurora. Suddenly, a swift shadow, like the fabulous flying-dragon, writhed through the air before her, and she felt herself instantly seized and borne aloft. It was that wild beast — the most savage and serpentine and subtle and fearless of our latitudes — known by hunters as the Indian Devil, and he held her in his clutches on the broad floor of a swinging fir-bough. His long sharp claws were caught in her clothing, he worried them sagaciously a little, then, finding that ineffectual to free them, he commenced licking her bare white arm with his rasping tongue and pouring over her the wide streams of his hot, fetid breath. So quick had this flashing action been that the woman had had no time for alarm; moreover, she was not of the screaming kind: but now, as she felt him endeavoring to disentangle his claws, and the horrid sense of her fate smote her, and she saw instinctively the fierce plunge of those weapons, the long strips of living flesh torn from her bones, the agony, the quivering disgust, itself a worse agony, — while by her side, and holding her in his great lithe embrace, the monster crouched, his white tusks whetting and gnashing, his eyes glaring through all the darkness like balls of red fire, — a shriek, that rang in every forest hollow, that startled every winter-housed thing, that stirred and woke the least needle of the tasseled pines, tore through her lips. A moment afterward, the beast left the arm, once white, now crimson, and looked up alertly.

She did not think at this instant to call upon God. She called upon her husband. It seemed to her that she had but one friend in the world; that was he; and again the cry, loud, clear, prolonged, echoed through the woods. It was not the shriek that disturbed the creature at his relish; he was not born in the woods to be scared of an owl, you know; what then? It must have been the echo, most musical, most resonant, repeated and yet repeated, dying with long sighs of sweet sound, vibrated from rock to river and back again from depth to depth of cave and cliff. Her thoughts flew after it; she knew, that, even if her husband heard it, he yet could not reach her in time; she saw that while the beast listened he would not gnaw, — and this she *felt* directly, when the rough, sharp, and multiplied stings of his tongue retouched her arm. Again her lips opened by instinct, but the sound that issued thence came by reason. She had heard that music charmed wild beasts, — just this point between life and death intensified every faculty, — and when she opened her lips the third time, it was not for shrieking, but for singing.

A little thread of melody stole out, a rill of tremulous motion; it was the cradle-song with which she rocked her baby; — how could she sing that? And then she remembered the baby sleeping rosily on the long settee before the fire, — the father cleaning his gun, with one foot on the green wooden rundle, — the merry light from the chimney dancing out and through the room, on the rafters of the ceiling with their tassels of onions and herbs, on the log walls painted with lichens and festooned with apples, on the king's-arm slung across the shelf with the old pirate's-cutlass, on the snow-pile of the bed, and on the great brass clock, — dancing, too, and lingering on the baby, with his fringed gentian eyes, his chubby fists clenched on the pillow, and his fine breezy hair fanning with the motion of his father's foot. All this struck her in one, and made a sob of her breath, and she ceased.

Immediately the long red tongue was thrust forth again. Before it touched, a song sprang to her lips, a wild sea-song, such as some sailor might be singing far out on trackless blue water that night, the shrouds whistling with frost and the sheets glued in ice, — a song with the wind in its burden and the spray in its chorus. The monster raised its head and flared the fiery eyeballs upon her, then fretted the imprisoned claws a moment and was quiet; only the breath like the vapor from some hell-pit still swathed her. Her voice, at first faint and fearful, gradually lost its quaver, grew under her control and subject to her modulation; it rose on long swells, it fell in subtle cadences, now and then its tones pealed out like bells from distant belfries on fresh sonorous mornings. She sung the song through, and, wondering lest his name of Indian Devil were not his true name, and if he would not detect her, she repeated it. Once or twice now, indeed, the beast stirred uneasily, turned, and made the bough sway at his movement. As she ended, he snapped his jaws together, and tore away the fettered member, curling it under him with a snarl, — when she burst into the gayest reel that ever answered a fiddle-bow. How many a time she had heard her husband play it on the homely fiddle made by himself from birch and cherry-wood! how many a time she had seen it danced on the floor of their one room, to the patter of wooden clogs and the rustle of homespun petticoat! how many a time she had danced it herself! — and did she not remember once, as they joined clasps for right-hands-round, how it had lent its gay, bright measure to her life? And here she was singing it alone, in the forest, at midnight, to a wild beast! As she sent her voice trilling up and down its quick oscillations between joy and pain, the creature who grasped her uncurled his paw and scratched the bark from the bough; she must vary the spell; and her voice spun leaping along the projecting points of tune of a hornpipe. Still singing, she felt herself twisted about with a low growl and a lifting of the red lip from the glittering teeth; she broke the hornpipe's thread, and commenced unraveling a lighter, livelier thing, an Irish jig. Up and down and round about her voice flew, the beast threw back his head so that the diabolical face fronted hers, and the torrent of his breath prepared her for his feast as the anaconda slimes his prey. Franticly she darted from tune to tune; his restless movements followed her. She tired herself with dancing and vivid national airs, growing feverish and singing spasmodically as she felt her horrid tomb yawning wider. Touching in this manner all the slogan and keen clan cries, the beast moved again, but only to lay the disengaged paw across her with heavy satisfaction. She did not dare to pause; through the clear cold air, the frosty starlight, she sang. If there were yet any tremor in the tone, it was not fear, —

she had learned the secret of sound at last; nor could it be chill, — far too high a fervor throbbed her pulses; it was nothing but the thought of the log-house and of what might be passing within it. She fancied the baby stirring in his sleep and moving his pretty lips, — her husband rising and opening the door, looking out after her, and wondering at her absence. She fancied the light pouring through the chink and then shut in again with all the safety and comfort and joy, her husband taking down the fiddle and playing lightly with his head inclined, playing while she sang, while she sang for her life to an Indian Devil. Then she knew he was fumbling for and finding some shining fragment and scoring it down the yellowing hair, and unconsciously her voice forsook the wild war-tunes and drifted into the half-gay, half-melancholy Rosin the Bow.

Suddenly she woke pierced with a pang, and the daggered tooth penetrated her flesh; — dreaming of safety, she had ceased singing and lost it. The beast had regained the use of all his limbs, and now, standing and raising his back, bristling and foaming, with sounds that would have been like hisses but for their deep and fearful sonority, he withdrew step by step toward the trunk of the tree, still with his flaming balls upon her. She was all at once free, on one end of the bough, twenty feet from the ground. She did not measure the distance, but rose to drop herself down, careless of any death, so that it were not this. Instantly, as if he scanned her thoughts, the creature bounded forward with a yell and caught her again in his dreadful hold. It might be that he was not greatly famished; for, as she suddenly flung up her voice again, he settled himself composedly on the bough, still clasping her with invincible pressure to his rough, ravenous breast, and listening in a fascination to the sad, strange U-la-lu that now moaned forth in loud, hollow tones above him. He half closed his eyes, and sleepily reopened and shut them again.

What rending pains were close at hand! Death! and what a death! worse than any other that is to be named! Water, be it cold or warm, that which buoys up blue ice-fields, or which bathes tropical coasts with currents of balmy bliss, is yet a gentle conqueror, kisses as it kills, and draws you down gently through darkening fathoms to its heart. Death at the sword is the festival of trumpet and bugle and banner, with glory ringing out around you and distant hearts thrilling through yours. No gnawing disease can bring such a hideous end as this; for that is a fiend bred of your own flesh, and this — is it a fiend, this living lump of appetites? What dread comes with the thought of perishing in flames! but fire, let it leap and hiss never so hotly, is something too remote, too alien, to inspire us with such loathly horror as a wild beast; if it have a life, that life is too utterly beyond our comprehension. Fire is not half ourselves; as it devours, arouses neither hatred nor disgust; is not to be known by the strength of our lower natures let loose; does not drip our blood into our faces from foaming chaps, nor mouth nor snarl above us with vitality. Let us be ended by fire, and we are ashes, for the winds to bear, the leaves to cover; let us be ended by wild beasts, and the base, cursed thing howls with us forever through the forest. All this she felt as she charmed him, and what force it lent to her song God knows. If her voice should fail! If the damp and cold should give her any fatal hoarseness! If all the silent powers of the forest did not conspire to help her! The dark, hollow night rose indifferently over her; the wide, cold air breathed rudely past her, lifted her wet hair and blew it down again; the great boughs swung with a ponderous strength, now and then clashed their iron lengths together and shook off a sparkle of icy spears or some long-lain weight of snow from their heavy shadows. The green depths were utterly cold and silent and stern. These beautiful haunts that all the summer were hers and rejoiced to share with her their bounty, these heavens that had yielded their largess, these stems that had thrust their blossoms into her hands, all these friends of three moons ago forgot her now and knew her no longer.

Feeling her desolation, wild, melancholy, forsaken songs rose thereon from that frightful aerie, — weeping, wailing tunes, that sob among the people from age to age, and overflow with otherwise unexpressed sadness, — all rude, mournful ballads, — old tearful strains, that Shakspeare heard the vagrants sing, and that rise and fall like the wind and tide, — sailor-songs, to be heard only in lone mid-watches beneath the moon and stars, — ghastly rhyming romances, such as that famous one of the "Lady Margaret," when

> She slipped on her gown of green
>   A piece below the knee, —
> And 'twas all a long, cold winter's night
>   A dead corse followed she.

Still the beast lay with closed eyes, yet never relaxing his grasp. Once a half-whine of enjoyment escaped him, — he fawned his fearful head upon her; once he scored her cheek with his tongue: savage caresses that hurt like wounds. How weary she was! and yet how terribly awake! How fuller and fuller of dismay grew the knowledge that she was only prolonging her anguish and playing with death! How appalling the thought that with her voice ceased her existence! Yet she could not sing forever; her throat was dry and hard; her very breath was a pain; her mouth was hotter than any desert-worn pilgrim's; — if she could but drop upon her burning tongue one atom of the ice that glittered about her! — but both of her arms were pinioned in the giant's vice. She remembered the winding-sheet, and for the first time in her life shivered with spiritual fear. Was it hers? She asked herself, as she sang, what sins she had committed, what life she had led, to find her punishment so soon and in these pangs, — and then she sought eagerly for some reason why her husband was not up and abroad to find her. He failed her, — her one sole hope in life; and without being aware of it, her voice forsook the songs of suffering and sorrow for old Covenanting hymns, — hymns with which her mother had lulled her, which the class-leader pitched in the chimney-corners, — grand and sweet Methodist hymns, brimming with melody and with all fantastic involutions of tune to suit that ecstatic worship, — hymns full of the beauty of holiness, steadfast, relying, sanctified by the salvation they had lent to those in worse extremity than hers, — for they had found themselves in the grasp of hell, while she was but in the jaws of death. Out of this strange music, peculiar to one character of faith, and than which there is none more beautiful in its degree nor owning a more potent sway of sound, her voice soared into the glorified chants of churches. What to her was death by cold or famine or wild beasts? "Though He slay me, yet will I trust in Him," she sang. High and clear through the frore fair night, the level moonbeams splintering in the wood, the scarce glints of stars in the shadowy roof of branches, these sacred anthems rose, — rose as a hope from despair, as some snowy spray of flower-bells from blackest mould. Was she not in God's hands? Did not the world swing at His will? If this were in His great plan of providence, was it not best, and should she not accept it?

"He is the Lord our God; His judgments are in all the earth."

Oh, sublime faith of our fathers, where utter self-sacrifice alone was true love, the fragrance of whose unrequired subjection was pleasant as that of golden censers swung in purple-vapored chancels!

Never ceasing in the rhythm of her thoughts, articulated in music as they thronged, the memory of her first communion flashed over her. Again she was in that distant place on that sweet spring morning. Again the congregation rustled out, and the few remained, and she trembled to find herself among them. How well she remembered the devout, quiet faces; too accustomed to the sacred feast to glow with their inner joy! how well the snowy linen at the altar, the silver vessels slowly and silently shifting! and as the cup approached and passed, how the sense of delicious perfume stole in and heightened the transport of her prayer, and she had seemed, looking up through the windows where the sky soared blue in constant freshness, to feel all heaven's balms dripping from the portals, and to scent the lilies of eternal peace! Perhaps another would not have felt so much ecstasy as satisfaction on that occasion; but it is a true, if a later disciple, who has said, "The Lord bestoweth his blessings there, where he findeth the vessels empty." — "And does it need the walls of a church to renew my communion?" she asked. "Does not every moment stand a temple four-square to God? And in that morning, with its buoyant sunlight, was I any dearer to the Heart of the World than now?" "My beloved is mine, and I am his," she sang over and over again, with all varied inflection and profuse tune. How gently all the winter-wrapt things bent toward her then! into what relation with her had they grown! how this common dependence was the spell of their intimacy! how at one with Nature had she become! how all the night and the silence and the forest seemed to hold its breath, and to send its soul up to God in her singing! It was no longer despondency, that singing. It was neither prayer not petition. She had left imploring, "How long wilt thou forget me, O Lord?" "Lighten mine eyes, lest I sleep the sleep of death!" "For in death there is no remembrance of thee"; — with countless other such fragments of supplication. She cried rather, "Yea, though I walk through the valley of the shadow of death, I will fear no evil: for thou art with me; thy rod and thy staff, they comfort me"; — and lingered, and repeated, and sang again, "I shall be satisfied, when I awake, with thy likeness."

Then she thought of the Great Deliverance, when he drew her up out of many waters, and the flashing old psalm pealed forth triumphantly: —

> The Lord descended from above,
>   and bow'd the heavens hie:
> And underneath his feet he cast
>   the darknesse of the skie.
> On cherubs and on cherubins
>   full royally he road:
> And on the wings of all the winds
>   came flying all abroad.

She forgot how recently, and with what a strange pity for her own shapeless form that was to be, she had quaintly sung, —

> Oh, lovely appearance of death!
>   What sight upon earth is so fair?
> Not all the gay pageants that breathe
>   Can with a dead body compare!

She remembered instead, — "In thy presence is fulness of joy; at thy right hand there are pleasures forevermore"; and, "God will redeem my soul from the power of the grave: for he shall receive me"; "He will swallow up death in victory." Not once now did she say, "Lord, how long wilt thou look on? rescue my soul from their destructions, my darling from the lions," — for she knew that "the young lions roar after their prey and seek their meat from God." "O Lord, thou preservest man and beast!" she said.

She had no comfort or consolation in this season, such as sustained the Christian martyrs in the amphitheatre. She was not dying for her faith; there were no palms in heaven for her to wave; but how many a time had she declared, — "I had rather be a doorkeeper in the house of my God, than to dwell in the tents of wickedness!" And as the broad rays here and there broke through the dense covert of shade and lay in rivers of lustre on crystal sheathing and frozen fretting of trunk and limb and on the great spaces of refraction, they builded up visibly that house, the shining city on the hill, and singing, "Beautiful for situation, the joy of the whole earth, is Mount Zion, on the sides of the North, the city of the Great King," her vision climbed to that higher picture where the angel shows the dazzling thing, the holy Jerusalem descending out of heaven from God, with its splendid battlements and gates of pearls, and its foundations, the eleventh a jacinth, the twelfth an amethyst, — with its great white throne, and the rainbow round about it, in sight like unto an emerald: — "And there shall be no night there, — for the Lord God giveth them light," she sang.

What whisper of dawn now rustled through the wilderness? How the night was passing! And still the beast crouched upon the bough, changing only the posture of his head, that again he might command her with those charmed eyes; — half their fire was gone; she could almost have released herself from his custody; yet, had she stirred, no one knows what malevolent instinct might have dominated anew. But of that she did not dream; long ago stripped of any expectation, she was experiencing in her divine rapture how mystically true it is that "he that dwelleth in the secret place of the Most High shall abide under the shadow of the Almighty."

Slow clarion cries now wound from the distance as the cocks caught the intelligence of day and reëchoed it faintly from farm to farm, — sleepy sentinels of night, sounding the foe's invasion, and translating that dim intuition to ringing notes of warning. Still she chanted on. A remote crash of brushwood told of some other beast on his depredations, or some night-belated traveler groping his way through the narrow path. Still she chanted on. The far, faint echoes of the chanticleers died into distance, — the crashing of the branches grew nearer. No wild beast that, but a man's step, — a man's form in the moonlight, stalwart and strong, — on one arm slept a little child, in the other hand he held his gun. Still she chanted on.

Perhaps, when her husband last looked forth, he was half ashamed to find what a fear he felt for her. He knew she would never leave the child so long but for some direst need, — and yet he may have laughed at himself, as he lifted and wrapped it with awkward care, and, loading his gun and strapping on his horn, opened the door again and closed it behind him, going out and plunging into the darkness and dangers of the forest. He was more singularly alarmed than he would have been willing to acknowledge; as he had sat with his bow hovering over the strings, he had half believed to hear her voice mingling gaily with the instrument, till he paused and listened if she were not about to lift the latch and enter. As he drew nearer the heart of the forest, that intimation of melody seemed to grow more actual, to take body and breath, to come and go on long swells and ebbs of the night-breeze, to increase with tune and words, till a strange, shrill singing grew ever clearer, and, as he stepped into an open space of moonbeams, far up in the branches, rocked by the wind, and singing, "How beautiful upon the mountains are the feet of him that bringeth good tidings, that publisheth peace," he saw his wife, — his wife, — but, great God in heaven! how? Some mad exclamation escaped him, but without diverting her. The child knew the singing voice, though never heard before in that unearthly key, and turned toward it through the veiling dreams. With a celerity almost instantaneous, it lay, in the twinkling of an eye, on the ground at the father's feet, while his gun was raised to his shoulder and levelled at the monster covering his wife with shaggy form and flaming gaze, — his wife so ghastly white, so rigid, so stained with blood, her eyes so fixedly bent above, and her lips, that had indurated into the chiselled pallor of marble, parted only with that flood of solemn song.

I do not know if it were the mother-instinct that for a moment lowered her eyes, — those eyes, so lately riveted on heaven, now suddenly seeing all life-long bliss possible. A thrill of joy pierced and shivered through her like a weapon, her voice trembled in its course, her glance lost its steady strength, fever-flushes chased each other over her face, yet she never once ceased chanting. She was quite aware, that, if her husband shot now, the ball must pierce her body before reaching any vital part of the beast, — and yet better that death, by his hand, than the other. But this her husband also knew, and he remained motionless, just covering the creature with the sight. He dared not fire, lest some wound not mortal should break the spell exercised by her voice, and the beast, enraged with pain, should rend her in atoms; moreover, the light was too uncertain for his aim. So he waited. Now and then he examined his gun to see if the damp were injuring its charge, now and then he wiped the great drops from his forehead. Again the cocks crowed with the passing hour, — the last time they were heard on that night. Cheerful home sound then, how full of safety and all comfort and rest it seemed! what sweet morning incidents of sparkling fire and sunshine, of gay household bustle, shining dresser, and cooing baby, of steaming cattle in the yard, and brimming milk-pails at the door! what pleasant voices! what laughter! what security! and here —

Now, as she sang on in the slow, endless, infinite moments, the fervent vision of God's peace was gone. Just as the grave had lost its sting, she was snatched back again into the arms of earthly hope. In vain she tried to sing, "There remaineth a rest for the people of God," — her eyes trembled on her husband's, and she could think only of him, and of the child, and of happiness that yet might be, but with what a dreadful gulf of doubt between! She shuddered now in the suspense; all calm forsook her; she was tortured with dissolving heats or frozen with icy blasts; her face contracted, growing small and pinched; her voice was hoarse and sharp, — every tone cut like a knife, — the notes became heavy to lift, — withheld by some hostile pressure, — impossible. One gasp, a convulsive effort, and there was silence, — she had lost her voice.

The beast made a sluggish movement, — stretched and fawned like one awaking, — then, as if he would have yet more of the enchantment, stirred her slightly with his muzzle. As he did so, a sidelong hint of the man standing below with the raised gun smote him; he sprung round furiously, and, seizing his prey, was about to leap into some unknown airy den of the topmost branches now waving to the slow dawn. The late moon had rounded through the sky so that her gleam at last fell full upon the bough with fairy frosting; the wintry morning light did not yet penetrate the gloom. The woman, suspended in mid-air an instant, cast only one agonized glance beneath, — but across and through it, ere the lids could fall, shot a withering sheet of flame, — a rifle-crack, half heard, was lost in the terrible yell of desperation that bounded after it and filled her ears with savage echoes, and in the wide arc of some eternal descent she was falling; — but the beast fell under her.

I think that the moment following must have been too sacred for us, and perhaps the three have no special interest again till they issue from the shadows of the wilderness upon the white hills that skirt their home. The father carries the child hushed again into slumber, the mother follows with no such feeble step as might be anticipated, — and as they slowly climb the steep under the clear gray sky and the paling morning star, she stops to gather a spray of the red-rose berries or a feathery tuft of dead grasses for the chimney-piece of the log-house, or a handful of brown ones for the child's play, — and of these quiet, happy folk you would scarcely dream how lately they had stolen from under the banner and encampment of the great King Death. The husband proceeds a step or two in advance; the wife lingers over a singular foot-print in the snow, stoops and examines it, then looks up with a hurried word. Her husband stands alone on the hill, his arms folded across the babe, his gun fallen, — stands defined against the pallid sky like a bronze. What is there in their home, lying below and yellowing in the light, to fix him with such a stare? She springs to his side. There is no home there. The log-house, the barns, the neighboring farms, the fences, are all blotted out and mingled in one smoking ruin. Desolation and death were indeed there, and beneficence and life in the forest. Tomahawk and scalping-knife, descended during that night, had left behind them only this work for their accomplished hatred and one subtle foot-print in the snow.

For the rest, — the world was all before them, where to choose.

Elizabeth Stoddard
The Prescription

Elizabeth Stoddard's "The Prescription" was published by *Harper's New Monthly Magazine* in May 1864, but surprisingly, it does not mention the Civil War, a subject that dominated most literature of the time. Instead, her story focuses on domestic conflict, gender issues with a new concern: mental illness. Trapped in a marriage to an overbearing husband, the wife in this case feels stifled and unfulfilled, and a sensitive physician offers his prescription for a cure. The drama proceeds from that moment. The dominant themes inherent in the events predict the work of Charlotte Perkins Gilman and Kate Chopin at the end of the century in their depiction of the self-realization and independence of women. Stoddard wrote about these ideas in scores of stories and in three novels, the best known of which is *The Morgesons* (1861).

Elizabeth Stoddard. "The Prescription," *Harper's New Monthly Magazine* 28 (May 1864): 794–800.

The Doctor said that change of air would do me good, and that the farther I went from home the better. It would be wise to go, he thought, beyond the reach of daily newspapers and Adams Express; an irregular mail would be advisable. "Choose a village," he added, "where there is no railroad, no telegraph wires, no barrack hotel, and no Gothic meeting-house."

"How long must she stay?" my husband asked.

The Doctor eyed him a moment, as if a reply was rising in his mind which he would like to give utterance to, but had a doubt whether it was best to do so. He answered presently, that I must stay out of the city till I was in a different condition from the one I was in at present.

When this conversation happened on a summer afternoon in my chamber, a torn Zouave jacket of white Marseilles was lying on the sofa where the Doctor sat. A few minutes before his arrival my husband, Gérard Fuller, entered the room and came to the table where I was drawing, and being very tall and very nearsighted bent his head over my shoulder; the gleam of the gilt buttons on the said jacket, which I had on, must have caught his eye, for he started back with the exclamation:

"Haven't I told you never to wear these things? Fast women only should wear them."

Before I could put my pencil down he cut the jacket open with his penknife, pulled it from my arms, tore it across and tossed it over on the sofa. I replaced it with a drab-colored barége, and seated myself at a distance from the table where Gérard stood contemplating my sketch, to await further demonstration from him, when a rap came on the door and the Doctor bustled in. It is possible that there might have been an unusual expression in our faces, for he only gave a queer "hem," and referred to his memorandum-book. After perusing it a while he remarked that he had been looking over, in his carriage, a clever little book by a Frenchman, who said, "that a woman may be loved for three things: for her superior intellect — a love serious but rare; for her beauty — a love vulgar and brief; for the qualities of her heart — a love lasting but monotonous." His eyes then dropped on the torn jacket, and without waiting for any comment on his quotation he asked me how I felt, and proposed change of air for me.

"Milk-and-water will be good for her, I suppose, in the out-of-the-way place you suggest," continued Gérard.

"Unless she finds the milk of human kindness there," the Doctor replied.

"Good, Doctor, but said by Grimaldi thirty years ago; and I believe he added something about the cream of the joke."

"I dare say. Mrs. Fuller," and the Doctor turned toward me, putting his fingers on my wrist, "when can you leave home?"

Gérard answered hastily that I could go any day, but he could not accompany me. Gérard is a cloth importer, and mid-summer is his busiest time; the Doctor knew this fact.

"I sent a patient," he said, "two years ago to a little town famous for its bad air, its disagreeable scenery, and the stupidity of its inhabitants. I wish you would allow your wife to go there" (here his eyes rested on the jacket again). "I am sure she can get in the same house where my patient boarded; and if you say so, I will write to my old friend, John Bowman, ancient mariner, who lives in it, and engage a room."

"Oh," said Gérard, in his roughest way, "I do not believe it is necessary to write your friend; he will be glad to take a boarder, and Caroline can go to-morrow if she chooses."

"Just so," answered the Doctor, rising. "It is understood then, Mrs. Fuller, that you will follow my directions."

"You had better make them more explicit," I answered.

"I'll drop in to-morrow to see how you are, and give you my final say."

"Where is that happy village?" inquired Gérard.

"Eighteen miles from the small city of Berford, on the sea-coast; its name is Marlow. Good-day."

Gérard left me immediately, and, naturally, I looked in the glass as soon as I was alone. I saw no difference in my appearance, and could not account for the Doctor's penetration; for I was convinced that he knew Gérard had torn off the jacket from me. Upon second thought, I remembered that he had shown the same manner once before. It was when Gérard happened to come home one day, in the beginning of my illness, with a carriage, to take me out with him. The Doctor, perceiving that I did not wish to go, said that I had better stay at home that day. Gérard flung about in wrath, and finally rushed out of the room and went off with the carriage. The Doctor asked me, suddenly, if I was nervous before I was married. "No," I said.

"Your grandmother," he remarked, "must be an old muff."

As Gérard had said the same thing frequently of her, I supposed it must be true that she was; but I was impressed with an idea that the Doctor had a different reason for thinking so from what Gérard had. I was not left alone much, was I? the Doctor questioned. What individual tastes or employments had I? Did I ever feel hemmed in by circumstances? He had often noticed that dyspeptic people felt that way. These, with many more strange questions, he asked, and I believe I answered him coherently, though, while I think of it now, I wonder that I was not embarrassed.

He came the next day after the episode of the jacket, and told me that he had already written to Mr. Bowman, who would be ready to receive me as soon as the letter reached him. He also gave me a prescription in a sealed envelope, adding that I need not open it till I had arrived in Marlow, for there was an apothecary's shop there.

"The Doctor has left nothing for me to arrange, I conclude," said Gérard, when he returned home that evening.

"He has even provided for me after I get there, in giving me a sealed prescription."

"Give it to me at once."

I offered it to him in silence.

"Take it," he said, after looking at it a moment; "do you imagine I wish to break the seal?"

I did imagine it, but did not say so.

"You will obey him, of course?"

"Shall I not?"

He shrugged his shoulders for reply.

It was several days before my traveling-dress came home and I was ready to go. Gérard continually wondered why the Doctor did not come to pack my trunk and order my carriage. He also begged me not to indulge in any sentimental twaddle on his account; which was entirely satirical on his part — for I never indulged in any thing of the kind in regard to him — and endeavored to torment me after the old fashion. He remained at home the day of my departure, but said little. He appeared interested in a novel, but I noticed that he was not so absorbed in it as to prevent his following me over the house, pursuing me from room to room with his book in his hand. He filled my purse, and a new carpet-bag was silently presented to me with various useful knickknacks in it, for which I expressed my gratitude. He accompanied me to the boat, and we had the pleasure of looking out from the opposite windows of the carriage on the drive thither. Depositing my carpet-bag and shawl on the cabin floor, he obtained a chair for me, and then stood before me in a rigid attitude. I untied my bonnet, pinned it to a berth curtain, took off my gloves, and fanned myself. He stared at my hands, oblivious of the crowd of people who hurried to and fro past us, till a man cried out, "All ashore that's going!" He pushed away my fan then, and whispered,

"It's a pity we are married."

In lieu of a reply I fanned myself with violence, for I did not know what reply to make.

"I love you, and I am tired of you; you fatigue me."

I fanned on.

"I wish the devil had that fan."

I shut it up. "Do you think it would cool him, Gérard?"

"Placid wit!"

"I am afraid the boat will start."

"Of course you are. I am going. Won't you say any thing? — send a message to your grandmother?"

I put out my hand without a word; he grasped it till I nearly cried out with pain, and was gone.

Before I had time to start a train of reflection upon the novelty of my situation the boat started; the stewardess put a bit of paper in my hand marked "37," and informed me that it was my berth; the Captain, perambulating the cabin, stopped and asked me if I would go down to supper; and a lady, with a cushion in a leather strap, asked me to exchange berths with her, as she preferred mine to hers. By this time the boat was rocking unpleasantly, my head ached, and I was glad to retire to "35," having at once given up 37 to the lady of the cushion. At sunrise we arrived in port. A train was waiting to convey passengers to different towns by a circuitous route. At the Berford station I alighted, and discovering there the Marlow mail wagon took passage therein.

"Mr. Bowman told me to look out for a lady," said the driver, "and I expect you are the invalid, or convalescent, or something of that sort boarder, ain't you?"

Somehow I felt that I had suddenly lost the claim to invalidism, and so I said that I was a convalescent.

"The air is strong in Marlow," he continued, "and no mistake; it kills or cures strangers. Mostly kills the folks that live there, too, before they get to old age. Old Bowman, though, is seventy; he's tough. Ever introduced to him? He is a first-rate man, and no mistake; he'll do what's right by you. As for myself, speaking of health, I am twenty-four, and I have had typhus fever, dysentery, inflammatory rheumatism, and no end of stoppages; but I calculate to enjoy myself for all that."

His loquacity continued and amused me till we reached John Bowman's house.

"There he is," said the driver, "awalking up and down in the sun."

"Hi yi!" said the old man, when the driver stopped; "have you brought somebody here, Ike?"

"That ere boarder, you know."

He approached the wagon, and lifting a white beaver hat, said:

"Your servant, marm."

"Bear a hand, will you," said the driver, "and unlash the trunk?"

Mr. Bowman propped his gold-headed cane against the paling, turned up the cuffs of his blue cloth jacket, and proceeded to unfasten the trunk. I observed that, in spite of his handsome beaver hat and gold-headed cane, he wore coarse gray trowsers, patched at the knees, and cow-hide shoes; and that he had a noble head, pale, dignified features, long gray hair rising from his forehead like a crown, and a diminutive figure. He interested me, and I felt no surprise at the fact of his being a friend of Doctor Brown's. I looked at the house before I entered it. It had been long built, and never painted; the martins were flying round the squat chimneys; and on the ridge-pole of the low porch several pigeons were daintily stepping to and fro. There was an iron knocker on the door, and before it a brick pavement, in the cracks of which tufts and seams of grass grew. The house interested me also.

"Now, then," said Mr. Bowman, smiting the dust from his hands, "we are ready, marm. Will you walk in? Mrs. Bowman's dinner is ready."

He opened the door softly, and preceding me, entered a room, where a tall, Roman-nosed old lady sat reading a green flannel-covered book, which I found afterward was Baxter's "Saint's Rest." Mr. Bowman waved his hand and said, "This is she;" and Mrs. Bowman rose, addressing me with a few precise words.

"Dinner, mother," he interrupted her with.

"Don't be impatient, father; let her get her things off."

He took my bonnet and shawl away, and placed me at the table. Mrs. Bowman went out, and returned with two covered dishes and a tea-pot, and we began dinner. She conversed during the meal; but her husband was silent for the most part, with the exception of a few "yi-hi's" and "pooh-pooh's," which did not seem to produce much effect upon her.

"What is the nature of your complaint?" she asked.

"Her complaint is going so fast she can't recall its name," he said.

"Father is so confident always," she remarked, with a smile of pity.

"Pooh! nonsense, mother."

"You remember what the Psalmist says, father?"

For answer he buried his face in a large mug which contained cold coffee, his constant drink, and draining it, rose from the table with twinkling eyes and went out. She gave a smiling sigh of superiority as he disappeared, and proceeded in a deliberate way to clear the table. I became interested in her performances, and declined her proposal that I should go to bed till tea-time. The remains of the dinner she disposed of in various bowls, and carried to the "cellar-way" to keep cool. She also prepared a hash for supper, and washed the dishes. I followed her into the kitchen to witness the final touch at her mid-day work, which was to scour the hooks and trammels which were already hanging on the crane as bright as steel. All this made me unmindful of the lapse of time, and I was surprised when Mr. Bowman came back with the announcement that it was going on for five o'clock.

"Hasn't she been up stairs yet, mother?" he exclaimed.

"No," she answered; "she said she was not tired."

"I will go now, Mr. Bowman, if you will show me the way," I said.

"I hope you won't mind the smell of the sea-weed when the tide is out," Mrs. Bowman remarked.

The tide! What could that have to do with going upstairs? I remembered catching a glimpse of a bay as we turned into the street where the house was situated, but there was no view of it in front.

"Nothing would tempt me," she continued, "to do my work or to stay in the back part of this house; but it is father's whim to stay here, with the butment all crumbled away, and he will stay till the underpinning goes."

He thumped the floor gently with his cane to attract my attention, and said:

"She's here for sea-weed, and the creek, and all. Don't Doctor Brown know what he is about, mother?"

He opened the door before she could reply, and I followed him. The stairs dividing on a platform about midway, we turned to the left, went up a few steps into a narrow passage, at the end of which was a door painted light blue. It was the door of my room.

"You'll like it," he said, as we entered, "because there is such a prospect from the window. It will do you good. *I* look out of it at odd times, and my mind goes out on my old voyages to Amsterdam, Leghorn, and Liverpool. I think you will like the prospect, I say."

I looked from the open window.

"Why, Mr. Bowman," I exclaimed. "your house is built on the sand!"

"Isn't it?" he chuckled, "and the floods don't wash it away either. Put your head out; streets in front of the house, seas behind; was there ever such a situation besides?"

I put my head out, and obtained a novel view. The house stood on the upper end of a marsh, half of its foundation on the border of it, and half on the solid ground of the street. A wide creek flowed past the underpinning of piles, whose channel had been divested by the "butment" now crumbling apart, but which still kept the creek from making further inroads into the spongy yards of the neighbors who lived higher up the street. Below the creek stretched the beautiful bay of Marlow, and beyond that rolled the ocean, over which Mr. Bowman's mind went on his old voyages.

"This is almost Venetian, Mr. Bowman; colorless Venice without architecture."

"I never went there; they have strange craft in that place I am told; the natives paddle their boats under the girls' windows. I went to St. Petersburg once, in the time of the Emperor Paul. Nothing will disturb you here, unless Gil Jones comes up in his punt at high tide to steal oysters. You'll hear the water splash sometimes; that's pleasant."

I must have looked tired or abstracted, for he made a hasty exit on tip-toe, without another word. I was weary; the sight of my unpacked trunk was discouraging. How could Gérard have allowed me to leave home alone? What occupation was I to find in this queer, lonely house with these strange, lonely old people?

After tea I unlocked my trunk, shook out my dresses, and looked over my stock of fineries. All at once I felt in better spirits; my clothes seemed to belong to me more than they had for a long time, and a strange sense of freedom stole over me when I recollected that I could keep the candle burning as long as I pleased, and sit up all night if I saw fit.

A sheet of dull, unbroken light hung before the shutterless window when I woke next morning. A mild silvery mist hid land and sea; immediately beneath the window I could see little pools of black water, and a bed of stones covered with a web of green viscous weeds. The tide was out. A faint breeze touched my face with dampness when I raised the sash, and a cloud of delicate mist edged itself into the room.

How different it was at noon!

Mr. Bowman was going across the bay to fish and so we dined early; by twelve o'clock he was hoisting sail at the one wharf Marlow could boast of. Mrs. Bowman went to a funeral several miles distant, and the house was left to me. I shut the windows below, bolted the outside doors, and betook myself to my room. Outside there was no shade, the pale marsh grass scorched in the sun, and the beach glittered as if every pebble was a precious stone. The water along the shore and at the mouth of the creek lay still and white, untouched by the breeze which ruffled the waters of the bay; its outlet spreading under the horizon was smooth and white also. It allured me like a magic mirror. If I should look steadfastly at it some strange mystery would be revealed to me.

It occurred to me while I stood gazing seaward to get the doctor's prescription. I opened the envelope and found on a bit of paper the following words:

"Comprehend yourself, then you will be able to comprehend others; to do this is necessary in your case."

My case! Was it pictured in yonder magic mirror and so reflected upon my mind, or were my mental eyes opening at last?

I passed several days in thinking that I was deep in thought, but I was simply in a chaos of feeling which made my brain turbid. I sat much by my window, and continually dropped into vague emotional dreams which produced as apparently a purposeless and futile agitation in my mind as the wind produces on the sea, stirring it up within its limits, but not able to move it an inch beyond. But the chaos was a process I was unaware of till it was completed by slight influences independent of my own will. One evening a tempest came up from the north, and I staid down stairs with the old people. For the most part we were silent, but as its lulls grew longer Mr. Bowman raised his voice, and his wife removed her finger from the place in the green flannel-covered book. When the tempest ceased, and all sounds had died away in the darkness of night, she remarked that she must take in the tubs she had put out to catch rain-water, and go round the house to wipe up the puddles that had leaked in.

"You are gaining, my dear," said Mr. Bowman, when she had gone.

"What am I gaining?"

"That is the secret of the sea. I knew you would go on just so, if you had the chance. I hadn't when I was young. I went hither and thither, on this voyage and that, doing the business of other men; do you think I minded what I was doing, hi yi? No, I didn't look into the sea, and the sea didn't look into me; but when the time of action was past, when my owners wanted younger captains and I sat me down here, my ships gone, my crews gone, then I looked into the sea, and the sea looked into me, and I learned what it is to live — late to be sure. You are alone for the first time in your life, I take it, for you are a young thing, and you are gaining. I knew you would like the prospect. Mother can't abear it; there's nothing of Baxter in it."

He laughed so loud that she was drawn back to the room to inquire if he had hysterics. I went to my room smiling too, but I felt as if there were tears in his eyes, for they were rising in mine. A band of moonlight crossed the floor, a portion of that which crossed the sea, and shimmered in long lines to the verge of the horizon.

"It is true," I reflected, "that I have been living and not thinking; nineteen years of unconscious doing what I have been directed to do. My biography is short, comprised in two facts. I lived with my grandmother, and married Gérard Fuller; there is little need to look into the sea in order to expatiate on these topics. But the sea looks into me, and reminds me of my eight months of married life. There is little to account for before that. We have always known Gérard; he is thirty years old; I remember him a grown man when I was a little girl — I always had to mind him. Grandmother wished me to marry him because he is the son of her old friend, for whom she still wears a mourning ring. Gérard was the only man ever intimate at our house. He was devoted to her, though she sometimes quarreled with him. He worried her into a consent to our marriage against her judgment, for she had a theory that a woman should not be married till she was twenty-five. We had not been married a month before he told me that he wished I had her character, and wondered if my marriage had really arrested my development. From that moment I felt myself the automaton he believed me to be. He began a series of experiments with me, ranging from the lively to the severe, always ending in the severe. I never retaliated, never showed anger, never remonstrated; I have more than once endeavored to pacify him, and have shaped my course entirely by his demands. His first experiment was melodramatic. His own friend, Ned Conover, happened to admire the way my hair was arranged one day. He had hardly left us when Gérard took my comb out, and pulled out the hair-pins, saying that he could not bear the way my hair was dressed. I remarked that he was hurting me, he replied that, as I was not thin-skinned, he did not believe it. But when he came home the next evening and saw that I had dressed my hair another way, he scowled and did not address a word to me for twenty-four hours. We were living with grandmother then, and I mentioned the incident to her; she looked aghast, but said nothing. Soon afterward he bought a house, and furnished it without consulting me: he supposed, he observed, that my tastes were the same as his, and that he need not trouble me. Grandmother was disappointed at our leaving her; but Gérard said that young people had better be by themselves, and she made no objection. She had several skirmishes with him, however, before we moved, and I was glad when the time came for us to go. He did not alter his behavior toward me when we lived alone. He was away from home more than formerly. Sometimes when he returned there was an inquiring expression on his face; he always went away again immediately when he wore that expression. There were times more pleasant, rare times though, when he asked me to read to him while he smoked in my chamber; I never took my eyes from my book that I did not find him perusing my face with a strange intentness. When he took me to the opera, and forgot almost that I was his wife, or to the theatre, where we could not fail to have the same chord of appreciation struck. Two months ago my health began to decline. Gérard said it was the coffee, and ordered tea for breakfast; but I did not improve. Then he said it was because I read too much, and I stopped reading. It must be sewing, he concluded, want of exercise, air, and fifty other things. But I grew worse, and Doctor Brown was called. He said little at first, and the medicine he gave was so mild that I am inclined to think it was sweetened water. Gérard stormed at him, maligned him, but succumbed to all he proposed; indeed, he carried out his directions with nervous haste. He watched me more closely than ever; how many times have I opened my eyes to see his face close to mine, full of eager anxiety! But how sullen he was if I spoke to him! At last I kept my eyes shut when I knew he bent over my pillow. It was irksome to suffer this espionage. Was it wise?"

The moon was setting behind the light-house across the bay, and the sea darkened. Whether I had been wise or foolish, it was time to go to bed.

The day after the tempest Mr. Bowman handed me a letter from Gérard.

"What has Brown's prescription done for you?" it abruptly opened with. "You are impatient to return, I know; but why should you be? you have the society that always suffices you — yourself."

I laid the letter aside without finishing it. "He is a brute," I said; "let me be free of him. I am free."

"Mr. Bowman," I said, when I went down stairs, "men are brutes."

"Yes, my dear, except when women tyrannize over them."

"What are they then, father?" his wife asked.

"Transformed into meek angels and saints. But why do you say so now particularly, my dear; did you hear me swearing at mother?"

"The old story-books on the shelves in the passage say so"

"So they do, my dear; hi yi, those stories went on more than one voyage with me."

"Poor kind of bread to cast on the waters, father," Mrs. Bowman observed.

"It returned though."

I left them arguing the point. It was evident that she did not consider Mr. Bowman one of the saved; but I knew that she thought him one of the wisest of men, and was happy with him.

I determined not to answer Gérard.

Within a week after the arrival of the letter I received one from Dr. Brown, which was more pithy even than Gérard's. It contained the following advice:

> Pursue your studies; I am inclined to believe that my prescription
> was a happy one. Let me know how you are. Physicians love intri-
> cate cases; besides, an account of the Bowmans will not come

amiss. Is Bowman satisfied with your progress? If he is, I shall be.
Be sure to stay till the September rains come on.

I divined that Gérard had applied to the Doctor to write to me, and decided not to answer the second letter also. But the two letters stirred my impulses: I began to wish the monotony of my life broken into by something tangible. I opened my port-folio, desiring to write to somebody, but what correspondent could I appeal to? I must write to myself — I would start a Diary. I commenced at once, with a motto, of course:

> Seldom should the morning's gold
> On the waters be unrolled:
> Or the troubled queen of night
> Lift her misty veil of light.
> Neither wholly dark nor bright,
> Gray by day and gray by night,
> That's the light, the sky for me,
> By the margent of the sea.

(Page first.)
The above motto is singularly inappropriate. It was in the vivid sunshine and clear moonlight which reigned over the sea that I tried to render the thoughts to the sea which it gave. In its light I saw images — not fantastic, airy shapes — but those of a plain man and woman named Gérard and Caroline. When will —
(Interruption.)
(Resume.)
Mr. Bowman came in to ask me to walk in the best street of Marlow, which has two rows of linden trees, short, thick, and vigorous in growth, in spite of the sea-wind, which gives them in infancy a slight slant to the northwest. Was glad to get back to my beloved Diary. How delightful it is to be able to express one's thoughts freely!
(Third page.)
I choose a new leaf each time I return to my Diary, because I do not feel that I have made a right beginning. I long to say something which is really important, and should never be seen by human eye. Some days have passed since I last wrote here. We have had rainy, dull weather. I staid down stairs, and sewed on Mrs. Bowman's patch-work, of the "Job's trouble" pattern, in red, yellow, and white calico. She has promised it for my bed next summer. Next summer! Shall I revisit these haunts again?

To-day it is clear, and Mr. Bowman is going to take me across the harbor in the *Polly.* What if I should be drowned? I think Gérard —

When we came back from our sail who should I see walking up and down the wharf but Gérard?

"Who upon 'arth is that?" queried Mr. Bowman.

"It looks like my husband."

"We are going to have a rush of strangers in Marlow," he said, embarrassed at his own surprise at the unexpected appearance of my husband. As the boat grated against the side of the wharf he stepped on the cap log, and extended his hand for the rope, which Mr. Bowman tossed toward him with, "Your servant, Sir; we are all right."

As Gérard turned it round a post he looked down at me with a curious expression, which indicated that he would wait for me to make a move, although he doubted whether I could do any thing original under his eye. Outwardly I was as calm as the water round the wharf, inwardly in a whirl. I contrived, however, by the time I put my foot on the gunwale to disentangle one idea, and that was, to take no pains to conceal the character of the relation between us, just as he was should he appear, as far as it lay in me to allow the truth to become apparent. I therefore took his hand to assist myself ashore, and dropped it immediately to walk in advance of him. Half-way up the wharf Mr. Bowman overtook me, and walked nimbly beside me with his basket of fish, while Gérard lingered behind, looking to the right and the left in admiration of the landscape.

"Does he read the 'Saint's Rest?'" Mr. Bowman slyly whispered. I shook my head, and the old man looked puzzled.

"For form's sake, Caroline," growled Gérard, on the other side, "you had better introduce me to your fisherman."

"For form's sake, Mr. Bowman, I introduce you to Mr. Fuller, but you already know him."

Gérard looked suspiciously at me.

"No occasion for an introduction," Mr. Bowman answered; "I knew him from his resemblance to you."

"Is it so striking?" I laughed, scanning Gérard with a nonchalant air, and meeting his eyes which were filled with astonishment and a certain expression which disturbed me, for it denoted approbation! He started a lively conversation on fish, which lasted till we reached our door. A large valise on the step met my view, and led my thoughts to speculate on the length of his stay. He must have come with an intention to remain. He seemed to understand my thoughts; for as we went in he said, with a meaning smile,

"You know how fond I am of fishing."

"It is too late in the season for that," I answered.

"Walk in, Sir," said Mr. Bowman. "This is my wife. Supper, mother."

For a wonder Mrs. Bowman was reading a pictorial newspaper, which served Gérard for a topic of talk with her. She grew lively in his presence. I saw at once that she would side with him if any contention should appear. I looked at Mr. Bowman, and detected a shade of sadness in his face. That he would sympathize with me I was sure. I put my hand on his brown fist as it lay beside his plate like a lump of brown bread. "My dear," he answered, with vivacity, "you are not well enough to go home yet."

"I am not going home."

Gérard raised his eyebrows.

"Father not having any children of his own alive is fond of young folks," Mrs. Bowman remarked.

"Yes," he replied, simply, "I love Mrs. Fuller."

"Don't you love children, ma'am?" Gérard asked, with some sharpness.

"I have been a mother."

"Do you love them, Gérard?" I asked, under my breath.

"Yes, but not the childish."

Had the sea told me all it might have told me? Or had it revealed but a one-sided story?

I slipped up stairs while he was engaged with the subject of the herring-fishery, and in my room saw the large valise again — the precursor of the coming of my lord and master. I took up my Diary and wrote in large letters the date of Gérard's arrival and these words —

    End of my Diary.

I then seated myself by the window. A breeze had sprung up since sunset, and the waves were lifting up their many voices in a melancholy dirge. The moon was not up, the stars were few, and the bay was hemmed in with darkness.

I heard Gérard's quick step along the passage; he opened my door.

"Shut that window," were his first words.

For reply I put my head tolerably far outside of it. After a moment's silence he began to unpack his valise, and laid out on the chairs a stock of shirts, handkerchiefs, and collars. He also approached my little table with an apparatus for shaving. The Diary caught his eye, and he deliberately read it.

"Equal to Miss Julia Mills's Diary," he commented. "But why do you end it?"

"Because you have come and would read whatever I might write."

He came toward me and offered his hand.

"Pooh, Gérard! what nonsense it is for me to take your hand."

He was silent again for a moment, and then ordered me once more to shut the window. It was damp, but I rose and left it open. As I walked across the room the impulse seized me to leave it to him; but he anticipated my thought, and caught me just as I put my hand on the latch.

"I dare say you will keep me here," I said, "but what will my staying avail you?"

"You are my wife; why shouldn't I compel you to stay?" and he favored me with Petruchio's opinion:

> She is my goods, my chattels, she is my house,
> My household stuff, my field, my barn,
> My horse, my ox, my ass, my any thing.

"He forgot to say aught about the *soul* of the shrew, didn't he?"

Cool enough to quote Shakspeare as he was, I saw that he was deeply agitated. I went on:

"Do you know that facts are no longer stubborn to me? I shall fight them, and conquer."

"What do you mean?"

"I mean there shall be something ideal in my life to live for — an ideal man, maybe."

"Where will you find him?"

"Yonder," I answered vaguely, looking toward the window.

"Did you ever have an ideal, Caroline, that you were disappointed in utterly?"

I never had, I said, but his question disturbed me. What if I were in fault somehow?

"Madam, I will leave you. There seems to be a lack of sofas in the house for one to sleep on, but I think I can manage the night."

"Before you go, let me give you a text to discourse upon. Doctor Brown sent me from under your tyranny."

"The tyranny of love," he said to himself.

"You nearly extinguished me."

"Did I?"

"I can't love you in your way."

"No?"

"And you wouldn't let me love in my way."

"Had you any way?"

"I might have had."

He darted out like an arrow, and I fell to crying.

When I opened my door the next morning he was beside it, leaning against the wall, very pale. My impulse was to stop; but I did not follow it, and walked down stairs. We entered the room, however, at the same time. Mr. Bowman looked at me over his spectacles till I felt uncomfortable; but he was uncommonly "chipper," to use his own expression, during breakfast.

The day ended as it began. Several days passed like it. I watched Gérard, and he watched me. It was strange, but I was obliged to acknowledge that I was making his acquaintance in this silent way. He was not the man I had known as my husband. His eyes often sought mine; perhaps he was making the same mental comments.

Mr. Bowman informed us one day that he was on the point of being very sick, and begged us to take care of him. I asked him what the matter was. He replied that the foolishness of two young people of his acquaintance was killing him by inches.

I believe I turned pale and looked weak; for Gérard dropped the book he was reading, and rushed toward me, exclaiming:

"It is not you who are foolish, Caroline; it is I!"

"No, it is not you, Gérard; it is me."

"Can you love a brute?"

"Brute!" Mr. Bowman exclaimed. "She knows the universal truth that Nature did not turn us out handsomely; reptile and four-legged rudiments cling to us yet."

"Caroline!"

"Gérard!"

"Now isn't this enough to make me down sick?" cried the old man. "Kiss each other and do better, and give my love to Brown."

Gérard told me afterward, with a queer smile, that his first night in Marlow was spent in looking for my "ideal man."

"And you found him," I answered.

4

Realism and Naturalism

Scholars traditionally date the era of Realism in American literature from historical rather than literary events, from the end of the Civil War in 1865 to the conclusion of World War I in 1918. The intervening years saw the most dramatic social transformation in national history as the population of the United States, swelled by extraordinary waves of immigration, rose from roughly 30,000,000 to over 100,000,000. Prompted by technical inventions and innovative means of capital formation that generated new manufacturing plants and businesses, the industrial revolution impelled the country to a leadership role in international politics, as the American Expeditionary Force in the First World War demonstrated. An industrial economy created employment in the major cities, and for the first time more citizens were urban than rural. The Jeffersonian ideal of a nation of yeoman farmers and villages had passed, and a vibrant new paradigm for the twentieth century took its place.

In the late nineteenth century, the nation was enriched by a diverse influx of people from scores of countries. By the end of the period New York City alone produced newspapers in over a hundred languages; even a fledgling metropolis such as Minneapolis had publications in sixteen. Virtually every religion could be found somewhere in the country, as could a myriad of customs, celebrations, phobias, resentments, and hopes. It was difficult to define an "American," and every day brought more changes and challenges. Never a society in stasis, the culture had so much dynamic energy it seemed at times ready to fly apart, but military conflict in Europe became a reason for the citizenry to finally unite in common purpose.

Related to these changes, other national transformations altered the consciousness, and the literature, of America. At the conclusion of the Civil War, the federal government freed the slaves and offered them education, work contracts, and social mobility, all administered during Reconstruction by the Freedman's Bureau. At the end of Reconstruction in 1877, the national agencies returned governmental authority to the individual states. Almost immediately, Southern Democrats, the previous

slave-owners, insured that a segregated South and Jim Crow laws replaced the programs that had been instituted under federal control. Black people moved north
into the major cities, and a new era had begun.

The Homestead Act of 1862 offered 160 acres of land to anyone who would work
the property, improve it, and live on it for five years. Millions of immigrants took advantage of the opportunity, and a vast migration to the Middle West and prairie states
soon began. The same year the Land Grant Act created universities funded by federal
property given to the states for educational purposes, land that could be rented, sold,
or simply farmed to produce income. The regulations required that these colleges
teach agriculture and military tactics in the Reserve Officers' Training Corps, known
as ROTC. A growing population needed a larger food supply, one produced with the
latest farming methods. America quickly became a major agricultural power. The military desired not simply officers but leaders, men who possessed a sense of moral
and social issues as well as skills in military strategy. Both programs were a dramatic
success. Middle-class families could now afford to send their children to college, and
increased education brought professional employment and prosperity for a new generation on a level their ancestors could only imagine.

For some arriving immigrants, life was a struggle to provide the essentials for
survival, and the poor huddled in the tenements of large cities. Other new arrivals
made their way to the frontier only to face blizzards in winter and scorching heat
throughout the summer. Many pioneers were driven out by drought or locusts, and
some even returned to Europe. But for millions of others, by far the majority, the
American dream offered genuine promise, and subsequent generations prospered.

During the period of Realism many other transformations had an impact on
daily life. After Thomas Edison's invention of the incandescent lamp in 1879, enormous dynamos produced enough electricity to light an entire city. With that source
of power came the electric streetcar, the telegraph, the telephone, and the phonograph, all within two decades. The Brooklyn Bridge opened in 1883, and people
stood in awe of what was now possible through modern engineering. Chicago
burned down in 1871, but it was rebuilt as an entirely new city that, in 1893, hosted
the Columbia Exposition, the world's fair. The Ford Motor Company began production in 1903, the same year the Wright brothers flew an airplane at Kitty Hawk,
North Carolina. In factories, the assembly-line method of production allowed for
affordable products, but with it came depersonalization, a sense that human beings were being reduced to simple mechanical functions. Charles Darwin's theory
of evolution swept the country, further suggesting that people were not the
anointed rulers of the earth but part of an evolutionary continuum that included all
of the lower creatures. A revivalist movement energized evangelical religion in
many parts of the country, but in literature it became the subject of satire and parody. The Anti-Saloon League arose in 1893 along with a parallel effort to achieve
women's suffrage, both of which would become law shortly after the Realist period.

New Forms of Literature

All of this social upheaval invigorated a new American literature, one based on principles that were quite different from those of Romanticism and addressed subjects and themes in innovative artistic modes. Various immigrant groups brought with them rich cultural and literary traditions, both oral and written, and these contributed to a new form of fiction, one informed by harsher ideas than the optimism that had driven Romanticism. Realism presented an honest portrait of everyday life for common people, and its conflicts grew from the problems Americans faced for themselves and their families. The narrators were often ordinary characters speaking a regional dialect, and the themes were familiar issues to the majority of citizens. Naturalism developed darker ideas derived from the concepts of pessimistic Determinism, Darwinian evolution, or the greed and corruption rampant in an unregulated economy.

These new forms of literature required expanded outlets to reach a growing readership. Just after the end of the war in 1865, changes in technology brought more rapid means of publication and circulation. The newspaper syndicate, for example, could have a story appear almost immediately in scores of newspapers across the country, and the author could be paid a handsome sum for such a work. The travels of young men to and from their military adventures had occasioned endless accounts of life in far regions of the country, and a market developed for narratives that portrayed a unique region with its dialect and folkways and unfamiliar setting. What followed was an explosion of interest in writing, and reading, American short fiction.

Southwestern Humor

The literary tastes and modes already established in American fiction persisted for many years, of course. The humor traditions that had begun as early as the 1820s continued to produce memorable tales, although many of them also depicted a localized setting, sometimes as remote as California, as in Mark Twain's "The Celebrated Jumping Frog of Calaveras County." Originally published as "Jim Smiley and His Jumping Frog" in 1865, it is the quintessential illustration of the aesthetics of Southwestern humor. In "How to Tell a Story," Twain explained the differences between the "comic" tale, one that depends on plot and punch line for its effects, and the "humorous" story, one that is funny throughout because of the nature of the telling. It needs to be told gravely, he said, with no awareness on the part of the narrator that there is anything even faintly ridiculous in what he is saying. Twain maintained that it is all the better if the teller is a garrulous old codger speaking to a sophisticated listener from the East. The tale traps the hearer in its aimless web. Twain said that the "humorous story may be spun out to great length, and may wander around as much as it pleases, and arrive nowhere in particular," which is often taken as an analysis of his own "Jumping Frog" tale.

However, "The Celebrated Jumping Frog of Calaveras County" is artful in subtle ways, beginning with the trick Artemus Ward plays on the frame narrator. He instructs him to ask old Simon Wheeler about Leonidas W. Smiley knowing that inquiry will trigger an interminable tale about "Jim" Smiley, who is no relation. Wheeler launches into his windy narrative and the narrator is caught. As Wheeler tells it, Jim Smiley's predilection for gambling on anything leads to absurd wagers: he even offers to bet a preacher that his wife will not recover from an illness. It is only at the end that Wheeler gets to the frog that is filled with lead shot and cannot get off the ground, restricted to hunching up his shoulders. Throughout it is the sincere attitude of the teller that generates the humor, not only the ridiculous events. Twain's brief tale, enriched by the Western vernacular, the frame "trick," and skillful dialogue, gave the American humor tradition its most famous story.

Local Colorism

As is evident in the localized background of "Jumping Frog," postwar literature emphasized regional settings as part of the national endeavor to define the social nature of the United States in a period of rapid change. Readers wanted descriptions of the geographical areas of the country, the people who lived in them, their language, traditions, and cultural values. The Northeast continued to be a frequent setting, but after the war there was a widespread fascination with the South. Indeed, immediately after the cessation of hostilities, *The Nation* in New York published a series of essays entitled "The South as It Is," and other magazines soon commissioned similar articles. In due course, other periodicals depicted all of the regions of the country in essays and short stories, and the Local Color movement had begun.

The term *Local Color* was not at all a term of condescension, as some scholars have mistakenly assumed. Indeed, the movement contains a good deal of the best fiction in American literature, including Twain's *Adventures of Huckleberry Finn,* often regarded as the greatest novel ever published in the United States. Sarah Orne Jewett's *The Country of the Pointed Firs* quickly took its place as one of the finest series of stories to emerge from New England. Similarly, Kate Chopin's *The Awakening* won recognition not only as a brilliant novel in the "New Woman" tradition, but also for its regional depiction of the unique life of Louisiana and the Creole elite. Her stories were equally celebrated, and Fred Lewis Pattee proclaimed her to be the great genius of American short fiction.

This sectional approach brought a localized richness to literature, subordinating plot to setting and regional character; it also captured local dialects, perhaps the most energizing aspect of the movement. The country was a liberal democracy that preached social equality, and it was appropriate that its fiction represent the speech of common folk. In *Crumbling Idols* in 1894, Hamlin Garland trumpeted the virtues of Local Colorism as the depiction of ordinary people and how they actually lived. He felt there could be no more important subject and called it the first original literary form the country had produced. Far from being a term of subordination, in its time Local Colorism expressed national pride, a belief that the ordinary citizens of this country were as important as people anywhere. Fiction that represented their lives accurately thus served a crucial national interest.

This movement energized the American story as nothing else had. Hundreds of monthly periodicals joined established newspapers as outlets for the new fiction. By 1885, 3,300 magazines served the country, many of them among the best in the world. *The Atlantic Monthly, The Nation, Harper's Monthly,* and *The Ladies Home Journal* all originated before the war, but now *Galaxy, Lippincott's Magazine, Appleton's Journal,* and *Scribner's Monthly* began publication. The size of the literate public dramatically increased as well, as the readership of the *New York World* indicates. In 1883 it had 20,000 subscribers; three years later, in 1886, that list had grown to 250,000, and much of this increase grew from the popularity of the Local Color movement.

Many of the finest writers of the day wrote in this mode, and they came from all parts of the nation. Harriet Beecher Stowe, Sarah Orne Jewett, and Mary Wilkins Freeman came from New England; Mark Twain and Charles Chesnutt depicted life in the South. Alice Dunbar-Nelson focused her work specifically on New Orleans, perhaps the most vibrant city in regional literature. Hamlin Garland set his dramatic stories in the Midwest, what he called the "middle border," and Bret Harte joined Mark Twain in establishing California as a setting for fiction. Women played as important a role in Local Colorism as did men, and writers from a broad spectrum of national and racial groups contributed to the movement.

The best of the stories from this tradition have remained classics for over a century. After Mark Twain's success with his "Jumping Frog" story, Bret Harte emerged as the great Local Colorist of California. He established his position with the publication of "The Luck of Roaring Camp" (1868) and "The Outcasts of Poker Flat" (1869), both of which used detailed geographical description, local dialects, and provincial character types in crafting tales that are at once sentimental and humorous. In the process, Harte popularized the device of using a sophisticated narrator to describe the activities of uncultivated characters. "The Outcasts of Poker Flat" presents a spectrum of interesting types: the ethical Gambler, who proves to be more deeply humane than the society that scorns him; the whore with a heart of gold, here personified by Mother Shipton; the town drunk who brings devastation to all around him; the innocent couple, naive and inexperienced, who connect with these people in a moment of crisis. Harte's work demonstrated that by the inception of regional fiction, writers had resolved the complex issues of advancing a plot, presenting characters, representing the language of common folk, and inventing a narrator to tell a coherent story.

Alice Dunbar-Nelson is part of the fascinating regional continuum from New

Orleans at the end of the nineteenth century. Kate Chopin, from St. Louis, lived in the area for many years and wrote with great insight about the rigid racial and gender traditions of Creole life, as had a host of other writers of the time. The best educated and perhaps most intellectually rigorous of the group was Dunbar-Nelson. She provided an African American perspective on the same region, but much of her best fiction involves characters of indeterminate racial identity who face issues not necessarily limited to ethnicity, class, and gender. In "M'Sieu Fortier's Violin," for example, the central drama grows from a love of music and a devotion to a fine instrument, even though poverty plays an important role in the motivation. Chopin and Dunbar-Nelson both contributed to the development of the short story, but their gifts were more in subject and theme than in technical innovation. Nevertheless, detailed descriptions of setting, dialect, and local customs are extremely important in the work of both writers, as is the rich cultural heritage of New Orleans.

Realism

Local Colorism contributed to the development of the American short story for works within the movement and provided the impetus for the inception of Realism in fiction. If regional literature was decidedly indigenous, Realism sprang from European sources. The term was first used in a review published in England in the *Westminster Review* in 1853, although the French had been using the term to describe a new wave in painting as well. Edmond Duranty founded a journal entitled *Réalisme* in 1856, and volumes of fiction added growing interest in the movement. The most celebrated books included Ivan Turgenev's *Sportsman's Sketches* in 1852, Leo Tolstoy's *Sevastopol* in 1856, and Gustave Flaubert's *Madame Bovary* the same year.

These works, and a wealth of others, were known by the immigrants flooding into the United States and were quickly translated into English. Realism offered a stronger plot line than Local Colorism, and these enriched dramas often centered on a moment of ethical crisis, a moral decision with profound consequences for the protagonist. Characters were believably drawn, and sentimentality was subordinated to a "normative" depiction of the way most people experienced life, although the use of regional dialects, which readers had found fascinating, continued.

This new literature dealt with ordinary characters struggling with the social, economic, ethnic, and moral issues of American life. Implicit in this idea was the notion that individuals have ethical sovereignty, that they are free to choose a course of action and thus bear responsibility for their choices. No intrusive supernatural agent saves the day. Fate does not predetermine the outcome of a predicament. The simplest form of Realism was mimetic representation, a journalistic "slice of life." The grandest type focused on moral issues and followed a character through a difficult decision. In William Dean Howells's *The Rise of Silas Lapham*, for example, the protagonist must choose deception or poverty. Huck Finn must decide between the values of his society and what he has learned through personal experience about Jim's humanity, and he elects to go to hell rather than betray his friend. These stories employed ethical crises of this kind, making them dramatic, compelling, and both socially and artistically important.

The aesthetics of Realism differ from those of Romanticism and Local Colorism. Fiction portraying conflicts in the lives of common people needs to be told by the characters themselves or, perhaps, by a limited third-person narrator identified with the mind of the protagonist. Realism rarely employs omniscience, a point-of-view that knows everything, nor does it use *symbols,* culturally established associations of objects and meaning. Rather, the movement works with metaphor and imagery, with meanings generated by context, not by the past. Unlike Romanticism, Realism does not use personified characters, portraying instead ordinary figures drawn from everyday life. Nature, a benevolent force in Romanticism, is indifferent in Realism, neither helpful nor hostile. None of the stories of the period fit this paradigm perfectly, since literary movements are more a matter of tendencies than absolutes, but the best fiction at the end of the century shared most of these attributes.

Sarah Orne Jewett's "A White Heron" is an example of a transitional work from Local Color to Realism that uses a localized setting, characters, and dialect. Despite the regional backdrop, however, the story is built around a moment of ethical crisis, one in which a young girl's allegiance to nature conflicts with her desire to win the admiration of a handsome young ornithologist.

Charles Chesnutt's "The Wife of His Youth" is a quintessential work of moral Realism set within the African American community. Published in *The Atlantic Monthly,* its enthusiastic reception in 1898 inspired Houghton Mifflin to entitle the author's collection of interrelated stories *The Wife of His Youth and Other Stories of the Color Line* the following year. All of the individual works in the book deal with race; all present a moral dilemma with dire consequences; all of them are artfully told, with complex narrative patterns and sophisticated modes of thematic development. Chesnutt was a literary artist, not a propagandist, and that fact made his work immensely popular in both the white and black readership of his day. It is typical of his work that the plot of "The Wife of His Youth" brings the protagonist, Mr. Ryder, to a decision point where he must choose between the woman he married during slavery and the beautiful and wealthy young lady he now intends to wed. Realistic stories often focus on such moments, but the consequences of the choice in this situation involve not simply Mr. Ryder's future but the complex racial past of American history.

Stephen Crane's "The Blue Hotel" presents perhaps the richest development of the theme of ethical responsibility in the short fiction of the era. A complex work, rewarding a number of perspectives, it can be interpreted as either a work of American Naturalism or Realism. From a Naturalistic perspective, the emphasis is on the forces influencing the fight in the hotel and another in a bar, where the Swede is killed by a gambler. Some scholars believe the murder is caused by the Swede's own paranoia; by the hostility of nature, expressed in the storm; or by the fragility of human existence. The Swede's fear is most often blamed for the tragedy, a powerful emotion that leads to the fight and to his encounter with the gambler. The protagonist is the only character who makes the transition from the hotel to the saloon, and thus he is the primary agent of his own demise. In contrast, a Realistic reading presumes that the men are free agents, able to choose to act in any manner they wish as guided by reason. This interpretation is supported by the conclusion, in which the Easterner reflects on the complex events that lead to the death of the Swede. The Easterner was reluctant to speak out when he knew that Johnny was cheating, and now a man is dead. He is at least partially responsible. However, Johnny is also guilty for cheating and fighting, the cowboy for heightening the violent tone, Scully for providing liquor, the Swede for confronting both Johnny and the gambler, and the gambler for knifing the Swede. Each of them is culpable, and there is no comfortable escape.

Many works of Realism, especially longer stories, presented more subtle moral conflicts. In "The Real Thing," Henry James demonstrated how the complexity of his novels could be used in his short fiction as well. This story is told by an artist looking back on an event that transformed his life. It deals with three interrelated themes all deriving from the moment when the Monarchs, an aristocratic couple who have lost their income, enter his studio and apply for work as models. They assume they can pose for the gentlemen and ladies frequently portrayed in the artist's sketches. Ironically, the Monarchs are unconvincing as representatives of the gentry, being too stiff. The artist's servants, the cockney Miss Churm and the Italian Oronte, are able to adapt themselves to a broad spectrum of parts, the "false" thing thus serving better for aesthetic purposes than the "real" thing. Eventually, the social roles of the elite couple and the servants are switched, the aristocrats doing menial tasks to earn a small wage. The artist witnesses this transformation and develops a new moral compassion, deepening his empathy for the Monarchs.

Realistic authors often dealt with military conflict in their works, a preoccupying subject for a century after the Civil War. Perhaps the greatest story on this subject is Ambrose Bierce's "An Occurrence at Owl Creek Bridge." It was written by a man who fought for the North during the Civil War, and yet the protagonist is a southern planter who sides with the Confederacy. In this sense, Bierce's fiction represents the literature of reconciliation, those stories and novels that embrace the common humanity of all regions of the country. In technical terms, what is significant is the different artistic method of each of the three numbered parts. The first is essentially Impressionistic, recording the sensations of an unnamed protagonist about to be hanged. The narrator does not know the background of the situation, does not reveal the name of the man, and presents what can be observed. The second section is omniscient: the narrator has full knowledge of what happened prior to the incident at the bridge. The third section is primarily subjective, as the narrator presents the thoughts of Peyton Farquhar in his final moments. Bierce handles all of this with such consummate skill that many readers, unaccustomed to shifts in narrative method, were mislead by the events until the final sentence. Bierce's methodology is part of the experimentation with Impressionism in fiction in the 1890s that leads to stream of consciousness in the twentieth century.

Realistic writers continued the emphasis on gender issues that originated in the eighteenth century. Mary Wilkins Freeman's "The Revolt of 'Mother,'" first published in *Harper's Magazine* in 1890, is one of the many stories focused on the subject. It depicts a confrontation between husband and wife over whether to build a new home or an additional barn. In the 1890s, gender concerns of this kind evolved to encompass the "New Woman" theme, one that emphasized independence, equality, and opportunity for women. Often the theme was explored in the negative, showing the consequences of stifling the capabilities of someone with creative imagination and intellectual potential.

Charlotte Perkins Gilman's "The Yellow Wallpaper" is among the most famous stories in this tradition. In subject it deals with emotional illness induced, at least in part, by the narrator's restricted life: she has not been allowed to read or write or engage in intellectual activities. Her insanity is a metaphorical protest against the lack of opportunity for women and the denial of full equality. Beyond the dramatic representation of mental illness, Gilman's fictional method demonstrates a great deal of artistic integrity. The first-person narrative method allows for direct self-revelation as she shows her innermost thoughts and feelings. The setting in an old mansion on the New England coast is Gothic in its suggestions. The imagery reflects the projection of her obsessions; the structure illustrates the progressive fragmentation of thought; and the themes grow naturally out of the action, which is almost entirely limited to the activity of the narrator.

Willa Cather's "A Wagner Matinée" explores the "submerged life" of a New England woman, Georgiana, who married and moved to a farm in Nebraska, far removed from the culture of her early years. The restricted world of a farm woman, with only a parlor organ for the music she dearly loves, reveals the limited options available to a rural mother with six children. In "The Other Two," Edith Wharton explores another dimension of changing gender roles at the turn of the century: divorce and remarriage. The rapid expansion of opportunities for women made it possible for a wife to leave an unhappy union and wed again, as Alice Waythorn does in this case. That a woman should have married three times and that all of her husbands should find themselves in her home at the same time provides the tension in this well-crafted story.

The gender theme in American Realism was rivaled in popularity by stories about racial issues, a topic evoking some of the best literature of the period. For example, beyond her work on women's issues, Kate Chopin also wrote a powerful story about race, "Désirée's Baby," which appeared in *Vogue* in 1893. Set in antebellum Louisiana, the area with the harshest codes for the treatment of slaves on the plantations, the impact of the story in 1893 was not for the eradication of slavery but for social and racial acceptance within the new South, a popular idea throughout American Realism. The plot involves the motifs of identity and parentage, common subjects in the period. Zitkala-Sä's "The Soft-Hearted Sioux," published in *Harper's Monthly Magazine* in 1901, deals with the conflict between Native American religion and Christianity. A Dakota woman, educated in schools for Indian children, Zitkala-Sä wrote of herself as adrift between two cultures, fully at home in neither. The plot concerns a father who dies and the confrontation of religious and social values that ensues. The narrative method is retrospective, told after the narrator is imprisoned for murder and about to be executed; the action reaches back to when he was sixteen and living with his parents, very much a member of his Dakota society.

The theme of race relations is tragically central in Paul Lawrence Dunbar's "The Lynching of Jube Benson," published in 1904. The narrative method employs a third-person frame around a first-person tale told by Dr. Melville, who is remembering his participation in the lynching of a black man many years before. Dr. Melville's dramatized telling (he speaks to friends sitting before him) emphasizes the crushing moral burden he carries for his participation in mob violence. Melville's reflections are ethical, well within the Realistic tradition. However, a reading with the emphasis on the title character stresses the Deterministic nature of the events, since Jube is caught in forces beyond his control, a Naturalistic concept. Scholars have disagreed about which of these ideas best describes the central theme of the story. Another twist on the racial theme in American fiction is Jessie Fauset's "Emmy," which appeared in the official magazine of the NAACP, *The Crisis*. Following the lead of Charles Chesnutt's work, the basic theme is more informational than confrontational. It flows from the idea that the racial "problem" in the United States would ultimately be solved through moral instruction and enlightenment, not through violence or political power. Emmy is presented as an innocent, young black woman who is barely conscious of her ethnic heritage, and all of the prejudice comes from the world around her.

One of the most remarkable "minority" writers of the turn of the century was John M. Oskison, of partial Cherokee descent, who earned a law degree from Stanford and went on to study literature at Harvard. "The Problem of Old Harjo," published in *The Southern Workman* in 1907, exemplifies his intellectual approach. It shows how the unquestioned values of Christian society can prove insufficient in a Native American cultural system. His Indian characters are not romanticized as noble savages, his portraits of white people are neither inherently evil nor coldly insensitive, and his plots do not follow standard expectations for the Western fiction so popular in the early twentieth century. Nevertheless, his stories of cultural collision are powerful and dramatic, and they remain some of the most sophisticated works of literature published in the early century.

Generally credited with being the first Asian American writer to publish in English about the Chinese experience in the United States, Sui Sin Far has emerged as an immensely popular figure in literary study. Despite the fact that she wrote only one book, *Mrs. Spring Fragrance* (1912), she is widely taught and has attracted a good deal of scholarly attention. The titular story, "Mrs. Spring Fragrance," originally appeared in 1910 in *Hampton's Magazine,* and it is significant for its subject, artistic sophistication, and the charm of its style. Millions of immigrants came to the new world during this period, and virtually every group wrote about its sense of cultural dislocation and struggles with a new language. However, the Asian experience was unique in the early twentieth century. The Chinese Exclusion Act was still in force, severely limiting the rate of entry into the United States, and in some areas new arrivals found discrimination and hostility based on race. Nevertheless, Sui Sin Far writes about these matters with only hints of bitterness in her references to Angel Island, the processing center on the West Coast, and other forms of overt racism practiced against her people. Her story of courtship in the New World, of assimilation, and of adjustment to American marriage is artistically rich. It features not only the charm of its style but the fascinating psychological portrait of Mrs. Spring Fragrance and her husband. The plot deals with moral conflicts as well as religious, racial, and emotional tensions.

María Cristina Mena's "The Education of Popo," published in *The Century Magazine* in 1914, also draws together themes of ethnicity and courtship rituals in a seemingly simple story of misunderstanding. Aesthetically, however, it is complex, especially in its point of view. The narrator first identifies with the collective minds of the Mexican hosts, showing their inflated conception of the proper way to entertain guests from the United States. Then the point of view reveals the Americans' naive pretensions to stature. Within the courtship that soon develops, both the young Mexican and the older Alicia are portrayed as being emotionally vulnerable. He is obsessed with his first infatuation, and she needs to feel desirable following a painful divorce. Popo's idealization of her leads to his "bruised heart," an outcome that seems inevitable from their first meeting. Mena's cultural insight and skill in handling a dramatic plot have helped sustain interest in this early Mexican American story.

Naturalism

Local Colorism and Realism were not the only important movements in the American short story during this period. Naturalism, an energizing force in the novel, also contributed scores of important stories. Primarily a movement that has its origins in science and sociology, Naturalism had its origins in a book by Claude Bernard entitled *An Introduction to the Study of Experimental Medicine,* which offered the idea that the duty of the physician is to construct the history of an illness and, by understanding its cause, cure the patient of a given ailment. From his point of view, human sickness was not an expression of divine retribution but the consequence of biological events that could be analyzed and manipulated. It was a rational approach to medicine, one in which appeals to supernatural powers were quite beside the point. Medicine was

changed on the basis of these controversial ideas, and so, to some extent, was literature. Impressed by this line of logic, the French novelist Emile Zola applied this thinking to fiction. In *The Experimental Novel,* he maintained that the responsibility of the
writer was to construct the history of social problems and suggest ways in which
poverty, discrimination, and injustice could be eliminated.

Other important ideas also contributed to the Naturalistic movement. In *The
Origin of the Species,* Charles Darwin maintained that human beings were not of divine origin but evolved from the animal kingdom over millions of years. People
were, he suggested, part of the continuum of life on earth from the simplest creatures to the most complex. Enormously influential, Darwin's theory spawned a
great deal of creative literature, fiction that portrayed life as a struggle against nature for survival. American writers often adapted the idea to society, showing the
predatory instincts at work in an unregulated economy. In political science, Socialist ideas about the exploitation of workers and the greed of capitalism inspired debate throughout Europe and the United States. Taken together, biological, social,
and economic Determinism were born from this thinking, a basic theme in Naturalism. Writers suggested that people were not free agents but victims swept along
by forces beyond their control. The depression of the 1890s made this logic seem
all the more pertinent, and the arrival of steady waves of impoverished immigrants
only exacerbated social tensions. The society could not create jobs fast enough to
absorb all of the new arrivals. The hopelessness of the poor was a problem that
cried out for immediate attention, and writers of the 1890s began to portray the
severity of the issue in their stories.

Frank Norris's "A Deal in Wheat" illustrates this effort. In this story, narrative
method, imagery, thematic development, and even historical accuracy are subordinated to the central idea of economic injustice, the exploitation of the poor by the
rich. A simple farmer, Sam Lewiston, goes bankrupt when commodities manipula-
tions drive the price of wheat down, forcing him to sell it for less than it costs him
to grow it. Driven off his farm, he moves to Chicago only to find that the market has
now moved the price up so high he cannot buy bread for his family. The five sections of the plot present a systematic history of economic injustice, one that shifts
about in time, geography, and character, a technique made possible by the omniscient narrator. Norris personalizes the greed of wealthy investors in Truslow and
Hornung, but historically the market fluctuations were driven by international
trade agreements and not simply by private speculators in the United States. Nevertheless, Norris presents a powerful drama of a poor man confronted by Deterministic forces, the very essence of Naturalistic themes.

Jack London's "To Build a Fire" uses an omniscient point of view with access to
the minds of both the protagonist and his dog. The narrator thus has knowledge of
the past as well as the present and the freedom to comment on the meaning of the
events. In the course of its three different publications in the first decade of the

twentieth century, the story became increasingly bitter. First appearing in a children's magazine, it was an adventure in the frozen north. The central character had a name, Tom Vincent, and his actions and limitations were his own. When the story later came out in *The Century Magazine* in 1908 and then as part of *Lost Face* in 1910, the protagonist had lost his name, becoming more a representative of humanity than a single person: his plight illustrates the human situation. The central theme of life as a struggle against a hostile nature, and of an evolutionary link between man and dog, became standard Naturalistic fare. It is ironic that, for purposes of survival, the dog's instinct proves better than the intelligence of the man.

Hamlin Garland's "The Return of a Private" exemplifies other Naturalistic principles. Garland had a long and diverse career, beginning as a Naturalistic populist and moving through popular romances, books on spiritualism, studies of Native Americans, and nine volumes of autobiography, winning the Pulitzer Prize for his memoir about his mother. But it is his early period that made the greatest contribution to short fiction, and many of his stories are essential to the development of Naturalism, especially "The Return of a Private." In this story, based on his father's experience in the Civil War, Garland rejects the stereotyped plot of the returning veteran and portrays the antiheroic situation of a typical poor farmer. He is "a private," not an officer or a military hero. In fact, arriving home, Edward Smith is up against forces too large for him to conquer: nature, economic injustice, greed, and social inequality. The three-part structure moves from companionship with comrades, to isolation, to reunion with his family. His wife's section provides thematic counterpoint in the middle of the action. The imagery is dehumanizing, atavistic, and pessimistic, consistent with the central ideas. Garland, an idealistic reformer, was also an artist who produced finely crafted fiction that rewards close examination, as it does in this case.

As a group these stories constitute a significant advance in the subjects, themes, and aesthetics of American short fiction, a development from which there was no turning back. Regional works contributed new locations and colorful characters, and the use of the vernacular changed the language of serious literature. Realism moved the story a step further in exploring issues of race, gender, and social identity that intensified in an era of massive immigration. Naturalism captured the harsh realities of a major depression in the 1890s. It also portrayed, for the first time, urban poverty as well as ethnic, national, and religious discrimination. The movement dramatized the plight of the poor and inspired social reforms in the early twentieth century. In addition, the "art" of the story developed. Writers exhibited more sophisticated narrative methods, better control of plot, imagery, and style, and more coherent means of structural organization. In short, the period of Realism and Naturalism greatly advanced the American short story. It is an era unrivaled for the sheer number of stories authors produced and for their energy, range of topics, and artistic skill.

Mark Twain
The Celebrated Jumping Frog of Calaveras County

The most famous example of the Southwestern humor tradition, Mark Twain's "The Celebrated Jumping Frog of Calaveras County" was originally published in the New York *Saturday Press* in 1865 under the title "Jim Smiley and His Jumping Frog." An immediate sensation, it was quickly revised and reprinted in a variety of newspapers and magazines until it was collected in *The Celebrated Jumping Frog of Calaveras County, and Other Stories* in 1867, where it was given its most common name. Deriving from regional oral folklore, it employs many of the devices of that form: a garrulous old codger of a narrator who outwits, and outlasts, the city slicker who listens to his tale; the deadpan recitation of an outlandish tale by a man who tells it in all earnestness, unaware that there is anything humorous about it; the emphasis on the teller and not the tale, since the manner of narration was the more important element. The multilayered strategy of rendition is another standard factor. It is Local Color in its setting, regional dialect, and circumstance, but in literary history the story is most important for its role in the American humor tradition.

Mark Twain, "The Celebrated Jumping Frog of Calaveras County," *The Celebrated Jumping Frog of Calaveras County, and Other Stories,* ed. John Paul (New York: C. H. Webb, Publisher, 1867), 7–19.

In compliance with the request of a friend of mine, who wrote me from the East, I called on good-natured, garrulous old Simon Wheeler, and inquired after my friend's friend, *Leonidas W.* Smiley, as requested to do, and I hereunto append the result. I have a lurking suspicion that *Leonidas W.* Smiley is a myth; that my friend never knew such a personage; and that he only conjectured that, if I asked old Wheeler about him, it would remind him of his infamous *Jim* Smiley, and he would go to work and bore me nearly to death with some infernal reminiscence of him as long and tedious as it should be useless to me. If that was the design, it certainly succeeded.

I found Simon Wheeler dozing comfortably by the bar-room stove of the old, dilapidated tavern in the ancient mining camp of Angel's, and I noticed that he was fat and bald-headed, and had an expression of winning gentleness and simplicity upon his tranquil countenance. He roused up and gave me good-day. I told him a friend of mine had commissioned me to make some inquiries about a cherished companion of his boyhood named *Leonidas W.* Smiley — *Rev. Leonidas W.* Smiley — a young minister of the Gospel, who he had heard was at one time a resident of Angel's Camp. I added that, if Mr. Wheeler could tell me any thing about this Rev. Leonidas W. Smiley, I would feel under many obligations to him.

Simon Wheeler backed me into a corner and blockaded me there with his chair, and then sat me down and reeled off the monotonous narrative which follows this paragraph. He never smiled, he never frowned, he never changed his voice from the gentle-flowing key to which he tuned the initial sentence, he never betrayed the slightest suspicion of enthusiasm; but all through the interminable narrative there ran a vein of impressive earnestness and sincerity, which showed me plainly that, so far from his imagining that there was any thing ridiculous or funny about his story, he regarded it as a really important matter, and admired its two heroes as men of transcendent genius in *finesse*. To me, the spectacle of a man drifting serenely along through such a queer yarn without ever smiling, was exquisitely absurd. As I said before, I asked him to tell me what he knew of Rev. Leonidas W. Smiley, and he replied as follows. I let him go on in his own way, and never interrupted him once:

§§

There was a feller here once by the name of *Jim* Smiley, in the winter of '49 — or may be it was the spring of '50 — I don't recollect exactly, somehow, though what makes me think it was one or the other is because I remember the big flume wasn't finished when he first came to the camp; but any way, he was the curiosest man about always betting on any thing that turned up you ever see, if he could get any body to bet on the other side; and if he couldn't, he'd change sides. Any way that suited the other man would suit him — any way just so's he got a bet, *he* was satisfied. But still he was lucky, uncommon lucky; he most always come out winner. He was always ready and laying for a chance; there couldn't be no solitry thing mentioned but that feller'd offer to bet on it, and take any side you please, as I was just telling you. If there was a horse-race, you'd find him flush, or you'd find him busted at the end of it; if there was a dog-fight, he'd bet on it; if there was a cat-fight, he'd bet on it; if there was a chicken-fight, he'd bet on it; why, if there was two birds setting on a fence, he would bet you which one would fly first; or if there was a camp-meeting, he would be there reg'lar, to bet on Parson Walker, which he judged to be the best exhorter about here, and so he was, too, and a good man. If he even seen a straddle-bug start to go anywheres, he would bet you how long it would take him to get wherever he was going to, and if you took him up, he would foller that straddle-bug to Mexico but what he would find out where he was bound for and how long he was on the road. Lots of the boys here has seen that Smiley, and can tell you about him. Why, it never made no difference to *him* — he would bet on *any* thing — the dangdest feller. Parson Walker's wife laid very sick once, for a good while, and it seemed as if they warn't going to save her; but one morning he come in, and Smiley asked how she was, and he said she was considerable better — thank the Lord for his inf'nit mercy — and coming on so smart that, with the blessing of Prov'dence, she'd get well yet; and Smiley, before he thought, says, "Well, I'll risk two-and-a-half that she don't any way."

Thish-yer Smiley had a mare — the boys called her the fifteen-minute nag, but that was only in fun, you know, because, of course, she was faster than that — and he used to win money on that horse, for all she was so slow and always had the asthma, or the distemper, or the consumption, or something of that kind. They used to give her two or three hundred yards start, and then pass her under way; but always at the fag-end of the race she'd get excited and desperate-like, and come cavorting and straddling up, and scattering her legs around limber, sometimes in the air, and sometimes out to one side amongst the fences, and kicking up m-o-r-e dust, and raising m-o-r-e racket with her coughing and sneez-ing and blowing her nose — and always fetch up at the stand just about a neck ahead, as near as you could cipher it down.

And he had a little small bull pup, that to look at him you'd think he wan't worth a cent, but to set around and look ornery, and lay for a chance to steal something. But as soon as money was up on him, he was a different dog; his under-jaw'd begin to stick out like the fo'castle of a steamboat, and his teeth would uncover, and shine savage like the furnaces. And a dog might tackle him, and bully-rag him, and bite him, and throw him over his shoulder two or three times, and Andrew Jackson — which was the name of the pup — Andrew Jackson would never let on but what *he* was satisfied, and hadn't expected nothing else — and the bets being doubled and doubled on the other side all the time, till the money was all up; and then all of a sudden he would grab that other dog jest by the j'int of his hind leg and freeze to it — not chaw, you understand, but only jest grip and hang on till they throwed up the sponge, if it was a year. Smiley always come out winner on that pup, till he harnessed a dog once that didn't have no hind legs, because they'd been sawed off by a circular saw, and when the thing had gone along far enough, and the money was all up, and he come to make a snatch for his pet holt, he saw in a minute how he'd been imposed on, and how the other dog had him in the door, so to speak, and he 'peared surprised, and then he looked sorter discouraged-like, and didn't try no more to win the fight, and so he got shucked out bad. He give Smiley a look, as much as to say his heart was broke, and it was *his* fault, for putting up a dog that hadn't no hind legs for him to take holt of, which was his main dependence in a fight, and then he limped off a piece and laid down and died. It was a good pup, was that Andrew Jackson, and would have made a name for hisself if he'd lived, for the stuff was in him, and he had genius — I know it, because he hadn't had no opportunities to speak of, and it don't stand to reason that a dog could make such a fight as he could under them circumstances, if he hadn't no talent. It always makes me feel sorry when I think of that last fight of his'n, and the way it turned out.

Well, thish-yer Smiley had rat-terriers, and chicken cocks, and tom-cats, and all them kind of things, till you couldn't rest, and you couldn't fetch nothing for him to bet on but he'd match you. He ketched a frog one day, and took him home, and said he cal'klated to edercate him; and so he never done nothing for three months but set in his back yard and learn that frog to jump. And you bet you he *did* learn him, too. He'd give him a little punch behind, and the next minute you'd see that frog whirling in the air like a doughnut — see him turn one summerset, or may be a couple, if he got a good start, and come down flat-footed and all right, like a cat. He got him up so in the matter of catching flies, and kept him in practice so constant, that he'd nail a fly every time as far as he could see him. Smiley said all a frog wanted was education, and he could do most any thing — and I believe him. Why, I've seen him set Dan'l Webster down here on this floor — Dan'l Webster was the name of the frog — and sing out, "Flies, Dan'l, flies!" and quicker'n you could wink, he'd spring straight up, and snake a fly off'n the counter there, and flop down on the floor again as solid as a gob of mud, and fall to scratching the side of his head with his hind foot as in-different as if he hadn't no idea he'd been doin' any more'n any frog might do. You never see a frog so modest and straightfor'ard as he was, for all he was so gifted. And when it come to fair and square jumping on a dead level, he could get over more ground at one straddle than any animal of his breed you ever see. Jumping on a dead level was his strong suit, you understand; and when it come to that, Smiley would ante up money on him as long as he had a red. Smiley was monstrous proud of his frog, and well he might be, for fellers that had traveled and been everywheres, all said he laid over any frog that ever *they* see.

Well, Smiley kept the beast in a little lattice box, and he used to fetch him down town sometimes and lay for a bet. One day a feller — a stranger in the camp, he was — come across him with his box, and says:

"What might it be that you've got in the box?"

And Smiley says, sorter indifferent like, "It might be a parrot, or it might be a canary, may be, but it an't — it's only just a frog."

And the feller took it, and looked at it careful, and turned it round this way and that, and says, "H'm — so 'tis. Well, what's *he* good for?"

"Well," Smiley says, easy and careless, "He's good enough for *one* thing, I should judge — he can outjump ary frog in Calaveras county."

The feller took the box again, and took another long, particular look, and gave it back to Smiley, and says, very deliberate, "Well, I don't see no p'ints about that frog that's any better'n any other frog."

"May be you don't," Smiley says. "May be you understand frogs, and may be you don't understand 'em; may be you've had experience, and may be you an't only a amature, as it were. Anyways, I've got *my* opinion, and I'll risk forty dollars that he can outjump any frog in Calaveras county."

And the feller studied a minute, and then says, kinder sad like, "Well, I'm only a stranger here, and I an't got no frog; but if I had a frog, I'd bet you."

And then Smiley says, "That's all right — that's all right — if you'll hold my box a minute, I'll go and get you a frog." And so the feller took the box, and put up his forty dollars along with Smiley's, and set down to wait.

So he set there a good while thinking and thinking to hisself, and then he got the frog out and prized his mouth open and took a teaspoon and filled him full of quail shot — filled him pretty near up to his chin — and set him on the floor. Smiley he went to the swamp and slopped around in the mud for a long time, and finally he ketched a frog, and fetched him in, and give him to this feller, and says:

"Now, if you're ready, set him alongside of Dan'l, with his fore-paws just even with Dan'l, and I'll give the word." Then he says, "One — two — three — jump!" and him and the feller touched up the frogs from behind, and the new frog hopped off, but Dan'l give a heave, and hysted up his shoulders — so — like a Frenchman, but it wan't no use — he couldn't budge; he was planted as solid as an anvil, and he couldn't no more stir than if he was anchored out. Smiley was a good deal surprised, and he was disgusted too, but he didn't have no idea what the matter was, of course.

The feller took the money and started away; and when he was going out at the door, he sorter jerked his thumb over his shoulders — this way — at Dan'l, and says again, very deliberate, "Well, *I* don't see no p'ints about that frog that's any better'n any other frog."

Smiley he stood scratching his head and looking down at Dan'l a long time, and at last he says, "I do wonder what in the nation that frog throw'd off for — I wonder if there an't something the matter with him — he 'pears to look mighty baggy, somehow." And he ketched Dan'l by the nap of the neck, and lifted him up and says, "Why, blame my cats, if he don't weigh five pound!" and turned him upside down, and he belched out a double handful of shot. And then he see how it was, and he was the maddest man — he set the frog down and took out after that feller, but he never ketched him. And ——

[Here Simon Wheeler heard his name called from the front yard, and got up to see what was wanted.] And turning to me as he moved away, he said: "Just set where you are, stranger, and rest easy — I an't going to be gone a second."

But, by your leave, I did not think that a continuation of the history of the enterprising vagabond *Jim* Smiley would be likely to afford me much information concerning the Rev. *Leonidas W.* Smiley, and so I started away.

At the door I met the sociable Wheeler returning, and he buttonholed me and recommenced:

"Well, thish-yer Smiley had a yaller one-eyed cow that didn't have no tail, only jest a short stump like a bannanner, and ——"

"Oh! hang Smiley and his afflicted cow!" I muttered, good-naturedly, and bidding the old gentleman good-day, I departed.

Bret Harte

The Outcasts of Poker Flat

One of Bret Harte's most celebrated examples of Local Color, "The Outcasts of Poker Flat" appeared in *The Overland Monthly* in 1869 and was included a year later in *The Luck of Roaring Camp and Other Sketches.* His work extended the settings for regionalism to California and the turbulent world of the gold rush. In "The Luck of Roaring Camp," which appeared only a few months before "The Outcasts," a rough and ready society is transformed through the birth of a child to the local prostitute. The scallywags, drunkards, and claim thieves that comprise the camp find the softer side of themselves in the presence of an infant, and this sentimental idea is characteristic of the author's work of the period. In the later story the setting and some of the characters are the same, as is the sentimental tone, but the action captures the moment a town is becoming "respectable" and forcing out the scarlet women and gamblers who were part of its founding. The use of an erudite narrator to describe the lives of the rustic characters, the dramatic plot, the elevation of setting over theme, and the stress on regional values, circumstances, and language all make "The Outcasts" a quintessential Local Color story.

Bret Harte, "The Outcasts of Poker Flat," *The Overland Monthly* 2 (January 1869): 40–47.

As Mr. John Oakhurst, gambler, stepped into the main street of Poker Flat on the morning of the twenty-third of November, 1850, he was conscious of a change in its moral atmosphere from the preceding night. Two or three men, conversing earnestly together, ceased as he approached, and exchanged significant glances. There was a Sabbath lull in the air, which, in a settlement unused to Sabbath influences, looked ominous.

Mr. Oakhurst's calm, handsome face betrayed small concern of these indications. Whether he was conscious of any predisposing cause, was another question. "I reckon they're after somebody," he reflected; "likely it's me." He returned to his pocket the handkerchief with which he had been whipping away the red dust of Poker Flat from his neat boots, and quietly discharged his mind of any further conjecture.

In point of fact, Poker Flat was "after somebody." It had lately suffered the loss of several thousand dollars, two valuable horses, and a prominent citizen. It was experiencing a spasm of virtuous reaction, quite as lawless and ungovernable as any of the acts that had provoked it. A secret committee had determined to rid the town of all improper persons. This was done permanently in regard to two men who were then hanging from the boughs of a sycamore in the gulch, and temporarily in the banishment of certain other objectionable characters. I regret to say that some of these were ladies. It is but due to the sex, however, to

state that their impropriety was professional, and it was only in such easily established standards of evil that Poker Flat ventured to sit in judgment.

Mr. Oakhurst was right in supposing that he was included in this category. A
few of the committee had urged hanging him as a possible example, and a sure
method of reimbursing themselves from his pockets of the sums he had won
from them. "It's agin justice," said Jim Wheeler, "to let this yer young man from
Roaring Camp — an entire stranger — carry away our money." But a crude sentiment of equity residing in the breasts of those who had been fortunate enough
to win from Mr. Oakhurst, overruled this narrower local prejudice.

Mr. Oakhurst received his sentence with philosophic calmness, none the less
coolly, that he was aware of the hesitation of his judges. He was too much of a
gambler not to accept Fate. With him life was at best an uncertain game, and he
recognized the usual percentage in favor of the dealer.

A body of armed men accompanied the deported wickedness of Poker Flat
to the outskirts of the settlement. Besides Mr. Oakhurst, who was known to be
a coolly desperate man, and for whose intimidation the armed escort was intended, the expatriated party consisted of a young woman familiarly known as
"The Duchess;" another, who had gained the infelicitous title of "Mother Shipton," and "Uncle Billy," a suspected sluice-robber and confirmed drunkard. The
cavalcade provoked no comments from the spectators, nor was any word uttered by the escort. Only when the gulch which marked the uttermost limit of
Poker Flat was reached, the leader spoke briefly and to the point. The exiles
were forbidden to return at the peril of their lives.

As the escort disappeared, their pent-up feelings found vent in a few hysterical tears from "The Duchess," some bad language from Mother Shipton, and a
Partheian volley of expletives from Uncle Billy. The philosophic Oakhurst alone
remained silent. He listened calmly to Mother Shipton's desire to cut somebody's heart out, to the repeated statements of "The Duchess" that she would
die in the road, and to the alarming oaths that seemed to be bumped out of Uncle Billy as he rode forward. With the easy good-humor characteristic of his
class, he insisted upon exchanging his own riding-horse, "Five Spot," for the
sorry mule which the Duchess rode. But even this act did not draw the party into
any closer sympathy. The young woman readjusted her somewhat draggled
plumes with a feeble, faded coquetry; Mother Shipton eyed the possessor of
"Five Spot" with malevolence, and Uncle Billy included the whole party in one
sweeping anathema.

The road to Sandy Bar — a camp that not having as yet experienced the regenerating influences of Poker Flat, consequently seemed to offer some invitation to the emigrants — lay over a steep mountain range. It was distant a day's
severe journey. In that advanced season, the party soon passed out of the moist,
temperate regions of the foot-hills, into the dry, cold, bracing air of the Sierras.
The trail was narrow and difficult. At noon the Duchess, rolling out of her

saddle upon the ground, declared her intention of going no further, and the party halted.

The spot was singularly wild and impressive. A wooded amphitheatre, surrounded on three sides by precipitous cliffs of naked granite, sloped gently toward the crest of another precipice that overlooked the valley. It was undoubtedly the most beautiful spot for a camp, had camping been advisable. But Mr. Oakhurst knew that scarcely half the journey to Sandy Bar was accomplished, and the party were not equipped or provisioned for delay. This fact he pointed out to his companions curtly, with a philosophic commentary on the folly of "throwing up their hand before the game was played out." But they were furnished with liquor, which in this emergency stood them in place of food, fuel, rest and prescience. In spite of his remonstrances, it was not long before they were more or less under its influence. Uncle Billy passed rapidly from a bellicose state into one of stupor, the Duchess became maudlin, and Mother Shipton snored. Mr. Oakhurst alone remained erect, leaning against a rock, calmly surveying them.

Mr. Oakhurst did not drink. It interfered with a profession which required coolness, impassiveness and presence of mind, and, in his own language, he "could n't afford it." As he gazed at his recumbent fellow-exiles, the loneliness begotten of his pariah-trade, his habits of life, his very vices, for the first time seriously oppressed him. He bestirred himself in dusting his black clothes, washing his hands and face, and other acts characteristic of his studiously neat habits, and for a moment forgot his annoyance. The thought of deserting his weaker and more pitiable companions never perhaps occurred to him. Yet he could not help feeling the want of that excitement, which singularly enough was most conducive to that calm equanimity for which he was notorious. He looked at the gloomy walls that rose a thousand feet sheer above the circling pines around him; at the sky, ominously clouded; at the valley below, already deepening into shadow. And doing so, suddenly he heard his own name called.

A horseman slowly ascended the trail. In the fresh, open face of the newcomer, Mr. Oakhurst recognized Tom Simson, otherwise known as "The Innocent" of Sandy Bar. He had met him some months before over a "little game," and had, with perfect equanimity, won the entire fortune — amounting to some forty dollars — of that guileless youth. After the game was finished, Mr. Oakhurst drew the youthful speculator behind the door and thus addressed him: "Tommy, you're a good little man, but you can't gamble worth a cent. Do n't try it over again." He then handed him his money back, pushed him gently from the room, and so made a devoted slave of Tom Simson.

There was a remembrance of this in his boyish and enthusiastic greeting of Mr. Oakhurst. He had started, he said, to go to Poker Flat to seek his fortune. "Alone?" No, not exactly alone; in fact — a giggle — he had run away with Piney Woods. Did n't Mr. Oakhurst remember Piney? She that used to wait on the table at the Temperance House? They had been engaged a long time, but old Jake Woods had objected, and so they had run away, and were going to Poker Flat to be married, and here they were. And they were tired out, and how lucky it was they had found a place to camp and company. All this The Innocent delivered, rapidly, while Piney — a stout, comely damsel of fifteen — emerged from behind the pine tree, where she had been blushing unseen, and rode to the side of her lover.

Mr. Oakhurst seldom troubled himself with sentiment. Still less with propriety. But he had a vague idea that the situation was not felicitous. He retained, however, his presence of mind sufficiently to kick Uncle Billy, who was about to say something, and Uncle Billy was sober enough to recognize in Mr. Oakhurst's kick a superior power that would not bear trifling. He then endeavored to dissuade Tom Simson from delaying further, but in vain. He even pointed out the fact that there was no provision, nor means of making a camp. But, unluckily, "The Innocent" met this objection by assuring the party that he was provided with an extra mule loaded with provisions, and by the discovery of a rude attempt at a log-house near the trail. "Piney can stay with Mrs. Oakhurst," said The Innocent, pointing to the Duchess, "and I can shift for myself."

Nothing but Mr. Oakhurst's admonishing foot saved Uncle Billy from bursting into a roar of laughter. As it was, he felt compelled to retire up the cañon until he could recover his gravity. There he confided the joke to the tall pine trees, with many slaps of his leg, contortions of his face, and the usual profanity. But when he returned to the party, he found them seated by a fire — for the air had grown strangely chill and the sky overcast — in apparently amicable conversation. Piney was actually talking in an impulsive, girlish fashion to the Duchess, who was listening with an interest and animation she had not shown for many days. The Innocent was holding forth, apparently with equal effect, to Mr. Oakhurst and Mother Shipton, who was actually relaxing into amiability. "Is this yer a d —— d picnic?" said Uncle Billy, with inward scorn, as he surveyed the sylvan group, the glancing fire-light and the tethered animals in the foreground. Suddenly an idea mingled with the alcoholic fumes that disturbed his brain. It was apparently of a jocular nature, for he felt impelled to slap his leg again and cram his fist into his mouth.

As the shadows crept slowly up the mountain, a slight breeze rocked the tops of the pine trees, and moaned through their long and gloomy aisles. The ruined cabin, patched and covered with pine boughs, was set apart for the ladies. As the lovers parted, they unaffectedly exchanged a parting kiss, so honest and sincere that it might have been heard above the swaying pines. The frail Duchess and the malevolent Mother Shipton were probably too stunned to remark upon this last evidence of simplicity, and so turned without a word to the hut. The fire was replenished, the men lay down before the door, and in a few minutes were asleep.

Mr. Oakhurst was a light sleeper. Toward morning he awoke benumbed and cold. As he stirred the dying fire, the wind, which was now blowing strongly, brought to his cheek that which caused the blood to leave it — snow!

He started to his feet with the intention of awakening the sleepers, for there was no time to lose. But turning to where Uncle Billy had been lying he found him gone. A suspicion leaped to his brain and a curse to his lips. He ran to the spot where the mules had been tethered; they were no longer there. The tracks were already rapidly disappearing in the snow.

The momentary excitement brought Mr. Oakhurst back to the fire with his usual calm. He did not waken the sleepers. The Innocent slumbered peacefully, with a smile on his good-humored, freckled face; the virgin Piney slept beside her frailer sisters as sweetly as though attended by celestial guardians, and Mr. Oakhurst, drawing his blanket over his shoulders, stroked his mustachios and waited for the dawn. It came slowly in a whirling mist of snowflakes, that dazzled and confused the eye. What could be seen of the landscape appeared magically changed. He looked over the valley, and summed up the present and future in two words —"Snowed in!"

ǫǫ

A careful inventory of the provisions, which, fortunately for the party, had been stored within the hut, and so escaped the felonious fingers of Uncle Billy, disclosed the fact that with care and prudence they might last ten days longer. "That is," said Mr. Oakhurst, *sotto voce* to The Innocent, "if you're willing to board us. If you aint — and perhaps you'd better not — you can wait till Uncle Billy gets back with provisions." For some occult reason, Mr. Oakhurst could not bring himself to disclose Uncle Billy's rascality, and so offered the hypothesis that he had wandered from the camp and had accidentally stampeded the animals. He dropped a warning to the Duchess and Mother Shipton, who of course knew the facts of their associate's defection. "They'll find out the truth about us *all,* when they find out anything," he added, significantly, "and there's no good frightening them now."

Tom Simson not only put all his worldly store at the disposal of Mr. Oakhurst, but seemed to enjoy the prospect of their enforced seclusion. "We'll have a good camp for a week, and then the snow'll melt, and we'll all go back together." The cheerful gayety of the young man and Mr. Oakhurst's calm infected the others. The Innocent, with the aid of pine boughs, extemporized a thatch for the roofless cabin, and the Duchess directed Piney in the rearrangement of the interior with a taste and tact that opened the blue eyes of that provincial maiden to their fullest extent. "I reckon now you're used to fine things at Poker Flat," said Piney. The Duchess turned away sharply to conceal something that reddened her cheeks through its professional tint, and Mother Shipton requested Piney not to "chatter." But when Mr. Oakhurst returned from a weary search for the trail, he heard the sound of happy laughter echoed from the rocks. He stopped in some alarm, and his thoughts first naturally reverted to the whiskey — which he had prudently *cachéd*. "And yet it do n't somehow sound like whiskey," said the gambler. It was not until he caught sight of the blazing fire through the still blinding storm, and the group around it, that he settled to the conviction that it was "square fun."

Whether Mr. Oakhurst had *cachéd* his cards with the whiskey as something debarred the free access of the community, I cannot say. It was certain that, in Mother Shipton's words, he "did n't say cards once" during that evening. Haply the time was beguiled by an accordeon, produced somewhat ostentatiously by Tom Simson, from his pack. Notwithstanding some difficulties attending the manipulation of this instrument, Piney Woods managed to pluck several reluctant melodies from its keys, to an accompaniment by The Innocent on a pair of bone castinets. But the crowning festivity of the evening was reached in a rude camp-meeting hymn, which the lovers, joining hands, sang with great earnestness and vociferation. I fear that a certain defiant tone and Covenanter's swing to its chorus, rather than any devotional quality, caused it to speedily infect the others, who at last joined in the refrain:

> I'm proud to live in the service of the Lord,
> And I'm bound to die in His army.

The pines rocked, the storm eddied and whirled above the miserable group, and the flames of their altar leaped heavenward, as if in token of the vow.

At midnight the storm abated, the rolling clouds parted, and the stars glittered keenly above the sleeping camp. Mr. Oakhurst, whose professional habits had enabled him to live on the smallest possible amount of sleep, in dividing the watch with Tom Simson, somehow managed to take upon himself the greater part of that duty. He excused himself to The Innocent, by saying that he had "often been a week without sleep." "Doing what?" asked Tom. "Poker!" replied Oakhurst, sententiously; "when a man gets a streak of luck — nigger-luck — he do n't get tired. The luck gives in first. Luck," continued the gambler, reflectively, "is a mighty queer thing. All you know about it for certain is that it's bound to change. And it's finding out when it's going to change that makes you. We've had a streak of bad luck since we left Poker Flat — you come along and slap you get into it, too. If you can hold your cards right along you're all right. For," added the gambler, with cheerful irrelevance,

> I'm proud to live in the service of the Lord,
> And I'm bound to die in His army.

The third day came, and the sun, looking through the white-curtained valley, saw the outcasts divide their slowly decreasing store of provisions for the morning meal. It was one of the peculiarities of that mountain climate that its rays diffused a kindly warmth over the wintry landscape, as if in regretful commiseration of the past. But it revealed drift on drift of snow piled high around the hut; a hopeless, uncharted, trackless sea of white lying below the rocky shores to which the castaways still clung. Through the marvelously clear air, the smoke of the pastoral village of Poker Flat rose miles away. Mother Shipton saw it, and from a remote pinnacle of her rocky fastness, hurled in that direction a final malediction. It was her last vituperative attempt, and perhaps for that reason was invested with a certain degree of sublimity. It did her good, she privately informed the Duchess. "Just you go out there and cuss, and see." She then set herself to the task of amusing "the child," as she and the Duchess were pleased to call Piney. Piney was no chicken, but it was a soothing and ingenious theory of the pair to thus account for the fact that she did n't swear and was n't improper.

When night crept up again through the gorges, the reedy notes of the accordeon rose and fell in fitful spasms and long-drawn gasps by the flickering campfire. But music failed to fill entirely the aching void left by insufficient food, and a new diversion was proposed by Piney — story-telling. Neither Mr. Oakhurst nor his female companions caring to relate their personal experiences, this plan would have failed, too, but for The Innocent. Some months before he had chanced upon a stray copy of Mr. Pope's ingenious translation of the Iliad. He now proposed to narrate the principal incidents of that poem — having thoroughly mastered the argument and fairly forgotten the words — in the current vernacular of Sandy Bar. And so for the rest of that night the Homeric demigods again walked the earth. Trojan bully and wily Greek wrestled in the winds, and the great pines in the cañon seemed to bow to the wrath of the son of Peleus. Mr. Oakhurst listened with quiet satisfaction. Most especially was he interested in the fate of "Ash-heels," as The Innocent persisted in denominating the "swift-footed Achilles."

So with small food and much of Homer and the accordeon, a week passed over the heads of the outcasts. The sun again forsook them, and again from leaden skies the snow-flakes were sifted over the land. Day by day closer around them drew the snowy circle, until at last they looked from their prison over drifted walls of dazzling white, that towered twenty feet above their heads. It became more and more difficult to replenish their fires, even from the fallen trees beside them, now half-hidden in the drifts. And yet no one complained. The lovers turned from the dreary prospect and looked into each other's eyes, and were happy. Mr. Oakhurst settled himself coolly to the losing game before him. The Duchess, more cheerful than she had been, assumed the care of Piney. Only Mother Shipton — once the strongest of the party — seemed to sicken and fade. At midnight on the tenth day she called Oakhurst to her side. "I'm going," she said, in a voice of querulous weakness, "but do n't say anything about it. Do n't waken the kids. Take the bundle from under my head and open it." Mr. Oakhurst did so. It contained Mother Shipton's rations for the last week, untouched. "Give 'em to the child," she said, pointing to the sleeping Piney. "You 've starved your-self," said the gambler. "That's what they call it," said the woman querulously, as she lay down again, and turning her face to the wall, passed quietly away.

The accordeon and the bones were put aside that day, and Homer was for-gotten. When the body of Mother Shipton had been committed to the snow, Mr. Oakhurst took The Innocent aside, and showed him a pair of snowshoes, which he had fashioned from the old pack-saddle. "There's one chance in a hundred to save her yet," he said, pointing to Piney; "but it's there," he added, pointing toward Poker Flat. "If you can reach there in two days she's safe. "And you?" asked Tom Simson. "I'll stay here," was the curt reply.

The lovers parted with a long embrace. "You are not going, too," said the Duchess, as she saw Mr. Oakhurst apparently waiting to accompany him. "As far as the cañon," he replied. He turned suddenly and kissed the Duchess, leaving her pallid face aflame, and her trembling limbs rigid with amazement.

Night came, but not Mr. Oakhurst. It brought the storm again and the whirling snow. Then the Duchess, feeding the fire, found that some one had qui-etly piled beside the hut enough fuel to last a few days longer. The tears rose to her eyes, but she hid them from Piney.

The women slept but little. In the morning, looking into each other's faces, they read their fate. Neither spoke; but Piney, accepting the position of the stronger, drew near and placed her arm around the Duchess's waist. They kept this attitude for the rest of the day. That night the storm reached its greatest fury, and rending asunder the protecting pines, invaded the very hut.

Toward morning they found themselves unable to feed the fire, which grad-ually died away. As the embers slowly blackened, the Duchess crept closer to Piney, and broke the silence of many hours: "Piney, can you pray?" "No, dear," said Piney, simply. The Duchess, without knowing exactly why, felt relieved, and putting her head upon Piney's shoulder, spoke no more. And so reclining, the younger and purer pillowing the head of her soiled sister upon her virgin breast, they fell asleep.

The wind lulled as if it feared to waken them. Feathery drifts of snow, shaken from the long pine boughs, flew like white-winged birds, and settled about them as they slept. The moon through the rifted clouds looked down upon what had been the camp. But all human stain, all trace of earthly travail, was hidden be-neath the spotless mantle mercifully flung from above.

They slept all that day and the next, nor did they waken when voices and footsteps broke the silence of the camp. And when pitying fingers brushed the snow from their wan faces, you could scarcely have told from the equal peace that dwelt upon them, which was she that had sinned. Even the Law of Poker Flat recognized this, and turned away, leaving them still locked in each other's arms.

But at the head of the gulch, on one of the largest pine trees, they found the deuce of clubs pinned to the bark with a bowie knife. It bore the following, written in pencil, in a firm hand:

†

BENEATH THIS TREE

LIES THE BODY

OF

JOHN OAKHURST,

WHO STRUCK A STREAK OF BAD LUCK

ON THE 23D OF NOVEMBER, 1850,

AND

HANDED IN HIS CHECKS

ON THE 7TH DECEMBER, 1850.

↓

And pulseless and cold, with a Derringer by his side and a bullet in his heart, though still calm as in life, beneath the snow, lay he who was at once the strongest and yet the weakest of the outcasts of Poker Flat.

Sarah Orne Jewett
A White Heron

Rejected by *The Atlantic Monthly* for being overly sentimental, "A White Heron" went on to become one of Sarah Orne Jewett's most renowned works of short fiction, widely celebrated more than a century after its publication. It first appeared in *A White Heron and Other Stories* in 1886, the year that Jewett became one of the founding members of the Board of Directors of the Massachusetts Audubon Society. One of the fundamental objectives of the group was the preservation of the snowy egret, commonly known as the white heron, which had been nearly eradicated by the desire of fashionable ladies to have bright feathers in their bonnets. Jewett objected to this destruction of nature, and she wrote "A White Heron" as a protest against the practice, a gesture that was successful, and the species was saved. Although there are inconsistencies with point of view in the story, there is much subtle artistry throughout, beginning with the name of the protagonist, Sylvia, a name derived from "Sylvan," which means forest. She is a creature of the woods, having moved away from the industrial world, and her first allegiance is to the world of nature, which the imagery strongly suggests. The moral conflict at the heart of the plot can be easily generalized to a broad theme about the relationship between civilization and the natural world, making this story an important comment in the history of American ecology.

Sarah Orne Jewett, "A White Heron," *A White Heron and Other Stories* (Boston: Houghton, Mifflin and Company, 1886), 1–22.

I

The woods were already filled with shadows one June evening, just before eight o'clock, though a bright sunset still glimmered faintly among the trunks of the trees. A little girl was driving home her cow, a plodding, dilatory, provoking creature in her behavior, but a valued companion for all that. They were going away from whatever light there was, and striking deep into the woods, but their feet were familiar with the path, and it was no matter whether their eyes could see it or not.

There was hardly a night the summer through when the old cow could be found waiting at the pasture bars; on the contrary, it was her greatest pleasure to hide herself away among the huckleberry bushes, and though she wore a loud bell she had made the discovery that if one stood perfectly still it would not ring. So Sylvia had to hunt for her until she found her, and call Co'! Co'! with never an answering Moo, until her childish patience was quite spent. If the creature had not given good milk and plenty of it, the case would have seemed very different to her owners. Besides, Sylvia had all the time there was, and very little use to make of it. Sometimes in pleasant weather it was a consolation to look upon the cow's pranks as an intelligent attempt to play hide and seek, and as the child had no playmates she lent herself to this amusement with a good deal of zest. Though this chase had been so long that the wary animal herself had given an unusual signal of her whereabouts, Sylvia had only laughed when she came upon Mistress Moolly at the swampside, and urged her affectionately homeward with a twig of birch leaves. The old cow was not inclined to wander farther, she even turned in the right direction for once as they left the pasture, and stepped along the road at a good pace. She was quite ready to be milked now, and seldom stopped to browse. Sylvia wondered what her grandmother would say because they were so late. It was a great while since she had left home at half-past five o'clock, but everybody knew the difficulty of making this errand a short one. Mrs. Tilley had chased the hornéd torment too many summer evenings herself to blame any one else for lingering, and was only thankful as she waited that she had Sylvia, nowadays, to give such valuable assistance. The good woman suspected that Sylvia loitered occasionally on her own account; there never was such a child for straying about out-of-doors since the world was made! Everybody said that it was a good change for a little maid who had tried to grow for eight years in a crowded manufacturing town, but, as for Sylvia herself, it seemed as if she never had been alive at all before she came to live at the farm. She thought often with wistful compassion of a wretched geranium that belonged to a town neighbor.

"'Afraid of folks,'" old Mrs. Tilley said to herself, with a smile, after she had made the unlikely choice of Sylvia from her daughter's houseful of children, and was returning to the farm. "'Afraid of folks,' they said! I guess she won't be troubled no great with 'em up to the old place!" When they reached the door of the lonely house and stopped to unlock it, and the cat came to purr loudly, and rub against them, a deserted pussy, indeed, but fat with young robins, Sylvia whispered that this was a beautiful place to live in, and she never should wish to go home.

❦

The companions followed the shady wood-road, the cow taking slow steps and the child very fast ones. The cow stopped long at the brook to drink, as if the pasture were not half a swamp, and Sylvia stood still and waited, letting her bare feet cool themselves in the shoal water, while the great twilight moths struck softly against her. She waded on through the brook as the cow moved away, and listened to the thrushes with a heart that beat fast with pleasure. There was a stirring in the great boughs overhead. They were full of little birds and beasts that seemed to be wide awake, and going about their world, or else saying good-night to each other in sleepy twitters. Sylvia herself felt sleepy as she walked along. However, it was not much farther to the house, and the air was soft and sweet. She was not often in the woods so late as this, and it made her feel as if she were a part of the gray shadows and the moving leaves. She was just think-ing how long it seemed since she first came to the farm a year ago, and wonder-ing if everything went on in the noisy town just the same as when she was there: the thought of the great red-faced boy who used to chase and frighten her made her hurry along the path to escape from the shadow of the trees.

Suddenly this little woods-girl is horror-stricken to hear a clear whistle not very far away. Not a bird's-whistle, which would have a sort of friendliness, but a boy's whistle, determined, and somewhat aggressive. Sylvia left the cow to whatever sad fate might await her, and stepped discreetly aside into the bushes, but she was just too late. The enemy had discovered her, and called out in a very cheerful and persuasive tone, "Halloa, little girl, how far is it to the road?" and trembling Sylvia answered almost inaudibly, "A good ways."

She did not dare to look boldly at the tall young man, who carried a gun over his shoulder, but she came out of her bush and again followed the cow, while he walked alongside.

"I have been hunting for some birds," the stranger said kindly, "and I have lost my way, and need a friend very much. Don't be afraid," he added gallantly. "Speak up and tell me what your name is, and whether you think I can spend the night at your house, and go out gunning early in the morning."

Sylvia was more alarmed than before. Would not her grandmother consider her much to blame? But who could have foreseen such an accident as this? It did not seem to be her fault, and she hung her head as if the stem of it were broken, but managed to answer "Sylvy," with much effort when her companion again asked her name.

Mrs. Tilley was standing in the doorway when the trio came into view. The cow gave a loud moo by way of explanation.

"Yes, you'd better speak up for yourself, you old trial! Where'd she tucked herself away this time, Sylvy?" But Sylvia kept an awed silence; she knew by instinct that her grandmother did not comprehend the gravity of the situation. She must be mistaking the stranger for one of the farmer-lads of the region.

The young man stood his gun beside the door, and dropped a lumpy game-bag beside it; then he bade Mrs. Tilley good-evening, and repeated his wayfarer's story, and asked if he could have a night's lodging.

"Put me anywhere you like," he said. "I must be off early in the morning, before day; but I am very hungry, indeed. You can give me some milk at any rate, that's plain."

"Dear sakes, yes," responded the hostess, whose long slumbering hospitality seemed to be easily awakened. "You might fare better if you went out to the main road a mile or so, but you 're welcome to what we 've got. I 'll milk right off, and you make yourself at home. You can sleep on husks or feathers," she proffered graciously. "I raised them all myself. There's good pasturing for geese just below here towards the ma'sh. Now step round and set a plate for the gentleman, Sylvy!" And Sylvia promptly stepped. She was glad to have something to do, and she was hungry herself.

It was a surprise to find so clean and comfortable a little dwelling in this New England wilderness. The young man had known the horrors of its most primitive housekeeping, and the dreary squalor of that level of society which does not rebel at the companionship of hens. This was the best thrift of an old-fashioned farmstead, though on such a small scale that it seemed like a hermitage. He listened eagerly to the old woman's quaint talk, he watched Sylvia's pale face and shining gray eyes with ever growing enthusiasm, and insisted that this was the best supper he had eaten for a month, and afterward the new-made friends sat down in the door-way together while the moon came up.

Soon it would be berry-time, and Sylvia was a great help at picking. The cow was a good milker, though a plaguy thing to keep track of, the hostess gossiped frankly, adding presently that she had buried four children, so Sylvia's mother, and a son (who might be dead) in California were all the children she had left. "Dan, my boy, was a great hand to go gunning," she explained sadly. "I never wanted for pa'tridges, or gray squer'ls while he was to home. He 's been a great wand'rer, I expect, and he 's no hand to write letters. There, I don't blame him, I 'd ha' seen the world myself if it had been so I could."

"Sylvy takes after him," the grandmother continued affectionately, after a minute's pause. "There ain't a foot o' ground she don't know her way over, and the wild creaturs counts her one o' themselves. Squer'ls she 'll tame to come an' feed right out o' her hands, and all sorts o' birds. Last winter she got the jaybirds to bangeing here, and I believe she 'd 'a' scanted herself of her own meals to have plenty to throw out amongst 'em, if I had n't kep' watch. Anything but crows, I tell her, I'm willin' to help suppport — though Dan he had a tamed one o' them that did seem to have reason same as folks. It was round here a good spell after he went away. Dan an' his father they did n't hitch, — but he never held up his head ag'in after Dan had dared him an' gone off."

The guest did not notice this hint of family sorrows in his eager interest in something else.

"So Sylvy knows all about birds, does she?" he exclaimed, as he looked round at the little girl who sat, very demure but increasingly sleepy, in the moonlight. "I am making a collection of birds myself. I have been at it ever since I was a boy." (Mrs. Tilley smiled.) "There are two or three very rare ones I have been hunting for these five years. I mean to get them on my own ground if they can be found."

"Do you cage 'em up?" asked Mrs. Tilley doubtfully, in response to this enthusiastic announcement.

"Oh no, they're stuffed and preserved, dozens and dozens of them," said the ornithologist, "and I have shot or snared every one myself. I caught a glimpse of a white heron a few miles from here on Saturday, and I have followed it in this direction. They have never been found in this district at all. The little white heron, it is," and he turned again to look at Sylvia with the hope of discovering that the rare bird was one of her acquaintances.

But Sylvia was watching a hop-toad in the narrow footpath.

"You would know the heron if you saw it," the stranger continued eagerly. "A queer tall white bird with soft feathers and long thin legs. And it would have a nest perhaps in the top of a high tree, made of sticks, something like a hawk's nest."

Sylvia's heart gave a wild beat; she knew that strange white bird, and had once stolen softly near where it stood in some bright green swamp grass, away over at the other side of the woods. There was an open place where the sunshine always seemed strangely yellow and hot, where tall, nodding rushes grew, and her grandmother had warned her that she might sink in the soft black mud underneath and never be heard of more. Not far beyond were the salt marshes just this side the sea itself, which Sylvia wondered and dreamed much about, but never had seen, whose great voice could sometimes be heard above the noise of the woods on stormy nights.

"I can't think of anything I should like so much as to find that heron's nest," the handsome stranger was saying. "I would give ten dollars to anybody who could show it to me," he added desperately, "and I mean to spend my whole vacation hunting for it if need be. Perhaps it was only migrating, or had been chased out of its own region by some bird of prey."

Mrs. Tilley gave amazed attention to all this, but Sylvia still watched the toad, not divining, as she might have done at some calmer time, that the creature wished to get to its hole under the door-step, and was much hindered by the unusual spectators at that hour of the evening. No amount of thought, that night, could decide how many wished-for treasures the ten dollars, so lightly spoken of, would buy.

⑤⑤

The next day the young sportsman hovered about the woods, and Sylvia kept him company, having lost her first fear of the friendly lad, who proved to be most kind and sympathetic. He told her many things about the birds and what they knew and where they lived and what they did with themselves. And he gave her a jack-knife, which she thought as great a treasure as if she were a desert-islander. All day long he did not once make her troubled or afraid except when he brought down some unsuspecting singing creature from its bough. Sylvia would have liked him vastly better without his gun; she could not understand why he killed the very birds he seemed to like so much. But as the day waned, Sylvia still watched the young man with loving admiration. She had never seen anybody so charming and delightful; the woman's heart, asleep in the child, was vaguely thrilled by a dream of love. Some premonition of that great power stirred and swayed these young creatures who traversed the solemn woodlands with soft-footed silent care. They stopped to listen to a bird's song; they pressed forward again eagerly, parting the branches — speaking to each other rarely and in whispers: the young man going first and Sylvia following, fascinated, a few steps behind, with her gray eyes dark with excitement.

She grieved because the longed-for white heron was elusive, but she did not lead the guest, she only followed, and there was no such thing as speaking first. The sound of her own unquestioned voice would have terrified her — it was hard enough to answer yes or no when there was need of that. At last evening began to fall, and they drove the cow home together, and Sylvia smiled with pleasure when they came to the place where she heard the whistle and was afraid only the night before.

II

Half a mile from home, at the farther edge of the woods, where the land was highest, a great pine-tree stood, the last of its generation. Whether it was left for a boundary mark, or for what reason, no one could say; the woodchoppers who had felled its mates were dead and gone long ago, and a whole forest of sturdy trees, pines and oaks and maples, had grown again. But the stately head of this old pine towered above them all and made a landmark for sea and shore miles and miles away. Sylvia knew it well. She had always believed that whoever climbed to the top of it could see the ocean; and the little girl had often laid her hand on the great rough trunk and looked up wistfully at those dark boughs that the wind always stirred, no matter how hot and still the air might be below. Now she thought of the tree with a new excitement, for why, if one climbed it at break of day could not one see all the world, and easily discover from whence the white heron flew, and mark the place, and find the hidden nest?

What a spirit of adventure, what wild ambition! What fancied triumph and delight and glory for the later morning when she could make known the secret! It was almost too real and too great for the childish heart to bear.

All night the door of the little house stood open and the whippoorwills came and sang upon the very step. The young sportsman and his old hostess were sound asleep, but Sylvia's great design kept her broad awake and watching. She forgot to think of sleep. The short summer night seemed as long as the winter darkness, and at last when the whippoorwills ceased, and she was afraid the morning would after all come too soon, she stole out of the house and followed the pasture path through the woods, hastening toward the open ground beyond, listening with a sense of comfort and companionship to the drowsy twitter of a half-awakened bird, whose perch she had jarred in passing. Alas, if the great wave of human interest which flooded for the first time this dull little life should sweep away the satisfactions of an existence heart to heart with nature and the dumb life of the forest!

There was the huge tree asleep yet in the paling moonlight, and small and silly Sylvia began with utmost bravery to mount to the top of it, with tingling, eager blood coursing the channels of her whole frame, with her bare feet and fingers, that pinched and held like bird's claws to the monstrous ladder reaching up, up, almost to the sky itself. First she must mount the white oak tree that grew alongside, where she was almost lost among the dark branches and the green leaves heavy and wet with dew; a bird fluttered off its nest, and a red squirrel ran to and fro and scolded pettishly at the harmless housebreaker. Sylvia felt her way easily. She had often climbed there, and knew that higher still one of the oak's upper branches chafed against the pine trunk, just where its lower boughs were set close together. There, when she made the dangerous pass from one tree to the other, the great enterprise would really begin.

She crept out along the swaying oak limb at last, and took the daring step across into the old pine-tree. The way was harder than she thought; she must reach far and hold fast, the sharp dry twigs caught and held her and scratched her like angry talons, the pitch made her thin little fingers clumsy and stiff as she went round and round the tree's great stem, higher and higher upward. The sparrows and robins in the woods below were beginning to wake and twitter to the dawn, yet it seemed much lighter there aloft in the pine-tree, and the child knew she must hurry if her project were to be of any use.

The tree seemed to lengthen itself out as she went up, and to reach farther and farther upward. It was like a great main-mast to the voyaging earth; it must truly have been amazed that morning through all its ponderous frame as it felt this determined spark of human spirit wending its way from higher branch to branch. Who knows how steadily the least twigs held themselves to advantage this light, weak creature on her way! The old pine must have loved his new dependent. More than all the hawks, and bats, and moths, and even the sweet voiced thrushes, was the brave, beating heart of the solitary gray-eyed child. And the tree stood still and frowned away the winds that June morning while the dawn grew bright in the east.

Sylvia's face was like a pale star, if one had seen it from the ground, when the last thorny bough was past, and she stood trembling and tired but wholly triumphant, high in the treetop. Yes, there was the sea with the dawning sun making a golden dazzle over it, and toward that glorious east flew two hawks with slow-moving pinions. How low they looked in the air from that height when one had only seen them before far up, and dark against the blue sky. Their gray feathers were as soft as moths; they seemed only a little way from the tree, and Sylvia felt as if she too could go flying away among the clouds. Westward, the woodlands and farms reached miles and miles into the distance; here and there were church steeples, and white villages, truly it was a vast and awesome world!

The birds sang louder and louder. At last the sun came up bewilderingly bright. Sylvia could see the white sails of ships out at sea, and the clouds that were purple and rose-colored and yellow at first began to fade away. Where was the white heron's nest in the sea of green branches, and was this wonderful sight and pageant of the world the only reward for having climbed to such a giddy height? Now look down again, Sylvia, where the green marsh is set among the shining birches and dark hemlocks; there where you saw the white heron once you will see him again; look, look! a white spot of him like a single floating feather comes up from the dead hemlock and grows larger, and rises, and comes close at last, and goes by the landmark pine with steady sweep of wing and outstretched slender neck and crested head. And wait! wait! do not move a foot or a finger, little girl, do not send an arrow of light and consciousness from your two eager eyes, for the heron has perched on a pine bough not far beyond yours, and cries back to his mate on the nest and plumes his feathers for the new day!

The child gives a long sigh a minute later when a company of shouting catbirds comes also to the tree, and vexed by their fluttering and lawlessness the solemn heron goes away. She knows his secret now, the wild, light, slender bird that floats and wavers, and goes back like an arrow presently to his home in the green world beneath. Then Sylvia, well satisfied, makes her perilous way down again, not daring to look far below the branch she stands on, ready to cry sometimes because her fingers ache and her lamed feet slip. Wondering over and over again what the stranger would say to her, and what he would think when she told him how to find his way straight to the heron's nest.

⁂

"Sylvy, Sylvy!" called the busy old grandmother again and again, but nobody answered, and the small husk bed was empty and Sylvia had disappeared.

The guest waked from a dream, and remembering his day's pleasure hurried to dress himself that might it sooner begin. He was sure from the way the shy little girl looked once or twice yesterday that she had at least seen the white heron, and now she must really be made to tell. Here she comes now, paler than ever, and her worn old frock is torn and tattered, and smeared with pine pitch. The grandmother and the sportsman stand in the door together and question her, and the splendid moment has come to speak of the dead hemlock-tree by the green marsh.

But Sylvia does not speak after all, though the old grandmother fretfully rebukes her, and the young man's kind, appealing eyes are looking straight in her own. He can make them rich with money; he has promised it, and they are poor now. He is so well worth making happy, and he waits to hear the story she can tell.

No, she must keep silence! What is it that suddenly forbids her and makes her dumb? Has she been nine years growing and now, when the great world for the first time puts out a hand to her, must she thrust it aside for a bird's sake? The murmur of the pine's green branches is in her ears, she remembers how the white heron came flying through the golden air and how they watched the sea and the morning together, and Sylvia cannot speak; she cannot tell the heron's secret and give its life away.

෪

Dear loyalty, that suffered a sharp pang as the guest went away disappointed later in the day, that could have served and followed him and loved him as a dog loves! Many a night Sylvia heard the echo of his whistle haunting the pasture path as she came home with the loitering cow. She forgot even her sorrow at the sharp report of his gun and the sight of thrushes and sparrows dropping silent to the ground, their songs hushed and their pretty feathers stained and wet with blood. Were the birds better friends than their hunter might have been, — who can tell? Whatever treasures were lost to her, woodlands and summer-time, remember! Bring your gifts and graces and tell your secrets to this lonely country child!

Hamlin Garland
The Return of a Private

Hamlin Garland's "The Return of a Private" was published in *Arena* magazine in December of 1890 prior to its inclusion in the celebrated *Main-Travelled Roads* the following year. That volume was enlarged and reprinted many times, ending in 1930, and Garland's stories were changed as he continued working on them in accord with his evolving aesthetic theories. In 1890, he was under the sway of Henry George and what became known as the *Populist movement,* an idealistic protest philosophy that attacked social and economic injustice as well as the cruel nature that midwestern farmers fought for their very survival. In "The Return of a Private,"

Garland drew on the experience of watching his wounded father return from the Civil War in 1865 only to resume the harsh struggle against the elements. The story is crafted in three parts: Private Smith's journey home among battle-worn comrades, all of whom face a hard life ahead; the family world of women and children, of generosity and community, of humane good will; and the heartfelt arrival, undercut by his not being recognized and by the degradation of the farm he had left when he enlisted. The tightly organized plot moves toward its understated conclusion in which resignation, rather than heroic triumph, is the only possible response for the simple but profoundly human protagonist.

Hamlin Garland, "The Return of a Private," *Arena* 3 (December 1890): 97–113.

I

The nearer the train drew toward La Crosse, the soberer the little group of "vets" became. On the long way from New Orleans they had beguiled tedium with jokes and friendly chaff; or with planning with elaborate detail what they were going to do now, after the war. A long journey, slowly, irregularly, yet persistently pushing northward. When they entered on Wisconsin Territory they gave a cheer, and another when they reached Madison, but after that they sank into a dumb expectancy. Comrades dropped off at one or two points beyond, until there were only four or five left who were bound for La Crosse County.

Three of them were gaunt and brown, the fourth was gaunt and pale, with signs of fever and ague upon him. One had a great scar down his temple; one limped; and they all had unnaturally large bright eyes, showing emaciation. There were no bands greeting them at the stations, no banks of gaily-dressed ladies waving handkerchiefs and shouting "bravo"; as they came in on the caboose of a freight train into the towns that had cheered and blared at them on their way to war. As they looked out or stepped upon the platform for a moment, as the train stood at the station, the loafers looked at them indifferently. Their blue coats, dusty and grimy, were too familiar now to excite notice, much less a friendly word. They were the last of the army to return, and the loafers were surfeited with such sights.

The train jogged forward so slowly that it seemed likely to be midnight before they should reach La Crosse. The little squad of "vets" grumbled and swore, but it was no use, the train would not hurry; and as a matter of fact, it was nearly two o'clock when the engine whistled "down brakes."

Most of the group were farmers, living in districts several miles out of the town, and all were poor.

"Now, boys," said Private Smith, he of the fever and ague, "we are landed in La Crosse in the night. We've got to stay somewhere till mornin'. Now I aint got no two dollars to waste on a hotel. I've got a wife and children, so I'm goin' to roost on a bench, and take the cost of a bed out of my hide."

"Same here," put in one of the other men. "Hide'll grow on again, dollars come hard. It's goin' to be mighty hot skirmishin' to find a dollar these days."

"Don't think they'll be a deputation of citizens waitin' to 'scort us to a hotel, eh?" said another. His sarcasm was too obvious to require an answer.

Smith went on: "Then at daybreak we'll start f'r home, at least I will."

"Well, I'll be dumned if I'll take two dollars out o'*my* hide," one of the younger men said. "I'm goin' to a hotel, ef I don't never lay up a cent."

"That'll do f'r you," said Smith; "but if you had a wife an' three young 'uns dependin' on yeh —"

"Which I aint, thank the Lord! and don't intend havin' while the court knows itself."

The station was deserted, chill, and dark, as they came into it at exactly a quarter to two in the morning. Lit by the oil lamps that flared a dull red light over the dingy benches, the waiting-room was not an inviting place. The younger man went off to look up a hotel, while the rest remained and prepared to camp down on the floor and benches. Smith was attended to tenderly by the other men, who spread their blankets on the bench for him, and by robbing themselves made quite a comfortable bed, though the narrowness of the bench made his sleeping precarious.

It was chill, though August, and the two men sitting with bowed heads grew stiff with cold and weariness, and were forced to rise now and again, and walk about to warm their stiffened limbs. It didn't occur to them, probably, to contrast their coming home with their going forth, or with the coming home of the generals, colonels, or even captains — but to Private Smith, at any rate, there came a sickness at heart almost deadly, as he lay there on his hard bed and went over his situation.

In the deep of the night, lying on a board in the town where he had enlisted three years ago, all elation and enthusiasm gone out of him, he faced the fact that with the joy of home coming was mingled the bitter juice of care. He saw himself sick, worn out, taking up the work on his half-cleared farm, the inevitable mortgage standing ready with open jaw to swallow half his earnings. He had given three years of his life for a mere pittance of pay, and now —

Morning dawned at last, slowly with a pale yellow dome of light rising silently above the bluffs which stand like some huge battlemented castle, just east of the city. Out to the left the great river swept on its massive, yet silent, way to the south. Jays called across the river from hillside to hillside, through the clear, beautiful air, and hawks began to skim the tops of the hills. The two vets were astir early, but Private Smith had fallen at last into a sleep, and they went out without waking him. He lay on his knapsack, his gaunt face turned toward the ceiling, his hands clasped on his breast, with a curious pathetic effect of weakness and appeal.

An engine switching near woke him at last, and he slowly sat up and stared about. He looked out of the window, and saw that the sun was lightening the hills across the river. He rose and brushed his hair as well as he could, folded his blankets up, and went out to find his companions. They stood gazing silently at the river and at the hills.

"Looks nat'ral, don't it?" they said, as he came out.

"That's what it does," he replied. "An' it looks good. D'yeh see that peak?" He pointed at a beautiful symmetrical peak, rising like a slightly truncated cone, so high that it seemed the very highest of them all. It was lighted by the morning sun til it glowed like a beacon, and a light scarf of gray morning fog was rolling up its shadowed side.

"My farm's just beyond that. Now, ef I can only ketch a ride, we'll be home by dinner time."

"I'm talkin' about breakfast," said one of the others.

"I guess it's one more meal o' hardtack f'r me," said Smith. They foraged around, and finally found a restaurant with a sleepy old German behind the counter, and procured some coffee, which they drank to wash down their hardtack.

"Time'll come," said Smith, holding up a piece by the corner, "when this'll be a curiosity."

"I hope to God it will! I bet I've chawed hardtack enough to shingle every house in the cooly. I've chawed it when my lampers was down, and when they wasn't. I've took it dry, soaked, and mashed. I've had it wormy, musty, sour, and blue-mouldy. I've had it in little bits and big bits; 'fore coffee an' after coffee. I'm ready f'r a change. I'd like t' git hol' jest about now o' some of the hot biscuits my wife c'n make when she lays herself out f'r company."

"Well, if you set there gablin', you'll never *see* yer wife."

"Come on," said Private Smith. "Wait a moment, boys; less take suthin'. It's on me." He led them to the rusty tin dipper which hung on a nail beside the wooden water pail, and they grinned and drank. (Things were primitive in La Crosse then.) Then shouldering their blankets and muskets, which they were "taking home to the boys," they struck out on their last march.

"They called that coffee, Jayvee," grumbled one of them, "but it never went by the road where government Jayvee resides. I reckon I know coffee from peas."

They kept together on the road along the turnpike, and up the winding road by the river, which they followed for some miles. The river was very lovely, curving down along its sandy beds, pausing now and then under broad basswood trees, or running in dark, swift, silent currents under tangles of wild grape-vines, and drooping alders, and haw trees. At one of these lovely spots the three vets sat down on the thick green sward to rest, "on Smith's account." The leaves of the trees were as fresh and green as June, the jays called cheery greetings to them, and kingfishers darted to and fro, with swooping, noiseless flight.

"I tell yeh, boys, this knocks the swamps of Loueesiana into kingdom come."

"You bet. All they c'n raise down there is snakes, niggers, and p'rticler hell."

"An' fightin' men," put in the older man.

"An' fightin' men. If I had a good hook an' line I'd sneak a pick'rel out o' that pond. Say, remember that time I shot that alligator —"

"I guess we'd better be crawlin' along," interrupted Smith, rising and shouldering his knapsack, with considerable effort, which he tried to hide.

"Say, Smith, lemme give you a lift on that."

"I guess I c'n manage," said Smith, grimly.

"'Course. But, yeh see, I may not have a chance right off to pay yeh back for the times ye've carried my gun and hull caboodle. Say, now, gimme that gun, anyway."

"All right, if yeh feel like it, Jim," Smith replied, and they trudged along doggedly in the sun, which was getting higher and hotter each half mile.

"Aint it queer they aint no teams comin' along?"

"Well, no, seein's it's Sunday."

"By jinks, that's a fact! It *is* Sunday. I'll git home in time f'r dinner, sure. She don't hev dinner usually till about *one* on Sundays." And he fell into a muse, in which he smiled.

"Well, I'll git home jest about six o'clock, jest about when the boys are milkin' the cows," said old Jim Cranby. "I'll step into the barn, an' then I'll say, 'He*ah!* why aint this milkin' done before this time o' day?' An' then won't they yell," he added, slapping his thigh in great glee.

Smith went on. "I'll jest go up the path. Old Rover'll come down the road to meet me. He won't bark; he'll know me, an' he'll come down waggin' his tail an' showin' his teeth. That's his way of laughin'. An' so I'll walk up to the kitchen door, an' I'll say, '*Dinner* f'r a hungry man!' An' then she'll jump up, an' —"

He couldn't go on. His voice choked at the thought of it. Saunders, the third man, hardly uttered a word. He walked silently behind the others. He had lost his wife the first year he was in the army. She died of pneumonia caught in the autumn rains, while working in the fields on his place.

They plodded along till at last they came to a parting of the ways. To the right the road continued up the main valley; to the left it went over the ridge.

"Well, boys," began Smith, as they grounded their muskets and looked away up the valley, "here's where we shake hands. We've marched together a good many miles, an' now I s'pose we're done."

"Yes, I don't think we'll do any more of it f'r a while. I don't want to, I know."

"I hope I'll see yeh, once in a while, boys, to talk over old times."

"Of course," said Saunders, whose voice trembled a little, too. "It aint *exactly* like dyin'."

"But we'd ought'r go home with you," said the younger man. "You never'll climb that ridge with all them things on yer back."

"Oh, I'm all right! Don't worry about me. Every step takes me nearer home, yeh see. Well, good-by, boys."

They shook hands. "Good-by. Good luck."

"Same to you. Lemme know how you find things at home."

He turned once before they passed out of sight, and waved his cap, and they did the same, and all yelled. Then all marched away with their long, steady, loping, veteran step. The solitary climber in blue walked on for a time, with his mind filled with the kindness of his comrades, and musing upon the many jolly days they had had together in camp and field.

He thought of his chum, Billy Tripp. Poor Billy! A "minie" ball fell into his breast one day, fell wailing like a cat, and tore a great ragged hole into his heart. He looked forward to a sad scene with Billy's mother and sweetheart. They would want to know all about it. He tried to recall all that Billy had said, and the particulars of it, but there was little to remember, just that wild wailing sound high in the air, a dull slap, a short, quick, expulsive groan, and the boy lay with his face in the dirt in the ploughed field they were marching across.

That was all. But all the scenes he had since been through had not dimmed the horror, the terror of that moment, when his boy comrade fell, with only a breath between a laugh and a death-groan. Poor handsome Billy! Worth millions of dollars was his young life.

These sombre recollections gave way at length to more cheerful feelings as he began to approach his home coulè. The fields and houses grew familiar, and in one or two he was greeted by people seated in the doorway. But he was in no mood to talk, and pushed on steadily, though he stopped and accepted a drink of milk once at the well-side of a neighbor.

The sun was getting hot on that slope, and his step grew slower, in spite of his iron resolution. He sat down several times to rest. Slowly he crawled up the rough, reddish brown road, which wound along the hillside, under great trees, through dense groves of jack oaks, with tree-tops far below him on his left hand, and the hills far above him on his right. He crawled along like some minute wingless variety of fly.

He ate some hardtack, sauced with wild berries, when he reached the summit of the ridge, and sat there for some time, looking down into his home coulè.

Sombre, pathetic figure! His wide, round gray eyes gazing down into the beautiful valley, seeing and not seeing, the splendid cloud-shadows sweeping over the western hills, and across the green and yellow wheat far below. His head drooped forward on his palm, his shoulders took on a tired stoop, his cheek bones showed painfully. An observer might have said, "He is looking down upon his own grave."

II

Sunday comes in a western wheat harvest with such sweet and sudden relaxation to man and beast, that it would be holy for that reason, if for no other. And Sundays are usually fair in harvest time. As one goes out into the field in the hot morning sunshine, with no sound abroad save the crickets and the indescribably pleasant, silken rustling of the ripened grain, the reaper and the very sheaves in the stubble seem to be resting, dreaming.

Around the house, in the shade of the trees, the men sit, smoking, dozing, or reading the papers, while the women, never resting, move about at the housework. The men eat on Sundays about the same as on any other days, and breakfast is no sooner over and out of the way than dinner begins.

But at the Smith farm there were no men dozing or reading. Mrs. Smith was alone with her three children, Mary, nine, Tommy, six, and little Ted, just past four. Her farm, rented to a neighbor, lay at the head of a coulè or narrow gulley, made at some far-off post-glacial period by the vast and angry floods of water which gullied these tremendous furrows in the level prairie — furrows so deep that undisturbed portions of the original level rose like hills on either side, — rose to quite considerable mountains.

The chickens wakened her as usual that Sabbath morning from dreams of her absent husband, from whom she had not heard for weeks. The shadows drifted over the hills, down the slopes, across the wheat, and up the opposite wall in leisurely ways, as if, being Sunday, they could "take it easy," also. The fowls clustered about the housewife as she went out into the yard. Fuzzy little chickens swarmed out from the coops where their clucking and perpetually disgruntled mothers tramped about, petulantly thrusting their heads through the spaces between the slats.

A cow called in a deep, musical bass, and a calf answered from a little pen near by, and a pig scurried guiltily out of the cabbages. Seeing all this, seeing the pig in the cabbages, the tangle of grass in the garden, the broken fence which she had mended again and again — the little woman, hardly more than a girl, sat down and cried. The bright Sabbath morning was only a mockery without him!

A few years ago they had bought this farm, paying part, mortgaging the rest in the usual way. Edward Smith was a man of terrible energy. He worked "nights and Sundays," as the saying goes, to clear the farm of its brush and of its insatiate mortgage. In the midst of his herculean struggle came the call for volunteers, and with the grim and unselfish devotion to his country which made the Eagle Brigade able to "whip its weight in wild cats," he threw down his scythe and his grub-axe, turned his cattle loose, and became a blue-coated cog in a vast machine for killing men, and not thistles. While the millionaire sent his money to England for safe keeping, this man, with his girl wife and three babies, left them on a mortgaged farm, and went away to fight for an idea. It was foolish, but it was sublime, for all that.

That was three years before, and the young wife, sitting on the well-curb on this bright Sabbath harvest morning, was righteously rebellious. It seemed to her that she had borne her share of the country's sorrow. Two brothers had been killed, the renter in whose hands her husband had left the farm had proved the villain, one year the farm was without crops, and now the over-ripe grain was waiting the tardy hand of the neighbor who had rented it, and who was cutting his own grain first.

About six weeks before she had received a letter saying, "We'll be discharged in a little while." But no other word had come from him. She had seen by the papers that his army was being discharged, and from day to day, other soldiers slowly percolated in blue streams back into the State and county, but still *her* private did not return.

Each week she had told the children that he was coming, and she had watched the road so long that it had become unconscious. As she stood at the well, or by the kitchen door, her eyes were fixed unthinkingly on the road that wound down the coulè. Nothing wears on the human soul like waiting. If the stranded mariner, searching the sun-bright seas, could once give up hope of a ship, that horrible grinding on his brain would cease. It was this waiting, hoping, on the edge of despair, that gave Emma Smith no rest.

Neighbors said, with kind intentions, "He's sick, maybe, an' can't start north just yet. He'll come along one o' these days."

"Why don't he write?" was her question, which silenced them all. This Sunday morning it seemed to her as if she couldn't stand it any longer. The house seemed intolerably lonely. So she dressed the little ones in their best calico dresses and home-made jackets, and closing up the house, set off down the coulè to old Mother Gray's.

"Old Widder Gray" lived at the "mouth of the coolly." She was a widow woman with a large family of stalwart boys and laughing girls. She was the visible incarnation of hospitality and optimistic poverty. With western openheartedness she fed every mouth that asked food of her, and worked herself to death as cheerfully as her girls danced in the neighborhood harvest dances.

She waddled down the path to meet Mrs. Smith with a smile on her face that would have made the countenance of a convict expand.

"Oh, you little dears! Come right to yer granny. Gimme a kiss! Come right in, Mis' Smith. How are yeh, anyway? Nice mornin', aint it? Come in an' set down. Everything's in a clutter, but that won't scare you any."

She led the way into the "best room," a sunny, square room, carpeted with a faded and patched rag carpet, and papered with a horrible white-and-green-striped wall paper, where a few ghastly effigies of dead members of the family hung in variously-sized oval walnut frames. The house resounded with singing, laughter, whistling, tramping of boots, and scufflings. Half-grown boys came to the door and crooked their fingers at the children, who ran out, and were soon heard in the midst of the fun.

"Don't s'pose you've heard from Ed?" Mrs. Smith shook her head. "He'll turn up some day, when you aint lookin' for 'm." The good old soul had said that so many times that poor Mrs. Smith derived no comfort from it any longer.

"Liz heard from Al the other day. He's comin' some day this week. Anyhow, they expect him."

"Did he say anything of —"

"No, he didn't," Mrs. Gray admitted. "But then, it was only a short letter, anyhow. Al aint much for ritin', anyhow. But come out and see my new cheese. I tell yeh, I don't believe I ever had better luck in my life. If Ed should come, I want you should take him up a piece of this cheese."

It was beyond human nature to resist the influence of that noisy, hearty, loving household, and in the midst of the singing and laughing, the wife forgot her anxiety, for the time at least, and laughed and sang with the rest.

About eleven o'clock a wagon-load more drove up to the door, and Bill Gray, the widow's oldest son, and his whole family from Sand Lake Coulè, piled out amid a good-natured uproar, as characteristic as it was ludicrous. Everyone talked at once, except Bill, who sat in the wagon with his wrists on his knees, a straw in his mouth, and an amused twinkle in his blue eyes.

"Aint heard nothin' o' Ed, I s'pose?" he asked in a kind of bellow. Mrs. Smith shook her head. Bill, with a delicacy very striking in such a great giant, rolled his quid in his mouth, and said: —

"Didn't know but you had. I hear two or three of the Sand Lake boys are comin'. Left New Orleenes some time this week. Didn't write nothin' about Ed, but no news is good news in such cases, mother always says."

"Well, go put out yer team," said Mrs. Gray, "an' go'n bring me in some taters, an', Sim, you go see if you c'n find some corn. Sadie, you put on the water to bile. Come now, hustle yer boots, all o' yeh. If I feed this yer crowd, we've got to have some raw materials. If y' think I'm goin' to feed yeh on pie —"

The children went off into the fields, the girls put dinner on to "bile," and then went to change their dresses and fix their hair. "Somebody might come," they said.

"Land sakes, *I hope* not! I don't know where in time I'd set 'em, 'less they'd eat at the secont table," Mrs. Gray laughed, in pretended dismay.

The two older boys, who had served their time in the army, lay out on the grass before the house, and whittled and talked desultorily about the war and the crops, and planned buying a threshing machine. The older girls and Mrs. Smith helped enlarge the table and put on the dishes, talking all the time in that cheery, incoherent, and meaningful way a group of such women have, — a conversation to be taken for its spirit rather than for its letter, though Mrs. Gray at last got the ear of them all and dissertated at length on girls.

"Girls in love aint no use in the whole blessed week," she said. "Sundays they're a lookin' down the road, expectin' he'll *come*. Sunday afternoons they can't think o' nothin' else, 'cause he's *here*. Monday mornin's they're sleepy and kind o' dreamy and slimpsy, and good f'r nothin' on Tuesday and Wednesday. Thursday they git absent-minded, an' begin to look off towards Sunday agin, an'mope aroun' and let the dish-water git cold, right under their noses. Friday they break dishes, and go off in the best room an' snivel, an' look out o' the winder. Saturdays they have queer spurts o' workin' like all p'sessed, an' spurts o' frizzin' their hair. An' Sunday they begin it all over agin."

The girls giggled and blushed all through this tirade from their mother, their broad faces and powerful frames anything but suggestive of lackadaisical sentiment. But Mrs. Smith said: —

"Now, Mrs. Gray, I hadn't ought to stay to dinner. You've got —"

"Now you set right down! If any of them girls' beaus comes, they'll have to take what's left, that's all. They aint s'posed to have much appetite, nohow. No, you're goin' to stay if they starve, an' they aint no danger o' that."

At one o'clock the long table was piled with boiled potatoes, cords of boiled corn on the cob, squash and pumpkin pies, hot biscuit, sweet pickles, bread and butter, and honey. Then one of the girls took down a conch shell from a nail, and going to the door blew a long, fine, free blast, that showed there was no weakness of lungs in her ample chest.

Then the children came out of the forest of corn, out of the crick, out of the loft of the barn, and out of the garden. The men shut up their jack-knives, and surrounded the horse-trough to souse their faces in the cold, hard water, and in a few moments the table was filled with a merry crowd, and a row of wistful-eyed youngsters circled the kitchen wall, where they stood first on one leg and then on the other, in impatient hunger.

"They come to their feed f'r all the world jest like the pigs when y' holler 'poo — ee!' See 'em scoot!" laughed Mrs. Gray, every wrinkle on her face shining with delight. "Now pitch in, Mrs. Smith," she said, presiding over the table. "You know these men critters. They'll eat every grain of it, if yeh give 'em a chance. I swan, they're made o' India-rubber, their stomachs is, I know it."

"Haf to eat to work," said Bill, gnawing a cob with a swift, circular motion that rivalled a corn-sheller in results.

"More like workin' to eat," put in one of the girls, with a giggle. "More eat 'n work with you."

"*You* needn't say anything, Net. Anyone that'll eat seven ears —"

"I didn't, no such thing. You piled your cobs on my plate."

"That'll do to tell Ed Varney. It won't go down here, where we know yeh."

"Good land! Eat all yeh want! They's plenty more in the fiel's, but I can't afford to give you young 'uns tea. The tea is for us women-folks, and 'specially f'r Mis' Smith an' Bill's wife. We're agoin' to tell fortunes by it."

One by one the men filled up and shoved back, and one by one the children slipped into their places, and by two o'clock the women alone remained around the debris-covered table, sipping their tea and telling fortunes.

As they got well down to the grounds in the cup, they shook them with a circular motion in the hand, and then turned them bottom-side-up quickly in the saucer, then twirled them three or four times one way, and three or four times the other, during a breathless pause. Then Mrs. Gray lifted the cup, and, gazing into it with profound gravity, pronounced the impending fate.

It must be admitted that to a critical observer, she had abundant preparation for hitting close to the mark; as when she told the girls that "somebody was coming." "It is a man," she went on gravely. "He is cross-eyed —"

"Oh, you hush!"

"He has red hair, and is death on biled corn and hot biscuit."

The others shrieked with delight.

"But he's goin' to get the mitten, that red-headed feller is, for I see a feller comin' up behind him."

"Oh, lemme see, lemme see," cried Nettie.

"Keep off," said the priestess, with a lofty gesture. "His hair is black. He don't eat so much, and he works more."

The girls exploded in a shriek of laughter, and pounded their sister on the back.

At last came Mrs. Smith's turn, and she was trembling with excitement as Mrs. Gray again composed her jolly face to what she considered a proper solemnity of expression.

"Somebody is comin' to *you*," she said after a long pause. "He's got a musket on his back. He's a soldier. He's almost here. See?"

She pointed at two little tea stems, which formed a faint suggestion of a man with a musket on his back. He had climbed nearly to the edge of the cup. Mrs. Smith grew pale with excitement. She trembled so she could hardly hold the cup in her hand as she gazed into it.

"It's Ed," cried the old woman. "He's on the way home. Heaven's an' earth! There he is now!" She turned and waved her hand out toward the road. They rushed to the door, and looked where she pointed.

A man in a blue coat, with a musket on his back, was toiling slowly up the hill, on the sun-bright, dusty road, toiling slowly, with bent head half hidden by a heavy knapsack. So tired it seemed that walking was indeed a process of falling. So eager to get home he would not stop, would not look aside, but plodded on, amid the cries of the locusts, the welcome of the crickets, and the rustle of the yellow wheat. Getting back to God's country, and his wife and babies!

Laughing, crying, trying to call him and the children at the same time, the little wife, almost hysterical, snatched her hat and ran out into the yard. But the soldier had disappeared over the hill into the hollow beyond, and, by the time she had found the children, he was too far away for her voice to reach him. And besides, she was not sure it was her husband, for he had not turned his head at their shouts. This seemed so strange. Why didn't he stop to rest at his old neighbor's house? Tortured by hope and doubt, she hurried up the coulè as fast as she could push the baby-wagon, the blue-coated figure just ahead pushing steadily, silently forward up the coulè.

When the excited, panting little group came in sight of the gate, they saw the blue-coated figure standing, leaning upon the rough rail fence, his chin on his palms, gazing at the empty house. His knapsack, canteen, blankets and musket lay upon the dusty grass at his feet.

He was like a man lost in a dream. His wide, hungry eyes devoured the scene. The rough lawn, the little unpainted house, the field of clear yellow wheat behind it, down across which streamed the sun, now almost ready to touch the high hill to the west, the crickets crying merrily, a cat on the fence near by, dreaming, unmindful of the stranger in blue.

How peaceful it all was. My God! How far removed from all camps, hospitals, battle-lines. A little cabin in a Wisconsin coulè, but it was majestic in its peace. How did he ever leave it for those years of tramping, thirsting, killing?

Trembling, weak with emotion, her eyes on the silent figure, Mrs. Smith hurried up to the fence. Her feet made no noise in the dust and grass, and they were close upon him before he knew of them. The oldest boy ran a little ahead. He will never forget that figure, that face. It will always remain as something epic, that return of the private. He fixed his eyes on the pale face, covered with a ragged beard.

"Who *are* you, sir?" asked the wife, or rather, started to ask, for he turned, stood a moment, and then cried: —

"Emma!"

"Edward!"

The children stood in a curious row to see their mother kiss this bearded, strange man, the elder girl sobbing sympathetically with her mother. Illness had left the soldier partly deaf, and this added to the strangeness of his manner.

But the boy of six years stood away, even after the girl had recognized her father and kissed him. The man turned then to the baby, and said in a curiously, unpaternal tone: —

"Come here, my little man, don't you know me?" But the baby backed away under the fence and stood peering at him critically.

"My little man!" What meaning in those words! This baby seemed like some other woman's child, and not the infant he had left in his wife's arms. The war had come between him and his baby — he was only "a strange man, with big eyes, dressed in blue, with mother hanging to his arm, and talking in a loud voice."

"And this is Tom," he said, drawing the oldest boy to him. "*He'll* come and see me. *He* knows his poor old pap when he comes home from the war."

The mother heard the pain and reproach in his voice, and hastened to apologize.

"You've changed so, Ed. He can't know yeh. This is papa, Teddy, come and kiss him, — Tom and Mary do. Come, won't you?" But Teddy still peered through the fence with solemn eyes, well out of reach. He resembled a half-wild kitten that hesitates, studying the tones of one's voice.

"I'll fix him," said the soldier, and sat down to undo his knapsack, out of which he drew three enormous and very red apples. After giving one to each of the older children, he said: —

"*Now* I guess he'll come. Eh, my little man? Now come see your pap."

Teddy crept slowly under the fence, assisted by the overzealous Tommy, and a moment later was kicking and squalling in his father's arms. Then they entered the house, into the sitting-room, poor, bare, art-forsaken little room, too, with its rag-carpet, its square clock, and its two or three chromos and pictures from *Harper's Weekly* pinned about.

"Emma, I'm all tired out," said Private Smith, as he flung himself down on the carpet as he used to do, while his wife brought a pillow to put under his head, and the children stood about, munching their apples.

"Tommy, you run and get me a pan of chips, and Mary you get the tea-kettle on, and I'll go and make some biscuit."

And the soldier talked. Question after question he poured forth about the crops, the cattle, the renter, the neighbors. He slipped his heavy government brogan shoes off his poor, tired, blistered feet, and lay out with utter, sweet relaxation. He was a free man again, no longer a soldier under command. At supper he stopped once, listened, and smiled. "That's old Spot. I know her voice. I s'pose that's her calf out there in the pen. I can't milk her to-night, though, I'm too tired; but I tell you, I'd like a drink o' her milk. What's become of old Rove?"

"He died last winter. Poisoned, I guess." There was a moment of sadness for them all. It was some time before the husband spoke again, in a voice that trembled a little.

"Poor old feller! He'd a known me a half a mile away. I expected him to come down the hill to meet me. It 'ud 'a' been more like comin' home if I could 'a' seen him comin' down the road an' waggin' his tail, an' laughin' that way he has. I tell yeh, it kin' o' took hold o' me to see the blinds down, an' the house shut up."

"But yeh see, we — we expected you'd write again 'fore you started. And then we thought we'd see you if you *did* come," she hastened to explain.

"Well, I aint worth a cent on writin'. Besides, it's just as well yeh didn't know when I was comin'. I tell yeh, it sounds good to hear them chickens out there, an' turkeys, an' the crickets. Do you know, they don't have just the same kind o' crickets down South. Who's Sam hired t' help cut yer grain?"

"The Ramsey boys."

"Looks like a good crop, but I'm afraid I won't do much gettin' it cut. This cussed fever an' ague has got me down pretty low. I don't know when I'll get red of it. I'll bet I've took twenty-five pounds of quinine, if I've taken a bit. Gimme another biscuit. I tell yeh, they taste good, Emma. I aint had anything like it — say, if you'd 'a' heard me braggin' to th' boys about your butter'n biscuits, I'll bet your ears 'ud 'a' burnt."

The Private's wife colored with pleasure. "Oh, you're always a braggin' about your things. Everybody makes good butter."

"Yes, old lady Snyder, for instance."

"Oh, well, she aint to be mentioned. She's Dutch."

"Or old Mis' Snively. One more cup o' tea, Mary. That's my girl! I'm feeling better already. I just b'lieve the matter with me is, I'm *starved.*"

This was a delicious hour, one long to be remembered. They were like lovers again. But their tenderness, like that of a typical American, found utterance in tones, rather than in words. He was praising her when praising her biscuit, and she knew it. They grew soberer when he showed where he had been struck, one ball burning the back of his hand, one cutting away a lock of hair from his temple, and one passing through the calf of his leg. The wife shuddered to think how near she had come to being a soldier's widow. Her waiting no longer seemed hard. This sweet, glorious hour effaced it all.

Then they rose, and all went out into the garden and down to the barn. He stood beside her while she milked old Spot. They began to plan fields and crops for next year. Here was the epic figure which Whitman has in mind, and which he calls the "common American soldier." With the livery of war on his limbs, this man was facing his future, his thoughts holding no scent of battle. Clean, clear-headed, in spite of physical weakness, Edward Smith, Private, turned future-ward with a sublime courage.

His farm was mortgaged, a rascally renter had run away with his machinery, "departing between two days," his children needed clothing, the years were coming upon him, he was sick and emaciated, but his heroic soul did not quail. With the same courage with which he faced his southern march, he entered upon a still more hazardous future.

Oh, that mystic hour! The pale man with big eyes standing there by the well, with his young wife by his side. The vast moon swinging above the eastern peaks, the cattle winding down the pasture slopes with jangling bells, the crickets singing, the stars blooming out sweet, and far, and serene, the katy-dids rhythmically calling, the little turkeys crying querulously, as they settled to roost in the poplar tree near the open gate. The voices at the well drop lower, the little ones nestle in their father's arms at last, and Teddy falls asleep there.

The common soldier of the American volunteer army had returned. His war with the South was over, and his war, his daily running fight with nature and against the injustice of his fellow-men was begun again. In the dusk of that far-off valley his figure looms vast, his personal peculiarities fade away, he rises into a magnificent type.

He is a gray-haired man of sixty now, and on the brown hair of his wife the white is also showing. They are fighting a hopeless battle, and must fight till God gives them furlough.

Mary Wilkins Freeman

The Revolt of "Mother"

Mary E. Wilkins married rather late in her life, becoming Mary Wilkins Freeman after she had published much of her best work. It was Mary Wilkins who first published "The Revolt of 'Mother'" in *Harper's Magazine* in 1890 and included it in *A New England Nun and Other Stories* the following year. Its strongly feminist theme has made it her most popular work of fiction, and it has received a great deal of scholarly attention. Freeman often wrote of strong women opposing the restrictions that circumscribe their lives, but few of them do so with the selfless determination of Sarah Penn, who desperately wants a decent home in which to host the wedding of her daughter. However, it is important to acknowledge that the plot involves a psychological transformation for both husband and wife. If Sarah, who is described in images of nobility and royalty, finds within herself the will to contravene the wishes of her husband, an act of extraordinary defiance in a New England household, her husband is also transformed by the gesture and brought to a new level of awareness of the needs and feelings of his wife. His loving humility is nowhere more evident than in the conclusion of this Local Color story.

Mary Wilkins Freeman, "The Revolt of 'Mother,'" *A New England Nun and Other Stories* (New York: Harper & Brothers Publishers, 1891), 448–68.

"Father!"

"What is it?"

"What are them men diggin' over there in the field for?"

There was a sudden dropping and enlarging of the lower part of the old man's face, as if some heavy weight had settled therein; he shut his mouth tight, and went on harnessing the great bay mare. He hustled the collar on to her neck with a jerk.

"Father!"

The old man slapped the saddle upon the mare's back.

"Look here, father, I want to know what them men are diggin' over in the field for, an' I'm goin' to know."

"I wish you'd go into the house, mother, an' 'tend to your own affairs," the old man said then. He ran his words together, and his speech was almost as inarticulate as a growl.

But the woman understood; it was her most native tongue. "I ain't goin' into the house till you tell me what them men are doin' over there in the field," said she.

Then she stood waiting. She was a small woman, short and straight-waisted like a child in her brown cotton gown. Her forehead was mild and benevolent between the smooth curves of gray hair; there were meek downward lines about her nose and mouth; but her eyes, fixed upon the old man, looked as if the meekness had been the result of her own will, never of the will of another.

They were in the barn, standing before the wide open doors. The spring air, full of the smell of growing grass and unseen blossoms, came in their faces. The deep yard in front was littered with farm wagons and piles of wood; on the edges, close to the fence and the house, the grass was a vivid green, and there were some dandelions.

The old man glanced doggedly at his wife as he tightened the last buckles on the harness. She looked as immovable to him as one of the rocks in his pastureland, bound to the earth with generations of blackberry vines. He slapped the reins over the horse, and started forth from the barn.

"Father!" said she.

The old man pulled up. "What is it?"

"I want to know what them men are diggin' over there in that field for."

"They're diggin' a cellar, I s'pose, if you've got to know."

"A cellar for what?"

"A barn."

"A barn? You ain't goin' to build a barn over there where we was goin' to have a house, father?"

The old man said not another word. He hurried the horse into the farm wagon, and clattered out of the yard, jouncing as sturdily on his seat as a boy.

The woman stood a moment looking after him, then she went out of the barn across a corner of the yard to the house. The house, standing at right angles with the great barn and a long reach of sheds and out-buildings, was infinitesimal compared with them. It was scarcely as commodious for people as the little boxes under the barn eaves were for doves.

A pretty girl's face, pink and delicate as a flower, was looking out of one of the house windows. She was watching three men who were digging over in the field which bounded the yard near the road line. She turned quietly when the woman entered.

"What are they digging for, mother?" said she. "Did he tell you?"

"They're diggin' for — a cellar for a new barn."

"Oh, mother, he ain't going to build another barn?"

"That's what he says."

A boy stood before the kitchen glass combing his hair. He combed slowly and painstakingly, arranging his brown hair in a smooth hillock over his forehead. He did not seem to pay any attention to the conversation.

"Sammy, did you know father was going to build a new barn?" asked the girl.

The boy combed assiduously.

"Sammy!"

He turned, and showed a face like his father's under his smooth crest of hair. "Yes, I s'pose I did," he said, reluctantly.

"How long have you known it?" asked his mother.

"'Bout three months, I guess."

"Why didn't you tell of it?"

"Didn't think 'twould do no good."

"I don't see what father wants another barn for," said the girl, in her sweet, slow voice. She turned again to the window, and stared out at the digging men in the field. Her tender, sweet face was full of a gentle distress. Her forehead was as bald and innocent as a baby's, with the light hair strained back from it in a row of curl-papers. She was quite large, but her soft curves did not look as if they covered muscles.

Her mother looked sternly at the boy. "Is he goin' to buy more cows?" said she.

The boy did not reply; he was tying his shoes.

"Sammy, I want you to tell me if he's goin' to buy more cows."

"I s'pose he is."

"How many?"

"Four, I guess."

His mother said nothing more. She went into the pantry, and there was a clatter of dishes. The boy got his cap from a nail behind the door, took an old arithmetic from the shelf, and started for school. He was lightly built, but clumsy. He went out of the yard with a curious spring in the hips, that made his loose home-made jacket tilt up in the rear.

The girl went to the sink, and began to wash the dishes that were piled up there. Her mother came promptly out of the pantry, and shoved her aside. "You wipe 'em!" said she; "I'll wash. There's a good many this mornin'."

The mother plunged her hands vigorously into the water, the girl wiped the plates slowly and dreamily. "Mother," said she, "don't you think it's too bad father's going to build that new barn, much as we need a decent house to live in?"

Her mother scrubbed a dish fiercely. "You ain't found out yet we're women-folks, Nanny Penn," said she. "You ain't seen enough of men-folks yet to. One of these days you'll find it out, an' then you'll know that we know only what men-folks think we do, so far as any use of it goes, an' how we'd ought to reckon men-folks in with Providence, an' not complain of what they do any more than we do of the weather."

"I don't care; I don't believe George is anything like that, anyhow," said

Nanny. Her delicate face flushed pink, her lips pouted softly, as if she were going to cry.

"You wait an' see. I guess George Eastman ain't no better than other men. You hadn't ought to judge father, though. He can't help it, 'cause he don't look at things jest the way we do. An' we've been pretty comfortable here, after all. The roof don't leak — ain't never but once — that's one thing. Father's kept it shingled right up."

"I do wish we had a parlor."

"I guess it won't hurt George Eastman any to come to see you in a nice clean kitchen. I guess a good many girls don't have as good a place as this. Nobody's ever heard me complain."

"I ain't complained either, mother."

"Well, I don't think you'd better, a good father an' a good home as you've got. S'pose your father made you go out an' work for your livin'? Lots of girls have to that ain't no stronger an' better able to than you be."

Sarah Penn washed the frying-pan with a conclusive air. She scrubbed the outside of it as faithfully as the inside. She was a masterly keeper of her box of a house. Her one living-room never seemed to have in it any of the dust which the friction of life with inanimate matter produces. She swept, and there seemed to be no dirt to go before the broom; she cleaned, and one could see no difference. She was like an artist so perfect that he has apparently no art. To-day she got out a mixing bowl and a board, and rolled some pies, and there was no more flour upon her than upon her daughter who was doing finer work. Nanny was to be married in the fall, and she was sewing on some white cambric and embroidery. She sewed industriously while her mother cooked, her soft milk-white hands and wrists showed whiter than her delicate work.

"We must have the stove moved out in the shed before long," said Mrs. Penn. "Talk about not havin' things, it's been a real blessin' to be able to put a stove up in that shed in hot weather. Father did one good thing when he fixed that stove-pipe out there."

Sarah Penn's face as she rolled her pies had that expression of meek vigor which might have characterized one of the New Testament saints. She was making mince-pies. Her husband, Adoniram Penn, liked them better than any other kind. She baked twice a week. Adoniram often liked a piece of pie between meals. She hurried this morning. It had been later than usual when she began, and she wanted to have a pie baked for dinner. However deep a resentment she might be forced to hold against her husband, she would never fail in sedulous attention to his wants.

Nobility of character manifests itself at loop-holes when it is not provided with large doors. Sarah Penn's showed itself to-day in flaky dishes of pastry. So she made the pies faithfully, while across the table she could see, when she glanced up from her work, the sight that rankled in her patient and steadfast soul — the digging of the cellar of the new barn in the place where Adoniram forty years ago had promised her their new house should stand.

The pies were done for dinner. Adoniram and Sammy were home a few minutes after twelve o'clock. The dinner was eaten with serious haste. There was never much conversation at the table in the Penn family. Adoniram asked a blessing, and they ate promptly, then rose up and went about their work.

Sammy went back to school, taking soft sly lopes out of the yard like a rabbit. He wanted a game of marbles before school, and feared his father would give him some chores to do. Adoniram hastened to the door and called after him, but he was out of sight.

"I don't see what you let him go for, mother," said he. "I wanted him to help me unload that wood."

Adoniram went to work out in the yard unloading wood from the wagon. Sarah put away the dinner dishes, while Nanny took down her curl-papers and changed her dress. She was going down to the store to buy some more embroidery and thread.

When Nanny was gone, Mrs. Penn went to the door. "Father!" she called.

"Well, what is it!"

"I want to see you jest a minute, father."

"I can't leave this wood nohow. I've got to git it unloaded an' go for a load of gravel afore two o'clock. Sammy had ought to helped me. You hadn't ought to let him go to school so early."

"I want to see you jest a minute."

"I tell ye I can't, nohow, mother."

"Father, you come here." Sarah Penn stood in the door like a queen; she held her head as if it bore a crown; there was that patience which makes authority royal in her voice. Adoniram went.

Mrs. Penn led the way into the kitchen, and pointed to a chair. "Sit down, father," said she; "I've got somethin' I want to say to you."

He sat down heavily; his face was quite stolid, but he looked at her with restive eyes. "Well, what is it, mother?"

"I want to know what you're buildin' that new barn for, father?"

"I ain't got nothin' to say about it."

"It can't be you think you need another barn?"

"I tell ye I ain't got nothin' to say about it, mother; an' I ain't goin' to say nothin'."

"Be you goin' to buy more cows?"

Adoniram did not reply; he shut his mouth tight.

"I know you be, as well as I want to. Now, father, look here" — Sarah Penn had not sat down; she stood before her husband in the humble fashion of a Scripture woman —"I'm goin' to talk real plain to you; I never have sence I married you, but I'm goin' to now. I ain't never complained, an' I ain't goin' to complain now, but I'm goin' to talk plain. You see this room here, father; you look at it well. You see there ain't no carpet on the floor, an' you see the paper is all dirty, an' droppin' off the walls. We ain't had no new paper on it for ten year, an' then I put it on myself, an' it didn't cost but ninepence a roll. You see this room, father; it's all the one I've had to work in an' eat in an' sit in sence we was married. There ain't another woman in the whole town whose husband ain't got half the means you have but what's got better. It's all the room Nanny's got to have her company in; an' there ain't one of her mates but what's got better, an' their fathers not so able as hers is. It's all the room she'll have to be married in. What would you have thought, father, if we had had our weddin' in a room no better than this? I was married in my mother's parlor, with a carpet on the floor, an' stuffed furniture, an' a mahogany card table. An' this is all the room my daughter will have to be married in. Look here, father!"

Sarah Penn went across the room as though it were a tragic stage. She flung open a door and disclosed a tiny bedroom, only large enough for a bed and bureau, with a path between. "There, father," said she —"there's all the room I've had to sleep in forty year. All my children were born there — the two that died, an' the two that's livin'. I was sick with a fever there."

She stepped to another door and opened it. It led into the small, ill-lighted pantry. "Here," said she, "is all the buttery I've got — every place I've got for my dishes, to set away my victuals in, an' to keep my milk-pans in. Father, I've been takin' care of the milk of six cows in this place, an' now you're goin' to build a new barn, an' keep more cows, an' give me more to do in it."

She threw open another door. A narrow crooked flight of stairs wound upward from it. "There, father," said she, "I want you to look at the stairs that go up to them two unfinished chambers that are all the places our son an' daughter have had to sleep in all their lives. There ain't a prettier girl in town nor a more ladylike one than Nanny, an' that's the place she has to sleep in. It ain't so good as your horse's stall; it ain't so warm an' tight."

Sarah Penn went back and stood before her husband. "Now, father," said she, "I want to know if you think you're doin' right an' accordin' to what you profess. Here, when we was married, forty year ago, you promised me faithful that we should have a new house build in that lot over in the field before the year was out. You said you had money enough, an' you wouldn't ask me to live in no such place as this. It is forty year now, an' you've been makin' more money, an' I've been savin' of it for you ever since, an' you ain't built no house yet. You've built sheds an' cow-houses an' one new barn, an' now you're goin' to build another. Father, I want to know if you think it's right. You're lodgin' your dumb beasts better than you are your own flesh an' blood. I want to know if you think it's right."

"I ain't got nothin' to say."

"You can't say nothin' without ownin' it ain't right, father. An' there's an-

other thing — I ain't complained; I've got along forty year, an' I s'pose I should
forty more, if it wa'n't for that — if we don't have another house. Nanny she
can't live with us after she's married. She'll have to go somewheres else to live
away from us, an' it don't seem as if I could have it so, noways, father. She wa'n't
ever strong. She's got considerable color, but there wa'n't never any backbone to
her. I've always took the heft of everything off her, an' she ain't fit to keep house
an' do everything herself. She'll be all worn out inside of a year. Think of her
doin' all the washin' an' ironin' an' bakin' with them soft white hands an' arms,
an' sweepin'! I can't have it so, noways, father."

Mrs. Penn's face was burning; her mild eyes gleamed. She had pleaded her
little cause like a Webster; she had ranged from severity to pathos; but her op-
ponent employed that obstinate silence which makes eloquence futile with
mocking echoes. Adoniram arose clumsily.

"Father, ain't you got nothin' to say?" said Mrs. Penn.

"I've got to go off after that load of gravel. I can't stan' here talkin' all day."

"Father, won't you think it over, an' have a house built there instead of a barn?"

"I ain't got nothin' to say."

Adoniram shuffled out. Mrs. Penn went into her bedroom. When she came
out, her eyes were red. She had a roll of unbleached cotton cloth. She spread it out
on the kitchen table, and began cutting out some shirts for her husband. The men
over in the field had a team to help them this afternoon; she could hear their halloos. She had a scanty pattern for the shirts; she had to plan and piece the sleeves.

Nanny came home with her embroidery, and sat down with her needlework.
She had taken down her curl-papers, and there was a soft roll of fair hair like an
aureole over her forehead; her face was as delicately fine and clear as porcelain.
Suddenly she looked up, and the tender red flamed all over her face and neck.
"Mother," said she.

"What say?"

"I've been thinking — I don't see how we're goin' to have any — wedding in
this room. I'd be ashamed to have his folks come if we didn't have anybody else."

"Mebbe we can have some new paper before then; I can put it on. I guess you
won't have no call to be ashamed of your belongin's."

"We might have the wedding in the new barn," said Nanny, with gentle pet-
tishness. "Why, mother, what makes you look so?"

Mrs. Penn had started, and was staring at her with a curious expression. She
turned again to her work, and spread out a pattern carefully on the cloth.
"Nothin'," said she.

Presently Adoniram clattered out of the yard in his two-wheeled dump cart,
standing as proudly upright as a Roman charioteer. Mrs. Penn opened the door
and stood there a minute looking out; the halloos of the men sounded louder.

It seemed to her all through the spring months that she heard nothing but
the halloos and the noises of saws and hammers. The new barn grew fast. It was

a fine edifice for this little village. Men came on pleasant Sundays, in their meeting suits and clean shirt bosoms, and stood around it admiringly. Mrs. Penn did not speak of it, and Adoniram did not mention it to her, although sometimes, upon a return from inspecting it, he bore himself with injured dignity.

"It's a strange thing how your mother feels about the new barn," he said, confidentially, to Sammy one day.

Sammy only grunted after an odd fashion for a boy; he had learned it from his father.

The barn was all completed ready for use by the third week in July. Adoniram had planned to move his stock in on Wednesday; on Tuesday he received a letter which changed his plans. He came in with it early in the morning. "Sammy's been to the post-office," said he, "an' I've got a letter from Hiram." Hiram was Mrs. Penn's brother, who lived in Vermont.

"Well," said Mrs. Penn, "what does he say about the folks?"

"I guess they're all right. He says he thinks if I come up country right off there's a chance to buy jest the kind of a horse I want." He stared reflectively out of the window at the new barn.

Mrs. Penn was making pies. She went on clapping the rolling-pin into the crust, although she was very pale, and her heart beat loudly.

"I dun' know but what I'd better go," said Adoniram. "I hate to go off jest now, right in the midst of hayin', but the ten-acre lot's cut, an' I guess Rufus an' the others can git along without me three or four days. I can't get a horse round here to suit me, nohow, an' I've got to have another for all that wood-haulin' in the fall. I told Hiram to watch out, an' if he got wind of a good horse to let me know. I guess I'd better go."

"I'll get out your clean shirt an' collar," said Mrs. Penn calmly.

She laid out Adoniram's Sunday suit and his clean clothes on the bed in the little bedroom. She got his shaving-water and razor ready. At last she buttoned on his collar and fastened his black cravat.

Adoniram never wore his collar and cravat except on extra occasions. He held his head high, with a rasped dignity. When he was all ready, with his coat and hat brushed, and a lunch of pie and cheese in a paper bag, he hesitated on the threshold of the door. He looked at his wife, and his manner was defiantly apologetic. "*If* them cows come to-day, Sammy can drive 'em into the new barn," said he, "an' when they bring the hay up, they can pitch it in there."

"Well," replied Mrs. Penn.

Adoniram set his shaven face ahead and started. When he had cleared the door-step, he turned and looked back with a kind of nervous solemnity. "I shall be back by Saturday if nothin' happens," said he.

"Do be careful, father," returned his wife.

She stood in the door with Nanny at her elbow and watched him out of sight. Her eyes had a strange, doubtful expression in them; her peaceful fore-

head was contracted. She went in, and about her baking again. Nanny sat
sewing. Her wedding-day was drawing nearer, and she was getting pale and thin
with her steady sewing. Her mother kept glancing at her.

"Have you got that pain in your side this mornin'?" she asked.

"A little."

Mrs. Penn's face, as she worked, changed, her perplexed forehead smoothed,
her eyes were steady, her lips firmly set. She formed a maxim for herself, although incoherently with her unlettered thoughts. "Unsolicited opportunities
are the guide-posts of the Lord to the new roads of life," she repeated in effect,
and she made up her mind to her course of action.

"S'posin' I *had* wrote to Hiram," she muttered once, when she was in the
pantry — "s'posin' I had wrote, an' asked him if he knew of any horse? But I
didn't, an' father's goin' wa'n't none of my doin'. It looks like a providence." Her
voice rang out quite loud at the last.

"What you talkin' about, mother?" called Nanny.

"Nothin'."

Mrs. Penn hurried her baking; at eleven o'clock it was all done. The load of
hay from the west field came slowly down the cart track, and drew up at the new
barn. Mrs. Penn ran out. "Stop!" she screamed — "stop!"

The men stopped and looked; Sammy upreared from the top of the load, and
stared at his mother.

"Stop!" she cried out again. "Don't you put the hay in that barn; put it in the
old one."

"Why, he said to put it in here," returned one of the haymakers, wonderingly. He was a young man, a neighbor's son, whom Adoniram hired by the year
to help on the farm.

"Don't you put the hay in the new barn; there's room enough in the old one,
ain't there?" said Mrs. Penn.

"Room enough," returned the hired man, in his thick, rustic tones. "Didn't
need the new barn, nohow, far as room's concerned. Well, I s'pose he changed
his mind." He took hold of the horses' bridles.

Mrs. Penn went back to the house. Soon the kitchen windows were darkened, and a fragrance like warm honey came into the room.

Nanny laid down her work. "I thought father wanted them to put the hay
into the new barn?" she said, wonderingly.

"It's all right," replied her mother.

Sammy slid down from the load of hay, and came in to see if dinner was ready.

"I ain't goin' to get a regular dinner to-day, as long as father's gone," said his
mother. "I've let the fire go out. You can have some bread an' milk an' pie. I
thought we could get along." She set out some bowls of milk, some bread, and
a pie on the kitchen table. "You'd better eat your dinner now," said she. "You
might jest as well get through with it. I want you to help me afterward."

Nanny and Sammy stared at each other. There was something strange in their mother's manner. Mrs. Penn did not eat anything herself. She went into the pantry, and they heard her moving dishes while they ate. Presently she came out with a pile of plates. She got the clothes-basket out of the shed, and packed them in it. Nanny and Sammy watched. She brought out cups and saucers, and put them in with the plates.

"What you goin' to do, mother?" inquired Nanny, in a timid voice. A sense of something unusual made her tremble, as if it were a ghost. Sammy rolled his eyes over his pie.

"You'll see what I'm goin' to do," replied Mrs. Penn. "If you're through, Nanny, I want you to go up-stairs an' pack up your things; an' I want you, Sammy, to help me take down the bed in the bedroom."

"Oh, mother, what for?" gasped Nanny.

"You'll see."

During the next few hours a feat was performed by this simple, pious New England mother which was equal in its way to Wolfe's storming of the Heights of Abraham. It took no more genius and audacity of bravery for Wolfe to cheer his wondering soldiers up those steep precipices, under the sleeping eyes of the enemy, than for Sarah Penn, at the head of her children, to move all their little household goods into the new barn while her husband was away.

Nanny and Sammy followed their mother's instructions without a murmur; indeed, they were overawed. There is a certain uncanny and superhuman quality about all such purely original undertakings as their mother's was to them. Nanny went back and forth with her light loads, and Sammy tugged with sober energy.

At five o'clock in the afternoon the little house in which the Penns had lived for forty years had emptied itself into the new barn.

Every builder builds somewhat for unknown purposes, and is in a measure a prophet. The architect of Adoniram Penn's barn, while he designed it for the comfort of four-footed animals, had planned better than he knew for the comfort of humans. Sarah Penn saw at a glance its possibilities. Those great box stalls, with quilts hung before them, would make better bedrooms than the one she had occupied for forty years, and there was a tight carriage-room. The harness-room, with its chimney and shelves, would make a kitchen of her dreams. The great middle space would make a parlor, by-and-by, fit for a palace. Up stairs there was as much room as down. With partitions and windows, what a house would there be! Sarah looked at the row of stanchions before the allotted space for cows, and reflected that she would have her front entry there.

At six o'clock the stove was up in the harness-room, the kettle was boiling, and the table set for tea. It looked almost as home-like as the abandoned house across the yard had ever done. The young hired man milked, and Sarah directed him calmly to bring the milk to the new barn. He came gaping, dropping little blots of foam from the brimming pails on the grass. Before the next morning he had spread the story of Adoniram Penn's wife moving into the new barn all over the little village. Men assembled in the store and talked it over, women with shawls over their heads scuttled into each other's houses before their work was done. Any deviation from the ordinary course of life in this quiet town was enough to stop all progress in it. Everybody paused to look at the staid, independent figure on the side track. There was a difference of opinion with regard to her. Some held her to be insane; some, of a lawless and rebellious spirit.

Friday the minister went to see her. It was in the forenoon, and she was at the barn door shelling pease for dinner. She looked up and returned his salutation with dignity, then she went on with her work. She did not invite him in. The saintly expression of her face remained fixed, but there was an angry flush over it.

The minister stood awkwardly before her, and talked. She handled the pease as if they were bullets. At last she looked up, and her eyes showed the spirit that her meek front had covered for a lifetime.

"There ain't no use talkin', Mr. Hersey," said she. "I've thought it all over an' over, an' I believe I'm doin' what's right. I've made it the subject of prayer, an' it's betwixt me an' the Lord an' Adoniram. There ain't no call for nobody else to worry about it."

"Well, of course, if you have brought it to the Lord in prayer, and feel satisfied that you are doing right, Mrs. Penn," said the minister, helplessly. His thin gray-bearded face was pathetic. He was a sickly man; his youthful confidence had cooled; he had to scourge himself up to some of his pastoral duties as relentlessly as a Catholic ascetic, and then he was prostrated by the smart.

"I think it's right jest as much as I think it was right for our forefathers to come over from the old country 'cause they didn't have what belonged to 'em," said Mrs. Penn. She arose. The barn threshold might have been Plymouth Rock from her bearing. "I don't doubt you mean well, Mr. Hersey," said she, "but there are things people hadn't ought to interfere with. I've been a member of the church for over forty year. I've got my own mind an' my own feet, an' I'm goin' to think my own thoughts an' go my own ways, an' nobody but the Lord is goin' to dictate to me unless I've a mind to have him. Won't you come in an' set down? How is Mis' Hersey?"

"She is well, I thank you," replied the minister. He added some more perplexed apologetic remarks; then he retreated.

He could expound the intricacies of every character study in the Scriptures, he was competent to grasp the Pilgrim Fathers and all historical innovators, but Sarah Penn was beyond him. He could deal with primal cases; but parallel ones worsted him. But, after all, although it was aside from his province, he wondered more how Adoniram Penn would deal with his wife than how the Lord would. Everybody shared the wonder. When Adoniram's four new cows arrived, Sarah ordered three to be put in the old barn, the other in the house shed where the cooking-stove had stood. That added to the excitement. It was whispered that all four cows were domiciled in the house.

Towards sunset on Saturday, when Adoniram was expected home, there was a knot of men in the road near the new barn. The hired man had milked, but he still hung around the premises. Sarah Penn had supper all ready. There were brown-bread and baked beans and a custard pie; it was the supper that Adoniram loved on a Saturday night. She had on a clean calico, and she bore herself imperturbably. Nanny and Sammy kept close at her heels. Their eyes were large, and Nanny was full of nervous tremors. Still there was to them more pleasant excitement than anything else. An inborn confidence in their mother over their father asserted itself.

Sammy looked out of the harness-room window. "There he is," he announced, in an awed whisper. He and Nanny peeped around the casing. Mrs. Penn kept on about her work. The children watched Adoniram leave the new horse standing in the drive while he went to the house door. It was fastened. Then he went around to the shed. That door was seldom locked, even when the family was away. The thought how her father would be confronted by the cow flashed upon Nanny. There was a hysterical sob in her throat. Adoniram emerged from the shed and stood looking about in a dazed fashion. His lips moved; he was saying something, but they could not hear what it was. The hired man was peeping around a corner of the old barn, but nobody saw him.

Adoniram took the new horse by the bridle and led him across the yard to the new barn. Nanny and Sammy slunk close to their mother. The barn doors rolled back, and there stood Adoniram, with the long mild face of the great Canadian farm horse looking over his shoulder.

Nanny kept behind her mother, but Sammy stepped suddenly forward, and stood in front of her.

Adoniram stared at the group. "What on airth you all down here for?" said he. "What's the matter over to the house?"

"We've come here to live, father," said Sammy. His shrill voice quavered out bravely.

"What" — Adoniram sniffed — "what is it smells like cookin?" said he. He stepped forward and looked in the open door of the harness-room. Then he turned to his wife. His old bristling face was pale and frightened. "What on airth does this mean, mother?" he gasped.

"You come in here, father," said Sarah. She led the way into the harness-room and shut the door. "Now, father," said she, "you needn't be scared. I ain't crazy. There ain't nothin' to be upset over. But we've come here to live, an' we're goin' to live here. We've got jest as good a right here as new horses an' cows. The house wa'n't fit for us to live in any longer, an' I made up my mind I wa'n't goin' to stay there. I've done my duty by you forty year, an' I'm goin' to do it now; but I'm goin' to live here. You've got to put in some windows and partitions; an' you'll have to buy some furniture."

"Why, mother!" the old man gasped.

"You'd better take your coat off an' get washed — there's the wash-basin — an' then we'll have supper."

☙☙

"Why, mother!"

Sammy went past the window leading the new horse to the old barn. The old man saw him, and shook his head speechlessly. He tried to take off his coat, but his arms seemed to lack the power. His wife helped him. She poured some water into the tin basin, and put in a piece of soap. She got the comb and brush, and smoothed his thin gray hair after he had washed. Then she put the beans, hot bread, and tea on the table. Sammy came in, and the family drew up. Adoniram sat looking dazedly at his plate, and they waited.

"Ain't you goin' to ask a blessin', father?" said Sarah.

And the old man bent his head and mumbled.

All through the meal he stopped eating at intervals, and stared furtively at his wife; but he ate well. The home food tasted good to him, and his old frame was too sturdily healthy to be affected by his mind. But after supper he went out, and sat down on the step of the smaller door at the right of the barn, through which he had meant his Jerseys to pass in stately file, but which Sarah designed for her front house door, and he leaned his head on his hands.

After the supper dishes were cleared away and the milk-pans washed, Sarah went out to him. The twilight was deepening. There was a clear green glow in the sky. Before them stretched the smooth level of field; in the distance was a cluster of hay-stacks like the huts of a village; the air was very cool and calm and sweet. The landscape might have been an ideal one of peace.

Sarah bent over and touched her husband on one of his thin, sinewy shoulders. "Father!"

The old man's shoulders heaved: he was weeping.

"Why, don't do so, father," said Sarah.

"I'll — put up the — partitions, an' — everything you — want, mother."

Sarah put her apron up to her face; she was overcome by her own triumph.

Adoniram was like a fortress whose walls had no active resistance, and went down the instant the right besieging tools were used. "Why, mother," he said, hoarsely, "I hadn't no idee you was so set on't as all this comes to."

Charlotte Perkins Gilman
The Yellow Wallpaper

When "The Yellow Wallpaper" first appeared in *The New England Magazine* in 1892, the author was still using the surname of her first husband, "Stetson," although her second union, to George Houghton Gilman, gave her the name by which she is known in literary history. A powerful example of the psychological Realism that was evolving through the 1890s, this story has been read on several levels: as an auto-biographical account of Gilman's own depression and "rest" cure under the treatment of S. Weir Mitchell, a leading physician of his day; as an imaginative dramatization of emotional pathology, partly iatrogenic, involving obsession, pro-jection, and hallucination; and as a metaphoric protest against the restriction women felt in a society that denied them full expression. However interpreted, it is masterful fiction, told in the first person by an unreliable narrator whose perspective is distorted by her disease. The structure reflects her progressive mental fragmen-tation as does the style and imagery. The development of the dominant themes per-vades every sentence of this tight and unforgettable work of short fiction.

Charlotte Perkins Gilman, "The Yellow Wallpaper," *The New England Magazine* 11 (January 1892): 647–56.

It is very seldom that mere ordinary people like John and myself secure ances-tral halls for the summer.

A colonial mansion, a hereditary estate, I would say a haunted house, and reach the height of romantic felicity — but that would be asking too much of fate!

Still I will proudly declare that there is something queer about it.

Else, why should it be let so cheaply? And why have stood so long untenanted?

John laughs at me, of course, but one expects that in marriage.

John is practical in the extreme. He has no patience with faith, an intense horror of superstition, and he scoffs openly at any talk of things not to be felt and seen and put down in figures.

John is a physician, and *perhaps* — (I would not say it to a living soul, of course, but this is dead paper and a great relief to my mind —) *perhaps* that is one reason I do not get well faster.

You see he does not believe I am sick!

And what can one do?

If a physician of high standing, and one's own husband, assures friends and relatives that there is really nothing the matter with one but temporary nervous depression — a slight hysterical tendency — what is one to do?

My brother is also a physician, and also of high standing, and he says the same thing.

So I take phosphates or phosphites — whichever it is, and tonics, and jour-neys, and air, and exercise, and am absolutely forbidden to "work" until I am well again.

Personally, I disagree with their ideas.

Personally, I believe that congenial work, with excitement and change, would do me good.

But what is one to do?

I did write for a while in spite of them; but it *does* exhaust me a good deal — having to be so sly about it, or else meet with heavy opposition.

I sometimes fancy that in my condition if I had less opposition and more so-ciety and stimulus — but John says the very worst thing I can do is to think about my condition, and I confess it always makes me feel bad.

So I will let it alone and talk about the house.

The most beautiful place! It is quite alone, standing well back from the road, quite three miles from the village. It makes me think of English places that you read about, for there are hedges and walls and gates that lock, and lots of sepa-rate little houses for the gardeners and people.

There is a *delicious* garden! I never saw such a garden — large and shady, full of box-bordered paths, and lined with long grape-covered arbors with seats un-der them.

There were greenhouses, too, but they are all broken now.

There was some legal trouble, I believe, something about the heirs and co-heirs; anyhow, the place has been empty for years.

That spoils my ghostliness, I am afraid, but I don't care — there is something strange about the house — I can feel it.

I even said so to John one moonlight evening, but he said what I felt was a *draught,* and shut the window.

I get unreasonably angry with John sometimes. I'm sure I never used to be so sensitive. I think it is due to this nervous condition.

But John says if I feel so, I shall neglect proper self-control; so I take pains to control myself — before him, at least, and that makes me very tired.

I don't like our room a bit. I wanted one downstairs that opened on the pi-azza and had roses all over the window, and such pretty old-fashioned chintz hangings! but John would not hear of it.

He said there was only one window and not room for two beds, and no near room for him if he took another.

He is very careful and loving, and hardly lets me stir without special direction.

I have a schedule prescription for each hour in the day; he takes all care from me, and so I feel basely ungrateful not to value it more.

He said we came here solely on my account, that I was to have perfect rest and all the air I could get. "Your exercise depends on your strength, my dear," said he, "and your food somewhat on your appetite; but air you can absorb all the time." So we took the nursery at the top of the house.

It is a big, airy room, the whole floor nearly, with windows that look all ways, and air and sunshine galore. It was nursery first and then playroom and gymna-sium, I should judge; for the windows are barred for little children, and there are rings and things in the walls.

The paint and paper look as if a boys' school had used it. It is stripped off — the paper — in great patches all around the head of my bed, about as far as I can reach, and in a great place on the other side of the room low down. I never saw a worse paper in my life.

One of those sprawling flamboyant patterns committing every artistic sin.

It is dull enough to confuse the eye in following, pronounced enough to constantly irritate and provoke study, and when you follow the lame uncertain curves for a little distance they suddenly commit suicide — plunge off at outrageous angles, destroy themselves in unheard of contradictions.

The color is repellant, almost revolting; a smouldering unclean yellow, strangely faded by the slow-turning sunlight.

It is a dull yet lurid orange in some places, a sickly sulphur tint in others.

No wonder the children hated it! I should hate it myself if I had to live in this room long.

There comes John, and I must put this away, — he hates to have me write a word.

§§

We have been here two weeks, and I haven't felt like writing before, since that first day.

I am sitting by the window now, up in this atrocious nursery, and there is nothing to hinder my writing as much as I please, save lack of strength.

John is away all day, and even some nights when his cases are serious.

I am glad my case is not serious!

But these nervous troubles are dreadfully depressing.

John does not know how much I really suffer. He knows there is no *reason* to suffer, and that satisfies him.

Of course it is only nervousness. It does weigh on me so not to do my duty in any way!

I meant to be such a help to John, such a real rest and comfort, and here I am a comparative burden already!

Nobody would believe what an effort it is to do what little I am able, — to dress and entertain, and order things.

It is fortunate Mary is so good with the baby. Such a dear baby!

And yet I *cannot* be with him, it makes me so nervous.

I suppose John never was nervous in his life. He laughs at me so about this wall-paper!

At first he meant to repaper the room, but afterwards he said that I was letting it get the better of me, and that nothing was worse for a nervous patient than to give way to such fancies.

He said that after the wall-paper was changed it would be the heavy bedstead, and then the barred windows, and then that gate at the head of the stairs, and so on.

"You know the place is doing you good," he said, "and really, dear, I don't care to renovate the house just for a three months' rental."

"Then do let us go downstairs," I said, "there are such pretty rooms there."

Then he took me in his arms and called me a blessed little goose, and said he would go down cellar, if I wished, and have it whitewashed into the bargain.

But he is right enough about the beds and windows and things.

It is an airy and comfortable room as any one need wish, and, of course, I would not be so silly as to make him uncomfortable just for a whim.

I'm really getting quite fond of the big room, all but that horrid paper.

Out of one window I can see the garden, those mysterious deep-shaded arbors, the riotous old-fashioned flowers, and bushes and gnarly trees.

Out of another I get a lovely view of the bay and a little private wharf belonging to the estate. There is a beautiful shaded lane that runs down there from the house. I always fancy I see people walking in these numerous paths and arbors, but John has cautioned me not to give way to fancy in the least. He says that with my imaginative power and habit of story-making, a nervous weakness like mine is sure to lead to all manner of excited fancies, and that I ought to use my will and good sense to check the tendency. So I try.

I think sometimes that if I were only well enough to write a little it would relieve the press of ideas and rest me.

But I find I get pretty tired when I try.

It is so discouraging not to have any advice and companionship about my work. When I get really well, John says we will ask Cousin Henry and Julia down for a long visit; but he says he would as soon put fireworks in my pillow-case as to let me have those stimulating people about now.

I wish I could get well faster.

But I must not think about that. This paper looks to me as if it *knew* what a vicious influence it had!

There is a recurrent spot where the pattern lolls like a broken neck and two bulbous eyes stare at you upside down.

I get positively angry with the impertinence of it and the everlastingness. Up and down and sideways they crawl, and those absurd, unblinking eyes are everywhere. There is one place where two breaths didn't match and the eyes go all up and down the line, one a little higher than the other.

I never saw so much expression in an inanimate thing before, and we all know how much expression they have! I used to lie awake as a child and get more entertainment and terror out of blank walls and plain furniture than most children could find in a toy-store.

I remember what a kindly wink the knobs of our big, old bureau used to have, and there was one chair that always seemed like a strong friend.

I used to feel that if any of the other things looked too fierce I could always hop into that chair and be safe.

The furniture in this room is no worse than inharmonious, however, for we had to bring it all from downstairs. I suppose when this was used as a playroom they had to take the nursery things out, and no wonder! I never saw such ravages as the children have made here.

The wall-paper, as I said before, is torn off in spots, and it sticketh closer than a brother — they must have had perseverance as well as hatred.

Then the floor is scratched and gouged and splintered, the plaster itself is dug out here and there, and this great heavy bed which is all we found in the room, looks as if it had been through the wars.

But I don't mind it a bit — only the paper.

There comes John's sister. Such a dear girl as she is, and so careful of me! I must not let her find me writing.

She is a perfect and enthusiastic housekeeper, and hopes for no better profession. I verily believe she thinks it is the writing which made me sick!

But I can write when she is out, and see her a long way off from these windows.

There is one that commands the road, a lovely shaded winding road, and one that just looks off over the country. A lovely country, too, full of great elms and velvet meadows.

This wallpaper has a kind of sub-pattern in a different shade, a particularly irritating one, for you can only see it in certain lights, and not clearly then.

But in the places where it isn't faded and where the sun is just so — I can see a strange, provoking, formless sort of figure, that seems to skulk about behind that silly and conspicuous front design.

There's sister on the stairs!

ॐ

Well, the Fourth of July is over! The people are all gone and I am tired out. John thought it might do me good to see a little company, so we just had mother and Nellie and the children down for a week.

Of course I didn't do a thing. Jennie sees to everything now.

But it tired me all the same.

John says if I don't pick up faster he shall send me to Weir Mitchell in the fall.

But I don't want to go there at all. I had a friend who was in his hands once, and she says he is just like John and my brother, only more so!

Besides, it is such an undertaking to go so far.

I don't feel as if it was worth while to turn my hand over for anything, and I'm getting dreadfully fretful and querulous.

I cry at nothing, and cry most of the time.

Of course I don't when John is here, or anybody else, but when I am alone.

And I am alone a good deal just now. John is kept in town very often by serious cases, and Jennie is good and lets me alone when I want her to.

So I walk a little in the garden or down that lovely lane, sit on the porch under the roses, and lie down up here a good deal.

I'm getting really fond of the room in spite of the wallpaper. Perhaps *because* of the wallpaper.

It dwells in my mind so!

I lie here on this great immovable bed — it is nailed down, I believe — and follow that pattern about by the hour. It is as good as gymnastics, I assure you. I start, we'll say, at the bottom, down in the corner over there where it has not been touched, and I determine for the thousandth time that I *will* follow that pointless pattern to some sort of a conclusion.

I know a little of the principle of design, and I know this thing was not arranged on any laws of radiation, or alternation, or repetition, or symmetry, or anything else that I ever heard of.

It is repeated, of course, by the breadths, but not otherwise.

Looked at in one way each breadth stands alone, the bloated curves and flourishes — a kind of "debased Romanesque" with *delirium tremens* — go waddling up and down in isolated columns of fatuity.

But, on the other hand, they connect diagonally, and the sprawling outlines run off in great slanting waves of optic horror, like a lot of wallowing seaweeds in full chase.

The whole thing goes horizontally, too, at least it seems so, and I exhaust myself in trying to distinguish the order of its going in that direction.

They have used a horizontal breadth for a frieze, and that adds wonderfully to the confusion.

There is one end of the room where it is almost intact, and there, when the crosslights fade and the low sun shines directly upon it, I can almost fancy radiation after all, — the interminable grotesque seem to form around a common centre and rush off in headlong plunges of equal distraction.

It makes me tired to follow it. I will take a nap I guess.

℞₠

I don't know why I should write this.

I don't want to.

I don't feel able.

And I know John would think it absurd. But I *must* say what I feel and think in some way — it is such a relief!

But the effort is getting to be greater than the relief.

Half the time now I am awfully lazy, and lie down ever so much.

John says I mustn't lose my strength, and has me take cod liver oil and lots of tonics and things, to say nothing of ale and wine and rare meat.

Dear John! He loves me very dearly, and hates to have me sick. I tried to have a real earnest reasonable talk with him the other day, and tell him how I wish he would let me go and make a visit to Cousin Henry and Julia.

But he said I wasn't able to go, nor able to stand it after I got there; and I did not make out a very good case for myself, for I was crying before I had finished.

It is getting to be a great effort for me to think straight. Just this nervous weakness I suppose.

And dear John gathered me up in his arms, and just carried me upstairs and laid me on the bed, and sat by me and read to me till it tired my head.

He said I was his darling and his comfort and all he had, and that I must take care of myself for his sake, and keep well.

He says no one but myself can help me out of it, that I must use my will and self-control and not let any silly fancies run away with me.

There's one comfort, the baby is well and happy, and does not have to occupy this nursery with the horrid wallpaper.

If we had not used it, that blessed child would have! What a fortunate escape! Why, I wouldn't have a child of mine, an impressionable little thing, live in such a room for worlds.

I never thought of it before, but it is lucky that John kept me here after all, I can stand it so much easier than a baby, you see.

Of course I never mention it to them any more — I am too wise, — but I keep watch of it all the same.

There are things in that paper that nobody knows but me, or ever will.

Behind that outside pattern the dim shapes get clearer every day.

It is always the same shape, only very numerous.

And it is like a woman stooping down and creeping about behind that pattern. I don't like it a bit. I wonder — I begin to think — I wish John would take me away from here!

ॐ

It is so hard to talk with John about my case, because he is so wise, and because he loves me so.

But I tried it last night.

It was moonlight. The moon shines in all around just as the sun does.

I hate to see it sometimes, it creeps so slowly, and always comes in by one window or another.

John was asleep and I hated to waken him, so I kept still and watched the moonlight on that undulating wallpaper till I felt creepy.

The faint figure behind seemed to shake the pattern, just as if she wanted to get out.

I got up softly and went to feel and see if the paper *did* move, and when I came back John was awake.

"What is it, little girl?" he said. "Don't go walking about like that — you'll get cold."

I thought it was a good time to talk, so I told him that I really was not gaining here, and that I wished he would take me away.

"Why, darling!" said he, "our lease will be up in three weeks, and I can't see how to leave before.

"The repairs are not done at home, and I cannot possibly leave town just now. Of course if you were in any danger, I could and would, but you really are better, dear, whether you can see it or not. I am a doctor, dear, and I know. You are gaining flesh and color, your appetite is better, I feel really much easier about you."

"I don't weigh a bit more," said I, "nor as much; and my appetite may be better in the evening when you are here, but it is worse in the morning when you are away!"

"Bless her little heart!" said he with a big hug, "she shall be as sick as she pleases! But now let's improve the shining hours by going to sleep, and talk about it in the morning!"

"And you won't go away?" I asked gloomily.

"Why, how can I, dear? It is only three weeks more and then we will take a nice little trip of a few days while Jennie is getting the house ready. Really dear you are better!"

"Better in body perhaps —" I began, and stopped short, for he sat up straight and looked at me with such a stern, reproachful look that I could not say another word.

"My darling," said he, "I beg of you, for my sake and for our child's sake, as well as for your own, that you will never for one instant let that idea enter your mind! There is nothing so dangerous, so fascinating, to a temperament like yours. It is a false and foolish fancy. Can you not trust me as a physician when I tell you so?"

So of course I said no more on that score, and we went to sleep before long. He thought I was asleep first, but I wasn't, and lay there for hours trying to decide whether that front pattern and the back pattern really did move together or separately.

ᔑᔓ

On a pattern like this, by daylight, there is a lack of sequence, a defiance of law, that is a constant irritant to a normal mind.

The color is hideous enough, and unreliable enough, and infuriating enough, but the pattern is torturing.

You think you have mastered it, but just as you get well underway in following, it turns a back-somersault and there you are. It slaps you in the face, knocks you down, and tramples upon you. It is like a bad dream.

The outside pattern is a florid arabesque, reminding one of a fungus. If you can imagine a toadstool in joints, an interminable string of toadstools, budding and sprouting in endless convolutions — why, that is something like it.

That is, sometimes!

There is one marked peculiarity about this paper, a thing nobody seems to notice but myself, and that is that it changes as the light changes.

When the sun shoots in through the east window — I always watch for that first long, straight ray — it changes so quickly that I never can quite believe it.

That is why I watch it always.

By moonlight — the moon shines in all night when there is a moon — I wouldn't know it was the same paper.

At night in any kind of light, in twilight, candlelight, lamplight, and worst of all by moonlight, it becomes bars! The outside pattern I mean and the woman behind it is as plain as can be.

I didn't realize for a long time what the thing was that showed behind, that dim sub-pattern, but now I am quite sure it is a woman.

By daylight she is subdued, quiet. I fancy it is the pattern that keeps her so still. It is so puzzling. It keeps me quiet by the hour.

I lie down ever so much now. John says it is good for me, and to sleep all I can.

Indeed he started the habit by making me lie down for an hour after each meal.

It is a very bad habit I am convinced, for you see I don't sleep.

And that cultivates deceit, for I don't tell them I'm awake — O no!

The fact is I am getting a little afraid of John.

He seems very queer sometimes, and even Jennie has an inexplicable look.

It strikes me occasionally, just as a scientific hypothesis, — that perhaps it is the paper!

I have watched John when he did not know I was looking, and come into the room suddenly on the most innocent excuses, and I've caught him several times *looking at the paper!* And Jennie too. I caught Jennie with her hand on it once.

She didn't know I was in the room, and when I asked her in a quiet, a very quiet voice, with the most restrained manner possible, what she was doing with the paper — she turned around as if she had been caught stealing, and looked quite angry — asked me why I should frighten her so!

Then she said that the paper stained everything it touched, that she had found yellow smooches on all my clothes and John's, and she wished we would be more careful!

Did not that sound innocent? But I know she was studying that pattern, and I am determined that nobody shall find it out but myself!

𝔖𝔢

Life is very much more exciting now than it used to be. You see I have some-thing more to expect, to look forward to, to watch. I really do eat better, and am more quiet than I was.

John is so pleased to see me improve! He laughed a little the other day, and said I seemed to be flourishing in spite of my wall-paper.

I turned it off with a laugh. I had no intention of telling him it was *because* of the wall-paper — he would make fun of me. He might even want to take me away.

I don't want to leave now until I have found it out. There is a week more, and I think that will be enough.

𝔖𝔢

I'm feeling ever so much better! I don't sleep much at night, for it is so inter-esting to watch developments; but I sleep a good deal in the daytime.

In the daytime it is tiresome and perplexing.

There are always new shoots on the fungus, and new shades of yellow all over it. I cannot keep count of them, though I have tried conscientiously.

It is the strangest yellow, that wall-paper! It makes me think of all the yellow things I ever saw — not beautiful ones like buttercups, but old foul, bad yellow things.

But there is something else about that paper — the smell! I noticed it the moment we came into the room, but with so much air and sun it was not bad. Now we have had a week of fog and rain, and whether the windows are open or not, the smell is here.

It creeps all over the house.

I find it hovering in the dining-room, skulking in the parlor, hiding in the hall, lying in wait for me on the stairs.

It gets into my hair.

Even when I go to ride, if I turn my head suddenly and surprise it — there is that smell!

Such a peculiar odor, too! I have spent hours in trying to analyze it, to find what it smelled like.

It is not bad — at first, and very gentle, but quite the subtlest, most enduring odor I ever met.

In this damp weather it is awful, I wake up in the night and find it hanging over me.

It used to disturb me at first. I thought seriously of burning the house — to reach the smell.

But now I am used to it. The only thing I can think of that it is like is the *color* of the paper! A yellow smell.

There is a very funny mark on this wall, low down, near the mopboard. A streak that runs round the room. It goes behind every piece of furniture, except the bed, a long, straight, even *smooch,* as if it had been rubbed over and over.

I wonder how it was done and who did it, and what they did it for. Round and round and round — round and round and round — it makes me dizzy!

§ê

I really have discovered something at last.

Through watching so much at night, when it changes so, I have finally found out.

The front pattern *does* move — and no wonder! The woman behind shakes it!

Sometimes I think there are a great many women behind, and sometimes only one, and she crawls around fast, and her crawling shakes it all over.

Then in the very bright spots she keeps still, and in the very shady spots she just takes hold of the bars and shakes them hard.

And she is all the time trying to climb through. But nobody could climb through that pattern — it strangles so; I think that is why it has so many heads.

They get through and then the pattern strangles them off and turns them upside down, and makes their eyes white!

If those heads were covered or taken off it would not be half so bad.

❦❧

I think that woman gets out in the daytime!

And I'll tell you why — privately — I've seen her!

I can see her out of every one of my windows!

It is the same woman, I know, for she is always creeping, and most women do not creep by daylight.

I see her in that long shaded lane, creeping up and down. I see her in those dark grape arbors, creeping all around the garden.

I see her on that long road under the trees, creeping along, and when a carriage comes she hides under the blackberry vines.

I don't blame her a bit. It must be very humiliating to be caught creeping by daylight!

I always lock the door when I creep by daylight. I can't do it at night, for I know John would suspect something at once.

And John is so queer now, that I don't want to irritate him. I wish he would take another room! Besides, I don't want anybody to get that woman out at night but myself.

I often wonder if I could see her out of all the windows at once.

But, turn as fast as I can, I can only see out of one at one time.

And though I always see her, she *may* be able to creep faster than I can turn!

I have watched her sometimes away off in the open country, creeping as fast as a cloud shadow in a high wind.

❦❧

If only that top pattern could be gotten off from the under one! I mean to try it, little by little.

I have found out another funny thing, but I shan't tell it this time! It does not do to trust people too much.

There are only two more days to get this paper off, and I believe John is beginning to notice. I don't like the look in his eyes.

And I heard him ask Jennie a lot of professional questions about me. She had a very good report to give.

She said I slept a good deal in the daytime.

John knows I don't sleep very well at night, for all I'm so quiet!

He asked me all sorts of questions, too, and pretended to be very loving and kind.

As if I couldn't see through him!

Still, I don't wonder he acts so, sleeping under this paper for three months.

It only interests me, but I feel sure John and Jennie are secretly affected by it.

❦

Hurrah! This is the last day, but it is enough. John to stay in town over night, and won't be out until this evening.

Jennie wanted to sleep with me — the sly thing! but I told her I should undoubtedly rest better for a night all alone.

That was clever, for really I wasn't alone a bit! As soon as it was moonlight and that poor thing began to crawl and shake the pattern, I got up and ran to help her.

I pulled and she shook, I shook and she pulled, and before morning we had peeled off yards of that paper.

A strip about as high as my head and half around the room.

And then when the sun came and that awful pattern began to laugh at me, I declared I would finish it to-day!

We go away to-morrow, and they are moving all my furniture down again to leave things as they were before.

Jennie looked at the wall in amazement, but I told her merrily that I did it out of pure spite at the vicious thing.

She laughed and said she wouldn't mind doing it herself, but I must not get tired.

How she betrayed herself that time!

But I am here, and no person touches this paper but me, — not *alive!*

She tried to get me out of the room — it was too patent! But I said it was so quiet and empty and clean now that I believed I would lie down again and sleep all I could; and not to wake me even for dinner — I would call when I woke.

So now she is gone, and the servants are gone, and the things are gone, and there is nothing left but that great bedstead nailed down, with the canvas mattress we found on it.

We shall sleep downstairs to-night, and take the boat home to-morrow.

I quite enjoy the room, now it is bare again.

How those children did tear about here!

This bedstead is fairly gnawed!

But I must get to work.

I have locked the door and thrown the key down into the front path.

I don't want to go out, and I don't want to have anybody come in, till John comes.

I want to astonish him.

I've got a rope up here that even Jennie did not find. If that woman does get out, and tries to get away, I can tie her!

But I forgot I could not reach far without anything to stand on!

This bed will *not* move!

I tried to lift and push it until I was lame, and then I got so angry I bit off a little piece at one corner — but it hurt my teeth.

Then I peeled off all the paper I could reach standing on the floor. It sticks horribly and the pattern just enjoys it! All those strangled heads and bulbous eyes and waddling fungus growths just shriek with derision!

I am getting angry enough to do something desperate. To jump out of the window would be admirable exercise, but the bars are too strong even to try.

Besides I wouldn't do it. Of course not. I know well enough that a step like that is improper and might be misconstrued.

I don't like to *look* out of the windows even — there are so many of those creeping women, and they creep so fast.

I wonder if they all come out of that wall-paper as I did?

But I am securely fastened now by my well-hidden rope — you don't get *me* out in the road there!

I suppose I shall have to get back behind the pattern when it comes night, and that is hard!

It is so pleasant to be out in this great room and creep around as I please!

I don't want to go outside. I won't, even if Jennie asks me to.

For outside you have to creep on the ground, and everything is green instead of yellow.

But here I can creep smoothly on the floor, and my shoulder just fits in that long smooch around the wall, so I cannot lose my way.

Why there's John at the door!

It is no use, young man, you can't open it!

How he does call and pound!

Now he's crying for an axe.

It would be a shame to break down that beautiful door!

"John dear!" said I in the gentlest voice, "the key is down by the front steps, under a plantain leaf!"

That silenced him for a few moments.

Then he said — very quietly indeed, "Open the door, my darling!"

"I can't," said I. "The key is down by the front door under a plantain leaf!"

And then I said it again, several times, very gently and slowly, and said it so often that he had to go and see, and he got it of course, and came in. He stopped short by the door.

"What is the matter?" he cried. "For God's sake, what are you doing!"

I kept on creeping just the same, but I looked at him over my shoulder.

"I've got out at last," said I, "in spite of you and Jane? And I've pulled off most of the paper, so you can't put me back!"

Now why should that man have fainted? But he did, and right across my path by the wall, so that I had to creep over him every time!

Henry James
The Real Thing

Henry James, Jr., born to one of the most celebrated families in America, lived much of his life in Europe, speaking fluent French and enjoying the cultural richness of the continent, a theme in many of his best novels. In his later years he lived in England, the setting for one of his most frequently read stories, "The Real Thing." First published in *Black & White* in 1892, this novella was incorporated into *The Real Thing and Other Tales* a year later, the title of the book testifying to the enthusiastic popularity of the story. James later wrote that the idea for it came to him when he heard from a friend about an aristocratic couple "who had been all their life stupid and well-dressed . . . now utterly unable to do anything, had no cleverness, no art nor craft," and he decided to use the situation in his fiction. What he constructed was a tale that functions on three thematic levels: the social concerns of the aristocrats who have become poor and useless in the new English economy, so ineffective that they eventually exchange functions with the servants who wait on the artist who employs them; the aesthetic where the "real" thing is revealed to be less convincing than pretense: the servants make better nobility than the Monarchs, who genuinely occupy the position; and the ethical, which deals with the growth of compassion the artist feels for the indignities the Monarchs face, their dismal prospects, the humiliation they must feel when he fires them. By the conclusion the artist, who narrates, has suffered in his craft even as he has grown immensely as a human being. Best known for his celebrated novels, including *The Wings of the Dove, The Ambassadors,* and *The Golden Bowl,* James demonstrates in "The Real Thing" how the thematic complexity of his longer works could be used to good advantage in his stories as well.

Henry James, "The Real Thing," *The Real Thing and Other Tales* (New York: Macmillan and Co., 1893), 1–41.

I

When the porter's wife (she used to answer the house-bell), announced "A gentleman — with a lady, sir," I had, as I often had in those days, for the wish was father to the thought, an immediate vision of sitters. Sitters my visitors in this case proved to be; but not in the sense I should have preferred. However, there was nothing at first to indicate that they might not have come for a portrait. The gentleman, a man of fifty, very high and very straight, with a moustache slightly grizzled and a dark grey walking-coat admirably fitted, both of which I noted professionally — I don't mean as a barber or yet as a tailor — would have struck me as a celebrity if celebrities often were striking. It was a truth of which I had for some time been conscious that a figure with a good deal of frontage was, as one might say, almost never a public institution. A glance at the lady helped to remind me of this paradoxical law: she also looked too distinguished to be a "personality." Moreover one would scarcely come across two variations together.

Neither of the pair spoke immediately — they only prolonged the preliminary gaze which suggested that each wished to give the other a chance. They were visibly shy; they stood there letting me take them in — which, as I afterwards perceived, was the most practical thing they could have done. In this way their embarrassment served their cause. I had seen people painfully reluctant to mention that they desired anything so gross as to be represented on canvas; but the scruples of my new friends appeared almost insurmountable. Yet the gentleman might have said "I should like a portrait of my wife," and the lady might have said "I should like a portrait of my husband." Perhaps they were not husband and wife — this naturally would make the matter more delicate. Perhaps they wished to be done together — in which case they ought to have brought a third person to break the news.

"We come from Mr. Rivet," the lady said at last, with a dim smile which had the effect of a moist sponge passed over a "sunk" piece of painting, as well as of a vague allusion to vanished beauty. She was as tall and straight, in her degree, as her companion, and with ten years less to carry. She looked as sad as a woman could look whose face was not charged with expression; that is her tinted oval mask showed friction as an exposed surface shows it. The hand of time had played over her freely, but only to simplify. She was slim and stiff, and so well-dressed, in dark blue cloth, with lappets and pockets and buttons, that it was clear she employed the same tailor as her husband. The couple had an indefinable air of prosperous thrift — they evidently got a good deal of luxury for their money. If I was to be one of their luxuries it would behove me to consider my terms.

"Ah, Claude Rivet recommended me?" I inquired; and I added that it was very kind of him, though I could reflect that, as he only painted landscape, this was not a sacrifice.

The lady looked very hard at the gentleman, and the gentleman looked round the room. Then staring at the floor a moment and stroking his moustache, he rested his pleasant eyes on me with the remark: "He said you were the right one."

"I try to be, when people want to sit."

"Yes, we should like to," said the lady anxiously.

"Do you mean together?"

My visitors exchanged a glance. "If you could do anything with *me*, I suppose it would be double," the gentleman stammered.

"Oh yes, there's naturally a higher charge for two figures than for one."

"We should like to make it pay," the husband confessed.

"That's very good of you," I returned, appreciating so unwonted a sympathy — for I supposed he meant pay the artist.

A sense of strangeness seemed to dawn on the lady. "We mean for the illustrations — Mr. Rivet said you might put one in."

"Put one in — an illustration?" I was equally confused.

"Sketch her off, you know," said the gentleman, colouring.

It was only then that I understood the service Claude Rivet had rendered me; he had told them that I worked in black and white, for magazines, for story-books, for sketches of contemporary life, and consequently had frequent employment for models. These things were true, but it was not less true (I may confess it now — whether because the aspiration was to lead to everything or to nothing I leave the reader to guess), that I couldn't get the honours, to say nothing of the emoluments, of a great painter of portraits out of my head. My "illustrations" were my pot-boilers; I looked to a different branch of art (far and away the most interesting it had always seemed to me), to perpetuate my fame. There was no shame in looking to it also to make my fortune; but that fortune was by so much further from being made from the moment my visitors wished to be "done" for nothing. I was disappointed; for in the pictorial sense I had immediately *seen* them. I had seized their type — I had already settled what I would do with it. Something that wouldn't absolutely have pleased them, I afterwards reflected.

"Ah, you're — you're — a — ?" I began, as soon as I had mastered my surprise. I couldn't bring out the dingy word "models"; it seemed to fit the case so little.

"We haven't had much practice," said the lady.

"We've got to *do* something, and we've thought that an artist in your line might perhaps make something of us," her husband threw off. He further mentioned that they didn't know many artists and that they had gone first, on the off-chance (he painted views of course, but sometimes put in figures — perhaps I remembered), to Mr. Rivet, whom they had met a few years before at a place in Norfolk where he was sketching.

"We used to sketch a little ourselves," the lady hinted.

"It's very awkward, but we absolutely *must* do something," her husband went on.

"Of course, we're not so *very* young," she admitted, with a wan smile.

With the remark that I might as well know something more about them, the husband had handed me a card extracted from a neat new pocket-book (their appurtenances were all of the freshest) and inscribed with the words "Major Monarch." Impressive as these words were they didn't carry my knowledge much further; but my visitor presently added: "I've left the army, and we've had the misfortune to lose our money. In fact our means are dreadfully small."

"It's an awful bore," said Mrs. Monarch.

They evidently wished to be discreet — to take care not to swagger because they were gentlefolks. I perceived they would have been willing to recognise this as something of a drawback, at the same time that I guessed at an underlying sense — their consolation in adversity — that they *had* their points. They certainly had; but these advantages struck me as preponderantly social; such for instance as would help to make a drawing-room look well. However, a drawing-room was always, or ought to be, a picture.

In consequence of his wife's allusion to their age Major Monarch observed: "Naturally, it's more for the figure that we thought of going in. We can still hold ourselves up." On the instant I saw that the figure was indeed their strong point. His "naturally" didn't sound vain, but it lighted up the question. "*She* has got the best," he continued, nodding at his wife, with a pleasant after-dinner absence of circumlocution. I could only reply, as if we were in fact sitting over our wine, that this didn't prevent his own from being very good; which led him in turn to rejoin: "We thought that if you ever have to do people like us, we might be something like it. *She,* particularly — for a lady in a book, you know."

I was so amused by them that, to get more of it, I did my best to take their point of view; and though it was an embarrassment to find myself appraising physically, as if they were animals on hire or useful blacks, a pair whom I should have expected to meet only in one of the relations in which criticism is tacit, I looked at Mrs. Monarch judicially enough to be able to exclaim, after a moment, with conviction: "Oh yes, a lady in a book!" She was singularly like a bad illustration.

"We'll stand up, if you like," said the Major; and he raised himself before me with a really grand air.

I could take his measure at a glance — he was six feet two and a perfect gentleman. It would have paid any club in process of formation and in want of a stamp to engage him at a salary to stand in the principal window. What struck me immediately was that in coming to me they had rather missed their vocation; they could surely have been turned to better account for advertising purposes. I couldn't of course see the thing in detail, but, I could see them make someone's fortune — I don't mean their own. There was something in them for a waistcoat-maker, an hotel-keeper or a soap-vendor. I could imagine "We always use it" pinned on their bosoms with the greatest effect; I had a vision of the promptitude with which they would launch a table d'hôte.

Mrs. Monarch sat still, not from pride but from shyness, and presently her husband said to her: "Get up my dear and show how smart you are." She obeyed, but she had no need to get up to show it. She walked to the end of the studio, and then she came back blushing, with her fluttered eyes on her husband. I was reminded of an incident I had accidentally had a glimpse of in Paris — being with a friend there, a dramatist about to produce a play — when an actress came to him to ask to be intrusted with a part. She went through her paces before him, walked up and down as Mrs. Monarch was doing. Mrs. Monarch did it quite as well, but I abstained from applauding. It was very odd to see such people apply for such poor pay. She looked as if she had ten thousand a year. Her husband had used the word that described her: she was, in the London current jargon, essentially and typically "smart." Her figure was, in the same order of ideas, conspicuously and irreproachably "good." For a woman of her age her waist was surprisingly small; her elbow moreover had the orthodox crook. She held her head at the conventional angle; but why did she come to *me?* She ought to have tried on jackets at a big shop. I feared my visitors were not only destitute, but "artistic" — which would be a great complication. When she sat down again I thanked her, observing that what a draughtsman most valued in his model was the faculty of keeping quiet.

"Oh, *she* can keep quiet," said Major Monarch. Then he added, jocosely: "I've always kept her quiet."

"I'm not a nasty fidget, am I?" Mrs. Monarch appealed to her husband.

He addressed his answer to me. "Perhaps it isn't out of place to mention — because we ought to be quite business-like, oughtn't we? — that when I married her she was known as the Beautiful Statue."

"Oh dear!" said Mrs. Monarch, ruefully.

"Of course I should want a certain amount of expression," I rejoined.

"Of *course!*" they both exclaimed.

"And then I suppose you know that you'll get awfully tired."

"Oh, we *never* get tired!" they eagerly cried.

"Have you had any kind of practice?"

They hesitated — they looked at each other. "We've been photographed, *immensely,*" said Mrs. Monarch.

"She means the fellows have asked us," added the Major.

"I see — because you're so good-looking."

"I don't know what they thought, but they were always after us."

"We always got our photographs for nothing," smiled Mrs. Monarch.

"We might have brought some, my dear," her husband remarked.

"I'm not sure we have any left. We've given quantities away," she explained to me.

"With our autographs and that sort of thing," said the Major.

"Are they to be got in the shops?" I inquired, as a harmless pleasantry.

"Oh, yes; *hers* — they used to be."

"Not now," said Mrs. Monarch, with her eyes on the floor.

II

I could fancy the "sort of thing" they put on the presentation-copies of their photographs, and I was sure they wrote a beautiful hand. It was odd how quickly I was sure of everything that concerned them. If they were now so poor as to have to earn shillings and pence, they never had had much of a margin. Their good looks had been their capital, and they had good-humouredly made the most of the career that this resource marked out for them. It was in their faces, the blankness, the deep intellectual repose of the twenty years of country-house visiting which had given them pleasant intonations. I could see the sunny drawing-rooms, sprinkled with periodicals she didn't read, in which Mrs. Monarch had continuously sat; I could see the wet shrubberies in which she had walked, equipped to admiration for either exercise. I could see the rich covers the Major had helped to shoot and the wonderful garments in which, late at night, he repaired to the smoking-room to talk about them. I could imagine their leggings and waterproofs, their knowing tweeds and rugs, their rolls of sticks and cases of tackle and neat umbrellas; and I could evoke the exact appearance of their servants and the compact variety of their luggage on the platforms of country stations.

They gave small tips, but they were liked; they didn't do anything themselves, but they were welcome. They looked so well everywhere; they gratified the general relish for stature, complexion and "form." They knew it without fatuity or vulgarity, and they respected themselves in consequence. They were not superficial; they were thorough and kept themselves up — it had been their line. People with such a taste for activity had to have some line. I could feel how, even in a dull house, they could have been counted upon for cheerfulness. At present something had happened — it didn't matter what, their little income had grown less, it had grown least — and they had to do something for pocket-money. Their friends liked them, but didn't like to support them. There was something about them that represented credit — their clothes, their manners, their type; but if credit is a large empty pocket in which an occasional chink reverberates, the chink at least must be audible. What they wanted of me was to help to make it so. Fortunately they had no children — I soon divined that. They would also perhaps wish our relations to be kept secret: this was why it was "for the figure" — the reproduction of the face would betray them.

I liked them — they were so simple; and I had no objection to them if they would suit. But, somehow, with all their perfections I didn't easily believe in them. After all they were amateurs, and the ruling passion of my life was the detestation of the amateur. Combined with this was another perversity — an innate preference for the represented subject over the real one: the defect of the real one was so apt to be a lack of representation. I liked things that appeared; then one was sure. Whether they *were* or not was a subordinate and almost always a profitless question. There were other considerations, the first of which was that I already had two or three people in use, notably a young person with big feet, in alpaca, from Kilburn, who for a couple of years had come to me regularly for my illustrations and with whom I was still — perhaps ignobly — satisfied. I frankly explained to my visitors how the case stood; but they had taken more precautions than I supposed. They had reasoned out their opportunity, for Claude Rivet had told them of the projected *édition de luxe* of one of the writers of our day — the rarest of the novelists — who, long neglected by the multitudinous vulgar and dearly prized by the attentive (need I mention Philip Vincent?) had had the happy fortune of seeing, late in life, the dawn and then the full light of a higher criticism — an estimate in which, on the part of the public, there was something really of expiation. The edition in question, planned by a publisher of taste, was practically an act of high reparation; the wood-cuts with which it was to be enriched were the homage of English art to one of the most independent representatives of English letters. Major and Mrs. Monarch confessed to me that they had hoped I might be able to work *them* into my share of the enterprise. They knew I was to do the first of the books, "Rutland Ramsay," but I had to make clear to them that my participation in the rest of the affair — this first book was to be a test — was to depend on the satisfaction I should give. If this should be limited my employers would drop me without a scruple. It was therefore a crisis for me, and naturally I was making special preparations, looking about for new people, if they should be necessary, and securing the best types. I admitted however that I should like to settle down to two or three good models who would do for everything.

"Should we have often to — a — put on special clothes?" Mrs. Monarch timidly demanded.

"Dear, yes — that's half the business."

"And should we be expected to supply our own costumes?"

"Oh, no; I've got a lot of things. A painter's models put on — or put off — anything he likes."

"And do you mean — a — the same?"

"The same?"

Mrs. Monarch looked at her husband again.

"Oh, she was just wondering," he explained, "if the costumes are in *general* use." I had to confess that they were, and I mentioned further that some of them (I had a lot of genuine, greasy last-century things), had served their time, a hundred years ago, on living, world-stained men and women. "We'll put on anything that *fits*," said the Major.

"Oh, I arrange that — they fit in the pictures."

"I'm afraid I should do better for the modern books. I would come as you like," said Mrs. Monarch.

"She has got a lot of clothes at home: they might do for contemporary life," her husband continued.

"Oh, I can fancy scenes in which you'd be quite natural." And indeed I could see the slipshod rearrangements of stale properties — the stories I tried to produce pictures for without the exasperation of reading them — whose sandy tracts the good lady might help to people. But I had to return to the fact that for this sort of work — the daily mechanical grind — I was already equipped; the people I was working with were fully adequate.

"We only thought we might be more like *some* characters," said Mrs. Monarch mildly, getting up.

Her husband also rose; he stood looking at me with a dim wistfulness that was touching in so fine a man. "Wouldn't it be rather a pull sometimes to have — a — to have — ?" He hung fire; he wanted me to help him by phrasing what he meant. But I couldn't — I didn't know. So he brought it out, awkwardly: "The *real* thing; a gentleman, you know, or a lady." I was quite ready to give a general assent — I admitted that there was a great deal in that. This encouraged Major Monarch to say, following up his appeal with an unacted gulp: "It's awfully hard — we've tried everything." The gulp was communicative; it proved too much for his wife. Before I knew it Mrs. Monarch had dropped again upon a divan and burst into tears. Her husband sat down beside her, holding one of her hands; whereupon she quickly dried her eyes with the other, while I felt embarrassed as she looked up at me. "There isn't a confounded job I haven't applied for — waited for — prayed for. You can fancy we'd be pretty bad first. Secretaryships and that sort of thing? You might as well ask for a peerage. I'd be *anything* — I'm strong; a messenger or a coalheaver. I'd put on a gold-laced cap and open carriage-doors in front of the haberdasher's; I'd hang about a station, to carry portmanteaus; I'd be a postman. But they won't *look* at you; there are thousands, as good as yourself, already on the ground. *Gentlemen*, poor beggars, who have drunk their wine, who have kept their hunters!"

I was as reassuring as I knew how to be, and my visitors were presently on their feet again while, for the experiment, we agreed on an hour. We were discussing it when the door opened and Miss Churm came in with a wet umbrella. Miss Churm had to take the omnibus to Maida Vale and then walk half-a-mile. She looked a trifle blowsy and slightly splashed. I scarcely ever saw her come in without thinking afresh how odd it was that, being so little in herself, she should yet be so much in others. She was a meagre little Miss Churm, but she was an ample heroine of romance. She was only a freckled cockney, but she could represent everything, from a fine lady to a shepherdess; she had the faculty, as she might have had a fine voice or long hair. She couldn't spell, and she loved beer, but she had two or three "points," and practice, and a knack, and mother-wit, and a kind of whimsical sensibility, and a love of the theatre, and seven sisters, and not an ounce of respect, especially for the *h*. The first thing my visitors saw was that her umbrella was wet, and in their spotless perfection they visibly winced at it. The rain had come on since their arrival.

"I'm all in a soak; there *was* a mess of people in the 'bus. I wish you lived near a styion," said Miss Churm. I requested her to get ready as quickly as possible, and she passed into the room in which she always changed her dress. But before going out she asked me what she was to get into this time.

"It's the Russian princess, don't you know?" I answered; "the one with the 'golden eyes,' in black velvet, for the long thing in the *Cheapside*."

"Golden eyes? I *say!*" cried Miss Churm, while my companions watched her with intensity as she withdrew. She always arranged herself, when she was late, before I could turn round; and I kept my visitors a little, on purpose, so that they might get an idea, from seeing her, what would be expected of themselves. I mentioned that she was quite my notion of an excellent model — she was really very clever.

"Do you think she looks like a Russian princess?" Major Monarch asked, with lurking alarm.

"When I make her, yes."

"Oh, if you have to *make* her — !" he reasoned, acutely.

"That's the most you can ask. There are so many that are not makeable."

"Well now, *here's* a lady" — and with a persuasive smile he passed his arm into his wife's — "who's already made!"

"Oh, I'm not a Russian princess," Mrs. Monarch protested, a little coldly. I could see that she had known some and didn't like them. There, immediately, was a complication of a kind that I never had to fear with Miss Churm.

This young lady came back in black velvet — the gown was rather rusty and very low on her lean shoulders — and with a Japanese fan in her red hands. I reminded her that in the scene I was doing she had to look over someone's head. "I forget whose it is; but it doesn't matter. Just look over a head."

"I'd rather look over a stove," said Miss Churm; and she took her station near the fire. She fell into position, settled herself into a tall attitude, gave a certain backward inclination to her head and a certain forward droop to her fan, and looked, at least to my prejudiced sense, distinguished and charming, foreign and dangerous. We left her looking so, while I went down-stairs with Major and Mrs. Monarch.

"I think I could come about as near it as that," said Mrs. Monarch.

"Oh, you think she's shabby, but you must allow for the alchemy of art."

However, they went off with an evident increase of comfort, founded on their demonstrable advantage in being the real thing. I could fancy them shuddering over Miss Churm. She was very droll about them when I went back, for I told her what they wanted.

"Well, if *she* can sit I'll tyke to bookkeeping," said my model.

"She's very lady-like," I replied, as an innocent form of aggravation.

"So much the worse for *you*. That means she can't turn round."

"She'll do for the fashionable novels."

"Oh yes, she'll *do* for them!" my model humorously declared. "Ain't they bad enough without her?" I had often sociably denounced them to Miss Churm.

III

It was for the elucidation of a mystery in one of these works that I first tried Mrs. Monarch. Her husband came with her, to be useful if necessary — it was sufficiently clear that as a general thing he would prefer to come with her. At first I wondered if this were for "propriety's" sake — if he were going to be jealous and meddling. The idea was too tiresome, and if it had been confirmed it would speedily have brought our acquaintance to a close. But I soon saw there was nothing in it and that if he accompanied Mrs. Monarch it was (in addition to the chance of being wanted), simply because he had nothing else to do. When she was away from him his occupation was gone — she never *had* been away from him. I judged, rightly, that in their awkward situation their close union was their main comfort and that this union had no weak spot. It was a real marriage, an encouragement to the hesitating, a nut for pessimists to crack. Their address was humble (I remember afterwards thinking it had been the only thing about them that was really professional), and I could fancy the lamentable lodgings in which the Major would have been left alone. He could bear them with his wife — he couldn't bear them without her.

He had too much tact to try and make himself agreeable when he couldn't be useful; so he simply sat and waited, when I was too absorbed in my work to talk. But I liked to make him talk — it made my work, when it didn't interrupt it, less sordid, less special. To listen to him was to combine the excitement of going out with the economy of staying at home. There was only one hindrance: that I seemed not to know any of the people he and his wife had known. I think he wondered extremely, during the term of our intercourse, whom the deuce I *did* know. He hadn't a stray sixpence of an idea to fumble for; so we didn't spin it very fine — we confined ourselves to questions of leather and even of liquor (saddlers and breeches-makers and how to get good claret cheap), and matters like "good trains" and the habits of small game. His lore on these last subjects was astonishing, he managed to interweave the station-master with the ornithologist. When he couldn't talk about greater things he could talk cheerfully about smaller, and since I couldn't accompany him into reminiscences of the fashionable world he could lower the conversation without a visible effort to my level.

So earnest a desire to please was touching in a man who could so easily have knocked one down. He looked after the fire and had an opinion on the draught of the stove, without my asking him, and I could see that he thought many of my arrangements not half clever enough. I remember telling him that if I were only rich I would offer him a salary to come and teach me how to live. Sometimes he gave a random sigh, of which the essence was: "Give me even such a bare old barrack as *this,* and I'd do something with it!" When I wanted to use him he came alone; which was an illustration of the superior courage of women. His wife could bear her solitary second floor, and she was in general more discreet; showing by various small reserves that she was alive to the propriety of keeping our relations markedly professional — not letting them slide into sociability. She wished it to remain clear that she and the Major were employed, not cultivated, and if she approved of me as a superior, who could be kept in his place, she never thought me quite good enough for an equal.

She sat with great intensity, giving the whole of her mind to it, and was capable of remaining for an hour almost as motionless as if she were before a photographer's lens. I could see she had been photographed often, but somehow the very habit that made her good for that purpose unfitted her for mine. At first I was extremely pleased with her lady-like air, and it was a satisfaction, on coming to follow her lines, to see how good they were and how far they could lead the pencil. But after a few times I began to find her too insurmountably stiff; do what I would with it my drawing looked like a photograph or a copy of a photograph. Her figure had no variety of expression — she herself had no sense of variety. You may say that this was my business, was only a question of placing her. I placed her in every conceivable position, but she managed to obliterate their differences. She was always a lady certainly, and into the bargain was always the same lady. She was the real thing, but always the same thing. There were moments when I was oppressed by the serenity of her confidence that she *was* the real thing. All her dealings with me and all her husband's were an implication that this was lucky for *me*. Meanwhile I found myself trying to invent types that approached her own, instead of making her own transform itself — in the clever way that was not impossible, for instance, to poor Miss Churm. Arrange as I would and take the precautions I would, she always, in my pictures, came out too tall — landing me in the dilemma of having represented a fascinating woman as seven feet high, which, out of respect perhaps to my own very much scantier inches, was far from my idea of such a personage.

The case was worse with the Major — nothing I could do would keep *him* down, so that he became useful only for the representation of brawny giants. I adored variety and range, I cherished human accidents, the illustrative note; I wanted to characterise closely, and the thing in the world I most hated was the danger of being ridden by a type. I had quarrelled with some of my friends about it — I had parted company with them for maintaining that one *had* to be, and that if the type was beautiful (witness Raphael and Leonardo), the servitude was only a gain. I was neither Leonardo nor Raphael; I might only be a presumptuous young modern searcher, but I held that everything was to be sacrificed sooner than character. When they averred that the haunting type in question could easily *be* character, I retorted, perhaps superficially: "Whose?" It couldn't be everybody's — it might end in being nobody's.

After I had drawn Mrs. Monarch a dozen times I perceived more clearly than before that the value of such a model as Miss Churm resided precisely in the fact that she had no positive stamp, combined of course with the other fact that what she did have was a curious and inexplicable talent for imitation. Her usual appearance was like a curtain which she could draw up at request for a capital performance. This performance was simply suggestive; but it was a word to the wise — it was vivid and pretty. Sometimes, even, I thought it, though she was plain herself, too insipidly pretty; I made it a reproach to her that the figures drawn from her were monotonously (*bêtement*, as we used to say) graceful. Nothing made her more angry: it was so much her pride to feel that she could sit for characters that had nothing in common with each other. She would accuse me at such moments of taking away her "reputytion."

It suffered a certain shrinkage, this queer quantity, from the repeated visits of my new friends. Miss Churm was greatly in demand, never in want of employment, so I had no scruple in putting her off occasionally, to try them more at my ease. It was certainly amusing at first to do the real thing — it was amusing to do Major Monarch's trousers. They *were* the real thing, even if he did come out colossal. It was amusing to do his wife's back hair (it was so mathematically neat,) and the particular "smart" tension of her tight stays. She lent herself especially to positions in which the face was somewhat averted or blurred; she abounded in lady-like back views and *profils perdus*. When she stood erect she took naturally one of the attitudes in which court-painters represent queens and princesses; so that I found myself wondering whether, to draw out this accomplishment, I couldn't get the editor of the *Cheapside* to publish a really royal romance, "A Tale of Buckingham Palace." Sometimes, however, the real thing and the make-believe came into contact; by which I mean that Miss Churm, keeping an appointment or coming to make one on days when I had much work in hand, encountered her invidious rivals. The encounter was not on their part, for they noticed her no more than if she had been the housemaid; not from intentional loftiness, but simply because, as yet professionally, they didn't know how to fraternise, as I could guess that they would have liked — or at least that the Major would. They couldn't talk about the omnibus — they always walked; and they didn't know what else to try — she wasn't interested in good trains or cheap claret. Besides, they must have felt — in the air — that she was amused at them, secretly derisive of their ever knowing how. She was not a person to conceal her scepticism if she had had a chance to show it. On the other hand Mrs. Monarch didn't think her tidy; for why else did she take pains to say to me (it was going out of the way, for Mrs. Monarch), that she didn't like dirty women?

One day when my young lady happened to be present with my other sitters (she even dropped in, when it was convenient, for a chat), I asked her to be so good as to lend a hand in getting tea — a service with which she was familiar and which was one of a class that, living as I did in a small way, with slender domestic resources, I often appealed to my models to render. They liked to lay hands on my property, to break the sitting, and sometimes the china — I made them feel Bohemian. The next time I saw Miss Churm after this incident she surprised me greatly by making a scene about it — she accused me of having wished to humiliate her. She had not resented the outrage at the time, but had seemed obliging and amused, enjoying the comedy of asking Mrs. Monarch, who sat vague and silent, whether she would have cream and sugar, and putting an exaggerated simper into the question. She had tried intonations — as if she too wished to pass for the real thing; till I was afraid my other visitors would take offence.

Oh, *they* were determined not to do this; and their touching patience was the measure of their great need. They would sit by the hour, uncomplaining, till I was ready to use them; they would come back on the chance of being wanted and would walk away cheerfully if they were not. I used to go to the door with them to see in what magnificent order they retreated. I tried to find other employment for them — I introduced them to several artists. But they didn't "take," for reasons I could appreciate, and I became conscious, rather anxiously, that after such disappointments they fell back upon me with a heavier weight. They did me the honour to think that it was I who was most *their* form. They were not picturesque enough for the painters, and in those days there were not so many serious workers in black and white. Besides, they had an eye to the great job I had mentioned to them — they had secretly set their hearts on supplying the right essence for my pictorial vindication of our fine novelist. They knew that for this undertaking I should want no costume-effects, none of the frippery of past ages — that it was a case in which everything would be contemporary and satirical and, presumably, genteel. If I could work them into it their future would be assured, for the labour would of course be long and the occupation steady.

One day Mrs. Monarch came without her husband — she explained his absence by his having had to go to the City. While she sat there in her usual anxious stiffness there came, at the door, a knock which I immediately recognized as the subdued appeal of a model out of work. It was followed by the entrance of a young man whom I easily perceived to be a foreigner and who proved in fact an Italian acquainted with no English word but my name, which he uttered in a way that made it seem to include all others. I had not then visited his country, nor was I proficient in his tongue; but as he was not so meanly constituted — what Italian is? — as to depend only on that member for expression he conveyed to me, in familiar but graceful mimicry, that he was in search of exactly the employment in which the lady before me was engaged. I was not struck with him at first, and while I continued to draw I emitted rough sounds of discouragement and dismissal. He stood his ground, however, not importunately, but with a dumb, dog-like fidelity in his eyes which amounted to innocent impudence — the manner of a devoted servant (he might have been in the house for years), unjustly suspected. Suddenly I saw that this very attitude and expression made a picture, whereupon I told him to sit down and wait till I should be free. There was another picture in the way he obeyed me, and I observed as I worked that there were others still in the way he looked wonderingly, with his head thrown back, about the high studio. He might have been crossing himself in St. Peter's. Before I finished I said to myself: "The fellow's a bankrupt orange-monger, but he's a treasure."

When Mrs. Monarch withdrew he passed across the room like a flash to open the door for her, standing there with the rapt, pure gaze of the young Dante spellbound by the young Beatrice. As I never insisted, in such situations, on the blankness of the British domestic, I reflected that he had the making of a servant (and I needed one, but couldn't pay him to be only that), as well as of a model; in short I made up my mind to adopt my bright adventurer if he would agree to officiate in the double capacity. He jumped at my offer, and in the event my rashness (for I had known nothing about him), was not brought home to me. He proved a sympathetic though a desultory ministrant, and had in a wonderful degree the *sentiment de la pose.* It was uncultivated, instinctive; a part of the happy instinct which had guided him to my door and helped him to spell out my name on the card nailed to it. He had had no other introduction to me than a guess, from the shape of my high north window, seen outside, that my place was a studio and that as a studio it would contain an artist. He had wandered to England in search of fortune, like other itinerants, and had embarked, with a partner and a small green hand-cart, on the sale of penny ices. The ices had melted away and the partner had dissolved in their train. My young man wore tight yellow trousers with reddish stripes and his name was Oronte. He was sallow but fair, and when I put him into some old clothes of my own he looked like an Englishman. He was as good as Miss Churm, who could look, when required, like an Italian.

IV

I thought Mrs. Monarch's face slightly convulsed when, on her coming back with her husband, she found Oronte installed. It was strange to have to recognise in a scrap of a lazzarone a competitor to her magnificent Major. It was she who scented danger first, for the Major was anecdotically unconscious. But Oronte gave us tea, with a hundred eager confusions (he had never seen such a queer process), and I think she thought better of me for having at last an "establishment." They saw a couple of drawings that I had made of the establishment, and Mrs. Monarch hinted that it never would have struck her that he had sat for them. "Now the drawings you make from *us,* they look exactly like us," she reminded me, smiling in triumph; and I recognized that this was indeed just their defect. When I drew the Monarchs I couldn't, somehow, get away from them — get into the character I wanted to represent; and I had not the least desire my model should be discoverable in my picture. Miss Churm never was, and Mrs. Monarch thought I hid her, very properly, because she was vulgar; whereas if she was lost it was only as the dead who go to heaven are lost — in the gain of an angel the more.

By this time I had got a certain start with "Rutland Ramsay," the first novel in the great projected series; that is I had produced a dozen drawings, several with the help of the Major and his wife, and I had sent them in for approval. My understanding with the publishers, as I have already hinted, had been that I was to be left to do my work, in this particular case, as I liked, with the whole book committed to me; but my connection with the rest of the series was only contingent. There were moments when, frankly, it *was* a comfort to have the real thing under one's hand; for there were characters in "Rutland Ramsay" that were very much like it. There were people presumably as straight as the Major and women of as good a fashion as Mrs. Monarch. There was a great deal of country-house life — treated, it is true, in a fine, fanciful, ironical, generalised way — and there was a considerable implication of knickerbockers and kilts. There were certain things I had to settle at the outset; such things for instance as the exact appearance of the hero; the particular bloom of the heroine. The author of course gave me a lead, but there was a margin for interpretation. I took the Monarchs into my confidence, I told them frankly what I was about, I mentioned my embarrassments and alternatives. "Oh, take *him!*" Mrs. Monarch murmured sweetly, looking at her husband; and "What could you want better than my wife?" the Major inquired, with the comfortable candour that now prevailed between us.

I was not obliged to answer these remarks — I was only obliged to place my sitters. I was not easy in mind, and I postponed, a little timidly perhaps, the solution of the question. The book was a large canvas, the other figures were numerous, and I worked off at first some of the episodes in which the hero and the heroine were not concerned. When once I had set *them* up I should have to stick to them — I couldn't make my young man seven feet high in one place and five feet nine in another. I inclined on the whole to the latter measurement, though the Major more than once reminded me that *he* looked about as young as anyone. It was indeed quite possible to arrange him, for the figure, so that it would have been difficult to detect his age. After the spontaneous Oronte had been with me a month, and after I had given him to understand several different times that his native exuberance would presently constitute an insurmountable barrier to our further intercourse, I waked to a sense of his heroic capacity. He was only five feet seven, but the remaining inches were latent. I tried him almost secretly at first, for I was really rather afraid of the judgment my other models would pass on such a choice. If they regarded Miss Churm as little better than a snare, what would they think of the representation by a person so little the real thing as an Italian street-vendor of a protagonist formed by a public school?

If I went a little in fear of them it was not because they bullied me, because they had got an oppressive foothold, but because in their really pathetic decorum and mysteriously permanent newness they counted on me so intensely. I was therefore very glad when Jack Hawley came home: he was always of such good counsel. He painted badly himself, but there was no one like him for putting his finger on the place. He had been absent from England for a year; he had been somewhere — I don't remember where — to get a fresh eye. I was in a good deal of dread of any such organ, but we were old friends; he had been away for months and a sense of emptiness was creeping into my life. I hadn't dodged a missile for a year.

He came back with a fresh eye, but with the same old black velvet blouse, and the first evening he spent in my studio we smoked cigarettes till the small hours. He had done no work himself, he had only got the eye; so the field was clear for the production of my little things. He wanted to see what I had done for the *Cheapside,* but he was disappointed in the exhibition. That at least seemed the meaning of two or three comprehensive groans which, as he lounged on my big divan, on a folded leg, looking at my latest drawings, issued from his lips with the smoke of the cigarette.

"What's the matter with you?" I asked.

"What's the matter with *you?*"

"Nothing save that I'm mystified."

"You are indeed. You're quite off the hinge. What's the meaning of this new fad?" And he tossed me, with visible irreverence, a drawing in which I happened to have depicted both my majestic models. I asked if he didn't think it good, and he replied that it struck him as execrable, given the sort of thing I had always represented myself to him as wishing to arrive at; but I let that pass, I was so anxious to see exactly what he meant. The two figures in the picture looked colossal, but I supposed this was *not* what he meant, inasmuch as, for aught he knew to the contrary, I might have been trying for that. I maintained that I was working exactly in the same way as when he last had done me the honour to commend me. "Well, there's a big hole somewhere," he answered; "wait a bit and I'll discover it." I depended upon him to do so: where else was the fresh eye? But he produced at last nothing more luminous than "I don't know — I don't like your types." This was lame, for a critic who had never consented to discuss with me anything but the question of execution, the direction of strokes and the mystery of values.

"In the drawings you've been looking at I think my types are very handsome."

"Oh, they won't do!"

"I've had a couple of new models."

"I see you have. *They* won't do."

"Are you very sure of that?"

"Absolutely — they're stupid."

"You mean *I* am — for I ought to get round that."

"You *can't* — with such people. Who are they?"

I told him, as far as was necessary, and he declared, heartlessly: *"Ce sont des gens qu'il faut mettre à la porte."*

"You've never seen them; they're awfully good," I compassionately objected.

"Not seen them? Why, all this recent work of yours drops to pieces with them. It's all I want to see of them."

"No one else has said anything against it — the *Cheapside* people are pleased."

"Everyone else is an ass, and the *Cheapside* people the biggest asses of all. Come, don't pretend, at this time of day, to have pretty illusions about the pub-

lic, especially about publishers and editors. It's not for *such* animals you work —
it's for those who know, *coloro che sanno;* so keep straight for *me* if you can't keep
straight for yourself. There's a certain sort of thing you tried for from the first —
and a very good thing it is. But this twaddle isn't *in* it." When I talked with Hawley later about "Rutland Ramsay" and its possible successors he declared that I
must get back into my boat again or I would go to the bottom. His voice in short
was the voice of warning.

I noted the warning, but I didn't turn my friends out of doors. They bored
me a good deal; but the very fact that they bored me admonished me not to sacrifice them — if there was anything to be done with them — simply to irritation. As I look back at this phase they seem to me to have pervaded my life not a
little. I have a vision of them as most of the time in my studio, seated, against the
wall, on an old velvet bench to be out of the way, and looking like a pair of
patient courtiers in a royal ante-chamber. I am convinced that during the coldest
weeks of the winter they held their ground because it saved them fire. Their
newness was losing its gloss, and it was impossible not to feel that they were objects of charity. Whenever Miss Churm arrived they went away, and after I was
fairly launched in "Rutland Ramsay" Miss Churm arrived pretty often. They
managed to express to me tacitly that they supposed I wanted her for the low life
of the book, and I let them suppose it, since they had attempted to study the
work — it was lying about the studio — without discovering that it dealt only
with the highest circles. They had dipped into the most brilliant of our novelists
without deciphering many passages. I still took an hour from them, now and
again, in spite of Jack Hawley's warning: it would be time enough to dismiss
them, if dismissal should be necessary, when the rigour of the season was over.
Hawley had made their acquaintance — he had met them at my fireside — and
thought them a ridiculous pair. Learning that he was a painter they tried to approach him, to show him too that they were the real thing; but he looked at
them, across the room, as if they were miles away: they were a compendium of
everything that he most objected to in the social system of his country. Such
people as that, all convention and patent-leather, with ejaculations that stopped
conversation, had no business in a studio. A studio was a place to learn to see,
and how could you see through a pair of feather beds?

The main inconvenience I suffered at their hands was that, at first, I was shy
of letting them discover how my artful little servant had begun to sit to me for
"Rutland Ramsay." They knew that I had been odd enough (they were prepared
by this time to allow oddity to artists,) to pick a foreign vagabond out of the
streets, when I might have had a person with whiskers and credentials; but it was
some time before they learned how high I rated his accomplishments. They
found him in an attitude more than once, but they never doubted I was doing
him as an organ-grinder. There were several things they never guessed, and one
of them was that for a striking scene in the novel, in which a footman briefly

figured, it occurred to me to make use of Major Monarch as the menial. I kept
putting this off, I didn't like to ask him to don the livery — besides the difficulty
of finding a livery to fit him. At last, one day late in the winter, when I was at
work on the despised Oronte (he caught one's idea in an instant), and was in the
glow of feeling that I was going very straight, they came in, the Major and his
wife, with their society laugh about nothing (there was less and less to laugh at),
like country-callers — they always reminded me of that — who have walked
across the park after church and are presently persuaded to stay to luncheon.
Luncheon was over, but they could stay to tea — I knew they wanted it. The fit
was on me, however, and I couldn't let my ardour cool and my work wait, with
the fading daylight, while my model prepared it. So I asked Mrs. Monarch if she
would mind laying it out — a request which, for an instant, brought all the blood
to her face. Her eyes were on her husband's for a second, and some mute teleg-
raphy passed between them. Their folly was over the next instant; his cheerful
shrewdness put an end to it. So far from pitying their wounded pride, I must add,
I was moved to give it as complete a lesson as I could. They bustled about together and got out the cups and saucers and made the kettle boil. I know they
felt as if they were waiting on my servant, and when the tea was prepared I said:
"He'll have a cup, please — he's tired." Mrs. Monarch brought him one where he
stood, and he took it from her as if he had been a gentleman at a party, squeezing a crush-hat with an elbow.

Then it came over me that she had made a great effort for me — made it
with a kind of nobleness — and that I owed her a compensation. Each time I saw
her after this I wondered what the compensation could be. I couldn't go on doing the wrong thing to oblige them. Oh, it *was* the wrong thing, the stamp of the
work for which they sat — Hawley was not the only person to say it now. I sent
in a large number of the drawings I had made for "Rutland Ramsay," and I received a warning that was more to the point than Hawley's. The artistic adviser
of the house for which I was working was of opinion that many of my illustrations were not what had been looked for. Most of these illustrations were the
subjects in which the Monarchs had figured. Without going into the question of
what *had* been looked for, I saw at this rate I shouldn't get the other books to do.
I hurled myself in despair upon Miss Churm, I put her through all her paces. I
not only adopted Oronte publicly as my hero, but one morning when the Major
looked in to see if I didn't require him to finish a figure for the *Cheapside,* for
which he had begun to sit the week before, I told him that I had changed my
mind — I would do the drawing from my man. At this my visitor turned pale
and stood looking at me. "Is *he* your idea of an English gentleman?" he asked.

I was disappointed, I was nervous, I wanted to get on with my work; so I
replied with irritation: "Oh, my dear Major — I can't be ruined for *you!*"

He stood another moment; then, without a word, he quitted the studio. I drew a long breath when he was gone, for I said to myself that I shouldn't see him again. I had not told him definitely that I was in danger of having my work rejected, but I was vexed at his not having felt the catastrophe in the air, read with me the moral of our fruitless collaboration, the lesson that, in the deceptive atmosphere of art, even the highest respectability may fail of being plastic.

I didn't owe my friends money, but I did see them again. They re-appeared together, three days later, and under the circumstances there was something tragic in the fact. It was a proof to me that they could find nothing else in life to do. They had threshed the matter out in a dismal conference — they had digested the bad news that they were not in for the series. If they were not useful to me even for the *Cheapside* their function seemed difficult to determine, and I could only judge at first that they had come, forgivingly, decorously, to take a last leave. This made me rejoice in secret that I had little leisure for a scene; for I had placed both my other models in position together and I was pegging away at a drawing from which I hoped to derive glory. It had been suggested by the passage in which Rutland Ramsay, drawing up a chair to Artemisia's piano-stool, says extraordinary things to her while she ostensibly fingers out a difficult piece of music. I had done Miss Churm at the piano before — it was an attitude in which she knew how to take on an absolutely poetic grace. I wished the two figures to "compose" together, intensely, and my little Italian had entered perfectly into my conception. The pair were vividly before me, the piano had been pulled out; it was a charming picture of blended youth and murmured love, which I had only to catch and keep. My visitors stood and looked at it, and I was friendly to them over my shoulder.

They made no response, but I was used to silent company and went on with my work, only a little disconcerted (even though exhilarated by the sense that *this* was at least the ideal thing), at not having got rid of them after all. Presently I heard Mrs. Monarch's sweet voice beside, or rather above me: "I wish her hair was a little better done." I looked up and she was staring with a strange fixedness at Miss Churm, whose back was turned to her. "Do you mind my just touching it?" she went on — a question which made me spring up for an instant, as with the instinctive fear that she might do the young lady a harm. But she quieted me with a glance I shall never forget — I confess I should like to have been able to paint *that* — and went for a moment to my model. She spoke to her softly, laying a hand upon her shoulder and bending over her; and as the girl, understanding, gratefully assented, she disposed her rough curls, with a few quick passes, in such a way as to make Miss Churm's head twice as charming. It was one of the most heroic personal services I have ever seen rendered. Then Mrs. Monarch turned away with a low sigh and, looking about her as if for something to do, stooped to the floor with a noble humility and picked up a dirty rag that had dropped out of my paint-box.

The Major meanwhile had also been looking for something to do and, wandering to the other end of the studio, saw before him my breakfast things, neglected, unremoved. "I say, can't I be useful *here?*" he called out to me with an irrepressible quaver. I assented with a laugh that I fear was awkward and for the next ten minutes, while I worked, I heard the light clatter of china and the tinkle of spoons and glass. Mrs. Monarch assisted her husband — they washed up my crockery, they put it away. They wandered off into my little scullery, and I afterwards found that they had cleaned my knives and that my slender stock of plate had an unprecedented surface. When it came over me, the latent eloquence of what they were doing, I confess that my drawing was blurred for a moment — the picture swam. They had accepted their failure, but they couldn't accept their fate. They had bowed their heads in bewilderment to the perverse and cruel law in virtue of which the real thing could be so much less precious than the unreal; but they didn't want to starve. If my servants were my models, my models might be my servants. They would reverse the parts — the others would sit for the ladies and gentlemen, and *they* would do the work. They would still be in the studio — it was an intense dumb appeal to me not to turn them out. "Take us on," they wanted to say — "we'll do *anything.*"

When all this hung before me the *afflatus* vanished — my pencil dropped from my hand. My sitting was spoiled and I got rid of my sitters, who were also evidently rather mystified and awestruck. Then, alone with the Major and his wife, I had a most uncomfortable moment. He put their prayer into a single sentence: "I say, you know — just let *us* do for you, can't you?" I couldn't — it was dreadful to see them emptying my slops; but I pretended I could, to oblige them, for about a week. Then I gave them a sum of money to go away; and I never saw them again. I obtained the remaining books, but my friend Hawley repeats that Major and Mrs. Monarch did me a permanent harm, got me into a second-rate trick. If it be true I am content to have paid the price — for the memory.

Kate Chopin
Désirée's Baby

In the early twentieth century, Fred Lewis Pattee, the leading American scholar of the day, proclaimed that Kate Chopin was the great genius of the short story, and his comment was joined by a chorus of other voices. Her novel *The Awakening* (1899) occasioned immense controversy and, in some circles, condemnation for its frank depiction of feminine sexual desires coupled with a rejection of motherhood. However, her stories were almost universally heralded for their subjects, their humane themes, and the grace of their artistry. None of them brought more solid praise than did "Désirée's Baby," which originally appeared in *Vogue* in 1893 under the title "The Father of Désirée's Baby," putting the emphasis on Armand, who has the moral crisis in the conclusion. Here marriage, a frequent topic for Chopin's writing, is linked to racial issues, a dominant concern in Louisiana fiction at the turn of the century. The deadly potential of blind prejudice is nowhere better exemplified than in this brief antebellum work, in which subtle hints of the ending are suggested throughout, making it less of a surprise than many readers have suggested.

Kate Chopin, "Désirée's Baby," *Bayou Folk* (Boston: Houghton, Mifflin and Company, 1894), 147–58.

As the day was pleasant, Madame Valmondé drove over to L'Abri to see Désirée and the baby.

It made her laugh to think of Désirée with a baby. Why, it seemed but yesterday that Désirée was little more than a baby herself; when Monsieur in riding through the gateway of Valmondé had found her lying asleep in the shadow of the big stone pillar.

The little one awoke in his arms and began to cry for "Dada." That was as much as she could do or say. Some people thought she might have strayed there of her own accord, for she was of the toddling age. The prevailing belief was that she had been purposely left by a party of Texans, whose canvas-covered wagon, late in the day, had crossed the ferry that Coton Maïs kept, just below the plantation. In time Madame Valmondé abandoned every speculation but the one that Désirée had been sent to her by a beneficent Providence to be the child of her affection, seeing that she was without child of the flesh. For the girl grew to be beautiful and gentle, affectionate and sincere, — the idol of Valmondé.

It was no wonder, when she stood one day against the stone pillar in whose shadow she had lain asleep, eighteen years before, that Armand Aubigny riding by and seeing her there, had fallen in love with her. That was the way all the Aubignys fell in love, as if struck by a pistol shot. The wonder was that he had not loved her before; for he had known her since his father brought him home from Paris, a boy of eight, after his mother died there. The passion that awoke in him that day, when he saw her at the gate, swept along like an avalanche, or like a prairie fire, or like anything that drives headlong over all obstacles.

Monsieur Valmondé grew practical and wanted things well considered: that is, the girl's obscure origin. Armand looked into her eyes and did not care. He was reminded that she was nameless. What did it matter about a name when he could give her one of the oldest and proudest in Louisiana? He ordered the *corbeille* from Paris, and contained himself with what patience he could until it arrived; then they were married.

Madame Valmondé had not seen Désirée and the baby for four weeks. When she reached L'Abri she shuddered at the first sight of it, as she always did. It was a sad looking place, which for many years had not known the gentle presence of a mistress, old Monsieur Aubigny having married and buried his wife in France, and she having loved her own land too well ever to leave it. The roof came down steep and black like a cowl, reaching out beyond the wide galleries that encircled the yellow stuccoed house. Big, solemn oaks grew close to it, and their thick-leaved, far-reaching branches shadowed it like a pall. Young Aubigny's rule was a strict one, too, and under it his negroes had forgotten how to be gay, as they had been during the old master's easy-going and indulgent lifetime.

The young mother was recovering slowly, and lay full length, in her soft white muslins and laces, upon a couch. The baby was beside her, upon her arm, where he had fallen asleep, at her breast. The yellow nurse woman sat beside a window fanning herself.

Madame Valmondé bent her portly figure over Désirée and kissed her, holding her an instant tenderly in her arms. Then she turned to the child.

"This is not the baby!" she exclaimed, in startled tones. French was the language spoken at Valmondé in those days.

"I knew you would be astonished," laughed Désirée, "at the way he has grown. The little *cochon de lait!* Look at his legs, mamma, and his hands and finger-nails, — real finger-nails. Zandrine had to cut them this morning. Isn't it true, Zandrine?"

The woman bowed her turbaned head majestically, "Mais si, Madame."

"And the way he cries," went on Désirée "is deafening. Armand heard him the other day as far away as La Blanche's cabin."

Madame Valmondé had never removed her eyes from the child. She lifted it and walked with it over to the window that was lightest. She scanned the baby narrowly, then looked as searchingly at Zandrine, whose face was turned to gaze across the fields.

"Yes, the child has grown, has changed;" said Madame Valmondé, slowly, as she replaced it beside its mother. "What does Armand say?"

Désirée's face became suffused with a glow that was happiness itself.

"Oh, Armand is the proudest father in the parish, I believe, chiefly because it is a boy, to bear his name; though he says not, — that he would have loved a girl as well. But I know it isn't true. I know he says that to please me. And mamma," she added, drawing Madame Valmondé's head down to her, and speaking in a whisper, "he hasn't punished one of them — not one of them — since baby is born. Even Négrillon, who pretended to have burnt his leg that he might rest from work — he only laughed, and said Négrillon was a great scamp. Oh, mamma, I'm so happy; it frightens me."

What Désirée said was true. Marriage, and later the birth of his son, had softened Armand Aubigny's imperious and exacting nature greatly. This was what made the gentle Désirée so happy, for she loved him desperately. When he frowned she trembled, but loved him. When he smiled, she asked no greater blessing of God. But Armand's dark, handsome face had not often been disfigured by frowns since the day he fell in love with her.

When the baby was about three months old, Désirée awoke one day to the conviction that there was something in the air menacing her peace. It was at first too subtle to grasp. It had only been a disquieting suggestion; an air of mystery among the blacks; unexpected visits from far-off neighbors who could hardly account for their coming. Then a strange, an awful change in her husband's manner, which she dared not ask him to explain. When he spoke to her, it was with averted eyes, from which the old love-light seemed to have gone out. He absented himself from home; and when there, avoided her presence and that of her child, without excuse. And the very spirit of Satan seemed suddenly to take hold of him in his dealings with the slaves. Désirée was miserable enough to die.

She sat in her room, one hot afternoon, in her *peignoir*, listlessly drawing through her fingers the strands of her long, silky brown hair that hung about her shoulders. The baby, half naked, lay asleep upon her own great mahogany bed, that was like a sumptuous throne, with its satin-lined half-canopy. One of La Blanche's little quadroon boys — half naked too — stood fanning the child slowly with a fan of peacock feathers. Désirée's eyes had been fixed absently and sadly upon the baby, while she was striving to penetrate the threatening mist that she felt closing about her. She looked from her child to the boy who stood beside him, and back again; over and over. "Ah!" It was a cry that she could not help; which she was not conscious of having uttered. The blood turned like ice in her veins, and a clammy moisture gathered upon her face.

She tried to speak to the little quadroon boy; but no sound would come, at first. When he heard his name uttered, he looked up, and his mistress was pointing to the door. He laid aside the great, soft fan, and obediently stole away, over the polished floor, on his bare tiptoes.

She stayed motionless, with gaze riveted upon her child, and her face the picture of fright.

Presently her husband entered the room, and without noticing her, went to a table and began to search among some papers which covered it.

"Armand," she called to him, in a voice which must have stabbed him, if he was human. But he did not notice. "Armand," she said again. Then she rose and tottered towards him. "Armand," she panted once more, clutching his arm, "look at our child. What does it mean? tell me."

He coldly but gently loosened her fingers from about his arm and thrust the hand away from him. "Tell me what it means!" she cried despairingly.

"It means," he answered lightly, "that the child is not white; it means that you are not white."

A quick conception of all that this accusation meant for her nerved her with unwonted courage to deny it. "It is a lie; it is not true, I am white! Look at my hair, it is brown; and my eyes are gray, Armand, you know they are gray. And my skin is fair," seizing his wrist. "Look at my hand; whiter than yours, Armand," she laughed hysterically.

"As white as La Blanche's," he returned cruelly; and went away leaving her alone with their child.

When she could hold a pen in her hand, she sent a despairing letter to Madame Valmondé.

"My mother, they tell me I am not white. Armand has told me I am not white. For God's sake tell them it is not true. You must know it is not true. I shall die. I must die. I cannot be so unhappy, and live."

The answer that came was as brief:

"My own Désirée: Come home to Valmondé; back to your mother who loves you. Come with your child."

When the letter reached Désirée she went with it to her husband's study, and laid it open upon the desk before which he sat. She was like a stone image: silent, white, motionless after she placed it there.

In silence he ran his cold eyes over the written words. He said nothing. "Shall I go, Armand?" she asked in tones sharp with agonized suspense.

"Yes, go."

"Do you want me to go?"

"Yes, I want you to go."

He thought Almighty God had dealt cruelly and unjustly with him; and felt, somehow, that he was paying Him back in kind when he stabbed thus into his wife's soul. Moreover he no longer loved her, because of the unconscious injury she had brought upon his home and his name.

She turned away like one stunned by a blow, and walked slowly towards the door, hoping he would call her back.

"Good-by, Armand," she moaned.

He did not answer her. That was his last blow at fate.

Désirée went in search of her child. Zandrine was pacing the sombre gallery with it. She took the little one from the nurse's arms with no word of explanation, and descending the steps, walked away, under the live-oak branches.

It was an October afternoon; the sun was just sinking. Out in the still fields the negroes were picking cotton.

Désirée had not changed the thin white garment nor the slippers which she wore. Her hair was uncovered and the sun's rays brought a golden gleam from its brown meshes. She did not take the broad, beaten road which led to the far-off plantation of Valmondé. She walked across a deserted field, where the stubble bruised her tender feet, so delicately shod, and tore her thin gown to shreds.

She disappeared among the reeds and willows that grew thick along the banks of the deep, sluggish bayou; and she did not come back again.

$\delta\delta$

Some weeks later there was a curious scene enacted at L'Abri. In the centre of the smoothly swept back yard was a great-bonfire. Armand Aubigny sat in the wide hallway that commanded a view of the spectacle; and it was he who dealt out to a half dozen negroes the material which kept this fire ablaze.

A graceful cradle of willow, with all its dainty furbishings, was laid upon the pyre, which had already been fed with the richness of a priceless *layette*. Then there were silk gowns, and velvet and satin ones added to these; laces, too, and embroideries; bonnets and gloves; for the *corbeille* had been of rare quality.

The last thing to go was a tiny bundle of letters; innocent little scribblings that Désirée had sent to him during the days of their espousal. There was the remnant of one back in the drawer from which he took them. But it was not Désirée's; it was part of an old letter from his mother to his father. He read it. She was thanking God for the blessing of her husband's love: —

"But, above all," she wrote, "night and day, I thank the good God for having so arranged our lives that our dear Armand will never know that his mother, who adores him, belongs to the race that is cursed with the brand of slavery."

Charles Chesnutt

The Wife of His Youth

Charles Chesnutt is an important figure in literary history as the first African American writer of fiction to attract a wide audience in both the black and white communities. Essentially a Realist who presented a mimetic portrait of racial issues with an emphasis on ethical conflicts, his work is well represented by "The Wife of His Youth." This story was first published in *The Atlantic Monthly* in 1898 and then incorporated into *The Wife of His Youth and Other Stories of the Color Line* the following year. In it are a series of moral dilemmas concerning race within white and black characters, which made the volume popular across the country. The titular story sets the crisis within a black character, Mr. Ryder, who must choose a course of action involving the return of his first wife just as he is about to marry his second. Within the main narrative there are a series of brief, retrospective accounts that clarify the tension in the plot, and the conclusion extends the resolution of the crisis to a broader audience. In 1905, Chesnutt, a lawyer, went on to become the first secretary of the NAACP and largely abandoned his literary career, but he is nonetheless considered one of the truly important writers of his era.

Charles Chesnutt, "The Wife of His Youth," *The Atlantic Monthly* 82 (July 1898): 55–61.

I

Mr. Ryder was going to give a ball. There were several reasons why this was an opportune time for such an event.

Mr. Ryder might aptly be called the dean of the Blue Veins. The original Blue Veins were a little society of colored persons organized in a certain Northern city shortly after the war. Its purpose was to establish and maintain correct social standards among a people whose social condition presented almost unlimited room for improvement. By accident, combined perhaps with some natural affinity, the society consisted of individuals who were, generally speaking, more white than black. Some envious outsider made the suggestion that no one was eligible for membership who was not white enough to show blue veins. The suggestion was readily adopted by those who were not of the favored few, and since that time the society, though possessing a longer and more pretentious name, had been known far and wide as the "Blue Vein Society," and its members as the "Blue Veins."

The Blue Veins did not allow that any such requirement existed for admission to their circle, but, on the contrary, declared that character and culture were the only things considered; and that if most of their members were light-colored, it was because such persons, as a rule, had had better opportunities to qualify themselves for membership. Opinions differed, too, as to the usefulness of the society. There were those who had been known to assail it violently as a glaring example of the very prejudice from which the colored race had suffered most; and later, when such critics had succeeded in getting on the inside, they had been heard to maintain with zeal and earnestness that the society was a lifeboat, an anchor, a bulwark and a shield, — a pillar of cloud by day and of fire by night, to guide their people through the social wilderness. Another alleged prerequisite for Blue Vein membership was that of free birth; and while there was really no such requirement, it is doubtless true that very few of the members would have been unable to meet it if there had been. If there were one or two of the older members who had come up from the South and from slavery, their history presented enough romantic circumstances to rob their servile origin of its grosser aspects.

While there were no such tests of eligibility, it is true that the Blue Veins had their notions on these subjects, and that not all of them were equally liberal in regard to the things they collectively disclaimed. Mr. Ryder was one of the most conservative. Though he had not been among the founders of the society, but had come in some years later, his genius for social leadership was such that he had speedily become its recognized adviser and head, the custodian of its standards, and the preserver of its traditions. He shaped its social policy, was active in providing for its entertainment, and when the interest fell off, as it sometimes did, he fanned the embers until they burst again into a cheerful flame.

There were still other reasons for his popularity. While he was not as white as some of the Blue Veins, his appearance was such as to confer distinction upon them. His features were of a refined type, his hair was almost straight; he was always neatly dressed; his manners were irreproachable, and his morals above suspicion. He had come to Groveland a young man, and obtaining employment in the office of a railroad company as messenger had in time worked himself up to the position of stationery clerk, having charge of the distribution of the office supplies for the whole company. Although the lack of early training had hindered the orderly development of a naturally fine mind, it had not prevented him from doing a great deal of reading or from forming decidedly literary tastes. Poetry was his passion. He could repeat whole pages of the great English poets; and if his pronunciation was sometimes faulty, his eye, his voice, his gestures, would respond to the changing sentiment with a precision that revealed a poetic soul and disarmed criticism. He was economical, and had saved money; he owned and occupied a very comfortable house on a respectable street. His residence was handsomely furnished, containing among other things a good library, especially rich in poetry, a piano, and some choice engravings. He generally shared his house with some young couple, who looked after his wants and were company for him; for Mr. Ryder was a single man. In the early days of his connection with the Blue Veins he had been regarded as quite a catch, and young ladies and their mothers had manœuvred with much ingenuity to capture him. Not, however, until Mrs. Molly Dixon visited Groveland had any woman ever made him wish to change his condition to that of a married man.

Mrs. Dixon had come to Groveland from Washington in the spring, and before the summer was over she had won Mr. Ryder's heart. She possessed many attractive qualities. She was much younger than he; in fact, he was old enough to have been her father, though no one knew exactly how old he was. She was whiter than he, and better educated. She had moved in the best colored society of the country, at Washington, and had taught in the schools in that city. Such a superior person had been eagerly welcomed to the Blue Vein Society, and had taken a leading part in its activities. Mr. Ryder had at first been attracted by her charms of person, for she was very good looking and not over twenty-five; then by her refined manners and the vivacity of her wit. Her husband had been a government clerk, and at his death had left a considerable life insurance. She was visiting friends in Groveland, and, finding the town and the people to her liking, had prolonged her stay indefinitely. She had not seemed displeased at Mr. Ryder's attentions, but on the contrary had given him every proper encouragement; indeed, a younger and less cautious man would long since have spoken. But he had made up his mind, and had only to determine the time when he would ask her to be his wife. He decided to give a ball in her honor, and at some time during the evening of the ball to offer her his heart and hand. He had no special fears about the outcome, but, with a little touch of romance, he wanted the surroundings to be in harmony with his own feelings when he should have received the answer he expected.

Mr. Ryder resolved that this ball should mark an epoch in the social history of Groveland. He knew, of course, — no one could know better, — the entertainments that had taken place in past years, and what must be done to surpass them. His ball must be worthy of the lady in whose honor it was to be given, and must, by the quality of its guests, set an example for the future. He had observed of late a growing liberality, almost a laxity, in social matters, even among members of his own set, and had several times been forced to meet in a social way persons whose complexions and callings in life were hardly up to the standard which he considered proper for the society to maintain. He had a theory of his own.

"I have no race prejudice," he would say, "but we people of mixed blood are ground between the upper and the nether millstone. Our fate lies between absorption by the white race and extinction in the black. The one doesn't want us yet, but may take us in time. The other would welcome us, but it would be for us a backward step. 'With malice towards none, with charity for all,' we must do the best we can for ourselves and those who are to follow us. Self-preservation is the first law of nature."

His ball would serve by its exclusiveness to counteract leveling tendencies, and his marriage with Mrs. Dixon would help to further the upward process of absorption he had been wishing and waiting for.

II

The ball was to take place on Friday night. The house had been put in order, the carpets covered with canvas, the halls and stairs decorated with palms and potted plants; and in the afternoon Mr. Ryder sat on his front porch, which the shade of a vine running up over a wire netting made a cool and pleasant lounging place. He expected to respond to the toast "The Ladies" at the supper, and from a volume of Tennyson — his favorite poet — was fortifying himself with apt quotations. The volume was open at "A Dream of Fair Women." His eyes fell on these lines, and he read them aloud to judge better of their effect: —

> At length I saw a lady within call,
>   Stiller than chisell'd marble, standing there;
> A daughter of the gods, divinely tall,
>   And most divinely fair.

He marked the verse, and turning the page read the stanza beginning, —

> O sweet pale Margaret,
>   O rare pale Margaret.

He weighed the passage a moment, and decided that it would not do. Mrs. Dixon was the palest lady he expected at the ball, and she was of a rather ruddy complexion, and of lively disposition and buxom build. So he ran over the leaves until his eye rested on the description of Queen Guinevere: —

> She seem'd a part of joyous Spring:
> A gown of grass-green silk she wore,
> Buckled with golden clasps before;
> A light-green tuft of plumes she bore
> Closed in a golden ring.
> • • • • • •

> She look'd so lovely, as she sway'd
> The rein with dainty finger-tips,
> A man had given all other bliss,
> And all his worldly worth for this,
> To waste his whole heart in one kiss
> Upon her perfect lips.

As Mr. Ryder murmured these words audibly, with an appreciative thrill, he heard the latch of his gate click, and a light footfall sounding on the steps. He turned his head, and saw a woman standing before his door.

She was a little woman, not five feet tall, and proportioned to her height. Although she stood erect, and looked around her with very bright and restless eyes, she seemed quite old; for her face was crossed and recrossed with a hundred wrinkles, and around the edges of her bonnet could be seen protruding here and there a tuft of short gray wool. She wore a blue calico gown of ancient cut, a little red shawl fastened around her shoulders with an old-fashioned brass brooch, and a large bonnet profusely ornamented with faded red and yellow artificial flowers. And she was very black, — so black that her toothless gums, revealed when she opened her mouth to speak, were not red, but blue. She looked like a bit of the old plantation life, summoned up from the past by the wave of a magician's wand, as the poet's fancy had called into being the gracious shapes of which Mr. Ryder had just been reading.

He rose from his chair and came over to where she stood.

"Good-afternoon, madam," he said.

"Good-evenin', suh," she answered, ducking suddenly with a quaint curtsy. Her voice was shrill and piping, but softened somewhat by age. "Is dis yere whar Mistuh Ryduh lib, suh?" she asked, looking around her doubtfully, and glancing into the open windows, through which some of the preparations for the evening were visible.

"Yes," he replied, with an air of kindly patronage, unconsciously flattered by her manner, "I am Mr. Ryder. Did you want to see me?"

"Yas, suh, ef I ain't 'sturbin' of you too much."

"Not at all. Have a seat over here behind the vine, where it is cool. What can I do for you?"

"'Scuse me, suh," she continued, when she had sat down on the edge of a chair, "'scuse me, suh, I's lookin' for my husban'. I heerd you wuz a big man an' had libbed heah a long time, an' I 'lowed you wouldn't min' ef I'd come roun' an' ax you ef you'd ever heerd of a merlatter man by de name er Sam Taylor 'quirin' roun' in de chu'ches ermongs' de people fer his wife 'Liza Jane?"

Mr. Ryder seemed to think for a moment.

"There used to be many such cases right after the war," he said, "but it has been so long that I have forgotten them. There are very few now. But tell me your story, and it may refresh my memory."

She sat back farther in her chair so as to be more comfortable, and folded her withered hands in her lap.

"My name's 'Liza," she began, "'Liza Jane. W'en I wuz young I us'ter b'long ter Marse Bob Smif, down in ole Missoura. I wuz bawn down dere. W'en I wuz a gal I wuz married ter a man named Jim. But Jim died, an' after dat I married a merlatter man named Sam Taylor. Sam wuz freebawn, but his mammy and daddy died, an' de w'ite folks 'prenticed him ter my marster fer ter work fer 'im 'tel he wuz growed up. Sam worked in de fiel', an' I wuz de cook. One day Ma'y Ann, ole miss's maid, came rushin' out ter de kitchen, an' says she, "Liza Jane, old marse gwine sell yo' Sam down de ribber.'

"'Go way f'm yere,' says I; 'my husban' 's free!'

"'Don' make no diff'ence. I heerd ole marse tell ole miss he wuz gwine take yo' Sam 'way wid 'im ter-morrow, fer he needed money, an' he knowed whar he could git a t'ousan' dollars fer Sam an' no questions axed.'

"W'en Sam come home f'm de fiel' dat night, I tole him 'bout ole marse gwine steal 'im, an' Sam run erway. His time wuz mos' up, an' he swo' dat w'en he wuz twenty-one he would come back an' he'p me run erway, er else save up de money ter buy my freedom. An' I know he'd 'a' done it, fer he thought a heap er me, Sam did. But w'en he come back he did n' fin' me, fer I wuz n' dere. Ole marse had heerd dat I warned Sam, so he had me whip' an' sol' down de ribber.

"Den de wah broke out, an' w'en it wuz ober de cullud folks wuz scattered. I went back ter de ole home; but Sam wuz n' dere, an' I could n' l'arn nuffin' 'bout 'im. But I knowed he'd be'n dere to look fer me an' had n' foun' me, an' had gone erway ter hunt fer me.

"I's be'n lookin' fer 'im eber sence," she added simply, as though twenty-five years were but a couple of weeks, "an' I knows he's be'n lookin' fer me. Fer he sot a heap er sto' by me, Sam did, an' I know he's be'n huntin' fer me all dese years, — 'less'n he's be'n sick er sump'n, so he could n' work, er out'n his head, so he could n' 'member his promise. I went back down de ribber, fer I 'lowed he'd gone down dere lookin' fer me. I's be'n ter Noo Orleens, an' Atlanty, an' Charleston, an' Richmon'; an' w'en I'd be'n all ober de Souf I come ter de Norf. Fer I knows I'll fin' 'im some er dese days," she added softly, "er he'll fin' me, an' den we'll bofe be as happy in freedom as we wuz in de ole days befo' de wah." A smile stole over her withered countenance as she paused a moment, and her bright eyes softened into a far-away look.

This was the substance of the old woman's story. She had wandered a little here and there. Mr. Ryder was looking at her curiously when she finished.

"How have you lived all these years? he asked.

"Cookin', suh. I's a good cook. Does you know anybody w'at needs a good cook, suh? I's stoppin' wid a cullud fam'ly roun' de corner yonder 'tel I kin git a place."

"Do you really expect to find your husband? He may be dead long ago."

She shook her head emphatically. "Oh no, he ain' dead. De signs an' de tokens tells me. I dremp three nights runnin' on'y dis las' week dat I foun' him."

"He may have married another woman. Your slave marriage would not have prevented him, for you never lived with him after the war, and without that your marriage doesn't count."

"Would n' make no diff'ence wid Sam. He would n' marry no yuther 'ooman 'tel he foun' out 'bout me. I knows it," she added. "Sump'n 's be'n tellin' me all dese years dat I's gwine fin' Sam 'fo' I dies."

"Perhaps he's outgrown you, and climbed up in the world where he wouldn't care to have you find him."

"No, indeed, suh," she replied. "Sam ain' dat kin' er man. He wuz good ter me, Sam wuz, but he wuz n' much good ter nobody e'se, fer he wuz one er de triflin'es' han's on de plantation. I 'spec's ter haf ter suppo't 'im w'en I fin' 'im, fer he nebber would work 'less'n he had ter. But den he wuz free, an' he did n' git no pay fer his work, an' I don' blame 'im much. Mebbe he's done better sence he run erway, but I ain' 'spectin' much."

"You may have passed him on the street a hundred times during the twenty-five years, and not have known him; time works great changes."

She smiled incredulously. "I'd know 'im 'mongs' a hund'ed men. Fer dey wuz n' no yuther merlatter man like my man Sam, an' I could n' be mistook. I's toted his picture roun' wid me twenty-five years."

"May I see it?" asked Mr. Ryder. "It might help me to remember whether I have seen the original."

As she drew a small parcel from her bosom he saw that it was fastened to a string that went around her neck. Removing several wrappers, she brought to light an old-fashioned daguerreotype in a black case. He looked long and intently at the portrait. It was faded with time, but the features were still distinct, and it was easy to see what manner of man it had represented.

He closed the case, and with a slow movement handed it back to her.

"I don't know of any man in town who goes by that name," he said, "nor have I heard of any one making such inquiries. But if you will leave me your address, I will give the matter some attention, and if I find out anything I will let you know."

She gave him the number of a house in the neighborhood, and went away, after thanking him warmly.

He wrote the address on the fly-leaf of the volume of Tennyson, and, when she had gone, rose to his feet and stood looking after her curiously. As she walked down the street with mincing step, he saw several persons whom she passed turn and look back at her with a smile of kindly amusement. When she had turned the corner, he went upstairs to his bedroom, and stood for a long time before the mirror of his dressing-case, gazing thoughtfully at the reflection of his own face.

III

At eight o'clock the ballroom was a blaze of light and the guests had begun to assemble; for there was a literary programme and some routine business of the society to be gone through with before the dancing. A black servant in evening dress waited at the door and directed the guests to the dressing-rooms.

The occasion was long memorable among the colored people of the city; not alone for the dress and display, but for the high average of intelligence and culture that distinguished the gathering as a whole. There were a number of school-teachers, several young doctors, three or four lawyers, some professional singers, an editor, a lieutenant in the United States army spending his furlough in the city, and others in various polite callings; these were colored, though most of them would not have attracted even a casual glance because of any marked difference from white people. Most of the ladies were in evening costume, and dress coats and dancing pumps were the rule among the men. A band of string music, stationed in an alcove behind a row of palms, played popular airs while the guests were gathering.

The dancing began at half past nine. At eleven o'clock supper was served. Mr. Ryder had left the ballroom some little time before the intermission, but reappeared at the supper-table. The spread was worthy of the occasion, and the guests did full justice to it. When the coffee had been served, the toast-master, Mr. Solomon Sadler, rapped for order. He made a brief introductory speech, complimenting host and guests, and then presented in their order the toasts of the evening. They were responded to with a very fair display of after-dinner wit.

"The last toast," said the toast-master, when he reached the end of the list, "is one which must appeal to us all. There is no one of us of the sterner sex who is not at some time dependent upon woman, — in infancy for protection, in manhood for companionship, in old age for care and comforting. Our good host has been trying to live alone, but the fair faces I see around me to-night prove that he too is largely dependent upon the gentler sex for most that makes life worth living, — the society and love of friends, — and rumor is at fault if he does not soon yield entire subjection to one of them. Mr. Ryder will now respond to the toast, — The Ladies."

There was a pensive look in Mr. Ryder's eyes as he took the floor and adjusted his eyeglasses. He began by speaking of woman as the gift of Heaven to man, and after some general observations on the relations of the sexes he said: "But perhaps the quality which most distinguishes woman is her fidelity and devotion to those she loves. History is full of examples, but has recorded none more striking than one which only to-day came under my notice."

He then related, simply but effectively, the story told by his visitor of the afternoon. He gave it in the same soft dialect, which came readily to his lips, while the company listened attentively and sympathetically. For the story had awakened a responsive thrill in many hearts. There were some present who had seen, and others who had heard their fathers and grandfathers tell, the wrongs and sufferings of this past generation, and all of them still felt, in their darker moments, the shadow hanging over them. Mr. Ryder went on: —

"Such devotion and confidence are rare even among women. There are many who would have searched a year, some who would have hoped ten years; but for twenty-five years this woman has retained her affection for and her faith in a man she has not seen or heard of in all that time.

"She came to me to-day in the hope that I might be able to help her find this long-lost husband. And when she was gone I gave my fancy rein, and imagined a case I will put to you.

"Suppose that this husband, soon after his escape, had learned that his wife had been sold away, and that such inquiries as he could make brought no information of her whereabouts. Suppose that he was young, and she much older than he; that he was light, and she was black; that their marriage was a slave marriage, and legally binding only if they chose to make it so after the war. Suppose, too, that he made his way to the North, as some of us have done, and there, where he had larger opportunities, had improved them, and had in the course of all these years grown to be as different from the ignorant boy who ran away from fear of slavery as the day is from the night. Suppose, even, that he had qualified himself, by industry, by thrift, and by study, to win the friendship and be considered worthy the society of such people as these I see around me to-night, gracing my board and filling my heart with gladness; for I am old enough to remember the day when such a gathering would not have been possible in this land. Suppose, too, that, as the years went by, this man's memory of the past grew more and more indistinct, until at last it was rarely, except in his dreams, that any image of this bygone period rose before his mind. And then suppose that accident should bring to his knowledge the fact that the wife of his youth, the wife he had left behind him, — not one who had walked by his side and kept pace with him in his upward struggle, but one upon whom advancing years and a laborious life had set their mark, — was alive and seeking him, but that he was absolutely safe from recognition or discovery, unless he chose to reveal himself. My friends, what would the man do? I will presume that he was one who loved honor, and tried to deal justly with all men. I will even carry the case further, and suppose that perhaps he had set his heart upon another, whom he had hoped to call his own. What would he do, or rather what ought he to do, in such a crisis of a lifetime?

"It seemed to me that he might hesitate, and I imagined that I was an old friend, a near friend, and that he had come to me for advice; and I argued the case with him. I tried to discuss it impartially. After we had looked upon the matter from every point of view, I said to him, in words that we all know: —

> This above all: to thine own self be true,
> And it must follow, as the night the day,
> Thou canst not then be false to any man.

Then, finally, I put the question to him, 'Shall you acknowledge her?'

"And now, ladies and gentlemen, friends and companions, I ask you, what should he have done?"

There was something in Mr. Ryder's voice that stirred the hearts of those who sat around him. It suggested more than mere sympathy with an imaginary situation; it seemed rather in the nature of a personal appeal. It was observed, too, that his look rested more especially upon Mrs. Dixon, with a mingled expression of renunciation and inquiry.

She had listened, with parted lips and streaming eyes. She was the first to speak: "He should have acknowledged her."

"Yes," they all echoed, "he should have acknowledged her."

"My friends and companions," responded Mr. Ryder, "I thank you, one and all. It is the answer I expected, for I knew your hearts."

He turned and walked toward the closed door of an adjoining room, while every eye followed him in wondering curiosity. He came back in a moment, leading by the hand his visitor of the afternoon, who stood startled and trembling at the sudden plunge into this scene of brilliant gayety. She was neatly dressed in gray, and wore the white cap of an elderly woman.

"Ladies and gentlemen," he said, "this is the woman, and I am the man, whose story I have told you. Permit me to introduce to you the wife of my youth."

Ambrose Bierce
An Occurrence at Owl Creek Bridge

Ambrose Bierce's "An Occurrence at Owl Creek Bridge," one of the most famous stories in English, was published in the *San Francisco Examiner* in 1890 and included in *Tales of Soldiers and Civilians* in 1891, a volume later entitled *In the Midst of Life*. The author was born in Ohio and fought for the Union Army in the Civil War, including the fierce engagement of the Battle of Shiloh, where he was wounded on the banks of Owl Creek. Later, when he was released from the hospital, he was promoted to regimental cartographer in Alabama, where he set the action of his celebrated story. The title is an ironic understatement, typical of the man who became known as "Bitter Bierce," as though death were so routine in wartime as to become simply an "occurrence." What makes the intense events so dramatic is the narrator's identification with the mind of the central character, his thoughts and sensations during the events that take place on the bridge. The domestic longings of this simple southern farmer, who was not a soldier of the Confederacy, are something that readers in all sections of the country could appreciate. The three parts of the story are markedly different from one another in narrative method, tone, and implication, and this structural manipulation accounts for much of the final impact.

Ambrose Bierce, "An Occurrence at Owl Creek Bridge," *In the Midst of Life* (New York: G. P. Putnam's Sons, 1898), 16–35.

I

A man stood upon a railroad bridge in Northern Alabama, looking down into the swift waters twenty feet below. The man's hands were behind his back, the wrists bound with a cord. A rope loosely encircled his neck. It was attached to a stout cross-timber above his head, and the slack fell to the level of his knees. Some loose boards laid upon the sleepers supporting the metals of the railway supplied a footing for him, and his executioners — two private soldiers of the Federal Army, directed by a sergeant, who in civil life may have been a deputy sheriff. At a short remove upon the same temporary platform was an officer in the uniform of his rank, armed. He was a captain. A sentinel at each end of the bridge stood with his rifle in the position known as "support," that is to say, vertical in front of the left shoulder, the hammer resting on the forearm thrown straight across the chest — a formal and unnatural position, enforcing an erect carriage of the body. It did not appear to be the duty of these two men to know what was occurring at the centre of the bridge; they merely blockaded the two ends of the foot plank which traversed it.

Beyond one of the sentinels, nobody was in sight; the railroad ran straight away into a forest for a hundred yards, then, curving, was lost to view. Doubtless there was an outpost farther along. The other bank of the stream was open ground — a gentle acclivity crowned with a stockade of vertical tree trunks, loopholed for rifles, with a single embrasure through which protruded the muzzle of a brass cannon commanding the bridge. Midway of the slope between bridge and fort were the spectators — a single company of infantry in line, at "parade rest," the butts of the rifles on the ground, the barrels inclining slightly backward against the right shoulder, the hands crossed upon the stock. A lieutenant stood at the right of the line, the point of his sword upon the ground, his left hand resting upon his right. Excepting the group of four at the centre of the bridge, not a man moved. The company faced the bridge, staring stonily, motionless. The sentinels, facing the banks of the stream, might have been statues to adorn the bridge. The captain stood with folded arms, silent, observing the work of his subordinates, but making no sign. Death is a dignitary who, when he comes announced, is to be received with formal manifestations of respect, even by those most familiar with him. In the code of military etiquette, silence and fixity are forms of deference.

The man who was engaged in being hanged was apparently about thirty-five years of age. He was a civilian, if one might judge from his habit, which was that of a planter. His features were good — a straight nose, firm mouth, broad forehead; from which his long, dark hair was combed straight back, falling behind his ears to the collar of his well-fitting frock-coat. He wore a mustache and pointed beard, but no whiskers; his eyes were large and dark gray and had a kindly expression which one would hardly have expected in one whose neck was in the hemp. Evidently this was no vulgar assassin. The liberal military code makes provision for hanging many kinds of persons, and gentlemen are not excluded.

The preparations being complete, the two private soldiers stepped aside and each drew away the plank upon which he had been standing. The sergeant turned to the captain, saluted, and placed himself immediately behind that officer, who in turn moved apart one pace. These movements left the condemned man and the sergeant standing on the two ends of the same plank, which spanned three of the cross-ties of the bridge. The end upon which the civilian stood almost, but not quite, reached a fourth. This plank had been held in place by the weight of the captain; it was now held by that of the sergeant. At a signal from the former, the latter would step aside, the plank would tilt and the condemned man go down between two ties. The arrangement commended itself to his judgment as simple and effective. His face had not been covered nor his eyes bandaged. He looked a moment at his "unsteadfast footing," then let his gaze wander to the swirling water of the stream racing madly beneath his feet. A piece of dancing driftwood caught his attention and his eyes followed it down the current. How slowly it appeared to move! What a sluggish stream!

He closed his eyes in order to fix his last thoughts upon his wife and children. The water, touched to gold by the early sun, the brooding mists under the banks at some distance down the stream, the fort, the soldiers, the piece of drift — all had distracted him. And now he became conscious of a new disturbance. Striking through the thought of his dear ones was a sound which he could neither ignore nor understand, a sharp, distinct, metallic percussion like the stroke of a blacksmith's hammer upon the anvil; it had the same ringing quality. He wondered what it was, and whether immeasurably distant or near by — it seemed both. Its recurrence was regular, but as slow as the tolling of a death knell. He awaited each stroke with impatience and — he knew not why — apprehension. The intervals of silence grew progressively longer; the delays became maddening. With their greater infrequency the sounds increased in strength and sharpness. They hurt his ear like the thrust of a knife; he feared he should shriek. What he heard was the ticking of his watch.

He unclosed his eyes and saw again the water below him. "If I could free my hands," he thought, "I might throw off the noose and spring into the stream. By diving I could evade the bullets, and, swimming vigorously, reach the bank, take to the woods, and get away home. My home, thank God, is as yet outside their lines; my wife and little ones are still beyond the invader's farthest advance."

As these thoughts, which have here to be set down in words, were flashed into the doomed man's brain rather than evolved from it, the captain nodded to the sergeant. The sergeant stepped aside.

II

Peyton Farquhar was a well-to-do planter, of an old and highly respected Alabama family. Being a slave owner, and, like other slave owners, a politician, he was naturally an original secessionist and ardently devoted to the Southern cause. Circumstances of an imperious nature, which it is unnecessary to relate here, had prevented him from taking service with the gallant army which had fought the disastrous campaigns ending with the fall of Corinth, and he chafed under the inglorious restraint, longing for the release of his energies, the larger life of the soldier, the opportunity for distinction. That opportunity, he felt, would come, as it comes to all in war time. Meanwhile he did what he could. No service was too humble for him to perform in aid of the South, no adventure too perilous for him to undertake if consistent with the character of a civilian who was at heart a soldier, and who in good faith and without too much qualification assented to at least a part of the frankly villainous dictum that all is fair in love and war.

One evening while Farquhar and his wife were sitting on a rustic bench near the entrance to his grounds, a gray-clad soldier rode up to the gate and asked for a drink of water. Mrs. Farquhar was only too happy to serve him with her own white hands. While she was gone to fetch the water her husband approached the dusty horseman and inquired eagerly for news from the front.

"The Yanks are repairing the railroads," said the man, "and are getting ready for another advance. They have reached the Owl Creek bridge, put it in order, and built a stockade on the north bank. The commandant has issued an order, which is posted everywhere, declaring that any civilian caught interfering with the railroad, its bridges, tunnels, or trains, will be summarily hanged. I saw the order."

"How far is it to the Owl Creek bridge?" Farquhar asked.

"About thirty miles."

"Is there no force on this side of the creek?"

"Only a picket post half a mile out, on the railroad, and a single sentinel at this end of the bridge."

"Suppose a man — a civilian and student of hanging — should elude the picket post and perhaps get the better of the sentinel," said Farquhar, smiling, "what could he accomplish?"

The soldier reflected. "I was there a month ago," he replied. "I observed that the flood of last winter had lodged a great quantity of driftwood against the wooden pier at this end of the bridge. It is now dry and would burn like tow."

The lady had now brought the water, which the soldier drank. He thanked her ceremoniously, bowed to her husband, and rode away. An hour later, after nightfall, he repassed the plantation, going northward in the direction from which he had come. He was a Federal scout.

III

As Peyton Farquhar fell straight downward through the bridge, he lost consciousness and was as one already dead. From this state he was awakened — ages later, it seemed to him — by the pain of a sharp pressure upon his throat, followed by a sense of suffocation. Keen, poignant agonies seemed to shoot from his neck downward through every fibre of his body and limbs. These pains appeared to flash along well-defined lines of ramification and to beat with an inconceivably rapid periodicity. They seemed like streams of pulsating fire heating him to an intolerable temperature. As to his head, he was conscious of nothing but a feeling of fulness — of congestion. These sensations were unaccompanied by thought. The intellectual part of his nature was already effaced; he had power only to feel; and feeling was torment. He was conscious of motion. Encompassed in a luminous cloud, of which he was now merely the fiery heart, without material substance, he swung through unthinkable arcs of oscillation, like a vast pendulum. Then all at once, with terrible suddenness, the light about him shot upward with the noise of a loud plash; a frightful roaring was in his ears, and all was cold and dark. The power of thought was restored; he knew that the rope had broken and he had fallen into the stream. There was no additional strangulation; the noose about his neck was already suffocating him and kept the water from his lungs. To die of hanging at the bottom of a river! — the idea seemed to him ludicrous. He opened his eyes in the darkness and saw above him a gleam of light, but how distant, how inaccessible! He was still sinking, for the light became fainter and fainter until it was a mere glimmer. Then it began to grow and brighten, and he knew that he was rising toward the surface — knew it with reluctance, for he was now very comfortable. "To be hanged and drowned," he thought, "that is not so bad; but I do not wish to be shot. No; I will not be shot; that is not fair."

He was not conscious of an effort, but a sharp pain in his wrists apprised him that he was trying to free his hands. He gave the struggle his attention, as an idler might observe the feat of a juggler, without interest in the outcome. What splendid effort! — what magnificent, what superhuman strength! Ah, that was a fine endeavor! Bravo! The cord fell away; his arms parted and floated upward, the hands dimly seen on each side in the growing light. He watched them with a new interest as first one and then the other pounced upon the noose at his neck. They tore it away and thrust it fiercely aside, its undulations resembling those of a water-snake. "Put it back, put it back!" He thought he shouted these words to his hands, for the undoing of the noose had been succeeded by the direst pang which he had yet experienced. His neck ached horribly; his brain was on fire; his heart, which had been fluttering faintly, gave a great leap, trying to force itself out at his mouth. His whole body was racked and wrenched with an insupportable anguish! But his disobedient hands gave no heed to the command. They beat the water vigorously with quick, downward strokes, forcing him to the surface. He felt his head emerge; his eyes were blinded by the sunlight; his chest expanded convulsively, and with a supreme and crowning agony his lungs engulfed a great draught of air, which instantly he expelled in a shriek!

He was now in full possession of his physical senses. They were, indeed, preternaturally keen and alert. Something in the awful disturbance of his organic system had so exalted and refined them that they made record of things never before perceived. He felt the ripples upon his face and heard their separate sounds as they struck. He looked at the forest on the bank of the stream, saw the individual trees, the leaves and the veining of each leaf — saw the very insects upon them, the locusts, the brilliant-bodied flies, the gray spiders stretching their webs from twig to twig. He noted the prismatic colors in all the dewdrops upon a million blades of grass. The humming of the gnats that danced above the eddies of the stream, the beating of the dragon-flies' wings, the strokes of the water-spiders' legs, like oars which had lifted their boat — all these made audible music. A fish slid along beneath his eyes and he heard the rush of its body parting the water.

He had come to the surface facing down the stream; in a moment the visible world seemed to wheel slowly round, himself the pivotal point, and he saw the bridge, the fort, the soldiers upon the bridge, the captain, the sergeant, the two privates, his executioners. They were in silhouette against the blue sky. They shouted and gesticulated, pointing at him; the captain had drawn his pistol, but did not fire; the others were unarmed. Their movements were grotesque and horrible, their forms gigantic.

Suddenly he heard a sharp report and something struck the water smartly within a few inches of his head, spattering his face with spray. He heard a second report, and saw one of the sentinels with his rifle at his shoulder, a light cloud of blue smoke rising from the muzzle. The man in the water saw the eye of the man on the bridge gazing into his own through the sights of the rifle. He observed that it was a gray eye, and remembered having read that gray eyes were keenest and that all famous marksmen had them. Nonetheless, this one had missed.

A counter swirl had caught Farquhar and turned him half round; he was again looking into the forest on the bank opposite the fort. The sound of a clear, high voice in a monotonous singsong now rang out behind him and came across the water with a distinctness that pierced and subdued all other sounds, even the beating of the ripples in his ears. Although no soldier, he had frequented camps enough to know the dread significance of that deliberate, drawling, aspirated chant; the lieutenant on shore was taking a part in the morning's work. How coldly and pitilessly — with what an even, calm intonation, presaging and enforcing tranquillity in the men — with what accurately measured intervals fell those cruel words:

"Attention, company! . . . Shoulder arms! . . . Ready! . . . Aim! . . . Fire!"

Farquhar dived — dived as deeply as he could. The water roared in his ears like the voice of Niagara, yet he heard the dulled thunder of the volley, and, rising again toward the surface, met shining bits of metal, singularly flattened, oscillating slowly downward. Some of them touched him on the face and hands, then fell away, continuing their descent. One lodged between his collar and neck; it was uncomfortably warm, and he snatched it out.

As he rose to the surface, gasping for breath, he saw that he had been a long time under water; he was perceptibly farther down stream — nearer to safety. The soldiers had almost finished reloading; the metal ramrods flashed all at once in the sunshine as they were drawn from the barrels, turned in the air, and thrust into their sockets. The two sentinels fired again, independently and ineffectually.

The hunted man saw all this over his shoulder; he was now swimming vigorously with the current. His brain was as energetic as his arms and legs; he thought with the rapidity of lightning.

"The officer," he reasoned, "will not make that martinet's error a second time. It is as easy to dodge a volley as a single shot. He has probably already given the command to fire at will. God help me, I cannot dodge them all!"

An appalling plash within two yards of him, followed by a loud, rushing sound, *diminuendo,* which seemed to travel back through the air to the fort and died in an explosion which stirred the very river to its deeps! A rising sheet of water, which curved over him, fell down upon him, blinded him, strangled him! The cannon had taken a hand in the game. As he shook his head free from the commotion of the smitten water, he heard the deflected shot humming through the air ahead, and in an instant it was cracking and smashing the branches in the forest beyond.

"They will not do that again," he thought; "the next time they will use a charge of grape. I must keep my eye upon the gun; the smoke will apprise me — the report arrives too late; it lags behind the missile. That is a good gun."

Suddenly he felt himself whirled round and round — spinning like a top. The water, the banks, the forest, the now distant bridge, fort and men — all were commingled and blurred. Objects were represented by their colors only; circular horizontal streaks of color — that was all he saw. He had been caught in a vortex and was being whirled on with a velocity of advance and gyration which made him giddy and sick. In a few moments he was flung upon the gravel at the foot of the left bank of the stream — the southern bank — and behind a projecting point which concealed him from his enemies. The sudden arrest of his motion, the abrasion of one of his hands on the gravel, restored him, and he wept with delight. He dug his fingers into the sand, threw it over himself in handfuls and audibly blessed it. It looked like diamonds, rubies, emeralds; he could think of nothing beautiful which it did not resemble. The trees upon the bank were giant garden plants; he noted a definite order in their arrangement, inhaled the fragrance of their blooms. A strange, roseate light shone through the spaces among their trunks, and the wind made their branches the music of æolian harps. He had no wish to perfect his escape, was content to remain in that enchanting spot until retaken.

A whiz and rattle of grapeshot among the branches high above his head roused him from his dream. The baffled cannoneer had fired him a random farewell. He sprang to his feet, rushed up the sloping bank, and plunged into the forest.

All that day he travelled, laying his course by the rounding sun. The forest seemed interminable; nowhere did he discover a break in it, not even a wood-man's road. He had not known that he lived in so wild a region. There was some-thing uncanny in the revelation.

By nightfall he was fatigued, footsore, famishing. The thought of his wife and children urged him on. At last he found a road which led him in what he knew to be the right direction. It was as wide and straight as a city street, yet it seemed untravelled. No fields bordered it, no dwelling anywhere. Not so much as the barking of a dog suggested human habitation. The black bodies of the trees formed a straight wall on both sides, terminating on the horizon in a point, like a diagram in a lesson in perspective. Overhead, as he looked up through this rift in the wood, shone great golden stars looking unfamiliar and grouped in strange constellations. He was sure they were arranged in some order which had a secret and malign significance. The wood on either side was full of singular noises, among which — once, twice, and again — he distinctly heard whispers in an unknown tongue.

His neck was in pain, and, lifting his hand to it, he found it horribly swollen. He knew that it had a circle of black where the rope had bruised it. His eyes felt congested; he could no longer close them. His tongue was swollen with thirst; he relieved its fever by thrusting it forward from between his teeth into the cool air. How softly the turf had carpeted the untravelled avenue — he could no longer feel the roadway beneath his feet!

Doubtless, despite his suffering, he had fallen asleep while walking, for now he sees another scene — perhaps he has merely recovered from a delirium. He stands at the gate of his own home. All is as he left it, and all bright and beauti-ful in the morning sunshine. He must have travelled the entire night. As he pushes open the gate and passes up the wide white walk, he sees a flutter of fe-male garments; his wife, looking fresh and cool and sweet, steps down from the veranda to meet him. At the bottom of the steps she stands waiting, with a smile of ineffable joy, an attitude of matchless grace and dignity. Ah, how beautiful she is! He springs forward with extended arms. As he is about to clasp her, he feels a stunning blow upon the back of the neck; a blinding white light blazes all about him, with a sound like the shock of a cannon — then all is darkness and silence!

Peyton Farquhar was dead; his body, with a broken neck, swung gently from side to side beneath the timbers of the Owl Creek bridge.

Stephen Crane
The Blue Hotel

Stephen Crane's "The Blue Hotel," one of the great Realistic works of short fiction, appeared first in *Collier's Weekly* in 1898 before its inclusion in *The Monster and Other Stories* a year later. The story grew out of a trip through the Midwest and South that he undertook as a journalist for the Bacheller newspaper syndicate, during which he stopped in Nebraska and observed a fight in a tavern. Celebrated since it first publication, the story is often read as a Naturalistic work stressing the Deterministic nature of the Swede's personality, the violence of the storm, and the hostility of the men in the hotel, all of which make tragedy inescapable. But a counterreading is suggested by the conclusion itself, in which the Easterner attempts to sort out the complex web of moral responsibility in the events that have taken place, the thematic substance of Realism. This approach assumes that human beings are free agents who chose their course of action and are accountable for it, for what they do, for what they fail to do, and even for what they fail to say. These assumptions lead to a rich interpretation of one of the finest American stories.

Stephen Crane, "The Blue Hotel," *The Monster and Other Stories* (New York: Harper & Brothers Publishers, 1899), 109–61.

I

The Palace Hotel at Fort Romper was painted a light blue, a shade that is on the legs of a kind of heron, causing the bird to declare its position against any background. The Palace Hotel, then, was always screaming and howling in a way that made the dazzling winter landscape of Nebraska seem only a gray swampish hush. It stood alone on the prairie, and when the snow was falling the town two hundred yards away was not visible. But when the traveller alighted at the railway station he was obliged to pass the Palace Hotel before he could come upon the company of the low clapboard houses which composed Fort Romper, and it was not to be thought that any traveller could pass the Palace Hotel without looking at it. Pat Scully, the proprietor, had proved himself a master of strategy when he chose his paints. It is true that on clear days, when the great trans-continental expresses, long lines of swaying Pullmans, swept through Fort Romper, passengers were overcome at the sight, and the cult that knows the brown-reds and the subdivisions of the dark greens of the East expressed shame, pity, horror, in a laugh. But to the citizens of this prairie town and to the people who would naturally stop there, Pat Scully had performed a feat. With this opulence and splendor, these creeds, classes, egotisms, that streamed through Romper on the rails day after day, they had no color in common.

As if the displayed delights of such a blue hotel were not sufficiently enticing, it was Scully's habit to go every morning and evening to meet the leisurely trains that stopped at Romper and work his seductions upon any man that he might see wavering, gripsack in hand.

One morning, when a snow-crusted engine dragged its long string of freight cars and its one passenger coach to the station, Scully performed the marvel of catching three men. One was a shaky and quick-eyed Swede, with a great shining cheap valise; one was a tall bronzed cowboy, who was on his way to a ranch near the Dakota line; one was a little silent man from the East, who didn't look it, and didn't announce it. Scully practically made them prisoners. He was so nimble and merry and kindly that each probably felt it would be the height of brutality to try to escape. They trudged off over the creaking board sidewalks in the wake of the eager little Irishman. He wore a heavy fur cap squeezed tightly down on his head. It caused his two red ears to stick out stiffly, as if they were made of tin.

At last, Scully, elaborately, with boisterous hospitality, conducted them through the portals of the blue hotel. The room which they entered was small. It seemed to be merely a proper temple for an enormous stove, which, in the centre, was humming with godlike violence. At various points on its surface the iron had become luminous and glowed yellow from the heat. Beside the stove Scully's son Johnnie was playing High-Five with an old farmer who had whiskers both gray and sandy. They were quarrelling. Frequently the old farmer turned his face towards a box of sawdust — colored brown from tobacco juice — that was behind the stove, and spat with an air of great impatience and irritation. With a loud flourish of words Scully destroyed the game of cards, and bustled his son up-stairs with part of the baggage of the new guests. He himself conducted them to three basins of the coldest water in the world. The cowboy and the Easterner burnished themselves fiery-red with this water, until it seemed to be some kind of a metal polish. The Swede, however, merely dipped his fingers gingerly and with trepidation. It was notable that throughout this series of small ceremonies the three travellers were made to feel that Scully was very benevolent. He was conferring great favors upon them. He handed the towel from one to the other with an air of philanthropic impulse.

Afterwards they went to the first room, and, sitting about the stove, listened to Scully's officious clamor at his daughters, who were preparing the mid-day meal. They reflected in the silence of experienced men who tread carefully amid new people. Nevertheless, the old farmer, stationary, invincible in his chair near the warmest part of the stove, turned his face from the sawdust box frequently and addressed a glowing commonplace to the strangers. Usually he was answered in short but adequate sentences by either the cowboy or the Easterner. The Swede said nothing. He seemed to be occupied in making furtive estimates of each man in the room. One might have thought that he had the sense of silly suspicion which comes to guilt. He resembled a badly frightened man.

Later, at dinner, he spoke a little, addressing his conversation entirely to Scully. He volunteered that he had come from New York, where for ten years he had worked as a tailor. These facts seemed to strike Scully as fascinating, and afterwards he volunteered that he had lived at Romper for fourteen years. The Swede asked about the crops and the price of labor. He seemed barely to listen to Scully's extended replies. His eyes continued to rove from man to man.

Finally, with a laugh and a wink, he said that some of these Western communities were very dangerous; and after his statement he straightened his legs under the table, tilted his head, and laughed again, loudly. It was plain that the demonstration had no meaning to the others. They looked at him wondering and in silence.

II

As the men trooped heavily back into the front-room, the two little windows presented views of a turmoiling sea of snow. The huge arms of the wind were making attempts — mighty, circular, futile — to embrace the flakes as they sped. A gate-post like a still man with a blanched face stood aghast amid this profligate fury. In a hearty voice Scully announced the presence of a blizzard. The guests of the blue hotel, lighting their pipes, assented with grunts of lazy masculine contentment. No island of the sea could be exempt in the degree of this little room with its humming stove. Johnnie, son of Scully, in a tone which defined his opinion of his ability as a card-player, challenged the old farmer of both gray and sandy whiskers to a game of High-Five. The farmer agreed with a contemptuous and bitter scoff. They sat close to the stove, and squared their knees under a wide board. The cowboy and the Easterner watched the game with interest. The Swede remained near the window, aloof, but with a countenance that showed signs of an inexplicable excitement.

The play of Johnnie and the gray-beard was suddenly ended by another quarrel. The old man arose while casting a look of heated scorn at his adversary. He slowly buttoned his coat, and then stalked with fabulous dignity from the room. In the discreet silence of all other men the Swede laughed. His laughter rang somehow childish. Men by this time had begun to look at him askance, as if they wished to inquire what ailed him.

A new game was formed jocosely. The cowboy volunteered to become the partner of Johnnie, and they all then turned to ask the Swede to throw in his lot with the little Easterner. He asked some questions about the game, and, learning that it wore many names, and that he had played it when it was under an alias, he accepted the invitation. He strode towards the men nervously, as if he expected to be assaulted. Finally, seated, he gazed from face to face and laughed shrilly. This laugh was so strange that the Easterner looked up quickly, the cowboy sat intent and with his mouth open, and Johnnie paused, holding the cards with still fingers.

Afterwards there was a short silence. Then Johnnie said, "Well, let's get at it. Come on now!" They pulled their chairs forward until their knees were bunched under the board. They began to play, and their interest in the game caused the others to forget the manner of the Swede.

The cowboy was a board-whacker. Each time that he held superior cards he whanged them, one by one, with exceeding force, down upon the improvised table, and took the tricks with a glowing air of prowess and pride that sent thrills of indignation into the hearts of his opponents. A game with a board-whacker in it is sure to become intense. The countenances of the Easterner and the Swede were miserable whenever the cowboy thundered down his aces and kings, while Johnnie, his eyes gleaming with joy, chuckled and chuckled.

Because of the absorbing play none considered the strange ways of the Swede. They paid strict heed to the game. Finally, during a lull caused by a new deal, the Swede suddenly addressed Johnnie: "I suppose there have been a good many men killed in this room." The jaws of the others dropped and they looked at him.

"What in hell are you talking about?" said Johnnie.

The Swede laughed again his blatant laugh, full of a kind of false courage and defiance. "Oh, you know what I mean all right," he answered.

"I'm a liar if I do," Johnnie protested. The card was halted, and the men stared at the Swede. Johnnie evidently felt that as the son of the proprietor he should make a direct inquiry. "Now, what might you be drivin' at, mister?" he asked. The Swede winked at him. It was a wink full of cunning. His fingers shook on the edge of the board. "Oh, maybe you think I have been to nowheres. Maybe you think I'm a tenderfoot?"

"I don't know nothin' about you," answered Johnnie, "and I don't give a damn where you've been. All I got to say is that I don't know what you're driving at. There hain't never been nobody killed in this room."

The cowboy, who had been steadily gazing at the Swede, then spoke: "What's wrong with you, mister?"

Apparently it seemed to the Swede that he was formidably menaced. He shivered and turned white near the corners of his mouth. He sent an appealing glance in the direction of the little Easterner. During these moments he did not forget to wear his air of advanced pot-valor. "They say they don't know what I mean," he remarked mockingly to the Easterner.

The latter answered after prolonged and cautious reflection. "I don't understand you," he said, impassively.

The Swede made a movement then which announced that he thought he had encountered treachery from the only quarter where he had expected sympathy, if not help. "Oh, I see you are all against me. I see —"

The cowboy was in a state of deep stupefaction. "Say," he cried, as he tumbled the deck violently down upon the board, "— say, what are you gittin' at, hey?"

The Swede sprang up with the celerity of a man escaping from a snake on the floor. "I don't want to fight!" he shouted. "I don't want to fight!"

The cowboy stretched his long legs indolently and deliberately. His hands were in his pockets. He spat into the sawdust box. "Well, who the hell thought you did?" he inquired.

The Swede backed rapidly towards a corner of the room. His hands were out protectingly in front of his chest, but he was making an obvious struggle to control his fright. "Gentlemen," he quavered, "I suppose I am going to be killed before I can leave this house! I suppose I am going to be killed before I can leave this house!" In his eyes was the dying-swan look. Through the windows could be seen the snow turning blue in the shadow of dusk. The wind tore at the house and some loose thing beat regularly against the clap-boards like a spirit tapping.

A door opened, and Scully himself entered. He paused in surprise as he noted the tragic attitude of the Swede. Then he said, "What's the matter here?"

The Swede answered him swiftly and eagerly: "These men are going to kill me."

"Kill you!" ejaculated Scully. "Kill you! What are you talkin'?"

The Swede made the gesture of a martyr.

Scully wheeled sternly upon his son. "What is this, Johnnie?"

The lad had grown sullen. "Damned if I know," he answered. "I can't make no sense to it." He began to shuffle the cards, fluttering them together with an angry snap. "He says a good many men have been killed in this room, or something like that. And he says he's goin' to be killed here too. I don't know what ails him. He's crazy, I shouldn't wonder."

Scully then looked for explanation to the cowboy, but the cowboy simply shrugged his shoulders.

"Kill you?" said Scully again to the Swede. "Kill you? Man, you're off your nut."

"Oh, I know," burst out the Swede. "I know what will happen. Yes, I'm crazy — yes. Yes, of course, I'm crazy — yes. But I know one thing —" There was a sort of sweat of misery and terror upon his face. "I know I won't get out of here alive."

The cowboy drew a deep breath, as if his mind was passing into the last stages of dissolution. "Well, I'm dog-goned," he whispered to himself.

Scully wheeled suddenly and faced his son. "You've been troublin' this man!"

Johnnie's voice was loud with its burden of grievance. "Why, good Gawd, I ain't done nothin' to 'im."

The Swede broke in. "Gentlemen, do not disturb yourselves. I will leave this house. I will go away because" — he accused them dramatically with his glance — "because I do not want to be killed."

Scully was furious with his son. "Will you tell me what is the matter, you young divil? What's the matter, anyhow? Speak out!"

"Blame it!" cried Johnnie in despair, "don't I tell you I don't know. He — he says we want to kill him, and that's all I know. I can't tell what ails him."

The Swede continued to repeat: "Never mind, Mr. Scully; never mind. I will leave this house. I will go away, because I do not wish to be killed. Yes, of course, I am crazy — yes. But I know one thing! I will go away. I will leave this house. Never mind, Mr. Scully; never mind. I will go away."

"You will not go 'way," said Scully. "You will not go 'way until I hear the reason of this business. If anybody has troubled you I will take care of him. This is my house. You are under my roof, and I will not allow any peaceable man to be troubled here." He cast a terrible eye upon Johnnie, the cowboy, and the Easterner.

"Never mind, Mr. Scully; never mind. I will go away. I do not wish to be killed." The Swede moved towards the door, which opened upon the stairs. It was evidently his intention to go at once for his baggage.

"No, no," shouted Scully peremptorily; but the white-faced man slid by him and disappeared. "Now," said Scully severely, "what does this mane?"

Johnnie and the cowboy cried together: "Why, we didn't do nothin' to 'im!"

Scully's eyes were cold. "No," he said, "you didn't?"

Johnnie swore a deep oath. "Why, this is the wildest loon I ever see. We didn't do nothin' at all. We were jest sittin' here playin' cards, and he —"

The father suddenly spoke to the Easterner. "Mr. Blanc," he asked, "what has these boys been doin'?"

The Easterner reflected again. "I didn't see anything wrong at all," he said at last, slowly.

Scully began to howl. "But what does it mane?" He stared ferociously at his son. "I have a mind to lather you for this, me boy."

Johnnie was frantic. "Well, what have I done?" he bawled at his father.

III

"I think you are tongue-tied," said Scully finally to his son, the cowboy, and the Easterner; and at the end of this scornful sentence he left the room.

Up-stairs the Swede was swiftly fastening the straps of his great valise. Once his back happened to be half turned towards the door, and, hearing a noise there, he wheeled and sprang up, uttering a loud cry. Scully's wrinkled visage showed gimly in the light of the small lamp he carried. This yellow effulgence, streaming upward, colored only his prominent features, and left his eyes, for instance, in mysterious shadow. He resembled a murderer.

"Man! man!" he exclaimed, "have you gone daffy?"

"Oh, no! Oh, no!" rejoined the other. "There are people in this world who know pretty nearly as much as you do — understand?"

For a moment they stood gazing at each other. Upon the Swede's deathly pale cheeks were two spots brightly crimson and sharply edged, as if they had been carefully painted. Scully placed the light on the table and sat himself on the edge of the bed. He spoke ruminatively. "By cracky, I never heard of such a thing in my life. It's a complete muddle. I can't, for the soul of me, think how you ever got this idea into your head." Presently he lifted his eyes and asked: "And did you sure think they were going to kill you?"

The Swede scanned the old man as if he wished to see into his mind. "I did," he said at last. He obviously suspected that this answer might precipitate an outbreak. As he pulled on a strap his whole arm shook, the elbow wavering like a bit of paper.

Scully banged his hand impressively on the foot-board of the bed. "Why, man, we're goin' to have a line of ilictric street-cars in this town next spring."

"'A line of electric street-cars,'" repeated the Swede, stupidly.

"And," said Scully, "there's a new railroad goin' to be built down from Broken Arm to here. Not to mintion the four churches and the smashin' big brick school-house. Then there's the big factory, too. Why, in two years Romper 'll be a met-tro-*pol*-is."

Having finished the preparation of his baggage, the Swede straightened himself. "Mr. Scully," he said, with sudden hardihood, "how much do I owe you?"

"You don't owe me anthin'," said the old man, angrily.

"Yes, I do," retorted the Swede. He took seventy-five cents from his pocket and tendered it to Scully; but the latter snapped his fingers in disdainful refusal. However, it happened that they both stood gazing in a strange fashion at three silver pieces on the Swede's open palm.

"I'll not take your money," said Scully at last. "Not after what's been goin' on here." Then a plan seemed to strike him. "Here," he cried, picking up his lamp and moving towards the door. "Here! Come with me a minute."

"No," said the Swede, in overwhelming alarm.

"Yes," urged the old man. "Come on! I want you to come and see a picter — just across the hall — in my room."

The Swede must have concluded that his hour was come. His jaw dropped and his teeth showed like a dead man's. He ultimately followed Scully across the corridor, but he had the step of one hung in chains.

Scully flashed the light high on the wall of his own chamber. There was revealed a ridiculous photograph of a little girl. She was leaning against a balustrade of gorgeous decoration, and the formidable bang to her hair was prominent. The figure was as graceful as an upright sled-stake, and, withal, it was of the hue of lead. "There," said Scully, tenderly, "that's the picter of my little girl that died. Her name was Carrie. She had the purtiest hair you ever saw! I was that fond of her, she —"

Turning then, he saw that the Swede was not contemplating the picture at all, but, instead, was keeping keen watch on the gloom in the rear.

"Look, man!" cried Scully, heartily. "That's the picter of my little gal that died. Her name was Carrie. And then here's the picter of my oldest boy, Michael. He's a lawyer in Lincoln, an' doin' well. I gave that boy a grand eddycation, and I'm glad for it now. He's a fine boy. Look at 'im now. Ain't he bold as blazes, him there in Lincoln, an honored an' respicted gintelman. An honored an' respected gintelman," concluded Scully with a flourish. And, so saying, he smote the Swede jovially on the back.

The Swede faintly smiled.

"Now," said the old man, "there's only one more thing." He dropped suddenly to the floor and thrust his head beneath the bed. The Swede could hear his muffled voice. "I'd keep it under me piller if it wasn't for that boy Johnnie. Then there's the old woman — Where is it now? I never put it twice in the same place. Ah, now come out with you!"

Presently he backed clumsily from under the bed, dragging with him an old coat rolled into a bundle. "I've fetched him," he muttered. Kneeling on the floor, he unrolled the coat and extracted from its heart a large yellow-brown whiskey bottle.

His first manœuvre was to hold the bottle up to the light. Reassured, apparently, that nobody had been tampering with it, he thrust it with a generous movement towards the Swede.

The weak-kneed Swede was about to eagerly clutch this element of strength, but he suddenly jerked his hand away and cast a look of horror upon Scully.

"Drink," said the old man affectionately. He had risen to his feet, and now stood facing the Swede.

There was a silence. Then again Scully said: "Drink!"

The Swede laughed wildly. He grabbed the bottle, put it to his mouth, and as his lips curled absurdly around the opening and his throat worked, he kept his glance, burning with hatred, upon the old man's face.

IV

After the departure of Scully the three men, with the card-board still upon their knees, preserved for a long time an astounded silence. Then Johnnie said: "That's the dod-dangest Swede I ever see."

"He ain't no Swede," said the cowboy, scornfully.

"Well, what is he then?" cried Johnnie. "What is he then?"

"It's my opinion," replied the cowboy deliberately, "he's some kind of a Dutchman." It was a venerable custom of the country to entitle as Swedes all light-haired men who spoke with a heavy tongue. In consequence the idea of the cowboy was not without its daring. "Yes, sir," he repeated. "It's my opinion this feller is some kind of a Dutchman."

"Well, he says he's a Swede, anyhow," muttered Johnnie, sulkily. He turned to the Easterner: "What do you think, Mr. Blanc?"

"Oh, I don't know," replied the Easterner.

"Well, what do you think makes him act that way?" asked the cowboy.

"Why, he's frightened." The Easterner knocked his pipe against a rim of the stove. "He's clear frightened out of his boots."

"What at?" cried Johnnie and the cowboy together.

The Easterner reflected over his answer.

"What at?" cried the others again.

"Oh, I don't know, but it seems to me this man has been reading dime-novels, and he thinks he's right out in the middle of it — the shootin' and stab-bin' and all."

"But," said the cowboy, deeply scandalized, "this ain't Wyoming, ner none of them places. This is Nebrasker."

"Yes," added Johnnie, "an' why don't he wait till he gits *out West?*"

The travelled Easterner laughed. "It isn't different there even — not in these days. But he thinks he's right in the middle of hell."

Johnnie and the cowboy mused long.

"It's awful funny," remarked Johnnie at last.

"Yes," said the cowboy. "This is a queer game. I hope we don't git snowed in, because then we'd have to stand this here man bein' around with us all the time. That wouldn't be no good."

"I wish pop would throw him out," said Johnnie.

Presently they heard a loud stamping on the stairs, accompanied by ringing jokes in the voice of old Scully, and laughter, evidently from the Swede. The men around the stove stared vacantly at each other. "Gosh!" said the cowboy. The door flew open, and old Scully, flushed and anecdotal, came into the room. He was jabbering at the Swede, who followed him, laughing bravely. It was the entry of two roisterers from a banquet-hall.

"Come now," said Scully sharply to the three seated men, "move up and give us a chance at the stove." The cowboy and the Easterner obediently sidled their chairs to make room for the new-comers. Johnnie, however, simply arranged himself in a more indolent attitude, and then remained motionless.

"Come! Git over, there," said Scully.

"Plenty of room on the other side of the stove," said Johnnie.

"Do you think we want to sit in the draught?" roared the father.

But the Swede here interposed with a grandeur of confidence. "No, no. Let the boy sit where he likes," he cried in a bullying voice to the father.

"All right! All right!" said Scully, deferentially. The cowboy and the Easterner exchanged glances of wonder.

The five chairs were formed in a crescent about one side of the stove. The Swede began to talk; he talked arrogantly, profanely, angrily. Johnnie, the cowboy, and the Easterner maintained a morose silence, while old Scully appeared to be receptive and eager, breaking in constantly with sympathetic ejaculations.

Finally the Swede announced that he was thirsty. He moved in his chair, and said that he would go for a drink of water.

"I'll git it for you," cried Scully at once.

"No," said the Swede, contemptuously. "I'll get it for myself." He arose and stalked with the air of an owner off into the executive parts of the hotel.

As soon as the Swede was out of hearing Scully sprang to his feet and whispered intensely to the others: "Up-stairs he thought I was tryin' to poison 'im."

"Say," said Johnnie, "this makes me sick. Why don't you throw 'im out in the snow?"

"Why, he's all right now," declared Scully. "It was only that he was from the East, and he thought this was a tough place. That's all. He's all right now."

The cowboy looked with admiration upon the Easterner. "You were straight," he said. "You were on to that there Dutchman."

"Well," said Johnnie to his father, "he may be all right now, but I don't see it. Other time he was scared, but now he's too fresh."

Scully's speech was always a combination of Irish brogue and idiom, Western twang and idiom, and scraps of curiously formal diction taken from the story-books and newspapers. He now hurled a strange mass of language at the head of his son. "What do I keep? What do I keep? What do I keep?" he demanded, in a voice of thunder. He slapped his knee impressively, to indicate that he himself was going to make reply, and that all should heed. "I keep a hotel," he shouted. "A hotel, do you mind? A guest under my roof has sacred privileges. He is to be intimidated by none. Not one word shall he hear that would prejudice him in favor of goin' away. I'll not have it. There's no place in this here town where they can say they iver took in a guest of mine because he was afraid to stay here." He wheeled suddenly upon the cowboy and the Easterner. "Am I right?"

"Yes, Mr. Scully," said the cowboy, "I think you're right."

"Yes, Mr. Scully," said the Easterner, "I think you're right."

V

At six o'clock supper, the Swede fizzed like a fire-wheel. He sometimes seemed on the point of bursting into riotous song, and in all his madness he was encouraged by old Scully. The Easterner was incased in reserve; the cowboy sat in wide-mouthed amazement, forgetting to eat, while Johnnie wrathily demolished great plates of food. The daughters of the house, when they were obliged to replenish the biscuits, approached as warily as Indians, and, having succeeded in their purpose, fled with ill-concealed trepidation. The Swede domineered the whole feast, and he gave it the appearance of a cruel bacchanal. He seemed to have grown suddenly taller; he gazed, brutally disdainful, into every face. His voice rang through the room. Once when he jabbed out harpoon-fashion with his fork to pinion a biscuit, the weapon nearly impaled the hand of the Easterner which had been stretched quietly out for the same biscuit.

After supper, as the men filed towards the other room, the Swede smote Scully ruthlessly on the shoulder. "Well, old boy, that was a good, square meal." Johnnie looked hopefully at his father; he knew that shoulder was tender from an old fall; and, indeed, it appeared for a moment as if Scully was going to flame out over the matter, but in the end he smiled a sickly smile and remained silent. The others understood from his manner that he was admitting his responsibility for the Swede's new view-point.

Johnnie, however, addressed his parent in an aside. "Why don't you license somebody to kick you down-stairs?" Scully scowled darkly by way of reply.

When they were gathered about the stove, the Swede insisted on another game of High-Five. Scully gently deprecated the plan at first, but the Swede turned a wolfish glare upon him. The old man subsided, and the Swede canvassed the others. In his tone there was always a great threat. The cowboy and the Easterner both remarked indifferently that they would play. Scully said that he would presently have to go to meet the 6.58 train, and so the Swede turned menacingly upon Johnnie. For a moment their glances crossed like blades, and then Johnnie smiled and said, "Yes, I'll play."

They formed a square, with the little board on their knees. The Easterner and the Swede were again partners. As the play went on, it was noticeable that the cowboy was not board-whacking as usual. Meanwhile, Scully, near the lamp, had put on his spectacles and, with an appearance curiously like an old priest, was reading a newspaper. In time he went out to meet the 6.58 train, and, despite his precautions, a gust of polar wind whirled into the room as he opened the door. Besides scattering the cards, it chilled the players to the marrow. The Swede cursed frightfully. When Scully returned, his entrance disturbed a cosey and friendly scene. The Swede again cursed. But presently they were once more intent, their heads bent forward and their hands moving swiftly. The Swede had adopted the fashion of board-whacking.

Scully took up his paper and for a long time remained immersed in matters which were extraordinarily remote from him. The lamp burned badly, and once he stopped to adjust the wick. The newspaper, as he turned from page to page, rustled with a slow and comfortable sound. Then suddenly he heard three terrible words: "You are cheatin'!"

Such scenes often prove that there can be little of dramatic import in environment. Any room can present a tragic front; any room can be comic. This little den was now hideous as a torture-chamber. The new faces of the men themselves had changed it upon the instant. The Swede held a huge fist in front of Johnnie's face, while the latter looked steadily over it into the blazing orbs of his accuser. The Easterner had grown pallid; the cowboy's jaw had dropped in an expression of bovine amazement which was one of his important mannerisms. After the three words, the first sound in the room was made by Scully's paper as it floated forgotten to his feet. His spectacles had also fallen from his nose, but by a clutch he had saved them in air. His hand, grasping the spectacles, now remained poised awkwardly and near his shoulder. He stared at the card-players.

Probably the silence was while a second elapsed. Then, if the floor had been suddenly twitched out from under the men they could not have moved quicker. The five had projected themselves headlong towards a common point. It happened that Johnnie, in rising to hurl himself upon the Swede, had stumbled slightly because of his curiously instinctive care for the cards and the board. The loss of the moment allowed time for the arrival of Scully, and also allowed the cowboy time to give the Swede a great push which sent him staggering back. The men found tongue together, and hoarse shouts of rage, appeal, or fear burst from every throat. The cowboy pushed and jostled feverishly at the Swede, and the Easterner and Scully clung wildly to Johnnie; but, through the smoky air, above the swaying bodies of the peace-compellers, the eyes of the two warriors ever sought each other in glances of challenge that were at once hot and steely.

Of course the board had been overturned, and now the whole company of cards was scattered over the floor, where the boots of the men trampled the fat and painted kings and queens as they gazed with their silly eyes at the war that was waging above them.

Scully's voice was dominating the yells. "Stop now? Stop, I say! Stop, now —"

Johnnie, as he struggled to burst through the rank formed by Scully and the Easterner, was crying, "Well, he says I cheated! He says I cheated! I won't allow no man to say I cheated! If he says I cheated, he's a —— ——!"

The cowboy was telling the Swede, "Quit, now! Quit, d'ye hear —"

The screams of the Swede never ceased: "He did cheat! I saw him! I saw him —"

As for the Easterner, he was importuning in a voice that was not heeded: "Wait a moment, can't you? Oh, wait a moment. What's the good of a fight over a game of cards? Wait a moment —"

In this tumult no complete sentences were clear. "Cheat" — "Quit" — "He says" — these fragments pierced the uproar and rang out sharply. It was remarkable that, whereas Scully undoubtedly made the most noise, he was the least heard of any of the riotous band.

Then suddenly there was a great cessation. It was as if each man had paused for breath; and although the room was still lighted with the anger of men, it could be seen that there was no danger of immediate conflict, and at once Johnnie, shouldering his way forward, almost succeeded in confronting the Swede. "What did you say I cheated for? What did you say I cheated for? I don't cheat, and I won't let no man say I do!"

The Swede said, "I saw you! I saw you!"

"Well," cried Johnnie, "I'll fight any man what says I cheat!"

"No, you won't," said the cowboy. "Not here."

"Ah, be still, can't you?" said Scully, coming between them.

The quiet was sufficient to allow the Easterner's voice to be heard. He was repeating, "Oh, wait a moment, can't you? What's the good of a fight over a game of cards? Wait a moment!"

Johnnie, his red face appearing above his father's shoulder, hailed the Swede again. "Did you say I cheated?"

The Swede showed his teeth. "Yes."

"Then," said Johnnie, "we must fight."

"Yes, fight," roared the Swede. He was like a demoniac. "Yes, fight! I'll show you what kind of man I am! I'll show you who you want to fight! Maybe you think I can't fight! Maybe you think I can't! I'll show you, you skin, you card-sharp! Yes, you cheated! You cheated! You cheated!"

"Well, let's go at it, then, mister," said Johnnie, coolly.

The cowboy's brow was beaded with sweat from his efforts in intercepting all sorts of raids. He turned in despair to Scully. "What are you goin' to do now?"

A change had come over the Celtic visage of the old man. He now seemed all eagerness; his eyes glowed.

"We'll let them fight," he answered, stalwartly. "I can't put up with it any longer. I've stood this damned Swede till I'm sick. We'll let them fight."

VI

The men prepared to go out-of-doors. The Easterner was so nervous that he had great difficulty in getting his arms into the sleeves of his new leather coat. As the cowboy drew his fur cap down over his ears his hands trembled. In fact, Johnnie and old Scully were the only ones who displayed no agitation. These preliminaries were conducted without words.

Scully threw open the door. "Well, come on," he said. Instantly a terrific wind caused the flame of the lamp to struggle at its wick, while a puff of black smoke sprang from the chimney-top. The stove was in mid-current of the blast, and its voice swelled to equal the roar of the storm. Some of the scarred and bedabbled cards were caught up from the floor and dashed helplessly against the farther wall. The men lowered their heads and plunged into the tempest as into a sea.

No snow was falling, but great whirls and clouds of flakes, swept up from the ground by the frantic winds, were streaming southward with the speed of bullets. The covered land was blue with the sheen of an unearthly satin, and there was no other hue save where, at the low, black railway station — which seemed incredibly distant — one light gleamed like a tiny jewel. As the men floundered into a thigh-deep drift, it was known that the Swede was bawling out something. Scully went to him, put a hand on his shoulder and projected an ear. "What's that you say?" he shouted.

"I say," bawled the Swede again, "I won't stand much show against this gang. I know you'll all pitch on me."

Scully smote him reproachfully on the arm. "Tut, man!" he yelled. The wind tore the words from Scully's lips and scattered them far alee.

"You are all a gang of —" boomed the Swede, but the storm also seized the remainder of his sentence.

Immediately turning their backs upon the wind, the men had swung around a corner to the sheltered side of the hotel. It was the function of the little house to preserve here, amid this great devastation of snow, an irregular V-shape of heavily incrusted grass, which crackled beneath the feet. One could imagine the great drifts piled against the windward side. When the party reached the comparative peace of this spot it was found that the Swede was still bellowing.

"Oh, I know what kind of thing this is! I know you'll all pitch on me. I can't lick you all!"

Scully turned upon him panther fashion. "You'll not have to whip all of us. You'll have to whip my son Johnnie. An' the man what troubles you durin' that time will have me to dale with."

The arrangements were swiftly made. The two men faced each other, obedient to the harsh commands of Scully, whose face, in the subtly luminous gloom, could be seen set in the austere impersonal lines that are pictured on the countenances of the Roman veterans. The Easterner's teeth were chattering, and he was hopping up and down like a mechanical toy. The cowboy stood rock-like.

The contestants had not stripped off any clothing. Each was in his ordinary attire. Their fists were up, and they eyed each other in a calm that had the elements of leonine cruelty in it.

During this pause, the Easterner's mind, like a film, took lasting impressions of three men — the iron-nerved master of the ceremony; the Swede, pale, motionless, terrible; and Johnnie, serene yet ferocious, brutish yet heroic. The entire prelude had in it a tragedy greater than the tragedy of action, and this aspect was accentuated by the long, mellow cry of the blizzard, as it sped the tumbling and wailing flakes into the black abyss of the south.

"Now!" said Scully.

The two combatants leaped forward and crashed together like bullocks. There was heard the cushioned sound of blows, and of a curse squeezing out from between the tight teeth of one.

As for the spectators, the Easterner's pent-up breath exploded from him with a pop of relief, absolute relief from the tension of the preliminaries. The cowboy bounded into the air with a yowl. Scully was immovable as from supreme amazement and fear at the fury of the fight which he himself had permitted and arranged.

For a time the encounter in the darkness was such a perplexity of flying arms that it presented no more detail than would a swiftly revolving wheel. Occasionally a face, as if illumined by a flash of light, would shine out, ghastly and marked with pink spots. A moment later, the men might have been known as shadows, if it were not for the involuntary utterance of oaths that came from them in whispers.

Suddenly a holocaust of warlike desire caught the cowboy, and he bolted forward with the speed of a bronco. "Go it, Johnnie! go it! Kill him! Kill him!"

Scully confronted him. "Kape back," he said; and by his glance the cowboy could tell that this man was Johnnie's father.

To the Easterner there was a monotony of unchangeable fighting that was an abomination. This confused mingling was eternal to his sense, which was concentrated in a longing for the end, the priceless end. Once the fighters lurched near him, and as he scrambled hastily backward he heard them breathe like men on the rack.

"Kill him, Johnnie! Kill him! Kill him! Kill him!" The cowboy's face was contorted like one of those agony masks in museums.

"Keep still," said Scully, icily.

Then there was a sudden loud grunt, incomplete, cut short, and Johnnie's body swung away from the Swede and fell with sickening heaviness to the grass. The cowboy was barely in time to prevent the mad Swede from flinging himself upon his prone adversary. "No, you don't," said the cowboy, interposing an arm. "Wait a second."

Scully was at his son's side. "Johnnie! Johnnie, me boy!" His voice had a quality of melancholy tenderness. "Johnnie! Can you go on with it?" He looked anxiously down into the bloody, pulpy face of his son.

There was a moment of silence, and then Johnnie answered in his ordinary voice, "Yes, I — it — yes."

Assisted by his father he struggled to his feet. "Wait a bit now till you git your wind," said the old man.

A few paces away the cowboy was lecturing the Swede. "No, you don't! Wait a second!"

The Easterner was plucking at Scully's sleeve. "Oh, this is enough," he pleaded. "This is enough! Let it go as it stands. This is enough!"

"Bill," said Scully, "git out of the road." The cowboy stepped aside. "Now." The combatants were actuated by a new caution as they advanced towards collision. They glared at each other, and then the Swede aimed a lightning blow that carried with it his entire weight. Johnnie was evidently half stupid from weakness, but he miraculously dodged, and his fist sent the over-balanced Swede sprawling.

The cowboy, Scully, and the Easterner burst into a cheer that was like a chorus of triumphant soldiery, but before its conclusion the Swede had scuffled agilely to his feet and come in berserk abandon at his foe. There was another perplexity of flying arms, and Johnnie's body again swung away and fell, even as a bundle might fall from a roof. The Swede instantly staggered to a little wind-waved tree and leaned upon it, breathing like an engine, while his savage and flame-lit eyes roamed from face to face as the men bent over Johnnie. There was a splendor of isolation in his situation at this time which the Easterner felt once when, lifting his eyes from the man on the ground, he beheld that mysterious and lonely figure, waiting.

"Are you any good yet, Johnnie?" asked Scully in a broken voice.

The son gasped and opened his eyes languidly. After a moment he answered, "No — I ain't — any good — any — more." Then, from shame and bodily ill, he began to weep, the tears furrowing down through the blood-stains on his face. "He was too — too — too heavy for me."

Scully straightened and addressed the waiting figure. "Stranger," he said, evenly, "it's all up with our side." Then his voice changed into that vibrant huskiness which is commonly the tone of the most simple and deadly announcements. "Johnnie is whipped."

Without replying, the victor moved off on the route to the front door of the hotel.

The cowboy was formulating new and unspellable blasphemies. The Easterner was startled to find that they were out in a wind that seemed to come direct from the shadowed arctic floes. He heard again the wail of the snow as it was flung to its grave in the south. He knew now that all this time the cold had been sinking into him deeper and deeper, and he wondered that he had not perished. He felt indifferent to the conditions of the vanquished man.

"Johnnie, can you walk?" asked Scully.

"Did I hurt — hurt him any?" asked the son.

"Can you walk, boy? Can you walk?"

Johnnie's voice was suddenly strong. There was a robust impatience in it. "I asked you whether I hurt him any!"

"Yes, yes, Johnnie," answered the cowboy, consolingly; "he's hurt a good deal."

They raised him from the ground, and as soon as he was on his feet he went tottering off, rebuffing all attempts at assistance. When the party rounded the corner they were fairly blinded by the pelting snow. It burned their faces like fire. The cowboy carried Johnnie through the drift to the door. As they entered some cards again rose from the floor and beat against the wall.

The Easterner rushed to the stove. He was so profoundly chilled that he almost dared to embrace the glowing iron. The Swede was not in the room. Johnnie sank into a chair, and folding his arms on his knees, buried his face in them.

Scully, warming one foot and then the other at a rim of the stove, muttered to himself with Celtic mournfulness. The cowboy had removed his fur cap, and with a dazed and rueful air he was running one hand through his tousled locks. From overhead they could hear the creaking of boards, as the Swede tramped here and there in his room.

The sad quiet was broken by the sudden flinging open of a door that led towards the kitchen. It was instantly followed by an inrush of women. They precipitated themselves upon Johnnie amid a chorus of lamentation. Before they carried their prey off to the kitchen, there to be bathed and harangued with that mixture of sympathy and abuse which is a feat of their sex, the mother straightened herself and fixed old Scully with an eye of stern reproach. "Shame be upon you, Patrick Scully!" she cried. "Your own son, too. Shame be upon you!"

"There, now! Be quiet, now!" said the old man, weakly.

"Shame be upon you, Patrick Scully!" The girls, rallying to this slogan, sniffed disdainfully in the direction of those trembling accomplices, the cowboy and the Easterner. Presently they bore Johnnie away, and left the three men to dismal reflection.

VII

"I'd like to fight this here Dutchman myself," said the cowboy, breaking a long silence.

Scully wagged his head sadly. "No, that wouldn't do. It wouldn't be right. It wouldn't be right."

"Well, why wouldn't it?" argued the cowboy. "I don't see no harm in it."

"No," answered Scully, with mournful heroism. "It wouldn't be right. It was Johnnie's fight, and now we mustn't whip the man just because he whipped Johnnie."

"Yes, that's true enough," said the cowboy; "but — he better not get fresh with me, because I couldn't stand no more of it."

"You'll not say a word to him," commanded Scully, and even then they heard the tread of the Swede on the stairs. His entrance was made theatric. He swept the door back with a bang and swaggered to the middle of the room. No one looked at him. "Well," he cried, insolently, at Scully, "I s'pose you'll tell me now how much I owe you?"

The old man remained stolid. "You don't owe me nothin'."

"Huh!" said the Swede, "huh! Don't owe 'im nothin'."

The cowboy addressed the Swede. "Stranger, I don't see how you come to be so gay around here."

Old Scully was instantly alert. "Stop!" he shouted, holding his hand forth, fingers upward. "Bill, you shut up!"

The cowboy spat carelessly into the sawdust-box. "I didn't say a word, did I?" he asked.

"Mr. Scully," called the Swede, "how much to I owe you?" It was seen that he was attired for departure, and that he had his valise in his hand.

"You don't owe me nothin'," repeated Scully in his same imperturbable way.

"Huh!" said the Swede. "I guess you're right. I guess if it was any way at all, you'd owe me somethin'. That's what I guess." He turned to the cowboy. "'Kill him! Kill him! Kill him!'" he mimicked, and then guffawed victoriously. "'Kill him!'" He was convulsed with ironical humor.

But he might have been jeering the dead. The three men were immovable and silent, staring with glassy eyes at the stove.

The Swede opened the door and passed into the storm, giving one derisive glance backward at the still group.

As soon as the door was closed, Scully and the cowboy leaped to their feet and began to curse. They tramped to and fro, waving their arms and smashing into the air with their fists. "Oh, but that was a hard minute! wailed Scully. "That was a hard minute! Him there leerin' and scoffin'! One bang at his nose was worth forty dollars to me that minute! How did you stand it, Bill?"

"How did I stand it?" cried the cowboy in a quivering voice. "How did I stand it? Oh!"

The old man burst into sudden brogue. "I'd loike to take that Swade," he wailed, "and hould 'im down on a shtone flure and bate 'im to a jelly wid a shtick!"

The cowboy groaned in sympathy. "I'd like to git him by the neck and ha-ammer him" — he brought his hand down on a chair with a noise like a pistol-shot — "hammer that there Dutchman until he couldn't tell himself from a dead coyote!"

"I'd bate 'im until he —"

"I'd show *him* some things —"

And then together they raised a yearning, frantic cry — "Oh-o-oh! if we only could —"

"Yes!"

"Yes!"

"And then I'd —"

"O-o-oh!"

VIII

The Swede, tightly gripping his valise, tacked across the face of the storm as if he carried sails. He was following a line of little naked, gasping trees, which he knew must mark the way of the road. His face, fresh from the pounding of John-nie's fists, felt more pleasure than pain in the wind and driving snow. A number of square shapes loomed upon him finally, and he knew them as the houses of the main body of the town. He found a street and made travel along it, leaning heavily upon the wind whenever, at a corner, a terrific blast caught him.

He might have been in a deserted village. We picture the world as thick with

conquering and elate humanity, but here, with the bugles of the tempest pealing, it was hard to imagine a peopled earth. One viewed the existence of man
then as a marvel, and conceded a glamour of wonder to these lice which were
caused to cling to a whirling, fire-smote, ice-locked, disease-stricken, space-lost
bulb. The conceit of man was explained by this storm to be the very engine of
life. One was a coxcomb not to die in it. However, the Swede found a saloon.

In front of it an indomitable red light was burning, and the snow-flakes were
made blood-color as they flew through the circumscribed territory of the lamp's
shining. The Swede pushed open the door of the saloon and entered. A sanded
expanse was before him, and at the end of it four men sat about a table drinking.
Down one side of the room extended a radiant bar, and its guardian was leaning
upon his elbows listening to the talk of the men at the table. The Swede dropped
his valise upon the floor, and, smiling fraternally upon the barkeeper, said,
"Gimme some whiskey, will you?" The man placed a bottle, a whiskey-glass, and
a glass of ice-thick water upon the bar. The Swede poured himself an abnormal
portion of whiskey and drank it in three gulps. "Pretty bad night," remarked the
bartender, indifferently. He was making the pretension of blindness which is
usually a distinction of his class; but it could have been seen that he was furtively
studying the half-erased blood-stains on the face of the Swede. "Bad night," he
said again.

"Oh, it's good enough for me," replied the Swede, hardily, as he poured himself some more whiskey. The barkeeper took his coin and manœuvred it
through its reception by the highly nickelled cash-machine. A bell rang; a card la-
belled "20 cts." had appeared.

"No," continued the Swede, "this isn't too bad weather. It's good enough
for me."

"So?" murmured the barkeeper, languidly.

The copious drams made the Swede's eyes swim, and he breathed a trifle
heavier. "Yes, I like this weather. I like it. It suits me." It was apparently his design
to impart a deep significance to these words.

"So?" murmured the bartender again. He turned to gaze dreamily at the
scroll-like birds and bird-like scrolls which had been drawn with soap upon the
mirrors at the back of the bar.

"Well, I guess I'll take another drink," said the Swede, presently. "Have
something?"

"No, thanks; I'm not drinkin'," answered the bartender. Afterwards he asked,
"How did you hurt your face?"

The Swede immediately began to boast loudly. "Why, in a fight. I thumped
the soul out of a man down here at Scully's hotel."

The interest of the four men at the table was at last aroused.

"Who was it?" said one.

"Johnnie Scully," blustered the Swede. "Son of the man what runs it. He will be pretty near dead for some weeks, I can tell you. I made a nice thing of him, I did. He couldn't get up. They carried him in the house. Have a drink?"

Instantly the men in some subtle way incased themselves in reserve. "No, thanks," said one. The group was of curious formation. Two were prominent local business men; one was the district-attorney; and one was a professional gambler of the kind known as "square." But a scrutiny of the group would not have enabled an observer to pick the gambler from the men of more reputable pursuits. He was, in fact, a man so delicate in manner, when among people of fair class, and so judicious in his choice of victims, that in the strictly masculine part of the town's life he had come to be explicitly trusted and admired. People called him a thoroughbred. The fear and contempt with which his craft was regarded was undoubtedly the reason that his quiet dignity shone conspicuous above the quiet dignity of men who might be merely hatters, billiard-markers, or grocery-clerks. Beyond the occasional unwary traveller, who came by rail, this gambler was supposed to prey solely upon reckless and senile farmers, who, when flush with good crops, drove into town in all the pride and confidence of an absolutely invulnerable stupidity. Hearing at times in circuitous fashion of the despoilment of such a farmer, the important men of Romper invariably laughed in contempt of the victim, and, if they thought of the wolf at all, it was with a kind of pride at the knowledge that he would never dare think of attacking their wisdom and courage. Besides, it was popular that this gambler had a real wife and two real children in a neat cottage in a suburb, where he led an exemplary home life; and when any one even suggested a discrepancy in his character, the crowd immediately vociferated descriptions of this virtuous family circle. Then men who led exemplary home lives, and men who did not lead exemplary home lives, all subsided in a bunch, remarking that there was nothing more to be said.

However, when a restriction was placed upon him — as, for instance, when a strong clique of members of the new Pollywog Club refused to permit him, even as a spectator, to appear in the rooms of the organization — the candor and gentleness with which he accepted the judgment disarmed many of his foes and made his friends more desperately partisan. He invariably distinguished between himself and a respectable Romper man so quickly and frankly that his manner actually appeared to be a continual broadcast compliment.

And one must not forget to declare the fundamental fact of his entire position in Romper. It is irrefutable that in all affairs outside of his business, in all matters that occur eternally and commonly between man and man, this thieving card-player was so generous, so just, so moral, that, in a contest, he could have put to flight the consciences of nine-tenths of the citizens of Romper.

And so it happened that he was seated in this saloon with the two prominent local merchants and the district-attorney.

The Swede continued to drink raw whiskey, meanwhile babbling at the bar-keeper and trying to induce him to indulge in potations. "Come on. Have a drink.

Come on. What — no? Well, have a little one, then. By gawd, I've whipped a man to-night, and I want to celebrate. I whipped him good, too. Gentlemen," the Swede cried to the men at the table, "have a drink?"

"Ssh!" said the barkeeper.

The group at the table, although furtively attentive, had been pretending to be deep in talk, but now a man lifted his eyes towards the Swede and said, shortly, "Thanks. We don't want any more."

At this reply the Swede ruffled out his chest like a rooster. "Well," he exploded, "it seems I can't get anybody to drink with me in this town. Seems so, don't it? Well!"

"Ssh!" said the barkeeper.

"Say," snarled the Swede, "don't you try to shut me up. I won't have it. I'm a gentleman, and I want people to drink with me. And I want 'em to drink with me now. *Now* — do you understand?" He rapped the bar with his knuckles.

Years of experience had calloused the bartender. He merely grew sulky. "I hear you," he answered.

"Well," cried the Swede, "listen hard then. See those men over there? Well, they're going to drink with me, and don't you forget it. Now you watch."

"Hi!" yelled the barkeeper, "this won't do!"

"Why won't it?" demanded the Swede. He stalked over to the table, and by chance laid his hand upon the shoulder of the gambler. "How about this?" he asked, wrathfully. "I asked you to drink with me."

The gambler simply twisted his head and spoke over his shoulder. "My friend, I don't know you."

"Oh, hell!" answered the Swede, "come and have a drink."

"Now, my boy," advised the gambler, kindly, "take your hand off my shoulder and go 'way and mind your own business." He was a little, slim man, and it seemed strange to hear him use this tone of heroic patronage to the burly Swede. The other men at the table said nothing.

"What! You won't drink with me, you little dude? I'll make you then! I'll make you!" The Swede had grasped the gambler frenziedly at the throat, and was dragging him from his chair. The other men sprang up. The barkeeper dashed around the corner of his bar. There was a great tumult, and then was seen a long blade in the hand of the gambler. It shot forward, and a human body, this citadel of virtue, wisdom, power, was pierced as easily as if it had been a melon. The Swede fell with a cry of supreme astonishment.

The prominent merchants and the district-attorney must have at once tumbled out of the place backward. The bartender found himself hanging limply to the arm of a chair and gazing into the eyes of a murderer.

"Henry," said the latter, as he wiped his knife on one of the towels that hung beneath the bar-rail, "you tell 'em where to find me. I'll be home, waiting for 'em." Then he vanished. A moment afterwards the barkeeper was in the street dinning through the storm for help, and, moreover, companionship.

The corpse of the Swede, alone in the saloon, had its eyes fixed upon a dreadful legend that dwelt atop of the cash-machine: "This registers the amount of your purchase."

IX

Months later, the cowboy was frying pork over the stove of a little ranch near the Dakota line, when there was a quick thud of hoofs outside, and presently the Easterner entered with the letters and the papers.

"Well," said the Easterner at once, "the chap that killed the Swede has got three years. Wasn't much, was it?"

"He has? Three years?" The cowboy poised his pan of pork, while he ruminated upon the news. "Three years. That ain't much."

"No. It was a light sentence," replied the Easterner as he unbuckled his spurs. "Seems there was a good deal of sympathy for him in Romper."

"If the bartender had been any good," observed the cowboy, thoughtfully, "he would have gone in and cracked that there Dutchman on the head with a bottle in the beginnin' of it and stopped all this here murderin'."

"Yes, a thousand things might have happened," said the Easterner, tartly.

The cowboy returned his pan of pork to the fire, but his philosophy continued. "It's funny, ain't it? If he hadn't said Johnnie was cheatin' he'd be alive this minute. He was an awful fool. Game played for fun, too. Not for money. I believe he was crazy."

"I feel sorry for that gambler," said the Easterner.

"Oh, so do I," said the cowboy. "He don't deserve none of it for killin' who he did."

"The Swede might not have been killed if everything had been square."

"Might not have been killed?" exclaimed the cowboy. "Everythin' square? Why, when he said that Johnnie was cheatin' and acted like such a jackass? And then in the saloon he fairly walked up to git hurt?" With these arguments the cowboy browbeat the Easterner and reduced him to rage.

"You're a fool!" cried the Easterner, viciously. "You're a bigger jackass than the Swede by a million majority. Now let me tell you one thing. Let me tell you something. Listen! Johnnie *was* cheating!"

"'Johnnie,'" said the cowboy, blankly. There was a minute of silence, and then he said, robustly, "Why, no. The game was only for fun."

"Fun or not," said the Easterner, "Johnnie was cheating. I saw him. I know it. I saw him. And I refused to stand up and be a man. I let the Swede fight it out alone. And you — you were simply puffing around the place and wanting to fight. And then old Scully himself! We are all in it! This poor gambler isn't even a noun. He is kind of an adverb. Every sin is the result of a collaboration. We, five of us, have collaborated in the murder of this Swede. Usually there are from a dozen to forty women really involved in every murder, but in this case it seems to be only five men — you, I, Johnnie, old Scully, and that fool of an unfortunate gambler came merely as a culmination, the apex of a human movement, and gets all the punishment."

The cowboy, injured and rebellious, cried out blindly into this fog of mysterious theory: "Well, I didn't do anythin', did I?"

Alice Dunbar-Nelson
M'sieu Fortier's Violin

Alice Dunbar-Nelson's "M'sieu Fortier's Violin" was published in *The Goodness of St. Rocque and Other Stories* in 1899, her most substantial volume of short fiction. As is true of many of her other works, it draws heavily on her early life in New Orleans and exposure to the Creole culture of Louisiana and the vibrant ethnic and linguistic intermingling of the most diverse city on the continent. She was born there in 1875 and educated in the public schools and at Straight University, where she trained to be a teacher, her profession throughout her life. She also played string instruments in the orchestra, especially the violin and the cello, an interest at issue in "M'sieu Fortier's Violin," and she became a devotee of the local opera, regarded as among the finest in the country. One of the remarkable dimensions of her fiction is that although she lived her life as a proud black woman, her characters are often of uncertain ethnic identity; their dialect is an unreliable indicator of their racial background because of the multilingual nature of their society. Her work is decidedly genteel and artistic, and her stories are elegant in their precision. Still, her fiction provides an African American perspective to the portrait of the complex society of New Orleans at the end of the nineteenth century.

Alice Dunbar-Nelson, "M'sieu Fortier's Violin," *The Goodness of St. Rocque and Other Stories* (New York: Dodd, Mead and Company, 1899), 67–82.

Slowly, one by one, the lights in the French Opera go out, until there is but a single glimmer of pale yellow flickering in the great dark space, a few moments ago all a-glitter with jewels and the radiance of womanhood and a-clash with music. Darkness now, and silence, and a great haunted hush over all, save for the distant cheery voice of a stage hand humming a bar of the opera.

The glimmer of gas makes a halo about the bowed white head of a little old man putting his violin carefully away in its case with aged, trembling, nervous fingers. Old M'sieu Fortier was the last one out every night.

Outside the air was murky, foggy. Gas and electricity were but faint splotches of light on the thick curtain of fog and mist. Around the opera was a mighty bustle of carriages and drivers and footmen, with a car gaining headway in the street now and then, a howling of names and numbers, the laughter and small talk of cloaked society stepping slowly to its carriages, and the more bourgeoisie vocalisation of the foot passengers who streamed along and hummed little bits of music. The fog's denseness was confusing, too, and at one moment it seemed that the little narrow street would become inextricably choked and remain so until some mighty engine would blow the crowd into atoms. It had been a crowded night. From around Toulouse Street, where led the entrance to the troisièmes, from the grand stairway, from the entrance to the quatrièmes, the human stream poured into the street, nearly all with a song on their lips.

M'sieu Fortier stood at the corner, blinking at the beautiful ladies in their carriages. He exchanged a hearty salutation with the saloon-keeper at the corner, then, tenderly carrying his violin case, he trudged down Bourbon Street, a little old, bent, withered figure, with shoulders shrugged up to keep warm, as though the faded brown overcoat were not thick enough.

Down on Bayou Road, not so far from Claiborne Street, was a house, little and old and queer, but quite large enough to hold M'sieu Fortier, a wrinkled dame, and a white cat. He was home but little, for on nearly every day there were rehearsals; then on Tuesday, Thursday, and Saturday nights, and twice Sundays there were performances, so Ma'am Jeanne and the white cat kept the house almost always alone. Then, when M'sieu Fortier was at home, why, it was practice, practice all the day, and smoke, snore, sleep at night. Altogether it was not very exhilarating.

M'sieu Fortier had played first violin in the orchestra ever since — well, no one remembered his not playing there. Sometimes there would come breaks in the seasons, and for a year the great building would be dark and silent. Then M'sieu Fortier would do jobs of playing here and there, one night for this ball, another night for that soirée dansante, and in the day, work at his trade, — that of a cigar-maker. But now for seven years there had been no break in the season, and the little old violinist was happy. There is nothing sweeter than a regular job and good music to play, music into which one can put some soul, some expression, and which one must study to understand. Dance music, of the frivolous, frothy kind deemed essential to soirées, is trivial, easy, uninteresting.

So M'sieu Fortier, Ma'am Jeanne, and the white cat lived a peaceful, uneventful existence out on Bayou Road. When the opera season was over in February, M'sieu went back to cigar-making, and the white cat purred none the less contentedly.

It had been a benefit to-night for the leading tenor, and he had chosen "Roland à Ronceveaux," a favourite this season, for his farewell. And, mon Dieu, mused the little M'sieu, but how his voice had rung out bell-like, piercing above the chorus of the first act! Encore after encore was given, and the bravos of the troisièmes were enough to stir the most sluggish of pulses.

> Superbes Pyrenées
> Qui dressez dans le ciel,
> Vos cimes couronnées
> D'un hiver éternelle,
> Pour nous livrer passage
> Ouvrez vos larges flancs,
> Faîtes taire l'orage,
> Voici, venir les Francs!

M'sieu quickened his pace down Bourbon Street as he sang the chorus to himself in a thin old voice, and then, before he could see in the thick fog, he had run into two young men.

"I — I — beg your pardon, — messieurs," he stammered.

"Most certainly," was the careless response; then the speaker, taking a second glance at the object of the rencontre, cried joyfully:

"Oh, M'sieu Fortier, is it you? Why, you are so happy, singing your love sonnet to your lady's eyebrow, that you did n't see a thing but the moon, did you? And who is the fair one who should clog your senses so?"

There was a deprecating shrug from the little man.

"Ma foi, but monsieur must know fo' sho', dat I am too old for love songs!"

"I know nothing save that I want that violin of yours. When is it to be mine, M'sieu Fortier?"

"Nevare, nevare!" exclaimed M'sieu, gripping on as tightly to the case as if he feared it might be wrenched from him. "Me a lovere, and to sell mon violon! Ah, so ver' foolish!"

"Martel," said the first speaker to his companion as they moved on up town, "I wish you knew that little Frenchman. He's a unique specimen. He has the most exquisite violin I've seen in years; beautiful and mellow as a genuine Cremona, and he can make the music leap, sing, laugh, sob, skip, wail, anything you like from under his bow when he wishes. It's something wonderful. We are good friends. Picked him up in my French-town rambles. I've been trying to buy that instrument since —"

"To throw it aside a week later?" lazily inquired Martel. "You are like the rest of these nineteenth-century vandals, you can see nothing picturesque that you do not wish to deface for a souvenir; you cannot even let simple happiness alone, but must needs destroy it in a vain attempt to make it your own or parade it as an advertisement."

As for M'sieu Fortier, he went right on with his song and turned into Bayou Road, his shoulders still shrugged high as though he were cold, and into the quaint little house, where Ma'am Jeanne and the white cat, who always waited up for him at nights, were both nodding over the fire.

It was not long after this that the opera closed, and M'sieu went back to his old out-of-season job. But somehow he did not do as well this spring and summer as always. There is a certain amount of cunning and finesse required to roll a cigar just so, that M'sieu seemed to be losing, whether from age or deterioration it was hard to tell. Nevertheless, there was just about half as much money coming in as formerly, and the quaint little pucker between M'sieu's eyebrows which served for a frown came oftener and stayed longer than ever before.

"Minesse," he said one day to the white cat, — he told all his troubles to her; it was of no use to talk to Ma'am Jeanne, she was too deaf to understand, — "Minesse, we are gettin' po'. You' père git h'old, an' hees han's dey go no mo' rapidement, an' dere be no mo' soirées dese day. Minesse, eef la saison don' hurry up, we shall eat ver' lil' meat."

And Minesse curled her tail and purred.

Before the summer had fairly begun, strange rumours began to float about in musical circles. M. Maugé would no longer manage the opera, but it would be turned into the hands of Americans, a syndicate. Bah! These English-speaking people could do nothing unless there was a trust, a syndicate, a company immense and dishonest. It was going to be a guarantee business, with a strictly financial basis. But worse than all this, the new manager, who was now in France, would not only procure the artists, but a new orchestra, a new leader. M'sieu Fortier grew apprehensive at this, for he knew what the loss of his place would mean to him.

September and October came, and the papers were filled with accounts of the new artists from France and of the new orchestra leader too. He was described as a most talented, progressive, energetic young man. M'sieu Fortier's heart sank at the word "progressive." He was anything but that. The New Orleans Creole blood flowed too sluggishly in his old veins.

November came; the opera reopened. M'sieu Fortier was not re-engaged.

"Minesse," he said with a catch in his voice that strongly resembled a sob, "Minesse, we mus' go hongry sometime. Ah, mon pauvre violon! Ah, mon Dieu, dey put us h'out, an' dey will not have us. Nev' min', we will sing anyhow." And drawing his bow across the strings, he sang in his thin, quavering voice, "Salut demeure, chaste et pure."

It is strange what a peculiar power of fascination former haunts have for the human mind. The criminal, after he has fled from justice, steals back and skulks about the scene of his crime; the employee thrown from work hangs about the place of his former industry; the schoolboy, truant or expelled, peeps in at the school-gate and taunts the good boys within. M'sieu Fortier was no exception. Night after night of the performances he climbed the stairs of the opera and sat, an attentive listener to the orchestra, with one ear inclined to the stage, and a quizzical expression on his wrinkled face. Then he would go home, and pat Minesse, and fondle the violin.

"Ah, Minesse, dose new player! Not one bit can dey play. Such tones, Minesse, such tones! All the time portemento, oh, so ver' bad! Ah, mon chere violon, we can play." And he would play and sing a romance, and smile tenderly to himself.

At first it used to be into the deuxièmes that M'sieu Fortier went, into the front seats. But soon they were too expensive, and after all, one could hear just as well in the fourth row as in the first. After a while even the rear row of the deuxièmes was too costly, and the little musician wended his way with the plebeians around on Toulouse Street, and climbed the long, tedious flight of stairs into the troisièmes. It makes no difference to be one row higher. It was more to the liking, after all. One felt more at home up here among the people. If one was thirsty, one could drink a glass of wine or beer being passed about by the libretto boys, and the music sounded just as well.

But it happened one night that M'sieu could not even afford to climb the Toulouse Street stairs. To be sure, there was yet another gallery, the quatrièmes, where the peanut boys went for a dime, but M'sieu could not get down to that yet. So he stayed outside until all the beautiful women in their warm wraps, a bright-hued chattering throng, came down the grand staircase to their carriages.

It was on one of these nights that Courcey and Martel found him shivering at the corner.

"Hello, M'sieu Fortier," cried Courcey, "are you ready to let me have that violin yet?"

"For shame!" interrupted Martel.

"Fifty dollars, you know," continued Courcey, taking no heed of his friend's interpolation.

M'sieu Fortier made a courtly bow. "Eef Monsieur will call at my 'ouse on de morrow, he may have mon violon," he said huskily; then turned abruptly on his heel, and went down Bourbon Street, his shoulders drawn high as though he were cold.

When Courcey and Martel entered the gate of the little house on Bayou Road the next day, there floated out to their ears a wordless song thrilling from the violin, a song that told more than speech or tears or gestures could have done of the utter sorrow and desolation of the little old man. They walked softly up the short red brick walk and tapped at the door. Within, M'sieu Fortier was caressing the violin, with silent tears streaming down his wrinkled gray face.

There was not much said on either side. Courcey came away with the instrument, leaving the money behind, while Martel grumbled at the essentially sordid, mercenary spirit of the world. M'sieu Fortier turned back into the room, after bowing his visitors out with old-time French courtliness, and turning to the sleepy white cat, said with a dry sob:

"Minesse, dere 's only me an' you now."

About six days later, Courcey's morning dreams were disturbed by the announcement of a visitor. Hastily doing a toilet, he descended the stairs to find M'sieu Fortier nervously pacing the hall floor.

"I come fo' bring back you' money, yaas. I cannot sleep, I cannot eat, I only cry, and t'ink, and weesh fo' mon violon; and Minesse, an' de ol' woman too, dey mope an' look bad too, all for mon violon. I try fo' to use dat money, but eet burn an' sting lak blood money. I feel lak' I done sol' my child. I cannot go at l'opera no mo', I t'ink of mon violon. I starve befo' I live widout. My heart, he is broke, I die for mon violon."

Courcey left the room and returned with the instrument.

"M'sieu Fortier," he said, bowing low, as he handed the case to the little man, "take your violin; it was a whim with me, a passion with you. And as for the money, why, keep that too; it was worth a hundred dollars to have possessed such an instrument even for six days."

Zitkala-Sä
The Soft-Hearted Sioux

"The Soft-Hearted Sioux," by the Dakota writer Zitkala-Sä, appeared in *Harper's Monthly Magazine* in March 1901. A year later she published "Why I Am a Pagan" in *The Atlantic Monthly* expressing some of her views on religion. In it she discusses the rich, natural religion of her people, who see divinity in all of nature and regard the simple things of the earth as being sacred. She contrasts this view with the harsh assumptions of Christianity, with the burning pits of eternal fire for sinners and redemption only through the sacrifice of Jesus Christ. She concludes, unabashedly, by asserting that she is a pagan, preferring the spirituality in the nature all around her to the abstract threats of a vengeful god. These ideas are present as well in "The Soft-Hearted Sioux." Zitkala-Sä adds to them the complex issue of cultural duality, a concept very popular at the turn of the century when hoards of immigrants were encountering, in somewhat different terms, many of the same conflicts. Here a young Dakota boy is educated in a mission school and converted to Christianity. When he returns to his village as a missionary, he is scorned and rejected, even by his dying father, and his internal battle of religious and social values leads to the profoundly dramatic conclusion.

Zitkala-Sä, "The Soft-Hearted Sioux," *Harper's Monthly Magazine* 102 (March 1901): 505–08.

I

Beside the open fire I sat within our tepee. With my red blanket wrapped tightly about my crossed legs, I was thinking of the coming season, my sixteenth winter.

On either side of the wigwam were my parents. My father was whistling a tune between his teeth while polishing with his bare hand a red stone pipe he had recently carved. Almost in front of me, beyond the centre fire, my old grandmother sat near the entranceway.

She turned her face toward her right and addressed most of her words to my mother. Now and then she spoke to me, but never did she allow her eyes to rest upon her daughter's husband, my father. It was only upon rare occasions that my grandmother said anything to him. Thus his ears were open and ready to catch the smallest wish she might express. Sometimes when my grandmother had been saying things which pleased him, my father used to comment upon them. At other times, when he could not approve of what was spoken, he used to work or smoke silently.

On this night my old grandmother began her talk about me. Filling the bowl of her red stone pipe with dry willow bark, she looked across at me.

"My grandchild, you are tall and are no longer a little boy." Narrowing her old eyes, she asked, "My grandchild, when are you going to bring here a handsome young woman?" I stared into the fire rather than meet her gaze. Waiting for my answer, she stooped forward and through the long stem drew a flame into the red stone pipe.

I smiled while my eyes were still fixed upon the bright fire, but I said nothing in reply. Turning to my mother, she offered her the pipe. I glanced at my grandmother. The loose buckskin sleeve fell off at her elbow and showed a wrist covered with silver bracelets. Holding up the fingers of her left hand, she named off the desirable young women of our village.

"Which one, my grandchild, which one?" she questioned.

"Hoh!" I said, pulling at my blanket in confusion. "Not yet!" Here my mother passed the pipe over the fire to my father. Then she too began speaking of what I should do.

"My son, be always active. Do not dislike a long hunt. Learn to provide much buffalo meat and many buckskins before you bring home a wife." Presently my father gave the pipe to my grandmother, and he took his turn in the exhortations.

"Ho, my son, I have been counting in my heart the bravest warriors of our people. There is not one of them who won his title in his sixteenth winter. My son, it is a great thing for some brave of sixteen winters to do."

Not a word had I to give in answer. I knew well the fame of my warrior father. He had earned the right of speaking such words, though even he himself was a brave only at my age. Refusing to smoke my grandmother's pipe because my heart was too much stirred by their words, and sorely troubled with a fear lest I should disappoint them, I arose to go. Drawing my blanket over my shoulders, I said, as I stepped toward the entranceway: "I go to hobble my pony. It is now late in the night."

II

Nine winters' snows had buried deep that night when my old grandmother, together with my father and mother, designed my future with the glow of a camp fire upon it.

Yet I did not grow up the warrior, huntsman, and husband I was to have been. At the mission school I learned it was wrong to kill. Nine winters I hunted for the soft heart of Christ, and prayed for the huntsmen who chased the buffalo on the plains.

In the autumn of the tenth year I was sent back to my tribe to preach Christianity to them. With the white man's Bible in my hand, and the white man's tender heart in my breast, I returned to my own people.

Wearing a foreigner's dress, I walked, a stranger, into my father's village.

Asking my way, for I had not forgotten my native tongue, an old man led me toward the teepee where my father lay. From my old companion I learned that my father had been sick many moons. As we drew near the teepee, I heard the chanting of a medicine-man within it. At once I wished to enter in and drive from my home the sorcerer of the plains, but the old warrior checked me. "Ho, wait outside until the medicine-man leaves your father," he said. While talking he scanned me from head to feet. Then he retraced his steps toward the heart of the camping-ground.

My father's dwelling was on the outer limits of the round-faced village. With every heart-throb I grew more impatient to enter the wigwam.

While I turned the leaves of my Bible with nervous fingers, the medicine-man came forth from the dwelling and walked hurriedly away. His head and face were closely covered with the loose robe which draped his entire figure.

He was tall and large. His long strides I have never forgot. They seemed to me then as the uncanny gait of eternal death. Quickly pocketing my Bible, I went into the teepee.

Upon a mat lay my father, with furrowed face and gray hair. His eyes and cheeks were sunken far into his head. His sallow skin lay thin upon his pinched nose and high cheek-bones. Stooping over him, I took his fevered hand. "How, Ate?" I greeted him. A light flashed from his listless eyes and his dried lips parted. "My son!" he murmured, in a feeble voice. Then again the wave of joy and recognition receded. He closed his eyes, and his hand dropped from my open palm to the ground.

Looking about, I saw an old woman sitting with bowed head. Shaking hands with her, I recognized my mother. I sat down between my father and mother as I used to do, but I did not feel at home. The place where my old grandmother used to sit was now unoccupied. With my mother I bowed my head. Alike our throats were choked and tears were streaming from our eyes; but far apart in spirit our ideas and faiths separated us. My grief was for the soul unsaved; and I thought my mother wept to see a brave man's body broken by sickness.

Useless was my attempt to change the faith in the medicine-man to that abstract power named God. Then one day I became righteously mad with anger that the medicine-man should thus ensnare my father's soul. And when he came to chant his sacred songs I pointed toward the door and bade him go! The man's eyes glared upon me for an instant. Slowly gathering his robe about him, he turned his back upon the sick man and stepped out of our wigwam. "Hā, hā, hā! my son, I cannot live without the medicine-man!" I heard my father cry when the sacred man was gone.

III

On a bright day, when the winged seeds of the prairie-grass were flying hither and thither, I walked solemnly toward the centre of the camping-ground. My heart beat hard and irregularly at my side. Tighter I grasped the sacred book I carried under my arm. Now was the beginning of life's work.

Though I knew it would be hard, I did not once feel that failure was to be my reward. As I stepped unevenly on the rolling ground, I thought of the warriors soon to wash off their war-paints and follow me.

At length I reached the place where the people had assembled to hear me preach. In a large circle men and women sat upon the dry red grass. Within the ring I stood, with the white man's Bible in my hand. I tried to tell them of the soft heart of Christ.

In silence the vast circle of bareheaded warriors sat under an afternoon sun. At last, wiping the wet from my brow, I took my place in the ring. The hush of the assembly filled me with great hope.

I was turning my thoughts upward to the sky in gratitude, when a stir called me to earth again.

A tall, strong man arose. His loose robe hung in folds over his right shoulder. A pair of snapping black eyes fastened themselves like the poisonous fangs of a serpent upon me. He was the medicine-man. A tremor played about my heart and a chill cooled the fire in my veins.

Scornfully he pointed a long forefinger in my direction and asked,

"What loyal son is he who, returning to his father's people, wears a foreigner's dress?" He paused a moment, and then continued: "The dress of that foreigner of whom a story says he bound a native of our land, and heaping dry sticks around him, kindled a fire at his feet!" Waving his hand toward me, he exclaimed, "Here is the traitor to his people!"

I was helpless. Before the eyes of the crowd the cunning magician turned my honest heart into a vile nest of treachery. Alas! the people frowned as they looked upon me.

"Listen!" he went on. "Which one of you who have eyed the young man can see through his bosom and warn the people of the nest of young snakes hatching there? Whose ear was so acute that he caught the hissing of snakes whenever the young man opened his mouth? This one has not only proven false to you, but even to the Great Spirit who made him. He is a fool! Why do you sit here giving ear to a foolish man who could not defend his people because he fears to kill, who could not bring venison to renew the life of his sick father? With his prayers, let him drive away the enemy! With his soft heart, let him keep off starvation! We shall go elsewhere to dwell upon an untainted ground."

With this he disbanded the people. When the sun lowered in the west and the winds were quiet, the village of cone-shaped tepees was gone. The medicine-man had won the hearts of the people.

Only my father's dwelling was left to mark the fighting-ground.

IV

From a long night at my father's bedside I came out to look upon the morning. The yellow sun hung equally between the snow-covered land and the cloudless blue sky. The light of the new day was cold. The strong breath of winter crusted the snow and fitted crystal shells over the rivers and lakes. As I stood in front of the tepee, thinking of the vast prairies which separated us from our tribe, and wondering if the high sky likewise separated the soft-hearted Son of God from us, the icy blast from the North blew through my hair and skull. My neglected hair had grown long and fell upon my neck.

My father had not risen from his bed since the day the medicine-man led the people away. Though I read from the Bible and prayed beside him upon my knees, my father would not listen. Yet I believed my prayers were not unheeded in heaven.

"Hā, hā, hā! my son," my father groaned upon the first snowfall. "My son, our food is gone. There is no one to bring me meat! My son, your soft heart has unfitted you for everything!" Then covering his face with the buffalo-robe, he said no more. Now while I stood out in that cold winter morning, I was starving. For two days I had not seen any food. But my own cold and hunger did not harass my soul as did the whining cry of the sick old man.

Stepping again into the tepee, I untied my snow-shoes, which were fastened to the tent-poles.

My poor mother, watching by the sick one, and faithfully heaping wood upon the centre fire, spoke to me:

"My son, do not fail again to bring your father meat, or he will starve to death."

"How, Ina," I answered, sorrowfully. From the tepee I started forth again to hunt food for my aged parents. All day I tracked the white level lands in vain. Nowhere, nowhere were there any other footprints but my own! In the evening of this third fast-day I came back without meat. Only a bundle of sticks for the fire I brought on my back. Dropping the wood outside, I lifted the door-flap and set one foot within the tepee.

There I grew dizzy and numb. My eyes swam in tears. Before me lay my old gray-haired father sobbing like a child. In his horny hands he clutched the buffalo-robe, and with his teeth he was gnawing off the edges. Chewing the dry stiff hair and buffalo-skin, my father's eyes sought my hands. Upon seeing them empty, he cried out:

"My son, your soft heart will let me starve before you bring me meat! Two hills eastward stand a herd of cattle. Yet you will see me die before you bring me food!"

Leaving my mother lying with covered head upon her mat, I rushed out into the night.

With a strange warmth in my heart and swiftness in my feet, I climbed over the first hill, and soon the second one. The moonlight upon the white country showed me a clear path to the white man's cattle. With my hand upon the knife in my belt, I leaned heavily against the fence while counting the herd.

Twenty in all I numbered. From among them I chose the best-fattened creature. Leaping over the fence, I plunged my knife into it.

My long knife was sharp, and my hands, no more fearful and slow, slashed off choice chunks of warm flesh. Bending under the meat I had taken for my starving father, I hurried across the prairie.

Toward home I fairly ran with the life-giving food I carried upon my back. Hardly had I climbed the second hill when I heard sounds coming after me. Faster and faster I ran with my load for my father, but the sounds were gaining upon me. I heard the clicking of snow-shoes and the squeaking of the leather straps at my heels; yet I did not turn to see what pursued me, for I was intent upon reaching my father. Suddenly like thunder an angry voice shouted curses and threats into my ear! A rough hand wrenched my shoulder and took the meat from me! I stopped struggling to run. A deafening whir filled my head. The moon and stars began to move. Now the white prairie was sky, and the stars lay under my feet. Now again they were turning. At last the starry blue rose up into place. The noise in my ears was still. A great quiet filled the air. In my hand I found my long knife dripping with blood. At my feet a man's figure lay prone in blood-red snow. The horrible scene about me seemed a trick of my senses, for I could not understand it was real. Looking long upon the blood-stained snow, the load of meat for my starving father reached my recognition at last. Quickly I tossed it over my shoulder and started again homeward.

Tired and haunted I reached the door of the wigwam. Carrying the food before me, I entered with it into the tepee.

"Father, here is food!" I cried, as I dropped the meat near my mother. No answer came. Turning about, I beheld my gray-haired father dead! I saw by the unsteady firelight an old gray-haired skeleton lying rigid and stiff.

Out into the open I started, but the snow at my feet became bloody.

V

On the day after my father's death, having led my mother to the camp of the medicine-man, I gave myself up to those who were searching for the murderer of the paleface.

They bound me hand and foot. Here in this cell I was placed four days ago.

The shrieking winter winds have followed me hither. Rattling the bars, they howl unceasingly: "Your soft heart! your soft heart will see me die before you bring me food!" Hark! something is clanking the chain on the door. It is being opened. From the dark night without a black figure crosses the threshold. . . . It is the guard. He comes to warn me of my fate. He tells me that tomorrow I must die. In his stern face I laugh aloud. I do not fear death.

Yet I wonder who shall come to welcome me in the realm of strange sight. Will the loving Jesus grant me pardon and give my soul a soothing sleep? or will my warrior father greet me and receive me as his son? Will my spirit fly upward to a happy heaven? or shall I sink into the bottomless pit, an outcast from a God of infinite love?

Soon, soon I shall know, for now I see the east is growing red. My heart is strong. My face is calm. My eyes are dry and eager for new scenes. My hands hang quietly at my side. Serene and brave, my soul awaits the men to perch me on the gallows for another flight. I go.

Frank Norris
A Deal in Wheat

Everybody's Magazine published Frank Norris's "A Deal in Wheat" in 1902 prior to its inclusion in *A Deal in Wheat and Other Stories of the New and Old West* the following year. It has long been regarded as the quintessential Naturalistic work in that it is told by an omniscient narrator who describes not only the backgrounds of characters but the social and economic context in expository passages that present the etiology of social pathology. The poverty and hopelessness experienced by a midwestern farmer are the result of forces beyond his control: nature, greed, and an economic system that allows for unfettered and unscrupulous manipulation. In dramatizing the situation Norris actually simplified the economic circumstances of the 1890s, in which trade policies with European countries caused the value of wheat to fluctuate much more violently than did speculation in the markets in Chicago. Still, the plight of Sam Lewiston is dramatic and poignant, and the story called attention to the extent to which commodities investors could impact the lives of farmers and consumers alike.

Frank Norris, "A Deal in Wheat," *Everybody's Magazine* 7 (August 1902): 173–80.

I. The Bear — Wheat at Sixty-Two

As Sam Lewiston backed the horse into the shafts of his buckboard and began hitching the tugs to the "whiffletree," his wife came out from the kitchen door of the house and drew near, and stood for some time at the horse's head, her arms folded and her apron rolled around them. For a long moment neither spoke. They had talked over the situation so long and so comprehensively the night before that there seemed to be nothing more to say.

The time was late in the summer, the place a ranch in southwestern Kansas, and Lewiston and his wife were two of a vast population of farmers, wheat growers, who at that moment were passing through a crisis — a crisis that at any moment might culminate in tragedy. Wheat was down to sixty-six.

At length Emma Lewiston spoke.

"Well," she hazarded, looking vaguely out across the ranch towards the horizon, leagues distant; "well, Sam, there's always that offer of brother Joe's. We can quit — and go to Chicago — if the worst comes."

"And give up!" exclaimed Lewiston, running the lines through the torrets. "Leave the ranch! Give up! After all these years!"

His wife made no reply for the moment. Lewiston climbed into the buckboard and gathered up the lines. "Well, here goes for the last try, Emmie," he said. "Good-bye, girl. Maybe things will look better in town to-day."

"Maybe," she said gravely. She kissed her husband good-bye and stood for some time looking after the buckboard travelling towards the town in a moving pillar of dust. "I don't know," she murmured at length; "I don't know just how we're going to make out."

When he reached town, Lewiston tied the horse to the iron railing in front of the Odd Fellows' Hall, the ground floor of which was occupied by the post-office, and went across the street and up the stairway of a building of brick and granite — quite the most pretentious structure of the town — and knocked at a door upon the first landing. The door was furnished with a pane of frosted glass, on which, in gold letters, was inscribed: "Bridges & Co., Grain Dealers."

Bridges himself, a middle-aged man who wore a velvet skull-cap and who was smoking a Pittsburg stogie, met the farmer at the counter and the two exchanged perfunctory greetings.

"Well," said Lewiston, tentatively, after a while.

"Well, Lewiston," said the other, "I can't take that wheat of yours at any better than sixty-two."

"Sixty-*two*."

"It's the Chicago price that does it, Lewiston. Truslow is bearing the stuff for all he's worth. It's Truslow and the bear clique that stick the knife into us. The price broke again this morning. We've just got a wire."

"Good heavens," murmured Lewiston, looking vaguely from side to side.

"That — that ruins me. I *can't* carry my grain any longer — what with storage charges and — and — Bridges, I don't see just how I'm going to make out. Sixty-two cents a bushel! Why, man, what with this and with that it's cost me nearly a dollar a bushel to raise that wheat, and now Truslow ——"

He turned away abruptly with a quick gesture of infinite discouragement.

He went down the stairs, and making his way to where his buckboard was hitched, got in, and, with eyes vacant, the reins slipping and sliding in his limp, half-open hands, drove slowly back to the ranch. His wife had seen him coming, and met him as he drew up before the barn.

"Well?" she demanded.

"Emmie," he said as he got out of the buckboard, laying his arm across her shoulder; "Emmie, I guess we'll take up with Joe's offer. We'll go to Chicago. We're cleaned out!"

II. The Bull — Wheat at a Dollar-Ten

. . . — and said Party of the Second Part further covenants and agrees to merchandize such wheat in foreign ports, it being understood and agreed between the Party of the First Part and the Party of the Second Part that the wheat hereinbefore mentioned is released and sold to the Party of the Second Part for export purposes only, and not for consumption or distribution within the boundaries of the United States of America or of Canada.

"Now, Mr. Gates, if you sign for Mr. Truslow I guess that'll be all," remarked Hornung when he had finished reading.

Hornung affixed his signature to the two documents and passed them over to Gates, who signed for his principal and client, Truslow — or, as he had been called ever since he had gone into the fight against Hornung's corner — the Great Bear. Hornung's secretary was called in and witnessed the signatures, and Gates thrust the contract into his Gladstone bag and stood up, smoothing his hat.

"You will deliver the warehouse receipts for the grain," — began Gates.

"I'll send a messenger to Truslow's office before noon," interrupted Hornung. "You can pay by certified check through the Illinois Trust people."

When the other had taken himself off, Hornung sat for some moments gazing abstractedly towards his office windows, thinking over the whole matter. He had just agreed to release to Truslow, at the rate of one dollar and ten cents per bushel, one hundred thousand out of the two million and odd bushels of wheat that he, Hornung, controlled, or actually owned. And for the moment he was wondering if, after all, he had done wisely in not goring the Great Bear to actual financial death. He had made him pay one hundred thousand dollars. Truslow was good for this amount. Would it not have been better to have put a prohibitive figure on the grain and forced the Bear into bankruptcy? True, Hornung would then be without his enemy's money, but Truslow would have been eliminated from the situation, and that — so Hornung told himself — was always a consummation most devoutly, strenuously and diligently to be striven for. Truslow once dead was dead, but the Bear was never more dangerous than when desperate.

"But so long as he can't get *wheat*," muttered Hornung at the end of his reflections, "he can't hurt me. And he can't get it. That I *know*."

For Hornung controlled the situation. So far back as the February of that year an "unknown bull" had been making his presence felt on the floor of the Board of Trade. By the middle of March the commercial reports of the daily press had begun to speak of "the powerful bull clique"; a few weeks later that legendary condition of affairs implied and epitomized in the magic words "Dollar Wheat" had been attained, and by the first of April, when the price had been boosted to one dollar and ten cents a bushel, Hornung had disclosed his hand, and in place of mere rumors, the definite and authoritative news that May wheat had been cornered in the Chicago pit went flashing around the world from Liverpool to Odessa and from Duluth to Buenos Ayres.

It was — so the veteran operators were persuaded — Truslow himself who had made Hornung's corner possible. The Great Bear had for once over-reached himself, and believing himself all-powerful, had hammered the price just the fatal fraction too far down. Wheat had gone to sixty-two — for the time, and, under the circumstances, an abnormal price. When the reaction came it was tremendous. Hornung saw his chance, seized it, and in a few months had turned the tables, had cornered the product, and virtually driven the bear clique out of the pit.

On the same day that the delivery of the hundred thousand bushels was made to Truslow, Hornung met his broker at his lunch club.

"Well," said the latter, "I see you let go that line of stuff to Truslow."

Hornung nodded; but the broker added:

"Remember, I was against it from the very beginning. I know we've cleared up over a hundred thou'. I would have fifty times preferred to have lost twice that and *smashed Truslow dead*. Bet you what you like he makes us pay for it somehow."

"Huh!" grunted his principal. "How about insurance, and warehouse charges, and carrying expenses on that lot? Guess we'd have had to pay those too if we'd held on."

But the other put up his chin, unwilling to be persuaded. "I won't sleep easy," he declared, "till Truslow is busted."

III. The Pit

Just as Going mounted the steps on the edge of the pit the great gong struck, a roar of a hundred voices developed with the swiftness of successive explosions, the rush of a hundred men surging downward to the centre of the pit filled the

air with the stamp and grind of feet, a hundred hands in eager strenuous gestures tossed upward from out the brown of the crowd, the official reporter in his
cage on the margin of the pit leaned far forward with straining ear to catch the
opening bid, and another day of battle was begun.

Since the sale of the hundred thousand bushels of wheat to Truslow, the
"Hornung crowd" had steadily shouldered the price higher, until on this particular morning it stood at one dollar and a half. That was Hornung's price. No one
else had any grain to sell.

But not ten minutes after the opening, Going was surprised out of all countenance to hear shouted from the other side of the pit these words:

"Sell May at one-fifty."

Going was for the moment touching elbows with Kimbark on one side and
with Merriam on the other, all three belonging to the "Hornung crowd." Their
answering challenge of *"Sold"* was as the voice of one man. They did not pause
to reflect upon the strangeness of the circumstance. (That was for afterwards.)
Their response to the offer was as unconscious as reflex action and almost as
rapid, and before the pit was well aware of what had happened the transaction
of one thousand bushels was down upon Going's trading-card, and fifteen hundred dollars had changed hands. But here was a marvel — the whole available
supply of wheat cornered, Hornung master of the situation, invincible, unassailable; yet behold a man willing to sell, a Bear bold enough to raise his head.

"That was Kennedy, wasn't it, who made that offer?" asked Kimbark, as Going noted down the trade — "Kennedy, that new man?"

"Yes; who do you suppose he's selling for; who's willing to go short at this
stage of the game?"

"Maybe he ain't short."

"Short! Great heavens, man, where'd he get the stuff?"

"Blamed if I know. We can account for every handful of May. Steady-oh,
there he goes again."

"Sell a thousand May at one-fifty," vociferated the bear broker, throwing out
his hand, one finger raised to indicate the number of "contracts" offered. This
time it was evident that he was attacking the Hornung crowd deliberately, for,
ignoring the jam of traders that swept towards him, he looked across the pit to
where Going and Kimbark were shouting *"Sold, sold,"* and nodded his head.

A second time Going made memoranda of the trade, and either the Hornung holdings were increased by two thousand bushels of May wheat, or the
Hornung bank account swelled by at least three thousand dollars of some unknown short's money.

Of late — so sure was the bull crowd of its position — no one had even
thought of glancing at the inspection sheet on the bulletin board. But now one
of Going's messengers hurried up to him with the announcement that this sheet
showed receipts at Chicago for that morning of twenty-five thousand bushels,

and not credited to Hornung. Some one had got hold of a line of wheat over-looked by the "clique," and was dumping it upon them.

"Wire the Chief," said Going over his shoulder to Merriam. This one struggled out of the crowd, and on a telegraph blank scribbled:

> Strong bear movement — New man — Kennedy — Selling in lots
> of five contracts — Chicago receipts twenty-five thousand.

The message was despatched, and in a few moments the answer came back, la-conic, of military terseness:

> Support the market.

And Going obeyed, Merriam and Kimbark following, the new broker fairly throwing the wheat at them in thousand-bushel lots.

"Sell May at 'fifty; sell May; sell May." A moment's indecision, an instant's hesitation, the first faint suggestion of weakness, and the market would have broken under them. But for the better part of four hours they stood their ground, taking all that was offered, in constant communication with the Chief, and from time to time stimulated and steadied by his brief, unvarying command:

"Support the market."

At the close of the session they had bought in the twenty-five thousand bushels of May. Hornung's position was as stable as a rock, and the price closed even with the opening figure — one dollar and a half.

But the morning's work was the talk of all La Salle Street. Who was back of the raid? What was the meaning of this unexpected selling? For weeks the pit-trading had been merely nominal. Truslow, the Great Bear, from whom the most serious attack might have been expected, had gone to his country seat at Geneva Lake, in Wisconsin, declaring himself to be out of the market entirely. He went bass fishing every day.

IV. The Belt Line

On a certain day towards the middle of the month, at a time when the mysteri-ous Bear had unloaded some eighty thousand bushels upon Hornung, a confer-ence was held in the library of Hornung's home. His broker attended it, and also a clean-faced, bright-eyed individual whose name of Cyrus Ryder might have been found upon the pay roll of a rather well-known detective agency. For up-wards of half an hour after the conference began, the detective spoke, the other two listening attentively, gravely.

"Then, last of all," concluded Ryder, "I made out I was a hobo, and began stealing rides on the Belt Line Railroad. Know the road? It just circles Chicago. Truslow owns it. Yes? Well, then I began to catch on. I noticed that cars of cer-tain numbers — thirty-three ought thirty-four, thirty-two one ninety — well, the numbers don't matter, but anyhow these cars were always switched onto the sidings by Mr. Truslow's main elevator D soon as they came in. The wheat was shunted in, and they were pulled out again. Well, I spotted one car and stole a ride on her. Say, look here, *that car went right around the city on the Belt, and came back to D again, and the same wheat in her all the time.* The grain was re-inspected — it was raw, I tell you — and the warehouse receipts made out just as though the stuff had come in from Kansas or Iowa."

"The same wheat all the time!" interposed Hornung.

"The same wheat — your wheat, that you sold to Truslow."

"Great snakes!" ejaculated Hornung's broker. "Truslow never took it abroad at all."

"Took it abroad! Say, he's just been running it around Chicago, like the supers in 'Shenandoah,' round an' round, so you'd think it was a new lot, an' selling it back to you again."

"No wonder we couldn't account for so much wheat."

"Bought it from us at $1.10, and made us buy it back — our own wheat — at $1.50."

Hornung and his broker looked at each other in silence for a moment. Then all at once Hornung struck the arm of his chair with his fist and exploded in a roar of laughter. The broker stared for one bewildered moment, then followed his example.

"Sold, sold," shouted Hornung almost gleefully. "Upon my soul it's as good as a Gilbert and Sullivan show. And we — Oh, Lord! Billy, shake on it, and hats off to my distinguished friend, Truslow. He'll be president some day. Hey! What? Prosecute him? Not I."

"He's done us out of a neat hatful of dollars for all that," observed the broker, suddenly grave.

"Billy, it's worth the price."

"We've got to make it up somehow."

"Well, tell you what. We were going to boost the price to one seventy-five next week, and make that our settlement figure."

"Can't do it now. Can't afford it."

"No. Here; we'll let out a big link; we'll put wheat at two dollars, and let it go at that."

"Two it is, then," said the broker.

V. The Bread Line

The street was very dark and absolutely deserted. It was a district on the "South Side," not far from the Chicago River, given up largely to wholesale stores, and after nightfall was empty of all life. The echoes slept but lightly hereabouts, and the slightest footfall, the faintest noise, woke them upon the instant and sent them clamoring up and down the length of the pavement between the iron shuttered fronts. The only light visible came from the side door of a certain "Vienna" bakery, where at one o'clock in the morning loaves of bread were given away to any who should ask. Every evening about nine o'clock the outcasts began to gather about the side door. The stragglers came in rapidly, and the line — the "bread line" as it was called — began to form. By midnight it was usually some hundred yards in length, stretching almost the entire length of the block.

Towards ten in the evening, his coat collar turned up against the fine drizzle that pervaded the air, his hands in his pockets, his elbows gripping his sides, Sam Lewiston came up and silently took his place at the end of the line.

Unable to conduct his farm upon a paying basis at the time when Truslow, the "Great Bear," had sent the price of grain down to 62 cents a bushel, Lewiston had turned over his entire property to his creditors, and, leaving Kansas for good, had abandoned farming, and had left his wife at her sister's boarding house in Topeka with the understanding that she was to join him in Chicago so soon as he had found a steady job. Then he had come to Chicago and had turned workman. His brother Joe conducted a small hat factory on Archer Avenue, and for a time he found there a meagre employment. But difficulties had occurred, times were bad, the hat factory was involved in debts, the repealing of a certain import duty on manufactured felt overcrowded the home market with cheap Belgian and French products, and in the end his brother had assigned and gone to Milwaukee.

Thrown out of work, Lewiston drifted aimlessly about Chicago, from pillar to post, working a little, earning here a dollar, there a dime, but always sinking, sinking, till at last the ooze of the lowest bottom dragged at his feet and the rush of the great ebb went over him and engulfed him and shut him out from the light, and a park bench became his home and the "bread-line" his chief makeshift of subsistence.

He stood now in the enfolding drizzle, sodden, stupefied with fatigue. Before and behind stretched the line. There was no talking. There was no sound. The street was empty. It was so still that the passing of a cable car in the adjoining thoroughfare grated like prolonged rolling explosions, beginning and ending at immeasurable distances. The drizzle descended incessantly. After a long time midnight struck.

There was something ominous and gravely impressive in this interminable line of dark figures, close-pressed, soundless; a crowd, yet absolutely still; a close-packed silent file, waiting, waiting in the vast deserted night-ridden street; waiting without a word, without a movement, there under the night and under the slow moving mists of rain.

Few in the crowd were professional beggars. Most of them were workmen, long since out of work, forced into idleness by long-continued "hard times," by ill luck, by sickness. To them the "bread-line" was a God-send. At least they could not starve. Between jobs here in the end was something to hold them up, a small platform, as it were, above the sweep of black water, where for a moment they might pause and take breath before the plunge.

The period of waiting on this night of rain seemed endless to those silent, hungry men; but at length there was a stir. The line moved. The side door opened. Ah, at last. They were going to hand out the bread.

But instead of the usual white-aproned undercook with his crowded hampers there now appeared in the doorway a new man — a young fellow, who looked like a bookkeeper's assistant. He bore in his hand a placard, which he tacked to the outside of the door. Then he disappeared within the bakery, locking the door after him.

A shudder of poignant despair, an unformed inarticulate sense of calamity, seemed to run from end to end of the line. What had happened? Those in the rear, unable to read the placard, surged forward, a sense of bitter disappointment clutching at their hearts.

The line broke up, disintegrated into a shapeless throng — a throng that crowded forward and collected in front of the shut door whereon the placard was affixed. Lewiston, with the others, pushed forward. On the placard he read these words:

> Owing to the fact that the price of grain has been increased to two dollars a bushel, there will be no distribution of bread from this bakery until further notice.

Lewiston turned away, dumb, bewildered. Till morning he walked the streets, going on without purpose, without direction. But now at last his luck had turned. Overnight the wheel of his fortunes had creaked and swung upon its axis, and before noon he had found a job in the street-cleaning brigade. In the course of time he rose to be first shift boss, then deputy-inspector, then inspector, promoted to the dignity of driving in a red wagon with rubber tires and drawing a salary instead of mere wages. The wife was sent for and a new start made.

♫♫

But Lewiston never forgot. Dimly he began to see the significance of things. Caught once in the cogs and wheels of a great and terrible engine, he had seen — none better — its workings. Of all the men who had vainly stood in the "bread-line" on that rainy night in early summer, he, perhaps, had been the only one who had struggled up to the surface again. How many others had gone down in the great ebb? Grim question; he dared not think how many.

He had seen the two ends of a great wheat operation, a battle between Bear and Bull. The stories (subsequently published in the city's press) of Truslow's counter-move in selling Hornung his own wheat, supplied the unseen section. The farmer — he who raised the wheat — was ruined upon one hand; the workingman — he who consumed it — was ruined upon the other. But between the two, the great operators, who never saw the wheat they traded in, bought and sold the world's food, gambled in the nourishment of entire nations, practised their tricks, their chicanery and oblique shifty "deals," were reconciled in their differences, and went on through their appointed way, jovial, contented, enthroned, and unassailable.

Paul Lawrence Dunbar
The Lynching of Jube Benson

Although he is primarily known as a poet, Paul Lawrence Dunbar also wrote a good deal of fiction, including several novels and four volumes of short stories. Born in Dayton, Ohio, where he was friends with Orville Wright, Dunbar went on to become one of the first African American writers to generate a wide readership within all races. "The Lynching of Jube Benson" appeared in *The Heart of Happy Hollow* in 1904 and became popular as a powerful work of protest against racial assumptions and mob violence. The central theme of moral responsibility, a matter of agonizing reflection by the internal narrator, places the story in the tradition of Realism, although some readers have emphasized the Deterministic power of racism that leads to the death of Jube Benson. Dunbar's skill in the rendering of dialect in his verse is here employed in the speech of the central character, linking the device to Local Color.

Paul Lawrence Dunbar, "The Lynching of Jube Benson," *The Heart of Happy Hollow* (New York: Dodd, Mead & Company, 1904), 223–40.

Gordon Fairfax's library held but three men, but the air was dense with clouds of smoke. The talk had drifted from one topic to another much as the smoke wreaths had puffed, floated, and thinned away. Then Handon Gay, who was an ambitious young reporter, spoke of a lynching story in a recent magazine, and the matter of punishment without trial put new life into the conversation.

"I should like to see a real lynching," said Gay rather callously.

"Well, I should hardly express it that way," said Fairfax, "but if a real, live lynching were to come my way, I should not avoid it."

"I should," spoke the other from the depths of his chair, where he had been puffing in moody silence. Judged by his hair, which was freely sprinkled with gray, the speaker might have been a man of forty-five or fifty, but his face, though lined and serious, was youthful, the face of a man hardly past thirty.

"What, you, Dr. Melville? Why, I thought that you physicians wouldn't weaken at anything."

"I have seen one such affair," said the doctor gravely, "in fact, I took a prominent part in it."

"Tell us about it," said the reporter, feeling for his pencil and note-book, which he was, nevertheless, careful to hide from the speaker.

The men drew their chairs eagerly up to the doctor's, but for a minute he did not seem to see them, but sat gazing abstractedly into the fire, then he took a long draw upon his cigar and began:

"I can see it all very vividly now. It was in the summer time and about seven years ago. I was practising at the time down in the little town of Bradford. It was a small and primitive place, just the location for an impecunious medical man, recently out of college.

"In lieu of a regular office, I attended to business in the first of two rooms which I rented from Hiram Daly, one of the more prosperous of the townsmen. Here I boarded and here also came my patients — white and black — whites from every section, and blacks from 'nigger town,' as the west portion of the place was called.

"The people about me were most of them coarse and rough, but they were simple and generous, and as time passed on I had about abandoned my intention of seeking distinction in wider fields and determined to settle into the place of a modest country doctor. This was rather a strange conclusion for a young man to arrive at, and I will not deny that the presence in the house of my host's beautiful young daughter, Annie, had something to do with my decision. She was a beautiful young girl of seventeen or eighteen, and very far superior to her surroundings. She had a native grace and a pleasing way about her that made everybody that came under her spell her abject slave. White and black who knew her loved her, and none, I thought, more deeply and respectfully than Jube Benson, the black man of all work about the place.

"He was a fellow whom everybody trusted; an apparently steady-going, grinning sort, as we used to call him. Well, he was completely under Miss Annie's thumb, and would fetch and carry for her like a faithful dog. As soon as he saw that I began to care for Annie, and anybody could see that, he transferred some of his allegiance to me and became my faithful servitor also. Never did a man have a more devoted adherent in his wooing than did I, and many a one of Annie's tasks which he volunteered to do gave her an extra hour with me. You can imagine that I liked the boy and you need not wonder any more that as both wooing and my practice waxed apace, I was content to give up my great ambitions and stay just where I was.

"It wasn't a very pleasant thing, then, to have an epidemic of typhoid break out in the town that kept me going so that I hardly had time for the courting that a fellow wants to carry on with his sweetheart while he is still young enough to call her his girl. I fumed, but duty was duty, and I kept to my work night and day. It was now that Jube proved how invaluable he was a coadjutor. He not only took messages to Annie, but brought sometimes little ones from her to me, and he would tell me little secret things that he had overheard her say that made me throb with joy and swear at him for repeating his mistress' conversation. But best of all, Jube was a perfect Cerberus, and no one on earth could have been more effective in keeping away or deluding the other young fellows who visited the Dalys. He would tell me of it afterwards, chuckling softly to himself. 'An', Doctah, I say to Mistah Hemp Stevens, "'Scuse us, Mistah Stevens, but Miss Annie, she des gone out," an' den he go outer de gate lookin' moughty lonesome. When Sam Elkins come, I say "Sh, Mistah Elkins, Miss Annie, she done tuk down," an' he say, "What, Jube, you don' reckon hit de ———" Den he stop an' look skeert, an' I say, "I feared hit is, Mistah Elkins," an' sheks my haid ez solemn. He goes outer de gate lookin' lak his bes' frien' done daid, an' all de time Miss Annie behine de cu'tain ovah de po'ch des' a laffin' fit to kill.'

"Jube was a most admirable liar, but what could I do? He knew that I was a young fool of a hypocrite, and when I would rebuke him for these deceptions, he would give way and roll on the floor in an excess of delighted laughter until from very contagion I had to join him — and, well, there was no need of my preaching when there had been no beginning to his repentance and when there must ensue a continuance of his wrong-doing.

"This thing went on for over three months, and then, pouf! I was down like a shot. My patients were nearly all up, but the reaction from overwork made me an easy victim of the lurking germs. Then Jube loomed up as a nurse. He put everyone else aside, and with the doctor, a friend of mine from a neighbouring town, took entire charge of me. Even Annie herself was put aside, and I was cared for as tenderly as a baby. Tom, that was my physician and friend, told me all about it afterward with tears in his eyes. Only he was a big, blunt man and his expressions did not convey all that he meant. He told me how my nigger had nursed me as if I were a sick kitten and he my mother. Of how fiercely he guarded his right to be the sole one to 'do' for me, as he called it, and how, when the crisis came, he hovered, weeping, but hopeful, at my bedside, until it was safely passed, when they drove him, weak and exhausted, from the room. As for me, I knew little about it at the time, and cared less. I was too busy in my fight with death. To my chimerical vision there was only a black but gentle demon that came and went, alternating with a white fairy, who would insist on coming in on her head, growing larger and larger and then dissolving. But the pathos and devotion in the story lost nothing in my blunt friend's telling.

"It was during the period of a long convalescence, however, that I came to know my humble ally as he really was, devoted to the point of abjectness. There were times when for very shame at his goodness to me, I would beg him to go away, to do something else. He would go, but before I had time to realise that I was not being ministered to, he would be back at my side, grinning and pottering just the same. He manufactured duties for the joy of performing them. He pretended to see desires in me that I never had, because he liked to pander to them, and when I became entirely exasperated, and ripped out a good round oath, he chuckled with the remark, 'Dah, now, you sholy is gittin' well. Nevah did hyeah a man anywhaih nigh Jo'dan's sho' cuss lak dat.'

"Why, I grew to love him, love him, oh, yes, I loved him as well — oh, what am I saying? All human love and gratitude are damned poor things; excuse me, gentlemen, this isn't a pleasant story. The truth is usually a nasty thing to stand.

"It was not six months after that that my friendship to Jube, which he had been at such great pains to win, was put to too severe a test.

"It was in the summer time again, and as business was slack, I had ridden over to see my friend, Dr. Tom. I had spent a good part of the day there, and it was past four o'clock when I rode leisurely into Bradford. I was in a particularly joyous mood and no premonition of the impending catastrophe oppressed me. No sense of sorrow, present or to come, forced itself upon me, even when I saw men hurrying through the almost deserted streets. When I got within sight of my home and saw a crowd surrounding it, I was only interested sufficiently to spur my horse into a jog trot, which brought me up to the throng, when something in the sullen, settled horror in the men's faces gave me a sudden, sick thrill. They whispered a word to me, and without a thought, save for Annie, the girl who had been so surely growing into my heart, I leaped from the saddle and tore my way through the people to the house.

"It was Annie, poor girl, bruised and bleeding, her face and dress torn from struggling. They were gathered round her with white faces, and, oh, with what terrible patience they were trying to gain from her fluttering lips the name of her murderer. They made way for me and I knelt at her side. She was beyond my skill, and my will merged with theirs. One thought was in our minds.

"'Who?' I asked.

"Her eyes half opened, 'That black —— ' She fell back into my arms dead.

"We turned and looked at each other. The mother had broken down and was weeping, but the face of the father was like iron.

"'It is enough,' he said; 'Jube has disappeared.' He went to the door and said to the expectant crowd, 'She is dead.'

"I heard the angry roar without swelling up like the noise of a flood, and then I heard the sudden movement of many feet as the men separated into searching parties, and laying the dead girl back upon her couch, I took my rifle and went out to join them.

"As if by intuition the knowledge had passed among the men that Jube Benson had disappeared, and he, by common consent, was to be the object of our search. Fully a dozen of the citizens had seen him hastening toward the woods and noted his skulking air, but as he had grinned in his old good-natured way they had, at the time, thought nothing of it. Now, however, the diabolical reason of his slyness was apparent. He had been shrewd enough to disarm suspicion, and by now was far away. Even Mrs. Daly, who was visiting with a neighbour, had seen him stepping out by a back way, and had said with a laugh, 'I reckon that black rascal's a-running off somewhere.' Oh, if she had only known.

"'To the woods! To the woods!' that was the cry, and away we went, each with the determination not to shoot, but to bring the culprit alive into town, and then to deal with him as his crime deserved.

"I cannot describe the feelings I experienced as I went out that night to beat the woods for this human tiger. My heart smouldered within me like a coal, and I went forward under the impulse of a will that was half my own, half some more malignant power's. My throat throbbed drily, but water nor whiskey would not have quenched my thirst. The thought has come to me since that now I could interpret the panther's desire for blood and sympathise with it, but then I thought nothing. I simply went forward, and watched, watched with burning eyes for a familiar form that I had looked for as often before with such different emotions.

"Luck or ill-luck, which you will, was with our party, and just as dawn was graying the sky, we came upon our quarry crouched in the corner of a fence. It was only half light, and we might have passed, but my eyes had caught sight of him, and I raised the cry. We levelled our guns and he rose and came toward us.

"'I t'ought you wa'n't gwine see me,' he said sullenly, 'I didn't mean no harm.'

"'Harm!'

"Some of the men took the word up with oaths, others were ominously silent.

"We gathered around him like hungry beasts, and I began to see terror dawning in his eyes. He turned to me, 'I's moughty glad you's hyeah, doc,' he said, 'you ain't gwine let 'em whup me.'

"'Whip you, you hound,' I said, 'I'm going to see you hanged,' and in the excess of my passion I struck him full on the mouth. He made a motion as if to resent the blow against even such great odds, but controlled himself.

"'W'y, doctah,' he exclaimed in the saddest voice I have ever heard, 'w'y, doctah! I ain't stole nuffin' o' yo'n, an' I was comin' back. I only run off to see my gal, Lucy, ovah to de Centah.'

"'You lie!' I said, and my hands were busy helping the others bind him upon a horse. Why did I do it? I don't know. A false education, I reckon, one false from the beginning. I saw his black face glooming there in the half light, and I could only think of him as a monster. It's tradition. At first I was told that the black man would catch me, and when I got over that, they taught me that the devil was black, and when I had recovered from the sickness of that belief, here were Jube and his fellows with faces of menacing blackness. There was only one conclusion: This black man stood for all the powers of evil, the result of whose machinations had been gathering in my mind from childhood up. But this has nothing to do with what happened.

"After firing a few shots to announce our capture, we rode back into town with Jube. The ingathering parties from all directions met us as we made our way up to the house. All was very quiet and orderly. There was no doubt that it was as the papers would have said, a gathering of the best citizens. It was a gathering of stern, determined men, bent on a terrible vengeance.

"We took Jube into the house, into the room where the corpse lay. At sight of it, he gave a scream like an animal's and his face went the colour of storm-blown water. This was enough to condemn him. We divined, rather than heard, his cry of 'Miss Ann, Miss Ann, oh, my God, doc, you don't t'ink I done it?'

"Hungry hands were ready. We hurried him out into the yard. A rope was ready. A tree was at hand. Well, that part was the least of it, save that Hiram Daly stepped aside to let me be the first to pull upon the rope. It was lax at first. Then it tightened, and I felt the quivering soft weight resist my muscles. Other hands joined, and Jube swung off his feet.

"No one was masked. We knew each other. Not even the culprit's face was covered, and the last I remember of him as he went into the air was a look of sad reproach that will remain with me until I meet him face to face again.

"We were tying the end of the rope to a tree, where the dead man might hang as a warning to his fellows, when a terrible cry chilled us to the marrow.

"'Cut 'im down, cut 'im down, he ain't guilty. We got de one. Cut him down, fu' Gawd's sake. Here's de man, we foun' him hidin' in de barn!'

"Jube's brother, Ben, and another Negro, came rushing toward us, half dragging, half carrying a miserable-looking wretch between them. Someone cut the rope and Jube dropped lifeless to the ground.

"'Oh, my Gawd, he's daid, he's daid!' wailed the brother, but with blazing eyes he brought his captive into the centre of the group, and we saw in the full light the scratched face of Tom Skinner — the worst white ruffian in the town — but the face we saw was not as we were accustomed to see it, merely smeared with dirt. It was blackened to imitate a Negro's.

"God forgive me; I could not wait to try to resuscitate Jube. I knew he was already past help, so I rushed into the house and to the dead girl's side. In the excitement they had not yet washed or laid her out. Carefully, carefully, I searched underneath her broken finger nails. There was skin there. I took it out, the little curled pieces, and went with it to my office.

"There, determinedly, I examined it under a powerful glass, and read my own doom. It was the skin of a white man, and in it were embedded strands of short, brown hair or beard.

"How I went out to tell the waiting crowd I do not know, for something kept crying in my ears, 'Blood guilty! Blood guilty!'

"The men went away stricken into silence and awe. The new prisoner attempted neither denial nor plea. When they were gone I would have helped Ben carry his brother in, but he waved me away fiercely, 'You he'ped murder my brothah, you dat was *his* frien', go 'way, go 'way! I'll tek him home myse'f.' I could only respect his wish, and he and his comrade took up the dead man and between them bore him up the street on which the sun was now shining full.

"I saw the few men who had not skulked indoors uncover as they passed, and I — I — stood there between the two murdered ones, while all the while something in my ears kept crying, 'Blood guilty! Blood guilty!'"

The doctor's head dropped into his hands and he sat for some time in silence, which was broken by neither of the men, then he rose, saying, "Gentlemen that was my last lynching."

Edith Wharton
The Other Two

Widely regarded as the most perfectly crafted of Edith Wharton's short fiction, "The Other Two" was published in *Collier's Weekly* in February 1904 prior to being collected in *The Descent of Man and Other Stories* later that year. It deals with divorce, a matter increasingly common at the turn of the century, when the new economic and social freedom for women had made terminating an unhappy marriage a viable option. Remarkably, however, the narrative perspective is allied with the third husband in the case, not with Alice Waythorn, and it is through his eyes, and within his sensibility, that the plot unravels. Wharton most often writes of feminist issues from the point of view of a woman, as she does in her most celebrated novels, including *The House of Mirth, The Age of Innocence, The Custom of the Country,* and *Summer*. But she also produced eleven volumes of short fiction admired for their carefully crafted plots, their adroit development of character, and their elegant style, which was often compared to that of Henry James. "The Other Two," which concentrates on the changing roles for women in the urban culture of New York, exemplifies the author's subtle exploration of the psychology of divorce and remarriage, a subject handled with gentle humor and emotional depth.

Edith Wharton, "The Other Two," *The Descent of Man and Other Stories* (New York: Charles Scribner's Sons, 1904), 71–105.

I

Waythorn, on the drawing-room hearth, waited for his wife to come down to dinner.

It was their first night under his own roof, and he was surprised at his thrill of boyish agitation. He was not so old, to be sure — his glass gave him little more than the five-and-thirty years to which his wife confessed — but he had fancied himself already in the temperate zone; yet here he was listening for her step with a tender sense of all it symbolised, with some old trail of verse about the garlanded nuptial door-posts floating through his enjoyment of the pleasant room and the good dinner just beyond it.

They had been hastily recalled from their honeymoon by the illness of Lily Haskett, the child of Mrs. Waythorn's first marriage. The little girl, at Waythorn's desire, had been transferred to his house on the day of her mother's wedding, and the doctor, on their arrival, broke the news that she was ill with typhoid, but declared that all the symptoms were favourable. Lily could show twelve years of unblemished health, and the case promised to be a light one. The nurse spoke as reassuringly, and after a moment of alarm Mrs. Waythorn had adjusted herself to the situation. She was very fond of Lily — her affection for the child had perhaps been her decisive charm in Waythorn's eyes — but she had the perfectly balanced nerves which her little girl had inherited, and no woman ever wasted less tissue in unproductive worry. Waythorn was therefore quite prepared to see her come in presently, a little late because of a last look at Lily, but as serene and well-appointed as if her good-night kiss had been laid on the brow of health. Her composure was restful to him; it acted as ballast to his somewhat unstable sensibilities. As he pictured her bending over the child's bed he thought how soothing her presence must be in illness: her very step would prognosticate recovery.

His own life had been a gray one, from temperament rather than circumstance, and he had been drawn to her by the unperturbed gaiety which kept her fresh and elastic at an age when most women's activities are growing either slack or febrile. He knew what was said about her; for, popular as she was, there had always been a faint undercurrent of detraction. When she had appeared in New York, nine or ten years earlier, as the pretty Mrs. Haskett whom Gus Varick had unearthed somewhere — was it in Pittsburg or Utica? — society, while promptly accepting her, had reserved the right to cast a doubt on its own indiscrimination. Enquiry, however, established her undoubted connection with a socially reigning family, and explained her recent divorce as the natural result of a runaway match at seventeen; and as nothing was known of Mr. Haskett it was easy to believe the worst of him.

Alice Haskett's remarriage with Gus Varick was a passport to the set whose recognition she coveted, and for a few years the Varicks were the most popular couple in town. Unfortunately the alliance was brief and stormy, and this time the husband had his champions. Still, even Varick's stanchest supporters admitted that he was not meant for matrimony, and Mrs. Varick's grievances were of a nature to bear the inspection of the New York courts. A New York divorce is in itself a diploma of virtue, and in the semi-widowhood of this second separation Mrs. Varick took on an air of sanctity, and was allowed to confide her wrongs to some of the most scrupulous ears in town. But when it was known that she was to marry Waythorn there was a momentary reaction. Her best friends would have preferred to see her remain in the rôle of the injured wife, which was as becoming to her as crape to a rosy complexion. True, a decent time had elapsed, and it was not even suggested that Waythorn had supplanted his predecessor. People shook their heads over him, however, and one grudging friend, to whom

he affirmed that he took the step with his eyes open, replied oracularly: "Yes —
and with your ears shut."

Waythorn could afford to smile at these innuendoes. In the Wall Street phrase,
he had "discounted" them. He knew that society has not yet adapted itself to the
consequences of divorce, and that till the adaptation takes place every woman
who uses the freedom the law accords her must be her own social justification.
Waythorn had an amused confidence in his wife's ability to justify herself. His expectations were fulfilled, and before the wedding took place Alice Varick's group
had rallied openly to her support. She took it all imperturbably: she had a way of
surmounting obstacles without seeming to be aware of them, and Waythorn
looked back with wonder at the trivialities over which he had worn his nerves thin.
He had the sense of having found refuge in a richer, warmer nature than his own,
and his satisfaction, at the moment, was humourously summed up in the thought
that his wife, when she had done all she could for Lily, would not be ashamed to
come down and enjoy a good dinner.

The anticipation of such enjoyment was not, however, the sentiment expressed by Mrs. Waythorn's charming face when she presently joined him.
Though she had put on her most engaging teagown she had neglected to assume the smile that went with it, and Waythorn thought he had never seen her
look so nearly worried.

"What is it?" he asked. "Is anything wrong with Lily?"

"No; I've just been in and she's still sleeping." Mrs. Waythorn hesitated. "But
something tiresome has happened."

He had taken her two hands, and now perceived that he was crushing a paper between them.

"This letter?"

"Yes — Mr. Haskett has written — I mean his lawyer has written."

Waythorn felt himself flush uncomfortably. He dropped his wife's hands.

"What about?"

"About seeing Lily. You know the courts —"

"Yes, yes," he interrupted nervously.

Nothing was known about Haskett in New York. He was vaguely supposed
to have remained in the outer darkness from which his wife had been rescued,
and Waythorn was one of the few who were aware that he had given up his business in Utica and followed her to New York in order to be near his little girl. In
the days of his wooing, Waythorn had often met Lily on the doorstep, rosy and
smiling, on her way "to see papa."

"I am so sorry," Mrs. Waythorn murmured.

He roused himself. "What does he want?"

"He wants to see her. You know she goes to him once a week."

"Well — he doesn't expect her to go to him now, does he?"

"No — he has heard of her illness; but he expects to come here."

"Here?"

Mrs. Waythorn reddened under his gaze. They looked away from each other.

"I'm afraid he has the right. . . . You'll see. . . ." She made a proffer of the letter.

Waythorn moved away with a gesture of refusal. He stood staring about the softly lighted room, which a moment before had seemed so full of bridal intimacy.

"I'm so sorry," she repeated. "If Lily could have been moved —"

"That's out of the question," he returned impatiently.

"I suppose so."

Her lip was beginning to tremble, and he felt himself a brute.

"He must come, of course," he said. "When is — his day?"

"I'm afraid — to-morrow."

"Very well. Send a note in the morning."

The butler entered to announce dinner.

Waythorn turned to his wife. "Come — you must be tired. It's beastly, but try to forget about it," he said, drawing her hand through his arm.

"You're so good, dear. I'll try," she whispered back.

Her face cleared at once, and as she looked at him across the flowers, between the rosy candle-shades, he saw her lips waver back into a smile.

"How pretty everything is!" she sighed luxuriously.

He turned to the butler. "The champagne at once, please. Mrs. Waythorn is tired."

In a moment or two their eyes met above the sparkling glasses. Her own were quite clear and untroubled: he saw that she had obeyed his injunction and forgotten.

II

Waythorn, the next morning, went down town earlier than usual. Haskett was not likely to come till the afternoon, but the instinct of flight drove him forth. He meant to stay away all day — he had thoughts of dining at his club. As his door closed behind him he reflected that before he opened it again it would have admitted another man who had as much right to enter it as himself, and the thought filled him with a physical repugnance.

He caught the "elevated" at the employés' hour, and found himself crushed between two layers of pendulous humanity. At Eighth Street the man facing him wriggled out, and another took his place. Waythorn glanced up and saw that it was Gus Varick. The men were so close together that it was impossible to ignore the smile of recognition on Varick's handsome overblown face. And after all — why not? They had always been on good terms, and Varick had been divorced before Waythorn's attentions to his wife began. The two exchanged a word on the perennial grievance of the congested trains, and when a seat at their side was miraculously left empty the instinct of self-preservation made Waythorn slip into it after Varick.

The latter drew the stout man's breath of relief. "Lord — I was beginning to feel like a pressed flower." He leaned back, looking unconcernedly at Waythorn. "Sorry to hear that Sellers is knocked out again."

"Sellers?" echoed Waythorn, starting at his partner's name.

Varick looked surprised. "You didn't know he was laid up with the gout?"

"No. I've been away — I only got back last night." Waythorn felt himself reddening in anticipation of the other's smile.

"Ah — yes; to be sure. And Sellers's attack came on two days ago. I'm afraid he's pretty bad. Very awkward for me, as it happens, because he was just putting through a rather important thing for me."

"Ah?" Waythorn wondered vaguely since when Varick had been dealing in "important things." Hitherto he had dabbled only in the shallow pools of speculation, with which Waythorn's office did not usually concern itself.

It occurred to him that Varick might be talking at random, to relieve the strain of their propinquity. That strain was becoming momentarily more apparent to Waythorn, and when, at Cortlandt Street, he caught sight of an acquaintance and had a sudden vision of the picture he and Varick must present to an initiated eye, he jumped up with a muttered excuse.

"I hope you'll find Sellers better," said Varick civilly, and he stammered back: "If I can be of any use to you —" and let the departing crowd sweep him to the platform.

At his office he heard that Sellers was in fact ill with the gout, and would probably not be able to leave the house for some weeks.

"I'm sorry it should have happened so, Mr. Waythorn," the senior clerk said with affable significance. "Mr. Sellers was very much upset at the idea of giving you such a lot of extra work just now."

"Oh, that's no matter," said Waythorn hastily. He secretly welcomed the pressure of additional business, and was glad to think that, when the day's work was over, he would have to call at his partner's on the way home.

He was late for luncheon, and turned in at the nearest restaurant instead of going to his club. The place was full, and the waiter hurried him to the back of the room to capture the only vacant table. In the cloud of cigar-smoke Waythorn did not at once distinguish his neighbours: but presently, looking about him, he saw Varick seated a few feet off. This time, luckily, they were too far apart for conversation, and Varick, who faced another way, had probably not even seen him; but there was an irony in their renewed nearness.

Varick was said to be fond of good living, and as Waythorn sat despatching his hurried luncheon he looked across half enviously at the other's leisurely degustation of his meal. When Waythorn first saw him he had been helping himself with critical deliberation to a bit of Camembert at the ideal point of liquefaction, and now, the cheese removed, he was just pouring his *café double* from its little two-storied earthen pot. He poured slowly, his ruddy profile bent above the task, and one beringed white hand steadying the lid of the coffee-pot; then he stretched his other hand to the decanter of cognac at his elbow, filled a liqueur-glass, took a tentative sip, and poured the brandy into his coffee-cup.

Waythorn watched him in a kind of fascination. What was he thinking of — only of the flavour of the coffee and the liqueur? Had the morning's meeting left no more trace in his thoughts than on his face? Had his wife so completely passed out of his life that even this odd encounter with her present husband, within a week after her remarriage, was no more than an incident in his day? And as Waythorn mused, another idea struck him: had Haskett ever met Varick as Varick and he had just met? The recollection of Haskett perturbed him, and he rose and left the restaurant, taking a circuitous way out to escape the placid irony of Varick's nod.

It was after seven when Waythorn reached home. He thought the footman who opened the door looked at him oddly.

"How is Miss Lily?" he asked in haste.

"Doing very well, sir. A gentleman —"

"Tell Barlow to put off dinner for half an hour," Waythorn cut him off, hurrying upstairs.

He went straight to his room and dressed without seeing his wife. When he reached the drawing-room she was there, fresh and radiant. Lily's day had been good; the doctor was not coming back that evening.

At dinner Waythorn told her of Sellers's illness and of the resulting complications. She listened sympathetically, adjuring him not to let himself be overworked, and asking vague feminine questions about the routine of the office. Then she gave him the chronicle of Lily's day; quoted the nurse and doctor, and told him who had called to inquire. He had never seen her more serene and unruffled. It struck him, with a curious pang, that she was very happy in being with him, so happy that she found a childish pleasure in rehearsing the trivial incidents of her day.

After dinner they went to the library, and the servant put the coffee and liqueurs on a low table before her and left the room. She looked singularly soft and girlish in her rosy pale dress, against the dark leather of one of his bachelor armchairs. A day earlier the contrast would have charmed him.

He turned away now, choosing a cigar with affected deliberation.

"Did Haskett come?" he asked, with his back to her.

"Oh, yes — he came."

"You didn't see him, of course?"

She hesitated a moment. "I let the nurse see him."

That was all. There was nothing more to ask. He swung round toward her, applying a match to his cigar. Well, the thing was over for a week, at any rate. He would try not to think of it. She looked up at him, a trifle rosier than usual, with a smile in her eyes.

"Ready for your coffee, dear?"

He leaned against the mantelpiece, watching her as she lifted the coffee-pot. The lamplight struck a gleam from her bracelets and tipped her soft hair with brightness. How light and slender she was, and how each gesture flowed into the next! She seemed a creature all compact of harmonies. As the thought of Haskett receded, Waythorn felt himself yielding again to the joy of possessorship. They were his, those white hands with their flitting motions, his the light haze of hair, the lips and eyes. . . .

She set down the coffee-pot, and reaching for the decanter of cognac, measured off a liqueur-glass and poured it into his cup.

Waythorn uttered a sudden exclamation.

"What is the matter?" she said, startled.

"Nothing; only — I don't take cognac in my coffee."

"Oh, how stupid of me," she cried.

Their eyes met, and she blushed a sudden agonised red.

III

Ten days later, Mr. Sellers, still house-bound, asked Waythorn to call on his way down town. The senior partner, with his swaddled foot propped up by the fire, greeted his associate with an air of embarrassment.

"I'm sorry, my dear fellow; I've got to ask you to do an awkward thing for me."

Waythorn waited, and the other went on, after a pause apparently given to the arrangement of his phrases: "The fact is, when I was knocked out I had just gone into a rather complicated piece of business for — Gus Varick."

"Well?" said Waythorn, with an attempt to put him at his ease.

"Well — it's this way: Varick came to me the day before my attack. He had evidently had an inside tip from somebody, and had made about a hundred thousand. He came to me for advice, and I suggested his going in with Vanderlyn."

"Oh, the deuce!" Waythorn exclaimed. He saw in a flash what had happened. The investment was an alluring one, but required negotiation. He listened quietly while Sellers put the case before him, and, the statement ended, he said: "You think I ought to see Varick?"

"I'm afraid I can't as yet. The doctor is obdurate. And this thing can't wait. I hate to ask you, but no one else in the office knows the ins and outs of it."

Waythorn stood silent. He did not care a farthing for the success of Varick's venture, but the honour of the office was to be considered, and he could hardly refuse to oblige his partner.

"Very well," he said, "I'll do it."

That afternoon, apprised by telephone, Varick called at the office. Waythorn, waiting in his private room, wondered what the others thought of it. The newspapers, at the time of Mrs. Waythorn's marriage, had acquainted their readers with every detail of her previous matrimonial ventures, and Waythorn could fancy the clerks smiling behind Varick's back as he was ushered in.

Varick bore himself admirably. He was easy without being undignified, and Waythorn was conscious of cutting a much less impressive figure. Varick had no experience of business, and the talk prolonged itself for nearly an hour while Waythorn set forth with scrupulous precision the details of the proposed transaction.

"I'm awfully obliged to you," Varick said as he rose. "The fact is I'm not used to having much money to look after, and I don't want to make an ass of myself —" He smiled, and Waythorn could not help noticing that there was something pleasant about his smile. "It feels uncommonly queer to have enough cash to pay one's bills. I'd have sold my soul for it a few years ago!"

Waythorn winced at the allusion. He had heard it rumoured that a lack of funds had been one of the determining causes of the Varick separation, but it did not occur to him that Varick's words were intentional. It seemed more likely that the desire to keep clear of embarrassing topics had fatally drawn him into one. Waythorn did not wish to be outdone in civility.

"We'll do the best we can for you," he said. "I think this is a good thing you're in."

"Oh, I'm sure it's immense. It's awfully good of you —" Varick broke off, embarrassed. "I suppose the thing's settled now — but if —"

"If anything happens before Sellers is about, I'll see you again," said Waythorn quietly. He was glad, in the end, to appear the more self-possessed of the two.

⚜

The course of Lily's illness ran smooth, and as the days passed Waythorn grew used to the idea of Haskett's weekly visit. The first time the day came round, he stayed out late, and questioned his wife as to the visit on his return. She replied at once that Haskett had merely seen the nurse downstairs, as the doctor did not wish any one in the child's sick-room till after the crisis.

The following week Waythorn was again conscious of the recurrence of the day, but had forgotten it by the time he came home to dinner. The crisis of the disease came a few days later, with a rapid decline of fever, and the little girl was pronounced out of danger. In the rejoicing which ensued the thought of Haskett passed out of Waythorn's mind, and one afternoon, letting himself into the house with a latchkey, he went straight to his library without noticing a shabby hat and umbrella in the hall.

In the library he found a small effaced-looking man with a thinnish gray beard sitting on the edge of a chair. The stranger might have been a piano-tuner, or one of those mysteriously efficient persons who are summoned in emergencies to adjust some detail of the domestic machinery. He blinked at Waythorn through a pair of gold-rimmed spectacles and said mildly: "Mr. Waythorn, I presume? I am Lily's father."

Waythorn flushed. "Oh —" he stammered uncomfortably. He broke off, disliking to appear rude. Inwardly he was trying to adjust the actual Haskett to the image of him projected by his wife's reminiscences. Waythorn had been allowed to infer that Alice's first husband was a brute.

"I am sorry to intrude," said Haskett, with his over-the-counter politeness.

"Don't mention it," returned Waythorn, collecting himself. "I suppose the nurse has been told?"

"I presume so. I can wait," said Haskett. He had a resigned way of speaking, as though life had worn down his natural powers of resistance.

Waythorn stood on the threshold, nervously pulling off his gloves.

"I'm sorry you've been detained. I will send for the nurse," he said; and as he opened the door he added with an effort: "I'm glad we can give you a good report of Lily." He winced as the *we* slipped out, but Haskett seemed not to notice it.

"Thank you, Mr. Waythorn. It's been an anxious time for me."

"Ah, well, that's past. Soon she'll be able to go to you." Waythorn nodded and passed out.

In his own room he flung himself down with a groan. He hated the womanish sensibility which made him suffer so acutely from the grotesque chances of life. He had known when he married that his wife's former husbands were both living, and that amid the multiplied contacts of modern existence there were a thousand chances to one that he would run against one or the other, yet he found himself as much disturbed by his brief encounter with Haskett as though the laws had not obligingly removed all difficulties in the way of their meeting.

Waythorn sprang up and began to pace the room nervously. He had not suffered half as much from his two meetings with Varick. It was Haskett's presence in his own house that made the situation so intolerable. He stood still, hearing steps in the passage.

"This way, please," he heard the nurse say. Haskett was being taken upstairs, then: not a corner of the house but was open to him. Waythorn dropped into another chair, staring vaguely ahead of him. On his dressing-table stood a photograph of Alice, taken when he had first known her. She was Alice Varick then — how fine and exquisite he had thought her! Those were Varick's pearls about her neck. At Waythorn's instance they had been returned before her marriage. Had Haskett ever given her any trinkets — and what had become of them, Waythorn wondered? He realised suddenly that he knew very little of Haskett's past or present situation; but from the man's appearance and manner of speech he could reconstruct with curious precision the surroundings of Alice's first marriage. And it startled him to think that she had, in the background of her life, a phase of existence so different from anything with which he had connected her. Varick, what-ever his faults, was a gentleman, in the conventional, traditional sense of the term: the sense which at that moment seemed, oddly enough, to have most meaning to Waythorn. He and Varick had the same social habits, spoke the same language, understood the same allusions. But this other man . . . it was grotesquely upper-most in Waythorn's mind that Haskett had worn a made-up tie attached with an elastic. Why should that ridiculous detail symbolise the whole man? Waythorn was exasperated by his own paltriness, but the fact of the tie expanded, forced it-self on him, became as it were the key to Alice's past. He could see her, as Mrs. Haskett, sitting in a "front parlour" furnished in plush, with a pianola, and a copy of "Ben Hur" on the centre-table. He could see her going to the theatre with Haskett — or perhaps even to a "Church Sociable" — she in a "picture hat" and Haskett in a black frock-coat, a little creased, with the made-up tie on an elastic. On the way home they would stop and look at the illuminated shop-windows, lingering over the photographs of New York actresses. On Sunday afternoons Haskett would take her for a walk, pushing Lily ahead of them in a white enam-elled perambulator, and Waythorn had a vision of the people they would stop and talk to. He could fancy how pretty Alice must have looked, in a dress adroitly con-structed from the hints of a New York fashion-paper, and how she must have looked down on the other women, chafing at her life, and secretly feeling that she belonged in a bigger place.

For the moment his foremost thought was one of wonder at the way in which she had shed the phase of existence which her marriage with Haskett im-plied. It was as if her whole aspect, every gesture, every inflection, every allu-sion, were a studied negation of that period of her life. If she had denied being married to Haskett she could hardly have stood more convicted of duplicity than in this obliteration of the self which had been his wife.

Waythorn started up, checking himself in the analysis of her motives. What right had he to create a fantastic effigy of her and then pass judgment on it? She had spoken vaguely of her first marriage as unhappy, had hinted, with becoming reti-cence, that Haskett had wrought havoc among her young illusions. . . . It was a pity for Waythorn's peace of mind that Haskett's very inoffensiveness shed a new light on the nature of those illusions. A man would rather think that his wife has been brutalised by her first husband than that the process has been reversed.

IV

"Mr. Waythorn, I don't like that French governess of Lily's."

Haskett, subdued and apologetic, stood before Waythorn in the library, re-volving his shabby hat in his hand.

Waythorn, surprised in his armchair over the evening paper, stared back per-plexedly at his visitor.

"You'll excuse my asking to see you," Haskett continued. "But this is my last visit, and I thought if I could have a word with you it would be a better way than writing to Mrs. Waythorn's lawyer."

Waythorn rose uneasily. He did not like the French governess either; but that was irrelevant.

"I am not so sure of that," he returned stiffly; "but since you wish it I will give your message to — my wife." He always hesitated over the possessive pronoun in addressing Haskett.

The latter sighed. "I don't know as that will help much. She didn't like it when I spoke to her."

Waythorn turned red. "When did you see her?" he asked.

"Not since the first day I came to see Lily — right after she was taken sick. I remarked to her then that I didn't like the governess."

Waythorn made no answer. He remembered distinctly that, after that first visit, he had asked his wife if she had seen Haskett. She had lied to him then, but she had respected his wishes since; and the incident cast a curious light on her character. He was sure she would not have seen Haskett that first day if she had divined that Waythorn would object, and the fact that she did not divine it was almost as disagreeable to the latter as the discovery that she had lied to him.

"I don't like the woman," Haskett was repeating with mild persistency. "She ain't straight, Mr. Waythorn — she'll teach the child to be underhand. I've noticed a change in Lily — she's too anxious to please — and she don't always tell the truth. She used to be the straightest child, Mr. Waythorn —" He broke off, his voice a little thick. "Not but what I want her to have a stylish education," he ended.

Waythorn was touched. "I'm sorry, Mr. Haskett; but frankly, I don't quite see what I can do."

Haskett hesitated. Then he laid his hat on the table, and advanced to the hearth-rug, on which Waythorn was standing. There was nothing aggressive in his manner, but he had the solemnity of a timid man resolved on a decisive measure.

"There's just one thing you can do, Mr. Waythorn," he said. "You can remind Mrs. Waythorn that, by the decree of the courts, I am entitled to have a voice in Lily's bringing up." He paused, and went on more deprecatingly: "I'm not the kind to talk about enforcing my rights, Mr. Waythorn. I don't know as I think a man is entitled to rights he hasn't known how to hold on to; but this business of the child is different. I've never let go there — and I never mean to."

⚭⚭

The scene left Waythorn deeply shaken. Shamefacedly, in indirect ways, he had been finding out about Haskett; and all that he had learned was favourable. The little man, in order to be near his daughter, had sold out his share in a profitable business in Utica, and accepted a modest clerkship in a New York manufacturing house. He boarded in a shabby street and had few acquaintances. His passion for Lily filled his life. Waythorn felt that this exploration of Haskett was like groping about with a dark-lantern in his wife's past; but he saw now that there were recesses his lantern had not explored. He had never enquired into the exact circumstances of his wife's first matrimonial rupture. On the surface all had been fair. It was she who had obtained the divorce, and the court had given her the child. But Waythorn knew how many ambiguities such a verdict might cover. The mere fact that Haskett retained a right over his daughter implied an unsuspected compromise. Waythorn was an idealist. He always refused to recognise unpleasant contingencies till he found himself confronted with them, and then he saw them followed by a spectral train of consequences. His next days were thus haunted, and he determined to try to lay the ghosts by conjuring them up in his wife's presence.

When he repeated Haskett's request a flame of anger passed over her face; but she subdued it instantly and spoke with a slight quiver of outraged motherhood.

"It is very ungentlemanly of him," she said.

The word grated on Waythorn. "That is neither here nor there. It's a bare question of rights."

She murmured: "It's not as if he could ever be a help to Lily —"

Waythorn flushed. This was even less to his taste. "The question is," he repeated, "what authority has he over her?"

She looked downward, twisting herself a little in her seat. "I am willing to see him — I thought you objected," she faltered.

In a flash he understood that she knew the extent of Haskett's claims. Perhaps it was not the first time she had resisted them.

"My objecting has nothing to do with it," he said coldly; "if Haskett has a right to be consulted you must consult him."

She burst into tears, and he saw that she expected him to regard her as a victim.

Haskett did not abuse his rights. Waythorn had felt miserably sure that he would not. But the governess was dismissed, and from time to time the little man demanded an interview with Alice. After the first outburst she accepted the situation with her usual adaptability. Haskett had once reminded Waythorn of the piano-tuner, and Mrs. Waythorn, after a month or two, appeared to class him with that domestic familiar. Waythorn could not but respect the father's tenacity. At first he had tried to cultivate the suspicion that Haskett might be "up to" something, that he had an object in securing a foothold in the house. But in his heart Waythorn was sure of Haskett's single-mindedness; he even guessed in the latter a mild contempt for such advantages as his relation with the Waythorns might offer. Haskett's sincerity of purpose made him invulnerable, and his successor had to accept him as a lien on the property.

⸎

Mr. Sellers was sent to Europe to recover from his gout, and Varick's affairs hung on Waythorn's hands. The negotiations were prolonged and complicated;

they necessitated frequent conferences between the two men, and the interests of the firm forbade Waythorn's suggesting that his client should transfer his business to another office.

Varick appeared well in the transaction. In moments of relaxation his coarse streak appeared, and Waythorn dreaded his geniality; but in the office he was concise and clear-headed, with a flattering deference to Waythorn's judgment. Their business relations being so affably established, it would have been absurd for the two men to ignore each other in society. The first time they met in a drawing-room, Varick took up their intercourse in the same easy key, and his hostess's grateful glance obliged Waythorn to respond to it. After that they ran across each other frequently, and one evening at a ball Waythorn, wandering through the remoter rooms, came upon Varick seated beside his wife. She coloured a little, and faltered in what she was saying; but Varick nodded to Waythorn without rising, and the latter strolled on.

In the carriage, on the way home, he broke out nervously: "I didn't know you spoke to Varick."

Her voice trembled a little. "It's the first time — he happened to be standing near me; I didn't know what to do. It's so awkward, meeting everywhere — and he said you had been very kind about some business."

"That's different," said Waythorn.

She paused a moment. "I'll do just as you wish," she returned pliantly. "I thought it would be less awkward to speak to him when we meet."

Her pliancy was beginning to sicken him. Had she really no will of her own — no theory about her relation to these men? She had accepted Haskett — did she mean to accept Varick? It was "less awkward," as she had said, and her instinct was to evade difficulties or to circumvent them. With sudden vividness Waythorn saw how the instinct had developed. She was "as easy as an old shoe" — a shoe that too many feet had worn. Her elasticity was the result of tension in too many different directions. Alice Haskett — Alice Varick — Alice Waythorn — she had been each in turn, and had left hanging to each name a little of her privacy, a little of her personality, a little of the inmost self where the unknown god abides.

"Yes — it's better to speak to Varick," said Waythorn wearily.

V

The winter wore on, and society took advantage of the Waythorns' acceptance of Varick. Harassed hostesses were grateful to them for bridging over a social difficulty, and Mrs. Waythorn was held up as a miracle of good taste. Some experimental spirits could not resist the diversion of throwing Varick and his former wife together, and there were those who thought he found a zest in the propinquity. But Mrs. Waythorn's conduct remained irreproachable. She neither avoided Varick nor sought him out. Even Waythorn could not but admit that she had discovered the solution of the newest social problem.

He had married her without giving much thought to that problem. He had fancied that a woman can shed her past like a man. But now he saw that Alice was bound to hers both by the circumstances which forced her into continued relation with it, and by the traces it had left on her nature. With grim irony Waythorn compared himself to a member of a syndicate. He held so many shares in his wife's personality and his predecessors were his partners in the business. If there had been any element of passion in the transaction he would have felt less deteriorated by it. The fact that Alice took her change of husbands like a change of weather reduced the situation to mediocrity. He could have forgiven her for blunders, for excesses; for resisting Haskett, for yielding to Varick; for anything but her acquiescence and her tact. She reminded him of a juggler tossing knives; but the knives were blunt and she knew they would never cut her.

And then, gradually, habit formed a protecting surface for his sensibilities. If he paid for each day's comfort with the small change of his illusions, he grew daily to value the comfort more and set less store upon the coin. He had drifted into a dulling propinquity with Haskett and Varick and he took refuge in the cheap revenge of satirising the situation. He even began to reckon up the advantages which accrued from it, to ask himself if it were not better to own a third of a wife who knew how to make a man happy than a whole one who had lacked opportunity to acquire the art. For it *was* an art, and made up, like all others, of concessions, eliminations and embellishments; of lights judiciously thrown and shadows skilfully softened. His wife knew exactly how to manage the lights, and he knew exactly to what training she owed her skill. He even tried to trace the source of his obligations, to discriminate between the influences which had combined to produce his domestic happiness: he perceived that Haskett's commonness had made Alice worship good breeding, while Varick's liberal construction of the marriage bond had taught her to value the conjugal virtues; so that he was directly indebted to his predecessors for the devotion which made his life easy if not inspiring.

From this phase he passed into that of complete acceptance. He ceased to satirise himself because time dulled the irony of the situation and the joke lost its humour with its sting. Even the sight of Haskett's hat on the hall table had ceased to touch the springs of epigram. The hat was often seen there now, for it had been decided that it was better for Lily's father to visit her than for the little girl to go to his boarding-house. Waythorn, having acquiesced in this arrangement, had been surprised to find how little difference it made. Haskett was never obtrusive, and the few visitors who met him on the stairs were unaware of his identity. Waythorn did not know how often he saw Alice, but with himself Haskett was seldom in contact.

One afternoon, however, he learned on entering that Lily's father was waiting to see him. In the library he found Haskett occupying a chair in his usual provisional way. Waythorn always felt grateful to him for not leaning back.

"I hope you'll excuse me, Mr. Waythorn," he said rising. "I wanted to see Mrs. Waythorn about Lily, and your man asked me to wait here till she came in."

"Of course," said Waythorn, remembering that a sudden leak had that morning given over the drawing-room to the plumbers.

He opened his cigar-case and held it out to his visitor, and Haskett's acceptance seemed to mark a fresh stage in their intercourse. The spring evening was chilly, and Waythorn invited his guest to draw up his chair to the fire. He meant to find an excuse to leave Haskett in a moment; but he was tired and cold, and after all the little man no longer jarred on him.

The two were enclosed in the intimacy of their blended cigar-smoke when the door opened and Varick walked into the room. Waythorn rose abruptly. It was the first time that Varick had come to the house, and the surprise of seeing him, combined with the singular inopportuneness of his arrival, gave a new edge to Waythorn's blunted sensibilities. He stared at his visitor without speaking.

Varick seemed too preoccupied to notice his host's embarrassment.

"My dear fellow," he exclaimed in his most expansive tone, "I must apologise for tumbling in on you in this way, but I was too late to catch you down town, and so I thought —"

He stopped short, catching sight of Haskett, and his sanguine colour deepened to a flush which spread vividly under his scant blond hair. But in a moment he recovered himself and nodded slightly. Haskett returned the bow in silence, and Waythorn was still groping for speech when the footman came in carrying a tea-table.

The intrusion offered a welcome vent to Waythorn's nerves. "What the deuce are you bringing this here for?" he said sharply.

"I beg your pardon, sir, but the plumbers are still in the drawing-room, and Mrs. Waythorn said she would have tea in the library." The footman's perfectly respectful tone implied a reflection on Waythorn's reasonableness.

"Oh, very well," said the latter resignedly, and the footman proceeded to open the folding tea-table and set out its complicated appointments. While this interminable process continued the three men stood motionless, watching it with a fascinated stare, till Waythorn, to break the silence, said to Varick: "Won't you have a cigar?"

He held out the case he had just tendered to Haskett, and Varick helped himself with a smile. Waythorn looked about for a match, and finding none, proffered a light from his own cigar. Haskett, in the background, held his ground mildly, examining his cigar-tip now and then, and stepping forward at the right moment to knock its ashes into the fire.

The footman at last withdrew, and Varick immediately began: "If I could just say half a word to you about this business —"

"Certainly," stammered Waythorn; "in the dining-room —"

But as he placed his hand on the door it opened from without, and his wife appeared on the threshold.

She came in fresh and smiling, in her street dress and hat, shedding a fragrance from the boa which she loosened in advancing.

"Shall we have tea in here, dear?" she began; and then she caught sight of Varick. Her smile deepened, veiling a slight tremor of surprise.

"Why, how do you do?" she said with a distinct note of pleasure.

As she shook hands with Varick she saw Haskett standing behind him. Her smile faded for a moment, but she recalled it quickly, with a scarcely perceptible side-glance at Waythorn.

"How do you do, Mr. Haskett?" she said, and shook hands with him a shade less cordially.

The three men stood awkwardly before her, till Varick, always the most self-possessed, dashed into an explanatory phrase.

"We — I had to see Waythorn a moment on business," he stammered, brick-red from chin to nape.

Haskett stepped forward with his air of mild obstinacy. "I am sorry to intrude; but you appointed five o'clock —" he directed his resigned glance to the timepiece on the mantel.

She swept aside their embarrassment with a charming gesture of hospitality.

"I'm so sorry — I'm always late; but the afternoon was so lovely." She stood drawing off her gloves, propitiatory and graceful, diffusing about her a sense of ease and familiarity in which the situation lost its grotesqueness. "But before talking business," she added brightly, "I'm sure every one wants a cup of tea."

She dropped into her low chair by the tea-table, and the two visitors, as if drawn by her smile, advanced to receive the cups she held out.

She glanced about for Waythorn, and he took the third cup with a laugh.

Willa Cather
A Wagner Matinée

One of Willa Cather's finest stories, "A Wagner Matinée" was published in *Everybody's Magazine* in 1904, revised for inclusion in *The Troll Garden* in 1905, and changed again to become part of *Youth and the Bright Medusa* in 1920. In each instance, the general effect of the alterations was to soften the portrait of the barren life Aunt Georgiana has faced since her move from Boston to Nebraska when she married thirty years before. Cather, who grew up on the prairies, wrote often of the restricted access to culture and the intellectual life endemic to the region, a theme that invests her masterpiece, *My Ántonia* (1918), and many of her shorter works of fiction. Indeed, a central idea in her stories is that art is essential for the soul, that a fulfilled life is dependent on exposure to creative work that moves her characters deeply, changing their very essence. This concept is especially poignant in this story of Aunt Georgiana, who enjoyed the richness of New England culture in her youth and now returns to it after three decades. Her nephew, who narrates, remembers the rude existence of the farm during the years he lived with her, and he now observes and describes the depths of her emotion as she enjoys an afternoon at the symphony. It is quintessential Cather, who wrote often of characters who desperately need music and culture to complete their humanity.

Willa Cather, "A Wagner Matinée," *Everybody's Magazine* 10 (March 1904): 325–28.

I received one morning a letter written in pale ink, on glassy, blue-lined notepaper, and bearing the postmark of a little Nebraska village. This communication, worn and rubbed, looking as though it had been carried for some days in a coat-pocket that was none too clean, was from my Uncle Howard. It informed me that his wife had been left a small legacy by a bachelor relative who had recently died, and that it had become necessary for her to come to Boston to attend to the settling of the estate. He requested me to meet her at the station, and render her whatever services might prove necessary. On examining the date indicated as that of her arrival, I found it no later than to-morrow. He had characteristically delayed writing until, had I been away from home for a day, I must have missed the good woman altogether.

The name of my Aunt Georgiana called up not alone her own figure, at once pathetic and grotesque, but opened before my feet a gulf of recollections so wide and deep that, as the letter dropped from my hand, I felt suddenly a stranger to all the present conditions of my existence, wholly ill at ease and out of place amid the surroundings of my study. I became, in short, the gangling farmer-boy my aunt had known, scourged with chilblains and bashfulness, my hands cracked and raw from the corn-husking. I felt the knuckles of my thumb tentatively, as though they were raw again. I sat again before her parlor organ, thumbing the scales with my stiff, red hands, while she beside me made canvas mittens for the huskers.

The next morning, after preparing my landlady somewhat, I set out for the station. When the train arrived I had some difficulty in finding my aunt. She was the last of the passengers to alight, and when I got her into the carriage she looked not unlike one of those charred, smoked bodies that firemen lift from the *débris* of a burned building. She had come all the way in a day coach; her linen duster had become black with soot and her black bonnet gray with dust during the journey. When we arrived at my boarding-house the landlady put her to bed at once, and I did not see her again until the next morning.

Whatever shock Mrs. Springer experienced at my aunt's appearance she considerately concealed. Myself, I saw my aunt's misshapen figure with that feeling of awe and respect with which we behold explorers who have left their ears and fingers north of Franz Josef Land, or their health somewhere along the Upper Congo. My Aunt Georgiana had been a music-teacher at the Boston Conservatory, somewhere back in the latter sixties. One summer, which she had spent in the little village in the Green Mountains where her ancestors had dwelt for generations, she had kindled the callow fancy of the most idle and shiftless of all the village lads, and had conceived for this Howard Carpenter one of those absurd and extravagant passions which a handsome country boy of twenty-one sometimes inspires in a plain, angular, spectacled woman of thirty. When she returned to her duties in Boston, Howard followed her; and the upshot of this inexplicable infatuation was that she eloped with him, eluding the reproaches of her family and the criticism of her friends by going with him to the Nebraska frontier. Carpenter, who of course had no money, took a homestead in Red Willow County, fifty miles from the railroad. There they measured off their eighty acres by driving across the prairie in a wagon, to the wheel of which they had tied a red cotton handkerchief, and counting its revolutions. They built a dugout in the red hillside, one of those cave dwellings whose inmates usually reverted to the conditions of primitive savagery. Their water they got from the lagoons where the buffalo drank, and their slender stock of provisions was always at the mercy of bands of roving Indians. For thirty years my aunt had not been farther than fifty miles from the homestead.

But Mrs. Springer knew nothing of all this, and must have been considerably shocked at what was left of my kinswoman. Beneath the soiled linen duster, which on her arrival was the most conspicuous feature of her costume, she wore a black stuff dress whose ornamentation showed that she had surrendered herself unquestioningly into the hands of a country dressmaker. My poor aunt's figure, however, would have presented astonishing difficulties to any dressmaker. Her skin was yellow as a Mongolian's from constant exposure to a pitiless wind, and to the alkaline water, which transforms the most transparent cuticle into a sort of flexible leather. She wore ill-fitting false teeth. The most striking thing about her physiognomy, however, was an incessant twitching of the mouth and eyebrows, a form of nervous disorder resulting from isolation and monotony, and from frequent physical suffering.

In my boyhood this affliction had possessed a sort of horrible fascination for me, of which I was secretly very much ashamed, for in those days I owed to this woman most of the good that ever came my way, and had a reverential affection for her. During the three winters when I was riding herd for my uncle, my aunt, after cooking three meals for half a dozen farm-hands, and putting the six children to bed, would often stand until midnight at her ironing-board, hearing me at the kitchen table beside her recite Latin declensions and conjugations, and gently shaking me when my drowsy head sank down over a page of irregular verbs. It was to her, at her ironing and mending, that I read my first Shakespeare; and her old text-book of mythology was the first that ever came into my empty hands. She taught me my scales and exercises, too, on the little parlor organ which her husband had bought her after fifteen years, during which she had not so much as seen any instrument except an accordion, that belonged to one of the Norwegian farm-hands. She would sit beside me by the hour, darning and counting, while I struggled with the *Harmonious Blacksmith*; but she seldom talked to me about music, and I understood why. She was a pious woman; she had the consolation of religion; and to her at least her martyrdom was not wholly sordid. Once when I had been doggedly beating out some passages from an old score of *Euryanthe* I had found among her music-books, she came up to me and, putting her hands over my eyes, gently drew my head back upon her shoulder, saying tremulously, "Don't love it so well, Clark, or it may be taken from you. Oh! dear boy, pray that whatever your sacrifice be it is not that."

When my aunt appeared on the morning after her arrival, she was still in a semi-somnambulent state. She seemed not to realize that she was in the city where she had spent her youth, the place longed for hungrily for half a lifetime. She had been so wretchedly train-sick throughout the journey that she had no recollection of anything but her discomfort, and, to all intents and purposes, there were but a few hours of nightmare between the farm in Red Willow County and my study on Newbury Street. I had planned a little pleasure for her that afternoon, to repay her for some of the glorious moments she had given me when we used to milk together in the straw-thatched cow-shed, and she, because I was more than usually tired, or because her husband had spoken sharply to me, would tell me of the splendid performance of Meyerbeer's *Huguenots* she had seen in Paris in her youth. At two o'clock the Boston Symphony Orchestra was to give a Wagner programme, and I intended to take my aunt, though as I conversed with her I grew doubtful about her enjoyment of it. Indeed, for her own sake, I could only wish her taste for such things quite dead, and the long struggle mercifully ended at last. I suggested our visiting the Conservatory and the Common before lunch, but she seemed altogether too timid to wish to venture out. She questioned me absently about various changes in the city, but she was chiefly concerned that she had forgotten to leave instructions about feeding half-skimmed milk to a certain weakling calf, "Old Maggie's calf, you know, Clark," she explained, evidently having forgotten how long I had been away. She was further troubled because she had neglected to tell her daughter about the freshly opened kit of mackerel in the cellar, that would spoil if it were not used directly.

I asked her whether she had ever heard any of the Wagnerian operas, and found that she had not, though she was perfectly familiar with their respective situations and had once possessed the piano score of *The Flying Dutchman*. I began to think it would have been best to get her back to Red Willow County without waking her, and regretted having suggested the concert.

From the time we entered the concert-hall, however, she was a trifle less passive and inert, and seemed to begin to perceive her surroundings. I had felt some trepidation lest she might become aware of the absurdities of her attire, or might experience some painful embarrassment at stepping suddenly into the world to which she had been dead for a quarter of a century. But again I found how superficially I had judged her. She sat looking about her with eyes as impersonal, almost as stony, as those with which the granite Rameses in a museum watches the froth and fret that ebbs and flows about his pedestal, separated from it by the lonely stretch of centuries. I have seen this same aloofness in old miners who drift into the Brown Hotel at Denver, their pockets full of bullion, their linen soiled, their haggard faces unshorn, and who stand in the thronged corridors as solitary as though they were still in a frozen camp on the Yukon, or in the yellow blaze of the Arizona desert, conscious that certain experiences have isolated them from their fellows by a gulf no haberdasher could conceal.

The audience was made up chiefly of women. One lost the contour of faces and figures, indeed any effect of line whatever, and there was only the color contrast of bodices past counting, the shimmer and shading of fabrics soft and firm, silky and sheer, resisting and yielding: red, mauve, pink, blue, lilac, purple, écru, rose, yellow, cream, and white, all the colors that an impressionist finds in a sunlit landscape, with here and there the dead black shadow of a frock-coat. My Aunt Georgiana regarded them as though they had been so many daubs of tube paint on a palette.

When the musicians came out and took their places, she gave a little stir of anticipation, and looked with quickening interest down over the rail at that invariable grouping; perhaps the first wholly familiar thing that had greeted her eye since she had left old Maggie and her weakling calf. I could feel how all those details sank into her soul, for I had not forgotten how they had sunk into mine when I came fresh from ploughing forever and forever between green aisles of corn, where, as in a treadmill, one might walk from daybreak to dusk without perceiving a shadow of change in one's environment. I reminded myself of the impression made on me by the clean profiles of the musicians, the gloss of their linen, the dull black of their coats, the beloved shapes of the instruments, the patches of yellow light thrown by the green-shaded stand-lamps on the smooth, varnished bellies of the 'cellos and the bass viols in the rear, the restless, wind-tossed forest of fiddle necks and bows; I recalled how, in the first orchestra I had ever heard, those long bow strokes seemed to draw the soul out of me, as a conjuror's stick reels out paper ribbon from a hat.

The first number was the *Tannhäuser* overture. When the violins drew out the first strain of the Pilgrims' chorus, my Aunt Georgiana clutched my coat-sleeve. Then it was that I first realized that for her this singing of basses and stinging frenzy of lighter strings broke a silence of thirty years, the inconceivable silence of the plains. With the battle between the two motifs, with the bitter frenzy of the Venusberg theme and its ripping of strings, came to me an overwhelming sense of the waste and wear we are so powerless to combat. I saw again the tall, naked house on the prairie, black and grim as a wooden fortress; the black pond where I had learned to swim, the rain-gullied clay about the naked house; the four dwarf ash-seedlings on which the dishcloths were always hung to dry before the kitchen door. The world there is the flat world of the ancients; to the east, a cornfield that stretched to daybreak; to the west, a corral that stretched to sunset; between, the sordid conquests of peace, more merciless than those of war.

The overture closed. My aunt released my coat-sleeve, but she said nothing. She sat staring at the orchestra through a dulness of thirty years, through the films made, little by little, by each of the three hundred and sixty-five days in every one of them. What, I wondered, did she get from it? She had been a good pianist in her day, I knew, and her musical education had been broader than that of most music-teachers of a quarter of a century ago. She had often told me of Mozart's operas and Meyerbeer's, and I could remember hearing her sing, years ago, certain melodies of Verdi's. When I had fallen ill with a fever she used to sit by my cot in the evening, while the cool night wind blew in through the faded mosquito-netting tacked over the window, and I lay watching a bright star that burned red above the cornfield, and sing "Home to our mountains, oh, let us return!" in a way fit to break the heart of a Vermont boy near dead of homesickness already.

I watched her closely through the prelude to *Tristan and Isolde*, trying vainly to conjecture what that warfare of motifs, that seething turmoil of strings and winds, might mean to her. Had this music any message for her? Did or did not a new planet swim into her ken? Wagner had been a sealed book to Americans before the sixties. Had she anything left with which to comprehend this glory that had flashed around the world since she had gone from it? I was in a fever of curiosity, but Aunt Georgiana sat silent upon her peak in Darien. She preserved this utter immobility throughout the numbers from the *Flying Dutchman*, though her fingers worked mechanically upon her black dress, as though of themselves they were recalling the piano score they had once played. Poor old hands! They were stretched and pulled and twisted into mere tentacles to hold, and lift, and knead with; the palms unduly swollen, the fingers bent and knotted, on one of them a thin worn band that had once been a wedding-ring. As I pressed and gently quieted one of those groping hands, I remembered, with quivering eyelids, their services for me in other days.

Soon after the tenor began the *Prize Song*, I heard a quick-drawn breath, and turned to my aunt. Her eyes were closed, but the tears were glistening on her cheeks, and I think in a moment more they were in my eyes as well. It never really dies, then, the soul? It withers to the outward eye only, like that strange moss which can lie on a dusty shelf half a century and yet, if placed in water, grows green again. My aunt wept gently throughout the development and elaboration of the melody.

During the intermission before the second half of the concert, I questioned my aunt and found that the *Prize Song* was not new to her. Some years before there had drifted to the farm in Red Willow County a young German, a tramp cow-puncher, who had sung in the chorus at Baireuth, when he was a boy, along with the other peasant boys and girls. Of a Sunday morning he used to sit on his blue gingham-sheeted bed in the hands' bedroom, which opened off the kitchen, cleaning the leather of his boots and saddle, and singing the *Prize Song*, while my aunt went about her work in the kitchen. She had hovered about him until she had prevailed upon him to join the country church, though his sole fitness for this step, so far as I could gather, lay in his boyish face and his possession of this divine melody. Shortly afterward he had gone to town on the Fourth of July, been drunk for several days, lost his money at a faro-table, ridden a saddled Texas steer on a bet, and disappeared with a fractured collar-bone.

"Well, we have come to better things than the old Trovatore at any rate, Aunt Georgie?" I queried, with well-meant jocularity.

Her lip quivered and she hastily put her handkerchief up to her mouth. From behind it she murmured, "And you've been hearing this ever since you left me, Clark?" Her question was the gentlest and saddest of reproaches.

"But do you get it, Aunt Georgiana, the astonishing structure of it all?" I persisted.

"Who could?" she said, absently; "why should one?"

The second half of the programme consisted of four numbers from the *Ring*. This was followed by the forest music from Siegfried, and the programme closed with Siegfried's funeral march. My aunt wept quietly, but almost continuously. I was perplexed as to what measure of musical comprehension was left to her, to her who had heard nothing for so many years but the singing of gospel hymns in Methodist services at the square frame school-house on Section Thirteen. I was unable to gauge how much of it had been dissolved in soapsuds, or worked into bread, or milked into the bottom of a pail.

The deluge of sound poured on and on; I never know what she found in the shining current of it; I never knew how far it bore her, or past what happy islands, or under what skies. From the trembling of her face I could well believe that the Siegfried march, at least, carried her out where the myriad graves are, out into the gray, burying-grounds of the sea; or into some world of death vaster yet, where, from the beginning of the world, hope has lain down with hope, and dream with dream and, renouncing, slept.

The concert was over; the people filed out of the hall chattering and laughing, glad to relax and find the living level again, but my kinswoman made no effort to rise. I spoke gently to her. She burst into tears and sobbed pleadingly, "I don't want to go, Clark, I don't want to go!"

I understood. For her, just outside the door of the concert-hall, lay the black pond with the cattle-tracked bluffs, the tall, unpainted house, naked as a tower, with weather-curled boards; the crook-backed ash-seedlings where the dish-cloths hung to dry, the gaunt, moulting turkeys picking up refuse about the kitchen door.

John M. Oskison
The Problem of Old Harjo

John M. Oskison's anthropological story "The Problem of Old Harjo" was published in *The Southern Workman* in 1907. The presentation of the characters and the central conflict between two cultures reflects much of the author's personal life. Born to an English father and a Cherokee mother, Oskison learned early to live and flourish in two vastly different worlds. Following the wishes of his parents, he graduated from Willie Halsell College in Oklahoma and went on to earn a law degree from Stanford. Then, driven by his own passion, he studied literature at Harvard until his first fiction appeared in *The Century Magazine*, and thereafter he devoted his life to his writing. He also served as an editor for several prestigious magazines and newspapers, including *Collier's Weekly* and the *New York Evening Post*. His fiction does not follow traditional expectations for Native American literature nor for the standard westerns of the day. Indeed, defying the standard treatment of the interaction between the races, in "The Problem of Old Harjo" he places the ethical conflict within the white outsider, who must evaluate Indian culture in ways not previously anticipated. The values of white, Christian society are here presented as inadequate to deal with the more complex traditions of the Cherokee, a matter powerfully dramatized in the conclusion.

John M. Oskison, "The Problem of Old Harjo," *The Southern Workman* 36 (April 1907): 235–41.

The Spirit of the Lord had descended upon old Harjo. From the new missionary, just out from New York, he had learned that he was a sinner. The fire in the new missionary's eyes and her gracious appeal had convinced old Harjo that this was the time to repent and be saved. He was very much in earnest, and he assured Miss Evans that he wanted to be baptized and received into the church at once. Miss Evans was enthusiastic and went to Mrs. Rowell with the news. It was Mrs. Rowell who had said that it was no use to try to convert the older Indians, and she, after fifteen years of work in Indian Territory missions, should have known. Miss Evans was pardonably proud of her conquest.

"Old Harjo converted!" exclaimed Mrs. Rowell. "Dear Miss Evans, do you know that old Harjo has two wives?" To the older woman it was as if some one had said to her "Madame, the Sultan of Turkey wishes to teach one of your mission Sabbath school classes."

"But," protested the younger woman, "he is really sincere, and —

"Then ask him," Mrs. Rowell interrupted a bit sternly, "if he will put away one of his wives. Ask him, before he comes into the presence of the Lord, if he is willing to conform to the laws of the country in which he lives, the country that guarantees his idle existence. Miss Evans, your work is not even begun." No one who knew Mrs. Rowell would say that she lacked sincerity and patriotism. Her own cousin was an earnest crusader against Mormonism, and had gathered a goodly share of that wagonload of protests that the Senate had been asked to read when it was considering whether a certain statesman of Utah should be allowed to represent his state at Washington.

In her practical, tactful way, Mrs. Rowell had kept clear of such embarrassments. At first, she had written letters of indignant protest to the Indian Office against the toleration of bigamy amongst the tribes. A wise inspector had been sent to the mission, and this man had pointed out that it was better to ignore certain things, "deplorable, to be sure," than to attempt to make over the habits of the old men. Of course, the young Indians would not be permitted to take more than one wife each.

So Mrs. Rowell had discreetly limited her missionary efforts to the young, and had exercised toward the old and bigamous only that strict charity which even a hopeless sinner might claim.

Miss Evans, it was to be regretted, had only the vaguest notions about "expediency;" so weak on matters of doctrine was she that the news that Harjo was living with two wives didn't startle her. She was young and possessed of but one enthusiasm — that for saving souls.

"I suppose," she ventured, "that old Harjo *must* put away one wife before he can join the church?"

"There can be no question about it, Miss Evans."

"Then I shall have to ask him to do it." Miss Evans regretted the necessity for forcing this sacrifice, but had no doubt that the Indian would make it an order to accept the gift of salvation which she was commissioned to bear to him.

Harjo lived in a "double" log cabin three miles from the mission. His ten acres of corn had been gathered into its fence-rail crib; four hogs that were to furnish his winter's bacon had been brought in from the woods and penned conveniently near to the crib; out in a corner of the garden, a fat mound of dirt rose where the crop of turnips and potatoes had been buried against the corrupting frost; and in the hayloft of his log stable were stored many pumpkins, dried corn, onions (suspended in bunches from the rafters) and the varied forage that Mrs. Harjo number one and Mrs. Harjo number two had thriftily provided. Three cows, three young heifers, two colts, and two patient, capable mares bore the Harjo brand, a fantastic "H-I" that the old man had designed. Materially, Harjo was solvent; and if the Government had ever come to his aid he could not recall the date.

This attempt to rehabilitate old Harjo morally, Miss Evans felt, was not one to be made at the mission; it should be undertaken in the Creek's own home where the evidences of his sin should confront him as she explained.

When Miss Evans rode up to the block in front of Harjo's cabin, the old Indian came out, slowly and with a broadening smile of welcome on his face. A clean gray flannel shirt had taken the place of the white collarless garment, with crackling stiff bosom, that he had worn to the mission meetings. Comfortable, well-patched moccasins had been substituted for creaking boots, and brown corduroys, belted in at the waist, for tight black trousers. His abundant gray hair fell down on his shoulders. In his eyes, clear and large and black, glowed the light of true hospitality. Miss Evans thought of the patriarchs as she saw him lead her horse out to the stable; thus Abraham might have looked and lived.

"Harjo," began Miss Evans before following the old man to the covered passageway between the disconnected cabins, "is it true that you have two wives?" Her tone was neither stern nor accusatory. The Creek had heard that question before, from scandalized missionaries and perplexed registry clerks when he went to Muscogee to enroll himself and his family in one of the many "final" records ordered to be made by the Government preparatory to dividing the Creek lands among the individual citizens.

For answer, Harjo called, first into the cabin that was used as a kitchen and then, in a loud, clear voice, toward the small field, where Miss Evans saw a flock of half-grown turkeys running about in the corn stubble. From the kitchen emerged a tall, thin Indian woman of fifty-five, with a red handkerchief bound severely over her head. She spoke to Miss Evans and sat down in the passageway. Presently, a clear, sweet voice was heard in the field; a stout, handsome woman, about the same age as the other, climbed the rail fence and came up to the house. She, also, greeted Miss Evans briefly. Then she carried a tin basin to the well near by, where she filled it to the brim. Setting it down on the horse block, she rolled back her sleeves, tucked in the collar of her gray blouse, and plunged her face in the water. In a minute she came out of the kitchen freshened and smiling. 'Liza Harjo had been pulling dried bean stalks at one end of the field, and it was dirty work. At last old Harjo turned to Miss Evans and said, "These two my wife — this one 'Liza, this one Jennie."

It was done with simple dignity. Miss Evans bowed and stammered. Three pairs of eyes were turned upon her in patient, courteous inquiry.

It was hard to state the case. The old man was so evidently proud of his women, and so flattered by Miss Evans' interest in them, that he would find it hard to understand. Still, it had to be done, and Miss Evans took the plunge.

"Harjo, you want to come into our church?" The old man's face lighted.

"Oh, yes, I would come to Jesus, please, my friend."

"Do you know, Harjo, that the Lord commanded that one man should mate with but one woman?" The question was stated again in simpler terms, and the Indian replied, "Me know that now, my friend. Long time ago" — Harjo plainly meant the whole period previous to his conversion — "me did not know. The Lord Jesus did not speak to me in that time and so I was blind. I do what blind man do."

"Harjo, you must have only one wife when you come into our church. Can't you give up one of these women?" Miss Evans glanced at the two, sitting by with smiles of polite interest on their faces, understanding nothing. They had not shared Harjo's enthusiasm either for the white man's God or his language.

"Give up my wife?" A sly smile stole over his face. He leaned closer to Miss Evans. "You tell me, my friend, which one I give up." He glanced from 'Liza to Jennie as if to weigh their attractions, and the two rewarded him with their pleasantest smiles. "You tell me which one," he urged.

"Why, Harjo, how can I tell you!" Miss Evans had little sense of humor; she had taken the old man seriously.

"Then," Harjo sighed, continuing the comedy, for surely the missionary was jesting with him, "'Liza and Jennie must say." He talked to the Indian women for a time, and they laughed heartily. 'Liza, pointing to the other, shook her head. At length Harjo explained, "My friend, they cannot say. Jennie, she would run a race to see which one stay, but 'Liza, she say no, she is fat and cannot run."

Miss Evans comprehended at last. She flushed angrily, and protested, "Harjo, you are making a mock of a sacred subject; I cannot allow you to talk like this."

"But did you not speak in fun, my friend?" Harjo queried, sobering. "Surely you have just said what your friend, the white woman at the mission (he meant Mrs. Rowell) would say, and you do not mean what you say."

"Yes, Harjo, I mean it. It is true that Mrs. Rowell raised the point first, but I agree with her. The church cannot be defiled by receiving a bigamist into its membership." Harjo saw that the young woman was serious, distressingly serious. He was silent for a long time, but at last he raised his head and spoke quietly, "It is not good to talk like that if it is not in fun."

He rose and went to the stable. As he led Miss Evans' horse up to the block it was champing a mouthful of corn, the last of a generous portion that Harjo had put before it. The Indian held the bridle and waited for Miss Evans to mount. She was embarrassed, humiliated, angry. It was absurd to be dismissed in this way by — "by an ignorant old bigamist!" Then the humor of it burst upon her, and its human aspect. In her anxiety concerning the spiritual welfare of the sinner Harjo, she had insulted the man Harjo. She began to understand why Mrs. Rowell had said that the old Indians were hopeless.

"Harjo," she begged, coming out of the passageway, "please forgive me. I do not want you to give up one of your wives. Just tell me why you took them."

"I will tell you that, my friend." The old Creek looped the reins over his arm and sat down on the block. "For thirty years Jennie has lived with me as my wife. She is of the Bear people, and she came to me when I was thirty-five and she was twenty-five. She could not come before, for her mother was old, very old, and Jennie, she stay with her and feed her.

"So, when I was thirty years old I took 'Liza for my woman. She is of the Crow people. She help me make this little farm here when there was no farm for many miles around.

"Well, five years 'Liza and me, we live here and work hard. But there was no child. Then the old mother of Jennie she died, and Jennie got no family left in this part of the country. So 'Liza say to me, 'Why don't you take Jennie in here?' I say, 'You don't care?' and she say, 'No, maybe we have children here then.' But we have no children — never have children. We do not like that, but God He would not let it be. So, we have lived here thirty years very happy. Only just now you make me sad."

"Harjo," cried Miss Evans, "forget what I said. Forget that you wanted to join the church." For a young mission worker with a single purpose always before her, Miss Evans was saying a strange thing. Yet she couldn't help saying it; all of her zeal seemed to have been dissipated by a simple statement of the old man.

"I cannot forget to love Jesus, and I want to be saved." Old Harjo spoke with solemn earnestness. The situation was distracting. On one side stood a convert eager for the protection of the church, asking only that he be allowed to fulfill the obligations of humanity and on the other stood the church, represented by Mrs. Rowell, that set an impossible condition on receiving old Harjo to itself. Miss Evans wanted to cry; prayer, she felt, would be entirely inadequate as a means of expression.

"Oh! Harjo," she cried out, "I don't know what to do. I must think it over and talk with Mrs. Rowell again."

But Mrs. Rowell could suggest no way out; Miss Evans' talk with her only gave the older woman another opportunity to preach the folly of wasting time on the old and "unreasonable" Indians. Certainly the church could not listen even to a hint of a compromise in this case. If Harjo wanted to be saved there was one way and only one — unless —

"Is either of the two women old? I mean, so old that she is — an —"

"Not at all," answered Miss Evans. "They're both strong and — yes, happy. I think they will outlive Harjo."

"Can't you appeal to one of the women to go away? I dare say we could provide for her." Miss Evans, incongruously, remembered Jennie's jesting proposal to race for the right to stay with Harjo. What could the mission provide as a substitute for the little home that 'Liza had helped to create there in the edge of the woods? What other home would satisfy Jennie?

"Mrs. Rowell, are you sure that we ought to try to take one of Harjo's women from him? I'm not sure that it would in the least advance morality amongst the tribe, but I'm certain that it would make three gentle people unhappy for the rest of their lives."

"You may be right, Miss Evans." Mrs. Rowell was not seeking to create unhappiness, for enough of it inevitably came to be pictured in the little mission building. "You may be right," she repeated, "but it is a grievous misfortune that old Harjo should wish to unite with the church."

No one was more regular in his attendance at the mission meetings than old Harjo. Sitting well forward, he was always in plain view of Miss Evans at the organ. Before the service began, and after it was over, the old man greeted the young woman. There was never a spoken question, but in the Creek's eyes was always a mute inquiry.

Once Miss Evans ventured to write to her old pastor in New York, and explain her trouble. This was what he wrote in reply: "I am surprised that you are troubled, for I should have expected you to rejoice, as I do, over this new and wonderful evidence of the Lord's reforming power. Though the church cannot receive the old man so long as he is confessedly a bigamist and violator of his country's just laws, you should be greatly strengthened in your work through bringing him to desire salvation."

"Oh! it's easy to talk when you're free from responsibility!" cried out Miss Evans. "But I woke him up to a desire for this water of salvation that he cannot take. I have seen Harjo's home, and I know how cruel and useless it would be to urge him to give up what he loves — for he does love those two women who have spent half their lives and more with him. What, what can be done!"

Month after month, as old Harjo continued to occupy his seat in the mission meetings, with that mute appeal in his eyes and a persistent light of hope on his face, Miss Evans repeated the question, "What can be done?" If she was sometimes tempted to say to the old man, "Stop worrying about your soul; you'll get to Heaven as surely as any of us," there was always Mrs. Rowell to remind her that she was not a Mormon missionary. She could not run away from her perplexity. If she should secure a transfer to another station, she felt that Harjo would give up coming to the meetings, and in his despair become a positive influence for evil amongst his people. Mrs. Rowell would not waste her energy on an obstinate old man. No, Harjo was her creation, her impossible convert, and throughout the years, until death — the great solvent which is not always a solvent — came to one of them, would continue to haunt her.

And meanwhile, what?

Sui Sin Far

Mrs. Spring Fragrance

Among the earliest Asian American works of fiction, Sui Sin Far's "Mrs. Spring Fragrance" appeared in *Hampton's Magazine* in 1910 prior to being incorporated into a volume using the same title. The story brings to the tradition of Realism a new dimension, the Asian perspective on the process of immigration, cultural duality, and the problems of assimilation inherent in linguistic, religious, and social transformation. Published at a time of intense apprehension about the potential for gigantic immigration from China, the United States had established restrictive policies allowing only small numbers of new arrivals each year, and other forms of discrimination were also common practice. Nevertheless, the story displays more charm than bitterness, more insight than outrage, more compassion than visceral hatred. Of special focus in this case are courtship rituals that differ dramatically from those of the native country, matters carried over into a new understanding of the relationships in a marriage as well.

Sui Sin Far, "Mrs. Spring Fragrance," *Hampton's Magazine* 24 (January 1910): 137–41.

When Mrs. Spring Fragrance first arrived in Seattle, she was unacquainted with even one word of the American language. Five years later, her husband, speaking of her, said: "There are no more American words for her learning." And everyone who knew Mrs. Spring Fragrance agreed with Mr. Spring Fragrance. This gentleman, whose business name was Sing Yook, was a young curio merchant. Though conservatively Chinese in many respects, he was at the same time what is called by the Westerners "Americanized." Mrs. Spring Fragrance was even more so — "Americanized."

Next door to the Spring Fragrances lived the Chin Yuens. Mrs. Chin Yuen was much older than Mrs. Spring Fragrance; but she had a daughter of eighteen with whom Mrs. Spring Fragrance was great friends. The daughter was a pretty girl, whose Chinese name was Mai Gwi Far (a rose), and whose American name was Laura. This daughter had a sweetheart, a youth named Kai Tzu. Kai Tzu, who was American born, and as ruddy and stalwart as any young Westerner, was noted among baseball players as one of the finest pitchers on the Coast. He could also sing "Drink to me only with thine eyes," to Laura's piano accompaniment.

Now, the only person who knew that Kai Tzu loved Laura and that Laura loved Kai Tzu was Mrs. Spring Fragrance. For though the Chin Yuen parents lived in a house furnished in American style and wore American clothes, they religiously observed many Chinese customs and their ideals of life were the ideals of their Chinese forefathers. Therefore, they had betrothed their daughter, Laura, at the age of fifteen, to the eldest son of the Chinese Government school-teacher in San Francisco. The time for the consummation of the betrothal was approaching.

"I have just had such a pretty walk," said Mrs. Spring Fragrance to Laura one day when the girl was very depressed. "I crossed the banks above the beach and came back by the long road. In the green grass the daffodils were blowing; in the cottage gardens the currant bushes were flowering, and in the air was the perfume of the wall flower. I wished, Laura, that you were with me."

Laura burst into tears. "That is the walk Kai Tzu and I so love," she sobbed, "but never, ah, never, can we take it together again."

"Now, Little Sister," comforted Mrs. Spring Fragrance, "you really must not grieve like that. Is there not a beautiful American poem written by a noble American named Tennyson which says: ''Tis better to have loved and lost, than never to have loved at all'?"

Mrs. Spring Fragrance was unaware that Mr. Spring Fragrance had returned from the city, tired with the day's business, and had thrown himself down on the bamboo settee on the veranda, and that though his eyes were engaged in scanning the pages of the *Chinese World,* his ears could not help receiving the words which were borne to him through the open window.

> 'Tis better to have loved and lost,
> Than never to have loved at all,

repeated Mr. Spring Fragrance. Not wishing to hear more of the secret talk of women, he arose and sauntered around the veranda to the other side of the house. Two pigeons circled around his head. He felt in his pocket for a li-chi which he usually carried for their picking. His fingers touched a little box. It contained a jade pendant which Mrs. Spring Fragrance had particularly admired the last time she was downtown. It was the fifth anniversary of Mr. and Mrs. Spring Fragrance's wedding day. Mr. Spring Fragrance pressed the little box into the depths of his pocket.

A young man came out of the back door of the house on Mr. Spring Fragrance's left-hand side.

"Good evening," said the young man.

"Good evening," returned Mr. Spring Fragrance.

"Will you please tell me," said Mr. Spring Fragrance, "the meaning of two lines of an American verse which I have heard?"

"Certainly," returned the young man with a genial smile. He was a star student at the University of Washington, and had not the slightest doubt that he could explain the meaning of all things in the universe.

"Well," said Mr. Spring Fragrance, "it is this:

> 'Tis better to have loved and lost,
> Than never to have loved at all.

"Ah!" responded the young man with an air of profound wisdom. "That, Mr. Spring Fragrance, means that it is a good thing to love anyway — even if we can't get what we love, or, as the poet tells us, lose what we love. Of course one needs some experience to feel the truth of this teaching."

"The truth of the teaching," echoed Mr. Spring Fragrance a little testily; "there is no truth in it whatever. It is disobedient to reason. Is it not better to have what you do not love than to love what you do not have?"

"That depends," answered the young man, "upon temperament."

"I thank you. Good evening," said Mr. Spring Fragrance. While he was musing upon the unwisdom of the American way of looking at things, inside the house Laura was refusing to be comforted.

"Ah, no! No!" cried she. "If I had not gone to school with Kai Tzu, nor talked and walked with him, nor played the accompaniments to his songs, then I might consider with complacency, or at least without horror, my approaching marriage with the son of Man You. But as it is, oh, as it is ——"

Mrs. Spring Fragrance knelt down beside the girl, who was rocking herself to and fro in heartfelt grief; clasping her arms around her neck, she cried in sympathy:

"Little Sister, O Little Sister! Dry your tears — do not despair. A moon has yet to pass before the marriage can take place. Who knows what the stars may have to say to one another during its passing. A little bird has whispered to me ——"

For a long time Mrs. Spring Fragrance talked. For a long time Laura listened. When the girl arose to go, there was a bright light in her eyes.

ॐ

Mrs. Spring Fragrance, in San Francisco on a visit to her cousin, the wife of the herb doctor of Clay Street, was having a good time. She was invited everywhere that the wife of an honorable Chinese merchant could go. There was much to see and hear, including more than a dozen babies who had been born in the families of her friends since she last visited the city of the Golden Gate. Mrs. Spring Fragrance loved babies. She had had two herself, but both had been transplanted into the spirit land before the completion of even one moon.

There were also many dinners and theater parties given in her honor. It was at one of the theater parties that Mrs. Spring Fragrance met Ah Oi, a young girl who had the reputation of being the prettiest Chinese girl in San Francisco and, according to Chinese gossip, the naughtiest. In spite of all the gossip, however, Mrs. Spring Fragrance took a great fancy to Ah Oi, and invited her to a *tête-à-tête* picnic on the following day. This invitation Ah Oi joyfully accepted. She was really a sort of bird girl and never felt so happy as when out in the park or woods.

On the day after the picnic Mrs. Spring Fragrance wrote to Laura Chin Yuen thus:

> My Precious Laura:
>   May the bamboo ever wave. Next week I accompany Ah Oi to the beauteous town of San Jose. There will we be met by the son

of the Illustrious Teacher, and in a little Mission, presided over by a benevolent American priest, the little Ah Oi and the son of the Illustrious Teacher will be joined together in love and harmony — two pieces of music made to complete one another.

The son of the Illustrious Teacher, having been through an American Hall of Learning, is well able to provide for his orphan bride, and fears not the displeasure of his parents, now that he is assured that your grief at his loss will not be inconsolable. He wishes me to waft to you and to Kai Tzu, and the little Ah Oi joins with him, ten thousand rainbow wishes for your happiness.

My respects to your honorable parents, and to yourself the heart of your loving friend,

Jade Spring Fragrance

To Mr. Spring Fragrance Mrs. Spring Fragrance also indited a letter, which read:

Great and Honored Man:

Greeting from your plum blossom, who is desirous of hiding herself from the sun of your presence for a week of seven days more. My honorable cousin is preparing for the Fifth Moon Festival, and wishes me to compound for the occasion some American "fudge," for which delectable sweet, made by my clumsy hands, you have sometimes shown a slight prejudice. I am enjoying a most agreeable visit, and American friends, as also our own, strive benevolently for the accomplishment of my pleasure. Mrs. Samuel Smith, an American lady, known to my cousin, asked for my accompaniment to a magniloquent lecture the other evening. The subject was "America, the Protector of China"! It was most exhilarating, and the effect of so much expression of benevolence leads me to beg of you to forget to remember that the barber charges you one dollar for a shave while he humbly submits to the American man a bill of fifteen cents. And murmur no more because your honored elder brother, on a visit to this country, is detained under the rooftree of this great Government instead of under your own humble roof. Console him with the reflection that he is protected under the wing of the Eagle, the Emblem of Liberty. What is the loss of ten hundred years or ten thousand times ten dollars compared with the happiness of knowing oneself so securely sheltered? All of this I have learned from Mrs. Samuel Smith, who is as brilliant and great of mind as one of your own superior sex.

For me, it is sufficient to know that the Golden Gate Park is most enchanting and the seals on the rocks at the Cliff House extremely entertaining and amiable. There is much feasting and merrymaking under the lanterns, in honor of your Stupid Thorn.

I have purchased for your smoking a pipe with an amber mouth. It is said to be very sweet to the lips and to emit a cloud of smoke fit for the gods to inhale.

Awaiting by the wonderful wire of the telegram message your gracious permission to remain for the celebration of the Fifth Moon Festival and the making of American fudge, I continue for ten thousand times ten thousand years,

Your ever loving and obedient woman,

Jade

P.S. Forget not to care for the cat, the birds, and the flowers. Do not eat too quickly nor fan too vigorously now that the weather is warming.

Mrs. Spring Fragrance smiled as she folded this last epistle. Even if he were old-fashioned, there was never a husband so good and kind as hers. Only on one occasion since their marriage had he slighted her wishes. That was when, on the last anniversary of their wedding, she had signified a desire for a certain jade pendant, and he had failed to satisfy that desire.

But Mrs. Spring Fragrance, being of a happy nature and disposed to look upon the bright side of things, did not allow her mind to dwell upon the jade pendant. Instead, she gazed complacently down upon her bejeweled fingers and folded in with her letter to Mr. Spring Fragrance a bright little sheaf of condensed love.

᎒᎒

Mr. Spring Fragrance sat on his doorstep reading his letters; there was one from Mrs. Spring Fragrance, and another from an elderly bachelor cousin in San Francisco. The one from the elderly bachelor cousin was a business letter, but it contained the following postscript:

"Tsen Hing, the son of the Government school-master, seems to be much in the company of your young wife. He is a good-looking youth. Pardon me, my dear cousin, but if women are allowed to stray at will from under their husband's mulberry roofs, what is to prevent them from becoming butterflies?"

"Sing Foon is old and cynical," said Mr. Spring Fragrance to himself. "Why should I pay any attention to him? This is America, where a man may speak to a woman, and a woman listen, without any thought of evil."

He destroyed his cousin's letter and reread his wife's. Then he became very thoughtful. Was the making of American fudge sufficient reason for a wife to wish to remain a week longer in a city where her husband was not?

The young man who lived in the next house came out to water the lawn.

"Good evening," said he. "Any news from Mrs. Spring Fragrance?"

"She is having a very good time," returned Mr. Spring Fragrance.

"Glad to hear it. I think you told me she was to return the end of this week."

"I have changed my mind about her," said Mr. Spring Fragrance. "I am bidding her remain a week longer, as I wish to give a smoking party during her absence. I hope I may have the pleasure of your company."

"I shall be delighted," returned the other. "But, Mr. Spring Fragrance, don't invite any other white fellows. If you do not, I shall be able to get in a scoop. You know, I'm a sort of honorary reporter for the *Gleaner*. I shall call it a high-class Chinese stag party!"

In spite of his melancholy mood, Mr. Spring Fragrance smiled.

"Everything is 'high class' in America," he observed.

"Sure!" cheerfully assented the young man. "Haven't you ever heard that all Americans are princes and princesses, and just as soon as a foreigner puts his foot upon our shores he also becomes of the nobility — I mean, the royal family."

Mr. Spring Fragrance puffed his pipe in silence for some moments. Weightier matters were troubling his mind.

At last he spoke. "Love," said he slowly and distinctly, "comes before the wedding in this country, does it not?"

"Yes, certainly."

"Presuming," continued Mr. Spring Fragrance, "presuming that some friend of your father's — living, presuming, in England — has a daughter that he arranges with your father to be your wife. Presuming that you have never seen that daughter, but that you marry her, knowing her not. Presuming that she marries you, knowing you not. After she marries you and knows you, will that woman love you?"

"Emphatically, no!" answered the young man.

"That is the way it would be in America — that the woman who marries the man like that would not love him?"

"Yes, that is the way it would be in America. Love, in this country, must be free, or it is not love at all."

"In China it is different!" mused Mr. Spring Fragrance.

"Oh, yes, I have no doubt that in China it is different."

"But the love is in the heart all the same," went on Mr. Spring Fragrance.

"Yes, all the same. Everybody falls in love some time or another. Some" — pensively — "many times."

Mr. Spring Fragrance arose.

"I must go downtown," said he.

As he walked down the street, he recalled the remark of a business acquaintance who had met his wife and had had some conversation with her: "She is just like an American woman."

He had felt somewhat flattered when this remark had been made. He looked upon it as a compliment to his wife's cleverness; but it rankled in his mind as he entered the telegraph office. If his wife was becoming like an American woman, would it not be possible for her to love, as an American woman, a man to whom she was not married? There also floated in his memory the verse which his wife had quoted to the daughter of Chin Yuen. Yet, when the telegraph clerk handed him a blank, he wrote this message:

"Remain as you wish, but remember that ''Tis better to have loved and lost, than never to have loved at all.'"

When Mrs. Spring Fragrance received this message, her laughter tinkled like falling water. How droll! How delightful! Here was her husband quoting American poetry in a telegram. Perhaps he had been reading her American poetry books since she had left him! She hoped so. They would lead him to understand her sympathy for her dear Laura and Kai Tzu. She need no longer keep from him their secret. How joyful! It had been such a hardship to refrain from confiding in him before. But discreetness had been most necessary, because Mr. Spring Fragrance entertained as old-fashioned notions concerning marriage as did the Chin Yuen parents. Strange that that should be so, since he had fallen in love with her picture before ever he had seen her, just as she had fallen in love with his! And when the marriage veil was lifted and each saw the other for the first time in the flesh, there had been no disillusion, no lessening of the respect and affection which those who had brought about the marriage had inspired in each young heart.

Mrs. Spring Fragrance began to wish she could fall asleep and wake to find herself, the week flown, in her own little home, pouring tea for Mr. Spring Fragrance.

$ð

Mr. Spring Fragrance was walking to business with Mr. Chin Yuen. As they walked they talked.

"Yes," said Mr. Chin Yuen, "the old order is passing away and the new order is taking its place, even with us who are Chinese. I have finally consented to give my daughter in marriage to young Kai Tzu."

Mr. Spring Fragrance expressed surprise. He had understood that the marriage between his neighbor's daughter and the San Francisco schoolteacher's son was all arranged.

"So 'twas," answered Mr. Chin Yuen; "but it seems the young renegade, without consultation or advice, has placed his affections upon some untrustworthy female, and is so under her influence that he refuses to fulfill his parents' promise to me for him."

"So!" said Mr. Spring Fragrance. The shadow on his brow deepened.

"But," said Mr. Chin Yuen with affable resignation, "it is all ordained by Heaven. Our daughter, as the wife of Kai Tzu, for whom she has long had a loving feeling, will not now be compelled to dwell with a mother-in-law and where her own mother is not. For that we are thankful, as she is our only one, and the conditions of life in this Western country are not as in China. Moreover, Kai Tzu, though not so much of a scholar as the teacher's son, has a keen eye for business and that, in America, is certainly much more desirable than scholarship. What do you think?"

"Eh! What!" exclaimed Mr. Spring Fragrance. The latter part of his companion's remarks had been lost upon him.

§ð

That day the shadow which had been following Mr. Spring Fragrance ever since he had heard his wife quote "'Tis better to have loved" became so heavy and deep that he quite lost himself within it. At home, in the evening, he fed the cat, the bird, and the flowers. Then, seating himself in a carved black chair — a present from his wife on his last birthday — he took out his pipe and smoked. The cat jumped into his lap. He stroked it softly and tenderly. It had been much fondled by Mrs. Spring Fragrance, and Mr. Spring Fragrance was under the impression that it missed her. "Poor thing!" said he, "I suppose you want her back." When he arose to go to bed he placed the animal carefully on the floor, and thus apostrophised it:

"O Wise and Silent One, your mistress returns to you, but her heart she leaves behind her with the Tommies in San Francisco."

The Wise and Silent One made no reply. He was not a jealous cat.

Mr. Spring Fragrance slept not that night; the next morning he ate not. Three days and three nights without sleep and food passed.

§ð

There was a springlike freshness in the air on the day that Mrs. Spring Fragrance came home. The skies overhead were as blue as Puget Sound stretching its gleaming length toward the mighty Pacific, and all the beautiful green world seemed to be throbbing with springing life. Mrs. Spring Fragrance was never so radiant.

"Oh," she cried light-heartedly, "is it not lovely to see the sun shining so clear and everything so bright to welcome me?"

Mr. Spring Fragrance did not smile. It was the morning after the fourth sleepless night.

"Everything — everyone is glad to see me but you," she declared, smiling up into his face.

"If my wife is glad to see me," quietly replied Mr. Spring Fragrance, "I also am glad to see her!"

Mrs. Spring Fragrance looked up into his face with honest and earnest eyes. There was something in his manner which touched her heart.

"Yen," said she, "you do not look well. You are not well. What is it?"

Something arose in Mr. Spring Fragrance's throat which prevented him from replying.

"O darling one! O sweetest one!" cried a girl's joyous voice. Laura Chin Yuen ran into the room and threw her arms around Mrs. Spring Fragrance's neck.

"I spied you from the window," said Laura, "and I couldn't rest until I told you. We are to be married next week, Kai Tzu and I. And all through you; all through you — the sweetest jade jewel in the world!"

"I must be downtown in half an hour," said Mr. Spring Fragrance, looking at his watch. Then he passed out of the room.

"So the son of the Government teacher and little Happy Love are already married," Laura cried, as she relieved Mrs. Spring Fragrance of her cloak, her hat, and her folding fan.

Mr. Spring Fragrance paused upon the doorstep.

"Sit down, Little Sister, and I will tell you all about it," said Mrs. Spring Fragrance, forgetting her husband for the moment.

When Laura Chin Yuen had danced away, Mr. Spring Fragrance came in and hung up his hat.

"You got back very soon," said Mrs. Spring Fragrance, covertly wiping away the tears which had begun to fall as soon as she thought herself alone. She could not understand being left at the moment of her arrival.

"I did not go," answered Mr. Spring Fragrance. "I have been listening to you and Laura."

"But if the business is very important, do not you think you should attend to it?" anxiously queried Mrs. Spring Fragrance.

"It is not important to me now," returned Mr. Spring Fragrance. "I would prefer to hear again about Ah Oi and Tsen Hing and Laura and Kai Tzu."

"How lovely of you to say that!" exclaimed Mrs. Spring Fragrance, who was easily made happy. And she began to chat away to her husband in the friendliest and wifeliest fashion possible. When she had finished she asked him if he were not glad to hear that those who loved as did the young lovers whose secrets she had been keeping were to be united; and he replied that indeed he was; that he would like every man to be as happy with his wife as he himself had ever been and ever would be.

"You did not always talk like that," said Mrs. Spring Fragrance slyly. "You must have been reading my American poetry books!"

"American poetry!" ejaculated Mr. Spring Fragrance almost fiercely. "American poetry is detestable, abhorrible!"

"Why! why!" exclaimed Mrs. Spring Fragrance, more and more surprised.

But the only explanation which Mr. Spring Fragrance vouchsafed was a jade-stone pendant.

Jack London
To Build a Fire

One of the most widely celebrated of the Naturalistic stories, Jack London's "To Build a Fire" had an enormous impact on the reading public of the early twentieth century. It first appeared as a story for children in *The Youth's Companion* in 1902 and was then revised for an adult audience before publication in *The Century Mag-*

azine in August 1908. Finally, in a revised form that generalized the protagonist by removing his name, London incorporated it in 1910 into a volume of stories, *Lost Face*. What is so gripping about the plot is the elemental presentation of life as a fight for survival against nature, a standard Naturalistic theme but one presented here in a highly personalized form, one man and his dog struggling with bitter cold. A swirl of related ideas enrich the situation, that the instinct of the dog serves it better than does the reason of the man, that simple miscalculation can lead to death, that human beings are small, impotent entities in the broad scheme of things. Widely read and analyzed, "To Build a Fire" has become one of the most famous of American stories.

Jack London, "To Build a Fire," *Lost Face* (New York: The Macmillan Company, 1910), 63–98.

Day had broken cold and gray, exceedingly cold and gray, when the man turned aside from the main Yukon trail and climbed the high earth-bank, where a dim and little-travelled trail led eastward through the fat spruce timberland. It was a steep bank, and he paused for breath at the top, excusing the act to himself by looking at his watch. It was nine o'clock. There was no sun nor hint of sun, though there was not a cloud in the sky. It was a clear day, and yet there seemed an intangible pall over the face of things, a subtle gloom that made the day dark, and that was due to the absence of sun. This fact did not worry the man. He was used to the lack of sun. It had been days since he had seen the sun, and he knew that a few more days must pass before that cheerful orb, due south, would just peep above the sky-line and dip immediately from view.

The man flung a look back along the way he had come. The Yukon lay a mile wide and hidden under three feet of ice. On top of this ice were as many feet of snow. It was all pure white, rolling in gentle, undulations where the ice-jams of the freeze-up had formed. North and south, as far as his eye could see, it was unbroken white, save for a dark hair-line that curved and twisted from around the spruce-covered island to the south, and that curved and twisted away into the north, where it disappeared behind another spruce-covered island. This dark hair-line was the trail — the main trail — that led south five hundred miles to the Chilcoot Pass, Dyea, and salt water; and that led north seventy miles to Dawson, and still on to the north a thousand miles to Nulato, and finally to St. Michael on Bering Sea, a thousand miles and half a thousand more.

But all this — the mysterious, far-reaching hair-line trail, the absence of sun from the sky, the tremendous cold, and the strangeness and weirdness of it all — made no impression on the man. It was not because he was long used to it. He was a newcomer in the land, a *chechaquo*, and this was his first winter. The trouble with him was that he was without imagination. He was quick and alert in the things of life, but only in the things, and not in the significances. Fifty degrees below zero meant eighty-odd degrees of frost. Such fact impressed him as being cold and uncomfortable, and that was all. It did not lead him to meditate upon his frailty as a creature of temperature, and upon man's frailty in general, able only to live within certain narrow limits of heat and cold; and from there on it did not lead him to the conjectural field of immortality and man's place in the universe. Fifty degrees below zero stood for a bite of frost that hurt and that must be guarded against by the use of mittens, ear-flaps, warm moccasins, and thick socks. Fifty degrees below zero was to him just precisely fifty degrees below zero. That there should be anything more to it than that was a thought that never entered his head.

As he turned to go on, he spat speculatively. There was a sharp, explosive crackle that startled him. He spat again. And again, in the air, before it could fall to the snow, the spittle crackled. He knew that at fifty below spittle crackled on the snow, but this spittle had crackled in the air. Undoubtedly it was colder than fifty below — how much colder he did not know. But the temperature did not matter. He was bound for the old claim on the left fork of Henderson Creek, where the boys were already. They had come over across the divide from the Indian Creek country, while he had come the roundabout way to take a look at the possibilities of getting out logs in the spring from the islands in the Yukon. He would be in to camp by six o'clock; a bit after dark, it was true, but the boys would be there, a fire would be going, and a hot supper would be ready. As for lunch, he pressed his hand against the protruding bundle under his jacket. It was also under his shirt, wrapped up in a handkerchief and lying against the naked skin. It was the only way to keep the biscuits from freezing. He smiled agreeably to himself as he thought of those biscuits, each cut open and sopped in bacon grease, and each enclosing a generous slice of fried bacon.

He plunged in among the big spruce trees. The trail was faint. A foot of snow had fallen since the last sled had passed over, and he was glad he was without a sled, travelling light. In fact, he carried nothing but the lunch wrapped in the handkerchief. He was surprised, however, at the cold. It certainly was cold, he concluded, as he rubbed his numb nose and cheek-bones with his mittened hand. He was a warm-whiskered man, but the hair on his face did not protect the high cheek-bones and the eager nose that thrust itself aggressively into the frosty air.

At the man's heels trotted a dog, a big native husky, the proper wolf-dog, gray-coated and without any visible or temperamental difference from its brother, the wild wolf. The animal was depressed by the tremendous cold. It knew that it was no time for travelling. Its instinct told it a truer tale than was told to the man by the man's judgment. In reality, it was not merely colder than fifty below zero; it was colder than sixty below, than seventy below. It was seventy-five below zero. Since the freezing-point is thirty-two above zero, it meant that one hundred and seven degrees of frost obtained. The dog did not know anything about thermometers. Possibly in its brain there was no sharp consciousness of a condition of very cold such as was in the man's brain. But the brute had its instinct. It experienced a vague but menacing apprehension that subdued it and made it slink along at the man's heels, and that made it question eagerly every unwonted movement of the man as if expecting him to go into camp or to seek shelter somewhere and build a fire. The dog had learned fire, and it wanted fire, or else to burrow under the snow and cuddle its warmth away from the air.

The frozen moisture of its breathing had settled on its fur in a fine powder of frost, and especially were its jowls, muzzle, and eyelashes whitened by its crystalled breath. The man's red beard and mustache were likewise frosted, but more solidly, the deposit taking the form of ice and increasing with every warm, moist breath he exhaled. Also, the man was chewing tobacco, and the muzzle of ice held his lips so rigidly that he was unable to clear his chin when he expelled the juice. The result was that a crystal beard of the color and solidity of amber was increasing its length on his chin. If he fell down it would shatter itself, like glass, into brittle fragments. But he did not mind the appendage. It was the penalty all tobacco-chewers paid in that country, and he had been out before in two cold snaps. They had not been so cold as this, he knew, but by the spirit thermometer at Sixty Mile he knew they had been registered at fifty below and at fifty-five.

He held on through the level stretch of woods for several miles, crossed a wide flat of nigger-heads, and dropped down a bank to the frozen bed of a small stream. This was Henderson Creek, and he knew he was ten miles from the forks. He looked at his watch. It was ten o'clock. He was making four miles an hour, and he calculated that he would arrive at the forks at half-past twelve. He decided to celebrate that event by eating his lunch there.

The dog dropped in again at his heels, with a tail drooping discouragement, as the man swung along the creek-bed. The furrow of the old sled-trail was plainly visible, but a dozen inches of snow covered the marks of the last runners. In a month no man had come up or down that silent creek. The man held steadily on. He was not much given to thinking, and just then particularly he had nothing to think about save that he would eat lunch at the forks and that at six o'clock he would be in camp with the boys. There was nobody to talk to; and, had there been, speech would have been impossible because of the ice-muzzle on his mouth. So he continued monotonously to chew tobacco and to increase the length of his amber beard.

Once in a while the thought reiterated itself that it was very cold and that he had never experienced such cold. As he walked along he rubbed his cheek-bones and nose with the back of his mittened hand. He did this automatically, now and again changing hands. But rub as he would, the instant he stopped his cheek-bones went numb, and the following instant the end of his nose went numb. He was sure to frost his cheeks; he knew that, and experienced a pang of regret that he had not devised a nose-strap of the sort Bud wore in cold snaps. Such a strap passed across the cheeks, as well, and saved them. But it didn't matter much, after all. What were frosted cheeks? A bit painful, that was all; they were never serious.

Empty as the man's mind was of thoughts, he was keenly observant, and he noticed the changes in the creek, the curves and bends and timber-jams, and always he sharply noted where he placed his feet. Once, coming around a bend, he shied abruptly, like a startled horse, curved away from the place where he had been walking, and retreated several paces back along the trail. The creek he knew was frozen clear to the bottom, — no creek could contain water in that arctic winter, — but he knew also that there were springs that bubbled out from the hillsides and ran along under the snow and on top the ice of the creek. He knew that the coldest snaps never froze these springs, and he knew likewise their danger. They were traps. They hid pools of water under the snow that might be three inches deep, or three feet. Sometimes a skin of ice half an inch thick covered them, and in turn was covered by the snow. Sometimes there were alternate layers of water and ice-skin, so that when one broke through he kept on breaking through for a while, sometimes wetting himself to the waist.

That was why he had shied in such panic. He had felt the give under his feet and heard the crackle of a snow-hidden ice-skin. And to get his feet wet in such a temperature meant trouble and danger. At the very least it meant delay, for he would be forced to stop and build a fire, and under its protection to bare his feet while he dried his socks and moccasins. He stood and studied the creek-bed and its banks, and decided that the flow of water came from the right. He reflected awhile, rubbing his nose and cheeks, then skirted to the left, stepping gingerly and testing the footing for each step. Once clear of the danger, he took a fresh chew of tobacco and swung along at his four-mile gait.

In the course of the next two hours he came upon several similar traps. Usually the snow above the hidden pools had a sunken, candied appearance that advertised the danger. Once again, however, he had a close call; and once, suspecting danger, he compelled the dog to go on in front. The dog did not want to go. It hung back until the man shoved it forward, and then it went quickly across the white, unbroken surface. Suddenly it broke through, floundered to one side, and got away to firmer footing. It had wet its forefeet and legs, and almost immediately the water that clung to it turned to ice. It made quick efforts to lick the ice off its legs, then dropped down in the snow and began to bite out the ice that had formed between the toes. This was a matter of instinct. To permit the ice to remain would mean sore feet. It did not know this. It merely obeyed the mysterious prompting that arose from the deep crypts of its being. But the man knew, having achieved a judgment on the subject, and he removed the mitten from his right hand and helped tear out the ice-particles. He did not expose his fingers more than a minute, and was astonished at the swift numbness that smote them.

It certainly was cold. He pulled on the mitten hastily, and beat the hand savagely across his chest.

At twelve o'clock the day was at its brightest. Yet the sun was too far south on its winter journey to clear the horizon. The bulge of the earth intervened between it and Henderson Creek, where the man walked under a clear sky at noon and cast no shadow. At half-past twelve, to the minute, he arrived at the forks of the creek. He was pleased at the speed he had made. If he kept it up, he would certainly be with the boys by six. He unbuttoned his jacket and shirt and drew forth his lunch. The action consumed no more than a quarter of a minute, yet in that brief moment the numbness laid hold of the exposed fingers. He did not put the mitten on, but, instead, struck the fingers a dozen sharp smashes against his leg. Then he sat down on a snow-covered log to eat. The sting that followed upon the striking of his fingers against his leg ceased so quickly that he was startled. He had had no chance to take a bite of biscuit. He struck the fingers repeatedly and returned them to the mitten, baring the other hand for the purpose of eating. He tried to take a mouthful, but the ice-muzzle prevented. He had forgotten to build a fire and thaw out. He chuckled at his foolishness, and as he chuckled he noted the numbness creeping into the exposed fingers. Also, he noted that the stinging which had first come to his toes when he sat down was already passing away. He wondered whether the toes were warm or numb. He moved them inside the moccasins and decided that they were numb.

He pulled the mitten on hurriedly and stood up. He was a bit frightened. He stamped up and down until the stinging returned into the feet. It certainly was cold, was his thought. That man from Sulphur Creek had spoken the truth when telling how cold it sometimes got in the country. And he had laughed at him at the time! That showed one must not be too sure of things. There was no mistake about it, it *was* cold. He strode up and down, stamping his feet and threshing his arms, until reassured by the returning warmth. Then he got out matches and proceeded to make a fire. From the undergrowth, where high water of the previous spring had lodged a supply of seasoned twigs, he got his fire-wood. Working carefully from a small beginning, he soon had a roaring fire, over which he thawed the ice from his face, and in the protection of which he ate his biscuits. For the moment the cold of space was outwitted. The dog took satisfaction in the fire, stretching out close enough for warmth and far enough away to escape being singed.

When the man had finished, he filled his pipe and took his comfortable time over a smoke. Then he pulled on his mittens, settled the earflaps of his cap firmly about his ears, and took the creek trail up the left fork. The dog was disappointed and yearned back toward the fire. This man did not know cold. Possibly all the generations of his ancestry had been ignorant of cold, of real cold, of cold one hundred and seven degrees below freezing-point. But the dog knew; all its ancestry knew, and it had inherited the knowledge. And it knew that it was not good to walk abroad in such fearful cold. It was the time to lie snug in a hole in the snow and wait for a curtain of cloud to be drawn across the face of outer space whence this cold came. On the other hand, there was no keen intimacy between the dog and the man. The one was the toil-slave of the other, and the only caresses it had ever received were the caresses of the whip-lash and of harsh and menacing throat-sounds that threatened the whip-lash. So the dog made no effort to communicate its apprehension to the man. It was not concerned in the welfare of the man; it was for its own sake that it yearned back toward the fire. But the man whistled, and spoke to it with the sound of whip-lashes, and the dog swung in at the man's heels and followed after.

The man took a chew of tobacco and proceeded to start a new amber beard. Also, his moist breath quickly powdered with white his mustache, eyebrows, and lashes. There did not seem to be so many springs on the left fork of the Henderson, and for half an hour the man saw no signs of any. And then it happened. At a place where there were no signs, where the soft, unbroken snow seemed to advertise solidity beneath, the man broke through. It was not deep. He wet himself halfway to the knees before he floundered out to the firm crust.

He was angry, and cursed his luck aloud. He had hoped to get into camp with the boys at six o'clock, and this would delay him an hour, for he would have to build a fire and dry out his foot-gear. This was imperative at that low temperature — he knew that much; and he turned aside to the bank, which he climbed. On top, tangled in the underbrush about the trunks of several small spruce trees, was a high-water deposit of dry fire-wood — sticks and twigs, principally, but also larger portions of seasoned branches and fine, dry, last-year's grasses. He threw down several large pieces on top of the snow. This served for a foundation and prevented the young flame from drowning itself in the snow it otherwise would melt. The flame he got by touching a match to a small shred of birch-bark that he took from his pocket. This burned even more readily than paper. Placing it on the foundation, he fed the young flame with wisps of dry grass and with the tiniest dry twigs.

He worked slowly and carefully, keenly aware of his danger. Gradually, as the flame grew stronger, he increased the size of the twigs with which he fed it. He squatted in the snow, pulling the twigs out from their entanglement in the brush and feeding directly to the flame. He knew there must be no failure. When it is seventy-five below zero, a man must not fail in his first attempt to build a fire — that is, if his feet are wet. If his feet are dry, and he fails, he can run along the trail for half a mile and restore his circulation. But the circulation of wet and freezing feet cannot be restored by running when it is seventy-five below. No matter how fast he runs, the wet feet will freeze the harder.

All this the man knew. The old-timer on Sulphur Creek had told him about it the previous fall, and now he was appreciating the advice. Already all sensation had gone out of his feet. To build the fire he had been forced to remove his mittens, and the fingers had quickly gone numb. His pace of four miles an hour had kept his heart pumping blood to the surface of his body and to all the extremities. But the instant he stopped, the action of the pump eased down. The cold of space smote the unprotected tip of the planet, and he, being on that unprotected tip, received the full force of the blow. The blood of his body recoiled before it. The blood was alive, like the dog, and like the dog it wanted to hide away and cover itself up from the fearful cold. So long as he walked four miles an hour, he pumped that blood, willy-nilly, to the surface; but now it ebbed away and sank down into the recesses of his body. The extremities were the first to feel its absence. His wet feet froze the faster, and his exposed fingers numbed the faster, though they had not yet begun to freeze. Nose and cheeks were already freezing, while the skin of all his body chilled as it lost its blood.

But he was safe. Toes and nose and cheeks would be only touched by the frost, for the fire was beginning to burn with strength. He was feeding it with twigs the size of his finger. In another minute he would be able to feed it with branches the size of his wrist, and then he could remove his wet foot-gear, and, while it dried, he could keep his naked feet warm by the fire, rubbing them at first, of course, with snow. The fire was a success. He was safe. He remembered the advice of the old-timer on Sulphur Creek, and smiled. The old-timer had been very serious in laying down the law that no man must travel alone in the Klondike after fifty below. Well, here he was; he had had the accident; he was alone; and he had saved himself. Those old-timers were rather womanish, some of them, he thought. All a man had to do was to keep his head, and he was all right. Any man who was a man could travel alone. But it was surprising, the rapidity with which his cheeks and nose were freezing. And he had not thought his fingers could go lifeless in so short a time. Lifeless they were, for he could scarcely make them move together to grip a twig, and they seemed remote from his body and from him. When he touched a twig, he had to look and see whether or not he had hold of it. The wires were pretty well down between him and his finger-ends.

All of which counted for little. There was the fire, snapping and crackling and promising life with every dancing flame. He started to untie his moccasins. They were coated with ice; the thick German socks were like sheaths of iron halfway to the knees; and the moccasin strings were like rods of steel all twisted and knotted as by some conflagration. For a moment he tugged with his numb fingers, then, realizing the folly of it, he drew his sheath-knife.

But before he could cut the strings, it happened. It was his own fault or, rather, his mistake. He should not have built the fire under the spruce tree. He should have built it in the open. But it had been easier to pull the twigs from the brush and drop them directly on the fire. Now the tree under which he had done this carried a weight of snow on its boughs. No wind had blown for weeks, and each bough was fully freighted. Each time he had pulled a twig he had communicated

a slight agitation to the tree — an imperceptible agitation, so far as he was concerned, but an agitation sufficient to bring about the disaster. High up in the tree
one bough capsized its load of snow. This fell on the boughs beneath, capsizing
them. This process continued, spreading out and involving the whole tree. It
grew like an avalanche, and it descended without warning upon the man and the
fire, and the fire was blotted out! Where it had burned was a mantle of fresh and
disordered snow.

The man was shocked. It was as though he had just heard his own sentence
of death. For a moment he sat and stared at the spot where the fire had been.
Then he grew very calm. Perhaps the old-timer on Sulphur Creek was right. If
he had only had a trail-mate he would have been in no danger now. The trail-
mate could have built the fire. Well, it was up to him to build the fire over again,
and this second time there must be no failure. Even if he succeeded, he would
most likely lose some toes. His feet must be badly frozen by now, and there
would be some time before the second fire was ready.

Such were his thoughts, but he did not sit and think them. He was busy all
the time they were passing through his mind. He made a new foundation for a
fire, this time in the open, where no treacherous tree could blot it out. Next, he
gathered dry grasses and tiny twigs from the high-water flotsam. He could not
bring his fingers together to pull them out, but he was able to gather them by the
handful. In this way he got many rotten twigs and bits of green moss that were
undesirable, but it was the best he could do. He worked methodically, even collecting an armful of the larger branches to be used later when the fire gathered
strength. And all the while the dog sat and watched him, a certain yearning wistfulness in its eyes, for it looked upon him as the fire-provider, and the fire was
slow in coming.

When all was ready, the man reached in his pocket for a second piece of
birch-bark. He knew the bark was there, and, though he could not feel it with his
fingers, he could hear its crisp rustling as he fumbled for it. Try as he would, he
could not clutch hold of it. And all the time, in his consciousness, was the
knowledge that each instant his feet were freezing. This thought tended to put
him in a panic, but he fought against it and kept calm. He pulled on his mittens
with his teeth, and threshed his arms back and forth, beating his hands with all
his might against his sides. He did this sitting down, and he stood up to do it; and
all the while the dog sat in the snow, its wolf-brush of a tail curled around
warmly over its forefeet, its sharp wolf-ears pricked forward intently as it
watched the man. And the man, as he beat and threshed with his arms and
hands, felt a great surge of envy as he regarded the creature that was warm and
secure in its natural covering.

After a time he was aware of the first far-away signals of sensation in his
beaten fingers. The faint tingling grew stronger till it evolved into a stinging ache
that was excruciating, but which the man hailed with satisfaction. He stripped

the mitten from his right hand and fetched forth the birch-bark. The exposed fingers were quickly going numb again. Next he brought out his bunch of sulphur matches. But the tremendous cold had already driven the life out of his fingers. In his effort to separate one match from the others, the whole bunch fell in the snow. He tried to pick it out of the snow, but failed. The dead fingers could neither touch nor clutch. He was very careful. He drove the thought of his freezing feet, and nose, and cheeks, out of his mind, devoting his whole soul to the matches. He watched, using the sense of vision in place of that of touch, and when he saw his fingers on each side the bunch, he closed them — that is, he willed to close them, for the wires were down, and the fingers did not obey. He pulled the mitten on the right hand, and beat it fiercely against his knee. Then, with both mittened hands, he scooped the bunch of matches, along with much snow, into his lap. Yet he was no better off.

After some manipulation he managed to get the bunch between the heels of his mittened hands. In this fashion he carried it to his mouth. The ice crackled and snapped when by a violent effort he opened his mouth. He drew the lower jaw in, curled the upper lip out of the way, and scraped the bunch with his upper teeth in order to separate a match. He succeeded in getting one, which he dropped on his lap. He was no better off. He could not pick it up. Then he devised a way. He picked it up in his teeth and scratched it on his leg. Twenty times he scratched before he succeeded in lighting it. As it flamed he held it with his teeth to the birch-bark. But the burning brimstone went up his nostrils and into his lungs, causing him to cough spasmodically. The match fell into the snow and went out.

The old-timer on Sulphur Creek was right, he thought in the moment of controlled despair that ensued: after fifty below, a man should travel with a partner. He beat his hands, but failed in exciting any sensation. Suddenly he bared both hands, removing the mittens with his teeth. He caught the whole bunch between the heels of his hands. His arm-muscles not being frozen enabled him to press the hand-heels tightly against the matches. Then he scratched the bunch along his leg. It flared into flame, seventy sulphur matches at once! There was no wind to blow them out. He kept his head to one side to escape the strangling fumes, and held the blazing bunch to the birch-bark. As he so held it, he became aware of sensation in his hand. His flesh was burning. He could smell it. Deep down below the surface he could feel it. The sensation developed into pain that grew acute. And still he endured it, holding the flame of the matches clumsily to the bark that would not light readily because his own burning hands were in the way, absorbing most of the flame.

At last, when he could endure no more, he jerked his hands apart. The blazing matches fell sizzling into the snow, but the birch-bark was alight. He began laying dry grasses and the tiniest twigs on the flame. He could not pick and choose, for he had to lift the fuel between the heels of his hands. Small pieces of rotten wood and green moss clung to the twigs, and he bit them off as well as he could with his teeth. He cherished the flame carefully and awkwardly. It meant life, and it must not perish. The withdrawal of blood from the surface of his body now made him begin to shiver, and he grew more awkward. A large piece of green moss fell squarely on the little fire. He tried to poke it out with his fingers, but his shivering flame made him poke too far, and he disrupted the nucleus of the little fire, the burning grasses and tiny twigs separating and scattering. He tried to poke them together again, but in spite of the tenseness of the effort, his shivering got away with him, and the twigs were hopelessly scattered. Each twig gushed a puff of smoke and went out. The fire-provider had failed. As he looked apathetically about him, his eyes chanced on the dog, sitting across the ruins of the fire from him, in the snow, making restless, hunching movements, slightly lifting one forefoot and then the other, shifting its weight back and forth on them with wistful eagerness.

The sight of the dog put a wild idea into his head. He remembered the tale of the man, caught in a blizzard, who killed a steer and crawled inside the carcass, and so was saved. He would kill the dog and bury his hands in the warm body until the numbness went out of them. Then he could build another fire. He spoke to the dog, calling it to him; but in his voice was a strange note of fear that frightened the animal, who had never known the man to speak in such way before. Something was the matter, and its suspicious nature sensed danger — it knew not what danger, but somewhere, somehow, in its brain arose an apprehension of the man. It flattened its ears down at the sound of the man's voice, and its restless, hunching movements and the liftings and shiftings of its forefeet became more pronounced; but it would not come to the man. He got on his hands and knees and crawled toward the dog. This unusual posture again excited suspicion, and the animal sidled mincingly away.

The man sat up in the snow for a moment and struggled for calmness. Then he pulled on his mittens, by means of his teeth, and got upon his feet. He glanced down at first in order to assure himself that he was really standing up, for the absence of sensation in his feet left him unrelated to the earth. His erect position in itself started to drive the webs of suspicion from the dog's mind; and when he spoke peremptorily, with the sound of whip-lashes in his voice, the dog rendered its customary allegiance and came to him. As it came within reaching distance, the man lost his control. His arms flashed out to the dog, and he experienced genuine surprise when he discovered that his hands could not clutch, that there was neither bend nor feeling in the fingers. He had forgotten for the moment that they were frozen and that they were freezing more and more. All this happened quickly, and before the animal could get away, he encircled its body with his arms. He sat down in the snow, and in this fashion held the dog, while it snarled and whined and struggled.

But it was all he could do, hold its body encircled in his arms and sit there. He realized that he could not kill the dog. There was no way to do it. With his help-less hands he could neither draw nor hold his sheath-knife nor throttle the animal. He released it, and it plunged wildly away, with tail between its legs, and still snarling. It halted forty feet away and surveyed him curiously, with ears sharply pricked forward. The man looked down at his hands in order to locate them, and found them hanging on the ends of his arms. It struck him as curious that one should have to use his eyes in order to find out where his hands were. He began threshing his arms back and forth, beating the mittened hands against his sides. He did this for five minutes, violently, and his heart pumped enough blood up to the surface to put a stop to his shivering. But no sensation was aroused in the hands. He had an impression that they hung like weights on the ends of his arms, but when he tried to run the impression down, he could not find it.

A certain fear of death, dull and oppressive, came to him. This fear quickly became poignant as he realized that it was no longer a mere matter of freezing his fingers and toes, or of losing his hands and feet, but that it was a matter of life and death with the chances against him. This threw him into a panic, and he turned and ran up the creek-bed along the old, dim trail. The dog joined in behind and kept up with him. He ran blindly, without intention, in fear such as he had never known in his life. Slowly, as he ploughed and floundered through the snow, he began to see things again, — the banks of the creek, the old timber-jams, the leafless aspens, and the sky. The running made him feel better. He did not shiver. Maybe, if he ran on, his feet would thaw out; and, anyway, if he ran far enough, he would reach camp and the boys. Without doubt he would lose some fingers and toes and some of his face; but the boys would take care of him, and save the rest of him when he got there. And at the same time there was another thought in his mind that said he would never get to the camp and the boys; that it was too many miles away, that the freezing had too great a start on him, and that he would soon be stiff and dead. This thought he kept in the background and refused to consider. Sometimes it pushed itself forward and demanded to be heard, but he thrust it back and strove to think of other things.

It struck him as curious that he could run at all on feet so frozen that he could not feel them when they struck the earth and took the weight of his body. He seemed to himself to skim along above the surface, and to have no connection with the earth. Somewhere he had once seen a winged Mercury, and he wondered if Mercury felt as he felt when skimming over the earth.

His theory of running until he reached camp and the boys had one flaw in it: he lacked the endurance. Several times he stumbled, and finally he tottered, crumpled up, and fell. When he tried to rise, he failed. He must sit and rest, he decided, and next time he would merely walk and keep on going. As he sat and regained his breath, he noted that he was feeling quite warm and comfortable.

He was not shivering, and it even seemed that a warm glow had come to his chest and trunk. And yet, when he touched his nose or cheeks, there was no sensation. Running would not thaw them out. Nor would it thaw out his hands and feet. Then the thought came to him that the frozen portions of his body must be extending. He tried to keep this thought down, to forget it, to think of something else; he was aware of the panicky feeling that it caused, and he was afraid of the panic. But the thought asserted itself, and persisted, until it produced a vision of his body totally frozen. This was too much, and he made another wild run along the trail. Once he slowed down to a walk, but the thought of the freezing extending itself made him run again.

And all the time the dog ran with him, at his heels. When he fell down a second time, it curled its tail over its forefeet and sat in front of him, facing him, curiously eager and intent. The warmth and security of the animal angered him, and he cursed it till it flattened down its ears appeasingly. This time the shivering came more quickly upon the man. He was losing in his battle with the frost. It was creeping into his body from all sides. The thought of it drove him on, but he ran no more than a hundred feet, when he staggered and pitched headlong. It was his last panic. When he had recovered his breath and control, he sat up and entertained in his mind the conception of meeting death with dignity. However, the conception did not come to him in such terms. His idea of it was that he had been making a fool of himself, running around like a chicken with its head cut off — such was the simile that occurred to him. Well, he was bound to freeze anyway, and he might as well take it decently. With this new-found peace of mind came the first glimmerings of drowsiness. A good idea, he thought, to sleep off to death. It was like taking an anæsthetic. Freezing was not so bad as people thought. There were lots worse ways to die.

He pictured the boys finding his body next day. Suddenly he found himself with them, coming along the trail and looking for himself. And, still with them, he came around a turn in the trail and found himself lying in the snow. He did not belong with himself any more, for even then he was out of himself, standing with the boys and looking at himself in the snow. It certainly was cold, was his thought. When he got back to the States he could tell the folks what real cold was. He drifted on from this to a vision of the old-timer on Sulphur Creek. He could see him quite clearly, warm and comfortable, and smoking a pipe.

"You were right, old hoss; you were right," the man mumbled to the old-timer of Sulphur Creek.

Then the man drowsed off into what seemed to him the most comfortable and satisfying sleep he had ever known. The dog sat facing him and waiting. The brief day drew to a close in a long, slow twilight. There were no signs of a fire to be made, and, besides, never in the dog's experience had it known a man to sit like that in the snow and make no fire. As the twilight drew on, its eager yearning for the fire mastered it, and with a great lifting and shifting of forefeet, it whined softly, then flattened its ears down in anticipation of being chidden by the man. But the man remained silent. Later, the dog whined loudly. And still later it crept close to the man and caught the scent of death. This made the animal bristle and back away. A little longer it delayed, howling under the stars that leaped and danced and shone brightly in the cold sky. Then it turned and trotted up the trail in the direction of the camp it knew, where were the other food-providers and fire-providers.

Jessie Fauset
Emmy

Jessie Fauset was born in 1882 into an affluent African American family and went on to become a pivotal figure in the Harlem Renaissance of the 1920s. Even before that, however, she had established herself as an important member of the literary community. The first black woman to attend Cornell University, where she graduated Phi Beta Kappa, she later took an M.A. in French from the University of Pennsylvania prior to continued study at the Sorbonne. After assuming a teaching post at what was later known as the Dunbar School in Washington, D.C., she produced a stream of essays, poems, and short stories followed by four novels, all issued by the leading publishers of the day. She was also active in the NAACP, including a stint as editor of its magazine, *The Crisis*. Her first short story, "Emmy," appeared there in 1912, and it deals with complex issues of race consciousness, passing, and subtle forms of discrimination. Carefully structured into scenes about Emmy and her intended, Archie, the alternating incidents reveal much about the social intricacies of black life in the early twentieth century.

Jessie Fauset, "Emmy," *The Crisis* 5, no. 2 (December 1912): 79–87; 5, no. 3 (January 1913): 135–42.

I

"There are five races," said Emmy confidently. "The white or Caucasian, the yellow or Mongolian, the red or Indian, the brown or Malay, and the black or Negro."

"Correct," nodded Miss Wenzel mechanically. "Now to which of the five do you belong?" And then immediately Miss Wenzel reddened.

Emmy hesitated. Not because hers was the only dark face in the crowded schoolroom, but because she was visualizing the pictures with which the geography had illustrated its information. She was not white, she knew that — nor had she almond eyes like the Chinese, nor the feathers which the Indian wore in his hair and which, of course, were to Emmy a racial characteristic. She regarded the color of her slim brown hands with interest — she had never thought of it before. The Malay was a horrid, ugly-looking thing with a ring in his nose. But he was brown, so she was, she supposed, really a Malay.

And yet the Hottentot, chosen with careful nicety to represent the entire Negro race, had on the whole a better appearance.

"I belong," she began tentatively, "to the black or Negro race."

"Yes," said Miss Wenzel with a sigh of relief, for if Emmy had chosen to ally herself with any other race except, of course, the white, how could she, teacher though she was, set her straight without embarrassment? The recess bell rang and she dismissed them with a brief but thankful "You may pass."

Emmy uttered a sigh of relief, too, as she entered the schoolyard. She had been terribly near failing.

"I was so scared," she breathed to little towheaded Mary Holborn. "Did you see what a long time I was answering? Guess Eunice Lecks thought for sure I'd fail and she'd get my place."

"Yes, I guess she did," agreed Mary. "I'm so glad you didn't fail — but, oh, Emmy, didn't you mind?"

Emmy looked up in astonishment from the orange she was peeling.

"Mind what? Here, you can have the biggest half. I don't like oranges anyway — sort of remind me of niter. Mind what, Mary?"

"Why, saying you were black and" — she hesitated, her little freckled face getting pinker and pinker — "a Negro, and all that before the class." And then mistaking the look on Emmy's face, she hastened on. "Everybody in Plainville says all the time that you're too nice and smart to be a — er — I mean, to be colored. And your dresses are so pretty, and your hair isn't all funny either." She seized one of Emmy's hands — an exquisite member, all bronze outside, and within a soft pinky white.

"Oh, Emmy, don't you think if you scrubbed real hard you could get some of the brown off?"

"But I don't want to," protested Emmy. "I guess my hands are as nice as yours, Mary Holborn. We're just the same, only you're white and I'm brown. But I don't see any difference. Eunice Lecks' eyes are green and yours are blue, but you can both see."

"Oh, well," said Mary Holborn, "if you don't mind —"

If she didn't mind — but why should she mind?

"Why should I mind, Archie," she asked that faithful squire as they walked home in the afternoon through the pleasant "main" street. Archie had brought her home from school ever since she could remember. He was two years older than she; tall, strong and beautiful, and her final arbiter.

Archie stopped to watch a spider.

"See how he does it, Emmy! See him bring that thread over! Gee, if I could swing a bridge across the pond as easy as that! What d'you say? Why should you mind? Oh, I don't guess there's anything for us to mind about. It's white people, they're always minding — I don't know why.

"If any of the boys in your class say anything to you, you let me know. I licked

Bill Jennings the other day for calling me a 'guiney.' Wish I were a good, sure-enough brown like you, and then everybody'd know just what I am."

Archie's clear olive skin and aquiline features made his Negro ancestry difficult of belief.

"But," persisted Emmy, "what difference does it make?"

"Oh, I'll tell you some other time," he returned vaguely. "Can't you ask questions though? Look, it's going to rain. That means uncle won't need me in the field this afternoon. See here, Emmy, bet I can let you run ahead while I count fifteen, and then beat you to your house. Want to try?"

They reached the house none too soon, for the soft spring drizzle soon turned into gusty torrents. Archie was happy — he loved Emmy's house with the long, high rooms and the books and the queer foreign pictures. And Emmy had so many sensible playthings. Of course, a great big fellow of 13 doesn't care for locomotives and blocks in the ordinary way, but when one is trying to work out how a bridge must be built over a lop-sided ravine, such things are by no means to be despised. When Mrs. Carrel, Emmy's mother, sent Céleste to tell the children to come to dinner, they raised such a protest that the kindly French woman finally set them a table in the sitting room, and left them to their own devices.

"Don't you love little fresh green peas?" said Emmy ecstatically. "Oh, Archie, won't you tell me now what difference it makes whether you are white or colored?" She peered into the vegetable dish. "Do you suppose Céleste would give us some more peas? There's only about a spoonful left."

"I don't believe she would," returned the boy, evading the important part of her question. "There were lots of them to start with, you know. Look, if you take up each pea separately on your fork — like that — they'll last longer. It's hard to do, too. Bet I can do it better than you."

And in the exciting contest that followed both children forgot all about the "problem."

II

Miss Wenzel sent for Emmy the next day. Gently but insistently, and altogether from a mistaken sense of duty, she tried to make the child see wherein her lot differed from that of her white schoolmates. She felt herself that she hadn't succeeded very well. Emmy, immaculate in a white frock, her bronze elfin face framed in its thick curling black hair, alert with interest, had listened very attentively. She had made no comments till toward the end.

"Then because I'm brown," she had said, "I'm not as good as you." Emmy was at all times severely logical.

"Well, I wouldn't — quite say that," stammered Miss Wenzel miserably. "You're really very nice, you know, especially nice for a colored girl, but — well, you're different."

Emmy listened patiently. "I wish you'd tell me how, Miss Wenzel," she began.

"Archie Ferrers is different, too, isn't he? And yet he's lots nicer than almost any of the boys in Plainville. And he's smart, you know. I guess he's pretty poor — I shouldn't like to be that — but my mother isn't poor, and she's handsome. I heard Céleste say so, and she has beautiful clothes. I think, Miss Wenzel, it must be rather nice to be different."

It was at this point that Miss Wenzel had desisted and, tucking a little tissue-wrapped oblong into Emmy's hands, had sent her home.

"I don't think I did any good," she told her sister wonderingly. "I couldn't make her see what being colored meant."

"I don't see why you didn't leave her alone," said Hannah Wenzel testily. "I don't guess she'll meet with much prejudice if she stays here in central Pennsylvania. And if she goes away she'll meet plenty of people who'll make it their business to see that she understands what being colored means. Those things adjust themselves."

"Not always," retorted Miss Wenzel, "and anyway, that child ought to know. She's got to have some of the wind taken out of her sails, some day, anyhow. Look how her mother dresses her. I suppose she does make pretty good money — I've heard that translating pays well. Seems so funny for a colored woman to be able to speak and write a foreign language." She returned to her former complaint.

"Of course it doesn't cost much to live here, but Emmy's clothes! White frocks all last winter, and a long red coat — broadcloth it was, Hannah. And big bows on her hair — she has got pretty hair, I must say."

"Oh, well," said Miss Hannah, "I suppose Céleste makes her clothes. I guess colored people want to look nice just as much as anybody else. I heard Mr. Holborn say Mrs. Carrel used to live in France; I suppose that's where she got all her stylish ways."

"Yes, just think of that," resumed Miss Wenzel vigorously, "a colored woman with a French maid. Though if it weren't for her skin you'd never tell by her actions what she was. It's the same way with that Archie Ferrers, too, looking for all the world like some foreigner. I must say I like colored people to look and act like what they are."

She spoke the more bitterly because of her keen sense of failure. What she had meant to do was to show Emmy kindly — oh, very kindly — her proper place, and then, using the object in the little tissue-wrapped parcel as a sort of text, to preach a sermon on humility without aspiration.

The tissue-wrapped oblong proved to Emmy's interested eyes to contain a motto of Robert Louis Stevenson, entitled: "A Task" — the phrases picked out in red and blue and gold, under glass and framed in passepartout. Everybody nowadays has one or more of such mottoes in his house, but the idea was new then to Plainville. The child read it through carefully as she passed by the lilac-scented "front yards." She read well for her age, albeit a trifle uncomprehendingly.

"To be honest, to be kind, to earn a little and to spend a little less;" —

"there," thought Emmy, "is a semi-colon — let's see — the semi-colon shows that the thought" — and she went on through the definition Miss Wenzel had given her, and returned happily to her motto:

"To make upon the whole a family happier for his presence" — thus far the lettering was in blue. "To renounce when that shall be necessary and not be embittered" — this phrase was in gold. Then the rest went on in red: "To keep a few friends, but these without capitulation; above all, on the same given condition to keep friends with himself — here is a task for all that a man has of fortitude and delicacy."

"It's all about some man," she thought with a child's literalness. "Wonder why Miss Wenzel gave it to me? That big word, cap-it-u-la-tion" — she divided it off into syllables, doubtfully — "must mean to spell with capitals I guess. I'll say it to Archie some time."

But she thought it very kind of Miss Wenzel. And after she had shown it to her mother, she hung it up in the bay window of her little white room, where the sun struck it every morning.

III

Afterward Emmy always connected the motto with the beginning of her own realization of what color might mean. It took her quite a while to find it out, but by the time she was ready to graduate from the high school she had come to recognize that the occasional impasse which she met now and then might generally be traced to color. This knowledge, however, far from embittering her, simply gave to her life keener zest. Of course she never met with any of the grosser forms of prejudice, and her personality was the kind to win her at least the respect and sometimes the wondering admiration of her schoolmates. For unconsciously she made them see that she was perfectly satisfied with being colored. She could never understand why anyone should think she would want to be white.

One day a girl — Elise Carter — asked her to let her copy her French verbs in the test they were to have later in the day. Emmy, who was both by nature and by necessity independent, refused bluntly.

"Oh, don't be so mean, Emmy," Elise had wailed. She hesitated. "If you'll let me copy them — I'll — I tell you what I'll do, I'll see that you get invited to our club spread Friday afternoon."

"Well, I guess you won't," Emmy had retorted. "I'll probably be asked anyway. 'Most everybody else has been invited already."

Elise jeered. "And did you think as a matter of course that we'd ask you? Well, you have got something to learn."

There was no mistaking the "you."

Emmy took the blow pretty calmly for all its unexpectedness. "You mean," she said slowly, the blood showing darkly under the thin brown of her skin, "because I'm colored?"

Elise hedged — she was a little frightened at such directness.

"Oh, well, Emmy, you know colored folks can't expect to have everything we have, or if they do they must pay extra for it."

"I — I see," said Emmy, stammering a little, as she always did when she was angry. "I begin to see for the first time why you think it's so awful to be colored. It's because you think we are willing to be mean and sneaky and" — with a sudden drop to schoolgirl vernacular — "soup-y. Why, Elise Carter, I wouldn't be in your old club with girls like you for worlds." There was no mistaking her sincerity.

"That was the day," she confided to Archie a long time afterward, "that I learned the meaning of making friends 'without capitulation.' Do you remember Miss Wenzel's motto, Archie?"

He assured her he did. "And of course you know, Emmy, you were an awful brick to answer that Carter girl like that. Didn't you really want to go to the spread?"

"Not one bit," she told him vigorously, "after I found out why I hadn't been asked. And look, Archie, isn't it funny, just as soon as she wanted something she didn't care whether I was colored or not."

Archie nodded. "They're all that way," he told her briefly.

"And if I'd gone she'd have believed that all colored people were sort of — well, you know, 'meachin' — just like me. It's so odd the ignorant way in which they draw their conclusions. Why, I remember reading the most interesting article in a magazine — the *Atlantic Monthly* I think it was. A woman had written it and at this point she was condemning universal suffrage. And all of a sudden, without any warning, she spoke of that 'fierce, silly, amiable creature, the uneducated Negro,' and — think of it, Archie — of 'his baser and sillier female.' It made me so angry. I've never forgotten it."

Archie whistled. "That was pretty tough," he acknowledged. "I suppose the truth is," he went on smiling at her earnestness, "she has a colored cook who drinks."

"That's just it," she returned emphatically. "She probably has. But, Archie, just think of all the colored people we've both seen here and over in Newtown, too; some of them just as poor and ignorant as they can be. But not one of them is fierce or base or silly enough for that to be considered his chief characteristic. I'll wager that woman never spoke to fifty colored people in her life. No, thank you, if that's what it means to belong to the 'superior race,' I'll come back, just as I am, to the fiftieth reincarnation."

Archie sighed. "Oh, well, life is very simple for you. You see, you've never been up against it like I've been. After all, you've had all you wanted practically — those girls even came around finally in the high school and asked you into their clubs and things. While I ——" he colored sensitively.

"You see, this plagued — er — complexion of mine, doesn't tell anybody what I am. At first — and all along, too, if I let them — fellows take me for a foreigner of some kind — Spanish or something, and they take me up hail-fellow-well-met. And then, if I let them know — I hate to feel I'm taking them in, you know, and besides that I can't help being curious to know what's going to happen ——"

"What does happen?" interrupted Emmy, all interest.

"Well, all sorts of things. You take that first summer just before I entered preparatory school. You remember I was working at that camp in Cottage City. All the waiters were fellows just like me, working to go to some college or other. At first I was just one of them — swam with them, played cards — oh, you know, regularly chummed with them. Well, the cook was a colored man — sure enough, colored you know — and one day one of the boys called him a — of course I couldn't tell you, Emmy, but he swore at him and called him a Nigger. And when I took up for him the fellow said — he was angry, Emmy, and he said it as the worst insult he could think of — 'Anybody would think you had black blood in your veins, too.'

"Anybody would think right," I told him.

"Well?" asked Emmy.

He shrugged his shoulders. "That was all there was to it. The fellows dropped me completely — left me to the company of the cook, who was all right enough as cooks go, I suppose, but he didn't want me any more than I wanted him. And finally the manager came and told me he was sorry, but he guessed I'd have to go." He smiled grimly as at some unpleasant reminiscence.

"What's the joke?" his listener wondered.

"He also told me that I was the blankest kind of a blank fool — oh, you couldn't dream how he swore, Emmy. He said why didn't I leave well enough alone.

"And don't you know that's the thought I've had ever since — why not leave well enough alone? — and not tell people what I am. I guess you're different from me," he broke off wistfully, noting her look of disapproval; "you're so complete and satisfied in yourself. Just being Emilie Carrel seems to be enough for you. But you just wait until color keeps you from the thing you want the most, and you'll see."

"You needn't be so tragic," she commented succinctly. "Outside of that one time at Cottage City, it doesn't seem to have kept you back."

For Archie's progress had been miraculous. In the seven years in which he had been from home, one marvel after another had come his way. He had found lucrative work each summer, he had got through his preparatory school in three years, he had been graduated number six from one of the best technical schools in the country — and now he had a position. He was to work for one of the biggest engineering concerns in Philadelphia.

This last bit of good fortune had dropped out of a clear sky. A guest at one of the hotels one summer had taken an interest in the handsome, willing bellboy and inquired into his history. Archie had hesitated at first, but finally, his eye alert for the first sign of dislike or superiority, he told the man of his Negro blood.

"If he turns me down," he said to himself boyishly, "I'll never risk it again."

But Mr. Robert Fallon — young, wealthy and quixotic — had become more interested than ever.

"So it's all a gamble with you, isn't it? By George! How exciting your life must be — now white and now black — standing between ambition and honor, what? Not that I don't think you're doing the right thing — it's nobody's confounded business anyway. Look here, when you get through look me up. I may be able to put you wise to something. Here's my card. And say, mum's the word, and when you've made your pile you can wake some fine morning and find yourself famous simply by telling what you are. All rot, this beastly prejudice, I say."

And when Archie had graduated, his new friend, true to his word, had gotten for him from his father a letter of introduction to Mr. Nicholas Fields in Philadelphia, and Archie was placed. Young Robert Fallon had gone laughing on his aimless, merry way.

"Be sure you keep your mouth shut, Ferrers," was his only enjoinment.

Archie, who at first had experienced some qualms, had finally completely acquiesced. For the few moments' talk with Mr. Fields had intoxicated him. The vision of work, plenty of it, his own chosen kind — and the opportunity to do it as a man — not an exception, but as a plain ordinary man among other men — was too much for him.

"It was my big chance, Emmy," he told her one day. He was spending his brief vacation in Plainville, and the two, having talked themselves out on other things, had returned to their old absorbing topic. He went on a little pleadingly, for she had protested. "I couldn't resist it. You don't know what it means to me. I don't care about being white in itself any more than you do — but I do care about a white man's chances. Don't let's talk about it any more though; here it's the first week in September and I have to go the 15th. I may not be back till Christmas. I should hate to think that you — you were changed toward me, Emmy."

"I'm not changed, Archie," she assured him gravely, "only somehow it makes me feel that you're different. I can't quite look up to you as I used. I don't like the idea of considering the end justified by the means."

She was silent, watching the falling leaves flutter like golden butterflies against her white dress. As she stood there in the old-fashioned garden, she seemed to the boy's adoring eyes like some beautiful but inflexible bronze goddess.

"I couldn't expect you to look up to me, Emmy, as though I were on a pedestal," he began miserably, "but I do want you to respect me, because — oh, Emmy, don't you see? I love you very much and I hope you will — I want you to — oh, Emmy, couldn't you like me a little? I — I've never thought ever of anyone but you. I didn't mean to tell you all about this now — I meant to wait until I really was successful, and then come and lay it all at your beautiful feet. You're so lovely, Emmy. But if you despise me ——" he was very humble.

For once in her calm young life Emmy was completely surprised. But she had to get to the root of things. "You mean," she faltered, "you mean you want" — she couldn't say it.

"I mean I want you to marry me," he said, gaining courage from her confusion. "Oh, have I frightened you, Emmy, dearest — of course you couldn't like me well enough for that all in a heap — it's different with me. I've always loved you, Emmy. But if you'd only think about it."

"Oh," she breathed, "there's Céleste. Oh, Archie, I don't know, it's all so funny. And we're so young. I couldn't really tell anything about my feelings anyway — you know, I've never seen anybody but you." Then as his face clouded — "Oh, well, I guess even if I had I wouldn't like him any better. Yes, Céleste, we're coming in. Archie, mother says you're to have dinner with us every night you're here, if you can."

There was no more said about the secret that Archie was keeping from Mr. Fields. There were too many other things to talk about — reasons why he had always loved Emmy; reasons why she couldn't be sure just yet; reasons why, if she were sure, she couldn't say yes.

Archie hung between high hope and despair, while Emmy, it must be confessed, enjoyed herself, albeit innocently enough, and grew distractingly pretty. On the last day as they sat in the sitting room, gaily recounting childish episodes, Archie suddenly asked her again. He was so grave and serious that she really became frightened.

"Oh, Archie, I couldn't — I don't really want to. It's so lovely just being a girl. I think I do like you — of course I like you lots. But couldn't we just be friends and keep going on — so?"

"No," he told her harshly, his face set and miserable; "no, we can't. And, Emmy — I'm not coming back any more — I couldn't stand it." His voice broke, he was fighting to keep back the hot boyish tears. After all he was only 21. "I'm sorry I troubled you," he said proudly.

She looked at him pitifully. "I don't want you to go away forever, Archie," she said tremulously. She made no effort to keep back the tears. "I've been so lonely this last year since I've been out of school — you can't think."

He was down on his knees, his arms around her. "Emmy, Emmy, look up — are you crying for me, dear? Do you want me to come back — you do — you mean it? Emmy, you must love me, you do — a little." He kissed her slim fingers.

"Are you going to marry me? Look at me, Emmy — you are! Oh, Emmy, do you know I'm — I'm going to kiss you."

The stage came lumbering up not long afterward, and bore him away to the train — triumphant and absolutely happy.

"My heart," sang Emmy rapturously as she ran up the broad, old-fashioned stairs to her room — "my heart is like a singing bird."

IV

The year that followed seemed to her perfection. Archie's letters alone would
have made it that. Emmy was quite sure that there had never been any other letters like them. She used to read them aloud to her mother.

Not all of them, though, for some were too precious for any eye but her own.
She used to pore over them alone in her room at night, planning to answer them
with an abandon equal to his own, but always finally evolving the same shy, almost timid epistle, which never failed to awaken in her lover's breast a sense
equally of amusement and reverence. Her shyness seemed to him the most exquisite thing in the world — so exquisite, indeed, that he almost wished it would
never vanish, were it not that its very disappearance would be the measure of
her trust in him. His own letters showed plainly his adoration.

Only once had a letter of his caused a fleeting pang of misapprehension.
He had been speaking of the persistent good fortune which had been his in
Philadelphia.

"You can't think how lucky I am anyway," the letter ran on. "The other day I
was standing on the corner of Fourth and Chestnut Streets at noon — you
ought to see Chestnut Street at 12 o'clock, Emmy — and someone came up,
looked at me and said: 'Well, if it isn't Archie Ferrers!' And guess who it was,
Emmy? Do you remember the Higginses who used to live over in Newtown? I
don't suppose you ever knew them, only they were so queer looking that you
must recall them. They were all sorts of colors from black with 'good' hair to
yellow with the red, kinky kind. And then there was Maude, clearly a Higgins,
and yet not looking like any of them, you know; perfectly white, with blue eyes
and fair hair. Well, this was Maude, and, say, maybe she didn't look good. I
couldn't tell you what she had on, but it was all right, and I was glad to take her
over to the Reading Terminal and put her on a train to New York.

"I guess you're wondering where my luck is in all this tale, but you wait. Just
as we started up the stairs of the depot, whom should we run into but young Peter Fields, my boss's son and heir, you know. Really, I thought I'd faint, and then
I remembered that Maude was whiter than he in looks, and that there was nothing to give me away. He wanted to talk to us, but I hurried her off to her train.
You know, it's a queer thing, Emmy; some girls are just naturally born stylish.
Now there are both you and Maude Higgins, brought up from little things in a
tiny inland town, and both of you able to give any of these city girls all sorts of
odds in the matter of dressing."

Emmy put the letter down, wondering what had made her grow so cold.

"I wonder," she mused. She turned and looked in the glass to be confronted
by a charming vision, slender — and dusky.

"I am black," she thought, "but comely." She laughed to herself happily. "Archie
loves you, girl," she said to the face in the glass, and put the little fear behind

her. It met her insistently now and then, however, until the next week brought a letter begging her to get her mother to bring her to Philadelphia for a week or so.

"I can't get off till Thanksgiving, dearest, and I'm so lonely and disappointed. You know, I had looked forward so to spending the 15th of September with you — do you remember that date, sweetheart? I wouldn't have you come now in all this heat — you can't imagine how hot Philadelphia is, Emmy — but it's beautiful here in October. You'll love it, Emmy. It's such a big city — miles and miles of long, narrow streets, rather ugly, too, but all so interesting. You'll like Chestnut and Market Streets, where the big shops are, and South Street, teeming with Jews and colored people, though there are more of these last on Lombard Street. You never dreamed of so many colored people, Emmy Carrel — or such kinds.

"And then there are the parks and the theatres, and music and restaurants. And Broad Street late at night, all silent with gold, electric lights beckoning you on for miles and miles. Do you think your mother will let me take you out by yourself, Emmy? You'd be willing, wouldn't you?"

If Emmy needed more reassurance than that she received it when Archie, a month later, met her and her mother at Broad Street station in Philadelphia. The boy was radiant. Mrs. Carrel, too, put aside her usual reticence, and the three were in fine spirits by the time they reached the rooms which Archie had procured for them on Christian Street. Once ensconced, the older woman announced her intention of taking advantage of the stores.

"I shall be shopping practically all day," she informed them. "I'll be so tired in the afternoons and evenings, Archie, that I'll have to get you to take my daughter off my hands."

Her daughter was delighted, but not more transparently so than her appointed cavalier. He was overjoyed at the thought of playing host and of showing Emmy the delights of city life.

"By the time I've finished showing you one-fifth of what I've planned you'll give up the idea of waiting 'way till next October and marry me Christmas. Say, do it anyway, Emmy, won't you?" He waited tensely, but she only shook her head.

"Oh, I couldn't, Archie, and anyway you must show me first your wonderful city."

They did manage to cover a great deal of ground, though their mutual absorption made its impression on them very doubtful. Some things though Emmy never forgot. There was a drive one wonderful, golden October afternoon along the Wissahickon. Emmy, in her perfectly correct gray suit and smart little gray hat, held the reins — in itself a sort of measure of Archie's devotion to her, for he was wild about horses. He sat beside her ecstatic, ringing all the changes from a boy's nonsense to the most mature kind of seriousness. And always he looked at her with his passionate though reverent eyes. They were very happy.

There was some wonderful music, too, at the Academy. That was by accident though. For they had started for the theatre — had reached there in fact. The usher was taking the tickets.

"This way, Emmy," said Archie. The usher looked up aimlessly, then, as his eyes traveled from the seeming young foreigner to the colored girl beside him, he flushed a little.

"Is the young lady with you?" he whispered politely enough. But Emmy, engrossed in a dazzling vision in a pink décolleté gown, would not in any event have heard him.

"She is," responded Archie alertly. "What's the trouble, isn't to-night the 17th?"

The usher passed over this question with another — who had bought the tickets? Archie of course had, and told him so, frankly puzzled.

"I see. Well, I'm sorry," the man said evenly, "but these seats are already occupied, and the rest of the floor is sold out besides. There's a mistake somewhere. Now if you'll take these tickets back to the office I can promise you they'll give you the best seats left in the balcony."

"What's the matter?" asked Emmy, tearing her glance from the pink vision at last. "Oh, Archie, you're hurting my arm; don't hold it that tight. Why — why are we going away from the theatre? Oh, Archie, are you sick? You're just as white!"

"There was some mistake about the tickets," he got out, trying to keep his voice steady. "And a fellow in the crowd gave me an awful dig just then; guess that's why I'm pale. I'm so sorry, Emmy — I was so stupid, it's all my fault."

"What was the matter with the tickets?" she asked, incuriously. "That's the Bellevue-Stratford over there, isn't it? Then the Academy of Music must be near here. See how fast I'm learning? Let's go there; I've never heard a symphony concert. And, Archie, I've always heard that the best way to hear big music like that is at a distance, so get gallery tickets."

He obeyed her, fearful that if there were any trouble this time she might hear it. Emmy enjoyed it all thoroughly, wondering a little, however, at his silence. "I guess he's tired," she thought. She would have been amazed to know his thoughts as he sat there staring moodily at the orchestra. "This damnation color business," he kept saying over and over.

That night as they stood in the vestibule of the Christian Street house Emmy, for the first time, volunteered him a kiss. "Such a nice, tired boy," she said gently. Afterward he stood for a long time bareheaded on the steps looking at the closed door. Nothing he felt could crush him as much as that kiss had lifted him up.

V

Not even for lovers can a week last forever. Archie had kept till the last day what he considered his choicest bit of exploring. This was to take Emmy down into old Philadelphia and show her how the city had grown up from the waterfront — and by means of what tortuous self-governing streets. It was a sight at once dear and yet painful to his methodical, mathematical mind. They had explored Dock and Beach Streets, and had got over into Shackamaxon, where he showed her Penn Treaty Park, and they had sat in the little pavilion overlooking the Delaware.

Not many colored people came through this vicinity, and the striking pair caught many a wondering, as well as admiring, glance. They caught, too, the aimless, wandering eye of Mr. Nicholas Fields as he lounged, comfortably smoking, on the rear of a "Gunner's Run" car, on his way to Shackamaxon Ferry. Something in the young fellow's walk seemed vaguely familiar to him, and he leaned way out toward the sidewalk to see who that he knew could be over in this cheerless, forsaken locality.

"Gad!" he said to himself in surprise, "if it isn't young Ferrers, with a lady, too! Hello, why it's a colored woman! Ain't he a rip? Always thought he seemed too proper. Got her dressed to death, too; so that's how his money goes!" He dismissed the matter with a smile and a shrug of his shoulders.

Perhaps he would never have thought of it again had not Archie, rushing into the office a trifle late the next morning, caromed directly into him.

"Oh, it's you," he said, receiving his clerk's smiling apology. "What d'you mean by knocking into anybody like that?" Mr. Fields was facetious with his favorite employees. "Evidently your Shackamaxon trip upset you a little. Where'd you get your black Venus, my boy? I'll bet you don't have one cent to rub against another at the end of a month. Oh, you needn't get red; boys will be boys, and everyone to his taste. Clarkson," he broke off, crossing to his secretary, "if Mr. Hunter calls me up, hold the 'phone and send over to the bank for me."

He had gone, and Archie, white now and shaken, entered his own little room. He sat down at the desk and sank his head in his hands. It had taken a moment for the insult to Emmy to sink in, but even when it did the thought of his own false position had held him back. The shame of it bit into him.

"I'm a coward," he said to himself, staring miserably at the familiar wall. "I'm a wretched cad to let him think that of Emmy — Emmy! and she the whitest angel that ever lived, purity incarnate." His cowardice made him sick. "I'll go and tell him," he said, and started for the door.

"If you do," whispered common sense, "you'll lose your job and then what would become of you? After all Emmy need never know."

"But I'll always know I didn't defend her," he answered back silently.

"He's gone out to the bank anyhow," went on the inward opposition. "What's the use of rushing in there and telling him before the whole board of directors?"

"Well, then, when he comes back," he capitulated, but he felt himself weaken.

But Mr. Fields didn't come back. When Mr. Hunter called him up, Clarkson connected him with the bank, with the result that Mr. Fields left for Reading in the course of an hour. He didn't come back for a week.

Meanwhile Archie tasted the depths of self-abasement. "But what am I to do?" he groaned to himself at nights. "If I tell him I'm colored he'll kick me out, and if I go anywhere else I'd run the same risk. If I'd only knocked him down! After all she'll never know and I'll make it up to her. I'll be so good to her — dear little Emmy! But how could I know that he would take that view of it — beastly low mind he must have!" He colored up like a girl at the thought of it.

He passed the week thus, alternately reviling and defending himself. He knew now though that he would never have the courage to tell. The economy of the thing he decided was at least as important as the principle. And always he wrote to Emmy letters of such passionate adoration that the girl for all her natural steadiness was carried off her feet.

"How he loves me," she thought happily. "If mother is willing I believe — yes, I will — I'll marry him Christmas. But I won't tell him till he comes Thanksgiving."

When Mr. Fields came back he sent immediately for his son Peter. The two held some rather stormy consultations, which were renewed for several days. Peter roomed in town, while his father lived out at Chestnut Hill. Eventually Archie was sent for.

"You're not looking very fit, my boy." Mr. Fields greeted him kindly; "working too hard I suppose over those specifications. Well, here's a tonic for you. This last week has shown me that I need someone younger than myself to take a hand in the business. I'm getting too old or too tired or something. Anyhow I'm played out.

"I've tried to make this young man here, — with an angry glance at his son — "see that the mantle ought to fall on him, but he won't hear of it. Says the business can stop for all he cares; he's got enough money anyway. Gad, in my day young men liked to work, instead of dabbling around in this filthy social settlement business — with a lot of old maids."

Peter smiled contentedly. "Sally in our alley, what?" he put in diabolically. The older man glared at him, exasperated.

"Now look here, Ferrers," he went on abruptly. "I've had my eye on you ever since you first came. I don't know a thing about you outside of Mr. Fallon's recommendation, but I can see you've got good stuff in you — and what's more, you're a born engineer. If you had some money, I'd take you into partnership at once, but I believe you told me that all you had was your salary." Archie nodded.

"Well, now, I tell you what I'm going to do. I'm going to take you in as a sort of silent partner, teach you the business end of the concern, and in the course of a few years, place the greater part of the management in your hands. You can see you won't lose by it. Of course I'll still be head, and after I step out Peter will take my place, though only nominally I suppose."

He sighed; his son's business defection was a bitter point with him. But that imperturbable young man only nodded.

"The boss guessed right the very first time," he paraphrased cheerfully. "You bet I'll be head in name only. Young Ferrers, there's just the man for the job. What d'you say, Archie?"

The latter tried to collect himself. "Of course I accept it, Mr. Fields, and I — I don't think you'll ever regret it." He actually stammered. Was there ever such wonderful luck?

"Oh, that's all right," Mr. Fields went on, "you wouldn't be getting this chance if you didn't deserve it. See here, what about your boarding out at Chestnut Hill for a year or two? Then I can lay my hands on you any time, and you can get hold of things that much sooner. You live on Green Street, don't you? Well, give your landlady a month's notice and quit the 1st of December. A young man coming on like you ought to be thinking of a home anyway. Can't find some nice girl to marry you, what?"

Archie, flushing a little, acknowledged his engagement.

"Good, that's fine!" Then with sudden recollection — "Oh, so you're reformed. Well, I thought you'd get over that. Can't settle down too soon. A lot of nice little cottages out there at Chestnut Hill. Peter, your mother says she wishes you'd come out to dinner to-night. The youngest Wilton girl is to be there, I believe. Guess that's all for this afternoon, Ferrers."

VI

Archie walked up Chestnut Street on air. "It's better to be born lucky than rich," he reflected. "But I'll be rich, too — and what a lot I can do for Emmy. Glad I didn't tell Mr. Fields now. Wonder what those 'little cottages' out to Chestnut Hill sell for. Emmy ——" He stopped short, struck by a sudden realization.

"Why, I must be stark, staring crazy," he said to himself, standing still right in the middle of Chestnut Street. A stout gentleman whom his sudden stopping had seriously incommoded gave him, as he passed by, a vicious prod with his elbow. It started him on again.

"If I hadn't clean forgotten all about it. Oh, Lord, what am I to do? Of course Emmy can't go out to Chestnut Hill to live — well, that would be a give-away. And he advised me to live out there for a year or two — and he knows I'm engaged, and — now — making more than enough to marry on."

He turned aimlessly down 19th Street, and spying Rittenhouse Square sat down in it. The cutting November wind swirled brown, crackling leaves right into his face, but he never saw one of them.

When he arose again, long after his dinner hour, he had made his decision. After all Emmy was a sensible girl; she knew he had only his salary to depend on. And, of course, he wouldn't have to stay out in Chestnut Hill forever. They could buy, or perhaps — he smiled proudly — even build now, far out in West Philadelphia, as far as possible away from Mr. Fields. He'd just ask her to postpone their marriage — perhaps for two years. He sighed a little, for he was very much in love.

"It seems funny that prosperity should make a fellow put off his happiness," he thought ruefully, swinging himself aboard a North 19th Street car.

He decided to go to Plainville and tell her about it — he could go up Saturday afternoon. "Let's see, I can get an express to Harrisburg, and a sleeper to Plainville, and come back Sunday afternoon. Emmy'll like a surprise like that." He thought of their improvised trip to the Academy and how she had made him buy gallery seats. "Lucky she has that little saving streak in her. She'll see through the whole thing like a brick." His simile made him smile. As soon as he reached home he scribbled her a note:

"I'm coming Sunday," he said briefly, "and I have something awfully important to ask you. I'll be there only from 3 to 7. 'When Time let's slip one little perfect hour,' that's that Omar thing you're always quoting, isn't it? Well, there'll be four perfect hours this trip."

All the way on the slow poky local from Harrisburg he pictured her surprise. "I guess she won't mind the postponement one bit," he thought with a brief pang "She never was keen on marrying. Girls certainly are funny. Here she admits she's in love and willing to marry, and yet she's always hung fire about the date." He dozed fitfully.

As a matter of fact Emmy had fixed the date. "Of course," she said to herself happily, "the 'something important' is that he wants me to marry him right away. Well, I'll tell him that I will, Christmas. Dear old Archie coming all this distance to ask me that. I'll let him beg me two or three times first, and then I'll tell him. Won't he be pleased? I shouldn't be a bit surprised if he went down on his knees again." She flushed a little, thinking of that first wonderful time.

"Being in love is just — dandy," she decided. "I guess I'll wear my red dress."

Afterward the sight of that red dress always caused Emmy a pang of actual physical anguish. She never saw it without seeing, too, every detail of that disastrous Sunday afternoon. Archie had come — she had gone to the door to meet him — they had lingered happily in the hall a few moments, and then she had brought him in to her mother and Céleste.

The old French woman had kissed him on both cheeks. "See, then it's thou, my cherished one!" she cried ecstatically. "How long a time it is since thou art here."

Mrs. Carrel's greeting, though not so demonstrative, was no less sincere, and when the two were left to themselves "the cherished one" was radiant.

"My, but your mother can make a fellow feel welcome, Emmy. She doesn't say much but what she does, goes."

Emmy smiled a little absently. The gray mist outside in the sombre garden, the fire crackling on the hearth and casting ruddy shadows on Archie's hair, the very red of her dress, Archie himself — all this was making for her a picture, which she saw repeated on endless future Sunday afternoons in Philadelphia. She sighed contentedly.

"I've got something to tell you, sweetheart," said Archie.

"It's coming," she thought. "Oh, isn't it lovely! Of all the people in the world — he loves me, loves me!" She almost missed the beginning of his story. For he was telling her of Mr. Fields and his wonderful offer.

When she finally caught the drift of what he was saying she was vaguely disappointed. He was talking business, in which she was really very little interested. The "saving streak" which Archie had attributed to her was merely sporadic, and was due to a nice girl's delicacy at having money spent on her by a man. But, of course, she listened.

"So you see the future is practically settled — there's only one immediate drawback," he said earnestly. She shut her eyes — it was coming after all.

He went on a little puzzled by her silence; "only one drawback, and that is that, of course, we can't be married for at least two years yet."

Her eyes flew open. "Not marry for two years! Why — why ever not?"

Even then he might have saved the situation by telling her first of his own cruel disappointment, for her loveliness, as she sat there, all glowing red and bronze in the firelit dusk, smote him very strongly.

But he only floundered on.

"Why, Emmy, of course, you can see — you're so much darker than I — anybody can tell at a glance what you — er — are." He was crude; he knew it, but he couldn't see how to help himself. "And we'd have to live at Chestnut Hill, at first, right there near the Fields', and there'd be no way with you there to keep people from knowing that I — that — oh, confound it all — Emmy, you must understand! You don't mind, do you? You know you never were keen on marrying anyway. If we were both the same color — why, Emmy, what is it?"

For she had risen and was looking at him as though he were someone entirely strange. Then she turned and gazed unseeingly out the window. So that was it — the "something important" — he was ashamed of her, of her color; he was always talking about a white man's chances. Why, of course, how foolish she'd been all along — how could he be white with her at his side? And she had thought he had come to urge her to marry him at once — the sting of it sent her head up higher. She turned and faced him, her beautiful silhouette distinctly outlined against the gray blur of the window. She wanted to hurt him — she was quite cool now.

"I have something to tell you, too, Archie," she said evenly. "I've been meaning to tell you for some time. It seems I've been making a mistake all along. I don't really love you" — she was surprised dully that the words didn't choke her — "so, of course, I can't marry you. I was wondering how I could get out of it — you can't think how tiresome it's all been." She had to stop.

He was standing, frozen, motionless like something carved.

"This seems as good an opportunity as any — oh, here's your ring," she finished, holding it out to him coldly. It was a beautiful diamond, small but flawless — the only thing he'd ever gone into debt for.

The statue came to life. "Emmy, you're crazy," he cried passionately, seizing her by the wrist. "You've got the wrong idea. You think I don't want you to marry me. What a cad you must take me for. I only asked you to postpone it a little while, so we'd be happier afterward. I'm doing it all for you, girl. I never dreamed — it's preposterous, Emmy! And you can't say you don't love me — that's all nonsense!"

But she clung to her lie desperately.

"No, really, Archie, I don't love you one bit; of course I like you awfully — let go my wrist, you can think how strong you are. I should have told you long ago, but I hadn't the heart — and it really was interesting." No grand lady on the stage could have been more detached. He should know, too, how it felt not to be wanted.

He was at her feet now, clutching desperately, as she retreated, at her dress — the red dress she had donned so bravely. He couldn't believe in her heartlessness. "You must love me, Emmy, and even if you don't you must marry me anyway. Why, you promised — you don't know what it means to me, Emmy — it's my very life — I've never even dreamed of another woman but you! Take it back, Emmy, you can't mean it."

But she convinced him that she could. "I wish you'd stop, Archie," she said wearily; "this is awfully tiresome. And, anyway, I think you'd better go now if you want to catch your train."

He stumbled to his feet, the life all out of him. In the hall he turned around: "You'll say good-by to your mother for me," he said mechanically. She nodded. He opened the front door. It seemed to close of its own accord behind him.

She came back into the sitting room, wondering why the place had suddenly grown so intolerably hot. She opened a window. From somewhere out of the gray mists came the strains of "Alice, Where Art Thou?" executed with exceeding mournfulness on an organ. The girl listened with a curious detached intentness.

"That must be Willie Holborn," she thought; "no one else could play as wretchedly as that." She crossed heavily to the armchair and flung herself in it. Her mind seemed to go on acting as though it were clockwork and she were watching it.

Once she said: "Now this, I suppose, is what they call a tragedy." And again: "He did get down on his knees."

VII

There was nothing detached or impersonal in Archie's consideration of his plight. All through the trip home, through the long days that followed and the still longer nights, he was in torment. Again and again he went over the scene.

"She was making a plaything out of me," he chafed bitterly. "All these months she's been only fooling. And yet I wonder if she really meant it, if she didn't just do it to make it easier for me to be white. If that's the case what an insufferable cad she must take me for. No, she couldn't have cared for me, because if she had she'd have seen through it all right away."

By the end of ten days he had worked himself almost into a fever. His burning face and shaking hands made him resolve, as he dressed that morning, to 'phone the office that he was too ill to come to work.

"And I'll stay home and write her a letter that she'll have to answer." For although he had sent her one and sometimes two letters every day ever since his return, there had been no reply.

"She must answer that," he said to himself at length, when the late afternoon shadows were creeping in. He had torn up letter after letter — he had been proud and beseeching by turns. But in this last he had laid his very heart bare.

"And if she doesn't answer it" — it seemed to him he couldn't face the possibility. He was at the writing desk where her picture stood in its little silver frame. It had been there all day. As a rule he kept it locked up, afraid of what it might reveal to his landlady's vigilant eye. He sat there, his head bowed over the picture, wondering dully how he should endure his misery.

Someone touched him on the shoulder.

"Gad, boy," said Mr. Nicholas Fields, "here I thought you were sick in bed, and come here to find you mooning over a picture. What's the matter? Won't the lady have you? Let's see who it is that's been breaking you up so." Archie watched him in fascinated horror, while he picked up the photograph and walked over to the window. As he scanned it his expression changed.

"Oh," he said, with a little puzzled frown and yet laughing, too, "it's your colored lady friend again. Won't she let you go? That's the way with these black women, once they get hold of a white man — bleed 'em to death. I don't see how you can stand them anyway; it's the Spanish in you, I suppose. Better get rid of her before you get married. Hello ——" he broke off.

For Archie was standing menacingly over him. "If you say another word about that girl I'll break every rotten bone in your body."

"Oh, come," said Mr. Fields, still pleasant, "isn't that going it a little too strong? Why, what can a woman like that mean to you?"

"She can mean," said the other slowly, "everything that the woman who has promised to be my wife ought to mean." The broken engagement meant nothing in a time like this.

Mr. Fields forgot his composure. "To be your wife! Why, you idiot, you — you'd ruin yourself — marry a Negro — have you lost your senses? Oh, I suppose it's some of your crazy foreign notions. In this country white gentlemen don't marry colored women."

Archie had not expected this loophole. He hesitated, then with a shrug he burnt all his bridges behind him. One by one he saw his ambitions flare up and vanish.

"No, you're right," he rejoined. "White gentlemen don't, but colored men do." Then he waited calmly for the avalanche.

It came. "You mean," said Mr. Nicholas Fields, at first with only wonder and then with growing suspicion in his voice, "you mean that you're colored?" Archie nodded and watched him turn into a maniac.

"Why, you low-lived young blackguard, you ——" he swore horribly. "And you've let me think all this time ——" He broke off again, hunting for something insulting enough to say. "You Nigger!" he hurled at him. He really felt there was nothing worse, so he repeated it again and again with fresh imprecations.

"I think," said Archie, "that that will do. I shouldn't like to forget myself, and I'm in a pretty reckless mood to-day. You must remember, Mr. Fields, you didn't ask me who I was, and I had no occasion to tell you. Of course I won't come back to the office."

"If you do," said Mr. Fields, white to the lips, "I'll have you locked up if I have to perjure my soul to find a charge against you. I'll show you what a white man can do — you ——"

But Archie had taken him by the shoulder and pushed him outside the door.

"And that's all right," he said to himself with a sudden heady sense of liberty. He surveyed himself curiously in the mirror. "Wouldn't anybody think I had changed into some horrible ravening beast. Lord, how that one little word changed him." He ruminated over the injustice — the petty, foolish injustice of the whole thing.

"I don't believe," he said slowly, "it's worth while having a white man's chances if one has to be like that. I see what Emmy used to be driving at now." The thought of her sobered him.

"If it should be on account of my chances that you're letting me go," he assured the picture gravely, "it's all quite unnecessary, for I'll never have another opportunity like that."

In which he was quite right. It even looked as though he couldn't get any work at all along his own line. There was no demand for colored engineers.

"If you keep your mouth shut," one man said, "and not let the other clerks know what you are I might try you for awhile." There was nothing for him to do but accept. At the end of two weeks — the day before Thanksgiving — he found out that the men beside him, doing exactly the same kind of work as his own, were receiving for it five dollars more a week. The old injustice based on color had begun to hedge him in. It seemed to him that his unhappiness and humiliation were more than he could stand.

VIII

But at least his life was occupied. Emmy, on the other hand, saw her own life stretching out through endless vistas of empty, useless days. She grew thin and listless, all the brightness and vividness of living toned down for her into one gray, flat monotony. By Thanksgiving Day the strain showed its effects on her very plainly.

Her mother, who had listened in her usual silence when her daughter told her the cause of the broken engagement, tried to help her.

"Emmy," she said, "you're probably doing Archie an injustice. I don't believe he ever dreamed of being ashamed of you. I think it is your own wilful pride that is at fault. You'd better consider carefully — if you are making a mistake you'll regret it to the day of your death. The sorrow of it will never leave you."

Emmy was petulant. "Oh, mother, what can you know about it? Céleste says you married when you were young, even younger than I — married to the man you loved, and you were with him, I suppose, till he died. You couldn't know how I feel." She fell to staring absently out the window. It was a long time before her mother spoke again.

"No, Emmy," she finally began again very gravely, "I wasn't with your father till he died. That is why I'm speaking to you as I am. I had sent him away — we had quarrelled — oh, I was passionate enough when I was your age, Emmy. He was jealous — he was a West Indian — I suppose Céleste has told you — and one day he came past the sitting room — it was just like this one, overlooking the garden. Well, as he glanced in the window he saw a man, a white man, put his arms around me and kiss me. When he came in through the side door the man had gone. I was just about to explain — no, tell him — for I didn't know he had seen me when he began." She paused a little, but presently went on in her even, dispassionate voice:

"He was furious, Emmy; oh, he was so angry, and he accused me — oh, my dear! He was almost insane. But it was really because he loved me. And then I became angry and I wouldn't tell him anything. And finally, Emmy, he struck me — you mustn't blame him, child; remember, it was the same spirit showing in both of us, in different ways. I was doing all I could to provoke him by keeping my silence and he merely retaliated in his way. The blow wouldn't have harmed a little bird. But — well, Emmy, I think I must have gone crazy. I ordered him from the house — it had been my mother's — and I told him never, never to let me see him again." She smiled drearily.

"I never did see him again. After he left Céleste and I packed up our things and came here to America. You were the littlest thing, Emmy. You can't remember living in France at all, can you? Well, when your father found out where I was he wrote and asked me to forgive him and to let him come back. 'I am on my knees,' the letter said. I wrote and told him yes — I loved him, Emmy; oh, child, you with your talk of color; you don't know what love is. If you really loved Archie you'd let him marry you and lock you off, away from all the world, just so long as you were with him.

"I was so happy," she resumed. "I hadn't seen him for two years. Well, he started — he was in Hayti then: he got to New York safely and started here. There was a wreck — just a little one — only five people killed, but he was one of them. He was so badly mangled, they wouldn't even let me see him."

"Oh!" breathed Emmy. "Oh, mother!" After a long time she ventured a question. "Who was the other man, mother?"

"The other man? Oh! that was my father; my mother's guardian, protector, everything, but not her husband. She was a slave, you know, in New Orleans, and he helped her to get away. He took her to Hayti first, and then, afterward, sent her over to France, where I was born. He never ceased in his kindness. After my mother's death I didn't see him for ten years, not till after I was married. That was the time Emile — you were named for your father, you know — saw him kiss me. Mr. Pechegru, my father, was genuinely attached to my mother, I think, and had come after all these years to make some reparation. It was through him I first began translating for the publishers. You know yourself how my work has grown."

She was quite ordinary and matter of fact again. Suddenly her manner changed.

"I lost him when I was 22. Emmy — think of it — and my life has been nothing ever since. That's why I want you to think — to consider ——" She was weeping passionately now.

Her mother in tears! To Emmy it was as though the world lay in ruins about her feet.

IX

As it happened Mrs. Carrel's story only plunged her daughter into deeper gloom.

"It couldn't have happened at all if we hadn't been colored," she told herself moodily. "If grandmother hadn't been colored she wouldn't have been a slave, and if she hadn't been a slave — That's what it is, color — color — it's wrecked mother's life and now it's wrecking mine."

She couldn't get away from the thought of it. Archie's words, said so long ago, came back to her: "Just wait till color keeps you from the thing you want the most," he had told her.

"It must be wonderful to be white," she said to herself, staring absently at the Stevenson motto on the wall of her little room. She went up close and surveyed it unseeingly. "If only I weren't colored," she thought. She checked herself angrily, enveloped by a sudden sense of shame. "It doesn't seem as though I could be the same girl."

A thin ray of cold December sunlight picked out from the motto a little gilded phrase: "To renounce when that shall be necessary and not be embittered." She read it over and over and smiled whimsically.

"I've renounced — there's no question about that," she thought, "but no one could expect me not to be bitter."

If she could just get up strength enough, she reflected, as the days passed by, she would try to be cheerful in her mother's presence. But it was so easy to be melancholy.

About a week before Christmas her mother went to New York. She would see her publishers and do some shopping and would be back Christmas Eve. Emmy was really glad to see her go.

"I'll spend that time in getting myself together," she told herself, "and when mother comes back I'll be all right." Nevertheless, for the first few days she was, if anything, more listless than ever. But Christmas Eve and the prospect of her mother's return gave her a sudden brace.

"Without bitterness," she kept saying to herself, "to renounce without bitterness." Well, she would — she would. When her mother came back she should be astonished. She would even wear the red dress. But the sight of it made her weak; she couldn't put it on. But she did dress herself very carefully in white, remembering how gay she had been last Christmas Eve. She had put mistletoe in her hair and Archie had taken it out.

"I don't have to have mistletoe," he had whispered to her proudly.

In the late afternoon she ran out to Holborn's. As she came back 'round the corner she saw the stage drive away. Her mother, of course, had come. She ran into the sitting room wondering why the door was closed.

"I will be all right," she said to herself, her hand on the knob, and stepped into the room — to walk straight into Archie's arms.

She clung to him as though she could never let him go.

"Oh, Archie, you've come back, you really wanted me."

He strained her closer. "I've never stopped wanting you," he told her, his lips on her hair.

Presently, when they were sitting by the fire, she in the armchair and he at her feet, he began to explain. She would not listen at first, it was all her fault, she said.

"No, indeed," he protested generously, "it was mine. I was so crude; it's a wonder you can care at all about anyone as stupid as I am. And I think I was too ambitious — though in a way it was all for you, Emmy; you must always believe that. But I'm at the bottom rung now, sweetheart; you see, I told Mr. Fields everything and — he put me out."

"Oh, Archie," she praised him, "that was really noble, since you weren't obliged to tell him."

"Well, but in one sense I was obliged to — to keep my self-respect, you know. So there wasn't anything very noble about it after all." He couldn't tell her what had really happened. "I'm genuinely poor now, dearest, but your mother sent for me to come over to New York. She knows some pretty all-right people there — she's a wonderful woman, Emmy — and I'm to go out to the Philippines. Could you — do you think you could come out there, Emmy?"

She could, she assured him, go anywhere. "Only don't let it be too long, Archie — I ——"

He was ecstatic. "Emmy — you — you don't mean you would be willing to start out there with me, do you? Why, that's only three months off. When ——" He stopped, peering out the window. "Who is that coming up the path?"

"It's Willie Holborn," said Emmy. "I suppose Mary sent him around with my present. Wait, I'll let him in."

But it wasn't Willie Holborn, unless he had been suddenly converted into a small and very grubby special-delivery boy.

"Mr. A. Ferrers," he said laconically, thrusting a book out at her. "Sign here."

She took the letter back into the pleasant room, and A. Ferrers, scanning the postmark, tore it open. "It's from my landlady; she's the only person in Philadelphia who knows where I am. Wonder what's up?" he said incuriously. "I know I didn't forget to pay her my bill. Hello, what's this?" For within was a yellow envelope — a telegram.

Together they tore it open.

> "Don't be a blooming idiot," it read; "the governor says come back and receive apologies and accept job. Merry Christmas.
>
> Peter Fields."

"Oh," said Emmy, "isn't it lovely? Why does he say 'receive apologies,' Archie?"

"Oh, I don't know," he quibbled, reflecting that if Peter hadn't said just that his return would have been as impossible as ever. "It's just his queer way of talking. He's the funniest chap! Looks as though I wouldn't have to go to the Philippines after all. But that doesn't alter the main question. How soon do you think you can marry me, Emmy?"

His voice was light, but his eyes —

"Well," said Emmy bravely, "what do you think of Christmas?"

María Cristina Mena

The Education of Popo

María Cristina Mena is widely regarded as the first Mexican American woman writer to have her fiction appear in the leading magazines in the United States. "The Education of Popo," for example, was published in *The Century Magazine* in 1914, and the ironic layers of its social satire have sustained interest even to the first decade of the twenty-first century. Mena was born in 1893 to a wealthy family in Mexico City but brought to America as a teenager. Her prominent social position allowed her to move among the literati of the day, including D. H. Lawrence, with whom she became friends. She married a successful playwright, Henry Chambers, and thoroughly assimilated into her new way of life. Nevertheless, her fiction most often reaches back to the themes of cultural interaction between the two societies on either side of the Rio Grande, exploring issues of linguistic division, cultural duality, and naive misunderstandings on both sides. In this work, for instance, there are misconceptions driven by a mutual desire for a profitable business negotiation. The Mexican hosts, the parents of Popo, entertain only the most inflated notions

of their American guests and the proper way to entertain such elevated personages, but it is a well-intentioned innocence, charming in its generosity. The passages in which the narrative intelligence reveals the thinking of the hosts are
rendered in absurdly formal language, a lexicon appropriate to the ceremonial ritual of the occasion. The satire of the Americans, conversely, reveals their lack of sophistication, their cultural simplicity, their pretense to stature. That the conflict
between these two points of view rests on the adolescent infatuation of young
Popo, whose heart is stolen by a divorced woman of another generation, suffuses
the drama with emotional exhilaration and unintended pain. Mena's story is an important early literary portrait of the collision of social conventions between Mexico
and the United States, a theme that would be more richly developed later in the
century.

María Cristina Mena, "The Education of Popo," *The Century Magazine* 87 (March
1914): 653–62.

Governor Fernando Arriola and his amiable señora were confronted with a critical problem in hospitality: it was nothing less than the entertaining of American
ladies, who by all means must be given the most favorable impressions of Mexican civilization.

Hence some unusual preparations. On the backs of men and beasts were arriving magnificent quantities, requisitioned from afar, of American canned
soups, fish, meats, sweets, hors-d'œuvres, and nondescripts; ready-to-serve cere-
als, ready-to-drink cocktails, a great variety of pickles, and much other cheer of
American manufacture. Even an assortment of can-openers had not been forgotten. Above all, an imperial call had gone out for ice, and precious consignments
of that exotic commodity were now being delivered in various stages of dissolution, to be installed with solicitude in cool places, and kept refreshed with a continual agitation of fans in the hands of superfluous servants. By such amiable
extremities it was designed to insure the ladies Cherry against all danger of going
hungry or thirsty for lack of conformable aliment or sufficiently frigid liquids.

The wife and daughter of that admirable Señor Montague Cherry of the
United States, who was manipulating the extension of certain important concessions in the State of which Don Fernando was governor, and with whose operations his Excellency found his own private interests to be pleasantly involved,
their visit was well-timed in a social way, for they would be present on the occasion of a great ball to be given by the governor. For other entertainment the Arriola family would provide as God might permit. Leonor, the only unmarried
daughter, was practising several new selections on the harp, her mama sagaciously conceiving that an abundance of music might ease the strain of conversation in the event of the visitors having no Spanish. And now Próspero, the only
son, aged fourteen, generally known as Popo, blossomed suddenly as the man of

the hour; for, thanks to divine Providence, he had been studying English, and could say prettily, although slowly, "What o'clock it is?" and "Please you this," and "Please you that," and doubtless much more if he were put to it.

Separately and in council the rest of the family impressed upon Popo that the honor of the house of Arriola, not to mention that of his native land, reposed in his hands, and he was conjured to comport himself as a true-born caballero. With a heavy sense of responsibility upon him, he bought some very high collars, burned much midnight oil over his English "method," and became suddenly censorious of his stockinged legs, which, accompanying him everywhere, decoyed his down-sweeping eyes and defied concealment or palliation. After anxious consideration, he put the case to his mama.

"Thou amiable companion of all my anguishes," he said tenderly, "thou knowest my anxiety to comport myself with credit in the view of the honored Meesees Cherry. Much English I have already, with immobile delivery the most authentic and distinguished. So far I feel myself modestly secure. But these legs, Mama — these legs of my nightmares —"

"*Chist, chist!* Thou hadst ever a symmetrical leg, Popo mine," expostulated Doña Elvira, whose soul of a young matron dreaded her boy's final plunge into manhood.

"But consider, little Mama," he cried, "that very soon I shall have fifteen years. Since the last day of my saint I have shaved the face scrupulously on alternate mornings; but that no longer suffices, for my maturing beard now asks for the razor every day, laughing to scorn these legs, which continue to lack the investment of dignity. Mother of my soul, for the honor of our family in the eyes of the foreign ladies, I supplicate thy consent that I should be of long pantaloons!"

Touched on the side of her obligations as an international hostess, Doña Elvira pondered deeply, and at length confessed with a sigh:

"It is unfortunately true, thou repose of my fatigues, that in long pantaloons thou wouldst represent more."

And it followed, as a crowning graciousness toward Mrs. Montague Cherry and her daughter, that Popo was promoted to trousers.

ᚨᚨ

When the visitors arrived, he essayed gallantly to dedicate himself to the service of the elder lady, in accordance with Mexican theories of propriety, but found his well-meaning efforts frustrated by the younger one, who, seeing no other young man thereabout, proceeded methodically to attach the governor's handsome little son to herself.

Popo found it almost impossible to believe that they were mother and daughter. By some magic peculiar to the highly original country of the *Yanquis,* their relation appeared to be that of an indifferent sisterliness, with a balance of authority in favor of the younger. That revolutionary arrangement would have scandalized Popo had he not perceived from the first that Alicia Cherry was entitled to extraordinary consideration. Never before had he seen a living woman with hair like daffodils, eyes like violets, and a complexion of coral and porcelain. It seemed to him that some precious image of the Virgin had been changed into a creature of sweet flesh and capricious impulses, animate with a fearless urbanity far beyond the dreams of the dark-eyed, demure, and now despised damsels of his own race. His delicious bewilderment was completed when Miss Cherry, after staring him in the face with a frank and inviting smile, turned to her mother and drawled laconically:

"He just simply talks with those eyes!"

There was a moon on the night of the day that the Cherrys arrived. There was also music, the bi-weekly *serenata* in the plaza fronting the governor's residence. The band swept sweetly into its opening number at the moment when Don Fernando, with Mrs. Cherry on his arm, stepped out upon his long balcony, and all the town began to move down there among the palms. Miss Cherry, who followed with Popo, exclaimed at the romantic strangeness of the scene, and you may be sure that a stir and buzzing passed through the crowd as it gazed up at the glittering coiffure and snowy shoulders of that angelic señorita from the United States.

Popo got her seated advantageously and leaned with somewhat exaggerated gallantry over her chair, answering her vivacious questions, and feeling as one translated to another and far superior planet. He explained as well as he could the social conventions of the *serenata* as unfolded before their eyes in a concerted coil of languid movement — how the ladies, when the music begins, rise and promenade slowly around the kiosk of the band, and how the gentlemen form an outer wheel revolving in the reverse direction, with constant interplay of salutations, compliments, seekings, avoidings, coquetries, intrigues, and a thousand other manifestations of the mysterious forces of attraction and repulsion.

Miss Cherry conceived a strong desire to go down and become merged in that moving coil. No, she would not dream of dragging Doña Elvira or Leonor or mama from the dignified repose of the balcony; but she did beg the privilege, however unprecedented, of promenading with a young gentleman at her side, and showing the inhabitants how such things were managed in America — beg pardon, the United States.

So they walked together under the palms, Alicia Cherry and Próspero Arriola, and although the youth's hat was in the air most of the time in acknowledgment of salutes, he did not really recognize those familiar and astonished faces, for his head was up somewhere near the moon, while his legs, in the proud shelter of their first trousers, were pleasantly afflicted with pins and needles as he moved on tiptoe beside the blonde Americana, a page beside a princess.

Miss Cherry was captivated by the native courtliness of his manners. She thought of a certain junior brother of her own, to whom the business of "tipping his hat," as he called it, to a lady occasioned such extreme anguish of mind that he would resort to the most laborious manœuvers to avoid occasions when the performance of that rite would be expected of him. As for Próspero, he had held the tips of her fingers lightly as they had descended the marble steps of his father's house, and then with a charming little bow had offered her his arm, which she with laughing independence had declined. And now she perused with sidelong glances the infantile curve of his chin, the April fluctuations of his lips, the occasional quiver of his thick lashes, and decided that he was an amazingly cute little cavalier.

With a deep breath she expelled everything disagreeable from her mind, and gave up her spirit to the enjoyment of finding herself for a little while among a warmer, wilder people, with gallant gestures and languorous smiles. And the aromatic air, the tantalizing music, the watchful fire that glanced from under the sombreros of the peons squatting in colorful lines between the benches — all the ardor and mystery of that unknown life caused a sudden fluttering in her breast, and almost unconsciously she took her escort's arm, pressing it impulsively to her side. His dark eyes flashed to hers, and for the first time failed to flutter and droop at the encounter; this time it was her own that lost courage and hastily veiled themselves.

"That waltz," she stammered, "is n't it delicious?"

He told her the name of the composer, and begged her to promise him the privilege of dancing that waltz with her at the ball, in two weeks' time. As she gave the promise, she perceived with amusement, and not without delight, that he trembled exceedingly.

Mrs. Cherry was a little rebellious when she and Alicia had retired to their rooms that night.

"Yes, I suppose it 's all very beautiful and romantic," she responded fretfully to her daughter's panegyrics, "but I 'm bound to confess that I could do with a little less moonlight for the sake of a few words of intelligible speech."

"One always feels that way at first in a foreign country," said Alicia, soothingly, "and it certainly is a splendid incentive to learn the language. You ought to adopt my plan, which is to study Spanish very hard every moment we 're here."

"If you continue studying the language," her mother retorted, "as industriously as you have been doing to-night, my dear, you will soon be speaking it like a native."

Alicia was impervious to irony. Critically inspecting her own pink-and-gold effulgence in the mirror, she went on:

"Of course this is also a splendid opportunity for Próspero to learn some real English, which will please the family very much, as they 've decided to send him to an American college. I do hope it won't spoil him. Is n't he a perfect darling?"

"I don't know, not having been given a chance to exchange three words with — 'Sh-h! Did you hear a noise?"

It had sounded like a sigh, followed by a stealthy shuffle. Alicia went to the door which had been left ajar, and looked out upon the moonlit gallery just in time to catch a glimpse of a fleeting figure, as Próspero raced for his English dictionary, to look up the strange word "darling."

"The little rascal!" she murmured to herself. "What a baby, after all!" But to her mother she only said, as she closed the door, "It was nothing, dear; just one of those biblical-looking servants covering a parrot's cage."

"Even the parrots here speak nothing but Spanish," Mrs. Cherry pursued fretfully. "Of course I am glad to sacrifice my own comfort to any extent to help your dear father in his schemes, although I do think the syndicate might make some graceful little acknowledgment of my social services; but I 'm sure that papa never dreamed of your monopolizing the only member of this household to whom it is possible to communicate the most primitive idea without screaming one's head off. I am too old to learn to gesticulate, and I refuse to dislodge all my hairpins in the attempt. And as for your studies in Spanish," she continued warmly, as Alicia laughed, "I 'd like to know how you reconcile that pretext with the fact that I distinctly heard you and that infant Lord Chesterfield chattering away together in French."

"French does come in handy at times," Alicia purred, "and if you were not so shy about your accent, Mama dear, you could have a really good time with Doña Elvira. I must ask her to encourage you."

"Don't do anything of the kind!" Mrs. Cherry exclaimed. "You know perfectly well that my French is not fit for foreign ears. And I do think, Alicia, that you might try to make things as easy as possible for me, after my giving way to you in everything, even introducing you here under false pretenses, so to speak."

"It is n't a case of false pretenses, Mama. I 've decided to resume my maiden name, and there was no necessity to enter into long explanations to these dear people, who, living as they do in a Catholic country, naturally know nothing about the blessings of divorce."

"So much the better for them!" retorted Mrs. Cherry. "However much of a blessing divorce may be, I 've noticed that since you got your decree your face has not had one atom of real enjoyment in it until to-night."

"Until to-night!" Alicia echoed with a stoical smile. "And to-night, because you see a spark of reviving interest in my face, you try to extinguish it with reproaches!"

"No, no, my darling. Forgive me. I 'm a little tired and nervous. And I can't help being anxious about you. It 's a very trying position for a woman to be in at your age. It 's trying for your mother, too. I could box that wretched Edward's ears."

"Not very hard, I 'm thinking. You wanted me to forgive him."

"No, my dear, only to take him back on probation. We can punish men for their favorite sins much more effectually by not giving them their freedom."

"I could n't be guilty of that meanness, and I shall never regret having shown some dignity. And I think that closes the subject, does n't it, dearest?" Alicia yawned.

"Poor Edward!" her mother persisted. "How he would have enjoyed this pic-turesque atmosphere with you!"

Alicia calmly creamed her face.

§ð

Próspero spent a great part of the night over his English dictionary. Again and again he conned the Spanish equivalents listed against that word "darling." A significant word, it seemed, heart-agitating, sky-transporting. He had not dreamed that the harsh, baffling English language could contain in seven letters a treasure so rare. *Predilecto, querido, favorito, amado* — which translation should he accept as defining his relation to Mees Cherry, avowed by her own lips? The patient compiler of that useful book could never have foreseen the ecstasy it would one day bring to a Mexican boy's heart.

He was living in a realm of enchantment. To think that already, on the very day of their meeting, he and his blonde Venus should have arrived at intimacies far transcending any that are possible in Mexico except between the wedded or the wicked! In stark freedom, miraculously unchaperoned, they had talked to-gether, walked together, boldly linked their very arms! In his ribs he still treas-ured the warmth of her; in his fingers throbbed the memory that for one electric instant their hands had fluttered, dove-like, each to each. Small enough, those tender contacts; yet by such is the life force unchained: Popo found himself look-ing into a seething volcano, which was his own manhood. That discovery, con-flicting as it did with the religious quality of his love, disturbed him mightily. Sublimely he invoked all his spiritual strength to subdue the volcano. And his tra-vail was richly rewarded. The volcano became transformed magically into a fount of pellucid purity in which, bathing his exhausted soul, young Popo became a saint.

In that interesting but arduous capacity he labored for many days, during which Miss Cherry created no further occasion for their being alone together, but seemed to throw him in the way of her mama, a trial which he endured with fiery fortitude. He was living the spiritual life with rigorous intensity, a victim of the eternal mandate that those fountains of purity into which idealism has power to transform the most troublesome of volcanoes should be of a temper-ature little short of the boiling-point.

His dark eyes kept his divinity faithfully informed of his anguish and his wor-ship, and her blue ones discreetly accepted the offering. Once or twice their hands met lightly, and it seemed that the shock might have given birth to flam-ing worlds. When alone with her mama, Alicia showed signs of an irritable ar-dor which Mrs. Cherry, with secret complacency, set down to regrets for the too hastily renounced blessings of matrimony.

"Poor old Ned!" the mother sighed one night. "Your father has seen him, and tells me that he looks dreadful."

§ð

On the morning of the night of the ball the entire party, to escape from the majordomo and his gang of hammering decorators, motored into the country on a visit to Popo's grandmother, whose house sheltered three priests and a score of orphan girls, and was noted for its florid magnificence of the Maximilian period.

Popo hoped that some mention might be made in Alicia's hearing of his grandmother's oft-expressed intention to bequeath the place to him, and he was much gratified when the saintly old lady, who wore a mustache *á la española,* brought up the subject, and dilated upon it at some length, telling Popo that he must continue to make the house blessed by the presence of the three padres, but that she would make provision for the orphans to be taken elsewhere, out of his way, a precaution she mentioned to an accompaniment of winks and innuendos which greatly amused all the company, including the padres, only Alicia and Popo showing signs of distress.

After dinner, which occurred early in the afternoon, Popo manœuvered Alicia apart from the others in the garden. His eyes telegraphed a desperate plea, to which hers consented, and he took her by the hand, and they ran through a green archway into a terraced Italian garden peopled with marble nymphs and fauns, from which they escaped by a little side gate into an avenue of orange-blossoms. Presently they were laboring over rougher ground, where their feet crushed the fat stems of lilies, and then they turned and descended a roughly cut path winding down the scarred, dripping face of a cliff into the green depth of a little cañon, at the upper end of which a cascade resembling a scarf flung over a wall sang a song of eternity, and baptized the tall tree ferns that climbed in disorderly rivalry for its kisses.

Alicia breathed deeply the cool, moss scented air. The trembling boy, suddenly appalled at the bounty of life in presenting him with this sovereign concatenation of the hour, the place, and the woman, could only stammer irrelevantly, as he switched at the leaves with his cane.

"There is a cave in there behind the waterfall. One looks through the moving water as through a thick window, but one gets wet. Sometimes I come here alone, all alone, without going to the house, and *mamagrande* never knows. The road we came by passes just below, crossing this little stream, where thou didst remark the tall bamboos before we saw the porter's lodge. The mud wall is low, and I tie my horse in the bamboo thicket."

"Why do you come here?" she asked, her eyes tracing the Indian character in the clear line of his profile and the dusky undertone of his cheek.

"It is my caprice to meditate here. From my childhood I have loved the *cañoncito* in a peculiar way. Thou wilt laugh at me — no? Well, I have always felt a presence here, unseen, a very quiet spirit that seemed to speak to me of — *quien sabe?* I never knew — never until now."

His voice thrilled, and his eyes lifted themselves to hers, as if for permission, before he continued in ringing exaltation:

"Now that thou hast come, now that thou appearest here in all thy lovely splendor, now I know that the spirit I once felt and loved in secret was a prophecy of thee. Yes, Alicia mine, for thee this place has waited long — for thee, thou adored image of all beauty, queen of my heart, object of my prayers, whose purity has sanctified my life."

Alicia, a confirmed matinée girl, wished that all her woman friends might have seen her at that moment (she had on a sweet frock and a perfectly darling hat), and that they might have heard the speech that had just been addressed to her by the leading man. He was a thought juvenile, to be sure, but he had lovely, adoring eyes and delightfully passionate tones in his voice; and, anyhow, it was simply delicious to be made love to in a foreign language.

She was extremely pleased, too, to note that her own heart was going pitapat in a fashion quite uncomfortable and sweet and girly. She would n't have missed that sensation for a good deal. What a comfort to a bruised heart to be loved like this! He was calling her his saint. If that Edward could only hear him! Perhaps, after all, she *was* a saint. Yes, she felt that she certainly was, or could be if she tried. Now he was repeating some verses that he had made to her in Spanish. Such musical words! One had to come to the hot countries to discover what emotion was; and as for love-making! How the child had suffered!

As he bowed his bared head before her she laid her hands, as in benediction, where a bronze light glanced upon the glossy, black waves of his hair; and that touch, so tender, felled Popo to the earth, where he groveled with tears and broken words and kisses for her little shoes, damp from the spongy soil. And she suddenly dropped her posings and her parasol, and forgot her complexion and her whalebones, and huddled down beside him in the bracken, hushing his sobs and wiping his face, with sweet epithets and sweeter assurances, finding a strange, wild comfort in mothering him recklessly, straight from the soul. At the height of which really promising situation she was startled by a familiar falsetto hail from her mama as the rest of the party descended into the *cañoncito,* whither it had been surmised that Popo had conducted Miss Cherry.

After flinging an artless yodel in response to the maternal signal, and while composing Popo and herself into lifelike attitudes suggestive of a mild absorption in the beauties of nature, she whispered in his ear:

"The next time you come here you shall have two horses to tie in the bamboos."

"*Ay Dios!* All blessings on thee! But when?" he pleaded. "Tell me when!"

"Well, to-morrow," she replied after quick thought; "as you would say, my dear, *mañana.* Yes, I 'll manage it. I 'm dying for a horseback ride, and I 've had such a lovely time to-day."

ॐ

To be the only blonde at a Mexican ball is to be reconciled for a few hours to the fate of being a woman. Alicia, her full-blown figure habited in the palest of pink, which seemed of the living texture of her skin, with a generous measure

of diamonds winking in effective constellations upon her golden head and dazzling bosom, absorbed through every pore the enravished admiration of the be-
holders, and beneficently poured it forth again in magnetic waves of the
happiness with which triumph enhances beauty. Popo almost swooned with rapture at this apotheosis of the being who, a few hours earlier, had actually hugged
him in the arms now revealed as those of a goddess. And to-morrow! With
swimming brain he repeated over and over, as if to convince himself of the incredible, *"Mañana!"*

Almost as acute as the emotions of Popo, in a different way, were those of a
foreign gentleman who had just been presented to the governor by the newly arrived Mr. Montague Cherry. So palpably moved was the stranger at the sight of
Alicia that Mrs. Cherry laid a soothing hand on his arm and whispered a conspirator's caution. Presently he and Alicia stood face to face. Had they been Mexican, there would have ensured an emotional and edifying scene. But all that
Alicia said, after one sharp inspiration of surprise, was, with an equivocal half
smile:

"Why, Edward! Of all people!"

And the gentleman addressed as Edward, finding his voice with difficulty,
blurted out hoarsely:

"How are you, Alicia?"

At which Alicia turned smilingly to compliment Doña Elvira on the decorations.

Mr. Edward P. Winterbottom was one of those fortunate persons who seem to
prefigure the ideal toward which their race is striving. A thousand conscientious
draftsmen, with that national ideal in their subconsciousness, were always hard at
work portraying his particular type in various romantic capacities, as those of
foot-ball hero, triumphant engineer, "well-known clubman," and pleased patron
of the latest collar, cigarette, sauce, or mineral water. Hence he would give you
the impression of having seen him before somewhere under very admirable auspices. Extremely good-looking, with long legs, a magnificent chin, and an expression of concentrated manhood, he had every claim to be classed as "wholesome,"
cherishing a set of opinions suitable to his excellent station in life, a proper reverence for the female of the species, and an adequate working assortment of simple
emotions easily predicable by a reasonably clever woman. Of the weaknesses
common to humanity he had fewer than the majority, and in the prostration of remorse and desire in which he now presented himself to Alicia he seemed to offer
timber capable of being made over into a prince of lifelong protectors.

Alicia had come to feel that she needed a protector, chiefly from herself.
Presently, without committing herself, however, she favored him with a waltz.
As they started off, she saw the agonized face of Popo, who had been trying to
reach her. She threw him a smile, which he lamentably failed to return. Not until then did she identify the music as that of the waltz she had promised him on
the night of that first *serenata*. After it was over she good-naturedly missed a

dance or two in search of him, meaning to make amends; but he was nowhere to be found.

ᔥᔥ

With many apologies, Doña Elvira mentioned to Alicia, when she appeared the following morning, that the household was somewhat perturbed over the disappearance of Próspero. No one could remember having seen him since early in the progress of the ball. He had not slept in his bed, and his favorite horse was missing from the stable. Don Fernando had set the police in motion. Moreover, *la mamagrande,* informed by telephone, was causing masses to be said for the safety of her favorite. God would undoubtedly protect him, and meanwhile the honored señorita and her mama would be so very gracious as to attribute any apparent neglect of the canons of hospitality to the anxieties of an unduly affectionate mother.

Alicia opened her mouth to reply to that tremulous speech, but, finding no voice, turned and bolted to her room, trying to shut out a vision of a slender boy lying self-slain among the ferns where he had received caresses and whispers of love from a goddess of light fancy and lighter faith. She had no doubt that he was there in his *cañoncito.* But perhaps he yet lived, waiting for her! She would go at once. Old Ned should escort her as far as the bamboos, to be within call in case of the worst.

Old Ned was so grateful for the privilege of riding into the blossoming country with his Alicia that she rewarded him with a full narration of the Popo episode; and he received the confidence with discreet respect, swallowing any qualms of jealousy, and extolling her for the high-minded sense of responsibility which now possessed her to the point of tears.

"It 's all your fault, anyway," she declared as they walked their horses up a long hill.

He accepted the blame with alacrity as a breath of the dear connubial days.

"One thing I 've demonstrated," she continued fretfully, "and that is that the summer flirtation of our happy land simply cannot be acclimated south of the Rio Grande. These people lack the necessary imperturbability of mind, which may be one good reason why they 're not permitted to hold hands before the marriage ceremony. To complicate matters, it seems that I 'm the first blonde with the slightest claim to respectability that ever invaded this part of Mexico, and although the inhabitants have a deluded idea that blue eyes are intensely spiritual, they get exactly the same Adam-and-Eve palpitations from them that we do from the lustrous black orbs of the languishing tropics."

"Did you — ah — did you get as far as — um — kissing?" Mr. Winterbottom inquired, with an admirable air of detachment.

"Not quite, Edward; that was where the rest of the folks came tagging along. But I promise you this: if I find that Popo alive, I 'm going to kiss him for all I 'm worth. The unfortunate child is entitled to nothing less."

"But would n't that — hum — add fuel to the flame?" he asked anxiously.

"It would give him back his self-respect," she declared. "It is n't healthy for a high-spirited boy to feel like a worm."

ൠ

Mr. Winterbottom, while waiting among the bamboos in company with three sociable horses, — Popo's was in possession when they arrived, — smoked one very long cigar and chewed another into pulpy remains. Alicia not having yodeled, he understood that she had found the boy alive, and he tried to derive comfort from that reflection. He had promised to preserve patience and silence, and such was his anxiety to propitiate Alicia that he managed to subjugate his native energy, although the process involved the kicking up of a good deal of soil. She reflected, when she noted on her return his carefully cheerful expression, that a long course of such discipline would go far toward regenerating him as a man and a husband.

"Well, how is our little patient today?" he inquired with gentle jocosity as he held the stirrup for her.

"I believe he 'll pull through now," Alicia responded gravely. "I 've sent him up to his grandmother's to be fed, and he 's going to telephone his mother right away."

"That 's bully," Mr. Winterbottom pronounced heartily; and for some moments, as they gained the road, nothing more was said. Alicia seemed thoughtful. Mr. Winterbottom was the first to speak.

"Poor little beggar must have been hungry," he hazarded.

"He had eaten a few bananas, but as they 're not recognized as food here, they only increased his humiliation. You know, banana-trees are just grown to shade the coffee-plants, which are delicate."

Mr. Winterbottom signified a proper interest in that phase of coffee culture, and Alicia took advantage of a level stretch of road to put her horse to the gallop. When he regained her side, half a mile farther on, he was agitated.

"Alicia, would you mind enlightening me on one point?" he asked. "Did you — give him back his self-respect?"

"Perhaps I 'd better tell you all that happened, Edward."

"By Jove! I wish you would!" he cried earnestly.

"Well, Popo was n't a bit surprised to see me. In fact, he was expecting me."

"Indeed? Had n't lost his assurance, then."

"He had simply worked out my probable actions, just as I had worked out his. Of course he looked like a wild thing, hair on end, eyes like a panther, regular young bandit. Well, I rag-timed up in my best tra-la-la style, but he halted me with a splendid gesture, and started a speech. You know what a command of language foreigners have, even the babies. He never fumbled for a word, and all his nouns had verbs waiting, and the climaxes just rolled over one another like waves. It was beautiful."

"But what was it about?"

"Me, of course: my iniquity, the treacherous falseness residing as ashes in the Dead Sea fruit of my beauty, with a lurid picture of the ruin I had made of his belief in woman, his capacity for happiness, and all that. And he wound up with a burst of denunciation in which he called me by a name which ought not to be applied to any lady in any language."

"Alicia!"

"Oh, I deserved it, Edward, and I told him so. I did n't care how badly he thought of me if I could only give him back his faith in love. It 's such a wonderful thing to get *that* back! So I sang pretty small about myself; and when I revealed my exact status as an ex-wife in process of being courted by her divorced husband, his eyes nearly dropped out of his head. You see, they don't play 'Tag! You 're it!' with marriage down here. That boy actually began to hand me out a line of missionary talk. He thinks I ought to remarry you, Ned."

"He must have splendid instincts, after all. So of course you did n't kiss him?"

"Wait a minute. After mentioning that I was eleven years older than he, and that my hair had been an elegant mouse-drab before I started touching it up —"

"Not at all. I liked its color — a very pretty shade of —"

"After that, I told him that he could thank his stars for the education I had given him, in view of the fact that he 's going to be sent to college in the U. S. A., and I gave him a few first-rate pointers on the college widow breed. And finally, Ned, I put it to him that I was anxious to do the square thing, and if he considered himself entitled to a few kisses while you were waiting, he could help himself."

"And he?" Mr. Winterbottom inquired with a pinched look.

"He looked so cute that I could have hugged him. But he nobly declined."

"That young fellow," said Mr. Winterbottom, taking off his hat and wiping his brow, "is worthy of being an American."

"Why, that was his Indian revenge, the little monkey! But he was tempted, Ned."

"Of course he was. If you 'd only tempt *me!* O Alicia, you 're a saint!"

"That 's what Popo called me yesterday, and it was neither more nor less true than what he called me to-day. I suppose we 're all mixtures of one kind and another. And I 've discovered, Ned, that it 's the healthiest kind of fun to be perfectly frank with — with an old pal. Let 's try it that way next time, shall we, dear?"

She offered her lips for the second time that day, and —

5

Modernism and Experimentation

World War I transformed Western civilization, an event with such enormous cultural and psychological implications for Europe and the United States that it altered virtually every level of society. The devastating Great War depersonalized military conflict with clouds of deadly gas that floated on the wind, killing whatever lay in their path, and artillery shells that carried over forty miles, reducing city blocks to rubble when they landed. Trench warfare lingered for months with regiments on both sides fighting for the same land over and over again. The American army invented dog tags to identify the bodies of men too mangled to recognize. Missing in action often meant that nothing at all could be found. Despite the fact that America resisted entry into the conflict until 1917, the country lost 119,000 men in infantry combat.

When the war was over, people on both sides of the conflict felt that the institutions that gave order and security to society had served them poorly, with a resulting loss of confidence in government, skepticism about religious faith, and questioning of the principles that served as the bedrock of middle-class life. Conventional ideas seemed ridiculous to the men coming home from Europe, especially when they were greeted by Prohibition and conservative attitudes about sex. Veterans found it difficult to return to the lives they had left behind, and many of the writers and artists who went back to the United States did not stay there very long.

Postwar America was embroiled in social transformations in other ways as well. The continued immigration into the country brought a broader range of nationalities and languages and religions to blend into society: Hasidic Jews expelled from Russia, Japanese and Chinese laborers, Scandinavian farmers, Polish and Bohemian urban poor, were all drawn to the American dream. Other changes came rapidly. The Eighteenth Amendment in 1919 established Prohibition, and with it came bootleg liquor, the rise of gangsterism, the speakeasy, and an enormous increase in the consumption of alcohol. The next year the Nineteenth Amendment gave women full voting privileges and participation in the democratic process.

Advances in technology altered daily life. The radio united the continent with news and entertainment, and an increasing number of homes enjoyed the conveniences of electricity and running water. The automobile became a staple of the middle class, and it changed social behavior, particularly among the young. Dating now involved cars and roadside nightclubs that sprang up on the periphery of cities and towns. Freudian psychology became increasingly popular, stressing repressed sexuality, and a Bohemian subculture in Greenwich Village published a manifesto of free love and unfettered artistic license. American cities held an increasing majority of the population, and industrial workers outnumbered those in agriculture. The modern world had arrived, and it offered enormous opportunities.

Literary Modernism

The American literary climate changed as well, especially regarding short fiction. Commercially as well as critically, the story boomed in the Modernist period, spurred in part by the burgeoning number of magazines willing to pay enormous prices for stories by established authors. As a result, many writers, F. Scott Fitzgerald and Katherine Anne Porter among them, turned their attention from novels to the shorter form. To the great periodicals established in the nineteenth century, such as *The Atlantic Monthly* and *Harper's Magazine,* were now added *The Saturday Evening Post, The Ladies' Home Journal, Cosmopolitan, The Kenyon Review,* and scores of others. As a result, the story form attracted much of the best creative energy in the country. Two important annual collections celebrated short fiction, *The Best American Short Stories* and the *O. Henry Memorial Award Prize Stories,* and there was no doubting the importance of the genre to the great publishing houses, most of which were located on the eastern seaboard.

A related phenomenon was the continued growth in popularity of the story cycle, volumes of interconnected stories. Virtually every writer of reputation produced such a book. Ernest Hemingway followed Sherwood Anderson's *Winesburg, Ohio* with *In Our Time,* for example, and Eudora Welty's *The Golden Apples,* William Faulkner's *Go Down, Moses,* and James Baldwin's *Going to Meet the Man* added to the list of more than a hundred important Modernist volumes of interrelated stories. Beyond such books, however, individual works of short fiction by a host of writers flooded the monthly magazines, capturing the attention of a swelling readership.

In some ways, the art and the subjects of American fiction in Modernism sustained the methodology developed during the period between the Civil War and World War I. Realism remained the dominant mode, depicting believable characters engaged in the conflicts of ordinary life. Most stories did not employ an omniscient narrator but an individualized point of view, using first person or third-person limited focused on the protagonist. The plots presumed free will for the characters, who thus took responsibility for the decisions they made. As a result, ethical dilemmas, expressed as internal struggles, became a central plot device, informing such stories as Faulkner's

"Barn Burning" and Philip Roth's "Defender of the Faith." Psychological growth or conflict was another common theme, as in Fitzgerald's "Winter Dreams," Hisaye Ya-mamoto's "The Legend of Miss Sasagawara," and James Baldwin's "Sonny's Blues."

The Naturalistic mode declined somewhat in the heyday of the Jazz Age of the 1920s but flourished again in the Depression years of the 1930s, depicting the limited options of impoverished characters caught in the sway of powerful Deterministic forces. Sherwood Anderson's "Death in the Woods," Tillie Olsen's "Help Her to Believe," and Ruth Suckow's "A Start in Life" portray women in such circumstances, and Arna Bontemps added racial overtones to the suicide of an elderly couple in "A Summer Tragedy." John Steinbeck's "The Chrysanthemums" dealt with the "submerged life" for a farm woman, the subject of Cather's earlier "A Wagner Matinée," portraying vulnerability as well as resignation to the empty existence a rural wife must endure.

The experimentation with Impressionism in fiction in the 1890s, led by Stephen Crane, Kate Chopin, and Ambrose Bierce, led to the Imagist movement in poetry in the middle of the second decade of the century. Its expression in fiction was called *polyphonic prose,* a somewhat disingenuous term because the most remarkable thing about it was not its multivoiced narration but rather its restriction to sensory experience, what became known as *minimalism* in Modernist stories.

The most celebrated practitioner of the mode was Ernest Hemingway, whose sparse but precise style rendered conflict through suggestion rather than explanation. He called one aspect of his method the "iceberg theory," wherein most of what is important in a story rests beneath the surface. In "Hills Like White Elephants," for example, a couple is clearly in the midst of an intense argument, but the subject is never mentioned, despite references to some vague medical procedure the man wants the woman to have. In context, the conflict derives from the woman's pregnancy, and the man wants her to have an abortion. There are hints, such as his having a drink alone, that after the operation he will leave her. She, on the other hand, wants a family, a quiet domestic life with the man she loves. The stakes are high in the dispute, and so are the emotions. But all of it is handled with restraint, with simple language, with only the slightest indication of the true nature of the quarrel. Hemingway's style was in many ways the dominant influence on fiction to emerge from the 1920s, and his portrayal of vulnerable characters confronting the pain of a violent world defined the postwar years in Europe and America.

Hemingway was the voice of the Lost Generation in France, a generation that had lived through the war and would never be free of the psychic impact of what they had witnessed. F. Scott Fitzgerald, especially after *The Great Gatsby* in 1925, was the spokesman for the Jazz Age in America. Perhaps the most celebrated American writer of the period of Prohibition and riotous celebration during the economic boom of the 1920s, Fitzgerald portrayed the era in terms of dancing in the country clubs of the major cities, driving open automobiles on the new highways, and engaging in endless flirtation and romance. In over a hundred short stories, his fiction explored the psychological complexity of idealized love, of striving for social advancement into the privileged classes, and of exposing the shallowness of the financial approach to the American dream. His typical protagonist, as in "Winter Dreams," couples romantic love with acceptance into country-club society, an advancement he believes promises emotional and economic fulfillment. The plot rests on the emotional impact of rejection and the destruction of Dexter Green's imaginings, those adolescent fantasies that motivated his youth. The story captures the romantic illusions of the era, its desperate longings and crushing disillusionment, ideas that have retained their appeal even in a vastly different period of American life.

The 1930s brought a swirl of ideas and themes to literature centered on the effects of the Great Depression, which saw nearly a third of the labor force unemployed and widespread poverty throughout the United States and Europe. Added to financial collapse, seven years of drought devastated the Midwest and plains states: food supplies diminished, prices fluctuated, and basic necessities became scarce. Socialist ideology emerged as part of the economic discourse of the country, and many Americans doubted that free enterprise could lead to recovery. A new literature developed to reflect these circumstances, drawing essentially on the Naturalism of the 1890s, when another economic depression inspired Stephen Crane, Frank Norris, Jack London, and others to deal with the plight of the poor. Among the important Naturalistic writers of the twentieth century, London remained a dominant force, but to that list were added significant new voices, John Steinbeck chief among them. His "The Chrysanthemums" concerns a woman trapped in restricted circumstances who yearns to be free, to live a richer life, a common theme in this mode. Sherwood Anderson's "Death in the Woods," Ruth Suckow's "A Start in Life," and Arna Bontemps's "A Summer Tragedy" are stories in the same tradition.

World War II was perhaps the most important event of the century, but it did not inspire as many great stories and novels as did the First World War, nor did that conflict generate the same level of disillusionment and despair. The use of atomic weapons for the first time created two decades of preoccupation with nuclear annihilation, but most of the fiction about the war dealt with bureaucracy, inefficiency, and domestic issues rather than international politics. Philip Roth's "Defender of the Faith" focused on ethnicity and moral conflict, and Hisaye Yamamoto's "The Legend of Miss Sasagawara" contributed a new dimension to American war fiction: the lives of Japanese Americans interred during the war. The 1950s were sometimes called the "placid" decade, but social changes began that would erupt a decade later, including the sexual revolution, the push for full equality for women, and the civil rights movement. Tillie Olson's "Help Her to Believe," later published under the title "I Stand Here Ironing," and James Baldwin's "Sonny's Blues" grew from these ideas.

Ethnic Themes

The Modernist era brought innovations in technique and subject as well as an expansion of the central subjects of Realistic stories. Ethnic themes, for example, exhibited greater insight into the ethical implications of belonging to an identifiable group while assimilating into full participation in society. Roth's "Defender of the Faith" is perhaps pre-eminent in its searching exploration of this idea. The issue of national identity is brought into sharp focus in this story, originally published in *The New Yorker* before inclusion in *Goodbye, Columbus* in 1959. The conflict between ethnic loyalty and fealty to country is the central emphasis in a philosophical plot that has been the subject of a great deal of critical controversy. At issue is the extent to which the protagonist, Sergeant Nathan Marx, should allow himself to be manipulated on the basis of race by Private Sheldon Grossbart. Few works of literature better present the psychology and morality of the conflict. Since Marx is also the narrator, there is constant access to his mind and values, to his resentments, predilections, realizations, and frustrations, including his disappointments with himself. Roth's contribution is thus a combination of the richness of the subject and the skill of his technique.

Not many authors addressed the complexity of the American Dream more directly than did Anzia Yezierska in her prize-winning "The Fat of the Land," published in 1919. Yezierska herself had emigrated from Russia in the last decade of the century, and she understood the hardship new arrivals faced during their initial years in the promised land, where the language, culture, economy, and topography were dramatically different. Writing in the wake of Abraham Cahan's Jewish stories from the 1890s, Yezierska addressed her work to the plight of urban women. Her protagonists have family responsibilities, restricted employment opportunities, and divided national loyalties, often preferring the familiar traditions of the old country to the freedom of the new.

Jean Toomer's "Blood-Burning Moon" represents both the highly experimental approach to literature representative of the 1920s and the celebration of African American themes at the heart of the Harlem Renaissance (1918 to 1940). Toomer's lyrical approach to fiction, his assemblage in *Cane* (1923) of related thematic work from three distinct genres, and his exploration of new forms and a fresh language to convey black experience all contribute to the innovation of Modernism. Perhaps the most memorable component of that book, "Blood-Burning Moon" uses a love triangle for its central conflict but expands the tension by making the romance interracial, giving an American twist to an old plot.

Arna Bontemps's stature derives from his reputation as a poet and erudite man of letters rather than from his fiction, but "A Summer Tragedy" won the award for the best short work of 1933 from *Opportunity* magazine, which carried the subtitle "Journal of Negro Life." This innovative story brought a fresh subject and methodology to fiction. It depicts the hopelessness of African American sharecroppers caught in a system in which their annual expenses exceed their income, making escape impossible. As in the case of Toomer's work, the aesthetic of Bontemps's fiction is often as important as the subject. His poetic style resonates with meaning throughout, such as the allusions to "Swing Low, Sweet Chariot" that become increasingly appropriate as the plot advances. The poignant characterizations reveal pride amid poverty, determination bred of misery, and affection that transcends the vicissitudes of life.

At the end of the 1950s, the fiction of James Baldwin brought fresh ideas to the African American story, concepts that had never been so directly explored, including the struggle of gay men to gain acceptance and equal rights. He also portrayed the complex relationship between race and artistic expression. Writing out of personal experience, he was able to give psychological depth to these themes without compromising the artistry of his work. "Sonny's Blues," for example, uses a point of view that puts as much emphasis on the speaker as on the main character being described. In this case, the narrator's internal conflict and transformation dominate the plot, not the activities of his younger brother, Sonny, the ostensible subject. The narrator's epiphany at the end, his new realization, is transformative, allowing him to understand the key events of his life. This transitional process generates even more poignancy through the shift of time in each of the six episodes, moving backward to explain the nature of the conflict between the two brothers and then returning to the narrative present at the end. The style reveals the sophistication of the narrator, a teacher, and his language suggests a supple mind, one capable of complex ideas.

All of the major characters in Hisaye Yamamoto's work are Japanese Americans. Most of her stories concern, to some degree, the internment of more than 100,000 Japanese Americans during World War II. She was among those sent to the camp in Poston, Arizona, and "The Legend of Miss Sasagawara" grows out of that experience. Yamamoto shows the psychological and moral complexity of the internment experience. The story, however, is much more than simple political protest; its intensity derives from its presentation of intergenerational conflict, the father's religious quest, and the price that his daughter pays for it. Her internal struggle as an aging ballet dancer who must deal with her repressed sexuality provides the center of the plot. In other circumstances, she might have found healthy expression for her feelings, but in the camp she resorts to fantasy and voyeurism, which eventually bring about her hospitalization in a mental institution. The sensitivity of the young woman who narrates enriches the conflict with subtle and complex insights, especially in portraying Miss Sasagawara, who appears only in fragments. Yamamoto writes with irony and emotional control: she begins her works with a specific event within a confined space and gradually expands the thematic parameters to encompass much broader implications, in this case a major social event in American history that has rarely been included in the nation's literature.

Gender Issues

In addition to ethnic concerns, gender issues, including the nature of marriage, continued to be a central focus in fiction. Indeed, many stories combined the two themes. Anzia Yezierska's story has implications for sexual roles as well as race, and Yamamoto's work has as much to do with a young woman's adjustment to her burgeoning sexuality as to the international conflict that has brought her to an internment camp. However, Ruth Suckow's "A Start in Life" focuses more purely on poverty and its effect on the life of a young girl, one undergoing a rude initiation into her station in society. It captures a transitional moment when Daisy Switzer journeys from her impoverished home to employment in the comfortable Kruse household. Suckow's structuring of the plot into discrete units, each of which contain a painful realization for the protagonist, culminates in a subdued epiphany at the end, one that reveals her resignation, hopelessness, and loneliness. Other writers explored poverty and its consequences in the cities, but Suckow set her work in the small towns and farms of the Midwest.

Eudora Welty's "Petrified Man" from 1939 gives another twist to the gender theme. In this story, women in a hairdresser shop reveal that they dominate their husbands and engage in appalling social conduct. The surface conversation has to do with the "freak show" and the deformed people on exhibit in it, including the supposedly "petrified" man later revealed to be as false as the women who are having their hair dyed during the conversation. Their attitudes about marriage, and even about pregnancy and motherhood, become more "monstrous" than the unfortunate man on exhibit. Welty's skill with dialogue enriches the style: the local idiom provides humor and depth to her portrait of Southern life.

Katherine Anne Porter's "Maria Concepción," her first important short fiction, also addresses marriage. Unlike Welty's story, however, the action takes place in Mexico and the conflict concerns not so much the husband as the wronged wife. Her murderous revenge, an act never punished legally nor morally, removes the competition for her husband. Indeed, the surrounding community, through its actions, condones the killing and awards Maria custody of the slaughtered woman's child. American readers of 1922 were fascinated by the anthropological dimensions of Porter's fiction, which was set in Mexico. María Christina Mena presented similar ideas in "The Education of Popo," but Porter's story develops ideas substantially at odds with the normative values of American readers.

Naturalistic writers approached gender issues from a different perspective. In many ways, the fictional techniques of Sherwood Anderson in "Death in the Woods" illustrate the extent to which they often emphasized plot and theme at the expense of other aspects of fiction, including style and narrative technique. The protagonist, a rural woman caught in a dehumanizing marriage, seems both unappreciated and dominated. She feeds the cattle, the chickens, and her husband. Even in death, the narrator implies, her body serves as food for the dogs. In presenting this shocking plot, the author employs a first-person retrospective point of view, an older man recalling an event from his youth, and yet what he tells exceeds the information that would have been available to him. He presents dialogue not heard, for example, and he shows events that took place when he was not present, including the description of the dogs tearing at the backpack worn by the dead woman. Still, the thematic force of the events resonated in the Naturalistic climate of the 1920s and 1930s, underlining the socioeconomic depravity of the world the woman lives in and the hostile environment of her own family life. The psychological effect of the woman's death on the narrator deepens his memories and his life. The conclusion reveals the painful realizations the experience forced onto his consciousness, compelling him to attempt to understand what he has remembered by telling about it.

Beyond Naturalistic approaches to the gender issue, perhaps the most celebrated Modern story on the theme is Tillie Olson's "Help Her to Believe" in 1956, later published as "I Stand Here Ironing." It depicts the plight of the single mother, living in poverty and despondency, who needs to assist her young daughter but who feels impotent to intervene without greater resources. As she irons, she thinks through the past and her limited options for intervention, and she decides to do nothing. Despite the fact that it was Olsen's first published story, composed for a creative writing class, its subtlety and sophistication have led readers to misinterpret it. The basic theme involves not so much an indictment of society as an intimate revelation of the mind of a mother, preoccupied with herself, who fails to guide or comfort her daughter in a moment of crisis. No financial resources are required to offer emotional support, for example, or to listen to the problems an adolescent faces. Often praised for its Modernist innovation in point of view, the story actually employs one of the oldest narrative techniques, a monologue, essentially the methodology of "The Speech of Miss Polly Baker" in 1747. Nevertheless, the temporal and tonal shifts, the dynamic interruptions in the telling, the unconscious expression of domestic failure, and the lapse in responsibility have all made the story widely read and discussed.

Other Modernist Approaches

Throughout the Modernist period a host of other subjects emerged in short fiction, including *social satire* and *situational comedy*. If Mark Twain enjoys recognition as the greatest American humorist of the nineteenth century, James Thurber occupies that position in the twentieth. Both writers use comedic situations and character portrayals that capture the social and psychological reality of everyday life, teasing laughter out of frustrating and humiliating situations. Thurber's standard protagonist copes ineffectually with the demands of his humdrum existence and his wife dominates him. The protagonist faces these circumstances in "The Secret Life of Walter Mitty," and his relief comes in his fantasies in which he can be a heroic figure drawn from film and literature. The social satire in this instance underscores the limitations of Mitty's imagination: the details of his dream episodes contain approximations of historic figures and scientific terms that have a ring of plausibility but are patently absurd. When Mitty imagines himself as a surgeon, for example, he hears that "coreopsis has set in." Coreopsis is a flower, not a medical condition. Apparently, he misremembers the countless scenes in film in which gangrene has set in to threaten the health of a patient. Even his deams betray the hapless Mitty and reveal him as no hero but an ordinary man in a mundane existence struggling through the travails of urban life.

William Faulkner's "Barn Burning" (1939) represents his experimentation in expanding the parameters of fiction in subject, theme, and methodology. Faulkner's work essentially traces three grand ideas, all resting on the social transformations brought by the Civil War: the collapse of the aristocratic class after slave labor was abolished, the lives of African Americans suddenly freed, and the rise of poor whites in the economic system that replaced the closed structure of the antebellum South. In this case he presents a boy from a sharecropper family whose values conflict with those of his father. When the father prepares to burn the barn of the landowner, the protagonist, Sarty Snopes, must choose one side or the other. His decision forms the climax of the action. As in this story, Faulkner's technical approach to fiction was inventive, challenging, and unparalleled in American literature. In passages of stream of consciousness, for example, he discards traditional syntax and punctuation to reflect the unbridled flow of thought; his plots frequently employ temporal shifts, often without markers of any kind, and his narrative methods change unpredictably, sometimes in the middle of a paragraph. Nevertheless, his readers have been enthralled by his fiction for more than seven decades.

In the strangely grotesque setting of another Southern writer, Flannery O'Connor, religious mysticism combines with sharply realistic evocations of a world in which Christian symbolism competes with experience for the minds of the central characters. In "The River," one of her most controversial stories, a young boy seeks salvation in a baptismal stream, hoping to find there the core of meaning absent from his daily life. The plot lends itself to multiple interpretations, all with some justification. At one pole of this debate, critics contend that the redemptive power of Christ offers genuine grace to those who seek it, and thus the boy's death in the river is a positive release from the sordid secular world that surrounds him. The alternative interpretation, embodied by Mr. Paradise, maintains that Christian fundamentalism offers no beneficial effects except ritual. Beyond the thematic concerns of religion, O'Connor's place in literary history is assured by her artistry, the modulations of narrative perspective that enrich the telling of her stories, the structural juxtapositions that provide irony and contrast, and the patterns of imagery that underscore the developing ideas of her fiction.

Conclusion

The Modernist period in the American story brought innovation, experimentation, and a broad spectrum of writers and subjects to the form. If ethnicity, gender, poverty, and the formation of identity continued to be central subjects, the writers of this era also portrayed characters with impressive sensitivity. By this time the basic problems of how to tell a story had long been solved, allowing for more emphasis on the subtlety of narration, structure, temporal shifts, and thematic development. Writers expanded the parameters of the traditional story to include important motifs that relate to the central idea. They addressed vital changes in society, among them civil rights and equal freedoms for women. The genre that had started as an amusement in a few magazines with extremely limited circulation played a major role in Modernist life and in the social transformations that were about to erupt in the 1960s.

Anzia Yezierska
The Fat of the Land

Anzia Yesierska is widely acknowledged as the first important female Jewish immigrant to gain a reputation as a writer in America. Born in Polish Russia in 1881, she came with her family to New York in the last decade of the century and worked in the garment industry on the east side of New York. Despite humble beginnings, she took a degree from Columbia University in 1904 and, after two failed marriages and a daughter, devoted the rest of her long life to literature, earning special praise for her short fiction. Her earliest recognition was for "The Fat of the Land," published in *The Century* in 1919, which won the O. Henry Award as the best story of the year. The following year the text was incorporated into *Hungry Hearts,* a series of tales about Jewish immigrants that was later made into a silent movie by Samuel Goldwyn in Hollywood. A novel, *Salome of the Tenements,* appeared in 1922, followed by a second collection of stories, *Children of Loneliness,* and her most famous book, *Bread Givers,* in 1925. Her work is important for its realistic treatment of tenement life for New York Jews, for its depiction of their idiom and culture. The protagonist of "The Fat of the Land," Hanneh Breineh, experiences the irony of the success of the American Dream as her children, who have ascended socially and financially, now feel ashamed of their backward mother. As the conclusion demonstrates, Hanneh finds herself suspended between two worlds, fitting into neither, unable to find in wealth the simple pleasures of community she had known in the poverty of her younger years.

Anzia Yezierska, "The Fat of the Land," *The Century* 98, no. 4 (August 1919): 433–79.

In an air-shaft so narrow that you could touch the next wall with your bare hands, Hanneh Breineh leaned out and knocked on her neighbor's window.

"Can you loan me your wash-boiler for the clothes?" she called.

Mrs. Pelz threw up the sash.

"The boiler? What's the matter with yours again? Did n't you tell me you had it fixed already last week?"

"A black year on him, the robber, the way he fixed it! If you have no luck in this world, then it 's better not to live. There I spent out fifteen cents to stop up one hole, and it runs out another. How I ate out my gall bargaining with him he should let it down to fifteen cents! He wanted yet a quarter, the swindler. *Gottuniu!* my bitter heart on him for every penny he took from me for nothing!"

"You got to watch all those swindlers, or they 'll steal the whites out of your eyes," admonished Mrs. Pelz. "You should have tried out your boiler before you paid him. Wait a minute till I empty out my dirty clothes in a pillow-case; then I'll hand it to you."

Mrs. Pelz returned with the boiler and tried to hand it across to Hanneh Breineh, but the soap-box refrigerator on the window-sill was in the way.

"You got to come in for the boiler yourself," said Mrs. Pelz.

"Wait only till I tie my Sammy on to the high-chair he should n't fall on me again. He 's so wild that ropes won't hold him."

Hanneh Breineh tied the child in the chair, stuck a pacifier in his mouth, and went in to her neighbor. As she took the boiler Mrs. Pelz said:

"Do you know Mrs. Melker ordered fifty pounds of chicken for her daughter's wedding? And such grand chickens! Shining like gold! My heart melted in me just looking at the flowing fatness of those chickens."

Hanneh Breineh smacked her thin, dry lips, a hungry gleam in her sunken eyes.

"Fifty pounds!" she gasped. "It ain't possible. How do you know?"

"I heard her with my own ears. I saw them with my own eyes. And she said she will chop the chicken livers with onions and eggs for an appetizer, and then she will buy twenty-five pounds of fish, and cook it sweet and sour with raisins, and she said she will bake all her strudels on pure chicken fat."

"Some people work themselves up in the world," sighed Hanneh Breineh. "For them is America flowing with milk and honey. In Savel Mrs. Melker used to get shriveled up from hunger. She and her children used to live on potato-peelings and crusts of dry bread picked out from the barrels; and in America she lives to eat chicken, and apple strudels soaking in fat."

"The world is a wheel always turning," philosophized Mrs. Pelz. "Those who were high go down low, and those who 've been low go up higher. Who will believe me here in America that in Poland I was a cook in a banker's house? I handled ducks and geese every day. I used to bake coffee-cake with cream so thick you could cut it with a knife."

"And do you think I was a nobody in Poland?" broke in Hanneh Breineh, tears welling in her eyes as the memories of her past rushed over her. "But what 's the use of talking? In America money is everything. Who cares who my father or grandfather was in Poland? Without money I 'm a living dead one. My head dries out worrying how to get for the children the eating a penny cheaper."

Mrs. Pelz wagged her head, a gnawing envy contracting her features.

"Mrs. Melker had it good from the day she came," she said begrudgingly. "Right away she sent all her children to the factory, and she began to cook meat for dinner every day. She and her children have eggs and buttered rolls for breakfast each morning like millionaires."

A sudden fall and a baby's scream, and the boiler dropped from Hanneh Breineh's hands as she rushed into her kitchen, Mrs. Pelz after her. They found the high-chair turned on top of the baby.

"*Gevalt!* Save me! Run for a doctor!" cried Hanneh Breineh as she dragged the child from under the highchair. "He 's killed! He 's killed! My only child! My precious lamb!" she shrieked as she ran back and forth with the scream-ing infant.

Mrs. Pelz snatched little Sammy from the mother's hands.

"*Meshugneh!* what are you running around like a crazy, frightening the child? Let me see. Let me tend to him. He ain't killed yet." She hastened to the sink to wash the child's face, and discovered a swelling lump on his forehead. "Have you a quarter in your house?" she asked.

"Yes, I got one," replied Hanneh Breineh, climbing on a chair. "I got to keep it on a high shelf where the children can't get it."

Mrs. Pelz seized the quarter Hanneh Breineh handed down to her.

"Now pull your left eyelid three times while I 'm pressing the quarter and you 'll see the swelling go down."

Hanneh Breineh took the child again in her arms, shaking and cooing over it and caressing it.

"Ah-ah-ah, Sammy! Ah-ah-ah-ah, little lamb! Ah-ah-ah, little bird! Ah-ah-ah-ah, precious heart! Oh, you saved my life; I thought he was killed," gasped Han-neh Breineh, turning to Mrs. Pelz. *Oi-i!*" she sighed, "a mother's heart! Always in fear over her children. The minute anything happens to them all life goes out of me. I lose my head and I don't know where I am any more."

"No wonder the child fell," admonished Mrs. Pelz. "You should have a red ribbon or red beads on his neck to keep away the evil eye. Wait. I got something in my machine-drawer."

Mrs. Pelz returned, bringing the boiler and a red string, which she tied about the child's neck while the mother proceeded to fill the boiler.

A little later Hanneh Breineh again came into Mrs. Pelz's kitchen, holding Sammy in one arm and in the other an apron full of potatoes. Putting the child down on the floor, she seated herself on the unmade kitchen-bed and began to peel the potatoes in her apron.

"Woe to me!" sobbed Hanneh Breineh. "To my bitter luck there ain't no end. With all my other troubles, the stove got broke'. I lighted the fire to boil the clothes, and it 's to get choked with smoke. I paid rent only a week ago, and the agent don't want to fix it. A thunder should strike him! He only comes for the rent, and if anything has to be fixed, then he don't want to hear nothing.

"Why comes it to me so hard?" went on Hanneh Breineh, the tears stream-ing down her cheeks. "I can't stand it no more. I came into you for a minute to run away from my troubles. It 's only when I sit myself down to peel potatoes or nurse the baby that I take time to draw a breath, and beg only for death."

Mrs. Pelz, accustomed to Hanneh Breineh's bitter outbursts, continued her scrubbing.

"*Ut!*" exclaimed Hanneh Breineh, irritated at her neighbor's silence, "what are you tearing up the world with your cleaning? What 's the use to clean up when everything only gets dirty again?"

"I got to shine up my house for the holidays."

"You've got it so good nothing lays on your mind but to clean your house. Look on this little blood-sucker," said Hanneh Breineh, pointing to the wizened child, made prematurely solemn from starvation and neglect. "Could anybody keep that brat clean? I wash him one minute, and he is dirty the minute after." Little Sammy grew frightened and began to cry. "Shut up!" ordered the mother, picking up the child to nurse it again. "Can't you see me take a rest for a minute?"

The hungry child began to cry at the top of its weakened lungs.

"*Na, na,* you glutton." Hanneh Breineh took out a dirty pacifier from her pocket and stuffed it into the baby's mouth. The grave, pasty-faced infant shrank into a panic of fear, and chewed the nipple nervously, clinging to it with both his thin little hands.

"For what did I need yet the sixth one?" groaned Hanneh Breineh, turning to Mrs. Pelz. "Was n't it enough five mouths to feed? If I did n't have this child on my neck, I could turn myself around and earn a few cents." She rang her hands in a passion of despair. "*Gottuniu!* the earth should only take it before it grows up!"

"Pshaw! pshaw!" reproved Mrs. Pelz. "Pity yourself on the child. Let it grow up already so long as it is here. See how frightened it looks on you." Mrs. Pelz took the child in her arms and petted it. "The poor little lamb! What did it done you should hate it so?"

Hanneh Breineh pushed Mrs. Pelz away from her.

"To whom can I open the wounds of my heart?" she moaned. "Nobody has pity on me. You don't believe me, nobody believes me until I 'll fall down like a horse in the middle of the street. *Oi weh!* mine life is so black for my eyes. Some mothers got luck. A child gets run over by a car, some fall from a window, some burn themselves up with a match, some get choked with diphtheria; but no death takes mine away."

"God from the world! stop cursing!" admonished Mrs. Pelz. "What do you want from the poor children? Is it their fault that their father makes small wages? Why do you let it all out on them?" Mrs. Pelz sat down beside Hanneh Breineh. "Wait only till your children get old enough to go to the shop and earn money," she consoled. "Push only through those few years while they are yet small; your sun will begin to shine, you will live on the fat of the land, when they begin to bring you in the wages each week."

Hanneh Breineh refused to be comforted.

"Till they are old enough to go to the shop and earn money they 'll eat the head off my bones," she wailed. "If you only knew the fights I got by each meal. Maybe I gave Abe a bigger piece of bread than Fanny. Maybe Fanny got a little more soup in her plate than Jake. Eating is dearer than diamonds. Potatoes went up a cent on a pound, and milk is only for millionaires. And once a week, when I buy a little meat for the Sabbath, the butcher weighs it for me like gold, with all the bones in it. When I come to lay the meat out on a plate and divide it up, there ain't nothing to it but bones. Before, he used to throw me in a piece of fat extra or a piece of lung, but now you got to pay for everything, even for a bone to the soup."

"Never mind; you 'll yet come out from all your troubles. Just as soon as your children get old enough to get their working papers the more children you got, the more money you 'll have."

"Why should I fool myself with the false shine of hope? Don't I know it 's already my black luck not to have it good in this world? Do you think American children will right away give everything they earn to their mother?"

"I know what is with you the matter," said Mrs. Pelz. "You did n't eat yet to-day. When it is empty in the stomach, the whole world looks black. Come, only let me give you something good to taste in the mouth; that will freshen you up." Mrs. Pelz went to the cupboard and brought out the saucepan of *gefülte* fish that she had cooked for dinner and placed it on the table in front of Hanneh Breineh. "Give a taste my fish," she said, taking one slice on a spoon, and handing it to Hanneh Breineh with a piece of bread. "I would n't give it to you on a plate because I just cleaned up my house, and I don't want to dirty up more dishes."

"What, am I a stranger you should have to serve me on a plate yet!" cried Hanneh Breineh, snatching the fish in her trembling fingers.

"*Oi weh!* how it melts through all the bones!" she exclaimed, brightening as she ate. "May it be for good luck to us all!" she exulted, waving aloft the last precious bite.

Mrs. Pelz was so flattered that she even ladled up a spoonful of gravy.

"There is a bit of onion and carrot in it," she said as she handed it to her neighbor.

Hanneh Breineh sipped the gravy drop by drop, like a connoisseur sipping wine.

"Ah-h-h! a taste of that gravy lifts me up to heaven!" As she disposed leisurely of the slice of onion and carrot she relaxed and expanded and even grew jovial. "Let us wish all our troubles on the Russian Czar! Let him burst with our worries for rent! Let him get shriveled with our hunger for bread! Let his eyes dry out of his head looking for work!"

"Pshaw! I 'm forgetting from everything," she exclaimed, jumping up. "It must be eleven or soon twelve, and my children will be right away out of school and fall on me like a pack of wild wolves. I better quick run to the market and see what cheaper I can get for a quarter."

Because of the lateness of her coming, the stale bread at the nearest bakeshop was sold out, and Hanneh Breineh had to trudge from shop to shop in search of the usual bargain, and spent nearly an hour to save two cents.

In the meantime the children returned from school, and, finding the door locked, climbed through the fire-escape, and entered the house through the window. Seeing nothing on the table, they rushed to the stove. Abe pulled a steaming potato out of the boiling pot, and so scalded his fingers that the potato fell to the floor; whereupon the three others pounced on it.

"It was my potato," cried Abe, blowing his burned fingers, while with the other hand and his foot he cuffed and kicked the three who were struggling on the floor. A wild fight ensued, and the potato was smashed under Abe's foot amid shouts and screams. Hanneh Breineh, on the stairs, heard the noise of her famished brood, and topped their cries with curses and invectives.

"They are here already, the savages! They are here already to shorten my life! They heard you all over the hall, in all the houses around!"

The children, disregarding her words, pounced on her market-basket, shouting ravenously: "Mama, I 'm hungry! What more do you got to eat?"

They tore the bread and herring out of Hanneh Breineh's basket and devoured it in starved savagery, clamoring for more.

"Murderers!" screamed Hannah Breineh, goaded beyond endurance. "What are you tearing from me my flesh? From where should I steal to give you more? Here I had already a pot of potatoes and a whole loaf of bread and two herrings, and you swallowed it down in the wink of an eye. I have to have Rockefeller's millions to fill your stomachs."

All at once Hanneh Breineh became aware that Benny was missing. "*Oi weh!*" she burst out, wringing her hands in a new wave of woe, "where is Benny? Did n't he come home yet from school?"

She ran out into the hall, opened the grime-coated window, and looked up and down the street; but Benny was nowhere in sight.

"Abe, Jake, Fanny, quick, find Benny!" entreated Hanneh Breineh as she rushed back into the kitchen. But the children, anxious to snatch a few minutes' play before the school-call, dodged past her and hurried out.

With the baby on her arm, Hanneh Breineh hastened to the kindergarten.

"Why are you keeping Benny here so long?" she shouted at the teacher as she flung open the door. "If you had my bitter heart, you would send him home long ago and not wait till I got to come for him."

The teacher turned calmly and consulted her record-cards.

"Benny Safron? He was n't present this morning."

"Not here?" shrieked Hanneh Breineh. "I pushed him out myself he should go. The children did n't want to take him, and I had no time. Woe is me! Where is my child?" She began pulling her hair and beating her breast as she ran into the street.

Mrs. Pelz was busy at a push-cart, picking over some spotted apples, when she heard the clamor of an approaching crowd. A block off she recognized Hanneh Breineh, her hair disheveled, her clothes awry, running toward her with her yelling baby in her arms, the crowd following.

"Friend mine," cried Hanneh Breineh, falling on Mrs. Pelz's neck. "I lost my Benny, the best child of all my children." Tears streamed down her red, swollen eyes as she sobbed. "Benny! mine heart, mine life! *Oi-i-i!*"

Mrs. Pelz took the frightened baby out of the mother's arms.

"Still yourself a little! See how you 're frightening your child."

"Woe to me! Where is my Benny? Maybe he 's killed already by a car. Maybe he fainted away from hunger. He did n't eat nothing all day long. *Gottuniu!* pity yourself on me!"

She lifted her hands full of tragic entreaty.

"People, my child! Get me my child! I 'll go crazy out of my head! Get me my child, or I 'll take poison before your eyes!"

"Still yourself a little!" pleaded Mrs. Pelz.

"Talk not to me!" cried Hanneh Breineh, wringing her hands. "You 're having all your children. I lost mine. Every good luck comes to other people. But I did n't live yet to see a good day in my life. Mine only joy, mine Benny, is lost away from me."

The crowd followed Hanneh Breineh as she wailed through the streets, leaning on Mrs. Pelz. By the time she returned to her house the children were back from school; but seeing that Benny was not there, she chased them out in the street, crying:

"Out of here, you robbers, gluttons! Go find Benny!" Hanneh Breineh crumpled into a chair in utter prostration. "*Oi weh!* he 's lost! Mine life; my little bird; mine only joy! How many nights I spent nursing him when he had the measles! And all that I suffered for weeks and months when he had the whooping-cough! How the eyes went out of my head till I learned him how to walk, till I learned him how to talk! And such a smart child! If I lost all the others, it would n't tear me so by the heart."

She worked herself up into such a hysteria, crying, and tearing her hair, and hitting her head with her knuckles, that at last she fell into a faint. It took some time before Mrs. Pelz, with the aid of neighbors, revived her.

"Benny, mine angel!" she moaned as she opened her eyes.

Just then a policeman came in with the lost Benny.

"*Na, na,* here you got him already!" said Mrs. Pelz. "Why did you carry on so for nothing? Why did you tear up the world like a crazy?"

The child's face was streaked with tears as he cowered, frightened and forlorn. Hanneh Breineh sprang toward him, slapping his cheeks, boxing his ears, before the neighbors could rescue him from her.

"Woe on your head!" cried the mother. "Where did you lost yourself? Ain't I got enough worries on my head than to go around looking for you? I did n't have yet a minute's peace from that child since he was born."

"See a crazy mother!" remonstrated Mrs. Pelz, rescuing Benny from another beating. "Such a mouth! With one breath she blesses him when he is lost, and with the other breath she curses him when he is found."

Hanneh Breineh took from the window-sill a piece of herring covered with swarming flies, and putting it on a slice of dry bread, she filled a cup of tea that had been stewing all day, and dragged Benny over to the table to eat.

But the child, choking with tears, was unable to touch the food.

"Go eat!" commanded Hanneh Breineh. "Eat and choke yourself eating!"

§§

"Maybe she won't remember me no more. Maybe the servant won't let me in," thought Mrs. Pelz as she walked by the brownstone house on Eighty-fourth Street where she had been told Hanneh Breineh now lived. At last she summoned up enough courage to climb the steps. She was all out of breath as she rang the bell with trembling fingers. "*Oi weh!* even the outside smells riches and plenty! Such curtains! And shades on all windows like by millionaires! Twenty years ago she used to eat from the pot to the hand, and now she lives in such a palace."

A whiff of steam-heated warmth swept over Mrs. Pelz as the door opened, and she saw her old friend of the tenements dressed in silk and diamonds like a being from another world.

"Mrs. Pelz, is it you!" cried Hanneh Breineh, overjoyed at the sight of her former neighbor. "Come right in. Since when are you back in New York?"

"We came last week," mumbled Mrs. Pelz as she was led into a richly carpeted reception-room.

"Make yourself comfortable. Take off your shawl," urged Hanneh Breineh.

But Mrs. Pelz only drew her shawl more tightly around her, a keen sense of her poverty gripping her as she gazed, abashed by the luxurious wealth that shone from every corner.

"This shawl covers up my rags," she said, trying to hide her shabby sweater.

"I 'll tell you what; come right into the kitchen," suggested Hanneh Breineh. "The servant is away for this afternoon, and we can feel more comfortable there. I can breathe like a free person in my kitchen when the girl has her day out."

Mrs. Pelz glanced about her in an excited daze. Never in her life had she seen anything so wonderful as a white tiled kitchen, with its glistening porcelain sink and the aluminum pots and pans that shone like silver.

"Where are you staying now?" asked Hanneh Breineh as she pinned an apron over her silk dress.

"I moved back to Delancey Street, where we used to live," replied Mrs. Pelz as she seated herself cautiously in a white enameled chair.

"*Oi weh!* what grand times we had in that old house when we were neighbors!" sighed Hanneh Breineh, looking at her old friend with misty eyes.

"You still think on Delancey Street? Have n't you more high-class neighbors up-town here?"

"A good neighbor is not to be found every day," deplored Hanneh Breineh. "Up-town here, where each lives in his own house, nobody cares if the person next door is dying or going crazy from loneliness. It ain't anything like we used to have it in Delancey Street, when we could walk into one another's rooms without knocking, and borrow a pinch of salt or a pot to cook in."

Hanneh Breineh went over to the pantry-shelf.

"We are going to have a bite right here on the kitchen-table like on Delancey Street. So long there 's no servant to watch us we can eat what we please."

"*Oi!* how it waters my mouth with appetite, the smell of the herring and onion!" chuckled Mrs. Pelz, sniffling the welcome odors with greedy pleasure.

Hanneh Breineh pulled a dish-towel from the rack and threw one end of it to Mrs. Pelz.

"So long there 's no servant around, we can use it together for a napkin. It 's dirty, anyhow. How it freshens up my heart to see you!" she rejoiced as she poured out her tea into a saucer. "If you would only know how I used to beg my daughter to write for me a letter to you; but these American children, what is to them a mother's feelings?"

"What are you talking!" cried Mrs. Pelz. "The whole world rings with you and your children. Everybody is envying you. Tell me how began your luck?"

"You heard how my husband died with consumption," replied Hanneh Breineh. "The five-hundred-dollars lodge money gave me the first lift in life, and I opened a little grocery store. Then my son Abe married himself to a girl with a thousand dollars. That started him in business, and now he has the biggest shirt-waist factory on West Twenty-ninth Street."

"Yes, I heard your son had a factory." Mrs. Pelz hesitated and stammered, "I 'll tell you the truth. What I came to ask you — I thought maybe you would beg your son Abe if he would give my husband a job."

"Why not?" said Hanneh Breineh. "He keeps more than five hundred hands. I 'll ask him he should take in Mr. Pelz."

"Long years on you, Hanneh Breineh! You 'll save my life if you could only help my husband get work."

"Of course my son will help him. All my children like to do good. My daughter Fanny is a milliner on Fifth Avenue, and she takes in the poorest girls in her shop and even pays them sometimes while they learn the trade." Hanneh Breineh's face lit up, and her chest filled with pride as she enumerated the successes of her children. "And my son Benny he wrote a play on Broadway and he gave away more than a hundred free tickets for the first night."

"Benny? The one who used to get lost from home all the time? You always did love that child more than all the rest. And what is Sammy your baby doing?"

"He ain't a baby no longer. He goes to college and quarterbacks the football team. They can't get along without him."

"And my son Jake, I nearly forgot him. He began collecting rent in Delancey Street, and now he is boss of renting the swellest apartment-houses on Riverside Drive."

"What did I tell you? In America children are like money in the bank," purred

Mrs. Pelz as she pinched and patted Hanneh Breineh's silk sleeve. "*Oi weh!* how it shines from you! You ought to kiss the air and dance for joy and happiness. It is such a bitter frost outside; a pail of coal is so dear, and you got it so warm with steam-heat. I had to pawn my feather-bed to have enough for the rent, and you are rolling in money."

"Yes, I got it good in some ways, but money ain't everything," sighed Hanneh Breineh.

"You ain't yet satisfied?"

"But here I got no friends," complained Hanneh Breineh.

"Friends?" queried Mrs. Pelz. "What greater friend is there on earth than the dollar?"

"*Oi!* Mrs. Pelz; if you could only look into my heart! I'm so choked up! You know they say, a cow has a long tongue, but can't talk." Hanneh Breineh shook her head wistfully, and her eyes filmed with inward brooding. "My children give me everything from the best. When I was sick, they got me a nurse by day and one by night. They bought me the best wine. If I asked for dove's milk, they would buy it for me; but — but — I can't talk myself out in their language. They want to make me over for an American lady, and I'm different." Tears cut their way under her eyelids with a pricking pain as she went on: "When I was poor, I was free, and could holler and do what I like in my own house. Here I got to lie still like a mouse under a broom. Between living up to my Fifth Avenue daughter and keeping up with the servants I am like a sinner in the next world that is thrown from one hell to another."

The door-bell rang, and Hanneh Breineh jumped up with a start.

"*Oi weh!* it must be the servant back already!" she exclaimed as she tore off her apron. "*Oi weh!* let's quickly put the dishes together in a dish-pan. If she sees I eat on the kitchen table, she will look on me like the dirt under her feet."

Mrs. Pelz seized her shawl in haste.

"I better run home quick in my rags before your servant sees me."

"I'll speak to Abe about the job," said Hanneh Breineh as she pushed a bill into the hand of Mrs. Pelz, who edged out as the servant entered.

৯৬

"I'm having fried potato *lotkes* special for you, Benny," said Hanneh Breineh as the children gathered about the table for the family dinner given in honor of Benny's success with his new play. "Do you remember how you used to lick the fingers from them?"

"O Mother!" reproved Fanny. "Anyone hearing you would think we were still in the push-cart district."

"Stop your nagging, Sis, and let ma alone," commanded Benny, patting his mother's arm affectionately. "I'm home only once a month. Let her feed me what she pleases. My stomach is bomb-proof."

"Do I hear that the President is coming to your play?" said Abe as he stuffed a napkin over his diamond-studded shirt-front.

"Why should n't he come?" returned Benny, "The critics say it 's the greatest antidote for the race hatred created by the war. If you want to know, he is coming to-night; and what 's more, our box is next to the President's."

"*Nu,* Mammeh," sallied Jake, "did you ever dream in Delancey Street that we should rub sleeves with the President?"

"I always said that Benny had more head than the rest of you," replied the mother.

As the laughter died away, Jake went on:

"Honor you are getting plenty; but how much *mezummen* does this play bring you? Can I invest any of it in real estate for you?"

"I'm getting ten per cent. royalties of the gross receipts," replied the youthful playwright.

"How much is that?" queried Hanneh Breineh.

"Enough to buy up all your fish-markets in Delancey Street," laughed Abe in good-natured raillery at his mother.

Her son's jest cut like a knife-thrust in her heart. She felt her heart ache with the pain that she was shut out from their successes. Each added triumph only widened the gulf. And when she tried to bridge this gulf by asking questions, they only thrust her back upon herself.

"Your fame has even helped me get my hat trade solid with the Four Hundred," put in Fanny. "You bet I let Mrs. Van Suyden know that our box is next to the President's. She said she would drop in to meet you. Of course she let on to me that she had n't seen the play yet, though my designer said she saw her there on the opening night."

"Oh, Gosh! the toadies!" sneered Benny. "Nothing so sickens you with success as the way people who once shoved you off the sidewalk come crawling to you on their stomachs begging you to dine with them."

"Say, that leading man of yours he's some class," cried Fanny. "That 's the man I 'm looking for. Will you invite him to supper after the theater?"

The playwright turned to his mother.

"Say, Ma," he said laughingly, "how would you like a real actor for a son-in-law?"

"She should worry," mocked Sam. "She 'll be discussing with him the future of the Greek drama. Too bad it does n't happen to be Warfield, or mother could give him tips on the 'Auctioneer.'"

Jake turned to his mother with a covert grin.

"I guess you 'd have no objection if Fanny got next to Benny's leading man. He makes at least fifteen hundred a week. That would n't be such a bad addition to the family, would it?"

Again the bantering tone stabbed Hanneh Breineh. Everything in her began to tremble and break lose.

"Why do you ask me?" she cried, throwing her napkin into her plate. "Do I count for a person in this house? If I 'll say something, will you even listen to me? What is to me the grandest man that my daughter could pick out? Another enemy in my house! Another person to shame himself from me!" She swept in her children in one glance of despairing anguish as she rose from the table. "What worth is an old mother to American children? The President is coming to-night to the theater, and none of you asked me to go." Unable to check the rising tears, she fled toward the kitchen and banged the door.

They all looked at one another guiltily.

"Say, Sis," Benny called out sharply, "what sort of frame-up is this? Have n't you told mother that she was to go with us to-night?"

"Yes — I —" Fanny bit her lips as she fumbled evasively for words. "I asked her if she wouldn't mind my taking her some other time."

"Now you have made a mess of it!" fumed Benny. "Mother 'll be too hurt to go now."

"Well, I don't care," snapped Fanny. "I can't appear with mother in a box at the theater. Can I introduce her to Mrs. Van Suyden? And suppose your leading man should ask to meet me?"

"Take your time, Sis. He has n't asked yet," scoffed Benny.

"The more reason I shouldn't spoil my chances. You know mother. She 'll spill the beans that we come from Delancey Street the minute we introduce her anywhere. Must I always have the black shadow of my past trailing after me?"

"But have you no feelings for mother?" admonished Abe.

"I 've tried harder than all of you to do my duty. I 've *lived* with her." She turned angrily upon them. "I 've borne the shame of mother while you bought her off with a present and a treat here and there. God knows how hard I tried to civilize her so as not to have to blush with shame when I take her anywhere. I dressed her in the most stylish Paris models, but Delancey Street sticks out from every inch of her. Whenever she opens her mouth, I 'm done for. You fellows had your chance to rise in the world because a man is free to go up as high as he can reach up to; but I, with all my style and pep, can't get a man my equal because a girl is always judged by her mother." .

They were silenced by her vehemence, and unconsciously turned to Benny.

"I guess we all tried to do our best for mother," said Benny, thoughtfully. "But wherever there is growth, there is pain and heartbreak. The trouble with us is that the Ghetto of the Middle Ages and the children of the twentieth century have to live under one roof, and —"

A sound of crashing dishes came from the kitchen, and the voice of Hanneh Breineh resounded through the dining-room as she wreaked her pent-up fury on the helpless servant.

"Oh, my nerves! I can't stand it any more! There will be no girl again for another week," cried Fanny.

"Oh, let up on the old lady," protested Abe. "Since she can't take it out on us any more, what harm is it if she cusses the servants?"

"If you fellows had to chase around employment agencies, you would n't see anything funny about it. Why can't we move into a hotel that will do away with the need of servants altogether?"

"I got it better," said Jake, consulting a note-book from his pocket. "I have on my list an apartment on Riverside Drive where there 's only a small kitchenette; but we can do away with the cooking, for there is a dining service in the building."

♋

The new Riverside apartment to which Hanneh Breineh was removed by her socially ambitious children was for the habitually active mother an empty desert of enforced idleness. Deprived of her kitchen, Hanneh Breineh felt robbed of the last reason for her existence. Cooking and marketing and puttering busily with pots and pans gave her an excuse for living and struggling and bearing up with her children. The lonely idleness of Riverside Drive stunned all her senses and arrested all her thoughts. It gave her that choked sense of being cut off from air, from life, from everything warm and human. The cold indifference, the each-for-himself look in the eyes of the people about her were like stinging slaps in the face. Even the children had nothing real or human in them. They were starched and stiff miniatures of their elders.

But the most unendurable part of the stifling life on Riverside Drive was being forced to eat in the public dining-room. No matter how hard she tried to learn polite table manners, she always found people staring at her, and her daughter rebuking her for eating with the wrong fork or guzzling the soup or staining the cloth.

In a fit of rebellion Hanneh Breineh resolved never to go down to the public dining-room again, but to make use of the gas-stove in the kitchenette to cook her own meals. That very day she rode down to Delancey Street and purchased a new market-basket. For some time she walked among the haggling push-cart venders, relaxing and swimming in the warm waves of her old familiar past.

A fish-peddler held up a large carp in his black, hairy hand and waved it dramatically:

"Women! Women! Fourteen cents a pound!"

He ceased his raucous shouting as he saw Hanneh Breineh in her rich attire approach his cart.

"How much?" she asked, pointing to the fattest carp.

"Fifteen cents, lady," said the peddler, smirking as he raised his price.

"Swindler! Did n't I hear you call fourteen cents?" shrieked Hanneh Breineh, exultingly, the spirit of the penny chase surging in her blood. Diplomatically,

Hanneh Breineh turned as if to go, and the fishman seized her basket in frantic fear.

"I should live; I'm losing money on the fish, lady," whined the peddler. "I'll let it down to thirteen cents for you only."

"Two pounds for a quarter, and not a penny more," said Hanneh Breineh, thrilling again with the rare sport of bargaining, which had been her chief joy in the good old days of poverty.

"*Nu*, I want to make the first sale for good luck." The peddler threw the fish on the scale.

As he wrapped up the fish, Hanneh Breineh saw the driven look of worry in his haggard eyes, and when he counted out for her the change from her dollar, she waved it aside.

"Keep it for your luck," she said, and hurried off to strike a new bargain at the push-cart of onions.

Hanneh Breineh returned triumphantly with her purchases. The basket under her arm gave forth the old, homelike odors of herring and garlic, while the scaly tail of a four-pound carp protruded from its newspaper wrapping. A gilded placard on the door of the apartment-house proclaimed that all merchandise must be delivered through the trade entrance in the rear; but Hanneh Breineh with her basket strode proudly through the marble-paneled hall and rang nonchalantly for the elevator.

The uniformed hall-man, erect, expressionless, frigid with dignity, stepped forward:

"Just a minute, Madam, I'll call a boy to take up your basket for you."

Hanneh Breineh, glaring at him, jerked the basket savagely from his hands.

"Mind your own business," she retorted. "I'll take it up myself. Do you think you're a Russian policeman to boss me in my own house?"

Angry lines appeared on the countenance of the representative of social decorum.

"It is against the rules, Madam," he said stiffly.

"You should sink into the earth with all your rules and brass buttons. Ain't this America? Ain't this a free country? Can't I take up in my own house what I buy with my own money?" cried Hanneh Breineh, reveling in the opportunity to shower forth the volley of invectives that had been suppressed in her for the weeks of deadly dignity of Riverside Drive.

In the midst of this uproar Fanny came in with Mrs. Van Suyden. Hanneh Breineh rushed over to her, crying:

"This bossy policeman won't let me take up my basket in the elevator."

The daughter, unnerved with shame and confusion, took the basket in her white-gloved hand and ordered the hall-boy to take it around to the regular delivery entrance.

Hanneh Breineh was so hurt by her daughter's apparent defense of the hall-man's rules that she utterly ignored Mrs. Van Suyden's greeting and walked up the seven flights of stairs out of sheer spite.

"You see the tragedy of my life?" broke out Fanny, turning to Mrs. Van Suyden.

"You poor child! You go right up to your dear, old lady mother, and I'll come some other time."

Instantly Fanny regretted her words. Mrs. Van Suyden's pity only roused her wrath the more against her mother.

Breathless from climbing the stairs, Hanneh Breineh entered the apartment just as Fanny tore the faultless millinery creation from her head and threw it on the floor in a rage.

"Mother, you are the ruination of my life! You have driven away Mrs. Van Suyden, as you have driven away all my best friends. What do you think we got this apartment for but to get rid of your fish smells and your brawls with the servants? And here you come with a basket on your arm as if you just landed from steerage! And this afternoon, of all times, when Benny is bringing his leading man to tea. When will you ever stop disgracing us?"

"When I'm dead," said Hanneh Breineh, grimly. "When the earth will cover me up, then you'll be free to go your American way. I'm not going to make myself over for a lady on Riverside Drive. I hate you and all your swell friends. I'll not let myself be choked up here by you or by that hall-boss-policeman that is higher in your eyes than your own mother."

"So that's your thanks for all we've done for you?" cried the daughter.

"All you've done for me?" shouted Hanneh Breineh. "What have you done for me? You hold me like a dog on a chain. It stands in the Talmud; some children give their mothers dry bread and water and go to heaven for it, and some give their mother roast duck and go to Gehenna because it's not given with love."

"You want me to love you yet?" raged the daughter. "You knocked every bit of love out of me when I was yet a kid. All the memories of childhood I have is your everlasting cursing and yelling that we were gluttons."

The bell rang sharply, and Hanneh Breineh flung open the door.

"Your groceries, ma'am," said the boy.

Hanneh Breineh seized the basket from him, and with a vicious fling sent it rolling across the room, strewing its contents over the Persian rugs and inlaid floor. Then seizing her hat and coat, she stormed out of the apartment and down the stairs.

Mr. and Mrs. Pelz sat crouched and shivering over their meager supper when the door opened, and Hanneh Breineh in fur coat and plumed hat charged into the room.

"I come to cry out to you my bitter heart," she sobbed. "Woe is me! It is so black for my eyes!"

"What is the matter with you, Hanneh Breineh?" cried Mrs. Pelz in bewildered alarm.

"I am turned out of my own house by the brass-buttoned policeman that bosses the elevator. *Oi-i-i-i! Weh-h-h-h!* what have I from my life? The whole world rings with my son's play. Even the President came to see it, and I, his mother, have not seen it yet. My heart is dying in me like in a prison," she went on wailing. "I am starved out for a piece of real eating. In that swell restaurant is nothing but napkins and forks and lettuce-leaves. There are a dozen plates to every bite of food. And it looks so fancy on the plate, but it 's nothing but straw in the mouth. I 'm starving, but I can't swallow down their American eating."

"Hanneh Breineh," said Mrs. Pelz, "you are sinning before God. Look on your fur coat; it alone would feed a whole family for a year. I never had yet a piece of fur trimming on a coat, and you are in a fur from the neck to the feet. I never had yet a piece of feather on a hat, and your hat is all feathers."

"What are you envying me?" protested Hanneh Breineh. "What have I from all my fine furs and feathers when my children are strangers to me? All the fur coats in the world can't warm up the loneliness inside my heart. All the grandest feathers can't hide the bitter shame in my face that my children shame themselves from me."

Hanneh Breineh suddenly loomed over them like some ancient, heroic figure of the Bible condemning unrighteousness.

"Why should my children shame themselves from me? From where did they get the stuff to work themselves up in the world? Did they get it from the air? How did they get all their smartness to rise over the people around them? Why don't the children of born American mothers write my Benny's plays? It is I, who never had a chance to be a person, who gave him the fire in his head. If I would have had a chance to go to school and learn the language, what could n't I have been? It is I and my mother and my mother's mother and my father and father's father who had such a black life in Poland; it is our choked thoughts and feelings that are flaming up in my children and making them great in America. And yet they shame themselves from me!"

For a moment Mr. and Mrs. Pelz were hypnotized by the sweep of her words. Then Hanneh Breineh sank into a chair in utter exhaustion. She began to weep bitterly, her body shaking with sobs.

"Woe is me! For what did I suffer and hope on my children? A bitter old age — my end. I 'm so lonely!"

All the dramatic fire seemed to have left her. The spell was broken. They saw the Hanneh Breineh of old, ever discontented, ever complaining even in the midst of riches and plenty.

"Hanneh Breineh," said Mrs. Pelz, "the only trouble with you is that you got it too good. People will tear the eyes out of your head because you're complaining yet. If I only had your fur coat! If I only had your diamonds! I have nothing. You have everything. You are living on the fat of the land. You go right back home and thank God that you don't have my bitter lot."

"You got to let me stay here with you," insisted Hanneh Breineh. "I 'll not go back to my children except when they bury me. When they will see my dead face, they will understand how they killed me."

Mrs. Pelz glanced nervously at her husband. They barely had enough covering for their one bed; how could they possibly lodge a visitor?

"I don't want to take up your bed," said Hanneh Breineh. "I don't care if I have to sleep on the floor or on the chairs, but I 'll stay here for the night."

Seeing that she was bent on staying, Mr. Pelz prepared to sleep by putting a few chairs next to the trunk, and Hanneh Breineh was invited to share the rickety bed with Mrs. Pelz.

The mattress was full of lumps and hollows. Hanneh Breineh lay cramped and miserable, unable to stretch out her limbs. For years she had been accustomed to hair mattresses and ample woolen blankets, so that though she covered herself with her fur coat, she was too cold to sleep. But worse than the cold were the creeping things on the wall. And as the lights were turned low, the mice came through the broken plaster and raced across the floor. The foul odors of the kitchen-sink added to the night of horrors.

"Are you going back home?" asked Mrs. Pelz as Hanneh Breineh put on her hat and coat the next morning.

"I don't know where I 'm going," she replied as she put a bill into Mrs. Pelz's hand.

For hours Hanneh Breineh walked through the crowded Ghetto streets. She realized that she no longer could endure the sordid ugliness of her past, and yet she could not go home to her children. She only felt that she must go on and on.

In the afternoon a cold, drizzling rain set in. She was worn out from the sleepless night and hours of tramping. With a piercing pain in her heart she at last turned back and boarded the subway for Riverside Drive. She had fled from the marble sepulcher of the Riverside apartment to her old home in the Ghetto; but now she knew that she could not live there again. She had outgrown her past by the habits of years of physical comforts, and these material comforts that she could no longer do without choked and crushed the life within her.

A cold shudder went through Hanneh Breineh as she approached the apartment-house. Peering through the plate glass of the door she saw the face of the uniformed hall-man. For a hesitating moment she remained standing in the drizzling rain, unable to enter and yet knowing full well that she would have to enter.

Then suddenly Hanneh Breineh began to laugh. She realized that it was the first time she had laughed since her children had become rich. But it was the hard laugh of bitter sorrow. Tears streamed down her furrowed cheeks as she walked slowly up the granite steps.

"The fat of the land!" muttered Hanneh Breineh, with a choking sob as the hall-man with immobile face deferentially swung open the door — "the fat of the land!"

Katherine Anne Porter
Maria Concepción

Katherine Anne Porter is unusual among American Modernists in that her reputation is largely dependent on her work in short fiction rather than on her only novel, *Ship of Fools*. Her other volumes, *Flowering Judas and Other Stories, Noon Wine, Pale Horse, Pale Rider,* and the *Collected Stories,* all demonstrate her prowess with the narrative compression of the story, a form she mastered from the very beginning. Born in Texas in 1890, Porter lived long enough to witness the seminal events of the twentieth century: two world wars; the social transformations brought by women's suffrage and the civil rights movement; technological advances of enormous proportions, including a landing on the moon; and the shift in literature from the concerns of Modernism to the more disquieting and disorienting ideas of the contemporary era. Her own work was formed by her residency in New York in the early 1920s and by her extended trips to Mexico, where she became interested in archaeology. She was fascinated by the complex society that confronted her, with its amalgam of Roman Catholicism and pagan beliefs, pre-Hispanic customs and modern reforms. Her first serious story, "Maria Concepción," rests on the simple plot of the avenging wife, but it is the subtle revelation of cultural and religious values that gives the story its charm and depth. Porter's skill in handling narration, imagery, and style all contribute to making her first story one of her finest.

Katherine Anne Porter, "Maria Concepción," *Century Illustrated Magazine* 105, no. 2 (December 1922): 224–39.

Maria Concepción walked carefully, keeping to the middle of the white, dusty road, where the maguey thorns and the treacherous curved spines of organa cactus had not gathered so profusely. She would have enjoyed resting for a moment in the dark shade by the roadside, but she had no time to waste drawing cactus needles from her feet. Juan and his *jefe* would be waiting for their food in the damp trenches of the buried city.

She carried about a dozen living fowls slung over her right shoulder, their feet fastened together. Half of them fell upon the flat of her back, the balance dangled uneasily over her breast. They wriggled their benumbed and swollen legs against her neck, they twisted their stupefied, half-blind eyes upward, seeming to peer into her face inquiringly. She did not see them or think of them. Her left arm was a trifle tired with the weight of the food basket, and she was hungry after her long morning's work.

Under her clean bright-blue cotton rebozo her straight back outlined itself strongly. Instinctive serenity softened her black eyes, shaped like almonds set far apart, and tilted a bit endwise. She walked with the free, natural, yet guarded, ease of the primitive woman carrying an unborn child. The shape of her body was easy, the swelling life was not a distortion, but the right, inevitable proportions of a woman. She was entirely contented, calmly filled with a sense of the goodness of life.

Her small house was half-way up a shallow hill, under a clump of peru-trees, a wall of organa cactus inclosing it on the side nearest the road. Now she came down into the valley, divided by the narrow spring, and crossed a bridge of loose stones near the hut where Maria Rosa the bee-keeper lived with her old godmother, Lupe, the medicine-woman. Maria Concepción had no faith in the charred owl bones, the singed rabbit fur, the messes and ointments sold by Lupe to the ailing of the village. She was a good Christian, and bought her remedies, bottled, with printed directions that she could not read, at the drug-store near the city market, where she went almost daily with her fowls. But she often purchased a jar of honey from young Maria Rosa, a pretty, shy child only fifteen years old.

Maria Concepción and her husband, Juan Villegas, were each a little past their eighteenth year. She had a good reputation with the neighbors as an energetic, religious woman. It was commonly known that if she wished to buy a new rebozo for herself or a shirt for Juan, she could bring out a sack of hard silver pesos for the purpose.

She had paid for the license, nearly a year ago, the potent bit of stamped paper which permits people to be married in the church. She had given money to the priest before she and Juan walked together up to the altar the Monday after Holy Week. It had been the adventure of the villagers to go, three Sundays one after another, to hear the banns called by the priest for Juan de Dios Villegas and Maria Concepción Guiterrez. After the wedding she had called herself Maria Concepción Guiterrez de Villegas, as though she owned a whole hacienda.

She paused on the bridge and dabbled her feet in the water, her eyes resting themselves from the sun-rays in a fixed, dreaming gaze to the far-off mountains, deeply blue under their hanging drift of clouds. It came to her that she would like a fresh crust of honey. The delicious aroma of bees, their slow, thrilling hum poured upon her, awakening a pleasant desire for a crisp flake of sweetness in her mouth.

"If I do not eat it now, I shall mark my child," she thought, peering through the crevices in the thick hedge of cactus that sheered up nakedly, like prodigious bared knife-blades cast protectingly around the small clearing. The place was so silent that she doubted if Maria Rosa and Lupe were at home.

The leaning *jacal* of dried rush-withes and corn-sheaves, bound to tall saplings thrust into the earth, roofed with yellowed maguey-leaves flattened and overlapping like shingles, sat drowsy and fragrant in the warmth of noonday. The hives, similarly constructed, were scattered toward the back of the clearing, like small mounds of clean vegetable refuse. Over each mound there hung a dusty golden shimmer of bees.

A light, gay scream of laughter rose from behind the hut; a man's short laugh joined in. "Ah, Maria Rosa has a *novio!*" Maria Concepción stopped short, smiling, shifted her burden slightly, bending forward to see more clearly through the hedge spaces, shading her eyes.

Maria Rosa ran, dodging between beehives, parting two stunted jasmine-bushes as she came, lifting her knees in swift leaps, looking over her shoulder and laughing in a quivering, excited way. A heavy jar, swung by the handle to her wrist, knocked against her thighs as she ran. Her toes pushed up sudden spurts of dust, her half-unbraided hair showered around her shoulders in long crinkled wisps.

Juan Villegas ran after her, also laughing strangely, his teeth set, both rows gleaming behind the small, soft black beard growing sparsely on his lips, his chin, leaving his brown cheeks girl-smooth. When he seized her, he clenched so hard that her chemise gave way and slipped off her shoulder. Frightened, she stopped laughing, pushed him away, and stood silent, trying to pull up the ripped sleeve with one hand. Her pointed chin and dark-red mouth moved in an uncertain way, as if she wished to laugh again; her long black lashes flickered with the tiny quick-moving lights in her half-hidden eyes.

Maria Concepción realized that she had not stirred or breathed for some seconds. Her forehead was cold, and yet boiling water seemed to be pouring slowly along her spine. An unaccountable pain was in her knees, as though pieces of ice had got into them. She was afraid Juan and Maria Rosa would feel her eyes fixed upon them, and find her there, unable to move. But they did not pass beyond the inclosure, or even glance toward the gap in the wall opening upon the road.

Juan lifted one of Maria Rosa's half-bound braids and slapped her neck with it, playfully. She smiled with soft, expectant shyness. Together they moved back through the hives of honey-comb. Juan flourished his wide hat back and forth, walking very proudly. Maria Rosa balanced her jar on one hip, and swung her long, full petticoats with every step.

Maria Concepción came out of the heavy darkness which seemed to enwrap her head and bind her at the throat, and found herself walking onward, keeping the road by instinct, feeling her way delicately, her ears strumming as if all Maria Rosa's bees had hived in them. Her careful sense of duty kept her moving toward the buried city where Juan's chief, the American archaeologist, was taking his midday rest, waiting for his dinner.

Juan and Maria Rosa! She burned all over now, as if a layer of those tiny fig-cactus bristles, as insidious and petty-cruel as spun glass, had crawled under her skin. She wished to sit down quietly and wait for her death without finishing what she had set out to do, remembering no more those two strange people, Juan and Maria Rosa, laughing and kissing in the sweet-smelling sunshine. Once, years before, when she was a young girl, she had returned from market to find her *jacal* burned to a pile of ash and her few pesos gone. An incredibly lost and empty feeling had possessed her; she had kept moving about the place, unbelieving, somehow expecting it all to take shape again before her eyes, restored unchanged. But it was all gone. And now here was a worse thing. This was something that could not happen. But it was true. Maria Rosa, that sinful girl, shameless!

She heard herself saying a harsh, true word about Maria Rosa, saying it aloud as if she expected some one to answer, "Yes, you are right." At this moment the gray, untidy head of Givens appeared over the edges of the newest trench he had caused to be dug in his field of excavations. The long, deep crevasses, in which a man might stand without being seen, lay criss-crossed like orderly gashes of a giant scalpel. Nearly all the men of the small community were employed by Givens in this work of uncovering the lost city of their ancestors. They worked all the year through and prospered, digging all day for those small clay heads and bits of pottery for which there was no use on earth, they being all broken and covered with earth. They themselves could make better ones, perfectly stout and new. But the unearthly delight of the *jefe* in finding these things was an endless puzzle. He would fairly roar for joy at times, waving a shattered pot or a human rib-bone above his head, shouting for his photographer to come and make a picture of this!

Now he emerged, and his young enthusiast's eyes welcomed Maria Concepción from his old-man face, covered with hard wrinkles, burned to the color of red earth under the countless suns of his explorer's life.

"I hope you 've brought me a nice fat one." He selected a fowl from the bunch dangling nearest him as Maria Concepción, wordless, leaned over the trench. "Dress it for me, there 's a good girl. I 'll broil it."

Maria Concepción took the fowl by the head, and silently, swiftly drew the knife across the throat, twisting off the head with the casual firmness one might use with the top of a beet.

"*Dios,* woman, but you have valor!" said Givens, watching her. "I can't do that. It makes me creep."

"My home country is Guadalajara," answered Maria Concepción, without bravado. "There we have valor for everything."

She stood and regarded Givens condescendingly, that diverting white man who had no woman to cook for him, and, moreover, appeared not to feel any loss of dignity in preparing his own food. He knelt now, eyes squinted tightly, nose wrinkled, trying to avoid the smoke, turning the roasting fowl busily on a stick. Juan's *jefe,* therefore to be humored, to be placated.

"The tortillas are fresh and hot, Señor," she murmured. "By permission, I will now go to market."

"Yes, yes, run along; bring me another to-morrow." Givens turned his head to look at her again. Her grand manner reminded him of royalty in exile. He noticed her unnatural paleness. "The sun is too hot, eh?" he asked.

"*Si,* Señor. Pardon me, but Juan will be here soon?"

"He should be, the scamp. Leave his food. The others will eat it."

She moved away; the blue of her rebozo became a dancing spot in the heat vibrations that appeared to rise from the gray-red soil. Givens considered her exceptionally intelligent. He liked to tell stories of Juan's escapades also, of how often he had saved him, within the last five years, from going to jail, or even from being shot, for his varied and highly imaginative misdemeanors.

"I am never a minute too soon," he would say indulgently. "Well, why not? He is a good worker. He never intentionally did harm in his life."

After Juan was married, he used to twit him, with exactly the right shade of condescension, on his many infidelities to Maria Concepción. He was fond of saying, "She 'll discover you yet, young demon!" which would please Juan immensely.

Maria Concepción did not think of telling Juan she had found him out, but she kept saying to herself, "If I had been a young girl like Maria Rosa, and a man had caught hold of me so, I would have broken my jar over his head." Her anger was all against Maria Rosa because she had not done this.

Less than a week after this the two culprits went away to war, Juan as a common soldier, Maria Rosa as his *soldadera.* She bowed her neck under a heavy and onerous yoke of duties; she carried the blankets and the cooking-pots, she slept on stones or dry branches, she marched ahead of the troops, with the battalion of experienced women of war, in search of provisions. She ate with them what was left after the men had eaten. After battles she went out on the field with the others to salvage clothing and guns and ammunition from the slain before they should begin to spoil in the heat.

This was the life the little bee-keeper found at the end of her runaway journey. There was no particular scandal in the village. People shrugged. It was far better for every one that they were gone. There was a popular belief among her neighbors that Maria Concepción was not so mild as she seemed.

When she learned about her man and that shameless girl she did not weep. Later, when the baby was born, and died within four days, she did not weep. "She is mere stone," said old Lupe, who had offered all her charms for the preservation of the little life, and had been rebuffed with a ferocity that appalled her.

If Maria Concepción had not gone so regularly to church, lighting candles before the saints and receiving holy communion at the altar every month, there might have been talk of her being devil-possessed, her face was so changed and blind-looking. But this was impossible when, after all, she had been married by the priest. It must be, they reasoned, that she was being punished for her pride. They decided this was the true reason: she was altogether too proud.

During the two years that Juan and Maria Rosa were gone Maria Concepción sold her fowls and looked after her house, and her sack of hard pesos grew. Lupe had no talent for bees, and the hives did not prosper. She used to see Maria Concepción in the market or at church, and afterward she always said that no one could tell by looking that she was a woman who had such a heavy grief.

"I pray God everything goes well with Maria Concepción from this out," she would say, "for she has had her share of trouble."

When some idle person repeated this to the deserted woman, she went down to Lupe's house and stood within the clearing, and called to the medicine-woman, who sat in her doorway stirring a jar of fresh snake's grease and rabbit blood, a cure for sores:

"Keep your prayers to yourself, Lupe, or offer them for others who need them. I will ask God for what I want in this world."

"And will you get it, you think, Maria Concepción?" asked Lupe, tittering cruelly, and smelling the mixture clinging to the wooden spoon. "Did you pray for what you have now?"

Afterward every one noticed that Maria Concepción went more often to church, and less to the village to talk with the other women as they sat along the curb, eating fruit and nursing their infants, at the end of the market-day.

"After all, she is wrong to take us for her enemies," said grave old Soledad, who always thought such things out. "All women have these troubles. Well, we should suffer together."

But Maria Concepción lived alone. She was thin, as if something was gnawing her away inside, her eyes were sunken, and she spoke no more than was necessary. She worked harder than ever, and her butchering knife was scarcely ever out of her hand.

Juan and Maria Rosa, tired of military life, came home one day without asking permission of any authority whatever. The field of war had unrolled itself, a long scroll of vexations, until the end had frayed out within twenty miles of Juan's village. So he and his *soldadera,* now as lean as a wolf, and burdened with a child daily expected, set out with no ostentation and walked home.

They arrived one morning about daybreak. Juan was picked up on sight by a group of military police from the small *cuartel* on the edge of town, who told him with impersonal cheerfulness that he would add one to a group of ten waiting to be shot next morning as deserters.

Maria Rosa, screaming, and falling on her face in the road, was taken under the armpits by two guards and helped briskly to her own *jacal,* now sadly run down. She was received with professional calm by Lupe, who hastily set about the business obviously in hand.

Limping with foot weariness, a layer of dust concealing his fine new clothes, got mysteriously from somewhere, Juan appeared before the captain of the *cuartel*. The captain recognized him as the chief digger for his good friend Givens. He despatched a note in haste to that kindly and eccentric person.

Shortly afterward, Givens showed up at the *cuartel*, and Juan was delivered to him, with the urgent request that nothing be made public about so humane and sensible an operation on the part of military authority.

Juan walked out of the rather stifling atmosphere of the drumhead court, a definite air of swagger about him. His hat, incredibly huge and embroidered with silver thread, hung over one eyebrow, secured at the back by a cord of silver dripping with cobalt-blue tassels. His shirt was of a checkerboard pattern in green and black, his white cotton trousers were bound by a belt of yellow leather tooled in red. His feet were bare, the beautifully arched and muscled feet of the Indian, with long, flexible toes.

He removed his cigarette from the corner of his full-lipped, wide mouth. He removed the splendid hat. His black hair, pressed damply to his forehead, sprang up suddenly in a cloudy thatch on his crown.

"You young devil," said Givens, a trifle shaken, "some day I shall be five minutes too late!"

Juan bowed to the officer, who appeared to be gazing at a vacuum. He swung his arm wide in a free circle up-soaring toward the prison window, where forlorn heads poked over the window-sill, hot eyes following the lucky departing one. Two or three of them flipped a hand in response, with a gallant effort to imitate his own casual and heady manner.

He kept up this insufferable pantomime until they rounded the first sheltering clump of fig-cactus. Then he seized Givens's hand, and his eyes blazed adoration and gratitude.

"With all my life, all my life, I thank thee!" he said. "It is nothing to be shot, *mi jefe*, — certainly you know I was not afraid — but to be shot in a drove of deserters, against a cold wall, by order of that —"

Glittering epithets tumbled over one another like explosions of a rocket. All the scandalous analogies from the animal and vegetable worlds were applied in a vivid, unique, and personal way to the life, loves, and family history of the harmless young officer who had just set him free. But Juan cared nothing for this; his gratitude to his *jefe* excluded all other possible obligations.

"What will Maria Concepción say to all this?" asked Givens. "You are very informal, Juan, for a man who was married in the church."

Juan put on his hat.

"Oh, Maria Concepción! That's nothing! Look you, *mi jefe*, to be married in the church is a great misfortune to a man. After that he is not himself any more. How can that woman complain when I do not drink, not even on days of fiesta, more than a glass of pulque? I do not beat her; never, never. We were always at peace. I say to her, 'Come here,' and she comes straight. I say, 'Go there,' and she goes quickly. Yet sometimes I looked at her and thought, 'Now I am married to that woman in the church,' and I felt a sinking inside, as if something were lying heavy on my stomach. With Maria Rosa it is all different. She is not silent; she talks. When she talks too much, I slap her and say, 'Silence, thou simpleton!' and she weeps. She is just a girl with whom I do as I please. You know how she used to keep those clean little bees in their hives? She always smelt of their honey. I swear it. I would not harm Maria Concepción because I am married to her in the church; but also, *mi jefe,* I will not leave Maria Rosa, because she pleases me more than any other woman."

"Let me tell you, Juan, Maria Concepción will some day take your head off with that sharp knife she uses on the fowls. Then you will remember what I have said."

Juan's expression was the proper blend of sentimental triumph and melancholy. It was pleasant to think of himself in the rôle of romantic hero to two such desirable women. His present situation was ineffably perfect. He had just escaped from the threat of a disagreeable end. His clothes were new and handsome. He was on his way to work and civilian life with his patient *jefe.* He was little more than twenty years old. Life tasted good, for a certainty. He fairly smacked his lips on its savor.

The early sunshine, the light, clear air, full of the good smell of ripening cactus-figs, peaches, and melons, of pungent pepper-berries dangling in bright red clusters on the peru-trees, the very smell of his cigarette, shook him with a merry ecstasy of good-will for all life, whatever it was.

"Señor," — he addressed his friend handsomely, as one man to another — "women are good things, but not at this moment. By your permission, I will now go to the village and eat. To-morrow morning very early I will come to the buried city and work. Let us forget Maria Concepción and Maria Rosa. Each one in her place. I will manage them when the time comes."

News of Juan's adventure soon got abroad, and Juan found many friends about him during the morning. They frankly commended his leaving the army. *Por Dios!* a man could do no better thing than that! The new hero ate a great deal and drank a little, the occasion being better than a feast-day. It was almost noon before he returned to visit Maria Rosa.

He found her sitting on a straw mat, rubbing oil on her three-hour-old son. Before this felicitous vision Juan's emotions so twisted him that he returned to the village and invited every man in the "Death and Resurrection" *pulqueria* to drink with him.

Having thus taken leave of his balance, he found himself unaccountably back in his own house after his long absence, attempting to beat Maria Concepción by way of reëstablishing himself in his legal household.

Maria Concepción, knowing what had happened in the withe hut of her enemy, knowing all the events of that unhappy day, refused to be beaten by Juan drunk when Juan sober had never thought of such a thing. She did not scream; she stood her ground and resisted; she even struck at him.

Juan, amazed, only half comprehending his own actions, stepped back and gazed at her questioningly through a leisurely whirling film which seemed to have lodged behind his eyes. Certainly here was a strange thing. He had not intended to touch her. Oh, well, no harm done. He gave up, turned away. Sleep was better. He lay down amiably in a shadowed corner and floated away dreamlessly.

Maria Concepción, seeing that Juan was quiet, began automatically to bind the legs of her fowls. It was market-day, and she would be late.

Her movements were quick and rigid, like a doll jerked about on strings. She fumbled and tangled the bits of cord in her haste, and set off across the plowed, heavy fields instead of taking the accustomed road. She ran grotesquely, in uneven, jolting leaps between furrows, a crazy panic in her head, in her stumbling legs. She seemed not to know her directions. Now and then she would stop and look about, trying to place herself, then proceed a few steps.

At once, with an inner quivering, she came to her senses completely, recognized the thing that troubled her so terribly, was certain of what she wanted. She sat down quietly under a sheltering thorny bush and gave herself over to her long and devouring sorrow; flinched and shuddered away for the first time from that pain in the heart that pressed and pressed intolerably, until she wished to tear out the heart with her hands to be eased of it. The thing which had for so long squeezed her whole body into a tight, dumb knot of suffering suddenly broke with painful and shocking violence. She jerked with the involuntary recoil of one who receives a blow, and the tears poured from her eyes as if the wounds of her whole life were shedding their salt ichor. Drawing her rebozo over her head, she bowed her forehead on her arms, folded upon her updrawn knees, and wept.

After a great while she sat up, throwing the rebozo off her face, and leaned against the clustered saplings of the bush, arms relaxed at her sides, her face still, her eyes swollen, the lids closed and heavy. She sat there in deadly silence and immobility, the tears still forming steadily under the lashes, as if poured from an inexhaustible, secret, slow-moving river. She seemed to be crying in her sleep. From time to time she would lift the corner of her rebozo to wipe her face dry; and silently the tears would run again, streaking her face, drenching the front of her chemise. She had that complete and horrifying realization of calamity which is not a thing of the mind, but a physical experience as sharp and certain as the bite of thorns. All her being was a dark, confused memory of an endless loss, of grief burning in the heart by night, of deadly baffled anger eating at her by day, until her feet were as heavy as if she were mired in the muddy roads during the time of rains.

Juan awakened slowly, with long yawns and grumblings, alternated with short relapses into sleep full of visions and clamorous noises. A blur of orange light seared his eyeballs when he tried to unseal his lids. There came from somewhere a rapid confusion of words, a low voice weeping without tears, speaking awful meaningless phrases over and over. He began to listen. He strained and tugged at the leash of his stupor, he sweated to grasp those words which should have fearful meanings, yet somehow he could not comprehend them. Then he came awake with frightening suddenness, sitting up, eyes straining at the long, lashing steak of gilded light piercing the corn-husk walls from the level, disappearing sun.

Maria Concepción stood in the doorway, looming colossally tall to his shocked eyes. She was talking quickly, calling to him. Then he saw her clearly.

"*Por Dios!*" thought Juan, frozen with amazement, "here I am facing my death!" for the long knife she wore habitually at her belt was in her hand. But instead, she threw it away, clear from her, and got down on her knees, crawling toward him as he had seen her crawl toward the shrine at Guadalupe many times. Never had she knelt before him! He watched her approach with superstitious horror. Falling forward upon her face, she kissed his feet. She huddled upon his knees, lips moving urgently in a thrilling whisper. Her words became clear, and Juan understood them all.

For a second he could not speak. He sat immovable. Then he took her head between both his hands, and supported her somewhat in this way, saying swiftly, anxiously reassuring, almost in a babble:

"Oh, thou poor creature! Oh, thou dear woman! Oh, my Maria Concepción, unfortunate! Listen! do not fear! Hear me! I will hide thee away, I, thy own man, will protect thee! Quiet! Not a sound!"

Trying to collect himself, he held and soothed her as they sat together in the new darkness. Maria Concepción bent over, face almost upon his knees, her feet folded under her, seeking security of him. For the first time in his careless, utterly unafraid existence Juan was aware of danger. This was danger. Maria Concepción would be dragged away between two gendarmes, with him helpless and unarmed, to spend her days in Belem Prison, maybe. Danger! The night was peopled with tangible menaces. He stood up, dragging the woman to her feet with him. She was silent now, perfectly rigid, holding to him with resistless strength, her hands frozen on his arms.

"Get me the knife," he told her in a whisper. She obeyed, her feet slipping along the hard earth floor, her shoulders straight, her arms stiffened downward. He lighted a candle. Maria Concepción held the knife out to him. It was stained and dark even to the end of the handle, a thick stain with a viscous gleam.

He frowned at her harshly, noting the same stains on her chemise and hands.

"Take off thy clothes and wash thy hands," he ordered. He washed the knife carefully, and threw the water wide of the doorway. She watched him, and did likewise with the bowl where she had bathed.

"Light thy brasero and cook food for me," he told her in the same peremptory tone. He took her garments and went out. When he returned, she was wearing an old soiled dress, and was fanning the fire in the charcoal-burner. Seating himself cross-legged near her, he stared at her as at a creature unknown to him, who bewildered him utterly, for whom there was no possible explanation. She did not turn her head, but kept an oblivious silence and stillness, save for the movement of her strong hands fanning the blaze which cast sparks and small jets of white smoke, flaring and dying rhythmically with the motion of the fan, lighting her face and leaving it in darkness by turns.

"*Tu mujer,*" — Juan's voice barely disturbed the silence — "listen now to me carefully, and answer my questions as I ask them, and later, when the gendarmes come here for us, thou shalt have nothing to fear. But there will be something to settle between us afterward."

She turned her head slowly at this. The light from the fire cast small red sparks into the corners of her eyes; a yellow phosphorescence glimmered behind the dark iris.

"For me it is all settled, *Juanito mio,*" she answered, without fear, in a tone so tender, so grave, so heavy with sorrow, that Juan felt his vitals contract. He wished to weep openly not as a man, but as a very small child. He could not fathom this woman, or the mysterious fortunes of life grown so instantly tangled where all had seemed so gay and simple. He felt, too, that she had become unique and invaluable, a woman without an equal in a million women, and he could not tell why. He drew an enormous sigh that rattled in his chest.

"*Si, si,* it is all settled. I shall not go away again. We shall stay here together, you and I, forever."

In whispers he questioned her, and she answered whispering, and he instructed her over and over until she had her lesson by heart. The profound blackness of the night encroached upon them, flowing over the narrow threshold, invading their hearts. It brought with it sighs and murmurs, the pad of ghostly feet in the near-by road, the sharp staccato whimper of wind through the cactus-leaves. All these familiar cadences were now invested with sinister terrors; a dread, formless and uncontrollable, possessed them both.

"Light another candle," said Juan, aloud, suddenly, in too resolute, in too hard a tone. "Let us eat now."

They sat facing each other and ate from the same dish, after their old habit. Neither tasted what they ate. With food half-way to his mouth, Juan listened. The sound of voices grew, spread, widened at the turn of the road, along the organa wall. A spray of lantern-light filtered through the hedge, a single voice slashed the blackness, literally ripped the fragile layer of stillness which hovered above the hut.

"Juan Villegas!"

"Pass, friends!" Juan cried cheerfully.

They stood in the doorway, simple, cautious gendarmes from the village, partly Indian themselves, personally known to all the inhabitants. They flashed their lanterns almost apologetically upon the pleasant, harmless scene of a man eating supper with his wife.

"Pardon, Brother," said the leader. "Some one has killed the woman Maria Rosa, and we must ask questions of all her neighbors and friends." He paused, and added with an attempt at severity, "Naturally!"

"Naturally," agreed Juan. "I was a good friend of Maria Rosa. I regret her bad fortune."

They all went away together, the men walking in a group, Maria Concepción following a trifle to one side, a few steps in the rear, but near Juan. This was the custom. There was no thought of changing it even for such an important occasion.

The two points of candle-light at Maria Rosa's head fluttered uneasily; the shadows shifted and dodged on the stained, darkened walls. To Maria Concepción everything in the smothering, inclosing room shared an evil restlessness. The watchful faces of those called as witnesses, those familiar faces of old friends, were made alien by that look of speculation in the eyes. The ridges of the rose-colored silk rebozo thrown over the body varied continually, as though the thing it covered was not perfectly in repose. Her eyes swerved over the body from the candle-tips at the head to the feet, jutting up thinly, the small, scarred soles protruding, freshly washed, a mass of crooked, half-healed wounds, thorn-pricks and cuts of sharp stones. Her gaze went back to the candle-flare, to Juan's eyes warning her, to the gendarmes talking among themselves. Her eyes would not be controlled.

With a leap that shook her her gaze settled upon the face of Maria Rosa. Instantly, her blood ran smoothly again: there was nothing to fear. Even the restless light could not give a look of life to that fixed countenance. She was dead. Maria Concepción felt her muscles give way softly; her heart began beating without effort. She knew no more rancor against that pitiable thing, lying indifferently on its new mat under the fine silk rebozo. The mouth drooped sharply at the corners in a grimace of weeping arrested half-way. The brows were strangely distressed; the dead could not cast off some dark, final obsession of terror. It was all finished. Maria Rosa had eaten too much honey and had had too much love. Now she must sit in hell, crying over her sins and her hard death forever and ever.

Old Lupe's cackling voice arose. She had spent the morning helping Maria Rosa. The child had spat blood the moment it was born, a bad sign. She thought then that bad luck would come to the house. Well, about sunset she was in the yard at the back of the house grinding tomatoes and pepper. She had left mother and babe asleep. She heard a strange noise in the house, a choking and smothered calling, like some one in the nightmare. Well, such a thing is only natural. But there followed a light, quick, thudding sound —

"Like the blows of a fist?" interrupted the officer.

"No, not at all like such a thing."

"How do you know?"

"I am acquainted with that sound, Señor," retorted Lupe. "This noise was something else."

But she was at a loss to describe it exactly. Immediately, there was a slight rattle of pebbles rolling and slipping under feet; then she knew some one had been there and was running away.

"Why did you wait so long before going to see?"

"I am old and hard in the joints," said Lupe; "I cannot run after people. I walked as fast as I could to the organa hedge, for it is only by this way that any one can enter. There was no one in the road, Señor, no one. Three cows, with a dog driving them; nothing else. When I got to Maria Rosa, she was lying all tangled up, and from her neck to her middle she was full of knife-holes. It was a sight to move the Blessed Image Himself! Her mouth and eyes were —"

"Never mind. Who came oftenest to her house? Who were her enemies?"

The old face congealed, closed. Her spongy skin drew into a network of secretive wrinkles. She turned withdrawn and expressionless eyes upon the gendarmes.

"I am an old woman; I do not see well; I cannot hurry on my feet. I did not see any one leave the clearing."

"You did not hear splashing in the spring near the bridge?"

"No, Señor."

"Why, then, do our dogs follow a scent there and lose it?"

"*Solo Dios sabe,* Señor. I am an old wo —"

"How did the footfalls sound?" broke in the officer, hastily.

"Like the tread of an evil spirit!" intoned Lupe in a swelling oracular tone startling to the listeners. The Indians stirred among themselves, watchfully. To them the medicine-woman was an incalculable force. They half expected her to pronounce a charm that would produce the evil spirit among them at once.

The gendarme's politeness began to wear thin.

"No, poor fool; I mean, were they heavy or light? The footsteps of a man or of a woman? Was the person shod or barefoot?"

A glance at the listening circle assured Lupe of their thrilled attention. She enjoyed the prominence, the menacing importance, of her situation. What she had not seen she could not describe, thank God! No one could harm her because her knees were stiff and she could not run even to seize a murderer. As for knowing the difference between footfalls, shod or bare, man or woman, nay, even as between devil and human, who ever heard of such madness?

"My ears are not eyes, Señor," she ended grandly; "but upon my heart I swear those footsteps fell as the tread of the spirit of evil!"

"*Loca!*" yapped the gendarme in a shrill voice. "Take her away somebody! Juan Villegas, tell me —"

Juan told him everything he knew, patiently, several times over. He had returned to his wife that day. She had gone to market as usual. He had helped her prepare her fowls. She had returned about mid-afternoon, they had talked, she had cooked, they had eaten. Nothing was amiss. Then the gendarmes came. That was all. Yes, Maria Rosa had gone away with him, but there had been no bad blood on this account between him and his wife or Maria Rosa. Everybody knew that his wife was a quiet woman.

Maria Concepción heard her own voice answering without a break. It was true at first she was troubled when her husband went away, but after that she had not cared. It was the way of men, she believed. Well, he had come home, thank God! She had gone to market, but had returned early, because now she had her man to cook for. That was all.

Other voices followed. A toothless old man said, "But she is a woman of good repute among us, and Maria Rosa was not." A smiling young mother, Anita, baby at breast, said: "But if no one thinks so, how can you accuse her? Should not a woman's own husband know best where she was at all times?" Another: "Maria Rosa had a strange life, apart from us. How do we know who may have wished her evil?"

Maria Concepción suddenly felt herself guarded, surrounded, upborne by her faithful friends. They were all about her, speaking for her, defending her, refusing to admit ill of her. The forces of life were ranged invincibly with her against the vanquished dead. Maria Rosa had forfeited her share in their loyalty. What did they really believe? How much had old Lupe seen? She looked from one to the other of the circling faces. Their eyes gave back reassurance, understanding, a secret and mighty sympathy.

The gendarmes were at a loss. They, too, felt that sheltering wall cast impenetrably around the woman they had meant to accuse of murder. They watched her closely. They questioned several people over again. There was no prying open the locked doors of their defenses.

A small bundle lying against the head of the body squirmed like an eel. A wail, a mere sliver of sound, issued. Maria Concepción took the almost forgotten son of Maria Rosa in her arms.

"He is mine," she said clearly; "I will take him with me."

No one assented in words, but she felt an approving nod, a bare breath of friendly agreement, run around the tight, hot room.

The gendarmes gave up. Nobody could be accused; there was not a shred of true evidence. Well, then, good night to everybody. Many pardons for having intruded. Good health!

Maria Concepción, carrying the child, followed Juan from the clearing. The hut was left with its lighted candles and a group of old women who would sit up all night, drinking coffee and smoking and relating pious tales of horror.

Juan's exaltation had burned down. There was not an ember of excitement left in him. He was tired; the high sense of adventure was faded. Maria Rosa was vanished, to come no more forever. Their days of marching, of eating, of fighting, of making love, were all over. To-morrow he would go back to dull and endless labor, he would descend into the trenches of the buried city as Maria Rosa would go into her grave. He felt his veins fill up with bitterness, with black and unendurable melancholy. *O Dios!* what strange fortunes overtake a man!

Well, there was no way out of it. For the moment he craved to forget in sleep. He found himself so drowsy he could hardly guide his feet. The occasional light touch of the woman at his elbow was unreal, as ghostly as the brushing of a leaf against his face. Having secured her safety, compelled by an instinct he could not in the least comprehend, he forgot her. There survived in him only a vast blind hurt like a covered wound.

He entered the *jacal,* and, without waiting to light a candle, threw off his clothing, sitting just within the door. He moved with lagging, half-awake hands, seeking to strip his outwearied body of its heavy finery. With a long groaning sigh of relief he fell straight back on the floor, almost instantly asleep, his arms flung up and out in the simple attitude of exhaustion.

Maria Concepción, a small clay jar in her hand, approached the gentle little mother goat tethered to a sapling, which gave and yielded as she pulled at the rope's-end after the farthest reaches of grass about her. The kid, tied up a few yards away, rose bleating, its feathery fleece shivering in the fresh wind. Sitting on her heels, holding his tether, she allowed him to suckle a few moments. Afterward — all her movements very deliberate and even — she drew a supply of milk for the child.

She sat against the wall of her house, near the doorway. The child, fed and asleep, was cradled in the hollow of her crossed legs. The silence over-filled the world, the skies flowed down evenly to the rim of the valley, the stealthy moon crept slantwise to the shelter of the mountains. She felt soft and warm all over; she dreamed that the newly born child was her own, and she was resting deliciously.

Maria Concepción could hear Juan's breathing. The sound vapored from the low doorway, calmly; the house seemed to be resting after a burdensome day. She breathed, too, very slowly and quietly, each inspiration saturating her with repose. The child's light, faint breath was a mere shadowy moth of sound flitting in the silver air. The night, the earth under her, seemed to swell and recede together with a vast, unhurried, benign breathing. She drooped and closed her eyes, feeling the slow rise and fall within her own body. She did not know what it was, but it eased her all through. Even as she was falling asleep, head bowed over the child, she was still aware of a strange, wakeful happiness.

Jean Toomer
Blood-Burning Moon

Jean Toomer's *Cane*, of which "Blood-Burning Moon" is a part, is widely regarded as representing the highest literary achievement of the Harlem Renaissance of the 1920s. Born of mixed parentage, and reared in wealthy white neighborhoods in Washington, D.C., Toomer seems to have regarded himself as an "American" rather than as a representative of any ethnic group, and his work is psychologically probing and dramatic rather than polemical. Educated at the University of Wisconsin, University of Chicago, New York University, and City College, and influenced by Henrik Ibsen, Johann Wolfgang von Goethe, and Sherwood Anderson, among other writers, Toomer's *oeuvre* defies traditional categorization. *Cane*, for example, is a composite book encompassing verse, fiction, and drama but unified by continuing themes about racial interactions in the South and the North. "Blood-Burning Moon" is an example of his utilization of a traditional love triangle in innovative ways, presenting interracial romance and the violence it inspires. Structured into three distinct sections, one with an emphasis on Louisa, a second dealing with Tom, and a third stressing the white Bob Stone, the story moves relentlessly toward confrontation and an unsettling resolution. Written in Toomer's typically lyrical prose, with a haunting refrain, this example of his short fiction illustrates why he is still highly regarded nearly a century after his most important book appeared.

Jean Toomer, "Blood-Burning Moon," *Cane* (New York: Boni and Liveright, 1923), 51–67.

1

Up from the skeleton stone walls, up from the rotting floor boards and the solid hand-hewn beams of oak of the pre-war cotton factory, dusk came. Up from the dusk the full moon came. Glowing like a fired pine-knot, it illumined the great door and soft showered the Negro shanties aligned along the single street of factory town. The full moon in the great door was an omen. Negro women improvised songs against its spell.

Louisa sang as she came over the crest of the hill from the white folks' kitchen. Her skin was the color of oak leaves on young trees in fall. Her breasts, firm and up-pointed like ripe acorns. And her singing had the low murmur of winds in fig trees. Bob Stone, younger son of the people she worked for, loved her. By the way the world reckons things, he had won her. By measure of that warm glow which came into her mind at thought of him, he had won her. Tom Burwell, whom the whole town called Big Boy, also loved her. But working in the fields all day, and far away from her, gave him no chance to show it. Though often enough of evenings he had tried to. Somehow, he never got along. Strong as he was with hands upon the ax or plow, he found it difficult to hold her. Or so he thought. But the fact was that he held her to factory town more firmly than he thought for. His black balanced, and pulled against, the white of Stone, when she thought of them. And her mind was vaguely upon them as she came over the crest of the hill, coming from the white folks' kitchen. As she sang softly at the evil face of the full moon.

A strange stir was in her. Indolently, she tried to fix upon Bob or Tom as the cause of it. To meet Bob in the canebrake, as she was going to do an hour or so later, was nothing new. And Tom's proposal which she felt on its way to her could be indefinitely put off. Separately, there was no unusual significance to either one. But for some reason, they jumbled when her eyes gazed vacantly at the rising moon. And from the jumble came the stir that was strangely within her. Her lips trembled. The slow rhythm of her song grew agitant and restless. Rusty black and tan spotted hounds, lying in the dark corners of porches or prowling around back yards, put their noses in the air and caught its tremor. They began plaintively to yelp and howl. Chickens woke up and cackled. Intermittently, all over the countryside dogs barked and roosters crowed as if heralding a weird dawn or some ungodly awakening. The women sang lustily. Their songs were cotton-wads to stop their ears. Louisa came down into factory town and sank wearily upon the step before her home. The moon was rising towards a thick cloud-bank which soon would hide it.

> Red nigger moon.   Sinner!
> Blood-burning moon.   Sinner!
> Come out that fact'ry door.

2

Up from the deep dusk of a cleared spot on the edge of the forest a mellow glow arose and spread fan-wise into the low-hanging heavens. And all around the air was heavy with the scent of boiling cane. A large pile of cane-stalks lay like ribboned shadows upon the ground. A mule, harnessed to a pole, trudged lazily round and round the pivot of the grinder. Beneath a swaying oil lamp, a Negro alternately whipped out at the mule, and fed cane-stalks to the grinder. A fat boy waddled pails of fresh ground juice between the grinder and the boiling stove. Steam came from the copper boiling pan. The scent of cane came from the copper pan and drenched the forest and the hill that sloped to factory town, beneath its fragrance. It drenched the men in circle seated around the stove. Some of them chewed at the white pulp of stalks, but there was no need for them to, if all they wanted was to taste the cane. One tasted it in factory town. And from factory town one could see the soft haze thrown by the glowing stove upon the low-hanging heavens.

Old David Georgia stirred the thickening syrup with a long ladle, and ever so often drew it off. Old David Georgia tended his stove and told tales about the white folks, about moonshining and cotton picking, and about sweet nigger gals, to the men who sat there about his stove to listen to him. Tom Burwell chewed cane-stalk and laughed with the others till someone mentioned Louisa. Till some one said something about Louisa and Bob Stone, about the silk stockings she must have gotten from him. Blood ran up Tom's neck hotter than the glow that flooded from the stove. He sprang up. Glared at the men and said, "She's my gal." Will Manning laughed. Tom strode over to him. Yanked him up and knocked him to the ground. Several of Manning's friends got up to fight for him. Tom whipped out a long knife and would have cut them to shreds if they hadnt ducked into the woods. Tom had had enough. He nodded to Old David Georgia and swung down the path to factory town. Just then, the dogs started barking and the roosters began to crow. Tom felt funny. Away from the fight, away from the stove, chill got to him. He shivered. He shuddered when he saw the full moon rising towards the cloud-bank. He who didnt give a godam for the fears of old women. He forced his mind to fasten on Louisa. Bob Stone. Better not be. He turned into the street and saw Louisa sitting before her home. He went towards her, ambling, touched the brim of a marvelously shaped, spotted, felt hat, said he wanted to say something to her, and then found that he didnt know what he had to say, or if he did, that he couldnt say it. He shoved his big fists in his overalls, grinned, and started to move off.

"Youall want me, Tom?"

"That's what us wants, sho, Louisa."

"Well, here I am —"

"An here I is, but that aint ahelpin none, all th same."

"You wanted to say something? . ."

"I did that, sho. But words is like th spots on dice: no matter how y fumbles em, there's times when they jes wont come. I dunno why. Seems like th love I feels fo yo done stole m tongue. I got it now. Whee! Louisa, honey, I oughtnt tell y, I feel I oughtnt cause yo is young and goes t church an I has had other gals, but Louisa I sho do love y. Lil gal, Ise watched y from them first days when youall sat right here befo you door befo th well an sang sometimes in a way that like t broke m heart. Ise carried y with me into th fields, day after day, an after that, an I sho can plow when yo is there, an I can pick cotton. Yassur! Come near beatin Barlo yesterday. I sho did. Yassur! An next year if old Stone'll trust me, I'll have a farm. My own. My bales will buy yo what y gets from white folks now. Silk stockings an purple dresses — course I dont believe what some folks been whisperin as t how y gets them things now. White folks always did do for niggers what they likes. An they jes cant help alikin yo, Louisa. Bob Stone likes y. Course he does. But not th way folks is awhisperin. Does he, hon?"

"I dont know what you mean, Tom."

"Course y dont. Ise already cut two niggers. Had t hon, t tell em so. Niggers always trying t make somethin out a nothin. An then besides, white folks aint up t them tricks so much nowadays. Godam better not be. Leastawise not with yo. Cause I wouldnt stand f it. Nassur."

"What would you do, Tom?"

"Cut him jes like I cut a nigger."

"No, Tom —"

"I said I would an there aint no mo to it. But that aint th talk f now. Sing, honey Louisa, an while I'm listenin t y I'll be makin love."

Tom took her hand in his. Against the tough thickness of his own, hers felt soft and small. His huge body slipped down to the step beside her. The full moon sank upward into the deep purple of the cloud-bank. An old woman brought a lighted lamp and hung it on the common well whose bulky shadow squatted in the middle of the road, opposite Tom and Louisa. The old woman lifted the well-lid, took hold the chain, and began drawing up the heavy bucket. As she did so, she sang. Figures shifted, restless-like, between lamp and window in the front rooms of the shanties. Shadows of the figures fought each other on the gray dust of the road. Figures raised the windows and joined the old woman in song. Louisa and Tom, the whole street, singing:

> Red nigger moon.   Sinner!
> Blood-burning moon.   Sinner!
> Come out that fact'ry door.

3

Bob Stone sauntered from his veranda out into the gloom of fir trees and magnolias. The clear white of his skin paled, and the flush of his cheeks turned purple. As if to balance this outer change, his mind became consciously a white man's. He passed the house with its huge open hearth which, in the days of slavery, was the plantation cookery. He saw Louisa bent over that hearth. He went in as a master should and took her. Direct, honest, bold. None of this sneaking that he had to go through now. The contrast was repulsive to him. His family had lost ground. Hell no, his family still owned the niggers, practically. Damned if they did, or he wouldnt have to duck around so. What would they think if they knew? His mother? His sister? He shouldnt mention them, shouldnt think of them in this connection. There in the dusk he blushed at doing so. Fellows about town were all right, but how about his friends up North? He could see them incredible, repulsed. They didnt know. The thought first made him laugh. Then, with their eyes still upon him, he began to feel embarrassed. He felt the need of explaining things to them. Explain hell. They wouldnt understand, and moreover, who ever heard of a Southerner getting on his knees to any Yankee, or anyone. No sir. He was going to see Louisa to-night, and love her. She was lovely — in her way. Nigger way. What way was that? Damned if he knew. Must know. He'd known her long enough to know. Was there something about niggers that you couldnt know? Listening to them at church didnt tell you anything. Looking at them didnt tell you anything. Talking to them didnt tell you anything — unless it was gossip, unless they wanted to talk. Of course, about farming, and licker, and craps — but those werent nigger. Nigger was something more. How much more? Something to be afraid of, more? Hell no. Who ever heard of being afraid of a nigger? Tom Burwell. Cartwell had told him that Tom went with Louisa after she reached home. No sir. No nigger had ever been with his girl. He'd like to see one try. Some position for him to be in. Him, Bob Stone, of the old Stone family, in a scrap with a nigger over a nigger girl. In the good old days . . . Ha! Those were the days. His family had lost ground. Not so much, though. Enough for him to have to cut through old Lemon's canefield by way of the woods, that he might meet her. She was worth it. Beautiful nigger gal. Why nigger? Why not, just gal? No, it was because she was nigger that he went to her. Sweet. . . The scent of boiling cane came to him. Then he saw the rich glow of the stove. He heard the voices of the men circled around it. He was about to skirt the clearing when he heard his own name mentioned. He stopped. Quivering. Leaning against a tree, he listened.

"Bad nigger. Yassur, he sho is one bad nigger when he gets started."

"Tom Burwell's been on th gang three times for cuttin men."

"What y think he's agwine t d t Bob Stone?"

"Dunno yet. He aint found out. When he does — Baby!"

"Aint no tellin."

"Young Stone aint no quitter an I ken tell y that. Blood of th old uns in his veins."

"Thats right. He'll scrap, sho."

"Be gettin too hot f niggers round this away."

"Shut up, nigger. Y dont know what y talking bout."

Bob Stone's ears burned as though he had been holding them over the stove. Sizzling heat welled up within him. His feet felt as if they rested on red-hot coals. They stung him to quick movement. He circled the fringe of the glowing. Not a twig cracked beneath his feet. He reached the path that led to factory town. Plunged furiously down it. Halfway along, a blindness within him veered him aside. He crashed into the bordering canebrake. Cane leaves cut his face and lips. He tasted blood. He threw himself down and dug his fingers in the ground. The earth was cool. Cane-roots took the fever from his hands. After a long while, or so it seemed to him, the thought came to him that it must be time to see Louisa. He got to his feet and walked calmly to their meeting place. No Louisa. Tom Burwell had her. Veins in his forehead bulged and distended. Saliva moistened the dried blood on his lips. He bit down on his lips. He tasted blood. Not his own blood; Tom Burwell's blood. Bob drove through the cane and out again upon the road. A hound swung down the path before him towards factory town. Bob couldnt see it. The dog loped aside to let him pass. Bob's blind rushing made him stumble over it. He fell with a thud that dazed him. The hound yelped. Answering yelps came from all over the countryside. Chickens cackled. Roosters crowed, heralding the bloodshot eyes of southern awakening. Singers in the town were silenced. They shut their windows down. Palpitant between the rooster crows, a chill hush settled upon the huddled forms of Tom and Louisa. A figure rushed from the shadow and stood before them. Tom popped to his feet.

"Whats y want?"

"I'm Bob Stone."

"Yassur — an I'm Tom Burwell. Whats y want?"

Bob lunged at him. Tom side-stepped, caught him by the shoulder, and flung him to the ground. Straddled him.

"Let me up."

"Yassur — but watch yo doins, Bob Stone."

A few dark figures, drawn by the sound of scuffle, stood about them. Bob sprang to his feet.

"Fight like a man, Tom Burwell, and I'll lick y."

Again he lunged. Tom side-stepped and flung him to the ground. Straddled him.

"Get off me, you godam nigger you."

"Yo sho has started somethin now. Get up."

Tom yanked him up and began hammering at him. Each blow sounded as if it smashed into a precious, irreplaceable soft something. Beneath them, Bob staggered back. He reached in his pocket and whipped out a knife.

"That's my game, sho."

Blue flash, a steel blade slashed across Bob Stone's throat. He had a sweetish sick feeling. Blood began to flow. Then he felt a sharp twitch of pain. He let his knife drop. He slapped one hand against his neck. He pressed the other on top of his head as if to hold it down. He groaned. He turned, and staggered towards the crest of the hill in the direction of white town. Negroes who had seen the fight slunk into their homes and blew the lamps out. Louisa, dazed, hysterical, refused to go indoors. She slipped, crumbled, her body loosely propped against the woodwork of the well. Tom Burwell leaned against it. He seemed rooted there.

Bob reached Broad Street. White men rushed up to him. He collapsed in their arms.

"Tom Burwell. . . ."

White men like ants upon a forage rushed about. Except for the taut hum of their moving, all was silent. Shotguns, revolvers, rope, kerosene, torches. Two high-powered cars with glaring search-lights. They came together. The taut hum rose to a low roar. Then nothing could be heard but the flop of their feet in the thick dust of the road. The moving body of their silence preceded them over the crest of the hill into factory town. It flattened the Negroes beneath it. It rolled to the wall of the factory, where it stopped. Tom knew that they were coming. He couldnt move. And then he saw the search-lights of the two cars glaring down on him. A quick shock went through him. He stiffened. He started to run. A yell went up from the mob. Tom wheeled about and faced them. They poured down on him. They swarmed. A large man with dead-white face and flabby cheeks came to him and almost jabbed a gun-barrel through his guts.

"Hands behind y, nigger."

Tom's wrists were bound. The big man shoved him to the well. Burn him over it, and when the woodwork caved in, his body would drop to the bottom. Two deaths for a godam nigger. Louisa was driven back. The mob pushed in. Its pressure, its momentum was too great. Drag him to the factory. Wood and stakes already there. Tom moved in the direction indicated. But they had to drag him. They reached the great door. Too many to get in there. The mob divided and flowed around the walls to either side. The big man shoved him through the door. The mob pressed in from the sides. Taut humming. No words. A stake was sunk into the ground. Rotting floor boards piled around it. Kerosene poured on the rotting floor boards. Tom bound to the stake. His breast was bare. Nails scratches let little lines of blood trickle down and mat into the hair. His face, his eyes were set and stony. Except for irregular breathing, one would have thought him already dead. Torches were flung onto the pile. A great flare muffled in black smoke shot upward. The mob yelled. The mob was silent. Now Tom could be seen within the flames. Only his head, erect, lean, like a blackened stone. Stench of burning flesh soaked the air. Tom's eyes popped. His head settled downward. The mob yelled. Its yell echoed against the skeleton stone walls and sounded like a hundred yells. Like a hundred mobs yelling. Its yell thudded against the thick front wall and fell back. Ghost of a yell slipped through the flames and out the great door of the factory. It fluttered like a dying thing down the single street of factory town. Louisa, upon the step before her home, did not hear it, but her eyes opened slowly. They saw the full moon glowing in the great door. The full moon, an evil thing, an omen, soft showering the homes of folks she knew. Where were they, these people? She'd sing, and perhaps they'd come out and join her. Perhaps Tom Burwell would come. At any rate, the full moon in the great door was an omen which she must sing to:

> Red nigger moon.   Sinner!
> Blood-burning moon.   Sinner!
> Come out that fact'ry door.

Sherwood Anderson
Death in the Woods

Despite a long list of novels published between 1916 and 1940, the literary reputation of Sherwood Anderson derives primarily from his short fiction, especially the quintessential story cycle *Winesburg, Ohio*. But there are also many frequently anthologized stories that support his stature, including "I Want to Know Why," "I'm a Fool," "The Egg," and "Death in the Woods," which first appeared in *The American Mercury* in 1926. It covers a situation described in the autobiographical *Tar: A Midwest Childhood*, also published in 1926, in which a woman, much exploited and reviled by her husband and son, dies in the snow and a pack of dogs circle around her. Anderson used these events from his childhood to inform the plot of "Death in the Woods," but beyond the tragedy of death, he shifted the emphasis to the emotional effect on the young boy who observes the discovery of the body. As a result, there is a double focus: the diminished life of a woman who, her body reveals, was still inherently lovely despite the contempt of her family; and the psychological effect of death for the narrator, who is prompted into difficult adult realizations by the experience.

Sherwood Anderson, "Death in the Woods," *The American Mercury* 9 (September 1926): 7–13.

I

She was an old woman and lived on a farm near the town in which I lived. All the country and small town people have seen such old women, but no one knows much about them. Such an old woman comes into town driving an old worn-out horse or she comes afoot carrying a basket. She may own a few hens and have eggs to sell. She brings them in a basket and takes them to a grocer. There she trades them in. She gets some salt pork and some beans. Then she gets a pound or two of sugar and some flour.

Afterwards she goes to the butcher's and asks for some dog-meat. She may spend ten or fifteen cents, but when she does she asks for something. In my day the butchers gave liver to anyone who wanted to carry it away. In our family we were always having it. Once one of my brothers got a whole cow's liver at the slaughter-house near the fair-grounds. We had it until we were sick of it. It never cost a cent. I have hated the thought of it ever since.

The old farm woman got some liver and a soup-bone. She never visited with anyone and as soon as she got what she wanted she lit out for home. It made quite a load for such an old body. No one gave her a lift. People drive right down a road and never notice an old woman like that.

There was such an old woman used to come into town past our house one

Summer and Fall when I was sick with what was called inflammatory rheumatism. She went home later carrying a heavy pack on her back. Two or three large gaunt-looking dogs followed at her heels.

The old woman was nothing special. She was one of the nameless ones that hardly anyone knows, but she got into my thoughts. I have just suddenly now, after all these years, remembered her and what happened. It is a story. Her name was, I think, Grimes, and she lived with her husband and son in a small unpainted house on the bank of a small creek four miles from town.

The husband and son were a tough lot. Although the son was but twenty-one, he had already served a term in jail. It was whispered about that the woman's husband stole horses and ran them off to some other county. Now and then, when a horse turned up missing, the man had also disappeared. No one ever caught him. Once, when I was loafing at Tom Whitehead's livery-barn, the man came there and sat on the bench in front. Two or three other men were there, but no one spoke to him. He sat for a few minutes and then got up and went away. When he was leaving he turned around and stared at the men. There was a look of defiance in his eyes. "Well, I have tried to be friendly. You don't want to talk to me. It has been so wherever I have gone in this town. If, some day, one of your fine horses turns up missing, well, then what?" He did not say anything actually. "I'd like to bust one of you on the jaw," was about what his eyes said. I remember how the look in his eyes made me shiver.

The old man belonged to a family that had had money once. His name was Grimes, Jake Grimes. It all comes back clearly now. His father, John Grimes, had owned a sawmill when the country was new and had made money. Then he got to drinking and running after women. When he died there wasn't much left.

Jake blew in the rest. Pretty soon there wasn't any more lumber to cut and his land was nearly all gone.

He got his wife off a German farmer, for whom he went to work one June day in the wheat harvest. She was a young thing then and scared to death. You see, the farmer was up to something with the girl — she was, I think, a bound girl and his wife had her suspicions. She took it out on the girl when the man wasn't around. Then, when the wife had to go off to town for supplies, the farmer got after her. She told young Jake that nothing really ever happened, but he didn't know whether to believe it or not.

He got her pretty easy himself, the first time he was out with her. He wouldn't have married her if the German farmer hadn't tried to tell him where to get off. He got her to go riding with him in his buggy one night when he was threshing on the place, and then he came for her the next Sunday night.

She managed to get out of the house without her employer's seeing, but when she was getting into the buggy he showed up. It was almost dark, and he just popped up suddenly at the horse's head. He grabbed the horse by the bridle and Jake got out his buggy whip.

They had it out all right! The German was a tough one. Maybe he didn't care whether his wife knew or not. Jake hit him over the face and shoulders with the buggy-whip, but the horse got to acting up and he had to get out.

Then the two men went for it. The girl didn't see it. The horse started to run away and went nearly a mile down the road before the girl got him stopped. Then she managed to tie him to a tree beside the road. (I wonder how I know all this. It must have stuck in my mind from small town tales when I was a boy.) Jake found her there after he got through with the German. She was huddled up in the buggy seat, crying, scared to death. She told Jake a lot of stuff, how the German had tried to get her, how he chased her once into the barn, how another time, when they happened to be alone in the barn together, he tore her dress open clear down the front. The German, she said, might have got her that time if he hadn't heard his old woman drive in at the gate. She had been off to town for supplies. Well, she would be putting the horse in the barn. The German managed to sneak off to the fields without his wife seeing. He told the girl he would kill her if she told. What could she do? She told a lie about ripping her dress in the barn when she was feeding the stock. I remember now that she was a bound girl and did not know where her father and mother were. Maybe she did not have any father. You know what I mean.

II

She married Jake and had a son and daughter but the daughter died.

Then she settled down to feed stock. That was her job. At the German's place she had cooked the food for the German and his wife. The wife was a strong woman with big hips and worked most of the time in the fields with her husband. She fed them and fed the cows in the barn, fed the pigs, the horses and the chickens. Every moment of every day as a young girl was spent feeding something.

Then she married Jake Grimes and he had to be fed. She was a slight thing and when she had been married for three or four years, and after the two children were born, her slender shoulders became stooped.

Jake always had a lot of big dogs around the house, that stood near the unused sawmill near the creek. He was always trading horses when he wasn't stealing something and had a lot of poor bony ones about. Also he kept three or four pigs and a cow. They were all pastured in the few acres left of the Grimes place and Jake did little.

He went into debt for a threshing outfit and ran it for several years, but it did not pay. People did not trust him. They were afraid he would steal the grain at night. He had to go a long way off to get work and it cost too much to get there. In the Winter he hunted and cut a little firewood, to be sold in some nearby town. When the boy grew up he was just like his father. They got drunk together. If there wasn't anything to eat in the house when they came home the old man gave his old woman a cut over the head. She had a few chickens of her own and had to kill one of them in a hurry. When they were all killed she wouldn't have any eggs to sell when she went to town, and then what would she do?

She had to scheme all her life about getting things fed, getting the pigs fed so they would grow fat and could be butchered in the Fall. When they were butchered her husband took most of the meat off to town and sold it. If he did not do it first the boy did. They fought sometimes and when they fought the old woman stood aside trembling.

She had got the habit of silence anyway — that was fixed. Sometimes, when she began to look old — she wasn't forty yet — and when the husband and son were both off, trading horses or drinking or hunting or stealing, she went around the house and the barnyard muttering to herself.

How was she going to get everything fed? — that was her problem. The dogs had to be fed. There wasn't enough hay in the barn for the horses and the cow. If she didn't feed the chickens how could they lay eggs? Without eggs to sell how could she get things in town, things she had to have to keep the life of the farm going? Thank heaven, she did not have to feed her husband — in a certain way. That hadn't lasted long after their marriage and after the babies came. Where he went on his long trips she did not know. Sometimes he was gone from home for weeks and after the boy grew up they went off together.

They left everything at home for her to manage and she had no money. She knew no one. No one ever talked to her in town. When it was Winter she had to gather sticks of wood for her fire, had to try to keep the stock fed with very little grain.

The stock in the barn cried to her hungrily, the dogs followed her about. In the Winter the hens laid few enough eggs. They huddled in the corners of the barn and she kept watching them. If a hen lays an egg in the barn in the Winter and you do not find it, it freezes and breaks.

One day in Winter the old woman went off to town with a few eggs and the dogs followed her. She did not get started until nearly three o'clock and the snow was heavy. She hadn't been feeling very well for several days and so she went muttering along, scantily clad, her shoulders stooped. She had an old grain bag in which she carried her eggs, tucked away down in the bottom. There weren't many of them, but in Winter the price of eggs is up. She would get a little meat for the eggs, some salt pork, a little sugar, and some coffee perhaps. It might be the butcher would give her a piece of liver.

When she had got to town and was trading in her eggs the dogs lay by the door outside. She did pretty well, got the things she needed, more than she had hoped. Then she went to the butcher and he gave her some liver and some dog-meat.

It was the first time anyone had spoken to her in a friendly way for a long time. The butcher was alone in his shop when she went in and was annoyed by the thought of such a sick-looking old woman out on such a day. It was bitter cold and the snow, that had let up during the afternoon, was falling again. The butcher said something about her husband and her son, swore at them, and the old woman stared at him, a look of mild surprise in her eyes as he talked. He said that if either the husband or the son were going to get any of the liver or the heavy bones with scraps of meat hanging to them that he had put into the grain bag, he'd see him starve first.

Starve, eh? Well things had to be fed. Men had to be fed, and the horses that weren't any good but maybe could be traded off, and the poor thin cow that hadn't given any milk for three months.

Horses, cows, pigs, dogs, men.

III

The old woman had to get back before darkness came if she could. The dogs followed at her heels, sniffing at the heavy grain bag she had fastened on her back. When she got to the edge of town she stopped by a fence and tied the bag on her back with a piece of rope she had carried in her dress-pocket for just that purpose. That was an easier way to carry it. Her arms ached. It was hard when she had to crawl over fences and once she fell over and landed in the snow. The dogs went frisking about. She had to struggle to get to her feet again but she made it. The point of climbing over the fences was that there was a short cut over a hill and through a wood. She might have gone around by the road, but it was a mile further that way. She was afraid she couldn't make it. And then, besides, the stock had to be fed. There was a little hay left, a little corn. Perhaps her husband and son would bring some home when they came. They had driven off in the only buggy the Grimes family had, a rickety thing, a rickety horse hitched to the buggy, two other rickety horses led by halters. They were going to trade horses, get a little money if they could. They might come home drunk. It would be well to have something in the house when they came back.

The son had an affair on with a woman at the county seat, fifteen miles away. She was a bad woman, a tough one. Once, in the Summer, the son had brought her to the house. Both she and the son had been drinking. Jake Grimes was away and the son and his woman ordered the old woman about like a servant. She didn't mind much; she was used to it. Whatever happened she never said anything. That was her way of getting along. She had managed that way when she was a young girl at the German's and ever since she had married Jake. That time her son brought his woman to the house they stayed all night, sleeping together just as though they were married. It hadn't shocked the old woman, not much. She had got past being shocked early in life.

With the pack on her back she went painfully along across an open field, wading in the deep snow, and got into the woods.

There was a path, but it was hard to follow. Just beyond the top of the hill, where the wood was thickest, there was a small clearing. Had someone once thought of building a house there? The clearing was as large as a building lot in town, large enough for a house and a garden. The path ran along the side of the clearing and when she got there the old woman sat down to rest at the foot of a tree.

It was a foolish thing to do. When she got herself placed, the pack against the tree's trunk, it was nice, but what about getting up again? She worried about that for a moment and then quietly closed her eyes.

She must have slept for a time. When you are about so cold you can't get any colder. The afternoon grew a little warmer and the snow came thicker than ever. Then after a time the weather cleared. The moon even came out.

There were four Grimes dogs that had followed Mrs. Grimes into town, all tall gaunt fellows. Such men as Jake Grimes and his son always keep just such dogs. They kick and abuse them, but they stay. The Grimes dogs, in order to keep from starving, had to do a lot of foraging for themselves, and they had been at it while the old woman slept with her back to the tree at the side of the clearing. They had been chasing rabbits in the woods and in adjoining fields and in their ranging had picked up three other farm dogs.

After a time all the dogs came back to the clearing. They were excited about something. Such nights, cold and clear and with a moon, do things to dogs. It may be that some old instinct, come down from the time when they were wolves and ranged the woods in packs on Winter nights, comes back into them.

The dogs in the clearing, before the old woman, had caught two or three rabbits and their immediate hunger had been satisfied. They began to play, running in circles in the clearing. Round and round they ran, each dog's nose at the tail of the next dog. In the clearing, under the snow-laden trees and under the wintry moon they made a strange picture, running thus silently, in a circle their running had beaten in the soft snow. The dogs made no sound. They ran around and around in the circle.

It may have been that the old woman saw them doing that before she died. She may have awakened once or twice and looked at the strange sight with dim old eyes.

She wouldn't be very cold now, just drowsy. Life hangs on a long time. Perhaps the old woman was out of her head. She may have dreamed of her girlhood, at the German's, and before that, when she was a child and before her mother lit out and left her.

Her dreams couldn't have been very pleasant. Not many pleasant things had happened to her. Now and then one of the Grimes dogs left the running circle and came to stand before her. The dog thrust his face close to her face. His red tongue was hanging out.

The running of the dogs may have been a kind of death ceremony. It may have been that the primitive instinct of the wolf, having been aroused in the dogs by the night and the running, made them somehow afraid.

"Now we are no longer wolves. We are dogs, the servants of men. Keep alive, man! When man dies we become wolves again."

When one of the dogs came to where the old woman sat with her back against the tree and thrust his nose close to her face he seemed satisfied and went back to run with the pack. All the Grimes dogs did it at some time during the evening, before she died. I knew all about it afterward, when I grew to be a man, because once in a wood on another Winter night I saw a pack of dogs act just like that. The dogs were waiting for me to die as they had waited for the old woman that night when I was a child, but when it happened to me I was a young man and had no intention whatever of dying.

The old woman died softly and quietly. When she was dead and when one of the Grimes dogs had come to her and had found her dead all the dogs stopped running.

They gathered about her.

Well, she was dead now. She had fed the Grimes dogs when she was alive, what about now?

There was the pack on her back, the grain bag containing the piece of salt pork, the liver the butcher had given her, the dog-meat, the soup bones. The butcher in town, having been suddenly overcome with a feeling of pity, had loaded her grain bag heavily. It had been a big haul for the old woman.

A big haul for the dogs now.

IV

One of the Grimes dogs sprang suddenly out from among the others and began worrying the pack on the old woman's back. Had the dogs really been wolves that one would have been the leader of the pack. What he did, all the others did.

All of them sank their teeth into the grain bag the old woman had fastened with ropes to her back.

They dragged the old woman's body out into the open clearing. The worn-out dress was quickly torn from her shoulders. When she was found, a day or two later, the dress had been torn from her body clear to the hips but the dogs had not touched her body. They had got the meat out of the grain bag, that was all. Her body was frozen stiff when it was found and the shoulders were so narrow and the body so slight that in death it looked like the body of some charming young girl.

Such things happened in towns of the Middle West, on farms near town, when I was a boy. A hunter out after rabbits found the old woman's body and did not touch it. Something, the beaten round path in the little snow-covered clearing, the silence of the place, the place where the dogs had worried the body trying to pull the grain bag away or tear it open — something startled the man and he hurried off to town.

I was in Main street with one of my brothers who was taking the afternoon papers to the stores. It was almost night.

The hunter came into a grocery and told his story. Then he went to a hardware-shop and into a drug-store. Men began to gather on the sidewalks. Then they started out along the road to the place in the wood.

My brother should have gone on about his business of distributing papers but he didn't. Everyone was going to the woods. The undertaker went and the town marshal. Several men got on a dray and rode out to where the path left the road and went into the woods, but the horses weren't very sharply shod and slid about on the slippery roads. They made no better time than those of us who walked.

The town marshal was a large man whose leg had been injured in the Civil War. He carried a heavy cane and limped rapidly along the road. My brother and I followed at his heels and as we went other men and boys joined the crowd.

It had grown dark by the time we got to where the old woman had left the road but the moon had come out. The marshal was thinking there might have been a murder. He kept asking the hunter questions. The hunter went along with his gun across his shoulders, a dog following at his heels. It isn't often a rabbit hunter has a chance to be so conspicuous. He was taking full advantage of it, leading the procession with the town marshal. "I didn't see any wounds. She was a beautiful young girl. Her face was buried in the snow. No, I didn't know her." As a matter of fact, the hunter had not looked closely at the body. He had been frightened. She might have been murdered and someone might spring out from behind a tree and murder him too. In a woods, in the late afternoon, when the trees are all bare and there is white snow on the ground, when all is silent, something creepy steals over the mind and body. If something strange or uncanny has happened in the neighborhood all you think about is getting away from there as fast as you can.

The crowd of men and boys had got to where the old woman crossed the field and went, following the marshal and the hunter up the slight incline and into the woods.

My brother and I were silent. He had his bundle of papers in a bag slung across his shoulder. When he got back to town he would have to go on distributing his papers before he went home to supper. If I went along, as he had no doubt already determined I should, we would both be late. Either mother or our younger sister would have to warm our supper.

Well, we would have something to tell. A boy did not get such a chance very often. It was lucky we just happened to go into the grocery when the hunter came in. The hunter was a country fellow. Neither of us had ever seen him before.

Now the crowd of men and boys had got to the clearing. Darkness comes quickly on such Winter nights but the full moon made everything clear. My brother and I stood near the trees, beneath which the old woman had died.

She did not look old, lying there frozen in that light. One of the men turned her over in the snow and I saw everything. My body trembled with some strange mystical feeling and so did my brother's. It might have been the cold.

Neither of us had ever seen a woman's body before. It may have been the snow, clinging to the frozen flesh, that made it look so white and lovely, so like marble. No woman had come with the party from town, but one of the men, he was the town blacksmith, took off his overcoat and spread it over her. Then he gathered her into his arms and started off to town, all the others following silently. At that time no one knew who she was.

V

I had seen everything, had seen the oval in the snow, like a miniature race-track, where the dogs had run, had seen how the men were mystified, had seen the white bare young-looking shoulders, had heard the whispered comments of the men.

The men were simply mystified. They took the body to the undertaker's, and when the blacksmith, the hunter, the marshal and several others had got inside they closed the door. If father had been there perhaps he could have got in, but we boys couldn't.

I went with my brother to distribute the rest of his papers and when we got home it was my brother who told the story.

I kept silent and went to bed early. It may have been I was not satisfied with the way he told it.

Later, in the town, I must have heard other fragments of the old woman's story. She was recognized the next day and there was an investigation.

The husband and son were found somewhere and brought to town and there was an attempt to connect them with the woman's death, but it did not work. They had perfect enough alibis.

However, the town was against them. They had to get out. Where they went I never heard.

I remember only the picture there in the forest, the men standing about, the naked girlish-looking figure, face down in the snow, the tracks made by the running dogs and the clear cold Winter sky above. White fragments of clouds were drifting across the sky. They went racing across the little open space among the trees.

The scene in the forest had become for me, without my knowing it, the foundation for the real story I am now trying to tell. The fragments, you see, had to be picked up slowly, long afterwards.

Things happened. When I was a young man I worked on the farm of a German. The hired-girl was afraid of her employer. The farmer's wife hated her.

I saw things at that place. Once later, I had a half-uncanny, mystical sort of adventure with dogs in a forest on a clear, moonlit Winter night. When I was a schoolboy, and on a Summer day, I went with a boy friend out along a creek some miles from town and came to the house where the old woman had lived. No one had lived in the house since her death. The doors were broken from the hinges, the window lights were all broken. As the boy and I stood in the road outside, two dogs, just roving farm dogs no doubt, came running around the corner of the house. The dogs were tall, gaunt fellows and came down to the fence and glared through at us, standing in the road.

The whole thing, the story of the old woman's death, was to me as I grew older like music heard from far off. The notes had to be picked up slowly one at a time. Something had to be understood.

The woman who died was one destined to feed animal life. Anyway, that is all she ever did. She was feeding animal life before she was born, as a child, as a young woman working on the farm of the German, after she married, when she grew old and when she died. She fed animal life in cows, in chickens, in pigs, in horses, in dogs, in men. Her daughter had died in childhood and with her one son she had no articulate relations. On the night when she died she was hurrying homeward, bearing on her body food for animal life.

She died in the clearing in the woods and even after her death continued feeding animal life.

You see it is likely that, when my brother told the story, that night when we got home and my mother and sister sat listening, I did not think he got the point. He was too young and so was I. A thing so complete has its own beauty.

I shall not try to emphasize the point. I am only explaining why I was dissatisfied then and have been ever since. I speak of that only that you may understand why I have been impelled to try to tell the simple story over again.

Ruth Suckow

A Start in Life

Ruth Suckow's "A Start in Life" first appeared in H. L. Mencken's *The American Mercury* in 1924 before its inclusion in *Iowa Interiors* two years later. After completion of her master's degree from the University of Denver, Suckow began a series of novels and stories dealing with family interactions, especially with the often painful process of self-realization for young women. "A Start in Life" is typical in its depiction of lower-class people in Iowa and the circumstances that require that the oldest daughter find work as a servant. What heightens the poignancy of the conclusion is the depiction of Daisy's gradual comprehension that she is not to be a "child" in her new household but merely a "helper" whose loneliness and pain are of no concern to anyone but herself. Suckow's work is quietly dramatic in its depiction of hopeless resignation.

Ruth Suckow, "A Start in Life," *Iowa Interiors* (New York: Alfred A. Knopf, 1926), 1–17.

1

The Switzers were scurrying around to get Daisy ready by the time that Elmer Kruse should get through in town. They had known all week that Elmer might be in for her any day. But they hadn't done a thing until he appeared. "Oh, it was so rainy to-day, the roads were so muddy, they hadn't thought he'd get in until maybe next week." It would have been the same any other day.

Mrs. Switzer was trying now at the last moment to get all of Daisy's things into the battered telescope that lay open on the bed. The bed had not "got made"; and just as soon as Daisy was gone, Mrs. Switzer would have to hurry off to the Woodworths' where she was to wash to-day. Daisy's things were scattered over the dark brown quilt and the rumpled sheet that were dingy and clammy in this damp weather. So was the whole bedroom, with its sloping ceiling and old-fashioned square-paned windows, the commode that they used for a dresser, littered with pin tray, curlers, broken comb, ribbons, smoky lamp, all mixed up together; the door of the closet open, showing the confusion of clothes and shabby shoes. . . . They all slept in this room — Mrs. Switzer and Dwight in the bed, the two girls in the cot against the wall.

"Mamma, I can't find the belt to that plaid dress."

"Oh, ain't it somewheres around? Well, I guess you'll have to let it go. If I come across it I can send it out to you. Someone'll be going past there."

She had meant to get Daisy all mended and "fixed up" before she went out to the country. But somehow . . . oh, there was always so much to see to when she came home. Gone all day, washing and cleaning for other people; it didn't leave her much time for her own house.

She was late now. The Woodworths liked to have her get the washing out early so that she could do some cleaning too before she left. But she couldn't help it. She would have to get Daisy off first. She had already had on her wraps ready to go, when Elmer came — her cleaning cap, of a blue faded almost into grey, and the ancient black coat with gathered sleeves that she wore over her work dress when she went out to wash.

"What's become of all your underclothes? They ain't all dirty, are they?"

"They are, too. You didn't wash for us last week, mamma."

"Well, you'll just have to take along what you've got. Maybe there'll be some way of getting the rest to you."

"Elmers come in every week, don't they?" Daisy demanded.

"Yes, but maybe they won't always be bringing you in."

She jammed what she could into the telescope, thinking with her helpless, anxious fatalism that it would have to do somehow.

"Daisy, you get yourself ready now."

"I am ready. Mamma, I want to put on my other ribbon."

"Oh, that's way down in the telescope somewhere. You needn't be so anxious to fix yourself up. This ain't like going visiting."

Daisy stood at the little mirror preening herself — such a homely child, "all Switzer," skinny, with pale sharp eyes set close together and thin, stringy, reddish hair. But she had never really learned yet how homely she was. She was the oldest, and she got the pick of what clothes were given to the Switzers. Goldie and Dwight envied her. She was important in her small world. She was proud of her blue coat that had belonged to Alice Brooker, the town lawyer's daughter. It hung unevenly about her bony little knees, and the buttons came down too far. Her mother had tried to make it over for her.

Mrs. Switzer looked at her, troubled, but not knowing how she could tell her all the things she ought to be told. Daisy had never been away before except to go to her Uncle Fred's at Lehigh. She seemed to think that this would be the same. She had so many things to learn. Well, she would find them out soon enough — only too soon. Working for other people — she would learn what that meant. Elmer and Edna Kruse were nice young people. They would mean well enough by Daisy. It was a good chance for her to start in. But it wasn't the same.

Daisy was so proud. She thought it was quite a thing to be "starting in to earn." She thought she could buy herself so much with that dollar and a half a week. The other children stood back watching her, round-eyed and impressed. They wished that they were going away, like Daisy.

They heard a car come splashing through the mud on low.

"There he is back! Have you got your things on? Goldie — go out and tell him she's coming."

"No, me tell him, me!" Dwight shouted jealously.

"Well — both of you tell him. Land! . . ."

She tried hastily to put on the cover of the bulging telescope and to fasten the straps. One of them broke.

"Well, you'll have to take it the way it is."

It was an old thing, hadn't been used since her husband, Mert, had "left off canvassing" before he died. And he had worn it all to pieces.

"Well, I guess you'll have to go now. He won't want to wait. I'll try and send you out what you ain't got with you." She turned to Daisy. Her face was working. There was nothing else to do, as everyone said. Daisy would have to help, and she might as well learn it now. Only, she hated to see Daisy go off, to have her starting in. She knew what it meant. "Well — you try and work good this summer, so they'll want you to stay. I hope they'll bring you in sometimes."

Daisy's homely little face grew pale with awe, suddenly, at the sight of her mother crying, at something that she dimly sensed in the pressure of her mother's thin strong arms. Her vanity in her new importance was somehow shamed and dampened.

Elmer's big new Buick, mud-splashed but imposing, stood tilted on the uneven road. Mud was thick on the wheels. It was a bad day for driving, with the roads a yellow mass, water lying in all the wheel ruts. This little road that led past these few houses on the outskirts of town, and up over the hill, had a cold rainy loneliness. Elmer sat in the front seat of the Buick, and in the back was a big box of groceries.

"Got room to sit in there?" he asked genially. "I didn't get out, it's so muddy here."

"No, don't get out," Mrs. Switzer said hastily. "She can put this right on the floor there in the back." She added, with a timid attempt at courtesy, "Ain't the roads pretty bad out that way?"

"Yes, but farmers get so they don't think so much about the roads."

"I s'pose that's so."

He saw the signs of tears on Mrs. Switzer's face, and they made him anxious to get away. She embraced Daisy hastily again. Daisy climbed over the grocery box and scrunched herself into the seat.

"I guess you'll bring her in with you some time when you're coming," Mrs. Switzer hinted.

"Sure. We'll bring her."

He started the engine. It roared, half died down as the wheels of the car spun in the thick wet mud.

In that moment, Daisy had a startled view of home — the small house standing on a rough rise of land, weathered to a dim colour that showed dark streaks from the rain; the narrow sloping front porch whose edge had a soaked gnawed look; the chickens, greyish-black, pecking at the wet ground; their playthings, stones, a wagon, some old pail covers littered about; a soaked, discoloured piece of underwear hanging on the line in the back yard. The yard was tussocky and overhung the road with shaggy long grass where the yellow bank was caved in under it. Goldie and Dwight were gazing at her solemnly. She saw her mother's face — a thin, weak, loving face, drawn with neglected weeping, with its reddened eyes and poor teeth . . . in the old coat and heavy shoes and cleaning-cap, her work-worn hand with its big knuckles clutching at her coat. She saw the playthings they had used yesterday, and the old swing that hung from one of the trees, the ropes sodden, the seat in crooked. . . .

The car went off, slipping on the wet clay. She waved frantically, suddenly understanding that she was leaving them. They waved at her.

Mrs. Switzer stood there a little while. Then came the harsh rasp of the old black iron pump that stood out under the box-elder tree. She was pumping water to leave for the children before she went off to work.

2

Daisy held on as the car skidded going down the short clay hill. Elmer didn't bother with chains. He was too used to the roads. But her eyes brightened with scared excitement. When they were down, and Elmer slowed up going along the tracks in the deep wet grass that led to the main road, she looked back, holding on her hat with her small scrawny hand.

Just down this little hill — and home was gone. The big car, the feel of her telescope under her feet, the fact that she was going out to the country, changed the looks of everything. She saw it all now.

Dunkels' house stood on one side of the road. A closed-up white house. The windows stared blank and cold between the old shutters. There was a chair with a broken straw seat under the fruit trees. The Dunkels were old Catholic people who seldom went anywhere. In the front yard was a clump of tall pines, the rough brown trunks wet, the green branches, dark and shining, heavy with rain, the ground underneath mournfully sodden and black.

The pasture on the other side. The green grass, lush, wet and cold, and the outcroppings of limestone that held little pools of rain-water in all the tiny holes. Beyond, the low hills gloomy with timber against the lowering sky.

They slid out on to the main road. They bumped over the small wooden bridge above the swollen creek that came from the pasture. Daisy looked down. She saw the little swirls of foam, the long grass that swished with the water, the old rusted tin cans lodged between the rocks.

She sat up straight and important, her thin, homely little face strained with excitement, her sharp eyes taking in everything. The watery mudholes in the road, the little thickets of plum-trees, low and wet, in dark interlacings. She held on fiercely, but made no sound when the car skidded.

She felt the grandeur of having a ride. One wet Sunday, Mr. Brooker had driven them all home from church, she and Goldie and Dwight packed tightly into the back seat of the car, shut in by the side curtains against which the rain lashed, catching the muddy scent of the roads. Sometimes they could plan to go to town just when Mr. Pattey was going to work in his Ford. Then they would run out and shout eagerly, "Mr. Pattey! Are you going through town?" Sometimes he didn't hear them. Sometimes he said, with curt good nature, "Well, pile in"; and they all hopped into the truck back. "He says we can go along with him."

She looked at the black wet fields through which little leaves of bright green corn grew in rows, at showery bushes of sumach along the roadside. A gasolene engine pumping water made a loud desolate sound. There were somber-looking cattle in the wet grass, and lonely, thick-foliaged trees growing here and there in the pastures. She felt her telescope on the floor of the car, the box of groceries beside her. She eyed these with a sharp curiosity. There was a fresh pine-apple — something the Switzers didn't often get at home. She wondered if Edna would have it for dinner. Maybe she could hint a little to Edna.

She was out in the country. She could no longer see her house even if she wanted to — standing dingy, streaked with rain, in its rough grass on the little hill. A lump came into her throat. She had looked forward to playing with Edna's children. But Goldie and Dwight would play all morning without her. She was still proud of her being the oldest, of going out with Elmer and Edna; but now there was a forlornness in the pride.

She wished she were in the front seat with Elmer. She didn't see why he hadn't put her there. She would have liked to know who all the people were who lived on these farms; how old Elmer's babies were; and if he and Edna always went to the movies when they went into town on Saturday nights. Elmer must have lots of money to buy a car like this. He had a new house on his farm, too, and Mrs. Metzinger had said that it had plumbing. Maybe they would take her to the movies, too. She might hint about that.

When she had gone to visit Uncle Fred, she had had to go on the train. She liked this better. She hoped they had a long way to go. She called out to Elmer:

"Say, how much farther is your place?"

"What's that?" He turned around. "Oh, just down the road a ways. Scared to drive in the mud?"

"No, I ain't scared. I like to drive most any way."

She looked at Elmer's back, the old felt hat crammed down carelessly on his head, the back of his neck with the golden hair on the sunburned skin above the blue of his shirt collar. Strong and easy and slouched a little over the steering-wheel that he handled so masterfully. Elmer and Edna were just young folks; but Mrs. Metzinger said that they had more to start with than most young farmers did, and that they were hustlers. Daisy felt that the pride of this belonged to her too, now.

"Here we are!"

"Oh, is this where you folks live?" Daisy cried eagerly.

The house stood back from the road beyond a space of bare yard with a little scattering of grass just starting — small, modern, painted a bright new white and yellow. The barn was new too, a big splendid barn of frescoed brick, with a silo of the same. There were no trees. A raw desolate wind blew across the back yard as they drove up beside the back door.

Edna had come out on the step. Elmer grinned at her as he took out the box of groceries, and she slightly raised her eyebrows. She said kindly enough:

"Well, you brought Daisy. Hello, Daisy, are you going to stay with us this summer?"

"I guess so," Daisy said importantly. But she suddenly felt a little shy and forlorn as she got out of the car and stood on the bare ground in the chilly wind.

"Yes, I brought her along," Elmer said.

"Are the roads very bad?"

"Kind of bad. Why?"

"Well, I'd like to get over to mamma's some time to-day."

"Oh, I guess they aren't too bad for that."

Daisy pricked up her sharp little ears. Another ride. That cheered her.

"Look in the door," Edna said in a low fond voice, motioning with her head.

Two little round, blond heads were pressed tightly against the screen door. There was a clamour of "Daddy, daddy!" Elmer grinned with a half bashful pride as he stood with the box of groceries, raising his eyebrows with mock surprise and demanding: "Who's this? What you shoutin' 'daddy' for? You don't think daddy's got anything for you, do you?" He and Edna were going into the kitchen together, until Edna remembered and called back hastily:

"Oh, come in, Daisy!"

Daisy stood, a little left out and solitary, there in the kitchen, as Billy, the older of the babies, climbed frantically over Elmer, demanding candy, and the little one toddled smilingly about. Her eyes took in all of it. She was impressed by the shining blue-and-white linoleum, the range with its nickel and enamel, the bright new woodwork. Edna was laughing and scolding at Elmer and the baby. Billy had made his father produce the candy. Daisy's sharp little eyes looked hungrily at the lemon drops until Edna remembered her.

"Give Daisy a piece of your candy," she said.

He would not go up to Daisy. She had to come forward and take one of the lemon drops herself. She saw where Edna put the sack, in a dish high in the cupboard. She hoped they would get some more before long.

"My telescope's out there in the car," she reminded them.

"Oh! Elmer, you go and get it and take it up for her," Edna said.

"What?"

"Her valise — or whatever it is — out in the car."

"Oh, sure," Elmer said with a cheerful grin.

"It's kind of an old telescope," Daisy said conversationally. "I guess it's been used a lot. My papa used to have it. The strap broke when mamma was fastening it this morning. We ain't got any suit-case. I had to take this because it was all there was in the house, and mamma didn't want to get me a new one."

Edna raised her eyebrows politely. She leaned over and pretended to spat the baby as he came toddling up to her, then rubbed her cheek against his round head with its funny fuzz of hair.

Daisy watched solemnly. "I didn't know both of your children was boys. I thought one of 'em was a girl. That's what there is at home now — one boy and one girl."

"Um-hm," Edna replied absently. "You can go up with Elmer and take off your things, Daisy," she said. "You can stop and unpack your valise now, I guess, if you'd like to. Then you can come down and help me in the kitchen. You know we got you to help me," she reminded.

Daisy, subdued, followed Elmer up the bright new stairs. In the upper hall, two strips of very clean rag rug were laid over the shining yellow of the floor. Elmer had put her telescope in one of the bedrooms.

"There you are!"

She heard him go clattering down the stairs, and then a kind of murmuring and laughing in the kitchen. The back door slammed. She hurried to the window in time to see Elmer go striding off toward the barn.

She looked about her room with intense curiosity. It too had a bright varnished floor. She had a bed all of her own — a small, old-fashioned bed, left from some old furnishings, that had been put in this room that had the pipes and the hot-water tank. She had to see everything, but she had a stealthy look as she tiptoed about, started to open the drawers of the dresser, looked out of her window. She put her coat and hat on the bed. She would rather be down in the kitchen with Edna than unpack her telescope now.

She guessed she would go down where the rest of them were.

3

Elmer came into the house for dinner. He brought in a cold, muddy, outdoor breath with him. The range was going, but the bright little kitchen seemed chilly, with the white oilcloth on the table, the baby's varnished high chair and his little fat, mottled hands.

Edna made a significant little face at Elmer. Daisy did not see. She was standing back from the stove, where Edna was at work, looking at the baby.

"He can talk pretty good, can't he? Dwight couldn't say anything but 'mamma' when he was that little."

Edna's back was turned. She said meaningly:

"Now, Elmer's come in to dinner, Daisy, we'll have to hurry. You must help me get on the dinner. You can cut bread and get things on the table. You must help, you know. That's what you are supposed to do."

Daisy looked startled, a little scared and resentful. "Well, I don't know where you keep your bread."

"Don't you remember where I told you to put it this morning? Right over in the cabinet, in that big box. You must watch, Daisy, and learn where things are."

Elmer, a little embarrassed at the look that Edna gave him, whistled as he began to wash his hands at the sink.

"How's daddy's old boy?" he said loudly, giving a poke at the baby's chin.

As Edna passed him, she shook her head, and her lips just formed: "Been like that all morning!"

He grinned comprehendingly. Then both their faces became expressionless.

Daisy had not exactly heard, but she looked from one to the other, silent and dimly wondering. The queer ache that had kept starting all through the morning, under her interest in Edna's things and doings, came over her again. She sensed something different in the atmosphere than she had ever known before — some queer difference between the position of herself and of the two babies, a faint notion of what mamma had meant when she had said that this would not be visiting.

"I guess I'm going to have the toothache again," she said faintly.

No one seemed to hear her.

Edna whisked off the potatoes, drained the water. . . . "You might bring me a dish, Daisy." Daisy searched a long time while Edna turned impatiently and pointed. Edna put the rest of the things on the table herself. Her young, fresh, capable mouth was tightly closed, and she was making certain resolutions.

Daisy stood hesitating in the middle of the room, a scrawny, unappealing little figure. Billy — fat, blond, in funny, dark blue union-alls — was trotting busily about the kitchen. Daisy swooped down upon him and tried to bring him to the table. He set up a howl. Edna turned, looked astonished, severe.

"I was trying to make him come to the table," Daisy explained weakly.

"You scared him. He isn't used to you. He doesn't like it. Don't cry, Billy. The girl didn't mean anything."

"Here, daddy'll put him in his place," Elmer said hastily.

Billy looked over his father's shoulder at Daisy with suffused, resentful blue eyes. She did not understand it, and felt strangely at a loss. She had been left with Goldie and Dwight so often. She had always made Dwight go to the table. She had been the boss.

Edna said in a cool, held-in voice, "Put these things on the table, Daisy."

They sat down. Daisy and the other children had always felt it a great treat to eat away from home instead of at their own scanty, hastily set table. They had hung around Mrs. Metzinger's house at noon, hoping to be asked to stay, not offended when told that "it was time for them to run off now." Her pinched little face had a hungry look as she stared at the potatoes and fried ham and pie. But they did not watch and urge her to have more, as Mrs. Metzinger did, and Mrs. Brooker when she took pity on the Switzers and had them there. Daisy wanted more pie. But none of them seemed to be taking more, and so she said nothing. She remembered what her mother had said, with now a faint comprehension: "You must remember you're out working for other folks, and it won't be like it is at home."

After dinner, Edna said: "Now you can wash the dishes, Daisy."

She went into the next room with the children. Daisy, as she went hesitatingly about the kitchen alone, could hear Edna's low contented humming as she sat in there rocking, the baby in her lap. The bright kitchen was empty and lonely now. Through the window, Daisy could see the great barn looming up against the rainy sky. She hoped that they would drive to Edna's mother's soon.

She finished as soon as she could, and went into the dining-room, where Edna was sewing on the baby's rompers. Edna went on sewing. Daisy sat down disconsolately. That queer low ache went all through her. She said in a small dismal voice:

"I guess I got the toothache again."

Edna bit off a thread.

"I had it awful hard a while ago. Mamma come pretty near taking me to the dentist."

"That's too bad," Edna murmured politely. But she offered no other condolence. She gave a secret little smile at the baby asleep on a blanket and a pillow in one corner of the shiny leather davenport.

"Is Elmer going to drive into town to-morrow?"

"To-morrow? I don't suppose so."

"Mamma couldn't find the belt of my plaid dress and I thought if he was, maybe I could go along and get it. I'd like to have it."

Daisy's homely mouth drooped at the corners. Her toothache did not seem to matter to anyone. Edna did not seem to want to see that anything was wrong with her. She had expected Edna to be concerned, to mention remedies. But it wasn't toothache, that strange lonesome ache all over her. Maybe she was going to be terribly sick. Mamma wouldn't come home for supper to be told about it.

She saw mamma's face as in that last glimpse of it — drawn with crying, and yet trying to smile, under the old cleaning-cap, her hand holding her coat together. . . .

Edna glanced quickly at her. The child was so mortally unattractive, unappealing even in her forlornness. Edna frowned a little, but said kindly:

"Now you might take Billy into the kitchen out of my way, Daisy, and amuse him."

"Well, he cries when I pick him up," Daisy said faintly.

"He won't cry this time. Take him out and help him play with his blocks. You must help me with the children, you know."

"Well, if he'll go with me."

"He'll go with you, won't he, Billy boy? Won't you go with Daisy, sweetheart?"

Billy stared and then nodded. Daisy felt a thrill of comfort as Billy put his little fat hand in hers and trotted into the kitchen beside her. He had the fattest hands, she thought. Edna brought the blocks and put the box down on the floor beside Daisy.

"Now, see if you can amuse him so that I can get my sewing done."

"Shall you and me play blocks, Billy?" Daisy murmured.

He nodded. Then he got hold of the box with one hand, tipped out all the blocks on the floor with a bang and a rattle, and looked at her with a pleased proud smile.

"Oh, no, Billy. You mustn't spill out the blocks. Look, you're too little to play with them. No, now — now wait! Let Daisy show you. Daisy'll build something real nice — shall she?"

He gave a solemn nod of consent.

Daisy set out the blocks on the bright linoleum. She had never had such blocks as these to handle before. Dwight's were only a few old, unmatched, broken ones. Her spirit of leadership came back, and she firmly put away that fat hand of Billy's whenever he meddled with her building. She could make something really wonderful with these blocks.

"No, Billy, you mustn't. See, when Daisy's got it all done, then you can see what the lovely building is."

She put the blocks together with great interest. She knew what she was going to make — it was going to be a new house; no, a new church. Just as she got the walls up, in came that little hand again, and then with a delighted grunt Billy swept the blocks pell-mell about the floor. At the clatter, he sat back, pursing up his mouth to give an ecstatic "Ooh!"

"Oh, Billy — you mustn't, the building wasn't done! Look, you've spoiled it. Now you've got to sit 'way off here while I try to build it over again."

Billy's look of triumph turned to surprise and then to vociferous protest as Daisy picked him up and firmly transplanted him to another corner of the room. He set up a tremendous howl. He had never been set aside like that before. Edna came hurrying out. Daisy looked at Edna for justification, but instinctively on the defensive.

"Billy knocked over the blocks. He spoiled the building."

"Wah! Wah!" Billy gave loud heart-broken sobs. The tears ran down his fat cheeks and he held out his arms piteously toward his mother.

"I didn't hurt him," Daisy said, scared.

"Never mind, lover," Edna was crooning. "Of course he can play with his blocks. They're Billy's blocks, Daisy," she said. "He doesn't like to sit and see you put up buildings. He wants to play, too. See, you've made him cry now."

"Do' wanna stay here," Billy wailed.

"Well, come in with mother then." She picked him up, wiping his tears.

"I didn't hurt him," Daisy protested.

"Well, never mind now. You can pick up the blocks and then sweep the floor, Daisy. You didn't do that when you finished the dishes. Never mind," she was saying to Billy. "Pretty soon daddy'll come in and we'll have a nice ride."

Daisy soberly picked up the blocks and got the broom. What had she done to Billy? He had tried to spoil her building. She always made Dwight keep back until she had finished. Of course it was Daisy, the oldest, who should lead and manage. There had been no one to hear her side. Everything was different. She winked back tears as she swept, poorly and carelessly.

Then she brightened up as Elmer came tramping up on the back porch and then through the kitchen.

"Edna!"

"She's in there," Daisy offered.

"Want to go now? What! Is the baby asleep?" he asked blankly.

Edna gave him a warning look and the door was closed.

Daisy listened hard. She swept very softly. She could catch only a little of what they said — "Kind of hate to go off . . . I know, but if we once start . . . not a thing all day . . . what we got her for . . ." She had no real comprehension of it. She hurried and put away the broom. She wanted to be sure and be ready to go.

Elmer tramped out, straight past her. She saw from the window that he was backing the car out of the shed. She could hear Edna and Billy upstairs, could hear the baby cry a little as he was wakened. Maybe she ought to go out and get on her wraps, too.

Elmer honked the horn. A moment later Edna came hurrying downstairs, in her hat and coat, and Billy in his knitted cap and red sweater crammed over his union-alls, so that he looked like a little Brownie. The baby had his little coat, too.

Edna called out: "Come in and get this boy, daddy." She did not look at Daisy, but said hurriedly: "We're going for a little ride, Daisy. Have you finished the sweeping? Well, then, you can pick up those pieces in the dining-room. We won't be gone so very long. When it's a quarter past five, you start the fire, like I showed you this noon, and slice the potatoes that were left, and the meat. And set the table."

The horn was honked again.

"Yes! Well, we'll be back, Daisy. Come, lover, daddy's in a hurry."

Daisy stood looking after them. Billy clamoured to sit beside his daddy. Edna took the baby from Elmer and put him beside her on the back seat. There was room — half of the big back seat. There wasn't anything, really, to be done at home. That was the worst of it. They just didn't want to take her. They all belonged together. They didn't want to take anyone else along. She was an outsider. They all — even the baby — had a freshened look of expectancy.

The engine roared — they had started; slipping on the mud of the drive, then forging straight ahead, around the turn, out of sight.

4

She went forlornly into the dining-room. The light from the windows was dim now in the rainy, late afternoon. The pink pieces from the baby's rompers were scattered over the gray rug. She got down on her hands and knees, slowly picking them up, sniffling a little. She heard the Big Ben clock in the kitchen ticking loudly.

That dreadful ache submerged her. No one would ask about it, no one would try to comfort her. Before, there had always been mamma coming home, anxious, scolding sometimes, but worried over them if they didn't feel right, caring about them. Mamma and Goldie and Dwight cared about her — but she was away out in the country, and they were at home. She didn't want to stay here, where she didn't belong. But mamma had told her that she must begin helping this summer.

Her ugly little mouth contorted into a grimace of weeping. But silent weeping, without any tears; because she already had the cold knowledge that no one would notice or comfort it.

F. Scott Fitzgerald
Winter Dreams

F. Scott Fitzgerald's "Winter Dreams" originally appeared in *Smart Set* in 1922 before its inclusion in *All the Sad Young Men* in 1926, a year after the publication of *The Great Gatsby*. The story is based on some of the same themes as Fitzgerald's greatest novel: the quest for social advancement, the romantic expectations of love, and the transforming disillusionment of the central character. It differs, however, in that it employs an intrusive omniscient narrator who presents more in expository comment than in dramatic action or dialogue. Still, it reflects some of the central concerns of the Jazz Age and much of its artifice and superficiality, especially with regard to surface appearance rather than internal substance. Fitzgerald's elegant style is everywhere apparent, as are the biographical details that invest much of his early work. He grew up in St. Paul, Minnesota, attended St. Paul Academy and then Princeton University (from which he was expelled), and spent summers in his youth enjoying the lush atmosphere of White Bear Lake, which he transforms, somewhat disingenuously, into Black Bear Lake in this story.

F. Scott Fitzgerald, "Winter Dreams," *All the Sad Young Men* (New York: Charles Scribner's Sons, 1926), 57–90.

I

Some of the caddies were poor as sin and lived in one-room houses with a neurasthenic cow in the front yard, but Dexter Green's father owned the second best grocery-store in Black Bear — the best one was "The Hub," patronized by the wealthy people from Sherry Island — and Dexter caddied only for pocket-money.

In the fall when the days became crisp and gray, and the long Minnesota winter shut down like the white lid of a box, Dexter's skis moved over the snow that hid the fairways of the golf course. At these times the country gave him a feeling of profound melancholy — it offended him that the links should lie in enforced fallowness, haunted by ragged sparrows for the long season. It was dreary, too, that on the tees where the gay colors fluttered in summer there were now only the desolate sand-boxes knee-deep in crusted ice. When he crossed the hills the wind blew cold as misery, and if the sun was out he tramped with his eyes squinted up against the hard dimensionless glare.

In April the winter ceased abruptly. The snow ran down into Black Bear Lake scarcely tarrying for the early golfers to brave the season with red and black balls. Without elation, without an interval of moist glory, the cold was gone.

Dexter knew that there was something dismal about this Northern spring, just as he knew there was something gorgeous about the fall. Fall made him clinch his hands and tremble and repeat idiotic sentences to himself, and make brisk abrupt gestures of command to imaginary audiences and armies. October filled him with hope which November raised to a sort of ecstatic triumph, and in this mood the fleeting brilliant impressions of the summer at Sherry Island were ready grist to his mill. He became a golf champion and defeated Mr. T. A. Hedrick in a marvellous match played a hundred times over the fairways of his imagination, a match each detail of which he changed about untiringly — sometimes he won with almost laughable ease, sometimes he came up magnificently from behind. Again, stepping from a Pierce-Arrow automobile, like Mr. Mortimer Jones, he strolled frigidly into the lounge of the Sherry Island Golf Club — or perhaps, surrounded by an admiring crowd, he gave an exhibition of fancy diving from the spring-board of the club raft. . . . Among those who watched him in open-mouthed wonder was Mr. Mortimer Jones.

And one day it came to pass that Mr. Jones — himself and not his ghost — came up to Dexter with tears in his eyes and said that Dexter was the —— best caddy in the club, and wouldn't he decide not to quit if Mr. Jones made it worth his while, because every other —— caddy in the club lost one ball a hole for him — regularly ——

"No, sir," said Dexter decisively, "I don't want to caddy any more." Then, after a pause: "I'm too old."

"You're not more than fourteen. Why the devil did you decide just this morning that you wanted to quit? You promised that next week you'd go over to the State tournament with me."

"I decided I was too old."

Dexter handed in his "A Class" badge, collected what money was due him from the caddy master, and walked home to Black Bear Village.

"The best —— caddy I ever saw," shouted Mr. Mortimer Jones over a drink that afternoon. "Never lost a ball! Willing! Intelligent! Quiet! Honest! Grateful!"

The little girl who had done this was eleven — beautifully ugly as little girls are apt to be who are destined after a few years to be inexpressibly lovely and bring no end of misery to a great number of men. The spark, however, was perceptible. There was a general ungodliness in the way her lips twisted down at the corners when she smiled, and in the — Heaven help us! — in the almost passionate quality of her eyes. Vitality is born early in such women. It was utterly in evidence now, shining through her thin frame in a sort of glow.

She had come eagerly out on to the course at nine o'clock with a white linen nurse and five small new golf-clubs in a white canvas bag which the nurse was carrying. When Dexter first saw her she was standing by the caddy house, rather ill at ease and trying to conceal the fact by engaging her nurse in an obviously unnatural conversation graced by startling and irrelevant grimaces from herself.

"Well, it's certainly a nice day, Hilda," Dexter heard her say. She drew down the corners of her mouth, smiled, and glanced furtively around, her eyes in transit falling for an instant on Dexter.

Then to the nurse:

"Well, I guess there aren't very many people out here this morning, are there?"

The smile again — radiant, blatantly artificial — convincing.

"I don't know what we're supposed to do now," said the nurse, looking nowhere in particular.

"Oh, that's all right. I'll fix it up."

Dexter stood perfectly still, his mouth slightly ajar. He knew that if he moved forward a step his stare would be in her line of vision — if he moved backward he would lose his full view of her face. For a moment he had not realized how young she was. Now he remembered having seen her several times the year before — in bloomers.

Suddenly, involuntarily, he laughed, a short abrupt laugh — then, startled by himself, he turned and began to walk quickly away.

"Boy!"

Dexter stopped.

"Boy ——"

Beyond question he was addressed. Not only that, but he was treated to that absurd smile, that preposterous smile — the memory of which at least a dozen men were to carry into middle age.

"Boy, do you know where the golf teacher is?"

"He's giving a lesson."

"Well, do you know where the caddy-master is?"

"He isn't here yet this morning."

"Oh." For a moment this baffled her. She stood alternately on her right and left foot.

"We'd like to get a caddy," said the nurse. "Mrs. Mortimer Jones sent us out to play golf, and we don't know how without we get a caddy."

Here she was stopped by an ominous glance from Miss Jones, followed immediately by the smile.

"There aren't any caddies here except me," said Dexter to the nurse, "and I got to stay here in charge until the caddy-master gets here."

"Oh."

Miss Jones and her retinue now withdrew, and at a proper distance from Dexter became involved in a heated conversation, which was concluded by Miss Jones taking one of the clubs and hitting it on the ground with violence. For further emphasis she raised it again and was about to bring it down smartly upon the nurse's bosom, when the nurse seized the club and twisted it from her hands.

"You damn little mean old *thing!*" cried Miss Jones wildly.

Another argument ensued. Realizing that the elements of the comedy were implied in the scene, Dexter several times began to laugh, but each time restrained the laugh before it reached audibility. He could not resist the monstrous conviction that the little girl was justified in beating the nurse.

The situation was resolved by the fortuitous appearance by the caddy-master, who was appealed to immediately by the nurse.

"Miss Jones is to have a little caddy, and this one says he can't go."

"Mr. McKenna said I was to wait here till you came," said Dexter quickly.

"Well, he's here now." Miss Jones smiled cheerfully at the caddy-master. Then she dropped her bag and set off at a haughty mince toward the first tee.

"Well?" The caddy-master turned to Dexter. "What you standing there like a dummy for? Go pick up the young lady's clubs."

"I don't think I'll go out to-day," said Dexter.

"You don't ——"

"I think I'll quit."

The enormity of his decision frightened him. He was a favorite caddy, and the thirty dollars a month he earned through the summer were not to be made elsewhere around the lake. But he had received a strong emotional shock, and his perturbation required a violent and immediate outlet.

It is not so simple as that, either. As so frequently would be the case in the future, Dexter was unconsciously dictated to by his winter dreams.

II

Now, of course, the quality and the seasonability of these winter dreams varied, but the stuff of them remained. They persuaded Dexter several years later to pass up a business course at the State university — his father, prospering now, would have paid his way — for the precarious advantage of attending an older and more famous university in the East, where he was bothered by his scanty funds. But do not get the impression, because his winter dreams happened to be concerned at first with musings on the rich, that there was anything merely snobbish in the boy. He wanted not association with glittering things and glittering people — he wanted the glittering things themselves. Often he reached out for the best without knowing why he wanted it — and sometimes he ran up against the mysterious denials and prohibitions in which life indulges. It is with one of those denials and not with his career as a whole that this story deals.

He made money. It was rather amazing. After college he went to the city from which Black Bear Lake draws its wealthy patrons. When he was only twenty-three and had been there not quite two years, there were already people who liked to say: "Now *there's* a boy ——" All about him rich men's sons were peddling bonds precariously, or investing patrimonies precariously, or plodding through the two dozen volumes of the "George Washington Commercial Course," but Dexter borrowed a thousand dollars on his college degree and his confident mouth, and bought a partnership in a laundry.

It was a small laundry when he went into it but Dexter made a specialty of learning how the English washed fine woollen golf-stockings without shrinking them, and within a year he was catering to the trade that wore knickerbockers. Men were insisting that their Shetland hose and sweaters go to his laundry just as they had insisted on a caddy who could find golf-balls. A little later he was doing their wives' lingerie as well — and running five branches in different parts of the city. Before he was twenty-seven he owned the largest string of laundries in his section of the country. It was then that he sold out and went to New York. But the part of his story that concerns us goes back to the days when he was making his first big success.

When he was twenty-three Mr. Hart — one of the gray-haired men who like to say "Now there's a boy" — gave him a guest card to the Sherry Island Golf Club for a week-end. So he signed his name one day on the register, and that afternoon played golf in a foursome with Mr. Hart and Mr. Sandwood and Mr. T. A. Hedrick. He did not consider it necessary to remark that he had once carried Mr. Hart's bag over this same links, and that he knew every trap and gully with his eyes shut — but he found himself glancing at the four caddies who trailed them, trying to catch a gleam or gesture that would remind him of himself, that would lessen the gap which lay between his present and his past.

It was a curious day, slashed abruptly with fleeting, familiar impressions. One minute he had the sense of being a trespasser — in the next he was impressed by the tremendous superiority he felt toward Mr. T. A. Hedrick, who was a bore and not even a good golfer any more.

Then, because of a ball Mr. Hart lost near the fifteenth green, an enormous thing happened. While they were searching the stiff grasses of the rough there was a clear call of "Fore!" from behind a hill in their rear. And as they all turned abruptly from their search a bright new ball sliced abruptly over the hill and caught Mr. T. A. Hedrick in the abdomen.

"By Gad!" cried Mr. T. A. Hedrick, "they ought to put some of these crazy women off the course. It's getting to be outrageous."

A head and a voice came up together over the hill:

"Do you mind if we go through?"

"You hit me in the stomach!" declared Mr. Hedrick wildly.

"Did I?" The girl approached the group of men. "I'm sorry. I yelled 'Fore!'"

Her glance fell casually on each of the men — then scanned the fairway for her ball.

"Did I bounce into the rough?"

It was impossible to determine whether this question was ingenuous or malicious. In a moment, however, she left no doubt, for as her partner came up over the hill she called cheerfully:

"Here I am! I'd have gone on the green except that I hit something."

As she took her stance for a short mashie shot, Dexter looked at her closely.

She wore a blue gingham dress, rimmed at throat and shoulders with a white edging that accentuated her tan. The quality of exaggeration, of thinness, which had made her passionate eyes and down-turning mouth absurd at eleven, was gone now. She was arrestingly beautiful. The color in her cheeks was centered like the color in a picture — it was not a "high" color, but a sort of fluctuating and feverish warmth, so shaded that it seemed at any moment it would recede and disappear. This color and the mobility of her mouth gave a continual impression of flux, of intense life, of passionate vitality — balanced only partially by the sad luxury of her eyes.

She swung her mashie impatiently and without interest, pitching the ball into a sand-pit on the other side of the green. With a quick, insincere smile and a careless "Thank you!" she went on after it.

"That Judy Jones!" remarked Mr. Hedrick on the next tee, as they waited — some moments — for her to play on ahead. "All she needs is to be turned up and spanked for six months and then to be married off to an old-fashioned cavalry captain."

"My God, she's good-looking!" said Mr. Sandwood, who was just over thirty.

"Good-looking!" cried Mr. Hedrick contemptuously, "she always looks as if she wanted to be kissed! Turning those big cow-eyes on every calf in town!"

It was doubtful if Mr. Hedrick intended a reference to the maternal instinct.

"She'd play pretty good golf if she'd try," said Mr. Sandwood.

"She has no form," said Mr. Hedrick solemnly.

"She has a nice figure," said Mr. Sandwood.

"Better thank the Lord she doesn't drive a swifter ball," said Mr. Hart, winking at Dexter.

Later in the afternoon the sun went down with a riotous swirl of gold and varying blues and scarlets, and left the dry, rustling night of Western summer. Dexter watched from the veranda of the Golf Club, watched the even overlap of the waters in the little wind, silver molasses under the harvest-moon. Then the moon held a finger to her lips and the lake became a clear pool, pale and quiet. Dexter put on his bathing-suit and swam out to the farthest raft, where he stretched dripping on the wet canvas of the springboard.

There was a fish jumping and a star shining and the lights around the lake were gleaming. Over on a dark peninsula a piano was playing the songs of last summer and of summers before that — songs from "Chin-Chin" and "The Count of Luxemburg" and "The Chocolate Soldier" — and because the sound of a piano over a stretch of water had always seemed beautiful to Dexter he lay perfectly quiet and listened.

The tune the piano was playing at that moment had been gay and new five years before when Dexter was a sophomore at college. They had played it at a prom once when he could not afford the luxury of proms, and he had stood outside the gymnasium and listened. The sound of the tune precipitated in him a sort of ecstasy and it was with that ecstasy he viewed what happened to him now. It was a mood of intense appreciation, a sense that, for once, he was magnificently attune to life and that everything about him was radiating a brightness and a glamour he might never know again.

A low, pale oblong detached itself suddenly from the darkness of the Island, spitting forth the reverberate sound of a racing motor-boat. Two white streamers of cleft water rolled themselves out behind it and almost immediately the boat was beside him, drowning out the hot tinkle of the piano in the drone of its spray. Dexter raising himself on his arms was aware of a figure standing at the wheel, of two dark eyes regarding him over the lengthening space of water — then the boat had gone by and was sweeping in an immense and purposeless circle of spray round and round in the middle of the lake. With equal eccentricity one of the circles flattened out and headed back toward the raft.

"Who's that?" she called, shutting off her motor. She was so near now that Dexter could see her bathing-suit, which consisted apparently of pink rompers.

The nose of the boat bumped the raft, and as the latter tilted rakishly he was precipitated toward her. With different degrees of interest they recognized each other.

"Aren't you one of those men we played through this afternoon?" she demanded.

He was.

"Well, do you know how to drive a motor-boat? Because if you do I wish you'd drive this one so I can ride on the surf-board behind. My name is Judy Jones" — she favored him with an absurd smirk — rather, what tried to be a smirk, for, twist her mouth as she might, it was not grotesque, it was merely beautiful — "and I live in a house over there on the Island, and in that house there is a man waiting for me. When he drove up at the door I drove out of the dock because he says I'm his ideal."

There was a fish jumping and a star shining and the lights around the lake were gleaming. Dexter sat beside Judy Jones and she explained how her boat was driven. Then she was in the water, swimming to the floating surf-board with a sinuous crawl. Watching her was without effort to the eye, watching a branch waving or a sea-gull flying. Her arms, burned to butternut, moved sinuously among the dull platinum ripples, elbow appearing first, casting the forearm back with a cadence of falling water, then reaching out and down, stabbing a path ahead.

They moved out into the lake; turning, Dexter saw that she was kneeling on the low rear of the now uptilted surf-board.

"Go faster," she called, "fast as it'll go."

Obediently he jammed the lever forward and the white spray mounted at the bow. When he looked around again the girl was standing up on the rushing board, her arms spread wide, her eyes lifted toward the moon.

"It's awful cold," she shouted. "What's your name?"

He told her.

"Well, why don't you come to dinner to-morrow night?"

His heart turned over like the fly-wheel of the boat, and, for the second time, her casual whim gave a new direction to his life.

III

Next evening while he waited for her to come down-stairs, Dexter peopled the soft deep summer room and the sun-porch that opened from it with the men who had already loved Judy Jones. He knew the sort of men they were — the men who when he first went to college had entered from the great prep schools with graceful clothes and the deep tan of healthy summers. He had seen that, in one sense, he was better than these men. He was newer and stronger. Yet in ac-knowledging to himself that he wished his children to be like them he was ad-mitting that he was but the rough, strong stuff from which they eternally sprang.

When the time had come for him to wear good clothes, he had known who were the best tailors in America, and the best tailors in America had made him the suit he wore this evening. He had acquired that particular reserve peculiar to his university, that set it off from other universities. He recognized the value to him of such a mannerism and he had adopted it; he knew that to be careless in dress and manner required more confidence than to be careful. But carelessness was for his children. His mother's name had been Krimslich. She was a Bohemian of the peasant class and she had talked broken English to the end of her days. Her son must keep to the set patterns.

At a little after seven Judy Jones came down-stairs. She wore a blue silk after-noon dress, and he was disappointed at first that she had not put on something more elaborate. This feeling was accentuated when, after a brief greeting, she went to the door of a butler's pantry and pushing it open called: "You can serve dinner, Martha." He had rather expected that a butler would announce dinner, that there would be a cocktail. Then he put these thoughts behind him as they sat down side by side on a lounge and looked at each other.

"Father and mother won't be here," she said thoughtfully.

He remembered the last time he had seen her father, and he was glad the par-ents were not to be here to-night — they might wonder who he was. He had been born in Keeble, a Minnesota village fifty miles farther north, and he always gave Keeble as his home instead of Black Bear Village. Country towns were well enough to come from if they weren't inconveniently in sight and used as foot-stools by fashionable lakes.

They talked of his university, which she had visited frequently during the past two years, and of the near-by city which supplied Sherry Island with its pa-trons, and whither Dexter would return next day to his prospering laundries.

During dinner she slipped into a moody depression which gave Dexter a feeling of uneasiness. Whatever petulance she uttered in her throaty voice worried him. Whatever she smiled at — at him, at a chicken liver, at nothing — it disturbed him that her smile could have no root in mirth, or even in amusement. When the scarlet corners of her lips curved down, it was less a smile than an invitation to a kiss.

Then, after dinner, she led him out on the dark sun-porch and deliberately changed the atmosphere.

"Do you mind if I weep a little?" she said.

"I'm afraid I'm boring you," he responded quickly.

"You're not. I like you. But I've just had a terrible afternoon. There was a man I cared about, and this afternoon he told me out of a clear sky that he was poor as a church-mouse. He'd never even hinted it before. Does this sound horribly mundane?"

"Perhaps he was afraid to tell you."

"Suppose he was," she answered. "He didn't start right. You see, if I'd thought of him as poor — well, I've been mad about loads of poor men, and fully intended to marry them all. But in this case, I hadn't thought of him that way, and my interest in him wasn't strong enough to survive the shock. As if a girl calmly informed her fiancé that she was a widow. He might not object to widows, but ——"

"Let's start right," she interrupted herself suddenly. "Who are you, anyhow?"

For a moment Dexter hesitated. Then:

"I'm nobody," he announced. "My career is largely a matter of futures."

"Are you poor?"

"No," he said frankly, "I'm probably making more money than any man my age in the Northwest. I know that's an obnoxious remark, but you advised me to start right."

There was a pause. Then she smiled and the corners of her mouth drooped and an almost imperceptible sway brought her closer to him, looking up into his eyes. A lump rose in Dexter's throat, and he waited breathless for the experiment, facing the unpredictable compound that would form mysteriously from the elements of their lips. Then he saw — she communicated her excitement to him, lavishly, deeply, with kisses that were not a promise but a fulfilment. They aroused in him not hunger demanding renewal but surfeit that would demand more surfeit . . . kisses that were like charity, creating want by holding back nothing at all.

It did not take him many hours to decide that he had wanted Judy Jones ever since he was a proud, desirous little boy.

IV

It began like that — and continued, with varying shades of intensity, on such a note right up to the dénouement. Dexter surrendered a part of himself to the most direct and unprincipled personality with which he had ever come in contact. Whatever Judy wanted, she went after with the full pressure of her charm. There was no divergence of method, no jockeying for position or premeditation of effects — there was a very little mental side to any of her affairs. She simply made men conscious to the highest degree of her physical loveliness. Dexter had no desire to change her. Her deficiencies were knit up with a passionate energy that transcended and justified them.

When, as Judy's head lay against his shoulder that first night, she whispered, "I don't know what's the matter with me. Last night I thought I was in love with a man and to-night I think I'm in love with you ——" — it seemed to him a beautiful and romantic thing to say. It was the exquisite excitability that for the moment he controlled and owned. But a week later he was compelled to view this same quality in a different light. She took him in her roadster to a picnic supper, and after supper she disappeared, likewise in her roadster, with another man. Dexter became enormously upset and was scarcely able to be decently civil to the other people present. When she assured him that she had not kissed the other man, he knew she was lying — yet he was glad that she had taken the trouble to lie to him.

He was, as he found before the summer ended, one of a varying dozen who circulated about her. Each of them had at one time been favored above all others — about half of them still basked in the solace of occasional sentimental revivals. Whenever one showed signs of dropping out through long neglect, she granted him a brief honeyed hour, which encouraged him to tag along for a year or so longer. Judy made these forays upon the helpless and defeated without malice, indeed half unconscious that there was anything mischievous in what she did.

When a new man came to town every one dropped out — dates were automatically cancelled.

The helpless part of trying to do anything about it was that she did it all herself. She was not a girl who could be "won" in the kinetic sense — she was proof against cleverness, she was proof against charm; if any of these assailed her too strongly she would immediately resolve the affair to a physical basis, and under the magic of her physical splendor the strong as well as the brilliant played her game and not their own. She was entertained only by the gratification of her desires and by the direct exercise of her own charm. Perhaps from so much youthful love, so many youthful lovers, she had come, in self-defense, to nourish herself wholly from within.

Succeeding Dexter's first exhilaration came restlessness and dissatisfaction. The helpless ecstasy of losing himself in her was opiate rather than tonic. It was fortunate for his work during the winter that those moments of ecstasy came infrequently. Early in their acquaintance it had seemed for a while that there was a deep and spontaneous mutual attraction — that first August, for example — three days of long evenings on her dusky veranda, of strange wan kisses through the late afternoon, in shadowy alcoves or behind the protecting trellises of the garden arbors, of mornings when she was fresh as a dream and almost shy at meeting him in the clarity of the rising day. There was all the ecstasy of an engagement about it, sharpened by his realization that there was no engagement. It was during those three days that, for the first time, he had asked her to marry him. She said "maybe some day," she said "kiss me," she said "I'd like to marry you," she said "I love you" — she said — nothing.

The three days were interrupted by the arrival of a New York man who visited at her house for half September. To Dexter's agony, rumor engaged them. The man was the son of the president of a great trust company. But at the end of a month it was reported that Judy was yawning. At a dance one night she sat all evening in a motor-boat with a local beau, while the New Yorker searched the club for her frantically. She told the local beau that she was bored with her visitor, and two days later he left. She was seen with him at the station, and it was reported that he looked very mournful indeed.

On this note the summer ended. Dexter was twenty-four, and he found himself increasingly in a position to do as he wished. He joined two clubs in the city and lived at one of them. Though he was by no means an integral part of the stag-lines at these clubs, he managed to be on hand at dances where Judy Jones was likely to appear. He could have gone out socially as much as he liked — he was an eligible young man, now, and popular with down-town fathers. His confessed devotion to Judy Jones had rather solidified his position. But he had no social aspirations and rather despised the dancing men who were always on tap for the Thursday or Saturday parties and who filled in at dinners with the younger married set. Already he was playing with the idea of going East to New York. He wanted to take Judy Jones with him. No disillusion as to the world in which she had grown up could cure his illusion as to her desirability.

Remember that — for only in the light of it can what he did for her be understood.

Eighteen months after he first met Judy Jones he became engaged to another girl. Her name was Irene Scheerer, and her father was one of the men who had always believed in Dexter. Irene was light-haired and sweet and honorable, and a little stout, and she had two suitors whom she pleasantly relinquished when Dexter formally asked her to marry him.

Summer, fall, winter, spring, another summer, another fall — so much he had given of his active life to the incorrigible lips of Judy Jones. She had treated him with interest, with encouragement, with malice, with indifference, with contempt. She had inflicted on him the innumerable little slights and indignities possible in such a case — as if in revenge for having ever cared for him at all. She had beckoned him and yawned at him and beckoned him again and he had responded often with bitterness and narrowed eyes. She had brought him ecstatic happiness and intolerable agony of spirit. She had caused him untold inconvenience and not a little trouble. She had insulted him, and she had ridden over him, and she had played his interest in her against his interest in his work — for fun. She had done everything to him except to criticise him — this she had not done — it seemed to him only because it might have sullied the utter indifference she manifested and sincerely felt toward him.

When autumn had come and gone again it occurred to him that he could not have Judy Jones. He had to beat this into his mind but he convinced himself at last. He lay awake at night for a while and argued it over. He told himself the trouble and the pain she had caused him, he enumerated her glaring deficiencies as a wife. Then he said to himself that he loved her, and after a while he fell asleep. For a week, lest he imagined her husky voice over the telephone or her eyes opposite him at lunch, he worked hard and late, and at night he went to his office and plotted out his years.

At the end of a week he went to a dance and cut in on her once. For almost the first time since they had met he did not ask her to sit out with him or tell her that she was lovely. It hurt him that she did not miss these things — that was all. He was not jealous when he saw that there was a new man to-night. He had been hardened against jealousy long before.

He stayed late at the dance. He sat for an hour with Irene Scheerer and talked about books and about music. He knew very little about either. But he was beginning to be master of his own time now, and he had a rather priggish notion that he — the young and already fabulously successful Dexter Green — should know more about such things.

That was in October, when he was twenty-five. In January, Dexter and Irene became engaged. It was to be announced in June, and they were to be married three months later.

The Minnesota winter prolonged itself interminably, and it was almost May when the winds came soft and the snow ran down into Black Bear Lake at last. For the first time in over a year Dexter was enjoying a certain tranquillity of spirit. Judy Jones had been in Florida, and afterward in Hot Springs, and somewhere she had been engaged, and somewhere she had broken it off. At first, when Dexter had definitely given her up, it had made him sad that people still linked them together and asked for news of her, but when he began to be placed at dinner next to Irene Scheerer people didn't ask him about her any more — they told him about her. He ceased to be an authority on her.

May at last. Dexter walked the streets at night when the darkness was damp as rain, wondering that so soon, with so little done, so much of ecstasy had gone from him. May one year back had been marked by Judy's poignant, unforgivable, yet forgiven turbulence — it had been one of those rare times when he fancied she had grown to care for him. That old penny's worth of happiness he had spent for this bushel of content. He knew that Irene would be no more than a curtain spread behind him, a hand moving among gleaming tea-cups, a voice calling to children . . . fire and loveliness were gone, the magic of nights and the wonder of the varying hours and seasons . . . slender lips, down-turning, dropping to his lips and bearing him up into a heaven of eyes. . . . The thing was deep in him. He was too strong and alive for it to die lightly.

In the middle of May when the weather balanced for a few days on the thin bridge that led to deep summer he turned in one night at Irene's house. Their engagement was to be announced in a week now — no one would be surprised at it. And to-night they would sit together on the lounge at the University Club and look on for an hour at the dancers. It gave him a sense of solidity to go with her — she was so sturdily popular, so intensely "great."

He mounted the steps of the brownstone house and stepped inside.

"Irene," he called.

Mrs. Scheerer came out of the living-room to meet him.

"Dexter," she said, "Irene's gone up-stairs with a splitting headache. She wanted to go with you but I made her go to bed."

"Nothing serious, I ——"

"Oh, no. She's going to play golf with you in the morning. You can spare her for just one night, can't you, Dexter?"

Her smile was kind. She and Dexter liked each other. In the living-room he talked for a moment before he said good-night.

Returning to the University Club, where he had rooms, he stood in the doorway for a moment and watched the dancers. He leaned against the doorpost, nodded at a man or two — yawned.

"Hello, darling."

The familiar voice at his elbow startled him. Judy Jones had left a man and crossed the room to him — Judy Jones, a slender enamelled doll in cloth of gold: gold in a band at her head, gold in two slipper points at her dress's hem. The fragile glow of her face seemed to blossom as she smiled at him. A breeze of warmth and light blew through the room. His hands in the pockets of his dinner-jacket tightened spasmodically. He was filled with sudden excitement.

"When did you get back?" he asked casually.

"Come here and I'll tell you about it."

She turned and he followed her. She had been away — he could have wept at the wonder of her return. She had passed through enchanted streets, doing things that were like provocative music. All mysterious happenings, all fresh and quickening hopes, had gone away with her, come back with her now.

She turned in the doorway.

"Have you a car here? If you haven't, I have."

"I have a coupé."

In then, with a rustle of golden cloth. He slammed the door. Into so many cars she had stepped — like this — like that — her back against the leather, so — her elbow resting on the door — waiting. She would have been soiled long since had there been anything to soil her — except herself — but this was her own self outpouring.

With an effort he forced himself to start the car and back into the street. This was nothing, he must remember. She had done this before, and he had put her behind him, as he would have crossed a bad account from his books.

He drove slowly down-town and, affecting abstraction, traversed the deserted streets of the business section, peopled here and there where a movie was giving out its crowd or where consumptive or pugilistic youth lounged in front of pool halls. The clink of glasses and the slap of hands on the bars issued from saloons, cloisters of glazed glass and dirty yellow light.

She was watching him closely and the silence was embarrassing, yet in this crisis he could find no casual word with which to profane the hour. At a convenient turning he began to zigzag back toward the University Club.

"Have you missed me?" she asked suddenly.

"Everybody missed you."

He wondered if she knew of Irene Scheerer. She had been back only a day — her absence had been almost contemporaneous with his engagement.

"What a remark!" Judy laughed sadly — without sadness. She looked at him searchingly. He became absorbed in the dashboard.

"You're handsomer than you used to be," she said thoughtfully. "Dexter, you have the most rememberable eyes."

He could have laughed at this, but he did not laugh. It was the sort of thing that was said to sophomores. Yet it stabbed at him.

"I'm awfully tired of everything, darling." She called every one darling, endowing the endearment with careless, individual comraderie. "I wish you'd marry me."

The directness of this confused him. He should have told her now that he was going to marry another girl, but he could not tell her. He could as easily have sworn that he had never loved her.

"I think we'd get along," she continued, on the same note, "unless probably you've forgotten me and fallen in love with another girl."

Her confidence was obviously enormous. She had said, in effect, that she found such a thing impossible to believe, that if it were true he had merely committed a childish indiscretion — and probably to show off. She would forgive him, because it was not a matter of any moment but rather something to be brushed aside lightly.

"Of course you could never love anybody but me," she continued, "I like the way you love me. Oh, Dexter, have you forgotten last year?"

"No, I haven't forgotten."

"Neither have I!"

Was she sincerely moved — or was she carried along by the wave of her own acting?

"I wish we could be like that again," she said, and he forced himself to answer: "I don't think we can."

"I suppose not. . . . I hear you're giving Irene Scheerer a violent rush."

There was not the faintest emphasis on the name, yet Dexter was suddenly ashamed.

"Oh, take me home," cried Judy suddenly; "I don't want to go back to that idiotic dance — with those children."

Then, as he turned up the street that led to the residence district, Judy began to cry quietly to herself. He had never seen her cry before.

The dark street lightened, the dwellings of the rich loomed up around them, he stopped his coupé in front of the great white bulk of the Mortimer Joneses house, somnolent, gorgeous, drenched with the splendor of the damp moonlight. Its solidity startled him. The strong walls, the steel of the girders, the breadth and beam and pomp of it were there only to bring out the contrast with the young beauty beside him. It was sturdy to accentuate her slightness — as if to show what a breeze could be generated by a butterfly's wing.

He sat perfectly quiet, his nerves in wild clamor, afraid that if he moved he would find her irresistibly in his arms. Two tears had rolled down her wet face and trembled on her upper lip.

"I'm more beautiful than anybody else," she said brokenly, "why can't I be happy?" Her moist eyes tore at his stability — her mouth turned slowly downward with an exquisite sadness: "I'd like to marry you if you'll have me, Dexter. I suppose you think I'm not worth having, but I'll be so beautiful for you, Dexter."

A million phrases of anger, pride, passion, hatred, tenderness fought on his lips. Then a perfect wave of emotion washed over him, carrying off with it a sediment of wisdom, of convention, of doubt, of honor. This was his girl who was speaking, his own, his beautiful, his pride.

"Won't you come in?" He heard her draw in her breath sharply.

Waiting.

"All right," his voice was trembling, "I'll come in."

V

It was strange that neither when it was over nor a long time afterward did he regret that night. Looking at it from the perspective of ten years, the fact that Judy's flare for him endured just one month seemed of little importance. Nor did it matter that by his yielding he subjected himself to a deeper agony in the end and gave serious hurt to Irene Scheerer and to Irene's parents, who had befriended him. There was nothing sufficiently pictorial about Irene's grief to stamp itself on his mind.

Dexter was at bottom hard-minded. The attitude of the city on his action was of no importance to him, not because he was going to leave the city, but because any outside attitude on the situation seemed superficial. He was completely indifferent to popular opinion. Nor, when he had seen that it was no use, that he did not possess in himself the power to move fundamentally or to hold Judy Jones, did he bear any malice toward her. He loved her, and he would love her until the day he was too old for loving — but he could not have her. So he tasted the deep pain that is reserved only for the strong, just as he had tasted for a little while the deep happiness.

Even the ultimate falsity of the grounds upon which Judy terminated the engagement that she did not want to "take him away" from Irene — Judy, who had wanted nothing else — did not revolt him. He was beyond any revulsion or any amusement.

He went East in February with the intention of selling out his laundries and settling in New York — but the war came to America in March and changed his plans. He returned to the West, handed over the management of the business to his partner, and went into the first officers' training-camp in late April. He was one of those young thousands who greeted the war with a certain amount of relief, welcoming the liberation from webs of tangled emotion.

VI

This story is not his biography, remember, although things creep into it which have nothing to do with those dreams he had when he was young. We are almost done with them and with him now. There is only one more incident to be related here, and it happens seven years farther on.

It took place in New York, where he had done well — so well that there were no barriers too high for him. He was thirty-two years old, and, except for one flying trip immediately after the war, he had not been West in seven years. A man named Devlin from Detroit came into his office to see him in a business way, and then and there this incident occurred, and closed out, so to speak, this particular side of his life.

"So you're from the Middle West," said the man Devlin with careless curiosity. "That's funny — I thought men like you were probably born and raised on Wall Street. You know — wife of one of my best friends in Detroit came from your city. I was an usher at the wedding."

Dexter waited with no apprehension of what was coming.

"Judy Simms," said Devlin with no particular interest; "Judy Jones she was once."

"Yes, I knew her." A dull impatience spread over him. He had heard, of course, that she was married — perhaps deliberately he had heard no more.

"Awfully nice girl," brooded Devlin meaninglessly, "I'm sort of sorry for her."

"Why?" Something in Dexter was alert, receptive, at once.

"Oh, Lud Simms has gone to pieces in a way. I don't mean he ill-uses her, but he drinks and runs around ——"

"Doesn't she run around?"

"No. Stays at home with her kids."

"Oh."

"She's a little too old for him," said Devlin.

"Too old!" cried Dexter. "Why, man, she's only twenty-seven."

He was possessed with a wild notion of rushing out into the streets and taking a train to Detroit. He rose to his feet spasmodically.

"I guess you're busy," Devlin apologized quickly. "I didn't realize ——"

"No, I'm not busy," said Dexter, steadying his voice. "I'm not busy at all. Not busy at all. Did you say she was — twenty-seven? No, I said she was twenty-seven."

"Yes, you did," agreed Devlin dryly.

"Go on, then. Go on."

"What do you mean?"

"About Judy Jones."

Devlin looked at him helplessly.

"Well, that's — I told you all there is to it. He treats her like the devil. Oh, they're not going to get divorced or anything. When he's particularly outrageous she forgives him. In fact, I'm inclined to think she loves him. She was a pretty girl when she first came to Detroit."

A pretty girl! The phrase struck Dexter as ludicrous.

"Isn't she — a pretty girl, any more?"

"Oh, she's all right."

"Look here," said Dexter, sitting down suddenly, "I don't understand. You say she was a 'pretty girl' and now you say she's 'all right.' I don't understand what you mean — Judy Jones wasn't a pretty girl, at all. She was a great beauty. Why, I knew her, I knew her. She was ——"

Devlin laughed pleasantly.

"I'm not trying to start a row," he said. "I think Judy's a nice girl and I like her. I can't understand how a man like Lud Simms could fall madly in love with her, but he did." Then he added: "Most of the women like her."

Dexter looked closely at Devlin, thinking wildly that there must be a reason for this, some insensitivity in the man or some private malice.

"Lots of women fade just like *that,*" Devlin snapped his fingers. "You must have seen it happen. Perhaps I've forgotten how pretty she was at her wedding. I've seen her so much since then, you see. She has nice eyes."

A sort of dullness settled down upon Dexter. For the first time in his life he felt like getting very drunk. He knew that he was laughing loudly at something Devlin had said, but he did not know what it was or why it was funny. When, in a few minutes, Devlin went he lay down on his lounge and looked out the window at the New York sky-line into which the sun was sinking in dull lovely shades of pink and gold.

He had thought that having nothing else to lose he was invulnerable at last — but he knew that he had just lost something more, as surely as if he had married Judy Jones and seen her fade away before his eyes.

The dream was gone. Something had been taken from him. In a sort of panic he pushed the palms of his hands into his eyes and tried to bring up a picture of the waters lapping on Sherry Island and the moonlit veranda, and gingham on the golf-links and the dry sun and the gold color of her neck's soft down. And her mouth damp to his kisses and her eyes plaintive with melancholy and her freshness like new fine linen in the morning. Why, these things were no longer in the world! They had existed and they existed no longer.

For the first time in years the tears were streaming down his face. But they were for himself now. He did not care about mouth and eyes and moving hands. He wanted to care, and he could not care. For he had gone away and he could never go back any more. The gates were closed, the sun was gone down, and there was no beauty but the gray beauty of steel that withstands all time. Even the grief he could have borne was left behind in the country of illusion, of youth, of the richness of life, where his winter dreams had flourished.

"Long ago," he said, "long ago, there was something in me, but now that thing is gone. Now that thing is gone, that thing is gone. I cannot cry. I cannot care. That thing will come back no more."

Ernest Hemingway
Hills Like White Elephants

In the course of his celebrated career, which included a Nobel Prize for literature, Ernest Hemingway wrote over a hundred stories, many of them among the most famous works of short fiction in English. First published in *transition* in 1927 prior to inclusion in *Men without Women* later that year, "Hills Like White Elephants" is often considered the finest example of Hemingway's "iceberg theory," in which important aspects of a situation are never directly revealed but are implied in context. Neither character in this story directly mentions abortion, for example, but that is clearly the conflict between the lovers. The controlled style, in which virtually every line is meaningful, is also indicative of his minimalist fiction, as is his skill in dialogue, in which speaker names are often not given; nor do adverbs clarify the tone or mood of the comments. Hemingway's work is subtle: the two landscapes of the opening, one barren, one fertile and productive, reflect the human drama that follows; the title carries connotations of a valuable but unwanted gift that will be a burden to retain and yet cannot be given away; the curtain in the conclusion refers not only to a practical doorway but to the beads of the rosary, implying that the woman is Roman Catholic and thus resists the concept of abortion. The ending is typically unsettled, not fully clarifying whether the woman's comment that she is "fine" reveals a tacit capitulation to the procedure or an ironic recognition that she, and her child, will have to form a life for themselves apart from the man who now lies to her about their future relationship. It is quintessential Hemingway in theme, style, and characterization.

Ernest Hemingway, "Hills Like White Elephants," *Men Without Women* (New York: Charles Scribner's Sons, 1927), 69–77.

The hills across the valley of the Ebro were long and white. On this side there was no shade and no trees and the station was between two lines of rails in the sun. Close against the side of the station there was the warm shadow of the building and a curtain, made of strings of bamboo beads, hung across the open door into the bar, to keep out flies. The American and the girl with him sat at a table in the shade, outside the building. It was very hot and the express from Barcelona would come in forty minutes. It stopped at this junction for two minutes and went on to Madrid.

"What should we drink?" the girl asked. She had taken off her hat and put it on the table.

"It's pretty hot," the man said.

"Let's drink beer."

"Dos cervezas," the man said into the curtain.

"Big ones?" the woman asked from the doorway.

"Yes. Two big ones."

The woman brought two glasses of beer and two felt pads. She put the felt pads and the beer glasses on the table and looked at the man and the girl. The girl was looking off at the line of hills. They were white in the sun and the country was brown and dry.

"They look like white elephants," she said.

"I've never seen one," the man drank his beer.

"No, you wouldn't have."

"I might have," the man said. "Just because you say I wouldn't have doesn't prove anything."

The girl looked at the bead curtain. "They've painted something on it," she said. "What does it say?"

"Anis del Toro. It's a drink."

"Could we try it?"

The man called "Listen" through the curtain. The woman came out from the bar.

"Four reales."

"We want two Anis del Toro."

"With water?"

"Do you want it with water?"

"I don't know," the girl said. "Is it good with water?"

"It's all right."

"You want them with water?" asked the woman.

"Yes, with water."

"It tastes like licorice," the girl said and put the glass down.

"That's the way with everything."

"Yes," said the girl. "Everything tastes of licorice. Especially all the things you've waited so long for, like absinthe."

"Oh, cut it out."

"You started it," the girl said. "I was being amused. I was having a fine time."

"Well, let's try and have a fine time."

"All right. I was trying. I said the mountains looked like white elephants. Wasn't that bright?"

"That was bright."

"I wanted to try this new drink. That's all we do, isn't it — look at things and try new drinks?"

"I guess so."

The girl looked across the hills.

"They're lovely hills," she said. "They don't really look like white elephants. I just meant the coloring of their skin through the trees."

"Should we have another drink?"

"All right."

The warm wind blew the bead curtain against the table.

"The beer's nice and cool," the man said.

"It's lovely," the girl said.

"It's really an awfully simple operation, Jig," the man said. "It's not really an operation at all."

The girl looked at the ground the table legs rested on.

"I know you wouldn't mind it, Jig. It's really not anything. It's just to let the air in."

The girl did not say anything.

"I'll go with you and I'll stay with you all the time. They just let the air in and then it's all perfectly natural."

"Then what will we do afterward?"

"We'll be fine afterward. Just like we were before."

"What makes you think so?"

"That's the only thing that bothers us. It's the only thing that's made us unhappy."

The girl looked at the bead curtain, put her hand out and took hold of two of the strings of beads.

"And you think then we'll be all right and be happy."

"I know we will. You don't have to be afraid. I've known lots of people that have done it."

"So have I," said the girl. "And afterward they were all so happy."

"Well," the man said, "if you don't want to you don't have to. I wouldn't have you do it if you didn't want to. But I know it's perfectly simple."

"And you really want to?"

"I think it's the best thing to do. But I don't want you to do it if you don't really want to."

"And if I do it you'll be happy and things will be like they were and you'll love me?"

"I love you now. You know I love you."

"I know. But if I do it, then it will be nice again if I say things are like white elephants, and you'll like it?"

"I'll love it. I love it now but I just can't think about it. You know how I get when I worry."

"If I do it you won't ever worry?"

"I won't worry about that because it's perfectly simple."

"Then I'll do it. Because I don't care about me."

"What do you mean?"

"I don't care about me."

"Well, I care about you."

"Oh, yes. But I don't care about me. And I'll do it and then everything will be fine."

"I don't want you to do it if you feel that way."

The girl stood up and walked to the end of the station. Across, on the other side, were fields of grain and trees along the banks of the Ebro. Far away, beyond the river, were mountains. The shadow of a cloud moved across the field of grain and she saw the river through the trees.

"And we could have all this," she said. "And we could have everything and every day we make it more impossible."

"What did you say?"

"I said we could have everything."

"We can have everything."

"No, we can't."

"We can have the whole world."

"No, we can't."

"We can go everywhere."

"No, we can't. It isn't ours any more."

"It's ours."

"No, it isn't. And once they take it away, you never get it back."

"But they haven't taken it away."

"We'll wait and see."

"Come on back in the shade," he said. "You mustn't feel that way."

"I don't feel any way," the girl said. "I just know things."

"I don't want you to do anything that you don't want to do ——"

"Nor that isn't good for me," she said. "I know. Could we have another beer?"

"All right. But you've got to realize ——"

"I realize," the girl said. "Can't we maybe stop talking?"

They sat down at the table and the girl looked across at the hills on the dry side of the valley and the man looked at her and at the table.

"You've got to realize," he said, "that I don't want you to do it if you don't want to. I'm perfectly willing to go through with it if it means anything to you."

"Doesn't it mean anything to you? We could get along."

"Of course it does. But I don't want anybody but you. I don't want any one else. And I know it's perfectly simple."

"Yes, you know it's perfectly simple."

"It's all right for you to say that, but I do know it."

"Would you do something for me now?"

"I'd do anything for you."

"Would you please please please please please please please stop talking?"

He did not say anything but looked at the bags against the wall of the station. There were labels on them from all the hotels where they had spent nights.

"But I don't want you to," he said, "I don't care anything about it."

"I'll scream," the girl said.

The woman came out through the curtains with two glasses of beer and put them down on the damp felt pads. "The train comes in five minutes," she said.

"What did she say?" asked the girl.

"That the train is coming in five minutes."

The girl smiled brightly at the woman, to thank her.

"I'd better take the bags over to the other side of the station," the man said. She smiled at him.

"All right. Then come back and we'll finish the beer."

He picked up the two heavy bags and carried them around the station to the other tracks. He looked up the tracks but could not see the train. Coming back, he walked through the barroom, where people waiting for the train were drinking. He drank an Anis at the bar and looked at the people. They were all waiting reasonably for the train. He went out through the bead curtain. She was sitting at the table and smiled at him.

"Do you feel better?" he asked.

"I feel fine," she said. "There's nothing wrong with me. I feel fine."

Arna Bontemps

A Summer Tragedy

Arna Bontemps was born in Louisiana in 1902 to Creole parents, the origin of the dialect he later employed in some of his fiction and verse. His father was a mason, his mother a teacher, and it was she who instilled in her son a lifelong love of literature. Educated at Pacific Union College, from which he graduated in 1923, he later took a masters degree in library science from the University of

Chicago. One of the prominent members of the Harlem Renaissance, he numbered among his friends such luminaries as Langston Hughes, Willa Cather, Jean Toomer, Katherine Anne Porter, Claude McKay, and Countee Cullen. Early in his career he taught at Harlem Academy, which put him in association with the urban literati, but in 1931 he moved to Oakwood Junior College in Huntsville, Alabama, where he wrote much of his important early work. A novel, *God Sends Sunday*, appeared that year, and "A Summer Tragedy" was published by *Opportunity* in 1933, winning the fiction award that year from the magazine, which stressed African American literature. Bontemps went on to become head librarian at Fisk University, where he developed extensive materials in black culture, but late in life he accepted a position at Yale University as curator of the James Weldon Johnson Collection. Bontemps earned wide recognition for his erudition and contributions to American culture, including the Alexander Pushkin Poetry Prize, a Guggenheim Fellowship, and a Rosenwald Fellowship, and he was celebrated as a humanitarian who sought dignity and freedom for people of all races and backgrounds. "A Summer Tragedy," his most frequently anthologized story, grows out of his Alabama experience, where he witnessed the hopeless poverty of people trapped in sharecropper farming, forever indebted to the landowner for the necessities of life. In this case, the protagonist, Jeff Patton, has had a stroke, and the future does not bode well for his health. His wife, Jennie, is blind, and they find only one way out of their dilemma. Their "trip" recalls the references to crossing Jordan River into heaven contained in folk spirituals, and their car becomes their "chariot," carrying them home to a better world than they have ever known.

Arna Bontemps, "A Summer Tragedy," *Opportunity* 11 (June 1933): 174–77, 190.

Old Jeff Patton, the black share farmer, fumbled with his bow tie. His fingers trembled and the high stiff collar pinched his throat. A fellow loses his hand for such vanities after thirty or forty years of simple life. Once a year, or maybe twice if there's a wedding among his kinfolks, he may spruce up; but generally fancy clothes do nothing but adorn the wall of the big room and feed the moths. That had been Jeff Patton's experience. He had not worn his stiff-bosomed shirt more than a dozen times in all his married life. His swallow-tailed coat lay on the bed beside him, freshly brushed and pressed, but it was as full of holes as the overalls, in which he worked on weekdays. The moths had used it badly. Jeff twisted his mouth into a hideous toothless grimace as he contended with the obstinate bow. He stamped his good foot and decided to give up the struggle.

"Jennie," he called.

"What's that, Jeff?" His wife's shrunken voice came out of the adjoining room like an echo. It was hardly bigger than a whisper.

"I reckon you'll have to he'p me wid this heah bow tie, baby," he said meekly. "Dog if I can hitch it up."

Her answer was not strong enough to reach him, but presently the old woman came to the door, feeling her way with a stick. She had a wasted, dead-leaf appearance. Her body, as scrawny and gnarled as a string bean, seemed less than nothing in the ocean of frayed and faded petticoats that surrounded her. These hung an inch or two above the tops of her heavy unlaced shoes and showed little grotesque piles where the stocking had fallen down from her negligible legs.

"You oughta could do a heap mo' wid a thing like that'n me — beingst as you got yo' good sight."

"Looks like I oughta could," he admitted. "But ma fingers is gone democrat on me. I get all mixed up in the looking glass an' can't tell wicha way to twist the devilish thing."

Jennie sat on the side of the bed and old Jeff Patton got down on one knee while she tied the bow knot. It was a slow and painful ordeal for each of them in this position. Jeff's bones cracked, his knee ached, and it was only after a half dozen attempts that Jennie worked a semblance of a bow into the tie.

"I got to dress maself now," the old woman whispered. "These is ma old shoes an' stockings, and I ain't so much as unwrapped ma dress."

"Well, don't worry 'bout me no mo', baby," Jeff said. "That 'bout finishes me. All I gotta do now is slip on that old coat 'n ves' an' I'll be fixed to leave."

Jennie disappeared again through the dim passage into the shed room. Being blind was no handicap to her in that black hole. Jeff heard the cane placed against the wall beside the door and knew that his wife was on easy ground. He put on his coat, took a battered top hat from the bedpost and hobbled to the front door. He was ready to travel. As soon as Jennie could get on her Sunday shoes and her old black silk dress, they would start.

Outside the tiny log house, the day was warm and mellow with sunshine. A host of wasps were humming with busy excitement in the trunk of a dead sycamore. Gray squirrels were searching through the grass for hickory nuts an blue jays were in the trees, hopping from branch to branch. Pine woods stretched away to the left like a black sea. Among them were scattered scores of log houses like Jeff's, houses of black share farmers. Cows and pigs wandered freely among the trees. There was no danger of loss. Each farmer knew his own stock and knew his neighbor's as well as he knew his neighbor's children.

Down the slope to the right were the cultivated acres on which the colored folks worked. They extended to the river, more than two miles away, and they were today green with the unmade cotton crop. A tiny thread of a road, which passed directly in front of Jeff's place, ran through these green fields like a pencil mark.

Jeff, standing outside the door, with his absurd hat in his left hand, surveyed the wide scene tenderly. He had been forty-five years on these acres. He loved them with the unexplained affection that others have for the countries to which they belong.

The sun was hot on his head, his collar still pinched his throat, and the Sunday clothes were intolerably hot. Jeff transfered the hat to his right hand and began fanning with it. Suddenly the whisper that was Jennie's voice came out of the shed room.

"You can bring the car round front whilst you's waitin'," it said feebly. There was a tired pause; then it added, "I'll soon be fixed to go."

"A'right, baby," Jeff answered. "I'll get it in a minute."

But he didn't move. A thought struck him that made his mouth fall open. The mention of the car brought to his mind, with new intensity, the trip he and Jennie were about to take. Fear came into his eyes; excitement took his breath. Lord Jesus!

"Jeff . . . . O Jeff," the old woman's whisper called.

He awakened with a jolt. "Hunh, baby?"

"What you doin'?"

"Nuthin. Jes studyin'. I jes been turnin' thing round 'n round in ma mind."

"You could be gettin' the car," she said.

"Oh yes, right away, baby."

He started round to the shed, limping heavily on his bad leg. There were three frizzly chickens in the yard. All his other chickens had been killed or stolen recently. But the frizzly chickens had been saved somehow. That was fortunate indeed, for these curious creatures had a way of devouring "poison" from the yard and in that way protecting against cunjure and bad luck and spells. But even the frizzly chickens seemed now to be in a stupor. Jeff thought they had some ailment; he expected all three of them to die shortly.

The shed in which the old T-model Ford stood was only a grass roof held up by four corner poles. It had been built by tremulous hands at a time when the little rattle trap car had been regarded as a peculiar treasure. And, miraculously, despite wind and downpour, it still stood.

Jeff adjusted the crank and put his weight upon it. The engine came to life with a sputter and bang that rattled the old car from radiator to tail light. Jeff hopped into the seat and put his foot on the accelerator. The sputtering and banging increased. The rattling became more violent. That was good. It was good banging, good sputtering and rattling, and it meant that the aged car was still in running condition. She could be depended on for this trip.

Again Jeff's thought halted as if paralyzed. The suggestion of the trip fell into the machinery of his mind like a wrench. He felt dazed and weak. He swung the car out into the yard, made a half turn and drove around to the front door.

When he took his hands off the wheel, he noticed that he was trembling violently. He cut off the motor and climbed to the ground to wait for Jennie.

A few moments later she was at the window, her voice rattling against the pane like a broken shutter.

"I'm ready, Jeff."

He did not answer, but limped into the house and took her by the arm. He led her slowly through the big room, down the step and across the yard.

"You reckon I'd oughta lock the do'?" he asked softly.

They stopped and Jennie weighed the question. Finally she shook her head.

"Ne' mind the do'," she said. "I don't see no cause to lock up things."

"You right," Jeff agreed. "No cause to lock up."

Jeff opened the door and helped his wife into the car. A quick shudder passed over him. Jesus! Again he trembled.

"How come you shaking so?" Jennie whispered.

"I don't know," he said.

"You mus' be scairt, Jeff."

"No, baby, I ain't scairt."

He slammed the door after her and went around to crank up again. The motor started easily. Jeff wished that it had not been so responsive. He would have liked a few more minutes in which to turn things around in his head. As it was, with Jennie chiding him about being afraid, he had to keep going. He swung the car into the little pencil-mark road and started off toward the river, driving very slowly, very cautiously.

Chugging across the green countryside, the small battered Ford seemed tiny indeed. Jeff felt a familiar excitement, a thrill, as they came down the first slope to the immense levels on which the cotton was growing. He could not help reflecting that the crops were good. He knew what that meant, too; he had made forty-five of them with his own hands. It was true that he had worn out nearly a dozen mules, but that was the fault of old man Stevenson, the owner of the land. Major Stevenson had the odd notion that one mule was all a share farmer needed to work a thirty-acre plot. It was an expensive notion, the way it killed mules from over work, but the old man held to it. Jeff thought it killed a good many share farmers as well as mules, but he had no sympathy for them. He had always been strong, and he had been taught to have no patience with weakness in men. Women or children might be tolerated if they were puny, but a weak man was a curse. Of course, his own children —

Jeff's thought halted there. He and Jennie never mentioned their dead children anymore. And naturally, he did not wish to dwell upon them in his mind. Before he knew it, some remark would slip out of his mouth and that would make Jennie feel blue. Perhaps she would cry. A woman like Jennie could not easily throw off the grief that comes from loosing five grown children within two years. Even Jeff was still staggered by the blow. His memory had not been much good recently. He frequently talked to himself. And, although he had kept it a secret, he knew that his courage had left him. He was terrified by the least unfamiliar sound at night. He was reluctant to venture far from home in the daytime. And that habit of trembling when he felt fearful was now far beyond his control. Sometimes he became afraid and trembled without knowing what had frightened him. The feeling would just come over him like a chill.

The car rattled slowly over the dusty road. Jennie sat erect and silent with a little absurd hat pinned to her hair. Her useless eyes seemed very large, very white in their deep sockets. Suddenly Jeff heard her voice, and he inclined his head to catch the words.

"Is we passed Delia Moore's house yet?" she asked.

"Not yet," he said.

"You must be drivin' mighty slow, Jeff."

"We jes as well take our time, baby."

There was a pause. A little puff of steam was coming out of the radiator of the car. Heat wavered above the hood. Delia Moore's house was nearly half a mile away. After a moment Jennie spoke again.

"You ain't really scairt, is you, Jeff?"

"Nah, baby, I ain't scairt."

"You know how we agreed — we gotta keep on goin.'"

Jewels of perspiration appeared on Jeff's forehead. His eyes rounded, blinked, became fixed on the road.

"I don't know," he said with a shiver, "I reckon it's the only thing to do."

"Hm."

A flock of guinea fowls, pecking in the road, were scattered by the passing car. Some of them took to their wings; others hid under bushes. A blue jay, swaying on a leafy twig, was annoying a roadside squirrel. Jeff held an even speed till he came near Delia's place. Then he slowed down noticeably.

Delia's house was really no house at all, but an abandoned store building converted into a dwelling. It sat near a crossroads, beneath a single black cedar tree. There Delia, a catish old creature of Jennie's age, lived alone. She had been there more years than anybody could remember, and long ago had won the disfavor of such women as Jennie. For in her young days Delia had been gayer, yellower and saucier than seemed proper in those parts. Her ways with menfolks had been dark and suspicious. And the fact that she had had as many husbands as children did not help her reputation.

"Yonder's old Delia," Jeff said as they passed.

"What she doin'?"

"Jes sittin' in the do'," he said.

"She see us?"

"Hm," Jeff said. "Musta did."

That relieved Jennie. It strengthened her to know that her old enemy had seen her pass in her best clothes. That would give the old she-devil something to chew her gums and fret about, Jennie thought. Wouldn't she have a fit if she didn't find out? Old evil Delia! This would be just the thing for her. It would pay her back for being so evil. It would also pay her, Jennie thought, for the way she used to grin at Jeff — long ago when her teeth were good.

The road became smooth and red, and Jeff could tell by the smell of the air that they were nearing the river. He could see the rise where the road turned and ran along parallel to the stream. The car chugged on monotonously. After a long silent spell, Jennie leaned against Jeff and spoke.

"How many bale o' cotton you think we got standin'?" she said.

Jeff wrinkled his forehead as he calculated.

"'Bout twenty-five, I reckon."

"How many you make las' year?"

"Twenty-eight," he said. "How come you ask that?"

"I's jes thinkin'," Jennie said quietly.

"It don't make a speck o' diff'ence though," Jeff reflected. "If we get much or if we get little, we still gonna be in debt to old man Stevenson when he gets through counting up again us. It's took us a long time to learn that."

Jennie was not listening to these words. She had fallen into a trance-like meditation. Her lips twitched. She chewed her gums and rubbed her old gnarled hands nervously. Suddenly, she leaned forward, buried her face in the nervous hands and burst into tears. She cried aloud in a dry cracked voice that suggested the rattle of fodder on dead stalks. She cried aloud like a child, for she had never learned to suppress a genuine sob. Her slight old frame shook heavily and seemed hardly able to sustain such violent grief.

"What's the matter, baby?" Jeff asked awkwardly. "Why you cryin' like all that?"

"I's jes thinkin'," she said.

"So you the one what's scairt now, hunh?"

"I ain't scairt, Jeff. I's jes tinkin' 'bout leavin' eve'thing like this — eve'thing we been used to. It's right sad-like."

Jeff did not answer, and presently Jennie buried her face again and cried.

The sun was almost overhead. It beat down furiously on the dusty wagon path road, on the parched roadside grass and the tiny battered car. Jeff's hands, gripping the wheels, became wet with perspiration; his forehead sparkled. Jeff's lips parted. His mouth shaped a hideous grimace. His face suggested the face of a man being burned. But the torture passed and his expression softened again.

"You mustn't cry, baby," he said to his wife. "We gotta be strong. We can't break down."

Jennie waited a few seconds, then said, "You reckon we oughta do it, Jeff? You reckon we oughta go 'head an' do it, really?"

Jeff's voice choked; his eyes blurred. He was terrified to hear Jennie say the thing that had been in his mind all morning. She had egged him on when he had wanted more than anything in the world to wait, to reconsider, and think things over a little longer. Now *she* was getting cold feet. Actually, there was no need of thinking the question through again. It would only end in making the same painful decision once more. Jeff knew that. There was no need of fooling around longer.

"We jes as well to do like we planned," he said. "They ain't nothin' else for us now — it's the bes' thing."

Jeff thought of the handicaps, the near impossibility of making another crop with his leg bothering him more and more each week. Then there was always the chance that he would have another stroke, like the one that had made him lame. Another one might kill him. The least it could do would be to leave him helpless. Jeff gasped . . . . Lord, Jesus! He could not bear to think of being helpless, like a baby, on Jennie's hands. Frail, blind Jennie.

The little pounding motor of the car worked harder and harder. The puff of steam from the cracked radiator became larger. Jeff realized that they were climbing a little rise. A moment later the road turned abruptly and he looked down upon the face of the river.

"Jeff."

"Hunh?"

"Is that the water I hear?"

"Hm. Tha's it."

"Well, which way you goin' now?"

"Down this-a way," he said. "The road runs 'long 'side' o' the water a lil piece."

She waited a while calmly. Then she said, "Drive faster."

"A'right, baby," Jeff said.

The water roared in the bed of the river. It was fifty or sixty feet below the level of the road. Between the road and the water there was a long smooth slope, sharply inclined. The slope was dry, the clay hardened by prolonged summer heat. The water below, roaring in a narrow channel, was noisy and wild.

"Jeff."

"Hunh?"

"How far you goin'?"

"Jes a lil piece down the road."

"You ain't scairt is you, Jeff?"

"Nah, baby," he said trembling. "I ain't scairt."

"Remember how we planned it, Jeff. We gotta do it like we said. Brave-like."

"Hm."

Jeff's brain darkened. Things suddenly seemed unreal, like figures in a dream. Thoughts swam in his mind foolishly, hysterically, like little blind fish in a pool within a dense cave. They rushed, crossed one another, jostled, collided, retreated and rushed again. Jeff soon became dizzy. He shuddered violently and turned to his wife.

"Jennie, I can't do it. I can't." His voice broke pitifully.

She did not appear to be listening. All the grief had gone from her face. She sat erect, her unseeing eyes wide open, strained and frightful. Her glossy black skin had become dull. She seemed as thin, as sharp and bony, as a starved bird. Now, having suffered and endured the sadness of tearing herself away from beloved things, she showed no anguish. She was absorbed with her own thoughts, and she didn't even hear Jeff's voice shouting in her ear.

Jeff said nothing more. For an instant there was light in his cavernous brain. The great chamber was, for less than a second, peopled by characters he knew and loved. They were simple, healthy creatures, and they behaved in a manner that he could understand. They had quality. But since he had already taken leave of them long ago, the remembrance did not break his heart again. Young Jeff Patton was among them, the Jeff Patton of fifty years ago who went down to New Orleans with a crowd of country boys to the *Mardi Gras* doings. The gay young crowd, boys with candy-striped shirts and rouged-brown girls in noisy silks, was like a picture in his head. Yet it did not make him sad. On that very trip Slim Burns had killed Joe Beasley — the crowd had been broken up. Since then Jeff Patton's world had been the Greenbriar Plantation. If there had been other *Mardi Gras* carnivals, he had not heard of them. Since then there had been no time; the years had fallen on him like waves. Now he was old, worn out. Another paralytic stroke (like the one he had already suffered) would put him on his back for keeps. In that condition, with a frail blind woman to look after him, he would be worse off than if he were dead.

Suddenly Jeff's hands became steady. He actually felt brave. He slowed down the motor of the car and carefully pulled off the road. Below, the water of the stream boomed, a soft thunder in the deep channel. Jeff ran the car onto the clay slope, pointed it directly toward the stream and put his foot heavily on the accelerator. The little car leaped furiously down the steep incline toward the water. The movement was nearly as swift and direct as a fall. The two old black folks, sitting quietly side by side, showed no excitement. In another instant the car hit the water and dropped immediately out of sight.

A little later it lodged in the mud of a shallow place. One wheel of the crushed and upturned little Ford became visible above the rushing water.

John Steinbeck
The Chrysanthemums

John Steinbeck, who won the Nobel Prize for literature in 1962, is justly regarded as one of the great novelists of the twentieth century, especially with regard to his masterpiece, *The Grapes of Wrath*. But his short fiction is also among the finest in the genre, especially "The Red Pony," "The Harness," and the opening segment of *The Long Valley*, "The Chrysanthemums." Steinbeck's work is essentially Naturalistic, depicting downtrodden characters trapped in circumstances they are powerless to change or escape. That idea is at the heart of this story, in which a farm wife reveals the depth of her submerged life as well as her longing to express more of what is inside her and explore her full potential for love and fulfillment. The hopelessness of her plight is revealed in her desperate hope that she might escape with the tradesman who visits her farm and who feigns interest in horticulture. The imagery throughout ties the woman to the natural world (she is at one point described as a "fawning dog"), and she has the capacity for affection, passion, and beauty, qualities the final line suggests will never be fully expressed.

John Steinbeck, "The Chrysanthemums," *The Long Valley* (New York: Viking Press, 1938), 3–18.

The high grey-flannel fog of winter closed off the Salinas Valley from the sky and from all the rest of the world. On every side it sat like a lid on the mountains and made of the great valley a closed pot. On the broad, level land floor the gang plows bit deep and left the black earth shining like metal where the shares had cut. On the foothill ranches across the Salinas River, the yellow stubble fields seemed to be bathed in pale cold sunshine, but there was no sunshine in the valley now in December. The thick willow scrub along the river flamed with sharp and positive yellow leaves.

It was a time of quiet and waiting. The air was cold and tender. A light wind blew up from the southwest so that the farmers were mildly hopeful of a good rain before long; but fog and rain do not go together.

Across the river, on Henry Allen's foothill ranch there was little work to be done, for the hay was cut and stored and the orchards were plowed up to receive the rain deeply when it should come. The cattle on the higher slopes were becoming shaggy and rough-coated.

Elisa Allen, working in her flower garden, looked down across the yard and saw Henry, her husband, talking to two men in business suits. The three of them stood by the tractor shed, each man with one foot on the side of the little Fordson. They smoked cigarettes and studied the machine as they talked.

Elisa watched them for a moment and then went back to her work. She was thirty-five. Her face was lean and strong and her eyes were as clear as water. Her figure looked blocked and heavy in her gardening costume, a man's black hat pulled low down over her eyes, clodhopper shoes, a figured print dress almost completely covered by a big corduroy apron with four big pockets to hold the snips, the trowel and scratcher, the seeds and the knife she worked with. She wore heavy leather gloves to protect her hands while she worked.

She was cutting down the old year's chrysanthemum stalks with a pair of short and powerful scissors. She looked down toward the men by the tractor shed now and then. Her face was eager and mature and handsome; even her work with the scissors was over-eager, over-powerful. The chrysanthemum stems seemed too small and easy for her energy.

She brushed a cloud of hair out of her eyes with the back of her glove, and left a smudge of earth on her cheek in doing it. Behind her stood the neat white farm house with red geraniums close-banked around it as high as the windows. It was a hard-swept looking little house with hard-polished windows, and a clean mud-mat on the front steps.

Elisa cast another glance toward the tractor shed. The strangers were getting into their Ford coupe. She took off a glove and put her strong fingers down into the forest of new green chrysanthemum sprouts that were growing around the old roots. She spread the leaves and looked down among the close-growing stems. No aphids were there, no sowbugs or snails or cutworms. Her terrier fingers destroyed such pests before they could get started.

Elisa started at the sound of her husband's voice. He had come near quietly, and he leaned over the wire fence that protected her flower garden from cattle and dogs and chickens.

"At it again," he said. "You've got a strong new crop coming."

Elisa straightened her back and pulled on the gardening glove again. "Yes. They'll be strong this coming year." In her tone and on her face there was a little smugness.

"You've got a gift with things," Henry observed. "Some of those yellow chrysanthemums you had this year were ten inches across. I wish you'd work out in the orchard and raise some apples that big."

Her eyes sharpened. "Maybe I could do it, too. I've a gift with things, all right. My mother had it. She could stick anything in the ground and make it grow. She said it was having planters' hands that knew how to do it."

"Well, it sure works with flowers," he said.

"Henry, who were those men you were talking to?"

"Why, sure, that's what I came to tell you. They were from the Western Meat Company. I sold those thirty head of three-year-old steers. Got nearly my own price, too."

"Good," she said. "Good for you."

"And I thought," he continued, "I thought how it's Saturday afternoon, and we might go into Salinas for dinner at a restaurant, and then to a picture-show — to celebrate, you see."

"Good," she repeated. "Oh, yes. That will be good."

Henry put on his joking tone. "There's fights tonight. How'd you like to go to the fights?"

"Oh, no," she said, breathlessly. "No, I wouldn't like fights."

"Just fooling, Elisa. We'll go to a movie. Let's see. It's two now. I'm going to take Scotty and bring down those steers from the hill. It'll take us maybe two hours. We'll go in town about five and have dinner at the Cominos Hotel. Like that?"

"Of course I'll like it. It's good to eat away from home."

"All right, then. I'll go get up a couple of horses."

She said, "I'll have plenty of time to transplant some of these sets, I guess."

She heard her husband calling Scotty down by the barn. And a little later she saw the two men ride up the pale yellow hillside in search of the steers.

There was a little square sandy bed kept for rooting the chrysanthemums. With her trowel she turned the soil over and over, and smoothed it and patted it firm. Then she dug ten parallel trenches to receive the sets. Back at the chrysanthemum bed she pulled out the little crisp shoots, trimmed off the leaves of each one with her scissors and laid it on a small orderly pile.

A squeak of wheels and plod of hoofs came from the road. Elisa looked up. The country road ran along the dense bank of willows and cottonwoods that bordered the river, and up this road came a curious vehicle, curiously drawn. It was an old spring-wagon, with a round canvas top on it like the cover of a prairie schooner. It was drawn by an old bay horse and a little grey-and-white burro. A big stubble-bearded man sat between the cover flaps and drove the crawling team. Underneath the wagon, between the hind wheels, a lean and rangy mongrel dog walked sedately. Words were painted on the canvas, in clumsy, crooked letters. "Pots, pans, knives, sisors, lawn mores, Fixed." Two rows of articles, and the triumphantly definitive "Fixed" below. The black paint had run down in little sharp points beneath each letter.

Elisa, squatting on the ground, watched to see the crazy, loose-jointed wagon pass by. But it didn't pass. It turned into the farm road in front of her house, crooked old wheels skirling and squeaking. The rangy dog darted from between the wheels and ran ahead. Instantly the two ranch shepherds flew out at him. Then all three stopped, and with stiff and quivering tails, with taut straight legs, with ambassadorial dignity, they slowly circled, sniffing daintily. The caravan pulled up to Elisa's wire fence and stopped. Now the newcomer dog, feeling outnumbered, lowered his tail and retired under the wagon with raised hackles and bared teeth.

The man on the wagon seat called out, "That's a bad dog in a fight when he gets started."

Elisa laughed. "I see he is. How soon does he generally get started?"

The man caught up her laughter and echoed it heartily. "Sometimes not for weeks and weeks," he said. He climbed stiffly down, over the wheel. The horse and the donkey drooped like unwatered flowers.

Elisa saw that he was a very big man. Although his hair and beard were greying, he did not look old. His worn black suit was wrinkled and spotted with grease. The laughter had disappeared from his face and eyes the moment his laughing voice ceased. His eyes were dark, and they were full of the brooding that gets in the eyes of teamsters and of sailors. The calloused hands he rested on the wire fence were cracked, and every crack was a black line. He took off his battered hat.

"I'm off my general road, ma'am," he said. "Does this dirt road cut over across the river to the Los Angeles highway?"

Elisa stood up and shoved the thick scissors in her apron pocket. "Well, yes, it does, but it winds around and then fords the river. I don't think your team could pull through the sand."

He replied with some asperity, "It might surprise you what them beasts can pull through."

"When they get started?" she asked.

He smiled for a second. "Yes. When they get started."

"Well," said Elisa. "I think you'll save time if you go back to the Salinas road and pick up the highway there."

He drew a big finger down the chicken wire and made it sing. "I ain't in any hurry, ma'am. I go from Seattle to San Diego and back every year. Takes all my time. About six months each way. I aim to follow nice weather."

Elisa took off her gloves and stuffed them in the apron pocket with the scissors. She touched the under edge of her man's hat, searching for fugitive hairs. "That sounds like a nice kind of a way to live," she said.

He leaned confidentially over the fence. "Maybe you noticed the writing on my wagon. I mend pots and sharpen knives and scissors. You got any of them things to do?"

"Oh, no," she said quickly. "Nothing like that." Her eyes hardened with resistance.

"Scissors is the worst thing," he explained. "Most people just ruin scissors trying to sharpen 'em, but I know how. I got a special tool. It's a little bobbit kind of thing, and patented. But it sure does the trick."

"No. My scissors are all sharp."

"All right, then. Take a pot," he continued earnestly, "a bent pot, or a pot with a hole. I can make it like new so you don't have to buy no new ones. That's a saving for you."

"No," she said shortly. "I tell you I have nothing like that for you to do."

His face fell to an exaggerated sadness. His voice took on a whining undertone. "I ain't had a thing to do today. Maybe I won't have no supper tonight. You see I'm off my regular road. I know folks on the highway clear from Seattle to San Diego. They save their things for me to sharpen up because they know I do it so good and save them money."

"I'm sorry," Elisa said irritably. "I haven't anything for you to do."

His eyes left her face and fell to searching the ground. They roamed about until they came to the chrysanthemum bed where she had been working. "What's them plants, ma'am?"

The irritation and resistance melted from Elisa's face. "Oh, those are chrysanthemums, giant whites and yellows. I raise them every year, bigger than anybody around here."

"Kind of a long-stemmed flower? Looks like a quick puff of colored smoke?" he asked.

"That's it. What a nice way to describe them."

"They smell kind of nasty till you get used to them," he said.

"It's a good bitter smell," she retorted, "not nasty at all."

He changed his tone quickly. "I like the smell myself."

"I had ten-inch blooms this year," she said.

The man leaned farther over the fence. "Look. I know a lady down the road a piece, has got the nicest garden you ever seen. Got nearly every kind of flower but no chrysanthemums. Last time I was mending a copper-bottom washtub for her (that's a hard job but I do it good), she said to me, 'If you ever run acrost some nice chrysanthemums I wish you'd try to get me a few seeds.' That's what she told me."

Elisa's eyes grew alert and eager. "She couldn't have known much about chrysanthemums. You *can* raise them from seed, but it's much easier to root the little sprouts you see there."

"Oh," he said. "I s'pose I can't take none to her, then."

"Why yes you can," Elisa cried. "I can put some in damp sand, and you can carry them right along with you. They'll take root in the pot if you keep them damp. And then she can transplant them."

"She'd sure like to have some, ma'am. You say they're nice ones?"

"Beautiful," she said. "Oh, beautiful." Her eyes shone. She tore off the battered hat and shook out her dark pretty hair. "I'll put them in a flower pot, and you can take them right with you. Come into the yard."

While the man came through the picket gate Elisa ran excitedly along the geranium-bordered path to the back of the house. And she returned carrying a big red flower pot. The gloves were forgotten now. She kneeled on the ground by the starting bed and dug up the sandy soil with her fingers and scooped it into the bright new flower pot. Then she picked up the little pile of shoots she had prepared. With her strong fingers she pressed them into the sand and tamped around them with her knuckles. The man stood over her. "I'll tell you what to do," she said. "You remember so you can tell the lady."

"Yes, I'll try to remember."

"Well, look. These will take root in about a month. Then she must set them out, about a foot apart in good rich earth like this, see?" She lifted a handful of dark soil for him to look at. "They'll grow fast and tall. Now remember this: In July tell her to cut them down, about eight inches from the ground."

"Before they bloom?" he asked.

"Yes, before they bloom." Her face was tight with eagerness. "They'll grow right up again. About the last of September the buds will start."

She stopped and seemed perplexed. "It's the budding that takes the most care," she said hesitantly. "I don't know how to tell you." She looked deep into his eyes, searchingly. Her mouth opened a little, and she seemed to be listening. "I'll try to tell you," she said. "Did you ever hear of planting hands?"

"Can't say I have, ma'am."

"Well, I can only tell you what it feels like. It's when you're picking off the buds you don't want. Everything goes right down into your fingertips. You watch your fingers work. They do it themselves. You can feel how it is. They pick and pick the buds. They never make a mistake. They're with the plant. Do you see? Your fingers and the plant. You can feel that, right up your arm. They know. They never make a mistake. You can feel it. When you're like that you can't do anything wrong. Do you see that? Can you understand that?"

She was kneeling on the ground looking up at him. Her breast swelled passionately.

The man's eyes narrowed. He looked away self-consciously. "Maybe I know," he said. "Sometimes in the night in the wagon there —"

Elisa's voice grew husky. She broke in on him. "I've never lived as you do, but I know what you mean. When the night is dark — why, the stars are sharp-pointed, and there's quiet. Why, you rise up and up! Every pointed star gets driven into your body. It's like that. Hot and sharp and — lovely."

Kneeling there, her hand went out toward his legs in the greasy black trousers. Her hesitant fingers almost touched the cloth. Then her hand dropped to the ground. She crouched low like a fawning dog.

He said, "It's nice, just like you say. Only when you don't have no dinner, it ain't."

She stood up then, very straight, and her face was ashamed. She held the flower pot out to him and placed it gently in his arms. "Here. Put it in your wagon, on the seat, where you can watch it. Maybe I can find something for you to do."

At the back of the house she dug in the can pile and found two old and battered aluminum saucepans. She carried them back and gave them to him. "Here, maybe you can fix these."

His manner changed. He became professional. "Good as new I can fix them." At the back of his wagon he set a little anvil, and out of an oily tool box dug a small machine hammer. Eliza came through the gate to watch him while he pounded out the dents in the kettles. His mouth grew sure and knowing. At a difficult part of the work he sucked his under-lip.

"You sleep right in the wagon?" Elisa asked.

"Right in the wagon, ma'am. Rain or shine I'm dry as a cow in there."

"It must be nice," she said. "It must be very nice. I wish women could do such things."

"It ain't the right kind of a life for a woman."

Her upper lip raised a little, showing her teeth. "How do you know? How can you tell?" she said.

"I don't know, ma'am," he protested. "Of course I don't know. Now here's your kettles, done. You don't have to buy no new ones."

"How much?"

"Oh, fifty cents'll do. I keep my prices down and my work good. That's why I have all them satisfied customers up and down the highway."

Elisa brought him a fifty-cent piece from the house and dropped it in his hand. "You might be surprised to have a rival some time. I can sharpen scissors, too. And I can beat the dents out of little pots. I could show you what a woman might do."

He put his hammer back in the oily box and shoved the little anvil out of sight. "It would be a lonely life for a woman, ma'am, and a scarey life, too, with animals creeping under the wagon all night." He climbed over the singletree, steadying himself with a hand on the burro's white rump. He settled himself in the seat, picked up the lines. "Thank you kindly, ma'am," he said. "I'll do like you told me; I'll go back and catch the Salinas road."

"Mind," she called, "if you're long in getting there, keep the sand damp."

"Sand, ma'am? . . . Sand? Oh, sure. You mean around the chrysanthemums. Sure I will." He clucked his tongue. The beasts leaned luxuriously into their collars. The mongrel dog took his place between the back wheels. The wagon turned and crawled out the entrance road and back the way it had come, along the river.

Elisa stood in front of her wire fence watching the slow progress of the caravan. Her shoulders were straight, her head thrown back, her eyes half-closed, so that the scene came vaguely into them. Her lips moved silently, forming the words "Good-bye — good-bye." Then she whispered, "That's a bright direction. There's a glowing there." The sound of her whisper startled her. She shook herself free and looked about to see whether anyone had been listening. Only the dogs had heard. They lifted their heads toward her from their sleeping in the dust, and then stretched out their chins and settled asleep again. Elisa turned and ran hurriedly into the house.

In the kitchen she reached behind the stove and felt the water tank. It was full of hot water from the noonday cooking. In the bathroom she tore off her soiled clothes and flung them into the corner. And then she scrubbed herself with a little block of pumice, legs and thighs, loins and chest and arms, until her skin was scratched and red. When she had dried herself she stood in front of the mirror in her bedroom and looked at her body. She tightened her stomach and threw out her chest. She turned and looked over her shoulder at her back.

After a while she began to dress, slowly. She put on her newest underclothing and her nicest stockings and the dress which was the symbol of her prettiness. She worked carefully on her hair, penciled her eyebrows and rouged her lips.

Before she was finished she heard the little thunder of hoofs and the shouts of Henry and his helper as they drove the red steers into the corral. She heard the gate bang shut and set herself for Henry's arrival.

His step sounded on the porch. He entered the house calling, "Elisa, where are you?"

"In my room, dressing. I'm not ready. There's hot water for your bath. Hurry up. It's getting late."

When she heard him splashing in the tub, Elisa laid his dark suit on the bed, and shirt and socks and tie beside it. She stood his polished shoes on the floor beside the bed. Then she went to the porch and sat primly and stiffly down. She looked toward the river road where the willow-line was still yellow with frosted leaves so that under the high grey fog they seemed a thin band of sunshine. This was the only color in the grey afternoon. She sat unmoving for a long time. Her eyes blinked rarely.

Henry came banging out of the door, shoving his tie inside his vest as he came. Elisa stiffened and her face grew tight. Henry stopped short and looked at her. "Why — why, Elisa. You look so nice!"

"Nice? You think I look nice? What do you mean by 'nice'?"

Henry blundered on. "I don't know. I mean you look different, strong and happy."

"I am strong? Yes, strong. What do you mean 'strong'?"

He looked bewildered. "You're playing some kind of a game," he said helplessly. "It's a kind of a play. You look strong enough to break a calf over your knee, happy enough to eat it like a watermelon."

For a second she lost her rigidity. "Henry! Don't talk like that. You didn't know what you said." She grew complete again. "I'm strong," she boasted. "I never knew before how strong."

Henry looked down toward the tractor shed, and when he brought his eyes back to her, they were his own again. "I'll get out the car. You can put on your coat while I'm starting."

Elisa went into the house. She heard him drive to the gate and idle down his motor, and then she took a long time to put on her hat. She pulled it here and pressed it there. When Henry turned the motor off she slipped into her coat and went out.

The little roadster bounced along on the dirt road by the river, raising the birds and driving the rabbits into the brush. Two cranes flapped heavily over the willow-line and dropped into the river-bed.

Far ahead on the road Elisa saw a dark speck. She knew.

She tried not to look as they passed it, but her eyes would not obey. She whispered to herself sadly, "He might have thrown them off the road. That wouldn't have been much trouble, not very much. But he kept the pot," she explained. "He had to keep the pot. That's why he couldn't get them off the road."

The roadster turned a bend and she saw the caravan ahead. She swung full around toward her husband so she could not see the little covered wagon and the mismatched team as the car passed them.

In a moment it was over. The thing was done. She did not look back.

She said loudly, to be heard above the motor, "It will be good, tonight, a good dinner."

"Now you've changed again," Henry complained. He took one hand from the wheel and patted her knee. "I ought to take you in to dinner oftener. It would be good for both of us. We get so heavy out on the ranch."

"Henry," she asked, "could we have wine at dinner?"

"Sure we could. Say! That will be fine."

She was silent for a while; then she said, "Henry, at those prize fights, do the men hurt each other very much?"

"Sometimes a little, not often. Why?"

"Well, I've read how they break noses, and blood runs down their chests. I've read how the fighting gloves get heavy and soggy with blood."

He looked around at her. "What's the matter, Elisa? I didn't know you read things like that." He brought the car to a stop, then turned to the right over the Salinas River bridge.

"Do any women ever go to the fights?" she asked.

"Oh, sure, some. What's the matter, Elisa? Do you want to go? I don't think you'd like it, but I'll take you if you really want to go."

She relaxed limply in the seat. "Oh, no. No. I don't want to go. I'm sure I don't." Her face was turned away from him. "It will be enough if we can have wine. It will be plenty." She turned up her coat collar so he could not see that she was crying weakly — like an old woman.

James Thurber
The Secret Life of Walter Mitty

James Thurber's most famous short story, "The Secret Life of Walter Mitty," first appeared in *The New Yorker* in 1939 prior to inclusion in *My World — and Welcome to It* in 1942. Thurber was the most celebrated American humorist of the twentieth century, and "Walter Mitty" contains the essence of his comic stance. His standard character is an ineffectual, urban man whose ineptitude makes even mundane tasks insurmountable. His domineering wife, who dictates every aspect of his daily life, further humiliates him at every turn. Mitty finds it difficult to drive a car, impossible to install snow chains, and beyond him to earn the approval of his spouse. He bristles at her suggestion that he purchase overshoes, but he does as he has been instructed. His compensatory fantasy world gives him the courage, stature, and satisfaction reality denies him, and the five brief daydreams in which he imagines himself in heroic circumstances are all derived from the stereotypes of film and the popular culture of the 1930s.

James Thurber, "The Secret Life of Walter Mitty," *The New Yorker* 15 (March 18, 1939): 19–20.

"We're going through!" The Commander's voice was like thin ice breaking. He wore his full-dress uniform, with the heavily braided white cap pulled down rakishly over one cold gray eye. "We can't make it, sir. It's spoiling for a hurricane, if you ask me." "I'm not asking you, Lieutenant Berg," said the Commander. "Throw on the power lights! Rev her up to 8,500! We're going through!" The pounding of the cylinders increased: ta-pocketa-pocketa-pocketa-*pocketa-pocketa*. The Commander stared at the ice forming on the pilot window. He walked over and twisted a row of complicated dials. "Switch on No. 8 auxiliary!" he shouted. "Switch on No. 8 auxiliary!" repeated Lieutenant Berg. "Full strength in No. 3 turret!" shouted the Commander. "Full strength in No. 3 turret!" The crew, bending to their various tasks in the huge, hurtling eight-engined Navy hydroplane, looked at each other and grinned. "The Old Man'll get us through," they said to one another. "The Old Man ain't afraid of Hell!" . . .

"Not so fast! You're driving too fast!" said Mrs. Mitty. "What are you driving so fast for?"

"Hmm?" said Walter Mitty. He looked at his wife, in the seat beside him, with shocked astonishment. She seemed grossly unfamiliar, like a strange woman who had yelled at him in a crowd. "You were up to fifty-five," she said. "You know I don't like to go more than forty. You were up to fifty-five." Walter Mitty drove on toward Waterbury in silence, the roaring of the SN202 through the worst storm in twenty years of Navy flying fading in the remote, intimate airways of his mind. "You're tensed up again," said Mrs. Mitty. "It's one of your days. I wish you'd let Dr. Renshaw look you over."

Walter Mitty stopped the car in front of the building where his wife went to have her hair done. "Remember to get those overshoes while I'm having my hair done," she said. "I don't need overshoes," said Mitty. She put her mirror back into her bag. "We've been all through that," she said, getting out of the car. "You're not a young man any longer." He raced the engine a little. "Why don't you wear your gloves? Have you lost your gloves?" Walter Mitty reached in a pocket and brought out the gloves. He put them on, but after she had turned and gone into the building and he had driven on to a red light, he took them off again. "Pick it up, brother!" snapped a cop as the light changed, and Mitty hastily pulled on his gloves and lurched ahead. He drove around the streets aimlessly for a time, and then he drove past the hospital on his way to the parking lot.

. . . . "It's the millionaire banker, Wellington McMillan," said the pretty nurse. "Yes?" said Walter Mitty, removing his gloves slowly. "Who has the case?" "Dr. Renshaw and Dr. Benbow, but there are two specialists here, Dr. Remington from New York and Dr. Pritchard-Mitford from London. He flew over." A door opened down a long, cool corridor and Dr. Renshaw came out. He looked distraught and haggard. "Hello, Mitty," he said. "We're having the devil's own time with McMillan, the millionaire banker and close personal friend of Roosevelt. Obstreosis of the ductal tract. Tertiary. Wish you'd take a look at him." "Glad to," said Mitty.

In the operating room there were whispered introductions: "Dr. Remington, Dr. Mitty. Dr. Pritchard-Mitford, Dr. Mitty." "I've read your book on streptothricosis," said Pritchard-Mitford, shaking hands. "A brilliant performance, sir."

"Thank you," said Walter Mitty. "Didn't know you were in the States, Mitty," grumbled Remington. "Coals to Newcastle, bringing Mitford and me up here for a tertiary." "You are very kind," said Mitty. A huge, complicated machine, connected to the operating table, with many tubes and wires, began at this moment to go pocketa-pocketa-pocketa. "The new anaesthetizer is giving way!" shouted an interne. "There is no one in the East who knows how to fix it!" "Quiet, man!" said Mitty, in a low, cool voice. He sprang to the machine, which was now going pocketa-pocketa-queep-pocketa-queep. He began fingering delicately a row of glistening dials. "Give me a fountain pen!" he snapped. Someone handed him a fountain pen. He pulled a faulty piston out of the machine and inserted the pen in its place. "That will hold for ten minutes," he said. "Get on with the operation." A nurse hurried over and whispered to Renshaw, and Mitty saw the man turn pale. "Coreopsis has set in," said Renshaw nervously. "If you would take over, Mitty?" Mitty looked at him and at the craven figure of Benbow, who drank, and at the grave, uncertain faces of the two great specialists. "If you wish," he said. They slipped a white gown on him; he adjusted a mask and drew on thin gloves; nurses handed him shining . . .

"Back it up, Mac! Look out for that Buick!" Walter Mitty jammed on the brakes. "Wrong lane, Mac," said the parking-lot attendant, looking at Mitty closely. "Gee. Yeh," muttered Mitty. He began cautiously to back out of the lane marked "Exit Only." "Leave her sit there," said the attendant. "I'll put her away." Mitty got out of the car. "Hey, better leave the key." "Oh," said Mitty, handing the man the ignition key. The attendant vaulted into the car, backed it up with insolent skill, and put it where it belonged.

They're so damn cocky, thought Walter Mitty, walking along Main Street; they think they know everything. Once he had tried to take his chains off, outside New Milford, and he had got them wound around the axles. A man had had to come out in a wrecking car and unwind them, a young, grinning garageman. Since then Mrs. Mitty always made him drive to a garage to have the chains taken off. The next time, he thought, I'll wear my right arm in a sling; they won't grin at me then. I'll have my right arm in a sling and they'll see I couldn't possibly take the chains off myself. He kicked at the slush on the sidewalk. "Overshoes," he said to himself, and he began looking for a shoe store.

When he came out into the street again, with the overshoes in a box under his arm, Walter Mitty began to wonder what the other thing was his wife had told him to get. She had told him, twice, before they set out from their house for Waterbury. In a way he hated these weekly trips to town — he was always getting something wrong. Kleenex, he thought, Squibb's, razor blades? No. Toothpaste, toothbrush, bicarbonate, carborundum, initiative and referendum? He gave it up. But she would remember it. "Where's the what's-its-name?" she would ask. "Don't tell me you forgot the what's-its-name." A newsboy went by shouting something about the Waterbury trial.

. . . . "Perhaps this will refresh your memory." The District Attorney suddenly thrust a heavy automatic at the quiet figure on the witness stand. "Have you ever seen this before?" Walter Mitty took the gun and examined it expertly. "This is my Webley-Vickers 50.80," he said calmly. An excited buzz ran around the courtroom. The Judge rapped for order. "You are a crack shot with any sort of firearms, I believe?" said the District Attorney, insinuatingly. "Objection!" shouted Mitty's attorney. "We have shown that the defendant could not have fired the shot. We have shown that he wore his right arm in a sling on the night of the fourteenth of July." Walter Mitty raised his hand briefly and the bickering attorneys were stilled. "With any known make of gun," he said evenly, "I could have killed Gregory Fitzhurst at three hundred feet *with my left hand*." Pandemonium broke loose in the courtroom. A woman's scream rose above the bedlam and suddenly a lovely, dark-haired girl was in Walter Mitty's arms. The District Attorney struck at her savagely. Without rising from his chair, Mitty let the man have it on the point of the chin. "You miserable cur!". . .

"Puppy biscuit," said Walter Mitty. He stopped walking and the buildings of Waterbury rose up out of the misty courtroom and surrounded him again. A woman who was passing laughed. "He said 'Puppy biscuit,'" she said to her companion. "That man said 'Puppy biscuit' to himself." Walter Mitty hurried on. He went into an A. & P., not the first one he came to but a smaller one farther up the street. "I want some biscuit for small, young dogs," he said to the clerk. "Any special brand, sir?" The greatest pistol shot in the world thought a moment. "It says 'Puppies Bark for It' on the box," said Walter Mitty.

♕

His wife would be through at the hairdresser's in fifteen minutes, Mitty saw in looking at his watch, unless they had trouble drying it; sometimes they had trouble drying it. She didn't like to get to the hotel first; she would want him to be there waiting for her as usual. He found a big leather chair in the lobby, facing a window, and he put the overshoes and the puppy biscuit on the floor beside it. He picked up an old copy of *Liberty* and sank down into the chair. "Can Germany Conquer the World Through the Air?" Walter Mitty looked at the pictures of bombing planes and of ruined streets.

. . . "The cannonading has got the wind up in young Raleigh, sir," said the sergeant. Captain Mitty looked up at him through touselled hair. "Get him to bed," he said wearily. "With the others. I'll fly alone." "But you can't, sir," said the sergeant anxiously. "It takes two men to handle that bomber and the Archies are pounding hell out of the air. Von Richtman's circus is between here and Saulier." "Somebody's got to get that ammunition dump," said Mitty. "I'm going over. Spot of brandy?" He poured a drink for the sergeant and one for himself. War thundered and whined around the dugout and battered at the door. There was a rending of wood and splinters flew through the room. "A bit of a near thing," said Captain Mitty carelessly. "The box barrage is closing in," said the sergeant. "We only live once, Sergeant," said Mitty, with his faint, fleeting smile. "Or do we?" He poured another brandy and tossed it off. "I never see a man could hold his brandy like you, sir," said the sergeant. "Begging your pardon, sir." Captain Mitty stood up and strapped on his huge Webley-Vickers automatic. "It's forty kilometers through hell, sir," said the sergeant. Mitty finished one last brandy. "After all," he said softly, "what isn't?" The pounding of the cannon increased; there was the rat-tat-tatting of machine guns, and from somewhere came the menacing pocketa-pocketa-pocketa of the new flame-throwers. Walter Mitty walked to the door of the dugout humming "Auprès de Ma Blonde." He turned and waved to the sergeant. "Cheerio!" he said. . . .

Something struck his shoulder. "I've been looking all over this hotel for you," said Mrs. Mitty. "Why do you have to hide in this old chair? How did you expect me to find you?" "Things close in," said Walter Mitty vaguely. "What?" Mrs. Mitty said. "Did you get the what's-its-name? The puppy biscuit? What's in that box?" "Overshoes," said Mitty. "Couldn't you have put them on in the store?" "I was thinking," said Walter Mitty. "Does it ever occur to you that I am sometimes thinking?" She looked at him. "I'm going to take your temperature when I get you home," she said.

§&§

They went out through the revolving doors that made a faintly derisive whistling sound when you pushed them. It was two blocks to the parking lot. At the drugstore on the corner she said, "Wait here for me. I forgot something. I won't be a minute." She was more than a minute. Walter Mitty lighted a cigarette. It began to rain, rain with sleet in it. He stood up against the wall of the drugstore, smoking. . . . He put his shoulders back and his heels together. "To hell with the handkerchief," said Walter Mitty scornfully. He took one last drag on his cigarette and snapped it away. Then, with that faint, fleeting smile playing about his lips, he faced the firing squad; erect and motionless, proud and disdainful, Walter Mitty the Undefeated, inscrutable to the last.

Eudora Welty
Petrified Man

A frequently anthologized story, Eudora Welty's "Petrified Man" first appeared in *The Southern Review* in 1939 prior to its inclusion in *Thirteen Stories* in 1965. Renowned for her skill in depicting southern dialect, Welty here is at her best, capturing a regional idiom that allows characters to reveal themselves at the same time they are gossiping about their neighbors. "Petrified Man" is a good example of the compression of the genre, since it takes place in a confined location during two sessions in a hairdressers shop. The social satire is directed not so much at the unfortunate beings described in the "freak show" but at the socially and morally deformed people who discuss them, the large, appalling women for whom pregnancy is an inconvenient embarrassment. The false presentation of themselves to the world (they dye their hair) is more important than marriage or motherhood. They live in a world of artifice and monstrous bad manners, and it is they who are ethically petrified, not the man in the show.

Eudora Welty, "Petrified Man," *The Southern Review* 4 (Spring 1939): 682–95.

"Reach in my purse and git me a cigarette without no powder in it if you kin, Mrs. Fletcher, honey," said Leota to her ten o'clock shampoo-and-set customer. "I don't like no perfumed cigarettes."

Mrs. Fletcher gladly reached over to the lavender shelf under the lavender-framed mirror, shook a hairnet loose from the clasp of the patent-leather bag, and slapped her hand down quickly on a powder-puff which burst out when the purse was opened.

"Why, look at the peanuts, Leota!" said Mrs. Fletcher in her marveling voice.

"Honey, them goobers has been in my purse a week if they's been in it a day. Mrs. Pike bought them peanuts."

"Who's Mrs. Pike?" asked Mrs. Fletcher, settling back. Hidden in this pretty den of curling fluid and henna packs, separated by a lavender swingdoor from the other customers, who were being gratified in other booths, she could give her curiosity its freedom. She looked expectantly at the black part in Leota's yellow curls as she bent to light the cigarette.

"Mrs. Pike is a lady from New Orleans," said Leota, puffing, and pressing into Mrs. Fletcher's scalp with strong red-nailed fingers. "A friend, not a customer. You see, like maybe I told you last time, me and Fred and Sal and Joe all had us a fuss, so Sal and Joe up and moved out, and we didn't open our mouths, only rented out their room, see. So we rented it to Mrs. Pike. And Mr. Pike." She flicked an ash into the basket of dirty towels. "Mrs. Pike is a very decided blonde. *She* bought me the peanuts."

"She must be cute," said Mrs. Fletcher.

"Honey, cute ain't the word for what she is. I'm tellin' you, Mrs. Pike is attractive. She has her a good time. She's got sharp eyes, Mrs. Pike has."

She dashed the comb through the air, and a cloud of Mrs. Fletcher's hennaed hair floated out of its lavender teeth like a small storm cloud.

"Hair fallin'."

"Aw, Leota!"

"Uh-huh, commencin' to fall out a blue streak," murmured Leota, combing again.

"Is it any dandruff in it?" Mrs. Fletcher was frowning, her hairline eyebrows diving down toward her nose and her wrinkled beady-lashed eyelids batting with concentration.

"Nope."

"Bet it was that last perm'nent you gave me did it," Mrs. Fletcher said cruelly.

"Naw, honey, couldn't be that," said Leota with finality.

"Bound to be somethin'," persisted Mrs. Fletcher. "I couldn'ta caught a thing like that from Mr. Fletcher, could I?"

"Well," Leota answered at last. "You know what I heard in here yestiddy: one of Thelma's ladies was settin' over yonda in Thelma's booth gittin' a perm'nent, and I don't mean to insist or insinuate or anything, Mrs. Fletcher, but Thelma's lady just happ'med to throw out that you was p-r-e-g — , and lots of times that'll make your hair do awful funny, fall out and God knows what all. It just ain't our fault, is the way I look at it."

There was a little pause. The women stared at each other in the mirror.

"Who was it?" demanded Mrs. Fletcher grimly.

"Honey, I really couldn't say," said Leota. "Not that you look it."

"Where's Thelma, I'll ask her," said Mrs. Fletcher.

"Now honey, I wouldn't go and git mad over a little thing like that," said Leota, combing hastily, as though to hold Mrs. Fletcher down by the hair. "Nobody'd ever know it. I'm sure it was somebody didn't mean no harm in the world."

But Mrs. Fletcher shrieked for Thelma.

"Thelma honey, throw your mind back to yestiddy if you kin," said Leota, drenching Mrs. Fletcher's hair with thick fluid and catching the overflow in a cold wet towel at her neck.

"Well, I got my lady half wound for a spiral," said Thelma doubtfully.

"This won't take but a minute," said Leota. "Just cast your mind back and try to remember who your lady was yestiddy who happ'med to mention that my customer was pregnant, that's all."

Thelma drooped her blood-red lips dolefully and combed her platinum hair with a pocket-comb. "Why, honey, I ain't got the faintest," she breathed, looking over Mrs. Fletcher's head into the mirror. "I really don't recollect the faintest. But I'm sure she meant no harm."

"Was it that Mrs. Hutchinson?" Mrs. Fletcher was tensely polite.

"Mrs. Hutchinson? Oh, Mrs. Hutchinson." Thelma batted her eyes. "Naw, dear, she come on Thursday and she didn't even mention your name. I doubt if she even knows you're pregnant."

"Thelma!" cried Leota staunchily.

"All I know is, whoever it is'll be sorry some day! Why, I just barely knew it myself!" cried Mrs. Fletcher. "Just let her wait."

"Why? What're you gonna do to her?"

It was a child's voice, and the women looked down. A little boy was making tents with water-wave combs on the floor under the sink.

"Billy Boy, hon, mustn't bother nice ladies," smiled Leota. She turned again to her customer and behind her back waved Thelma out of the booth. "Ain't Billy Boy a sight. Only three years old, and already just nuts about the beauty-parlor business."

"I haven't seen him here before," said Mrs. Fletcher still unmollified.

"He ain't been here before, that's how come," said Leota. "He belongs to Mrs. Pike. She got her a job but it was Ward's third floor millinery. He oughtn't to wear those ladies' hats, they come down over his eyes like I don't know what. They just look ridiculous, that's what, an' a course he's gonna put 'em on; they didn't like him hangin' around there. Here, he couldn't hurt a thing."

"Well! I don't like children that much," said Mrs. Fletcher.

"Well!" said Leota moodily.

"Well, I'm almost tempted not to have this one," said Mrs. Fletcher. "That Mrs. Hutchinson! Just looks straight through you when she sees you on the street, an' then spits at you behind your back."

"Mr. Fletcher would beat you on the head if you didn't have it now," said Leota. "After goin' this far."

Mrs. Fletcher sat up straight. "Mr. Fletcher can't do a thing with me."

"He can't?" Leota winked at herself in the mirror.

"No siree, he can't. If he so much as raises his voice against me he knows good and well I'll have one of my sick headaches. They're awful. And if I really look so pregnant already —"

"Well, now, honey, I just want you to know — I habm't told any of my ladies and I ain't goin' to tell 'em, evem about your hair fallin' out. What they don't know don't hurt nobody, as Mrs. Pike says."

"Did you tell Mrs. Pike?" asked Mrs. Fletcher sulkily.

"Well, Mrs. Fletcher, look, you ain't ever goin' to lay eyes on Mrs. Pike or her lay eyes on you, so what diffunce does it make in the long run?"

"I knew it!" Mrs. Fletcher deliberately nodded her head so as to destroy a ringlet Leota was working on behind her ear. "Mrs. Pike!"

Leota sighed. "I reckon I might as well tell you. It wasn't any more Thelma's lady told me you was pregnant than a bat."

"Not Mrs. Hutchinson?"

"Naw. It was Mrs. Pike."

"Mrs. Pike!" Mrs. Fletcher could only sputter, although curling fluid was rolling into her ear. "How could Mrs. Pike possibly know I was pregnant, when she doesn't even know me? The nerve of some people."

"Well, here's how it was. Sunday — remember?"

"Yes," said Mrs. Fletcher.

"Sunday, Mrs. Pike an' me was all by ourself, Mr. Pike and Fred had gone over to Eagle Lake sayin' they was goin' to catch 'em some fish, but they didn't. So we was settin' in Mrs. Pike's car, is a 1933 Dodge —"

"1933, eh," said Mrs. Fletcher.

" — And we was gettin' us a Jax beer apiece, that's the beer that Mrs. Pike says is made in New Orleans so she won't drink no other kind. So I seen you drive up to the drugstore and run in for just a secont and come out with what looked like a perscription. So I says to Mrs. Pike, just to be makin' conversation like, 'Right yonder's Mrs. Fletcher, she's one of my regular customers,' I says."

"I had on a figured print," said Mrs. Fletcher tentatively.

"You sure did," agreed Leota. "So Mrs. Pike she give you a good look, she's very observant, a good judge of character — cute as a minute, you know — and she says, 'I bet you another Jax that lady's three months on the way.'"

"What gall!" said Mrs. Fletcher. "Mrs. Pike!"

"Mrs. Pike ain't goin' to bite you," said Leota. "Mrs. Pike is a lovely girl. Can't sit still a minute. We went to the travelin' freak show yestiddy after work, down in the vacant store on South Main. What, you ain't been?"

"No, I despise freaks," declared Mrs. Fletcher.

"Well, honey, talkin' about bein' pregnant an' all, you ought to see those twins in a bottle, you really owe it to yourself."

"What twins?" asked Mrs. Fletcher out of the side of her mouth.

"Well honey, they got these two twins in a bottle, see, born joined plum together, dead a course." Leota dropped her voice into a soft lyrical hum. "They was about this long — pardon — must have been full time all right, wouldn't you say, an' they had these two heads and two faces and four arms and four legs, all kind of joined *here*. See, this face looked this-a-way, and the other face looked that-a-way, over their shoulder, see. Kinda pathetic."

"Glah!" said Mrs. Fletcher disapprovingly.

"Well, ugly? Honey, I mean to tell you. Their parents was first cousins, and things like that. Billy Boy, git me a fresh towel from off Thelma's stack, this'n's wringin'-wet, and quit ticklin' my ankles with that curler. I declare! He don't miss nothin'."

"Me and Mr. Fletcher ain't one speck of kin, or he could never of had me," said Mrs. Fletcher placidly.

"Of course not!" protested Leota. "Neither is me and Fred, not that we know of. Well honey, what Mrs. Pike liked was the pygmies. They've got these pygmies down there, too, an' Mrs. Pike was just wild about 'em. You know, the tiniest people in the universe? Well honey, they can just rest back on their little bohunkus and roll around and you can't hardly tell if they're sittin' or standin'. That'll give you some idea. They're about forty-two years old. Just suppose it was your husband!"

"Well, my husband is five foot nine and a half," said Mrs. Fletcher quickly.

"Fred's five foot ten," said Leota, "but I tell him he's a shrimp and he knows it. Account of I'm so tall." She made a deep wave over Mrs. Fletcher's temple with the comb. "Well these pygmies are a kind of dark brown, Mrs. Fletcher. Not bad looking for what they are, you know."

"I wouldn't care for them," said Mrs. Fletcher. "What does that Mrs. Pike see in them?"

"Aw I don't know," said Leota. "She's just cute, that's all. But they got this man, this petrified man, that everything ever since he was nine years old, when it goes through his digestion, see, somehow Mrs. Pike says it goes to his joints and has been turning to stone."

"How awful!" said Mrs. Fletcher.

"He's forty-two, too. That looks like a bad age."

"Who said so, that Mrs. Pike?" Mrs. Fletcher flared up.

"Naw, Mrs. Pike didn't like the petrified man much," said Leota. "Not as much as some of the others, she didn't. He could move his head, like this; a course his head and mind ain't a joint, so to speak, and I guess his stomach ain't either, not yet anyways. See — his food, he eats it, and it goes down, see, and then he digests it —" Leota rose on her toes for an instant; "and it goes out to his joints, and before you know it it's stone, pure stone. He's turning to stone. How'd you like to be married to a guy like that? He can move his head like this. A course he *looks* just *terrible!*"

"I should think he would," said Mrs. Fletcher frostily. "Mr. Fletcher takes bending exercises every night of the world. I make him."

"All Fred does is lay around the house like a rug. The petrified man can move his head like this, though," said Leota reminiscently, turning her own head a few inches to one side. "But Mrs. Pike couldn't stand him: she likes a man to be a good dresser and all that."

"Is Mr. Pike a good dresser?" asked Mrs. Fletcher skeptically.

"Oh, well, yeah," said Leota. "But he's twelve-fourteen years older'n her. She ast Lady Evangeline about him."

"Who's Lady Evangeline?" asked Mrs. Fletcher.

"Well it's this mindreader they got in the freak show," said Leota. "Was real good. Lady Evangeline's her name and if I had another dollar I'd go straight back and have my other palm read. A course I ought not to. She has what Mrs. Pike said was the sixth mind, though."

"What did she tell Mrs. Pike?" asked Mrs. Fletcher.

"She told her Mr. Pike was true to her, all right," said Leota.

"Humph!" said Mrs. Fletcher.

"She didn't tell me nothin' extra about my nature, or anything, but she said . . . Well, I tell you, Mrs. Fletcher, I use to go with this boy got married last September to this girl, see. About three and a half years ago, that was when you was still goin' to the Robert E. Lee Beauty Shop in Jackson. He married her for her money. Another fortune teller tole me that at the time. So I'm not in love with him any more anyway, besides bein' married to Fred, but Mrs. Pike thought just for the sport of the thing, see, to ask Lady Evangeline —"

"Does Mrs. Pike know everything about you already?" Mrs. Fletcher asked unbelievingly. "Good fathers above."

"Oh yeah, I told her ever'thing about ever'thing, from now on back to I don't know when: to when I first started goin' out," said Leota. "So I ast Lady Evangeline was he happily married, and she says 'Honey,' she says, 'naw he idn't. You write down this day, March eight, 1937,' she says, 'and mock it down like I say, three years from today him an' her won't be occupyin' the same bed,' and she says, 'You ought to be glad you didn't git him, because he's so mercenary.' So I'm glad I married Fred. She says, 'There's fairer fields for you, dearie.' I guess that meant Fred."

"Did Mrs. Pike believe in what the fortune teller said?" asked Mrs. Fletcher in a superior tone of voice.

"Lord yes, she's from New Orleans. She knows they've got this sixth mind for a fact. One of them in New Orleans says to Mrs. Pike one summer she was goin' to go from state to state and meet some gray-headed men, and sure enough, she says she went on a beautician convention up to Chicago —"

"Oh," said Mrs. Fletcher, "is Mrs. Pike a beautician too?"

"Oh, lord, yes!" protested Leota. "That's one thing right off the bat . . . I'm goin' to git her in here if I can. Before she married. But it's kind of left her, you know. So she says sure enough, there was three men who was a very large part of making her trip what it was, and they all three had gray hair and they went in six states. Got Christmas cards from 'em. A course Mrs. Pike says they was married men, and she didn't care for them in that way, but still. Billy Boy, go see if Thelma's got any dry cotton. Look how Mrs. Fletcher's a-drippin'."

"Where did Mrs. Pike meet Mr. Pike?" asked Mrs. Fletcher primly.

"On another train," said Leota.

"I met Mr. Fletcher, or rather he met me, in a rental library," said Mrs. Fletcher with dignity.

"Honey, me and Fred, we met in a rumble seat eight months ago and we was practically what you might call on the way to the altar inside of a half an hour," said Leota in a guttural voice and bit a bobbie-pin open. "Course it didn't last. Mrs. Pike says nothin' like that ever lasts."

"Mr. Fletcher and myself are as much in love as the day we married." said Mrs. Fletcher belligerently.

"Mrs. Pike says it don't last," repeated Leota. "Now go git under the dryer. I'll come back and comb you out. Durin' lunch time I promised to give Mrs. Pike a facial. You know, free. Her bein' in the business, so to speak."

"I bet she needs one," remarked Mrs. Fletcher, letting the swinging door fly back against Leota as she followed her out. "Oh, pardon me."

ᨏᨎ

A week later, on time for her appointment, Mrs. Fletcher sank heavily into Leota's chair and looked in a discouraged way into the mirror.

"You can tell it when I'm sittin' down, all right," she said.

Leota looked preoccupied and stood shaking out a lavender cloth. She began to pin it around Mrs. Fletcher's neck in silence.

"I said you sure can tell it when I'm sittin' straight on comin' at you this way," Mrs. Fletcher said.

"Why, honey, naw you can't," said Leota gloomily. "Why, I'd never know. If somebody was to come up to me on the street an' say, 'Mrs. Fletcher is lookin' pregnant,' I'd say, 'Hec, she don't look it to me!'"

"If a certain party hadn't found it out and spread it around, it wouldn't be too late even now," said Mrs. Fletcher frostily, but Leota was almost choking her with the cloth, pinning it so tight, and she couldn't even speak clearly. She paddled her hands in the air until Leota wearily loosened her.

"Listen, honey, you're just a virgin compared with Mrs. Montjoy," Leota was going on, still absent-minded. She bent Mrs. Fletcher backwards in the chair, and sighing, tossed liquid soap from a teacup onto her head and dug both hands into her scalp. "You know Mrs. Montjoy: her husband's that premature-gray-headed fella?"

"She's in the Trojan Needlework Society, is all I know," said Mrs. Fletcher.

"Well, honey," said Leota, but in a weary voice, "she come in here not the week before and not the day before she had her baby, she come in here the very selfsame day, I mean to tell you. Child, we was all plum scared to death. There she was! Come for her shampoo an' set. Why Mrs. Fletcher, in an hour and twenty minutes she was layin' up there in the Babtist Hospital with a seb'm pound son. It was that close a shave."

"What gall," said Mrs. Fletcher. "I never knew her at all well."

"See, her husband was waitin' outside in the car and her bags was all packed an' in the back seat, and she was all ready, 'cept she wanted a shampoo an' set. An' havin' one pain right after another. Her husband kep' comin' in here, scared-like, but couldn't do nothin' with her a course. She yelled bloodymurder too, but she always yelled her head off when I give her a perm'nent."

"She must have been crazy," said Mrs. Fletcher. "How did she look?"

"Shoot!" said Leota deprecatingly.

"Well, I can guess," said Mrs. Fletcher. "Awful."

"Just wanted to look pretty while she was havin' her baby, is all," said Leota airily. "Course we was glad to give the lady what she was after, that's our motto, but I bet a hour later she wasn't payin' no mind to them little end-curls. I bet she wasn't thinkin' about she ought to have on a net. It wouldn't of done her no good if she had. Yeah man, she was a-yellin'. Just like when I give her a perm'-nent, if possible."

"Her husband ought to could make her behave, don't it seem that way to you?" asked Mrs. Fletcher. "He ought to put his foot down."

"Shoot," said Leota. "A lot he could do. Maybe some women is soft."

"Oh, you mistake me, I don't mean for her to get soft, I don't think of myself as soft!" cried Mrs. Fletcher. "But I ask Mr. Fletcher's advice now and then. Especially on perm'nents. He says what does he know about perm'nents — go ahead."

"Huh! If I ever taken Fred's advice, we'd be livin' out in a houseboat on the

Yazoo River or somethin' by this time," said Leota. "I'm sick of Fred. I tole him to go over to Vicksburg."

"Is he going?" demanded Mrs. Fletcher.

"Sure. See, the fortune teller — went back and had my other palm read since we got to rent the room agin — said my lover was goin' to work in Vicksburg, so I don't know who else she could mean. And Fred sure ain't workin' here."

"Is he really going?" asked Mrs. Fletcher, "and —"

"If he lives an' don't nothin' happ'm between now and tomorrow," said Leota grimly. "He don't want to go but I ain't gonna put up with nothin' like that. Lays around the house an' bulls — did bull — with that good-for-nothin' Mr. Pike. Billy Boy, take Mrs. Grover that Screen Secrets, and leg it."

Mrs. Fletcher heard stomping footsteps go out the door.

"Is that that Mrs. Pike's little boy here again?" she asked, sitting up gingerly.

"Yeah, that's still him," Leota stuck out her tongue.

Mrs. Fletcher could hardly believe her eyes. "Well! How's Mrs. Pike, your attractive new friend with the sharp eyes who spreads it around town that everybody's pregnant so they can't do anything about it?" she asked in a sweetened voice.

"Oh, Mrs. Pike." Leota combed Mrs. Fletcher's hair with heavy strokes. "Did I tell you about the awful luck we had, me and Fred? Well, you know, we rented out our room to this Mr. and Mrs. Pike from New Orleans when Sal and Joe Fentress got mad at us 'cause they drank up some beer we had in the closet, Sal and Joe did. Well, a week ago Sat'day Mr. and Mrs. Pike moved in. And I kinda fixed up the room, you know, put a sofa-pilla on the couch and picked some ragged robins, but they never did say they appreciated it. Anyway, then I put some old magazines on the table."

"I think that was lovely," said Mrs. Fletcher.

"Wait. So come night 'fore last, Fred and this Mr. Pike was back from they said they was fishin', bein' as neither one of 'em has got a job to his name, and we was all settin' around in their room. So Mrs. Pike was settin' there readin' a old Startlin' Detective that was mine, mind you, I'd bought it my own self, and all of a sudden she jumps! — into the air — you'd a-thought she'd set on a spider, an' says 'Canfield' — ain't that silly, that's Mr. Pike — 'Canfield, my God amighty,' she says, 'honey,' she says, 'we're rich, and you won't have to work.' Not that he turned one hand anyway. Well, me and Fred rushes over to her, and Mr. Pike too, and there she sets, pointin' her finger at a photo in my copy of Startlin' Detective. 'See that man,' yells Mrs. Pike, 'remember him, Canfield?' 'Well, why shouldn't I, dear,' says Mr. Pike, 'it's Mr. Petrie, that we stayed with him in the apartment next to ours in Toulouse Street in New Orleans for six weeks. Mr. Petrie.' 'Well!' Mrs. Pike says, like she can't hold out one secont longer, 'Mr. Petrie is wanted for five hundred dollars cash, for rapin' four women in California, and I know where he is.'"

"Mercy!" said Mrs. Fletcher. "Where was he?"

"Know where he was?" Leota flung a towel around her customer's head and wrapped it into a turban. "Nowhere else but in that freak show! I saw him just as plain as Mrs. Pike. *He* was the Petrified Man!"

"Who would ever have thought that!" cried Mrs. Fletcher sympathetically.

"So Mr. Pike says, 'Well whatta you know about that,' an' he looks real hard at the photo and whistles. And she starts dancin' and singin' about their good luck. She meant our bad luck! Can you beat it? That magazine was layin' around the house for a month and there was five hundred dollars in it for somebody. And there was the freak show goin' night an' day not two steps away from my own beauty parlor, with Mr. Petrie just settin' there waitin'. And it had to be Mr. and Mrs. Pike: almost perfect strangers."

"What gall," said Mrs. Fletcher. Leota was snagging and pulling her hair dreadfully in her distraction, combing it dry, but she did not mind.

"She goes around actin' like she thinks she was Mrs. God," said Leota. "So they're goin' to leave tomorrow. And in the meantime, I've got to keep that dirty filthy little ole kid here, gettin' under my feet ever' minute of the day an' talkin' back too."

"Have they gotten the five hundred dollars for the reward already?" asked Mrs. Fletcher.

"Well," said Leota, "at first Mr. Pike didn't want to do anything about it — can you feature that? Said he kinda liked that old bird and said he was real nice to 'em, lent 'em money or somethin'. But Mrs. Pike simply tole him he could just go to hell, and I can see her point. She says, 'You ain't worked a lick in six months and here I make five hundred dollars in two seconts, and what thanks do I get for it? You go to hell,' she says. So," Leota went on in a despondent voice, "they called up the cops and they caught the old bird all right, right there in the freak show where I saw him with my own eyes, thinkin' he was petrified. He's the one. Did it under his real name: Mr. Petrie. Four women in California, last August. So Mrs. Pike gits five hundred dollars. And my magazine, and right next door to my beauty parlor. I cried all night, but Fred said it wasn't a bit of use, because the whole thing was just a sort of coincidence — you know: can't do nothin' about it. But he says it put him clean out of the notion of goin' to Vicksburg till we rent out the room agin — no tellin' who we'll git this time. Somebody else to take advantage."

"But can you imagine them knowing this old man, that's raped four women?" persisted Mrs. Fletcher, and shuddered audibly. "Did Mrs. Pike *speak* to him when she met him in the freak show?"

"Well, I says to her, I says, 'I didn't notice you fallin' on his neck when he was the Petrified Man. Don't tell me you didn't recognize your old friend?' And she says, 'I didn't recognize him with that white powder all over his face. He just looked familiar,' Mrs. Pike says, 'and lots of people look familiar.' But she says that old petrified man did put her in mind of somebody. She wondered who it was. Kep' her awake, which man she'd ever knew it reminded her of. So when she seen the photo, it all come to her. Like a flash. Mr. Petrie. The way he'd turn to look at her when she took him in his breakfast."

"Took him in his breakfast!" shrieked Mrs. Fletcher. "Listen — don't tell me. I'd a-felt something."

"Four women. I guess those women didn't have the faintest notion at the time they'd be worth a hunderd an' twenty-five bucks apiece some day to Mrs. Pike. We ast her how old the fella was then, and she says he musta had one foot in the grave at least. Can you beat it?"

"Not really petrified at all, of course," said Mrs. Fletcher meditatively. She drew herself up in fully restored superiority. "I'd a-felt something," she said proudly.

"Shoot! I did feel somethin'," said Leota. "I tole Fred when I got home I felt so funny. I said, 'Fred, that ole petrified man sure did leave me with a funny feelin'.' He says, 'Funny-haha or funny-peculiar?' and I says, 'Funny-peculiar.'" She pointed her comb into the air emphatically.

"I'll bet you did," said Mrs. Fletcher.

They both heard a crackling noise.

Leota screamed, "Billy Boy! What you doin' in my purse?"

"Aw, I'm just eatin' these old stale peanuts up," said Billy Boy.

"You come here to me!" screamed Leota, throwing the wet towel recklessly over Mrs. Fletcher's half-set waves. "I've had enough out of you men — this is the last straw!"

She picked up a hairbrush and bent toward the child.

"I caught him! I caught him!" giggled Mrs. Fletcher. "I'll hold him on my lap. You bad, bad boy, you!"

Leota paddled him heartily with the brush, while he gave angry but belittling screams which penetrated beyond the swinging door and filled the whole curious beauty parlor, and the wild-haired ladies began to gather around to watch. Billy Boy kicked both Leota and Mrs. Fletcher as hard as he could.

"There, my little man," gasped Leota. "You won't be able to set down for a week, if I knew what I was doin'."

Billy Boy stomped through the ladies and went out the door, but flung back the words, "If you're so smart, why ain't you rich?"

William Faulkner
Barn Burning

One of William Faulkner's most celebrated works of short fiction, "Barn Burning" first appeared in *Harper's Magazine* in 1939 and was included in *O. Henry Memorial Award Prize Stories of 1939*. In subject, it deals with a conflict within a young boy who must choose between his own innate sense of what is right and his father's vindictive approach to personal justice. The boy, Sarty Snopes, comes from a poor white family, sharecroppers constantly at odds with the plantation owners who employ them. In Faulkner's work, the Snopes family is relentlessly ambitious, rising economically through ruthless and unprincipled means, a trajectory outlined in three novels: *The Hamlet, The Town,* and *The Mansion.* This story represents one of the few times that the protagonist is set against the values of his family, but Sarty, named Colonel Sartoris Snopes after a distinguished officer in the Civil War, seems to have absorbed the ethics of a social class not his own. His internal struggle, revealed in a narrative method identified with his thoughts, gives depth and meaning to this quintessential Faulkner story.

William Faulkner, "Barn Burning," *Harper's Magazine* 179 (June 1939): 86–96.

The store in which the Justice of the Peace's court was sitting smelled of cheese. The boy, crouched on his nail keg at the back of the crowded room, knew he smelled cheese, and more: from where he sat he could see the ranked shelves close-packed with the solid, squat, dynamic shapes of tin cans whose labels his stomach read, not from the lettering which meant nothing to his mind but from the scarlet devils and the silver curve of fish — this, the cheese which he knew he smelled and the hermetic meat which his intestines believed he smelled coming in intermittent gusts momentary and brief between the other constant one, the smell and sense just a little of fear because mostly of despair and grief, the old fierce pull of blood. He could not see the table where the Justice sat and before which his father and his father's enemy (*our enemy* he thought in that despair; *ourn! mine and hisn both! He's my father!*) stood, but he could hear them, the two of them that is, because his father had said no word yet:

"But what proof have you, Mr. Harris?"

"I told you. The hog got into my corn. I caught it up and sent it back to him. He had no fence that would hold it. I told him so, warned him. The next time I put the hog in my pen. When he came to get it I gave him enough wire to patch up his pen. The next time I put the hog up and kept it. I rode down to his house and saw the wire I gave him still rolled on to the spool in his yard. I told him he could have the hog when he paid me a dollar pound fee. That evening a nigger came with the dollar and got the hog. He was a strange nigger. He said, 'He say to tell you wood and hay kin burn.' I said, 'What?' 'That whut he say to tell you,' the nigger said. 'Wood and hay kin burn.' That night my barn burned. I got the stock out but I lost the barn."

"Where is the nigger? Have you got him?"

"He was a strange nigger, I tell you. I don't know what became of him."

"But that's not proof. Don't you see that's not proof?"

"Get that boy up here. He knows." For a moment the boy thought too that the man meant his older brother until Harris said, "Not him. The little one. The boy," and, crouching, small for his age, small and wiry like his father, in patched and faded jeans even too small for him, with straight, uncombed, brown hair and eyes gray and wild as storm scud, he saw the men between himself and the table part and become a lane of grim faces, at the end of which he saw the Justice, a shabby, collarless, graying man in spectacles, beckoning him. He felt no floor under his bare feet; he seemed to walk beneath the palpable weight of the grim turning faces. His father, stiff in his black Sunday coat donned not for the trial but for the moving, did not even look at him. *He aims for me to lie,* he thought, again with that frantic grief and despair. *And I will have to do hit.*

"What's your name, boy?" the Justice said.

"Colonel Sartoris Snopes," the boy whispered.

"Hey?" the Justice said. "Talk louder. Colonel Sartoris? I reckon anybody named for Colonel Sartoris in this country can't help but tell the truth, can they?" The boy said nothing. *Enemy! Enemy!* he thought; for a moment he could not even see, could not see that the Justice's face was kindly nor discern that his voice was troubled when he spoke to the man named Harris: "Do you want me to question this boy?" But he could hear, and during those subsequent long seconds while there was absolutely no sound in the crowded little room save that of quiet and intent breathing it was as if he had swung outward at the end of a grape vine, over a ravine, and at the top of the swing had been caught in a prolonged instant of mesmerized gravity, weightless in time.

"No!" Harris said violently, explosively. "Damnation! Send him out of here!" Now time, the fluid world, rushed beneath him again, the voices coming to him again through the smell of cheese and sealed meat, the fear and despair and the old grief of blood:

"This case is closed. I can't find against you, Snopes, but I can give you advice. Leave this country and don't come back to it."

His father spoke for the first time, his voice cold and harsh, level, without emphasis: "I aim to. I don't figure to stay in a country among people who . . ." he said something unprintable and vile, addressed to no one.

"That'll do," the Justice said. "Take your wagon and get out of this country before dark. Case dismissed."

His father turned, and he followed the stiff black coat, the wiry figure walking a little stiffly from where a Confederate provost's man's musket ball had taken him in the heel on a stolen horse thirty years ago, followed the two backs now, since his older brother had appeared from somewhere in the crowd, no taller than the father but thicker, chewing tobacco steadily, between the two lines of grim-faced men and out of the store and across the worn gallery and down the sagging steps and among the dogs and half-grown boys in the mild May dust, where as he passed a voice hissed:

"Barn burner!"

Again he could not see, whirling; there was a face in a red haze, moonlike, bigger than the full moon, the owner of it half again his size, he leaping in the red haze toward the face, feeling no blow, feeling no shock when his head struck the earth, scrabbling up and leaping again, feeling no blow this time either and tasting no blood, scrabbling up to see the other boy in full flight and himself already leaping into pursuit as his father's hand jerked him back, the harsh, cold voice speaking above him: "Go get in the wagon."

It stood in a grove of locusts and mulberries across the road. His two hulking sisters in their Sunday dresses and his mother and her sister in calico and sunbonnets were already in it, sitting on and among the sorry residue of the dozen and more movings which even the boy could remember — the battered stove, the broken beds and chairs, the clock inlaid with mother-of-pearl, which would not run, stopped at some fourteen minutes past two o'clock of a dead and forgotten day and time, which had been his mother's dowry. She was crying, though when she saw him she drew her sleeve across her face and began to descend from the wagon. "Get back," the father said.

"He's hurt. I got to get some water and wash his . . ."

"Get back in the wagon," his father said. He got in too, over the tail-gate. His father mounted to the seat where the older brother already sat and struck the gaunt mules two savage blows with the peeled willow, but without heat. It was not even sadistic; it was exactly that same quality which in later years would cause his descendants to over-run the engine before putting a motor car into motion, striking and reining back in the same movement. The wagon went on, the store with its quiet crowd of grimly watching men dropped behind; a curve in the road hid it. *Forever* he thought. *Maybe he's done satisfied now, now that he has . . .* stopping himself, not to say it aloud even to himself. His mother's hand touched his shoulder.

"Does hit hurt?" she said.

"Naw," he said. "Hit don't hurt. Lemme be."

"Can't you wipe some of the blood off before hit dries?"

"I'll wash to-night," he said. "Lemme be, I tell you."

The wagon went on. He did not know where they were going. None of them ever did or ever asked, because it was always somewhere, always a house of sorts waiting for them a day or two days or even three days away. Likely his father had already arranged to make a crop on another farm before he . . . Again he had to stop himself. He (the father) always did. There was something about his wolflike independence and even courage when the advantage was at least neutral which impressed strangers, as if they got from his latent ravening ferocity not so much a sense of dependability as a feeling that his ferocious conviction in the rightness of his own actions would be of advantage to all whose interest lay with his.

That night they camped, in a grove of oaks and beeches where a spring ran. The nights were still cool and they had a fire against it, of a rail lifted from a nearby fence and cut into lengths — a small fire, neat, niggard almost, a shrewd fire; such fires were his father's habit and custom always, even in freezing weather. Older, the boy might have remarked this and wondered why not a big one; why should not a man who had not only seen the waste and extravagance of war, but who had in his blood an inherent voracious prodigality with material not his own, have burned everything in sight? Then he might have gone a step farther and thought that that was the reason: that niggard blaze was the living fruit of nights passed during those four years in the woods hiding from all men, blue or gray, with his string of horses (captured horses, he called them). And older still, he might have divined the true reason: that the element of fire spoke to some deep mainspring of his father's being, as the element of steel or of powder spoke to other men, as the one weapon for the preservation of integrity, else breath were not worth the breathing, and hence to be regarded with respect and used with discretion.

But he did not think this now and he had seen those same niggard blazes all his life. He merely ate his supper beside it and was already half asleep over his iron plate when his father called him, and once more he followed the stiff back, the stiff and ruthless limp, up the slope and on to the starlit road where, turning, he could see his father against the stars but without face or depth — a shape black, flat, bloodless as though cut from tin in the iron folds of the frockcoat which had not been made for him, the voice harsh like tin and without heat like tin:

"You were fixing to tell them. You would have told him." He didn't answer. His father struck him with the flat of his hand on the side of the head, hard but without heat, exactly as he had struck the two mules at the store, exactly as he would strike either of them with any stick in order to kill a horse fly, his voice still without heat or anger: "You're getting to be a man. You got to learn. You got to learn to stick to your own blood or you ain't going to have any blood to stick to you. Do you think either of them, any man there this morning, would? Don't you know all they wanted was a chance to get at me because they knew I had them beat? Eh?" Later, twenty years later, he was to tell himself, "If I had said they wanted only truth, justice, he would have hit me again." But now he said nothing. He was not crying. He just stood there. "Answer me," his father said.

"Yes," he whispered. His father turned.

"Get on to bed. We'll be there to-morrow."

To-morrow they were there. In the early afternoon the wagon stopped before a paintless two-room house identical almost with the dozen others it had stopped before even in the boy's ten years, and again, as on the other dozen occasions, his mother and aunt got down and began to unload the wagon, although his two sisters and his father and brother had not moved.

"Likely hit ain't fitten for hawgs," one of the sisters said.

"Nevertheless, fit it will and you'll hog it and like it," his father said. "Get out of them chairs and help your Ma unload."

The two sisters got down, big, bovine, in a flutter of cheap ribbons; one of them drew from the jumbled wagon bed a battered lantern, the other a worn broom. His father handed the reins to the older son and began to climb stiffly over the wheel. "When they get unloaded, take the team to the barn and feed them." Then he said, and at first the boy thought he was still speaking to his brother: "Come with me."

"Me?" he said.

"Yes," his father said. "You."

"Abner," his mother said. His father paused and looked back — the harsh level stare beneath the shaggy, graying, irascible brows.

"I reckon I'll have a word with the man that aims to begin to-morrow owning me body and soul for the next eight months."

They went back up the road. A week ago — or before last night, that is — he would have asked where they were going, but not now. His father had struck him before last night but never before had he paused afterward to explain why; it was as if the blow and the following calm, outrageous voice still rang, repercussed, divulging nothing to him save the terrible handicap of being young, the light weight of his few years, just heavy enough to prevent his soaring free of the world as it seemed to be ordered but not heavy enough to keep him footed solid in it, to resist it and try to change the course of its events.

Presently he could see the grove of oaks and cedars and the other flowering trees and shrubs where the house would be, though not the house yet. They walked beside a fence massed with honeysuckle and Cherokee roses and came to a gate swinging open between two brick pillars, and now, beyond a sweep of drive, he saw the house for the first time and at that instant he forgot his father and the terror and despair both, even when he remembered his father again (who had not stopped) the terror and despair did not return. Because, for all the twelve movings, they had sojourned until now in a poor country, a land of small farms and fields and houses, and he had never seen a house like this before. *Hit's big as a courthouse* he thought quietly, with a surge of peace and joy whose reason he could not have thought into words, being too young for that; *They are safe from him. People whose lives are a part of this peace and dignity are beyond his touch, he no more to them than a buzzing wasp: capable of stinging for a little moment but that's all; the spell of this peace and dignity rendering even the barns and stable and cribs which belong to it impervious to the puny flames he might contrive . . . this,* the peace and joy, ebbing for an instant as he looked again at the stiff black back, the stiff and implacable limp of the figure which was not dwarfed by the house, for the reason that it had never looked big anywhere and which now, against this serene columned backdrop, had more than ever that impervious quality of something cut ruthlessly from tin, depthless, as though, sidewise to the sun, it would cast no shadow. Watching him, the boy remarked the absolutely undeviating course which his father held and saw the stiff foot come squarely down in a pile of fresh droppings where a horse had stood in the drive and which his father could have avoided by a simple change of stride. But it ebbed only for a moment, though he could not have thought this into words either, walking on in the spell of the house, which he could even want but without envy, without sorrow, certainly never with that ravening and jealous rage which unknown to him walked in the ironlike black coat before him: *Maybe he will feel it too. Maybe it will even change him now from what maybe he couldn't help but be.*

They crossed the portico. Now he could hear his father's stiff foot as it came down on the boards with clocklike finality, a sound out of all proportion to the displacement of the body it bore and which was not dwarfed either by the white door before it, as though it had attained to a sort of vicious and ravening minimum not to be dwarfed by anything — the flat, wide, black hat, the formal coat of broadcloth which had once been black but which had now that friction-glazed greenish cast of the bodies of old house flies, the lifted sleeve which was too large, the lifted hand like a curled claw. The door opened so promptly that the boy knew the negro must have been watching them all the time, an old man with neat grizzled hair, in a linen jacket, who stood barring the door with his body, saying, "Wipe yo foots, white man, fo you come in here. Major ain't home nohow."

"Get out of my way, nigger," his father said, without heat too, flinging the door back and the negro also and entering, his hat still on his head. And now the boy saw the prints of the stiff foot on the doorjamb and saw them appear on the pale rug behind the machinelike deliberation of the foot which seemed to bear (or transmit) twice the weight which the body compassed. The negro was shouting "Miss Lula! Miss Lula!" somewhere behind them, then the boy, deluged as though by a warm wave by a suave turn of carpeted stair and a pendant glitter of chandeliers and a mute gleam of gold frames, heard the swift feet and saw her too, a lady — perhaps he had never seen her like before either — in a gray, smooth gown with lace at the throat and an apron tied at the waist and the sleeves turned back, wiping cake or biscuit dough from her hands with a towel as she came up the hall, looking not at his father at all but at the tracks on the blond rug with an expression of incredulous amazement.

"I tried," the negro cried. "I tole him to . . ."

"Will you please go away?" she said in a shaking voice. "Major de Spain is not at home. Will you please go away?"

His father had not spoken again. He did not speak again. He did not even look at her. He just stood stiff in the center of the rug, in his hat, the shaggy iron-gray brows twitching slightly above the pebble-colored eyes as he appeared to examine the house with brief deliberation. Then with the same deliberation he turned; the boy watched him pivot on the good leg and saw the stiff foot drag round the arc of the turning, leaving a final long and fading smear. His father never looked at it, he never once looked down at the rug. The negro held the door. It closed behind them, upon the hysteric and indistinguishable woman-wail. His father stopped at the top of the steps and scraped his boot clean on the edge of it. At the gate he stopped again. He stood for a moment, planted stiffly on the stiff foot, looking back at the house. "Pretty and white, ain't it?" he said. "That's sweat. Nigger sweat. Maybe it ain't white enough yet to suit him. Maybe he wants to mix some white sweat with it."

Two hours later the boy was chopping wood behind the house within which his mother and aunt and the two sisters (the mother and aunt, not the two girls, he knew that; even at this distance and muffled by walls the flat loud voices of the two girls emanated an incorrigible idle inertia) were setting up the stove to prepare a meal, when he heard the hooves and saw the linen-clad man on a fine sorrel mare, whom he recognized even before he saw the rolled rug in front of the negro youth following on a fat bay carriage horse — a suffused, angry face vanishing, still at full gallop, beyond the corner of the house where his father and brother were sitting in the two tilted chairs; and a moment later, almost before he could have put the axe down, he heard the hooves again and watched the sorrel mare go back out of the yard, already galloping again. Then his father began to shout one of the sisters' names, who presently emerged backward from the kitchen door dragging the rolled rug along the ground by one end while the other sister walked behind it.

"If you ain't going to tote, go on and set up the wash pot," the first said.

"You, Sarty!" the second shouted. "Set up the wash pot!" His father appeared at the door, framed against that shabbiness, as he had been against that other bland perfection, impervious to either, the mother's anxious face at his shoulder.

"Go on," the father said. "Pick it up." The two sisters stooped, broad, lethargic; stooping, they presented an incredible expanse of pale cloth and a flutter of tawdry ribbons.

"If I thought enough of a rug to have to git hit all the way from France I wouldn't keep hit where folks coming in would have to tromp on hit," the first said. They raised the rug.

"Abner," the mother said. "Let me do it."

"You go back and git dinner," his father said. "I'll tend to this."

From the woodpile through the rest of the afternoon the boy watched them, the rug spread flat in the dust beside the bubbling wash-pot, the two sisters stooping over it with that profound and lethargic reluctance, while the father stood over them in turn, implacable and grim, driving them though never raising his voice again. He could smell the harsh homemade lye they were using; he saw his mother come to the door once and look toward them with an expression not anxious now but very like despair; he saw his father turn, and he fell to with the axe and saw from the corner of his eye his father raise from the ground a flattish fragment of field stone and examine it and return to the pot, and this time his mother actually spoke: "Abner. Abner. Please don't. Please, Abner."

Then he was done too. It was dusk; the whippoorwills had already begun. He could smell coffee from the room where they would presently eat the cold food remaining from the mid-afternoon meal, though when he entered the house he realized they were having coffee again probably because there was a fire on the hearth, before which the rug now lay spread over the backs of the two chairs. The tracks of his father's foot were gone. Where they had been were now long, water-cloudy scoriations resembling the sporadic course of a lilliputian mowing machine.

It still hung there while they ate the cold food and then went to bed, scattered without order or claim up and down the two rooms, his mother in one bed, where his father would later lie, the older brother in the other, himself, the aunt, and the two sisters on pallets on the floor. But his father was not in bed yet. The last thing the boy remembered was the depthless, harsh silhouette of the hat and coat bending over the rug and it seemed to him that he had not even closed his eyes when the silhouette was standing over him, the fire almost dead behind it, the stiff foot prodding him awake. "Catch up the mule," his father said.

When he returned with the mule his father was standing in the black door, the rolled rug over his shoulder. "Ain't you going to ride?" he said.

"No. Give me your foot."

He bent his knee into his father's hand, the wiry, surprising power flowed smoothly, rising, he rising with it, on to the mule's bare back (they had owned a saddle once; the boy could remember it though not when or where) and with the same effortlessness his father swung the rug up in front of him. Now in the starlight they retraced the afternoon's path, up the dusty road rife with honeysuckle, through the gate and up the black tunnel of the drive to the lightless house, where he sat on the mule and felt the rough warp of the rug drag across his thighs and vanish.

"Don't you want me to help?" he whispered. His father did not answer and now he heard again that stiff foot striking the hollow portico with that wooden and clocklike deliberation, that outrageous overstatement of the weight it carried. The rug, hunched, not flung (the boy could tell that even in the darkness) from his father's shoulder struck the angle of wall and floor with a sound unbelievably loud, thunderous, then the foot again, unhurried and enormous; a light came on in the house and the boy sat, tense, breathing steadily and quietly and just a little fast, though the foot itself did not increase its beat at all, descending the steps now; now the boy could see him.

"Don't you want to ride now?" he whispered. "We kin both ride now," the light within the house altering now, flaring up and sinking. *He's coming down the stairs now,* he thought. He had already ridden the mule up beside the horse block; presently his father was up behind him and he doubled the reins over and slashed the mule across the neck, but before the animal could begin to trot the hard, thin arm came round him, the hard, knotted hand jerking the mule back to a walk.

In the first red rays of the sun they were in the lot, putting plow gear on the mules. This time the sorrel mare was in the lot before he heard it at all, the rider collarless and even bareheaded, trembling, speaking in a shaking voice as the woman in the house had done, his father merely looking up once before stooping again to the hame he was buckling, so that the man on the mare spoke to his stooping back:

"You must realize you have ruined that rug. Wasn't there anybody here, any of your women . . ." he ceased, shaking, the boy watching him, the older brother leaning now in the stable door, chewing, blinking slowly and steadily at nothing apparently. "It cost a hundred dollars. But you never had a hundred dollars. You never will. So I'm going to charge you twenty bushels of corn against your crop. I'll add it in your contract and when you come to the commissary you can sign it. That won't keep Mrs. de Spain quiet but maybe it will teach you to wipe your feet off before you enter her house again."

Then he was gone. The boy looked at his father, who still had not spoken or even looked up again, who was now adjusting the logger-head in the hame.

"Pap," he said. His father looked at him — the inscrutable face, the shaggy brows beneath which the gray eyes glinted coldly. Suddenly the boy went toward him, fast, stopping as suddenly. "You done the best you could!" he cried. "If he wanted hit done different why didn't he wait and tell you how? He won't git no twenty bushels! He won't git none! We'll gather hit and hide hit! I kin watch . . ."

"Did you put the cutter back in that straight stock like I told you?"

"No, sir," he said.

"Then go do it."

That was Wednesday. During the rest of that week he worked steadily, at what was within his scope and some which was beyond it, with an industry that did not need to be driven nor even commanded twice; he had this from his mother, with the difference that some at least of what he did he liked to do, such as splitting wood with the half-size axe which his mother and aunt had earned, or saved money somehow, to present him with at Christmas. In company with the two older women (and on one afternoon, even one of the sisters), he built pens for the shoat and the cow which were a part of his father's contract with the landlord, and one afternoon, his father being absent, gone somewhere on one of the mules, he went to the field.

They were running a middle buster now, his brother holding the plow straight while he handled the reins, and walking beside the straining mule, the rich black soil shearing cool and damp against his bare ankles, he thought *Maybe this is the end of it. Maybe even that twenty bushels that seems hard to have to pay for just a rug will be a cheap price for him to stop forever and always from being what he used to be;* thinking, dreaming now, so that his brother had to speak sharply to him to mind the mule: *Maybe he even won't collect the twenty bushels. Maybe it will all add up and balance and vanish — corn, rug, fire; the terror and grief, the being pulled two ways like between two teams of horses — gone, done with for ever and ever.*

Then it was Saturday; he looked up from beneath the mule he was harnessing and saw his father in the black coat and hat. "Not that," his father said. "The wagon gear." And then, two hours later, sitting in the wagon bed behind his father and brother on the seat, the wagon accomplished a final curve, and he saw the weathered paintless store with its tattered tobacco- and patent-medicine posters and the tethered wagons and saddle animals below the gallery. He mounted the gnawed steps behind his father and brother, and there again was the lane of quiet, watching faces for the three of them to walk through. He saw the man in spectacles sitting at the plank table and he did not need to be told this was a Justice of the Peace; he sent one glare of fierce, exultant, partisan defiance at the man in collar and cravat now, whom he had seen but twice before in his life, and that on a galloping horse, who now wore on his face an expression not of rage but of amazed unbelief which the boy could not have known was at the incredible circumstance of being sued by one of his own tenants, and came and stood against his father and cried at the Justice: "He ain't done it! He ain't burnt . . ."

"Go back to the wagin," his father said.

"Burnt?" the Justice said. "Do I understand this rug was burned too?"

"Does anybody here claim it was?" his father said. "Go back to the wagon."
But he did not, he merely retreated to the rear of the room, crowded as that other had been, but not to sit down this time, instead, to stand pressing among the motionless bodies, listening to the voices:

"And you claim twenty bushels of corn is too high for the damage you did to the rug?"

"He brought the rug to me and said he wanted the tracks washed out of it. I washed the tracks out and took the rug back to him."

"But you didn't carry the rug back to him in the same condition it was in before you made the tracks on it."

His father did not answer, and now for perhaps half a minute there was no sound at all save that of breathing, the faint, steady suspiration of complete and intent listening.

"You decline to answer that, Mr. Snopes?" Again his father did not answer. "I'm going to find against you, Mr. Snopes. I'm going to find that you were responsible for the injury to Major de Spain's rug and hold you liable for it. But twenty bushels of corn seems a little high for a man in your circumstances to have to pay. Major de Spain claims it cost a hundred dollars. October corn will be worth about fifty cents. I figure that if Major de Spain can stand a ninety-five dollar loss on something he paid cash for, you can stand a five-dollar loss you haven't earned yet. I hold you in damages to Major de Spain to the amount of ten bushels of corn over and above your contract with him, to be paid to him out of your crop at gathering time. Court adjourned."

It had taken no time hardly, the morning was but half begun. He thought they would return home and perhaps back to the field, since they were late, far behind all other farmers. But instead his father passed on behind the wagon, merely indicating with his hand for the older brother to follow with it, and crossed the road toward the blacksmith shop opposite, pressing on after his father, overtaking him, speaking, whispering up at the harsh, calm face beneath the weathered hat: "He won't git no ten bushels neither. He won't git one. We'll . . ." until his father glanced for an instant down at him, the face absolutely calm, the grizzled eyebrows tangled above the cold eyes, the voice almost pleasant, almost gentle:

"You think so? Well, we'll wait till October anyway."

The matter of the wagon — the setting of a spoke or two and the tightening of the tires — did not take long either, the business of the tires accomplished by driving the wagon into the spring branch behind the shop and letting it stand there, the mules nuzzling into the water from time to time, and the boy on the seat with the idle reins, looking up the slope and through the sooty tunnel of the shed where the slow hammer rang and where his father sat on an upended cypress bolt, easily, either talking or listening, still sitting there when the boy brought the dripping wagon up out of the branch and halted it before the door.

"Take them on to the shade and hitch," his father said. He did so and returned. His father and the smith and a third man squatting on his heels inside the door were talking, about crops and animals; the boy, squatting too in the ammoniac dust and hoof-parings and scales of rust, heard his father tell a long and unhurried story out of the time before the birth of the older brother even when he had been a professional horse trader. And then his father came up beside him where he stood before a tattered last year's circus poster on the other side of the store, gazing rapt and quiet at the scarlet horses, the incredible poisings and convolutions of tulle and tights and the painted leers of comedians, and said, "It's time to eat."

But not at home. Squatting beside his brother against the front wall, he watched his father emerge from the store and produce from a paper sack a segment of cheese and divide it carefully and deliberately into three with his pocket knife and produce crackers from the same sack. They all three squatted on the gallery and ate, slowly, without talking; then in the store again, they drank from a tin dipper tepid water smelling of the cedar bucket and of living beech trees. And still they did not go home. It was a horse lot this time, a tall rail fence upon and along which men stood and sat and out of which one by one horses were led, to be walked and trotted and then cantered back and forth along the road while the slow swapping and buying went on and the sun began to slant westward, they — the three of them — watching, and listening, the older brother with his muddy eyes and his steady, inevitable tobacco, the father commenting now and then on certain of the animals, to no one in particular.

It was after sundown when they reached home. They ate supper by lamplight, then, sitting on the doorstep, the boy watched the night fully accomplish, listening to the whippoorwills and the frogs, when he heard his mother's voice:

"Abner! No! No! Oh, God. Oh, God. Abner!" and he rose, whirled, and saw the altered light through the door where a candle stub now burned in a bottle neck on the table and his father, still in the hat and coat, at once formal and burlesque as though dressed carefully for some shabby and ceremonial violence, emptying the reservoir of the lamp back into the five-gallon kerosene can from which it had been filled, while the mother tugged at his arm until he shifted the lamp to the other hand and flung her back, not savagely or viciously, just hard, into the wall, her hands flung out against the wall for balance, her mouth open and in her face the same quality of hopeless despair as had been in her voice. Then his father saw him standing in the door.

"Go to the barn and get that can of oil we were oiling the wagon with," he said. The boy did not move. Then he could speak.

"What . . ." he cried. "What are you . . ."

"Go get that oil," his father said. "Go."

Then he was moving, running, outside the house, toward the stable: this the old habit, the old blood which he had not been permitted to choose for himself, which had been bequeathed him willy nilly and which had run for so long (and who knew where, battening on what of outrage and savagery and lust) before it came to him. *I could keep on,* he thought. *I could run on and on and never look back, never need to see his face again. Only I can't. I can't,* the rusted can in his hand now, the liquid sploshing in it as he ran back to the house and into it, into the sound of his mother's weeping in the next room, and handed the can to his father.

"Ain't you going to even send a nigger?" he cried. "At least you sent a nigger before!"

This time his father didn't strike him. The hand came even faster than the blow had, the same hand which had set the can on the table with almost excruciating care flashing from the can toward him too quick for him to follow it, gripping him by the back of his shirt and on to tiptoe before he had seen it quit the can, the face stooping at him in breathless and frozen ferocity, the cold, dead voice speaking over him to the older brother who leaned against the table, chewing with that steady, curious, sidewise motion of cows:

"Empty the can into the big one and go on. I'll catch up with you."

"Better tie him up to the bedpost," the brother said.

"Do like I told you," the father said. Then the boy was moving, his bunched shirt and the hard, bony hand between his shoulder-blades, his toes just touching the floor, across the room and into the other one, past the sisters sitting with spread heavy thighs on the two chairs over the cold hearth, and to where his mother and aunt sat side by side on the bed, the aunt's arms about his mother's shoulders.

"Hold him," the father said. The aunt made a startled movement. "Not you," the father said. "Lennie. Take hold of him. I want to see you do it." His mother took him by the wrist. "You'll hold him better than that. If he gets loose don't you know what he is going to do? He will go up yonder." He jerked his head toward the road. "Maybe I'd better tie him."

"I'll hold him," my mother whispered.

"See you do then." Then his father was gone, the stiff foot heavy and measured upon the boards, ceasing at last.

Then he began to struggle. His mother caught him in both arms, he jerking and wrenching at them. He would be stronger in the end, he knew that. But he had no time to wait for it. "Lemme go!" he cried. "I don't want to have to hit you!"

"Let him go!" the aunt said. "If he don't go, before God, I am going up there myself!"

"Don't you see I can't?" his mother cried. "Sarty! Sarty! No! No! Help me, Lizzie!"

Then he was free. His aunt grasped at him but it was too late. He whirled, running, his mother stumbled forward on to her knees behind him, crying to the nearer sister: "Catch him, Net! Catch him!" But that was too late too, the sister (the sisters were twins, born at the same time, yet either of them now gave the impression of being, encompassing as much living meat and volume and weight as any other two of the family) not yet having begun to rise from the chair, her head, face alone merely turned, presenting to him in the flying instant an astonishing expanse of young female features untroubled by any surprise even, wearing only an expression of bovine interest. Then he was out of the room, out of the house, in the mild dust of the starlit road and the heavy rifeness of honeysuckle, the pale ribbon unspooling with terrific slowness under his running feet, reaching the gate at last and turning in, running, his heart and lungs drumming, on up the drive toward the lighted house, the lighted door. He did not knock, he burst in, sobbing for breath, incapable for the moment of speech; he saw the astonished face of the negro in the linen jacket without knowing when the negro had appeared.

"De Spain!" he cried, panted. "Wher's . . ." then he saw the white man too emerging from a white door down the hall. "Barn!" he cried. "Barn!"

"What?" the white man said. "Barn?"

"Yes!" the boy cried. "Barn!"

"Catch him!" the white man shouted.

But it was too late this time too. The negro grasped his shirt, but the entire sleeve, rotten with washing, carried away, and he was out that door too and in the drive again, and had actually never ceased to run even while he was screaming into the white man's face.

Behind him the white man was shouting, "My horse! Fetch my horse!" and he thought for an instant of cutting across the park and climbing the fence into the road, but he did not know the park nor how high the vine-massed fence

might be and he dared not risk it. So he ran on down the drive, blood and breath
roaring; presently he was in the road again though he could not see it. He could
not hear either: the galloping mare was almost upon him before he heard her,
and even then he held his course, as if the very urgency of his wild grief and
need must in a moment more find him wings, waiting until the ultimate instant
to hurl himself aside into the weed-choked roadside ditch as the horse thundered past and on, for an instant in furious silhouette against the stars, the tranquil early summer night sky which, even before the shape of the horse and rider
vanished, stained abruptly and violently upward: a long, swirling roar incredible
and soundless, blotting the stars, and he springing up and into the road again,
running again, knowing it was too late yet still running even after he heard the
shot and, an instant later, two shots, pausing now without knowing he had
ceased to run, crying "Pap! Pap!", running again before he knew he had begun
to run, stumbling, tripping over something and scrabbling up again without
ceasing to run, looking backward over his shoulder at the glare as he got up, running on among the invisible trees, panting, sobbing, "Father! Father!"

At midnight he was sitting on the crest of a hill. He did not know it was midnight and he did not know how far he had come. But there was no glare behind
him now and he sat now, his back toward what he had called home for four days
anyhow, his face toward the dark woods which he would enter when breath was
strong again, small, shaking steadily in the chill darkness, hugging himself into
the remainder of his thin, rotten shirt, the grief and despair now no longer terror and fear but just grief and despair. *Father. My father,* he thought. "He was
brave!" he cried suddenly, aloud but not loud, no more than a whisper: "He was!
He was in the war! He was in Colonel Sartoris' cav'ry!" not knowing that his father had gone to that war a private in the fine old European sense, wearing no
uniform, admitting the authority of and giving fidelity to no man or army or
flag, going to war as Malbrouck himself did: for booty — it meant nothing and
less than nothing to him if it were enemy booty or his own.

The slow constellations wheeled on. It would be dawn and then sun-up after
a while and he would be hungry. But that would be to-morrow and now he was
only cold, and walking would cure that. His breathing was easier now and he decided to get up and go on, and then he found that he had been asleep because he
knew it was almost dawn, the night almost over. He could tell that from the
whippoorwills. They were everywhere now among the dark trees below him,
constant and inflectioned and ceaseless, so that, as the instant for giving over to
the day birds drew nearer and nearer, there was no interval at all between them.
He got up. He was a little stiff, but walking would cure that too as it would the
cold, and soon there would be the sun. He went on down the hill, toward the
dark woods within which the liquid silver voices of the birds called unceasing —
the rapid and urgent beating of the urgent and quiring heart of the late spring
night. He did not look back.

Hisaye Yamamoto

The Legend of Miss Sasagawara

Hisaye Yamamoto was born in Redondo Beach, California, a Nisei, a second-generation Japanese immigrant. Despite her family's patriotism (her brother was killed in World War II in Italy), she and her parents were forced to leave their home for an internment camp in Poston, Arizona, the setting for one of her great stories, "The Legend of Miss Sasagawara." First published in *The Kenyon Review* in 1950 prior to inclusion in *Seventeen Syllables and Other Stories* in 1988, it emphasizes not what might be expected, the unjust treatment of Japanese Americans during the war, but more subtle issues of religion, sexuality, and psychology. The father, for example, is a devout Buddhist who seeks a divine spiritual state in persistent meditation; at the same time he is emotionally remote to his daughter, insensitive to her needs, and negligent of his duties as a parent. The daughter, a ballet dancer somewhat past her prime, struggles with her sexuality, which, given the circumstances of the camp, manifests as voyeurism and eventually causes her emotional breakdown. The narrator, also a member of the camp, observes and reflects on her own experience and what she has observed in the lives of those around her. Yamamoto captures a regrettable but nonetheless significant part of the American experience of the period, and no one has portrayed it in more compelling fiction. It is part of what made her one of the most important Japanese American writers to emerge after the conclusion of World War II.

Hisaye Yamamoto, "The Legend of Miss Sasagawara," *The Kenyon Review* 12, no. 1 (1950): 99–115.

Even in that unlikely place of wind, sand, and heat, it was easy to imagine Miss Sasagawara a decorative ingredient of some ballet. Her daily costume, brief and fitting closely to her trifling waist, generously billowing below, and bringing together arrestingly rich colors like mustard yellow and forest green, appeared to have been cut from a coarse-textured homespun; her shining hair was so long it wound twice about her head to form a coronet; her face was delicate and pale, with a fine nose, pouting bright mouth, and glittering eyes; and her measured walk said, "Look, I'm *walking!*" as though walking were not a common but a rather special thing to be doing. I first saw her so one evening after mess, as she was coming out of the women's latrine, going towards her barracks, and after I thought she was out of hearing, I imitated the young men of the Block (No. 33), and gasped, "Wow! How much does *she* weigh?"

"Oh, haven't you heard?" said my friend Elsie Kubo, knowing very well I had not. "That's Miss Sasagawara."

It turned out Elsie knew all about Miss Sasagawara, who with her father was new to Block 33. Where had she accumulated all her items? Probably a morsel here and a morsel there, and, anyway, I forgot to ask her sources, because the picture she painted was so distracting: Miss Sasagawara's father was a Buddhist minister, and the two had gotten permission to come to this Japanese evacuation camp in Arizona from one farther north, after the death there of Mrs. Sasagawara. They had come here to join the Rev. Sasagawara's brother's family, who lived in a neighboring Block, but there had been some trouble between them, and just this week the immigrant pair had gotten leave to move over to Block 33. They were occupying one end of the Block's lone empty barracks, which had not been chopped up yet into the customary four apartments. The other end had been taken over by a young couple, also newcomers to the Block, who had moved in the same day.

"And do you know what, Kiku?" Elsie continued. "Oooh, that gal is really temperamental. I guess it's because she was a ballet dancer before she got stuck in camp, I hear people like that are temperamental. Anyway, the Sasakis, the new couple at the other end of the barracks, think she's crazy. The day they all moved in, the barracks was really dirty, all covered with dust from the dust storms and everything, so Mr. Sasaki was going to wash the whole barracks down with a hose, and he thought he'd be nice and do the Sasagawara's side first. You know, do them a favor. But do you know what? Mr. Sasaki got the hose attached to the faucet outside and started to go in the door, and he said all the Sasagawaras' suitcases and things were on top of the Army cots and Miss Sasagawara was trying to clean the place out with a pail of water and a broom. He said, 'Here let me flush the place out with a hose for you; it'll be faster.' And she turned right around and screamed at him, 'What are you trying to do? Spy on me? Get out of here or I'll throw this water on you!' He said he was so surprised he couldn't move for a minute, and before he knew it, Miss Sasagawara just up and threw that water at him, pail and all. Oh, he said he got out of that place fast, but fast. Madwoman, he called her."

But Elsie had already met Miss Sasagawara, too, over at the apartment of the Murakamis, where Miss Sasagawara was borrowing Mrs. Murakami's Singer, and had found her quite amiable. "She said she was thirty-nine years old — imagine, thirty-nine, she looks so young, more like twenty-five; but she said she wasn't sorry she never got married, because she's had her fun. She said she got to go all over the country a couple of times, dancing in the ballet."

And after we emerged from the latrine, Elsie and I, slapping mosquitoes in the warm, gathering dusk, sat on the stoop of her apartment and talked awhile, jealously of the scintillating life Miss Sasagawara had led until now and nostalgically of a few ballets we had seen in the world outside (how faraway Los Angeles seemed!), but we ended up as we always did, agreeing that our mission in life, pushing twenty as we were, was first to finish college somewhere when and if the war ever ended, and we were free again, and then to find good jobs and two nice, clean young men, preferably handsome, preferably rich, who would cherish us forever and a day.

My introduction, less spectacular, to the Rev. Sasagawara came later, as I noticed him, a slight and fragile-looking old man, in the Block mess hall (where I worked as a waitress, and Elsie, too) or laundry room or going to and from the latrine. Sometimes he would be farther out, perhaps going to the post-office or canteen or to visit friends in another Block or on some business to the Administration buildings, but wherever he was headed, however doubtless his destination, he always seemed to be wandering lostly. This may have been because he walked so slowly, with such negligible steps, or because he wore perpetually an air of bemusement, never talking directly to a person, as though, being what he was, he could not stop for an instant his meditation on the higher life.

I noticed, too, that Miss Sasagawara never came to the mess hall herself. Her father ate at the tables reserved for the occupants, mostly elderly, of the end barracks known as the bachelors' dormitory. After each meal, he came up to the counter and carried away a plate of food, protected with one of the pinkish apple wrappers we waitresses made as wrinkleless as possible and put out for napkins, and a mug of tea or coffee. Sometimes Miss Sasagawara could be seen rinsing her empties at the one double-tub in the laundry that was reserved for private dishwashing.

If any one in the Block or in the entire camp of 15,000 or so people had talked at any length with Miss Sasagawara (everyone happening to speak of her called her that, although her first name, Mari, was simple enough and rather pretty) after her first and only visit to use Mrs. Murakami's sewing machine, I never heard of it. Nor did she ever willingly use the shower room, just off the latrine, when anyone else was there. Once, when I was up past midnight writing letters and went for my shower, I came upon her under the full needling force of a steamy spray, but she turned her back to me and did not answer my surprised hello. I hoped my body would be as smooth and spare and well-turned when I was thirty-nine. Another time, Elsie and I passed in front of the Sasagawara apartment, which was really only a cubicle because the once-empty barracks had soon been partitioned off into six units for families of two, and we saw her there on the wooden steps, sitting with her wide, wide skirt spread splendidly about her. She was intent on peeling a grapefruit, which her father had probably brought to her from the mess hall that morning, and Elsie called out, "Hello there!" Miss Sasagawara looked up and stared, without recognition. We were almost out of earshot when I heard her call, "Do I know you?" and I could have almost sworn that she sounded hopeful, if not downright wistful, but Elsie, already miffed at having expended friendliness so unprofitably, seemed not to have heard, and that was that.

Well, if Miss Sasagawara was not one to speak to, she was certainly one to speak of, and she came up quite often as topic for the endless conversations which helped along the monotonous days. My mother said she had met the late Mrs. Sasagawara once, many years before the war, and to hear her tell it, a sweeter, kindlier woman there never was. "I suppose," said my mother, "that I'll never meet anyone like her again; she was a lady in every sense of the word." Then she reminded me that I had seen the Rev. Sasagawara before. Didn't I remember him as one of the three bhikshus who had read the sutras at Grandfather's funeral?

I could not say that I did. I barely remembered Grandfather, my mother's father. The only thing that came back with clarity was my nausea at the wake and the funeral, the first and only ones I had ever had occasion to attend, because it had been reproduced several times since — each time, in fact, that I had crossed again the actual scent or a suspicion of burning incense. Dimly I recalled the inside of the Buddhist temple in Los Angeles, an immense, murky auditorium whose high and huge platform had held, centered in the background, a great golden shrine touched with black and white. Below this platform, Grandfather, veiled by gauze, had slept in a long, grey box which just fitted him. There had been flowers, oh, such flowers, everywhere. And right in front of Grandfather's box had been the incense stand, upon which squatted two small bowls, one with a cluster of straw-thin sticks sending up white tendrils of smoke, the other containing a heap of coarse, grey powder. Each mourner in turn had gone up to the stand, bowing once, his palms touching in prayer, before he reached it; had bent in prayer over the stand; had taken then a pinch of incense from the bowl of crumbs and, bowing over it reverently, cast it into the other, the active bowl; had bowed, the hands praying again; had retreated a few steps and bowed one last time, the hands still joined, before returning to his seat. (I knew the ceremony well for having been severely coached in it on the evening of the wake.) There had been tears and tears and here and there a sudden sob.

And all this while, three men in black robes had been on the platform, one standing in front of the shining altar, the others sitting on either side, and the entire trio incessantly chanting a strange, mellifluous language in unison. From time to time there had reverberated through the enormous room, above the singsong, above the weeping, above the fragrance, the sharp, startling whang of the gong.

So, one of those men had been Miss Sasagawara's father. . . . This information brought him closer to me, and I listened with interest later when it was told that he kept here in his apartment a small shrine, much more intricately constructed than that kept by the usual Buddhist household, before which, at regular hours of the day, he offered incense and chanted, tinkling (in lieu of the gong) a small bell. What did Miss Sasagawara do at these prayer periods, I wondered; did she participate, did she let it go in one ear and out the other, or did she abruptly go out on the steps, perhaps to eat a grapefruit?

◈◈

Elsie and I tired one day of working in the mess hall. And this desire for greener fields came almost together with the Administration announcement that henceforth all wages of residents doing truly vital labor, such as in the hospital or on the garbage trucks that went from mess hall to mess hall, would be upped to nineteen dollars a month instead of the common sixteen.

"Oh, I've always wanted to be a nurse!" Elsie confided, as the Block manager sat down to his breakfast after reading out the day's bulletin in English and Japanese.

"What's stopped you?" I asked.

"Mom," Elsie said. "She thinks it's dirty work. And she's afraid I'll catch something. But I'll remind her of the extra three dollars."

"It's never appealed to me much, either," I confessed. "Why don't we go over to garbage? It's the same pay."

Elsie would not even consider it. "Very funny. Well, you don't have to be a nurse's aide, Kiku. The hospital's short all kinds of help. Dental assistants, receptionists. . . . Let's go apply after we finish this here."

So, willy-nilly, while Elsie plunged gleefully into the pleasure of wearing a trim blue-and-white striped seersucker, into the duties of taking temperatures and carrying bed-pans, and into the fringe of medical jargon (she spoke very casually now of catheters, enemas, primiparas, multiparas), I became a relief receptionist at the hospital's front desk, taking my hours as they were assigned. And it was on one of my midnight-to-morning shifts that I spoke to Miss Sasagawara for the first time.

The cooler in the corridor window was still whirring away (for that desert heat in Summer had a way of lingering intact through the night to merge with the warmth of the morning sun), but she entered bundled in an extraordinarily long black coat, her face made petulant, not unprettily, by lines of pain.

"I think I've got appendicitis," she said breathlessly, without preliminary.

"May I have your name and address?" I asked, unscrewing my pen.

Annoyance seemed to outbalance agony for a moment, but she answered soon enough, in a cold rush, "Mari Sasagawara. Thirty-three-seven C."

It was necessary also to learn her symptoms, and I wrote down that she had chills and a dull aching at the back of her head, as well as these excruciating flashes in her lower right abdomen.

"I'll have to go wake up the doctor. Here's a blanket, why don't you lie down over there on the bench until he comes?" I suggested.

She did not answer, so I tossed the Army blanket on the bench, and when I returned from the doctors' dormitory, after having tapped and tapped on the door of young Dr. Moritomo, who was on night duty, she was still standing where I had left her, immobile and holding onto the wooden railing shielding the desk.

"Dr. Moritomo's coming right away," I said. "Why don't you sit down at least?"

Miss Sasagawara said, "Yes," but did not move.

"Did you walk all the way?" I asked incredulously, for Block 33 was a good mile off, across the canal.

She nodded, as if that were not important, also as if to thank me kindly to mind my own business.

Dr. Moritomo (technically, the title was premature; evacuation had caught him with a few months to go on his degree), wearing a maroon bathrobe, shuffled in sleepily and asked her to come into the emergency room for an examination. A short while later, he guided her past my desk into the laboratory, saying he was going to take her blood count.

When they came out, she went over to the electric fountain for a drink of water, and Dr. Moritomo said reflectively, "Her count's all right. Not appendicitis. We should keep her for observation, but the general ward is pretty full, isn't it? Hm, well, I'll give her something to take. Will you tell one of the boys to take her home?"

This I did, but when I came back from arousing George, one of the ambulance boys, Miss Sasagawara was gone, and Dr. Moritomo was coming out of the laboratory where he had gone to push out the lights. "Here's George, but that girl must have walked home," I reported helplessly.

"She's in no condition to do that. George, better catch up with her and take her home," Dr. Moritomo ordered.

Shrugging, George strode down the hall; the doctor shuffled back to bed; and soon there was the shattering sound of one of the old Army ambulances backing out of the hospital drive.

George returned in no time at all to say that Miss Sasagawara had refused to get on the ambulance. "She wouldn't even listen to me. She just kept walking and I drove alongside and told her it was Dr. Moritomo's orders, but she wouldn't even listen to me."

"She wouldn't?"

"I hope Doc didn't expect me to drag her into the ambulance."

"Oh, well," I said. "I guess she'll get home all right. She walked all the way up here."

"Cripes, what a dame!" George complained, shaking his head as he started back to the ambulance room. "I never heard of such a thing. She wouldn't even listen to me."

∮ఠ

Miss Sasagawara came back to the hospital about a month later. Elsie was the one who rushed up to the desk where I was on day duty to whisper, "Miss Sasagawara just tried to escape from the hospital!"

"Escape? What do you mean, escape?" I said.

"Well, she came in last night, and they didn't know what was wrong with her, so they kept her for observation. And this morning, just now, she ran out of the ward in just a hospital nightgown and the orderlies chased after her and caught her and brought her back. Oh, she was just fighting them. But once they got her back to bed, she calmed down right away, and Miss Morris asked her what was the big idea, you know, and do you know what she said? She said she didn't want any more of those doctors pawing her. *Pawing* her, imagine!"

After an instant's struggle with self-mockery, my curiosity led me down the entrance corridor after Elsie, into the longer, wider corridor admitting to the general ward. The whole hospital staff appeared to have gathered in the room to get a look at Miss Sasagawara, and the other patients, or those of them that could, were sitting up attentively in their high, white, and narrow beds. Miss Sasagawara had the corner bed to the left as we entered and, covered only by a brief hospital apron, she was sitting on the edge with her legs dangling over the side. With her head slightly bent, she was staring at a certain place on the floor, and I knew she must be aware of that concentrated gaze, of trembling old Dr. Kawamoto (he had retired several years before the war, but he had been drafted here), of Miss Morris, the head nurse, of Miss Bowman, the nurse in charge of the general ward during the day, of the other patients, of the nurse's aides, of the orderlies, and of everyone else who tripped in and out abashedly on some pretext or other in order to pass by her bed. I knew this by her smile, for as she continued to look at that same piece of floor, she continued, unexpectedly, to seem wryly amused with the entire proceedings. I peered at her wonderingly through the triangular peep-hole created by someone's hand on hip, while Dr. Kawamoto, Miss Morris, and Miss Bowman tried to persuade her to lie down and relax. She was as smilingly immune to tactful suggestions as she was to tactless gawking.

There was no future to watching such a war of nerves as this, and besides, I was supposed to be at the front desk, so I hurried back in time to greet a frantic young mother and father, the latter carrying their small son who had had a hemorrhage this morning after a tonsillectomy yesterday in the out-patient clinic.

A couple of weeks later, on the late shift, I found George, the ambulance driver, in high spirits. This time he had been the one selected to drive a patient to Phoenix, where special cases were occasionally sent under escort, and he was looking forward to the moment when, for a few hours, the escort would permit him to go shopping around the city and perhaps take in a new movie. He showed me the list of things his friends had asked him to bring back for them, and we laughed together over the request of one plumpish nurse's aide for the biggest, richest chocolate cake he could find.

"You ought to have seen Mabel's eyes while she was describing the kind of cake she wanted," he said. "Man, she looked like she was eating it already!"

Just then one of the other drivers, Bobo Kunitomi, came up and nudged George, and they withdrew a few steps from my desk.

"Oh, I ain't particularly interested in that," I heard George saying.

There was some murmuring from Bobo, of which I caught the words, "Well, hell, you might as well, just as long as you're getting to go out there."

George shrugged, then nodded, and Bobo came over to the desk and asked for pencil and paper. "This is a good place. . . ." he said, handing George what he had written.

Was it my imagination, or did George emerge from his chat with Bobo a little ruddier than usual? "Well, I guess I better go get ready," he said, taking leave. "Oh, anything you want, Kiku? Just say the word."

"Thanks, not this time," I said. "Well, enjoy yourself."

"Don't worry," he said. "I will!"

He had started down the hall when I remembered to ask, "Who are you taking, anyway?"

George turned around. "Miss Sa-sa-ga-wa-ra," he said, accenting every syllable. "Remember that dame? The one who wouldn't let me take her home?"

"Yes," I said. "What's the matter with her?"

George, saying not a word, pointed at his head and made several circles in the air with his first finger.

"Really?" I asked.

Still mum, George nodded in emphasis and pity before he turned to go.

❦❦

How long was she away? It must have been several months, and when, towards late Autumn, she returned at last from the sanitarium in Phoenix, everyone in Block 33 was amazed at the change. She said hello and how are you as often and easily as the next person, although many of those she greeted were surprised and suspicious, remembering the earlier rebuffs. There were some who never did get used to Miss Sasagawara as a friendly being.

One evening when I was going toward the latrine for my shower, my youngest sister, ten-year-old Michi, almost collided with me and said excitedly, "You going for your shower now, Kiku?"

"You want to fight about it?" I said, making fists.

"Don't go now, don't go now! Miss Sasagawara's in there," she whispered wickedly.

"Well," I demanded. "What's wrong with that, honey?"

"She's scary. Us kids were in there and she came in and we finished, so we got out, and she said, 'Don't be afraid of me. I won't hurt you.' Gee, we weren't even afraid of her, but when she said that, gee!"

"Oh, go on home and go to bed," I said.

Miss Sasagawara was indeed in the shower and she welcomed me with a smile. "Aren't you the girl who plays the violin?"

I giggled and explained. Elsie and I, after hearing Menuhin on the radio, had, in a fit of madness, sent to Sears and Roebuck for beginners' violins that cost five dollars each. We had received free instruction booklets, too, but, unable to make heads or tails from them, we contented ourselves with occasionally taking the violins out of their paper bags and sawing every whichway away.

Miss Sasagawara laughed aloud — a lovely sound. "Well, you're just about as good as I am. I sent for a Spanish guitar. I studied it about a year once, but that was so long ago I don't remember the first thing and I'm having to start all over again. We'd make a fine orchestra."

That was the only time we really exchanged words, and some weeks later, I understood she had organized a dancing class from among the younger girls in the Block. My sister Michi, becoming one of her pupils, got very attached to her and spoke of her frequently at home. So I knew Miss Sasagawara and her father had decorated their apartment to look oh, so pretty, that Miss Sasagawara had a whole big suitcase full of dancing costumes, and that Miss Sasagawara had just lots and lots of books to read.

The fruits of Miss Sasagawara's patient labor were put on show at the Block Christmas party, the second such observance in camp. Again, it was a gay, if odd, celebration. The mess hall was hung with red and green crêpe-paper streamers and the greyish mistletoe that grew abundantly on the ancient mesquite surrounding the camp. There were even electric decorations on the token Christmas tree. The oldest occupant of the bachelors' dormitory gave a tremulous monologue in an exaggerated Hiroshima dialect, one of the young boys wore a bowtie and whispered a popular song while the girls shrieked and pretended to be growing faint, my mother sang an old Japanese song, four of the girls wore similar blue dresses and harmonized on a sweet tune, a little girl in a grass skirt and superfluous brassiere did a hula, and the chief cook came out with an ample saucepan and, assisted by the waitresses, performed the familiar *dojo-sukui,* the comic dance about a man who is merely trying to scoop up a few loaches from an uncooperative lake. Then Miss Sasagawara shooed her eight little girls, including Michi, in front, and while they formed a stiff pattern and waited, self-conscious in the rustly crêpe-paper dresses they had made themselves, she set up a portable phonograph on the floor and vigorously turned the crank.

Something was past its prime, either the machine or the record or the needle, for what came out was a feeble rasp but distantly related to the Mozart minuet it was supposed to be. After a bit I recognized the melody; I had learned it as a child to the words,

> When dames wore hoops and powdered hair,
> And very strict was e-ti-quette,
> When men were brave and ladies fair,
> They danced the min-u-et. . . .

And the little girls, who might have curtsied and stepped gracefully about under Miss Sasagawara's eyes alone, were all elbows and knees as they felt the Block's one-hundred-and-fifty or more pairs of eyes on them. Although there was sustained applause after their number, what we were benevolently approving was the great effort, for the achievement had been undeniably small. Then Santa came with a pillow for a stomach, his hands each dragging a bulging burlap bag. Church people outside had kindly sent these gifts, Santa announced, and every recipient must write and thank the person whose name he would find on an enclosed slip. So saying, he called by name each Block child under twelve and ceremoniously presented each eleemosynary package, and a couple of the youngest children screamed in fright at this new experience of a red and white man with a booming voice.

At the last, Santa called, "Miss Mari Sasagawara!" and when she came forward in surprise, he explained to the gathering that she was being rewarded for her help with the Block's younger generation. Everyone clapped and Miss Sasagawara, smiling graciously, opened her package then and there. She held up her gift, a peach-colored bath towel, so that it could be fully seen, and everyone clapped again.

♪♪

Suddenly, I put this desert scene behind me. The notice I had long awaited, of permission to relocate to Philadelphia to attend college, finally came, and there was a prodigious amount of packing to do, leave papers to sign, and goodbyes to say. And once the wearying, sooty train trip was over, I found myself in an intoxicating new world of daily classes, afternoon teas, and evening concerts, from which I dutifully emerged now and then to answer the letters from home. When the beautiful semester was over, I returned to Arizona, to that glowing heat, to the camp, to the family, for although the war was still on, it had been decided to close down the camps, and I had been asked to go back and spread the good word about higher education among the young people who might be dispersed in this way.

Elsie was still working in the hospital, although she had applied for entrance into the cadet nurse corps and was expecting acceptance any day, and the long conversations we held were mostly about the good old days, the good old days when we had worked in the mess hall together, the good old days when we had worked in the hospital together.

"What ever became of Miss Sasagawara?" I asked one day, seeing the Rev. Sasagawara go abstractly by. "Did she relocate somewhere?"

"I didn't write you about her, did I?" Elsie said meaningfully. "Yes, she's relocated all right. Haven't seen her around, have you?"

"Where did she go?"

Elsie answered offhandedly. "California."

"California?" I exclaimed. "We can't go back to California. What's she doing in California?"

So Elsie told me: Miss Sasagawara had been sent back there to a state institution, oh, not so very long after I had left for school. She had begun slipping back into her aloof ways almost immediately after Christmas, giving up the dancing class and not speaking to people. Then Elsie had heard a couple of very strange, yes, very strange things about her. One thing had been told by young Mrs. Sasaki, the next-door neighbor of the Sasagawaras.

Mrs. Sasaki said she had once come upon Miss Sasagawara sitting, as was her habit, on the porch. Mrs. Sasaki had been shocked to the core to see that the face of this thirty-nine-year-old woman (or was she forty now?) wore a beatific expression as she watched the activity going on in the doorway of her neighbors across the way, the Yoshinagas. This activity had been the joking and loud laughter of Joe and Frank, the young Yoshinaga boys, and three or four of their friends. Mrs. Sasaki would have let the matter go, were it not for the fact that Miss Sasagawara was so absorbed a spectator of this horseplay that her head was bent to one side and she actually had one finger in her mouth as she gazed, in the manner of a shy child confronted with a marvel. "What's the matter with you, watching the boys like that?" Mrs. Sasaki had cried. "You're old enough to be their mother!" Startled, Miss Sasagawara had jumped up and dashed back into her apartment. And when Mrs. Sasaki had gone into hers, adjoining the Sasagawaras', she had been terrified to hear Miss Sasagawara begin to bang on the wooden walls with something heavy like a hammer. The banging, which sounded as though Miss Sasagawara was using all her strength on each blow, had continued wildly for at least five minutes. Then all had been still.

The other thing had been told by Joe Yoshinaga, who lived across the way from Miss Sasagawara. Joe and his brother slept on two Army cots pushed together on one side of the room, while their parents had a similar arrangement on the other side. Joe had standing by his bed an apple crate for a shelf, and he was in the habit of reading his sports and western magazines in bed and throwing them on top of the crate before he went to sleep. But one morning he had noticed his magazines all neatly stacked inside the crate, when he was sure he had carelessly thrown some on top the night before, as usual. This happened several times, and he finally asked his family whether one of them had been putting his magazines away after he fell asleep. They had said no and laughed, telling him he must be getting absent-minded. But the mystery had been solved late one night, when Joe gradually awoke in his cot with the feeling that he was being watched. Warily, he had opened one eye slightly and had been thoroughly awakened and chilled, in the bargain, by what he saw. For what he saw was Miss Sasagawara sitting there on his apple crate, her long hair all undone and flowing about her. She was dressed in a white nightgown and her hands were clasped on her lap. And all she was doing was sitting there watching him, Joe Yoshinaga. He could not help it, he had sat up and screamed. His mother, a light sleeper, came running to see what had happened, just as Miss Sasagawara was running out the door, the door they had always left unlatched, or even wide open in Summer. In the morning, Mrs. Yoshinaga had gone straight to the Rev. Sasagawara and asked him to do something about his daughter. The Rev. Sasagawara, sympathizing with her indignation in his benign but vague manner, had said he would have a talk with Mari.

And, concluded Elsie, Miss Sasagawara had gone away not long after. I was impressed, although Elsie's sources were not what I would ordinarily pay much attention to, Mrs. Sasaki, that plump and giggling young woman who always felt called upon to explain that she was childless by choice, and Joe Yoshinaga, who had a knack of blowing up, in his drawling voice, any incident in which he personally played even a small part (I could imagine the field day he had had with this one). Elsie puzzled aloud over the cause of Miss Sasagawara's derangement, and I, who had so newly had some contact with the recorded explorations into the virgin territory of the human mind, sagely explained that Miss Sasagawara had no doubt looked upon Joe Yoshinaga as the image of either the lost lover or the lost son. But my words made me uneasy by their glibness, and I began to wonder seriously about Miss Sasagawara for the first time.

Then there was this last word from Miss Sasagawara herself, making her strange legend as complete as I, at any rate, would probably ever know it. This came some time after I had gone back to Philadelphia and the family had joined me there, when I was neck deep in research for my final paper. I happened one day to be looking through the last issue of a small poetry magazine that had suspended publication midway through the war. I felt a thrill of recognition in the name, Mari Sasagawara, signed to a long poem, introduced as ". . . the first published poem of a Japanese-American woman who is, at present, an evacuee from the West Coast making her home in a War Relocation center in Arizona."

It was a *tour de force,* erratically brilliant and, through the first readings, tantalizingly obscure. It appeared to be about a man whose lifelong aim had been to achieve Nirvana, that saintly state of moral purity and universal wisdom. This man had in his way certain handicaps, all stemming from his having acquired, when young and unaware, a family for which he must provide. The day came at last, however, when his wife died and other circumstances made it unnecessary for him to earn a competitive living. These circumstances were considered by those about him as sheer imprisonment, but he had felt free for the first time in his long life. It became possible for him to extinguish within himself all unworthy desire and consequently all evil, to concentrate on that serene, eight-fold path of highest understanding, highest mindedness, highest speech, highest action, highest livelihood, highest recollectedness, highest endeavor, and highest meditation.

This man was certainly noble, the poet wrote, this man was beyond censure. The world was doubtless enriched by his presence. But say that someone else, someone sensitive, someone admiring, someone who had not achieved this sublime condition and who did not wish to, were somehow called to companion such a man. Was it not likely that the saint, blissfully bent on cleansing from his already radiant soul the last imperceptible blemishes (for, being perfect, would he not humbly suspect his own flawlessness?) would be deaf and blind to the human passions rising, subsiding, and again rising, perhaps in anguished silence, within the selfsame room? The poet could not speak for others, of course; she could only speak for herself. But she would describe this man's devotion as a sort of madness, the monstrous sort which, pure of itself and so with immunity, might possibly bring troublous, scented scenes to recur in the other's sleep.

Flannery O'Connor

The River

Flannery O'Connor's controversial story "The River" was published in the *Sewanee Review* in 1953 prior to its inclusion in *A Good Man Is Hard to Find and Other Stories* two years later. It is typical of her fiction in its utilization of Christian mythology, which often has both comic and tragic implications. Nearly all of her work ends in devastating circumstances, despite the heavy emphasis on grace as a redemptive religious principle. Born in 1925 to a Roman Catholic family in Savannah, O'Connor was raised in Milledgeville, where she enrolled in Georgia State College before further study in the Writer's Workshop at the University of Iowa. Her first book was a novel, *Wise Blood,* followed by a collection of nine stories under the title *A Good Man Is Hard to Find and Other Stories.* Her novel *The Violent Bear It Away* preceded another story collection, *Everything That Rises Must Converge,* a year after her death. In 1971, *The Complete Stories of Flannery O'Connor* won the National Book Award, solidifying her stature as one of the preeminent writers of short fiction. Beyond the grotesque evocation of the mysteries of religion, her work is characterized by artistic subtlety and complexity, a reflection of her interest in the New Critical theories of the midcentury. As a result, her fiction often employs narrative modulations, patterns of imagery that underscore thematic development, and structural parallelism. In "The River," for example, the third-person perspective is identified primarily with the mind of the young boy, but it shifts to provide other views of events: the boys at the pig pen, Mr. Paradise in the river. The changes in setting are also meaningful, from the secular dissipation of the Ashfield home, the poverty and yet domestic richness of the Connin family, and the mystical confusion of the baptismal scene in the stream. Religion means something quite different in each context, and the ironic perspective of Mr. Paradise provides yet another assessment. It is dramatically appropriate that it is he, the skeptic, who attempts to preserve life at the end.

Flannery O'Connor, "The River," *Sewanee Review* 61, no. 3 (Summer 1953): 455–75.

The child stood glum and limp in the middle of the dark living room while his father pulled him into a plaid coat. His right arm was hung in the sleeve but the father buttoned the coat anyway and pushed him forward toward a pale spotted hand that stuck through the half-open door.

"He ain't fixed right," a loud voice said from the hall.

"Well then for Christ's sake fix him," the father muttered. "It's six o'clock in the morning." He was in his bathrobe and barefooted. When he got the child to the door and tried to shut it, he found her looming in it, a speckled skeleton in a long pea-green coat and felt helmet.

"And his and my carfare," she said. "It'll be twict we have to ride the car."

He went in the bedroom again to get the money and when he came back, she and the boy were both standing in the middle of the room. She was taking stock. "I couldn't smell those dead cigarette butts long if I was ever to come sit with you," she said, shaking him down in his coat.

"Here's the change," the father said. He went to the door and opened it wide and waited.

After she had counted the money she slipped it somewhere inside her coat and walked over to a watercolor hanging near the phonograph. "I know what time it is," she said, peering closely at the black lines crossing into broken planes of violent color. "I ought to. My shift goes on at 10 P.M. and don't get off till 5 and it takes me one hour to ride the Vine Street car."

"Oh, I see," he said; "well, we'll expect him back tonight, about eight or nine?"

"Maybe later," she said. "We're going to the river to a healing. This particular preacher don't get around this way often. I wouldn't have paid for that," she said, nodding at the painting, "I would have drew it myself."

"All right, Mrs. Connin, we'll see you then," he said, drumming on the door.

A toneless voice called from the bedroom, "Bring me an icepack."

"Too bad his mamma's sick," Mrs. Connin said. "What's her trouble?"

"We don't know," he muttered.

"We'll ask the preacher to pray for her. He's healed a lot of folks. The Reverend Bevel Summers. Maybe she ought to see him sometime."

"Maybe so," he said. "We'll see you tonight," and he disappeared into the bedroom and left them to go.

The little boy stared at her silently, his nose and eyes running. He was four or five. He had a long face and bulging chin and half-shut eyes set far apart. He seemed mute and patient, like an old sheep waiting to be let out.

"You'll like this preacher," she said. "The Reverend Bevel Summers. You ought to hear him sing."

The bedroom door opened suddenly and the father stuck his head out and said, "Good-by, old man. Have a good time."

"Good-by," the little boy said and jumped as if he had been shot.

Mrs. Connin gave the watercolor another look. Then they went out into the hall and rang for the elevator. "I wouldn't have drew it," she said.

Outside the gray morning was blocked off on either side by the unlit empty buildings. "It's going to fair up later," she said, "but this is the last time we'll be able to have any preaching at the river this year. Wipe your nose, Sugar Boy."

He began rubbing his sleeve across it but she stopped him. "That ain't nice," she said. "Where's your handkerchief?"

He put his hands in his pockets and pretended to look for it while she waited. "Some people don't care how they send one off," she murmured to her reflection in the coffee shop window. "You pervide." She took a red and blue flowered handkerchief out of her pocket and stooped down and began to work on his nose. "Now blow," she said and he blew. "You can borry it. Put it in your pocket."

He folded it up and put it in his pocket carefully and they walked on to the corner and leaned against the side of a closed drugstore to wait for the car. Mrs. Connin turned up her coat collar so that it met her hat in the back. Her eyelids began to droop and she looked as if she might go to sleep against the wall. The little boy put a slight pressure on her hand.

"What's your name?" she asked in a drowsy voice. "I don't know but only your last name. I should have found out your first name."

His name was Harry Ashfield and he had never thought at any time before of changing it. "Bevel," he said.

Mrs. Connin raised herself from the wall. "Why ain't that a coincident!" she said. "I told you that's the name of this preacher!"

"Bevel," he repeated.

She stood looking down at him as if he had become a marvel to her. "I'll have to see you meet him today," she said. "He's no ordinary preacher. He's a healer. He couldn't do nothing for Mr. Connin though. Mr. Connin didn't have the faith but he said he would try anything once. He had this griping in his gut."

The trolley appeared as a yellow spot at the end of the deserted street.

"He's gone to the government hospital now," she said, "and they taken one-third of his stomach. I tell him he better thank Jesus for what he's got left but he says he ain't thanking nobody. Well I declare," she murmured, "Bevel!"

They walked out to the tracks to wait. "Will he heal me?" Bevel asked.

"What you got?"

"I'm hungry," he decided finally.

"Didn't you have your breakfast?"

"I didn't have time to be hungry yet then," he said.

"Well when we get home we'll both have us something," she said. "I'm ready myself."

They got on the car and sat down a few seats behind the driver and Mrs. Connin took Bevel on her knees. "Now you be a good boy," she said, "and let me get some sleep. Just don't get off my lap." She lay her head back and as he watched, gradually her eyes closed and her mouth fell open to show a few long scattered teeth, some gold and some darker than her face; she began to whistle and blow like a musical skeleton. There was no one in the car but themselves and the driver and when he saw she was asleep, he took out the flowered handkerchief and unfolded it and examined it carefully. Then he folded it up again and unzipped a place in the innerlining of his coat and hid it in there and shortly he went to sleep himself.

Her house was a half-mile from the end of the car line, set back a little from the road. It was tan paper brick with a porch across the front of it and a tin top. On the porch there were three little boys of different sizes with identical speckled faces and one tall girl who had her hair up in so many aluminum curlers that it glared like the roof. The three boys followed them inside and closed in on Bevel. They looked at him silently, not smiling.

"That's Bevel," Mrs. Connin said, taking off her coat. "It's a coincident he's named the same as the preacher. These boys are J. C., Spivey, and Sinclair, and that's Sarah Mildred on the porch. Take off that coat and hang it on the bed post, Bevel."

The three boys watched him while he unbuttoned the coat and took it off. Then they watched him hang it on the bed post and then they stood, watching the coat. They turned abruptly and went out the door and had a conference on the porch.

Bevel stood looking around him at the room. It was part kitchen and part bedroom. The entire house was two rooms and two porches. Close to his foot the tail of a light-colored dog moved up and down between two floor boards as he scratched his back on the underside of the house. Bevel jumped on it but the hound was experienced and had already withdrawn when his feet hit the spot.

The walls were filled with pictures and calendars. There were two round photographs of an old man and woman with collapsed mouths and another picture of a man whose eyebrows dashed out of two bushes of hair and clashed in a heap on the bridge of his nose; the rest of his face stuck out like a bare cliff to fall from. "That's Mr. Connin," Mrs. Connin said, standing back from the stove for a second to admire the face with him, "but it don't favor him any more." Bevel turned from Mr. Connin to a colored picture over the bed of a man wearing a white sheet. He had long hair and a gold circle around his head and he was sawing on a board while some children stood watching him. He was going to ask who that was when the three boys came in again and motioned for him to follow them. He thought of crawling under the bed and hanging onto one of the legs but the three boys only stood there, speckled and silent, waiting, and after a second he followed them at a little distance out on the porch and around the corner of the house. They started off through a field of rough yellow weeds to the hog pen, a five-foot boarded square full of shoats, which they intended to ease him over into. When they reached it, they turned and waited silently, leaning against the side.

He was coming very slowly, deliberately bumping his feet together as if he had trouble walking. Once he had been beaten up in the park by some strange boys when his sitter forgot him, but he hadn't known anything was going to happen that time until it was over. He began to smell a strong odor of garbage and to hear the noises of a wild animal. He stopped a few feet from the pen and waited, pale but dogged.

The three boys didn't move. Something seemed to have happened to them. They stared over his head as if they saw something coming behind him but he was afraid to turn his own head and look. Their speckles were pale and their eyes were still and gray as glass. Only their ears twitched slightly. Nothing happened. Finally, the one in the middle said, "She'd kill us," and turned, dejected and hacked, and climbed up on the pen and hung over, staring in.

Bevel sat down on the ground, dazed with relief, and grinned up at them.

The one sitting on the pen glanced at him severely. "Hey you," he said after a second, "if you can't climb up and see these pigs you can lift that bottom board off and look in thataway." He appeared to offer this as a kindness.

Bevel had never seen a real pig but he had seen a pig in a book and knew they were small fat pink animals with curly tails and round grinning faces and bow ties. He leaned forward and pulled eagerly at the board.

"Pull harder," the littlest boy said. "It's nice and rotten. Just life out thet nail."

He eased a long reddish nail out of the soft wood.

"Now you can lift up on the board and put your face to the . . ." a quiet voice began.

He had already done it and another face, gray, wet and sour, was pushing into his, knocking him down and back as it scraped out under the plank. Something snorted over him and charged back again, rolling him over and pushing him up from behind and then sending him forward, screaming through the yellow field, while it bounded behind.

The three Connins watched from where they were. The one sitting on the pen held the loose board back with is dangling foot. Their stern faces didn't brighten any but they seemed to become less taut, as if some great need had been partly satisfied. "Maw ain't going to like him lettin out thet hawg," the smallest one said.

Mrs. Connin was on the back porch and caught Bevel up as he reached the steps. The hog ran under the house and subsided, panting, but the child screamed for five minutes. When she had finally calmed him down, she gave him his breakfast and let him sit on her lap while he ate it. The shoat climbed the two steps onto the back porch and stood outside the screen door, looking in with his head lowered sullenly. He was long-legged and hump-backed and part of one of his ears had been bitten off.

"Git away!" Mrs. Connin shouted. "That one yonder favors Mr. Paradise that has the gas station," she said. "You'll see him today at the healing. He's got the cancer over his ear. He always comes to show he ain't been healed."

The shoat stood squinting a few seconds longer and then moved off slowly. "I don't want to see him," Bevel said.

♪♪

They walked to the river, Mrs. Connin in front with him and the three boys strung out behind and Sarah Mildred, the tall girl, at the end to holler if one of them ran out on the road. They looked like the skeleton of an old boat with two pointed ends, sailing slowly on the edge of the highway. The white Sunday sun followed at a little distance, climbing fast through a scum of gray cloud as if it meant to overtake them. Bevel walked on the outside edge, holding Mrs. Connin's hand and looking down into the orange and purple gulley that dropped off from the concrete.

It occurred to him that he was lucky this time that they had found Mrs. Connin who would take you away for the day instead of an ordinary sitter who only sat where you lived or went to the park. You found out more when you left where you lived. He had found out already this morning that he had been made by a carpenter named Jesus Christ. Before he had thought it had been a doctor named Sladewall, a fat man with a yellow mustache who gave him shots and thought his name was Herbert, but this must have been a joke. They joked a lot where he lived. If he had thought about it before, he would have thought Jesus Christ was a word like "oh" or "damm" or "God," or maybe somebody who had cheated them out of something sometime. When he had asked Mrs. Connin who the man in the sheet in the picture over her bed was, she had looked at him a while with her mouth open. Then she had said, "That's Jesus," and she had kept on looking at him.

In a few minutes she had got up and got a book out of the other room. "See here," she said, turning over the cover, "this belonged to my great grand-mamma. I wouldn't part with it for nothing on earth." She ran her finger under some brown writing on a spotted page. "Emma Stevens Oakley, 1832," she said. "Ain't that something to have? And every word of it the gospel truth." She turned the next page and read him the name: "The Life of Jesus Christ for Readers Under Twelve." Then she read him the book.

It was a small book, pale brown on the outside with gold edges and a smell like old putty. It was full of pictures, one of the carpenter driving a crowd of pigs out of a man. They were real pigs, gray and sour-looking, and Mrs. Connin said Jesus had driven them all out of this one man. When she finished reading, she let him sit on the floor and look at the pictures again.

Just before they left for the healing, he had managed to get the book inside his innerlining without her seeing him. Now it made his coat hang down a little farther on one side than the other. His mind was dreamy and serene as they walked along and when they turned off the highway onto a long red clay road winding between banks of honeysuckle, he began to make wild leaps and pull forward on her hand as if he wanted to dash off and snatch the sun which was rolling away ahead of them now.

They walked on the dirt road for a while and then they crossed a field stippled with purple weeds and entered the shadows of a wood where the ground was covered with thick pine needles. He had never been in woods before and he walked carefully, looking from side to side as if he were entering a strange country. They moved along a bridle path that twisted downhill through crackling red leaves, and once, catching at a branch to keep himself from slipping, he looked into two frozen green-gold eyes enclosed in the darkness of a tree hole. At the bottom of the hill, the woods opened suddenly onto a pasture dotted here and there with black and white cows and sloping down, tier after tier, to a broad orange stream where the reflection of the sun was set like a diamond.

There were people standing on the near bank in a group, singing. Long tables were set up behind them and a few cars and trucks were parked in a road that came up by the river. They crossed the pasture, hurrying, because Mrs. Connin, using her hand for a shed over her eyes, saw the preacher already standing out in the water. She dropped her basket on one of the tables and pushed the three boys in front of her into the knot of people so that they wouldn't linger by the food. She kept Bevel by the hand and eased her way up to the front.

The preacher was standing about ten feet out in the stream where the water came up to his knees. He was a tall youth in khaki trousers that he had rolled up higher than the water. He had on a blue shirt and a red scarf around his neck but no hat and his light-colored hair was cut in sideburns that curved into the hollows of his cheeks. His face was all bone and red light reflected from the river. He looked as if he might have been nineteen years old. He was singing in a high twangy voice, above the singing on the bank, and he kept his hands behind him and his head tilted back.

He ended the hymn on a high note and stood silent, looking down at the water and shifting his feet in it. Then he looked up at the people on the bank. They stood close together, waiting; their faces were solemn but expectant and every eye was on him. He shifted his feet again.

"Maybe I know why you come," he said in the twangy voice, "maybe I don't."

"If you ain't come for Jesus, you ain't come for me. If you just come to see can you leave your pain in the river, you ain't come for Jesus. You can't leave your pain in the river," he said. "I never told nobody that." He stopped and looked down at his knees.

"I seen you cure a woman oncet!" a sudden high voice shouted from the hump of people. "Seen that woman git up and walk out straight where she had limped in!"

The preacher lifted one foot and then the other. He seemed almost but not quite to smile. "You might as well go home if that's what you come for," he said.

Then he lifted his head and arms and shouted, "Listen to what I got to say, you people! There ain't but one river and that's the River of Life, made out of Jesus' Blood. That's the river you have to lay your pain in, in the River of Faith, in the River of Life, in the River of Love, in the rich red river of Jesus' Blood, you people!"

His voice grew soft and musical. "All the rivers come from that one River and go back to it like it was the ocean sea and if you believe, you can lay your pain in that River and get rid of it because that's the River that was made to carry sin. It's a River full of pain itself, pain itself, moving toward the Kingdom of Christ, to be washed away, slow, you people, slow as this here old red water river round my feet."

"Listen," he sang, "I read in Mark about an unclean man, I read in Luke about a blind man, I read in John about a dead man! Oh you people hear! The same blood that makes this River red, made that leper clean, made that blind man stare, made that dead man leap! You people with trouble," he cried, "lay it in that River of Blood, lay it in that River of Pain, and watch it move away toward the Kingdom of Christ."

While he preached, Bevel's eyes followed drowsily the slow circles of two silent birds revolving high in the air. Across the river there was a low red and gold grove of sassafras with hills of dark blue trees behind it and an occasional pine jutting over the skyline. Behind, in the distance, the city rose like a cluster of warts on the side of the mountain. The birds revolved downward and dropped lightly in the top of the highest pine and sat hunch-shouldered as if they were supporting the sky.

"If it's this River of Life you want to lay your pain in, then come up," the preacher said, "and lay your sorrow here. But don't be thinking this is the last of it because this old red river don't end here. This old red suffering stream goes on, you people, slow to the Kingdom of Christ. This old red river is good to Baptize in, good to lay your faith in, good to lay your pain in, but it ain't this muddy water here that saves you. I been all up and down this river this week," he said. "Tuesday I was in Fortune Lake, next day in Ideal, Friday me and my wife drove to Lulawillow to see a sick man there. Them people didn't see no healing," he said and his face burned redder for a second. "I never said they would."

While he was talking a fluttering figure had begun to move forward with a kind of butterfly movement — an old woman with flapping arms whose head wobbled as if it might fall off any second. She managed to lower herself at the edge of the bank and let her arms churn in the water. Then she bent farther and pushed her face down in it and raised herself up finally, streaming wet; and still flapping, she turned a time or two in a blind circle until someone reached out and pulled her back into the group.

"She's been that way for thirteen years," a rough voice shouted, "Pass the hat and give this kid his money. That's what he's here for." The shout, directed out to the boy in the river, came from a huge old man who sat like a humped stone on the bumper of a long ancient gray automobile. He had on a gray hat that was turned down over one ear and up over the other to expose a purple bulge on his left temple. He sat bent forward with his hands hanging between his knees and his small eyes half closed.

Bevel stared at him once and then moved into the folds of Mrs. Connin's coat and hid himself.

The boy in the river glanced at the old man quickly and raised his fist. "Believe Jesus or the devil!" he cried. "Testify to one or the other!"

"I know from my own self-experience," a woman's mysterious voice called from the knot of people, "I know from it that this preacher can heal. My eyes have been opened! I testify to Jesus!"

The preacher lifted his arms quickly and began to repeat all that he had said before about the River and the Kingdom of Christ and the old man sat on the bumper, fixing him with a narrow squint. From time to time Bevel stared at him again from around Mrs. Connin.

A man in overalls and a brown coat leaned forward and dipped his hand in the water quickly and shook it and leaned back, and a woman held a baby over the edge of the bank and splashed its feet with water. One man moved a little distance away and sat down on the bank and took off his shoes and waded out into the stream; he stood there for a few minutes with his face tilted as far back as it would go, then he waded back and put on his shoes. All this time, the preacher sang and did not appear to watch what went on.

As soon as he stopped singing, Mrs. Connin lifted Bevel up and said, "Listen here, preacher, I got a boy from town today that I'm keeping. His mamma's sick and he wants you to pray for her. And this is a coincident — his name is Bevel! Bevel," she said, turning to look at the people behind her, "same as his. Ain't that a coincident, though?"

There were some murmurs and Bevel turned and grinned over her shoulder at the faces looking at him. "Bevel," he said in a loud jaunty voice.

"Listen," Mrs. Connin said, "have you ever been Baptized, Bevel?"

He only grinned.

"I suspect he ain't ever been Baptized," Mrs. Connin said, raising her eyebrows at the preacher.

"Swang him over here," the preacher said and took a stride forward and caught him.

He held him in the crook of his arm and looked at the grinning face. Bevel rolled his eyes in a comical way and thrust his face forward, close to the preacher's. "My name is Bevvvuuuuul," he said in a loud deep voice and let the tip of his tongue slide across his mouth.

The preacher didn't smile. His bony face was rigid and his narrow gray eyes reflected the almost colorless sky. There was a loud laugh from the old man sitting on the car bumper and Bevel grasped the back of the preacher's collar and held it tightly. The grin had already disappeared from his face. He had the sudden feeling that this was not a joke. Where he lived everything was a joke. From the preacher's face, he knew immediately that nothing the preacher said or did was a joke. "My mother named me that," he said quickly.

"Have you ever been Baptized?" the preacher asked.

"What's that?" he murmured.

"If I Baptize you," the preacher said, "you'll be able to go to the Kingdom of Christ. You'll be washed in the river of suffering, son, and you'll go by the deep river of life. Do you want that?"

"Yes," the child said, and thought, I won't go back to the apartment then, I'll go under the river.

"You won't be the same again," the preacher said. "You'll count." Then he turned his face to the people and began to preach and Bevel looked over his shoulder at the pieces of the white sun scattered in the river. Suddenly the preacher said, "All right, I'm going to Baptize you now," and without more warning, he tightened his hold and swung him upside down and plunged his head into the water. He held him under while he said the words of Baptism and then he jerked him up again and looked sternly at the gasping child. Bevel's eyes were dark and dilated. "You count now," the preacher said. "You didn't even count before."

The little boy was too shocked to cry. He spit out the muddy water and rubbed his wet sleeve into his eyes and over his face.

"Don't forget his mamma," Mrs. Connin called. "He wants you to pray for his mamma. She's sick."

"Lord," the preacher said, "we pray for somebody in affliction who isn't here to testify. Is your mother sick in the hospital?" he asked. "Is she in pain?"

The child stared at him. "She hasn't got up yet," he said in a high dazed voice. "She has a hangover." The air was so quiet he could hear the broken pieces of the sun knocking in the water.

The preacher looked angry and startled. The red drained out of his face and the sky appeared to darken in his eyes. There was a loud guffaw from the bank and Mr. Paradise shouted, "Haw! Cure the afflicted woman with the hangover!" and began to beat his knee with his fist.

§≈

"He's had a long day," Mrs. Connin said, standing with him in the door of the apartment and looking sharply into the room where the party was going on. "I reckon it's past his regular bedtime." One of Bevel's eyes was closed and the other half closed; his nose was running and he kept his mouth open and breathed through it. The damp plaid coat dragged down on one side.

That would be her, Mrs. Connin decided, in the black britches — long black satin britches and barefoot sandals and red toenails. She was lying on half the sofa, with her knees crossed in the air and her head propped on the arm. She didn't get up.

"Hello Harry," she said. "Did you have a big day?" She had a long pale face, smooth and blank, and straight sweet-potato-colored hair, pulled back.

The father went off to get the money. There were two other couples. One of the men, blond with little violet-blue eyes, leaned out of his chair and said, "Well Harry, old man, have a big day?"

"His name ain't Harry. It's Bevel," Mrs. Connin said.

"His name is Harry," *she* said from the sofa. "Whoever heard of anybody named Bevel?"

The little boy seemed to be going to sleep on his feet, his head drooping farther and farther forward; he pulled it back suddenly and opened one eye; the other was stuck.

"He told me this morning his name was Bevel," Mrs. Connin said in a shocked voice. "The same as our preacher. We been all day at a preaching and healing at the river. He said his name was Bevel, the same as the preacher's. That's what he told me."

"Bevel!" his mother said. "My God! what a name."

"This preacher is name Bevel and there's no better preacher around," Mrs. Connin said. "And furthermore," she added in a defiant tone, "he Baptized this child this morning!"

His mother sat straight up. "Well the nerve!" she muttered.

"Furthermore," Mrs. Connin said, "he's a healer and he prayed for you to be healed."

"Healed!" she almost shouted. "Healed of what for Christ's sake?"

"Of your affliction," Mrs. Connin said icily.

The father had returned with the money and was standing near Mrs. Connin waiting to give it to her. His eyes were lined with red threads. "Go on, go on," he said, "I want to hear more about her affliction. The exact nature of it has escaped . . ." He waved the bill and his voice trailed off. "Healing by prayer is mighty inexpensive," he murmured.

Mrs. Connin stood a second, staring into the room, with a skeleton's appearance of seeing everything. Then, without taking the money, she turned and shut the door behind her. The father swung around, smiling vaguely, and shrugged. The rest of them were looking at Harry. The little boy began to shamble toward the bedroom.

"Come here, Harry," his mother said. He automatically shifted his direction toward her without opening his eye any farther. "Tell me what happened today," she said when he reached her. She began to pull off his coat.

"I don't know," he muttered.

"Yes you do know," she said, feeling the coat heavier on one side. She unzipped the innerlining and caught the book and a dirty handkerchief as they fell out. "Where did you get these?"

"I don't know," he said and grabbed for them. "They're mine. She gave them to me."

She threw the handkerchief down and held the book too high for him to reach and began to read it, her face after a second assuming an exaggerated comical expression. The others moved around and looked at it over her shoulder. "My God," somebody said.

One of the men peered at it sharply from behind a thick pair of glasses. "That's valuable," he said. "That's a collector's item," and he took it away from the rest of them and retired to another chair.

"Don't let George go off with that," his girl said.

"I tell you it's valuable," George said. "1832."

Bevel shifted his direction again toward the room where he slept. He shut the door behind him and moved slowly in the darkness to the bed and sat down and took off his shoes and got under the cover. After a minute a shaft of light let in the tall silhouette of his mother. She tiptoed lightly across the room and sat down on the edge of his bed. "What did that dolt of a preacher say about me?" she whispered. "What lies have you been telling today, honey?"

He shut his eye and heard her voice from a long way away, as if he were under the river and she on top of it. She shook his shoulder. "Harry," she said, leaning down and putting her mouth to his ear, "tell me what he said." She pulled him into a sitting position and he felt as if he had been drawn up from under the river. "Tell me," she whispered and her bitter breath covered his face.

He saw the pale oval close to him in the dark. "He said I'm not the same now," he muttered. "I count."

After a second, she lowered him by his shirt front onto the pillow. She hung over him an instant and brushed her lips against his forehead. Then she got up and moved away, swaying her hips lightly through the shaft of light.

♦♦

He didn't wake up early but the apartment was still dark and close when he did. For a while he lay there, picking his nose and eyes. Then he sat up in bed and looked out the window. The sun came in palely, stained gray by the glass. Across the street at the Empire Hotel, a colored cleaning woman was looking down from an upper window, resting her face on her folded arms. He got up and put on his shoes and went to the bathroom and then into the front room. He ate two crackers spread with anchovy paste, that he found on the coffee table, and drank some ginger ale left in a bottle and looked around for his book but it was not there.

The apartment was silent except for the faint humming of the refrigerator. He went into the kitchen and found some raisin bread heels and spread a half jar of peanut butter between them and climbed up on the tall kitchen stool and sat chewing the sandwich slowly, wiping his nose every now and then on his shoulder. When he finished he found some chocolate milk and drank that. He would rather have had the ginger ale he saw but they left the bottle openers where he couldn't reach them. He studied what was left in the refrigerator for a while — some shriveled vegetables that she had forgot were there and a lot of brown oranges that she bought and didn't squeeze; there were three or four kinds of cheese and something fishy in a paper bag; the rest was a pork bone. He left the refrigerator door open and wandered back into the dark living room and sat down on the sofa.

He decided they would be out cold until one o'clock and that they would all have to go to a restaurant for lunch. He wasn't high enough for the table yet and the waiter would bring a highchair and he was too big for a highchair. He sat in the middle of the sofa, kicking it with his heels. Then he got up and wandered around the room, looking into the ashtrays at the butts as if this might be a habit. In his own room he had picture books and blocks but they were for the most part torn up; he found the way to get new ones was to tear up the ones he had. There was very little to do at any time but eat; however, he was not a fat boy.

He decided he would empty a few of the ashtrays on the floor. If he only emptied a few, she would think they had fallen. He emptied two, rubbing the ashes carefully into the rug with his finger. Then he lay on the floor for a while, studying his feet which he held up in the air. His shoes were still damp and he began to think about the river.

Very slowly, his expression changed as if he were gradually seeing appear what he didn't know he'd been looking for. Then all of a sudden he knew what he wanted to do.

He got up and tiptoed into their bedroom and stood in the dim light there, looking for her pocketbook. His glance passed her long pale arm hanging off the edge of the bed down to the floor, and across the white mound his father made, and past the crowded bureau, until it rested on the pocketbook hung on the back of a chair. He took a car-token out of it and half a package of Life Savers. Then he left the apartment and caught the car at the corner. He hadn't taken a suitcase because there was nothing from there he wanted to keep.

He got off the car at the end of the line and started down the road he and Mrs. Connin had taken the day before. He knew there wouldn't be anybody at her house because the three boys and the girl went to school and Mrs. Connin had told him she went out to clean. He passed her yard and walked on the way they had gone to the river. The paper brick houses were far apart and after a while the dirt place to walk on ended and he had to walk on the edge of the highway. The sun was pale yellow and high and hot.

He passed a shack with an orange gas pump in front of it but he didn't see the old man looking out at nothing in particular from the doorway. Mr. Paradise was having an orange drink. He finished it slowly, squinting over the bottle at the small plaid-coated figure disappearing down the road. Then he set the empty bottle on a bench and, still squinting, wiped his sleeve over his mouth. He went in the shack and picked out a peppermint stick, a foot long and two inches thick, from the candy shelf, and stuck it in his hip pocket. Then he got in his car and drove slowly down the highway after the boy.

By the time Bevel came to the field speckled with purple weeds, he was dusty and sweating and he crossed it at a trot to get into the woods as fast as he could. Once inside, he wandered from tree to tree, trying to find the path they had taken yesterday. Finally he found a line worn in the pine needles and followed it until he saw the steep trail twisting down through the trees.

Mr. Paradise had left his automobile back some way on the road and had walked to the place where he was accustomed to sit almost every day, holding an unbaited fishline in the water while he stared at the river passing in front of him. Anyone looking at him from a distance would have seen an old boulder half hidden in the bushes.

Bevel didn't see him at all. He only saw the river, shimmering reddish yellow, and bounded into it with his shoes and his coat on and took a gulp. He swallowed some and spit the rest out and then he stood there in water up to his chest and looked around him. The sky was a clear pale blue, all in one piece — except for the hole the sun made — and fringed around the bottom with treetops. His coat floated to the surface and surrounded him like a strange gay lily pad and he stood grinning in the sun. He intended not to fool with preachers any more but to Baptize himself and to keep on going this time until he found the Kingdom of Christ in the river. He didn't mean to waste any more time. He put his head under the water at once and pushed forward.

In a second he began to gasp and sputter and his head reappeared on the surface; he started under again and the same thing happened. The river wouldn't have him. He tried again and came up, choking. This was the way it had been when the preacher held him under — he had had to fight with something that pushed him back in the face. He stopped and thought suddenly: it's another joke, it's just another joke! He thought how far he had come for nothing and he began to hit and splash and kick the filthy river. His feet were already treading on nothing. He gave one low cry of pain and indignation. Then he heard a shout and turned his head and saw something like a giant pig bounding after him, shaking a red and white club and shouting. He plunged under once and this time, the waiting current caught him like a long gentle hand and pulled him swiftly forward and down. For an instant he was overcome with surprise; then since he was moving quickly and knew that he was getting somewhere, all his fury and his fear left him.

Mr. Paradise's head appeared from time to time on the surface of the water. Finally, far downstream, the old man rose like some ancient water monster and stood empty-handed, staring with his dull eyes as far down the river line as he could see.

Tillie Olsen

Help Her to Believe [I Stand Here Ironing]

Tillie Olsen's "Help Her to Believe" first appeared in the *Pacific Spectator* in 1956 before it was published in *Tell Me a Riddle* in 1961 under the title "I Stand Here Ironing." The two titles carry somewhat differing implications: the first suggests a mother's concern for her daughter, whom she feels needs to believe she can lead a fulfilling life, something beyond the drudgery of ironing that the mother faces; the second expresses the mother's preoccupation with herself, with her years of poverty and hopelessness, with her inability to do anything to guide her daughter. In either form, it gives expression to a unique central character, a single mother, impoverished, who recites her monologue while ironing, a repetitive activity that allows her mind to wander. The issue is a moment of familial crisis when her daughter, Emily, clearly needs help in school, but the narrator's preoccupation with her own life prevents her from giving any guidance or emotional support beyond "let her be." The story was an assignment for a creative writing class at San Francisco State University, and the skill of its narration and style led to additional stories and a novel, *Yonnondio: From the Thirties.* Born into a family of Russian immigrants in 1913, Olsen grew up in Omaha, Nebraska, where she was exposed to a spectrum of religious and linguistic groups, expanding her lexicon and giving her an understanding of the diversity of the country. Her work reflects her deep knowledge of the psychology of parenting and of living in a diverse and complex modern world.

Tillie Olsen, "Help Her to Believe," *Pacific Spectator* 10, no. 1 (Winter 1956): 55–63.

I stand here ironing, and what you asked of me moves tormented back and forth with the iron.

"I wish you would manage the time to come in and talk with me about your daughter. I'm sure you can help me understand her. She's a youngster who needs help and whom I'm deeply interested in helping."

"Who needs help?" Even if I came what good would it do? You think because I'm her mother I have a key, or that in some way you could use me as a key? She has lived for nineteen years. There is all that life that has happened outside of me, beyond me.

And when is there time to remember, to sift, to weigh, to estimate, to total? I will start and there will be an interruption and I will have to gather it all together again. Or I will become engulfed with all I did or did not do, with what should have been and what cannot be helped.

She was a beautiful baby. The first and only one of our five that was beautiful at birth. You do not guess how new and uneasy her tenancy in her now-loveliness. You did not know her all those years she was thought homely, or see her poring over her baby pictures, making me tell her over and over how beautiful she had been — and would be, I would tell her — and was now, to the seeing eye. But the seeing eyes were few or nonexistent. Including mine.

I nursed her. They feel that's important nowadays. I nursed all the children, but with her, with all the fierce rigidity of first motherhood, I did like the books said. Though her cries battered me to trembling and my breasts ached with swollenness, I waited till the clock decreed.

Why do I put that first? I do not even know if it matters, or if it explains anything.

She was a beautiful baby. She blew shining bubbles of sound. She loved motion, loved light, loved color and music and textures. She would lie on the floor in her blue overalls patting the surface so hard in ecstacy her hands and feet would blur. She was a miracle to me, but when she was eight months old I had to leave her daytimes with the woman downstairs to whom she was no miracle at all, for I worked or looked for work and for Emily's father, who "could no longer endure" (he wrote in his good-bye note) "sharing want with us."

I was nineteen. It was the pre-relief, pre-WPA world of the depression. I would start running as soon as I got off the streetcar, running up the stairs, the place smelling sour, and awake or asleep to startle awake, when she saw me she would break into a clogged weeping that could not be comforted, a weeping I can hear yet.

After a while I found a job hashing at night so I could be with her days, and it was better. But it came to where I had to bring her to his family and leave her.

It took a long time to raise the money for her fare back. Then she got chicken pox and I had to wait longer. When she finally came, I hardly knew her, walking quick and nervous like her father, looking like her father, thin, and dressed in a shoddy red that yellowed her skin and glared at the pock marks. All the baby loveliness gone.

She was two. Old enough for nursery school they said, and I did not know then what I know now — the fatigue of the long day, and the lacerations of group life in nurseries that are only parking places for children.

Except that it would have made no difference if I had known. It was the only place there was. It was the only way we could be together, the only way I could hold a job.

And even without knowing, I knew. I knew the teacher that was evil because all these years it has curdled into my memory, the little boy hunched in the corner, her rasp, "why aren't you outside, because Alvin hits you? that's no reason, go out coward." I knew Emily hated it even if she did not clutch and implore "don't go mommy" like the other children, mornings.

She always had a reason why we should stay home. Momma, you look sick, momma. I feel sick. Momma, the teachers aren't there today, they're sick. Momma there was a fire there last night. Momma it's a holiday today, no school, they told me.

But never a direct protest, never rebellion. I think of our others in their three-, four-year-oldness — the explosions, the tempers, the denunciations, the demands —

and I feel suddenly ill. I stop the ironing. What in me demanded that goodness in her? And what was the cost, the cost to her of such goodness?

The old man living in the back once said in his gentle way: "You should smile at Emily more when you look at her." What *was* in my face when I looked at her? I loved her. There were all the acts of love.

It was only with the others I remembered what he said, so that it was the face of joy, and not of care or tightness or worry I turned to them — but never to Emily. She does not smile easily, let alone almost always as her brothers and sisters do. Her face is closed and somber, but when she wants, how fluid. You must have seen it in her pantomimes, you spoke of her rare gift for comedy on the stage that rouses a laughter out of the audience so dear they applaud and applaud and do not want to let her go.

Where does it come from, that comedy? There was none of it in her when she came back to me that second time, after I had had to send her away again. She had a new daddy now to learn to love, and I think perhaps it was a better time. Except when we left her alone nights, telling ourselves she was old enough.

"Can't you go some other time mommy, like tomorrow?" she would ask, "will it be just a little while you'll be gone?"

The time we came back, the front door open, the clock on the floor in the hall. She rigid awake. "It wasn't just a little while. I didn't cry. I called you a little, just three times, and then I went downstairs to open the door so you could come faster. The clock talked loud, I threw it away, it scared me what it talked."

She said the clock talked loud that night I went to the hospital to have Susan. She was delirious with the fever that comes before red measles, but she was fully conscious all the week I was gone and the week after we were home when she could not come near the baby or me.

She did not get well. She stayed skeleton thin, not wanting to eat, and night after night she had nightmares. She would call for me, and I would sleepily call back, "you're all right, darling, go to sleep, it's just a dream," and if she still called, in a sterner voice, "now go to sleep Emily, there's nothing to hurt you." Twice, only twice, when I had to get up for Susan anyhow, I went in to sit with her.

Now when it's too late (as if she would let me hold and comfort her like I do the others) I get up and go to her at her moan or restless stirring. "Are you awake? Can I get you something?" And the answer is always the same: "No, I'm all right, go back to sleep mother."

They persuaded me at the clinic to send her away to a convalescent home in the country where "she can have the kind of food and care you can't manage for her, and you'll be free to concentrate on the new baby." They still send children to that place. I see pictures on the society page of sleek young women planning affairs to raise money for it, or dancing at the affairs, or decorating Easter eggs or filling Christmas stockings for the children.

They never have a picture of the children so I do not know if they still wear those gigantic red bows and the ravaged looks on the every other Sunday when parents can come to visit "unless otherwise notified" — as we were notified the first six weeks.

Oh it is a handsome place, green lawns and tall trees and fluted flower beds. High up on the balconies of each cottage the children stand, the girls in their red bows and white dresses, the boys in white suits and giant red ties. The parents stand below shrieking up to be heard and the children shriek down to be heard, and between them the invisible wall. "Not To Be Contaminated By Parental Germs or Physical Affection."

There was a tiny girl who always stood hand in hand with Emily. Her parents never came. One visit she was gone. "They moved her to Rose Cottage," Emily shouted in explanation. "They don't like you to love anybody here."

She wrote once a week, the labored writing of a seven-year-old. "I am fine. How is the baby. If I write my leter nicly I will have a star. Love." There never was a star. We wrote every other day, letters she could never hold or keep but only hear read — once. "We simply do not have room for children to keep any personal possessions," they patiently explained when we pieced one Sunday's shrieking together to plead how much it would mean to Emily to keep her letters and cards.

Each visit she looked frailer. "She isn't eating," they told us. (They had runny eggs for breakfast or mush with lumps, Emily said later, I'd hold it in my mouth and not swallow. Nothing ever tasted good, just when they had chicken.)

It took us eight months to get her released home, and only the fact that she gained back so little of her seven lost pounds, convinced the social worker.

I used to try to hold and love her after she came back, but her body would stay stiff, and after a while she'd push away. She ate little. Food sickened her, and I think much of life too. Oh she had physical lightness and brightness, twinkling by on skates, bouncing like a ball up and down up and down over the jump rope, skimming over the hill; but these were momentary.

She fretted about her appearance, thin and dark and foreign looking at a time when every little girl was supposed to look or thought she should look a chubby blonde replica of Shirley Temple. The doorbell sometimes rang for her, but no one seemed to come and play in the house or be a best friend. Maybe because we moved so much.

There was a boy she loved painfully through two school semesters. Months later she told me how she had taken pennies from my purse to buy him candy. "Licorice was his favorite and I brought him some every day, but he still liked Jennifer better'n me. Why mommy why?" A question I could never answer.

School was a worry to her. She was not glib or quick in a world where glibness and quickness were easily confused with ability to learn. To her overworked and exasperated teachers she was an overconscientious "slow learner" who kept trying to catch up and was absent entirely too often.

I let her be absent, though sometimes the illness was imaginary. How different from my now-strictness about attendance with the others. I wasn't working.

We had a new baby, I was home anyhow. Sometimes, after Susan grew old enough, I would keep her home from school, too, to have them all together.

Mostly Emily had asthma, and her breathing, harsh and labored, would fill the house with a curiously tranquil sound. I would bring the two old dresser mirrors and her boxes of collections to her bed. She would select beads and single earrings, bottle tops and shells, dried flowers and pebbles, old postcards and scraps, oh all sorts of oddments; then she and Susan would play Kingdom, setting up landscapes and furniture, peopling them with action.

Those were the only times of peaceful companionship between her and Susan. I have edged away from it, that poisonous feeling between them, that terrible balancing of hurts and needs I had to do between them, and did so badly, those earlier years.

Oh there are conflicts between the others too, each one human, needing, demanding, hurting, taking — but only between Emily and Susan, no, Emily towards Susan that corroding resentment. It seems so obvious on the surface, yet it is not obvious. Susan, the second child, Susan, golden and curly haired and chubby, quick and articulate and assured, everything in appearance and manner Emily was not; Susan, not able to resist Emily's precious things, losing or sometimes clumsily breaking them; Susan telling jokes and riddles to company for applause while Emily sat silent (to say to me later: that was *my* riddle, mother, I told it to Susan); Susan, who for all the five years' difference in age was just a year behind Emily in developing physically.

I am glad for that slow physical development that widened the difference between her and her contemporaries, though she suffered over it. She was too vulnerable for that terrible world of youthful competition, of preening and parading, of constant measuring of yourself against every other, of envy, "If I had that copper hair," or "If I had that skin . . ." She tormented herself enough about not looking like the others, there was enough of the unsureness, the having to be conscious of words before you speak, the constant caring — what are they thinking of me? what kind of an impression am I making — there was enough without having it all magnified unendurably by the merciless physical drives.

Ronnie is calling. He is wet and I change him. It is rare there is such a cry now. That time of motherhood is almost behind me when the ear is not one's own but must always be racked and listening for the child cry, the child call. We sit for a while and I hold him, looking out over the city spread in charcoal with its soft aisles of light. "Shuggily" he breathes. A funny word, a family word, inherited from Emily, invented by her to say comfort.

In this and other ways she leaves her seal, I say aloud. And startle at my saying it. What do I mean? What did I start to gather together, to try and make coherent? I was at the terrible, growing years. War years. I do not remember them well. I was working, there were four smaller ones now, there was not time for her. She had to help be a mother, and housekeeper, and shopper. She had to set her seal. Mornings of crisis and near hysteria trying to get lunches packed, hair combed, coats and shoes found, everyone to school or Child Care on time, the baby ready for transportation. And always the paper scribbled on by a smaller one, the book looked at by Susan then mislaid, the homework not done. Running out to that huge school where she was one, she was lost, she was a drop; suffering over the unpreparedness, stammering and unsure in her classes.

There was so little time left at night after the kids were bedded down. She would struggle over books, always eating (it was in those years she developed her enormous appetite that is legendary in our family) and I would be ironing, or preparing food for the next day, or writing V-mail to Bill, or tending the baby. Sometimes, to make me laugh, or out of her despair, she would imitate happenings or types at school.

I think I said once: "Why don't you do something like this in the school amateur show?" One morning she phoned me at work, hardly understandable through her weeping: "Mother, I did it. I won, I won; they gave me first prize; they clapped and clapped and wouldn't let me go."

Now suddenly she was Somebody, and as imprisoned in her difference as in anonymity.

She began to be asked to perform at other high schools, even in colleges, then at city and state-wide affairs. The first one we went to, I only recognized her that first moment when thin, shy, she almost drowned herself into the curtains. Then: Was this Emily? the control, the command, the convulsing and deadly clowning, the spell, then the roaring, stamping audience, unwilling to let this rare and precious laughter out of their lives.

Afterwards: You ought to do something about her with a gift like that — but without money or knowing how, what does one do? We have left it all to her, and the gift has as often eddied inside, clogged and clotted as been used and growing.

She is coming. She runs up the stairs two at a time with her light graceful step, and I know she is happy tonight. Whatever it was that occasioned your call did not happen today.

"Aren't you ever going to finish the ironing, mother? Whistler painted his mother in a rocker. I'd have to paint mine standing over an ironing board." This is one of her communicative nights and she tells me everything and nothing as she fixes herself a plate of food out of the icebox.

She is so lovely. Why did you want me to come in at all? Why were you concerned? She will find her way.

She starts up the stairs to bed. "Don't get me up with the rest in the morning." "But I thought you were having midterms." "Oh, those," she comes back in and says quite lightly, "in a couple of years when we'll all be atom-dead they won't matter a bit."

She has said it before. She believes it. But because I have been dredging the past, and all that compounds a human being is so heavy and meaningful in me, I cannot endure it tonight.

I will never total it all now. I will never come in to say: She was a child seldom smiled at. Her father left me before she was a year old. I worked her first six years when there was work, or I sent her home and to his relatives. There were years she had care she hated. She was dark and thin and foreign looking in a world where the prestige went to blondness and curly hair and dimples, slow where glibness was prized. She was a child of anxious, not proud, love. We were poor and could not afford for her the soil of easy growth. I was a young mother, I was a distracted mother. There were the other children pushing up, demanding. Her younger sister was all that she was not. She did not like me to touch her. She kept too much in herself, her life was such she had to keep too much in herself. My wisdom came too late. She has much in her and probably nothing will come of it. She is a child of her age, of depression, of war, of fear.

Let her be. So all that is in her will not bloom — but in how many does it? There is still enough left to live by. Only help her to believe — help make it so there is cause for her to believe that she is more than this dress on the ironing board, helpless before the iron.

Philip Roth
Defender of the Faith

Philip Roth is best known for a series of sensational novels that brought him international recognition and numerous literary prizes, including the National Book Award, both the Guggenheim and Rockefeller Fellowships, and the PEN/Faulkner Award. But before *Portnoy's Complaint*, or *Letting Go*, or *When She Was Good*, Roth published a notable volume of short stories under the title *Goodbye, Columbus*. Perhaps the most famous piece of short fiction to come out of that book is "Defender of the Faith," often reprinted and widely analyzed. It takes its title from the phrase the pope bestowed upon Henry VIII shortly before the king rejected Catholicism and established his own Church of England. In it the central character, who is also the narrator, must struggle with the conflict between his loyalty to his ethnicity as opposed to his sense of national responsibility, between his duty as a soldier and his feelings as a man. Although the narrator, Nathan Marx, spends most of his time talking about Private Sheldon Grossbart, who seeks constantly to manipulate his superiors on the basis of religion and cultural identity, it is Marx himself who has the internal discord and who bears the accountability in the conclusion. The skillful handling of point of view, revealing the depth of the ethical and philosophical struggle the narrator must face, is remarkable, as is the significance of his final act, which resolves his sense of being maneuvered by Grossbart but leaves Marx with a profound sense of moral responsibility. It is Roth at his fictional best.

Philip Roth, "Defender of the Faith," *Goodbye, Columbus* (Boston: Houghton Mifflin, 1959), 161–200.

In May of 1945, only a few weeks after the fighting had ended in Europe, I was rotated back to the States, where I spent the remainder of the war with a training company at Camp Crowder, Missouri. Along with the rest of the Ninth Army, I had been racing across Germany so swiftly during the late winter and spring that when I boarded the plane, I couldn't believe its destination lay to the west. My mind might inform me otherwise, but there was an inertia of the spirit that told me we were flying to a new front, where we would disembark and continue our push eastward — eastward until we'd circled the globe, marching through villages along whose twisting, cobbled streets crowds of the enemy would watch us take possession of what, up till then, they'd considered their own. I had changed enough in two years not to mind the trembling of the old people, the crying of the very young, the uncertainty and fear in the eyes of the once arrogant. I had been fortunate enough to develop an infantryman's heart, which, like his feet, at first aches and swells but finally grows horny enough for him to travel the weirdest paths without feeling a thing.

Captain Paul Barrett was my C.O. in Camp Crowder. The day I reported for duty, he came out of his office to shake my hand. He was short, gruff, and fiery, and — indoors or out — he wore his polished helmet liner pulled down to his little eyes. In Europe, he had received a battlefield commission and a serious chest wound, and he'd been returned to the States only a few months before. He spoke easily to me, and at the evening formation he introduced me to the troops. "Gentlemen," he said, "Sergeant Thurston, as you know, is no longer with this company. Your new first sergeant is Sergeant Nathan Marx, here. He is a veteran of the European theater, and consequently will expect to find a company of soldiers here, and not a company of *boys*."

I sat up late in the orderly room that evening, trying half-heartedly to solve the riddle of duty rosters, personnel forms, and morning reports. The Charge of Quarters slept with his mouth open on a mattress on the floor. A trainee stood reading the next day's duty roster, which was posted on the bulletin board just inside the screen door. It was a warm evening, and I could hear radios playing dance music over in the barracks. The trainee, who had been staring at me whenever he thought I wouldn't notice, finally took a step in my direction.

"Hey, Sarge — we having a G.I. party tomorrow night?" he asked. A G.I. party is a barracks cleaning.

"You usually have them on Friday nights?" I asked him.

"Yes," he said, and then he added, mysteriously, "that's the whole thing."

"Then you'll have a G.I. party."

He turned away, and I heard him mumbling. His shoulders were moving, and I wondered if he was crying.

"What's your name, soldier?" I asked.

He turned, not crying at all. Instead, his green-speckled eyes, long and narrow, flashed like fish in the sun. He walked over to me and sat on the edge of my desk. He reached out a hand. "Sheldon," he said.

"Stand on your feet, Sheldon."

Getting off the desk, he said, "Sheldon Grossbart." He smiled at the familiarity into which he'd led me.

"You against cleaning the barracks Friday night, Grossbart?" I said. "Maybe we shouldn't have G.I. parties. Maybe we should get a maid." My tone startled me. I felt I sounded like every top sergeant I had ever known.

"No, Sergeant." He grew serious, but with a seriousness that seemed to be only the stifling of a smile. "It's just — G.I. parties on Friday night, of all nights."

He slipped up onto the corner of my desk again — not quite sitting, but not quite standing, either. He looked at me with those speckled eyes flashing, and then made a gesture with his hand. It was very slight — no more than a movement back and forth of the wrist — and yet it managed to exclude from our affairs everything else in the orderly room, to make the two of us the center of the world. It seemed, in fact, to exclude everything even about the two of us except our hearts.

"Sergeant Thurston was one thing," he whispered, glancing at the sleeping C.Q., "but we thought that with you here things might be a little different."

"We?"

"The Jewish personnel."

"Why?" I asked, harshly. "What's on your mind?" Whether I was still angry at the "Sheldon" business, or now at something else, I hadn't time to tell, but clearly I was angry.

"We thought you — Marx, you know, like Karl Marx. The Marx Brothers. Those guys are all — M-a-r-x. Isn't that how *you* spell it, Sergeant?"

"M-a-r-x."

"Fishbein said —" He stopped. "What I mean to say, Sergeant —" His face and neck were red, and his mouth moved but no words came out. In a moment, he raised himself to attention, gazing down at me. It was as though he had suddenly decided he could expect no more sympathy from me than from Thurston, the reason being that I was of Thurston's faith, and not his. The young man had managed to confuse himself as to what my faith really was, but I felt no desire to straighten him out. Very simply, I didn't like him.

When I did nothing but return his gaze, he spoke, in an altered tone. "You see, Sergeant," he explained to me, "Friday nights, Jews are supposed to go to services."

"Did Sergeant Thurston tell you you couldn't go to them when there was a G.I. party?"

"No."

"Did he say you had to stay and scrub the floors?"

"No, Sergeant."

"Did the Captain say you had to stay and scrub the floors?"

"That isn't it, Sergeant. It's the other guys in the barracks." He leaned toward me. "They think we're goofing off. But we're not. That's when Jews go to services, Friday night. We have to."

"Then go."

"But the other guys make accusations. They have no right."

"That's not the Army's problem, Grossbart. It's a personal problem you'll have to work out yourself."

"But it's un*fair.*"

I got up to leave. "There's nothing I can do about it," I said.

Grossbart stiffened and stood in front of me. "But this is a matter of *religion,* sir."

"Sergeant," I said.

"I mean 'Sergeant,'" he said, almost snarling.

"Look, go see the chaplain. You want to see Captain Barrett, I'll arrange an appointment."

"No, no. I don't want to make trouble, Sergeant. That's the first thing they throw up to you. I just want my rights!"

"Damn it, Grossbart, stop whining. You have your rights. You can stay and scrub floors or you can go to shul —"

The smile swam in again. Spittle gleamed at the corners of his mouth. "You mean church, Sergeant."

"I mean shul, Grossbart!"

I walked past him and went outside. Near me, I heard the scrunching of a guard's boots on gravel. Beyond the lighted windows of the barracks, young men in T shirts and fatigue pants were sitting on their bunks, polishing their rifles. Suddenly there was a light rustling behind me. I turned and saw Grossbart's dark frame fleeing back to the barracks, racing to tell his Jewish friends that they were right — that, like Karl and Harpo, I was one of them.

❦❦

The next morning, while chatting with Captain Barrett, I recounted the incident of the previous evening. Somehow, in the telling, it must have seemed to the Captain that I was not so much explaining Grossbart's position as defending it. "Marx, I'd fight side by side with a nigger if the fella proved to me he was a man. I pride myself," he said, looking out the window, "that I've got an open mind. Consequently, Sergeant, nobody gets special treatment here, for the good *or* the bad. All a man's got to do is prove himself. A man fires well on the range, I give him a weekend pass. He scores high in P.T., he gets a weekend pass. He *earns* it." He turned from the window and pointed a finger at me. "You're a Jewish fella, am I right, Marx?"

"Yes, sir."

"And I admire you. I admire you because of the ribbons on your chest. I judge a man by what he shows me on the field of battle, Sergeant. It's what he's got *here,*" he said, and then, though I expected he would point to his chest, he jerked a thumb toward the buttons straining to hold his blouse across his belly. "Guts," he said.

"O.K., sir. I only wanted to pass on to you how the men felt."

"Mr. Marx, you're going to be old before your time if you worry about how the men feel. Leave that stuff to the chaplain — that's his business, not yours. Let's us train these fellas to shoot straight. If the Jewish personnel feels the other men are accusing them of goldbricking — well, I just don't know. Seems awful funny that suddenly the Lord is calling so loud in Private Grossman's ear he's just got to run to church."

"Synagogue," I said.

"Synagogue is right, Sergeant. I'll write that down for handy reference. Thank you for stopping by."

That evening, a few minutes before the company gathered outside the orderly room for the chow formation, I called the C.Q., Corporal Robert LaHill, in to see me. LaHill was a dark, burly fellow whose hair curled out of his clothes wherever it could. He had a glaze in his eyes that made one think of caves and dinosaurs. "LaHill," I said, "when you take the formation, remind the men that they're free to attend church services *whenever* they are held, provided they report to the orderly room before they leave the area."

LaHill scratched his wrist, but gave no indication that he'd heard or understood.

"LaHill," I said, "*church.* You remember? Church, priest, Mass, confession."

He curled one lip into a kind of smile; I took it for a signal that for a second he had flickered back up into the human race.

"Jewish personnel who want to attend services this evening are to fall out in front of the orderly room at 1900," I said. Then, as an afterthought, I added, "By order of Captain Barrett."

A little while later, as the day's last light — softer than any I had seen that year — began to drop over Camp Crowder, I heard LaHill's thick, inflectionless voice outside my window: "Give me your ears, troopers. Toppie says for me to tell you that at 1900 hours all Jewish personnel is to fall out in front, here, if they want to attend the Jewish Mass."

જીજી

At seven o'clock, I looked out the orderly-room window and saw three soldiers in starched khakis standing on the dusty quadrangle. They looked at their watches and fidgeted while they whispered back and forth. It was getting dimmer, and, alone on the otherwise deserted field, they looked tiny. When I opened the door, I heard the noises of the G.I. party coming from the surrounding barracks — bunks being pushed to the walls, faucets pounding water into buckets, brooms whisking at the wooden floors, cleaning the dirt away for Saturday's inspection. Big puffs of cloth moved round and round on the windowpanes. I walked outside, and the moment my foot hit the ground I thought I heard Grossbart call to the others, "'Ten-*hut!*'" Or maybe, when they all three jumped to attention, I imagined I heard the command.

Grossbart stepped forward. "Thank you, sir," he said.

"'Sergeant,' Grossbart," I reminded him. "You call officers 'sir.' I'm not an officer. You've been in the Army three weeks — you know that."

He turned his palms out at his sides to indicate that, in truth, he and I lived beyond convention. "Thank you, anyway," he said.

"Yes," a tall boy behind him said. "Thanks a lot."

And the third boy whispered, "Thank you," but his mouth barely fluttered, so that he did not alter by more than a lip's movement his posture of attention.

"For what?" I asked.

Grossbart snorted happily. "For the announcement. The Corporal's announcement. It helped. It made it —"

"Fancier." The tall boy finished Grossbart's sentence.

Grossbart smiled. "He means formal, sir. Public," he said to me. "Now it won't seem as though we're just taking off — goldbricking because the work has begun."

"It was by order of Captain Barrett," I said.

"Aaah, but you pull a little weight," Grossbart said. "So we thank you." then he turned to his companions. "Sergeant Marx, I want you to meet Larry Fishbein."

The tall boy stepped forward and extended his hand. I shook it. "You from New York?" he asked.

"Yes."

"Me, too." He had a cadaverous face that collapsed inward from his cheekbone to his jaw, and when he smiled — as he did at the news of our communal attachment — revealed a mouthful of bad teeth. He was blinking his eyes a good deal, as though he were fighting back tears. "What borough?" he asked.

I turned to Grossbart. "It's five after seven. What time are services?"

"Shul," he said, smiling, "is in ten minutes. I want you to meet Mickey Halpern. This is Nathan Marx, our sergeant."

The third boy hopped forward. "Private Michael Halpern." He saluted.

"Salute officers, Halpern," I said. The boy dropped his hand, and, on its way down, in his nervousness, checked to see if his shirt pockets were buttoned.

"Shall I march them over, sir?" Grossbart asked. "Or are you coming along?"

From behind Grossbart, Fishbein piped up. "Afterward, they're having refreshments. A ladies' auxiliary from St. Louis, the rabbi told us last week."

"The chaplain," Halpern whispered.

"You're welcome to come along," Grossbart said.

To avoid his plea, I looked away, and saw, in the windows of the barracks, a cloud of faces staring out at the four of us. "Hurry along, Grossbart," I said.

"O.K., then," he said. He turned to the others. "Double time, *march!*"

They started off, but ten feet away Grossbart spun around and, running backward, called to me, "good *shabbus*, sir!" And then the three of them were swallowed into the alien Missouri dusk.

Even after they had disappeared over the parade ground, whose green was now a deep blue, I could hear Grossbart singing the double-time cadence, and as it grew dimmer and dimmer, it suddenly touched a deep memory — as did the slant of the light — and I was remembering the shrill sounds of a Bronx playground where, years ago, beside the Grand Concourse, I had played on long spring evenings such as this. It was a pleasant memory for a young man so far from peace and home, and it brought so many recollections with it that I began to grow exceedingly tender about myself. In fact, I indulged myself in a reverie so strong that I felt as though a hand were reaching down inside me. It had to reach so very far to touch me! It had to reach past those days in the forests of Belgium, and past the dying I'd refused to weep over; past the nights in German farmhouses whose books we'd burned to warm us; past endless stretches when I had shut off all softness I might feel for my fellows, and had managed even to deny myself the posture of a conqueror — the swagger that I, as a Jew, might well have worn as my boots whacked against the rubble of Wesel, Münster, and Braunschweig.

But now one night noise, one rumor of home and time past, and memory plunged down through all I had anesthetized, and came to what I suddenly remembered was myself. So it was not altogether curious that, in search of more of me, I found myself following Grossbart's tracks to Chapel No. 3, where the Jewish services were being held.

I took a seat in the last row, which was empty. Two rows in front of me sat Grossbart, Fishbein, and Halpern, holding little white Dixie cups. Each row of seats was raised higher than the one in front of it, and I could see clearly what was going on. Fishbein was pouring the contents of his cup into Grossbart's, and Grossbart looked mirthful as the liquid made a purple arc between Fishbein's hand and his. In the glaring yellow light, I saw the chaplain standing on the platform at the front; he was chanting the first line of the responsive reading. Grossbart's prayer book remained closed on his lap; he was swishing the cup around. Only Halpern responded to the chant by praying. The fingers of his right hand were spread wide across the cover of his open book. His cap was pulled down low onto his brow, which made it round, like a yarmulke. From time to time, Grossbart wet his lips at the cup's edge; Fishbein, his long yellow face a dying light bulb, looked from here to there, craning forward to catch sight of the faces down the row, then of those in front of him, then behind. He saw me, and his eyelids beat a tattoo. His elbow slid into Grossbart's side, his neck inclined toward his friend, he whispered something, and then, when the congregation next responded to the chant, Grossbart's voice was among the others. Fishbein looked into his book now, too; his lips, however, didn't move.

Finally, it was time to drink the wine. The chaplain smiled down at them as Grossbart swigged his in one long gulp, Halpern sipped, meditating, and Fishbein faked devotion with an empty cup. "As I look down amongst the congregation" — the chaplain grinned at the word — "this night, I see many new faces, and I want to welcome you to Friday-night services here at Camp Crowder. I am Major Leo Ben Ezra, your chaplain." Though an American, the chaplain spoke deliberately — syllable by syllable, almost — as though to communicate, above all, with the lip readers in his audience. "I have only a few words to say before we adjourn to the refreshment room, where the kind ladies of the Temple Sinai, St. Louis, Missouri, have a nice setting for you."

Applause and whistling broke out. After another momentary grin, the chaplain raised his hands, palms out, his eyes flicking upward a moment, as if to remind the troops where they were and Who Else might be in attendance. In the sudden silence that followed, I thought I heard Grossbart cackle, "Let the goyim clean the floors!" Were those the words? I wasn't sure, but Fishbein, grinning, nudged Halpern. Halpern looked dumbly at him, then went back to his prayer book, which had been occupying him all through the rabbi's talk. One hand tugged at the black kinky hair that stuck out under his cap. His lips moved.

The rabbi continued. "It is about the food that I want to speak to you for a moment. I know, I know, I know," he intoned, wearily, "how in the mouths of most of you the *trafe* food tastes like ashes. I know how you gag, some of you, and how your parents suffer to think of their children eating foods unclean and offensive to the palate. What can I tell you? I can only say, close your eyes and swallow as best you can. Eat what you must to live, and throw away the rest. I wish I could help more. For those of you who find this impossible, may I ask that you try and try, but then come to see me in private. If your revulsion is so great, we will have to seek aid from those higher up."

A round of chatter rose and subsided. Then everyone sang "Ain Kelohainu"; after all those years, I discovered I still knew the words. Then, suddenly, the service over, Grossbart was upon me. "Higher up? He means the General?"

"Hey, Shelly," Fishbein said, "he means God." He smacked his face and looked at Halpern. "How high can you go!"

"Sh-h-h!" Grossbart said. "What do you think, Sergeant?"

"I don't know," I said. "You better ask the chaplain."

"I'm going to. I'm making an appointment to see him in private. So is Mickey."

Halpern shook his head. "No, no, Sheldon —"

"You have rights, Mickey," Grossbart said. "They can't push us around."

"It's O.K.," said Halpern. "It bothers my mother, not me."

Grossbart looked at me. "Yesterday he threw up. From the hash. It was all ham and God knows what else."

"I have a cold — that was why," Halpern said. He pushed his yarmulke back into a cap.

"What about you, Fishbein?" I asked. "You kosher, too?"

He flushed. "A little. But I'll let it ride. I have a very strong stomach, and I don't eat a lot anyway." I continued to look at him, and he held up his wrist to reinforce what he'd just said; his watch strap was tightened to the last hole, and he pointed that out to me.

"But services are important to you?" I asked him.

He looked at Grossbart. "Sure, sir."

"Sergeant."

"Not so much at home," said Grossbart, stepping between us, "but away from home it gives one a sense of his Jewishness."

"We have to stick together," Fishbein said.

I started to walk toward the door; Halpern stepped back to make way for me.

"That's what happened in Germany," Grossbart was saying, loud enough for me to hear. "They didn't stick together. They let themselves get pushed around."

I turned. "Look, Grossbart. This is the Army, not summer camp."

He smiled. "So?"

Halpern tried to sneak off, but Grossbart held his arm.

"Grossbart, how old are you?" I asked.

"Nineteen."

"And you?" I said to Fishbein.

"The same. The same month, even."

"And what about him?" I pointed to Halpern, who had by now made it safely to the door.

"Eighteen," Grossbart whispered. "But like he can't tie his shoes or brush his teeth himself. I feel sorry for him."

"I feel sorry for all of us, Grossbart," I said, "but just act like a man. Just don't overdo it."

"Overdo what, sir?"

"The 'sir' business, for one thing. Don't overdo that," I said.

I left him standing there. I passed by Halpern, but he did not look at me. Then I was outside, but, behind, I heard Grossbart call, "Hey, Mickey, my *leben,* come on back. Refreshments!"

"*Leben!*" My grandmother's word for me!

※

One morning a week later, while I was working at my desk, Captain Barrett shouted for me to come into his office. When I entered, he had his helmet liner squashed down so far on his head that I couldn't even see his eyes. He was on the phone, and when he spoke to me, he cupped one hand over the mouthpiece. "Who the hell is Grossbart?"

"Third platoon, Captain," I said. "A trainee."

"What's all this stink about food? His mother called a goddam congressman about the food." He uncovered the mouthpiece and slid his helmet up until I could see his bottom eyelashes. "Yes, sir," he said into the phone. "Yes, sir. I'm still here, sir. I'm asking Marx, here, right now —"

He covered the mouthpiece again and turned his head back toward me. "Lightfoot Harry's on the phone," he said, between his teeth. "This congressman calls General Lyman, who calls Colonel Sousa, who calls the Major, who calls me. They're just dying to stick this thing on me. Whatsa matter?" He shook the phone at me. "I don't feed the troops? What is this?"

"Sir, Grossbart is strange —" Barrett greeted that with a mockingly indulgent smile. I altered my approach. "Captain, he's a very orthodox Jew, and so he's only allowed to eat certain foods."

"He throws up, the congressman said. Every time he eats something, his mother says, he throws up!"

"He's accustomed to observing the dietary laws, Captain."

"So why's his old lady have to call the White House?"

"Jewish parents, sir — they're apt to be more protective than you expect. I mean, Jews have a very close family life. A boy goes away from home, sometimes the mother is liable to get very upset. Probably the boy mentioned something in a letter, and his mother misinterpreted."

"I'd like to punch him one right in the mouth," the Captain said. "There's a war on, and he wants a silver platter!"

"I don't think the boy's to blame, sir. I'm sure we can straighten it out by just asking him. Jewish parents worry —"

"*All* parents worry, for Christ's sake. But they don't get on their high horse and start pulling strings —"

I interrupted, my voice higher, tighter than before. "The home life, Captain, is very important — but you're right, it may sometimes get out of hand. It's a very wonderful thing, Captain, but because it's so close, this kind of thing . . ."

He didn't listen any longer to my attempt to present both myself and Lightfoot Harry with an explanation for the letter. He turned back to the phone. "Sir?" he said. "Sir — Marx, here, tells me Jews have a tendency to be pushy. He says he thinks we can settle it right here in the company. . . . Yes, sir. . . . I *will* call back, sir, soon as I can." He hung up. "Where are the men, Sergeant?"

"On the range."

With a whack on the top of his helmet, he crushed it down over his eyes again, and charged out of his chair. "We're going for a ride," he said.

§§

The Captain drove, and I sat beside him. It was a hot spring day, and under my newly starched fatigues I felt as though my armpits were melting down onto my sides and chest. The roads were dry, and by the time we reached the firing range, my teeth felt gritty with dust, though my mouth had been shut the whole trip. The Captain slammed the brakes on and told me to get the hell out and find Grossbart.

I found him on his belly, firing wildly at the five-hundred-feet target. Waiting their turns behind him were Halpern and Fishbein. Fishbein, wearing a pair of steel-rimmed G.I. glasses I hadn't seen on him before, had the appearance of an old peddler who would gladly have sold you his rifle and the cartridges that were slung all over him. I stood back by the ammo boxes, waiting for Grossbart to finish spraying the distant targets. Fishbein straggled back to stand near me.

"Hello, Sergeant Marx," he said.

"How are you?" I mumbled.

"Fine, thank you. Sheldon's really a good shot."

"I didn't notice."

"I'm not so good, but I think I'm getting the hang of it now. Sergeant, I don't mean to, you know, ask what I shouldn't —" The boy stopped. He was trying to speak intimately, but the noise of the shooting forced him to shout at me.

"What is it?" I asked. Down the range, I saw Captain Barrett standing up in the jeep, scanning the line for me and Grossbart.

"My parents keep asking and asking where we're going," Fishbein said. "Everybody says the Pacific. I don't care, but my parents — If I could relieve their minds, I think I could concentrate more on my shooting."

"I don't know where, Fishbein. Try to concentrate anyway."

"Sheldon says you might be able to find out."

"I don't know a thing, Fishbein. You just take it easy, and don't let Sheldon —"

"*I'm* taking it easy, Sergeant. It's at home —"

Grossbart had finished on the line, and was dusting his fatigues with one hand. I called to him, "Grossbart, the Captain wants to see you."

He came towards us. His eyes blazed and twinkled. "Hi!"

"Don't point that rifle!" I said.

"I wouldn't shoot you, Sarge." He gave me a smile as wide as a pumpkin, and turned the barrel aside.

"Damn you, Grossbart, this is no joke! Follow me."

I walked ahead of him, and had the awful suspicion that, behind me, Grossbart was *marching,* his rifle on his shoulder, as though he were a one-man detachment. At the jeep, he gave the Captain a rifle salute, "Private Sheldon Grossbart, sir."

"At ease, Grossman." The Captain sat down, slid over into the empty seat, and, crooking a finger, invited Grossbart closer.

"Bart, sir. Sheldon Gross*bart.* It's a common error." Grossbart nodded at me; *I* understood, he indicated. I looked away just as the mess truck pulled up to the range, disgorging a half-dozen K.P.'s with rolled-up sleeves. The mess sergeant screamed at them while they set up the chow-line equipment.

"Grossbart, your mama wrote some congressman that we don't feed you right. Do you know that?" the Captain said.

"It was my father, sir. He wrote to Representative Franconi that my religion forbids me to eat certain foods."

"What religion is that, Grossbart?"

"Jewish."

"'Jewish, *sir*,'" I said to Grossbart.

"Excuse me, sir. Jewish, sir."

"What have you been living on?" the Captain asked. "You've been in the Army a month already. You don't look to me like you're falling to pieces."

"I eat because I have to, sir. But Sergeant Marx will testify to the fact that I don't eat one mouthful more than I need to in order to survive."

"Is that so, Marx?" Barrett asked.

"I've never seen Grossbart eat, sir," I said.

"But you heard the rabbi," Grossbart said. "He told us what to do, and I listened."

The Captain looked at me. "Well, Marx?"

"I still don't know what he eats and doesn't eat, sir."

Grossbart raised his arms to plead with me, and it looked for a moment as though he were going to hand me his weapon to hold. "But, Sergeant —"

"Look, Grossbart, just answer the Captain's questions," I said sharply.

Barrett smiled at me, and I resented it. "All right, Grossbart," he said. "What is it you want? The little piece of paper? You want out?"

"No, sir. Only to be allowed to live as a Jew. And for the others, too."

"What others?"

"Fishbein, sir, and Halpern."

"They don't like the way we serve, either?"

"Halpern throws up, sir. I've seen it."

"I thought *you* throw up."

"Just once, sir. I didn't know the sausage was sausage."

"We'll give menus, Grossbart. We'll show training films about the food, so you can identify when we're trying to poison you."

Grossbart did not answer. The men had been organized into two long chow lines. At the tail end of one, I spotted Fishbein — or, rather, his glasses spotted me. They winked sunlight back at me. Halpern stood next to him, patting the inside of his collar with a khaki handkerchief. They moved with the line as it began to edge up toward the food. The mess sergeant was still screaming at the K.P.s. For a moment, I was actually terrified by the thought that somehow the mess sergeant was going to become involved in Grossbart's problem.

"Marx," the Captain said, "you're a Jewish fella — am I right?"

I played straight man. "Yes, sir."

"How long you been in the Army? Tell this boy."

"Three years and two months."

"A year in combat, Grossbart. Twelve goddam months in combat all through Europe. I admire this man." The Captain snapped a wrist against my chest. "Do you hear him peeping about the food? Do you? I want an answer, Grossbart. Yes or no."

"No, sir."

"And why not? He's a Jewish fella."

"Some things are more important to some Jews than other things to other Jews."

Barrett blew up. "Look, Grossbart. Marx, here, is a good man — a goddam hero. When you were in high school, Sergeant Marx was killing Germans. Who does more for the Jews — you, by throwing up over a lousy piece of sausage, a piece of first-cut meat, or Marx, by killing those Nazi bastards? If I was a Jew, Grossbart, I'd kiss this man's feet. He's a goddam hero, and *he* eats what we give him. Why do you have to cause trouble is what I want to know! What is it you're buckin' for — a discharge?"

"No, sir."

"I'm talking to a wall! Sergeant, get him out of my way." Barrett swung himself back into the driver's seat. "I'm going to see the chaplain." The engine roared, the jeep spun around in a whirl of dust, and the Captain was headed back to camp.

For a moment, Grossbart and I stood side by side, watching the jeep. Then he looked at me and said, "I don't want to start trouble. That's the first thing they toss up to us."

When he spoke, I saw that his teeth were white and straight, and the sight of them suddenly made me understand that Grossbart actually did have parents — that once upon a time someone had taken little Sheldon to the dentist. He was their son. Despite all the talk about his parents, it was hard to believe in Grossbart as a child, an heir — as related by blood to anyone, mother, father, or, above all, to me. This realization led me to another.

"What does your father do, Grossbart?" I asked as we started to walk back toward the chow line.

"He's a tailor."

"An American?"

"Now, yes. A son in the Army," he said, jokingly.

"And your mother?" I asked.

He winked. "A *ballabusta*. She practially sleeps with a dustcloth in her hand."

"She's also an immigrant?"

"All she talks is Yiddish, still."

"And your father, too?"

"A little English. 'Clean,' 'Press,' 'Take the pants in.' That's the extent of it. But they're good to me."

"Then, Grossbart —" I reached out and stopped him. He turned toward me, and when our eyes met, his seemed to jump back, to shiver in their sockets. "Grossbart — you were the one who wrote that letter, weren't you?"

It took only a second or two for his eyes to flash happy again. "Yes." He walked on, and I kept pace. "Its what my father *would* have written if he had known how. It was his name, though. *He* signed it. He even mailed it. I sent it home. For the New York postmark."

I was astonished, and he saw it. With complete seriousness, he thrust his right arm in front of me. "Blood is blood, Sergeant," he said, pinching the blue vein in his wrist.

"What the hell *are* you trying to do, Grossbart?" I asked. "I've seen you eat. Do you know that? I told the Captain I don't know what you eat, but I've seen you eat like a hound at chow."

"We work hard, Sergeant. We're in training. For a furnace to work, you've got to feed it coal."

"Why did you say in the letter that you threw up all the time?"

"I was really talking about Mickey there. I was talking *for* him. He would never write, Sergeant, though I pleaded with him. He'll waste away to nothing if I don't help. Sergeant, I used my name — my father's name — but it's Mickey, and Fishbein, too, I'm watching out for."

"You're a regular Messiah, aren't you?"

We were at the chow line now.

"That's a good one, Sergeant," he said, smiling. "But who knows? Who can tell? Maybe you're the Messiah — a little bit. What Mickey says is the Messiah is a collective idea. He went to Yeshiva, Mickey, for a while. He says *together* we're the Messiah. Me a little bit, you a little bit. You should hear the kid talk, Sergeant, when he gets going."

"Me a little bit, you a little bit," I said. "You'd like to believe that, wouldn't you, Grossbart? That would make everything so clean for you."

"It doesn't seem too bad a thing to believe, Sergeant. It only means we should all *give* a little, is all."

I walked off to eat my rations with the other noncoms.

♪♪

Two days later, a letter addressed to Captain Barrett passed over my desk. It had come through the chain of command — from the office of Congressman Franconi, where it had been received, to General Lyman, to Colonel Sousa, to Major Lamont, now to Captain Barrett. I read it over twice. It was dated May 14, the day Barrett had spoken with Grossbart on the rifle range.

> Dear Congressman:
>   First let me thank you for your interest in behalf of my son, Private Sheldon Grossbart. Fortunately, I was able to speak with

Sheldon on the phone the other night, and I think I've been able to solve our problem. He is, as I mentioned in my last letter, a very religious boy, and it was only with the greatest difficulty that I could persuade him that the religious thing to do — what God Himself would want Sheldon to do — would be to suffer the pangs of religious remorse for the good of his country and all mankind. It took some doing, Congressman, but finally he saw the light. In fact, what he said (and I wrote down the words on a scratch pad so as never to forget), what he said was "I guess you're right, Dad. So many millions of my fellow-Jews gave up their lives to the enemy, the least I can do is live for a while minus a bit of my heritage so as to help end this struggle and regain for all the children of God dignity and humanity." That, Congressman, would make any father proud.

By the way, Sheldon wanted me to know — and to pass on to you — the name of a soldier who helped him reach this decision: SERGEANT NATHAN MARX. Sergeant Marx is a combat veteran who is Sheldon's first sergeant. This man has helped Sheldon over some of the first hurdles he's had to face in the Army, and is in part responsible for Sheldon's changing his mind about the dietary laws. I know Sheldon would appreciate any recognition Marx could receive.

Thank you and good luck. I look forward to seeing your name on the next election ballot.

Respectfully,
Samuel E. Grossbart

Attached to the Grossbart communiqué was another, addressed to General Marshall Lyman, the post commander, and signed by Representative Charles E. Franconi, of the House of Representatives. The communiqué informed General Lyman that Sergeant Nathan Marx was a credit to the U.S. Army and the Jewish people.

What was Grossbart's motive in recanting? Did he feel he'd gone too far? Was the letter a strategic retreat — a crafty attempt to strengthen what he considered our alliance? Or had he actually changed his mind, via an imaginary dialogue between Grossbart *père* and Grossbart *fils?* I was puzzled, but only for a few days — that is, only until I realized that, whatever his reasons, he had actually decided to disappear from my life; he was going to allow himself to become just another trainee. I saw him at inspection, but he never winked; at chow formations, but he never flashed me a sign. On Sundays, with the other trainees, he would sit around watching the noncoms' softball team, for which I pitched, but not once did he speak an unnecessary word to me. Fishbein and Halpern retreated, too — at

Grossbart's command, I was sure. Apparently he had seen that wisdom lay in turning back before he plunged over into the ugliness of privilege undeserved. Our separation allowed me to forgive him our past encounters, and, finally, to admire him for his good sense.

⚘

Meanwhile, free of Grossbart, I grew used to my job and my administrative tasks. I stepped on a scale one day, and discovered I had truly become a noncombatant; I had gained seven pounds. I found patience to get past the first three pages of a book. I thought about the future more and more, and wrote letters to girls I'd known before the war. I even got a few answers. I sent away to Columbia for a Law School catalogue. I continued to follow the war in the Pacific, but it was not my war. I thought I could see the end, and sometimes, at night, I dreamed that I was walking on the streets of Manhattan — Broadway, Third Avenue, 116th Street, where I had lived the three years I attended Columbia. I curled myself around these dreams and I began to be happy.

And then, one Sunday, when everybody was away and I was alone in the orderly room reading a month-old copy of the *Sporting News*, Grossbart reappeared.

"You a baseball fan, Sergeant?"

I looked up. "How are you?"

"Fine," Grossbart said. "They're making a soldier out of me."

"How are Fishbein and Halpern?"

"Coming along," he said. "We've got no training this afternoon. They're at the movies."

"How come you're not with them?"

"I wanted to come over and say hello."

He smiled — a shy, regular-guy smile, as though he and I well knew that our friendship drew its sustenance from unexpected visits, remembered birthdays, and borrowed lawnmowers. At first it offended me, and then the feeling was swallowed by the general uneasiness I felt at the thought that everyone on the post was locked away in a dark movie theater and I was here alone with Grossbart. I folded up my paper.

"Sergeant," he said. "I'd like to ask a favor. It is a favor, and I'm making no bones about it."

He stopped, allowing me to refuse him a hearing — which, of course, forced me into a courtesy I did not intend. "Go ahead."

"Well, actually it's two favors."

I said nothing.

"The first one's about these rumors. Everybody says we're going to the Pacific."

"As I told your friend Fishbein, I don't know," I said. "You'll just have to wait to find out. Like everybody else."

"You think there's a chance of any of us going East?"

"Germany?" I said. "Maybe."

"I meant New York."

"I don't think so, Grossbart. Offhand."

"Thanks for the information, Sergeant," he said.

"It's not information, Grossbart. Just what I surmise."

"It certainly would be good to be near home. My parents — you know." He took a step toward the door and then turned back. "Oh, the other thing. May I ask the other?"

"What is it?"

"The other thing is — I've got relatives in St. Louis, and they say they'll give me a whole Passover dinner if I can get down there. God, Sergeant, that'd mean an awful lot to me."

I stood up. "No passes during basic, Grossbart."

"But we're off from now till Monday morning, Sergeant. I could leave the post and no one would even know."

"I'd know. You'd know."

"But that's all. Just the two of us. Last night, I called my aunt, and you should have heard her. 'Come — come,' she said. 'I got gefilte fish, *chrain* — the works!' Just a day, Sergeant. I'd take the blame if anything happened."

"The Captain isn't here to sign a pass."

"You could sign."

"Look, Grossbart —"

"Sergeant, for two months, practically, I've been eating *trafe* till I want to die."

"I thought you'd made up your mind to live with it. To be minus a little bit of heritage."

He pointed a finger at me. "You!" he said. "That wasn't for you to read."

"I read it. So what?"

"That letter was addressed to a congressman."

"Grossbart, don't feed me any baloney. You *wanted* me to read it."

"Why are you persecuting me, Sergeant?"

"Are you kidding!"

"I've run into this before," he said, "but never from my own!"

"Get out of here, Grossbart! Get the hell out of my sight!"

He did not move. "Ashamed, that's what you are," he said. "So you take it out on the rest of us. They say Hitler himself was half a Jew. Hearing you, I wouldn't doubt it."

"What are you trying to do with me, Grossbart?" I asked him. "What are you after? You want me to give you special privileges, to change the food, to find out about your orders, to give you weekend passes."

"You even talk like a goy!" Grossbart shook his fist. "Is this just a weekend pass I'm asking for? Is a Seder sacred, or not?"

Seder! It suddenly occurred to me that Passover had been celebrated weeks before. I said so.

"That's right," he replied. "Who says no? A month ago — and I was in the field eating hash! And now all I ask is a simple favor. A Jewish boy I thought would understand. My aunt's willing to go out of her way — to make a Seder a month later. . . ." He turned to go, mumbling.

"Come back here!" I called. He stopped and looked at me. "Grossbart, why can't you be like the rest? Why do you have to stick out like a sore thumb?"

"Because I'm a Jew, Sergeant. I *am* different. Better, maybe not. But different."

"This is a war, Grossbart. For the time being *be* the same."

"I refuse."

"What?"

"I refuse. I can't stop being me. That's all there is to it." Tears came to his eyes. "It's a hard thing to be a Jew. But now I understand what Mickey says — it's a harder thing to stay one." He raised a hand sadly toward me. "Look at *you*."

"Stop crying!"

"Stop this, stop that, stop the other thing! *You* stop, Sergeant. Stop closing your heart to your own!" And, wiping his face with his sleeve, he ran out the door. "The least we can do for one another — the least . . ."

An hour later, looking out of the window, I saw Grossbart headed across the field. He wore a pair of starched khakis and carried a little leather ditty bag. I went out into the heat of the day. It was quiet; not a soul was in sight except, over by the mess hall, four K.P.s sitting around a pan, sloping forward from their waists, gabbing and peeling potatoes in the sun.

"Grossbart!" I called.

He looked toward me and continued walking.

"Grossbart, get over here!"

He turned and came across the field. Finally, he stood before me.

"Where are you going?" I asked.

"St. Louis. I don't care."

"You'll get caught without a pass."

"So I'll get caught without a pass."

"You'll go to the stockade."

"I'm *in* the stockade." He made an about-face and headed off.

I let him go only a step or two. "Come back here," I said, and he followed me into the office, where I typed out a pass and signed the Captain's name, and my own initials after it.

He took the pass and then, a moment later, reached out and grabbed my hand. "Sergeant, you don't know how much this means to me."

"O.K.," I said. "Don't get in any trouble."

"I wish I could show you how much this means to me."

"Don't do me any favors. Don't write any more congressmen for citations."

He smiled. "You're right. I won't. But let me do something."

"Bring me a piece of that gefilte fish. Just get out of here."

"I will!" he said. "With a slice of carrot and a little horseradish. I won't forget."

"All right. Just show your pass at the gate. And don't tell *anybody.*"

"I won't. It's a month late, but a good Yom Tov to you."

"Good Yom Tov, Grossbart," I said.

"You're a good Jew, Sergeant. You like to think you have a hard heart, but underneath, you're a fine, decent man. I mean that."

Those last three words touched me more than any words from Grossbart's mouth had the right to. "All right, Grossbart," I said. "Now call me 'sir,' and get the hell out of here."

He ran out the door and was gone. I felt very pleased with myself; it was a great relief to stop fighting Grossbart, and it had cost me nothing. Barrett would never find out, and if he did, I could manage to invent some excuse. For a while, I sat at my desk, comfortable in my decision. Then the screen door flew back and Grossbart burst in again. "Sergeant!" he said. Behind him I saw Fishbein and Halpern both in starched khakis, both carrying ditty bags like Grossbart's.

"Sergeant, I caught Mickey and Larry coming out of the movies. I almost missed them."

"Grossbart — did I say to tell no one?" I said.

"But my aunt said I could bring friends. That I should, in fact."

"*I'm* the Sergeant, Grossbart — not your aunt!"

Grossbart looked at me in disbelief. He pulled Halpern up by his sleeve. "Mickey, tell the Sergeant what this would mean to you."

Halpern looked at me and, shrugging, said, "A lot."

Fishbein stepped forward without prompting. "This would mean a great deal to me and my parents, Sergeant Marx."

"No!" I shouted.

Grossbart was shaking his head. "Sergeant, I could see you denying me, but how you can deny Mickey, a Yeshiva boy — that's beyond me."

"I'm not denying Mickey anything," I said. "You just pushed a little too hard, Grossbart. *You* denied him."

"I'll give him my pass, then," Grossbart said. "I'll give him my aunt's address and a little note. At least let him go."

In a second, he had crammed the pass into Halpern's pants pocket. Halpern looked at me, and so did Fishbein. Grossbart was at the door, pushing it open. "Mickey, bring me a piece of gelfilte fish, at least," he said, and then he was outside again.

The three of us looked at one another, and then I said, "Halpern, hand that pass over."

He took it from his pocket and gave it to me. Fishbein had now moved to the doorway, where he lingered. He stood there for a moment with his mouth slightly open, and then he pointed to himself. "And me?" he asked.

His utter ridiculousness exhausted me. I slumped down in my seat and felt pulses knocking at the back of my eyes. "Fishbein," I said, "you understand I'm not trying to deny you anything, don't you? If it was my Army, I'd serve gefilte fish in the mess hall. I'd sell *kugel* in the PX, honest to God."

Halpern smiled.

"You understand, don't you, Halpern?"

"Yes, Sergeant."

"And you, Fishbein? I don't want enemies. I'm just like you — I want to serve my time and go home. I miss the same things you miss."

"Then, Sergeant," Fishbein said, "why don't you come, too?"

"Where?"

"To St. Louis. To Shelly's aunt. We'll have a regular Seder. Play hide-the-matzoh." He gave me a broad, black-toothed smile.

I saw Grossbart again, on the other side of the screen.

"Pst!" He waved a piece of paper. "Mickey, here's the address. Tell her I couldn't get away."

Halpern did not move. He looked at me, and I saw the shrug moving up his arms into his shoulders again. I took the cover off my typewriter and made out passes for him and Fishbein. "Go," I said. "The three of you."

I thought Halpern was going to kiss my hand.

§§

That afternoon, in a bar in Joplin, I drank beer and listened with half an ear to the Cardinal game. I tried to look squarely at what I'd become involved in, and began to wonder if perhaps the struggle with Grossbart wasn't as much my fault as his. What was I that I had to *muster* generous feelings? Who was I to have been feeling so grudging, so tight-hearted? After all, I wasn't being asked to move the world. Had I a right, then, or a reason, to clamp down on Grossbart, when that meant clamping down on Halpern, too? And Fishbein — that ugly, agreeable soul? Out of the many recollections of my childhood that had tumbled over me these past few days I heard my grandmother's voice: "What are you making a *tsimmes?*" It was what she would ask my mother when, say, I had cut myself while doing something I shouldn't have done, and her daughter was busy bawling me out. I needed a hug and a kiss, and my mother would moralize. But my grandmother knew — mercy overrides justice. I should have known it, too. Who was Nathan Marx to be such a penny pincher with kindness? Surely, I thought, the Messiah himself — if He should ever come — won't niggle over nickels and dimes. God willing, he'll hug and kiss.

The next day, while I was playing softball over on the parade ground, I decided to ask Bob Wright, who was noncom in charge of Classification and Assignment, where he thought our trainees would be sent when their cycle ended, in two weeks. I asked casually, between innings, and he said "They're pushing them all into the Pacific. Shulman cut the orders on your boys the other day."

The news shocked me, as though I were the father of Halpern, Fishbein, and Grossbart.

ॐ

That night, I was just sliding into sleep when someone tapped on my door. "Who is it?" I asked.

"Sheldon."

He opened the door and came in. For a moment, I felt his presence without being able to see him. "How was it?" I asked.

He popped into sight in the near-darkness before me. "Great, Sergeant." Then he was sitting on the edge of the bed. I sat up.

"How about you?" he asked. "Have a nice weekend?"

"Yes."

"The others went to sleep." He took a deep, paternal breath. We sat silent for a while, and a homey feeling invaded my ugly little cubicle; the door was locked, the cat was out, the children were safely in bed.

"Sergeant, can I tell you something? Personal?"

I did not answer, and he seemed to know why. "Not about me. About Mickey, Sergeant. I never felt for anybody like I feel for him. Last night I heard Mickey in the bed next to me. He was crying so, it could have broken your heart. Real sobs."

"I'm sorry to hear that."

"I had to talk to him to stop him. He held my hand, Sergeant — he wouldn't let it go. He was almost hysterical. He kept saying if he only knew where we were going. Even if he knew it *was* the Pacific, that would be better than nothing. Just to know."

Long ago, someone had taught Grossbart the sad rule that only lies can get the truth. Not that I couldn't believe in the fact of Halpern's crying; his eyes *always* seemed red-rimmed. But, fact or not, it became a lie when Grossbart uttered it. He was entirely strategic. But then — it came with the force of indictment — so was I! There are strategies of aggression, but there are strategies of retreat as well. And so, recognizing that I myself had not been without craft and guile, I told him what I knew. "It is the Pacific."

He let out a small gasp, which was not a lie. "I'll tell him. I wish it was otherwise."

"So do I."

He jumped on my words. "You mean you think you could do something? A change, maybe?"

"No, I couldn't do a thing."

"Don't you know anybody over at C. and A.?"

"Grossbart, there's nothing I can do," I said. "If your orders are for the Pacific, then it's the Pacific."

"But Mickey —"

"Mickey, you, me — everybody, Grossbart. There's nothing to be done. Maybe the war'll end before you go. Pray for a miracle."

"But —"

"Good night, Grossbart." I settled back, and was relieved to feel the springs unbend as Grossbart rose to leave. I could see him clearly now; his jaw had dropped, and he looked like a dazed prizefighter. I noticed for the first time a little paper bag in his hand.

"Grossbart." I smiled. "My gift?"

"Oh, yes, Sergeant. Here — from all of us." He handed me the bag. "It's egg roll."

"Egg roll?" I accepted the bag and felt a damp grease spot on the bottom. I opened it, sure that Grossbart was joking.

"We thought you'd probably like it. You know — Chinese egg roll. We thought you'd probably have a taste for —"

"Your aunt served egg roll?"

"She wasn't home."

"Grossbart, she invited you. You told me she invited you and your friends."

"I know," he said. "I just reread the letter. *Next* week."

I got out of bed and walked to the window. "Grossbart," I said. But I was not calling to him.

"What?"

"What are you, Grossbart? Honest to God, what are you?"

I think it was the first time I'd asked him a question for which he didn't have an immediate answer.

"How can you do this to people?" I went on.

"Sergeant, the day away did us all a world of good. Fishbein, you should see him, he *loves* Chinese food."

"But the Seder," I said.

"We took the second best, Sergeant."

Rage came charging at me. I didn't sidestep. "Grossbart, you're a liar!" I said. "You're a schemer and a crook. You've got no respect for anything. Nothing at all. Not for me, for the truth — not even for poor Halpern! You use us all —"

"Sergeant, Sergeant, I feel for Mickey. Honest to God, I do. I *love* Mickey. I try —"

"You try! You feel!" I lurched toward him and grabbed his shirt front. I shook him furiously. "Grossbart, get out! Get out and stay the hell away from me. Because if I see you, I'll make your life miserable. *You understand that?*"

"Yes."

I let him free, and when he walked from the room, I wanted to spit on the floor where he had stood. I couldn't stop the fury. It engulfed me, owned me, till it seemed I could only rid myself of it with tears or an act of violence. I snatched from the bed the bag Grossbart had given me and, with all my strength, threw it out the window. And the next morning, as the men policed the area around the barracks, I heard a great cry go up from one of the trainees, who had been anticipating only his morning handful of cigarette butts and candy wrappers. "Egg roll!" he shouted. "Holy Christ, Chinese goddam egg roll!"

δδ

A week later, when I read the orders that had come down from C. and A., I couldn't believe my eyes. Every single trainee was to be shipped to Camp Stoneman, California, and from there to the Pacific — every trainee but one. Private Sheldon Grossbart. He was to be sent to Fort Monmouth, New Jersey. I read the mimeographed sheet several times. Dee, Farrell, Fishbein, Fuselli, Fylypowycz, Glinicki, Gromke, Gucwa, Halpern, Hardy, Helebrandt, right down to Anton Zygadlo — all were to be headed West before the month was out. All except Grossbart. He had pulled a string, and I wasn't it.

I lifted the phone and called C. and A.

The voice on the other end said smartly, "Corporal Shulman, sir."

"Let me speak to Sergeant Wright."

"Who is this calling, sir?"

"Sergeant Marx."

And, to my surprise, the voice said, *"Oh!"* Then, "Just a minute, Sergeant."

Shulman's *"Oh!"* stayed with me while I waited for Wright to come to the phone. Why *"Oh!"* Who was Shulman? And then, so simply, I knew I'd discovered the string that Grossbart had pulled. In fact, I could hear Grossbart the day he'd discovered Shulman in the PX, or in the bowling alley, or maybe even at services. "Glad to meet you. Where you from? Bronx? Me, too. Do you know So-and-So? And So-and-So? Me, too! You work at C. and A.? Really? Hey, how's chances of getting East? Could you do something? Change something? Swindle, cheat, lie? We gotta help each other, you know. If the Jews in Germany . . ."

Bob Wright answered the phone. "How are you, Nate? How's the pitching arm?"

"Good. Bob, I wonder if you could do me a favor." I heard clearly my own words, and they so reminded me of Grossbart that I dropped more easily than I could have imagined into what I had planned. "This may sound crazy, Bob, but I got a kid here on orders to Monmouth who wants them changed. He had a brother killed in Europe, and he's hot to go to the Pacific. Says he'd feel like a coward if he wound up Stateside. I don't know, Bob — can anything be done? Put somebody else in the Monmouth slot?"

"Who?" he asked cagily.

"Anybody. First guy in the alphabet. I don't care. The kid just asked if something could be done."

"What's his name?"

"Grossbart, Sheldon."

Wright didn't answer.

"Yeah," I said. "He's a Jewish kid, so he thought I could help him out. You know."

"I guess I can do something," he finally said. "The Major hasn't been around here for weeks. Temporary duty to the golf course. I'll try, Nate, that's all I can say."

"I'd appreciate it, Bob. See you Sunday." And I hung up, perspiring.

The following day, the corrected orders appeared: Fishbein, Fuselli, Fyly-powycz, Glinicki, Gromke, Grossbart, Gucwa, Halpern, Hardy . . . Lucky Private Harley Alton was to go to Fort Monmouth, New Jersey, where for some reason or other, they wanted an enlisted man with infantry training.

After chow that night, I stopped back at the orderly room to straighten out the guard-duty roster. Grossbart was waiting for me. He spoke first.

"You son of a bitch!"

I sat down at my desk, and while he glared at me, I began to make the necessary alterations in the duty roster.

"What do you have against me?" he cried. "Against my family? Would it kill you for me to be near my father, God knows how many months he has left to him?"

"Why so?"

"His heart," Grossbart said. "He hasn't had enough troubles in a lifetime, you've got to add to them. I curse the day I ever met you, Marx! Shulman told me what happened over there. There's no limit to your anti-Semitism, is there? The damage you've done here isn't enough. You have to make a special phone call! You really want me dead!"

I made the last few notations in the duty roster and got up to leave. "Good night, Grossbart."

"You owe me an explanation!" He stood in my path.

"Sheldon, you're the one who owes explanations."

He scowled. "To *you*?"

"To me, I think so — yes. Mostly to Fishbein and Halpern."

"That's right, twist things around. I owe nobody nothing, I've done all I could do for them. Now I think I've got the right to watch out for myself."

"For each other we have to learn to watch out, Sheldon. You told me yourself."

"You call this watching out for me — what you did?"

"No. For all of us."

I pushed him aside and started for the door. I heard his furious breathing behind me, and it sounded like steam rushing from an engine of terrible strength.

"*You'll* be all right," I said from the door. And, I thought, so would Fishbein and Halpern be all right, even in the Pacific, if only Grossbart continued to see — in the obsequiousness of the one, the soft spirituality of the other — some profit for himself.

I stood outside the orderly room, and I heard Grossbart weeping behind me. Over in the barracks, in the lighted windows, I could see the boys in their T shirts sitting on their bunks talking about their orders, as they'd been doing for the past two days. With a kind of quiet nervousness, they polished shoes, shined belt buckles, squared away underwear, trying as best they could to accept their fate. Behind me, Grossbart swallowed hard, accepting his. And then, resisting with all my will an impulse to turn and seek pardon for my vindictiveness, I accepted my own.

James Baldwin
Sonny's Blues

One of the outstanding figures of modern literature, James Baldwin's work ranges from such celebrated novels as *Go Tell It on the Mountain* and *Giovanni's Room* to two plays, *Blues for Mister Charlie* and *The Amen Corner,* to volumes of essays, among them *Notes of a Native Son* and *Nobody Knows My Name.* He published only one collection of short fiction, but the eight stories that comprised *Going to Meet the Man* in 1965 have become widely studied and discussed. The most famous of these is "Sonny's Blues," which first appeared in the *Partisan Review* in 1957. Baldwin's work addresses a range of central subjects, among them the quest for dignity and respect for gay African Americans; another basic theme is the complexity of racial identity and the ways in which it impinges upon artistic expression, an idea central to this story. It is significant that the aesthetic form at issue is the blues, a lyrical mode with both personal and social implications expressing pain and travail on several levels. Also key is the first-person narrative stance, for it is the narrator, not the titular character, who has the internal struggle, the conflict, the epiphany, and the psychological and emotional growth at the end. In the process, the unnamed speaker comes to terms with the important transformational events in his life, among them the death of his daughter and his difficult relationship with his younger brother, Sonny. The plot is structured in six episodes with temporal modulations moving from the present into the past and back to the time of the telling. This arrangement brings into focus the narrator's empathetic admission into the musical expression of his brother, whom he comes to understand only in the poignant final paragraphs.

James Baldwin, "Sonny's Blues," *Going to Meet the Man* (New York: The Dial Press, 1965), 103–41.

I read about it in the paper, in the subway, on my way to work. I read it, and I couldn't believe it, and I read it again. Then perhaps I just stared at it, at the newsprint spelling out his name, spelling out the story. I stared at it in the swinging lights of the subway car, and in the faces and bodies of the people, and in my own face, trapped in the darkness which roared outside.

It was not to be believed and I kept telling myself that, as I walked from the subway station to the high school. And at the same time I couldn't doubt it. I was scared, scared for Sonny. He became real to me again. A great block of ice got settled in my belly and kept melting there slowly all day long, while I taught my classes algebra. It was a special kind of ice. It kept melting, sending trickles of ice water all up and down my veins, but it never got less. Sometimes it hardened and seemed to expand until I felt my guts were going to come spilling out or that I was going to choke or scream. This would always be at a moment when I was re-membering some specific thing Sonny had once said or done.

When he was about as old as the boys in my classes his face had been bright and open, there was a lot of copper in it; and he'd had wonderfully direct brown eyes, and great gentleness and privacy. I wondered what he looked like now. He had been picked up, the evening before, in a raid on an apartment downtown, for peddling and using heroin.

I couldn't believe it: but what I mean by that is that I couldn't find any room for it anywhere inside me. I had kept it outside me for a long time. I hadn't wanted to know. I had had suspicions, but I didn't name them, I kept putting them away. I told myself that Sonny was wild, but he wasn't crazy. And he'd al-ways been a good boy, he hadn't ever turned hard or evil or disrespectful, the way kids can, so quick, so quick, especially in Harlem. I didn't want to believe that I'd ever see my brother going down, coming to nothing, all that light in his face gone out, in the condition I'd already seen so many others. Yet it had hap-pened and here I was, talking about algebra to a lot of boys who might, every one of them for all I knew, be popping off needles every time they went to the head. Maybe it did more for them than algebra could.

I was sure that the first time Sonny had ever had horse, he couldn't have been much older than these boys were now. These boys, now, were living as we'd been living then, they were growing up with a rush and their heads bumped abruptly against the low ceiling of their actual possibilities. They were filled with rage. All they really knew were two darknesses, the darkness of their lives, which was now closing in on them, and the darkness of the movies, which had blinded them to that other darkness, and in which they now, vindictively, dreamed at once more together than they were at any other time, and more alone.

When the last bell rang, the last class ended, I let out my breath. It seemed I'd been holding it for all that time. My clothes were wet — I may have looked as though I'd been sitting in a steam bath, all dressed up, all afternoon. I sat alone in the classroom a long time. I listened to the boys outside, downstairs, shouting and cursing and laughing. Their laughter struck me for perhaps the first time. It was not the joyous laughter which — God knows why — one associates with children. It was mocking and insular, its intent was to denigrate. It was disen-chanted, and in this, also, lay the authority of their curses. Perhaps I was listen-ing to them because I was thinking about my brother and in them I heard my brother. And myself.

One boy was whistling a tune, at once very complicated and very simple, it seemed to be pouring out of him as though he were a bird, and it sounded very cool and moving through all that harsh, bright air, only just holding its own through all those other sounds.

I stood up and walked over to the window and looked down into the courtyard. It was the beginning of the spring and the sap was rising in the boys. A teacher passed through them every now and again, quickly, as though he or she couldn't wait to get out of that courtyard, to get those boys out of their sight and off their minds. I started collecting my stuff. I thought I'd better get home and talk to Isabel.

The courtyard was almost deserted by the time I got downstairs. I saw this boy standing in the shadow of a doorway, looking just like Sonny. I almost called his name. Then I saw that it wasn't Sonny, but somebody we used to know, a boy from around our block. He'd been Sonny's friend. He'd never been mine, having been too young for me, and, anyway, I'd never liked him. And now, even though he was a grown-up man, he still hung around that block, still spent hours on the street corners, was always high and raggy. I used to run into him from time to time and he'd often work around to asking me for a quarter or fifty cents. He always had some real good excuse, too, and I always gave it to him, I don't know why.

But now, abruptly, I hated him. I couldn't stand the way he looked at me, partly like a dog, partly like a cunning child. I wanted to ask him what the hell he was doing in the school courtyard.

He sort of shuffled over to me, and he said, "I see you got the papers. So you already know about it."

"You mean about Sonny? Yes, I already know about it. How come they didn't get you?"

He grinned. It made him repulsive and it also brought to mind what he'd looked like as a kid. "I wasn't there. I stay away from them people."

"Good for you." I offered him a cigarette and I watched him through the smoke. "You come all the way down here just to tell me about Sonny?"

"That's right." He was sort of shaking his head and his eyes looked strange, as though they were about to cross. The bright sun deadened his damp dark brown skin and it made his eyes look yellow and showed up the dirt in his kinked hair. He smelled funky. I moved a little away from him and I said, "Well, thanks. But I already know about it and I got to get home."

"I'll walk you a little ways," he said. We started walking. There were a couple of kids still loitering in the courtyard and one of them said goodnight to me and looked strangely at the boy beside me.

"What're you going to do?" he asked me. "I mean, about Sonny?"

"Look. I haven't seen Sonny for over a year, I'm not sure I'm going to do anything. Anyway, what the hell *can* I do?"

"That's right," he said quickly, "ain't nothing you can do. Can't much help old Sonny no more, I guess."

It was what I was thinking and so it seemed to me he had no right to say it.

"I'm surprised at Sonny, though," he went on — he had a funny way of talking, he looked straight ahead as though he were talking to himself — "I thought Sonny was a smart boy, I thought he was too smart to get hung."

"I guess he thought so too," I said sharply, "and that's how he got hung. And how about you? You're pretty goddamn smart, I bet."

Then he looked directly at me, just for a minute. "I ain't smart," he said. "If I was smart, I'd have reached for a pistol a long time ago."

"Look. Don't tell *me* your sad story, if it was up to me, I'd give you one." Then I felt guilty — guilty, probably, for never having supposed that the poor bastard *had* a story of his own, much less a sad one, and I asked, quickly, "What's going to happen to him now?"

He didn't answer this. He was off by himself some place. "Funny thing," he said, and from his tone we might have been discussing the quickest way to get to Brookyn, "when I saw the papers this morning, the first thing I asked myself was if I had anything to do with it. I felt sort of responsible."

I began to listen more carefully. The subway station was on the corner, just before us, and I stopped. He stopped, too. We were in front of a bar and he ducked slightly, peering in, but whoever he was looking for didn't seem to be there. The juke box was blasting away with something black and bouncy and I half watched the barmaid as she danced her way from the juke box to her place behind the bar. And I watched her face as she laughingly responded to something someone said to her, still keeping time to the music. When she smiled one saw the little girl, one sensed the doomed, still-struggling woman beneath the battered face of the semi-whore.

"I never *give* Sonny nothing," the boy said finally, "but a long time ago I come to school high and Sonny asked me how it felt." He paused, I couldn't bear to watch him, I watched the barmaid, and I listened to the music which seemed to be causing the pavement to shake. "I told him it felt great." The music stopped, the barmaid paused and watched the juke box until the music began again. "It did."

All this was carrying me some place I didn't want to go. I certainly didn't want to know how it felt. It filled everything, the people, the houses, the music, the dark, quicksilver barmaid, with menace; and this menace was their reality.

"What's going to happen to him now?" I asked again.

"They'll send him away some place and they'll try to cure him." He shook his head. "Maybe he'll even think he's kicked the habit. Then they'll let him loose" — he gestured, throwing his cigarette into the gutter. "That's all."

"What do you mean, that's *all*?"

But I knew what he meant.

"I *mean,* that's *all*." He turned his head and looked at me, pulling down the corners of his mouth. "Don't you know what I mean?" he asked, softly.

"How the hell *would* I know what you mean?" I almost whispered it, I don't know why.

"That's right," he said to the air, "how would *he* know what I mean?" He turned toward me again, patient and calm, and yet I somehow felt him shaking, shaking as though he were going to fall apart. I felt that ice in my guts again, the dread I'd felt all afternoon; and again I watched the barmaid, moving about the bar, washing glasses, and singing. "Listen. They'll let him out and then it'll just start all over again. That's what I mean."

"You mean — they'll let him out. And then he'll just start working his way back in again. You mean he'll never kick the habit. Is that what you mean?"

"That's right," he said, cheerfully. "*You* see what I mean."

"Tell me," I said at last, "why does he want to die? He must want to die, he's killing himself, why does he want to die?"

He looked at me in surprise. He licked his lips. "He don't want to die. He wants to live. Don't nobody want to die, ever."

Then I wanted to ask him — too many things. He could not have answered, or if he had, I could not have borne the answers. I started walking. "Well, I guess it's none of my business."

"It's going to be rough on old Sonny," he said. We reached the subway station. "This is your station?" he asked. I nodded. I took one step down. "Damn!" he said, suddenly. I looked up at him. He grinned again. "Damn it if I didn't leave all my money home. You ain't got a dollar on you, have you? Just for a couple of days, is all."

All at once something inside gave and threatened to come pouring out of me. I didn't hate him any more. I felt that in another moment I'd start crying like a child.

"Sure," I said. "Don't sweat." I looked in my wallet and didn't have a dollar, I only had a five. "Here," I said. "That hold you?"

He didn't look at it — he didn't want to look at it. A terrible, closed look came over his face, as though he were keeping the number on the bill a secret from him and me. "Thanks," he said, and now he was dying to see me go. "Don't worry about Sonny. Maybe I'll write him or something."

"Sure," I said. "You do that. So long."

"Be seeing you," he said. I went on down the steps.

♫

And I didn't write Sonny or send him anything for a long time. When I finally did, it was just after my little girl died, he wrote me back a letter which made me feel like a bastard.

Here's what he said:

> Dear brother,
>
> You don't know how much I needed to hear from you. I wanted to write you many a time but I dug how much I must have hurt you and so I didn't write. But now I feel like a man who's been

trying to climb up out of some deep, real deep and funky hole and just saw the sun up there, outside. I got to get outside.

I can't tell you much about how I got here. I mean I don't know how to tell you. I guess I was afraid of something or I was trying to escape from something and you know I have never been very strong in the head (smile). I'm glad Mama and Daddy are dead and can't see what's happened to their son and I swear if I'd known what I was doing I would never have hurt you so, you and a lot of other fine people who were nice to me and who believed in me.

I don't want you to think it had anything to do with me being a musician. It's more than that. Or maybe less than that. I can't get anything straight in my head down here and I try not to think about what's going to happen to me when I get outside again. Sometime I think I'm going to flip and *never* get outside and sometime I think I'll come straight back. I tell you one thing, though, I'd rather blow my brains out than go through this again. But that's what they all say, so they tell me. If I tell you when I'm coming to New York and if you could meet me, I sure would appreciate it. Give my love to Isabel and the kids and I was sure sorry to hear about little Gracie. I wish I could be like Mama and say the Lord's will be done, but I don't know it seems to me that trouble is the one thing that never does get stopped and I don't know what good it does to blame it on the Lord. But maybe it does some good if you believe it.

> Your brother,
> Sonny

Then I kept in constant touch with him and I sent him whatever I could and I went to meet him when he came back to New York. When I saw him many things I thought I had forgotten came flooding back to me. This was because I had begun, finally, to wonder about Sonny, about the life that Sonny lived inside. This life, whatever it was, had made him older and thinner and it had deepened the distant stillness in which he had always moved. He looked very unlike my baby brother. Yet, when he smiled, when we shook hands, the baby brother I'd never known looked out from the depths of his private life, like an animal waiting to be coaxed into the light.

"How you been keeping?" he asked me.

"All right. And you?"

"Just fine." He was smiling all over his face. "It's good to see you again."

"It's good to see you."

The seven years' difference in our ages lay between us like a chasm: I wondered if these years would ever operate between us as a bridge. I was remembering, and it made it hard to catch my breath, that I had been there when he was born; and I had heard the first words he had ever spoken. When he started to walk, he walked from our mother straight to me. I caught him just before he fell when he took the first steps he ever took in this world.

"How's Isabel?"

"Just fine. She's dying to see you."

"And the boys?"

"They're fine, too. They're anxious to see their uncle."

"Oh, come on. You know they don't remember me."

"Are you kidding? Of course they remember you."

He grinned again. We got into a taxi. We had a lot to say to each other, far too much to know how to begin.

As the taxi began to move, I asked, "You still want to go to India?"

He laughed. "You still remember that. Hell, no. This place is Indian enough for me."

"It used to belong to them," I said.

And he laughed again. "They damn sure knew what they were doing when they got rid of it."

Years ago, when he was around fourteen, he'd been all hipped on the idea of going to India. He read books about people sitting on rocks, naked, in all kinds of weather, but mostly bad, naturally, and walking barefoot through hot coals and arriving at wisdom. I used to say that it sounded to me as though they were getting away from wisdom as fast as they could. I think he sort of looked down on me for that.

"Do you mind," he asked, "if we have the driver drive alongside the park? On the west side — I haven't seen the city in so long."

"Of course not," I said. I was afraid that I might sound as though I were humoring him, but I hoped he wouldn't take it that way.

So we drove along, between the green of the park and the stony, lifeless elegance of hotels and apartment buildings, toward the vivid, killing streets of our childhood. These streets hadn't changed, though housing projects jutted up out of them now like rocks in the middle of a boiling sea. Most of the houses in which we had grown up had vanished, as had the stores from which we had stolen, the basements in which we had first tried sex, the rooftops from which we had hurled tin cans and bricks. But houses exactly like the houses of our past yet dominated the landscape, boys exactly like the boys we once had been found themselves smothering in these houses, came down into the streets for light and air and found themselves encircled by disaster. Some escaped the trap, most didn't. Those who got out always left something of themselves behind, as some animals amputate a leg and leave it in the trap. It might be said, perhaps, that I had escaped, after all, I was a school teacher; or that Sonny had, he hadn't lived in Harlem for years. Yet, as the cab moved uptown through streets which seemed, with a rush, to darken with dark people, and as I covertly studied Sonny's face, it came to me that what we both were seeking through our separate cab windows was that part of ourselves which had been left behind. It's always at the hour of trouble and confrontation that the missing member aches.

We hit 110th Street and started rolling up Lenox Avenue. And I'd known this avenue all my life, but it seemed to me again, as it had seemed on the day I'd first heard about Sonny's trouble, filled with a hidden menace which was its very breath of life.

"We almost there," said Sonny.

"Almost." We were both too nervous to say anything more.

We live in a housing project. It hasn't been up long. A few days after it was up it seemed uninhabitably new, now, of course, it's already rundown. It looks like a parody of the good, clean, faceless life — God knows the people who live in it do their best to make it a parody. The beat-looking grass lying around isn't enough to make their lives green, the hedges will never hold out the streets, and they know it. The big windows fool no one, they aren't big enough to make space out of no space. They don't bother with the windows, they watch the TV screen instead. The playground is most popular with the children who don't play at jacks, or skip rope, or roller skate, or swing, and they can be found in it after dark. We moved in partly because it's not too far from where I teach, and partly for the kids; but it's really just like the houses in which Sonny and I grew up. The same things happen, they'll have the same things to remember. The moment Sonny and I started into the house I had the feeling that I was simply bringing him back into the danger he had almost died trying to escape.

Sonny has never been talkative. So I don't know why I was sure he'd be dying to talk to me when supper was over the first night. Everything went fine, the oldest boy remembered him, and the youngest boy liked him, and Sonny had remembered to bring something for each of them; and Isabel, who is really much nicer than I am, more open and giving, had gone to a lot of trouble about dinner and was genuinely glad to see him. And she's always been able to tease Sonny in a way that I haven't. It was nice to see her face so vivid again and to hear her laugh and watch her make Sonny laugh. She wasn't, or, anyway, she didn't seem to be, at all uneasy or embarrassed. She chatted as though there were no subject which had to be avoided and she got Sonny past his first, faint stiffness. And thank God she was there, for I was filled with that icy dread again. Everything I did seemed awkward to me, and everything I said sounded freighted with hidden meaning. I was trying to remember everything I'd heard about dope addiction and I couldn't help watching Sonny for signs. I wasn't doing it out of malice. I was trying to find out something about my brother. I was dying to hear him tell me he was safe.

"Safe!" my father grunted, whenever Mama suggested trying to move to a neighborhood which might be safer for children. "Safe, hell! Ain't no place safe for kids, nor nobody."

He always went on like this, but he wasn't, ever, really as bad as he sounded, not even on weekends, when he got drunk. As a matter of fact, he was always on the lookout for "something a little better," but he died before he found it. He died suddenly, during a drunken weekend in the middle of the war, when Sonny was fifteen. He and Sonny hadn't ever got on too well. And this was partly because Sonny was the apple of his father's eye. It was because he loved Sonny so much and was frightened for him, that he was always fighting with him. It doesn't do any good to fight with Sonny. Sonny just moves back, inside himself, where he can't be reached. But the principal reason that they never hit it off is that they were so much alike. Daddy was big and rough and loud-talking, just the opposite of Sonny, but they both had — that same privacy.

Mama tried to tell me something about this, just after Daddy died. I was home on leave from the army.

This was the last time I ever saw my mother alive. Just the same, this picture gets all mixed up in my mind with pictures I had of her when she was younger. The way I always see her is the way she used to be on a Sunday afternoon, say, when the old folks were talking after the big Sunday dinner. I always see her wearing pale blue. She'd be sitting on the sofa. And my father would be sitting in the easy chair, not far from her. And the living room would be full of church folks and relatives. There they sit, in chairs all around the living room, and the night is creeping up outside, but nobody knows it yet. You can see the darkness growing against the windowpanes and you hear the street noises every now and again, or maybe the jangling beat of a tambourine from one of the churches close by, but it's real quiet in the room. For a moment nobody's talking, but every face looks darkening, like the sky outside. And my mother rocks a little from the waist, and my father's eyes are closed. Everyone is looking at something a child can't see. For a minute they've forgotten the children. Maybe a kid is lying on the rug, half asleep. Maybe somebody's got a kid in his lap and is absent-mindedly stroking the kid's head. Maybe there's a kid, quiet and big-eyed, curled up in a big chair in the corner. The silence, the darkness coming, and the darkness in the faces frightens the child obscurely. He hopes that the hand which strokes his forehead will never stop — will never die. He hopes that there will never come a time when the old folks won't be sitting around the living room, talking about where they've come from, and what they've seen, and what's happened to them and their kinfolk.

But something deep and watchful in the child knows that this is bound to end, is already ending. In a moment someone will get up and turn on the light. Then the old folks will remember the children and they won't talk any more that day. And when light fills the room, the child is filled with darkness. He knows that every time this happens he's moved just a little closer to that darkness out-side. The darkness outside is what the old folks have been talking about. It's what they've come from. It's what they endure. The child knows that they won't talk any more because if he knows too much about what's happened to *them,* he'll know too much too soon, about what's going to happen to *him.*

The last time I talked to my mother, I remember I was restless. I wanted to get out and see Isabel. We weren't married then and we had a lot to straighten out between us.

There Mama sat, in black, by the window. She was humming an old church song, *Lord, you brought me from a long ways off.* Sonny was out somewhere. Mama kept watching the streets.

"I don't know," she said, "if I'll ever see you again, after you go off from here. But I hope you'll remember the things I tried to teach you."

"Don't talk like that," I said, and smiled. "You'll be here a long time yet."

She smiled, too, but she said nothing. She was quiet for a long time. And I said, "Mama, don't you worry about nothing. I'll be writing all the time, and you be getting the checks. . . ."

"I want to talk to you about your brother," she said, suddenly. "If anything happens to me he ain't going to have nobody to look out for him."

"Mama," I said, "ain't nothing going to happen to you *or* Sonny. Sonny's all right. He's a good boy and he's got good sense."

"It ain't a question of his being a good boy," Mama said, "nor of his having good sense. It ain't only the bad ones, nor yet the dumb ones that gets sucked un-der." She stopped, looking at me. "Your Daddy once had a brother," she said, and she smiled in a way that made me feel she was in pain. "You didn't never know that, did you?"

"No," I said, "I never knew that," and I watched her face.

"Oh, yes," she said, "your Daddy had a brother." She looked out of the win-dow again. "I know you never saw your Daddy cry. But *I* did — many a time, through all these years."

I asked her, "What happened to his brother? How come nobody's ever talked about him?"

This was the first time I ever saw my mother look old.

"His brother got killed," she said, "when he was just a little younger than you are now. I knew him. He was a fine boy. He was maybe a little full of the devil, but he didn't mean nobody no harm."

Then she stopped and the room was silent, exactly as it had sometimes been on those Sunday afternoons. Mama kept looking out into the streets.

"He used to have a job in the mill," she said, "and, like all young folks, he just liked to perform on Saturday nights. Saturday nights, him and your father would drift around to different places, go to dances and things like that, or just sit around with people they knew, and your father's brother would sing, he had a fine voice, and play along with himself on his guitar. Well, this particular Saturday night, him and your father was coming home from some place, and they were both a little drunk and there was a moon that night, it was bright like day. Your father's brother was feeling kind of good, and he was whistling to himself, and he had his guitar slung over his shoulder. They was coming down a hill and beneath them was a road that turned off from the highway. Well, your father's brother, being always kind of frisky, decided to run down this hill, and he did, with that guitar banging and clanging behind him, and he ran across the road, and he was making water behind a tree. And your father was sort of amused at him and he was still coming down the hill, kind of slow. Then he heard a car motor and that same minute his brother stepped from behind the tree, into the road, in the moonlight. And he started to cross the road. And your father started to run down the hill, he says he don't know why. This car was full of white men. They was all drunk, and when they seen your father's brother they let out a great whoop and holler and they aimed the car straight at him. They was having fun, they just wanted to scare him, the way they do sometimes, you know. But they was drunk. And I guess the boy, being drunk, too, and scared, kind of lost his head. By the time he jumped it was too late. Your father says he heard his brother scream when the car rolled over him, and he heard the wood of that guitar when it give, and he heard them strings go flying, and he heard them white men shouting, and the car kept on a-going and it ain't stopped till this day. And, time your father got down the hill, his brother weren't nothing but blood and pulp."

Tears were gleaming on my mother's face. There wasn't anything I could say.

"He never mentioned it," she said, "because I never let him mention it before you children. Your Daddy was like a crazy man that night and for many a night thereafter. He says he never in his life seen anything as dark as that road after the lights of that car had gone away. Weren't nothing, weren't nobody on that road, just your Daddy and his brother and that busted guitar. Oh, yes. Your Daddy never did really get right again. Till the day he died he weren't sure but that every white man he saw was the man that killed his brother."

She stopped and took out her handkerchief and dried her eyes and looked at me.

"I ain't telling you all this," she said, "to make you scared or bitter or to make you hate nobody. I'm telling you this because you got a brother. And the world ain't changed."

I guess I didn't want to believe this. I guess she saw this in my face. She turned away from me, toward the window again, searching those streets.

"But I praise my Redeemer," she said at last, "that He called your Daddy home before me. I ain't saying it to throw no flowers at myself, but, I declare, it keeps me from feeling too cast down to know I helped your father get safely through this world. Your father always acted like he was the roughest, strongest man on earth. And everybody took him to be like that. But if he hadn't had *me* there — to see his tears!"

She was crying again. Still, I couldn't move. I said, "Lord, Lord, Mama, I didn't know it was like that."

"Oh, honey," she said, "there's a lot that you don't know. But you are going to find it out." She stood up from the window and came over to me. "You got to hold on to your brother," she said, "and don't let him fall, no matter what it looks like is happening to him and no matter how evil you gets with him. You going to be evil with him many a time. But don't you forget what I told you, you hear?"

"I won't forget," I said. "Don't you worry, I won't forget. I won't let nothing happen to Sonny."

My mother smiled as though she were amused at something she saw in my face. Then, "You may not be able to stop nothing from happening. But you got to let him know you's *there*."

§§

Two days later I was married, and then I was gone. And I had a lot of things on my mind and I pretty well forgot my promise to Mama until I got shipped home on a special furlough for her funeral.

And, after the funeral, with just Sonny and me alone in the empty kitchen, I tried to find out something about him.

"What do you want to do?" I asked him.

"I'm going to be a musician," he said.

For he had graduated, in the time I had been away, from dancing to the juke box to finding out who was playing what, and what they were doing with it, and he had bought himself a set of drums.

"You mean, you want to be a drummer?" I somehow had the feeling that being a drummer might be all right for other people but not for my brother Sonny.

"I don't think," he said, looking at me very gravely, "that I'll ever be a good drummer. But I think I can play a piano."

I frowned. I'd never played the role of the older brother quite so seriously before, had scarcely ever, in fact, *asked* Sonny a damn thing. I sensed myself in the presence of something I didn't really know how to handle, didn't understand. So I made my frown a little deeper as I asked: "What kind of musician do you want to be?"

He grinned. "How many kinds do you think there are?"

"Be *serious*," I said.

He laughed, throwing his head back, and then looked at me. "I *am* serious."

"Well, then, for Christ's sake, stop kidding around and answer a serious question. I mean, do you want to be a concert pianist, you want to play classical music and all that, or — or what?" Long before I finished he was laughing again. "For Christ's *sake,* Sonny!"

He sobered, but with difficulty. "I'm sorry. But you sound so — *scared!*" and he was off again.

"Well, you may think it's funny now, baby, but it's not going to be so funny when you have to make your living at it, let me tell you *that.*" I was furious because I knew he was laughing at me and I didn't know why.

"No," he said, very sober now, and afraid, perhaps, that he'd hurt me, "I don't want to be a classical pianist. That isn't what interests me. I mean" — he paused, looking hard at me, as though his eyes would help me to understand, and then gestured helplessly, as though perhaps his hand would help — "I mean, I'll have a lot of studying to do, and I'll have to study *everything,* but, I mean, I want to play *with* — jazz musicians." He stopped. "I want to play jazz," he said.

Well, the word had never before sounded as heavy, as real, as it sounded that afternoon in Sonny's mouth. I just looked at him and I was probably frowning a real frown by this time. I simply couldn't see why on earth he'd want to spend his time hanging around nightclubs, clowning around on bandstands, while people pushed each other around a dance floor. It seemed — beneath him, somehow. I had never thought about it before, had never been forced to, but I suppose I had always put jazz musicians in a class with what Daddy called "good-time people."

"Are you *serious?*"

"Hell, *yes,* I'm serious."

He looked more helpless than ever, and annoyed, and deeply hurt.

I suggested, helpfully: "You mean — like Louis Armstrong?"

His face closed as though I'd struck him. "No. I'm not talking about none of that old-time, down home crap."

"Well, look, Sonny, I'm sorry, don't get mad. I just don't altogether get it, that's all. Name somebody — you know, a jazz musician you admire."

"Bird."

"Who?"

"Bird! Charlie Parker! Don't they teach you nothing in the goddamn army?"

I lit a cigarette. I was surprised and then a little amused to discover that I was trembling. "I've been out of touch," I said. "You'll have to be patient with me. Now. Who's this Parker character?"

"He's just one of the greatest jazz musicians alive," said Sonny, sullenly, his hands in his pockets, his back to me. "Maybe *the* greatest," he added, bitterly, "that's probably why *you* never heard of him."

"All right," I said, "I'm ignorant. I'm sorry. I'll go out and buy all the cat's records right away, all right?"

"It don't," said Sonny, with dignity, "make any difference to me. I don't care what you listen to. Don't do me no favors."

I was beginning to realize that I'd never seen him so upset before. With another part of my mind I was thinking that this would probably turn out to be one of those things kids go through and that I shouldn't make it seem important by pushing it too hard. Still, I didn't think it would do any harm to ask: "Doesn't all this take a lot of time? Can you make a living at it?"

He turned back to me and half leaned, half sat, on the kitchen table. "Everything takes time," he said, "and — well, yes, sure, I can make a living at it. But what I don't seem to be able to make you understand is that it's the only thing I want to do."

"Well, Sonny," I said, gently, "you know people can't always do exactly what they *want* to do —"

"No, I don't know that," said Sonny, surprising me. "I think people *ought* to do what they want to do, what else are they alive for?"

"You getting to be a big boy," I said desperately, "it's time you started thinking about your future."

"I'm thinking about my future," said Sonny, grimly. "I think about it all the time."

I gave up. I decided, if he didn't change his mind, that we could always talk about it later. "In the meantime," I said, "you got to finish school." We had already decided that he'd have to move in with Isabel and her folks. I knew this wasn't the ideal arrangement because Isabel's folks are inclined to be dicty and they hadn't especially wanted Isabel to marry me. But I didn't know what else to do. "And we have to get you fixed up at Isabel's."

There was a long silence. He moved from the kitchen table to the window. "That's a terrible idea. You know it yourself."

"Do you have a *better* idea?"

He just walked up and down the kitchen for a minute. He was as tall as I was. He had started to shave. I suddenly had the feeling that I didn't know him at all.

He stopped at the kitchen table and picked up my cigarettes. Looking at me with a kind of mocking, amused defiance, he put one between his lips. "You mind?"

"You smoking already?"

He lit the cigarette and nodded, watching me through the smoke. "I just wanted to see if I'd have the courage to smoke in front of you." He grinned and blew a great cloud of smoke to the ceiling. "It was easy." He looked at my face. "Come on, now. I bet you was smoking at my age, tell the truth."

I didn't say anything but the truth was on my face, and he laughed. But now there was something very strained in his laugh. "Sure. And I bet that ain't all you was doing."

He was frightening me a little. "Cut the crap," I said. "We already decided that you was going to go and live at Isabel's. Now what's got into you all of a sudden?"

"*You* decided it," he pointed out. "*I* didn't decide nothing." He stopped in front of me, leaning against the stove, arms loosely folded. "Look, brother. I don't want to stay in Harlem no more, I really don't." He was very earnest. He looked at me, then over toward the kitchen window. There was something in his eyes I'd never seen before, some thoughtfulness, some worry all his own. He rubbed the muscle of one arm. "It's time I was getting out of here."

"Where do you want to go, Sonny?"

"I want to join the army. Or the navy, I don't care. If I say I'm old enough, they'll believe me."

Then I got mad. It was because I was so scared. "You must be crazy. You goddamn fool, what the hell do you want to go and join the *army* for?"

"I just told you. To get out of Harlem."

"Sonny, you haven't even finished *school*. And if you really want to be a musician, how do you expect to study if you're in the *army*?"

He looked at me, trapped, and in anguish. "There's ways. I might be able to work out some kind of deal. Anyway, I'll have the G.I. Bill when I come out."

"*If* you come out." We stared at each other. "Sonny, please. Be reasonable. I know the setup is far from perfect. But we got to do the best we can."

"I ain't learning nothing in school," he said. "Even when I go." He turned away from me and opened the window and threw his cigarette out into the narrow alley. I watched his back. "At least, I ain't learning nothing you'd want me to learn." He slammed the window so hard I thought the glass would fly out, and turned back to me. "And I'm sick of the stink of these garbage cans!"

"Sonny," I said, "I know how you feel. But if you don't finish school now, you're going to be sorry later that you didn't." I grabbed him by the shoulders. "And you only got another year. It ain't so bad. And I'll come back and I swear I'll help you do *whatever* you want to do. Just try to put up with it till I come back. Will you please do that? For me?"

He didn't answer and he wouldn't look at me.

"Sonny. You hear me?"

He pulled away. "I hear you. But you never hear anything I say."

I didn't know what to say to that. He looked out of the window and then back at me. "OK," he said, and sighed. "I'll try."

Then I said, trying to cheer him up a little, "They got a piano at Isabel's. You can practice on it."

And as a matter of fact, it did cheer him up for a minute. "That's right," he said to himself. "I forgot that." His face relaxed a little. But the worry, the thoughtfulness, played on it still, the way shadows play on a face which is staring into the fire.

❦❧

But I thought I'd never hear the end of that piano. At first, Isabel would write me, saying how nice it was that Sonny was so serious about his music and how, as soon as he came in from school, or wherever he had been when he was supposed to be at school, he went straight to that piano and stayed there until suppertime. And, after supper, he went back to that piano and stayed there until everybody went to bed. He was at the piano all day Saturday and all day Sunday. Then he bought a record player and started playing records. He'd play one record over and over again, all day long sometimes, and he'd improvise along with it on the piano. Or he'd play one section of the record, one chord, one change, one progression, then he'd do it on the piano. Then back to the record. Then back to the piano.

Well, I really don't know how they stood it. Isabel finally confessed that it wasn't like living with a person at all, it was like living with sound. And the sound didn't make any sense to her, didn't make any sense to any of them — naturally. They began, in a way, to be afflicted by this presence that was living in their home. It was as though Sonny were some sort of god, or monster. He moved in an atmosphere which wasn't like theirs at all. They fed him and he ate, he washed himself, he walked in and out of their door; he certainly wasn't nasty or unpleasant or rude, Sonny isn't any of those things; but it was as though he were all wrapped up in some cloud, some fire, some vision all his own; and there wasn't any way to reach him.

At the same time, he wasn't really a man yet, he was still a child, and they had to watch out for him in all kinds of ways. They certainly couldn't throw him out. Neither did they dare to make a great scene about that piano because even they dimly sensed, as I sensed, from so many thousands of miles away, that Sonny was at that piano playing for his life.

But he hadn't been going to school. One day a letter came from the school board and Isabel's mother got it — there had, apparently, been other letters but Sonny had torn them up. This day, when Sonny came in, Isabel's mother showed him the letter and asked where he'd been spending his time. And she finally got it out of him that he'd been down in Greenwich Village, with musicians and other characters, in a white girl's apartment. And this scared her and she started to scream at him and what came up, once she began — though she denies it to this day — was what sacrifices they were making to give Sonny a decent home and how little he appreciated it.

Sonny didn't play the piano that day. By evening, Isabel's mother had calmed down but then there was the old man to deal with, and Isabel herself. Isabel says she did her best to be calm but she broke down and started crying. She says she just watched Sonny's face. She could tell, by watching him, what was happening with him. And what was happening was that they penetrated his cloud, they had reached him. Even if their fingers had been a thousand times more gentle than human fingers ever are, he could hardly help feeling that they had stripped him naked and were spitting on that nakedness. For he also had to see that his presence, that music, which was life or death to him, had been torture for them and that they had endured it, not at all for his sake, but only for mine. And Sonny couldn't take that. He can take it a little better today than he could then but he's still not very good at it and, frankly, I don't know anybody who is.

The silence of the next few days must have been louder than the sound of all the music ever played since time began. One morning, before she went to work, Isabel was in his room for something and she suddenly realized that all of his records were gone. And she knew for certain that he was gone. And he was. He went as far as the navy would carry him. He finally sent me a postcard from some place in Greece and that was the first I knew that Sonny was still alive. I didn't see him any more until we were both back in New York and the war had long been over.

He was a man by then, of course, but I wasn't willing to see it. He came by the house from time to time, but we fought almost every time we met. I didn't like the way he carried himself, loose and dreamlike all the time, and I didn't like his friends, and his music seemed to be merely an excuse for the life he led. It sounded just that weird and disordered.

Then we had a fight, a pretty awful fight, and I didn't see him for months. By and by I looked him up, where he was living, in a furnished room in the Village, and I tried to make it up. But there were lots of other people in the room and Sonny just lay on his bed, and he wouldn't come downstairs with me, and he treated these other people as though they were his family and I weren't. So I got mad and then he got mad, and then I told him that he might just as well be dead as live the way he was living. Then he stood up and he told me not to worry about him any more in life, that he *was* dead as far as I was concerned. Then he pushed me to the door and the other people looked on as though nothing were happening, and he slammed the door behind me. I stood in the hallway, staring at the door. I heard somebody laugh in the room and then the tears came to my eyes. I started down the steps, whistling to keep from crying, I kept whistling to myself, *You going to need me, baby, one of these cold, rainy days.*

♫♫

I read about Sonny's trouble in the spring. Little Grace died in the fall. She was a beautiful little girl. But she only lived a little over two years. She died of polio and she suffered. She had a slight fever for a couple of days, but it didn't seem like anything and we just kept her in bed. And we would certainly have called the doctor, but the fever dropped, she seemed to be all right. So we thought it had just been a cold. Then, one day, she was up, playing, Isabel was in the kitchen fixing lunch for the two boys when they'd come in from school, and she heard Grace fall down in the living room. When you have a lot of children you don't always start running when one of them falls, unless they start screaming or something. And, this time, Grace was quiet. Yet, Isabel says that when she heard that *thump* and then that silence, something happened in her to make her afraid. And she ran to the living room and there was little Grace on the floor, all twisted up, and the reason she hadn't screamed was that she couldn't get her breath. And when she did scream, it was the worst sound, Isabel says, that she'd ever heard in all her life, and she still hears it sometimes in her dreams. Isabel will sometimes wake me up with a low, moaning, strangled sound and I have to be quick to awaken her and hold her to me and where Isabel is weeping against me seems a mortal wound.

I think I may have written Sonny the very day that little Grace was buried. I was sitting in the living room in the dark, by myself, and I suddenly thought of Sonny. My trouble made his real.

◈◈

One Saturday afternoon, when Sonny had been living with us, or, anyway, been in our house, for nearly two weeks, I found myself wandering aimlessly about the living room, drinking from a can of beer, and trying to work up the courage to search Sonny's room. He was out, he was usually out whenever I was home, and Isabel had taken the children to see their grandparents. Suddenly I was standing still in front of the living room window, watching Seventh Avenue. The idea of searching Sonny's room made me still. I scarcely dared to admit to myself what I'd be searching for. I didn't know what I'd do if I found it. Or if I didn't.

On the sidewalk across from me, near the entrance to a barbecue joint, some people were holding an old-fashioned revival meeting. The barbecue cook, wearing a dirty white apron, his conked hair reddish and metallic in the pale sun, and a cigarette between his lips, stood in the doorway, watching them. Kids and older people paused in their errands and stood there, along with some older men and a couple of very tough-looking women who watched everything that happened on the avenue, as though they owned it, or were maybe owned by it. Well, they were watching this, too. The revival was being carried on by three sisters in black, and a brother. All they had were their voices and their Bibles and a tambourine. The brother was testifying and while he testified two of the sisters stood together, seeming to say, amen, and the third sister walked around with the tambourine outstretched and a couple of people dropped coins into it. Then the brother's testimony ended and the sister who had been taking up the collection dumped the coins into her palm and transferred them to the pocket of her long black robe. Then she raised both hands, striking the tambourine against the air, and then against one hand, and she started to sing. And the two other sisters and the brother joined in.

It was strange, suddenly, to watch, though I had been seeing these street meetings all my life. So, of course, had everybody else down there. Yet, they paused and watched and listened and I stood still at the window. *"Tis the old ship of Zion,"* they sang, and the sister with the tambourine kept a steady, jangling beat, *"it has rescued many a thousand!"* Not a soul under the sound of their voices was hearing this song for the first time, not one of them had been rescued. Nor had they seen much in the way of rescue work being done around them. Neither did they especially believe in the holiness of the three sisters and the brother, they knew too much about them, knew where they lived, and how. The woman with the tambourine, whose voice dominated the air, whose face was bright with joy, was divided by very little from the woman who stood watching her, a cigarette between her heavy, chapped lips, her hair a cuckoo's nest, her face scarred and swollen from many beatings, and her black eyes glittering like coal. Perhaps they both knew this, which was why, when, as rarely, they addressed each other, they addressed each other as Sister. As the singing filled the air the watching, listening faces underwent a change, the eyes focusing on something within; the music seemed to soothe a poison out of them; and time seemed, nearly, to fall away from the sullen, belligerent, battered faces, as though they were fleeing back to their first condition, while dreaming of their last. The barbecue cook half shook his head and smiled, and dropped his cigarette and disappeared into his joint. A man fumbled in his pockets for change and stood holding it in his hand impatiently, as though he had just remembered a pressing appointment further up the avenue. He looked furious. Then I saw Sonny, standing on the edge of the crowd. He was carrying a wide, flat notebook with a green cover, and it made him look, from where I was standing, almost like a schoolboy. The coppery sun brought out the copper in his skin, he was very faintly smiling, standing very still. Then the singing stopped, the tambourine turned into a collection plate again. The furious man dropped in his coins and vanished, so did a couple of the women, and Sonny dropped some change in the plate, looking directly at the woman with a little smile. He started across the avenue, toward the house. He has a slow, loping walk, something like the way Harlem hipsters walk, only he's imposed on this his own half-beat. I had never really noticed it before.

I stayed at the window, both relieved and apprehensive. As Sonny disappeared from my sight, they began singing again. And they were still singing when his key turned in the lock.

"Hey," he said.

"Hey, yourself. You want some beer?"

"No. Well, maybe." But he came up to the window and stood beside me, looking out. "What a warm voice," he said.

They were singing *If I could only hear my mother pray again!*

"Yes," I said, "and she can sure beat that tambourine."

"But what a terrible song," he said, and laughed. He dropped his notebook on the sofa and disappeared into the kitchen. "Where's Isabel and the kids?"

"I think they went to see their grandparents. You hungry?"

"No." He came back into the living room with his can of beer. "You want to come some place with me tonight?"

I sensed, I don't know how, that I couldn't possibly say no. "Sure. Where?"

He sat down on the sofa and picked up his notebook and started leafing through it. "I'm going to sit in with some fellows in a joint in the Village."

"You mean, you're going to play, tonight?"

"That's right." He took a swallow of his beer and moved back to the window. He gave me a sidelong look. "If you can stand it."

"I'll try," I said.

He smiled to himself and we both watched as the meeting across the way broke up. The three sisters and the brother, heads bowed, were singing *God be with you till we meet again.* The faces around them were very quiet. Then the song ended. The small crowd dispersed. We watched the three women and the lone man walk slowly up the avenue.

"When she was singing before," said Sonny, abruptly, "her voice reminded me for a minute of what heroin feels like sometimes — when it's in your veins. It makes you feel sort of warm and cool at the same time. And distant. And — and sure." He sipped his beer, very deliberately not looking at me. I watched his face. "It makes you feel — in control. Sometimes you've got to have that feeling."

"Do you?" I sat down slowly in the easy chair.

"Sometimes." He went to the sofa and picked up his notebook again. "Some people do."

"In order," I asked, "to play?" And my voice was very ugly, full of contempt and anger.

"Well" — he looked at me with great, troubled eyes, as though, in fact, he hoped his eyes would tell me things he could never otherwise say — "they *think* so. And *if* they think so — !"

"And what do *you* think?" I asked.

He sat on the sofa and put his can of beer on the floor. "I don't know," he said, and I couldn't be sure if he were answering my question or pursuing his thoughts. His face didn't tell me. "It's not so much to *play.* It's to *stand* it, to be able to make it at all. On any level." He frowned and smiled: "In order to keep from shaking to pieces."

"But these friends of yours," I said, "they seem to shake themselves to pieces pretty goddamn fast."

"Maybe." He played with the notebook. And something told me that I should curb my tongue, that Sonny was doing his best to talk, that I should listen. "But of course you only know the ones that've gone to pieces. Some don't — or at least they haven't *yet* and that's just about all *any* of us can say." He paused. "And then there are some who just live, really, in hell, and they know it and they see what's happening and they go right on. I don't know." He sighed, dropped the notebook, folded his arms. "Some guys, you can tell from the way they play, they on something *all* the time. And you can see that, well, it makes something real for them. But of course," he picked up his beer from the floor and sipped it and put the can down again, "they *want* to, too, you've got to see that. Even some of them that say they don't — *some,* not all."

"And what about you?" I asked — I couldn't help it. "What about you? Do *you* want to?"

He stood up and walked to the window and remained silent for a long time. Then he sighed. "Me," he said. Then: "While I was downstairs before, on my way here, listening to that woman sing, it struck me all of a sudden how much suffering she must have had to go through — to sing like that. It's *repulsive* to think you have to suffer that much."

I said: "But there's no way not to suffer — is there, Sonny?"

"I believe not," he said and smiled, "but that's never stopped anyone from trying." He looked at me. "Has it?" I realized, with his mocking look, that there stood between us, forever, beyond the power of time or forgiveness, the fact that I had held silence — so long! — when he needed human speech to help him. He turned back to the window. "No, there's no way not to suffer. But you try all kinds of ways to keep from drowning in it, to keep on top of it, and to make it seem — well, like *you*. Like you did something, all right, and now you're suffering for it. You know?" I said nothing. "Well you know," he said, impatiently, "why *do* people suffer? Maybe it's better to do something to give it a reason, *any* reason."

"But we just agreed," I said, "that there's no way not to suffer. Isn't it better, then, just to — take it?"

"But nobody just takes it," Sonny cried, "that's what I'm telling you! *Everybody* tries not to. You're just hung up on the *way* some people try — it's not *your* way!"

The hair on my face began to itch, my face felt wet. "That's not true," I said, "that's not true. I don't give a damn what other people do, I don't even care how they suffer. I just care how *you* suffer." And he looked at me. "Please believe me," I said, "I don't want to see you — die — trying not to suffer."

"I won't," he said, flatly, "die trying not to suffer. At least, not any faster than anybody else."

"But there's no need," I said, trying to laugh, "is there? in killing yourself."

I wanted to say more, but I couldn't. I wanted to talk about will power and how life could be — well, beautiful. I wanted to say that it was all within; but was it? or, rather, wasn't that exactly the trouble? And I wanted to promise that I would never fail him again. But it would all have sounded — empty words and lies.

So I made the promise to myself and prayed that I would keep it.

"It's terrible sometimes, inside," he said, "that's what's the trouble. You walk these streets, black and funky and cold, and there's not really a living ass to talk to, and there's nothing shaking, and there's no way of getting it out — that storm inside. You can't talk it and you can't make love with it, and when you finally try to get with it and play it, you realize *nobody's* listening. So *you've* got to listen. You got to find a way to listen."

And then he walked away from the window and sat on the sofa again, as though all the wind had suddenly been knocked out of him. "Sometimes you'll do *any-thing* to play, even cut your mother's throat." He laughed and looked at me. "Or your brother's." Then he sobered. "Or your own." Then: "Don't worry. I'm all right now and I think I'll *be* all right. But I can't forget — where I've been. I don't mean just the physical place I've been, I mean where I've *been*. And *what* I've been."

"What have you been, Sonny?" I asked.

He smiled — but sat sideways on the sofa, his elbow resting on the back, his fingers playing with his mouth and chin, not looking at me. "I've been something I didn't recognize, didn't know I could be. Didn't know anybody could be." He stopped, looking inward, looking helplessly young, looking old. "I'm not talking about it now because I feel *guilty* or anything like that — maybe it would be better if I did, I don't know. Anyway, I can't really talk about it. Not to you, not to anybody," and now he turned and faced me. "Sometimes, you know, and it was actually when I was most *out* of the world, I felt that I was in it, that I was *with* it, really, and I could play or I didn't really have to *play,* it just came out of me, it was there. And I don't know how I played, thinking about it now, but I know I did awful things, those times, sometimes, to people. Or it wasn't that I *did* anything to them — it was that they weren't real." He picked up the beer can; it was empty; he rolled it between his palms: "And other times — well, I needed a fix, I needed to find a place to lean, I needed to clear a space to *listen* — and I couldn't find it, and I — went crazy, I did terrible things to *me,* I was terrible *for* me." He began pressing the beer can between his hands, I watched the metal began to give. It glittered, as he played with it, like a knife, and I was afraid he would cut himself, but I said nothing. "Oh well. I can never tell you. I was all by myself at the bottom of something, stinking and sweating and crying and shaking, and I smelled it, you know? *my* stink, and I thought I'd die if I couldn't get away from it and yet, all the same, I knew that everything I was doing was just locking me in with it. And I didn't know," he paused, still flattening the beer can, "I didn't know, I still *don't* know, something kept telling me that maybe it was good to smell your own stink, but I didn't think that *that* was what I'd been trying to do — and — who can stand it?" and he abruptly dropped the ruined beer can, looking at me with a small, still smile, and then rose, walking to the window as though it were the lodestone rock. I watched his face, he watched the avenue. "I couldn't tell you when Mama died — but the reason I wanted to leave Harlem so bad was to get away from drugs. And then, when I ran away, that's what I was running from — really. When I came back, nothing had changed, I hadn't changed, I was just — older." And he stopped, drumming with his fingers on the windowpane. The sun had vanished, soon darkness would fall. I watched his face. "It can come again," he said, almost as though speaking to himself. Then he turned to me. "It can come again," he repeated. "I just want you to know that."

"All right," I said, at last. "So it can come again, All right."

He smiled, but the smile was sorrowful. "I had to try to tell you," he said.

"Yes," I said. "I understand that."

"You're my brother," he said, looking straight at me, and not smiling at all.

"Yes," I repeated, "yes. I understand that."

He turned back to the window, looking out. "All that hatred down there," he said, "all that hatred and misery and love. It's a wonder it doesn't blow the avenue apart."

⅗℩

We went to the only nightclub on a short, dark street, downtown. We squeezed through the narrow, chattering, jam-packed bar to the entrance of the big room, where the bandstand was. And we stood there for a moment, for the lights were very dim in this room and we couldn't see. Then, "Hello, boy," said a voice and an enormous black man, much older than Sonny or myself, erupted out of all that atmospheric lighting and put an arm around Sonny's shoulder. "I been sitting right here," he said, "waiting for you."

He had a big voice, too, and heads in the darkness turned toward us.

Sonny grinned and pulled a little away, and said, "Creole, this is my brother. I told you about him."

Creole shook my hand. "I'm glad to meet you, son," he said, and it was clear that he was glad to meet me *there*, for Sonny's sake. And he smiled, "You got a real musician in *your* family," and he took his arm from Sonny's shoulder and slapped him, lightly, affectionately, with the back of his hand.

"Well. Now I've heard it all," said a voice behind us. This was another musician, and a friend of Sonny's, a coal-black, cheerful-looking man, built close to the ground. He immediately began confiding to me, at the top of his lungs, the most terrible things about Sonny, his teeth gleaming like a lighthouse and his laugh coming up out of him like the beginning of an earthquake. And it turned out that everyone at the bar knew Sonny, or almost everyone; some were musicians, working there, or nearby, or not working, some were simply hangers-on, and some were there to hear Sonny play. I was introduced to all of them and they were all very polite to me. Yet, it was clear that, for them, I was only Sonny's brother. Here, I was in Sonny's world. Or, rather: his kingdom. Here, it was not even a question that his veins bore royal blood.

They were going to play soon and Creole installed me, by myself, at a table in a dark corner. Then I watched them, Creole, and the little black man, and Sonny, and the others, while they horsed around, standing just below the bandstand. The light from the bandstand spilled just a little short of them and, watching them laughing and gesturing and moving about, I had the feeling that they, nevertheless, were being most careful not to step into that circle of light too suddenly: that if they moved into the light too suddenly, without thinking, they would perish in flame. Then, while I watched, one of them, the small, black man, moved into the light and crossed the bandstand and started fooling around with his drums. Then — being funny and being, also, extremely ceremonious — Creole took Sonny by the arm and led him to the piano. A woman's voice called Sonny's name and a few hands started clapping. And Sonny, also being funny and being ceremonious, and so touched, I think, that he could have cried, but neither hiding it nor showing it, riding it like a man, grinned, and put both hands to his heart and bowed from the waist.

Creole then went to the bass fiddle and a lean, very bright-skinned brown man jumped up on the bandstand and picked up his horn. So there they were, and the atmosphere on the bandstand and in the room began to change and tighten. Someone stepped up to the microphone and announced them. Then there were all kinds of murmurs. Some people at the bar shushed others. The waitress ran around, frantically getting in the last orders, guys and chicks got closer to each other, and the lights on the bandstand, on the quartet, turned to a kind of indigo. Then they all looked different there. Creole looked about him for the last time, as though he were making certain that all his chickens were in the coop, and then he — jumped and struck the fiddle. And there they were.

All I know about music is that not many people ever really hear it. And even then, on the rare occasions when something opens within, and the music enters, what we mainly hear, or hear corroborated, are personal, private, vanishing evocations. But the man who creates the music is hearing something else, is dealing with the roar rising from the void and imposing order on it as it hits the air. What is evoked in him, then, is of another order, more terrible because it has no words, and triumphant, too, for that same reason. And his triumph, when he triumphs, is ours. I just watched Sonny's face. His face was troubled, he was working hard, but he wasn't with it. And I had the feeling that, in a way, everyone on the bandstand was waiting for him, both waiting for him and pushing him along. But as I began to watch Creole, I realized that it was Creole who held them all back. He had them on a short rein. Up there, keeping the beat with his whole body, wailing on the fiddle, with his eyes half closed, he was listening to everything, but he was listening to Sonny. He was having a dialogue with Sonny. He wanted Sonny to leave the shoreline and strike out for the deep water. He was Sonny's witness that deep water and drowning were not the same thing — he had been there, and he knew. And he wanted Sonny to know. He was waiting for Sonny to do the things on the keys which would let Creole know that Sonny was in the water.

And, while Creole listened, Sonny moved, deep within, exactly like someone in torment. I had never before thought of how awful the relationship must be between the musician and his instrument. He has to fill it, this instrument, with the breath of life, his own. He has to make it do what he wants it to do. And a piano is just a piano. It's made out of so much wood and wires and little hammers and big ones, and ivory. While there's only so much you can do with it, the only way to find this out is to try; to try and make it do everything.

And Sonny hadn't been near a piano for over a year. And he wasn't on much better terms with his life, not the life that stretched before him now. He and the piano stammered, started one way, got scared, stopped; started another way, panicked, marked time, started again; then seemed to have found a direction, panicked again, got stuck. And the face I saw on Sonny I'd never seen before. Everything had been burned out of it, and, at the same time, things usually hidden were being burned in, by the fire and fury of the battle which was occurring in him up there.

Yet, watching Creole's face as they neared the end of the first set, I had the feeling that something had happened, something I hadn't heard. Then they finished, there was scattered applause, and then, without an instant's warning, Creole started into something else, it was almost sardonic, it was *Am I Blue.* And, as though he commanded, Sonny began to play. Something began to happen. And Creole let out the reins. The dry, low, black man said something awful on the drums, Creole answered, and the drums talked back. Then the horn insisted, sweet and high, slightly detached perhaps, and Creole listened, commenting now and then, dry, and driving, beautiful and calm and old. Then they all came together again, and Sonny was part of the family again. I could tell this from his face. He seemed to have found, right there beneath his fingers, a damn brand-new piano. It seemed that he couldn't get over it. Then, for awhile, just being happy with Sonny, they seemed to be agreeing with him that brand-new pianos certainly were a gas.

Then Creole stepped forward to remind them that what they were playing was the blues. He hit something in all of them, he hit something in me, myself, and the music tightened and deepened, apprehension began to beat the air. Creole began to tell us what the blues were all about. They were not about anything very new. He and his boys up there were keeping it new, at the risk of ruin, destruction, madness, and death, in order to find new ways to make us listen. For, while the tale of how we suffer, and how we are delighted, and how we may triumph is never new, it always must be heard. There isn't any other tale to tell, it's the only light we've got in all this darkness.

And this tale, according to that face, that body, those strong hands on those strings, has another aspect in every country, and a new depth in every generation. Listen, Creole seemed to be saying, listen. Now these are Sonny's blues. He made the little black man on the drums know it, and the bright, brown man on the horn. Creole wasn't trying any longer to get Sonny in the water. He was wishing him Godspeed. Then he stepped back, very slowly, filling the air with the immense suggestion that Sonny speak for himself.

Then they all gathered around Sonny and Sonny played. Every now and again one of them seemed to say, amen. Sonny's fingers filled the air with life, his life. But that life contained so many others. And Sonny went all the way back, he really began with the spare, flat statement of the opening phrase of the song. Then he began to make it his. It was very beautiful because it wasn't hurried and it was no longer a lament. I seemed to hear with what burning he had made it his, with what burning we had yet to make it ours, how we could cease lamenting. Freedom lurked around us and I understood, at last, that he could help us to be free if we would listen, that he would never be free until we did. Yet, there was no battle in his face now. I heard what he had gone through, and would continue to go through until he came to rest in earth. He had made it his: that long line, of which we knew only Mama and Daddy. And he was giving it back, as everything must be given back, so that, passing through death, it can live forever. I saw my mother's face again, and felt, for the first time, how the stones of the road she had walked on must have bruised her feet. I saw the moonlit road where my father's brother died. And it brought something else back to me, and carried me past it, I saw my little girl again and felt Isabel's tears again, and I felt my own tears begin to rise. And I was yet aware that this was only a moment, that the world waited outside, as hungry as a tiger, and that trouble stretched above us, longer than the sky.

Then it was over. Creole and Sonny let out their breath, both soaking wet, and grinning. There was a lot of applause and some of it was real. In the dark, the girl came by and I asked her to take drinks to the bandstand. There was a long pause, while they talked up there in the indigo light and after awhile I saw the girl put a Scotch and milk on top of the piano for Sonny. He didn't seem to notice it, but just before they started playing again, he sipped from it and looked toward me, and nodded. Then he put it back on top of the piano. For me, then, as they began to play again, it glowed and shook above my brother's head like the very cup of trembling.

6

The Contemporary
Expansion of the Genre

The election of John F. Kennedy in 1960 signaled a new era for America. He was the first president born in the twentieth century, and his youthful vigor appealed to a younger generation that identified with him, emulated his accent, endorsed his vision for the future, and accepted his domestic and international objectives. He established the Peace Corps, spoke eloquently on behalf of civil rights for African Americans, and inspired citizens to a more athletic life, recalling the muscular Christianity of Theodore Roosevelt. But the era of "Camelot," of optimism and patriotism, was brought to an end with the assassination of President Kennedy in late 1963 and the deaths of Martin Luther King Jr. and Robert Kennedy in 1968. A period of social unrest followed, exacerbated by opposition to the war in Vietnam and racial tensions in the major cities.

But American society offered positive signs as well. Social and political transformations provided reassurance that responsible citizens could work together for the common good. Medical research developed a vaccine for polio, for example, and surgeons transplanted human organs to prolong life. The Vietnam War concluded, a man walked on the moon, and, in due course, President Ronald Reagan and Premier Mikhail Gorbachev would end the cold war and establish a new period of cooperation. Congress passed the Civil Rights Act in 1964 and educational and social institutions soon became open to people of all races, religions, and economic backgrounds. The Voting Rights Act eliminated poll taxes and other regulations that had prevented minorities from participation in national elections, and Thurgood Marshall became the first African American to serve on the U.S. Supreme Court, followed two decades later by Clarence Thomas. In 1965, the Immigration Act abolished long-standing quotas restricting admission, and people swarmed into the country in enormous numbers, changing the culture and adding new languages. By some estimates, by the end of the twentieth century more immigrants had come to America than had moved anywhere in the collective history of the world. Mexican arrivals outpaced all others, but significant numbers came from Southeast Asia and Africa.

Medicare and Medicaid became part of President Lyndon Johnson's Great Society programs, and Congress initiated the National Endowment for the Arts and for the Humanities.

The passage of Title IX in 1972 opened athletics on all levels of education to women students in numbers equal to that of men. The women's movement began in earnest, demanding an equal role in social, economic, and political life, and in 1977 a National Women's Conference convened in Houston. *Ms.* magazine published its inaugural issue in 1981, and Sandra Day O'Connor became the first woman to serve on the U.S. Supreme Court. Other breakthroughs soon followed: Geraldine Ferraro ran for vice president, Janet Reno served as head of the Department of Justice, and Condoleezza Rice succeeded Colin Powell as secretary of state. The computer age and the Internet changed forever the ways in which information could be shared, and cell phones, airline travel, cable television news, and international competition in athletics made the world seem a smaller place, more of a global community.

The era also saw a dramatic alteration of the people who were writing fiction, and women emerged as the majority voice in literature. Jewish and African American writers dominated for several decades, winning Nobel Prizes and holding influential chairs in creative writing at major universities throughout the country. Native American authors became an important force for the first time, joined by Latinos and Asian Americans. Gay and lesbian writers staked their claim to a position in the literary spectrum, as did transgendered and disabled writers, and virtually every segment of society wanted to participate in the formation of a new national canon. In no genre was that participation more influential than in the short story.

Continuity and Change

Not all of the important short fiction of the contemporary era was aesthetically innovative. Andre Dubus's style and approach to narrative are traditional, recalling, in some respects, Ernest Hemingway's emphasis on the psychological dimensions of violent confrontations. Dubus is not a minimalist, but his themes of familial cruelty and bloodshed are presented in understated prose, implying that powerful emotions are just below the surface, as in "Killings." Dubus often concludes his stories with a moral quandary, suggesting that in the complex modern world what is legal is often at odds with what is psychologically and morally "correct," and the tension between these concepts drives his powerful plots. Bobbie Ann Mason's fiction also employs traditional methods, including a standard third-person narrator who presents a psychological conflict within a family. Her innovations have more to do with subject and theme than with aesthetics. The commonplace details on the surface of her work often convey an emotional significance as ordinary characters struggle for self-realization and their place in the world. "Shiloh," published in *The New Yorker* in 1980, reflects Mason's meticulous handling of details as it opens and closes with the same image of pectoral exercise, an "envelope" structural device. The narrative method is restrained, the language direct and concrete, the plot controlled and relentless.

Some of the work in the period reaches back in methodology to early Modernist experimentation, such as Donald Barthelme's "Views of My Father Weeping," considered to be among the best of the stories in his seven volumes of short fiction. His fragmented style, leaving key events uncertain, has been hailed as an innovative postmodern method, a technique that expresses the incoherence of contemporary life. Actually, however, this mode in many respects duplicates the prose of the Imagist movement of the teens and 1920s. Indeed, the many volumes of fiction in that tradition were even more indecipherable, presenting sensory data without clear organization, thematic development, or definable plot. Barthelme would have been aware of the contributions of Amy Lowell, Ezra Pound, and D. H. Lawrence to this mode, the literary expression of the ideas of visual Impressionism, especially as they relate to the ideas of postmodern collage. Barthelme, however, blends historical authenticity with fictional drama, setting the action at King's New Square in Copenhagen, the cultural center of the capital of Denmark. It is here that a carriage accident occurs, killing a bystander, the key event of the story. The alternating passages of information about the incident and scenes of the narrator's memories and reflections constitute the narrative flow, which proceeds with growing thematic power despite the ambiguity of the conclusion. The result is fiction that seems to suggest that life is indecipherable, incoherent, and fragmented and that there is no solid point from which to arrest its constant change. Art, it implies, should reflect an awareness of the lack of certainty in contemporary times.

Susan Minot's fiction is also reminiscent of that of Ernest Hemingway's minimalist stories in the 1920s, especially in her highly controlled style. *Monkeys* is an example of a collection of stories that work very nicely in isolation but depend upon context within the volume for their full meaning. Such *story-cycles* are typically unified by setting, character, theme, or point of view, and the component works are enriched by intertextual reference, as in this case. The opening story in *Monkeys*, "Hiding," functions in isolation, a complete story with a dramatic conclusion. However, the full implications of the subtle events are not evident until the subsequent stories are included. When it first appeared in *Grand Street* in 1983, there was no way to know the significance of the family outing to Castle Hill, for example. There Mum tells the local legend about a woman who would meet her lover surreptitiously in the garden. When he failed to appear one evening, she felt betrayed and committed suicide by jumping off a cliff. Later, in subsequent episodes, Mum takes a lover, is betrayed by him, and kills herself by driving into a railroad train near her home. Within "Hiding" itself, the conflicts are abundantly evident. Mum and Dad have an emotional estrangement. She needs warmth and connection, and he needs independence and private space. Mum is absorbed with her children, her "monkeys," while Dad finds them a distraction. Mum, from Irish South Boston, is

Roman Catholic; Dad, product of a Brahmin background and most likely Anglican, grew up in the tony suburbs, went to Harvard, and, in effect, "married down." It is significant that one of the children, Sophie, narrates in first person because it provides an "innocent eye" perspective, allowing for suggestions she does not fully comprehend.

The Vietnam War

The social upheaval brought on by the war in Vietnam inspired a great deal of literary attention, especially by Tim O'Brien and Robert Olen Butler, both of whom actually served in Southeast Asia. O'Brien's "Sweetheart of the Song Tra Bong" involves military conflict and gender. He introduces an innocent female teenager, Mary Anne Bell, into the middle of the action despite the fact that during this war women were not allowed to serve in combat. Nevertheless, the plot follows her progressive transformation from purity to utter corruption, a metaphor for what was happening to hundreds of thousands of soldiers in the course of the engagement. Her change is both fascinating and horrifying, but it is the young woman who undergoes moral deterioration, suggesting that exposure to such a brutal conflict can destroy anyone.

Butler's fiction is unique in work about the war in that it deals in large measure with Vietnamese immigrants living in the United States after the end of hostilities. Thus, the scenes set in Vietnam occur in memory, the Louisiana material takes place in the present. "Open Arms" is a rich and troubling piece of short fiction about a communist defector, Thập, and it is told by a narrator struggling to understand this deeply sensitive man dedicated to a sense of personal purity. Thập defected after the communists killed his wife and children, but he retains his code of proper conduct, his basic moral values, and his sense of personal honor. Although he now shares many of the military objectives of the Australian and American troops, he cannot accept their social principles. The incident that precipitates the violence of the conclusion is not political but ethical — Thập's sense of sexual propriety has been deeply offended by a pornographic film. The narrator's speculations about Thập's feelings and motivations constitute an impressively complex portrait of human psychology in the aftermath of war.

Native American Stories

In contemporary literature, African American and Native American writers have found an audience fascinated by the complex issues in their work. In Native American literature, the inventiveness evident in Leslie Marmon Silko's "Storyteller," published in *Puerto del Sol* in 1975, derives from her experiences with the oral tradition, in which poetic images and allusions are interwoven in the narrative, the speaker giving voice to a community as well as an individual. Such tales are generally fragmentary and nonsequential, dominated by recurring mythic images, and their subjects are as much spiritual as they are social and psychological. "Storyteller" falls into this tradition, rendering the thoughts and memories of a Yupik woman in Alaska who is awaiting trial for murder. Her reflections constitute the heart of the story. The action in the present, in other words, is static, a woman thinking in her cell. Her memories, on the other hand, are dramatic and emotionally wrenching, as she reflects on the deaths of her parents, her grandmother, and the old man who lived in their house with them. But central to "Storyteller" is the haunting narrative the old man relates, obsessively, never quite completing what he has to say, never explaining its significance except in the act of telling itself. Similarly, the protagonist's need to tell her story seems to reside in a desire for closure, to come to terms with the heritage of her people, their lives intertwined with nature and the oppressive cold that surrounds them. In contrast, the white characters, called "Gussucks," are motivated by greed and practicality. The Russians originally came for fur and fish, and now the whites of the lower United States come for oil in a world they little understand.

"The Red Convertible" is one of fourteen works in Louise Erdrich's *Love Medicine* of 1984. The story was first published in the *Mississippi Valley Review* in 1982, in which version it is narrated by a character named Marty and concerns an older brother named Stephen. In the book, it is told by Lyman Lamartine, a member of one of the continuing families of Erdrich's fictional world, and many of the dates and places had to be altered from the magazine text to coordinate with action in other episodes. The plot deals with Lyman's brother Henry Jr., and, in typical fashion, the motivation for his action is contained in the other stories, including the fact that he suffers from post-traumatic stress syndrome brought on by the Vietnam War, in which he was a prisoner. Ironically, his father is not Henry Sr. but his uncle, who, in another story, enjoyed a tryst with the mother, Lulu, the very day of her husband's funeral. Indeed, none of Lulu's children are born of her husband, which may have motivated his suicide and now plays a role in the death of his son.

Sherman Alexie's work also plays an important role in Native literature. He is a proponent of "reservation fiction," portraits of people fixed in government dependency, their dignity and self-respect stripped away, their sense of identity destroyed by racism, poverty, and alcoholism. As is the case in "The Lone Ranger and Tonto Fistfight in Heaven," his fictional techniques reach back to oral methods of narration, shifting perspectives and time schemes, building themes incrementally rather than through a single plot line. In this story, the narrator reveals his aimless, lonely life through a series of brief scenes as simple as buying ice cream at a convenience store. Even in such basic action, however, his obsessions intrude, especially the end of his romance with a white girl, whom he loved but left for reasons he cannot fully comprehend. Preoccupied with racial identity and the historical injustices to his people, he seems unable to function in the present, thinking of himself as a contemporary warrior with no one to fight but himself.

Susan Power's fiction about Dakota characters is less lyrical and not nearly as angry as Sherman Alexie's work, but she is more analytical in her psychological insights and in the clarity of her themes. Based on the Native American oral tradition as well as on the deep fascination her white father had for English literature, which inspired her own, Power's stories are powerful and far-ranging, exploring the inner life of her characters and showing, through temporal modulations, how their lives intersect with those of their ancestors. Her plots do not follow a simple chronological line of development but shift forward and back in time, tracing developments of several characters at once, filling in broken moments in family memories that now impinge on the present. "Morse Code," which originally appeared in *The Atlantic Monthly* in 1994 prior to inclusion in the award-winning *The Grass Dancer* the same year, is a fascinating revelation of two generations of the Thunder family. Power's fiction is in some ways traditional in narrative method and plot development, but it draws on Sioux modes of handling non-linear time to reveal the central conflicts of Native American life in the twentieth century.

African American Short Fiction

Among the contributions of African American writers to the genre, Alice Walker's "Everyday Use" is an example of the ways in which a single work can inspire multiple interpretations. In one sense, it deals with the return of a sophisticated daughter, Dee, to the home of her youth. Her education, wealth, and condescension are everywhere evident, especially in contrast with her uneducated sister, Maggie, and her long-suffering mother. The conflict arises out of who is to inherit a quilt made by the grandmother, one containing remnants of discarded clothing worn by the women in the family. One view of the quilt is that it embodies the African American past, the emergence from slavery and the discrimination of the Jim Crow years to full participation in the larger life of the country. The counter approach rejects the "American" legacy to celebrate a distant "African" heritage, a point of view adopted by Dee, who has changed her name to "Wangero." The grandmother is essentially a representative of the American tradition, knowing and caring nothing of Africa and tied directly to her immediate family. Maggie perpetuates this orientation. Wangero represents the idealization of the African past, a commitment that leads to the denigration of her own people. That conflict, very much at the center of a debate within the African American community at the time the story was published, helps explain the charged atmosphere within the family.

Jamaica Kincaid's *Annie John* is composed of eight pieces previously published in *The New Yorker* in 1983 and 1984, the year the book appeared. As a collective entity, the volume traces the life of young Annie from the age of ten to seventeen, when she leaves the island of Antigua to begin an independent life. Along the way she encounters the classic conflicts of growing up: a reliance on her parents that gradually melds into a struggle for personal sovereignty; an awkward and uncertain acceptance of puberty and its attendant confusion; the depths of love, first for family, then for friends, then for members of the opposite gender. But the most contentious transformation occurs in "Columbus in Chains" because it involves not only her personal situation but the realization that the voyage of Columbus led to the enslavement of African people, their domination by British cultural and educational norms, and her family's poverty and lack of opportunity. Her rebellion here takes on a larger meaning, resisting the celebration of Queen Victoria's birthday as an indication of a rejection of colonial psychology.

Contemporary Latina Writers

Building on the work of María Cristina Mena a century earlier, Latina writers became a significant literary force in the last decades of the century, writing with power and artistic sophistication about problems of assimilation experienced by characters from Mexico and Puerto Rico. Sandra Cisneros's *The House on Mango Street,* in which "Red Clowns" appeared in 1983, is a book that traces the development of the central character, Esperanza Cordero. A young girl who lives in a violent multiracial area, she longs for the security of a nice home in a quiet neighborhood, the longing suggested in the title of the book. It is she who narrates "Red Clowns," and she who, after numerous situations involving sexual menace in previous stories, is raped and left painfully disillusioned.

Judith Ortiz Cofer's "Nada" presents a rich evocation of urban life for Puerto Rican immigrants during the time of the Vietnam War. It is traditional in narrative technique and innovative in characterization, subject, and theme, presenting the cultural ambiguity of life in the *barrio.* The important characters in this story, which first appeared in *The Georgia Review* in 1992, are poor immigrants sharing life in a tenement while preserving the values and customs of Puerto Rican society. Their language, which adds an increment of charm for an English-speaking readership, suggests the depth of their investment in Latino culture, even as the Anglo world around them impinges on their lives in tragically important ways.

Asian American Writers

Perhaps the ethnic minority that increased its contribution to short fiction most impressively at the end of the twentieth century is Asian American, especially first- and second-generation immigrants. Although Sui Sin Far wrote about the same subject a century earlier, her central ideas were given fresh expression by new writers within a vibrant and highly educated Chinese community.

One of the most powerful voices in this group of writers is Frank Chin, a product of the Iowa Writer's Workshop. His work essentially revisits history to redraw the portrait of the Chinese immigrant from that of a compliant workman building the cross-continental railroad to a new heroic figure, a "Chinatown Cowboy," one who is assertive, sensuous, and strong. Chin's eight stories were collected in *The Chinaman Pacific & Frisco R. R. Co.* in 1988, winning the National Book Award for challenging narratives that are achronological, utilizing multiple narrative lines simultaneously. "Railroad Standard Time," first published in *City Lights* in 1978, follows a young man named Tampax Lum on a drive from Seattle to San Francisco to attend his mother's funeral. There is little action in the narrative present, but his mind imagines his grandfather's work on the railroad and the many years he carried the very watch Lum now wears. In the process Lum must search for direction and meaning, a matter of confusion and uncertainty.

Amy Tan's "Four Directions" was first published in *The Joy Luck Club* in 1989. The title of the story reflects the complexity of Tan's work, referring not only to mahjong but to Waverly Jong's technique in chess, the varying approaches to survival in contemporary society, and to the Four Directions Restaurant where mother and daughter have lunch. Two concerns, among many, are central: the ongoing struggle for dominance between mother and daughter, and Waverly's decision to marry a white man.

A century after Sui Sin Far wrote her stories of Chinese immigrants struggling to retain their traditional culture while at the same time being accepted into American society, Gish Jen has produced her own remarkable short fiction dealing with the same ideas. Jen's work is more complex in that she situates her Asian characters in multicultural circumstances, encountering Jewish or Irish or African American neighbors, each with their own religion and values. In "Who's Irish?" for example, the narrator is a Chinese woman whose daughter has married into an Irish family, and the collision of social assumptions could hardly be more pronounced. As is often the case in Jen's stories, the major characters are women, three generations of them, and the conflicts and reconciliations that develop are as unpredictable as they are uniquely that of the United States. Indeed, central to her fiction is the concept of the formation of an American identity, an idea that, in an increasingly eclectic population, almost defies definition. Jen has said that she very much doubts if there are any citizens who feel "unequivocally American," a perceptive comment that underlines the themes of her work. She explores these kinds of subjects in fresh and challenging ways, even though her fundamental artistic techniques are conventional in virtually every aspect. As "Who's Irish?" demonstrates most dramatically, the central literary concerns of the end of the nineteenth century continue to enrich contemporary literature.

Yiyun Li explores the complexity of forming an American identity in her innovative stories, collected in *A Thousand Years of Good Prayers,* which won the PEN/Hemingway award for the best first book of fiction in 2005. Part of this collection, "The Princess of Nebraska" involves three central characters: Boshen is a gay physician who emigrated from China by virtue of a token marriage, one that betrayed his lover, Yang, who remained in Beijing. Boshen, who still longs for the beautiful young man, finds himself attracted to Sasha, who is carrying Yang's child.

Sasha, a Mongolian with a Russian name, feels herself of a race separate from the Chinese who befriend her, which further complicates her efforts to find a place in the complex ethnic patterns of midwestern American society. What finally emerges are conflicts of ethnicity on two levels: the problems of international homosexuality in cultures not fully accepting of sexual freedoms, and a central love triangle that cuts across all of these matters. The irony is that these richly contemporary and innovative themes are presented in the most conventional of narrative methodologies, an omniscient point of view that enters the minds of multiple characters and ranges forward and backward in time, linking related conflicts thematically.

Conclusion

It is clear that the American story enters the twenty-first century with vitality and an expanding range of writers and fresh ideas. Although the basic aesthetic of the form took shape at the end of the nineteenth century, the innovative contributions of a legion of new writers brought energy and original subjects to short fiction at the end of the twentieth. Virtually every segment of society contributed to the burgeoning popularity of the genre, and these authors found expression for innovative subjects and themes, some of them exhibiting startling insights into social issues in the United States. The short story in the early twenty-first century is robust, fresh, and ever more popular as a literary form.

The genre that grew in the New World as it had on no other soil continues to dramatize the most salient issues of its heterogeneous population, absorbing concepts from citizens from every country, racial background, and religious orientation, a rich and fascinating aesthetic tradition that reaches back before the Revolutionary War for its origins. At that time, writers were in danger of being ostracized for deigning to write in the scandalous new form, and nearly all early short fiction was anonymous. By the end of the twentieth century, authors of the genre were among the most celebrated, and most generously supported, artists in the country, as the $60,000 Frank O'Connor International Short Story Award to Yiyun Li would indicate. Every important writer of fiction in the United States produced a significant body of stories, and university students everywhere are familiar with them. Many such works, including Ambrose Bierce's "An Occurrence at Owl Creek Bridge," Andre Dubus's "Killings," Edgar Allan Poe's "The Fall of the House of Usher," Herman Melville's "Bartleby, the Scrivener," and James Thurber's "The Secret Life of Walter Mitty," have been made into celebrated motion pictures, attracting an even wider audience. Surely it could be said that the story, as is true of jazz in music, has become the most "American" of literary genres. There is every indication in the breadth of its creators, and in the sweep of its vibrant themes, that the form will become an even more exciting form of aesthetic expression in the new millennium.

Donald Barthelme
Views of My Father Weeping

Often considered the typical postmodern story, "Views of My Father Weeping" first appeared in *The New Yorker* in 1969 and has been frequently reprinted ever since. Born in 1931 in Philadelphia but raised in Texas, Donald Barthelme was educated at the University of Houston, where he returned many years later as the Cullen Distinguished Professor of English. In the course of his career, he published seven collections of stories and four novels, work that challenged many of the prevailing conventions of fiction, breaking narrative sequence, leaving central conflicts unresolved, blending social realism with abstraction and dislocation. In "See the Moon," one of his characters says that "fragments are the only form I trust," a comment that has often been applied to the author's own work. Certainly "Views of My Father Weeping" proceeds through brief and incomplete structural units, but despite this technique there is narrative order. The units that reveal the events inherent in the carriage accident that killed the narrator's father proceed chronologically, giving progressively more information about what "may" have happened. These sections are interspersed with the personal reflections of the narrator about himself, his memories, fantasies, pain, despair. The central events have an accretive indeterminacy: it is not clear, for example, if the narrator sees a supernatural father weeping on the bed, whether he remembers having seen such an incident, or whether what is conveyed is actually a projection by the narrator (that it is "he" who is weeping, not the father at all). Similarly, the account given by the carriage driver, Lars Bang, is called into question by the dark-haired girl, with the result that there is no assurance that any of the information is reliable. Remarkably, Barthelme sets the action in a genuine place, the center of Copenhagen, the King's New Square (Kongens Nytorv), near the Royal Academy of Fine Arts, the Charlottenborg Palace, the Royal Theater, and the numerous opera companies. It is, indeed, a place where a titled "aristocrat" might venture, and the Lensgreve af Ahlefeldt (slightly misspelled in the text) would be a member of the Danish nobility. Thus Barthelme grounds innovative abstraction in historical authenticity, a hallmark of his demanding short fiction.

Donald Barthelme, "Views of My Father Weeping," *The New Yorker* 45 (December 6, 1969): 56–60.

An Aristocrat was riding down the street in his carriage. He ran over my father.

★ ★ ★

After the ceremony I walked back to the city. I was trying to think of the reason my father had died. Then I remembered: He was run over by a carriage.

★ ★ ★

I telephoned my mother and told her of my father's death. She said she supposed it was the best thing. I too supposed it was the best thing. His enjoyment was diminishing. I wondered if I should attempt to trace the aristocrat whose carriage had run him down. There were said to have been one or two witnesses.

★ ★ ★

Yes it is possible that it is not my father who sits there in the center of the bed weeping. It may be someone else — the mailman, the man who delivers the groceries, an insurance salesman or tax collector, who knows. However, I must say, it resembles my father. The resemblance is very strong. He is not smiling through his tears but frowning through them. I remember once we were out on the ranch shooting peccadillos (result of a meeting, on the plains of the West, of the collared peccary and the nine-banded armadillo). My father shot and missed. He wept. This weeping resembles that weeping.

★ ★ ★

"Did you see it?" "Yes but only part of it. Part of the time I had my back turned." The witness was a little girl, eleven or twelve. She lived in a very poor quarter and I could not imagine that, were she to testify, anyone would credit her. "Can you recall what the man in the carriage looked like?" "Like an aristocrat," she said.

★ ★ ★

The first witness declares that the man in the carriage looked "like an aristocrat." But that might be simply the carriage itself. Any man sitting in a handsome carriage with a driver on the box and perhaps one or two footmen up behind tends to look like an aristocrat. I wrote down her name and asked her to call me if she remembered anything else. I gave her some candy.

★ ★ ★

I stood in the square where my father was killed and asked people passing by if they had seen, or knew of anyone who had seen, the incident. At the same time I felt the effort was wasted. Even if I found the man whose carriage had done the job, what would I say to him? "You killed my father." "Yes," the aristocrat would say, "but he ran right in under the legs of the horses. My man tried to stop but it happened too quickly. There was nothing anyone could do." Then perhaps he would offer me a purse full of money.

★ ★ ★

The man sitting in the center of the bed looks very much like my father. He is weeping, tears coursing down his cheeks. One can see that he is upset about something. Looking at him I see that something is wrong. He is spewing like a fire hydrant with its lock knocked off. His yammer darts in and out of all the rooms. In a melting mood I lay my paw on my breast and say, "Father." This does not distract him from his plaint, which rises to a shriek, sinks to a pule. His range is great, his ambition commensurate. I say again, "Father," but he ignores me. I don't know whether it is time to flee or will not be time to flee until later. He may suddenly stop, assume a sternness. I have kept the door open and nothing between me and the door, and moreover the screen unlatched, and on top of that the motor running, in the Mustang. But perhaps it is not my father weeping there, but another father: Tom's father, Phil's father, Pat's father, Pete's father, Paul's father. Apply some sort of test, voiceprint reading or . . .

★ ★ ★

My father throws his ball of knitting up in the air. The orange wool hangs there.

★ ★ ★

My father regards the tray of pink cupcakes. Then he jams his thumb into each cupcake, into the top. Cupcake by cupcake. A thick smile spreads over the face of each cupcake.

★ ★ ★

Then a man volunteered that he had heard two other men talking about the accident in a shop. "What shop?" The man pointed it out to me, a draper's shop on the south side of the square. I entered the shop and made inquiries. "It was your father, eh? He was bloody clumsy if you ask me." This was the clerk behind the counter. But another man standing nearby, well-dressed, even elegant, a gold watchchain stretched across his vest, disagreed. "It was the fault of the driver," the second man said. "He could have stopped them if he had cared to." "Nonsense," the clerk said, "not a chance in the world. If your father hadn't been drunk—" "He wasn't drunk," I said. "I arrived on the scene soon after it happened and I smelled no liquor."

★ ★ ★

This was true. I had been notified by the police, who came to my room and fetched me to the scene of the accident. I bent over my father, whose chest was crushed, and laid my cheek against his. His cheek was cold. I smelled no liquor but blood from his mouth stained the collar of my coat. I asked the people standing there how it had happened. "Run down by a carriage," they said. "Did the driver stop?" "No, he whipped up the horses and went off down the street and then around the corner at the end of the street, toward King's New Square." "You have no idea as to whose carriage . . ." "None." Then I made the arrangements for the burial. It was not until several days later that the idea of seeking the aristocrat in the carriage came to me.

★ ★ ★

I had had in my life nothing to do with aristocrats, did not even know in what part of the city they lived, in their great houses. So that even if I located someone who had seen the incident and could identify the particular aristocrat involved, I would be faced with the further task of finding his house and gaining admittance (and even then, might he not be abroad?). "No, the driver was at fault," the man with the gold watchchain said. "Even if your father was drunk — and I can't say about that, one way or another, I have no opinion — even if your father was drunk, the driver could have done more to avoid the accident. He was dragged, you know. The carriage dragged him about forty feet." I had noticed that my father's clothes were torn in a peculiar way. "There was one thing," the clerk said, "don't tell anyone I told you, but I can give you one hint. The driver's livery was blue and green."

★ ★ ★

It is someone's father. That much is clear. He is fatherly. The gray in the head. The puff in the face. The droop in the shoulders. The flab on the gut. Tears falling. Tears falling. Tears falling. Tears falling. More tears. It seems that he intends to go further along this salty path. The facts suggest that this is his program, weeping. He has something in mind, more weeping. O lud lud! But why remain? Why watch it? Why tarry? Why not fly? Why subject myself? I could be somewhere else, reading a book, watching the telly, stuffing a big ship into a little bottle, dancing the Pig. I could be out in the streets feeling up eleven-year-old girls in their soldier drag, there are thousands, as alike as pennies, and I could be — Why doesn't he stand up, arrange his clothes, dry his face? He's trying to embarrass us. He wants attention. He's trying to make himself interesting. He wants his brow wrapped in cold cloths perhaps, his hands held perhaps, his back rubbed, his neck kneaded, his wrists patted, his elbows anointed with rare oils, his toenails painted with tiny scenes representing God blessing America. I won't do it.

★ ★ ★

My father has a red bandana tied around his face covering the nose and mouth. He extends his right hand in which there is a water pistol. "Stick 'em up!" he says.

★ ★ ★

But blue and green livery is not unusual. A blue coat with green trousers, or the reverse — if I saw a coachman wearing such livery I would take no particular notice. It is true that most livery tends to be blue and buff, or blue and white, or blue and a sort of darker blue (for the trousers). But in these days one often finds a servant aping the more exquisite color combinations affected by his masters. I have even seen them in red trousers although red trousers used to be reserved, by unspoken agreement, for the aristocracy. So that the colors of the driver's livery were not of much consequence. Still it was something. I could now go about in the city, especially in stables and gin shops and such places, keeping a weather eye for the livery of the lackeys who gathered there. It was possible that more than one of the gentry dressed his servants in this blue and green livery, but on the other hand, unlikely that there were as many as half a dozen. So that in fact the draper's clerk had offered a very good clue indeed, had one the energy to pursue it vigorously.

★ ★ ★

There is my father, standing alongside an extremely large dog, a dog ten hands high at the very least. My father leaps on the dog's back, straddles him. My father kicks the large dog in the ribs with his heels. "Giddyap!"

★ ★ ★

My father has written on the white wall with his crayons.

★ ★ ★

I was stretched out on my bed when someone knocked at the door. It was the small girl to whom I had given candy when I had first begun searching for the aristocrat. She looked frightened, yet resolute; I could see that she had some information for me. "I know who it was," she said. "I know his name." "What is it?" "First you must give me five crowns." Luckily I had five crowns in my pocket, had she come later in the day, after I had eaten, I would have had nothing to give her. I handed over the money and she said, "Lars Bang." I looked at her in some surprise. "What sort of name is that for an aristocrat?" "His coachman," she said. "The coachman's name is Lars Bang." Then she fled.

★ ★ ★

When I heard this name, which in its sound and appearance is rude, vulgar, not unlike my own name, I was seized with repugnance, thought of dropping the whole business, although the piece of information she had brought had just cost me five crowns. When I was seeking him and he was yet nameless, the aristocrat and, by extension, his servants, seemed vulnerable: they had, after all, been responsible for a crime, or a sort of crime. My father was dead and they were responsible, or at least involved; and even though they were of the aristocracy or servants of the aristocracy, still common justice might be sought for; they might be required to make reparation, in some measure, for what they had done. Now, having the name of the coachman, and being thus much closer to his master than when I merely had the clue of the blue-and-green livery, I became afraid. For, after all, the unknown aristocrat must be a very powerful man, not at all accustomed to being called to account by people like me; indeed, his contempt for people like me was so great that, when one of us was so foolish as to stray into the path of his carriage, the aristocrat dashed him down, or permitted his coachman to do so, dragged him along the cobblestones for as much as forty feet, and then went gaily on his way, toward King's New Square. Such a man, I reasoned, was not very likely to take kindly to what I had to say to him. Very possibly there would be no purse of money at all, not a crown, not an öre, but rather he would, with an abrupt, impatient nod of his head, set his servants upon me. I would be beaten, perhaps killed. Like my father.

★ ★ ★

But if it is not my father sitting there in the bed weeping, why am I standing before the bed, in an attitude of supplication? Why do I desire with all my heart that this man, my father, cease what he is doing, which is so painful to me? Is it only that my position is a familiar one? That I remember, before, desiring with all my heart that this man, my father, cease what he is doing?

★ ★ ★

Why! . . . there's my father! . . . sitting in the bed there! . . . and he's *weeping!* . . . as though his heart would burst! . . . Father! . . . how is this? . . . who has wounded you? . . . name the man! . . . why I'll . . . I'll . . . here, Father, take this handkerchief! . . . and this handkerchief! . . . and this handkerchief! . . . I'll run for a towel . . . for a doctor . . . for a priest . . . for a good fairy . . . is there . . . can you . . . can I . . . a cup of hot tea? . . . bowl of steaming soup? . . . shot of Calvados? . . . a joint? . . . a red jacket? . . . a blue jacket? . . . Father, please! . . . look at me, Father . . . who has insulted you? . . . are you, then, compromised? . . . ruined? . . . a slander is going around? . . . an obloquy? . . . a traducement? . . . 'sdeath! . . . I won't permit it! . . . I won't abide it! . . . I'll . . . move every mountain . . . climb every river . . . etc.

★ ★ ★

My father is playing with the salt and pepper shakers, and with the sugar bowl. He lifts the cover off the sugar bowl, and shakes pepper into it.

★ ★ ★

Or: My father thrusts his hand through a window of the doll's house. His hand knocks over the doll's chair, knocks over the doll's chest of drawers, knocks over the doll's bed.

★ ★ ★

The next day, just before noon, Lars Bang himself came to my room. "I understand that you are looking for me." He was very much of a surprise. I had expected a rather burly, heavy man, of a piece with all of the other coachmen one saw sitting up on the box; Lars Bang was, instead, slight, almost feminine-looking, more the type of the secretary or valet than the coachman. He was not threatening at all, contrary to my fears; he was almost helpful, albeit with the slightest hint of malice in his helpfulness. I stammeringly explained that my father, a good man although subject to certain weaknesses, including a love of the bottle, had been run down by an aristocrat's coach, in the vicinity of King's New Square, not very many days previously; that I had information that the coach had dragged him some forty feet; and that I was eager to establish certain facts about the case. "Well then," Lars Bang said, with a helpful nod, "I'm your man, for it was my coach that was involved. A sorry business! Unfortunately I haven't the time right now to give you the full particulars, but if you will call round at the address written on this card, at six o'clock in the evening, I believe I will be able to satisfy you." So saying, he took himself off, leaving me with the card in my hand.

★ ★ ★

I spoke to Miranda, quickly sketching what had happened. She asked to see the white card; I gave it to her, for the address meant nothing to me. "Oh my," she said. "17 rue du Bac, that's over by the Vixen Gate — a very special quarter. Only aristocrats of the highest rank live there, and common people are not even allowed into the great park that lies between the houses and the river. If you are found wandering about there at night, you are apt to earn yourself a very severe beating." "But I have an appointment," I said. "An appointment with a coachman!" Miranda cried, "how foolish you are! Do you think the men of the watch will believe that, or even if they believe it (you have an honest enough face) will allow you to prowl that rich quarter, where so many thieves would dearly love to be set free for an hour or so, after dark? Go to!" Then she advised me that I must carry something with me — a pannier of beef or some dozen bottles of wine, so that if apprehended by the watch, I could say that I was delivering to such and such a house, and thus be judged an honest man on an honest errand, and escape a beating. I saw that she was right; and going out, I purchased at the wine merchant's a dozen bottles of a rather good claret (for it would never do to be delivering wine no aristocrat would drink); this cost me thirty crowns, which I had borrowed from Miranda. The bottles we wrapped round with straw, to prevent them banging into one another, and the whole we arranged in a sack — which I could carry on my back. I remember thinking, how they rhymed, fitted together, *sack* and *back*. In this fashion I set off across the city.

* * *

There is my father's bed. In it, my father. Attitude of dejection. Graceful as a mule deer once, the same large ears. For a nanosecond, there is a nanosmile. Is he having me on? I remember once we went out on the ups and downs of the West (out past Vulture's Roost) to shoot. First we shot up a lot of old beer cans, then we shot up a lot of old whiskey bottles, better because they shattered. Then we shot up some mesquite bushes and some parts of a Ford pickup somebody'd left lying around. But no animals came to our party (it was noisy, I admit it). A long list of animals failed to arrive — no deer, quail, rabbit, seals, sea lions, condylarths. It was pretty boring shooting up mesquite bushes, so we hunkered down behind some rocks, Father and I, he hunkered down behind his rocks and I hunkered down behind my rocks, and we commenced to shooting at each other. That was interesting.

* * *

My father is looking at himself in a mirror. He is wearing a large hat (straw) on which there are a number of blue and yellow plastic jonquils. He says: "How do I look?"

* * *

Lars Bang took the sack from me and without asking permission reached inside, withdrawing one of the straw-wrapped bottles of claret. "Here's something!" he exclaimed, reading the label. "A gift for the master, I don't doubt!" Then, regarding me steadily all the while, he took up an awl and lifted the cork. There were two other men seated at the pantry table, dressed in the blue-and-green livery, and with them a dark-haired, beautiful girl, quite young, who said nothing and looked at no one. Lars Bang obtained glasses, kicked a chair in my direction, and poured drinks all round. "To your health!" he said (with what I thought an ironical overtone) and we drank. "This young man," Lars Bang said, nodding at me, "is here seeking our advice on a very complicated business. A murder, I believe you said?" "I said nothing of the kind. I seek information about an accident." The claret was soon exhausted. Without looking at me, Lars Bang opened a second bottle and set it in the center of the table. The beautiful dark-haired girl ignored me along with all the others. For my part, I felt I had conducted myself rather well thus far. I had not protested when the wine was made free of (after all, they would be accustomed to levying a sort of tax on anything entering through the back door). But also I had not permitted his word "murder" to be used, but instead specified the use of the word "accident." Therefore I was, in general, comfortable sitting at the table drinking the wine, for which I have no better head than had my father. "Well," said Lars Bang at length, "I will relate the circumstances of the accident, and you may judge for yourself as to whether myself and my master, the Lensgreve Aklefeldt, were at fault." I absorbed this news with a slight shock. A count! I had selected a man of very high rank indeed to put my question to. In a moment my accumulated self-confidence drained away. A count! Mother of God, have mercy on me.

★ ★ ★

There is my father, peering through an open door into an empty house. He is accompanied by a dog (small dog; not the same dog as before). He looks into the empty room. He says: "Anybody home?"

★ ★ ★

There is my father, sitting in his bed, weeping.

★ ★ ★

"It was a Friday," Lars Bang began, as if he were telling a tavern story. "The hour was close upon noon and my master directed me to drive him to King's New Square, where he had some business. We were proceeding there at a modest easy pace, for he was in no great hurry. Judge of my astonishment when, passing through the draper's quarter, we found ourselves set upon by an elderly man, thoroughly drunk, who flung himself at my lead pair and began cutting at their legs with a switch, in the most vicious manner imaginable. The poor dumb brutes reared, of course, in fright and fear, for," Lars Bang said piously, "they are accustomed to the best of care, and never a blow do they receive from me, or from the other coachman, Rik, for the count is especially severe upon this point, that his animals be well-treated. The horses, then, were rearing and plunging; it was all I could do to hold them; I shouted at the man, who fell back for an instant. The count stuck his head out of the window, to inquire as to the nature of the trouble, and I told him that a drunken man had attacked our horses. Your father, in his blindness, being not content with the mischief he had already worked, ran back in again, close to the animals, and began madly cutting at their legs with his stick. At this renewed attack the horses, frightened out of their wits, jerked the reins from my hands, and ran headlong over your father, who fell beneath their hooves. The heavy wheels of the carriage passed over him (I felt two quite distinct thumps), his body caught upon a projection under the boot, and he was dragged some forty feet, over the cobblestones. I was attempting, with all my might, merely to hang on to the box, for, having taken the bit between their teeth, the horses were in no mood to tarry; nor could any human agency have stopped them. We flew down the street . . ."

★ ★ ★

My father is attending a class in good behavior.

"Do the men rise when friends greet us while we are sitting in a booth?"

"The men do not rise when they are seated in a booth," he answers, "although they may half-rise and make apologies for not fully rising."

★ ★ ★

". . . the horses turning into the way that leads to King's New Square; and it was not until we reached that place that they stopped and allowed me to quiet them. I wanted to go back and see what had become of the madman, your father, who had attacked us; but my master, vastly angry and shaken up, forbade it. I have never seen him in so fearful a temper as that day; if your father had survived, and my master got his hands on him, it would have gone ill with your father, that's a certainty. And so, you are now in possession of all the facts. I trust you are satisfied, and will drink another bottle of this quite fair claret you have brought us, and be on your way." Before I had time to frame a reply, the dark-haired girl spoke. "Bang is an absolute bloody liar," she said.

★ ★ ★

Etc.

Alice Walker
Everyday Use

Alice Walker has built a distinguished record among contemporary American writers based on her five novels, five volumes of verse, two essay collections, and two books containing short stories. Perhaps her most celebrated single work, *The Color Purple*, published in 1982, won the Pulitzer Prize and was made into a Hollywood motion picture. "Everyday Use," which first appeared in 1973 and was then part of In *Love and Trouble: Stories of Black Women*, is among her most studied pieces of short fiction, and it attracted special attention for its implementation of the metaphor of "quilting," an activity that not only makes something beautiful and useful out of discarded cloth but that links generations of women together, in this case, African American women. Quilting is a folk art that honors the maternal lineage, and it celebrates the ability of poor people to create something out of nothing, the central circumstance of their lives. "Everyday Use" is narrated by a woman, and it concerns the lives of women across a spectrum of attitudes. The mother values her family, both present and past, and she has sacrificed all for the welfare of her children. Her daughter Maggie is scarred from a fire and seems not to value herself as a human being with a role to play in the household. Dee, the daughter with a college education, has rejected her background, changed her name, and now sees the familial artifacts as cultural objects, not as treasured memories of ancestral pride. Interestingly, the name Dee has chosen for herself, "Wangero," was the name given to Walker herself during a trip to Africa. Although Walker was born into a sharecropper family in Georgia, in many ways she lived a privileged life, attending Spelman College before graduating from Sarah Lawrence in 1963. After marriage to a white attorney, and their subsequent divorce, she taught and wrote with support from a Guggenheim fellowship, a Radcliffe Institute fellowship, and a grant from the National Endowment for the Arts. Her work has brought her respect and adulation, and she has taken her rightful place as one of the most venerated writers in the United States.

Alice Walker, "Everyday Use," *Harper's Magazine* 246 (April 1973): 74–81.

I will wait for her in the yard that Maggie and I made so clean and wavy yesterday afternoon. A yard like this is more comfortable than most people know. It is not just a yard. It is like an extended living room. When the hard clay is swept clean as a floor and the fine sand around the edges lined with tiny, irregular grooves, anyone can come and sit and look up into the elm tree and wait for the breezes that never come inside the house.

Maggie will be nervous until after her sister goes: she will stand hopelessly in corners, homely and ashamed of the burn scars down her arms and legs, eyeing her sister with a mixture of envy and awe. She thinks her sister has held life always in the palm of one hand, that "no" is a word the world never learned to say to her.

You've no doubt seen those TV shows where the child who has "made it" is confronted, as a surprise, by his own mother and father, tottering in weakly from backstage. (A pleasant surprise, of course: what would they do if parent and child came on the show only to curse out and insult each other?) On TV mother and child embrace and smile into each other's faces. Sometimes the mother and father weep, the child wraps them in his arms and leans across the table to tell how he would not have made it without their help. I have seen these programs.

Sometimes I dream a dream in which Dee and I are suddenly brought together on a TV program of this sort. Out of a dark and soft-seated limousine I am ushered into a bright room filled with many people. There I meet a smiling, gray, sporty man like Johnny Carson who shakes my hand and tells me what a fine girl I have. Then we are on the stage and Dee is embracing me with tears in her eyes. She pins on my dress a large orchid, even though she has told me once that she thinks orchids are tacky flowers.

In real life I am a large big-boned woman with rough, man-working hands. In the winter I wear flannel nightgowns to bed and overalls during the day. I can kill and clean a hog as mercilessly as a man. My fat keeps me hot in zero weather. I can work outside all day, breaking ice to get water for washing; I can eat pork liver cooked over the open fire minutes after it comes steaming from the hog. One winter I knocked a bull calf straight in the brain between the eyes with a sledgehammer and had the meat hung up to chill before nightfall. But of course all this does not show on television. I am the way my daughter would want me to be; a hundred pounds lighter, my skin like an uncooked barley pancake. My hair glistens in the hot bright lights. Johnny Carson has much to do to keep up with my quick and witty tongue.

But that is a mistake. I know even before I wake up. Who ever knew a Johnson with a quick tongue? Who can even imagine me looking a strange white man in the eye? It seems to me I have talked to them always with one foot raised in flight, with my head turned in whichever way is farthest from them. Dee, though. She would always look anyone in the eye. Hesitation was no part of her nature.

ᔥᔢ

How do I look, Mama?" Maggie says, showing just enough of her thin body enveloped in pink skirt and red blouse for me to know she's there almost hidden by the door.

"Come out into the yard," I say.

Have you ever seen a lame animal, perhaps a dog run over by some careless person rich enough to own a car, sidle up to someone who is ignorant enough to be kind to him? That is the way my Maggie walks. She has been like this, chin on chest, eyes on ground, feet in shuffle, ever since the fire that burned the other house to the ground.

Dee is lighter than Maggie, with nicer hair and a fuller figure. She's a woman now, though sometimes I forget. How long ago was it that the other house burned? Ten, twelve years? Sometimes I can still hear the flames and feel Maggie's arms sticking to me, her hair smoking and her dress falling off her in little black papery flakes. Her eyes seemed stretched open, blazed open by the flames reflected in them. And Dee. I see her standing off under the sweetgum tree she used to dig gum out of; a look of concentration on her face as she watched the last dingy gray board of the house fall in toward the red-hot brick chimney. Why don't you do a dance around the ashes? I'd wanted to ask her. She had hated the house that much.

I used to think she hated Maggie too. But that was before we raised the money, the church and me, to send her to Augusta to school. She used to read to us without pity; forcing words, lies, other folks' habits, whole lives upon us two, sitting trapped and ignorant underneath her voice. She washed us in a river of make-believe, burned us with a lot of knowledge we didn't necessarily need to know. Pressed us to her with the serious way she read, to shove us away, like dimwits, at just the moment we seemed about to understand.

Dee wanted nice things. A yellow organdy dress to wear to her graduation from high school; black pumps to match a green suit she'd made from an old suit somebody gave me. She was determined to stare down any disaster in her efforts. Her eyelids would not flicker for minutes at a time. Often I fought off the temptation to shake her. At sixteen she had a style of her own: and knew what style was.

I never had an education myself. After second grade the school was closed down. Don't ask me why: in 1927 colored asked fewer questions than they do now. Sometimes Maggie reads to me. She stumbles along good-naturedly but can't see well. She knows she is not bright. Like good looks and money, quickness passed her by. She will marry John Thomas (who has mossy teeth in an earnest face), and then I'll be free to sit here and I guess just sing church songs to myself. Although I never was a good singer. Never could carry a tune. I was always better at a man's job. I used to love to milk till I was hooked in the side in '49. Cows are soothing and slow and don't bother you, unless you try to milk them the wrong way.

I have deliberately turned my back on the house. It is three rooms, just like the one that burned, except the roof is tin; they don't make shingle roofs anymore. There are no real windows, just some holes cut in the sides, like the portholes in a ship, but not round and not square, with rawhide holding the shutters up on the outside. This house is in a pasture too, like the other one. No doubt when Dee sees it she will want to tear it down. She wrote me once that no matter where we "choose" to live, she will manage to come see us. But she will never bring her friends. Maggie and I thought about this and Maggie asked me, "Mama, when did Dee ever *have* any friends?"

She had a few. Furtive boys in pink shirts hanging about on washday after school. Nervous girls who never laughed. Impressed with her they worshiped the well-turned phrase, the cute shape, the scalding humor that erupted like bubbles in lye. She read to them.

When she was courting Jimmy T she didn't have much time to pay to us, but turned all her fault-finding power on him. He *flew* to marry a cheap city girl from a family of ignorant flashy people. She hardly had time to recompose herself.

ॐ

When she comes I will meet . . . but there they are!

Maggie attempts to make a dash for the house, in her shuffling way, but I stay her with my hand. "Come back here," I say. And she stops and tries to dig a well in the sand with her toe.

It is hard to see them clearly through the strong sun. But even the first glimpse of leg out of the car tells me it is Dee. Her feet were always neat looking, as if God himself had shaped them with a certain style. From the other side of the car comes a short, stocky man. Hair is all over his head a foot long and hanging from his chin like a kinky mule tail. I hear Maggie suck in her breath. "Uhnnnh," is what it sounds like. Like when you see the wriggling end of a snake just in front of your foot on a road. "Uhnnnh."

Dee, next. A dress down to the ground, in this hot weather. A dress so loud it hurts my eyes. There are yellows and oranges enough to throw back the light of the sun. I feel my whole face warming from the heat waves it throws out. Earrings gold too, and hanging down to her shoulders. Bracelets dangling and making noises when she moves her arm up to shake the folds of the dress out of her armpits. The dress is loose and flows, and as she walks closer, I like it. I hear Maggie go "Uhnnnh" again. It is her sister's hair. It stands straight up like the wool on a sheep. It is black as night and around the edges are two long pigtails that rope about like small lizards disappearing behind her ears.

"Wa-su-zo-Tean-o!" she says, coming on in that gliding way the dress makes her move. The short stocky fellow with the hair to his navel is all grinning and he follows up with, "Asalamalakim, my mother and sister!" He moves to hug Maggie but she falls back, right up against the back of my chair. I feel her trembling there, and when I look up I see the perspiration falling off her skin.

"Don't get up," says Dee. Since I am stout it takes something of a push. You can see me trying to move a second or two before I make it. She turns, showing white heels through her sandals, and goes back to the car. Out she peeks next with a Polaroid. She stoops down quickly and snaps off picture after picture of me sitting there in front of the house with Maggie cowering behind me. She never takes a shot without making sure the house is included. When a cow comes nibbling around the edge of the yard she snaps it and me and Maggie *and* the house. Then she puts the Polaroid on the back seat of the car, and comes up and kisses me on the forehead.

Meanwhile Asalamalakim is going through motions with Maggie's hand. Maggie's hand is as limp as a fish, and probably as cold, despite the sweat, and she keeps trying to pull it back. It looks like Asalamalakim wants to shake hands but wants to do it fancy. Or maybe he don't know how people shake hands. Anyhow, he soon gives up on Maggie.

"Well," I say. "Dee."

"No, Mama," she says. "Not 'Dee,' Wangero Leewanika Kemanjo!"

"What happened to 'Dee'?" I wanted to know.

"She's dead," Wangero said. "I couldn't bear it any longer, being named after the people who oppress me."

"You know well as me you was named after your aunt Dicie," I said. Dicie is my sister. She named Dee. We called her "Big Dee" after Dee was born.

"But who was *she* named after?" asked Wangero.

"I guess after Grandma Dee," I said.

"And who was she named after?" asked Wangero.

"Her mother," I said, and saw Wangero was getting tired. "That's about as far back as I can trace it," I said. Though, in fact, I probably could have carried it back beyond the Civil War through the branches.

"Well," said Asalamalakim, "there you are."

"Uhnnnh," I heard Maggie say.

"There I was not," I said, "before 'Dicie' cropped up in our family, so why should I try to trace it that far back?"

He just stood there grinning, looking down on me like somebody inspecting a Model A car. Every once in a while he and Wangero sent eye signals over my head.

"How do you pronounce this name?" I asked.

"You don't have to call me by it if you don't want to," said Wangero.

"Why shouldn't I?" I asked. "If that's what you want us to call you, we'll call you."

"I know it might sound awkward at first," said Wangero.

"I'll get used to it," I said. "Ream it out again."

Well, soon we got the name out of the way. Asalamalakim had a name twice as long and three times as hard. After I tripped over it two or three times he told me to just call him Hakim-a-barber. I wanted to ask him was he a barber, but I didn't really think he was, so I didn't ask.

"You must belong to those beef cattle peoples down the road," I said. They said "Asalamalakim" when they met you too, but they didn't shake hands. Always too busy: feeding the cattle, fixing the fences, putting up salt-lick shelters, throwing down hay. When the white folks poisoned some of the herd, the men stayed up all night with rifles in their hands. I walked a mile and a half just to see the sight.

Hakim-a-barber said, "I accept some of their doctrines, but farming and raising cattle is not my style." They didn't tell me, and I didn't ask, whether Wangero (Dee) had really gone and married him.

We sat down to eat and right away he said he didn't eat collards and pork was unclean. Wangero, though, went on through the chitlins and corn bread, the greens and everything else. She talked a blue streak over the sweet potatoes. Everything delighted her. Even the fact that we still used the benches her daddy made for the table when we couldn't afford to buy chairs.

"Oh, Mama!" she cried. Then turned to Hakim-a-barber. "I never knew how lovely these benches are. You can feel the rump prints," she said, running her hands underneath her and along the bench. Then she gave a sigh and her hand closed over Grandma Dee's butter dish. "That's it!" she said. "I knew there was something I wanted to ask you if I could have." She jumped up from the table and went over in the corner where the churn stood, the milk in it clabber by now. She looked at the churn and looked at it.

"This churn top is what I need," she said. "Didn't Uncle Buddy whittle it out of a tree you all used to have?"

"Yes," I said.

"Uh huh," she said happily. "And I want the dasher too."

"Uncle Buddy whittle that too?" asked the barber.

Dee (Wangero) looked up at me.

"Aunt Dee's first husband whittled the dash," said Maggie so low you almost couldn't hear her. "His name was Henry, but they called him Stash."

"Maggie's brain is like an elephant's," Wangero said, laughing. "I can use the churn top as a centerpiece for the alcove table," she said, sliding a plate over the churn, "and I'll think of something artistic to do with the dasher."

When she finished wrapping the dasher the handle stuck out. I took it for a moment in my hands. You didn't even have to look close to see where hands pushing the dasher up and down to make butter had left a kind of sink in the wood. In fact, there were a lot of small sinks; you could see where thumbs and fingers had sunk into the wood. It was beautiful light yellow wood, from a tree that grew in the yard where Big Dee and Stash had lived.

After dinner Dee (Wangero) went to the trunk at the foot of my bed and started rifling through it. Maggie hung back in the kitchen over the dishpan. Out came Wangero with two quilts. They had been pieced by Grandma Dee, and then Big Dee and me had hung them on the quilt frames on the front porch and quilted them. One was in the Lone Star pattern. The other was Walk Around the Mountain. In both of them were scraps of dresses Grandma Dee had worn fifty and more years ago. Bits and pieces of Grandpa Jarrell's paisley shirts. And one teeny faded blue piece, about the size of a penny matchbox, that was from Great Grandpa Ezra's uniform that he wore in the Civil War.

"Mama," Wangero said sweet as a bird. "Can I have these old quilts?"

I heard something fall in the kitchen, and a minute later the kitchen door slammed.

"Why don't you take one or two of the others?" I asked. "These old things was just done by me and Big Dee from some tops your grandma pieced before she died."

"No," said Wangero. "I don't want those. They are stitched around the borders by machine."

"That'll make them last better," I said.

"That's not the point," said Wangero. "These are all pieces of dresses Grandma used to wear. She did all this stitching by hand. Imagine!" She held the quilts securely in her arms, stroking them.

"Some of the pieces, like those lavender ones, come from old clothes her mother handed down to her," I said, moving up to touch the quilts. Dee (Wangero) moved back just enough so that I couldn't reach the quilts. They already belonged to her.

"Imagine!" she breathed again, clutching them closely to her bosom.

"The truth is," I said, "I promised to give them quilts to Maggie, for when she marries John Thomas."

She gasped, like a bee had stung her.

"Maggie can't appreciate these quilts!" she said. "She'd probably be backward enough to put them to everyday use."

"I reckon she would," I said. "God knows I been saving 'em for long enough with nobody using 'em. I hope she will!" I didn't want to bring up how I had offered Dee (Wangero) a quilt when she went away to college. Then she had told me they were old-fashioned, out of style.

"But they're *priceless*!" she was saying now, furiously; for she has a temper.

"Maggie would put them on the bed and in five years they'd be in rags. Less than that!"

"She can always make some more," I said. "Maggie knows how to quilt."

Dee (Wangero) looked at me with hatred. "You just will not understand. The point is these quilts, *these* quilts!"

"Well," I said, stumped, "what would *you* do with them?"

"Hang them," she said. As if that was the only thing you *could* do with quilts.

༺༻

Maggie, by now, was standing in the door. I could almost hear the sound her feet made as they scraped over each other.

"She can have them, Mama," she said, like somebody used to never winning anything, of having anything reserved for her. "I can 'member Grandma Dee without the quilts."

I looked at her hard. She had filled her bottom lip with checkerberry snuff, and it gave her face a kind of dopey, hangdog look. It was Grandma Dee and Big Dee who taught her how to quilt herself. She stood there with her scarred hands hidden in the folds of her skirt. She looked at her sister with something like fear, but she wasn't mad at her. This was Maggie's portion. This was the way she knew God to work.

When I looked at her like that something hit me in the top of my head and ran down to the soles of my feet. Just like when I'm in church and the spirit of God touches me and I get happy and shout. I did something I never had done before: hugged Maggie to me, then dragged her on into the room, snatched the quilts out of Miss Wangero's hands and dumped them into Maggie's lap. Maggie just sat there on my bed with her mouth open.

"Take one or two of the others," I said to Dee.

But she turned without a word and went out to Hakim-a-barber.

༺༻

"You just don't understand," she said, as Maggie and I came out to the car.

"What don't I understand?" I wanted to know.

"Your heritage," she said. And then she turned to Maggie, kissed her, and said, "You ought to try to make something of yourself too, Maggie. It's really a new day for us. But from the way you and Mama still live you'd never know it."

She put on some sunglasses that hid everything above the tip of her nose and her chin.

Maggie smiled; maybe at the sunglasses. But a real smile, not scared. After we watched the car dust settle I asked Maggie to bring me a dip of snuff. And then the two of us sat there just enjoying, until it was time to go in the house and go to bed.

Leslie Marmon Silko
Storyteller

Leslie Marmon Silko is one of the celebrated writers of the 1970s who constitute what has been called the Native American Renaissance, a period of extraordinary productivity within her ethnic tradition. Born in 1948 of mixed racial heritage, Silko was raised on the Laguna Pueblo Reservation in New Mexico, where she learned about the oral tradition of narrative from her immediate family. She was an English major at the University of New Mexico and then attended law school before committing herself to literature. A volume of verse, *Laguna Woman,* appeared in 1974, after which she lived for two years in Alaska, the origin of her fiction set in that region. Her first novel, *Ceremony,* was published in 1977, a book that breaks genre borders by weaving poetry and fictional narrative together. In 1981, *Storyteller* followed, similarly eclectic in its nature, with prose narratives, autobiographical comments, verse, and photographs, all exploring the Indian experience in America. A flood of other books issued forth after that, including *Almanac of the Dead, Sacred Water: Narratives and Pictures, Yellow Woman and a Beauty of the Spirit,* and *Gardens in the Dunes: A Novel.* Her work has been supported by the largess of numerous universities and foundations, and she has received grants from the National Endowment for the Arts and the MacArthur Foundation. "Storyteller" first appeared in *Puerto del Sol* in 1975 prior to inclusion in the volume bearing the same name in *1981.* What is remarkable about it is an iconoclastic expansion of what short fiction can do. The central narrative stance is that of a Yupik woman in jail awaiting arraignment for murder, and as she sits in solitude her mind wanders, achronologically, back through salient events in her life: the deaths of her parents, her life with her grandmother and the old man, the oral narrative he tells relentlessly about bear hunting, and her involvement with whites ("Gussucks," a residual term for the Russian Cossacks who first encountered Eskimo culture), which leads to the death of the storekeeper. Sequential time has little significance in this circumstance, but language, heritage, nature, and the art of storytelling mean everything, the central issues of this challenging narrative.

Leslie Marmon Silko, "Storyteller," *Puerto del Sol* 14, no. 1 (1975): 11–25.

I

Every day the sun came up a little lower on the horizon, moving more slowly until one day she got excited and started calling the jailer. She realized she had been sitting there for many hours, yet the sun had not moved from the center of the sky. The color of the sky had not been good lately; it had been pale blue, almost white, even when there were no clouds. She told herself it wasn't a good sign for the sky to be indistinguishable from the river ice, frozen solid and white against the earth. The tundra rose up behind the river but all the boundaries between the river and hills and sky were lost in the density of the pale ice.

She yelled again, this time some English words which came randomly into her mouth, probably swear words she'd heard from the oil drilling crews last winter. The jailer was an Eskimo, but he would not speak Yupik to her. She had watched people in the other cells; when they spoke to him in Yupik he ignored them until they spoke English.

He came and stared at her. She didn't know if he understood what she was telling him until he glanced behind her at the small high window. He looked at the sun, and turned and walked away. She could hear the buckles on his heavy snowmobile boots jingle as he walked to the front of the building.

It was like the other buildings that white people, the Gussucks, brought with them: BIA and school buildings, portable buildings that arrived sliced in halves, on barges coming up the river. Squares of metal panelling bulged out with the layers of insulation stuffed inside. She had asked once what it was and someone told her it was to keep out the cold. She had not laughed then, but she did now. She walked over to the small double-pane window and she laughed out loud. They thought they could keep out the cold with stringy yellow wadding. Look at the sun. It wasn't moving; it was frozen, caught in the middle of the sky. Look at the sky, solid as the river with ice which had trapped the sun. It had not moved for a long time; in a few more hours it would be weak, and heavy frost would begin to appear on the edges and spread across the face of the sun like a mask. Its light was pale yellow, worn thin by the winter.

She could see people walking down the snow-packed roads, their breath steaming out from their parka hoods, faces hidden and protected by deep ruffs of fur. There were no cars or snowmobiles that day so she calculated it was fifty below zero, the temperature which silenced their machines. The metal froze; it split and shattered. Oil hardened and moving parts jammed solidly. She had seen it happen to their big yellow machines and the giant drill last winter when they came to drill their test holes. The cold stopped them, and they were helpless against it.

Her village was many miles upriver from this town, but in her mind she could see it clearly. Their house was not near the village houses. It stood alone on the bank upriver from the village. Snow had drifted to the eaves of the roof on the north side, but on the west side, by the door, the path was almost clear. She had nailed scraps of red tin over the logs last summer. She had done it for the bright red color, not for added warmth the way the village people had done. This final winter had been coming down even then; there had been signs of its approach for many years.

II

She went because she was curious about the big school where the Government sent all the other girls and boys. She had not played much with the village children while she was growing up because they were afraid of the old man, and they ran when her grandmother came. She went because she was tired of being alone with the old woman whose body had been stiffening for as long as the girl could remember. Her knees and knuckles were swollen grotesquely, and the pain had squeezed the brown skin of her face tight against the bones; it left her eyes hard like river stone. The girl asked once, what it was that did this to her body, and the old woman had raised up from sewing a sealskin boot, and stared at her.

"The joints," the old woman said in a low voice, whispering like wind across the roof, "the joints are swollen with anger."

Sometimes she did not answer and only stared at the girl. Each year she spoke less and less, but the old man talked more — all night sometimes not to anyone but himself: in a soft deliberate voice, he told stories, moving his smooth brown hands above the blankets. He had not fished or hunted with the other men for many years although he was not crippled or sick. He stayed in his bed, smelling like dry fish and urine, telling stories all winter; and when warm weather came, he went to his place on the river bank. He sat with a long willow stick, poking at the smoldering moss he burned against the insects while he continued with the stories.

The trouble was that she had not recognized the warnings in time. She did not see what the Gussuck school would do to her until she walked into the dormitory and realized that the old man had not been lying about the place. She thought he had been trying to scare her as he used to when she was very small and her grandmother was outside cutting up fish. She hadn't believed what he told her about the school because she knew he wanted to keep her there in the log house with him. She knew what he wanted.

The dormitory matron pulled down her underpants and whipped her with a leather belt because she refused to speak English.

"Those backwards village people," the matron said, because she was an Eskimo who had worked for the BIA a long time, "they kept this one until she was too big to learn." The other girls whispered in English. They knew how to work the showers, and they washed and curled their hair at night. They ate Gussuck food. She laid on her bed and imagined what her grandmother might be sewing, and what the old man was eating in his bed. When summer came, they sent her home.

The way her grandmother had hugged her before she left for school had been a warning too, because the old woman had not hugged or touched her for many years. Not like the old man, whose hands were always hunting, like ravens circling lazily in the sky, ready to touch her. She was not surprised when the priest and the old man met her at the landing strip, to say that the old lady was gone. The priest asked her where she would like to stay. He referred to the old man as her grandfather, but she did not bother to correct him. She had already been thinking about it; if she went with the priest, he would send her away to a school. But the old man was different. She knew he wouldn't send her back to school. She knew he wanted to keep her.

III

He told her one time, that she would get too old for him faster than he got too old for her; but again she had not believed him because sometimes he lied. He had lied about what he would do with her if she came into his bed. But as the years passed, she realized what he said was true. She was restless and strong. She had no patience with the old man who had never changed his slow smooth motions under the blankets.

The old man was in his bed for the winter; he did not leave it except to use the slop bucket in the corner. He was dozing with his mouth open slightly; his lips quivered and sometimes they moved like he was telling a story even while he dreamed. She pulled on the sealskin boots, the mukluks with the bright red flannel linings her grandmother had sewn for her, and she tied the braided red yarn tassels around her ankles over the gray wool pants. She zipped the wolfskin parka. Her grandmother had worn it for many years, but the old man said that before she died, she instructed him to bury her in an old black sweater, and to give the parka to the girl. The wolf pelts were creamy colored and silver, almost white in some places, and when the old lady had walked across the tundra in the winter, she disappeared into the snow.

She walked toward the village, breaking her own path through the deep snow. A team of sled dogs tied outside a house at the edge of the village leaped against their chains to bark at her. She kept walking, watching the dusky sky for the first evening stars. It was warm and the dogs were alert. When it got cold again, the dogs would lie curled and still, too drowsy from the cold to bark or pull at the chains. She laughed loudly because it made them howl and snarl. Once the old man had seen her tease the dogs and he shook his head. "So that's the kind of woman you are," he said, "in the wintertime the two of us are no different from those dogs. We wait in the cold for someone to bring us a few dry fish."

She laughed out loud again, and kept walking. She was thinking about the Gussuck oil drillers. They were strange; they watched her when she walked near their machines. She wondered what they looked like underneath their quilted goosedown trousers; she wanted to know how they moved. They would be something different from the old man.

☙❧

The old man screamed at her. He shook her shoulders so violently that her head bumped against the log wall. "I smelled it!" he yelled, "as soon as I woke up!

I am sure of it now. You can't fool me!" His thin legs were shaking inside the baggy wool trousers; he stumbled over her boots in his bare feet. His toe nails were long and yellow like bird claws; she had seen a gray crane last summer fighting another in the shallow water on the edge of the river. She laughed out loud and pulled her shoulder out of his grip. He stood in front of her. He was breathing hard and shaking; he looked weak. He would probably die next winter.

"I'm warning you," he said, "I'm warning you." He crawled back into his bunk then, and reached under the old soiled feather pillow for a piece of dry fish. He lay back on the pillow, staring at the ceiling and chewed dry strips of salmon. "I don't know what the old woman told you," he said, "but there will be trouble." He looked over to see if she was listening. His face suddenly relaxed into a smile, his dark slanty eyes were lost in wrinkles of brown skin. "I could tell you, but you are too good for warnings now. I can smell what you did all night with the Gussucks."

❧❧

She did not understand why they came there, because the village was small and so far upriver that even some Eskimos who had been away to school would not come back. They stayed downriver in the town. They said the village was too quiet. They were used to the town where the boarding school was located, with electric lights and running water. After all those years away at school, they had forgotten how to set nets in the river and where to hunt seals in the fall. Those who left did not say it, but their confidence had been destroyed. When she asked the old man why the Gussucks bothered to come to the village, his narrow eyes got bright with excitement.

"They only come when there is something to steal. The fur animals are too difficult for them to get now, and the seals and fish are hard to find. Now they come for oil deep in the earth. But this is the last time for them." His breathing was wheezy and fast; his hands gestured at the sky. "It is approaching. As it comes, ice will push across the sky." His eyes were open wide and he stared at the low ceiling rafters for hours without blinking. She remembered all this clearly because he began the story that day, the story he told from that time on. It began with a giant bear which he described muscle by muscle, from the curve of the ivory claws to the whorls of hair at the top of the massive skull. And for eight days he did not sleep, but talked continuously of the giant bear whose color was pale blue glacier ice.

IV

The snow was dirty and worn down in a path to the door. On either side of the path, the snow was higher than her head. In front of the door there were jagged yellow stains melted into the snow where men had urinated. She stopped in the entry way and kicked the snow off her boots. The room was dim; a kerosene lantern by the cash register was burning low. The long wooden shelves were jammed with cans of beans and potted meats. On the bottom shelf a jar of mayonnaise was broken open, leaking oily white clots on the floor. There was no one in the room except the yellowish dog sleeping in front of the long glass display case. A reflection made it appear to be lying on the knives and ammunition inside the case. Gussucks kept dogs inside their houses with them; they did not seem to mind the odors which seeped out of the dogs. "They tell us we are dirty for the food we eat — raw fish and fermented meat. But we do not live with dogs," the old man once said. She heard voices in the back room, and the sound of bottles set down hard on tables.

They were always confident. The first year they waited for the ice to break up on the river, and then they brought their big yellow machines up river on barges. They planned to drill their test holes during the summer to avoid the freezing. But the imprints and graves of their machines were still there, on the edge of the tundra above the river, where the summer mud had swallowed them before they ever left sight of the river. The village people had gathered to watch the white men, and to laugh as they drove the giant machines, one by one, off the steel ramp into the bogs; as if sheer numbers of vehicles would somehow make the tundra solid. But the old man said they behaved like desperate people, and they would come back again. When the tundra was frozen solid, they returned.

Village women did not even look through the door to the back room. The priest had warned them. The storeman was watching her because he didn't let Eskimos or Indians sit down at the tables in the back room. But she knew he couldn't throw her out if one of his Gussuck customers invited her to sit with him. She walked across the room. They stared at her, but she had the feeling she was walking for someone else, not herself, so their eyes did not matter. The red-haired man pulled out a chair and motioned for her to sit down. She looked back at the storeman while the red-haired man poured her a glass of red sweet wine. She wanted to laugh at the storeman the way she laughed at the dogs, straining against their chains, howling at her.

The red-haired man kept talking to the other Gussucks sitting around the table, but he slid one hand off the top of the table to her thigh. She looked over at the storeman to see if he was still watching her. She laughed out loud at him and the red-haired man stopped talking and turned to her. He asked if she wanted to go. She nodded and stood up.

Someone in the village had been telling him things about her, he said as they walked down the road to his trailer. She understood that much of what he was saying, but the rest she did not hear. The whine of the big generators at the construction camp sucked away the sound of his words. But English was of no concern to her anymore, and neither was anything the Christians in the village might say about her or the old man. She smiled at the effect of the subzero air on the electric lights around the trailers; they did not shine. They left only flat yellow holes in the darkness.

It took him a long time to get ready, even after she had undressed for him. She waited in the bed with the blankets pulled close, watching him. He adjusted the thermostat and lit candles in the room, turning out the electric lights. He searched through a stack of record albums until he found the right one. She was not sure about the last thing he did: he taped something on the wall behind the bed where he could see it while he laid on top of her. He was shrivelled and white from the cold; he pushed against her body for warmth. He guided her hands to his thighs; he was shivering.

She had returned a last time because she wanted to know what it was he stuck on the wall above the bed. After he finished each time, he reached up and pulled it loose, folding it carefully so that she could not see it. But this time she was ready; she waited for his fast breathing and sudden collapse on top of her. She slid out from under him and stood up beside the bed. She looked at the picture while she got dressed. He did not raise his face from the pillow, and she thought she heard teeth rattling together as she left the room.

♦♦

She heard the old man move when she came in. After the Gussuck's trailer, the log house felt cool. It smelled like dry fish and cured meat. The room was dark except for the blinking yellow flame in the mica window of the oil stove. She squatted in front of the stove and watched the flames for a long time before she walked to the bed where her grandmother had slept. The bed was covered with a mound of rags and fur scraps the old woman had saved. She reached into the mound until she felt something cold and solid wrapped in a wool blanket. She pushed her fingers around it until she felt smooth stone. Long ago, before the Gussucks came, they had burned whale oil in the big stone lamp which made light and heat as well. The old woman had saved everything they would need when the time came.

In the morning, the old man pulled a piece of dry caribou meat from under the blankets and offered it to her. While she was gone, men from the village had brought a bundle of dry meat. She chewed it slowly, thinking about the way they still came from the village to take care of the old man and his stories. But she had a story now, about the red-haired Gussuck. The old man knew what she was thinking, and his smile made his face seem more round than it was.

"Well," he said, "what was it?"

"A woman with a big dog on top of her."

He laughed softly to himself and walked over to the water barrel. He dipped the tin cup into the water.

"It doesn't surprise me," he said.

V

"Grandma," she said, "there was something red in the grass that morning. I remember." She had not asked about her parents before. The old woman stopped splitting the fish bellies open for the willow drying racks. Her jaw muscles pulled so tightly against her skull, the girl thought the old woman would not be able to speak.

"They bought a tin can full of it from the storeman. Late at night. He told them it was alcohol safe to drink. They traded a rifle for it." The old woman's voice sounded like each word stole strength from her. "It made no difference about the rifle. That year the Gussuck boats had come, firing big guns at the walrus and seals. There was nothing left to hunt after that anyway. So," the old lady said, in a low soft voice the girl had not heard for a long time, "I didn't say anything to them when they left that night."

"Right over there," she said, pointing at the fallen poles, half buried in the river sand and tall grass, "in the summer shelter. The sun was high half the night then. Early in the morning when it was still low, the policeman came around. I told the interpreter to tell him that the storeman had poisoned them." She made outlines in the air in front of her, showing how their bodies laid twisted on the sand; telling the story was like laboring to walk through deep snow; sweat shone in the white hair around her forehead. "I told the priest too, after he came. I told him the storeman lied." She turned away from the girl. She held her mouth even tighter, set solidly, not in sorrow or anger, but against the pain, which was all that remained. "I never believed," she said, "not much anyway. I wasn't surprised when the priest did nothing."

The wind came off the river and folded the tall grass into itself like river waves. She could feel the silence the story left, and she wanted to have the old woman go on.

"I heard sounds that night, grandma. Sounds like someone was singing. It was light outside. I could see something red on the ground." The old woman did not answer her; she moved to the tub full of fish on the ground beside the work bench. She stabbed her knife into the belly of a whitefish and lifted it onto the bench. "The Gussuck storeman left the village right after that," the old woman said as she pulled the entrails from the fish, "otherwise, I could tell you more." The old woman's voice flowed with the wind blowing off the river; they never spoke of it again.

When the willows got their leaves and the grass grew tall along the river banks and around the sloughs, she walked early in the morning. While the sun was still low on the horizon, she listened to the wind off the river; its sound was like the voice that day long ago. In the distance, she could hear the engines of the machinery the oil drillers had left the winter before, but she did not go near the village or the store. The sun never left the sky and the summer became the same long day, with only the winds to fan the sun into brightness or allow it to slip into twilight.

She sat beside the old man at his place on the river bank. She poked the smoky fire for him, and felt herself growing wide and thin in the sun as if she had been split from belly to throat and strung on the willow pole in preparation for the winter to come. The old man did not speak anymore. When men from the village brought him fresh fish he hid them deep in the river grass where it was cool. After he went inside, she split the fish open and spread them to dry on the willow frame the way the old woman had done. Inside, he dozed and talked to himself. He had talked all winter, softly and incessantly about the giant polar bear stalking a lone man across Bering Sea ice. After all the months the old man had been telling the story, the bear was within a hundred feet of the man; but the ice fog had closed in on them now and the man could only smell the sharp ammonia odor of the bear, and hear the edge of the snow crust crack under the giant paws.

One night she listened to the old man tell the story all night in his sleep, describing each crystal of ice and the slightly different sounds they made under each paw; first the left and then the right paw, then the hind feet. Her grandmother was there suddenly, a shadow around the stove. She spoke in her low wind voice and the girl was afraid to sit up to hear more clearly. Maybe what she said had been to the old man because he stopped telling the story and began to snore softly the way he had long ago when the old woman had scolded him for telling his stories while others in the house were trying to sleep. But the last words she heard clearly: "It will take a long time, but the story must be told. There must not be any lies." She pulled the blankets up around her chin, slowly, so that her movements would not be seen. She thought her grandmother was talking about the old man's bear story; she did not know about the other story then.

She left the old man wheezing and snoring in his bed. She walked through river grass glistening with frost; the bright green summer color was already fading. She watched the sun move across the sky, already lower on the horizon, already moving away from the village. She stopped by the fallen poles of the summer shelter where her parents had died. Frost glittered on the river sand too; in a few more weeks there would be snow. The predawn light would be the color of an old woman. An old woman sky full of snow. There had been something red lying on the ground the morning they died. She looked for it again, pushing aside the grass with her foot. She knelt in the sand and looked under the fallen structure for some trace of it. When she found it, she would know what the old woman had never told her. She squatted down close to the gray poles and leaned her back against them. The wind made her shiver.

The summer rain had washed the mud from between the logs; the sod blocks stacked as high as her belly next to the log walls had lost their square-cut shape and had grown into soft mounds of tundra moss and stiff-bladed grass bending with clusters of seed bristles. She looked at the northwest, in the direction of the Bering Sea. The cold would come down from there to find narrow slits in the mud, rainwater holes in the outer layer of sod which protected the log house. The dark green tundra stretched away flat and continuous. Somewhere the sea and the land met; she knew by their dark green colors there were no boundaries between them. That was how the cold would come: when the boundaries were gone the polar ice would range across the land into the sky. She watched the horizon for a long time. She would stand in that place on the north side of the house and she would keep watch on the northwest horizon, and eventually she would see it come. She would watch for its approach in the stars, and hear it come with the wind. These preparations were unfamiliar, but gradually she recognized them as she did her own footprints in the snow.

ॐ

She emptied the slop jar beside his bed twice a day and kept the barrel full of water melted from river ice. He did not recognize her anymore, and when he spoke to her, he called her by her grandmother's name and talked about people and events from long ago, before he went back to telling the story. The giant bear was creeping across the new snow on its belly, close enough now that the man could hear the rasp of its breathing. On and on in a soft singing voice, the old man caressed the story, repeating the words again and again like gentle strokes.

The sky was gray like a river crane's egg; its destiny curved into the thin crust of frost already covering the land. She looked at the bright red color of the tin against the ground and the sky and she told the village men to bring the pieces for the old man and her. To drill the test holes in the tundra, the Gussucks had used hundreds of barrels of fuel. The village people split open the empty barrels that were abandoned on the river bank, and pounded the red tin into flat sheets. The village people were using the strips of tin to mend walls and roofs for winter. But she nailed it on the log walls for its color. When she finished, she walked away with the hammer in her hand, not turning around until she was far away, on the ridge above the river banks, and then she looked back. She felt a chill when she saw how the sky and the land were already losing their boundaries, already becoming lost in each other. But the red tin penetrated the thick white color of earth and sky; it defined the boundaries like a wound revealing the ribs and heart of a great caribou about to bolt and be lost to the hunter forever. That night the wind howled and when she scratched a hole through the heavy frost on the inside of the window, she could see nothing but the impenetrable white; whether it was blowing snow or snow that had drifted as high as the house, she did not know.

It had come down suddenly, and she stood with her back to the wind looking at the river, its smoky water clotted with ice. The wind had blown the snow over the frozen river, hiding thin blue streaks where fast water ran under ice translucent and fragile as memory. But she could see shadows of boundaries, outlines of paths which were slender branches of solidity reaching out from the earth. She spent days walking on the river, watching the colors of ice that would safely hold her, kicking the heel of her boot into the snow crust, listening for a solid sound. When she could feel the paths through the soles of her feet, she went to the middle of the river where the fast gray water churned under a thin pane of ice. She looked back. On the river bank in the distance she could see the red tin nailed to the log house, something not swallowed up by the heavy white belly of the sky or caught in the folds of the frozen earth. It was time.

ᚼᚼ

The wolverine fur around the hood of her parka was white with the frost from her breathing. The warmth inside the store melted it, and she felt tiny drops of water on her face. The storeman came in from the back room. She unzipped the parka and stood by the oil stove. She didn't look at him, but stared instead at the yellowish dog, covered with scabs of matted hair, sleeping in front of the stove. She thought of the Gussuck's picture, taped on the wall above the bed and she laughed out loud. The sound of her laughter was piercing; the yellow dog jumped to its feet and the hair bristled down its back. The storeman was watching her. She wanted to laugh again because he didn't know about the ice. He did not know that it was prowling the earth, or that it had already pushed its way into the sky to seize the sun. She sat down in the chair by the stove and shook her long hair loose. He was like a dog tied up all winter, watching while the others got fed. He remembered how she had gone with the oil drillers, and his blue eyes moved like flies crawling over her body. He held his thin pale lips like he wanted to spit on her. He hated the people because they had something of value, the old man said, something which the Gussucks could never have. They thought they could take it, suck it out of the earth or cut it from the mountains; but they were fools.

There was a matted hunk of dog hair on the floor by her foot. She thought of the yellow insulation coming unstuffed: their defense against the freezing going to pieces as it advanced on them. The ice was crouching on the northwest horizon like the old man's bear. She laughed out loud again. The sun would be down now; it was time.

The first time he spoke to her, she did not hear what he said, so she did not answer or even look up at him. He spoke to her again but his words were only noises coming from his pale mouth, trembling now as his anger began to unravel. He jerked her up and the chair fell over behind her. His arms were shaking and she could feel his hands tense up, pulling the edges of the parka tighter. He raised his fist to hit her, his thin body quivering with rage; but the fist collapsed with the desire he had for the valuable things, which, the old man had rightly said, was the only reason they came. She could hear his heart pounding as he held her close and arched his hips against her, groaning and breathing in spasms. She twisted away from him and ducked under his arms.

She ran with a mitten over her mouth, breathing through the fur to protect her lungs from the freezing air. She could hear him running behind her, his heavy breathing, the occasional sound of metal jingling against metal. But he ran without his parka or mittens, breathing the frozen air; its fire squeezed the lungs against the ribs and it was enough that he could not catch her near his store. On the river bank he realized how far he was from his stove, and the wads of yellow stuffing that held off the cold. But the girl was not able to run very fast through the deep drifts at the edge of the river. The twilight was luminous and he could still see clearly for a long distance; he knew he could catch her so he kept running.

When she neared the middle of the river she looked over her shoulder. He was not following her tracks; he went straight across the ice, running the short-est distance to reach her. He was close then: his face was twisted and scarlet from the exertion and the cold. There was satisfaction in his eyes; he was sure he could outrun her.

She was familiar with the river, down to the instant the ice flexed into hair-line fractures, and the cracking bone-sliver sounds gathered momentum with the opening ice until the sound of the churning gray water was set free. She stopped and turned to the sound of the river and the rattle of swirling ice frag-ments where he fell through. She pulled off a mitten and zipped the parka to her throat. She was conscious then of her own rapid breathing.

She moved slowly, kicking the ice ahead with the heel of her boot, feeling for sinews of ice to hold her. She looked ahead and all around herself; in the twi-light, the dense white sky had merged into the flat snow-covered tundra. In the frantic running she had lost her place on the river. She stood still. The east bank of the river was lost in the sky; the boundaries had been swallowed by the freez-ing white. And then, in the distance, she saw something red, and suddenly it was as she had remembered it all those years.

VI

She sat on her bed and while she waited, she listened to the old man. The man had found a small jagged knoll on the ice. He pulled his beaver fur cap off his head; the fur inside it steamed with his body heat and sweat. He left it upside down on the ice for the great bear to stalk, and he waited downwind on top of the ice knoll; he was holding the jade knife.

She thought she could see the end of his story in the way he wheezed out the words; but still he reached into his cache of dry fish and dribbled water into his mouth from the tin cup. All night she listened to him describe each breath the man took, each motion of the bear's head as it tried to catch the sound of the man's breathing, and tested the wind for his scent.

ᏚᏓ

The state trooper asked her questions, and the women who cleaned house for the priest translated them into Yupik. They wanted to know what happened to the storeman, the Gussuck who had been seen running after her down the road onto the river late last evening. He had not come back, and the Gussuck boss in Anchorage was concerned about him. She did not answer for a long time because the old man suddenly sat up in his bed and began to talk excitedly, looking at all of them — the trooper in his dark glasses and the housekeeper in her corduroy parka. He kept saying, "The story! The story! Eh-ya! The great bear! The hunter!"

They asked her again, what happened to the man from the Northern Commercial store. "He lied to them. He told them it was safe to drink. But I will not lie." She stood up and put on the gray wolfskin parka. "I killed him," she said, "but I don't lie."

§§

The attorney came back again, and the jailer slid open the steel doors and opened the cell to let him in. He motioned for the jailer to stay to translate for him. She laughed when she saw how the jailer would be forced by this Gussuck to speak Yupik to her. She liked the Gussuck attorney for that, and for the thinning hair on his head. He was very tall, and she liked to think about the exposure of his head to the freezing; she wondered if he would feel the ice descending from the sky before the others did. He wanted to know why she told the state trooper she had killed the storeman. Some village children had seen it happen, he said, and it was an accident. "That's all you have to say to the judge: it was an accident." He kept repeating it over and over again to her, slowly in a loud but gentle voice: "It was an accident. He was running after you and he fell through the ice. That's all you have to say in court. That's all. And they will let you go home. Back to your village." The jailer translated the words sullenly, staring down at the floor. She shook her head. "I will not change the story, not even to escape this place and go home. I intended that he die. The story must be told as it is." The attorney exhaled loudly; his eyes looked tired. "Tell her that she could not have killed him that way. He was a white man. He ran after her without a parka or mittens. She could not have planned that." He paused and turned toward the cell door. "Tell her I will do all I can for her. I will explain to the judge that her mind is confused." She laughed out loud when the jailer translated what the attorney said. The Gussucks did not understand the story; they could not see the way it must be told, year after year as the old man had done, without lapse or silence.

She looked out the window at the frozen white sky. The sun had finally broken loose from the ice but it moved like a wounded caribou running on strength which only dying animals find, leaping and running on bullet-shattered lungs. Its light was weak and pale; it pushed dimly through the clouds. She turned and faced the Gussuck attorney.

"It began a long time ago," she intoned steadily, "in the summertime. Early in the morning, I remember, something red in the tall river grass. . . ."

§§

The day after the old man died, men from the village came. She was sitting on the edge of her bed, across from the woman the trooper hired to watch her. They came into the room slowly and listened to her. At the foot of her bed they left a king salmon that had been split open wide and dried last summer. But she did not pause or hesitate; she went on with the story, and she never stopped, not even when the woman got up to close the door behind the village men.

⬧⬧

The old man would not change the story even when he knew the end was approaching. Lies could not stop what was coming. He thrashed around on the bed, pulling the blankets loose, knocking bundles of dried fish and meat on the floor. The man had been on the ice for many hours. The freezing winds on the ice knoll had numbed his hands in the mittens, and the cold had exhausted him. He felt a single muscle tremor in his hand that he could not suppress, and the jade knife fell; it shattered on the ice, and the blue glacier bear turned slowly to face him.

Frank Chin
Railroad Standard Time

Ever since the production of his play *The Chickencoop Chinaman* opened in New York in 1972, Frank Chin has been regarded as an important and controversial Asian American writer. His work embraces a book widely taught in universities, *Aiiieeee! An Anthology of Asian American Writers,* two novels, a collection of essays, and a volume of short stories. Educated at the University of California at Berkeley, University of California at Santa Barbara, and the Writers' Workshop at the University of Iowa, he emerged from these institutions with a loathing of white society and a contempt for "Chinatown" Asians who have assimilated into the mainstream, married people of other races, and assumed comfortable lives largely free of ethnic concerns. In Chin's work the protagonists are often "Chinatown Cowboys," as he calls them, strong males aware of their heroic past and eager to assert themselves in the modern present, especially in terms of sexual conquests. His stories, collected in *The Chinaman Pacific & Frisco R. R. Co.,* which won the National Book Award, address these issues in heavily autobiographical narratives that mingle temporal levels among several plot lines. "Railroad Standard Time," which first appeared in *City Lights* in 1978, moves forward and backward in time and shifts concerns from the protagonist's journey to attend his mother's funeral; to speculations about his grandfather, who owned the watch he now possesses; to his own attempt to understand himself and his place in the world.

Frank Chin, "Railroad Standard Time," *The Chinaman Pacific & Frisco R. R. Co.* (Minneapolis: Coffee House Press, 1988), 1–7.

"This was your grandfather's" Ma said. I was twelve, maybe fourteen years old when Grandma died. Ma put it on the table. The big railroad watch, Elgin. Nineteen-jewel movement. American made. Lever set. Stem wound. Glass facecover. Railroad standard all the way. It ticked on the table between stacks of dirty dishes and cold food. She brought me in here to the kitchen, always to the kitchen to loose her thrills and secrets, as if the sound of running water and breathing the warm soggy ghosts of stale food, floating grease, old spices, ever comforted her, as if the kitchen was a paradise for conspiracy, sanctuary for us *juk sing* Chinamen from the royalty of pure-talking China-born Chinese, old, mourning, and belching in the other rooms of my dead grandmother's last house. Here, private, to say in Chinese, "This was your grandfather's," as if now that her mother had died and she'd been up all night long, not weeping, tough and lank, making coffee and tea and little foods for the brokenhearted family in her mother's kitchen, Chinese would be easier for me to understand. As if my mother would say all the important things of the soul and blood to her son, me, only in Chinese from now on. Very few people spoke the language at me the way she did. She chanted a spell up over me that conjured the meaning of what she was saying in the shape of old memories come to call. Words I'd never heard before set me at play in familiar scenes new to me, and ancient.

She lay the watch on the table, eased it slowly off her fingertips down to the tabletop without a sound. She didn't touch me, but put it down and held her hands in front of her like a bridesmaid holding an invisible bouquet and stared at the watch. As if it were talking to her, she looked hard at it, made faces at it, and did not move or answer the voices of the old, calling her from other rooms, until I picked it up.

A two-driver, high stepping locomotive ahead of a coal tender and baggage car, on double track between two semaphores showing a stop signal was engraved on the back.

"Your grandfather collected railroad watches," Ma said. "This one is the best." I held it in one hand and then the other, hefted it, felt out the meaning of "the best," words that rang of meat and vegetables, oils, things we touched, smelled, squeezed, washed, and ate, and I turned the big cased thing over several times. "Grandma gives it to you now," she said. It was big in my hand. Gold. A little greasy. Warm.

I asked her what her father's name had been, and the manic heat of her all-night burnout seemed to go cold and congeal. "Oh," she finally said, "it's one of those Chinese names I . . ." in English, faintly from another world, woozy and her throat and nostrils full of bubbly sniffles, the solemnity of the moment gone, the watch in my hand turned to cheap with the mumbling of a few awful English words. She giggled herself down to nothing but breath and moving lips. She shuffled backward, one step at a time, fox trotting dreamily backwards, one hand dragging on the edge of the table, wobbling the table, rattling the dishes, spilling cold soup. Back down one side of the table, she dropped her butt a little with each step then muscled it back up. There were no chairs in the kitchen tonight. She knew, but still she looked. So this dance and groggy mumbling about the watch being no good, in strange English, like an Indian medicine man in a movie.

I wouldn't give it back or trade it for another out of the collection. This one was mine. No other. It had belonged to my grandfather. I wore it braking on the Southern Pacific, though it was two jewels short of new railroad standard and an outlaw watch that could get me fired. I kept it on me, arrived at my day-off courthouse wedding to its time, wore it as a railroad relic/family heirloom/grin-bringing affectation when I was writing background news in Seattle, reporting from the shadows of race riots, grabbing snaps for the 11:00 P.M., timing today's happenings with a nineteenth-century escapement. (Ride with me, Grandmother.) I was wearing it on my twenty-seventh birthday, the Saturday I came home to see my son asleep in the back of a strange station wagon, and Sarah inside, waving, shouting through an open window, "Goodbye Daddy," over and over.

I stood it. Still and expressionless as some good Chink, I watched Barbara drive off, leave me, like some blonde white goddess going home from the jungle with her leather patches and briar pipe sweetheart writer and my kids. I'll learn to be a sore loser. I'll learn to hit people in the face. I'll learn to cry when I'm hurt and go for the throat instead of being polite and worrying about being obnoxious to people walking out of my house with my things, taking my kids away. I'll be more than quiet, embarrassed. I won't be likable anymore.

I hate my novel about a Chinatown mother like mine dying, now that Ma's dead. But I'll keep it. I hated after reading *Father and Glorious Descendant, Fifth Chinese Daughter, The House That Tai Ming Built.* Books scribbled up by a sad legion of snobby autobiographical Chinatown saps all on their own. Christians who never heard of each other, hardworking people who sweat out the exact same Chinatown book, the same cunning "Confucius says" joke, just like me. I kept it then and I'll still keep it. Part cookbook, memories of Mother in the kitchen slicing meat paper-thin with a cleaver. Mumbo jumbo about spices and steaming. The secret of Chinatown rice. The hands come down toward the food. The food crawls with culture. The thousand-year-old living Chinese meat makes dinner a safari into the unknown, a blood ritual. Food pornography. Black magic. Between the lines, I read a madman's detailed description of the preparation of shrunken heads. I never wrote to mean anything more than word fun with the food Grandma cooked at home. Chinese food. I read a list of what I remembered eating at my grandmother's table and knew I'd always be known by what I ate, that we come from a hungry tradition. Slop eaters following the wars on all fours. Weed cuisine and mud gravy in the shadow of corpses. We plundered the dust for fungus. Buried things. Seeds plucked out of the wind to feed a race of lace-boned skinnys, in high-school English, become transcendental Oriental art to make the dyke-ish spinster teacher cry. We always come to fake art and write the Chinatown book like bugs come to fly in the light. I hate my book now that ma's dead, but I'll keep it. I know she's not the woman I wrote up like my mother, and dead, in a book that was like everybody else's Chinatown book. Part word map of Chinatown San Francisco, shop to shop down Grant Avenue. Food again. The wind sucks the shops out and you breathe warm roast ducks dripping fat, hooks into the neck, through the head, out an eye. Stacks of iced fish, blue and fluorescent pink in the neon. The air is thin soup, sharp up the nostrils.

All mention escape from Chinatown into the movies. But we all forgot to mention how stepping off the streets into a faceful of Charlie Chaplin or a Western on a ripped and stained screen that became caught in the grip of winos breathing in unison in their sleep and billowed in and out, that shuddered when cars went by . . . we all of us Chinamans watched our own MOVIE ABOUT ME! I learned how to box watching movies shot by James Wong Howe. Cartoons were our nursery rhymes. Summers inside those neon-and-stucco downtown hole-in-the-wall Market Street Frisco movie houses blowing three solid hours of full-color seven-minute cartoons was school, was rows and rows of Chinamans learning English in a hurry from Daffy Duck.

When we ate in the dark and recited the dialogue of cartoon mice and cats out loud in various tones of voice with our mouths full, we looked like people singing hymns in church. We learned to talk like everybody in America. Learned to need to be afraid to stay alive, keep moving. We learned to run, to be cheerful losers, to take a sudden pie in the face, talk American with a lot of giggles. To us a cartoon is a desperate situation. Of the movies, cartoons were the high art of our claustrophobia. They understood us living too close to each other. How, when you're living too close to too many people, you can't wait for one thing more without losing your mind. Cartoons were a fine way out of waiting in Chinatown around the rooms. Those of our Chinamans who every now and then break a reverie with, "Thank you, Mighty Mouse," mean it. Other folks thank Porky Pig, Snuffy Smith, Woody Woodpecker.

The day my mother told me I was to stay home from Chinese school one day a week starting today, to read to my father and teach him English while he was captured in total paralysis from a vertebra in the neck on down, I stayed away from cartoons. I went to a matinee in a white neighborhood looking for the MOVIE ABOUT ME and was the only Chinaman in the house. I liked the way Peter Lorre ran along non-stop routine hysterical. I came back home with Peter Lorre. I turned out the lights in Pa's room. I put a candle on the dresser and wheeled Pa around in his chair to see me in front of the dresser mirror, reading Edgar Allan Poe out loud to him in the voice of Peter Lorre by candlelight.

The old men in the Chinatown books are all fixtures for Chinese ceremonies. All the same. Loyal filial children kowtow to the old and whiff food laid out for the dead. The dead eat the same as the living but without the sauces. White food. Steamed chicken. Rice we all remember as children scrambling down to the ground, to all fours and bonking our heads on the floor, kowtowing to a dead chicken.

My mother and aunts said nothing about the men of the family except they were weak. I like to think my grandfather was a good man. Even the kiss-ass steward service, I like to think he was tough, had a few laughs and ran off with his pockets full of engraved watches. Because I never knew him, not his name, nor anything about him, except a photograph of him as a young man with something of my mother's face in his face, and a watch chain across his vest. I kept his watch in good repair and told everyone it would pass to my son some-day, until the day the boy was gone. Then I kept it like something of his he'd loved and had left behind, saving it for him maybe, to give to him when he was a man. But I haven't felt that in a long time.

The watch ticked against my heart and pounded my chest as I went too fast over bumps in the night and the radio on, on an all-night run downcoast, down country, down old Highway 99, Interstate 5, I ran my grandfather's time down past road signs that caught a gleam in my headlights and came at me out of the night with the names of forgotten high school girlfriends, BELLEVUE KIRKLAND, ROBERTA GERBER, AURORA CANBY, and sang with the radio to Jonah and Sarah in Berkeley, my Chinatown in Oakland and Frisco, to raise the dead. Ride with me, Grandfather, this is your grandson the ragmouth, called Tampax, the burned scarred boy, called Barbecue, going to San Francisco to bury my mother, your daughter, and spend Chinese New Year's at home. When we were sitting down and into our dinner after Grandma's funeral, and ate in front of the table set with white food for the dead, Ma said she wanted no white food and money burning after her funeral. Her sisters were there. Her sisters took charge of her funeral and the dinner afterwards. The dinner would most likely be in a Chinese restaurant in Frisco. Nobody had these dinners at home anymore. I wouldn't mind people having dinner at my place after my funeral, but no white food.

The whiz goes out of the tires as their roll bites into the steel grating of the Carquinez Bridge. The noise of the engine groans and echoes like a bomber in flight through the steel roadway. Light from the water far below shines through the grate, and I'm driving high, above a glow. The voice of the tires hums a shrill rubber screechy mosquito hum that vibrates through the chassis and frame of the car into my meatless butt, into my tender asshole, my pelvic bones, the roots of my teeth. Over the Carquinez Bridge to CROCKETT MARTINEZ closer to home, roll the tires of Ma's Chevy, my car now, carrying me up over the water southwest toward rolls of fog. The fat man's coming home on a sneaky breeze. Dusk comes a drooly mess of sunlight, a slobber of cheap pawnshop gold, a slow building heat across the water, all through the milky air through the glass of the window into the closed atmosphere of a driven car, into one side of my bomber's face. A bomber, flying my mother's car into the unknown charted by the stars and the ra-dio, feels the coming of some old night song climbing hand over hand, bass notes plunking as steady and shady as reminiscence to get on my nerves one stupid beat after the other crossing the high rhythm six-step of the engine. I drive through the shadows of the bridge's steel structure all over the road. Fine day. I've been on the road for sixteen hours straight down the music of Seattle, Spokane, Salt Lake, Sacramento, Los Angeles, and Wolfman Jack lurking in odd hours of darkness, at peculiar altitudes of darkness, favoring the depths of certain Oregon valleys and heat and moonlight of my miles. And I'm still alive. Country 'n' western music for the night road. It's pure white music. Like "The Star-Spangled Banner," it was the first official American music out of school into my jingling earbones sung by sighing white big tits in front of the climbing promise of FACE and Every Good Boy Does Fine chalked on the blackboard.

She stood up singing, one hand cupped in the other as if to catch drool slipping off her lower lip. Our eyes scouted through her blouse to elastic straps, lacy stuff, circular stitching, buckles, and in the distance, finally some skin. The color of her skin spread through the stuff of her blouse like melted butter through bread nicely to our tongues and was warm there. She sat flopping them on the keyboard as she breathed, singing "Home on the Range" over her shoulder, and pounded the tune out with her palms. The lonesome prairie was nothing but her voice, some hearsay country she stood up to sing *a capella* out of her. Simple music you can count. You can hear the words clear. The music's run through Clorox and Simonized, beating so insistently right and regular that you feel to sing it will deodorize you, make you clean. The hardhat hit parade. I listen to it a lot on the road. It's that get-outta-town beat and tune that makes me go.

Mrs. Morales was her name. Aurora Morales. The music teacher us boys liked to con into singing for us. Come-on opera, we wanted from her, not them Shirley Temple tunes the girls wanted to learn, but big notes, high long ones up from the navel that drilled through plaster and steel and skin and meat for bone marrow and electric wires on one long titpopping breath.

This is how I come home, riding a mass of spasms and death throes, warm and screechy inside, itchy, full of ghostpiss, as I drive right past what's left of Oakland's dark wooden Chinatown and dark streets full of dead lettuce and trampled carrot tops, parallel all the time in line with the tracks of the Western Pacific and Southern Pacific railroads.

Andre Dubus

Killings

Andre Dubus is considered to be a literary descendant of Ernest Hemingway in exploring the psychological effects of violence, especially that within families. Writing direct prose in a plain style, his unpretentious approach to fiction has earned him a substantial reputation that has grown from his first book in 1967. Born of Cajun descent in Lake Charles, Louisiana, he was educated at McNeese State College, where he took a B.A. in English, and at the Iowa Writers' Workshop, where he earned an M.F.A. For two decades he taught English at Bradford College in Massachusetts, the setting for much of his work. In 1986 he was struck by a car while assisting a stranded driver north of Boston, and he spent the rest of his life in a wheelchair, dying in 1999. His fiction has attracted not only a wide audience but prestigious awards as well, including a MacArthur fellowship, a Guggenheim fellowship, and a National Endowment for the Arts grant. One of his most celebrated stories, "Killings" first appeared in the *Sewannee Review* in 1979 and was collected in *Finding a Girl in America: Ten Stories and a Novella* the following year. In 2001 it was made into a major motion picture under the title *In the Bedroom.* In a strong narrative line, it explores the morality of murder and revenge, the psychic weight a man of conscience must carry to bring justice and peace to his family. The plurality of "killings" suggested by the title points to the contrasting meaning of the two murders in the story and the dramatic consequences that flow from each of them.

Andre Dubus, "Killings," *Finding a Girl in America: Ten Stories and a Novella* (Boston: David R. Godine, 1980), 3–20.

On the August morning when Matt Fowler buried his youngest son, Frank, who had lived for twenty-one years, eight months, and four days, Matt's older son, Steve, turned to him as the family left the grave and walked between their friends, and said: "I should kill him." He was twenty-eight, his brown hair starting to thin in front where he used to have a cowlick. He bit his lower lip, wiped his eyes, then said it again. Ruth's arm, linked with Matt's, tightened; he looked at her. Beneath her eyes there was swelling from the three days she had suffered. At the limousine Matt stopped and looked back at the grave, the casket, and the Congregationalist minister who he thought had probably had a difficult job with the eulogy though he hadn't seemed to, and the old funeral director who was saying something to the six young pallbearers. The grave was on a hill and overlooked the Merrimack, which he could not see from where he stood; he looked at the opposite bank, at the apple orchard with its symmetrically planted trees going up a hill.

Next day Steve drove with his wife back to Baltimore where he managed the branch office of a bank, and Cathleen, the middle child, drove her husband back to Syracuse. They had left the grandchildren with friends. A month after the funeral Matt played poker at Willis Trottier's because Ruth, who knew this was the second time he had been invited, told him to go, he couldn't sit home with her for the rest of her life, she was all right. After the game Willis went outside to tell everyone goodnight and, when the others had driven away, he walked with Matt to his car. Willis was a short, silver-haired man who had opened a diner after World War II, his trade then mostly very early breakfast, which he cooked, and then lunch for the men who worked at the leather and shoe factories. He now owned a large restaurant.

"He walks the Goddamn streets," Matt said.

"I know. He was in my place last night, at the bar. With a girl."

"I don't see him. I'm in the store all the time. Ruth sees him. She sees him too much. She was at Sunnyhurst today getting cigarettes and aspirin, and there he was. She can't even go out for cigarettes and aspirin. It's killing her."

"Come back in for a drink."

Matt looked at his watch. Ruth would be asleep. He walked with Willis back into the house, pausing at the steps to look at the starlit sky. It was a cool summer night; he thought vaguely of the Red Sox, did not even know if they were at home tonight; since it happened he had not been able to think about any of the small pleasures he believed he had earned, as he had earned also what was shattered now forever: the quietly harried and quietly pleasurable days of fatherhood. They went inside. Willis's wife, Martha, had gone to bed hours ago, in the rear of the large house which was rigged with burglar and fire alarms. They went downstairs to the game room: the television set suspended from the ceiling, the pool table, the poker table with beer cans, cards, chips, filled ashtrays, and the six chairs where Matt and his friends had sat, the friends picking up the old banter as though he had only been away on vacation; but he could see the affection and courtesy in their eyes. Willis went behind the bar and mixed them each a Scotch and soda; he stayed behind the bar and looked at Matt sitting on the stool.

"How often have you thought about it?" Willis said.

"Every day since he got out. I didn't think about bail. I thought I wouldn't have to worry about him for years. She sees him all the time. It makes her cry."

"He was in my place a long time last night. He'll be back."

"Maybe he won't."

"The band. He likes the band."

"What's he doing now?"

"He's tending bar up to Hampton Beach. For a friend. Ever notice even the worst bastard always has friends? He couldn't get work in town. It's just tourists and kids up to Hampton. Nobody knows him. If they do, they don't care. They drink what he mixes."

"Nobody tells me about him."

"I hate him, Matt. My boys went to school with him. He was the same then. Know what he'll do? Five at the most. Remember that woman about seven years ago? Shot her husband and dropped him off the bridge in the Merrimack with a hundred pound sack of cement and said all the way through it that nobody helped her. Know where she is now? She's in Lawrence now, a secretary. And whoever helped her, where the hell is he?"

"I've got a .38 I've had for years. I take it to the store now. I tell Ruth it's for the night deposits. I tell her things have changed: we got junkies here now too. Lots of people without jobs. She knows though."

"What does she know?"

"She knows I started carrying it after the first time she saw him in town. She knows it's in case I see him, and there's some kind of a situation —"

He stopped, looked at Willis, and finished his drink. Willis mixed him another.

"What kind of a situation?"

"Where he did something to me. Where I could get away with it."

"How does Ruth feel about that?"

"She doesn't know."

"You said she does, she's got it figured out."

He thought of her that afternoon: when she went into Sunnyhurst, Strout was waiting at the counter while the clerk bagged the things he had bought; she turned down an aisle and looked at soup cans until he left.

"Ruth would shoot him herself, if she thought she could hit him."

"You got a permit?"

"No."

"I do. You could get a year for that."

"Maybe I'll get one. Or maybe I won't. Maybe I'll just stop bringing it to the store."

⁂

Richard Strout was twenty-six years old, a high school athlete, football scholarship to the University of Massachusetts where he lasted for almost two semesters before quitting in advance of the final grades that would have forced him not to return. People then said: Dickie can do the work; he just doesn't want to. He came home and did construction work for his father but refused his father's offer to learn the business; his two older brothers had learned it, so that Strout and Sons trucks going about town, and signs on construction sites, now slashed wounds into Matt Fowler's life. Then Richard married a young girl and became a bartender, his salary and tips augmented and perhaps sometimes matched by his father, who also posted his bond. So his friends, his enemies (he had those: fist fights or, more often, boys and then young men who had not fought him when they thought they should have), and those who simply knew him by face and name, had a series of images of him which they recalled when they heard of the killing: the high school running back, the young drunk in bars, the oblivious hard-hatted young man eating lunch at a counter, the bartender who could perhaps be called courteous but not more than that: as he tended bar, his dark eyes and dark, wide-jawed face appeared less sullen, near blank.

One night he beat Frank. Frank was living at home and waiting for September, for graduate school in economics, and working as a lifeguard at Salisbury Beach, where he met Mary Ann Strout, in her first month of separation. She spent most days at the beach with her two sons. Before ten o'clock one night Frank came home; he had driven to the hospital first, and he walked into the living room with stitches over his right eye and both lips bright and swollen.

"I'm all right," he said, when Matt and Ruth stood up, and Matt turned off the television, letting Ruth get to him first: the tall, muscled but slender sun-tanned boy. Frank tried to smile at them but couldn't because of his lips.

"It was her husband, wasn't it?" Ruth said.

"Ex," Frank said. "He dropped in."

Matt gently held Frank's jaw and turned his face to the light, looked at the stitches, the blood under the white of the eye, the bruised flesh.

"Press charges," Matt said.

"No."

"What's to stop him from doing it again? Did you hit him at all? Enough so he won't want to next time?"

"I don't think I touched him."

"So what are you going to do?"

"Take karate," Frank said, and tried again to smile.

"That's not the problem," Ruth said.

"You know you like her," Frank said.

"I like a lot of people. What about the boys? Did they see it?"

"They were asleep."

"Did you leave her alone with him?"

"He left first. She was yelling at him. I believe she had a skillet in her hand."

"Oh for God's sake," Ruth said.

Matt had been dealing with that too: at the dinner table on evenings when Frank wasn't home, was eating with Mary Ann; or, on the other nights — and Frank was with her every night — he talked with Ruth while they watched television, or lay in bed with the windows open and he smelled the night air and imagined, with both pride and muted sorrow, Frank in Mary Ann's arms. Ruth didn't like it because Mary Ann was in the process of divorce, because she had two children, because she was four years older than Frank, and finally — she told this in bed, where she had during all of their marriage told him of her deepest feelings: of love, of passion, of fears about one of the children, of pain Matt had caused her or she had caused him — she was against it because of what she had heard: that the marriage had gone bad early, and for most of it Richard and Mary Ann had both played around.

"That can't be true," Matt said. "Strout wouldn't have stood for it."

"Maybe he loves her."

"He's too hot-tempered. He couldn't have taken that."

But Matt knew Strout had taken it, for he had heard the stories too. He wondered who had told them to Ruth; and he felt vaguely annoyed and isolated: living with her for thirty-one years and still not knowing what she talked about with her friends. On these summer nights he did not so much argue with her as try to comfort her, but finally there was no difference between the two: she had concrete objections, which he tried to overcome. And in his attempt to do this, he neglected his own objections, which were the same as hers, so that as he spoke to her he felt as disembodied as he sometimes did in the store when he helped a man choose a blouse or dress or piece of costume jewelry for his wife.

"The divorce doesn't mean anything," he said. "She was young and maybe she liked his looks and then after a while she realized she was living with a bastard. I see it as a positive thing."

"She's not divorced yet."

"It's the same thing. Massachusetts has crazy laws, that's all. Her age is no problem. What's it matter when she was born? And that other business: even if it's true, which it probably isn't, it's got nothing to do with Frank, it's in the past. And the kids are no problem. She's been married six years; she ought to have kids. Frank likes them. He plays with them. And he's not going to marry her anyway, so it's not a problem of money."

"Then what's he doing with her?"

"She probably loves him, Ruth. Girls always have. Why can't we just leave it at that?"

"He got home at six o'clock Tuesday morning."

"I didn't know you knew. I've already talked to him about it."

Which he had: since he believed almost nothing he told Ruth, he went to Frank with what he believed. The night before, he had followed Frank to the car after dinner.

"You wouldn't make much of a burglar," he said.

"How's that?"

Matt was looking up at him; Frank was six feet tall, an inch and a half taller than Matt, who had been proud when Frank at seventeen outgrew him; he had only felt uncomfortable when he had to reprimand or caution him. He touched Frank's bicep, thought of the young taut passionate body, believed he could sense the desire, and again he felt the pride and sorrow and envy too, not knowing whether he was envious of Frank or Mary Ann.

"When you came in yesterday morning, I woke up. One of these mornings your mother will. And I'm the one who'll have to talk to her. She won't interfere with you. Okay? I know it means —" But he stopped, thinking: I know it means getting up and leaving that suntanned girl and going sleepy to the car, I know —

"Okay," Frank said, and touched Matt's shoulder and got into the car.

There had been other talks, but the only long one was their first one: a night driving to Fenway Park, Matt having ordered the tickets so they could talk, and knowing when Frank said yes, he would go, that he knew the talk was coming too. It took them forty minutes to get to Boston, and they talked about Mary Ann until they joined the city traffic along the Charles River, blue in the late sun. Frank told him all the things that Matt would later pretend to believe when he told them to Ruth.

"It seems like a lot for a young guy to take on," Matt finally said.

"Sometimes it is. But she's worth it."

"Are you thinking about getting married?"

"We haven't talked about it. She can't for over a year. I've got school."

"I *do* like her," Matt said.

He did. Some evenings, when the long summer sun was still low in the sky, Frank brought her home; they came into the house smelling of suntan lotion and the sea, and Matt gave them gin and tonics and started the charcoal in the backyard, and looked at Mary Ann in the lawn chair: long and very light brown hair (Matt thinking that twenty years ago she would have dyed it blonde), and the long brown legs he loved to look at; her face was pretty; she had probably never in her adult life gone unnoticed into a public place. It was in her wide brown eyes that she looked older than Frank; after a few drinks Matt thought what he saw in her eyes was something erotic, testament to the rumors about her; but he knew it wasn't that, or all that: she had, very young, been through a sort of pain that his children, and he and Ruth, had been spared. In the moments of his recognizing that pain, he wanted to tenderly touch her hair, wanted with some gesture to give her solace and hope. And he would glance at Frank, and hope they would love each other, hope Frank would soothe that pain in her heart, take it from her eyes; and her divorce, her age, and her children did not matter at all. On the first two evenings she did not bring her boys, and then Ruth asked her to bring them next time. In bed that night Ruth said, "She hasn't brought them because she's embarrassed. She shouldn't feel embarrassed."

§§

Richard Strout shot Frank in front of the boys. They were sitting on the living room floor watching television, Frank sitting on the couch, and Mary Ann just returning from the kitchen with a tray of sandwiches. Strout came in the front door and shot Frank twice in the chest and once in the face with a 9 mm. automatic. Then he looked at the boys and Mary Ann, and went home to wait for the police.

It seemed to Matt that from the time Mary Ann called weeping to tell him until now, a Saturday night in September, sitting in the car with Willis, parked beside Strout's car, waiting for the bar to close, that he had not so much moved through his life as wandered through it, his spirit like a dazed body bumping into furniture and corners. He had always been a fearful father: when his children were young, at the start of each summer he thought of them drowning in a pond or the sea, and he was relieved when he came home in the evenings and they were there; usually that relief was his only acknowledgment of his fear, which he never spoke of, and which he controlled within his heart. As he had when they were very young and all of them in turn, Cathleen too, were drawn to the high oak in the backyard, and had to climb it. Smiling, he watched them, imagining the fall: and he was poised to catch the small body before it hit the earth. Or his legs were poised; his hands were in his pockets or his arms were folded and, for the child looking down, he appeared relaxed and confident while his heart beat with the two words he wanted to call out but did not: *Don't fall.* In winter he was less afraid: he made sure the ice would hold him before they skated, and he brought or sent them to places where they could sled without ending in the street. So he and his children had survived their childhood, and he only worried about them when he knew they were driving a long distance, and then he lost Frank in a way no father expected to lose his son, and he felt that all the fears he had borne while they were growing up, and all the grief he had been afraid of, had backed up like a huge wave and struck him on the beach and swept him out to sea. Each day he felt the same and when he was able to forget how he felt, when he was able to force himself not to feel that way, the eyes of his clerks and customers defeated him. He wished those eyes were oblivious, even cold; he felt he was withering in their tenderness. And beneath his listless wandering, every day in his soul he shot Richard Strout in the face; while Ruth, going about town on errands, kept seeing him. And at nights in bed she would hold Matt and cry, or sometimes she was silent and Matt would touch her tightening arm, her clenched fist.

As his own right fist was now, squeezing the butt of the revolver, the last of the drinkers having left the bar, talking to each other, going to their separate cars which were in the lot in front of the bar, out of Matt's vision. He heard their voices, their cars, and then the ocean again, across the street. The tide was in and sometimes it smacked the sea wall. Through the windshield he looked at the dark red side wall of the bar, and then to his left, past Willis, at Strout's car, and through its windows he could see the now-emptied parking lot, the road, the sea wall. He could smell the sea.

The front door of the bar opened and closed again and Willis looked at Matt then at the corner of the building; when Strout came around it alone Matt got out of the car, giving up the hope he had kept all night (and for the past week) that Strout would come out with friends, and Willis would simply drive away; thinking: *All right then. All right*; and he went around the front of Willis's car, and at Strout's he stopped and aimed over the hood at Strout's blue shirt ten feet away. Willis was aiming too, crouched on Matt's left, his elbow resting on the hood.

"Mr. Fowler," Strout said. He looked at each of them, and at the guns. "Mr. Trottier."

Then Matt, watching the parking lot and the road, walked quickly between the car and the building and stood behind Strout. He took one leather glove from his pocket and put it on his left hand.

"Don't talk. Unlock the front and back and get in."

Strout unlocked the front door, reached in and unlocked the back, then got in, and Matt slid into the back seat, closed the door with his gloved hand, and touched Strout's head once with the muzzle.

"It's cocked. Drive to your house."

When Strout looked over his shoulder to back the car, Matt aimed at his temple and did not look at his eyes.

"Drive slowly," he said. "Don't try to get stopped."

They drove across the empty front lot and onto the road, Willis's headlights shining into the car; then back through town, the sea wall on the left hiding the beach, though far out Matt could see the ocean; he uncocked the revolver; on the right were the places, most with their neon signs off, that did so much business in summer: the lounges and cafés and pizza houses, the street itself empty of traffic, the way he and Willis had known it would be when they decided to take Strout at the bar rather than knock on his door at two o'clock one morning and risk that one insomniac neighbor. Matt had not told Willis he was afraid he could not be alone with Strout for very long, smell his smells, feel the presence of his flesh, hear his voice, and then shoot him. They left the beach town and then were on the high bridge over the channel: to the left the smacking curling white at the breakwater and beyond that the dark sea and the full moon, and down to his right the small fishing boats bobbing at anchor in the cove. When they left the bridge, the sea was blocked by abandoned beach cottages, and Matt's left hand was sweating in the glove. Out here in the dark in the car he believed Ruth knew. Willis had come to his house at eleven and asked if he wanted a nightcap; Matt went to the bedroom for his wallet, put the gloves in one trouser pocket and the .38 in the other and went back to the living room, his hand in his pocket covering the bulge of the cool cylinder pressed against his fingers, the butt against his palm. When Ruth said goodnight she looked at his face, and he felt she could see in his eyes the gun, and the night he was going to. But he knew he couldn't trust what he saw. Willis's wife had taken her sleeping pill, which gave her eight hours — the reason, Willis had told Matt, he had the alarms installed, for nights when he was late at the restaurant — and when it was all done and Willis got home he would leave ice and a trace of Scotch and soda in two glasses in the game room and tell Martha in the morning that he had left the restaurant early and brought Matt home for a drink.

"He was making it with my wife." Strout's voice was careful, not pleading.

Matt pressed the muzzle against Strout's head, pressed it harder than he wanted to, feeling through the gun Strout's head flinching and moving forward; then he lowered the gun to his lap.

"Don't talk," he said.

Strout did not speak again. They turned west, drove past the Dairy Queen closed until spring, and the two lobster restaurants that faced each other and were crowded all summer and were now also closed, onto the short bridge crossing the tidal stream, and over the engine Matt could hear through his open window the water rushing inland under the bridge; looking to his left he saw its swift moonlit current going back into the marsh which, leaving the bridge, they entered: the salt marsh stretching out on both sides, the grass tall in patches but mostly low and leaning earthward as though windblown, a large dark rock sitting as though it rested on nothing but itself, and shallow pools reflecting the bright moon.

Beyond the marsh they drove through woods, Matt thinking now of the hole he and Willis had dug last Sunday afternoon after telling their wives they were going to Fenway Park. They listened to the game on a transistor radio, but heard none of it as they dug into the soft earth on the knoll they had chosen because elms and maples sheltered it. Already some leaves had fallen. When the hole was deep enough they covered it and the piled earth with dead branches, then cleaned their shoes and pants and went to a restaurant farther up in New Hampshire where they ate sandwiches and drank beer and watched the rest of the game on television. Looking at the back of Strout's head he thought of Frank's grave; he had not been back to it; but he would go before winter, and its second burial of snow.

He thought of Frank sitting on the couch and perhaps talking to the children as they watched television, imagined him feeling young and strong, still warmed from the sun at the beach, and feeling loved, hearing Mary Ann moving about in the kitchen, hearing her walking into the living room; maybe he looked up at her and maybe she said something, looking at him over the tray of sandwiches, smiling at him, saying something the way women do when they offer food as a gift, then the front door opening and this son of a bitch coming in and Frank seeing that he meant the gun in his hand, this son of a bitch and his gun the last person and thing Frank saw on earth.

When they drove into town the streets were nearly empty: a few slow cars, a policeman walking his beat past the darkened fronts of stores. Strout and Matt both glanced at him as they drove by. They were on the main street, and all the stoplights were blinking yellow. Willis and Matt had talked about that too: the lights changed at midnight, so there would be no place Strout had to stop and where he might try to run. Strout turned down the block where he lived and Willis's headlights were no longer with Matt in the back seat. They had planned that too, had decided it was best for just the one car to go to the house, and again Matt had said nothing about his fear of being alone with Strout, especially in his house: a duplex, dark as all the houses on the street were, the street itself lit at the corner of each block. As Strout turned into the driveway Matt thought of the one insomniac neighbor, thought of some man or woman sitting alone in the dark living room, watching the all-night channel from Boston. When Strout stopped the car near the front of the house, Matt said: "Drive it to the back."

He touched Strout's head with the muzzle.

"You wouldn't have it cocked, would you? For when I put on the brakes."

Matt cocked it, and said: "It is now."

Strout waited a moment; then he eased the car foward, the engine doing little more than idling, and as they approached the garage he gently braked. Matt opened the door, then took off the glove and put it in his pocket. He stepped out and shut the door with his hip and said: "All right."

Strout looked at the gun, then got out, and Matt followed him across the grass, and as Strout unlocked the door Matt looked quickly at the row of small backyards on either side, and scattered tall trees, some evergreens, others not, and he thought of the red and yellow leaves on the trees over the hole, saw them falling soon, probably in two weeks, dropping slowly, covering. Strout stepped into the kitchen.

"Turn on the light."

Strout reached to the wall switch, and in the light Matt looked at his wide back, the dark blue shirt, the white belt, the red plaid pants.

"Where's your suitcase?"

"My suitcase?"

"Where is it."

"In the bedroom closet."

"That's where we're going then. When we get to a door you stop and turn on the light."

They crossed the kitchen, Matt glancing at the sink and stove and refrigerator: no dishes in the sink or even the dish rack beside it, no grease splashings on the stove, the refrigerator door clean and white. He did not want to look at any more but he looked quickly at all he could see: in the living room magazines and newspapers in a wicker basket, clean ashtrays, a record player, the records shelved next to it, then down the hall where, near the bedroom door, hung a color photograph of Mary Ann and the two boys sitting on a lawn — there was no house in the picture — Mary Ann smiling at the camera or Strout or whoever held the camera, smiling as she had on Matt's lawn this summer while he waited for the charcoal and they all talked and he looked at her brown legs and at Frank touching her arm, her shoulder, her hair; he moved down the hall with her smile in his mind, wondering: was that when they were both playing around and she was smiling like that at him and they were happy, even sometimes, making it worth it? He recalled her eyes, the pain in them, and he was conscious of the circles of love he was touching with the hand that held the revolver so tightly now as Strout stopped at the door at the end of the hall.

"There's no wall switch."

"Where's the light?"

"By the bed."

"Let's go."

Matt stayed a pace behind, then Strout leaned over and the room was lighted: the bed, a double one, was neatly made; the ashtray on the bedside table clean, the bureau top dustless, and no photographs; probably so the girl — who *was* she? — would not have to see Mary Ann in the bedroom she believed was theirs. But because Matt was a father and a husband, though never an ex-husband, he knew (and did not want to know) that this bedroom had never been theirs alone. Strout turned around; Matt looked at his lips, his wide jaw, and thought of Frank's doomed and fearful eyes looking up from the couch.

"Where's Mr. Trottier?"

"He's waiting. Pack clothes for warm weather."

"What's going on?"

"You're jumping bail."

"Mr. Fowler —"

He pointed the cocked revolver at Strout's face. The barrel trembled but not much, not as much as he had expected. Strout went to the closet and got the suitcase from the floor and opened it on the bed. As he went to the bureau, he said: "He was making it with my wife. I'd go pick up my kids and he'd be there. Sometimes he spent the night. My boys told me."

He did not look at Matt as he spoke. He opened the top drawer and Matt stepped closer so he could see Strout's hands: underwear and socks, the socks rolled, the underwear folded and stacked. He took them back to the bed, arranged them neatly in the suitcase, then from the closet he was taking shirts and trousers and a jacket; he laid them on the bed and Matt followed him to the bathroom and watched from the door while he packed his shaving kit; watched in the bedroom as he folded and packed those things a person accumulated and that became part of him so that at times in the store Matt felt he was selling more than clothes.

"I wanted to try to get together with her again." He was bent over the suitcase. "I couldn't even talk to her. He was always with her. I'm going to jail for it; if I ever get out I'll be an old man. Isn't that enough?"

"You're not going to jail."

Strout closed the suitcase and faced Matt, looking at the gun. Matt went to his rear, so Strout was between him and the lighted hall; then using his handkerchief he turned off the lamp and said: "Let's go."

They went down the hall, Matt looking again at the photograph, and through the living room and kitchen, Matt turning off the lights and talking, frightened that he was talking, that he was telling this lie he had not planned: "It's the trial. We can't go through that, my wife and me. So you're leaving. We've got you a ticket, and a job. A friend of Mr. Trottier's. Out west. My wife keeps seeing you. We can't have that anymore."

Matt turned out the kitchen light and put the handkerchief in his pocket, and they went down the two brick steps and across the lawn. Strout put the suitcase on the floor of the back seat, then got into the front seat and Matt got in the back and put on his glove and shut the door.

"They'll catch me. They'll check passenger lists."

"We didn't use your name."

"They'll figure that out too. You think I wouldn't have done it myself if it was that easy?"

He backed into the street, Matt looking down the gun barrel but not at the profiled face beyond it.

"You were alone," Matt said. "We've got it worked out."

"There's no planes this time of night, Mr. Fowler."

"Go back through town. Then north on 125."

They came to the corner and turned, and now Willis's headlights were in the car with Matt.

"Why north, Mr. Fowler?"

"Somebody's going to keep you for a while. They'll take you to the airport." He uncocked the hammer and lowered the revolver to his lap and said wearily: "No more talking."

As they drove back through town, Matt's body sagged, going limp with his spirit and its new and false bond with Strout, the hope his lie had given Strout. He had grown up in this town whose streets had become places of apprehension and pain for Ruth as she drove and walked, doing what she had to do; and for him too, if only in his mind as he worked and chatted six days a week in his store; he wondered now if his lie would have worked, if sending Strout away would have been enough; but then he knew that just thinking of Strout in Montana or whatever place lay at the end of the lie he had told, thinking of him walking the streets there, loving a girl there (who *was* she?) would be enough to slowly rot the rest of his days. And Ruth's. Again he was certain that she knew, that she was waiting for him.

They were in New Hampshire now, on the narrow highway, passing the shopping center at the state line, and then houses and small stores and sandwich shops. There were few cars on the road. After ten minutes he raised his tembling hand, touched Strout's neck with the gun, and said: "Turn in up here. At the dirt road."

Strout flicked on the indicator and slowed.

"Mr. Fowler?"

"They're waiting here."

Strout turned very slowly, easing his neck away from the gun. In the moonlight the road was light brown, lighter and yellowed where the headlights shone; weeds and a few trees grew on either side of it, and ahead of them were the woods.

"There's nothing back here, Mr. Fowler."

"It's for your car. You don't think we'd leave it at the airport, do you?"

He watched Strout's large, big-knuckled hands tighten on the wheel, saw

Frank's face that night: not the stitches and bruised eye and swollen lips, but his own hand gently touching Frank's jaw, turning his wounds to the light. They rounded a bend in the road and were out of sight of the highway: tall trees all around them now, hiding the moon. When they reached the abandoned gravel pit on the left, the bare flat earth and steep pale embankment behind it, and the black crowns of trees at its top, Matt said: "Stop here."

Strout stopped but did not turn off the engine. Matt pressed the gun hard against his neck, and he straightened in the seat and looked in the rearview mirror, Matt's eyes meeting his in the glass for an instant before looking at the hair at the end of the gun barrel.

"Turn it off."

Strout did, then held the wheel with two hands, and looked in the mirror.

"I'll do twenty years, Mr. Fowler; at least. I'll be forty-six years old."

"That's nine years younger than I am," Matt said, and got out and took off the glove and kicked the door shut. He aimed at Strout's ear and pulled back the hammer. Willis's headlights were off and Matt heard him walking on the soft thin layer of dust, the hard earth beneath it. Strout opened the door, sat for a moment in the interior light, then stepped out onto the road. Now his face was pleading. Matt did not look at his eyes, but he could see it in the lips.

"Just get the suitcase. They're right up the road."

Willis was beside him now, to his left. Strout looked at both guns. Then he opened the back door, leaned in, and with a jerk brought the suitcase out. He was turning to face them when Matt said: "Just walk up the road. Just ahead."

Strout turned to walk, the suitcase in his right hand, and Matt and Willis followed; as Strout cleared the front of his car he dropped the suitcase and, ducking, took one step that was the beginning of a sprint to his right. The gun kicked in Matt's hand, and the explosion of the shot surrounded him, isolated him in a nimbus of sound that cut him off from all his time, all his history, isolated him standing absolutely still on the dirt road with the gun in his hand, looking down at Richard Strout squirming on his belly, kicking one leg behind him, pushing himself forward, toward the woods. Then Matt went to him and shot him once in the back of the head.

ۏۏ

Driving south to Boston, wearing both gloves now, staying in the middle lane and looking often in the rearview mirror at Willis's headlights, he relived the suitcase dropping, the quick dip and turn of Strout's back, and the kick of the gun, the sound of the shot. When he walked to Strout, he still existed within the first shot, still trembled and breathed with it. The second shot and the burial seemed to be happening to someone else, someone he was watching. He and Willis each held an arm and pulled Strout face-down off the road and into the woods, his bouncing sliding belt white under the trees where it was so dark that when they stopped at the top of the knoll, panting and sweating, Matt could not see where

Strout's blue shirt ended and the earth began. They pulled off the branches then dragged Strout to the edge of the hole and went behind him and lifted his legs and pushed him in. They stood still for a moment. The woods were quiet save for their breathing, and Matt remembered hearing the movements of birds and small animals after the first shot. Or maybe he had not heard them. Willis went down to the road. Matt could see him clearly out on the tan dirt, could see the glint of Strout's car and, beyond the road, the gravel pit. Willis came back up the knoll with the suitcase. He dropped it in the hole and took off his gloves and they went down to his car for the spades. They worked quietly. Sometimes they paused to listen to the woods. When they were finished Willis turned on his flashlight and they covered the earth with leaves and branches and then went down to the spot in front of the car, and while Matt held the light Willis crouched and sprinkled dust on the blood, backing up till he reached the grass and leaves, then he used leaves until they had worked up to the grave again. They did not stop. They walked around the grave and through the woods, using the light on the ground, looking up through the trees to where they ended at the lake. Neither of them spoke above the sounds of their heavy and clumsy strides through low brush and over fallen branches. Then they reached it: wide and dark, lapping softly at the bank, pine needles smooth under Matt's feet, moonlight on the lake, a small island near its middle, with black, tall evergreens. He took out the gun and threw for the island: taking two steps back on the pine needles, striding with the throw and going to one knee as he followed through, looking up to see the dark shapeless object arcing downward, splashing.

℔℔

They left Strout's car in Boston, in front of an apartment building on Commonwealth Avenue. When they got back to town Willis drove slowly over the bridge and Matt threw the keys into the Merrimack. The sky was turning light. Willis let him out a block from his house, and walking home he listened for sounds from the houses he passed. They were quiet. A light was on in his living room. He turned it off and undressed in there, and went softly toward the bedroom; in the hall he smelled the smoke, and he stood in the bedroom doorway and looked at the orange of her cigarette in the dark. The curtains were closed. He went to the closet and put his shoes on the floor and felt for a hanger.

"Did you do it?" she said.

He went down the hall to the bathroom and in the dark he washed his hands and face. Then he went to her, lay on his back, and pulled the sheet up to his throat.

"Are you all right?" she said.

"I think so."

Now she touched him, lying on her side, her hand on his belly, his thigh.

"Tell me," she said.

He started from the beginning, in the parking lot at the bar; but soon with his eyes closed and Ruth petting him, he spoke of Strout's house: the order, the woman presence, the picture on the wall.

"The way she was smiling," he said.

"What about it?"

"I don't know. Did you ever see Strout's girl? When you saw him in town?"

"No."

"I wonder who she was."

Then he thought: *not was: is. Sleeping now she is his girl.* He opened his eyes, then closed them again. There was more light beyond the curtains. With Ruth now he left Strout's house and told again his lie to Strout, gave him again that hope that Strout must have for a while believed, else he would have to believe only the gun pointed at him for the last two hours of his life. And with Ruth he saw again the dropping suitcase, the darting move to the right: and he told of the first shot, feeling her hand on him but his heart isolated still, beating on the road still in that explosion like thunder. He told her the rest, but the words had no images for him, he did not see himself doing what the words said he had done; he only saw himself on that road.

"We can't tell the other kids," she said. "It'll hurt them, thinking he got away. But we mustn't."

"No."

She was holding him, wanting him, and he wished he could make love with her but he could not. He saw Frank and Mary Ann making love in her bed, their eyes closed, their bodies brown and smelling of the sea; the other girl was faceless, bodiless, but he felt her sleeping now; and he saw Frank and Strout, their faces alive; he saw red and yellow leaves falling to the earth, then snow: falling and freezing and falling; and holding Ruth, his cheek touching her breast, he shuddered with a sob that he kept silent in his heart.

Bobbie Ann Mason
Shiloh

Bobbie Ann Mason has emerged as the contemporary champion of "shopping mall" realism, a portrait of lower middle-class characters living in a mundane world of popular culture and cheap linoleum. But the details of this world, which she often catalogues as though some particular fact will define a character or clarify an issue, should not obscure the subtle psychological transformations that are at the center of her fiction, giving depth to ordinary people. "Shiloh," which was first published in *The New Yorker* in 1980 and then included in *Shiloh and Other Stories* two years later, works in just this way. In it a husband and wife are both undergoing psychic adjustments. Leroy, a trucker, is injured and spends his time at home, gradually taking on "feminine" pursuits, needlepoint, for example. His wife, Norma Jean, is becoming masculine, working on her pectorals, becoming more independent and assertive. She takes classes to improve her mind and works out to strengthen her body, and it is evident she is growing rapidly while he is more static, left behind in the life they used to share. The uncertainty of the conclusion is typical of Mason's stories, if Norma Jean's final gesture indicates a severing of marital ties or whether Leroy's movement toward her holds out hope of reconciliation. Born in Kentucky in 1940, Mason earned a B.A. in English at the State University of New York in Binghamton before she took a Ph.D. at the University of Connecticut. Throughout the 1970s, she taught in the English department at Mansfield State College in Pennsylvania. Nonetheless, the setting for her fiction is nearly always Kentucky, as it is in her most frequently anthologized story, "Shiloh."

Bobbie Ann Mason, "Shiloh," *The New Yorker* 56 (October 20, 1980): 50–57.

Leroy Moffitt's wife, Norma Jean, is working on her pectorals. She lifts three-pound dumbbells to warm up, then progresses to a twenty-pound barbell. Standing with her legs apart, she reminds Leroy of Wonder Woman.

"I'd give anything if I could just get these muscles to where they're real hard," says Norma Jean. "Feel this arm. It's not as hard as the other one."

"That's 'cause you're right-handed," says Leroy, dodging as she swings the barbell in an arc.

"Do you think so?"

"Sure."

Leroy is a truck driver. He injured his leg in a highway accident four months ago, and his physical therapy, which involves weights and a pulley, prompted Norma Jean to try building herself up. Now she is attending a body-building class. Leroy has been collecting temporary disability since his tractor-trailer jackknifed in Missouri, badly twisting his left leg in its socket. He has a steel pin in his hip. He will probably not be able to drive his rig again. It sits in the back yard, like a gigantic bird that has flown home to roost. Leroy has been home in Kentucky for three months, and his leg is almost healed, but the accident frightened him and he does not want to drive any more long hauls. He is not sure what to do next. In the meantime, he makes things from craft kits. He started by building a miniature log cabin from notched Popsicle sticks. He varnished it and placed it on the TV set, where it remains. It reminds him of a rustic Nativity scene. Then he tried string art (sailing ships on black velvet), a macrame owl kit, a snap-together B-17 Flying Fortress, and a lamp made out of a model truck with a light fixture screwed in the top of the cab. At first the kits were diversions, something to kill time, but now he is thinking about building a full-scale log house from a kit. It would be considerably cheaper than building a regular house, and besides, Leroy has grown to appreciate how things are put together. He has begun to realize that in all the years he was on the road he never took time to examine anything. He was always flying past scenery.

"They won't let you build a log cabin in any of the new subvisions," Norma Jean tells him.

"They will if I tell them it's for you," he says, teasing her. Ever since they were married, he has promised Norma Jean he would build her a new home one day. They have always rented, and the house they live in is small and nondescript. It does not even feel like a home, Leroy realizes now.

Norma Jean works at the Rexall drugstore, and she has acquired an amazing amount of information about cosmetics. When she explains to Leroy the three stages of complexion care, involving creams, toners, and moisturizers, he thinks happily of other petroleum products — axle grease, diesel fuel. This is a connection between himself and Norma Jean. Since he has been home, he has felt unusually tender about his wife and guilty over his long absences. But he can't tell what she feels about him. Norma Jean has never complained about his travelling; she has never made hurt remarks, like calling his truck a "widow-maker." He is reasonably certain she has been faithful to him, but he wishes she would celebrate his permanent homecoming more happily. Norma Jean is often startled to find Leroy at home, and he thinks she seems a little disappointed about it. Perhaps he reminds her too much of the early days of their marriage, before he went on the road. They had a child who died as an infant, years ago. They never speak about their memories of Randy, which have almost faded, but now that Leroy is home all the time they sometimes feel awkward around each other, and Leroy wonders if one of them should mention the child. He has the feeling that they are waking up out of a dream together — that they must create a new marriage, start afresh. They are lucky they are still married. Leroy has read that for most people losing a child destroys the marriage — or else he heard this on "Donahue." He can't always remember where he learns things anymore.

At Christmas, Leroy bought an electric organ for Norma Jean. She used to play the piano when she was in high school. "It don't leave you," she told him once. "It's like riding a bicycle."

The new instrument had so many keys and buttons that she was bewildered by it at first. She touched the keys tentatively, pushed some buttons, then pecked out "Chopsticks." It came out in an amplified foxtrot rhythm, with marimba sounds.

"It's an orchestra!" she cried.

The organ had a pecan-look finish and eighteen pre-set chords, with optional flute, violin, trumpet, clarinet, and banjo accompaniments. Norma Jean mastered the organ almost immediately. At first she played Christmas songs. Then she bought "The Sixties Songbook" and learned every tune in it, adding variations to each with the rows of brightly colored buttons.

"I didn't like these old songs back then," she said. "But I have this crazy feeling I missed something."

"You didn't miss a thing," said Leroy.

Leroy likes to lie on the couch and smoke a joint and listen to Norma Jean play "Can't Take My Eyes Off You" and "I'll Be Back." He is back again. After fifteen years on the road, he is finally settling down with the woman he loves. She is still pretty. Her skin is flawless. Her frosted curls resemble pencil trimmings.

♪♪

Now that Leroy has come home to stay, he notices how much the town has changed. Subdivisions are spreading across western Kentucky like an oil slick. The sign at the edge of town says "Pop: 10,500" — only seven hundred more than it said twenty years ago. Leroy can't figure out who is living in all the new houses. The farmers who used to gather around the courthouse square on Saturday afternoons to play checkers and spit tobacco juice have gone. It has been years since Leroy has thought about the farmers, and they have disappeared without his noticing.

Leroy meets a kid named Stevie Hamilton in the parking lot at the new shopping center. While they pretend to be strangers meeting over a stalled car, Stevie tosses an ounce of marijuana under the front seat of Leroy's car. Stevie is wearing orange jogging shoes and a T-shirt that says "CHATTAHOOCHEE SUPER-RAT." His father is a prominent doctor who lives in one of the expensive subdivisions in a new white-columned brick house that looks like a funeral parlor. In the phone book under his name there is a separate number, with the listing "Teenagers."

"Where do you get this stuff?" asks Leroy. "From your pappy?"

"That's for me to know and you to find out," Stevie says. He is slit-eyed and skinny.

"What else you got?"

"What you interested in?"

"Nothing special. Just wondered."

Leroy used to take speed on the road. Now he has to go slowly. He needs to be mellow. He leans back against the car and says, "I'm aiming to build me a log house, soon as I get time. My wife, though, I don't think she likes the idea."

"Well, let me know when you want me again," Stevie says. He has a cigarette in his cupped palm, as though sheltering it from the wind. He takes a long drag, then stomps it on the asphalt and slouches away.

Stevie's father was two years ahead of Leroy in high school. Leroy is thirty-four. He married Norma Jean when they were both eighteen, and their child Randy was born a few months later, but he died at the age of four months and three days. He would be about Stevie's age now. Norma Jean and Leroy were at the drive-in, watching a double feature ("Dr. Strangelove" and "Lover Come Back"), and the baby was sleeping in the back seat. When the first movie ended, the baby was dead. It was the sudden-infant-death syndrome. Leroy remembers handing Randy to a nurse at the emergency room, as though he were offering her a large doll as a present. A dead baby feels like a sack of flour. "It just happens sometimes," said the doctor, in what Leroy always recalls as a nonchalant tone. Leroy can hardly remember the child anymore, but he still sees vividly a scene from "Dr. Strangelove" in which the President of the United States was talking in a folksy voice on the hot line to the Soviet Premier about the bombers accidentally headed toward Russia. He was in the War Room, and the world map was lit up. Leroy remembers Norma Jean standing catatonically beside him in the hospital and himself thinking, Who is this strange girl? He had forgotten who she was. Now scientists are saying that crib death is caused by a virus. Nobody knows anything, Leroy thinks. The answers are always changing.

When Leroy gets home from the shopping center, Norma Jean's mother, Mabel Beasley, is there. Until this year, Leroy has not realized how much time she spends with Norma Jean. When she visits, she inspects the closets and then the plants, informing Norma Jean when a plant is droopy or yellow. Mabel calls the plants "flowers," although there are never any blooms. She always notices if Norma Jean's laundry is piling up. Mabel is a short, overweight woman whose tight, brown-dyed curls look more like a wig than the actual wig she sometimes wears. Today she has brought Norma Jean an off-white dust ruffle she made for the bed; Mabel works in a custom-upholstery shop.

"This is the tenth one I made this year," Mabel says. "I got started and couldn't stop."

"It's real pretty," says Norma Jean.

"Now we can hide things under the bed," says Leroy, who gets along with his mother-in-law primarily by joking with her. Mabel has never really forgiven him for disgracing her by getting Norma Jean pregnant. When the baby died, she said that fate was mocking her.

"What's that thing?" Mabel says to Leroy in a loud voice, pointing to a tangle of yarn on a piece of canvas.

Leroy holds it up for Mabel to see. "It's my needlepoint," he explains. "This is a 'Star Trek' pillow cover."

"That's what a woman would do," says Mabel. "Great day in the morning!"

"All the big football players on TV do it," he says.

"Why, Leroy, you're always trying to fool me. I don't believe you for one minute. You don't know what to do with yourself — that's the whole trouble. Sewing!"

"I'm aiming to build us a log house," says Leroy. "Soon as my plans come."

"Like *heck* you are," says Norma Jean. She takes Leroy's needlepoint and shoves it into a drawer. "You have to find a job first. Nobody can afford to build now anyway."

Mabel straightens her girdle and says, "I still think before you get tied down y'all ought to take a little run to Shiloh."

"One of these days, Mama," Norma Jean says impatiently.

Mabel is talking about Shiloh, Tennessee. For the past few years, she has been urging Leroy and Norma Jean to visit the Civil War battleground there. Mabel went there on her honeymoon — the only real trip she ever took. Her husband died of a perforated ulcer when Norma Jean was ten, but Mabel, who was accepted into the United Daughters of the Confederacy in 1975, is still preoccupied with going back to Shiloh.

"I've been to kingdom come and back in that truck out yonder," Leroy says to Mabel, "but we never yet set foot in that battleground. Ain't that something? How did I miss it?"

"It's not even that far," Mabel says.

After Mabel leaves, Norma Jean reads to Leroy from a list she has made. "Things you could do," she announces. "You could get a job as a guard at Union Carbide, where they'd let you set on a stool. You could get on at the lumberyard. You could do a little carpenter work, if you want to build so bad. You could —"

"I can't do something where I'd have to stand up all day."

"You ought to try standing up all day behind a cosmetics counter. It's amazing that I have strong feet, coming from two parents that never had strong feet at all." At the moment, Norma Jean is holding on to the kitchen counter, raising her knees one at a time as she talks. She is wearing two-pound ankle weights.

"Don't worry," says Leroy. "I'll do something."

"You could truck calves to slaughter for somebody. You wouldn't have to drive any big old truck for that."

"I'm going to build you this house," says Leroy. "I want to make you a real home."

"I don't want to live in any log cabin."

"It's not a cabin. It's a house."

"I don't care. It looks like a cabin."

"You and me together could lift those logs. It's just like lifting weights."

Norma Jean doesn't answer. Under her breath, she is counting. Now she is marching through the kitchen. She is doing goose steps.

𝔖𝔢

Before his accident, when Leroy came home he used to stay in the house with Norma Jean, watching TV in bed and playing cards. She would cook fried chicken, picnic ham, chocolate pie — all his favorites. Now he is home alone much of the time. In the mornings, Norma Jean disappears, leaving a cooling place in the bed. She eats a cereal called Body Buddies, and she leaves the bowl on the table, with the soggy tan balls floating in a milk puddle. He sees things about Norma Jean that he never realized before. When she chops onions, she stares off into a corner, as if she can't bear to look. She puts on her house slippers almost precisely at nine o'clock every evening and nudges her jogging shoes under the couch. She saves bread heels for the birds. Leroy watches the birds at the feeder. He notices the peculiar way goldfinches fly past the window. They close their wings, then fall, then spread their wings to catch and lift themselves. He wonders if they close their eyes when they fall. Norma Jean closes her eyes when they are in bed. She wants the lights turned out. Even then, he is sure she closes her eyes.

He goes for long drives around town. He tends to drive a car rather carelessly. Power steering and an automatic shift make a car feel so small and inconsequential that his body is hardly involved in the driving process. His injured leg stretches out comfortably. Once or twice he has almost hit something, but even the prospect of an accident seems minor in a car. He cruises the new subdivisions, feeling like a criminal rehearsing for a robbery. Norma Jean is probably right about a log house being inappropriate here in the new subdivisions. All the houses look grand and complicated. They depress him.

One day when Leroy comes home from a drive he finds Norma Jean in tears. She is in the kitchen making a potato and mushroom-soup casserole, with grated-cheese topping. She is crying because her mother caught her smoking.

"I didn't hear her coming. I was standing here puffing away pretty as you please," Norma Jean says, wiping her eyes.

"I knew it would happen sooner or later," says Leroy, putting his arm around her.

"She don't know the meaning of the word 'knock,'" says Norma Jean. "It's a wonder she hadn't caught me years ago."

"Think of it this way," Leroy says. "What if she caught me with a joint?"

"You better not let her!" Norma Jean shrieks. "I'm warning you, Leroy Moffitt!"

"I'm just kidding. Here, play me a tune. That'll help you relax."

Norma Jean puts the casserole in the oven and sets the timer. Then she plays a ragtime tune, with horns and banjo, as Leroy lights up a joint and lies on the couch, laughing to himself about Mabel's catching him at it. He thinks of Stevie Hamilton — a doctor's son pushing grass. Everything is funny. The whole town seems crazy and small. He is reminded of Virgil Mathis, a boastful policeman Leroy used to shoot pool with. Virgil recently led a drug bust in a back room at a bowling alley, where he seized ten thousand dollars' worth of marijuana. The newspaper had a picture of him holding up the bags of grass and grinning widely. Right now, Leroy can imagine Virgil breaking down the door and arresting him with a lungful of smoke. Virgil would probably have been alerted to the scene because of all the racket Norma Jean is making. Now she sounds like a hard-rock band. Norma Jean is terrific. When she switches to a Latin-rhythm version of "Sunshine Superman," Leroy hums along. Norma Jean's foot goes up and down, up and down.

"Well, what do you think?" Leroy says, when Norma Jean pauses to search through her music.

"What do I think about what?"

His mind has gone blank. Then he says, "I'll sell my rig and build us a house." That wasn't what he wanted to say. He wanted to know what she thought — what she *really* thought — about them.

"Don't start in on that again," says Norma Jean. She begins playing "Who'll Be the Next in Line?"

Leroy used to tell hitchhikers his whole life story — about his travels, his home town, the baby. He would end with a question: "Well, what do you think?" It was just a rhetorical question. In time, he had the feeling that he'd been telling the same story over and over to the same hitchhikers. He quit talking to hitchhikers when he realized how his voice sounded — whining and self-pitying, like some teen-age-tragedy song. Now Leroy has the sudden impulse to tell Norma Jean about himself, as if he had just met her. They have known each other so long they have forgotten a lot about each other. They could become reacquainted. But when the oven timer goes off and she runs to the kitchen, he forgets why he wants to do this.

𝔰𝔢

The next day, Mabel drops by. It is Saturday and Norma Jean is cleaning. Leroy is studying the plans of his log house, which have finally come in the mail. He has them spread out on the table — big sheets of stiff blue paper, with diagrams and numbers printed in white. While Norma Jean runs the vacuum, Mabel drinks coffee. She sets her coffee cup on a blueprint.

"I'm just waiting for time to pass," she says to Leroy, drumming her fingers on the table.

As soon as Norma Jean switches off the vacuum, Mabel says in a loud voice, "Did you hear about the datsun dog that killed the baby?"

Norma Jean says, "The word is 'dachshund.'"

"They put the dog on trial. It chewed the baby's legs off. The mother was in the next room all the time." She raises her voice. "They thought it was neglect."

Norma Jean is holding her ears. Leroy manages to open the refrigerator and get some Diet Pepsi to offer Mabel. Mabel still has some coffee and she waves away the Pepsi.

"Datsuns are like that," Mabel says. "They're jealous dogs. They'll tear a place to pieces if you don't keep an eye on them."

"You better watch out what you're saying, Mabel," says Leroy.

"Well, facts is facts."

Leroy looks out the window at his rig. It is like a huge piece of furniture gathering dust in the back yard. Pretty soon it will be an antique. He hears the vacuum cleaner. Norma Jean seems to be cleaning the living-room rug again.

Later, she says to Leroy, "She just said that about the baby because she caught me smoking. She's trying to pay me back."

"What are you talking about?" Leroy says, nervously shuffling blueprints.

"You know good and well," Norma Jean says. She is sitting in a kitchen chair with her feet up and her arms wrapped around her knees. She looks small and helpless. She says, "The very idea, her bringing up a subject like that! Saying it was neglect."

"She didn't mean that," Leroy says.

"She might not have *thought* she meant it. She always says things like that. You don't know how she goes on."

"But she didn't really mean it. She was just talking."

Leroy opens a king-sized bottle of beer and pours it into two glasses, dividing it carefully. He hands a glass to Norma Jean and she takes it from him mechanically. For a long time, they sit by the kitchen window watching the birds at the feeder.

ба

Something is happening. Norma Jean is going to night school. She has graduated from her six-week body-building course and now she is taking an adult-education course in composition at Paducah Community College. She spends her evenings outlining paragraphs.

"First you have a topic sentence," she explains to Leroy. "Then you divide it up. Your secondary topic has to be connected to your primary topic."

To Leroy, this sounds intimidating. "I never was any good in English," he says.

"It makes a lot of sense."

"What are you doing this for anyhow?"

She shrugs. "It's something to do." She stands up and lifts her dumbbells a few times.

"Driving a rig, nobody cared about my English."

"I'm not criticizing your English."

Norma Jean used to say, "If I lose ten minutes' sleep, I just drag all day." Now she stays up late, writing compositions. She got a B on her first paper — a how-to theme on soup-based casseroles. Recently Norma Jean has been cooking unusual foods — tacos, lasagna, Bombay duck. She doesn't play the organ anymore, though her second paper was called "Why Music Is Important to Me." She sits at the kitchen table, concentrating on her outlines while Leroy plays with his log-house plans, practicing with a set of Lincoln Logs. The thought of getting a truckload of notched, numbered logs scares him, and he wants to be prepared. As he and Norma Jean work together at the kitchen table, Leroy has the hopeful thought that they are sharing something, but he knows he is a fool to think this. Norma Jean is miles away. He knows he is going to lose her. Like Mabel, he is just waiting for time to pass.

One day Mabel is there before Norma Jean gets home from work, and Leroy finds himself confiding in her. Mabel, he realizes, must know Norma Jean better than he does.

"I don't know what's got into that girl," Mabel says. "She used to go to bed with the chickens. Now you say she's up all hours. Plus her a-smoking. I like to died."

"I want to make her this beautiful home," Leroy says, indicating the Lincoln Logs. "I don't think she even wants it. Maybe she was happier with me gone."

"She don't know what to make of you, coming home like this."

"Is that it?"

Mabel takes the roof off his Lincoln Log cabin. "You couldn't get *me* in a log cabin," she says. "I was raised in one. It's no picnic, let me tell you."

"They're different now," says Leroy.

"I tell you what," Mabel says, smiling oddly at Leroy.

"What?"

"Take her on down to Shiloh. Y'all need to get out together, stir a little. Her brain's all balled up over them books."

Leroy can see traces of Norma Jean's features in her mother's face. Mabel's worn face has the texture of crinkled cotton, but suddenly she looks pretty. It occurs to Leroy that Mabel has been hinting all along that she wants them to take her with them to Shiloh.

"Let's all go to Shiloh," he says, "You and me and her. Come Sunday."

Mabel throws up her hands in protest. "Oh, no, not me. Young folks want to be by theirselves."

When Norma Jean comes in with groceries, Leroy says excitedly, "Your mama here's been dying to go to Shiloh for thirty-five years. It's about time we went, don't you think?"

"I'm not going to butt in on anybody's second honeymoon," Mabel says.

"Who's going on a honeymoon, for Christ's sake?" Norma Jeans says loudly.

"I never raised no daughter of mine to talk that-a-way," Mabel says.

"You ain't seen nothing yet," says Norma Jean. She starts putting away boxes and cans, slamming cabinet doors.

"There's a log cabin at Shiloh," Mabel says. "It was there during the battle. There's bullet holes in it."

"When are you going to *shut up* about Shiloh, Mama?" asks Norma Jean.

"I always thought Shiloh was the prettiest place, so full of history," Mabel goes on. "I just hoped y'all could see it once before I die, so you could tell me about it." Later, she whispers to Leroy, "You do what I said. A little change is what she needs."

ও ও

"Your name means 'the king,'" Norma Jean says to Leroy that evening. He is trying to get her to go to Shiloh, and she is reading a book about another century.

"Well, I reckon I ought to be right proud."

"I guess so."

"Am I still king around here?"

Norma Jean flexes her biceps and feels them for hardness. "I'm not fooling around with anybody, if that's what you mean," she says.

"Would you tell me if you were?"

"I don't know."

"What does *your* name mean?"

"It was Marilyn Monroe's real name."

"No kidding!"

"Norma comes from the Normans. They were invaders," she says. She closes her book and looks hard at Leroy. "I'll go to Shiloh with you if you'll stop staring at me."

ᎦᎬ

On Sunday, Norma Jean packs a picnic and they go to Shiloh. To Leroy's relief, Mabel says she does not want to come with them. Norma Jean drives, and Leroy, sitting beside her, feels like some boring hitchhiker she has picked up. He tries some conversation, but she answers him in monosyllables. At Shiloh, she drives aimlessly through the park, past bluffs and trails and steep ravines. Shiloh is an immense place, and Leroy cannot see it as a battleground. It is not what he expected. He thought it would look like a golf course. Monuments are everywhere, showing through the thick clusters of trees. Norma Jean passes the log cabin Mabel mentioned. It is surrounded by tourists looking for bullet holes.

"That's not the kind of log house I've got in mind," says Leroy apologetically.

"I know *that*."

"This is a pretty place. Your mama was right."

"It's O.K.," says Norma Jean. "Well, we've seen it. I hope she's satisfied."

They burst out laughing together.

At the park museum, a movie on Shiloh is shown every half hour, but they decide that they don't want to see it. They buy a souvenir Confederate flag for Mabel, and then they find a picnic spot near the cemetery. Norma Jean has brought a Styrofoam cooler, with pimiento sandwiches, soft drinks, and Yodels. Leroy eats a sandwich and then smokes a joint, hiding it behind the picnic cooler. Norma Jean has quit smoking altogether. She is picking cake crumbs from the cellophane wrapper, like a fussy bird.

Leroy says, "So the boys in gray ended up in Corinth. The Union soldiers zapped 'em finally. April 7, 1862."

They both know that he doesn't know any history; he is just talking about some of the historical plaques they have read. He feels awkward, like a boy on a date with an older girl. They are still just making conversation.

"Corinth is where Mama eloped to," says Norma Jean.

They sit in silence and stare at the cemetery for the Union dead and, beyond, at a tall cluster of trees. Campers are parked nearby bumper to bumper, and small children in bright clothing are cavorting and squealing. Norma Jean wads up the cake wrapper and squeezes it tightly in her hand. Without looking at Leroy, she says, "I want to leave you."

Leroy takes a bottle of Coke out of the cooler and flips off the cap. He holds the bottle poised near his mouth but cannot remember to take a drink. Finally he says, "No, you don't."

"Yes, I do."

"I won't let you."

"You can't stop me."

"Don't do me that way."

Leroy knows Norma Jean will have her own way. "Didn't I promise to be home from now on?" he says.

"In some ways, a woman prefers a man who wanders," says Norma Jean. "That sounds crazy, I know."

"You're not crazy."

Leroy remembers to drink from his Coke. Then he says, "Yes, you *are* crazy. You and me could start all over again. Right back at the beginning."

"We *have* started all over again," says Norma Jean. "And this is how it turned out."

"What did I do wrong?"

"Nothing."

"Is this one of those women's-lib things?" Leroy asks.

"Don't be funny."

The cemetery, a green slope dotted with white markers, looks like a subdivision site. Leroy is trying to comprehend that his marriage is breaking up, but for some reason he is wondering about white slabs in a graveyard.

"Everything was fine till Mama caught me smoking," says Norma Jean, standing up. "That set something off."

"What are you talking about?"

"*She* won't leave me alone — *you* won't leave me alone." Norma Jean seems to be crying, but she is looking away from him. "I feel eighteen again. I can't face that all over again." She starts walking away. "No, it *wasn't* fine. I don't know what I'm saying. Forget it."

Leroy takes a lungful of smoke and closes his eyes as Norma Jean's words sink in. He tries to focus on the fact that thirty-five hundred soldiers died on the grounds around him. He can only think of that war as a board game with plastic soldiers. Leroy almost smiles, as he compares the Confederates' daring attack on the Union camps and Virgil Mathis's raid on the bowling alley. General Grant, drunk and furious, shoved the Southerners back to Corinth, where Mabel and Jet Beasley were married years later, when Mabel was still thin and good-looking. The next day, Mabel and Jet visited the battleground, and then Norma Jean was born, and then she married Leroy and they had a baby, which they lost, and now Leroy and Norma Jean are here at the same battleground. Leroy knows he is leaving out a lot. He is leaving out the insides of history. History was always just names and dates to him. It occurs to him that building a house out of logs is similarly empty — too simple. And the real inner workings of a marriage, like most of history, have escaped him. Now he sees that building a log house is the dumbest idea he could have had. It was clumsy of him to think Norma Jean would want a log house. It was a crazy idea. He'll have to think of something else, quickly. He will wad the blueprints into tight balls and fling them into the lake. Then he'll get moving again. He opens his eyes. Norma Jean has moved away and is walking through the cemetery, following a serpentine brick path.

Leroy gets up to follow his wife, but his good leg is asleep and his bad leg still hurts him. Norma Jean is far away, walking rapidly toward the bluff by the river, and he tries to hobble toward her. Some children run past him, screaming noisily. Norma Jean has reached the bluff, and she is looking out over the Tennessee River. Now she turns toward Leroy and waves her arms. Is she beckoning to him? She seems to be doing an exercise for her chest muscles. The sky is unusually pale — the color of the dust ruffle Mabel made for their bed.

Sandra Cisneros
Red Clowns

The life of Sandra Cisneros is a study in opportunity and success. Born in Chicago in 1954 to a Chicana mother and a Mexican father, she went on to graduate from Loyola University and to earn an M.F.A. from the Iowa Writers' Workshop in 1978. There, as one of her projects, she wrote one of the most celebrated books in contemporary literature, *The House on Mango Street,* which won the American Book Award. This prestigious prize was followed by a grant from the National Endowment for the Arts and by a MacArthur Fellowship, the most generous honor available for writers and artists. In the course of her career she has published a volume of verse, *Bad Boys,* along with her fiction in *My Wicked, Wicked Ways, Woman Hollering Creek,* and *Mango Street,* which first appeared from Arte Publico Press in 1983. "Red Clowns," included in that book, can be fully understood only in terms of the other stories in the volume, a short-story cycle. In context, the narrator, Esperanza, lives in a physically threatening world, one made all the more so by the machismo ethic of the men around her. As she matures in the course of the forty-four stories, the sexual danger becomes increasingly more evident, as a series of men taunt and menace her. Ironically, in "Red Clowns" it would seem that the boys who rape her are Caucasian, since they call her "Spanish girl." With the exception of this story, white America is almost entirely absent in the book. Esperanza's retrospective rendition of events is typically poetic and fragmentary for Cisneros's work, and through indirection it conveys the disillusionment, despair, and sense of abandonment of this young woman, coming of age in an environment she desperately longs to escape.

Sandra Cisernos, "Red Clowns," *The House on Mango Street* (Houston: Arte Publico Press, 1983), 93–94.

Sally, you lied. It wasn't what you said at all. What he did. Where he touched me. I didn't want it, Sally. The way they said it, the way it's supposed to be, all the storybooks and movies, why did you lie to me?

I was waiting by the red clowns. I was standing by the tilt-a-whirl where you said. And anyway I don't like carnivals. I went to be with you because you laugh on the tilt-a-whirl, you throw your head back and laugh. I hold your change, wave, count how many times you go by. Those boys that look at you because you're pretty. I like to be with you, Sally. You're my friend. But that big boy, where did he take you? I waited such a long time. I waited by the red clowns, just like you said, but you never came, you never came for me.

Sally Sally a hundred times. Why didn't you hear me when I called? Why didn't you tell them to leave me alone? The one who grabbed me by the arm, he wouldn't let me go. He said I love you, Spanish girl, I love you, and pressed his sour mouth to mine.

Sally, make him stop. I couldn't make them go away. I couldn't do anything but cry. I don't remember. It was dark. I don't remember. I don't remember. Please don't make me tell it all.

Why did you leave me all alone? I waited my whole life. You're a liar. They all lied. All the books and magazines, everything that told it wrong. Only his dirty fingernails against my skin, only his sour smell again. The moon that watched. The tilt-a-whirl. The red clowns laughing their thick-tongue laugh.

Then the colors began to whirl. Sky tipped. Their high black gym shoes ran. Sally, you lied, you lied. He wouldn't let me go. He said I love you, I love you, Spanish girl.

Louise Erdrich
The Red Convertible

Louise Erdrich was born in Little Falls, Minnesota, to a father of German descent and a mother who was a quarter Chippewa, but she grew up in North Dakota, where her parents both taught at the Wahpeton Indian School. Erdrich, however, attended the local public high school before going on to Dartmouth for a B.A. and Johns Hopkins for an M.A. in English in 1979. Two years later she married Michael Dorris, a professor at Dartmouth and a writer, and they went on to inspire each other on a series of important books including her volume of poetry, *Jacklight*, published in 1984. It was followed later that year by a collection of interrelated stories dealing with Native American life, *Love Medicine*, which won the National Book Award for fiction. Two years later another story cycle, *The Beet Queen*, appeared; *Tracks*, a novel, was published in 1988, *The Bingo Palace* in 1994, and *Tales of Burning Love* two years later. Since then several additional volumes have added to her important work, which somewhat resembles that of William Faulkner in the creation of a fictional geographic area populated by characters who appear repeatedly in various books. Erdrich's narrative methods often employ a series of speakers, a community of tellers rather than a single voice. The plots of her stories are achronological, shifting forward and back, linking thematic episodes rather than sequential action. Each story picks up ideas and characters from the previous ones, using storytelling in the Chippewa tradition of binding speakers into a society that regards the rendition of a story to be a profoundly important act. "The Red Convertible" was first published in the *Mississippi Valley Review* in 1982 prior to inclusion in *Love Medicine*. It concerns activity that takes place after Henry Lamartine, Jr. returns from the Vietnam War suffering from post-traumatic stress disorder, and his relationship with his brother Lyman is the central issue in this dramatic and tragic short story.

Louise Erdrich, "The Red Convertible," *Love Medicine* (New York: Holt, Rinehart and Winston, 1984), 143–54.

Lyman Lamartine

I was the first one to drive a convertible on my reservation. And of course it was red, a red Olds. I owned that car along with my brother Henry Junior. We owned it together until his boots filled with water on a windy night and he bought out my share. Now Henry owns the whole car, and his younger brother Lyman (that's myself), Lyman walks everywhere he goes.

How did I earn enough money to buy my share in the first place? My one talent was I could always make money. I had a touch for it, unusual in a Chippewa. From the first I was different that way, and everyone recognized it. I was the only kid they let in the American Legion Hall to shine shoes, for example, and one Christmas I sold spiritual bouquets for the mission door to door. The nuns let me keep a percentage. Once I started, it seemed the more money I made the easier the money came. Everyone encouraged it. When I was fifteen I got a job washing dishes at the Joliet Café, and that was where my first big break happened.

It wasn't long before I was promoted to busing tables, and then the short-order cook quit and I was hired to take her place. No sooner than you know it I was managing the Joliet. The rest is history. I went on managing. I soon became part owner, and of course there was no stopping me then. It wasn't long before the whole thing was mine.

After I'd owned the Joliet for one year, it blew over in the worst tornado ever seen around here. The whole operation was smashed to bits. A total loss. The fryalator was up in a tree, the grill torn in half like it was paper. I was only sixteen. I had it all in my mother's name, and I lost it quick, but before I lost it I had every one of my relatives, and their relatives, to dinner, and I also bought that red Olds I mentioned, along with Henry.

ꙸ

The first time we saw it! I'll tell you when we first saw it. We had gotten a ride up to Winnipeg, and both of us had money. Don't ask me why, because we never mentioned a car or anything, we just had all our money. Mine was cash, a big bankroll from the Joliet's insurance. Henry had two checks — a week's extra pay for being laid off, and his regular check from the Jewel Bearing Plant.

We were walking down Portage anyway, seeing the sights, when we saw it. There it was, parked, large as life. Really as *if* it was alive. I thought of the word *repose*, because the car wasn't simply stopped, parked, or whatever. That car reposed, calm and gleaming, a FOR SALE sign in its left front window. Then, before we had thought it over at all, the car belonged to us and our pockets were empty. We had just enough money for gas back home.

We went places in that car, me and Henry. We took off driving all one whole summer. We started off toward the Little Knife River and Mandaree in Fort Berthold and then we found ourselves down in Wakpala somehow, and then suddenly we were over in Montana on the Rocky Boy, and yet the summer was not even half over. Some people hang on to details when they travel, but we didn't let them bother us and just lived our everyday lives here to there.

I do remember this one place with willows. I remember I laid under those trees and it was comfortable. So comfortable. The branches bent down all around me like a tent or a stable. And quiet, it was quiet, even though there was a powwow close enough so I could see it going on. The air was not too still, not too windy either. When the dust rises up and hangs in the air around the dancers like that, I feel good. Henry was asleep with his arms thrown wide. Later on, he woke up and we started driving again. We were somewhere in Montana, or maybe on the Blood Reserve — it could have been anywhere. Anyway it was where we met the girl.

ꙸ

All her hair was in buns around her ears, that's the first thing I noticed about her. She was posed alongside the road with her arm out, so we stopped. That girl was short, so short her lumber shirt looked comical on her, like a nightgown. She had jeans on and fancy moccasins and she carried a little suitcase.

"Hop on in," says Henry. So she climbs in between us.

"We'll take you home," I says. "Where do you live?"

"Chicken," she says.

"Where the hell's that?" I ask her.

"Alaska."

"Okay," says Henry, and we drive.

We got up there and never wanted to leave. The sun doesn't truly set there in summer, and the night is more a soft dusk. You might doze off, sometimes, but before you know it you're up again, like an animal in nature. You never feel like you have to sleep hard or put away the world. And things would grow up there. One day just dirt or moss, the next day flowers and long grass. The girl's name was Susy. Her family really took to us. They fed us and put us up. We had our own tent to live in by their house, and the kids would be in and out of there all day and night. They couldn't get over me and Henry being brothers, we looked so different. We told them we knew we had the same mother, anyway.

One night Susy came in to visit us. We sat around in the tent talking of this and that. The season was changing. It was getting darker by that time, and the cold was even getting just a little mean. I told her it was time for us to go. She stood up on a chair.

"You never seen my hair," Susy said.

That was true. She was standing on a chair, but still, when she unclipped her buns the hair reached all the way to the ground. Our eyes opened. You couldn't tell how much hair she had when it was rolled up so neatly. Then my brother Henry did something funny. He went up to the chair and said, "Jump on my shoulders." So she did that, and her hair reached down past his waist, and he started twirling, this way and that, so her hair was flung out from side to side.

"I always wondered what it was like to have long pretty hair," Henry says. Well we laughed. It was a funny sight, the way he did it. The next morning we got up and took leave of those people.

§§

On to greener pastures, as they say. It was down through Spokane and across Idaho then Montana and very soon we were racing the weather right along under the Canadian border through Columbus, Des Lacs, and then we were in Bottineau County and soon home. We'd made most of the trip, that summer, without putting up the car hood at all. We got home just in time, it turned out, for the army to remember Henry had signed up to join it.

I don't wonder that the army was so glad to get my brother that they turned him into a Marine. He was built like a brick outhouse anyway. We liked to tease him that they really wanted him for his Indian nose. He had a nose big and sharp as a hatchet, like the nose on Red Tomahawk, the Indian who killed Sitting Bull, whose profile is on signs all along the North Dakota highways. Henry went off to training camp, came home once during Christmas, then the next thing you know we got an overseas letter from him. It was 1970, and he said he was stationed up in the nothern hill country. Whereabouts I did not know. He wasn't such a hot letter writer, and only got off two before the enemy caught him. I could never keep it straight, which direction those good Vietnam soldiers were from.

I wrote him back several times, even though I didn't know if those letters would get through. I kept him informed all about the car. Most of the time I had it up on blocks in the yard or half taken apart, because that long trip did a hard job on it under the hood.

I always had good luck with numbers, and never worried about the draft myself. I never even had to think about what my number was. But Henry was never lucky in the same way as me. It was at least three years before Henry came home. By then I guess the whole war was solved in the government's mind, but for him it would keep on going. In those years I'd put his car into almost perfect shape. I always thought of it as his car while he was gone, even though when he left he said, "Now it's yours," and threw me his key.

"Thanks for the extra key," I'd said. "I'll put it up in your drawer just in case I need it." He laughed.

ჽბ

When he came home, though, Henry was very different, and I'll say this: the change was no good. You could hardly expect him to change for the better, I know. But he was quiet, so quiet, and never comfortable sitting still anywhere but always up and moving around. I thought back to times we'd sat still for whole afternoons, never moving a muscle, just shifting our weight along the ground, talking to whoever sat with us, watching things. He'd always had a joke, then, too, and now you couldn't get him to laugh, or when he did it was more the sound of a man choking, a sound that stopped up the throats of other people around him. They got to leaving him alone most of the time, and I didn't blame them. It was a fact: Henry was jumpy and mean.

I'd bought a color TV set for my mom and the rest of us while Henry was away. Money still came very easy. I was sorry I'd ever bought it though, because of Henry. I was also sorry I'd bought color, because with black-and-white the pictures seem older and farther away. But what are you going to do? He sat in front of it, watching it, and that was the only time he was completely still. But it was the kind of stillness that you see in a rabbit when it freezes and before it will bolt. He was not easy. He sat in his chair gripping the armrests with all his might, as if the chair itself was moving at a high speed and if he let go at all he would rocket forward and maybe crash right through the set.

Once I was in the room watching TV with Henry and I heard his teeth click at something. I looked over, and he'd bitten through his lip. Blood was going down his chin. I tell you right then I wanted to smash that tube to pieces. I went over to it but Henry must have known what I was up to. He rushed from his chair and shoved me out of the way, against the wall. I told myself he didn't know what he was doing.

My mom came in, turned the set off real quiet, and told us she had made something for supper. So we went and sat down. There was still blood going down Henry's chin, but he didn't notice it and no one said anything, even though every time he took a bite of his bread his blood fell onto it until he was eating his own blood mixed in with the food.

ふ

While Henry was not around we talked about what was going to happen to him. There were no Indian doctors on the reservation, and my mom couldn't come around to trusting the old man, Moses Pillager, because he courted her long ago and was jealous of her husbands. He might take revenge through her son. We were afraid that if we brought Henry to a regular hospital they would keep him.

"They don't fix them in those places," Mom said; "they just give them drugs."

"We wouldn't get him there in the first place," I agreed, "so let's just forget about it."

Then I thought about the car.

Henry had not even looked at the car since he'd gotten home, though like I said, it was in tip-top condition and ready to drive. I thought the car might bring the old Henry back somehow. So I bided my time and waited for my chance to interest him in the vehicle.

One night Henry was off somewhere. I took myself a hammer. I went out to that car and I did a number on its underside. Whacked it up. Bent the tail pipe double. Ripped the muffler loose. By the time I was done with the car it looked worse than any typical Indian car that has been driven all its life on reservation roads, which they always say are like government promises — full of holes. It just about hurt me, I'll tell you that! I threw dirt in the carburetor and I ripped all the electric tape off the seats. I made it look just as beat up as I could. Then I sat back and waited for Henry to find it.

Still, it took him over a month. That was all right, because it was just getting warm enough, not melting, but warm enough to work outside.

"Lyman," he says, walking in one day, "that red car looks like shit."

"Well it's old," I says. "You got to expect that."

"No way!" says Henry. "That car's a classic! But you went and ran the piss right out of it, Lyman, and you know it don't deserve that. I kept that car in A-one shape. You don't remember. You're too young. But when I left, that car was running like a watch. Now I don't even know if I can get it to start again, let alone get it anywhere near its old condition."

"Well you try," I said, like I was getting mad, "but I say it's a piece of junk."

Then I walked out before he could realize I knew he'd strung together more than six words at once.

ふ

After that I thought he'd freeze himself to death working on that car. He was out there all day, and at night he rigged up a little lamp, ran a cord out the window, and had himself some light to see by while he worked. He was better than he had been before, but that's still not saying much. It was easier for him to do the things the rest of us did. He ate more slowly and didn't jump up and down during the meal to get this or that or look out the window. I put my hand in the back of the TV set, I admit, and fiddled around with it good, so that it was almost impossible now to get a clear picture. He didn't look at it very often anyway. He was always out with that car or going off to get parts for it. By the time it was really melting outside, he had it fixed.

I had been feeling down in the dumps about Henry around this time. We had always been together before. Henry and Lyman. But he was such a loner now that I didn't know how to take it. So I jumped at the chance one day when Henry seemed friendly. It's not that he smiled or anything. He just said, "Let's take that old shitbox for a spin." Just the way he said it made me think he could be coming around.

We went out to the car. It was spring. The sun was shining very bright. My only sister, Bonita, who was just eleven years old, came out and made us stand together for a picture. Henry leaned his elbow on the red car's windshield, and he took his other arm and put it over my shoulder, very carefully, as though it was heavy for him to lift and he didn't want to bring the weight down all at once.

"Smile," Bonita said, and he did.

◊◊

That picture. I never look at it anymore. A few months ago, I don't know why, I got his picture out and tacked it on the wall. I felt good about Henry at the time, close to him. I felt good having his picture on the wall, until one night when I was looking at television. I was a little drunk and stoned. I looked up at the wall and Henry was staring at me. I don't know what it was, but his smile had changed, or maybe it was gone. All I know is I couldn't stay in the same room with that picture. I was shaking. I got up, closed the door, and went into the kitchen. A little later my friend Ray came over and we both went back into that room. We put the picture in a brown bag, folded the bag over and over tightly, then put it way back in a closet.

I still see that picture now, as if it tugs at me, whenever I pass that closet door. The picture is very clear in my mind. It was so sunny that day Henry had to squint against the glare. Or maybe the camera Bonita held flashed like a mirror, blinding him, before she snapped the picture. My face is right out in the sun, big and round. But he might have drawn back, because the shadows on his face are deep as holes. There are two shadows curved like little hooks around the ends of his smile, as if to frame it and try to keep it there — that one, first smile that looked like it might have hurt his face. He has his field jacket on and the worn-in clothes he'd come back in and kept wearing ever since. After Bonita took the picture, she went into the house and we got into the car. There was a full cooler in the trunk. We started off, east, toward Pembina and the Red River because Henry said he wanted to see the high water.

🕭

The trip over there was beautiful. When everything starts changing, drying up, clearing off, you feel like your whole life is starting. Henry felt it, too. The top was down and the car hummed like a top. He'd really put it back in shape, even the tape on the seats was very carefully put down and glued back in layers. It's not that he smiled again or even joked, but his face looked to me as if it was clear, more peaceful. It looked as though he wasn't thinking of anything in particular except the bare fields and windbreaks and houses we were passing.

The river was high and full of winter trash when we got there. The sun was still out, but it was colder by the river. There were still little clumps of dirty snow here and there on the banks. The water hadn't gone over the banks yet, but it would, you could tell. It was just at its limit, hard swollen, glossy like an old gray scar. We made ourselves a fire, and we sat down and watched the current go. As I watched it I felt something squeezing inside me and tightening and trying to let go all at the same time. I knew I was not just feeling it myself; I knew I was feeling what Henry was going through at that moment. Except that I couldn't stand it, the closing and opening. I jumped to my feet. I took Henry by the shoulders and I started shaking him. "Wake up," I says, "wake up, wake up, wake up!" I didn't know what had come over me. I sat down beside him again.

His face was totally white and hard. Then it broke, like stones break all of a sudden when water boils up inside them.

"I know it," he says. "I know it. I can't help it. It's no use."

We start talking. He said he knew what I'd done with the car. It was obvious it had been whacked out of shape and not just neglected. He said he wanted to give the car to me for good now, it was no use. He said he'd fixed it just to give it back and I should take it.

"No way," I says. "I don't want it."

"That's okay," he says, "you take it."

"I don't want it, though," I says back to him, and then to emphasize, just to emphasize, you understand, I touch his shoulder. He slaps my hand off.

"Take that car," he says.

"No," I say. "Make me," I say, and then he grabs my jacket and rips the arm loose. That jacket is a class act, suede with tags and zippers. I push Henry backwards, off the log. He jumps up and bowls me over. We go down in a clinch and come up swinging hard, for all we're worth, with our fists. He socks my jaw so hard I feel like it swings loose. Then I'm at his rib cage and land a good one under his chin so his head snaps back. He's dazzled. He looks at me and I look at him and then his eyes are full of tears and blood and at first I think he's crying. But no, he's laughing. "Ha! Ha!" he says. "Ha! Ha! Take good care of it."

"Okay," I says. "Okay, no problem. Ha! Ha!"

I can't help it, and I start laughing, too. My face feels fat and strange, and after a while I get a beer from the cooler in the trunk, and when I hand it to Henry he takes his shirt and wipes my germs off. "Hoof-and-mouth disease," he says. For some reason this cracks me up, and so we're really laughing for a while, and then we drink all the rest of the beers one by one and throw them in the river and see how far, how fast, the current takes them before they fill up and sink.

"You want to go on back?" I ask after a while. "Maybe we could snag a couple nice Kashpaw girls."

He says nothing. But I can tell his mood is turning again.

"They're all crazy, the girls up here, every damn one of them."

"You're crazy too," I say, to jolly him up. "Crazy Lamartine boys!"

He looks as though he will take this wrong at first. His face twists, then clears, and he jumps up on his feet. "That's right!" he says. "Crazier 'n hell. Crazy Indians!"

I think it's the old Henry again. He throws off his jacket and starts springing his legs up from the knees like a fancy dancer. He's down doing something between a grass dance and a bunny hop, no kind of dance I ever saw before, but neither has anyone else on all this green growing earth. He's wild. He wants to pitch whoopee! He's up and at me and all over. All this time I'm laughing so hard, so hard my belly is getting tied up in a knot.

"Got to cool me off!" he shouts all of a sudden. Then he runs over to the river and jumps in.

There's boards and other things in the current. It's so high. No sound comes from the river after the splash he makes, so I run right over. I look around. It's getting dark. I see he's halfway across the water already, and I know he didn't swim there but the current took him. It's far. I hear his voice, though, very clearly across it.

"My boots are filling," he says.

He says this in a normal voice, like he just noticed and he doesn't know what to think of it. Then he's gone. A branch comes by. Another branch. I go in.

§ð

By the time I get out of the river, off the snag I pulled myself onto, the sun is down. I walk back to the car, turn on the high beams, and drive it up the bank. I put it in first gear and then I take my foot off the clutch. I get out, close the door, and watch it plow softly into the water. The headlights reach in as they go down, searching, still lighted even after the water swirls over the back end. I wait. The wires short out. It is all finally dark. And then there is only the water, the sound of it going and running and going and running and running.

Jamaica Kincaid
Columbus in Chains

Jamaica Kincaid was born Elaine Potter Richardson in St. John's, Antigua in 1949 and changed her name when she started writing in New York. She has explained that she wished to retain a connection with the Caribbean by choosing "Jamaica," and her fiction is infused with the region of her birth. In the course of her career, she has published three volumes of short stories, *At the Bottom of the River* (1983), *Annie John* (1985), and *Lucy* (1990), the last two made up entirely of work previously published in *The New Yorker*. In addition, her *Autobiography of My Mother, A Small Place,* and *My Brother* have attracted considerable attention from her readers, and transcend racial and geographic limitations. Kincaid has won the Morton Dauwen Zabel Award from the American Academy and Institute of Arts and Letters, and she has been a finalist for numerous other recognitions, including the Ritz Paris Hemingway Award. *Annie John* is a story cycle consisting of eight works of short fiction published in *The New Yorker* in 1983 and 1984. As a collective entity, they constitute a *Bildungsroman* of a young woman in Antigua moving from childhood through rebellion against her mother to her final departure from the island at the end of the book. The stories in the magazine are not identical to those in the volume. Numerous details, including names, dates, and places, were changed in each of the constituent stories to coordinate them into a coherent sequence tracing Annie's development into a young woman. "Columbus in Chains" is the fifth episode in a progression of events that transform young Annie from a dependent child of ten to a rebellious adolescent determined to establish her own autonomous life. Especially as revised for inclusion in the collection, this story is vital in that it contains her racial, social, and political enlightenment inspired by a history lesson about the voyages of Columbus to the Caribbean. It is here that, at the age of twelve, she first realizes what the West Indies meant to the African peoples: a history of slavery, domination by British culture, and the background of her family in Antigua. It is a crucial epiphany, and it adds a critical social component to what had been primarily a personal journey toward maturity.

Jamaica Kincaid, "Columbus in Chains," *Annie John* (New York: Farrar, Straus and Giroux, 1985), 72–84.

Outside, as usual, the sun shone, the trade winds blew; on her way to put some starched clothes on the line, my mother shooed some hens out of her garden; Miss Dewberry baked the buns, some of which my mother would buy for my father and me to eat with our afternoon tea; Miss Henry brought the milk, a glass of which I would drink with my lunch, and another glass of which I would drink with the bun from Miss Dewberry; my mother prepared our lunch; my father noted some perfectly idiotic thing his partner in housebuilding, Mr. Oatie, had done, so that over lunch he and my mother could have a good laugh.

    The Anglican church bell struck eleven o'clock — one hour to go before lunch. I was then sitting at my desk in my classroom. We were having a history lesson — the last lesson of the morning. For taking first place over all the other girls, I had been given a prize, a copy of a book called *Roman Britain*, and I was made prefect of my class. What a mistake the prefect part had been, for I was among the worst-behaved in my class and did not at all believe in setting myself up as a good example, the way a prefect was supposed to do. Now I had to sit in the prefect's seat — the first seat in the front row, the seat from which I could stand up and survey quite easily my classmates. From where I sat I could see out the window. Sometimes when I looked out, I could see the sexton going over to the minister's house. The sexton's daughter, Hilarene, a disgusting model of good behavior and keen attention to scholarship, sat next to me, since she took second place. The minister's daughter, Ruth, sat in the last row, the row reserved for all the dunce girls. Hilarene, of course, I could not stand. A girl that good would never do for me. I would probably not have cared so much for first place if I could be sure it would not go to her. Ruth I liked, because she was such a dunce and came from England and had yellow hair. When I first met her, I used to walk her home and sing bad songs to her just to see her turn pink, as if I had spilled hot water all over her.

Our books, *A History of the West Indies,* were open in front of us. Our day had begun with morning prayers, then a geometry lesson, then it was over to the science building for a lesson in "Introductory Physics" (not a subject we cared much for), taught by the most dingy-toothed Mr. Slacks, a teacher from Canada, then precious recess, and now this, our history lesson. Recess had the usual drama: this time, I coaxed Gwen out of her disappointment at not being allowed to join the junior choir. Her father — how many times had I wished he would become a leper and so be banished to a leper colony for the rest of my long and happy life with Gwen — had forbidden it, giving as his reason that she lived too far away from church, where choir rehearsals were conducted, and that it would be dangerous for her, a young girl, to walk home alone at night in the dark. Of course, all the streets had lamplight, but it was useless to point that out to him. Oh, how it would have pleased us to press and rub our knees together as we sat in our pew while pretending to pay close attention to Mr. Simmons, our choirmaster, as he waved his baton up and down and across, and how it would have pleased us even more to walk home together, alone in the "early dusk" (the way Gwen had phrased it, a ready phrase always on her tongue), stopping, if there was a full moon, to lie down in a pasture and expose our bosoms in the moonlight. We had heard that full moonlight would make our breasts grow to a size we would like. Poor Gwen! When I first heard from her that she was one of ten children, right on the spot I told her that I would love only her, since her mother already had so many other people to love.

Our teacher, Miss Edward, paced up and down in front of the class in her usual way. In front of her desk stood a small table, and on it stood the dunce cap. The dunce cap was in the shape of a coronet, with an adjustable opening in the back, so that it could fit any head. It was made of cardboard with a shiny gold paper covering and the word "DUNCE" in shiny red paper on the front. When the sun shone on it, the dunce cap was all aglitter, almost as if you were being tricked into thinking it a desirable thing to wear. As Miss Edward paced up and down, she would pass between us and the dunce cap like an eclipse. Each Friday morning, we were given a small test to see how well we had learned the things taught to us all week. The girl who scored lowest was made to wear the dunce cap all day the following Monday. On many Mondays, Ruth wore it — only, with her short yellow hair, when the dunce cap was sitting on her head she looked like a girl attending a birthday party in *The Schoolgirl's Own Annual*.

It was Miss Edward's way to ask one of us a question the answer to which she was sure the girl would not know and then put the same question to another girl who she was sure would know the answer. The girl who did not answer correctly would then have to repeat the correct answer in the exact words of the other girl. Many times, I had heard my exact words repeated over and over again, and I liked it especially when the girl doing the repeating was one I didn't care about very much. Pointing a finger at Ruth, Miss Edward asked a question the answer to which was "On the third of November 1493, a Sunday morning, Christopher Columbus discovered Dominica." Ruth, of course, did not know the answer, as she did not know the answer to many questions about the West Indies. I could hardly blame her. Ruth had come all the way from England. Perhaps she did not want to be in the West Indies at all. Perhaps she wanted to be in England, where no one would remind her constantly of the terrible things her ancestors had done; perhaps she had felt even worse when her father was a missionary in Africa. I could see how Ruth felt from looking at her face. Her ancestors had been the masters, while ours had been the slaves. She had such a lot to be ashamed of, and by being with us every day she was always being reminded. We could look everybody in the eye, for our ancestors had done nothing wrong except just sit somewhere, defenseless. Of course, sometimes, what with our teachers and our books, it was hard for us to tell on which side we really now belonged — with the masters or the slaves — for it was all history, it was all in the past, and everybody behaved differently now; all of us celebrated Queen Victoria's birthday, even though she had been dead a long time. But we, the descendants of the slaves, knew quite well what had really happened, and I was sure that if the tables had been turned we would have acted differently; I was sure that if our ancestors had gone from Africa to Europe and come upon the people living there, they would have taken a proper interest in the Europeans on first seeing them, and said, "How nice," and then gone home to tell their friends about it.

I was sitting at my desk, having these thoughts to myself. I don't know how long it had been since I lost track of what was going on around me. I had not noticed that the girl who asked the question after Ruth failed — a girl named Hyacinth — had only got a part of the answer correct. I had not noticed that after these two attempts Miss Edward had launched into a harangue about what a worthless bunch we were compared to girls of the past. In fact, I was no longer on the same chapter we were studying. I was way ahead, at the end of the chapter about Columbus's third voyage. In this chapter, there was a picture of Columbus that took up a whole page, and it was in color — one of only five color pictures in the book. In this picture, Columbus was seated in the bottom of a ship. He was wearing the usual three-quarter trousers and a shirt with enormous sleeves, both the trousers and shirt made of maroon-colored velvet. His hat, which was cocked up on one side of his head, had a gold feather in it, and his black shoes had huge gold buckles. His hands and feet were bound up in chains, and he was sitting there staring off into space, looking quite dejected and miserable. The picture had as a title "Columbus in Chains," printed at the bottom of the page. What had happened was that the usually quarrelsome Columbus had got into a disagreement with people who were even more quarrelsome, and a man named Bobadilla, representing King Ferdinand and Queen Isabella, had sent him back to Spain fettered in chains attached to the bottom of a ship. What just deserts, I thought, for I did not like Columbus. How I loved this picture — to see the usually triumphant Columbus, brought so low, seated at the bottom of a boat just watching things go by. Shortly after I first discovered it in my history book, I heard my mother read out loud to my father a letter she had received from her sister, who still lived with her mother and father in the very same Dominica, which is where my mother came from. Ma Chess was fine, wrote my aunt, but Pa Chess was not well. Pa Chess was having a bit of trouble with his limbs; he was not able to go about as he pleased; often he had to depend on someone else to do one thing or another for him. My mother read the letter in quite a state, her voice rising to a higher pitch with each sentence. After she read the part about Pa Chess's stiff limbs, she turned to my father and laughed as she said, "So the great man can no longer just get up and go. How I would love to see his face now!" When I next saw the picture of Columbus sitting there all locked up in his chains, I wrote under it the words "The Great Man Can No Longer Just Get Up and Go." I had written this out with my fountain pen, and in Old English lettering — a script I had recently mastered. As I sat there looking at the picture, I traced the words with my pen over and over, so that the letters grew big and you could read what I had written from not very far away. I don't know how long it was before I heard that my name, Annie John, was being said by this bellowing dragon in the form of Miss Edward bearing down on me.

I had never been a favorite of hers. Her favorite was Hilarene. It must have pained Miss Edward that I so often beat out Hilarene. Not that I liked Miss Edward and wanted her to like me back, but all my other teachers regarded me with much affection, would always tell my mother that I was the most charming student they had ever had, beamed at me when they saw me coming, and were very sorry when they had to write some version of this on my report card: "Annie is an unusually bright girl. She is well behaved in class, at least in the presence of her masters and mistresses, but behind their backs and outside the classroom quite the opposite is true." When my mother read this or something like it, she would burst into tears. She had hoped to display, with a great flourish, my report card to her friends, along with whatever prize I had won. Instead, the report card would have to take a place at the bottom of the old trunk in which she kept any important thing that had to do with me. I became not a favorite of Miss Edward's in the following way: Each Friday afternoon, the girls in the lower forms were given, instead of a last lesson period, an extra-long recess. We were to use this in ladylike recreation — walks, chats about the novels and poems we were reading, showing each other the new embroidery stitches we had learned to master in home class, or something just as seemly. Instead, some of the girls would play a game of cricket or rounders or stones, but most of us would go to the far end of the school grounds and play band. In this game, of which teachers and parents disapproved and which was sometimes absolutely forbidden, we would place our arms around each other's waist or shoulders, forming lines of ten or so girls, and then we would dance from one end of the school grounds to the other. As we danced, we would sometimes chant these words: "Tee la la la, come go. Tee la la la, come go." At other times we would sing a popular calypso song which usually had lots of unladylike words to it. Up and down the schoolyard, away from our teachers, we would dance and sing. At the end of recess — forty-five minutes — we were missing ribbons and other ornaments from our hair, the pleats of our linen tunics became unset, the collars of our blouses were pulled out, and we were soaking wet all the way down to our bloomers. When the school bell rang, we would make a whooping sound, as if in a great panic, and then we would throw ourselves on top of each other as we laughed and shrieked. We would then run back to our classes, where we prepared to file into the auditorium for evening prayers. After that, it was home for the weekend. But how could we go straight home after all that excitement? No sooner were we on the street than we would form little groups, depending on the direction we were headed in. I was never keen on joining them on the way home, because I was sure I would run into my mother. Instead, my friends and I would go to our usual place near the back of the churchyard and sit on the tombstones of people who had been buried there way before slavery was abolished, in 1833. We would sit and sing bad songs, use forbidden words, and, of course, show each other various parts of our bodies. While some of us watched, the others would walk up and down on the large tombstones showing off their legs. It was immediately a popular idea; everybody soon wanted to do it. It wasn't long before many girls — the ones whose mothers didn't pay strict attention to what they were doing — started to come to school on Fridays wearing not bloomers under their uniforms but underpants trimmed with lace and satin frills. It also wasn't long before an end came to all that. One Friday afternoon, Miss Edward, on her way home from school, took a shortcut through the churchyard. She must have heard the commotion we were making, because there she suddenly was, saying, "What is the meaning of this?" — just the very thing someone like her would say if she came unexpectedly on something like us. It was obvious that I was the ringleader. Oh, how I wished the ground would open up and take her in, but it did not. We all, shamefacedly, slunk home, I with Miss Edward at my side. Tears came to my mother's eyes when she heard what I had done. It was apparently such a bad thing that my mother couldn't bring herself to repeat my misdeed to my father in my presence. I got the usual punishment of dinner alone, outside under the breadfruit tree, but added on to that, I was not allowed to go to the library on Saturday, and on Sunday, after Sunday school and dinner, I was not allowed to take a stroll in the botanical gardens, where Gwen was waiting for me in the bamboo grove.

♪♪

That happened when I was in the first form. Now here Miss Edward stood. Her whole face was on fire. Her eyes were bulging out of her head. I was sure that at any minute they would land at my feet and roll away. The small pimples on her face, already looking as if they were constantly irritated, now ballooned into huge, on-the-verge-of-exploding boils. Her head shook from side to side. Her strange bottom, which she carried high in the air, seemed to rise up so high that it almost touched the ceiling. Why did I not pay attention, she said. My impertinence was beyond endurance. She then found a hundred words for the different forms my impertinence took. On she went. I was just getting used to this amazing bellowing when suddenly she was speechless. In fact, everything stopped. Her eyes stopped, her bottom stopped, her pimples stopped. Yes, she had got close enough so that her eyes caught a glimpse of what I had done to my textbook. The glimpse soon led to closer inspection. It was bad enough that I had defaced my schoolbook by writing in it. That I should write under the picture of Columbus "The Great Man . . ." etc. was just too much. I had gone too far this time, defaming one of the great men in history, Christopher Columbus, discoverer of the island that was my home. And now look at me. I was not even hanging my head in remorse. Had my peers ever seen anyone so arrogant, so blasphemous?

I was sent to the headmistress, Miss Moore. As punishment, I was removed from my position as prefect, and my place was taken by the odious Hilarene. As an added punishment, I was ordered to copy Books I and II of *Paradise Lost*, by John Milton, and to have it done a week from that day. I then couldn't wait to get home to lunch and the comfort of my mother's kisses and arms. I had nothing to worry about there yet; it would be a while before my mother and father heard of my bad deeds. What a terrible morning! Seeing my mother would be such a tonic! — something to pick me up.

When I got home, my mother kissed me absent-mindedly. My father had got home ahead of me, and they were already deep in conversation, my father regaling her with some unusually outlandish thing the oaf Mr. Oatie had done. I washed my hands and took my place at table. My mother brought me my lunch. I took one smell of it, and I could tell that it was the much hated breadfruit. My mother said not at all, it was a new kind of rice imported from Belgium, and not breadfruit, mashed and forced through a ricer, as I thought. She went back to talking to my father. My father could hardly get a few words out of his mouth before she was a jellyfish of laughter. I sat there, putting my food in my mouth. I could not believe that she couldn't see how miserable I was and so reach out a hand to comfort me and caress my cheek, the way she usually did when she sensed that something was amiss with me. I could not believe how she laughed at everything he said, and how bitter it made me feel to see how much she liked him. I ate my meal. The more I ate of it, the more I was sure that it was bread-fruit. When I finished, my mother got up to remove my plate. As she started out the door, I said, "Tell me, really, the name of the thing I just ate."

My mother said, "You just ate some breadfruit. I made it look like rice so that you would eat it. It's very good for you, filled with lots of vitamins." As she said this, she laughed. She was standing half inside the door, half outside. Her body was in the shade of our house, but her head was in the sun. When she laughed, her mouth opened to show off big, shiny, sharp white teeth. It was as if my mother had suddenly turned into a crocodile.

Susan Minot
Hiding

Susan Minot's "Hiding" was first published in *Grand Street* in 1983 prior to its inclusion in *Monkeys*, a collection of nine interrelated stories about events in the Vincent family from February of 1966 to May of 1979. Collectively, these nine episodes dramatize moments of domestic interaction around several unifying themes: alienation and poignant longing, isolation, growing up, and the class and religious differences between the two parents, referred to as "Mum" and "Dad." "Hiding" opens the volume, establishing the characters and the central conflicts of the book, and is told by one of the children, ten-year-old Sophie, who does not understand all that she observes but is sensitive to the emotional implications of everything that happens. The book was widely heralded in reviews and criticism, and it won Minot the first of her awards, the *Prix Fémina Étranger* in France. Born in Massachusetts in 1956, Minot studied creative writing at Brown before taking a B.F.A. from Columbia. After *Monkeys*, she went on to publish *Lust and Other Stories*, short fiction on the theme of erotic desire; a historical novel, *Folly*; and two other novels on the theme of romantic love, *Rapture* and *Evening*. She also collaborated with Bernardo Bertolucci on the screenplay for *Stealing Beauty*. Regarded as a minimalist in direct descent from Ernest Hemingway, Minot's fiction is subtle, rewarding close attention to gesture, dialogue, and what is left unsaid. The issues in "Hiding" involve Dad's distance from his family, Mum's nurturing warmth and need for affection, and the sensitivity of Sophie in observing the interactions between them.

Susan Minot, "Hiding," *Monkeys* (New York: E. P. Dutton, 1986), 1–22.

Our father doesn't go to church with us but we're all downstairs in the hall at the same time, bumbling, getting ready to go. Mum knuckles the buttons of Chicky's snowsuit till he's knot-tight, crouching, her heels lifted out of the backs of her shoes, her nylons creased at the ankles. She wears a black lace veil that stays on her hair like magic. Sherman ripples by, coat flapping, and Mum grabs him by the hood, reeling him in, and zips him up with a pinch at his chin. Gus stands there with his bottom lip out, waiting, looking like someone's smacked him except not that hard. Even though he's seven, he still wants Mum to do him up. Delilah comes half-hurrying down the stairs, late, looking like a ragamuffin with her skirt slid down to her hips and her hair all slept on wrong. Caitlin says, "It's about time." Delilah sweeps along the curve of the banister, looks at Caitlin, who's all ready to go herself with her pea jacket on and her loafers and bare legs, and tells her, "You're going to freeze." Everyone's in a bad mood because we just woke up.

Dad's outside already on the other side of the French doors, waiting for us to go. You can tell it's cold out there by his white breath blowing by his cheek in spurts. He just stands on the porch, hands shoved in his black parka, feet pressed together, looking at the crusty snow on the lawn. He doesn't wear a hat but that's because he barely feels the cold. Mum's the one who's warm-blooded. At skiing, she'll take you in when your toes get numb. You sit there with hot chocolate and a carton of french fries and the other mothers and she rubs your foot to get the circulation back. Down on the driveway the car is warming up and the exhaust goes straight up, disappearing in thin white curls.

"Okay, monkeys," says Mum filing us out the door. Chicky starts down the steps one red boot at a time till Mum whisks him up under a wing. The driveway is wrinkled over with ice so we take little shuffle steps across it, blinking at how bright it is, still only half-awake. Only the station wagon can fit everybody. Gus and Sherman scamper in across the huge backseat. Caitlin's head is the only one that shows over the front. (Caitlin is the oldest and she's eleven. I'm next, then Delilah, then the boys.) Mum rubs her thumbs on the steering wheel so that her gloves are shiny and round at the knuckles. Dad is doing things like checking the gutters, waiting till we leave. When we finally barrel down the hill, he turns and goes back into the house, which is big and empty now and quiet.

We keep our coats on in church. Except for the O'Shaunesseys, we have the most children in one pew. Dad only comes on Christmas and Easter, because he's not Catholic. A lot of times you only see the mothers there. When Dad stays at home, he does things like cuts prickles in the woods or tears up thorns, or rakes leaves for burning, or just stands around on the other side of the house by the lilacs, surveying his garden, wondering what to do next. We usually sit up near the front and there's a lot of kneeling near the end. One time Gus got his finger stuck in the diamond-shaped holes of the heating vent and Mum had to yank it out. When the man comes around for the collection, we each put in a nickel or a dime and the handle goes by like a rake. If Mum drops in a five-dollar bill, she'll pluck out a couple of bills for her change.

The church is huge. Out loud in the dead quiet, a baby blares out "Dah-Dee." We giggle and Mum goes "Ssshhh" but smiles too. A baby always yells at the quietest part. Only the girls are old enough to go to Communion; you're not allowed to chew it. The priest's neck is peeling and I try not to look. "He leaves me cold," Mum says when we leave, touching her forehead with a fingertip after dipping it into the holy water.

On the way home, we pick up the paper at Cage's and a bag of eight lollipops — one for each of us, plus Mum and Dad, even though Dad never eats his. I choose root beer. Sherman crinkles his wrapper, shifting his eyes around to see if anyone's looking. Gus says, "Sherman, you have to wait till after breakfast." Sherman gives a fierce look and shoves it in his mouth. Up in front, Mum, flicking on the blinker, says, "Take that out," with eyes in the back of her head.

Depending on what time of year it is, we do different things on the weekends. In the fall we might go to Castle Hill and stop by the orchard in Ipswich for cider and apples and red licorice. Castle Hill is closed after the summer so there's nobody else there and it's all covered with leaves. Mum goes up to the windows on the terrace and tries to peer in, cupping her hands around her eyes and seeing curtains. We do things like roll down the hills, making our arms stiff like mummies, or climb around on the marble statues, which are really cold, or balance along the edge of the fountains without falling. Mum says "Be careful" even though there's no water in them, just red leaves plastered against the sides. When Dad notices us he yells, "Get down."

One garden has a ghost, according to Mum. A lady used to sneak out and meet her lover in the garden behind the grape trellis. Or she'd hide in the garden somewhere and he'd look for her and find her. But one night she crept out and he didn't come and didn't come and finally when she couldn't stand it any longer, she went crazy and ran off the cliff and killed herself and now her ghost comes back and keeps waiting. We creep into the boxed-in place, smelling the yellow berries and the wet bark, and Delilah jumps — "What was that?" — trying to scare us. Dad shakes the wood to see if it's rotten. We run ahead and hide in a pile of leaves. Little twigs get in your mouth and your nostrils; we hold still underneath listening to the brittle ticking leaves. When we hear Mum and Dad get close, we burst up to surprise them, all the leaves fluttering down, sputtering from the dust and tiny grits that get all over your face like gray ash, like Ash Wednesday. Mum and Dad just keep walking. She brushes a pine needle from his collar and he jerks his head, thinking of something else, probably that it's a fly. We follow them back to the car in a line, all scruffy with leaf scraps.

After church, we have breakfast because you're not allowed to eat before. Dad comes in for the paper or a sliver of bacon. One thing about Dad, he has the weirdest taste. Spam is his favorite thing or this cheese that no one can stand the smell of. He barely sits down at all, glancing at the paper with his feet flat down on either side of him, ready to get up any minute to go back outside and sprinkle white fertilizer on the lawn. After, it looks like frost.

৯৹

This Sunday we get to go skating at Ice House Pond. Dad drives. "Pipe down," he says into the backseat. Mum faces him with white fur around her hood. She calls him Uncs, short for Uncle, a kind of joke, I guess, calling him Uncs while he calls her Mum, same as we do. We are making a racket.

"Will you quit it?" Caitlin elbows Gus.

"What? I'm not doing anything."

"Just taking up all the room."

Sherman's in the way back. "How come Chicky always gets the front?"

"'Cause he's the baby." Delilah is always explaining everything.

"I en not a baby," says Chicky without turning around.

Caitlin frowns at me. "Who said you could wear my scarf?"

I ask into the front seat, "Can we go to the Fairy Garden?" even though I know we won't.

"Why couldn't Rummy come?"

Delilah says, "Because Dad didn't want him to."

Sherman wants to know how old Dad was when he learned how to skate.

Dad says, "About your age." He has a deep voice.

"Really?" I think about that for a minute, about Dad being Sherman's age.

"What about Mum?" says Caitlin.

This isn't his department so he just keeps driving. Mum shifts her shoulders more toward us but still looks at Dad.

"When I was a little girl on the Boston Common." Her teeth are white and she wears fuchsia lipstick. "We used to have skating parties."

Caitlin leans close to Mum's fur hood, crossing her arms into a pillow. "What? With dates?"

Mum bats her eyelashes. "Oh sure. Lots of beaux." She smiles, acting like a flirt. I look at Dad but he's concentrating on the road.

We saw one at a football game once. He had a huge mustard overcoat and a bow tie and a pink face like a ham. He bent down to shake our tiny hands, half-looking at Mum the whole time. Dad was someplace else getting the tickets. His name was Hank. After he went, Mum put her sunglasses on her head and told us she used to watch him play football at BC. Dad never wears a tie except to work. One time Gus got lost. We waited until the last people had trickled out and the stadium was practically empty. It had started to get dark and the headlights were crisscrossing out of the parking field. Finally Dad came back carrying him, walking fast, Gus's head bobbing around and his face all blotchy. Dad rolled his eyes and made a kidding groan to Mum and we laughed because Gus was always getting lost. When Mum took him, he rammed his head onto her shoulder and hid his face while we walked back to the car, and under Mum's hand you could see his back twitching, trying to hide his crying.

We have Ice House Pond all to ourselves. In certain places the ice is bumpy and if you glide on it going *Aauuuuhhhh* in a low tone, your voice wobbles and vibrates. Every once in a while, a crack shoots across the pond, echoing just beneath the surface, and you feel something drop in the hollow of your back. It sounds like someone's jumped off a steel wire and left it twanging in the air.

I try to teach Delilah how to skate backwards but she's flopping all over the ice, making me laugh, with her hat lopsided and her mittens dangling on strings out of her sleeves. When Gus falls, he just stays there, polishing the ice with his mitten. Dad sees him and says, "I don't care if my son is a violin player," kidding.

Dad played hockey in college and was so good his name is on a plaque that's right as you walk into the Harvard rink. He can go really fast. He takes off — *whoosh* — whizzing, circling at the edge of the pond, taking long strides, then gliding, chopping his skates, crossing over in little jumps. He goes zipping by and we watch him: his hands behind him in a tight clasp, his face as calm as if he were just walking along, only slightly forward. When he sweeps a corner, he tips in, then rolls into a hunch, and starts the long side-pushing again. After he stops, his face is red and the tears leak from the sides of his eyes and there's a white smudge around his mouth like frostbite. Sherman, copying, goes chopping forward on collapsed ankles and it sounds like someone sharpening knives.

Mum practices her 3s from when she used to figure skate. She pushes forward on one skate, turning in the middle like a petal flipped suddenly in the wind. We always make her do a spin. First she does backward crossovers, holding her wrists like a tulip in her fluorescent pink parka, then stops straight up on her toes, sucking in her breath and dips, twisted, following her own tight circle, faster and faster, drawing her feet together. Whirring around, she lowers into a crouch, ventures out one balanced leg, a twirling whirlpool, hot pink, rises again, spinning, into a blurred pillar or a tornado, her arms going above her head and her hands like the eye of a needle. Then suddenly: stop. Hiss of ice shavings, stopped. We clap our mittens. Her hood has slipped off and her hair is spread across her shoulders like when she's reading in bed, and she takes white breaths with her teeth showing and her pink mouth smiling. She squints over our heads. Dad is way off at the car, unlacing his skates on the tailgate but he doesn't turn. Mum's face means that it's time to go.

Chicky stands in the front seat leaning against Dad. Our parkas crinkle in the cold car. Sherman has been chewing on his thumb and it's a pointed black witch's hat. A rumble goes through the car like a monster growl and before we back up Dad lifts Chicky and sets him leaning against Mum instead.

The speed bumps are marked with yellow stripes and it's like sea serpents have crawled under the tar. When we bounce, Mum says, "Thank-you-ma'am" with a lilt in her voice. If it was only Mum, the radio would be on and she'd turn it up on the good ones. Dad snaps it off because there's enough racket already. He used to listen to opera when he got home from work but not anymore. Now we give him hard hugs and he changes upstairs then goes into the TV room to the same place on the couch, propping his book on his crossed knees and reaching for his drink without looking up. At supper, he comes in for a handful of onion-flavored bacon crisps or a dish of miniature corn-on-the-cobs pickled. Mum keeps us in the kitchen longer so he can have a little peace and quiet. Ask him what he wants for Christmas and he'll say, "No more arguing." When Mum clears our plates, she takes a bite of someone's hot dog or a quick spoonful of peas before dumping the rest down the pig.

In the car, we ask Dad if we can stop at Shucker's for candy. When he doesn't answer, it means *No*. Mum's eyes mean *Not today*. She says, "It's treat night anyway." Treats are ginger ale and vanilla ice cream.

On Sunday nights we have treats and BLTs and get to watch Ted Mack and Ed Sullivan. There are circus people on almost every time, doing cartwheels or flips or balancing. We stand up in our socks and try some of it. Delilah does an imitation of Elvis by making jump-rope handles into a microphone. Girls come on with silver shoes and their stomachs showing and do clappity tap dances. "That's a cinch," says Mum behind us.

"Let's see you then," we say and she goes over to the brick in front of the fireplace to show us. She bangs the floor with her sneakers, pumping and kicking, thudding her heels in smacks, not like clicking at all, swinging her arms out in front of her like she's wading through the jungle. She speeds up, staring straight at Dad who's reading his book, making us laugh even harder. He's always like that. Sometimes for no reason, he'll snap out of it, going "What? What? What's all this? What's going on?" as if he's emerged from a dark tunnel, looking like he does when we wake him up and he hasn't put on his glasses yet, sort of angry. He sits there before dinner, popping black olives into his mouth one at a time, eyes never leaving his book. His huge glass mug is from college and in the lamplight you can see the liquid separate. One layer is beer, the rest is gin. Even smelling it makes you gag.

Dad would never take us to Shucker's for candy. With him, we do things outside. If there's a storm we go down to the rocks to see the waves — you have to yell — and get sopped. Or if Mum needs a nap, we go to the beach. In the spring it's wild and windy as anything, which I love. The wind presses against you and you kind of choke but in a good way. Sherman and I run, run, run! Couples at the end are so far away you can hardly tell they're moving. Rummy races around with other dogs, flipping his rear like a goldfish, snapping at the air, or careening in big looping circles across the beach. Caitlin jabs a stick into the wet part and draws flowers. Chicky smells the seaweed by smushing it all over his face. Delilah's dark bangs jitter across her forehead like magnets and she yells back to Gus lagging behind. Dad looks at things far away. He points out birds — a great blue heron near the breakers as thin as a safety pin or an osprey in the sky, tilting like a paper cutout. We collect little things. Delilah holds out a razor shell on one sandy palm for Dad to take and he says "Uh-huh" and calls Rummy. When Sherman, grinning, carries a dead seagull to him, Dad says, "Cut that out." Once in Maine, I found a triangle of blue and white china and showed it to Dad. "Ah yes, a bit of crockery," he said.

"Do you think it's from the Indians?" I whispered. They had made the arrowheads we found on the beach.

"I think it's probably debris," he said and handed it back to me. According to Mum, debris is the same thing as litter, as in Don't Be a Litterbug.

When we get home from skating, it's already started to get dark. Sherman runs up first and beats us to the door but can't open it himself. We are all used to how warm it was in the car so everybody's going "Brrr," or "Hurry up," banging our feet on the porch so it thunders. The sky is dark blue glass and the railing seems whiter and the fur on Mum's hood glows. From the driveway Dad yells, "I'm going downtown. Be right back," slamming the door and starting the car again.

Delilah yells, "Can I come?" and Gus goes, "Me too!" as we watch the car back up.

"Right back," says his deep voice through the crack in the window and he rounds the side of the house.

"How come he didn't stop on the way home?" asks Caitlin, sticking out her chin.

"Yah," says Delilah. "How come?" We look at Mum.

She kicks the door with her boot. "In we go, totsies," she says instead of answering and drops someone's skate on the porch because she's carrying so much stuff.

Gus gets in a bad mood, standing by the door with his coat on, not moving a muscle. His hat has flaps over the ears. Delilah flops onto the hall sofa, her neck bent, ramming her chin into her chest. "Why don't you take off your coat and stay awhile?" she says, drumming her fingers on her stomach as slow as a spider.

"I don't have to."

"Yah," Sherman butts in. "Who says you're the boss?" He's lying on the marble tile with Rummy, scissor-kicking his legs like windshield wipers.

"No one," says Delilah, her fingers rippling along.

On the piano bench, Caitlin is picking at her split ends. We can hear Mum in the kitchen putting the dishes away.

Banging on the piano fast because she knows it by heart, Caitlin plays "Walking in a Winter Wonderland." Delilah sits up and imitates her behind her back, shifting her hips from side to side, making us all laugh. Caitlin whips around. "What?"

"Nothing." But we can't help laughing.

"Nothing what?" says Mum coming around the corner, picking up mittens and socks from the floor, snapping on the lights.

Delilah stiffens her legs. "We weren't doing anything," she says.

We make room for Mum on the couch and huddle. Gus perches at the edge, sideways.

"When's Dad coming back?" he says.

"You know your father," says Mum vaguely, smoothing Delilah's hair on her lap, daydreaming at the floor but thinking about something. When Dad goes to the store, he only gets one thing, like a can of black bean soup or watermelon rind.

"What shall we play?" says Sherman, strangling Rummy in a hug.

"Yah. Yah. Let's do something," we say and turn to Mum.

She narrows her eyes into spying slits. "All rightee. I might have a little idea."

"What?" we all shout, excited. "What?" Mum hardly ever plays with us because she has to do everything else.

She rises, slowly, lifting her eyebrows, hinting. "You'll see."

"What?" says Gus and his bottom lip loosens nervously.

Delilah's dark eyes flash like jumping beans. "Yah, Mum. What?"

"Just come with me," says Mum in a singsong and we scamper after her. At the bottom of the stairs, she crouches in the middle of us. Upstairs behind her, it's dark.

"Where are we going?" asks Caitlin, and everybody watches Mum's face, thinking of the darkness up there.

"Hee hee hee," she says in her witch voice. "We're going to surprise your father, play a little trick."

"What?" asks Caitlin again, getting ready to worry, but Mum's already creeping up the stairs so we follow, going one mile per hour like her, not making a peep even though there's no one in the house to hear us.

Suddenly she wheels around. "We're going to hide," she cackles.

"Where?" we all want to know, sneaking along like burglars.

Her voice is hushed. "Just come with me."

At the top of the stairs it is dark and we whisper.

"How about your room?" says Delilah. "Maybe under the bed."

"No," says Sherman breathlessly. "In the fireplace." We all laugh because we could never fit in there.

Standing in the hall, Mum opens the door to the linen closet and pulls the light-string. "How about right here?" The light falls across our faces. On the shelves are stacks of bedcovers and rolled puffs, red and white striped sheets and pink towels, everything clean and folded and smelling of soap.

All of a sudden Caitlin gasps, "Wait — I hear the car!"

Quickly we all jumble and scramble around, bumbling and knocking and trying to cram ourselves inside. Sherman makes whimpering noises like an excited dog. "Ssshhh," we say or "Hurry, Hurry," or "Wait." I knee up to a top shelf and Sherman gets a boost after me and then Delilah comes grunting up. We play in here sometimes. Gus and Chicky crawl into the shelf underneath, wedging themselves in sideways. Caitlin half-sits on molding with her legs dangling and one hand braced against the door-frame. When the rushing settles, Mum pulls out the light and hikes herself up on the other ledge. Everyone is off the ground then, and quiet.

Delilah giggles. Caitlin says "Ssshhh" and I say "Come on" in a whisper. Only when Mum says "Hush" do we all stop and listen. Everyone is breathing; a shelf creaks. Chicky knocks a towel off and it hits the ground like a pillow. Gus says, "I don't hear anything." "Ssshhh," we say. Mum touches the door and light widens and we listen. Nothing.

"False alarm," says Sherman.

Our eyes start to get used to the dark. Next to me Delilah gurgles her spit.

"What do you think he'll do?" whispers Caitlin. We all smile, curled up in the darkness with Mum, thinking how fooled he'll be, coming back and not a soul anywhere, standing in the hall with all the lights glaring not hearing a sound.

"Where will he think we've gone?" We picture him looking around for a long time, till finally we all pour out of the closet.

"He'll find out," Mum whispers. Someone laughs at the back of his throat, like a cricket quietly ticking.

Delilah hisses, "Wait —"

"Forget it," says Caitlin, who knows it's a false alarm.

"What will he do?" we ask Mum.

She's in the darkest part of the closet, on the other side of the light slant. We hear her voice. "We'll see."

"My foot's completely fallen asleep," says Caitlin.

"Kick it," says Mum's voice.

"Ssshhh," lisps Chicky, and we laugh at him copying everybody.

Gus's muffled voice comes from under the shelf. "My head's getting squished."

"Move it," says Delilah.

"Quiet!"

And then we really do hear the car.

"Silence, monkeys," says Mum, and we all hush, holding our breaths. The car hums up the hill.

The motor dies and the car shuts off. We hear the door crack, then clip shut. Footsteps bang up the echoing porch, loud, toe-hard and scuffing. The glass panes rattle when the door opens, resounding in the empty hall, and then the door slams in the dead quiet, reverberating through the whole side of the house. Someone in the closet squeaks like a hamster. Downstairs there isn't a sound.

"Anybody home?" he bellows, and we try not to giggle.

Now what will he do? He strides across the deep hall, going by the foot of the stairs, obviously wondering where everybody's gone, stopping at the hooks to hang up his parka.

"What's he doing?" whispers Caitlin to herself.

"He's by the mitten basket," says Sherman. We all have smiles, our teeth like watermelon wedges, grinning in the dark.

He yells toward the kitchen, "Hello?" and we hunch our shoulders to keep from laughing, holding on to something tight like our toes or the shelf, or biting the side of our mouths.

He starts back into the hall.

"He's getting warmer," whispers Mum's voice, far away. We all wait for his footsteps on the stairs.

But he stops by the TV room doorway. We hear him rustling something, a paper bag, taking out what he's bought, the bag crinkling, setting something down on the hall table, then crumpling up the bag and pitching it in the wastebasket. Gus says, "Why doesn't he — ?" "Ssshhh," says Mum like spitting and we all freeze. He moves again — his footsteps turn and bang on the hollow threshold into the TV room where the rug pads the sound.

Next we hear the TV click on, the sound swelling and the dial switching *tickah tikka tikka tick* till it lands on a crowd roar, a football game. We can hear the announcer's voice and the hiss-breath behind it of cheering.

Then it's the only sound in the house.

"What do we do now?" says Delilah only half-whispering. Mum slips down from her shelf and her legs appear in the light, touching down.

Still hushed, Sherman goes, "Let's keep hiding."

The loud thud is from Caitlin jumping down. She uses her regular voice. "Forget it. I'm sick of this anyway." Everyone starts to rustle. Chicky panics, "I can't get down," as if we're about to desert him.

"Stop being such a baby," says Delilah, disgusted.

Mum doesn't say anything, just opens the door all the way. Past the banister in the hall it is yellow and bright. We climb out of the closet, feet-feeling our way down backward, bumping out one at a time, knocking down blankets and washcloths by mistake. Mum guides our backs and checks our landings. We don't leave the narrow hallway. The light from downstairs shines up through the railing and casts shadows on the wall — bars of light and dark like a fence. Standing in it we have stripes all over us. "Hey look," we say whispering, with the football drone in the background, even though this isn't anything new — we always see this, holding out your arms and seeing the stripes. Lingering near the linen closet, we wait. Mum picks up the tumbled things, restacking the stuff we knocked down, folding things, clinching a towel with her chin, smoothing it over her stomach and then matching the corners left and right, like crossing herself, patting everything into neat piles. The light gets like this every night after we've gone to bed and we creep into the hall to listen to Mum and Dad downstairs. The bands of shadows go across our nightgowns and pajamas and we press our foreheads against the railing trying to hear the mumbling of what Mum and Dad are saying down there. Then we hear the deep boom of Dad clearing his throat and look up at Mum. Though she is turned away, we still can see the wince on her face like when you are waiting to be hit or right after you have been. So we keep standing there, our hearts pounding, waving our hands through the flickered stripes, suddenly interested the way you get when it's time to take a bath and you are mesmerized by something. We're stalling, waiting for Mum to finish folding, waiting to see what she's going to do next because we don't want to go downstairs yet, where Dad is, without her.

Amy Tan
Four Directions

Amy Tan was born in Oakland, California in 1952. Her parents, both Chinese immigrants, came to America in the 1940s, her father working as an electrical engineer as well as in the Baptist clergy. After his death, her mother took the family to Europe, where Tan completed high school in Montreux, Switzerland. Returning to the United States, she attended Linfield College and then San José State University, earning a degree in English. She then made a living creating technical manuals for the electronics industry (one of them, for IBM, was entitled *Telecommunications and You*) while studying creative writing in the evening, an activity that changed her life. After completion of her first three pieces of short fiction, she was offered a contract for *The Joy Luck Club,* which quickly became one of the most celebrated books in contemporary literature and the subject of a major Hollywood motion picture. Her subsequent volumes include *The Kitchen God's Wife, The Hundred Secret Senses, The Bonesetter's Daughter,* and, in 2005, *Saving Fish from Drowning.* Her fiction is renowned for its sensitive portrayal of cultural duality within Chinese American families, who attempt to retain the language, customs, and sense of identity associated with the mother country while at the same time becoming fully part of their new society. Equally as important is the dynamic between mothers and daughters, who struggle for dominance or freedom, control or independence, often with devastating emotional consequences. That issue informs "Four Directions," which also involves a humorous ethnic conflict when the protagonist, Waverly Jong, brings her white boyfriend to dinner with her Chinese family. The ironic tension of that scene is at the center of the action even as a swirl of other issues enriches the thematic strands of one of Tan's finest short stories.

Amy Tan, "Four Directions," *The Joy Luck Club* (New York: G.P. Putnam's Sons, 1989), 166–84.

I had taken my mother out to lunch at my favorite Chinese restaurant in hopes of putting her in a good mood, but it was a disaster.

When we met at the Four Directions Restaurant, she eyed me with immediate disapproval. *"Ai-ya!* What's the matter with your hair?" she said in Chinese.

"What do you mean, 'What's the matter,'" I said. "I had it cut." Mr. Rory had styled my hair differently this time, an asymmetrical blunt-line fringe that was shorter on the left side. It was fashionable, yet not radically so.

"Looks chopped off," she said. "You must ask for your money back."

I sighed. "Let's just have a nice lunch together, okay?"

She wore her tight-lipped, pinched-nose look as she scanned the menu, muttering, "Not too many good things, this menu." Then she tapped the waiter's arm, wiped the length of her chopsticks with her finger, and sniffed: "This greasy thing, do you expect me to eat with it?" She made a show of washing out her rice bowl with hot tea, and then warned other restaurant patrons seated near us to do the same. She told the waiter to make sure the soup was very hot, and of course, it was by her tongue's expert estimate "not even *lukewarm*."

"You shouldn't get so upset," I said to my mother after she disputed a charge of two extra dollars because she had specified chrysanthemum tea, instead of the regular green tea. "Besides, unnecessary stress isn't good for your heart."

"Nothing is wrong with my heart," she huffed as she kept a disparaging eye on the waiter.

And she was right. Despite all the tension she places on herself — and others — the doctors have proclaimed that my mother, at age sixty-nine, has the blood pressure of a sixteen-year-old and the strength of a horse. And that's what she is. A Horse, born in 1918, destined to be obstinate and frank to the point of tactlessness. She and I make a bad combination, because I'm a Rabbit, born in 1951, supposedly sensitive, with tendencies toward being thin-skinned and skittery at the first sign of criticism.

After our miserable lunch, I gave up the idea that there would ever be a good time to tell her the news: that Rich Schields and I were getting married.

§ᔰ

"Why are you so nervous?" my friend Marlene Ferber had asked over the phone the other night. "It's not as if Rich is the scum of the earth. He's a tax attorney like you, for Chrissake. How can she criticize that?"

"You don't know my mother," I said. "She never thinks anybody is good enough for anything."

"So elope with the guy," said Marlene.

"That's what I did with Marvin." Marvin was my first husband, my high school sweetheart.

"So there you go," said Marlene.

"So when my mother found out, she threw her shoe at us," I said. "And that was just for openers."

§ᔰ

My mother had never met Rich. In fact, every time I brought up his name — when I said, for instance, that Rich and I had gone to the symphony, that Rich had taken my four-year-old daughter, Shoshana, to the zoo — my mother found a way to change the subject.

"Did I tell you," I said as we waited for the lunch bill at Four Directions, "what a great time Shoshana had with Rich at the Exploratorium? He —"

"Oh," interrupted my mother, "I didn't tell you. Your father, doctors say maybe need exploratory surgery. But no, now they say everything normal, just too much constipated." I gave up. And then we did the usual routine.

I paid for the bill, with a ten and three ones. My mother pulled back the dollar bills and counted out exact change, thirteen cents, and put that on the tray instead, explaining firmly: "No tip!" She tossed her head back with a triumphant smile. And while my mother used the restroom, I slipped the waiter a five-dollar bill. He nodded to me with deep understanding. While she was gone, I devised another plan.

"*Choszle!*" — Stinks to death in there! — muttered my mother when she returned. She nudged me with a little travel package of Kleenex. She did not trust other people's toilet paper. "Do you need to use?"

I shook my head. "But before I drop you off, let's stop at my place real quick. There's something I want to show you."

⌘

My mother had not been to my apartment in months. When I was first married, she used to drop by unannounced, until one day I suggested she should call ahead of time. Ever since then, she has refused to come unless I issue an official invitation.

And so I watched her, seeing her reaction to the changes in my apartment — from the pristine habitat I maintained after the divorce, when all of a sudden I had too much time to keep my life in order — to this present chaos, a home full of life and love. The hallway floor was littered with Shoshana's toys, all bright plastic things with scattered parts. There was a set of Rich's barbells in the living room, two dirty snifters on the coffee table, the disemboweled remains of a phone that Shoshana and Rich took apart the other day to see where the voices came from.

"It's back here," I said. We kept walking, all the way to the back bedroom. The bed was unmade, dresser drawers were hanging out with socks and ties spilling over. My mother stepped over running shoes, more of Shoshana's toys, Rich's black loafers, my scarves, a stack of white shirts just back from the cleaner's.

Her look was one of painful denial, reminding me of a time long ago when she took my brothers and me down to a clinic to get our polio booster shots. As the needle went into my brother's arm and he screamed, my mother looked at me with agony written all over her face and assured me, "Next one doesn't hurt."

But now, how could my mother *not* notice that we were living together, that this was serious and would not go away even if she didn't talk about it? She had to say something.

I went to the closet and then came back with a mink jacket that Rich had given me for Christmas. It was the most extravagant gift I had ever received.

I put the jacket on. "It's sort of a silly present," I said nervously. "It's hardly ever cold enough in San Francisco to wear mink. But it seems to be a fad, what people are buying their wives and girlfriends these days."

My mother was quiet. She was looking toward my open closet, bulging with racks of shoes, ties, my dresses, and Rich's suits. She ran her fingers over the mink.

"This is not so good," she said at last. "It is just leftover strips. And the fur is too short, no long hairs."

"How can you criticize a gift!" I protested. I was deeply wounded. "He gave me this from his heart."

"That is why I worry," she said.

And looking at the coat in the mirror, I couldn't fend off the strength of her will anymore, her ability to make me see black where there was once white, white where there was once black. The coat looked shabby, an imitation of romance.

"Aren't you going to say anything else?" I asked softly.

"What I should say?"

"About the apartment? About *this*?" I gestured to all the signs of Rich lying about.

She looked around the room, toward the hall, and finally she said, "You have career. You are busy. You want to live like mess, what I can say?"

♪♪

My mother knows how to hit a nerve. And the pain I feel is worse than any other kind of misery. Because what she does always comes as a shock, exactly like an electric jolt, that grounds itself permanently in my memory. I still remember the first time I felt it.

♪♪

I was ten years old. Even though I was young, I knew my ability to play chess was a gift. It was effortless, so easy. I could see things on the chessboard that other people could not. I could create barriers to protect myself that were invisible to my opponents. And this gift gave me supreme confidence. I knew what my opponents would do, move for move. I knew at exactly what point their faces would fall when my seemingly simple and childlike strategy would reveal itself as a devastating and irrevocable course. I loved to win.

And my mother loved to show me off, like one of my many trophies she polished. She used to discuss my games as if she had devised the strategies.

"I told my daughter, Use your horses to run over the enemy," she informed one shopkeeper. "She won very quickly this way." And of course, she had said this before the game — that and a hundred other useless things that had nothing to do with my winning.

To our family friends who visited she would confide, "You don't have to be so smart to win chess. It is just tricks. You blow from the North, South, East, and West. The other person becomes confused. They don't know which way to run."

I hated the way she tried to take all the credit. And one day I told her so, shouting at her on Stockton Street, in the middle of a crowd of people. I told her she didn't know anything, so she shouldn't show off. She should shut up. Words to that effect.

That evening and the next day she wouldn't speak to me. She would say stiff words to my father and brothers, as if I had become invisible and she was talking about a rotten fish she had thrown away but which had left behind its bad smell.

I knew this strategy, the sneaky way to get someone to pounce back in anger and fall into a trap. So I ignored her. I refused to speak and waited for her to come to me.

After many days had gone by in silence, I sat in my room, staring at the sixty-four squares of my chessboard, trying to think of another way. And that's when I decided to quit playing chess.

Of course I didn't mean to quit forever. At most, just for a few days. And I made a show of it. Instead of practicing in my room every night, as I always did, I marched into the living room and sat down in front of the television set with my brothers, who stared at me, an unwelcome intruder. I used my brothers to further my plan; I cracked my knuckles to annoy them.

"Ma!" they shouted. "Make her stop. Make her go away."

But my mother did not say anything.

Still I was not worried. But I could see I would have to make a stronger move. I decided to sacrifice a tournament that was coming up in one week. I would refuse to play in it. And my mother would certainly have to speak to me about this. Because the sponsors and the benevolent associations would start calling her, asking, shouting, pleading to make me play again.

And then the tournament came and went. And she did not come to me, crying, "Why are you not playing chess?" But I was crying inside, because I learned that a boy whom I had easily defeated on two other occasions had won.

I realized my mother knew more tricks than I had thought. But now I was tired of her game. I wanted to start practicing for the next tournament. So I decided to pretend to let her win. I would be the one to speak first.

"I am ready to play chess again," I announced to her. I had imagined she would smile and then ask me what special thing I wanted to eat.

But instead, she gathered her face into a frown and stared into my eyes, as if she could force some kind of truth out of me.

"Why do you tell me this?" she finally said in sharp tones. "You think it is so easy. One day quit, next day play. Everything for you is this way. So smart, so easy, so fast."

"I said I'll play," I whined.

"No!" she shouted, and I almost jumped out of my scalp. "It is not so easy anymore."

I was quivering, stunned by what she said, in not knowing what she meant. And then I went back to my room. I stared at my chessboard, its sixty-four squares, to figure out how to undo this terrible mess. And after staring like this for many hours, I actually believed that I had made the white squares black and the black squares white, and everything would be all right.

And sure enough, I won her back. That night I developed a high fever, and she sat next to my bed, scolding me for going to school without my sweater. In the morning she was there as well, feeding me rice porridge flavored with chicken broth she had strained herself. She said she was feeding me this because I had the chicken pox and one chicken knew how to fight another. And in the afternoon, she sat in a chair in my room, knitting me a pink sweater while telling me about a sweater that Auntie Suyuan had knit for her daughter June, and how it was most unattractive and of the worst yarn. I was so happy that she had become her usual self.

But after I got well, I discovered that, really, my mother had changed. She no longer hovered over me as I practiced different chess games. She did not polish my trophies every day. She did not cut out the small newspaper item that mentioned my name. It was as if she had erected an invisible wall and I was secretly groping each day to see how high and how wide it was.

At my next tournament, while I had done well overall, in the end the points were not enough. I lost. And what was worse, my mother said nothing. She seemed to walk around with this satisfied look, as if it had happened because she had devised this strategy.

I was horrified. I spent many hours every day going over in my mind what I had lost. I knew it was not just the last tournament. I examined every move, every piece, every square. And I could no longer see the secret weapons of each piece, the magic within the intersection of each square. I could see only my mistakes, my weaknesses. It was as though I had lost my magic armor. And everybody could see this, where it was easy to attack me.

Over the next few weeks and later months and years, I continued to play, but never with that same feeling of supreme confidence. I fought hard, with fear and desperation. When I won, I was grateful, relieved. And when I lost, I was filled with growing dread, and then terror that I was no longer a prodigy, that I had lost the gift and had turned into someone quite ordinary.

When I lost twice to the boy whom I had defeated so easily a few years before, I stopped playing chess altogether. And nobody protested. I was fourteen.

§§

"You know, I really don't understand you," said Marlene when I called her the night after I had shown my mother the mink jacket. "You can tell the IRS to piss up a rope, but you can't stand up to your own mother."

"I always intend to and then she says these little sneaky things, smoke bombs and little barbs, and . . ."

"Why don't you tell her to stop torturing you," said Marlene. "Tell her to stop ruining your life. Tell her to shut up."

"That's hilarious," I said with a half-laugh. "You want me to tell my mother to shut up?"

"Sure, why not?"

"Well, I don't know if it's explicitly stated in the law, but you can't *ever* tell a Chinese mother to shut up. You could be charged as an accessory to your own murder."

I wasn't so much afraid of my mother as I was afraid for Rich. I already knew what she would do, how she would attack him, how she would criticize him. She would be quiet at first. Then she would say a word about something small, something she had noticed, and then another word, and another, each one flung out like a little piece of sand, one from this direction, another from behind, more and more, until his looks, his character, his soul would have eroded away. And even if I recognized her strategy, her sneak attack, I was afraid that some unseen speck of truth would fly into my eye, blur what I was seeing and transform him from the divine man I thought he was into someone quite mundane, mortally wounded with tiresome habits and irritating imperfections.

This happened to my first marriage, to Marvin Chen, with whom I had eloped when I was eighteen and he was nineteen. When I was in love with Marvin, he was nearly perfect. He graduated third in his class at Lowell and got a full scholarship to Stanford. He played tennis. He had bulging calf muscles and one hundred forty-six straight black hairs on his chest. He made everyone laugh and his own laugh was deep, sonorous, masculinely sexy. He prided himself on having favorite love positions for different days and hours of the week; all he had to whisper was "Wednesday afternoon" and I'd shiver.

But by the time my mother had had her say about him, I saw his brain had shrunk from laziness, so that now it was good only for thinking up excuses. He chased golf and tennis balls to run away from family responsibilities. His eye wandered up and down other girls' legs, so he didn't know how to drive straight home anymore. He liked to tell big jokes to make other people feel little. He made a loud show of leaving ten-dollar tips to strangers but was stingy with presents to family. He thought waxing his red sports car all afternoon was more important than taking his wife somewhere in it.

My feelings for Marvin never reached the level of hate. No, it was worse in a way. It went from disappointment to contempt to apathetic boredom. It wasn't until after we separated, on nights when Shoshana was asleep and I was lonely, that I wondered if perhaps my mother had poisoned my marriage.

Thank God, her poison didn't affect my daughter, Shoshana. I almost aborted her, though. When I found out I was pregnant, I was furious. I secretly referred to my pregnancy as my "growing resentment," and I dragged Marvin down to the clinic so he would have to suffer through this too. It turned out we went to the wrong kind of clinic. They made us watch a film, a terrible bit of puritanical brainwash. I saw those little things, babies they called them even at seven weeks, and they had tiny, tiny fingers. And the film said that the baby's translucent fingers could *move,* that we should imagine them clinging for life, grasping for a chance, this miracle of life. If they had shown *anything else* except tiny fingers — so thank God they did. Because Shoshana really was a miracle. She was perfect. I found every detail about her to be remarkable, especially the way she flexed and curled her fingers. From the very moment she flung her fist away from her mouth to cry, I knew my feelings for her were inviolable.

But I worried for Rich. Because I knew my feelings for him were vulnerable to being felled by my mother's suspicions, passing remarks, and innuendos. And I was afraid of what I would then lose, because Rich Schields adored me in the same way I adored Shoshana. His love was unequivocal. Nothing could change it. He expected nothing from me; my mere existence was enough. And at the same time, he said that he had changed — for the *better* — because of me. He was embarrassingly romantic; he insisted he never was until he met me. And this confession made his romantic gestures all the more ennobling. At work, for example, when he would staple "FYI — For Your Information" notes to legal briefs and corporate returns that I had to review, he signed them at the bottom: "FYI — Forever You & I." The firm didn't know about our relationship, and so that kind of reckless behavior on his part thrilled me.

The sexual chemistry was what really surprised me, though. I thought he'd be one of those quiet types who was awkwardly gentle and clumsy, the kind of mild-mannered guy who says, "Am I hurting you?" when I can't feel a thing. But he was so attuned to my every movement I was sure he was reading my mind. He had no inhibitions, and whatever ones he discovered I had he'd pry away from me like little treasures. He saw all those private aspects of me — and I mean not just sexual private parts, but my darker side, my meanness, my pettiness, my self-loathing — all the things I kept hidden. So that with him I was completely naked, and when I was, when I was feeling the most vulnerable — when the wrong word would have sent me flying out the door forever — he always said exactly the right thing at the right moment. He didn't allow me to cover myself up. He would grab my hands, look me straight in the eye and tell me something new about why he loved me.

I'd never known love so pure, and I was afraid that it would become sullied by my mother. So I tried to store every one of these endearments about Rich in my memory, and I planned to call upon them again when the time was necessary.

❧❧

After much thought, I came up with a brilliant plan. I concocted a way for Rich to meet my mother and win her over. In fact, I arranged it so my mother would want to cook a meal especially for him. I had some help from Auntie Suyuan. Auntie Su was my mother's friend from way back. They were very close, which meant they were ceaselessly tormenting each other with boasts and secrets. And I gave Auntie Su a secret to boast about.

After walking through North Beach one Sunday, I suggested to Rich that we stop by for a surprise visit to my Auntie Su and Uncle Canning. They lived on Leavenworth, just a few blocks west of my mother's apartment. It was late afternoon, just in time to catch Auntie Su preparing Sunday dinner.

"Stay! Stay!" she had insisted.

"No, no. It's just that we were walking by," I said.

"Already cooked enough for you. See? One soup, four dishes. You don't eat it, only have to throw it away. Wasted!"

How could we refuse? Three days later, Auntie Suyuan had a thank-you letter from Rich and me. "Rich said it was the best Chinese food he has ever tasted," I wrote.

And the next day, my mother called me, to invite me to a belated birthday dinner for my father. My brother Vincent was bringing his girlfriend, Lisa Lum. I could bring a friend, too.

❧❦

I knew she would do this, because cooking was how my mother expressed her love, her pride, her power, her proof that she knew more than Auntie Su. "Just be sure to tell her later that her cooking was the best you ever tasted, that it was far better than Auntie Su's." I told Rich. "Believe me."

The night of the dinner, I sat in the kitchen watching her cook, waiting for the right moment to tell her about our marriage plans, that we had decided to get married next July, about seven months away. She was chopping eggplant into wedges, chattering at the same time about Auntie Suyuan: "She can only cook looking at a recipe. My instructions are in my fingers. I know what secret ingredients to put in just by using my nose!" And she was slicing with such a ferocity, seemingly inattentive to her sharp cleaver, that I was afraid her fingertips would become one of the ingredients of the red-cooked eggplant and shredded pork dish.

I was hoping she would say something first about Rich. I had seen her expression when she opened the door, her forced smile as she scrutinized him from head to toe, checking her appraisal of him against that already given to her by Auntie Suyuan. I tried to anticipate what criticisms she would have.

Rich was not only *not* Chinese, he was a few years younger than I was. And unfortunately, he looked much younger with his curly red hair, smooth pale skin, and the splash of orange freckles across his nose. He was a bit on the short side, compactly built. In his dark business suits, he looked nice but easily forgettable, like somebody's nephew at a funeral. Which was why I didn't notice him the first year we worked together at the firm. But my mother noticed everything.

"So what do you think of Rich?" I finally asked, holding my breath.

She tossed the eggplant in the hot oil and it made a loud, angry hissing sound. "So many spots on his face," she said.

I could feel the pinpricks on my back. "They're freckles. Freckles are good luck, you know," I said a bit too heatedly in trying to raise my voice above the din of the kitchen.

"Oh?" she said innocently.

"Yes, the more spots the better. Everybody knows that."

She considered this a moment and then smiled and spoke in Chinese: "Maybe this is true. When you were young, you got the chicken pox. So many spots, you had to stay home for ten days. So lucky, you thought."

I couldn't save Rich in the kitchen. And I couldn't save him later at the dinner table.

He had brought a bottle of French wine, something he did not know my parents could not appreciate. My parents did not even own wineglasses. And then he also made the mistake of drinking not one but two frosted glasses full, while everybody else had a half-inch "just for taste."

When I offered Rich a fork, he insisted on using the slippery ivory chopsticks. He held them splayed like the knock-kneed legs of an ostrich while picking up a large chunk of sauce-coated eggplant. Halfway between his plate and his open mouth, the chunk fell on his crisp white shirt and then slid into his crotch. It took several minutes to get Shoshana to stop shrieking with laughter.

And then he had helped himself to big portions of the shrimp and snow peas, not realizing he should have taken only a polite spoonful, until everybody had had a morsel.

He had declined the sautéed new greens, the tender and expensive leaves of bean plants plucked before the sprouts turn into beans. And Shoshana refused to eat them also, pointing to Rich: "He didn't eat them! He didn't eat them!"

He thought he was being polite by refusing seconds, when he should have followed my father's example, who made a big show of taking small portions of seconds, thirds, and even fourths, always saying he could not resist another bite of something or other, and then groaning that he was so full he thought he would burst.

But the worst was when Rich criticized my mother's cooking, and he didn't even know what he had done. As is the Chinese cook's custom, my mother always made disparaging remarks about her own cooking. That night she chose to direct it toward her famous steamed pork and preserved vegetable dish, which she always served with special pride.

"Ai! This dish not salty enough, no flavor," she complained, after tasting a small bite. "It is too bad to eat."

This was our family's cue to eat some and proclaim it the best she had ever made. But before we could do so, Rich said, "You know, all it needs is a little soy sauce." And he proceeded to pour a riverful of the salty black stuff on the platter, right before my mother's horrified eyes.

And even though I was hoping throughout the dinner that my mother would somehow see Rich's kindness, his sense of humor and boyish charm, I knew he had failed miserably in her eyes.

Rich obviously had had a different opinion on how the evening had gone.

When we got home that night, after we put Shoshana to bed, he said modestly, "Well. I think we hit it off *A-o-kay.*" He had the look of a dalmatian, panting, loyal, waiting to be petted.

"Uh-hmm," I said. I was putting on an old nightgown, a hint that I was not feeling amorous. I was still shuddering, remembering how Rich had firmly shaken both my parents' hands with that same easy familiarity he used with nervous new clients. "Linda, Tim," he said, "we'll see you again soon, I'm sure." My parents' names are Lindo and Tin Jong, and nobody, except a few older family friends, ever calls them by their first names.

"So what did she say when you told her?" And I knew he was referring to our getting married. I had told Rich earlier that I would tell my mother first and let her break the news to my father.

"I never had a chance," I said, which was true. How could I have told my mother I was getting married, when at every possible moment we were alone, she seemed to remark on how much expensive wine Rich liked to drink, or how pale and ill he looked, or how sad Shoshana seemed to be.

Rich was smiling. "How long does it take to say, Mom, Dad, I'm getting married?"

"You don't understand. You don't understand my mother."

Rich shook his head. "Whew! You can say that again. Her English was *so* bad. You know, when she was talking about that dead guy showing up on *Dynasty,* I thought she was talking about something that happened in China a long time ago."

ஒ

That night, after the dinner, I lay in bed, tense. I was despairing over this latest failure, made worse by the fact that Rich seemed blind to it all. He looked so pathetic. *So pathetic,* those words! My mother was doing it again, making me see black where I once saw white. In her hands, I always became the pawn. I could only run away. And she was the queen, able to move in all directions, relentless in her pursuit, always able to find my weakest spots.

I woke up late, with teeth clenched and every nerve on edge. Rich was already up, showered, and reading the Sunday paper. "Morning, doll," he said between noisy munches of cornflakes. I put on my jogging clothes and headed out the door, got into the car, and drove to my parents' apartment.

Marlene was right. I had to tell my mother — that I knew what she was doing, her scheming ways of making me miserable. By the time I arrived, I had enough anger to fend off a thousand flying cleavers.

My father opened the door and looked surprised to see me. "Where's Ma?" I asked, trying to keep my breath even. He gestured to the living room in back.

I found her sleeping soundly on the sofa. The back of her head was resting on a white embroidered doily. Her mouth was slack and all the lines in her face were gone. With her smooth face, she looked like a young girl, frail, guileless, and innocent. One arm hung limply down the side of the sofa. Her chest was still. All her strength was gone. She had no weapons, no demons surrounding her. She looked powerless. Defeated.

And then I was seized with a fear that she looked like this because she was dead. She had died when I was having terrible thoughts about her. I had wished her out of my life, and she had acquiesced, floating out of her body to escape my terrible hatred.

"Ma!" I said sharply. "Ma!" I whined, starting to cry.

And her eyes slowly opened. She blinked. Her hands moved with life. "*Shemma?* Meimei-ah? Is that you?"

I was speechless. She had not called me Meimei, my childhood name, in many years. She sat up and the lines in her face returned, only now they seemed less harsh, soft creases of worry. "Why are you here? Why are you crying? Something has happened!"

I didn't know what to do or say. In a matter of seconds, it seemed, I had gone from being angered by her strength, to being amazed by her innocence, and then frightened by her vulnerability. And now I felt numb, strangely weak, as if someone had unplugged me and the current running through me had stopped.

"Nothing's happened. Nothing's the matter. I don't know why I'm here," I said in a hoarse voice. "I wanted to talk to you. . . . I wanted to tell you . . . Rich and I are getting married."

I squeezed my eyes shut, waiting to hear her protests, her laments, the dry voice delivering some sort of painful verdict.

"*Jrdaule*" — I already know this — she said, as if to ask why I was telling her this again.

"You know?"

"Of course. Even if you didn't tell me," she said simply.

This was worse than I had imagined. She had known all along, when she criticized the mink jacket, when she belittled his freckles and complained about his drinking habits. She disapproved of him. "I know you hate him," I said in a quavering voice. "I know you think he's not good enough, but I . . ."

"Hate? Why do you think I hate your future husband?"

"You never want to talk about him. The other day, when I started to tell you about him and Shoshana at the Exploratorium, you . . . you changed the subject . . . you started talking about Dad's exploratory surgery and then . . ."

"What is more important, explore fun or explore sickness?"

I wasn't going to let her escape this time. "And then when you met him, you said he had spots on his face."

She looked at me, puzzled. "Is this not true?"

"Yes, but, you said it just to be mean, to hurt me, to . . ."

"Ai-ya, why do you think these bad things about me?" Her face looked old and full of sorrow. "So you think your mother is this bad. You think I have a secret meaning. But it is you who has this meaning. Ai-ya! She thinks I am this bad!" She sat straight and proud on the sofa, her mouth clamped tight, her hands clasped together, her eyes sparkling with angry tears.

Oh, her strength! her weakness! — both pulling me apart. My mind was flying one way, my heart another. I sat down on the sofa next to her, the two of us stricken by the other.

I felt as if I had lost a battle, but one that I didn't know I had been fighting. I was weary. "I'm going home," I finally said. "I'm not feeling too good right now."

"You have become ill?" she murmured, putting her hand on my forehead.

"No," I said. I wanted to leave. "I . . . I just don't know what's inside me right now."

"Then I will tell you," she said simply. And I stared at her. "Half of everything inside you," she explained in Chinese, "is from your father's side. This is natural. They are the Jong clan, Cantonese people. Good, honest people. Although sometimes they are bad-tempered and stingy. You know this from your father, how he can be unless I remind him."

And I was thinking to myself, Why is she telling me this? What does this have to do with anything? But my mother continued to speak, smiling broadly, sweeping her hand. "And half of everything inside you is from me, your mother's side, from the Sun clan in Taiyuan." She wrote the characters out on the back of an envelope, forgetting that I cannot read Chinese.

"We are a smart people, very strong, tricky, and famous for winning wars. You know Sun Yat-sen, hah?"

I nodded.

"He is from the Sun clan. But his family moved to the south many centuries ago, so he is not exactly the same clan. My family has always live in Taiyuan, from before the days of even Sun Wei. Do you know Sun Wei?"

I shook my head. And although I still didn't know where this conversation was going, I felt soothed. It seemed like the first time we had had an almost normal conversation.

"He went to battle with Genghis Khan. And when the Mongol soldiers shot at Sun Wei's warriors — heh! — their arrows bounced off the shields like rain on stone. Sun Wei had made a kind of armor so strong Genghis Khan believed it was magic!"

"Genghis Khan must have invented some magic arrows, then," I said. "After all, he conquered China."

My mother acted as if she hadn't heard me right. "This is true, we always know how to win. So now you know what is inside you, almost all good stuff from Taiyuan."

"I guess we've evolved to just winning in the toy and electronics market," I said.

"How do you know this?" she asked eagerly.

"You see it on everything. Made in Taiwan."

"Ai!" she cried loudly. "I'm not from Taiwan!"

And just like that, the fragile connection we were starting to build snapped.

"I was born in China, in *Taiyuan*," she said. "Taiwan is not China."

"Well, I only thought you said 'Taiwan' because it sounds the same," I argued, irritated that she was upset by such an unintentional mistake.

"Sound is completely different! Country is completely different!" she said in a huff. "People there only dream that it is China, because if you are Chinese you can never let go of China in your mind."

We sank into silence, a stalemate. And then her eyes lighted up. "Now listen. You can also say the name of Taiyuan is Bing. Everyone from that city calls it that. Easier for you to say. Bing, it is a nickname."

She wrote down the character, and I nodded as if this made everything perfectly clear. "The same as here," she added in English. "You call Apple for New York. Frisco for San Francisco."

"Nobody calls San Francisco that!" I said, laughing. "People who call it that don't know any better."

"Now you understand my meaning," said my mother triumphantly.

I smiled.

And really, I did understand finally. Not what she had just said. But what had been true all along.

I saw what I had been fighting for: It was for me, a scared child, who had run away a long time ago to what I had imagined was a safer place. And hiding in this place, behind my invisible barriers, I knew what lay on the other side: Her side attacks. Her secret weapons. Her uncanny ability to find my weakest spots. But in the brief instant that I had peered over the barriers I could finally see what was really there: an old woman, a wok for her armor, a knitting needle for her sword, getting a little crabby as she waited patiently for her daughter to invite her in.

෧ඦ

Rich and I have decided to postpone our wedding. My mother says July is not a good time to go to China on our honeymoon. She knows this because she and my father have just returned from a trip to Beijing and Taiyuan.

"It is too hot in the summer. You will only grow more spots and then your whole face will become red!" she tells Rich. And Rich grins, gestures his thumb toward my mother, and says to me, "Can you believe what comes out of her mouth? Now I know where you get your sweet, tactful nature."

"You must go in October. That is the best time. Not too hot, not too cold. I am thinking of going back then too," she says authoritatively. And then she hastily adds: "Of course not with you!"

I laugh nervously, and Rich jokes: "That'd be great, Lindo. You could translate all the menus for us, make sure we're not eating snakes or dogs by mistake." I almost kick him.

"No, this is not my meaning," insists my mother. "Really, I am not asking."

And I know what she really means. She would love to go to China with us. And I would hate it. Three weeks' worth of her complaining about dirty chopsticks and cold soup, three meals a day — well, it would be a disaster.

Yet part of me also thinks the whole idea makes perfect sense. The three of us, leaving our differences behind, stepping on the plane together, sitting side by side, lifting off, moving West to reach the East.

Tim O'Brien
Sweetheart of the Song Tra Bong

Tim O'Brien was born in Austin, Minnesota, in 1946 but grew up in Worthington in the southern part of the state, a setting that figures in much of his fiction. He graduated from Macalester College in 1968, having been a political science major and student body president, and he was quickly drafted and sent to Vietnam. There he served in the infamous Americal division, a unit involved in horrifying combat including the My Lai massacre, in which scores of civilians were executed. He fulfilled his tour of duty, was promoted, and returned home to write *If I Die in a Combat Zone,* a nonfictional account of his experience. But it was his fiction that attracted the greatest adulation. A collection of stories about the war, *The Things They Carried,* was a finalist for the Pulitzer Prize and for the National Book Award. *Going After Cacciato,* a novel, won that recognition, and a host of other prizes soon followed. O'Brien has been given awards from the Guggenheim Foundation, the American Academy of Arts and Letters, and the National Endowment for the Arts. His other books include *Northern Lights, In the Lake of the Woods,* and *July, July,* all novels. "Sweetheart of the Song Tra Bong," included in *The Things They Carried,* is one of his most celebrated stories about Vietnam. It is typical of O'Brien's work in its narrative complexity, since information comes from multiple sources, all of which are potentially unreliable, and the result is a swirl of concerns, rumors, and uncertain accounts. The key figure is Mary Anne Bell, an innocent American teenager who flies to Southeast Asia to be with her boyfriend. Her transition from an innocent to a killing machine is dramatic and metaphoric, suggesting that what became of her is emblematic of what happened to all the young men who served as grunts in the war. The observer of this frightening psychic transformation is the fictional character "Tim O'Brien," not synonymous with the writer, who serves as a central narrator. But much of the information comes from Rat Kiley, who witnessed some of it, heard about some, and imagined the rest. It is a nightmare episode of degradation and inhumanity, but it is a powerful representation of the ethical and psychological reality of that disputed military conflict.

Tim O'Brien, "Sweetheart of the Song Tra Bong," *The Things They Carried* (New York: Broadway Books, 1990), 89–116.

Vietnam was full of strange stories, some improbable, some well beyond that, but the stories that will last forever are those that swirl back and forth across the border between trivia and bedlam, the mad and the mundane. This one keeps returning to me. I heard it from Rat Kiley, who swore up and down to its truth, although in the end, I'll admit, that doesn't amount to much of a warranty. Among the men in Alpha Company, Rat had a reputation for exaggeration and overstatement, a compulsion to rev up the facts, and for most of us it was normal procedure to discount sixty or seventy percent of anything he had to say. If Rat told you, for example, that he'd slept with four girls one night, you could figure it was about a girl and a half. It wasn't a question of deceit. Just the opposite: he wanted to heat up the truth, to make it burn so hot that you would feel exactly what he felt. For Rat Kiley, I think, facts were formed by sensation, not the other way around, and when you listened to one of his stories, you'd find yourself performing rapid calculations in your head, subtracting superlatives, figuring the square root of an absolute and then multiplying by maybe.

Still, with this particular story, Rat never backed down. He claimed to have witnessed the incident with his own eyes, and I remember how upset he became one morning when Mitchell Sanders challenged him on its basic premise.

"It can't happen," Sanders said. "Nobody ships his honey over to Nam. It don't ring true. I mean, you just can't import your own personal poontang."

Rat shook his head, "I *saw* it, man. I was right there. This guy did it."

"His girlfriend?"

"Straight on. It's a fact." Rat's voice squeaked a little. He paused and looked at his hands. "Listen, the guy sends her the money. Flies her over. This cute blonde — just a kid, just barely out of high school — she shows up with a suitcase and one of those plastic cosmetic bags. Comes right out to the boonies. I swear to God, man, she's got on culottes. White culottes and this sexy pink sweater. There she *is*."

I remember Mitchell Sanders folding his arms. He looked over at me for a second, not quite grinning, not saying a word, but I could read the amusement in his eyes.

Rat saw it, too.

"No lie," he muttered. "Culottes."

ऽ ऽ

When he first arrived in-country, before joining Alpha Company, Rat had been assigned to a small medical detachment up in the mountains west of Chu Lai, near the village of Tra Bong, where along with eight other enlisted men he ran an aid station that provided basic emergency and trauma care. Casualties were flown in by helicopter, stabilized, then shipped out to hospitals in Chu Lai or Danang. It was gory work, Rat said, but predictable. Amputations, mostly — legs and feet. The area was heavily mined, thick with Bouncing Betties and homemade booby traps. For a medic, though, it was ideal duty, and Rat counted himself lucky. There was plenty of cold beer, three hot meals a day, a tin roof over his head. No humping at all. No officers, either. You could let your hair grow, he said, and you didn't have to polish your boots or snap off salutes or put up with the usual rear-echelon nonsense. The highest ranking NCO was an E-6 named Eddie Diamond, whose pleasures ran from dope to Darvon, and except for a rare field inspection there was no such thing as military discipline.

As Rat described it, the compound was situated at the top of a flat-crested hill along the northern outskirts of Tra Bong. At one end was a small dirt helipad; at the other end, in a rough semicircle, the mess hall and medical hootches overlooked a river called the Song Tra Bong. Surrounding the place were tangled rolls of concertina wire, with bunkers and reinforced firing positions at staggered intervals, and base security was provided by a mixed unit of RFs, PFs, and ARVN infantry. Which is to say virtually no security at all. As soldiers, the ARVNs were useless; the Ruff-and-Puffs were outright dangerous. And yet even with decent troops the place was clearly indefensible. To the north and west the country rose up in thick walls of wilderness, triple-canopied jungle, mountains unfolding into higher mountains, ravines and gorges and fast-moving rivers and waterfalls and exotic butterflies and steep cliffs and smoky little hamlets and great valleys of bamboo and elephant grass. Originally, in the early 1960s, the place had been set up as a Special Forces outpost, and when Rat Kiley arrived nearly a decade later, a squad of six Green Berets still used the compound as a base of operations. The Greenies were not social animals. Animals, Rat said, but far from social. They had their own hootch at the edge of the perimeter, fortified with sandbags and a metal fence, and except for the bare essentials they avoided contact with the medical detachment. Secretive and suspicious, loners by nature, the six Greenies would sometimes vanish for days at a time, or even weeks, then late in the night they would just as magically reappear, moving like shadows through the moonlight, filing in silently from the dense rain forest off to the west. Among the medics there were jokes about this, but no one asked questions.

While the outpost was isolated and vulnerable, Rat said, he always felt a curious sense of safety there. Nothing much ever happened. The place was never mortared, never taken under fire, and the war seemed to be somewhere far away. On occasion, when casualties came in, there were quick spurts of activity, but otherwise the days flowed by without incident, a smooth and peaceful time. Most mornings were spent on the volleyball court. In the heat of midday the men would head for the shade, lazing away the long afternoons, and after sundown there were movies and card games and sometimes all-night drinking sessions.

It was during one of those late nights that Eddie Diamond first brought up the tantalizing possibility. It was an offhand comment. A joke, really. What they should do, Eddie said, was pool some bucks and bring in a few mama-sans from Saigon, spice things up, and after a moment one of the men laughed and said, "Our own little EM club," and somebody else said, "Hey, yeah, we pay our fuckin' dues, don't we?" It was nothing serious. Just passing time, playing with the possibilities, and so for a while they tossed the idea around, how you could actually get away with it, no officers or anything, nobody to clamp down, then they dropped the subject and moved on to cars and baseball.

Later in the night, though, a young medic named Mark Fossie kept coming back to the subject.

"Look, if you think about it," he said, "it's not that crazy. You could actually do it."

"Do what?" Rat said.

"You know. Bring in a girl. I mean, what's the problem?"

Rat shrugged. "Nothing. A war."

"Well, see, that's the thing," Mark Fossie said. "No war *here*. You could really do it. A pair of solid brass balls, that's all you'd need."

There was some laughter, and Eddie Diamond told him he'd best strap down his dick, but Fossie just frowned and looked at the ceiling for a while and then went off to write a letter.

Six weeks later his girlfriend showed up.

The way Rat told it, she came in by helicopter along with the daily resupply shipment out of Chu Lai. A tall, big-boned blonde. At best, Rat said, she was seventeen years old, fresh out of Cleveland Heights Senior High. She had long white legs and blue eyes and a complexion like strawberry ice cream. Very friendly, too.

At the helipad that morning, Mark Fossie grinned and put his arm around her and said, "Guys, this is Mary Anne."

The girl seemed tired and somewhat lost, but she smiled.

There was a heavy silence. Eddie Diamond, the ranking NCO, made a small motion with his hand, and some of the others murmured a word or two, then they watched Mark Fossie pick up her suitcase and lead her by the arm down to the hootches. For a long while the men were quiet.

"That fucker," somebody finally said.

At evening chow Mark Fossie explained how he'd set it up. It was expensive, he admitted, and the logistics were complicated, but it wasn't like going to the moon. Cleveland to Los Angeles, LA to Bangkok, Bangkok to Saigon. She'd hopped a C-130 up to Chu Lai and stayed overnight at the USO and the next morning hooked a ride west with the resupply chopper.

"A cinch," Fossie said, and gazed down at his pretty girlfriend. "Thing is, you just got to *want* it enough."

Mary Anne Bell and Mark Fossie had been sweethearts since grammar school. From the sixth grade on they had known for a fact that someday they would be married, and live in a fine gingerbread house near Lake Erie, and have three healthy yellow-haired children, and grow old together, and no doubt die in each other's arms and be buried in the same walnut casket. That was the plan. They were very much in love, full of dreams, and in the ordinary flow of their lives the whole scenario might well have come true.

On the first night they set up house in one of the bunkers along the perimeter, near the Special Forces hootch, and over the next two weeks they stuck together like a pair of high school steadies. It was almost disgusting, Rat said, the way they mooned over each other. Always holding hands, always laughing over some private joke. All they needed, he said, were a couple of matching sweaters. But among the medics there was some envy. It was Vietnam, after all, and Mary Anne Bell was an attractive girl. Too wide in the shoulders, maybe, but she had terrific legs, a bubbly personality, a happy smile. The men genuinely liked her. Out on the volleyball court she wore cut-off blue jeans and a black swimsuit top, which the guys appreciated, and in the evenings she liked to dance to music from Rat's portable tape deck. There was a novelty to it; she was good for morale. At times she gave off a kind of come-get-me energy, coy and flirtatious, but apparently it never bothered Mark Fossie. In fact he seemed to enjoy it, just grinning at her, because he was so much in love, and because it was the sort of show that a girl will sometimes put on for her boyfriend's entertainment and education.

Though she was young, Rat said, Mary Anne Bell was no timid child. She was curious about things. During her first days in-country she liked to roam around the compound asking questions: What exactly was a trip flare? How did a Claymore work? What was behind those scary green mountains to the west? Then she'd squint and listen quietly while somebody filled her in. She had a good quick mind. She paid attention. Often, especially during the hot afternoons, she would spend time with the ARVNs out along the perimeter, picking up little phrases of Vietnamese, learning how to cook rice over a can of Sterno, how to eat with her hands. The guys sometimes liked to kid her about it — our own little native, they'd say — but Mary Anne would just smile and stick out her tongue. "I'm here," she'd say, "I might as well learn something."

The war intrigued her. The land, too, and the mystery. At the beginning of her second week she began pestering Mark Fossie to take her down to the village at the foot of the hill. In a quiet voice, very patiently, he tried to tell her that it was a bad idea, way too dangerous, but Mary Anne kept after him. She wanted to get a feel for how people lived, what the smells and customs were. It did not impress her that the VC owned the place.

"Listen, it can't be that bad," she said. "They're human beings, aren't they? Like everybody else?"

Fossie nodded. He loved her.

And so in the morning Rat Kiley and two other medics tagged along as security while Mark and Mary Anne strolled through the ville like a pair of tourists. If the girl was nervous, she didn't show it. She seemed comfortable and entirely at home; the hostile atmosphere did not seem to register. All morning Mary Anne chattered away about how quaint the place was, how she loved the thatched roofs and naked children, the wonderful simplicity of village life. A strange thing to watch, Rat said. This seventeen-year-old doll in her goddamn culottes, perky and fresh-faced, like a cheerleader visiting the opposing team's locker room. Her pretty blue eyes seemed to glow. She couldn't get enough of it. On their way back up to the compound she stopped for a swim in the Song Tra Bong, stripping down to her underwear, showing off her legs while Fossie tried to explain to her about things like ambushes and snipers and the stopping power of an AK-47.

The guys, though, were impressed.

"A real tiger," said Eddie Diamond. "D-cup guts, trainer-bra brains."

"She'll learn," somebody said.

Eddie Diamond gave a solemn nod. "There's the scary part. I promise you, this girl will most definitely learn."

ॐॐ

In parts, at least, it was a funny story, and yet to hear Rat Kiley tell it you'd almost think it was intended as straight tragedy. He never smiled. Not even at the crazy stuff. There was always a dark, far-off look in his eyes, a kind of sadness, as if he were troubled by something sliding beneath the story's surface. Whenever we laughed, I remember, he'd sigh and wait it out, but the one thing he could not tolerate was disbelief. He'd get edgy if someone questioned one of the details. "She *wasn't* dumb," he'd snap. "I never said that. Young, that's all I said. Like you and me. A *girl,* that's the only difference, and I'll tell you something: it didn't amount to jack. I mean, when we first got here — all of us — we were real young and innocent, full of romantic bullshit, but we learned pretty damn quick. And so did Mary Anne."

Rat would peer down at his hands, silent and thoughtful. After a moment his voice would flatten out.

"You don't believe it?" he'd say. "Fine with me. But you don't know human nature. You don't know Nam."

Then he'd tell us to listen up.

ॐॐ

A good sharp mind, Rat said. True, she could be silly sometimes, but she picked up on things fast. At the end of the second week, when four casualties came in, Mary Anne wasn't afraid to get her hands bloody. At times, in fact, she seemed fascinated by it. Not the gore so much, but the adrenaline buzz that went with the job, that quick hot rush in your veins when the choppers settled down and you had to do things fast and right. No time for sorting through options, no thinking at all; you just stuck your hands in and started plugging up holes. She was quiet and steady. She didn't back off from the ugly cases. Over the next day or two, as more casualties trickled in, she learned how to clip an artery and pump up a plastic splint and shoot in morphine. In times of action her face took on a sudden new composure, almost serene, the fuzzy blue eyes narrowing into a tight, intelligent focus. Mark Fossie would grin at this. He was proud, yes, but also amazed. A different person, it seemed, and he wasn't sure what to make of it.

Other things, too. The way she quickly fell into the habits of the bush. No cosmetics, no fingernail filing. She stopped wearing jewelry, cut her hair short and wrapped it in a dark green bandanna. Hygiene became a matter of small consequence. In her second week Eddie Diamond taught her how to disassemble an M-16, how the various parts worked, and from there it was a natural progression to learning how to use the weapon. For hours at a time she plunked away at C-ration cans, a bit unsure of herself, but as it turned out she had a real knack for it. There was a new confidence in her voice, a new authority in the way she carried herself. In many ways she remained naive and immature, still a kid, but Cleveland Heights now seemed very far away.

Once or twice, gently, Mark Fossie suggested that it might be time to think about heading home, but Mary Anne laughed and told him to forget it. "Everything I want," she said, "is right here."

She stroked his arm, and then kissed him.

On one level things remained the same between them. They slept together. They held hands and made plans for after the war. But now there was a new imprecision in the way Mary Anne expressed her thoughts on certain subjects. Not necessarily three kids, she'd say. Not necessarily a house on Lake Erie. "Naturally we'll still get married," she'd tell him, "but it doesn't have to be right away. Maybe travel first. Maybe live together. Just test it out, you know?"

Mark Fossie would nod at this, even smile and agree, but it made him uncomfortable. He couldn't pin it down. Her body seemed foreign somehow — too stiff in places, too firm where the softness used to be. The bubbliness was gone. The nervous giggling, too. When she laughed now, which was rare, it was only when something struck her as truly funny. Her voice seemed to reorganize itself at a lower pitch. In the evenings, while the men played cards, she would sometimes fall into long elastic silences, her eyes fixed on the dark, her arms folded, her foot tapping out a coded message against the floor. When Fossie asked about it one evening, Mary Anne looked at him for a long moment and then shrugged. "It's nothing," she said. "Really nothing. To tell the truth, I've never been happier in my whole life. Never."

Twice, though, she came in late at night. Very late. And then finally she did not come in at all.

Rat Kiley heard about it from Fossie himself. Before dawn one morning, the kid shook him awake. He was in bad shape. His voice seemed hollow and stuffed up, nasal-sounding, as if he had a bad cold. He held a flashlight in his hand, clicking it on and off.

"Mary Anne," he whispered, "I can't *find* her."

Rat sat up and rubbed his face. Even in the dim light it was clear that the boy was in trouble. There were dark smudges under his eyes, the frayed edges of somebody who hadn't slept in a while.

"Gone," Fossie said. "Rat, listen, she's sleeping with somebody. Last night, she didn't even . . . I don't know what to *do*."

Abruptly then, Fossie seemed to collapse. He squatted down, rocking on his heels, still clutching the flashlight. Just a boy — eighteen years old. Tall and blond. A gifted athlete. A nice kid, too, polite and good-hearted, although for the moment none of it seemed to be serving him well.

He kept clicking the flashlight on and off.

"All right, start at the start," Rat said. "Nice and slow. Sleeping with who?"

"I don't know who. Eddie Diamond."

"Eddie?"

"Has to be. The guy's always there, always hanging on her."

Rat shook his head. "Man, I don't know. Can't say it strikes a right note, not with Eddie."

"Yes, but he's —"

"Easy does it," Rat said. He reached out and tapped the boy's shoulder. "Why not just check some bunks? We got nine guys. You and me, that's two, so there's seven possibles. Do a quick body count."

Fossie hesitated. "But I can't . . . If she's there, I mean, if she's with some-body —"

"Oh, Christ."

Rat pushed himself up. He took the flashlight, muttered something, and moved down to the far end of the hootch. For privacy, the men had rigged up curtained walls around their cots, small makeshift bedrooms, and in the dark Rat went quickly from room to room, using the flashlight to pluck out the faces. Eddie Diamond slept a hard deep sleep — the others, too. To be sure, though, Rat checked once more, very carefully, then he reported back to Fossie.

"All accounted for. No extras."

"Eddie?"

"Darvon dreams." Rat switched off the flashlight and tried to think it out. "Maybe she just — I don't know — maybe she camped out tonight. Under the stars or something. You search the compound?"

"Sure I did."

"Well, come on," Rat said. "One more time."

Outside, a soft violet light was spreading out across the eastern hillsides. Two or three ARVN soldiers had built their breakfast fires, but the place was mostly quiet and unmoving. They tried the helipad first, then the mess hall and supply hootches, then they walked the entire six hundred meters of perimeter.

"Okay," Rat finally said. "We got a problem."

⅋

When he first told the story, Rat stopped there and looked at Mitchell Sanders for a time.

"So what's your vote? Where was she?"

"The Greenies," Sanders said.

"Yeah?"

Sanders smiled. "No other option. That stuff about the Special Forces — how they used the place as a base of operations, how they'd glide in and out — all that had to be there for a *reason*. That's how stories work, man."

Rat thought about it, then shrugged.

"All right, sure, the Greenies. But it's not what Fossie thought. She wasn't sleeping with any of them. At least not exactly. I mean, in a way she was sleeping with *all* of them, more or less, except it wasn't sex or anything. They was just lying together, so to speak, Mary Anne and these six grungy weirded-out Green Berets."

"Lying down?" Sanders said.

"You got it."

"Lying down how?"

Rat smiled. "Ambush. All night long, man, Mary Anne's out on fuckin' *ambush*."

ॐ

Just after sunrise, Rat said, she came trooping in through the wire, tired-looking but cheerful as she dropped her gear and gave Mark Fossie a brisk hug. The six Green Berets did not speak. One of them nodded at her, and the others gave Fossie a long stare, then they filed off to their hootch at the edge of the compound.

"Please," she said. "Not a word."

Fossie took a half step forward and hesitated. It was as though he had trouble recognizing her. She wore a bush hat and filthy green fatigues; she carried the standard M-16 automatic assault rifle; her face was black with charcoal.

Mary Anne handed him the weapon. "I'm exhausted," she said. "We'll talk later."

She glanced over at the Special Forces area, then turned and walked quickly across the compound toward her own bunker. Fossie stood still for a few seconds. A little dazed, it seemed. After a moment, though, he set his jaw and whispered something and went after her with a hard, fast stride.

"Not later!" he yelled. "Now!"

What happened between them, Rat said, nobody ever knew for sure. But in the mess hall that evening it was clear that an accommodation had been reached. Or more likely, he said, it was a case of setting down some new rules. Mary Anne's hair was freshly shampooed. She wore a white blouse, a navy blue skirt, a pair of plain black flats. Over dinner she kept her eyes down, poking at her food, subdued to the point of silence. Eddie Diamond and some of the others tried to nudge her into talking about the ambush — What was the feeling out there? What exactly did she see and hear? — but the questions seemed to give her trouble. Nervously, she'd look across the table at Fossie. She'd wait a moment, as if to receive some sort of clearance, then she'd bow her head and mumble out a vague word or two. There were no real answers.

Mark Fossie, too, had little to say.

"Nobody's business," he told Rat that night. Then he offered a brief smile. "One thing for sure, though, there won't be any more ambushes. No more late nights."

"You laid down the law?"

"Compromise," Fossie said. "I'll put it this way — we're officially engaged."
Rat nodded cautiously.

"Well hey, she'll make a sweet bride," he said. "Combat ready."

❦❦

Over the next several days there was a strained, tightly wound quality to the way they treated each other, a rigid correctness that was enforced by repetitive acts of willpower. To look at them from a distance, Rat said, you would think they were the happiest two people on the planet. They spent the long afternoons sunbathing together, stretched out side by side on top of their bunker, or playing backgammon in the shade of a giant palm tree, or just sitting quietly. A model of togetherness, it seemed. And yet at close range their faces showed the tension. Too polite, too thoughtful. Mark Fossie tried hard to keep up a self-assured pose, as if nothing had ever come between them, or ever could, but there was a fragility to it, something tentative and false. If Mary Anne happened to move a few steps away from him, even briefly, he'd tighten up and force himself not to watch her. But then a moment later he'd be watching.

In the presence of others, at least, they kept on their masks. Over meals they talked about plans for a huge wedding in Cleveland Heights — a two-day bash, lots of flowers. And yet even then their smiles seemed too intense. They were too quick with their banter; they held hands as if afraid to let go.

It had to end, and eventually it did.

Near the end of the third week Fossie began making arrangements to send her home. At first, Rat said, Mary Anne seemed to accept it, but then after a day or two she fell into a restless gloom, sitting off by herself at the edge of the perimeter. She would not speak. Shoulders hunched, her blue eyes opaque, she seemed to disappear inside herself. A couple of times Fossie approached her and tried to talk it out, but Mary Anne just stared out at the dark green mountains to the west. The wilderness seemed to draw her in. A haunted look, Rat said — partly terror, partly rapture. It was as if she had come up on the edge of something, as if she were caught in that no-man's-land between Cleveland Heights and deep jungle. Seventeen years old. Just a child, blond and innocent, but then weren't they all?

The next morning she was gone. The six Greenies were gone, too.

In a way, Rat said, poor Fossie expected it, or something like it, but that did not help much with the pain. The kid couldn't function. The grief took him by the throat and squeezed and would not let go.

"Lost," he kept whispering.

❦❦

It was nearly three weeks before she returned. But in a sense she never returned. Not entirely, not all of her.

By chance, Rat said, he was awake to see it. A damp misty night, he couldn't sleep, so he'd gone outside for a quick smoke. He was just standing there, he said, watching the moon, and then off to the west a column of silhouettes appeared as if by magic at the edge of the jungle. At first he didn't recognize her — a small, soft shadow among six other shadows. There was no sound. No real substance either. The seven silhouettes seemed to float across the surface of the earth, like spirits, vaporous and unreal. As he watched, Rat said, it made him think of some weird opium dream. The silhouettes moved without moving. Silently, one by one, they came up the hill, passed through the wire, and drifted in a loose file across the compound. It was then, Rat said, that he picked out Mary Anne's face. Her eyes seemed to shine in the dark — not blue, though, but a bright glowing jungle green. She did not pause at Fossie's bunker. She cradled her weapon and moved swiftly to the Special Forces hootch and followed the others inside.

Briefly, a light came on, and someone laughed, then the place went dark again.

ॐ

Whenever he told the story, Rat had a tendency to stop now and then, interrupting the flow, inserting little clarifications or bits of analysis and personal opinion. It was a bad habit, Mitchell Sanders said, because all that matters is the raw material, the stuff itself, and you can't clutter it up with your own half-baked commentary. That just breaks the spell. It destroys the magic. What you have to do, Sanders said, is trust your own story. Get the hell out of the way and let it tell itself.

But Rat Kiley couldn't help it. He wanted to bracket the full range of meaning.

"I know it sounds far-out," he'd tell us, "but it's not like *impossible* or anything. We all heard plenty of wackier stories. Some guy comes back from the bush, tells you he saw the Virgin Mary out there, she was riding a goddamn goose or something. Everybody buys it. Everybody smiles and asks how fast was they going, did she have spurs on. Well, it's not like that. This Mary Anne wasn't no virgin but at least she was real. I saw it. When she came in through the wire that night, I was right there, I saw those eyes of hers, I saw how she wasn't even the same person no more. What's so impossible about that? She was a girl, that's all. I mean, if it was a guy, everybody'd say, Hey, no big deal, he got caught up in the Nam shit, he got seduced by the Greenies. See what I mean? You got these blinders on about women. How gentle and peaceful they are. All that crap about how if we had a pussy for president there wouldn't be no more wars. Pure garbage. You got to get rid of that sexist attitude."

Rat would go on like that until Mitchell Sanders couldn't tolerate it any longer. It offended his inner ear.

"The story," Sanders would say. "The whole tone, man, you're wrecking it."

"Tone?"

"The *sound*. You need to get a consistent sound, like slow or fast, funny or sad. All these digressions, they just screw up your story's *sound*. Stick to what happened."

Frowning, Rat would close his eyes.

"Tone?" he'd say. "I didn't know it was all that complicated. The girl joined the zoo. One more animal — end of story."

"Yeah, fine. But tell it right."

♫

At daybreak the next morning, when Mark Fossie heard she was back, he stationed himself outside the fenced-off Special Forces area. All morning he waited for her, and all afternoon. Around dusk Rat brought him something to eat.

"She has to come out," Fossie said. "Sooner or later, she has to."

"Or else what?" Rat said.

"I go get her. I bring her out."

Rat shook his head. "Your decision. I was you, though, no way I'd mess around with any Greenie types, not for nothing."

"It's Mary Anne in there."

"Sure, I know that. All the same, I'd knock real extra super polite."

Even with the cooling night air Fossie's face was slick with sweat. He looked sick. His eyes were bloodshot; his skin had a whitish, almost colorless cast. For a few minutes Rat waited with him, quietly watching the hootch, then he patted the kid's shoulder and left him alone.

It was after midnight when Rat and Eddie Diamond went out to check on him. The night had gone cold and steamy, a low fog sliding down from the mountains, and somewhere out in the dark they heard music playing. Not loud but not soft either. It had a chaotic, almost unmusical sound, without rhythm or form or progression, like the noise of nature. A synthesizer, it seemed, or maybe an electric organ. In the background, just audible, a woman's voice was half singing, half chanting, but the lyrics seemed to be in a foreign tongue.

They found Fossie squatting near the gate in front of the Special Forces area. Head bowed, he was swaying to the music, his face wet and shiny. As Eddie bent down beside him, the kid looked up with dull eyes, ashen and powdery, not quite in register.

"Hear that?" he whispered. "You *hear*? It's Mary Anne."

Eddie Diamond took his arm. "Let's get you inside. Somebody's radio, that's all it is. Move it now."

"Mary Anne. Just listen."

"Sure, but —"

"Listen!"

Fossie suddenly pulled away, twisting sideways, and fell back against the gate. He lay there with his eyes closed. The music — the noise, whatever it was — came from the hootch beyond the fence. The place was dark except for a small glowing window, which stood partly open, the panes dancing in bright reds and yellows as though the glass were on fire. The chanting seemed louder now. Fiercer, too, and higher pitched.

Fossie pushed himself up. He wavered for a moment then forced the gate open. "That voice," he said. "Mary Anne."

Rat took a step forward, reaching out for him, but Fossie was already moving fast toward the hootch. He stumbled once, caught himself, and hit the door hard with both arms. There was a noise — a short screeching sound, like a cat — and the door swung in and Fossie was framed there for an instant, his arms stretched out, then he slipped inside. After a moment Rat and Eddie followed quietly. Just inside the door they found Fossie bent down on one knee. He wasn't moving.

Across the room a dozen candles were burning on the floor near the open window. The place seemed to echo with a weird deep-wilderness sound — tribal music — bamboo flutes and drums and chimes. But what hit you first, Rat said, was the smell. Two kinds of smells. There was a topmost scent of joss sticks and incense, like the fumes of some exotic smokehouse, but beneath the smoke lay a deeper and much more powerful stench. Impossible to describe, Rat said. It paralyzed your lungs. Thick and numbing, like an animal's den, a mix of blood and scorched hair and excrement and the sweet-sour odor of moldering flesh — the stink of the kill. But that wasn't all. On a post at the rear of the hootch was the decayed head of a large black leopard; strips of yellow-brown skin dangled from the overhead rafters. And bones. Stacks of bones — all kinds. To one side, propped up against a wall, stood a poster in neat black lettering: ASSEMBLE YOUR OWN GOOK!! FREE SAMPLE KIT!! The images came in a swirl, Rat said, and there was no way you could process it all. Off in the gloom a few dim figures lounged in hammocks, or on cots, but none of them moved or spoke. The background music came from a tape deck near the circle of candles, but the high voice was Mary Anne's.

After a second Mark Fossie made a soft moaning sound. He started to get up but then stiffened.

"Mary Anne?" he said.

Quietly then, she stepped out of the shadows. At least for a moment she seemed to be the same pretty young girl who had arrived a few weeks earlier. She was barefoot. She wore her pink sweater and a white blouse and a simple cotton skirt.

For a long while the girl gazed down at Fossie, almost blankly, and in the candlelight her face had the composure of someone perfectly at peace with herself. It took a few seconds, Rat said, to appreciate the full change. In part it was her eyes: utterly flat and indifferent. There was no emotion in her stare, no sense of the person behind it. But the grotesque part, he said, was her jewelry. At the girl's throat was a necklace of human tongues. Elongated and narrow, like pieces of blackened leather, the tongues were threaded along a length of copper wire, one overlapping the next, the tips curled upward as if caught in a final shrill syllable.

Briefly, it seemed, the girl smiled at Mark Fossie.

"There's no sense talking," she said. "I know what you think but it's not . . . it's not *bad*."

"Bad?" Fossie murmured.

"It's not."

In the shadows there was laughter.

One of the Greenies sat up and lighted a cigar. The others lay silent.

"You're in a place," Mary Anne said softly, "where you don't belong."

She moved her hand in a gesture that encompassed not just the hootch but everything around it, the entire war, the mountains, the mean little villages, the trails and trees and rivers and deep misted-over valleys.

"You just don't *know*," she said. "You hide in this little fortress, behind wire and sandbags, and you don't know what it's all about. Sometimes I want to *eat* this place. Vietnam. I want to swallow the whole country — the dirt, the death — I just want to eat it and have it there inside me. That's how I feel. It's like . . . this appetite. I get scared sometimes — lots of times — but it's not *bad*. You know? I feel close to myself. When I'm out there at night, I feel close to my own body, I can feel my blood moving, my skin and my fingernails, everything, it's like I'm full of electricity and I'm glowing in the dark — I'm on fire almost — I'm burning away into nothing — but it doesn't matter because I know exactly who I am. You can't feel like that anywhere else."

All this was said softly, as if to herself, her voice slow and impassive. She was not trying to persuade. For a few moments she looked at Mark Fossie, who seemed to shrink away, then she turned and moved back into the gloom.

There was nothing to be done.

Rat took Fossie's arm, helped him up, and led him outside. In the darkness there was that weird tribal music, which seemed to come from the earth itself, from the deep rain forest, and a woman's voice rising up in a language beyond translation.

Mark Fossie stood rigid.

"Do something," he whispered. "I can't just let her go like that."

Rat listened for a time, then shook his head.

"Man, you must be deaf. She's already gone."

♪♪

Rat Kiley stopped there, almost in midsentence, which drove Mitchell Sanders crazy.

"What next?" he said.

"Next?"

"The girl. What happened to her?"

Rat made a small, tired motion with his shoulders. "Hard to tell for sure. Maybe three, four days later I got orders to report here to Alpha Company. Jumped the first chopper out, that's the last I ever seen of the place. Mary Anne, too."

Mitchell Sanders stared at him.

"You can't do that."

"Do what?"

"Jesus Christ, it's against the *rules*," Sanders said. "Against human *nature*. This elaborate story, you can't say, Hey, by the way, I don't know the *ending*. I mean, you got certain obligations."

Rat gave a quick smile. "Patience, man. Up to now, everything I told you is from personal experience, the exact truth, but there's a few other things I heard secondhand. Thirdhand, actually. From here on it gets to be . . . I don't know what the word is."

"Speculation."

"Yeah, right." Rat looked off to the west, scanning the mountains, as if expecting something to appear on one of the high ridgelines. After a second he shrugged. "Anyhow, maybe two months later I ran into Eddie Diamond over in Bangkok — I was on R&R, just this fluke thing — and he told me some stuff I can't vouch for with my own eyes. Even Eddie didn't really see it. He heard it from one of the Greenies, so you got to take this with a whole shakerful of salt."

Once more, Rat searched the mountains, then he sat back and closed his eyes.

"You know," he said abruptly, "I loved her."

"Say again?"

"A lot. We all did, I guess. The way she looked, Mary Anne made you think about those girls back home, how clean and innocent they all are, how they'll never understand any of this, not in a billion years. Try to tell them about it, they'll just stare at you with those big round candy eyes. They won't understand zip. It's like trying to tell somebody what chocolate tastes like."

Mitchell Sanders nodded. "Or shit."

"There it is, you got to taste it, and that's the thing with Mary Anne. She was *there*. She was up to her eyeballs in it. After the war, man, I promise you, you won't find nobody like her."

Suddenly, Rat pushed up to his feet, moved a few steps away from us, then stopped and stood with his back turned. He was an emotional guy.

"Got hooked, I guess," he said. "I loved her. So when I heard from Eddie about what happened, it almost made me . . . Like you say, it's pure speculation."

"Go on," Mitchell Sanders said. "Finish up."

❦❧

What happened to her, Rat said, was what happened to all of them. You come over clean and you get dirty and then afterward it's never the same. A question of degree. Some make it intact, some don't make it at all. For Mary Anne Bell, it seemed, Vietnam had the effect of a powerful drug: that mix of unnamed terror and unnamed pleasure that comes as the needle slips in and you know you're risking something. The endorphins start to flow, and the adrenaline, and you hold your breath and creep quietly through the moonlit nightscapes; you become intimate with danger; you're in touch with the far side of yourself, as though it's another hemisphere, and you want to string it out and go wherever the trip takes you and be host to all the possibilities inside yourself. Not *bad*, she'd said. Vietnam made her glow in the dark. She wanted more, she wanted to penetrate deeper into the mystery of herself, and after a time the wanting became needing, which turned then to craving.

According to Eddie Diamond, who heard it from one of the Greenies, she took a greedy pleasure in night patrols. She was good at it; she had the moves. All camouflaged up, her face smooth and vacant, she seemed to flow like water through the dark, like oil, without sound or center. She went barefoot. She stopped carrying a weapon. There were times, apparently, when she took crazy, death-wish chances — things that even the Greenies balked at. It was as if she were taunting some wild creature out in the bush, or in her head, inviting it to show itself, a curious game of hide-and-go-seek that was played out in the dense terrain of a nightmare. She was lost inside herself. On occasion, when they were taken under fire, Mary Anne would stand quietly and watch the tracer rounds snap by, a little smile at her lips, intent on some private transaction with the war. Other times she would simply vanish altogether — for hours, for days.

And then one morning, all alone, Mary Anne walked off into the mountains and did not come back.

No body was ever found. No equipment, no clothing. For all he knew, Rat said, the girl was still alive. Maybe up in one of the high mountain villes, maybe with the Montagnard tribes. But that was guesswork.

There was an inquiry, of course, and a week-long air search, and for a time the Tra Bong compound went crazy with MP and CID types. In the end, however, nothing came of it. It was a war and the war went on. Mark Fossie was busted to PFC, shipped back to a hospital in the States, and two months later received a medical discharge. Mary Anne Bell joined the missing.

But the story did not end there. If you believed the Greenies, Rat said, Mary Anne was still somewhere out there in the dark. Odd movements, odd shapes. Late at night, when the Greenies were out on ambush, the whole rain forest seemed to stare in at them — a watched feeling — and a couple of times they almost saw her sliding through the shadows. Not quite, but almost. She had crossed to the other side. She was part of the land. She was wearing her culottes, her pink sweater, and a necklace of human tongues. She was dangerous. She was ready for the kill.

Robert Olen Butler

Open Arms

Robert Olen Butler was born in Illinois in 1945, went to Northwestern University as a theater major, and then studied playwriting at the University of Iowa. He served in the army during the Vietnam War as a sergeant in military intelligence, where he developed a fluency in Vietnamese. After his service, he worked for a time in publishing until 1981, when he wrote his first novel about the war, *The Alleys of Eden.* *Sun Dogs,* another novel about Vietnam, followed a year later. His best book relating to the subject appeared in 1992, *A Good Scent from a Strange Mountain,* which won the Pulitzer Prize for fiction. In all, Butler has published a dozen books bringing him numerous prestigious recognitions, including a Guggenheim Fellowship, a National Endowment for the Arts Fellowship, and a National Magazine Award for fiction. "Open Arms," part of *A Good Scent from a Strange Mountain,* first appeared in the *Missouri Review* in 1990, and it has attracted significant critical comment. The title suggests a rich ambiguity, the open arms of the American military in receiving defectors from the opposition, and the open arms of the prostitute in the pornographic film that precipitates the conclusion. "Arms" refers both to weapons and to human appendages, to destruction and to amorous embrace. As is typical of Butler, the narrative itself has a double focus. In one sense it is an exercise in self-revelation: the Vietnamese narrator, now living in Louisiana, evaluating himself, his motives, feelings, values. But the story is also about Thập, who defected from the communist forces after they killed his wife and children. His portrait is a deeply humane one, conveying his sense of decency, his political philosophy, his code of honor. The narrator primarily observes him and comes to understand him, making "Open Arms" more of a psychological and ethical study than one of military conflict.

Robert Olen Butler, "Open Arms," *A Good Scent from a Strange Mountain* (New York: Henry Holt and Company, 1992), 1–15.

I have no hatred in me. I'm almost certain of that. I fought for my country long enough to lose my wife to another man, a cripple. This was because even though I was alive, I was dead to her, being far away. Perhaps it bothers me a little that his deformity was something he was born with and not earned in the war. But even that doesn't matter. In the end, my country itself was lost and I am no longer there and the two of them are surely suffering, from what I read in the papers about life in a unified Vietnam. They mean nothing to me, really. It seems strange even to mention them like this, and it is stranger still to speak of them before I speak of the man who suffered the most complicated feeling I could imagine. It is he who makes me feel sometimes that I am sitting with my legs crossed in an attitude of peace and with an acceptance of all that I've been taught about the suffering that comes from desire.

There are others I could hate. But I feel sorry for my enemies and the enemies of my country. I live on South Mary Poppins Drive in Gretna, Louisiana, and since I speak perfect English, I am influential with the others who live here, the Westbank Vietnamese. We are all of us from South Vietnam. If you go across the bridge and into New Orleans and you take the interstate north and then turn on a highway named after a chef, you will come to the place called Versailles.

There you will find the Vietnamese who are originally from the North. They are Catholics in Versailles. I am a Buddhist. But what I know now about things, I learned from a communist one dark evening in the province of Phu'ó'c Tuy in the Republic of South Vietnam.

I was working as an interpreter for the Australians in their base camp near Núi Ð'ât. The Australians were different from Americans when they made a camp. The Americans cleared the land, cut it and plowed it and leveled it and strung their barbed wire and put up their tin hootches. The Australians put up tents. They lived under canvas with wooden floors and they didn't cut down the trees. They raised their tents under the trees and you could hear the birds above you when you woke in the morning, and I could think of home that way. My village was far away, up-country, near Pleiku, but my wife was still my wife at that time. I could lie in a tent under the trees and think of her and that would last until I was in the mess hall and I was faced with eggs and curried sausages and beans for breakfast.

The Australians made a good camp, but I could not understand their food, especially at the start of the day. The morning I met Ðặng Văn Thập, I first saw him across the mess hall staring at a tray full of this food. He had the commanding officer at one elbow and the executive officer at his other, so I knew he was important, and I looked at Thập closely. His skin was dark, basic peasant blood like me, and he wore a sport shirt of green and blue plaid. He could be anybody on a motor scooter in Saigon or hustling for xích-lộ fares in Vũng Tàu. But I knew there was something special about him right away.

His hair was wildly fanned on his head, the product of VC field-barbering, but there was something else about him that gave him away. He sat between these two Australian officers who were nearly a head taller, and he was hunched forward a little bit. But he seemed enormous, somehow. The people in our village believe in ghosts. Many people in Vietnam have this belief. And sometimes a ghost will appear in human form and then vanish. When that happens and you think back on the encounter, you realize that all along you felt like you were near something enormous, like if you came upon a mountain in the dark and could not see it but knew it was there. I had something of that feeling as I looked at Thập for the first time. Not that I believed he was a ghost. But I knew he was much bigger than the body he was in as he stared at the curried sausages.

Then there was a stir to my left, someone sitting down, but I didn't look right away because Thập held me. "You'll have your chance with him, mate," a voice said in a loud whisper, very near my ear. I turned and it was Captain Townsend, the intelligence officer. His mustache, waxed and twirled to two sharp points, twitched as it usually did when he and I were in the midst of an interrogation and he was getting especially interested in what he heard. But it was Thập now causing the twitch. Townsend's eyes had slid away from me and back across the mess hall, and I followed his gaze. Another Vietnamese was arriving with a tray, an ARVN major, and the C.O. slid over and let the new man sit next to Thập. The major said a few words to Thập and Thập made some sort of answer and the major spoke to the C.O.

"He's our new bushman scout," Townsend said. "The major there is heading back to division after breakfast and then we can talk to him."

I'd heard that a new scout was coming in, but he would be working mostly with the units out interdicting the infiltration routes and so I hadn't given him much thought. Townsend was fumbling around for something and I glanced over. He was pulling a slip of paper out of his pocket. He read a name off the paper, but he butchered the tones and I had no idea what he was saying. I took the paper from him and read Thập's name. Townsend said, "They tell me he's a real smart little bastard. Political cadre. Before that he was a sapper. Brains and a killer, too. Hope this conversion of his is for real."

I looked up and it was the ARVN major who was doing all the talking. He was in fatigues that were so starched and crisp they could sit there all by themselves, and his hair was slicked into careful shape and rose over his forehead in a pompadour the shape of the front fender on the elegant old Citroën sedans you saw around Saigon. Thập had sat back in his chair now and he was watching the major talk, and if I was the major I'd feel very nervous, because the man beside him had the mountain shadow and the steady look of the ghost of somebody his grandfather had cheated or cuckolded or murdered fifty years ago and he was back to take him.

It wasn't until the next day that Captain Townsend dropped Thập's file into the center of my desk. The desk was spread with a dozen photographs, different angles on two dead woodcutters that an Australian patrol had shot yesterday. The woodcutters had been in a restricted area, and when they ran, they were killed. The photos were taken after the two had been laid out in their cart, their arms sprawled, their legs angled like they were leaping up and clicking their heels. The fall of Thập's file scattered the photos, fluttered them away. Townsend said, "Look this over right away, mate. We'll have him here in an hour."

The government program that allowed a longtime, hard-core Viet Cong like Thập to switch sides so easily had a stiff name in Vietnamese but it came to be known as "Open Arms." An hour later, when Thập came through the door with Townsend, he filled the room and looked at me once, knowing everything about me that he wished, and the idea of our opening our arms to him, exposing our chests, our hearts, truly frightened me. In my village you ran from a ghost because if he wants you, he can reach into that chest of yours and pull out not only your heart but your soul as well.

I knew the facts about Thập from the file, but I wondered what he would say about some of these things I'd just read. The things about his life, about the terrible act that turned him away from the cause he'd been fighting for. But Townsend grilled him, through me, for an hour first. He asked him all the things an intelligence captain would be expected to ask, even though the file already had the answers to these questions as well. The division interrogation had already learned all that Thập knew about the locations and strengths of the VC units in our area, the names of shadow government cadre in the villages, things like that. But Thập patiently repeated his answers, smoking one Chesterfield cigarette after another, careful about keeping his ash from falling on the floor, never really looking at either of us, not in the eye, only occasionally at our hands, a quick glance, like he expected us to suddenly be holding a weapon, and he seemed very small now, no less smart and skilled in killing, but a man, at last, in my eyes.

So when Captain Townsend was through, he gave me a nod and, as we'd arranged, he stepped out for me to chat with Thập informally. Townsend figured that Thập might feel more comfortable talking with his countryman one on one. I had my doubts about that. Still, I was interested in this man, though not for the reasons Townsend was. At that moment I didn't care about the tactical intelligence my boss wanted, and so even before he was out of the room I intended to ignore it. But I felt no guilt. He had all he needed already.

As soon as the Australian was gone, Thập lifted his face high for the first time and blew a puff of smoke toward the ceiling. This stopped me cold, like he'd just sprung an ambush from the undergrowth where he'd been crouching very low. He did not look at me. He watched the smoke rise and he waited, his face placid. Finally I felt my voice would come out steady and I said, "We are from the same region. I am from Pleiku Province." The file said that Thập was from Kontum, the next province north, bordering both Cambodia and Laos. He said nothing, though he lowered his face a little. He looked straight ahead and took another drag on his cigarette, a long one, the ash lengthening visibly, doubling in size, as he drew the smoke in.

I knew from the file the sadness he was bearing, but I wanted to make him show it to me, speak of it. I knew I should talk with him indirectly, at least for a time. But I could only think of the crude approach, and to my shame, I took it. I said, "Do you have family there?"

His face turned to me now, and I could not draw a breath. I thought for a moment that my first impression of him had been correct. He was a ghost and this was the moment he would carry me away with him. My breath was gone, never to return. But he did not dissolve into the air. His eyes fixed me and then they went down to the file on the desk, as if to say that I asked what I already knew. He had been sent to Phu'ó'c Tuy Province to indoctrinate the villagers. He was a master, our other sources said, of explaining the communist vision of the world to the woodcutters and fishermen and rice farmers. And meanwhile, in Kontum, the tactics had changed, as they always do, and three months ago the VC made a lesson out of a little village that had a chief with a taste for American consumer goods and information to trade for them. This time the lesson was severe and the ones who did not run were all killed. Thập's wife and two children expected to be safe because someone was supposed to know whose family they were. They stayed and they were murdered by the VC and Thập made a choice.

His eyes were still on the file and my breath had come back to me and I said, "Yes, I know."

He turned away again and he stared at the cigarette, watched the curl of smoke without drawing it into him. I said, "But isn't that just the war? I thought you were a believer."

"I still am," he said and then he looked at me and smiled faintly, but the smile was only for himself, like he knew what I was thinking. And he did. "This is nothing new," he said. "I confessed to the same thing at your division headquarters. I believe in the government caring for all the people, the poor before the rich. I believe in the state of personal purity that makes this possible. But I finally came to believe that the government these men from the north want to set up can't be controlled by the very people it's supposed to serve."

"And what do you think of these people you've joined to fight with now?" I said.

He took a last drag on his cigarette and then leaned forward to stub it out in an ashtray at the corner of my desk. He sat back and folded his hands in his lap and his face grew still, his mouth drew down in placid seriousness. "I understand them," he said. "The Americans, too. I learned about their history. What they believe is good."

I admit that my first impulse at this was to challenge him. He didn't know anything about the history of Western democracy until after he'd left the communists. They killed his wife and his children and he wanted to get them. But I knew that what he said was also true. He was a believer. I could see his Buddist upbringing in him. The communists could appeal to that. They couldn't touch the Catholics, but the Buddhists who didn't believe in all the mysticism were well prepared for communism. The communists were full of right views, right intentions, right speech, and all that. And Buddha's second Truth, about the thirst of the passions being the big trap, the communists were real strict about that, real prudes. If a VC got caught by his superiors with a pinup, just a girl in a bathing suit even, he'd be in very deep trouble.

That thing Thập said about personal purity. After it sank in a little bit, it pissed me off. But this is a weakness of my own, I guess, though at times I can't quite see it as a weakness. I'm not that good a Buddhist. I live in America and things just don't look the way my mother and my grandmother explained them to me. But Thập suddenly seemed a little too smug. And I wasn't frightened by him anymore. He was a communist prude and I even had trouble figuring out how he'd brought himself to make a couple of kids. Then, to my shame, I said, "You miss being with your wife, do you?" What I almost said was, "Do you miss sleeping with your wife?" but I wasn't quite that heartless, even with this smug true believer who until very recently had been a bitter enemy of my country.

Changing my question as I did, even as I spoke it, I thought I would never get the answer to what I really wanted to know. As soon as the words were out of my mouth, I felt a flush spread from under my chin and up my face. It was only a minor attack of shame until I saw what was happening before me. I suppose it was the suddenness of this question, its unexpectedness, that caught him off guard. It's an old interrogation trick. But Thập's hands rose gently from his lap and I knew they were remembering her. It all happened in a few seconds and the hands simply lifted up briefly, but I knew without any doubt that his palms, his fingertips, were stunned by the memory of touching her. Then the hands returned to his lap and he said in a low voice, "Of course I miss her."

I asked him no more questions, and after he was gone, my own hands, lying on the desktop, grew restless, rose and then hid in my lap and burned with their own soft memories. I still had a wife and she had not been my wife for long before I'd had to leave her. I knew that Thập was no ghost but a man and he loved his wife and desired her as I loved and desired mine and that was within the bounds of his purity. He was a man, but I wished from then on only to stay far away from him. The infantry guys had their own interpreter and I wouldn't have to deal with Thập and I was very glad for that.

Less than a week later, however, I saw him again. It was on a Sunday. Early that morning there'd been some contact out in the Long Khánh Mountains just to the east of us. First there was the popping of small arms for a few minutes and then a long roar, the mini-guns on the Cobras as they swooped in, and then there was silence.

In the afternoon the enlisted men played cricket and I sat beneath a tree with my eyes on them but not really following this strange game, just feeling the press of the tree's shade and listening to the thunk of the ball on the bat and the smatterings of applause, and I let the breeze bring me a vision of my wife wearing her aó dài, the long silk panels fluttering, as if lifted by this very breeze, as if she was nearby, waiting for me. And a few times as I sat there, I thought of Thập. Maybe it was my wife who brought him to me, the link of our yearning hands. But it wasn't until the evening that I actually saw him.

It was in the officers' club. Sometimes they had a film to show and this was one of the nights. Captain Townsend got me there early to help him move the wicker chairs around to face the big bed sheet they'd put up at one end for a screen. Townsend wouldn't tell me what the film was. When I asked him, he just winked and said, "You'll like it, mate," and I figured it was another of the Norman Wisdom films. This little man, Wisdom, was forever being knocked down and tormented by a world of people bigger than him. Townsend knew I didn't like these films, and so I decided that was what the wink was all about.

Thập came in with a couple of the infantry officers and I was sorry to see that their interpreter wasn't with them. I couldn't understand why they had him here. I guess they were trying to make him feel welcome, a part of their world. I still think that. They just didn't understand what sort of man he was. They clapped him on the back and pointed to the screen and the projector, and they tried their own few words of Vietnamese with him and some of that baby talk, the pidgin English that sounded so ridiculous to me, even with English being my second language. I didn't think Thập would like Norman Wisdom either. Thập and I were both little men.

But when he came in, the thing I was most concerned about was that since I was the only other Vietnamese in the club, Thập would seek me out for help. But he didn't. He glanced at me once and that was it. The two infantry officers took him up to the front row and sat him between them, and when Thập was settled, my attention shifted enough that I finally realized that something was going on here out of the ordinary. The Aussies were unusually boisterous, poking at one another and laughing, and one of them yelled to Townsend, "You intelligence boys have to smuggle this stuff in?"

Townsend laughed and said, "It was too bloody hot even for us, mate."

I didn't know what he was talking about and I was evidently staring at Captain Townsend with my confusion clear on my face. He looked at me and then put his arm around my shoulders. "You'll see," he said. "It's for all us boys who are missing our little ladies." He nodded me toward the chairs and I went and sat a couple of rows behind Thập and a little to his left. I could see only the back of his head, the spray of his hair, his deep brown neck, the collar of his plaid shirt. He raised his face to the screen and the lights went out and the films began.

There were nine of them, each lasting about twenty minutes. The first began without any credits. A man was walking along a country path. He was a large, blond-haired man, Swedish I later learned, though at the time it simply struck me that this wasn't the sort of man who would be in a Norman Wisdom movie. He was dressed in tight blue jeans and a flannel shirt that was unbuttoned, exposing his bare chest. I had never seen an Englishman dressed like that. Or an Australian either. And Wisdom's movies were all in black and white. This one was in grainy color and the camera was quaking just a little bit and then I realized that all I was hearing were the sounds of the projector clicking away and the men beginning to laugh. There was no soundtrack on this film. Someone shouted something that I didn't catch, then someone else. I thought at first that there'd been a mistake. This was the wrong film and the men were telling Townsend to stop the show, put on little Norman. But then the camera turned to a young woman standing by a fence with cows in the background and she was wearing shorts that were cut high up into her crotch and she shook her long hair and the Australians whooped. The camera returned to the man and he was clearly agitated and the club filled with cries that I could understand now: Go for her, mate; put it to her, mate; get on with it.

I glanced at Thập and his face was lifted to the screen, but of course he did not know what was about to happen. I looked up, too, and the man and woman were talking with each other and then they kissed. Not for long. The woman pulled back and knelt down before the man and she unsnapped and unzipped his blue jeans and she pulled them down and he still had his underpants on. I discovered, a little to my surprise, that I could not breathe very well and I felt weak in my arms. I had never seen a film like this, though I'd heard things about them. But there was a moment, when the man remained clad in his underpants, that I thought there was still some boundary here, that this was not a true example of the films I'd heard about.

But the woman squeezed at him there, playfully, smiling, like this was wonderful fun for her, and then she stripped off his underpants. His body was ready for her and that was very clear there, right on the screen, and she seemed truly happy about this and she brought her face near to this part of him and I drew in a sudden breath as she did a thing that I had never even asked my wife to do, though seeing it now made me weak with desire for her.

And then I looked at Thập. It was simply a reflex. I still had not put together what was happening in this club and what Thập was and what had happened to him in his life and what he believed. I looked to him and his face was still lifted; he was watching, and I glanced up and the woman's eyes lifted, too; she looked at the man even as she did this for him, and I returned to Thập and now his face was coming down, very slowly. His head bowed low and it remained bowed and I watched him for as long as I could.

I must admit, to my shame, that it was not very long. I was distracted. I said before, speaking of Thập's "personal purity," that an indifference to this notion is a weakness of mine. I have never remarried, and I must admit that it pleases me to look at the pictures in some of the magazines easily available in America. The women are so naked I feel I know them very well and the looks on their faces are usually so pleasant that they seem somehow willing for me to know them this way — me personally. It's a childish fantasy, I realize, hardly the right intentions, and I suppose someday this little desire will lead to unhappiness. But I am susceptible to that. And on that dark night, in that Australian tent in the province of Phước Tuy, I was filled with desire, and I watched all nine films, desiring my wife — mostly her, I think — but at times, too, briefly desiring one of these long-haired women who took such pleasure in the passing farmer, the sailor on the town, the delivery man, even the elderly and rather small doctor.

Three more times I looked at Thập. The first time, his head was still bowed. The second time, he was, to my surprise, looking at the screen. He was watching as the camera settled on the face of a dark-haired woman who was being made love to in the only way I had ever known to do it, and for a time all we could see was her face, turned a little to the side, jarred again and again, her eyes closed. But on her face was a smile, quiet, full of love, but a little sad, like she knew her man would soon have to leave her. I know I was reading this into her from my own life. She was a Swedish prostitute making a pornographic movie, and the smile was nothing of this sort. It was fake. And I know that it's the same with all the smiles in the magazines. The smiles of these naked women are the smiles of money, of fame, of a hope to break into movies or buy some cocaine or whatever. But on that night in the Australian tent, Thập and I looked at this woman's face and I know what I felt and something told me that Thập was feeling that, too. He watched for a long time, his face lifted, his hands, I know, yearning.

He was still watching as I turned my own face back to the screen. There were two more films after that, and I viewed them carefully. But my mind was now on Thập. I knew that a few rows in front of me he was suffering. This man had been my sworn enemy till a week ago. The others in this room had been my friends. But Thập was my countryman in some deeper way. And it had nothing to do with his being Vietnamese, either. I knew what was happening inside him. He was desiring his wife, just as I was desiring mine. Except on that night I thought I would one day be with my wife again, and his was newly dead.

But if that was all of it, I don't think he would have made this impression on me that does not leave. These films he saw sucked at his desire, brought the feel of his wife to him, made his hands rise before him. He was a man, after all. I watched the films till there were no more and I felt bad for Thập, his wanting a woman, wanting his wife, his being drawn by that very yearning to a vision of her body as ashes now and bits of bone. The third time I looked at him, his head was bowed again and it probably remained bowed. It was bowed still when the lights went on and Captain Townsend was called to the front of the room and was hailed for his show with wild applause and cheers.

And as we all shuffled out of the tent I saw Thập's face briefly, between his two Australian mates, the two infantry officers who had made him feel like he was really part of the gang. Thập's face told me how it would all end. His eyes were wildly restless, like he'd been on a sapper mission and a flare had just gone off and he suddenly found himself here in the midst of his enemy.

That night he went to a tent and killed one of the two infantry officers, the one, no doubt, who had insisted on his coming to the club. Then Thập killed himself, a bullet in his brain. It was lucky for Townsend that Thập didn't understand the cheers at the end or the captain might have been chosen instead of the infantry officer. Thập's desire for his wife had made him very unhappy. But it alone did not drive him to his final act. That was a result of a history lesson. Thập was a true believer, and that night he felt that he had suddenly understood the democracies he was trying to believe in. He felt that the communists whom he had rightly broken with, who had killed his wife and shown him their own fatal flaw, nevertheless had been right about all the rest of us. The fact that the impurity of the West had touched Thập directly, had made him feel something strongly for his dead wife, had only made things worse. He'd had no choice.

And as for myself, I live my life in the United States of America. I work in a bank. I have my own apartment with my own furniture and I have saved more money than I expect ever to need, if I can keep my job. And there's no worry about that. It's a big bank and they like me there. I can talk to the Vietnamese customers, and they think I'm a good worker beyond that. I read the newspapers. I subscribe to several magazines, and in one of them beautiful women smile at me each month. I no longer think of my wife. I go to the movies. I own a VCR and at last I saw the movie *Mary Poppins.* The street I live on is one of four named after Mary Poppins in our neighborhood. This is true. You can look it up on any street map.

The Vietnamese on the Westbank do not like the Vietnamese in Versailles. The ones on the Westbank point out that for the ones in Versailles, freedom only means the freedom to make money They are cold people, driving people, Northerners. The Southerners say that for them, freedom means the freedom to think, to enjoy life. The Vietnamese in Versailles do not like the Southerners. We are lazy people, to them. Unfocused. Greedy but not capable of working hard together for what we want. They say that they are the ones who understand America and how to succeed here. There are many on the Westbank and in Versailles who are full of hatred.

I say that desire can lead to unhappiness, and so can a strong belief. I can sit for long hours from the late afternoon and into the darkness of night and I do not feel compelled to watch anything or hear anything or do anything. I can think about Thập and I can fold my hands together and at those times there is no hatred at all within me.

Judith Ortiz Cofer
Nada

Judith Ortiz Cofer was born in Puerto Rico in 1952 but came to Patterson, New Jersey with her family when she was a child. Her father served in the United States Navy, and upon his retirement they moved to Augusta, Georgia, where she completed high school and graduated from Augusta College in 1974. She went on to take an M.A. in English from Florida Atlantic University, writing a thesis on Lillian Hellman's Southern plays, and she is now the Franklin Professor of English and Creative Writing at the University of Georgia. A prolific author, she has produced numerous books of verse, fiction, and autobiography, all drawing on the dual culture of her background, a subject that enriches the subjects and themes of her work. Among the best known of her volumes of fiction are *The Meaning of Consuelo, An Island Like You: Stories of the Barrio,* and *The Line of the Sun,* nominated for a Pulitzer Prize. *The Latin Deli* contains both fiction and verse, and *Silent Dancing: A Partial Remembrance of a Puerto Rican Childhood* is highly regarded as among her best creative nonfiction. She has won the Pushcart Prize and the Georgia Author of the Year award, and she has received grants from the Rockefeller Foundation and the National Endowment for the Arts. One of her most famous stories, "Nada" was published in *The Georgia Review* in 1992. It presents a social and linguistic evocation of life in the *barrio* for Puerto Rican immigrants to urban New Jersey while at the same time offering a protest against the unpopular war in Vietnam. It is told by an unnamed narrator, who speaks first in the plural *we* to represent the generalized view of the residents of a tenement and then moves to the singular *I* to reveal her empathy and personal emotions. The focus is on Doña Ernestina, who suffers multiple loses, all deeply felt, until she is left with nothing, with "nada." The revelation of a close community of women from the same ethnic tradition is central to the action, as is the ineffectuality of religion and the complexity of courtship and marriage. All of these themes deepen the incremental development of this remarkable American story.

Judith Ortiz Cofer, "Nada," *The Georgia Review* 46, no. 4 (1992): 754–62.

Almost as soon as Doña Ernestina got the telegram about her son having been killed in Vietnam, she started giving her possessions away. At first we didn't realize what she was doing. By the time we did, it was too late.

The Army people had comforted Doña Ernestina with the news that her son's "remains" would have to be "collected and shipped" back to New Jersey at some later date, since other "personnel" had also been lost on the same day. In other words, she would have to wait until Tony's body could be processed.

Processed. Doña Ernestina spoke that word like a curse when she told us. We were all down in *El Basement* — that's what we called the cellar of our apartment building: no windows for light, boilers making such a racket that you could scream bloody murder and almost no one would hear you. Some of us had started meeting here on Saturday mornings — as much to talk as to wash our clothes — and over the years it became a sort of women's club, where we could catch up on a week's worth of gossip. That Saturday, however, I had dreaded going down the cement steps. All of us had just heard the news about Tony the night before.

I should have known the minute I saw her, holding court in her widow's costume, that something had cracked inside Doña Ernestina. She was in full *luto* — black from head to toe, including a mantilla. In contrast, Lydia and Isabelita were both in rollers and bathrobes: our customary uniform for these Saturday-morning gatherings — maybe our way of saying "No Men Allowed." As I approached them, Lydia stared at me with a scared-rabbit look in her eyes.

Doña Ernestina simply waited for me to join the other two leaning against the machines before she continued explaining what had happened when the news of Tony had arrived at her door the day before. She spoke calmly, a haughty expression on her face, looking like an offended duchess in her beautiful black dress. She was pale, pale, but she had a wild look in her eyes. The officer had told her that — when the time came — they would bury Tony with "full military honors"; for now they were sending her the medal and a flag. But she had said, "No, gracias," to the funeral, and she sent the flag and medals back marked *Y a no vive aquí:* Does not live here anymore. "Tell the Mr. President of the United States what I say: *No, gracias.*"

Then she waited for our response.

Lydia shook her head, indicating that she was speechless. And Elenita looked pointedly at me, forcing me to be the one to speak the words of sympathy for all of us, to reassure Doña Ernestina that she had done exactly what any of us would have done in her place: Yes, we would have all said *No, gracias* to any president who had actually tried to pay for a son's life with a few trinkets and a folded flag.

Doña Ernestina nodded gravely. Then she picked up the stack of neatly folded men's shirts from the sofa (a discard we had salvaged from the sidewalk) and walked regally out of El Basement.

Lydia, who had gone to high school with Tony, burst into tears as soon as Doña Ernestina was out of sight. Elenita and I sat her down between us on the sofa and held her until she had let most of it out. Lydia is still young — a woman not yet visited too often by *la muerte.* Her husband of six months had just gotten his draft notice, and they have been trying for a baby — trying very hard. The walls of El Building are thin enough so that it has become a secret joke (kept only from Lydia and Roberto) that he is far more likely to escape the draft due to acute exhaustion than by becoming a father.

"Doesn't Doña Ernestina feel *anything?*" Lydia asked in between sobs. "Did you see her, dressed up like an actress in a play — and not one tear for her son?"

"We all have different ways of grieving," I said, though I couldn't help thinking that there *was* a strangeness to Doña Ernestina, and that Lydia was right when she said that the woman seemed to be acting out a part. "I think we should wait and see what she is going to do."

"Maybe," said Elenita. "Did you get a visit from *El Padre* yesterday?"

We nodded, not surprised to learn that all of us had gotten personal calls from Padre Alvaro, our painfully shy priest, after Doña Ernestina had frightened him away. Apparently El Padre had come to her apartment immediately after hearing about Tony, expecting to comfort the woman as he had when Don Antonio died suddenly a year ago. Her grief then had been understandable in its immensity, for she had been burying not only her husband but also the dream shared by many of the barrio women her age — that of returning with her man to the Island after retirement, of buying a *casita* in the old pueblo, and of being buried on native ground alongside *la familia.* People *my* age — those of us born or raised here — have had our mothers drill this fantasy into our brains all of our lives. So when Don Antonio dropped his head on the dominoes table, scattering the ivory pieces of the best game of the year, and when he was laid out in his best black suit at Ramirez' Funeral Home, all of us knew how to talk to the grieving widow.

That was the last time we saw both her men. Tony was there — home on a two-day pass from basic training — and he cried like a little boy over his father's handsome face, calling him *Papi, Papi*. Doña Ernestina had had a full mother's duty then, taking care of the hysterical boy. It was a normal chain of grief, the strongest taking care of the weakest. We buried Don Antonio at Garden State Memorial Park, where there are probably more Puerto Ricans than on the Island. Padre Alvaro said his sermon in a soft, trembling voice that was barely audible over the cries of the boy being supported on one side by his mother, impressive in her quiet strength and dignity, and on the other by Cheo, owner of the *bodega* where Don Antonio had played dominoes with other barrio men of his age for over twenty years.

Just about everyone from El Building had attended that funeral, and it had been done right. Doña Ernestina had sent her son off to fight for America and then had started collecting her widow's pension. Some of us asked Doña Iris (who knew how to read cards) about Doña Ernestina's future, and Doña Iris had said: "A long journey within a year" — which fit with what we had thought would happen next: Doña Ernestina would move back to the Island and wait with her relatives for Tony to come home from the war. Some older women actually went home when they started collecting social security or pensions, but that was rare. Usually, it seemed to me, somebody had to die before the island dream would come true for women like Doña Ernestina. As for my friends and me, we talked about "vacations" in the Caribbean. But we knew that if life was hard for us in this barrio, it would be worse in a pueblo where no one knew us (and had maybe only heard of our parents before they came to *los estados unidos de América,* where most of us had been brought as children).

When Padre Alvaro had knocked softly on my door, I yanked it open, thinking it was that ex-husband of mine asking for a second chance again. (That's just the way Miguel knocks when he's sorry for leaving me — about once a week — when he wants a loan.) So I was wearing my Go-to-Hell face when I threw open the door, and the poor priest nearly jumped out of his skin. I saw him take a couple of deep breaths before he asked me in his slow way — he tries to hide his stutter by dragging out his words — if I knew whether or not Doña Ernestina was ill. After I said, "No, not that I know," Padre Alvaro just stood there looking pitiful until I asked him if he cared to come in. I had been sleeping on the sofa and watching TV all afternoon, and I really didn't want him to see the mess, but I had nothing to fear. The poor man actually took one step back at my invitation. No, he was in a hurry, he had a few other parishioners to visit, etc. These were difficult times, he said, so-so-so many young people lost to drugs or dying in the wa-wa-war. I asked him if *he* thought Doña Ernestina was sick, but he just shook his head. The man looked like an orphan at my door with those sad, brown eyes. He was actually appealing in a homely way: that long nose nearly touched the tip of his chin when he smiled, and his big crooked teeth broke my heart.

"She does not want to speak to me," Padre Alvaro said as he caressed a large silver crucifix that hung on a thick chain around his neck. He seemed to be dragged down by its weight, stoop-shouldered and skinny as he was.

I felt a strong impulse to feed him some of my chicken soup, still warm on the stove from my supper. Contrary to what Lydia says about me behind my back, I like living by myself. And I could not have been happier to have that mama's boy Miguel back where he belonged — with his mother who thought that he was still her baby. But this scraggly thing at my door needed home cooking and maybe even something more than a hot meal to bring a little spark into his life. (I mentally asked God to forgive me for having thoughts like these about one of his priests. *Ay bendito,* but they too are made of flesh and blood.)

"Maybe she just needs a little more time, Padre," I said in as comforting a voice as I could manage. Unlike the other women in El Building, I am not convinced that priests are truly necessary — or even much help — in times of crisis.

"*Sí, hija,* perhaps you're right," he muttered sadly — calling me "daughter" even though I'm pretty sure I'm five or six years older. (Padre Alvaro seems so "untouched" that it's hard to tell *his* age. I mean, when you live, it shows. He looks hungry for love, starving himself by choice.) I promised him that I would look in on Doña Ernestina. Without another word, he made the sign of the cross in the air between us and turned away. As I heard his slow steps descending the creaky stairs, I asked myself: What do priests dream about?

When El Padre's name came up again during that Saturday meeting in El Basement, I asked my friends what *they* thought a priest dreamed about. It was a fertile subject, so much so that we spend the rest of our laundry time coming up with scenarios. Before the last dryer stopped we all agreed that we could not receive communion the next day at Mass unless we went to confession that afternoon and told another priest, not Alvaro, about our "unclean thoughts."

As for Doña Ernestina's situation, we agreed that we should be there for her if she called, but the decent thing to do, we decided, was give her a little more time alone. Lydia kept repeating, in that childish way of hers, that "something is wrong with the woman," but she didn't volunteer to go see what it was that was making Doña Ernestina act so strangely. Instead she complained that she and Roberto had heard pots and pans banging and things being moved around for hours in 4-D last night — they had hardly been able to sleep. Isabelita winked at me behind Lydia's back. Lydia and Roberto still had not caught on: if they could hear what was going on in 4-D, the rest of us could also get an earful of what went on in 4-A. They were just kids who thought they had invented sex. I tell you, a *telenovela* could be made from the stories in El Building.

On Sunday Doña Ernestina was not at the Spanish mass, and I avoided Padre Alvaro so he would not ask me about her. But I was worried. Doña Ernestina was a church *cucaracha* — a devout Catholic who, like many of us, did not always do what the priests and the pope ordered, but who knew where God lived.

Only a serious illness or tragedy could keep her from attending mass, so afterward I went straight to her apartment and knocked on her door. There was no answer, although I heard scraping and dragging noises, like furniture being moved around. At least she was on her feet and active. Maybe housework was what she needed to snap out of her shock. I decided to try again the next day.

As I went by Lydia's apartment, the young woman opened her door — I knew she had been watching me through the peephole — to tell me about more noises from across the hall during the night. Lydia was in her baby-doll pajamas. Although she stuck only her nose out, I could see Roberto in his jockey underwear, doing something in the kitchen. I couldn't help thinking about Miguel and me when we had first gotten together. We were an explosive combination. After a night of passionate lovemaking, I would walk around thinking: Do not light cigarettes around me. No open flames. Highly combustible materials being transported. But when his mamá showed up at our door, the man of fire turned into a heap of ashes at her feet.

"Let's wait and see what happens," I told Lydia again.

We did not have to wait for long. On Monday Doña Ernestina called to invite us to a wake for Tony, a *velorio,* in her apartment. The word spread fast. Everyone wanted to do something for her. Cheo donated fresh chickens and island produce of all kinds. Several of us got together and made *arroz con pollo,* plus flan for dessert. And Doña Irish made two dozen *pasteles* and wrapped the meat pies in banana leaves that she had been saving in her freezer for her famous Christmas parties. We women carried in our steaming plates, while the men brought in their bottles of Palo Viejo rum for themselves and candy-sweet Manischewitz wine for us. We came ready to spend the night saying our rosaries and praying for Tony's soul.

Doña Ernestina met us at the door and led us into her living room, where the lights were off. A photograph of Tony and one of her deceased husband Don Antonio were sitting on top of a table, surrounded by at least a dozen candles. It was a spooky sight that caused several of the older women to cross themselves. Doña Ernestina had arranged folding chairs in front of this table and told us to sit down. She did not ask us to take our food and drinks to the kitchen. She just looked at each of us individually, as if she were taking attendance in a class, and then said: "I have asked you here to say good-bye to my husband Antonio and my son Tony. You have been my friends and neighbors for twenty years, but they were my life. Now that they are gone, I have *nada. Nada. Nada.*"

I tell you, that word is like a drain that sucks everything down. Hearing her say *nada* over and over made me feel as if I were being yanked into a dark pit. I could feel the others getting nervous too, but here was a woman deep into her pain: we had to give her a little space. She looked around the room, then walked out without saying another word.

As we sat there in silence, stealing looks at each other, we began to hear the sounds of things being moved around in other rooms. One of the older women took charge then, and soon the drinks were poured, the food served — all this while the strange sounds kept coming from different rooms in the apartment. Nobody said much, except once when we heard something like a dish fall and break. Doña Iris pointed her index finger at her ear and made a couple of circles — and out of nervousness, I guess, some of us giggled like schoolchildren.

It was a long while before Doña Ernestina came back out to us. By then we were gathering our dishes and purses, having come to the conclusion that it was time to leave. Holding two huge Sears shopping bags, one in each hand, Doña Ernestina took her place at the front door as if she were a society hostess in a receiving line. Some of us women hung back to see what was going on. But Tito, the building's super, had had enough and tried to get past her. She took his hand, putting in it a small ceramic poodle with a gold chain around its neck. Tito gave the poodle a funny look, glanced at Doña Ernestina as though he were scared, and hurried away with the dog in his hand.

We were let out of her place one by one, but not until she had forced one of her possessions on each of us. She grabbed without looking from her bags. Out came her prized *miniaturas,* knickknacks that take a woman a lifetime to collect. Out came ceramic and porcelain items of all kinds, including vases and ashtrays. Out came kitchen utensils, dishes, forks, knives, spoons. Out came old calendars and every small item that she had touched or been touched by in the last twenty years. Out came a bronzed baby shoe — I got that.

As we left the apartment, Doña Iris said "Psst" to some of us, so we followed her down the hallway. "Doña Ernestina's faculties are temporarily out of order," she said very seriously. "It is due to the shock of her son's death."

We all said *"Sí"* and nodded our heads.

"But what can we do?" Lydia said, her voice cracking a little. "What should I do with this?" She was holding one of Tony's baseball trophies in her hand: 1968 Most Valuable Player, for the Pocos Locos, our barrio's team.

Doña Iris said, "Let us keep her things safe for her until she recovers her senses. And let her mourn in peace. These things take time. If she needs us, she will call us." Doña Iris shrugged her shoulders, *"Así es la vida, hijas:* that's the way life is."

As I passed Tito on the stairs, he shook his head while looking up at Doña Ernestina's door: "I say she needs a shrink. I think somebody should call the social worker." He did not look at me when he mumbled these things. By "somebody" he meant one of us women. He didn't want trouble in his building, and he expected one of us to get rid of the problems. I just ignored him.

In my bed I prayed to the Holy Mother that she would find peace for Doña Ernestina's troubled spirit, but things got worse. All that week Lydia saw strange things happening through the peephole on her door. Every time people came to Doña Ernestina's apartment — to deliver flowers, or telegrams from the Island, or anything — the woman would force something on them. She pleaded with them to take this or that; if they hesitated, she commanded them with those tragic eyes to accept a token of her life.

And they did, walking out of our apartment building carrying cushions, lamps, doilies, clothing, shoes, umbrellas, wastebaskets, schoolbooks, and notebooks: things of value and things of no worth at all to anyone but to the person who had owned them. Eventually winos and street people got the news of the great giveaway in 4-D, and soon there was a line down the stairs and out the door. Nobody went home empty-handed; it was like a soup kitchen. Lydia was afraid to step out of her place because of all the dangerous-looking characters hanging out on that floor. And the smell! Entering our building was like coming into a cheap bar and public urinal combined.

Isabelita, living alone with her two little children and fearing for their safety, was the one who finally called a meeting of the residents. Only the women attended, since the men were truly afraid of Doña Ernestina. It isn't unusual for men to be frightened when they see a woman go crazy. If they are not the cause of her madness, then they act as if they don't understand it, and usually leave us alone to deal with our "woman's problems." This is just as well.

Maybe I *am* just bitter because of Miguel — I know what is said behind my back. But this is a fact: When a woman is in trouble, a man calls in her mamá, her sisters, or her friends, and then he makes himself scarce until it's all over. This happens again and again. At how many bedsides of women have I sat? How many times have I made the doctor's appointment, taken care of the children, and fed the husbands of my friends in the barrio? It is not that men can't do these things; it's just that they know how much women help each other. Maybe the men even suspect that we know one another better than they know their own wives. As I said, it is just as well that they stay out of our way when there is trouble. It makes things simpler for us.

At the meeting, Isabelita said right away that we should go up to 4-D and try to reason with *la pobre* Doña Ernestina. Maybe we could get her to give us a relative's address in Puerto Rico — the woman obviously needed to be taken care of. What she was doing was putting us all in a very difficult situation. There were no dissenters this time. We voted to go as a group to talk to Doña Ernestina the next morning.

But that night we were all awakened by crashing noises down on the street. In the light of the full moon, I could see that the air was raining household goods: kitchen chairs, stools, a small TV, a nightstand, pieces of a bed frame. Everything was splintering as it landed on the pavement. People were running for cover and yelling up at our building. The problem, I knew instantly, was in Apartment 4-D.

Putting on my bathrobe and slippers, I stepped out into the hallway. Lydia and Roberto were rushing down the stairs, but on the flight above my landing I caught up with Doña Iris and Isabelita, heading toward 4-D. Out of breath, we stood in the fourth-floor hallway, listening to police sirens approaching our building in front. We could hear the slamming of car doors and yelling — in both Spanish and English. Then we tried the door to 4-D. It was unlocked.

We came into a room virtually empty. Even the pictures had been taken down from the walls; all that was left were the nail holes and the lighter places on the paint where the framed photographs had been for years. We took a few seconds to spot Doña Ernestina: she was curled up in the farthest corner of the living room, naked.

"Como salió a éste mundo," said Doña Iris, crossing herself.

Just as she had come into the world. Wearing nothing. Nothing around her except a clean, empty room. Nada. She had left nothing behind — except the bottles of pills, the ones the doctors give to ease the pain, to numb you, to make you feel nothing when someone dies.

The bottles were empty too, and the policemen took them. But we didn't let them take Doña Ernestina until we each had brought up some of our own best clothes and dressed her like the decent woman that she was. *La decencia.* Nothing can ever change that — not even *la muerte.* This is the way life is. *Así es la vida.*

Sherman Alexie

The Lone Ranger and Tonto Fistfight in Heaven

Sherman Alexie was born in 1966 in Spokane, Washington to a largely Native American family, although his mother was part white. He was educated at Gonzaga University and at Washington State University, where he studied creative writing. Inspired by the program, he became a committed author almost at once, and he has published in nearly all of the leading periodicals in the country. Writing in several genres, he has been awarded a National Endowment for the Arts Fellowship for poetry and the PEN/Hemingway Award for the best first book of fiction. His work reflects his ethnic heritage, drawing on the oral tradition for narrative methods, structure, and, most powerfully, subject and theme. He writes about the cultural dislocation of Native Americans who live in their own land, an issue particularly acute on the reservation, the setting for much of his work. He deals with broken families, rampant alcoholism, and the infantilizing dependency and ineffectuality that derive from permanent government support. His stories are lyrical, reflecting his success with verse, and they are often joined within a volume with poems, as in *The Business of Fancydancing,* a pessimistic look at tribal life. *First Indian on the Moon,* another mixed book, brought him critical praise, but it was *The Lone Ranger and Tonto Fistfight in Heaven* that made him widely respected as an international literary figure. These stories use traditional oral techniques of rendition, shifting from first person to the intimacy of direct address in second person, for example, or shifting time schemes between memory and present activity. His novels, among them *Reservation Blues* and *Indian Killer,* deal with persistent racism, the construction of identity, and the difficulties of living simultaneously in two worlds. These are also the central issues in "The Lone Ranger and Tonto Fistfight in Heaven," a component of the 1993 volume of that title. It features an unnamed, depersonalized narrator and protagonist who seeks to define himself through the act of telling his story. What he relates is largely retrospective, with flashbacks to scenes with his estranged girlfriend, with a dream sequence, and with one comment about the future success of a white basketball player. The narrator is constantly aware of his heritage, which defines his sense of identity, and even though he was able to find love with a white woman, his depression and confusion make it impossible for him to be happy or fulfilled. He knows how all his dreams will end.

Sherman Alexie, "The Lone Ranger and Tonto Fistfight in Heaven," *The Lone Ranger and Tonto Fistfight in Heaven* (New York: Atlantic Monthly Press, 1993), 181–90.

Too hot to sleep so I walked down to the Third Avenue 7-11 for a Creamsicle and the company of a graveyard-shift cashier. I know that game. I worked graveyard for a Seattle 7-11 and got robbed once too often. The last time the bastard locked me in the cooler. He even took my money and my basketball shoes.

The graveyard-shift worker in the Third Avenue 7-11 looked like they all do. Acne scars and a bad haircut, work pants that showed off his white socks, and those cheap black shoes that have no support. My arches still ache from my year at the Seattle 7-11.

"Hello," he asked when I walked into his store. "How you doing?"

I gave him a half-wave as I headed back to the freezer. He looked me over so he could describe me to the police later. I knew the look. One of my old girlfriends said I started to look at her that way, too. She left me not long after that. No, I left her and don't blame her for anything. That's how it happened. When one person starts to look at another like a criminal, then the love is over. It's logical.

ა◌ტ

"I don't trust you," she said to me. "You get too angry."

She was white and I lived with her in Seattle. Some nights we fought so bad that I would just get in my car and drive all night, only stop to fill up on gas. In fact, I worked the graveyard shift to spend as much time away from her as possible. But I learned all about Seattle that way, driving its back ways and dirty alleys.

Sometimes, though, I would forget where I was and get lost. I'd drive for hours, searching for something familiar. Seems like I'd spent my whole life that way, looking for anything I recognized. Once, I ended up in a nice residential neighborhood and somebody must have been worried because the police showed up and pulled me over.

"What are you doing out here?" the police officer asked me as he looked over my license and registration.

"I'm lost."

"Well, where are you supposed to be?" he asked me, and I knew there were plenty of places I wanted to be, but none where I was supposed to be.

"I got in a fight with my girlfriend," I said. "I was just driving around, blowing off steam, you know?"

"Well, you should be more careful where you drive," the officer said. "You're making people nervous. You don't fit the profile of the neighborhood."

I wanted to tell him that I didn't really fit the profile of the country but I knew it would just get me into trouble.

♪♪

"Can I help you?" the 7-11 clerk asked me loudly, searching for some response that would reassure him that I wasn't an armed robber. He knew this dark skin and long, black hair of mine was dangerous. I had potential.

"Just getting a Creamsicle," I said after a long interval. It was a sick twist to pull on the guy, but it was late and I was bored. I grabbed my Creamsicle and walked back to the counter slowly, scanned the aisles for effect. I wanted to whistle low and menacingly but I never learned to whistle.

"Pretty hot out tonight?" he asked, that old rhetorical weather bullshit question designed to put us both at ease.

"Hot enough to make you go crazy," I said and smiled. He swallowed hard like a white man does in those situations. I looked him over. Same old green, red, and white 7-11 jacket and thick glasses. But he wasn't ugly, just misplaced and marked by loneliness. If he wasn't working there that night, he'd be at home alone, flipping through channels and wishing he could afford HBO or Showtime.

"Will this be all?" he asked me, in that company effort to make me do some impulse shopping. Like adding a clause onto a treaty. *We'll take Washington and Oregon and you get six pine trees and a brand-new Chrysler Cordoba.* I knew how to make and break promises.

"No," I said and paused. "Give me a Cherry Slushie, too."

"What size?" he asked, relieved.

"Large," I said, and he turned his back to me to make the drink. He realized his mistake but it was too late. He stiffened, ready for the gunshot or the blow behind the ear. When it didn't come, he turned back to me.

"I'm sorry," he said. "What size did you say?"

"Small," I said and changed the story.

"But I thought you said large."

"If you knew I wanted a large, then why did you ask me again?" I asked him and laughed. He looked at me, couldn't decide if I was giving him serious shit or just goofing. There was something about him I liked, even if it was three in the morning and he was white.

"Hey," I said. "Forget the Slushie. What I want to know is if you know all the words to the theme from 'The Brady Bunch'?"

He looked at me, confused at first, then laughed.

"Shit," he said. "I was hoping you weren't crazy. You were scaring me."

"Well, I'm going to get crazy if you don't know the words."

He laughed loudly then, told me to take the Creamsicle for free. He was the graveyard-shift manager and those little demonstrations of power tickled him. All seventy-five cents of it. I knew how much everything cost.

"Thanks," I said to him and walked out the door. I took my time walking home, let the heat of the night melt the Creamsicle all over my hand. At three in the morning I could act just as young as I wanted to act. There was no one around to ask me to grow up.

ॐ

In Seattle, I broke lamps. She and I would argue and I'd break a lamp, just pick it up and throw it down. At first she'd buy replacement lamps, expensive and beautiful. But after a while she'd buy lamps from Goodwill or garage sales. Then she just gave up the idea entirely and we'd argue in the dark.

"You're just like your brother," she'd yell. "Drunk all the time and stupid."

"My brother don't drink that much."

She and I never tried to hurt each other physically. I did love her, after all, and she loved me. But those arguments were just as damaging as a fist. Words can be like that, you know? Whenever I get into arguments now, I remember her and I also remember Muhammad Ali. He knew the power of his fists but, more importantly, he knew the power of his words, too. Even though he only had an IQ of 80 or so, Ali was a genius. And she was a genius, too. She knew exactly what to say to cause me the most pain.

But don't get me wrong. I walked through that relationship with an executioner's hood. Or more appropriately, with war paint and sharp arrows. She was a kindergarten teacher and I continually insulted her for that.

"Hey, schoolmarm," I asked. "Did your kids teach you anything new today?"

And I always had crazy dreams. I always have had them, but it seemed they became nightmares more often in Seattle.

In one dream, she was a missionary's wife and I was a minor war chief. We fell in love and tried to keep it secret. But the missionary caught us fucking in the barn and shot me. As I lay dying, my tribe learned of the shooting and attacked the whites all across the reservation. I died and my soul drifted above the reservation.

Disembodied, I could see everything that was happening. Whites killing Indians and Indians killing whites. At first it was small, just my tribe and the few whites who lived there. But my dream grew, intensified. Other tribes arrived on horseback to continue the slaughter of whites, and the United States Cavalry rode into battle.

The most vivid image of that dream stays with me. Three mounted soldiers played polo with a dead Indian woman's head. When I first dreamed it, I thought it was just a product of my anger and imagination. But since then, I've read similar accounts of that kind of evil in the old West. Even more terrifying, though, is the fact that those kinds of brutal things are happening today in places like El Salvador.

All I know for sure, though, is that I woke from that dream in terror, packed up all my possessions, and left Seattle in the middle of the night.

"I love you," she said as I left her. "And don't ever come back."

I drove through the night, over the Cascades, down into the plains of central Washington, and back home to the Spokane Indian Reservation.

§§

When I finished the Creamsicle that the 7-11 clerk gave me, I held the wooden stick up into the air and shouted out very loudly. A couple lights flashed on in windows and a police car cruised by me a few minutes later. I waved to the men in blue and they waved back accidentally. When I got home it was still too hot to sleep so I picked up a week-old newspaper from the floor and read.

There was another civil war, another terrorist bomb exploded, and one more plane crashed and all aboard were presumed dead. The crime rate was rising in every city with populations larger than 100,000, and a farmer in Iowa shot his banker after foreclosure on his 1,000 acres.

A kid from Spokane won the local spelling bee by spelling the word *rhinoceros*.

§§

When I got back to the reservation, my family wasn't surprised to see me. They'd been expecting me back since the day I left for Seattle. There's an old Indian poet who said that Indians can reside in the city, but they can never live there. That's as close to truth as any of us can get.

Mostly I watched television. For weeks I flipped through channels, searched for answers in the game shows and soap operas. My mother would circle the want ads in red and hand the paper to me.

"What are you going to do with the rest of your life?" she asked.

"Don't know," I said, and normally, for almost any other Indian in the country, that would have been a perfectly fine answer. But I was special, a former college student, a smart kid. I was one of those Indians who was supposed to make it, to rise above the rest of the reservation like a fucking eagle or something. I was the new kind of warrior.

For a few months I didn't even look at the want ads my mother circled, just left the newspaper where she had set it down. After a while, though, I got tired of television and started to play basketball again. I'd been a good player in high school, nearly great, and almost played at the college I attended for a couple years. But I'd been too out of shape from drinking and sadness to ever be good again. Still, I liked the way the ball felt in my hands and the way my feet felt inside my shoes.

At first I just shot baskets by myself. It was selfish, and I also wanted to learn the game again before I played against anybody else. Since I had been good before and embarrassed fellow tribal members, I knew they would want to take revenge on me. Forget about the cowboys versus Indians business. The most intense competition on any reservation is Indians versus Indians.

But on the night I was ready to play for real, there was this white guy at the gym, playing with all the Indians.

"Who is that?" I asked Jimmy Seyler.

"He's the new BIA chief's kid."

"Can he play?"

"Oh, yeah."

And he could play. He played Indian ball, fast and loose, better than all the Indians there.

"How long's he been playing here?" I asked.

"Long enough."

I stretched my muscles, and everybody watched me. All these Indians watched one of their old and dusty heroes. Even though I had played most of my ball at the white high school I went to, I was still all Indian, you know? I was Indian when it counted, and this BIA kid needed to be beaten by an Indian, any Indian.

I jumped into the game and played well for a little while. It felt good. I hit a few shots, grabbed a rebound or two, played enough defense to keep the other team honest. Then that white kid took over the game. He was too good. Later, he'd play college ball back East and would nearly make the Knicks team a couple years on. But we didn't know any of that would happen. We just knew he was better that day and every other day.

The next morning I woke up tired and hungry, so I grabbed the want ads, found a job I wanted, and drove to Spokane to get it. I've been working at the high school exchange program ever since, typing and answering phones. Sometimes I wonder if the people on the other end of the line know that I'm Indian and if their voices would change if they did know.

One day I picked up the phone and it was her, calling from Seattle.

"I got your number from your mom," she said. "I'm glad you're working."

"Yeah, nothing like a regular paycheck."

"Are you drinking?"

"No, I've been on the wagon for almost a year."

"Good."

The connection was good. I could hear her breathing in the spaces between our words. How do you talk to the real person whose ghost has haunted you? How do you tell the difference between the two?

"Listen," I said. "I'm sorry for everything."

"Me, too."

"What's going to happen to us?" I asked her and wished I had the answer for myself.

"I don't know," she said. "I want to change the world."

ॐ

These days, living alone in Spokane, I wish I lived closer to the river, to the falls where ghosts of salmon jump. I wish I could sleep. I put down my paper or book and turn off all the lights, lie quietly in the dark. It may take hours, even years, for me to sleep again. There's nothing surprising or disappointing in that.

I know how all my dreams end anyway.

Susan Power

Morse Code

Susan Power was born in Chicago in 1961, the daughter of a Dakota Sioux mother and a white father whose ancestor had been governor of New Hampshire during the Civil War. She went on to a distinguished educational career, graduating with a B.A. in psychology from Harvard before taking a law degree, with highest honors, from the same university. A few years of legal work inspired her to apply to the M.F.A. program at the Iowa Writers' Workshop, a course she completed in 1992. It was there that she began the series of stories that would become *The Grass Dancer,* which won the 1995 PEN/Hemingway Award for the best first book of fiction. This volume of interconnecting tales, of which "Morse Code" is a part, traces the lives of generations of Native American characters, shifting temporally in the manner of the oral tradition to link meaningful events together. "Morse Code," originally published in *The Atlantic Monthly* in 1994, is short fiction in this mode. It is told in first person by Crystal Thunder, a Dakota high school girl, and it traces her romance and marriage to the Swedish farmer and artist Martin Lundstrom. The counterplot, never far from the surface, is Crystal's account of her mother, Anna Thunder, and her amorous adventures that give new meaning to the title of the story. Related in a series of brief episodes that revolve around the central events. Power develops powerful themes of racial and religious identity, genuine love across ethnic barriers, and the ancient pull of tradition on Native Americans living in the contemporary world. Her most recent book is *Roofwalker* (2004), a mixture of stories and non-fiction pieces about Dakota characters living in the twenty-first century.

Susan Power, "Morse Code," *The Atlantic Monthly* 273 (June 1994): 88–90, 92–94, 96–100.

Martin Lundstrom was white, a North Dakota Swede in the heart of farm country, but he was nevertheless an outcast. He had not one cowlick but three, a trinity of bristling tufts of hair rising from his brown head like three horns. His face was attractive (*I* found it pleasing), nearly sharp-featured, but softened by beauty marks at his temple and chin, and when he smiled, seldom though it was, a delightful dimple puckered his left cheek. The others called him "Tiny Tim," because he walked with a pronounced limp, only partly corrected by a thick orthopedic shoe. When I say "the others," I don't mean the Indians, the Dakota students from our reservation. We Indians were outcasts on our own turf, and left the Germans and Scandinavians to torture one another as they saw fit. We avoided them as much as possible.

By the time I was a senior at Saint Mary's High School, I was a misfit myself, shunned by tribesmen because my mother had too many boyfriends and was rumored to practice Indian medicine. Regina Red Horn became a rude, annoying shadow, and would stare at me in the hall as she sucked on the end of her black braid. Her faction of wistful cheerleader candidates — pretty, athletic girls too swarthy to be selected, but persistently hopeful — pointed at me as they whispered, until I felt speared in the back by their sharp fingernails. In exasperation I dug out the leather pouch containing my old jacks and rubber ball, and wore it to school. When Regina resumed her aloof surveillance, I went up to her, clutching the pouch in my hand. I squeezed so hard I could feel the spiky metal jacks.

"I'll take your eyes," I told her, "and wear them in my bundle. You better aim them somewhere else." I heard her gasp, and very quickly Regina Red Horn and her graceful flock migrated to the other end of the hall. Their disapproval was so potent I could smell it, a metallic odor like scorched gunpowder, but after it passed in a smoky cloud, all I smelled was the soap on their skin.

I admired Martin Lundstrom from afar, considered him a talented artist and coveted the sketches he scribbled in notebooks. He was forever ripping them out of his binders and throwing them in the wastebasket, from which I retrieved them when no one was looking. I liked the way he drew horses, capturing the weary, cynical posture of stocky farm horses, their heads down and muscles straining, while his elegant, slim-ankled Indian ponies reared at the edge of the page, poised to leap off the paper.

I followed a trail of these drawings straight to the source after weeks of collecting them, smoothing them out, memorizing their lines. I approached him in the school cafeteria, painfully aware that my footsteps echoed in the great room, which had once been a chapel. I looked up and up at the high ceiling, determined to keep my destination a secret until I arrived. Martin Lundstrom occupied the seat closest to the garbage cans. He was alone, as usual, staring at nothing as he ate a slice of yellow cake. I heard him say, with his mouth quite full, "She's coming over." I paused. I squeezed the drawings too tightly, and they crumpled in my hand.

"She stopped," he said, to no one in particular. I closed the space between us.

"She's here," I told Martin Lundstrom, and he smiled. "I'm Crystal Thunder. I think you can really draw."

He looked at me then, not staring exactly, but with concentration, as if trying to decide the best way to sketch my features. I had a flat, pancake face and glistening eyes I hoped made up for it. I was all one shade, brown hair, brown eyes, dusky skin, the only spot of color being the odd crimson birthmark on my forehead, perfectly bowed in the shape of a horseshoe. At least I had coaxed my straight hair into a stylish shoulder-length flip. I thought he might be pleased to sketch those lines. Martin ended his inspection and gestured to the nearest chair.

"Have a seat." I was still clutching his discarded pages as I sat down, and he held out his hand for them. "So, she likes my work?"

What was this "she" business?, I wondered. He could have read my mind.

"I don't talk to people much," he said, apologizing. "I tend to think aloud. I've fallen into bad habits." Martin plucked a stub of charcoal from his pants pocket and turned over one of his wrinkled sketches. "Hold still."

His eyes probed me like hooks, and I opened my mouth once or twice; I was a great gasping fish. To ease the tension I crossed my eyes and saw the steep ridge of my nose dividing a world consisting entirely of pairs.

"She shouldn't do that," Martin scolded, so I stopped. His eyes never left my face. I'm certain of it, though I noticed his hand jerking across the paper. What his fingers accomplished, they did using their own vision. He finished as Sister Francis rang a small silver handbell, signaling the end of lunch. He gave me the drawing and then quickly stuffed his hands in his pockets and lurched away. Surely this wasn't my face, which I well know is as round as a griddle and nearly as flat. This face was lovely in its symmetry: cheekbones as neat as equilateral triangles, a firm, rectangular chin, perfectly matched elliptical eyes, irises glittering like faceted gemstones. Even the birthmark was transfigured, into the delicate lips of a rosebud.

ба

Saint Mary's was scandalized by my relationship with Martin Lundstrom. When we walked down the hall together, we heard rustling on both sides, mouths working overtime.

"Sounds like a plague of grasshoppers chewing a wheatfield," Martin said.

Sister Nora asked me to stay after class one day to help her wash down the blackboards. As I applied a wet rag to the slate, I heard her wheeze behind me.

"You're a young girl to be so serious about a boy," she breathed. Her congested lungs strangled the words.

"I'm seventeen," I told her. I wouldn't make her task an easy one.

"Have you spoken to your mother about this?"

"Yes," I lied.

"Well, she can't approve. It's a delicate matter for a girl. Her reputation. Remember that." I nodded my head, which didn't satisfy Sister Nora. "Will you?" she pressed.

"Yes, Sister." But what I understood was something different. Most of my classmates were dating, pinned by college men or given a heavy ID bracelet to wear, a ritual I thought was like the tagging of cows. No one cared when Germans dated Swedes or Dakotas dated Assiniboines, as long as like courted like. So Martin and I moved in our own space and ignored the gossip whirling around us, spinning as furiously as dust devils.

ба

Martin's widowed mother worked as a phone operator in Bismarck. He said, "She listens in when she can and gets involved in the problems of strangers. I think they're all the problems she can handle, the ones at a distance."

We agreed to keep our feelings secret from our mothers, a promise I was relieved to make. My mother might not care that Martin was white, but I was certain she would resent his influence over me. She begrudged Jesus the space He took up in my soul, though I promised her it was only a corner. In my mind He stood off to the side and pinched one edge of my spirit between His cold fingers, as if making ready to fold it.

"So, who should be inside there?" I had once asked her.

"I am your spirit until the day comes when you understand me, and then you should take over."

If I lived to be ninety, I would never understand my mother, all her secrets and memories and desires. She was claiming my soul for all time.

δδ

A few weeks before graduating from high school Martin bought himself a sleek black Thunderbird.

"The first one I've seen in these parts," he said. "A fish out of water."

I hadn't seen another of its kind — this was pickup country — but it didn't look at all out of place. It was meant to swerve down gravel roads like a black snake, and stalk its own shadow across white fields of needlegrass.

"How'd you pay for it?" I asked him.

"I've had a job. No one knows but my mother. No one knows it's me."

He told me he had been designing catalogue covers for Will's Bismarck Seed House since he was fifteen.

"Those covers keep getting more popular. They tell me sales are up," Martin said with a shrug.

I went to the library to look at past issues and spread them out on a heavy oak table. Martin Lundstrom's hormones were loose upon the land. The rural scenes he painted were sensual, pulsing with the desperate energy of puberty. On one cover two women were drawn standing before a lurid sun, carrying baskets of corn in their arms. Their upper lips were damp with tiny beads of perspiration, as sweet as seed pearls, and long tresses of wavy hair clung to their bodies. In another painting a tower silo rose from the ground like a man's organ plunging for the sky. I could sense the movement, feel the earth quiver. I realized why the pictures were so successful. I could just imagine an elderly farmer — one long considered a pillar of the community — carrying a rolled-up catalogue in his back pocket. Now and again he'd reach back to finger the tube, rub it like a good-luck piece. His dreams would be spiced for weeks, as hot as chili peppers, causing him to blush through breakfast and reach more often for his wife.

δδ

Martin was cautious and gentle with me; he handled me like a wild horse. Not until June did he risk a kiss on the mouth, and as our lips brushed, his eyes snapped wide open, alert for signs of distress.

"It's okay," I murmured. I ran my hands through his hair and paused to finger the cowlicks growing against the grain.

We were parked on a dirt road that bisected a flat plain of mixed grass. Martin had spread an old wool blanket on the hood of his car, and we curled there, gradually relaxing as the heat of the car's engine warmed the blanket and melted our bodies. The sky was a flat stretch of blue and white, a weightless spring quilt settled on our bed. Slowly we undressed, folding our clothes, tucking socks in our shoes and placing the bundles on the roof of the car. As we moved together, I saw my face reflected in Martin's gray eyes. The beautiful girl from his sketch peered back at me, her eyes blinking and filling with tears. I turned my head to the side so that Martin wouldn't see me cry, and I noticed a box elder, our sole witness, perched on a gentle slope. It seemed to be waving at me, branch arms raised high, its gray bark deeply furrowed with worry lines. It frightened me, and I clung tightly to Martin.

"Crystal," he moaned, and I wanted to hush him.

Don't speak our names aloud, I was tempted to warn. *We aren't alone.* But I could guess how foolish that would sound. Martin would laugh if I told him the bare truth: *That glaring tree is my mother.* She watched us from the slope, her hair wild and fingers snapping, her thick roots buried deep in the earth, so deep they reached that place of nothing but heat and magma — all the planet's churning anger.

♪♫

I learned that my mother was different when I was five. I was seated on old Mrs. Elk Nation's lap, for she was kind, and allowed me to trail behind her at powwows. Her spine impressed me: it was so straight that I liked to think she was born with a sapling backbone, a flexible whip that stiffened to an erect trunk by middle age. She was a good dancer, one of the best, like a tree with elastic roots springing up and down in time to the music. I perched on her lap with pride and enjoyed the way she smoothed back the loose hair at my temples. She must have thought I was hypnotized by the soft touch of her hands, or too young to follow her conversation.

"I feel for this one," she told Emma Two Bulls, a Pine Ridge Sioux who was visiting cousins on our reservation. "This one belongs to that Thunder woman."

"*Ohan,*" said Mrs. Two Bulls. "I heard of her. She messes with things you should leave alone."

"Bad medicine," Mrs. Elk Nation whispered. I could feel her moist gossip breath slide across the part in my hair. "You check which dish she puts out for the feed, and don't you taste any of it."

I scooted to the end of Mrs. Elk Nation's lap and slid off her knees.

"Restless?" she asked me. "Ready to dance again?"

I told her I was hungry, which wasn't true but gave me an excuse to move away from those words. I even rubbed the top of my head to brush off any that had caught in my hair with their mean little thorns.

Until that day I had never doubted my mother. I accepted her presence as easily as my own, and I hadn't missed a father. My earliest memories of her were warm. I could remember being an infant strapped to a cradleboard and tipped against the wall of her kitchen, where I could watch her bead. She used the lazy stitch, picking up nine beads at a time to decorate leggings, moccasins, the yokes of buckskin dresses, purses, pipe bags, and the tapered handles of eagle-feather fans. She had beaded the turtle amulet that dangled from the top of my cradle-board. Sometimes I reached for its stiff horsehair tail and she would tell me, "No, don't touch." She gave me a small beaded lizard to squeeze in my hands, and I could play with it as long as I didn't pop it into my mouth. Later I learned that my umbilical cord was sewn inside the turtle's shell to bring me good health and a long life. The lizard amulet was a decoy for harmful spirits, meant to confuse them should they try to steal my protection.

Back then I didn't need amulets, only my tall mother with her beautiful lined face. I wanted to touch her straight nose and crescent eyebrows, run a finger along her chapped, bitten lips. But she was across the room from me, busy with her silver needle and nylon thread, her movements so quick she looked as though she were spinning a web.

Mrs. Elk Nation's words put questions in my head, and they became a nuisance. I thought I could hear them knock together, tumble and click like gambling bones tossed against the back of my cranium. I wondered who my father was, where he was. I wondered why no one on our reservation wore the garments my mother beaded. Her customers were white collectors or Indians of other tribes: Chippewa, Cheyenne, Crow — *never* Dakota. Click. Click. The questions accumulated, without relief. I could not interrogate Anna Thunder, my tall mother who seemed to know everything in the world. I had seen her crush potato bugs and snap the delicate pods of sweet peas. She had never struck me, but I was in awe of her efficient hands.

As the years passed, my questions — too many to keep inside my head — remained unanswered. They spilled out, raising a painful rash on my arms. I fingered the bumps and recognized them for what they were: evidence of my curiosity. Perhaps someone with sensitive fingertips, or someone familiar with Braille, the tactile language, could have read my arms like a book. My mother never trailed a finger along my broken flesh but covered the area with clean white rags, wrapping me like a mummy.

⚬⚬

That fall, when my figure swelled and I had to sew elastic bands into the waists of my slacks, Martin said, "She should marry me."

"*Who* should?" I asked. I wanted Martin to be quite clear on this.

"Crystal Thunder should become Crystal Lundstrom." Martin poked his finger through the coil of my flip, and the starched hair curled around it.

"Please," he whispered. "Please." I placed my hands on his shoulders and felt him tremble. His shorter leg was planted behind him and he leaned forward, his weight on the good leg. He looked ready for a fight.

"We'll have to tell our mothers," I said. I didn't ask him, *Where will we go? What will we do for a living?* I knew we could work, and that eventually we would be able to rent our own little place. The only obstacle for me was my fierce mother, Anna Thunder, who could stretch an animal hide with her sharp pegs, scrape it clean, and then work it until the skin was pliable velvet. This was how she worked a person's soul, gaining entry through the eyes. Anna Thunder never blinked. Her wide owl stare penetrated and then smothered.

"My mother won't allow it," I said.

"How can she stop us? We're of age. Crystal can do whatever Crystal wants."

I shook my head, but I told Martin, "Yes. Yes, I will marry you."

He dipped toward me, wrapped his arms around me, and stroked my stiff hair. I wanted to make him happy this last time, give him the answer he wanted, and speak aloud my own dearest wish.

⸙

I discovered my mother beading a small amulet in the shape of a turtle. Its shell was a spiral of red, yellow, and blue beads. I stood behind her in the kitchen doorway, looking over her shoulder as the needle stabbed and disappeared and re-emerged.

"You're carrying a girl," she said. She snipped the nylon thread.

I stumbled forward and grabbed the back of a kitchen chair. Its thatched seat was coming loose; straw poked in every direction. I dropped silently into the chair.

My mother pointed her needle at me. She said, "You've been messing with that lame Swede. I saw you. Now he wants you to run away." I looked at the needle and would not raise my eyes to hers. I wouldn't let her in, not this time.

"He isn't lame. He loves me," I said, in that ridiculous order.

Anna spat into one of the tissues she kept crumpled in her apron pocket.

"He loves you — as if it matters." Laughter rose from her chest. "His feelings are useless dust!"

"I want to marry him," I said, so quietly I thought she couldn't hear me.

"You do whatever you like. Run off with that lame Swede and bear him a dozen peg-leg brats with even less sense than you have. Waste yourself, go ahead. But don't you waste that child." She poked me in the navel. "A soul for a soul."

I was so cold my limbs clenched and shivered, my fingernails turned blue.

"I haven't begun to teach you," she said. "You haven't come into your power, girl; you don't know what you're capable of. You could have your pick of any man, and wouldn't have to settle on just one. I have so much to teach you — ancient ways passed down from the dead to the living."

My teeth chattered and I hugged myself. "I want to be Crystal Lundstrom," I said between cracked lips.

My mother slapped her beadwork on the table and rose from her seat. "You will not waste that child," she promised me. "A soul for a soul."

⸙

I wrote to Martin Lundstrom, my intended, that I would join him once the child was born. I told him that my mother would help with the pregnancy, but only if I kept to the house and didn't see him until then.

Martin took to driving his Thunderbird right up to the back steps of Anna's square house. "Crystal!" he would shout. "Come to the window!"

And I always did, but hidden by Anna's heavy drapes, so that my poor intended couldn't catch a glimpse of me. If he set foot on the stairs, Anna would open the door and fill its frame, her hefty arms crossed beneath the rock ledge of her chest. She never spoke a word to him; the most she would do was flick her fingers, the rudest gesture a Dakota Indian can make. Eventually Martin would withdraw, clumping noisily down the steps in his mismatched shoes. To my eyes he was as graceful as a goshawk; he floated. One time he sat in the car for a solid hour and I stood just as long behind the curtain, watching his face, touching it, as best I could, with my eyes.

My feelings for Martin hadn't changed, they had just been set aside, somewhere to the left of those for my mother, who now filled the empty places in me. She had never been so patient and affectionate before. She was a dream mother come true. Each night she bathed me in her claw-footed tub, soaped my back and washed my hair, her hands moving in warm circles. She combed my hair with the stiff head of a purple coneflower, a hundred tender strokes, and plaited it in two French braids. She took my feet in her lap and counted the bones, smoothing each one with her thumb. She fed me wild turnips and leafy kale, cabbage stew, fried potatoes, corn on the cob glistening with butter, and moist lemon cake sprinkled with powdered sugar. At night we slept on her wide brass bed, so that she could watch over me even then. I think she sorted out my dreams, teased the unpleasant images from the harmless ones so that I never waked until morning, and the first thing I saw, once I opened my eyes, was my mother's concerned face hovering inches away, her breath as sweet as mint, moving against my cheek.

We passed the long winter indoors, snug beneath blankets of snow. I had my mother to myself; she had banished her boyfriends for the duration, although Roger Bonnin turned up now and again to shovel snow off the roof, clear our chimney, and plow a tunnel from our back door to the gravel road. I felt protected, hidden. I remembered stories the nuns had told us about the catacombs constructed by early Christians. At first I didn't miss the sun, which blazed somewhere above the snow walls. By March, however, I had dark circles under my eyes, a permanent shadow I attributed to the gloom. I missed the broad sky and bright colors, craved the wind and fragrant grasses.

The first thaw came in March, a week before I was due. The snowbanks still rose on either side of the house, twenty feet high in some places. I could see only a channel of light above our tunnel, a slim band as narrow as a bracelet. I was surrounded by colorless white and was reluctant to step outdoors, for fear it would swallow me up in its nothingness.

"Mama," I called, my pleading voice as high as a child's. "I can't *see* anything."

My mother helped me into bed and told me to take a nap. "I'll take care of it," she said.

I awakened late in the afternoon, and my mother was there, as if she had never stepped away. I know a song called "Stairway to the Sky," and I have seen religious paintings of stairways lit by God's finger and thronged with pious Christians, but none could compare to the steps Anna Thunder had carved out of a snowbank, using an ax and a shovel. Her dress was soaked through from the effort and her palms blistered.

"Let's go while there's still sun," she said. She wrapped me in an old Pendleton blanket and guided me up the steep block steps. She pushed from behind, supporting most of my weight until I reached the chilly summit.

The sun's light washed over me and pressed itself into my body. I closed my eyes and tipped my face toward the sun's heat.

"Thank you, Mama. Thank you for this," I murmured. The baby fluttered a little, moved her hands and feet. "She likes it too," I said. "It really woke her up."

I turned in all directions, searching for a swatch of color. "There." My mother pointed to the distant road, which had been cleared by plows. Pushing up from the road's edge was a cluster of hardy crocuses, thriving despite the cold. They looked like a set of elegant lavender teacups, lonesome for a picnic.

I said, "They're a month early." But my mother didn't seem at all surprised.

"They came out to see you," she told me. "They know how important it is." She held out her hand, offering me a peppermint candy. "Take this in your mouth; when it melts, we should get back inside."

The descent was trickier than the climb. My mother went ahead of me so that I could balance myself by clutching her shoulders. The baby kicked me all the way down, restless, disappointed. *Can't we stay a while longer?*, I imagined her pleading. She was furious with me, and by the time we entered the house, she had tensed her plump body and was fighting for release.

§‰

Old Mrs. Elk Nation had told me three years earlier that my father was buried in the Catholic cemetery. "I pass him all the time on my way to visit Albert," she said. "They'd be side by side except for a good-sized chokecherry tree sprouting right between them. I know they enjoy that fruit."

"What's his name? How do you know it's him?" I would have shouted at her, but I didn't have the air.

"Everybody knows," she said. She patted my arm with her crippled hand, frozen with arthritis and as heavy as stone. "Now you're growing up, it's about time somebody told you. Shouldn't be the last to hear. And you have the mark of sadness on you. I want to wash it away." I didn't know whether she meant my expression or the birthmark on my forehead.

"What's his name?" I asked again. I was whispering now.

"Clive Broken Rope," she said. "Born 1918, died 1946."

"The year I was born."

"That's right. That's all I'm going to say now. You ask your mother about the rest. She's the only one who knows for sure."

Mrs. Elk Nation smiled at me and walked away, hoisted her shawl higher across her shoulders, and joined a line of older women dancing at the edge of the pow-wow circle. They danced close together and matched their movements in perfect time to the drum. I liked the way their shawl fringe overlapped, connecting them like beads strung on a necklace. I made myself watch to push the name back. Clive Broken Rope. If I weren't careful, I would hear ripe chokecherries fall from the tree and strike hollow ground, making my father's bones rattle, his teeth chatter. I think Mrs. Elk Nation meant well, meant to do right by me. After all, I was fifteen years old and I wanted some of those answers I had scratched up my sore arms longing for. But now I was in a deeper hole — in the red, as they say — because those answers had split up into more questions, multiplying like rabbits.

Ask your mother about the rest. I couldn't imagine her telling me secrets. I still saw her the way I had as a child: across miles of cracked linoleum, as massive as a statue, part of the great unknown.

I found my mother in the garden, on her knees in the black dirt. She cast a broad shadow across the plants, as threatening as a storm cloud. She was tending not the vegetables we grew to put on our table but the several varieties of weeds, roots, wildflowers, and herbs that were her private pharmacy. Over the years she had taught me the healing properties of each plant, and made me recite the cure recipes to test my memory: bloodwort for whooping cough or rashes, sweet flag for diabetes, wild onion for bee sting, purple coneflower for rabies or snakebite, fleabane for rheumatism, wild licorice for fever, and on and on.

In a separate plot of land behind our house she grew tall stalks of prairie larkspurs, as high as my waist, the white blossoms sprouting in every direction like a spray of stars.

"Look out for these," she had warned a long time ago, looking pleased as she pinched a creamy petal. "They can be poison." Beside them she had pointed out feathery bundles of prairie parsley. "If you know how to use this plant, you can control weak minds." She broke off the end of one hollow stem and chewed the tiny leaves as if to say she had a strong mind that nothing could bend. I wondered if this was the ingredient she used to capture the affections of young, good-looking men. I could picture her sprinkling their corn soup with the green flakes, watching as, sip after sip, their minds opened to her, peeled back like a nutshell to expose the tasty meat. My mother had a trail of young Sioux men go through her bedroom, men just a scratch older than boys, young enough to be the sons she never had. She didn't collect them for long. They were here one day, gone the next, and I was accustomed to their silent arrival and empty eyes, to seeing her clamp her hands on their wrists, fingers pinching as tight as shackles, to lead them upstairs. If the herb helped her to win power over them, it would be the only plant I'd known her to use. She had a garden full of remedies, but she never attempted to heal anyone. She could have plucked flat clusters of bloodwort, chewed it to a paste, and prepared a poultice for my sore arms, but the plants remained rooted in soil. *I* could have done it, but somehow I understood that the garden was hers and not mine, her collection of hoarded knowledge. I felt she was as greedy about the shoots and stems as whites about their gold. Maybe she counted the buds and leaves, and knew exactly what she owned, how much she had coaxed from the fickle ground.

Mrs. Elk Nation was probably still dancing with her friends at the powwow grounds, but I thought I saw her staring at me.

"Ma," I said to my mother's hunched back. She still crouched on the ground. She looked up at me. "Ma," I whispered. The questions nearly choked me; they filled my throat and hammered my teeth. Why couldn't I peel them from my tongue?

"Clive Broken Rope," I said. I blinked my eyes then, flinching in anticipation of a big reaction. But my mother's usual vaguely annoyed expression never changed. She put out her hand and I helped her up. She slapped her cotton dress to dust it.

"Those biddies must be squawking," she said to herself. To me she said, "Clive Broken Rope is a long story, and I don't like the way it ends up."

I thought that was the end of it, and started planning ways to get the information from Mrs. Elk Nation. But my mother surprised me. "I'll make us some horsemint tea and then I'll tell you," she said.

My mother blew on her tea, and the steam hid her face. She looked like a ghost. "When your father came to me, he was a dead man. He wanted me to breathe life into him, jump-start his blood. I met him straight out of the Army, when we had an honor dance for all our Second World War heroes. He was in one of those tank regiments that liberated the concentration camps in Germany, and he told me his hair turned white from what he saw, pure white in just a couple of days."

As white as the larkspur, I was thinking. I saw his head bobbing like the bell of a flower.

"All I had to do was cook him a meal, let him talk about his experiences, and he was happy. He said it made him a new man. He started smiling after a bit, and then he could laugh again. He tried to make me laugh, but it wasn't easy. The best trick he knew was imitating that Little Tramp from the silent movies, the one with the Hitler moustache. He wore his big Army boots and turned them out so he could waddle like a duck. He looked like a drunk sick bird. I almost wet my pants every time he did that routine — imagine, a Sioux warrior goofing like that.

"People talked, the way they do, because he was younger. But we didn't care. We married Indian way."

I knew my mother meant "lived in sin," but she wasn't Catholic like me. She didn't have to go to the Catholic reservation school where the old-crow nuns pecked our souls to pieces.

"Your father wasn't wounded in the war, but he came back damaged. At first I didn't notice it; I thought he was getting better all the time. But once he found out I was carrying, the holes in him opened up. I think he was afraid of what he might pass on to you. I don't know. All I know is the memories of that war chewed his mind away."

I wished I could tell her to stop. I could see it all too clearly: my father's skull empty and gleaming, licked clean from the inside. I heard the sound my mother makes when she cracks bones and eats the marrow.

"You were afraid of him," my mother told me. "Every time he put his hand out to touch my belly, you flipped over. When you got too big to move that much, you kicked his hand away. You already knew something was wrong.

"Your father hit me just once, and that was enough. 'That's the last mistake you'll ever make,' I told him. I didn't care if he was half crazy or had left his mind in Germany, blown to bits like everything else. Nobody does that to me, or mine." My mother got up and poured herself more of the smooth tea. It smelled as cool and clean as virgin snow.

"Some little thing upset him. I don't remember what. He howled and scratched his face so deep that he was bleeding into his collar. I grabbed his hands to stop him, but he knocked me down. When I tried to get up, he kicked me right here." My mother touched her thick middle. "So he kicked you as well. The toe of his boot left that mark on your face."

My hand lifted to the birthmark and massaged the area above my left eye. It was just a birthmark, nothing more, certainly not the pointed edge of my father's boot, tattooing my flesh with his crazy anger. I knew the claim wasn't true, but I believed it.

"Your father died a week before you were born," my mother said.

It was all she would tell me.

I stood up and went to the kitchen window for a breath of fresh air. Waving below me in the soft wind were neat rows of prairie larkspurs. Their white faces nodded at me until I became dizzy and had to look away.

ಶಿ

I married Martin Lundstrom on March 10, 1964, in a tiny office at the state capitol. I had always been impressed by the nineteen-story skyscraper constructed of smooth limestone, but on my wedding day clouds massed behind my eyes, making the sky look bleak and overcast, transforming the majestic building into a cold tower. I wasn't excited by the rare elevator ride, and I was impatient with employees of the state who gawked openly at us. I reached for Martin's hand, straightened my spine, even tilted my chin at a haughty angle. One pink secretary, looking as fluffy as a lamb in a cashmere dress, stared the longest, her jaw creaked open so wide I could count her fillings. Just before we turned a corner and left her sight, I flicked my fingers at her.

Martin grabbed my hand. "Don't be bothered, Crystal. They're just ignorant."

He lifted my hand to his lips and warmed it with a soft kiss. "No," he said, "they're just jealous."

Our witnesses were strangers on a coffee break, and every mouth was set in a flat line of grim disapproval. A storm swept through my head, and I needed a great effort of concentration to get through the brief ceremony, hear enough of it to respond properly. Once it was over, the chaos descended: thunder cracked in my eardrums, and needles of lightning flashed through my skull. Hailstones the size of jelly beans pounded my brain, shattering my thoughts. I leaned against my new husband. I gave up the future to him.

ॐॐ

I am a weak vessel, I told myself as I peered out the rain-streaked windows of Martin's Thunderbird.

"The state sure hates to see us go; it's crying its eyes out," he said. He clutched my knee.

I am a weak vessel chanted silently in my head, the drone of a familiar prayer.

"We'll hit Chicago tomorrow," Martin told me. "Things'll get better, just wait. How about some music?"

It was Sunday, so all we could tune in were gospel shows or music hours filled with mournful hymns as oppressive as dirges: *I'll cling to the old rugged cross, and exchange it someday for a crown.*

Voices soaked with tears of passion swelled in the car, the harmonies strained and nearly collapsed. We drove through a great bath of tears until we reached Minnesota.

"Now we've found the sun!" Martin cried. He rolled down his window and thrust his pale hand into the light. "The sun always makes a difference."

I believe I nodded my head, but it was a useless gesture. The voice of my thoughts was stuck in a groove: rain or shine, it bumped over the same ground.

I am a weak vessel, it sputtered, over and over again.

ॐॐ

Martin and I rented a two-bedroom apartment on Belmont Avenue, not far from the harbor full of crisp white sailboats, webbed with intricate rigging. Because of a glowing reference letter written by the manager of Will's Bismarck Seed House, Martin was able to secure a position in the advertising department of the *Chicago Tribune*. We were suddenly respectable, saving our money and attending company parties where only a handful of people seemed aware of our clashing colors.

I was determined to make Martin happy in the small ways left to me. My hair was once again firmly pressed into a flip, and I added depth to my face using a dark-brown eyebrow pencil and a tube of coral-red lipstick. I cleaned the apartment regularly and thoroughly, paying attention to even the smallest details. I starched our linen so that it had snap to it and a crisp fragrance, and the creamy white curtains I'd sewn by hand billowed spotlessly at each open window. Potpourri scented every bureau drawer. I scoured the ceilings with a rag-wrapped broom to discourage cobwebs, and I polished our two fluted wineglasses until they sparkled from the recesses of the kitchen cabinet, though we had yet to use them.

Isabel Lundstrom appeared at our front door on the first Monday in June, while I was beating rugs on our back porch, dust and lint powdering me like pollen. I heard the knock and ran through the long chain of rooms, slinging the door open so suddenly that I frightened Martin's mother, and even myself. We both started.

"Oh," she gasped. "Oh." I had never met Isabel Lundstrom, but I recognized her from a photograph Martin had placed on our mantel.

"Come in, Mrs. Lundstrom, please. Let me help you." She had an alarming number of suitcases and shopping bags scattered around her feet. I wondered how she had managed the two flights. "I hope you didn't haul these upstairs yourself."

"No, a cabdriver helped me," she said. She finally stepped inside the apartment, and I wrangled with her bags, carrying them into the spare bedroom. One shopping bag was torn at the bottom, and the contents spilled to the floor with a great clatter.

"Not to worry, it's just the *plättpanna*." Isabel pointed to a huge iron pancake pan. I was lucky it hadn't landed on my foot. Despite the heat she was wearing a heavy woolen overcoat, which I helped her remove. Beneath it she wore a brown cardigan and a yellow scarf tied at her throat. When she cocked her head to the side, I nearly tittered; she was the very picture of a stout meadowlark.

We sat in the narrow kitchen with a view of back porches that looked as precarious as a stack of Legos, our faces hanging over the pot of tea so that we could inhale the steam.

"Smells wonderful," Isabel said, but she didn't look as though she meant it. "I hope a visit won't be inconvenient. Martin is very young, and I want to be certain he's eating properly. His appetite was always poor. I battled so hard to get him to eat any fruit — I sometimes feared he would suffer the shame of scurvy."

Isabel left the table, and I heard her rummaging through her shopping bags. She returned with a sack of oranges in one hand and a tin of tasty, brittle gingersnaps in the other. "These are Martin's all-time favorite cookie. I usually make them only at Christmas, but I wanted to bring him something special."

"This is certainly a treat," I assured her.

She decided to take a nap so that she would be refreshed by the time Martin returned from work. "Just a catnap," she said. "Please wake me one half hour before you think he'll be here. Two days sitting up on the train, I must surely be a wreck. No, don't tell me different. I'm puffed and strained and creaking."

Isabel swept into the spare bedroom, and I put my head down on the table. I needed time to digest this new development, this sudden hitch, but I had dinner to prepare and was still covered with a thick layer of dust. In moments Isabel's dainty snores issued forth from her room, whistling in my ears like a kind of tune. I found I couldn't form a single coherent thought. Just as one floated toward consciousness, as fragile as a bubble, Isabel's piercing note popped it mercilessly, and I remained bewildered.

Martin's arrival sparked a squall of tears; a typhoon washed over him, embraced him, and only reluctantly let him go. Isabel had aged ten years in the time he took to cross the threshold. Her mouth went slack, and her hands developed a subtle tremble.

"She's made such a long trip!" he said — to her, not to me. "Oh, she must be exhausted!"

"Well, yes. My recovery time isn't what it was, but I have only to look at you and all will be well."

This threatened to be a prolonged visit, and I decided then and there that I would be pleasant about it. Isabel would be my penance, my hair shirt, and I willingly shouldered the burden of her visit. Foolishly, I hadn't thought to alter our usual Monday-night menu in honor of Isabel's arrival. I realized my mistake when I began to put the food on the table. It seemed to me bright and ridiculous: clowns' food, fit for a child's birthday party. I served spicy sloppy Joes, a bowl of peas, grape-flavored Kool-Aid, and butterscotch pudding for dessert.

Isabel nibbled at the peas and picked a few morsels of hamburger from the orange sauce. "Very nice," she said. "Very tasty."

After dinner she offered to wash the dishes. "The cook mustn't do everything," she scolded. "You need your rest after such a spread."

We struggled over a dish — I insisted that she should visit with her son and leave the task to me — and we both relented at the same moment, letting the dish crash to the floor.

"I'll get it!" we both cried, and nearly knocked heads in our haste to pick up the pieces.

Martin poked his head into the kitchen. "Is everything okay?" He didn't wait for an answer but limped toward us, his arms spread wide so that he could embrace us simultaneously. "It's grand to have everyone together!" he said. And for just a moment I *was* reminded of Tiny Tim, as disloyal as that felt. He was beaming, bouncing a little on the balls of his feet. He never noticed the look that passed between his mother and his wife.

§§

My life quickly became one long home-economics course. I majored in smorgasbord and minored in patience. I learned to make Swedish pancakes with lingonberry jam, potato griddle cakes, spiced red cabbage, fried salt herring, home-cured ham and pork sausage, limpa bread, shortbread, cardamom coffee cake, almond tortes, and walnut meringues. Martin gained five pounds, and one evening, before he switched off the bedroom light, he thanked me for being so kind to his mother.

"She's getting old," he said.

"Well, sixty-two," I reminded him.

"That's old for some people, especially when they're alone. I think she's doing better with us than she ever did before."

I kissed his mouth to quiet him, and yanked on his cowlicks. Lately they threatened to disappear, so I trained them when I could, bullied them into maintaining their former rebellion.

"Don't ever change," I told my husband.

❦❦

I discovered an eerie parallel between mother and son. Evidently Martin's reluctance to address people directly was an inherited trait. Isabel wouldn't say anything to correct me, but instead left little notes around the kitchen to guide me. I came to despise her fancy rounded script.

Needs more salt, she taped to casserole lids. Or, *I saved this from burning to a crisp. Cake fell!!* she wrote, when the rebuke was hardly necessary. I even found a note in the bathtub, after I had nearly washed it down the drain. *Too much grit,* she admonished. I switched to another cleanser.

I found her most agreeable when she was dressing her hair for the day. The procedure was complicated, involving the careful pinning of waves, the arrangement of tortoiseshell combs, and the twisting of fine silver-blonde hair. For those twenty minutes she was solemn and quiet and never offered an opinion — written or otherwise — on any subject. I liked to watch her fuss with her waist-length tresses; it was her single vanity. Gradually I came to notice that the ritual was difficult for her, painful. Sometimes her fingers slipped and she'd have to begin again. I offered to help, and for the longest time she refused. Not until autumn, when the damp cold must have penetrated her bones, did she sigh in defeat.

"A simple bun will do," she told me.

"I'm not good at this," I admitted. "But if you help me, tell me what to do, I think I'll get it right eventually."

I think she appreciated the effort and so made one of her own: forcing herself to speak directions, to interrupt my movements with a helpful comment. We managed best when she sat at a low dressing table that Martin had bought from The Salvation Army. We both faced the old warped mirror and watched as her hair was transformed from a tangled mass into a sculpted crown. By December, Isabel allowed me to brush her hair before we dressed it, and I could tell she enjoyed the sensation, for she closed her eyes and her wrinkles smoothed as I applied a hundred tender strokes.

The week before Christmas, Isabel took the brush from my hand as I made ready to fix her hair. She covered my hand with her own. We stared into the mirror, gray eyes finding brown, our hands clasped together and our breathing perfectly still. Her palm was rough from so many years of housework but the touch didn't chafe; her raw hands felt like silk to me.

"I want to show you something," she said. Isabel opened a little drawer in the center of her dressing table and removed a black velvet box.

She said, "My grandmother made this when she first came to this country."

The box opened with a whine, revealing a tiny painted bird's egg, no larger than a thimble. "Isn't it cunning?" she asked. She lifted it from the fabric nest and placed it in my hands. "You see, it's a miniature globe." The egg was blue and its continents worked in cheerful vermilion, each line as delicate as thread.

"She must have used an eyelash," I said, awed by the careful work.

"I don't know how she did it, my mother never told me, but I'd like to tell you a story connected with this little egg."

"You'd better take it first," I said. "I don't want to squash it — it's so fine." We settled the egg back in the box but left the lid open so that we could admire it from a safe distance. I took a seat on Isabel's bed, and she turned her stool to face me.

"I had twin sisters," she said, and then stopped. She fingered the thick yarn fringe of her shawl. "Their names were Beatrice and Dagmar, but everyone just called them 'the angels,' because they were such beautiful little girls. They had thick blonde ringlets like gold coins, and green eyes Mother said were emeralds stolen from Africa. I adored them, plain and simple. They were five years younger, but I never thought they were a nuisance underfoot. I liked to make up stories to tell them late at night, when they had trouble falling asleep. 'Bell,' they called me. 'Tell us something, Bell.'"

Isabel paused, caressing the egg with one finger. "Mother and I always saved the milk for them to drink. The rest of us drank water. The milk cow must have eaten a toxic weed one time, because she suffered like a poisoned thing, thrashed on the ground, and took forever to die. We didn't kill her, because we kept hoping she'd recover. Cows were so valuable back then.

"When the girls got sick, the doctor came and gave Mother paregoric for the colic. 'But they're poisoned,' Father said. Doctors were like God in those days, and when our doctor said they weren't poisoned, well, they weren't. The angels died no more than an hour after he left. The end was terrible, but they never let go of each other's hands, and my parents ordered a special coffin so they could be buried like that, side by side."

Isabel pinched her nightgown between her fingers. "My parents were distraught. My mother said she would have no life without the angels. I was so strange, I couldn't cry. I missed them, but I couldn't cry at all. Mother decided to bury Grandmother's egg with the angels. 'It passes from mother to daughter,' she said, 'and now is the end of the line.' Mother lifted the white satin coverlet we had spread over them and placed the egg beneath their clasped hands. I was set to watch over my sisters while Father took care of Mother. I guess you know

I robbed them. I was wrong, but Crystal, I would do it again. Mother shouldn't have forgotten that I existed."

Isabel rose and shut the lid of the box. "It wasn't the end of the line, and it still isn't. I pass this on to you."

I now possessed two objects I prized above all others: Isabel's painted egg and a beaded turtle amulet I kept hidden beneath my slips. I set them both out on my bureau, one beside the other, and meant to leave them there together. I quickly decided not to. Something about the turtle unnerved me: it looked so alive, so capable of cracking the egg's delicate shell with its hinged jaws, devouring the globe and its vivid continents and slippery oceans.

🕭🕭

I had given birth to a baby girl. I know this because Anna Thunder said, her voice triumphant, "I *knew* it would be a girl!"

I asked for the umbilical cord so that I could slip it in the turtle amulet I wore around my neck. My mother handed it to me. "I'll stitch it up later," she said. "I'm busy."

Then she cleaned the baby with a warm washcloth and wrapped her in flannel.

Now I'll get to hold her, I thought. But Anna left the room with my baby caught up in her arms.

"Mama, what are you doing?" I cried. She returned moments later with a drink like spiced cider. It soothed me, helped me to relax.

"Everything is fine," she said. "Fine and dandy, just like candy."

Had I heard wrong? My mother sounded foolish, girlish. The world broke apart, and when I tried to fit the pieces back together, I got it wrong. I thought I saw my mother waltzing with the baby. She spun toward the ceiling in defiance of gravity, and I was looking at the soles of her shoes. Then I was flying, or floating, out the window, onto a feather mattress settled in the bed of a pickup truck. Roger Bonnin's face swooped toward mine and then swelled to fill the horizon. I wanted to scream, but my tongue was thick cotton. Snow sparkled in the air, it was crushed diamonds, and its dust covered me until my staring eyes went blind.

Martin found me curled in the back seat of his Thunderbird, empty, wrapped in quilts. When he asked me what had happened, I knew, even though I couldn't remember. My spirit belonged to me, free and clear, for the first time since I had grown in the bowl of my mother's womb. But the price was my daughter's soul. Anna Thunder had stolen my child to raise, to cast in her own image so that she would never die. My hand shook as I reached inside my nightgown. Was anything left? Then relief washed through me; the beaded turtle was there.

"Where is the baby?" Martin asked me. He was digging through the quilts as if she might be nestled there. I covered his warm hands with mine. I sent a chill through him because my touch was ice.

"The baby is dead," I told him.

🕭🕭

I do not know my daughter's name, or the shape of her face. In dreams she stands with her back to me, her hair in tight braids, stiff like black ropes.

"Ina," she says, "Mama," but she is speaking to my own mother, who sits before her and looks at me over my daughter's head. Anna smiles. "Such a good girl," she says in these dreams, and although she is looking at me, straight into my eyes, I know she doesn't mean me.

Sometimes I wear the turtle amulet Anna made for my baby. Coiled inside the beaded shell is her umbilical cord, a dry piece of flesh that keeps me tied to the small girl with black braids poking down her back like sharp spears. The amulet is meant to keep her from ill health and other calamities, but I have taken it because a mother must keep her child safe. If I protect the amulet, then surely I will protect the girl. At least, this is the story I tell myself when I wake up from those dreams where my daughter keeps her back to me and will not turn when I call, will not tip her face in my direction so that I can see if she looks anything like me.

❦❦

For as long as I could remember my mother was preoccupied with her boyfriends. She had a great hunger that was never satisfied. They marched up her stairs, as awkward as puppets, their empty eyes proof of some troubled magic. Those eyes were spilled ink, drained of love and hope. If they reflected anything at all, it was surely fear, and not my mother's beautiful lined face.

I understand now that my mother's lovemaking was despair, but when I was little, I thought it was her great adventure. The sounds fascinated me: animal cries, the shrill creak of her brass bed, but mostly the *tap tap* of her knee knocking against the wall. I was on the other side of that barrier, and I liked to press my hands against the flaking plaster and feel the vibrations.

I came to believe that her rhythmic knock was a hidden message, a kind of code. In the library I discovered a thick book on a secret language called International Morse Code: a series of dots and dashes, short raps and long thumps. Finally I could translate my mother's most potent signal, her purest magic. The next night I listened carefully at my post, ear against the wall, jotting marks on a yellow tablet. A pattern was forming, a regular series of sounds played over and over like a song with many verses:

Dash-Dash-Dot / Dot-Dash-Dot / Dot-Dash / Dot-Dot-Dot / Dot-Dot-Dot

Grass, she said. My mother's knee spelled *grass.* I collapsed with disappointment. Was this the great secret I had so eagerly anticipated? I flung the book to the floor and pulled the covers over my head.

Grass. I couldn't escape the word; its still tattoo pounded against my wall. I could not make sense of it until I imagined my mother on the plains, surrounded by tall grass, perhaps little bluestem, rising to her shoulder. I could see her move with the stalks, ripple in the wind, her hands in the air and fingers spread like wispy flowers. My mother's roots drilled deep, and she would not be plucked. I thought that if anyone tried, he would tear up the earth and a tongue of flame would shoot from the core, straight to his heart.

Okay, I told myself. *Mama is the grass.* And me? I couldn't have said as a child. But now I know that I am not like Anna Thunder. I am one of those seeds that will push up tentative shoots wherever I land.

Gish Jen

Who's Irish?

Gish Jen was born Lillian Jen on Long Island in 1955, the daughter of Chinese immigrants who came to the United States in the 1940s. An English major, she graduated from Harvard in 1977 and later earned an M.F.A. from the Iowa Writers' Workshop. Following a Bunting Fellowship at Radcliffe, she began publishing her short stories in the leading magazines almost immediately; a novel, *Typical American,* appeared in 1991 and another, *Mona in the Promised Land,* came out in 1996, both tracing the lives of the extended Chang family. Her most complex novel, *The Love Wife,* received sustained acclaim when it was reviewed in 2004, and she has taken her place as one of the foremost American writers dealing with ethnic issues, a subject often presented in complex circumstances in her fiction. She has said that she has been most influenced by Jewish writers, for example, and her characters often interact across national and racial boundaries, encountering social and religious traditions alien to their own. That is the central situation in one of her most famous stories, "Who's Irish?" which was featured in *The New Yorker* in 1999 prior to being collected in the volume *Who's Irish?* later that year. It deals with her typical situation, a Chinese immigrant dealing with issues of cultural duality, language, and self-definition whose daughter marries into an Irish family. The conflicts of religion, customs, food, and attitudes about work that ensue are humorous and yet distinctly American. Jen's fiction is rich in humanistic depth rather than the bitterness that invests some contemporary fiction, and it has brought her a wide audience of admiring readers from virtually every background.

Gish Jen, "Who's Irish?" *Who's Irish?* (New York: Vintage, 1999), 3–16.

In China, people say mixed children are supposed to be smart, and definitely my granddaughter Sophie is smart. But Sophie is wild, Sophie is not like my daughter Natalie, or like me. I am work hard my whole life, and fierce besides. My husband always used to say he is afraid of me, and in our restaurant, busboys and cooks all afraid of me too. Even the gang members come for protection money, they try to talk to my husband. When I am there, they stay away. If they come by mistake, they pretend they are come to eat. They hide behind the menu, they order a lot of food. They talk about their mothers. Oh, my mother have some arthritis, need to take herbal medicine, they say. Oh, my mother getting old, her hair all white now.

I say, Your mother's hair used to be white, but since she dye it, it become black again. Why don't you go home once in a while and take a look? I tell them, Confucius say a filial son knows what color his mother's hair is.

My daughter is fierce too, she is vice president in the bank now. Her new house is big enough for everybody to have their own room, including me. But Sophie take after Natalie's husband's family, their name is Shea. Irish. I always thought Irish people are like Chinese people, work so hard on the railroad, but now I know why the Chinese beat the Irish. Of course, not all Irish are like the Shea family, of course not. My daughter tell me I should not say Irish this, Irish that.

How do you like it when people say the Chinese this, the Chinese that, she say.

You know, the British call the Irish heathen, just like they call the Chinese, she say.

You think the Opium War was bad, how would you like to live right next door to the British, she say.

And that is that. My daughter have a funny habit when she win an argument, she take a sip of something and look away, so the other person is not embarrassed. So I am not embarrassed. I do not call anybody anything either. I just happen to mention about the Shea family, an interesting fact: four brothers in the family, and not one of them work. The mother, Bess, have a job before she got sick, she was executive secretary in a big company. She is handle everything for a big shot, you would be surprised how complicated her job is, not just type this, type that. Now she is a nice woman with a clean house. But her boys, every one of them is on welfare, or so-called severance pay, or so-called disability pay. Something. They say they cannot find work, this is not the economy of the fifties, but I say, Even the black people doing better these days, some of them live so fancy, you'd be surprised. Why the Shea family have so much trouble? They are white people, they speak English. When I come to this country, I have no money and do not speak English. But my husband and I own our restaurant before he die. Free and clear, no mortgage. Of course, I understand I am just lucky, come from a country where the food is popular all over the world. I understand it is not the Shea family's fault they come from a country where everything is boiled. Still, I say.

She's right, we should broaden our horizons, say one brother, Jim, at Thanksgiving. Forget about the car business. Think about egg rolls.

Pad thai, say another brother, Mike. I'm going to make my fortune in pad thai. It's going to be the new pizza.

I say, You people too picky about what you sell. Selling egg rolls not good enough for you, but at least my husband and I can say, We made it. What can you say? Tell me. What can you say?

Everybody chew their tough turkey.

I especially cannot understand my daughter's husband John, who has no job but cannot take care of Sophie either. Because he is a man, he say, and that's the end of the sentence.

Plain boiled food, plain boiled thinking. Even his name is plain boiled: John. Maybe because I grew up with black bean sauce and hoisin sauce and garlic sauce, I always feel something is missing when my son-in-law talk.

But, okay: so my son-in-law can be man, I am baby-sitter. Six hours a day, same as the old sitter, crazy Amy, who quit. This is not so easy, now that I am sixty-eight, Chinese age almost seventy. Still, I try. In China, daughter take care of mother. Here it is the other way around. Mother help daughter, mother ask, Anything else I can do? Otherwise daughter complain mother is not supportive. I tell daughter, We do not have this word in Chinese, *supportive*. But my daughter too busy to listen, she has to go to meeting, she has to write memo while her husband go to the gym to be a man. My daughter say otherwise he will be depressed. Seems like all his life he has this trouble, depression.

No one wants to hire someone who is depressed, she say. It is important for him to keep his spirits up.

Beautiful wife, beautiful daughter, beautiful house, oven can clean itself automatically. No money left over, because only one income, but lucky enough, got the baby-sitter for free. If John lived in China, he would be very happy. But he is not happy. Even at the gym things go wrong. One day, he pull a muscle. Another day, weight room too crowded. Always something.

Until finally, hooray, he has a job. Then he feel pressure.

I need to concentrate, he say. I need to focus.

He is going to work for insurance company. Salesman job. A paycheck, he say, and at least he will wear clothes instead of gym shorts. My daughter buy him some special candy bars from the health-food store. They say THINK! on them, and are supposed to help John think.

John is a good-looking boy, you have to say that, especially now that he shave so you can see his face.

I am an old man in a young man's game, say John.

I will need a new suit, say John.

This time I am not going to shoot myself in the foot, say John.

Good, I say.

She means to be supportive, my daughter say. Don't start the send her back to China thing, because we can't.

ᵊᵊ

Sophie is three years old American age, but already I see her nice Chinese side swallowed up by her wild Shea side. She looks like mostly Chinese. Beautiful black hair, beautiful black eyes. Nose perfect size, not so flat looks like something fell down, not so large looks like some big deal got stuck in wrong face. Everything just right, only her skin is a brown surprise to John's family. So brown, they say. Even John say it. She never goes in the sun, still she is that color, he say. Brown. They say, Nothing the matter with brown. They are just surprised. So brown. Nattie is not that brown, they say. They say, It seems like Sophie should be a color in between Nattie and John. Seems funny, a girl named Sophie Shea be brown. But she is brown, maybe her name should be Sophie Brown. She never go in the sun, still she is that color, they say. Nothing the matter with brown. They are just surprised.

The Shea family talk is like this sometimes, going around and around like a Christmas-tree train.

Maybe John is not her father, I say one day, to stop the train. And sure enough, train wreck. None of the brothers ever say the word *brown* to me again.

Instead, John's mother, Bess, say, I hope you are not offended.

She say, I did my best on those boys. But raising four boys with no father is no picnic.

You have a beautiful family, I say.

I'm getting old, she say.

You deserve a rest, I say. Too many boys make you old.

I never had a daughter, she say. You have a daughter.

I have a daughter, I say. Chinese people don't think a daughter is so great, but you're right. I have a daughter.

I was never against the marriage, you know, she say. I never thought John was marrying down. I always thought Nattie was just as good as white.

I was never against the marriage either, I say. I just wonder if they look at the whole problem.

Of course you pointed out the problem, you are a mother, she say. And now we both have a granddaughter. A little brown granddaughter, she is so precious to me.

I laugh. A little brown granddaughter, I say. To tell you the truth, I don't know how she came out so brown.

We laugh some more. These days Bess need a walker to walk. She take so many pills, she need two glasses of water to get them all down. Her favorite TV show is about bloopers, and she love her bird feeder. All day long, she can watch that bird feeder, like a cat.

I can't wait for her to grow up, Bess say. I could use some female company.

Too many boys, I say.

Boys are fine, she say. But they do surround you after a while.

You should take a break, come live with us, I say. Lots of girls at our house.

Be careful what you offer, say Bess with a wink. Where I come from, people mean for you to move in when they say a thing like that.

❦

Nothing the matter with Sophie's outside, that's the truth. It is inside that she is like not any Chinese girl I ever see. We go to the park, and this is what she does. She stand up in the stroller. She take off all her clothes and throw them in the fountain.

Sophie! I say. Stop!

But she just laugh like a crazy person. Before I take over as baby-sitter, Sophie has that crazy-person sitter, Amy the guitar player. My daughter thought this Amy very creative — another word we do not talk about in China. In China, we talk about whether we have difficulty or no difficulty. We talk about whether life is bitter or not bitter. In America, all day long, people talk about creative. Never mind that I cannot even look at this Amy, with her shirt so short that her belly button showing. This Amy think Sophie should love her body. So when Sophie take off her diaper, Amy laugh. When Sophie run around naked, Amy say she wouldn't want to wear a diaper either. When Sophie go *shu-shu* in her lap, Amy laugh and say there are no germs in pee. When Sophie take off her shoes, Amy say bare feet is best, even the pediatrician say so. That is why Sophie now walk around with no shoes like a beggar child. Also why Sophie love to take off her clothes.

Turn around! say the boys in the park. Let's see that ass!

Of course, Sophie does not understand. Sophie clap her hands, I am the only one to say, No! This is not a game.

It has nothing to do with John's family, my daughter say. Amy was too permissive, that's all.

But I think if Sophie was not wild inside, she would not take off her shoes and clothes to begin with.

You never take off your clothes when you were little, I say. All my Chinese friends had babies, I never saw one of them act wild like that.

Look, my daughter say. I have a big presentation tomorrow.

John and my daughter agree Sophie is a problem, but they don't know what to do.

You spank her, she'll stop, I say another day.

But they say, Oh no.

In America, parents not supposed to spank the child.

It gives them low self-esteem, my daughter say. And that leads to problems later, as I happen to know.

My daughter never have big presentation the next day when the subject of spanking come up.

I don't want you to touch Sophie, she say. No spanking, period.

Don't tell me what to do, I say.

I'm not telling you what to do, say my daughter. I'm telling you how I feel.

I am not your servant, I say. Don't you dare talk to me like that.

My daughter have another funny habit when she lose an argument. She spread out all her fingers and look at them, as if she like to make sure they are still there.

My daughter is fierce like me, but she and John think it is better to explain to Sophie that clothes are a good idea. This is not so hard in the cold weather. In the warm weather, it is very hard.

Use your words, my daughter say. That's what we tell Sophie. How about if you set a good example.

As if good example mean anything to Sophie. I am so fierce, the gang members who used to come to the restaurant all afraid of me, but Sophie is not afraid.

I say, Sophie, if you take off your clothes, no snack.

I say, Sophie, if you take off your clothes, no lunch.

I say, Sophie, if you take off your clothes, no park.

Pretty soon we are stay home all day, and by the end of six hours she still did not have one thing to eat. You never saw a child stubborn like that.

I'm hungry! she cry when my daughter come home.

What's the matter, doesn't your grandmother feed you? My daughter laugh.

No! Sophie say. She doesn't feed me anything!

My daughter laugh again. Here you go, she say.

She say to John, Sophie must be growing.

Growing like a weed, I say.

Still Sophie take off her clothes, until one day I spank her. Not too hard, but she cry and cry, and when I tell her if she doesn't put her clothes back on I'll spank her again, she put her clothes back on. Then I tell her she is good girl, and give her some food to eat. The next day we go to the park and, like a nice Chinese girl, she does not take off her clothes.

She stop taking off her clothes, I report. Finally!

How did you do it? my daughter ask.

After twenty-eight years experience with you, I guess I learn something, I say.

It must have been a phase, John say, and his voice is suddenly like an expert.

His voice is like an expert about everything these days, now that he carry a leather briefcase, and wear shiny shoes, and can go shopping for a new car. On the company, he say. The company will pay for it, but he will be able to drive it whenever he want.

A free car, he say. How do you like that.

It's good to see you in the saddle again, my daughter say. Some of your family patterns are scary.

At least I don't drink, he say. He say, And I'm not the only one with scary family patterns.

That's for sure, say my daughter.

§§

Everyone is happy. Even I am happy, because there is more trouble with Sophie, but now I think I can help her Chinese side fight against her wild side. I teach her to eat food with fork or spoon or chopsticks, she cannot just grab into the middle of a bowl of noodles. I teach her not to play with garbage cans. Sometimes I spank her, but not too often, and not too hard.

Still, there are problems. Sophie like to climb everything. If there is a railing, she is never next to it. Always she is on top of it. Also, Sophie like to hit the mommies of her friends. She learn this from her playground best friend, Sinbad, who is four. Sinbad wear army clothes every day and like to ambush his mommy. He is the one who dug a big hole under the play structure, a foxhole he call it, all by himself. Very hardworking. Now he wait in the foxhole with a shovel full of wet sand. When his mommy come, he throw it right at her.

Oh, it's all right, his mommy say. You can't get rid of war games, it's part of their imaginative play. All the boys go through it.

Also, he like to kick his mommy, and one day he tell Sophie to kick his mommy too.

I wish this story is not true.

Kick her, kick her! Sinbad say.

Sophie kick her. A little kick, as if she just so happened was swinging her little leg and didn't realize that big mommy leg was in the way. Still I spank Sophie and make Sophie say sorry, and what does the mommy say?

Really, it's all right, she say. It didn't hurt.

After that, Sophie learn she can attack mommies in the playground, and some will say, Stop, but others will say, Oh, she didn't mean it, especially if they realize Sophie will be punished.

δ℮

This is how, one day, bigger trouble come. The bigger trouble start when Sophie hide in the foxhole with that shovel full of sand. She wait, and when I come look for her, she throw it at me. All over my nice clean clothes.

Did you ever see a Chinese girl act this way?

Sophie! I say. Come out of there, say you're sorry.

But she does not come out. Instead, she laugh. Naaah, naah-na, naaa-naaa, she say.

I am not exaggerate: millions of children in China, not one act like this.

Sophie! I say. Now! Come out now!

But she know she is in big trouble. She know if she come out, what will happen next. So she does not come out. I am sixty-eight, Chinese age almost seventy, how can I crawl under there to catch her? Impossible. So I yell, yell, yell, and what happen? Nothing. A Chinese mother would help, but American mothers, they look at you, they shake their head, they go home. And, of course, a Chinese child would give up, but not Sophie.

I hate you! she yell. I hate you, Meanie!

Meanie is my new name these days.

Long time this goes on, long long time The foxhole is deep, you cannot see

too much, you don't know where is the bottom. You cannot hear too much either. If she does not yell, you cannot even know she is still there or not. After a
while, getting cold out, getting dark out. No one left in the playground, only us.

Sophie, I say. How did you become stubborn like this? I am go home without
you now.

I try to use a stick, chase her out of there, and once or twice I hit her, but still
she does not come out. So finally I leave. I go outside the gate.

Bye-bye! I say. I'm go home now.

But still she does not come out and does not come out. Now it is dinnertime,
the sky is black. I think I should maybe go get help, but how can I leave a little
girl by herself in the playground? A bad man could come. A rat could come. I go
back in to see what is happen to Sophie. What if she have a shovel and is making
a tunnel to escape?

Sophie! I say.

No answer.

Sophie!

I don't know if she is alive. I don't know if she is fall asleep down there. If she
is crying, I cannot hear her.

So I take the stick and poke.

Sophie! I say. I promise I no hit you. If you come out, I give you a lollipop.

No answer. By now I worried. What to do, what to do, what to do? I poke
some more, even harder, so that I am poking and poking when my daughter and
John suddenly appear.

What are you doing? What is going on? say my daughter.

Put down that stick! say my daughter.

You are crazy! say my daughter.

John wiggle under the structure, into the foxhole, to rescue Sophie.

She fell asleep, say John the expert. She's okay. That is one big hole.

Now Sophie is crying and crying.

Sophia, my daughter say, hugging her. Are you okay, peanut? Are you okay?

She's just scared, say John.

Are you okay? I say too. I don't know what happen, I say.

She's okay, say John. He is not like my daughter, full of questions. He is full
of answers until we get home and can see by the lamplight.

Will you look at her? he yell then. What the hell happened?

Bruises all over her brown skin, and a swollen-up eye.

You are crazy! say my daughter. Look at what you did! You are crazy!

I try very hard, I say.

How could you use a stick? I told you to use your words!

She is hard to handle, I say.

She's three years old! You cannot use a stick! say my daughter.

She is not like any Chinese girl I ever saw, I say.

I brush some sand off my clothes. Sophie's clothes are dirty too, but at least she has her clothes on.

Has she done this before? ask my daughter. Has she hit you before?

She hits me all the time, Sophie say, eating ice cream.

Your family, say John.

Believe me, say my daughter.

ᔥᔥ

A daughter I have, a beautiful daughter. I took care of her when she could not hold her head up. I took care of her before she could argue with me, when she was a little girl with two pigtails, one of them always crooked. I took care of her when we have to escape from China, I took care of her when suddenly we live in a country with cars everywhere, if you are not careful your little girl get run over. When my husband die, I promise him I will keep the family together, even though it was just two of us, hardly a family at all.

But now my daughter take me around to look at apartments. After all, I can cook, I can clean, there's no reason I cannot live by myself, all I need is a telephone. Of course, she is sorry. Sometimes she cry, I am the one to say everything will be okay. She say she have no choice, she doesn't want to end up divorced. I say divorce is terrible, I don't know who invented this terrible idea. Instead of live with a telephone, though, surprise, I come to live with Bess. Imagine that. Bess make an offer and, sure enough, where she come from, people mean for you to move in when they say things like that. A crazy idea, go to live with someone else's family, but she like to have some female company, not like my daughter, who does not believe in company. These days when my daughter visit, she does not bring Sophie. Bess say we should give Nattie time, we will see Sophie again soon. But seems like my daughter have more presentation than ever before, every time she come she have to leave.

I have a family to support, she say, and her voice is heavy, as if soaking wet. I have a young daughter and a depressed husband and no one to turn to.

When she say no one to turn to, she mean me.

These days my beautiful daughter is so tired she can just sit there in a chair and fall asleep. John lost his job again, already, but still they rather hire a baby-sitter than ask me to help, even they can't afford it. Of course, the new baby-sitter is much younger, can run around. I don't know if Sophie these days is wild or not wild. She call me Meanie, but she like to kiss me too, sometimes. I remember that every time I see a child on TV. Sophie like to grab my hair, a fistful in each hand, and then kiss me smack on the nose. I never see any other child kiss that way.

The satellite TV has so many channels, more channels than I can count, including a Chinese channel from the Mainland and a Chinese channel from Taiwan, but most of the time I watch bloopers with Bess. Also, I watch the bird feeder — so many, many kinds of birds come. The Shea sons hang around all the time, asking when will I go home, but Bess tell them, Get lost.

She's a permanent resident, say Bess. She isn't going anywhere.

Then she wink at me, and switch the channel with the remote control.

Of course, I shouldn't say Irish this, Irish that, especially now I am become honorary Irish myself, according to Bess. Me! Who's Irish? I say, and she laugh. All the same, if I could mention one thing about some of the Irish, not all of them of course, I like to mention this: Their talk just stick. I don't know how Bess Shea learn to use her words, but sometimes I hear what she say a long time later. *Permanent resident. Not going anywhere.* Over and over I hear it, the voice of Bess.

Yiyun Li

The Princess of Nebraska

Yiyun Li, a welcome new voice among American writers, was born in China in 1974 and grew up in Beijing, studying immunology at Peking University. She came to the United States in 1996 to continue her work in medicine, eventually receiving a master's degree, but she shifted her interests to the writing of stories, earning an M.F.A. from the Iowa Writers' Workshop. Her work was soon appearing in the most prestigious magazines, including *The Paris Review, The New Yorker, Ploughshares, The Gettysburg Review,* and *The New York Times Magazine.* When these pieces were brought together in *A Thousand Years of Good Prayers* in 2005, the volume won the richest literary prize in the world for short fiction, the Frank O'Connor International Short Story Award of $60,000, an astonishing accomplishment for a Chinese immigrant who did not speak English when she left her homeland. "The Princess of Nebraska," first published in *Ploughshares* in 2004, well represents the complex texture of her fiction, introducing multiple layers of action involving three intriguing characters. It is told in a traditional omniscient perspective, with access to the minds of the two central figures. Boshen is a middle-aged physician who immigrated to America, leaving his gay lover behind in China, and Sasha is a young woman of twenty-one who is carrying the child of the lover, Yang. He is, in one sense, the "princess" of the title since his profession is that of *Nan Dan,* playing female roles on stage with the Peking Opera. On another level, it is Sasha herself who is the princess in that she has come to Chicago from Nebraska to have an abortion. The complex love triangle that this situation presents is only the beginning of the interwoven pattern of the plot, which ranges forward and backward in time, from action in Chicago to flashbacks to events in China, from the way Boshen perceives the situation to Sasha's changing point of view about her life, her baby, and the promise of the American dream.

Yiyun Li, "The Princess of Nebraska," *A Thousand Years of Good Prayers* (New York: Random House, 2005), 68–91.

Sasha looked at Boshen in the waiting line for a moment before turning her eyes to the window. She wished that she would never have to see Boshen again after this trip. She had run to the bathroom the moment they entered the McDonald's, leaving him to order for them both. He had suggested a good meal in Chinatown, and she had refused. She wanted to see downtown Chicago before going to the clinic at Planned Parenthood the next morning. It was the only reason for her to ride the Greyhound bus all day from Nebraska. Kansas City would have been a wiser choice, closer, cheaper, but there was nothing to see there — the trip was not meant for sightseeing, but Sasha hoped to get at least something out of it. She did not want to spend all her money only to remember a drugged sleep in a dreary motel in the middle of nowhere. Sasha had grown up in a small town in Inner Mongolia; vast and empty landscapes depressed her.

"You must be tired," Boshen said as he pushed the tray of food to Sasha, who had taken a table by the window. She looked tiny in the oversized sweatshirt. Her face was slightly swollen, and the way she checked out the customers in the store, her eyes staying on each face a moment too long, moved him. She was twenty-one, a child still.

"I got a fish sandwich for you," Boshen said when Sasha did not answer him.

"I haven't seen one happy face since arriving," Sasha said. "What's the other one?"

"Chicken."

Sasha threw the fish sandwich across the table and grabbed the chicken sandwich from Boshen's tray. "I hate fish," she said.

"It's good for you now," Boshen said.

"Now will be over soon," Sasha said. She looked forward to the moment when she was ready to move on. "Moving on" was a phrase she just learned, an American concept that suited her well. It was such a wonderful phrase that Sasha could almost see herself stapling her Chinese life, one staple after another around the pages until they became one solid block that nobody would be able to open and read. She would have a fresh page then, for her American life. She was four months late already.

Boshen said nothing and unwrapped the fish sandwich. It was a change — sitting at a table and having an ordered meal — after months of eating in the kitchen of the Chinese restaurant where he worked as a helper to the Sichuan chef. Boshen had come to America via a false marriage to a friend five months earlier, when he had been put under house arrest for his correspondence with a Western reporter regarding a potential AIDS epidemic in a central province. He had had to publish a written confession of his wrongdoing to earn his freedom. A lesbian friend, a newly naturalized American citizen herself, had offered to marry him out of China. Before that, he had lived an openly gay life in Beijing, madly in love with Yang, an eighteen-year-old boy. Boshen had tried different ways to contact Yang since he had arrived in America, but the boy never responded. The checks Boshen sent him were not cashed, either.

They ate without speaking. Sasha swallowed her food fast, and waited for Boshen to finish his. Outside the window, more and more people appeared, all moving toward downtown, red reindeer's antlers on the heads of children who sat astride their fathers' shoulders. Boshen saw the question in Sasha's eyes and told her that there was a parade that evening, and all the trees on Michigan Avenue would light up for the coming Thanksgiving and Christmas holidays. "Do you want to stay for it?" he asked halfheartedly, hoping that she would choose instead to rest after the long bus ride.

"Why not?" Sasha said, and put on her coat.

Boshen folded the sandwich wrapper like a freshly ironed napkin. "I wonder if we could talk for a few minutes here," he said.

Sasha sighed. She never liked Boshen, whom she had met only once and who had struck her as the type of man as fussy as an old hen. She had not hesitated, however, to call him and ask for help when she had found his number through an acquaintance. She had spoken in a dry, matter-of-fact way about her pregnancy, which had gone too long for an abortion in the state of Nebraska. Yang had fathered the baby; she had told Boshen this first in their phone call. She had had no intention of sparing Boshen the truth; in a way, she felt Boshen was responsible for her misfortune, too.

"Have you, uh, made up your mind about the operation?" Boshen asked.

"What do you think I'm here for?" Sasha said. Over the past week Boshen had called her twice, bringing up the possibility of keeping the baby. Both times she had hung up right away. Whatever interest he had in the baby was stupid and selfish, Sasha had decided.

The easiest solution may not be the best one in life, Boshen thought of telling Sasha, but then, what right did he have to talk about options, when the decisions he had made for his life were all compromises? At thirty-eight, Boshen felt he had achieved less than he had failed. He was a mediocre doctor before he was asked politely to leave the hospital for establishing the first counseling hotline for homosexuals in the small Chinese city where he lived. He moved to Beijing and took on a part-time job at a private clinic while working as an activist for gay rights. After a few visits from the secret police, however, he realized that, in the post-Tiananmen era, talk of any kind of human rights was dangerous. He decided to go into a less extreme and more practical area, advocating for AIDS awareness, but even that he had to give up after pressure from the secret police and his family. He was in love with a boy twenty years younger, and he thought he could make a difference in the boy's life. In the end, he was the one to marry a woman and leave. Boshen had thought of adopting the baby — half of her blood came from Yang, after all — but Sasha's eyes, sharp and unrelenting, chilled him. He smiled weakly and said, "I just wanted to make sure."

Sasha wrapped her head in a shawl and stood up. Boshen did not move, and when she asked him if he was leaving, he said, "I've heard from my friends that Yang is prostituting again."

Not a surprise, Sasha thought, but the man at the table, too old for a role as a heartbroken lover and too serious for it, was pitiful. In a kinder voice she said, "Then we'll have to live with that, no?"

�჻

Boshen was not the first man to have fallen in love with Yang, but he believed, for a long time, that he was the only one to have seen and touched the boy's soul. Since the age of seven, Yang had been trained as a *Nan Dan* — a male actor who plays female roles on stage in the Peking Opera — and had lived his life in the opera school. At seventeen, when he was discovered going out with a male lover, he was expelled. Boshen had written several articles about the incident, but he had not met Yang until he had become a *money boy*. Yang could've easily enticed a willing man to keep him for a good price, but rumors were that the boy was interested only in selling after his first lover abandoned him.

The day Boshen heard about Yang's falling into prostitution, he went to the park where men paid for such services. It was near dusk when he arrived, and men of all ages slipped into the park like silent fish. Soon night fell; beneath the lampposts, transactions started in whispers, familiar scenarios for Boshen, but standing in the shade of a tree — a customer instead of researcher — made him tremble. It was not difficult to recognize Yang in the moon-white-colored silk shirt and pants he was reputed to wear every day to the park. Boshen looked at the boy, too beautiful for the grimy underground, a white lotus blossom untouched by the surrounding mud.

After watching the boy for several days, Boshen finally offered to pay Yang's asking price. The night Yang came home with Boshen, he became drunk on his own words. For a long time he talked about his work, his dream of bringing an end to injustice and building a more tolerant world; Yang huddled on the couch and listened. Boshen thought of shutting up, but the more he talked, the more he despaired at the beautiful and impassive face of Yang — in the boy's eyes he must be the same as all the other men, so full of themselves. Finally Boshen said, "Someday I'll make you go back to the stage."

"An empty promise of a man keeps a woman's heart full," Yang recited in a low voice.

"But this," Boshen said, pointing to the pile of paperwork on his desk. "This is the work that will make it illegal for them to take you away from the stage because of who you are."

Yang's face softened. Boshen watched the unmistakable hope in the boy's eyes. Yang was too young to hide his pain, despite years of wearing female masks and portraying others' tragedies onstage. Boshen wanted to save him from his suffering. After a few weeks of pursuing, Boshen convinced Yang to try a new life. Boshen redecorated the apartment with expensive hand-painted curtains that featured the costumes of the Peking Opera and huge paper lanterns bearing the Peking Opera masks. He sold a few pieces of furniture to make space, and borrowed a rug from a friend for Yang to practice on. Yang fit into the quiet life like the most virtuous woman he had played on stage. He got up early every morning, stretching his body into unbelievable positions, and dancing the most intricate choreography. He trained his voice, too, in the shower so that the neighbors would not hear him. Always Boshen stood outside and listened, Yang's voice splitting the waterfall, the bath curtain, the door, and the rest of the dull world like a silver knife. At those moments Boshen was overwhelmed by gratitude — he was not the only one to have been touched by the boy's beauty, but he was the one to guard and nurture it. That alone lifted him above his mundane, disappointing life.

When Boshen was at work, Yang practiced painting and calligraphy. Sometimes they went out to parties, but most evenings they stayed home. Yang never performed for Boshen, and he dared not ask him to. Yang was an angel falling out of the heavens, and every day Boshen dreaded that he would not be able to return the boy to where he belonged.

Such a fear, as it turned out, was not unfounded. Two months into the relationship, Yang started to show signs of restlessness. During the day he went out more than before, and he totally abandoned painting and calligraphy. Boshen wondered if the boy was suffocated by the stillness of their life.

One day shortly before Boshen was expelled from Beijing and put under house arrest in his hometown, Yang asked him casually how his work was going. Fine, Boshen said, feeling uneasy. Yang had never asked him anything about his work; it was part of the ugly world that Boshen had wanted to shelter Yang from.

"What are you working on?" Yang asked.

"Why, the usual stuff," Boshen said.

"I heard you were working on AIDS," Yang said. "What has that to do with you?"

Stunned, Boshen tried to find an explanation. Finally he said, "You don't understand, Yang."

"I'm not a child," Yang said. "Why are you concerned with that dirty disease? The more you work on it, the more people will connect it with gay people. What good does it do for me?"

"I'm trying to help more people," Boshen said.

"But you've promised to help me get back to the stage," Yang said. "If you insist on working on something irrelevant, you'll never fulfill your promise."

Boshen could not answer Yang. Afterward, Yang started to go out more often, and a few days later, he did not come home for the first time in their relationship. Boshen thought of all the predators waiting to set their fangs and claws on Yang, and he did not sleep that night.

"There's nothing for you to worry about," Yang said with a strange smile when Boshen confronted him. "You're not as endangered as you imagine."

"At least you should've let me know where you were," Boshen said.

"I was with a girl," Yang said, and mentioned the name Sasha, which sounded slightly familiar to Boshen. They had met her at a party, Yang reminded Boshen, but he did not remember who she was; he did not understand why Yang was going out with her, either.

"Why? What a silly question," Yang said. "You do things when you feel like it, no?"

୬୧

The first time Sasha met Yang, at a party, she felt that she was looking into a mirror that reflected not her own face, but that of someone she could never become. She watched the ballet of his long fingers across the table while he listened absentmindedly to the conversation of others around the table. She looked at the innocent half-moons on his fingernails; her own fingers were plump and blunt. His cream-colored face, his delicate nose and mouth reminded her of an exquisite china doll. Later, when they sat closer, she saw the melancholy in his eyes and decided that he was more like a statue of Kuanyin, the male Buddha in a female body, the goddess who listened and responded to the prayers of suffering women and children. Sitting next to him, Sasha felt like a mass-produced rubber doll.

The uneasy feeling lasted only for a moment. Sasha had heard of his stories, and was glad to see him finally in person. She leaned toward him and asked, as if picking up from a conversation they had dropped somewhere, "What do you think of girls, then?"

He looked up at her, and she saw a strange light in his eyes. They reminded her of a wounded sparrow she had once kept during a cold Mongolian winter. Sparrows were an obstinate species that would never eat and drink once they were caged, her mother told her. Sasha did not believe it. She locked up the bird for days, and it kept bumping into the cage until its head started to go bald. Still she refused to release it, mesmerized by its eyes, wild but helplessly tender, too. She nudged the little bowl of soaked millet closer to the sparrow, but the bird was blind to her hospitality. Cheap birds, a neighbor told her; only cheap birds would be so stubborn. Have a canary, the neighbor said, and she would be singing for you every morning by now.

The boy lowered his eyes at Sasha's scrutiny, and she felt the urge to chase the beautiful eyes, a huntress of that strange light. "You must have known some girls, no?" she said. "When you went to the opera school, were there girls in the school?"

"Yes," the boy said, his voice reminding her of a satin dress.

"So?"

"We didn't talk. They played handmaids and nannies, background roles."

"So you were the princess, huh?" Sasha laughed and saw the boy blush, with anger perhaps, but it made her more curious and insistent in cornering him. "What's your name?" she said.

"Which name?"

"How many names do you have?"

"Two. One given by my parents. One given by the opera school."

"What are they?"

He dipped one finger into a glass of orange juice and wrote on the dark marble tabletop. She followed the wet trace of his finger. It was Yang, a common boy's name with the character for the sun, the masculine principle of nature, the opposite of Yin.

"A so-so name. What's your opera name?"

"Sumeng," he said. A serene and pure dreamer, it meant.

"Worse. Sounds like a weepy name from a romance novel," Sasha said. "You need a better name. I'll have to think of one for you."

In the end she did not use either name, and did not find a better one for him. She called him "my little *Nan Dan,*" and that was what he was to her, a boy destined to play a woman's part. She paged him often, and invited him to movies and walks in the park. She made decisions for them both, and he let her. She tried to pry him open with questions — she was so curious about him — and slowly he started to talk, about the man he had loved and men who loved him. He never said anything about the opera school or his stage life, and she learned not to push him. He was so vain, Sasha thought when he spent a long time fixing his hair or when he put on an expression of aloofness at the slightest attention of a stranger; she teased him, and then felt tender and guilty when he did not defend himself. She made fun of the other people in Yang's life, too: his lover, Boshen, whom she believed to be a useless dreamer, and the men who boldly asked him for his number. She believed she was the first person in his life who did not worship him in any way, and he must be following her around because of that. It pleased her.

Was she dating the boy? Sasha's classmates asked when they saw her with Yang more than once. Of course not, she said. In a month, Sasha was to go to America for graduate school, and it was pointless to start a relationship now. Besides, how smart was it to date a boy who loved no one but himself?

♪♪

Even the wind could not cut through the warm bodies lined up on both sides of Michigan Avenue. Sasha pushed through the crowd. They looked so young and carefree, these Americans, happy as a group of pupils on a field trip. She envied these people, who would stand in a long line in front of a popcorn shop waiting for a bag of fresh popcorn, lovers leaning into each other, children hanging on to their parents. They were born to be themselves, naive and contented with their naivety.

"I would trade my place with any one of them," Sasha said to Boshen, but when he raised his voice and asked her to repeat her words, she shook her head.

If only there were a law in America binding her to where her baby belonged so that the baby would have a reason to live!

Sasha herself had once been used by the law to trap her mother in the grassland. One of the thousands of high school students sent down from Beijing to Inner Mongolia for labor reeducation, her mother, in order to join the Party, married a Mongolian herdsman, one of the model interracial marriages that were broadcast across the grassland. Five years later, at the end of the Cultural Revolution, all of the students were allowed to return to Beijing. Sasha's mother, however, was forced to stay, even after she divorced her Mongolian husband. Their two daughters, born in the grassland, did not have legal residency in Beijing, and the mother had to stay where the children belonged.

Sasha pushed forward, looking at every store window. Silky scarves curved around the mannequins' necks with soft obedience. Diamonds glistened on dark velvet. At a street corner, children gathered and watched the animated story displayed in the windows of Marshall Field's. If only her baby were a visa that would admit her into this prosperity, Sasha thought, saddened by the memories of Nebraska and Inner Mongolia, the night skies of both places black with lonely, lifeless stars.

"There's an open spot there," Boshen said. "Do you want to stand there?"

Sasha nodded, and Boshen followed her. Apart from the brief encounter at the party in Beijing and a few phone calls, he did not know her. He had thought about her often after she had called him about the pregnancy. What kind of girl, he had wondered, would've made Yang a father? He had imagined a mature and understanding girl. Beautiful, too. He had made up a perfect woman for Yang and for his own peace of mind, but Sasha had disappointed him. When they settled along the curb, he said, "So, what's your plan after the operation?"

Sasha stood on tiptoe like a child, and looked in the direction where the parade would start. Boshen regretted right away speaking with such animosity. Seeing nothing, she turned to him and said, "What's *your* plan in America? Where's your new wife, anyway?"

Boshen frowned. He had told Yang that the marriage would be used as a cover, and his departure was meant only to be a temporary one. He had promised Yang other things, too, money he would send, help he would seek in the overseas Chinese community for Yang's return to the stage. Not a day since he had arrived did he forget his promises, but Sasha's words stung him. His marriage must have been an unforgivable betrayal, in Sasha's and Yang's eyes alike. "I can't defend myself," Boshen said finally.

"Of course not. You were the one sending him back to the street," Sasha said.

"It's been a troubled time," Boshen said, struggling over the words. "It's been difficult for all of us. But we certainly should try to help him out."

Sasha turned to look at Boshen with an amused smile. "You speak like the worst kind of politician," she said. "Show me the solution."

"I am thinking." Boshen hesitated, and said, "I've been thinking — if we can tell him that he'll be able to perform in America, maybe he would want to leave Beijing?"

"And then?"

"We will try here. There's a *Nan Dan* master in New York. Maybe we can contact him and ask for his help. But the first thing we do is to get Yang out of the country."

"Does that 'we' include me?"

"If you could marry Yang, he would be here in no time. I know him. If there's one percent chance to go back to the stage, he'll try."

"A very nice plan, Boshen," Sasha said. "But why should I agree to the proposal? What's in it for me?"

Boshen looked away from Sasha and watched a couple kiss at the other side of the street. After a long moment, he turned to Sasha and tried to look into her eyes. "You must have loved him at least once, Sasha," he said, his voice trembling.

♉

Sasha had not planned for love, or even an affair. The friendship was out of whimsy, a convenience for the empty days immediately before graduating from college. The movie they watched one night in July was not planned, either. It was ten o'clock when Sasha purchased the tickets, at the last minute. Yang looked at the clock in the ticket booth and wondered aloud if it was too late, and Sasha laughed, asking him if he was a child and if his lover had a curfew for him.

The movie was *Pretty Woman,* with almost unreadable Chinese subtitles. When they came out to the midnight street, Sasha said, "Don't you just love Julia Roberts?"

"What's to love about her?" Yang said.

Sasha glanced at Yang. He was quiet throughout the movie — he did not understand English, but Sasha thought at least he could've enjoyed the beautiful actress. "She's pretty, and funny, and so — American," Sasha said. "America is a good place. Everything could happen there. A prostitute becomes a princess; a crow turns into a swan overnight."

"A prostitute never becomes a princess," Yang said.

"How do you know?" Sasha said. "If only you could come with me to America and take a look at it yourself."

After a long moment, Yang said, "Every place is a good place. Only time goes wrong."

Sasha said nothing. She did not want to spend the night philosophizing. When they walked past a small hotel, she asked Yang if he wanted to come in with her. Just for the fun of staying out for a night, she said; he needn't have to report to his lover anyway, she added. Yang hesitated, and she grabbed his hand and pulled him into the foyer with her. A middle-aged woman at the reception opened the window and said, "What do you want?"

"Comrade, do you have a single room for two persons?" Sasha said.

The woman threw out a pad for registration and shut the window. Sasha filled in the form. The woman scanned the pad. "Your ID?" she asked.

Sasha handed her ID to the woman. The woman looked at it for a long time, and pointed to Yang with her chin. "His ID?"

"He's my cousin from Inner Mongolia," Sasha said in a cheerful voice. "He forgot to bring his ID with him."

"Then there's no room tonight." The woman threw out Sasha's ID and closed the window.

"Comrade." Sasha tapped on the glass.

The woman opened the window. "Go away," she said. "Your cousin? Let me tell you — either you have a marriage license and I will give you a room, or you go out and do that shameless thing in the street and let the cops arrest you. Don't you think I don't know girls like you?"

Sasha dragged Yang out the door, his lips quavering. "I don't believe I can't find a room for us," Sasha said finally.

Yang looked at Sasha with a baffled look. "Why do we have to do this?" he said.

"Ha, you're afraid now. Go ahead if you don't want to come," Sasha said, and started to walk. Yang followed Sasha to an even smaller hotel at the end of a narrow lane. An old man was sitting behind a desk, playing poker with himself. "Grandpapa," Sasha said, handing her ID to the old man. "Do you have a single room for my brother and me?"

The old man looked at Sasha and then Yang. "He's not fifteen yet so he doesn't have an ID," Sasha said, and Yang smiled shyly at the old man, his white teeth flashing in the dark.

The old man nodded and handed a registration pad to Sasha. Five minutes later they were granted a key. It was a small room on the second floor, with two single beds, a rusty basin stand with two basins, and a window that did not have a curtain. Roaches scurried to find a hiding place when Sasha turned on the light. They stood just inside the door, and all of a sudden she did not know what the excitement was of spending a night together in a filthy hotel. "Why don't we just go home?" Yang said behind her.

"Where's the place you call home?" Sasha snapped. She turned off the light and lay down on a bed without undressing. "Go back to the man who keeps you if this is not a place for a princess like you," she said.

Yang stood for a long moment before he got into the other bed. Sasha waited for him to speak, and when he did not, she became angry with him, and with herself.

The next morning, when the city stirred to life, they both lay awake in their own beds. The homing pigeons flew across the sky, the small brass whistles bound to their tails humming in a harmonious low tone. Not far away, Tao music played on a tape recorder, calling for the early risers to join the practice of tai chi. Old men, the fans of Peking Opera, sang their favorite parts of the opera, their voices cracking at high notes. Then the doors down the lane creaked open, releasing the shouting children headed to school, and adults to work, their bicycle bells clanking.

Later, someone turned on a record player and music blasted across the alley. Sasha sat up and looked out the window. A young man was setting up a newspaper stand at the end of the alley, making theatrical movements along with a song in which a rock singer was yelling, "Oh, Genghis Khan, Genghis Khan, he's a powerful old man. He's rich, he's strong, and I want to marry him."

Sasha listened to the song repeat and said, "I don't understand why these people think they have the right to trash Genghis Khan."

"Their ears are dead to real music," Yang said.

"When I was little, my father taught me a song about Genghis Khan. It's the only Mongolian song I remember now," Sasha said, and opened her mouth to sing the song. The melody was in her mind, but no words came to her tongue. She had forgotten almost all of the Mongolian words she had learned, after her parents' divorce; she had not seen her father for fifteen years. "Well, I don't remember it anymore."

"*The broken pillars, the slanted roof, they once saw the banqueting days; the dying trees, the withering peonies, they once danced in the heavenly music. The young girls dreamed of their lovers who were enlisted to fight the Huns. They did not know the loved ones had become white bones glistening in the moonlight,*" Yang chanted in a low voice to the ceiling. "Our masters say that real arts never die. Real arts are about remembrance."

"What's the point of remembering the song anyway? I don't even remember what my father looked like." Sasha thought about her father, one of the offspring of Genghis Khan. Genghis Khan was turned into a clown in the pop song. Mongolia was once the biggest empire in the world, and now it was a piece of meat, sandwiched by China and Russia.

"We live in a wrong time," Yang said.

Sasha turned to look at Yang. He lay on his hands and stared at the ceiling, his face taking on the resigned look of an old man. It hurt her, and scared her too, to glimpse a world beneath his empty beauty. "We were born into a wrong place, is what our problem is," she said, trying to cheer him and herself up. "Why don't you come to America with me, Yang?"

Yang smiled. "Who am I to follow you?"

"A husband, a lover, a brother, I don't care. Why don't you get out of Beijing and have a new life in America?" The words, once said, hung in the room like heavy fog, and Sasha wondered if Yang, too, had difficulty breathing. Outside the window, a vendor was sharpening a chopper with a whetstone, the strange sound making their mouths water unpleasantly. Then the vendor started to sing in a drawn-out voice about his tasty pig heads.

"Sasha," Yang said finally. "Is Sasha a Mongolian name?"

"Not really. It's Russian, a name of my mom's favorite heroine in a Soviet war novel."

"That's why it doesn't sound Chinese. I would rather it is a Mongolian name," Yang said. "Sasha, the princess of Mongolia."

Sasha walked barefoot to Yang's bed and knelt beside him. He did not move, and let Sasha hold his face with both hands. "Come to America with me," she said. "We'll be the prince and princess of Nebraska."

"I was not trained to play a prince," Yang said.

"The script is changed," Sasha said. "From today on."

Yang turned to look at Sasha. She tried to kiss him, but he pushed her away gently. *"A beautiful body is only a bag of bones,"* he sang in a low voice.

Sasha had never seen Yang perform, and could not imagine him onstage; he had played princesses and prostitutes, but he did not have to live with the painted mask and the silk costume. "The Peking Opera is dead," she said. "Why don't you give it up?"

"Who are you to say that about the Peking Opera?" Yang said, his face turning suddenly stern.

Sasha saw the iciness in Yang's eyes and let the topic drop. Afterward, neither mentioned anything about the stay in the hotel. A week later, when Boshen was escorted away from Beijing, Sasha was relieved and scared. There was, all of a sudden, time for them to fill. To her relief and disappointment, Yang seemed to have forgotten the moment when they were close, so close that they were almost in love.

ʃ&

The parade started with music and laughter, colorful floats moving past, on which happy people waved to the happy audience. Boshen looked at Sasha's face, lit up by curiosity, and sighed. Despite her willfulness and unfriendliness, the thought of the baby — Yang's baby — made him eager to forgive her. "Do you still not want to tell Yang about the baby?" he said.

"You've asked this the hundredth time," Sasha said. "Why should I?"

"He might want to come to the U.S. if he learned about the baby," Boshen said.

"There'll be no baby after tomorrow," Sasha said. She had tried Yang's phone number when she had learned of the pregnancy; she had tried his pager, too. At first it was measured by hours and days, and then it became weeks since she had left the message on his pager. He might be living in another apartment with a new telephone number. The pager might no longer belong to him. She knew he had every reason for not getting her message, but she could not forgive his silence. In the meantime, her body changed. She felt the growth inside her and she was disgusted by it. Sometimes she hated it from morning till night, hoping that it would finally go away, somehow, surrendering to the strength of her resentment. Other times she kept her mind away for as long as she could, thinking that it would disappear as if it had never existed. Still, in the end, it required her action. In the end, she thought, it was just a chunk of flesh and blood.

"But why was there a baby in the first place?" Boshen said. Why and how it happened were the questions that had been haunting him since he had heard from Sasha. He wanted to ask her if she, too, had been dazzled by the boy's body, smooth, lithe, perfectly shaped. He wanted to know if she had loved him as he had, but in that case, how could she have the heart to discard what had been left with her?

Sasha turned to Boshen. For the first time, she studied the man with curiosity. Not handsome or ugly, he had a candid face that Sasha thought she could not fall in love with but nonetheless could trust. A man like Boshen should have an ordinary life, boring and comfortable, yet his craze for Yang made him a more interesting man than he deserved to be. But that must be what was Yang's value — he made people fall in love with him, and the love led them astray, willingly, from their otherwise tedious paths. Yang had been the one to bring up the idea of spending a night together again, and Sasha the one to ask a friend for the use of her rented room, a few days before Sasha's flight. It was one of the soggiest summer evenings. After their lovemaking, sweet and short and uneventful, they stayed on the floor, on top of the blanket Sasha had brought for the purpose, an arm's length between them, each too warm to touch the other. Outside, the landlady's family and two other neighbor families were sitting in the courtyard and watching a TV program, their voices mixed with the claps of their hands killing the mosquitoes. Sasha turned to look at Yang, who was lying with his back to her. The little pack of condoms she had bought was tucked underneath the blanket, unopened. She had suggested it and he had refused. A rubber was for people who touched without loving each other, Yang had said; his words had made her hopeful again. "Do you want to come to America with me now?" she asked, tracing his back with one finger.

"What am I going to do in America? Be kept as a canary by you?" Yang said and moved farther away from her finger.

"You can spent some time learning English, and get a useful degree in America."

"Useful? Don't you already know that I am useless? Besides, nothing humiliates a man more than living as a parasite on his woman," Yang said, and reached for a silk robe he had packed with him. Before Sasha had the time to stop him, he walked out the door. Sasha jumped to her feet and watched from behind the curtain; Yang walked with a calculated laziness, not looking at the people who turned their eyes away from the television to stare at him. When he reached the brick sink in the middle of the courtyard, he sat on the edge and raised his bare legs to the tap. The water had run for a long moment before the landlady recovered from her shock and said, "Hey, the water costs me money."

Yang smiled. "It's so hot," he said in a pleasant voice.

"Indeed," the landlady agreed.

Yang turned off the tap and walked back to the room, with the same grace and idleness, knowing that the people in the courtyard were all watching him, his willowy body wrapped in the moon white robe. Sasha stood by the window, cold with disappointment. She became his audience, one of the most difficult to capture, perhaps, but he succeeded after all.

A Disney float approached the corner where Sasha and Boshen stood. "Look," Sasha said and pointed at a giant glove of Mickey Mouse moving ahead of the float. "There're only four fingers."

"I didn't know that," Boshen said.

"Yang needs us no more than that glove needs us for our admiration," Sasha said.

"But our love is the only thing to protect him, and to save him, too."

Sasha turned and looked into Boshen's eyes. "It's people like us who have destroyed him, isn't it? Why was there *Nan Dan* in the Peking Opera in the first place? *Men loved him because he was playing a woman; women loved him because he was a man playing,*" she said.

"That's totally wrong."

"Why else do you want so much to put him back on the stage? Don't think I'm happy to see him fall. Believe me, I wanted to help him as much as you do. He didn't have to be a man playing a woman — I thought I would make him understand. But what did I end up with? You're not the one who has a baby inside; he's not the one having an abortion," Sasha said, and started to cry.

Boshen held out his hand and touched Sasha's shoulder hesitantly. If only she could love the boy one more time. Yang could choose to live with either of them; he could choose not to love them at all but their love would keep him safe and intact; they could — the three of them — bring up the baby together. Yang would remain the princess, exiled, yes, but a true princess, beautiful in a foreign land. If only he knew how to make Sasha love Yang again, Boshen thought.

Sasha did not move away when Boshen put an arm around her shoulder. They must look like the most ordinary couple to strangers, a nervous husband comforting his moody wife after an argument. They might as well be a couple, out of love, he caring only for the baby inside her, she having no feeling left for anything, her unborn child included.

As if responding, the baby moved. A tap, and then another one, gentle and tentative, the first greeting that Sasha had wished she would never have to answer, but it seemed impossible, once it happened, not to hope for more. After a long moment, people in the street shouted, and children screamed out of excitement. Sasha looked up — the lights were lit up in the trees, thousands of stars forming a constellation. She thought about the small Mongolian town where her mother lived alone now, her long shadow trailing behind her as she walked home along the dimly lit alley. Her mother had been born into a wrong time, lived all her adult life in a wrong place, yet she had never regretted the births of her two daughters. Sasha held her breath and waited for more of the baby's messages. America was a good country, she thought, a right place to be born into, even though the baby had come at a wrong time. Everything was possible in America, she thought, and imagined a baby possessing the beauty of her father but happier, and luckier. Sasha smiled, but then when the baby moved again, she burst into tears. Being a mother must be the saddest yet the most hopeful thing in the world, falling into a love that, once started, would never end.

APPENDIX A: List of Sources

Alexie, Sherman. "The Lone Ranger and Tonto Fistfight in Heaven." *The Lone Ranger and Tonto Fistfight in Heaven* (New York: Atlantic Monthly Press, 1993), 181–90.

Anderson, Sherwood. "Death in the Woods." *The American Mercury* 9 (September 1926): 7–13.

Anonymous. "Adventure of a Young English Officer among the Abenakee Savages." *Royal American Magazine* 2 (February 1775): 59–61.

Anonymous. "Amelia; or, The Faithless Briton. An Original Novel, Founded upon Recent Events." *Columbian Magazine, or Monthly Miscellany* 1 (October 1787): 676–82; supplement to vol. 1 (October 1787): 877–80.

Anonymous. "Anecdote [An Argument against the Ownership of Slaves]." *American Museum* 7, no. 6 (June 1790): 332–33.

Anonymous. "The Calamities of War and the Effects of Unbridled Passion." *Boston Magazine* (February 1784): 127–29.

Anonymous. "Indian Fidelity." *Columbian Magazine, or Monthly Miscellany* 2 (August 1788): 421–22.

Anonymous. "Intrepidity of a Negro Woman." *Massachusetts Magazine* 3 (December 1791): 728.

Anonymous. "The Negro." *The Weekly Magazine of Original Essays, Fugitive Pieces, and Interesting Intelligence* 1 (February 3, 1798): 11–12.

Anonymous. "Three Days after Marriage: or, the History of Ned Easy and Mrs. Manlove. A Story Founded in Fact." *Gentlemen and Ladies Town and Country Magazine* 6 (February 1789): 19–21.

Anonymous. "The Wretched Taillah: An African Story." *Massachusetts Magazine* 4 (April 1792): 250–51.

Austin, William. "Peter Rugg, the Missing Man." *Literary Papers of William Austin, with a Biographical Sketch by His Son, James Walker Austin* (Boston: Little, Brown Company, 1890), 3–17. Originally published in the *New England Galaxy* 7 (September 10, 1824): 32.

Baldwin, James. "Sonny's Blues." *Going to Meet the Man* (New York: The Dial Press, 1965), 103–41.

Barthelme, Donald. "Views of My Father Weeping." *The New Yorker* 45 (December 6, 1969): 56–60.

Bellamy, Thomas. "The Fatal Effects of Seduction, Exemplified in a Letter from the Reformed Edmund, to His Friend." *Gentlemen and Ladies Town and Country Magazine* 6 (June 1789): 250–51.

Bierce, Ambrose. "An Occurrence at Owl Creek Bridge." *In the Midst of Life* (New York: G. P. Putnam's Sons, 1898), 16–35.

Bontemps, Arna. "A Summer Tragedy." *Opportunity* 11 (June 1933): 174–77, 190.

Butler, Robert Olen. "Open Arms." *A Good Scent from a Strange Mountain* (New York: Henry Holt and Company, 1992), 1–15.

Cather, Willa. "A Wagner Matinée." *Everybody's Magazine* 10 (March 1904): 325–28.

Chesnutt, Charles. "The Wife of His Youth." *The Atlantic Monthly* 82 (July 1898): 55–61.

Child, Lydia Maria. "The Indian Wife." *The Legendary* 1 (1828): 197–207.

Chin, Frank. "Railroad Standard Time." *The Chinaman Pacific & Frisco R. R. Co.* (Minneapolis: Coffee House Press, 1988), 1–7.

Chopin, Kate. "Désirée's Baby." *Bayou Folk* (Boston: Houghton, Mifflin and Company, 1894), 147–58.

Cisneros, Sandra. "Red Clowns." *The House on Mango Street* (Houston: Arte Publico Press, 1983), 93–94.

Cofer, Judith Ortiz. "Nada." *The Georgia Review* 46, no. 4 (1992): 754–62.

Colla, Ruri. "The Story of the Captain's Wife and an Aged Woman." *Gentlemen and Ladies Town and Country Magazine* 6 (October 1789): 483–85; 6 (November 1789): 520–21.

Crane, Stephen. "The Blue Hotel." *The Monster and Other Stories* (New York: Harper & Brothers Publishers, 1899), 109–61.

Dunbar, Paul Lawrence. "The Lynching of Jube Benson." *The Heart of Happy Hollow* (New York: Dodd, Mead and Company, 1904), 223–40.

Dunbar-Nelson, Alice. "M'sieu Fortier's Violin." *The Goodness of St. Rocque and Other Stories* (New York: Dodd, Mead and Company, 1899), 67–82.

Dubus, Andre. "Killings." *Finding a Girl in America: Ten Stories and a Novella* (Boston: David R. Godine, 1980), 3–20.

Erdrich, Louise. "The Red Convertible." *Love Medicine* (New York: Holt, Rinehart and Winston, 1984), 143–54.

Far, Sui Sin. "Mrs. Spring Fragrance." *Hampton's Magazine* 24 (January 1910): 137–41.

Faulkner, William. "Barn Burning." *Harper's Magazine* 179 (June 1939): 86–96.

Fauset, Jessie. "Emmy." *The Crisis* 5, no. 2 (December 1912): 79–87; 5, no. 3 (January 1913): 135–42.

Fitzgerald, F. Scott. "Winter Dreams." *All the Sad Young Men* (New York: Charles Scribner's Sons, 1926), 57–90.

Franklin, Benjamin. "The Speech of Miss Polly Baker." *The General Advertiser* (April 15, 1747): 1.

Freeman, Mary Wilkins. "The Revolt of 'Mother.'" *A New England Nun and Other Stories* (New York: Harper & Brothers Publishers, 1891), 448–68.

Garland, Hamlin. "The Return of a Private." *Arena* 3 (December 1890): 97–113.

Gilman, Charlotte Perkins. "The Yellow Wallpaper." *The New England Magazine* 11 (January 1892): 647–56.

Harper, Frances Ellen Watkins. "The Two Offers." *Anglo-African Magazine* 1 (September 1859): 288–91; 1 (October 1859): 311–13.

Harte, Bret. "The Outcasts of Poker Flat." *The Overland Monthly* 2 (January 1869): 40–47.

Hawthorne, Nathaniel. "Rappaccini's Daughter." *Mosses from an Old Manse* (Boston: Houghton, Mifflin and Company, 1846), 1: 85–118.

Hawthorne, Nathaniel. "Young Goodman Brown." *Mosses from an Old Manse* (Boston: Houghton, Mifflin and Company, 1846), 1: 69–84.

Hemingway, Ernest. "Hills Like White Elephants." *Men Without Women* (New York: Charles Scribner's Sons, 1927), 69–77.

Irving, Washington. "Rip Van Winkle." *The Sketch Book of Geoffrey Crayon, Gent.* (New York: Putnam, 1848), 27–41.

James, Henry. "The Real Thing." *The Real Thing and Other Tales* (New York: Macmillan and Co., 1893), 1–41.

Jen, Gish. "Who's Irish?" *Who's Irish?* (New York: Vintage, 1999), 3–16.

Jewett, Sarah Orne. "A White Heron." *A White Heron and Other Stories* (Boston: Houghton, Mifflin and Company, 1886), 1–22.

Kincaid, Jamaica. "Columbus in Chains." *Annie John* (New York: Farrar, Straus and Giroux, 1985), 72–84.

Li, Yiyun. "The Princess of Nebraska." *A Thousand Years of Good Prayers* (New York: Random House, 2005), 68–91.

London, Jack. "To Build a Fire." *Lost Face* (New York: The Macmillan Company, 1910), 63–98.

Longstreet, Augustus Baldwin. "The Horse Swap." *Georgia Scenes, Characters, Incidents &c. in the First Half Century of the Republic* (Augusta: S. R. Sentinel Office, 1835), 23–31.

Mason, Bobbie Ann. "Shiloh." *The New Yorker* 56 (October 20, 1980): 50–57.

Melville, Herman. "Bartleby, the Scrivener." *Putnam's Monthly Magazine* 2, no. 11 (November 1853): 546–57; 2, no. 12 (December 1853): 609–15.

Melville, Herman. "Benito Cereno." *The Piazza Tales* (New York: Dix & Edwards, 1856), 109–270.

Mena, María Cristina. "The Education of Popo." *The Century Magazine* 87 (March 1914): 653–62.

Minot, Susan. "Hiding." *Monkeys* (New York: E. P. Dutton, 1986), 1–22.

Norris, Frank. "A Deal in Wheat." *Everybody's Magazine* 7 (August 1902): 173–80.

O'Brien, Tim. "Sweetheart of the Song Tra Bong." *The Things They Carried* (New York: Broadway Books, 1990), 89–116.

O'Connor, Flannery. "The River." *Sewanee Review* 61, no. 3 (Summer 1953): 455–75.

Olsen, Tillie. "Help Her to Believe." *Pacific Spectator* 10, no. 1 (Winter 1956): 55–63.

Oskison, John M. "The Problem of Old Harjo." *The Southern Workman* 36 (April 1907): 235–41.

Poe, Edgar Allan. "The Cask of Amontillado." *Godey's Lady's Book* 33 (November 1846): 216–18.

Poe, Edgar Allan. "The Fall of the House of Usher." *Burton's Gentleman's Magazine* 5 (September 1839): 145–52.

Porter, Katherine Anne. "Maria Concepción." *Century Illustrated Magazine* 105, no. 2 (December 1922): 224–39.

Power, Susan. "Morse Code." *Atlantic Monthly* 273 (June 1994): 88–90, 92–94, 96–100.

Richardson, William. "The Indians: A Tale." *Philadelphia Monthly Magazine; or, Universal Repository* 1 (January 1798): 23–27; 1 (February 1798): 74–77.

Roth, Philip. "Defender of the Faith." *Goodbye, Columbus* (Boston: Houghton Mifflin, Co., 1959), 161–200.

Silko, Leslie Marmon. "Storyteller." *Puerto del Sol* 14, no. 1 (1975): 11–25.

Spofford, Harriet Prescott. "Circumstance." *The Atlantic Monthly* 5 (May 1860): 558–65.

Steinbeck, John. "The Chrysanthemums." *The Long Valley* (New York: Viking Press, 1938), 3–18.

Stoddard, Elizabeth. "The Prescription." *Harper's New Monthly Magazine* 28 (May 1864): 794–800.

Stowe, Harriet Beecher. "The Two Altars; or, Two Pictures in One." *The New-York Evangelist and New-York Presbyterian* 22, no. 24 (June 12, 1851): 3–4; 22, no. 25 (June 19, 1851): 97–98.

Suckow, Ruth. "A Start in Life." *Iowa Interiors* (New York: Alfred A. Knopf, 1926), 1–17.

Tan, Amy. "Four Directions." *The Joy Luck Club* (New York: G. P. Putnam's Sons, 1989), 166–84.

Thorpe, Thomas Bangs. "The Big Bear of Arkansas." *Spirit of the Times* 11 (March 27, 1841): 43–51.

Thurber, James. "The Secret Life of Walter Mitty." *The New Yorker* 15 (March 18, 1939): 19–20.

Toomer, Jean. "Blood-Burning Moon." *Cane* (New York: Boni and Liveright, 1923), 51–67.

Twain, Mark. "The Celebrated Jumping Frog of Calaveras County." *The Celebrated Jumping Frog of Calaveras County, and Other Stories,* ed. John Paul (New York: C. H. Webb, Publisher, 1867), 7–19.

Walker, Alice. "Everyday Use." *Harper's Magazine* 246 (April 1973): 74–81.

Welty, Eudora. "Petrified Man." *The Southern Review* 4 (Spring 1939): 682–95.

Wharton, Edith. "The Other Two." *The Descent of Man and Other Stories* (New York: Charles Scribner's Sons, 1904), 71–105.

Yezierska, Anzia. "The Fat of the Land." *The Century* 98, no. 4 (August 1919): 433–79.

Yamamoto, Hisaye. "The Legend of Miss Sasagawara." *The Kenyon Review* 12, no. 1 (1950): 99–115.

Zitkala-Sä. "The Soft-Hearted Sioux." *Harper's Monthly Magazine* 102 (March 1901): 505–08.

APPENDIX B: Selected Books for the Study of the American Short Story

Allen, Walter. *The Short Story in English.* Oxford: Clarendon, 1981.

Ammons, Elizabeth. *Conflicting Stories: American Women Writers at the Turn into the Twentieth Century.* New York: Oxford University Press, 1991.

Aycock, Wendell M. *The Teller and the Tale: Aspects of the Short Story.* Lubbock: Texas Tech University Press, 1982.

Bone, Robert. *Down Home: Origin of the Afro-American Short Story.* New York: Columbia University Press, 1988.

Bonheim, Helmut. *The Narrative Modes: Techniques of the Short Story.* Cambridge: Cambridge University Press, 1982.

Brown, Julie, ed. *Ethnicity and the American Short Story.* New York: Garland, 1997.

Canby, Henry S. *The Short Story in English.* New York: Holt, 1932.

Coltelli, Laura. *Winged Words: American Indian Writers Speak.* Lincoln: University of Nebraska Press, 1990.

Crowley, Donald. *The American Short Story, 1850–1900.* Boston: Twayne, 1982.

Curnutt, Kirk. *Wise Economies: Brevity and Storytelling in American Short Stories.* Moscow: University of Idaho Press, 1997.

Current-Garcia, Eugene. *The American Short Story before 1850.* Boston: Twayne, 1985.

Foster, David William. *Studies in the Contemporary Spanish-American Short Story.* Columbia: University of Missouri Press, 1979.

Fusco, Richard. *Maupassant and the American Short Story.* University Park: Pennsylvania State University Press, 1994.

Gerlach, John. *Toward the End: Closure and Structure in the American Short Story.* Tuscaloosa: University of Alabama Press, 1985.

Herrera-Sobek, Maria, and Helena Maria Viramontes, eds. *Chicana Creativity and Criticism: New Frontiers in American Literature.* Albuquerque: University of New Mexico Press, 1996.

Ingram, Forrest L. *Representative Short Story Cycles of the Twentieth Century.* The Hague: Mouton, 1971.

Kennedy, J. Gerald. *Modern American Short Story Sequences: Composite Fictions and Fictive Communities.* Cambridge: Cambridge University Press, 1995.

Kim, Elaine. *Asian American Literature: An Introduction to the Writings and Their Social Context.* Philadelphia: Temple University Press, 1982.

Levy, Andrew. *The Culture and Commerce of the American Short Story.* Cambridge: Cambridge University Press, 1993.

Lohafer, Susan. *Coming to Terms with the Short Story.* Baton Rouge: Louisiana State University Press, 1983.

Lohafer, Susan, and Jo Ellyn Clarey, eds. *Short Story Theory at a Crossroads.* Baton Rouge: Louisiana State University Press, 1989.

Lundén, Rolf. *The United Stories of America: Studies in the Short Story Composite.* Amsterdam: Rodopi, 1999.

Mann, Susan Garland. *The Short Story Cycle: A Genre Companion and Reference Guide*. Westport: Greenwood, 1989.

Matthews, Brander. *The Philosophy of the Short-Story*. New York: Longmans, 1901.

Nagel, James. *The Contemporary American Short-Story Cycle: The Ethnic Resonance of Genre*. Baton Rouge: Louisiana State University Press, 2001.

O'Brien, Edward J. *The Advance of the American Short Story*. New York: Dodd, 1931.

O'Connor, Frank. *The Lonely Voice: A Study of the Short Story*. Cleveland: World, 1963.

Pattee, Fred Lewis. *The Development of the American Short Story: An Historical Survey*. New York: Harper, 1923.

Pattee, Fred Lewis. *A History of American Literature since 1870*. New York: Century, 1915.

Peden, William. *The American Short Story: Front Line in the National Defense of Literature*. Boston: Houghton Mifflin, 1964.

Reynolds, Margaret, ed. *The Penguin Book of Lesbian Short Stories*. New York: Penguin, 1994.

Rhode, Robert D. *Setting in the American Short Story of Local Color: 1865–1900*. The Hague: Mouton, 1975.

Sollors, Werner, ed. *Multilingual America: Transnationalism, Ethnicity, and the Languages of American Literature*. New York: New York University Press, 1998.

Stevick, Philip, ed. *The American Short Story, 1900–1945*. Boston: Twayne, 1984.

Voss, Arthur. *The American Short Story: A Critical Survey*. Norman: University of Oklahoma Press, 1973.

Walker, Warren S. *Twentieth-Century Short Story Explication, 1900–1975*. 3rd ed. Hamden: Shoe String, 1977.

Ward, Alfred C. *Aspects of the Modern Short Story: English and American*. London: University of London Press, 1924.

Weaver, Gordon, ed. *The American Short Story, 1945–1980: A Critical History*. Boston: Twayne, 1983.

Weixlmann, Joe. *American Short-Fiction Criticism and Scholarship, 1959–1977*. Chicago: Swallow, 1982.

West, Ray B. *The Short Story in America: 1900–1955*. Chicago: Regnery, 1952.

Winther, Per, Jakob Lothe, and Hans H. Skei, eds. *The Art of Brevity: Excursions in Short Fiction Theory and Analysis*. Columbia: University of South Carolina Press, 2005.

Wright, Austin. *The American Short Story in the Twenties*. Chicago: University of Chicago Press, 1961.

Yin, Xiao-huang. *Chinese American Literature since the 1850s*. Carbondale: Southern Illinois University Press, 2000.

Zyla, Wolodymyr T., and Wendell M. Aycock, eds. *Ethnic Literature since 1776: The Many Voices of America*. Lubbock: Texas Tech University Press, 1978.

Credits

Alexie, Sherman "The Lone Ranger and Tonto Fistfight in Heaven," from *The Lone Ranger and Tonto Fistfight in Heaven* by Sherman Alexie. Copyright © 1993 by Sherman Alexie. Used by permission of Grove/Atlantic, Inc.

Anderson, Sherwood, "Death in the Woods," from *Portable Sherwood Anderson*. Reprinted by permission of Harold Ober Associates Incorporated. Copyright 1926 by Sherwood Anderson. Copyright renewed 1953 by Eleanor Copenhaver Anderson.

Baldwin, James, "Sonny's Blues," © 1957 by James Baldwin was originally published in *Partisan Review.* Copyright renewed. Collected in *Going to Meet the Man,* published by Vintage Books. Reprinted by arrangement with the James Baldwin Estate.

Barthelme, Donald "Views of My Father Weeping," first published in *The New Yorker.* Copyright © 1969 by Donald Barthelme, reprinted with the permission of the Wylie Agency.

Bontemps, Arna "A Summer Tragedy," is reprinted by permission of Harold Ober Associates Incorporated. First published in *Opportunity,* 11 (June 1933). Copyright 1933 by Arna Bontemps.

Butler, Robert Olen "Open Arms," from *A Good Scent from a Strange Mountain* by Robert Olen Butler, © 1992 by Robert Olen Butler. Reprinted by permission of Henry Holt and Company, LLC.

Chin, Frank "Railroad Standard Time," from *The Chinamen Pacific & Frisco R. R. Co.* Copyright © 1988 by Frank Chin. Reprinted with the permission of Coffee House Press, Minneapolis, MN.

Cisneros, Sandra "Red Clowns," from *The House on Mango Street.* Copyright © 1984 by Sandra Cisneros. Published by Vintage Books, a division of Random House, Inc., New York, and in hardcover by Alfred A. Knopf in 1994. Reprinted by permission of Susan Bergholz Literary Services, New York. All rights reserved.

Cofer, Judith Ortiz "Nada," from *The Latin Deli: Prose & Poetry* by Judith Ortiz Cofer. Copyright 1993 by Judith Ortiz Cofer. Reprinted by permission of the University of Georgia Press.

Dubus, Andre "Killings," from *Finding a Girl in America* by Andre Dubus. Reprinted by permission of David R. Godine, Publisher, Inc. Copyright © 1980 by Andre Dubus.

Erdrich, Louise "The Red Convertible," from *Love Medicine* (new and expanded edition) by Louise Erdrich. © 1984, 1993 by Louise Erdrich. Reprinted by permission of Henry Holt and Company, LLC.

Faulkner, William "Barn Burning," copyright © 1950 by Random House, Inc. Copyright renewed 1977 by Jill Faulkner Summers, from *Collected Stories of William Faulkner* by William Faulkner. Used by permission of Random House, Inc.

Fitzgerald, F. Scott "Winter Dreams," reprinted with the permission of Scribner, a Division of Simon & Schuster Adult Publishing Group, from *The Short Stories of F. Scott Fitzgerald,* edited by Matthew J. Bruccoli. Copyright © 1922 by Metropolitan Publications, Inc. Copyright © renewed 1950 by Frances Scott Fitzgerald Lanahan.

Index of Authors and Titles